Third Edition

Business Applications Software for IBM and Compatible Microcomputers

Lon Ingalsbe
Portland State University

Merrill Publishing Company
Columbus Toronto London Melbourne

Cover transparency showing School of Athens, Vatican, provided by Scala/ Art Resource. Computer-aided imaging using the Scitex system executed by Magna Graphic, Lexington, KY.

Module opening photo provided by Larry Hamill.

The first and second editions of this book were published under the title *Business Application Software for the IBM PC.*

Published by
Merrill Publishing Company
Columbus, Ohio 43216

This book was set in Univers and Century Schoolbook.

Administrative editor: Vern Anthony
Production coordinator: Pam Bennett
Text designer: Anne Daly
Cover designer: Brian Deep

Library of Congress Catalog Card Number: 89-63964
International Standard Book Number: 0-675-21175-1
Printed in the United States of America
1 2 3 4 5 6 7 8 9—93 92 91 90

To my wife Marita,
and our children Marguerite, Claire, and Brent.

THE MERRILL SERIES IN COMPUTER AND INFORMATION SYSTEMS

BARKER	*Developing Business Expert Systems with LEVEL5,* 20951-X
BROQUARD/WESTLEY	*Fundamentals of Assembler Language Programming for the IBM PC and XT,* 21058-5
CAFOLLA/KAUFFMAN	*Turbo Prolog: Step by Step,* 20816-5
CHANDLER/LIANG	*Developing Expert Systems for Business Applications,* 21102-6
CHIRLIAN	*Programming in C++,* 21007-0
	Turbo Prolog: An Introduction, 20846-7
	UNIX for the IBM PC: An Introduction, 20785-1
DENOIA	*Data Communication: Fundamentals and Applications,* 20368-6
ERICKSON/ISAAK	*Easy Ventura: A Guide to Learning Ventura Desktop Publishing for the IBM PC,* 21304-5
GEE	*A Programmer's Guide to RPG II and RPG III,* 20908-0
HOBART/OCTERNAUD/ SYTSMA	*Hands-On Computing Using WordPerfect 5.0, Lotus 1-2-3 and dBase IV,* 21110-7
HOUSTON	*Looking into C,* 20845-9
INGALSBE	*Using Computers and Applications Software Featuring VP-Planner, dBase III/III Plus, and WordPerfect,* 21097-6
	Using Computers and Applications Software Featuring Lotus 1-2-3, dBase III/III Plus, and WordPerfect, 21179-4
	Business Applications Software for the IBM PC Alternate Edition with VP-Planner, dBase III/III Plus, and WordPerfect, 21000-3
	Business Applications Software for the IBM PC Alternate Edition with Lotus 1-2-3, dBase III/III Plus, and WordPerfect, 21042-9
KHAN	*Beginning Structured COBOL,* 21174-3
LETRAUNIK	*MVS/XA JCL: A Practical Approach,* 20916-1
LIPNER/KALMAN	*Computer Law: Cases and Materials,* 21104-2
MELLARD	*Introduction to Business Programming Using Pascal,* 20547-6
MORGAN	*Introduction to Structured Programming Using Turbo Pascal Version 5.0 on the IBM PC,* 20770-3
MORIBER	*Structured BASIC Programming, Second Edition,* 20715-0
REYNOLDS/RIECKS	*Introduction to Business Telecommunications, Second Edition,* 20815-7
ROSEN	*Office Automation and Information Systems,* 20557-3
SCHATT	*Microcomputers in Business and Society,* 20862-9
SPRANKLE	*Problem Solving and Programming Concepts,* 20867-X
STARK	*The Complete Textbook of Lotus 1-2-3,* 21103-4
SZYMANSKI	*Computers and Information Systems in Business,* 20905-6
SZYMANSKI/	*Computers and Application Software,* 20904-8
SZYMANSKI/MORRIS/ PULSCHEN	*Introduction to Computers and Information Systems,* 20768-1

PREFACE

The advent of the microcomputer continues to bring revolutionary changes to the information environment of today's organizations. As these changes continue to affect every aspect of the organization, many individuals, untrained in the discipline of programming theory, will be expected to use microcomputers to perform their everyday tasks.

This text is designed for any course in information systems where learning to use applications software as a problem-solving tool is necessary. The text has been carefully conceived to provide students with extensive hands-on experience in using microcomputers. Every portion of the text has been thoroughly tested with students of varying degrees of technical sophistication with microcomputers. The result is a text that will work equally well with students who have significant microcomputer background as with those who have little or no exposure to the computer and to computer fundamentals.

SCOPE AND SEQUENCE

This text has been organized into six self-contained modules that take the student command-by-command through the use of the software, its capabilities, and its advantages/disadvantages for given applications. The modular format allows the instructor to choose which software to teach and in what order.

Each software module has been organized in an easy-to-follow format that has been developed for maximum flexibility.

- Each software module begins with an introduction that provides the student with an understanding of the software's fundamental application and the key terminology associated with it.
- *Tutorial Lessons* take the student step-by-step through the basics of the software, introducing its essential commands, concepts, and structures. The objective of this section is to bring the student to an initial level of competency with the software.
- Several *Exercises* are included to provide a problem-solving environment in which the student can continue to learn about the software. The exercises are designed to reinforce previously learned material and to bridge the prescriptive approach found in the tutorial lessons with the descriptive approach found in the command summary.
- *Cases* provide the ultimate challenge to the problem-solving skills of the student. Here the processes of analysis, design, testing, and implementation are combined with the student's technical expertise in the completion of a task.
- The *Hints and Hazards* section presents tips for improving efficiency and avoiding frustrating pitfalls in the use of the software.
- *Study Questions* test the student's understanding with carefully thought-out questions that focus on conceptual issues involved in using the software.
- *Additional Topics* are covered to explore important advanced topics that are more appropriately taught by example-based discussions than by tutorial or command summary presentations.
- An *Operation and Command Summary* found at the end of each module provides an extensive reference for the student. The summary includes brief explanations and examples in the use of the software's commands, functions, and control keys.

TEXT ORGANIZATION

The text begins with a comprehensive, yet concise, discussion of microcomputer hardware, software, and the process involved in applying the microcomputer system to accomplishing tasks. The objective of the introduction is to provide a general knowledge base upon which students may begin to build an understanding of data processing and their microcomputer skills.

Software Coverage

- *WordPerfect* (Version 5.0) is one of the most popular word processing software in use today. Learning to use a word processing application is immediately useful to students, who will use it to write papers, résumés, and written assignments.
- *Lotus 1-2-3* (Version 2.1) is the most popular spreadsheet software. Knowing how to use Lotus is rapidly becoming a job requirement for many organizations, and a growing number of college courses are requiring the use of Lotus 1-2-3 in their college work.
- *dBASE III Plus* is perhaps the most important software for students to learn since the majority of the data processing problems faced by today's organizations concern effectively managing, storing, and retrieving database-type data.

The *Data Transfer between Applications Software* module introduces a subject neglected in other texts of this type. It provides instruction on how to move data from one software application to another. This module provides the opportunity to gain a conceptual understanding of data structures as well as the ability to use applications software to the greatest extent of its processing power.

The final module of the manual details the features of one of the most commonly used programming languages, BASICA. This module is included to give students a basic understanding of structured programming theory to enhance their use of applications software.

Several important appendices are included in the manual. Two of these, *Appendix A, The Basics of DOS,* and *Appendix C, Expressions,* explore the important topics of the microcomputer's operating system and use of computer expressions. Since the materials are not necessarily introductory in nature, they were placed into appendices so that they can be covered at any time during the course. Two other appendices, *Appendix D, Lotus 1-2-3 Release 2.2 and 3,* and *Appendix E, Using VP-Planner Plus with This Manual,* have been included to allow users of these software packages to use the text successfully.

DESIGN FEATURES

Because it is important for students to check their work against what is happening on the computer screen while they are learning, we have included accurate representations of the screens throughout every instructional step of each tutorial module. These screen representations provide immediate feedback regarding student's correct interaction with the software, as well as signaling errors or hazards that may have occurred while the student was inputting data. These should be checked at every stage while the student is working through the software.

The use of color in this text has been designed for maximum instructional benefit. Every time the text signals hands-on work at the keyboard, the type appears in blue rather than black type. The explanations, then, are distinct from the tutorial sections, and students are easily prompted as to when they are next expected to enter data with the keyboard. Further, the use of color separates the computer's response from the user's input, making it easy for students to see the results of their input.

ACKNOWLEDGMENTS

In 1982, the Chiles Foundation provided a grant to the School of Business Administration, Portland State University, for the purchase of a microcomputing laboratory to be used by students and faculty. Without this far-sighted action and the Foundation's continued support, this manual would not have been written.

After several years of use at PSU, the material in this text has evolved through five rewrites to its present form. Its continued success at reaching its learning objectives is due largely to the constructive feedback of several thousand PSU students and their instructors.

Special acknowledgment must be given to Brent Simonson, School of Business Administration PSU 1989 graduate. Brent's research, writing, technical expertise, and standards of excellence are largely responsible for the quality of the material in this manual.

When it became time to have the manual published, a new group of individuals became involved in helping produce the finished product.

These individuals reviewed the manuscript and provided many valuable comments and suggestions: Rosario Arevalo, Golden Gate University; Glen Boswell, San Antonio College; James Buchan, Yuba College; Francis Cecil, Yuba College; James Davis, Marywood College; Steve Deam, Milwaukee Area Technical College; Beth Defoor, Eastern New Mexico University; Richard Ender, University of Alaska-Anchorage; Alex Ephraim, Monroe Business Institute; Richard Ernst, Sullivan Junior College; Barbara Felty, Harrisburg Area Community College; Pat Fenton, West Valley College; Vicki Giordano, Nova University; Patricia Green, Temple Jr. College; David Hale, Texas Technical University; Edward Hanning, Marywood College; Phyllis Helms, Randolph College; David Hemenway, Montgomery College; James Horn, Vincennes University; Wes Jones, DeVry Institute of Technology; Douglas Kerley, Florida Community College; Candice Marble, Wentworth Military Academy; John Miller, Williamsport Area Community College; J. D. Oliver, Prairie View A & M; Gene Rathswohl, University of San Diego; Linda Rosenberg, Layola College; Vivek Shah, South West Texas State; Duane Shelton, Layola College; Gene Taylor, Central Oregon Community College; Ed Thomas, Stanly Tech; Megan Tucker, Vermont Community College; William Viereck, Saint Joseph's University; and G. W. Willis, Baylor University.

Finally, the staff of Merrill Publishing Company deserves special recognition for their efforts to produce this text. Their attention to detail, concern for pedagogical issues, and commitment of resources have resulted in producing the best possible finished product. In particular, we would like to thank Pam Bennett, Production Coordinator, and Vern Anthony, Acquisitions Editor, for their efforts.

CONTENTS

dBASE III Plus Version 1.1

BASICA

Appendices

Business Applications Software for IBM and Compatible Microcomputers

Fundamentals of Using Microcomputers

FUNDAMENTALS OF USING MICROCOMPUTERS

The microcomputer is a tool—a means to an end. Every tool holds functional properties that make it the "more appropriate" or "best" tool to use in accomplishing a given task or solving a particular problem. A hammer, for instance, is an excellent tool for driving nails, but is nearly impossible to use for correctly driving screws. It is the responsibility of the tool user to decide which tools are appropriate for accomplishing a certain task or reaching a desired objective. To make such decisions, the user must have access to a selection of alternate tools and an understanding of each tool's functional properties.

The computer's basic value as a tool lies in its ability to rapidly organize or calculate data items into a useful or meaningful form. The end results (the organized or calculated data) of using the tool are referred to as *information.* The original (unorganized/uncalculated) data items are referred to as *data,* and the computer's act of organizing or calculating the data items is called *data processing* (DP) or *electronic data processing* (EDP).

The scope and variety of tasks to which the microcomputer can be applied are immense. For this reason, the microcomputer can be considered a general purpose tool—one which provides the user with the means to accomplish many different ends. The microcomputer obtains its flexible nature from the fact that it operates within a system of component elements.

The three major components of any microcomputer system are its hardware, software, and user(s). Microcomputer systems differ from other computer systems because they usually are designed for a single user. In this manual you will be considered the user. Your role is to gain a functional understanding of how you can use the hardware and software covered here to solve organizational problems.

Microcomputer Hardware

The tangible (or physical) part of a microcomputer system is a piece of equipment with individual mechanical and electronic parts. The equipment and its parts are referred to as computer *hardware.* The hardware of a microcomputer system consists of at least five basic devices, as shown in the following drawing.

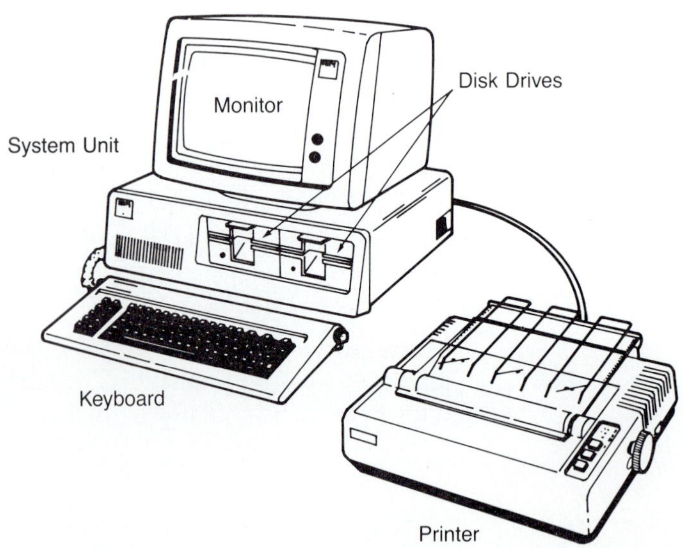

The System Unit

The *system unit* is the central hardware component. It is the device that contains the microprocessor and integrated circuit (IC) chips that perform the manipulations (organization and calculation) of data items.

Within the circuit chips of the system unit, data items are represented by electrical patterns of high and low voltages. A single voltage pattern element is called a *bit* (binary digit). Its current state (high or low voltage) is usually represented by a 1 for high voltage and a 0 for low voltage. Eight bits are combined to create a single pattern called a *byte*. In general, it takes a byte (a single pattern of eight bits) to represent one character of data in the circuit chips of the system unit.

Computing standards have been established to specify the bit patterns to be used when representing certain data characters. For instance, one well-known standard called ASCII (American Standard Code for Information Interchange) establishes that the upper-case A character is represented by the seven-bit pattern 1000001. (When the ASCII standard was established, one particular bit in the byte was used to check for errors in the byte's pattern of bits, and did not appear as an element of the pattern itself. This one bit is called the *parity check bit*.)

The byte is the basic data unit of the computer. One measure of a system unit's computing capacity is the number of bytes of data its circuit chips are able to hold at one time. The capacity to hold data is referred to as being the system's *memory* (or *primary storage*), which is usually described in 1,024 byte (*kilobytes* or K) or 1,048,576 byte (*megabyte* or M) quantities. That is, a microcomputer having 640K of memory is able to hold 655,360 characters of data in memory.

Another measure of a system unit's computing performance is the speed at which it can perform the individual manipulations of data. A microcomputer's speed is a function of two main factors: the rate at which it performs the manipulations (determined by the system's *clock speed*) and the number of adjacent bits it can manipulate at one time (called the *word size*). The system unit's clock speed is rated in millions of cycles per second (megahertz or MHz). Clock speeds between 4 and 16 MHz are common, with 16 MHz being four times faster than 4 MHz. Word size refers to the number of bits the microprocessor manipulates at once. Common word sizes for microcomputer processors are 8, 16, and 32 bits. In general, the larger the bit processor, the faster the microcomputer.

The Microcomputer Keyboard

The microcomputer's *keyboard* (also called the console) provides the user with a way to enter characters of data to be held in the microcomputer's memory. In addition to the keys you would normally find on a standard typewriter, a microcomputer's keyboard includes control keys, function keys, cursor movement keys, and a numeric keypad for 10-key data entry.

There are two common styles of keyboards currently used with the IBM and compatible microcomputers. The keyboards differ mainly in the location of their keys, as shown in the following illustrations.

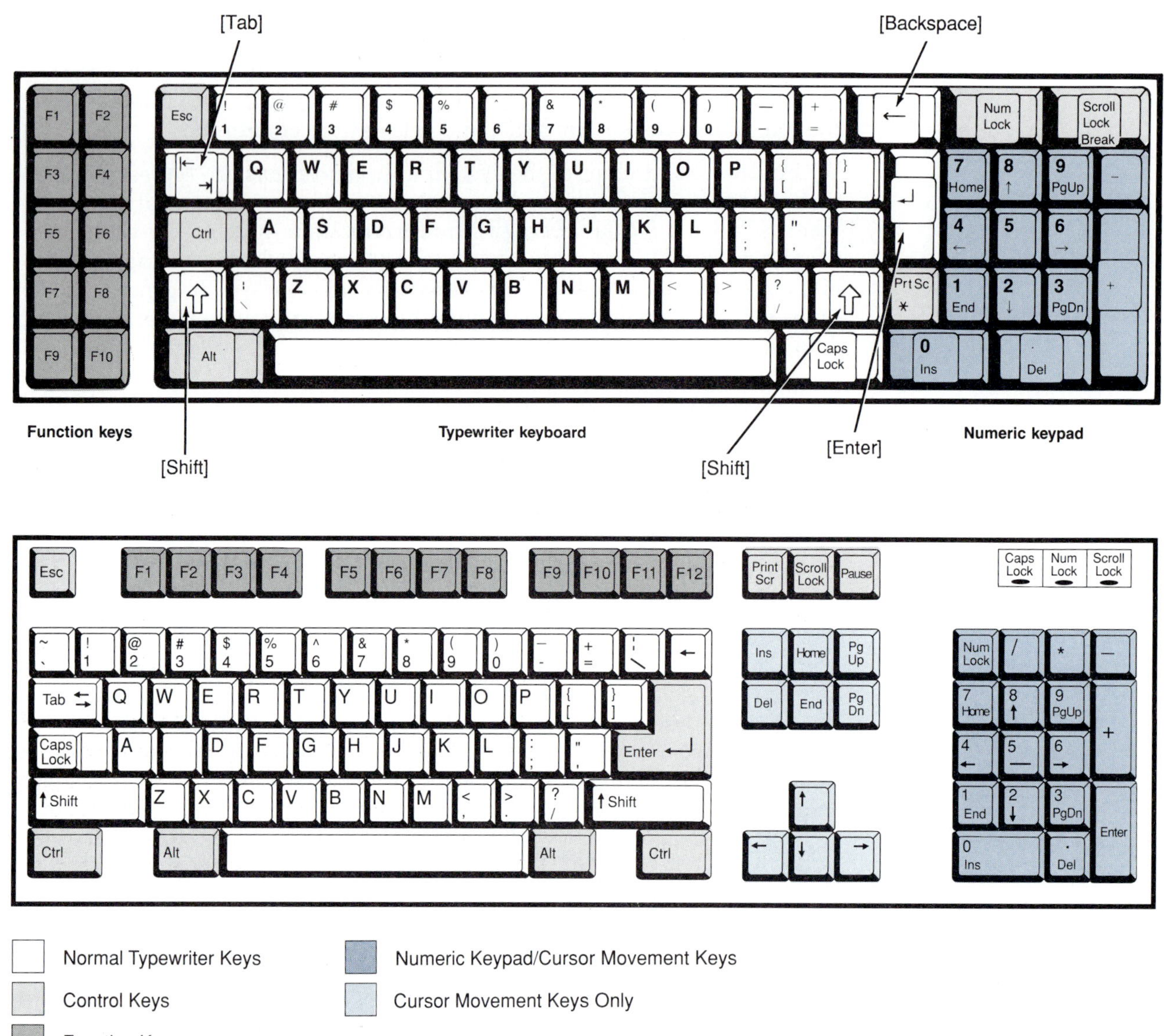

The Microcomputer Monitor

The microcomputer *monitor* is used to display an image of the data being transmitted between the user and the rest of the microcomputer system. The most popular type of monitor (one that uses a cathode-ray tube or *CRT*) produces an image on a phosphor-coated screen by passing an electronic beam across it. A fairly new type of monitor called a flat screen monitor uses liquid crystal display *(LCD)* technology to produce its image of the data.

Monitor quality is often expressed in units of screen resolution called *pixels.* A pixel describes the smallest discrete image that the monitor is able to produce. The resolution of the monitor is defined by the number of pixels on a screen. For instance, a high-resolution monitor has a display of 640 pixels horizontally by 460 pixels vertically. The following illustration shows an arrangement of pixels used to create upper- and lower-case images of the letter A on a high-resolution monitor screen.

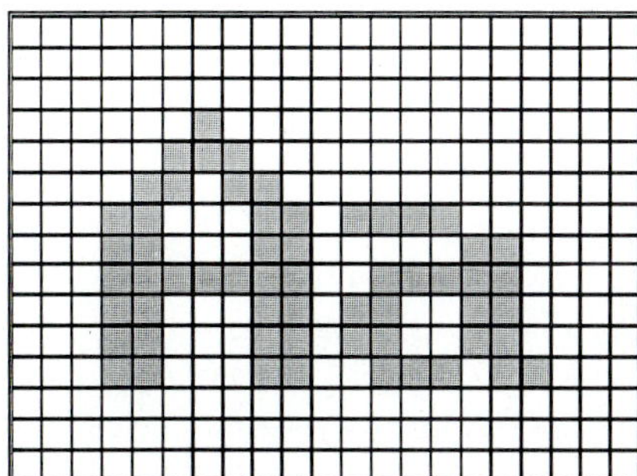

The Microcomputer Disk Drives

The microcomputer's *disk drive* devices are usually mounted in the front of (or inside of) the system unit. They are, nonetheless, hardware components considered separate from the system unit.

As mentioned earlier, data are represented in the microcomputer's memory (primary storage) in patterns of high and low voltages. When the electrical power to the system unit is disrupted, the patterns cease to exist. To help overcome the volatility of the microcomputer's primary storage, disk drives are used to provide what is called *secondary storage.*

Secondary storage involves a process of recording (copying) the patterns of data currently in memory onto a medium made of material coated with iron oxide (called *magnetic storage media*). The process is quite similar to recording sounds (patterns of vibration) onto an audio-cassette tape. The act of copying data from memory onto magnetic storage media is termed a *write operation.* The process of copying data from magnetic storage into memory is termed a *read operation.*

Secondary Storage Types

A microcomputer's magnetic storage media usually comes in the form of a flat, circular disk that is placed into the disk drive. To copy the data currently in memory onto the disk (or vice versa), the disk drive spins the disk while it moves a *read/write head* (the disk drive's read/write mechanism) back and forth across the surface of the disk. A disk's capacity to hold data is usually expressed in kilobyte or megabyte quantities in the same manner as memory's capacity to hold data. Two types of disks are now commonly used—*floppy disks* and *hard disks.*

Floppy Disks Floppy disks are made of oxide-coated mylar and are enclosed in a cover (called a *disk jacket*). For the IBM and compatible microcomputers, floppy disks come in two different sizes—5¼″ and 3½″ disks.

The two sizes of floppy disks require different types of disk drives to read and write their data. The 5¼″ floppy disks are usually capable of holding 360K of data. Although smaller in size, the newer 3½″ floppy disks may hold up to 1.44M (or 1,440K) of data. Floppy disks have a hub ring or hub spindle which the disk drive grasps in order to spin the disk within its jacket.

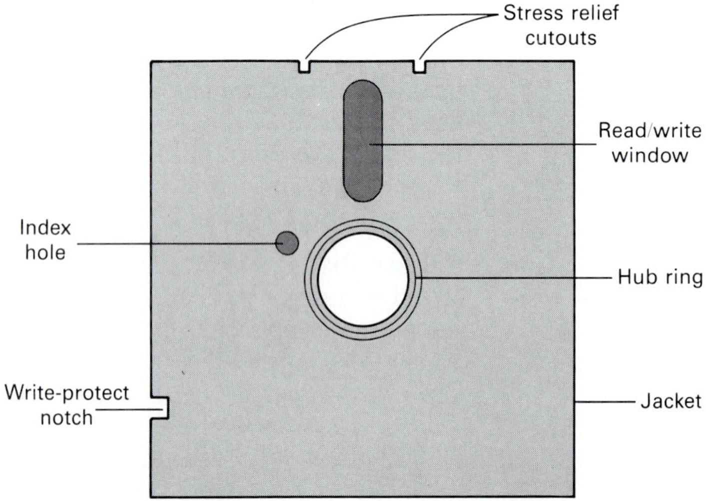

Both styles of disk have a *read/write window* which allows the disk drive's read/write head to access the magnetic storage media. On the 5¼″ disk, the read/write window exposes a portion of the disk, and so care must be taken not to touch or soil the exposed area. On the 3½″ disk, the read/write window is protected with a metal shutter which is automatically pushed open when the disk is inserted into the disk drive. On the 5¼″ disk an *index hole* is used to determine the relative rotational position of the disk as it is spinning.

The 5¼″ disk has a *write-protect notch* in the disk jacket that, when covered with a piece of tape, prevents the microcomputer from writing data onto the disk. The microcomputer, however, is still able to read data from the disk. The 3½″ disk has a write-protect switch that performs the same function.

Hard Disks Hard disks are platters usually made of an oxide-coated metal (such as aluminum). They are permanently built into the disk drive that performs the hard disk read/write operations. (Several disk platters may be used to constitute one hard disk.) The hard-disk drive and its hard disk are usually installed inside the case that surrounds the system unit. Although hard disks vary in their storage capacities, all hard disks have substantially greater storage capacity than do floppy disks. The lowest capacity hard disk today can hold about 20M (20,000K) of data. Hard disks exceeding 160M (160,000K) are available for microcomputers.

One measure of any disk drive's performance is the storage capacity of the disks it is designed to read and write. Another measure of performance is the speed at which it reads and writes data to and from the disk (called the *average access time*). The access time for a disk drive depends, in part, on the speed at which the disk drive spins the disk. A typical disk drive, designed to access a 5¼″ disk, spins the disk at a rate of 300 revolutions per minute (rpm). A typical hard-disk drive spins its disk at a rate of 3,600 rpm.

Another important factor that affects access time is the distance the read/write head must move in order to access the data on a disk. Since a 3½″ disk holds more data in less space than a 5¼″ disk (that is, the data are more densely packed on a 3½″ disk), the time it takes to move the read/write head to specific data on the smaller disk is substantially reduced.

A new disk (and disk drive) that is being developed using optical laser technology promises dramatic improvements in both storage capacity and average access time.

The Printer

The *printer's* function is to produce printed copies of the data or information held in the memory of the microcomputer. Such copies are called *hard copies* since they are not electrical or magnetic in nature. Of all the microcomputer hardware components, printers vary the most in the number of types available. Printer performance is usually measured in terms of print resolution (quality) and speed. However, other factors such as graphics and color capabilities, number of paper sizes and shapes that can be fed through the printer, variety of available fonts, and noise made while printing often are important considerations in evaluating printers. The three major types of printers in use today are *impact printers, nonimpact printers,* and *plotter printers.*

Impact Printers

Impact printers strike an ink ribbon to produce a printed image in the same manner as a conventional typewriter does. The two most popular types of impact printers are *dot matrix printers* and *daisy wheel printers.*

Dot matrix printers strike the ink ribbon with a *print head* that contains from 9 to 24 *pins.* To print a character-size image of data, the printer determines which pins will be used to strike the ink ribbon. In general, the more pins contained in the print head of a dot matrix printer, the greater the resolution of the printed characters will be. Most dot matrix printers sold today are capable of printing microcomputer graphics. Dot matrix printers vary in the speed at which they are able to print—from 80 characters per second (cps) to about 450 cps. Printing speed decreases dramatically when graphic images are being printed with a dot matrix printer.

Daisy wheel printers use interchangeable print wheels which have radiating spokes. Each spoke has one or more characters physically cast into its outer end. A daisy wheel produces its printed characters by striking the appropriate spoke with a print hammer. The spoke then strikes the ink ribbon. Since they use a cast image to produce a printed character, daisy wheel printers produce very high-quality printed text. However, daisy wheel printers are typically slow (10 to 60 cps), noisy, and are unable to print microcomputer graphic images.

Nonimpact Printers

The most popular nonimpact printer is the *laser jet printer,* a printer that bonds liquid toner (ink) to a sheet of paper using the heat of a laser beam. The toner sticks to areas on the page that are holding an electrical charge which also is produced by the printer. The printing technology used in the laser jet printer is the same technology used in the modern office copier. Laser jet printers have very high resolution, are quiet, and are fast, printing between 8 and 10 pages of text per minute. They also are able to print very high-resolution graphics.

Plotter Printers

A plotter is a type of printer that moves ink pens across a page to produce printed images. Most plotters allow for several pens of different colors to be used while printing. Plotters are most useful in preparing presentation-quality graphs, charts, maps, and so on. They have very high-quality print and are about as fast as dot matrix printers at producing printed microcomputer graphics.

MICROCOMPUTER SOFTWARE

Software is the second required element of a microcomputer system. Software can be defined as a set of instructions that directs and controls the operation of the microcomputer's hardware. Software is held in the microcomputer's memory while it controls the system's hardware devices. By placing different software into memory at different times, the microcomputer system acquires its flexibility and becomes a general purpose tool.

Software can be divided into five general, although not clear-cut, categories: operating systems, programming languages, canned programs, utility software, and applications software. The first category, operating systems, includes a type of software that must be in memory prior to using any of the other software listed here. The operating system software covered later in this manual is IBM's disk operating system or DOS (see Appendix A for a discussion of DOS). The last category, applications software, is by far the most popular type of software used with microcomputers. The following is a brief discussion of the three general types of applications software: *spreadsheets, word processing,* and *database management systems.*

Spreadsheets

Spreadsheet applications software enable the microcomputer user to create an electronic version of the accountant's standard spreadsheet. Lotus 1-2-3 is the product name for one popular spreadsheet software.

With spreadsheet software, text, numbers, and formulas (data items) are entered into a two-dimensional grid (or matrix) which is presented on the monitor screen. The formulas in the spreadsheet are calculated by the software, and their locations on the screen display the calculated results, as shown in the following spreadsheet.

```
A1: [W12]                                                          READY

         A            B                C               D          E
1
2
3              Beginning Sales   $100,000.00     in January
4              Growth in Sales          5.0%     Per Month
5              Cost of Goods           75.0%      of Sales
6
7
8                                   COST OF
9                   SALES         GOODS SOLD        NET
10
11      January   $100,000.00     $75,000.00     $25,000.00
12     February   $105,000.00     $78,750.00     $26,250.00
13        March   $110,250.00     $82,687.50     $27,562.50
14        April   $115,762.50     $86,821.88     $28,940.63
15          May   $121,550.63     $91,162.97     $30,387.66
16         June   $127,628.16     $95,721.12     $31,907.04
17         July   $134,009.56    $100,507.17     $33,502.39
18
19
20
07-Jan-90   11:09 AM
```

In this spreadsheet, text has been entered to describe the various columns and rows of numbers. The three numbers at the top of the screen representing beginning sales ($100,000), growth in sales (5%), and cost of goods (75%) have been entered as *key values*—numbers from which spreadsheet formulas derive their displayed values. The values displayed in the table portion of the spreadsheet are generated by formulas that have been entered into the spreadsheet.

A spreadsheet formula usually is composed of references to other locations in the spreadsheet. The locations use column letters and row numbers (seen on the border of the spreadsheet) to describe where the values included in the formula may be found. For instance, the formula in the location C14 (April's Cost of Goods Sold) is entered in a form similar to B14*C5 (April's Sales times the Cost of Goods percentage).

When the key values of a spreadsheet are changed, the formulas within the spreadsheet are automatically recalculated to display their new values. Therefore, when the data processing task can be described or solved with a number- or formula-based model, the task is a likely candidate for spreadsheet applications software.

Word Processing

Word processing applications software enables the microcomputer user to create sentences, paragraphs, and pages of text. WordPerfect is the product name of one popular word processing software.

With word processing software, the user is presented with a blank "page" on the monitor screen where sentences and paragraphs may be entered by using the microcomputer's keyboard. Whatever the user types on the keyboard appears on the monitor screen, much as it would appear on a piece of paper in a typewriter. An example of how the monitor screen might appear follows.

```
JEROME C. FAIRFAX

              P.O. Box 198  Portland, OR 97207
            (503) 244-8733 H    (503) 229-2724 W

EDUCATION

      Bachelor of Arts, Business Administration - Marketing
      Bachelor of Arts, Spanish
      Certificate of International Business Studies
      PORTLAND STATE UNIVERSITY, Portland, OR  June 1990

EXPERIENCE

      Front Desk/Public Relations
      Center Court Athletic club, Portland, OR.  Greet and register
      members and guests.  Conduct tours of facility and explain
      benefits.  Attend to members needs, serve snack bar items and
      make reservations.  Promote club programs, answer telephone
      inquiries, collect and process payments on accounts.
      (September 1988 to present)

      Manager
      Coffee House Juice Bar, Portland, OR.  Directed set-up and
A:\RESUME                                 Doc 2 Pg 1 Ln 0.5" Pos 1"
```

The main difference between using a typewriter and using word processing software is that with word processing the act of typing text is separate from printing it. In word processing, the text may be printed after the user has finished typing the text. The advantage of word processing is that nothing is "committed" until it is printed. The user can move freely through the text "pages" shown on the monitor screen, stopping wherever it is appropriate to insert, delete, copy, or move a word, group of words, or even entire pages of text.

With word processing the user may format the text in professional, attractive, and efficient ways. Paragraphs already typed may be automatically adjusted to fit within new margins. Entirely separate texts or parts of texts may be merged to form new composites for form letters, contracts, or résumés. Topic headings may be automatically centered on the page, key words may be typed boldface or underlined, and line spacing may be changed at any time.

Today's word processing software typically include features for finding spelling errors and typographical errors, providing synonyms for words (a thesaurus feature), and automatically inserting inside addresses and proper names at the appropriate places in form letters or contracts. When the data processing task can be described as being the professional presentation of text, the task is a likely candidate for word processing applications software.

Database Management Systems

Database management systems (DBMS) applications software enable the microcomputer user to manipulate data that are record-like in nature. Examples of such data may include employee records, customer/client records, shipping and receiving invoices, and production reports. dBASE III PLUS is the product name for one popular DBMS applications software.

The data items entered by the user of a DBMS software are held in fields that comprise records that together constitute a set of data called a *database file.* A database file is shown in the following screen.

LSTNAME-----	FSTNAME--	ADDRESS----------------------	CITY------	STATE	ZIP--
Anderson	Terry	2525 N.E 34th	Portland	OR	97206
Anderson	Ken	1235 S.W Wedgewood Dr.	Portland	OR	97201
Bennett	Molly	3356 S.E Dale St.	Portland	OR	97214
Brown	Anthony	5926 S.E Stark Street	Portland	OR	97230
Campbell	Carl	559 N. Hayden Bay Dr.	Portland	OR	97034
Chin	Connie	8765 N. Hill Dr.	Portland	OR	97215
Cochran	Debra	12390 S.W. Hall Blvd.	Beaverton	OR	97543
Davis	Brad	1010 N.E. Jove	Portland	OR	97202
Douglas	Terri	18763 N.E 180th	Portland	OR	97450
Hilmes	Lori	918 S.W. Pine #3	Portland	OR	97201
House	Don	2109 Andresen Road	Vancouver	WA	98682
Johnson	David	4829 N.E 48th	Portland	OR	97211
Johnson	Sharon	18106 S.W Shaw	Aloha	OR	97007
Johnson	Bill	775 S.W. Main	Beaverton	OR	97005
Jones	Tom	32990 N.W. Dawn St.	Portland	OR	97203
Kilmes	Sara	9073 N.W. Halsey	Portland	OR	97201
Kuhn	Edward	309 N.W. Everett	Portland	OR	97210

BROWSE <B:> EMPS Rec: 8/28 Ins

View and edit fields.

Once a database file has been created, the DBMS allows the user to rapidly produce reports on those records which meet certain criteria. For instance, a report based on the example database shown here might include the first and last names for all people living in the state of Washington. The criteria for such extractions of information from database files may be substantially more complex. For instance, a DBMS software command similar to

```
REPORT FORM Names FOR city = "Portland" .AND. ZIP > "97207" .OR.
city = "Beaverton"
```

may be used to produce a report that lists the names of all people living in Portland who have ZIP code numbers greater than 97207 as well as the names of all people living in Beaverton.

There are two related advantages to maintaining database files with a microcomputer system. The first advantage is the ability of the microcomputer to reorganize the records in the database. A DBMS software is able to organize (sort) the records in the database by any of the data items in a record. The second advantage is the ability of the DBMS software to quickly perform counting and totaling operations for the records in the database. When the data processing task can be described as the selective treatment of record-type data, the task is a likely candidate for database management systems applications software.

THE EVOLUTION OF HARDWARE/SOFTWARE

It is important to note that any precise description of microcomputer hardware or software merely represents a "snapshot" in time. Just a few years ago, system units with 64K memory with one 160K floppy disk drive were considered state of the art, and few people could imagine a need for more computing capacity in a microcomputer. VisiCalc and WordStar Version 1.0 (two now-extinct versions of software) amazed microcomputer users in 1982, yet the same software would be considered quite primitive by today's standards.

In the preceding discussions, various categories and definitions have been presented to facilitate an initial understanding of the nature of the microcomputer as a tool. Such categories and definitions have a tendency to "degrade" over time. For example, in the past it was clear that spreadsheet, word processing, and DBMS software were fundamentally different software designed to perform fundamentally different data processing tasks. While this general rule still holds true, there is a trend in today's applications software to cross over the functional lines. For instance, WordPerfect Version 5.0 is an exceptionally good word processing applications software; however, it is now able to perform simple and limited spreadsheet and DBMS-type data processing functions.

There is a cyclical pattern to the evolution of microcomputer technology. The first event to occur in the pattern is the development and production of new hardware. To date, the most important of such developments have provided greater processing speed and primary/secondary storage. The next event to occur is the development of software having features that use the improved performance of the hardware. The last event in the cycle is the training (or upgrading) of the user—which is the objective of this text. The user will be the final microcomputer system element discussed here.

The role of the user in a microcomputer system is best described by examining how the elements of a microcomputer system interrelate during the process of applying the tool to a task. The examples and concepts presented here provide an overview of generalities concerned with using the microcomputer.

EXAMPLE SESSION STEP 1
Getting Started

The user begins by sitting down at the microcomputer and inserting a disk into a disk drive. The user next turns on the microcomputer and its monitor. After a few moments a light on the disk drive comes on and a "whirring" sound is heard. Shortly, an A> (A prompt) appears on the monitor screen. The user has just booted DOS.

Computer Memory

Inside the system unit are circuit chips that provide the microcomputer's memory. There are two types of memory in the system unit—read only memory *(ROM)* and random access memory *(RAM)*.

ROM is a portion of memory that holds special sets of instructions that are sometimes called *firmware*. Firmware consists of instruction sets that are permanently etched into ROM circuit chips. That is, the data held in ROM is nonvolatile—it does not disappear when the power to the system unit is disrupted.

The instruction sets (or *programs*) in ROM relate, in large part, directly to the microcomputer's internal operations. You can consider ROM a sort of subconscious memory for the microcomputer.

RAM can be thought of as memory space which is available to hold software, data entered by the user, and information created by processing the data. Before the microcomputer is turned on, RAM can be thought of as empty space. The model here and its subsequent development illustrate the concept.

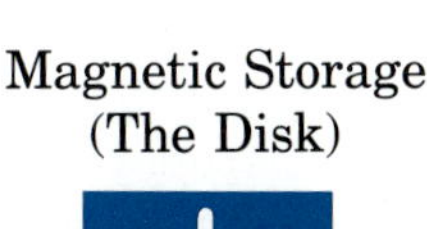

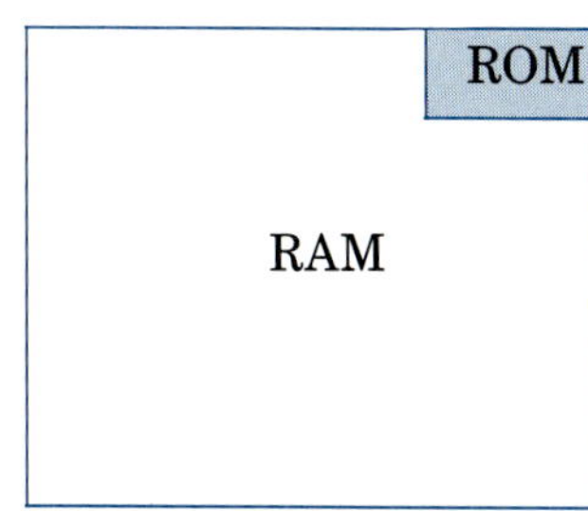

When the microcomputer is first turned on, there is a short wait while ROM helps the microcomputer get started. The programs in ROM instruct the microcomputer to check its parts to see if any are missing or not working, to check to see if any attachments are connected, and to perform other "housekeeping" chores necessary for the microcomputer to function properly while it is being used. ROM then instructs the microcomputer to check the disk drive(s) for the presence of a disk. At this point the microcomputer is looking for an operating system software.

The Operating System Software

If a software is stored on a disk, it is stored there as a distinct set of instructions under a specific name. The set of instructions is called a *file,* and the name is referred to as its *filename.*

DOS is the operating system software for the IBM microcomputer. When the microcomputer checks its disk drive(s), it has been instructed by ROM to look for a file with the filename COMMAND.COM. This file is one part of an interlinked group of files collectively called DOS.

DOS software instructs the microcomputer on how to operate its disk drives so that it can find other files that may be on a disk. It also instructs the microcomputer on how to respond if the user types certain messages (called DOS commands) on the keyboard. The DOS software must be in RAM before any other applications software may be used with the microcomputer.

When the microcomputer starts its search for the DOS software, it begins by checking the first floppy disk drive to see if a disk is inserted there. The first floppy disk drive has the hardware device name A: and is called the *A: drive.* If there is another floppy disk drive, it will usually have the hardware device name B: (or *B: drive*). When there is a disk in the A: drive, but the disk does not have the DOS software stored on it, the microcomputer will respond with a message similar to:

```
Non-System disk or disk error
Replace and strike any key when ready
```

The message simply means that the disk in the A: drive does not have the DOS software (the "system") on it, and that the microcomputer is pausing for the user to insert a disk holding the DOS software into the A: disk drive.

If there is no disk in the A: drive and the microcomputer has a hard-disk drive, it will next search for DOS on the hard disk. A hard-disk drive usually has the device name C: (or *C: drive*).

The user knows the microcomputer has found and automatically read DOS into RAM when an A> or C> (the letter of the prompt depends on the disk drive where DOS was found) appears on the monitor screen. In the example above, the A> on the screen indicates that DOS was on the disk that the user placed in the first floppy disk drive (A:).

The act of reading DOS into RAM is a copying process referred to as booting, reading, or loading the system. The software is not physically moved off the disk, but rather the microcomputer creates a copy of the software and places the copy into RAM.

The DOS Operating Level

Reading DOS from the disk into RAM uses up part of the space available there to hold data, as illustrated in the following.

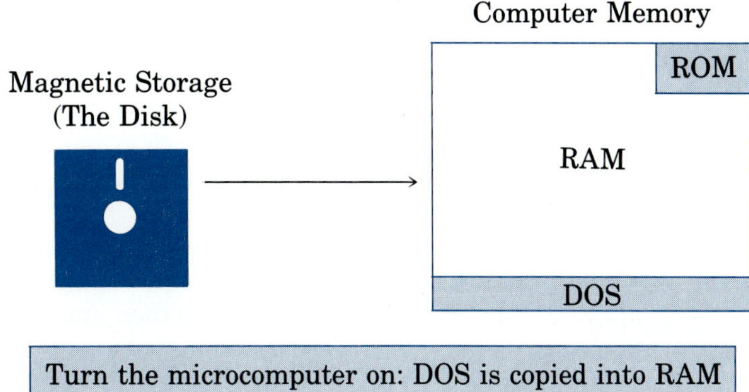

Turn the microcomputer on: DOS is copied into RAM

At this point the microcomputer system is said to be at the *DOS operating level* or the *system level.* The microcomputer is now able to perform several small but important tasks, including reading other software into RAM.

EXAMPLE SESSION STEP 2
Using the Microcomputer at the DOS Operating Level

After the user sees the A> (DOS prompt) on the monitor screen, the keyboard is used to type **DIR.** The user then presses the Enter key. The microcomputer responds by putting the following on the monitor screen.

```
A>DIR

 Volume in drive A has no label
 Directory of  A:\

COMMAND  COM    25307  3-17-87  12:00p
WP       EXE   251904  9-23-88   5:37p
        2 File(s)    452608 bytes free

A>
```

The DOS *drive*> Prompt

DOS's *drive*> prompt indicates that it is the user's turn to use the microcomputer's keyboard to send commands to the microcomputer. The microcomputer system uses the monitor screen to display the commands being given to it and to display the results of executing commands. Commands are sent to the microcomputer when the user presses the Enter key (a keystroke represented in this text with the ↵ character).

Entering a DOS Command

In the example, the user used the keyboard to type **DIR,** and then sent the command to the microcomputer system by typing ↵. **DIR** is the DOS command that causes the microcomputer to list the directory of the files found on a disk. The listed directory includes the filenames, size of the files (measured in bytes), and the date/time stamp of each of the file's date of creation and/or latest modification.

COMMAND.COM was the first filename listed on the screen, and it is the filename for the DOS software already mentioned. The directory tells the user that the file's size is about 25,000 bytes (which is roughly equivalent to 25,000 characters of data) and that it originally was dated during March of 1987.

EXAMPLE SESSION STEP 3
Reading Software into RAM

After viewing the directory of the disk on the monitor screen, the user types WP↵. Once more the disk drive light comes on and a "whirring" sound is heard. In a moment the screen appears similar to the following.

```
-











                                              Doc 1 Pg 1 Ln 1" Pos 1"
```

Loading Software into RAM

The second filename listed in the disk's directory, WP.EXE, is the filename for WordPerfect, the word processing applications software used in this example. (In reality, the WordPerfect software is composed of several files that are usually stored together on a hard disk. For the sake of example, however, it will be assumed that the software consists of one file named WP.EXE, and that the software file is stored on the floppy disk now in the A: drive.)

When the user typed WP↵, the microcomputer system did not recognize the message as a DOS command. Therefore, it set out to do the second thing that the microcomputer can do at the DOS level of operation—it started spinning the disk in the disk drive to look for a software file with the filename WP. When the microcomputer found the file, it read (copied) the software into RAM.

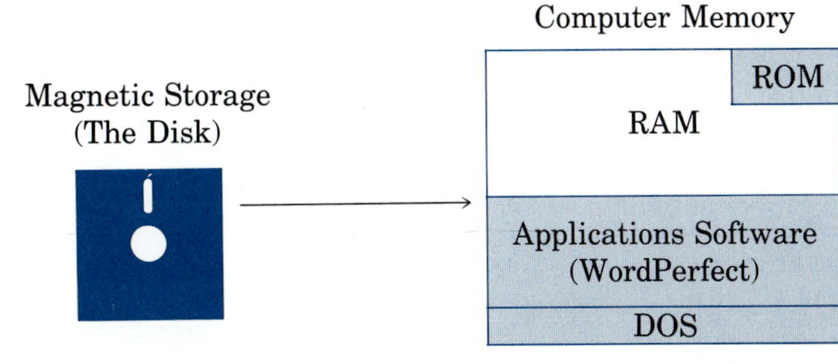

Type the filename of a software: The software is copied into RAM

The Software Operating Level

Once the software named WP was read into RAM, the screen became transformed into the editing screen of a word processing software. The microcomputer is now said to be at the *software operating level,* the level at which the user may use the commands of the software currently held in RAM.

As the software's commands are used, the user usually ends up creating something—a spreadsheet, letter, or database file. To proceed with the example here, the user will create the beginning of a report.

EXAMPLE SESSION STEP 4
Creating a File

The screen now appears as a mostly blank area with a blinking *cursor* located in the top left corner. The cursor indicates where the characters typed by the user will appear on the screen. The user begins the report by typing the following.

```
                              Introduction

Word Processing has long been an integral part of many business
organizations.  Webster defines Word Processing as "the production
of typewritten documents (as business letters) with automated and
usually computerized typing and text-editing equipment".  The
equipment may range from typewriters with memory, correction and
mag card features to dedicated word processing equipment to general
purpose computers using specialized word processing software._




A:\REPORT                                    Doc 1 Pg 1 Ln 2.5" Pos 7.1"
```

The user next moves the cursor to the top of the screen, presses and holds the keyboard's Shift key, and then types the key marked F8. The monitor screen changes to present the following.

```
Format

    1 - Line
            Hyphenation                      Line Spacing
            Justification                    Margins Left/Right
            Line Height                      Tab Set
            Line Numbering                   Widow/Orphan Protection

    2 - Page
            Center Page (top to bottom)      New Page Number
            Force Odd/Even Page              Page Numbering
            Headers and Footers              Paper Size/Type
            Margins Top/Bottom               Suppress

    3 - Document
            Display Pitch                    Redline Method
            Initial Codes/Font               Summary

    4 - Other
            Advance                          Overstrike
            Conditional End of Page          Printer Functions
            Decimal Characters               Underline Spaces/Tabs
            Language

Selection: 0
```

The user continues by typing the keystrokes necessary to change the line spacing in the report. When the user is finished typing the keystrokes, the screen returns to displaying the report being written; however, the text in the report is now double spaced.

```
                              Introduction


Word Processing has long been an integral part of many business

organizations.  Webster defines Word Processing as "the production

of typewritten documents (as business letters) with automated and

usually computerized typing and text-editing equipment".  The

equipment may range from typewriters with memory, correction and

mag card features to dedicated word processing equipment to general

purpose computers using specialized word processing software.



A:\REPORT                                     Doc 1 Pg 1 Ln 1" Pos 1"
```

Creating a Data File

In the example session here, the user created a short document by typing characters on the keyboard. The data items entered in the example consisted of characters, words, sentences, and so on. As the data were entered, a file was created in RAM. The files created while using a software occupy a portion of RAM and can be represented in the model as follows.

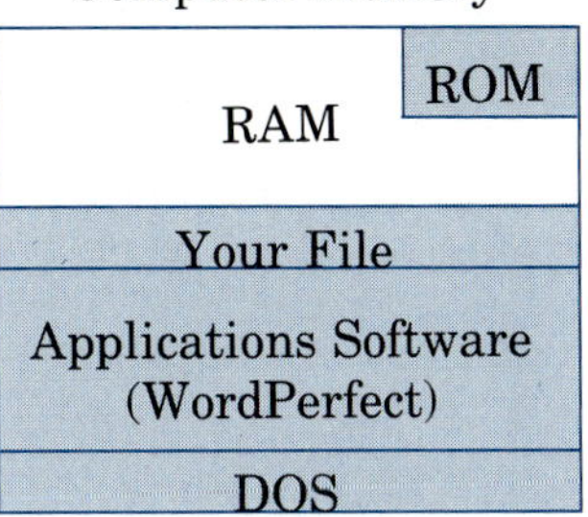

Enter data: The data are held as a file in RAM

Data Entry versus Command Modes

When the microcomputer system is used to create a spreadsheet, text, or database file, the user will be either directly entering data for the file or using the software's commands.

When text for the document was being typed in the example here, data were being directly entered into the file. However, as soon as the user typed the **Shift-F8** keystroke, the screen changed and the user began using WordPerfect commands. Until finished using the commands, the user was unable to directly enter data into the text file. There are two modes in every applications software, a data entry mode and a command mode. Beginning users can avoid many common problems if they understand this fundamental concept and remain aware of it while they use the microcomputer.

EXAMPLE SESSION STEP 5
Saving Data Files

The user is satisfied with the beginning of the report and would like to continue writing at a later time. To prepare to end the editing session, the user replaces the software disk in the A: drive with a newly *formatted disk* that will be used to hold the data file. The user then types the key marked F7. The microcomputer enters the command mode and the following message appears at the bottom of the screen.

```
Save document? (Y/N)
```

The user next types Y, and the following message appears at the bottom of the screen.

```
Document to be saved:
```

The user responds to the message by typing REPORT↵ and notices that the light on the floppy disk drive turns on for a few seconds. The next message to appear on the screen is

```
Exit WP? (Y/N)
```

The user answers this prompt by typing Y. In a few moments the DOS prompt (A>) appears on the screen. The user next types **DIR** ↵ and the following appears on the screen.

```
A>DIR

 Volume in drive A has no label
 Directory of  A:\

REPORT            1202    1-13-89   11:18a
        1 File(s)    1456128 bytes free

A>
```

Saving Your Work

As previously mentioned, RAM is known as volatile memory. *Volatile* is defined as "easily turned to vapor." Any software or data being held in RAM is lost the instant the microcomputer is turned off.

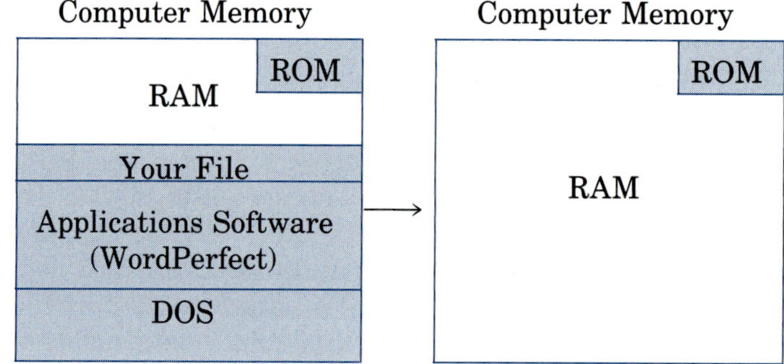

Turn the microcomputer off: All software and data in RAM are lost

With software such as DOS and WordPerfect, this is not a problem—both already exist in a permanent form on a disk. If the software are erased from RAM, the user need only have the microcomputer read them back into RAM. The user's files, however, are created in RAM and must be saved in a permanent form to be used again later.

Naming a File

Every applications software has commands that are used to save a copy of the files in RAM onto a disk. In every case the user must name the file in order to save it. Similarly, every applications software has commands to read the user's files back into RAM. The microcomputer uses the name given to the file to determine which file to retrieve from the disk.

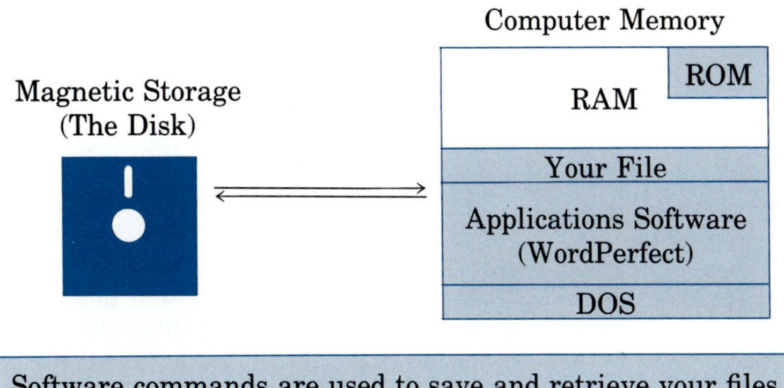

Saving and Resaving Data Files

The beginning user may be confused about what the microcomputer does when it saves data files onto a disk, and this confusion can lead to unnecessary work. The microcomputer rarely physically moves data. Instead, it makes a copy of the data and then places that copy in the new location. In the example here, after the user entered the commands to save the text file and the microcomputer executed the commands, there were two identical sets of data—one still in RAM and a copy now stored on the disk.

The data file copied onto the disk was a copy of the data in RAM at that time. If after saving the file any changes are made to the text in RAM, the changes will not automatically be made to the copy of the file on the disk. In most cases, the user needs to save the data again (re-execute the save commands) in order for the changes to be included in the copy of the file on the disk.

Saving the data file again with the same filename used previously (REPORT) updates the copy on the disk with any changes made to the copy in RAM. That is, when a file is resaved, the old copy on the disk is replaced by a new copy of the file in RAM. It is highly recommended that you resave your data file (update the copy on the disk) every 15 minutes or so when you are using the microcomputer.

How the Microcomputer Saves Data

Although the software's commands are used to save a file, it is actually DOS and the instruction sets in ROM that perform the save operation. (Together, DOS and the instruction sets in ROM may be referred to as simply the *operating system.*) When a data file is saved on a disk, the operating system divides the file into 512 byte-size blocks of data and then looks for room on the disk to save each block. The blocks are saved one at a time. As the operating system stores the blocks of data on the disk, it records where they can be found and where they came from (the name of the file) in a special area of the disk called the file allocation table *(FAT)*. When the user later wants a data file read back into RAM, the operating system uses the FAT to locate the individual blocks of data that make up the file. It then copies the blocks into RAM in the order in which they were stored on the disk.

Formatted Disks

The term *formatted* was used to describe the disk that the user inserted into the disk drive in the example. When a disk is first purchased, it is unformatted. Before DOS can save blocks of data onto a disk, the disk must be formatted.

Formatting a disk establishes where data may or may not be stored on the disk, configures the file allocation table for the disk, and marks defective areas (if any) so that data will not be saved there. A special utility software with the filename FORMAT.COM is found on the DOS disk purchased with the computer. The FORMAT software is used to format a new disk to the specifications of the IBM or compatible microcomputer and to the version of DOS being used. A disk only needs to be formatted once, but until it is formatted the computer will not be able to save data on it. (You may refer to Appendix A section "Formatting a Disk" for more information on the format process.)

Erasing Data Files and Software from RAM

In the example session, after the user saved the data file, WordPerfect presented the prompt

```
Exit WP? (Y/N)
```

which the user answered by typing Y. If N for *No* had been typed instead, the monitor screen would have been cleared of all text and the user would have been left at the point where WordPerfect was first read into RAM.

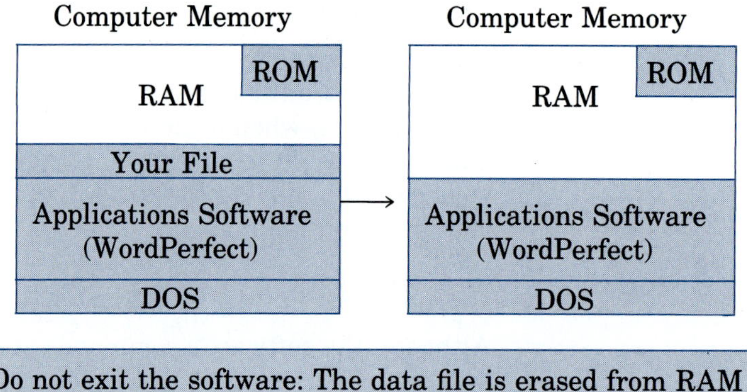

Erasing only the data file from RAM allows the user to begin creating a new data file by using the software that still resides there.

By typing Y to the "Exit WP?" prompt, as was done in the example session, the user caused both the data file and the WordPerfect software to be erased from RAM.

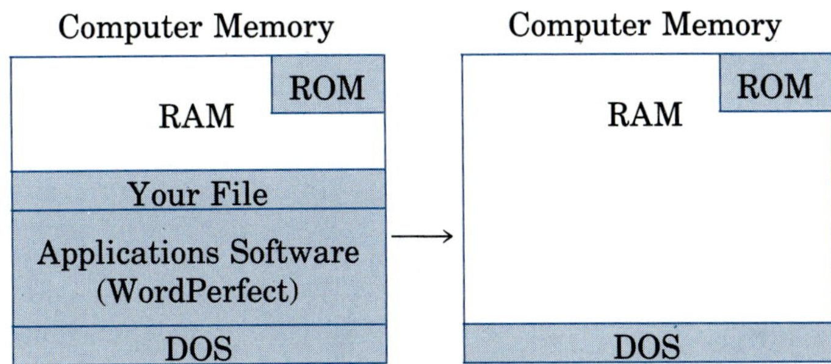

Exit the software: The data file and software are both erased from RAM

The commands to either erase the current data file from RAM so that a new data file may be created or to erase the data file and the software from RAM and return to the DOS operating level are available (and often used) commands common to all applications software.

Returning to DOS

In the final step of the example the user typed the DOS command **DIR↵**. The directory displayed on the screen showed that the file created using WordPerfect was saved onto the disk under the name given it, and that it used up approximately 1,200 bytes of the space available to hold data on the disk.

SUMMARY

This section of the manual provides an overview of the microcomputer and the process of using it. The various hardware components have been described in light of function and performance factors. The principal types of applications software have been discussed in terms of the data processing tasks to which they are best suited. Finally, a simplified example session was used to describe the major processes involved when the three elements of a microcomputer system are brought together to become a productivity tool.

Before you begin studying the commands and features of the applications software covered in this manual, you may find it helpful to read the contents of Appendix A, "The Basics of DOS." There you will find a discussion that expands on the fundamentals presented in this section.

STUDY QUESTIONS

1. Name the five basic devices that compose a standard microcomputer hardware system.

   ______________ ______________ ______________

   ______________ ______________

2. If *input* is defined as placing data into the computer's RAM, which two of the hardware devices would most likely be considered input devices?

   ______________ ______________

3. If *output* is defined as copying data held in RAM to another hardware device, which two devices would most likely be considered output devices?

   ______________ ______________

4. Which device functions as both an input and output device?

   ____

5. The hardware component that performs the manipulations and calculations of data items is called the ______________.
6. The rate at which a microcomputer is able to perform data item manipulations is a function of its ______________ and ______________.
7. A read operation describes the process of ______________.
8. One character of data is represented in RAM with a pattern of high and low voltages called a ______________.
9. A microcomputer's capacity to hold data in RAM is usually expressed in ______________ or ______________ quantities.
10. The smallest discrete image displayed on a monitor screen is called a ______________.
11. One measure of a monitor's performance is its ______________ which is expressed in ______________.
12. Describe how primary storage differs from secondary storage.

    ____

    ____

    ____

    ____

13. Names two measures of performance associated with microcomputer disk drives.

    ____

    ____

14. Name two measures of performance associated with microcomputer printers.

    ____

    ____

15. When a task can be described as being primarily number- or formula-based, which applications software is most likely the appropriate one to use?

____

16. When a task can be described as being the professional presentation of text, which applications software is most likely the appropriate one to use?

____

17. When a task can be described as being concerned with the selective organization of records, which applications software is most likely the appropriate one to use?

____

18. What software must first be in RAM before any applications software may be placed there?

____

19. While at the system level (A> or C>), the user is able to enter _______________ or _______________ for the computer to act upon.

20. While at the software operating level, the user is able to _______________ or use the software's _______________.

21. In order to alter a data file, such as adding a word to a memo or adding a formula to a spreadsheet, where must the data to be modified be currently stored?

____

22. After having made an alteration to a data file, what must occur in order for the change to be permanently recorded?

____

23. You sit down at the computer, boot DOS, load an applications software, and then use its commands to load a file you previously saved on a disk. Just then, someone accidentally kicks the power cord to your computer out of the outlet and your computer shuts down. Have you lost your data?

____

24. You sit down at the computer, boot DOS, load an applications software, and then accidentally use the software's command to save a file when you meant to load a set of data previously saved. You used the same filename and completed the command. Have you lost your data?

____

25. You use a software's commands to load a set of data you saved previously. You then make several changes to the data and are now ready to leave. However, you are not sure if you want the changes made to the copy of your data on the disk. You would like to wait and make up your mind tomorrow. How can you do this?

____

THE FUNDAMENTALS KEY TERM GLOSSARY

A: Drive The hardware device name for the first floppy disk drive.

Average Access Time Speed at which disk drive reads and writes data to and from the disk.

B: Drive The hardware device name for the second floppy disk drive.

Bit A single electrical pattern of high or low voltage that represents a data item.

Byte A single pattern of eight bits that usually represents one character of data.

C: Drive The hardware device name for a hard-disk drive.

Clock Speed Rate at which data manipulations are performed.

CRT Cathode ray tube used in the most popular type of monitor.

Cursor A small blinking line that indicates where characters will appear on the screen as they are typed.

Daisy Wheel Printer A printer that strikes a spoke with a die cast character against an ink ribbon to produce a printed character.

Data Original data items that are unorganized/uncalculated.

Data Processing The computer's act of organizing or calculating data items.

Database File Data items held in fields that comprise records that together constitute a set of data.

Database Management Systems Software Used to manipulate data that are in record-like structure.

Disk Drive Hardware device that provides a means for secondary storage.

Disk Jacket Cover that encloses and protects a floppy disk.

DOS Operating system software for the IBM microcomputer.

DOS Operating Level The microcomputer has read DOS into RAM.

Dot Matrix Printer A printer that strikes an ink ribbon with various pins of a print head to produce printed characters and graphics.

Electronic Data Processing See data processing.

FAT File allocation table.

File A distinct set of software instructions under a specific name.

Filename The specific name identifying a set of software instructions.

Firmware Instruction sets permanently etched into ROM circuit chips.

Floppy Disk Magnetic storage media made of oxide-coated mylar and enclosed in a disk jacket.

Formatted Disk A disk that has been initialized by establishing where data may or may not be stored, configuring the file allocation table, and marking any defective areas.

Hard Copies Printed copies of data or information held in memory.

Hard Disk Magnetic storage media made of an oxide-coated metal that is permanently built into the disk drive.

Hardware The physical part of a microcomputer system.

Impact Printer A printer that strikes an ink ribbon to produce a printed image.

Index Hole Used on 5¼″ disk to determine the relative rotational position as the disk is spinning.

Information Organized or calculated data.

Key Values Spreadsheet numbers from which formulas derive their displayed values.

Keyboard Hardware that allows the user to enter characters of data into the computer's memory.

Kilobyte 1,024 bytes.

Laser Jet Printer Bonds liquid toner to a sheet of paper with the heat of laser beam to produce printed characters or graphics.

LCD Liquid crystal display used in a new type of monitor.

Magnetic Storage Media Material coated with iron oxide and used for secondary storage.

Megabyte 1,048,576 bytes.

Memory Capacity to hold data, expressed as number of bytes.

Monitor Hardware used to display an image of the data being transmitted between the user and the microcomputer system.

Nonimpact Printer Bonds toner to paper using heat without physically striking the paper.

Operating System DOS and the instruction sets in ROM.

Parity Check Bit One bit in the byte that was used to check for errors in the byte's pattern of bits.

Pins Used in print head on dot matrix printers to print characters. The more pins contained in the print head, the greater the resolution of the printed characters.

Pixel The smallest discrete image a monitor can produce.

Plotter Printer A printer that moves ink pen(s) across a page to produce printed images.

Primary Storage The system's memory capacity.

Print Head Mechanism for a dot matrix printer containing 9 to 24 pins which are used to strike the ink ribbon.

Printer Hardware that produces printed copies of data or information held in the memory of a microcomputer or on a disk.

Programs Instruction sets for the computer.

RAM Random access memory.

Read Operation Process of copying data from magnetic storage into memory.

Read/Write Head The disk drive's read/write mechanism.

Read/Write Window Allows the disk drive's read/write head to access the magnetic storage media.

ROM Read only memory.

Secondary Storage Magnetic storage media such as hard and floppy disks used to store data in a permanent form.

Software Set of instructions that directs and controls the operation of the microcomputer's hardware.

Software Operating Level DOS has read another software into RAM and the commands of the software may be used.

Spreadsheet Software An electronic version of the accountant's standard spreadsheet.

System Unit Hardware that performs data manipulations.

Word Processing Software Used to create sentences, paragraphs, and pages of text.

Word Size Number of adjacent bits that can be manipulated at one time.

Write Operation Act of copying data from memory onto magnetic storage media.

Write-Protect Notch/Switch Prevents the microcomputer from writing data onto the disk.

WordPerfect Version 5.0

INTRODUCTION

WordPerfect is an applications software designed to do word processing. It allows the user to create text by typing characters on the microcomputer's keyboard. As the text is typed, it is entered into RAM. The microcomputer then can be used to manipulate the data. Manipulating text data is the primary function of word processing software. When the text has been manipulated into its finished form, the word processing software's commands can be used to print the text.

This module begins with a brief discussion of WordPerfect basics and file handling. It continues with a set of introductory tutorial lessons that presents the basic operations used to create, edit, format, and print a text file. The tutorial lessons then present the commands and techniques used in a set of timesaving procedures called *block operations*. Here the tutorial provides you with the opportunity to practice the word processing operations covered earlier. The introductory tutorial is followed by several short exercises and cases designed to introduce and reinforce the use of additional WordPerfect features, commands, and operations.

At the end of this module you will find a WordPerfect operation and command summary, which briefly describes WordPerfect's full range of commands and control key operations. You also will find a convenient WordPerfect quick reference command index that lists the most commonly used WordPerfect commands.

As you progress through the material, you may notice slight differences between the menus and commands presented in the text and those shown on your monitor screen. The differences occur because of minor changes made to various versions of WordPerfect or differences among the hardware being used.

WORDPERFECT BASICS

Typing on Electronic Pages

WordPerfect is designed primarily to process text data. When you type the data on the keyboard, your words, sentences, and paragraphs appear on the monitor screen much as they would on a piece of paper in a typewriter. A small blinking cursor on the screen indicates where the next character that you type will appear.

As you continue to type, the lines of text begin to scroll on the monitor screen in the same way that paper feeds through a typewriter when the carriage return is pressed. When one screen's worth of text is complete, the text at the top of the screen scrolls up and disappears to make room at the bottom of the screen for new lines of text. Although the text disappears from view, the computer continues to hold it as part of the data in the file. You may use various WordPerfect commands to scroll text back and forth to review text that is not currently displayed on the screen.

When you have typed a printed page's worth of text (default of 54 lines), WordPerfect displays a line of dashes across the screen (called a *page break*) to indicate that a new printed page is about to begin. The "electronic pages" of text are connected as new pages are added for every 54 lines of text typed.

WordPerfect refers to the text files you create in this manner as *documents* or document files.

Manipulating Text Data

As you enter text, you may move the cursor to edit any previously entered word, sentence, or paragraph. *Editing* a document involves either revising data by changing the written content of the text or formatting data by changing the appearance of the text. *Revising* includes operations such as deleting words, inserting words, moving paragraphs, and correcting misspellings. *Formatting* includes such operations as centering text, changing line spacing and margins, boldfacing, and underlining. WordPerfect's commands enable you to perform such text data manipulations.

WordPerfect Command Structure

WordPerfect provides menu commands to accomplish the revising and formatting operations. The command mode of WordPerfect is entered by typing certain keystrokes and keystroke combinations. The first keystroke in a menu command keystroke combination will be the **Ctrl, Shift,** or **Alt** key. The second keystroke in a keystroke combination will be a Function key (**F1** through **F10.)**

The Keyboard Command Template

WordPerfect provides a keyboard template to place over the Function keys on the keyboard. The template is essential to a beginning WordPerfect user because it lists the 40 main commands of WordPerfect—essentially it can be thought of as WordPerfect's main menu of commands. There are four such commands for each of the 10 Function keys. The four commands for each Function key are color coded to describe the keystroke or keystroke combination used to execute them:

Red = **Ctrl**
Green = **Shift**
Blue = **Alt**
Black = **Function keys 1–10**

To execute a command shown in red, green, or blue, you first press and hold the appropriate key (Ctrl, Shift, or Alt), and then press the Function key. To execute a command shown in black, you simply press the appropriate Function key.

WordPerfect Command Menus

When many of the WordPerfect commands are executed, they present menus of additional commands. The additional commands are selected by typing their number or letter. For instance, on the keyboard template next to Function key 8, the command "Format" is shown in green. If you press and hold the **Shift** key and then press the **F8** key, the following menu will be displayed on the screen.

```
Format

     1 - Line
             Hyphenation                    Line Spacing
             Justification                  Margins Left/Right
             Line Height                    Tab Set
             Line Numbering                 Widow/Orphan Protection

     2 - Page
             Center Page (top to bottom)    New Page Number
             Force Odd/Even Page            Page Numbering
             Headers and Footers            Paper Size/Type
             Margins Top/Bottom             Suppress

     3 - Document
             Display Pitch                  Redline Method
             Initial Codes/Font             Summary

     4 - Other
             Advance                        Overstrike
             Conditional End of Page        Printer Functions
             Decimal Characters             Underline Spaces/Tabs
             Language

Selection: 0
```

Here, there are four menu items (commands) listed to the left on the screen. Each command is preceded with a number and has one of its letters highlighted. You may select a command by either typing the command number or the highlighted letter in its name. In this example, if you typed **1** or **L** (**L**ine), the following menu would appear:

```
Format: Line

     1 - Hyphenation                      Off

     2 - Hyphenation Zone - Left          10%
                            Right         4%

     3 - Justification                    Yes

     4 - Line Height                      Auto

     5 - Line Numbering                   No

     6 - Line Spacing                     1

     7 - Margins - Left                   1"
                   Right                  1"

     8 - Tab Set                          0", every 0.5"

     9 - Widow/Orphan Protection          No

Selection: 0
```

If your intention was to change the line spacing in the document, you would next type **6** or **S** (Line **S**pacing).

Command Name Conventions

In this module, the full command used to complete an operation will be presented as the sequence (or path) of commands necessary to complete the operation. For instance, the full command to change line spacing will be stated in the form

Shift-F8 (Format),**L**ine,Line **S**pacing

Command Menu Trees

Later in the text, you will find command menu trees that graphically describe the command paths to a final completed operation. For instance, the small portion of the Format command tree that includes the operation of changing line spacing in a document will appear as follows:

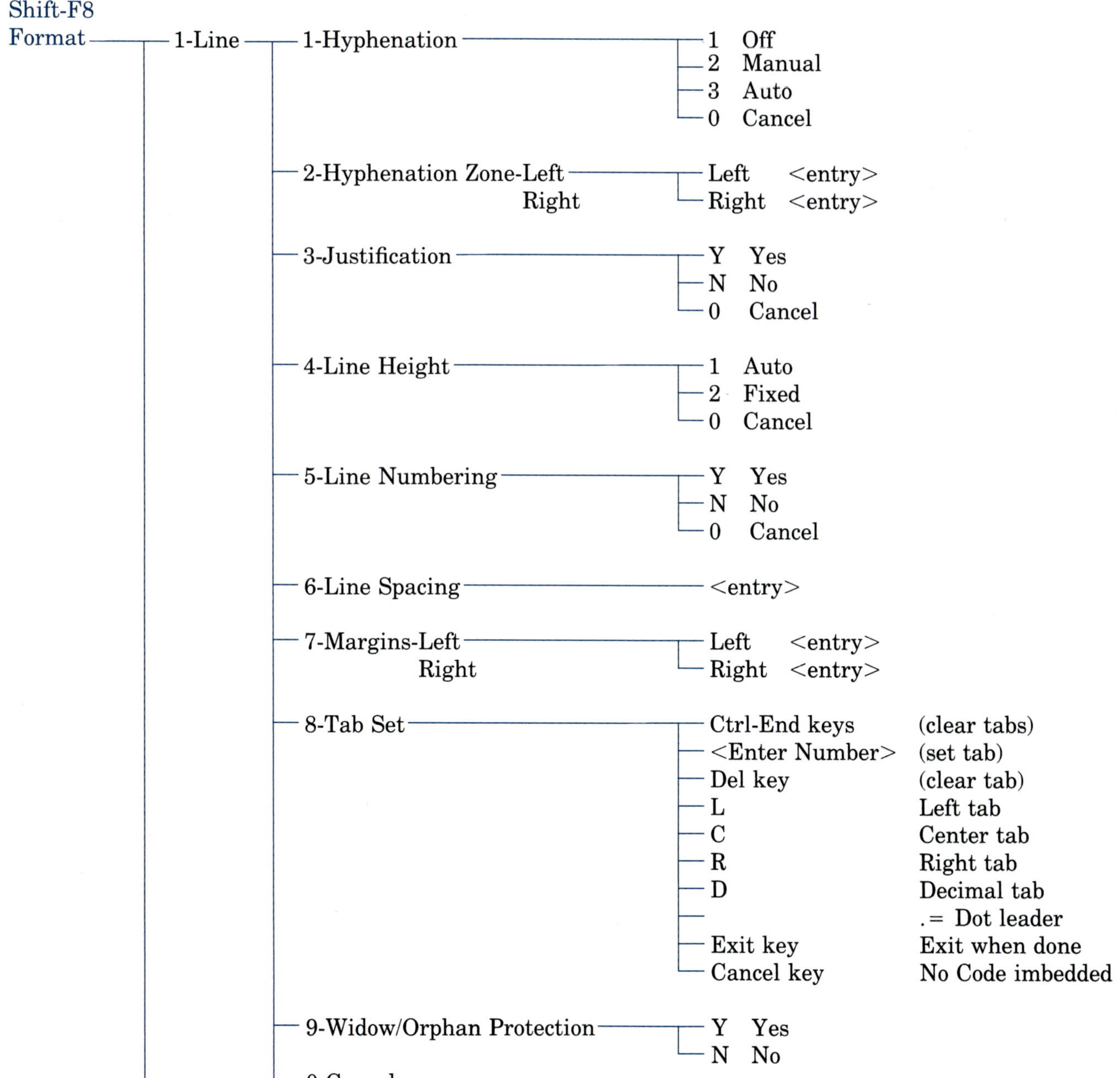

Command Index

The WordPerfect command summary also includes an index of completed operations. The index may be used to reference the appropriate command tree for further information, or simply to get you started towards successfully completing an operation while you are at the computer. An example of the index reference for line spacing appears as follows:

Italic Font	**Ctrl-F8**(Font)
Justification (on/off)	**Shift-F8,1** (Format),**L**ine
Kerning	**Shift-F8,4** (Format),**O**ther
Keyboard Layout	**Shift-F1** (Setup)
Line	
Graphics	**Alt-F9** (Graphics)
Draw	**Ctrl-F3** (Screen)
Height	**Shift-F8,1** (Format),**L**ine
Numbering	**Shift-F8,1** (Format),**L**ine
Spacing	**Shift-F8,1** (Format),**L**ine
Lists Feature	**Alt-F5** (Mark Text)

Command Keystroke Conventions

In this module, the keystrokes used to execute a command are shown with a dash (-) to indicate keystroke combinations. Commas are used to separate the keystrokes. For instance, in the last example the keystrokes used to change line spacing will be shown in the manual as **Shift-F8,1,6.**

WordPerfect's File Handling

WordPerfect, with all of its features, is a large software that could consume a considerable amount of RAM. In addition, as document files become several pages long, they rapidly use up RAM. WordPerfect circumvents the memory's size limits by keeping in RAM only the data currently needed. The rest of the data are maintained on disks and are brought into RAM as necessary.

How WordPerfect is Loaded into RAM

To use the full extent of its commands, the WordPerfect software requires that eight floppy disks be available during editing. The floppy disks are labeled WordPerfect 1, WordPerfect 2, Speller, Thesaurus, Learning, Fonts/Graphics, PTR Program, and Conversion.

The basic word processing software of WordPerfect is kept on the WordPerfect 1 and WordPerfect 2 floppy disks. During normal editing operations, the WordPerfect 2 floppy disk must be kept in the disk drive. Software comprising other features of WordPerfect, such as its spelling checker, thesaurus, and graphics, are kept individually on the other floppy disks. To use the other features of WordPerfect, the other floppy disks must be inserted into the disk drive when needed.

Because of its total size, WordPerfect is best suited for computers having a hard disk. By copying all of the data files comprising WordPerfect onto the hard disk, you eliminate the need to change disks each time you use a special feature of the software.

How Document Files Are Loaded and Saved

When you first load WordPerfect into RAM, the software allows you to immediately begin entering text to create a document file. As you type, the data you enter begins to use up memory. When the memory of the computer becomes full, WordPerfect begins to save parts (blocks) of the document onto temporary files on the WordPerfect disk or directory. Once a block of data is copied onto a disk file, the space it has occupied in RAM may be erased to make room for new data.

If you move backwards in the text to correct errors or add data, and the section on which you want to work is not in RAM, WordPerfect copies what is in RAM onto the disk. It then reads the section on which you want to work into the memory space that was freed up. A current file being moved between RAM and disk storage in this fashion is called an *open file.*

When you are through creating and editing a document, you must use the appropriate WordPerfect commands to *close* the file. Closing a file causes all data in the document to be saved to your disk. The document will be saved under the name you give it at the time you save it.

Learning WordPerfect

WordPerfect is best learned by using it. Although you may be able to learn the fundamentals of creating and editing standard document files in just a few hours, the full set of WordPerfect commands and operations may take months to learn.

Getting Help

One WordPerfect command, **F3** (Help), provides an extensive on-line summary of information on the various commands of WordPerfect. To use the Help facility, you type **F3** (Help) and then follow the instructions shown to access various command topics. The data used to provide the Help facility are on the WordPerfect 1 floppy disk. You may need to reinsert the WordPerfect 1 floppy disk into the disk drive to use the **F3** (Help) command. When finished with the Help facility, you press the Space or ↵ key to return to the editing mode.

REQUIRED PREPARATION

The tutorial lessons and exercises in this module will give you experience using the commands and features of WordPerfect. Before you begin the "hands-on" learning experience, however, you will need to complete a few initial steps and gain some preliminary information in order to be adequately prepared.

Initial Steps

1. Obtain a floppy disk appropriate for the microcomputer you will be using to complete your course assignments. Your instructor or laboratory staff will be able to tell you which kind of disk to purchase.

   Size: ____________________

   Sides: ____________________

   Density: ____________________

2. Format your disk to the specifications of the DOS and microcomputer hardware you will be using to complete your course assignments. Your instructor or laboratory staff will be able to tell you the steps to follow. **Caution:** Formatting a disk erases all files that may exist on that disk.

Steps to Format a Disk: ______________________________

3. Each time you use the WordPerfect software, you will want to be sure that your text (data) files are saved on your disk. There will be certain steps to follow, either when you first load WordPerfect into RAM or immediately afterwards, to ensure that your files are automatically saved on your disk. Your instructor or laboratory staff will be able to tell you the steps to follow.

Starting a WordPerfect Editing Session: ______________________________

REQUIRED MATERIALS

1. An IBM DOS floppy disk (or hard-disk directory containing the DOS software)
2. A WordPerfect 1 and a WordPerfect 2 floppy disk (or hard-disk directory containing the software)
3. A formatted disk (your files disk)
4. A WordPerfect keyboard command template
5. This manual
6. Other ______________________________

TUTORIAL CONVENTIONS

During the introductory WordPerfect tutorial you will create text files using various WordPerfect commands. The following are the conventions the tutorial's instructions will use.

↵	The bent arrow means to type the Enter key located on the right side of the keyboard.
Key-Key	Key combinations using a hyphen indicate that you should press and hold the first key, then type the next key shown.
Key, Key	Key combinations using a comma indicate that you should type the first key and then type the second key.
‖ ‖	Do not type the double lines; type only what is inside them.

NOTE: Here drive *means type the letter (A, B, etc.) for the disk drive in which your files disk is kept.*

HOW TO GET OUT OF TROUBLE

If you want to:	*Then:*
■ Backspace and erase characters to the left of the cursor . . .	■ Type the Backspace key located on the right top side of keyboard.
■ Erase a line of text . . .	■ Move the cursor to the line to be erased and type Home,Home,Left,Ctrl-End.
■ Stop a command operation and return to editing the document . . .	■ Type **F1** (Cancel).
■ Leave the Reveal Codes screen to resume normal editing . . .	■ Type **Alt-F3** (Reveal Codes).
■ Stop the tutorial to continue later . . .	■ Type **F7** (Exit),**Y**,*drive*:WPTUT1↵, **Y.**
■ Continue with the tutorial after stopping . . .	■ After loading WordPerfect, type **Shift-F10** (Retrieve),*drive*:WPTUT1↵.

NOTE: During the tutorial exercises, you may see references made to screen positions that do not exactly match the positions displayed on your monitor. For instance, the text here may display a position of Ln 1.67" (line 1.67 inches) while your screen displays Ln 1.66" (line 1.66 inches). Such minor variations (1/100th of an inch) should be of no concern.

Throughout the tutorial lessons you will see the following symbol.

It indicates an opportune time to save your file(s) and quit the microcomputer session if you so desire.

GETTING STARTED

The proper "getting started" procedures require information specific to the hardware and software you are using. Refer to your notes in the preceding "Required Preparation" section for the specific information. The following is a general procedure for getting started; however, you may need to refer to Appendix A, "The Basics of DOS," to understand some of the terminology used here.

You will need to know in which disk drive (A: or B:) your files disk will be and where (disk drive and path) the WordPerfect software will be.

1. Load DOS from a floppy disk or hard disk, or return to the DOS operating level from the current software operating level.
2. Put the WordPerfect keyboard template over the Function keys on the keyboard.
3. Put your files floppy disk into the proper disk drive (drive name ______:).
4. When you see DOS's "*drive:*\>" prompt on the screen, change the current disk drive to where your files disk is by typing *drive:*↵.
5. If necessary, put the WordPerfect 1 disk in the proper disk drive (drive name ______:).
6. Now enter the drive, path, and filename for WordPerfect by typing *drive:**path*\\WP↵.
7. If necessary, follow WordPerfect's instructions until the screen appears as follows.

Doc 1 Pg 1 Ln 1" Pos 1"

LESSON 1 Creating a Document File

When WordPerfect is first loaded, you are presented with a blank screen onto which you may enter text. A blinking cursor should appear on the first position of the first line on the screen. At the bottom of the screen, a *status line* appears, which is used to display various messages about current editing operations. This is where many of WordPerfect's menus of commands will appear.

Entering Text

You are going to type part of a form letter prepared for prospective renters inquiring about units in a townhouse complex. As you enter the following text, be certain to type ↵ (Enter) only when the tutorial indicates that you are to do so. To correct typing errors as you go, use the Backspace key (top row, right side of keyboard) to backspace and erase characters you have typed. Also, use two spaces to separate sentences in the text.

1. Type ‖ ↵↵Thank you for your interest in Vista Ridge Townhouses. We feel that our one and two bedroom deluxe townhouse apartments offer adult living at its finest.↵↵Each large unit has wall-to-wall carpeting, drapes, private patio and sun deck with a breathtaking view. In addition you will find the townhouse of your choice equipped with self-defrosting refrigerator, self-cleaning oven, dishwasher and garbage disposal unit.↵↵ ‖

At this point the screen should appear as

```
Thank you for your interest in Vista Ridge Townhouses.  We feel
that our one and two bedroom deluxe townhouse apartments offer
adult living at its finest.

Each large unit has wall-to-wall carpeting, drapes, private patio
and sun deck with a breathtaking view.  In addition you will find
the townhouse of your choice equipped with self-defrosting
refrigerator, self-cleaning oven, dishwasher and garbage disposal
unit.

_

                                        Doc 1 Pg 1 Ln 3" Pos 1"
```

How WordPerfect Manipulates String Data as It Is Entered

As you enter text, WordPerfect's *word wrap* feature automatically begins a new line when the right margin of the current line is reached. If you want to begin a new line of text before you have reached the end of the previous line (such as when you want to begin a new paragraph), you must type the Enter key. Typing the Enter key stops the word wrap and moves the cursor forward to the next line.

Hard and Soft Returns

When a line is automatically wrapped to the next line by WordPerfect, the line is ended with what is known as a *soft return.* Groups of lines having soft return endings are considered by WordPerfect to be paragraphs of words. When a line is ended by typing ↵ (Enter), the line is ended by what is known as a *hard return.* A hard return separates paragraphs in WordPerfect.

Adding Text to a File

You will now finish the body of the text of the form letter.

2. Enter the text necessary to bring this document to the form shown in the following screen.

```
Thank you for your interest in Vista Ridge Townhouses. We feel
that our one and two bedroom deluxe townhouse apartments offer
adult living at its finest.

Each large unit has wall-to-wall carpeting, drapes, private patio
and sun deck with a breathtaking view. In addition you will find
the townhouse of your choice equipped with self-defrosting
refrigerator, self-cleaning oven, dishwasher and garbage disposal
unit.

Every tenant enjoys year-round swimming and sauna plus use of our
recreation room and tennis courts.

We are located in the South West Heights area, close to shopping,
city parks and University campus. For an appointment to view one
of our fine townhouse apartments and a tour of the grounds, please
call Mr. Smith at (503) 244-7163.

                                    Doc 1 Pg 1 Ln 4.33" Pos 1"
```

LESSON 2 WordPerfect's Basic Editing Operations

The basic editing operations of WordPerfect are revisional in nature. They allow you to change the content of the text by deleting and inserting characters, words, and larger units of text. To perform such operations, certain keystrokes are used. The general steps involved are

1. Move the cursor to the location where the change is to be made.
2. Use the appropriate keystrokes to make the change.

Moving the Cursor through a Document

The right side of the keyboard has a keypad that contains four keys with arrows on them. These keys (cursor control keys) may be used to move the cursor one character to the left or right and one line up or down by typing the key with the appropriate directional arrow on it. The printed page position of the cursor is displayed at the bottom of the screen in vertical (Ln) and horizontal (Pos) inches.

1. Use the cursor control keys to move the cursor to the *c* in *city* by following the path indicated in the following text.

```
We are located in the South West Heights area, close to shopping,
city parks and University campus. For an appointment to view one
of our fine townhouse apartments and a tour of the grounds, please
call Mr. Smith at (503) 244-7163.

_
```

NOTE: If numbers appear on the screen at this time, type the Num Lock key once, and then use the Backspace key to erase the numbers and continue.

2. Watch the cursor move as you type the cursor left key (←) three or four times. Now type the cursor right key (→) five or six times.

Notice that when you attempt to move the cursor past the left or right margins of text, the cursor follows the word wrap path (either backwards or forwards) that was set when you entered the text.

Where the Cursor May Not Be Moved

WordPerfect's various cursor movement commands may be used to move the cursor anywhere on the screen where characters of text exist. The cursor may not be moved to areas where there are no text characters. To demonstrate, do the following.

3. Move the cursor to the *r* in *our* in the third paragraph.

```
Every tenant enjoys year-round swimming and sauna plus use of our
recreation room and tennis courts.

We are located in the South West Heights area, close to shopping,
```

4. Type the cursor down key (↓), then type it again.

Notice that the cursor jumped to the last character entered in the line to which it was being moved.

5. Now, with the cursor at 3.33″ vertical (the status line displays the current cursor's (Ln) location), try to move the cursor to the right.

Since no characters are entered into the line, the cursor moves to the next line down following the word wrap.

When you want to move the cursor to an area of the screen where no characters exist, you may use the Space bar or Tab key to enter spaces or tabs (which are characters) into a line of text to move the cursor to the desired position (displayed as Pos on the status line).

WordPerfect Cursor Control Keys

Several keystrokes and keystroke combinations may be used to move the cursor around in a document. Although the WordPerfect keyboard template summarizes some of them, it is best to memorize the full list in order to use the word processing software most efficiently. To gain experience in some of the cursor control key operations, do the following.

6. Read the following table and practice using the cursor control keystrokes that are highlighted below.

Cursor Movement	Keystrokes
Character Left	Left ←
Character Right	Right →
Line Up	Up ↑
Line Down	Down ↓
Word Left	Ctrl-Left
Word Right	Ctrl-Right
Forward to Character *a*	Ctrl-Home,*a*
Beginning of Line	Home,Left
End of Line	Home,Right
Top of File	Home, Home,Up
Bottom of File	Home, Home,Down
To Page *nn*	Ctrl-Home,*nn*↵
Screen Up	− (Numeric Keypad)
Screen Down	+ (Numeric Keypad)
Page Up	Page Up (PgUp)
Page Down	Page Down (PgDn)
Previous Position	Ctrl-Home,Ctrl-Home
Column Left	Ctrl-Home,Left
Column Right	Ctrl-Home,Right

Revising a Paragraph of Text

Now that you are able to move the cursor throughout your document, you are ready to learn the basic word processing commands that allow you to revise text by inserting, deleting, or typing over characters, words, or lines of text.

Insert or Typeover Text

On the right-hand side of the keyboard there is a key marked "Ins" for insert. This key is used to switch WordPerfect between one of two editing modes, *Insert* or *Typeover*. The default mode is Insert.

7. If you see the Typeover message displayed on the left side of the status line, type the Ins key to switch WordPerfect back to the Insert mode.
8. Move the cursor to the first line of the second paragraph, and then to the *u* in *unit.*

```
Each large unit has wall-to-wall carpeting, drapes, private patio
and sun deck with a breathtaking view.  In addition you will find
the townhouse of your choice equipped with self-defrosting
refrigerator, self-cleaning oven, dishwasher and garbage disposal
unit.
```

9. Now type ||apartment||.

The paragraph now should appear as

```
Each large apartment unit has wall-to-wall carpeting, drapes, private patio
and sun deck with a breathtaking view.  In addition you will find
the townhouse of your choice equipped with self-defrosting
refrigerator, self-cleaning oven, dishwasher and garbage disposal
unit.
```

When the Insert mode is on, any characters that you type will be inserted into the text to the left of the cursor.

10. Now move the cursor with one of the cursor control keys.

```
Each large apartment unit has wall-to-wall carpeting, drapes,
private patio and sun deck with a breathtaking view.  In addition
you will find the townhouse of your choice equipped with self-
defrosting refrigerator, self-cleaning oven, dishwasher and garbage
disposal unit.
```

Notice that WordPerfect automatically rewraps the lines in a paragraph when revisions are made to it. This is referred to by WordPerfect as its *screen rewrite* feature.

11. Type the Ins key once.

Notice that the Typeover message appears on the left side of the status line.

12. Now move the cursor to the *a* in *apartment* and type ||townhouse||.

The paragraph now should appear as

```
Each large townhouse_unit has wall-to-wall carpeting, drapes,
private patio and sun deck with a breathtaking view.  In addition
you will find the townhouse of your choice equipped with self-
defrosting refrigerator, self-cleaning oven, dishwasher and garbage
disposal unit.
```

When the Typeover mode is on, any characters that you type will type over (overwrite) existing characters of text.

Deleting Text

There are several keystrokes and keystroke combinations that may be used to delete text from a document. The following table describes many of them.

Delete Operation	Keystrokes
Current Character	Delete (Del)
Previous Character	Backspace
Current Word	Ctrl-Backspace
Current Word Left	Home,Backspace
Current Word Right	Home,Delete (Del)
End of Line	Ctrl-End
End of Page	Ctrl-Page Down (PgDn)

Deleting Characters

13. Move the cursor down one line and to the *w* in *with.*

```
Each large townhouse unit has wall-to-wall carpeting, drapes,
private patio and sun deck with a breathtaking view.  In addition
you will find the townhouse of your choice equipped with self-
defrosting refrigerator, self-cleaning oven, dishwasher and garbage
disposal unit.
```

The Delete or Del key found on the right-hand side of the keyboard may be used to delete the character at the cursor position.

14. Type the Delete or Del key three times.

The Backspace key is used to delete the character to the immediate left of the cursor. If the Typeover mode is on, the characters are replaced with spaces. If the Insert mode is on, the characters are deleted from the text and the space is closed up.

15. Move the cursor four characters to the right (to the *b* in *breathtaking*). Use the Ins key to make sure the Insert mode is on, and then type the Backspace key four times.

Deleting Words

Another delete operation uses the keystroke combination Ctrl-Backspace to delete the word at the cursor location. A word is defined by WordPerfect to be a group of characters separated from other groups by spaces, or the group of spaces to the right of the cursor.

16. Move the cursor to the middle of the word *breathtaking* and type Ctrl-Backspace.

```
Each large townhouse unit has wall-to-wall carpeting, drapes,
private patio and sun deck view.  In addition you will
find the townhouse of your choice equipped with self-defrosting
refrigerator, self-cleaning oven, dishwasher and garbage disposal
unit.
```

Deleting Lines of Text

The final delete operation to be discussed here is one which deletes the line to the right of the cursor. The keystroke combination used is Ctrl-End. Although this tutorial does not include a demonstration of the operation, you will find the keystroke combination to be very useful when you need to delete small sections of text.

The **F1** (Cancel) Command—WordPerfect's Panic Button

One of the first commands you should become familiar with is WordPerfect's **F1** (Cancel) command. The Cancel command may be used to abort and exit other WordPerfect commands. The Cancel command also may be used to recover any or all of the last three text deletions or Typeover text.

Recovering Deleted Text

To recover deleted text, you move the cursor to the position where you want the recovered text to appear and then type **F1** (Cancel). The most recent deletion will appear on the screen at the cursor location. The **2 P**revious Deletion command may be used to continuously scroll through the last three deletions, with each deletion appearing on the screen in order. When the appropriate deletion is displayed on the screen, you type **1** or **R** (**R**estore) to recover it, or type **F1** (Cancel) to abort the recovery operation.

17. Move the cursor to the *s* in *sun* (second paragraph, second line), and then type **F1.**

```
Thank you for your interest in Vista Ridge Townhouses.  We feel
that our one and two bedroom deluxe townhouse apartments offer
adult living at its finest.

Each large townhouse unit has wall-to-wall carpeting, drapes,
private patio and breathtaking sun deck view.  In addition you will
find the townhouse of your choice equipped with self-defrosting
refrigerator, self-cleaning oven, dishwasher and garbage disposal
unit.

Every tenant enjoys year-round swimming and sauna plus use of our
recreation room and tennis courts.

We are located in the South West Heights area, close to shopping,
city parks and University campus.  For an appointment to view one
of our fine townhouse apartments and a tour of the grounds, please
call Mr. Smith at (503) 244-7163.




Undelete: 1 Restore; 2 Previous Deletion: 0
```

At the bottom of the screen you will see the menu for the Cancel command.

18. Type **2** or **P** several times.

Notice how the last three sections of deleted text appear on the screen in the order they were deleted.

19. Continue typing **2** or **P** until the word *breathtaking* appears again, and then type **1** or **R** to restore the deleted text.

LESSON 3
Practice Revisions

1. Use the methods of your choice to insert, overwrite, and/or delete the words in the paragraph so that it appears as follows.

```
Each spacious townhouse unit has wall-to-wall carpeting, drapes,
private patio and sun deck.  You will also find the townhouse of
your choice equipped with a completely modern kitchen including a
self-defrosting refrigerator, self-cleaning oven, dishwasher and
garbage disposal unit.
```

LESSON 4
Formatting Text

WordPerfect Format Codes

When WordPerfect commands and keystrokes are used to format text, codes are imbedded into the document. The codes that format text tend to fall into three general categories: *hard codes* and *soft codes; format forward codes;* and *start and stop codes*. The following section discusses each category as it presents the more important or most used formatting commands and keystrokes in WordPerfect.

Hard and Soft Codes

Soft codes are, for the most part, codes which WordPerfect generates and automatically inserts into a document. Hard codes are generated by the user. For instance, you learned earlier that WordPerfect inserts soft returns at the end of lines when it wraps text, and that typing the Enter key produces a hard return at the end of a line. The soft return is flexible; it can be (and is) moved about when a paragraph is rewritten. A hard return is inflexible; WordPerfect will not automatically move or remove it from the end of a line.

*The **Alt-F3** (Reveal Codes) Command*

The **Alt-F3** (Reveal Codes) command allows you to edit your document while its imbedded codes are visible on the screen.

1. Move the cursor to the *E* in *Every* (first letter, third paragraph) and type the **Alt-F3** (Reveal Codes) command.

The screen will appear as follows.

```
Thank you for your interest in Vista Ridge Townhouses.  We feel
that our one and two bedroom deluxe townhouse apartments offer
adult living at its finest.

Each spacious townhouse unit has wall-to-wall carpeting, drapes,
private patio and sun deck.  You will also find the townhouse of
your choice equipped with a completely modern kitchen including a
self-defrosting refrigerator, self-cleaning oven, dishwasher and
garbage disposal unit.

Every tenant enjoys year-round swimming and sauna plus use of our
                                          Doc 1 Pg 1 Ln 3" Pos 1"
{   ▲   ▲   ▲   ▲   ▲   ▲   ▲   ▲   ▲   ▲   ▲   ▲   }   ▲   ▲
garbage disposal unit.[HRt]
[HRt]
Every tenant enjoys year[-]round swimming and sauna plus use of our[SRt]
recreation room and tennis courts.[HRt]
[HRt]
We are located in the South West Heights area, close to shopping,[SRt]
city parks and University campus.  For an appointment to view one[SRt]
of our fine townhouse apartments and a tour of the grounds, please[SRt]
call Mr. Smith at (503) 244[-]7163.[HRt]
[HRt]

Press Reveal Codes to restore screen
```

The top portion of the Reveal Codes screen displays your document as it appears during normal editing. The bottom portion of the screen displays the same text with its imbedded codes. Such codes will be highlighted and enclosed in brackets. The code [SRt] indicates a soft return and the code [HRt] indicates a hard return.

The cursors E and E appearing in the top and bottom portions of the screen may be moved at the same time (synchronously) using the cursor control keys. This feature allows you to move about and scroll through the text without leaving the Reveal Codes screen.

2. Watch the bottom portion of the screen and move the cursor left two characters.

The bottom cursor should now be on the [HRt] code at the end of the line ending with *unit.*

```
private patio and sun deck.  You will also find the townhouse of
your choice equipped with a completely modern kitchen including a
self-defrosting refrigerator, self-cleaning oven, dishwasher and
garbage disposal unit._

Every tenant enjoys year-round swimming and sauna plus use of our
                                        Doc 1 Pg 1 Ln 2.67" Pos 3.2"
{   ▲   ▲   ▲   ▲   ▲   ▲   ▲   ▲   ▲   ▲   ▲   ▲   }   ▲   ▲
your choice equipped with a completely modern kitchen including a[SRt]
self[-]defrosting refrigerator, self[-]cleaning oven, dishwasher and[SRt]
garbage disposal unit.[HRt]
[HRt]
Every tenant enjoys year[-]round swimming and sauna plus use of our[SRt]
recreation room and tennis courts.[HRt]
[HRt]
```

All of the editing and command features of WordPerfect are available to you while in the Reveal Codes screen. Since most of WordPerfect's formatting operations place hidden (imbedded) codes into the document, the Reveal Codes screen can be most useful for ensuring proper placement of such codes and for later finding and deleting unwanted codes from a document. For instance, the Del and Backspace keys may be used to delete codes from a document while you are in the Reveal Codes screen.

3. Type the Del key once. Then type it again.

```
Each spacious townhouse unit has wall-to-wall carpeting, drapes,
private patio and sun deck.  You will also find the townhouse of
your choice equipped with a completely modern kitchen including a
self-defrosting refrigerator, self-cleaning oven, dishwasher and
garbage disposal unit.Every tenant enjoys year-round swimming and
sauna plus use of our recreation room and tennis courts.

                                     Doc 1 Pg 1 Ln 2.67" Pos 3.2"
{ ▲ ▲ ▲ ▲ ▲ ▲ ▲ ▲ ▲ ▲ ▲ ▲ } ▲ ▲
your choice equipped with a completely modern kitchen including a[SRt]
self[-]defrosting refrigerator, self[-]cleaning oven, dishwasher and[SRt]
garbage disposal unit.Every tenant enjoys year[-]round swimming and[SRt]
sauna plus use of our recreation room and tennis courts.[HRt]
[HRt]
```

By deleting the two hard returns ([HRt]s) that were separating the second and third paragraphs, you were able to combine them into one paragraph.

4. To give you experience in editing a document from the Reveal Codes screen, revise the second paragraph to read as in the following.

```
Each spacious townhouse unit has wall-to-wall carpeting, drapes,
private patio and sun deck.  You will find the townhouse of your
choice equipped with a completely modern kitchen including a self-
defrosting refrigerator, self-cleaning oven, dishwasher and garbage
disposal unit.  In addition, every Vista Ridge tenant enjoys year-
round swimming and sauna plus use of our recreation room and tennis
courts._

                                          Doc 1 Pg 1 Ln 3" Pos 1.7"
{ ▲ ▲ ▲ ▲ ▲ ▲ ▲ ▲ ▲ ▲ ▲ ▲ } ▲ ▲
disposal unit.  In addition, every Vista Ridge tenant enjoys year[-]
round swimming and sauna plus use of our recreation room and tennis[SRt]
courts.[HRt]
[HRt]
```

5. When finished, type the **Alt-F3** (Reveal Codes) command to exit the Reveal Codes screen.

Other Hard and Soft Codes

Hard and Soft Page Breaks. WordPerfect generates soft page breaks ([SPg]) every 54 lines of text. You can force a page break to occur by typing Ctrl-↵. A [HPg] code will be inserted into the text.

Hard Spaces and Hard Hyphens. If you do not want two or more words to be separated from each other when WordPerfect wraps a line in a paragraph, you can insert *hard spaces* between the words. Similarly, if you want a hyphenated word to remain whole, you can insert a *hard hyphen* into the word. To produce a hard space, you type the keys Home,Space. A [ ] code will be inserted into the text. To produce a hard hyphen, you type the keys Home,—. A hard hyphen appears in the text as simply a — (dash) in the Reveal Codes screen; a hyphen typed without the Home key appears as a [—] code in the Reveal Codes screen.

All of the hard codes can be directly deleted with the Backspace or Del keys without using the Reveal Codes screen. This is not true for other types of codes.

Format Forward Codes

Many of the codes imbedded into a document by WordPerfect are format forward in nature. In general, the procedure is to first move the cursor to where you want the code to be placed in your document, and then execute the WordPerfect command which will generate the imbedded code. To demonstrate how such codes work, you will use a command to imbed a code that changes the left and right margins into the document.

Changing Left and Right Margins

6. Move the cursor to the beginning of the second paragraph and then to the *E* in *Each.*
7. Type the **Shift-F8** (Format) command.

The following screen should appear.

```
Format

   1 - Line
          Hyphenation                    Line Spacing
          Justification                  Margins Left/Right
          Line Height                    Tab Set
          Line Numbering                 Widow/Orphan Protection

   2 - Page
          Center Page (top to bottom)    New Page Number
          Force Odd/Even Page            Page Numbering
          Headers and Footers            Paper Size/Type
          Margins Top/Bottom             Suppress

   3 - Document
          Display Pitch                  Redline Method
          Initial Codes/Font             Summary

   4 - Other
          Advance                        Overstrike
          Conditional End of Page        Printer Functions
          Decimal Characters             Underline Spaces/Tabs
          Language

Selection: 0
```

The **Shift-F8** (Format) command presents a menu of commands. The option to set Margins Left/Right can be found to the right of the menu command **1 - L**ine.

8. Type **1** or **L** to select the **Shift-F8** (Format),**L**ine command.

The following menu of commands should appear on the screen.

```
Format: Line

   1 - Hyphenation                    Off

   2 - Hyphenation Zone - Left        10%
                          Right       4%

   3 - Justification                  Yes

   4 - Line Height                    Auto

   5 - Line Numbering                 No

   6 - Line Spacing                   1

   7 - Margins - Left                 1"
                 Right                1"

   8 - Tab Set                        0", every 0.5"

   9 - Widow/Orphan Protection        No


Selection: 0
```

Here you see that the **Margins** command is option **7** on the (Format),**Line** command menu. You can see the current settings or values for each command on the menu to the right of the command.

9. Type **7** or **M** to select the **Margins** command.

By default, WordPerfect measures margins in printed page inches. In most cases the characters are printed in 10 pitch—that is, there are 10 characters per inch occurring on a printed line. This means that one inch of margin amounts to 10 characters.

10. Reset the current left and right margins by typing ‖ 2↵2↵ ‖ .

In some cases, WordPerfect does not immediately return you to editing your document after a command has been executed. Here you have finished changing the margins for the document, but the Format,**Line** command menu screen is still present. As a general rule, when a WordPerfect command puts a 0 (zero) over the menu selection cursor as it has here, typing ↵ will return you to the normal editing mode. At other times, the **F7** (Exit) command is used to return you to editing.

11. Type ‖ ↵↵ ‖ , and then type the cursor down key once to cause WordPerfect to rewrite the screen.

```
Thank you for your interest in Vista Ridge Townhouses.  We feel
that our one and two bedroom deluxe townhouse apartments offer
adult living at its finest.

          Each spacious townhouse unit has wall-to-wall
          carpeting, drapes, private patio and sun deck.
          You will find the townhouse of your choice
          equipped with a completely modern kitchen
          including a self-defrosting refrigerator, self-
          cleaning oven, dishwasher and garbage disposal
          unit.  In addition, every Vista Ridge tenant
          enjoys year-round swimming and sauna plus use
          of our recreation room and tennis courts.

          We are located in the South West Heights area,
          close to shopping, city parks and University
          campus.  For an appointment to view one of our
          fine townhouse apartments and a tour of the
          grounds, please call Mr. Smith at (503) 244-
          7163.

                                    Doc 1 Pg 1 Ln 2.17" Pos 2"
```

When the **Shift-F8** (Format),**Line**,**Margins** command was executed, WordPerfect inserted a [L/R Mar:2″,2″] code into the document at the cursor location.

12. Type **Alt-F3** (Reveal Codes) to see the imbedded code. When finished, type **Alt-F3** (Reveal Codes) again to return to the normal editing screen.

Notice that all of the text following the [L/R Mar:2″,2″] code was rewritten to fit the new left and right margins. A format forward code affects all of the following text up to the end of the document, or until another similar code, in this case another [L/R Mar:n",n"], is encountered.

13. Move the cursor to the *W* in *We* in the last paragraph and repeat the previous steps to set the margins Left = 1.5", Right = 1.5" (one-and-a-half inches each). Type ‖ ↵↵ ‖ to return to editing, and then type the cursor down key to rewrite the screen.

```
Thank you for your interest in Vista Ridge Townhouses.  We feel
that our one and two bedroom deluxe townhouse apartments offer
adult living at its finest.

          Each spacious townhouse unit has wall-to-wall
          carpeting, drapes, private patio and sun deck.
          You will find the townhouse of your choice
          equipped with a completely modern kitchen
          including a self-defrosting refrigerator, self-
          cleaning oven, dishwasher and garbage disposal
          unit.  In addition, every Vista Ridge tenant
          enjoys year-round swimming and sauna plus use
          of our recreation room and tennis courts.

     We are located in the South West Heights area, close to
     shopping, city parks and University campus.  For an
     appointment to view one of our fine townhouse apartments
     and a tour of the grounds, please call Mr. Smith at (503)
     244-7163.

                                       Doc 1 Pg 1 Ln 1" Pos 1"
```

Deleting Format Forward Codes

You may use the Reveal Codes screen to delete codes that affect the document in a format forward manner, or you may often delete them using the Backspace or Del keys without entering the Reveal Codes screen.

14. Move the cursor to the *E* in *Each* in the second paragraph and type the Backspace key.

Notice the message "Delete [L/R Mar:2",2"]? (Y/N) No" at the bottom of the screen. If you now type **Y,** the code will be deleted from the document. If you type any other key, the code will not be deleted.

15. Use the method of your choice to delete the two [L/R Mar:n",n"] codes that are in the document.
16. Now move to the top line on the screen (to the beginning of the document file) and use the **Shift-F8** (Format),**L**ine,**M**argins command to set the left margin to 1.5" and the right margin to 1.5". Remember that moving the cursor down will cause the screen to be rewritten for the new margins.

Changing Line Spacing

The **Shift-F8** (Format),**L**ine,**L**ine **S**pacing command is another useful formatting command.

17. With the cursor at the top of the document, type the **Shift-F8** (Format),**L**ine,**L**ine **S**pacing command.

18. Change the current line spacing to two by typing ‖ 2↵ ‖ . Then type ‖ ↵↵ ‖ to return to the normal editing mode.

19. Next use the Reveal Codes command to view the two format forward codes that are now imbedded at the beginning of your text.

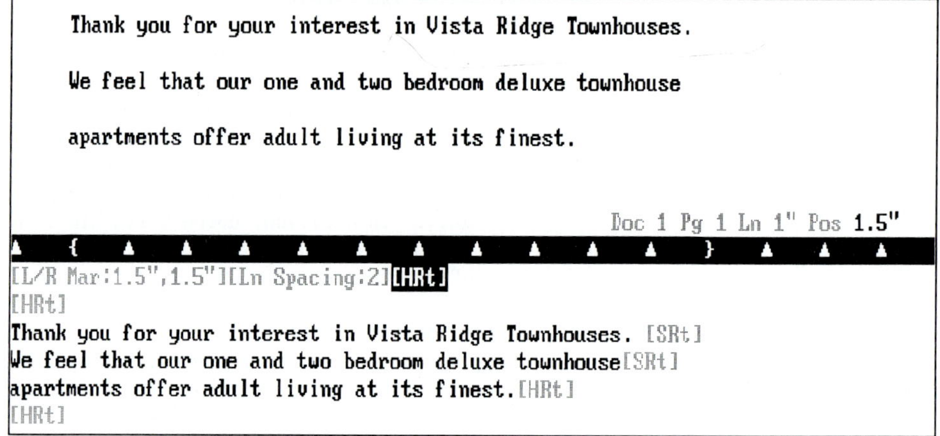

Start and Stop Codes

In general, commands that generate start and stop codes imbed two codes into the document. The text between the two codes is the segment of text affected by the command's format.

Centering Text

WordPerfect's **Shift-F6** (Center) command inserts start and stop codes to center text between them. To give you experience in using the command, do the following.

20. Use the Reveal Codes screen to move the cursor to the [Ln Spacing:2] code imbedded in the text.

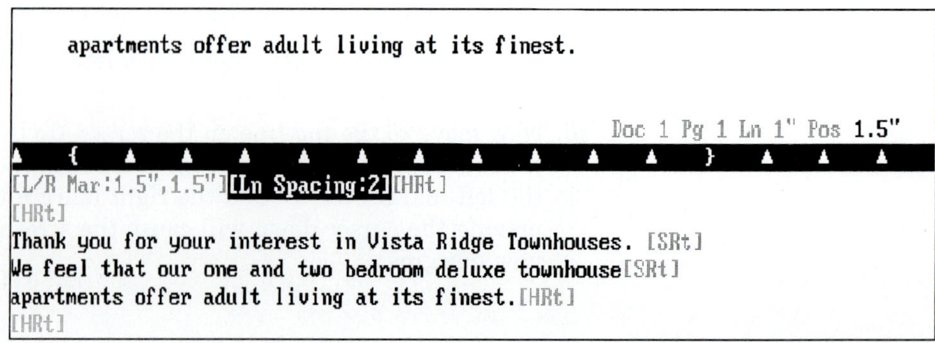

21. Now type ‖ ↵↵ ‖ to insert one blank line between the [L/R Mar:1.5",1.5"] code and the [Ln Spacing:2] code. Then move the cursor to that blank line.

```
    We feel that our one and two bedroom deluxe townhouse

    apartments offer adult living at its finest.
                                           Doc 1 Pg 1 Ln 1.17" Pos 1.5"
[L/R Mar:1.5",1.5"][HRt]
[HRt]
[Ln Spacing:2][HRt]
[HRt]
Thank you for your interest in Vista Ridge Townhouses. [SRt]
We feel that our one and two bedroom deluxe townhouse[SRt]
apartments offer adult living at its finest.[HRt]
[HRt]
```

22. Next, type **Shift-F6** (Center) to begin the Center command.

Notice the start code [Cntr] appears to the left of the cursor. Text now typed on this line will appear centered between the current margins.

23. Now type ‖ Vista Ridge Townhouses↵ ‖ .

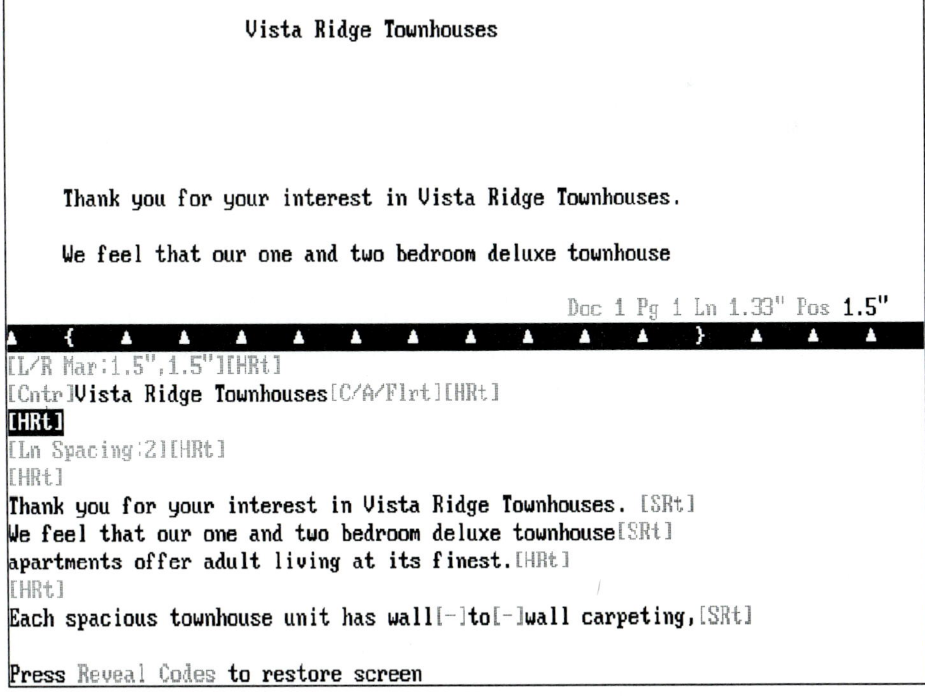

When using the **Shift-F6** (Center) command in this manner, typing ↵, moving the cursor Up or Down, or typing **Shift-F6** (Center) again completes the command operation and causes the stop code [C/A/Flrt] to be placed in the document on the same line. The text between the Center command's start and stop codes is the text which will be centered by the command.

Bold Type and Underline

Two other WordPerfect commands that insert start and stop codes into the document in the same manner as the **Shift-F6** (Center) command are the **F6** (Bold) command, which is used to print text darker than normal, and the **F8** (Underline) command, which is used to underline text when it is printed.

To boldface or underline text you may type, respectively, the **F6** or **F8** keys (Bold or Underline) to begin the command, type the text to be boldfaced or underlined, and then type the **F6** or **F8** keys (Bold or Underline) again to stop the command.

Deleting Start and Stop Codes

You may delete start and stop codes in the same manner as you delete format forward codes, with or without the Reveal Codes screen. However, with start and stop codes, only one of the two codes need be deleted; the other will automatically be deleted.

LESSON 5 Practice Reformatting the Document

1. Use the commands and operations discussed so far to:
   - a. Set the left margin to 2″ and the right margin to 2″ for the entire document.
   - b. Complete the centered letterhead as shown here:

     Vista Ridge Townhouse
     ~~~~~~~~~~~~~~~~~~~~~~~~~~
     1800 S.W. Sunset View Avenue
     Portland, OR 97207

   - c. Keep the line spacing at 1 for the letterhead and 2 for the rest of the document.
   - d. Underline the phone number. Note that the underlined text will appear underlined and/or highlighted on the screen and will print underlined.
   - e. Use a hard space (Home,Space) and a hard hyphen (Home,Hyphen) to prevent WordPerfect from separating the area code, prefix, and phone number when it wraps the last line of the last paragraph.
   - f. Delete all unnecessary codes from your document.

The finished document appears on the screen as on the following page.
     ~~~~~~~~~~~~~~~~~~~~~~~~~~

```
                 Vista Ridge Townhouses
                 ~~~~~~~~~~~~~~~~~~~~~~
              1800 S.W. Sunset View Avenue
                   Portland, OR 97207

      Thank you for your interest in Vista Ridge

      Townhouses.  We feel that our one and two

      bedroom deluxe townhouse apartments offer adult

      living at its finest.


      Each spacious townhouse unit has wall-to-wall

      carpeting, drapes, private patio and sun deck.

      You will find the townhouse of your choice

      equipped with a completely modern kitchen

      including a self-defrosting refrigerator, self-

      cleaning oven, dishwasher and garbage disposal

      unit.  In addition, every Vista Ridge tenant

      enjoys year-round swimming and sauna plus use

      of our recreation room and tennis courts.


      We are located in the South West Heights area,

      close to shopping, city parks and University

      campus.  For an appointment to view one of our

      fine townhouse apartments and a tour of the

      grounds, please call Mr. Smith at

      (503) 244-7163.
Typeover                          Doc 1 Pg 1 Ln 8.83" Pos 3.5"
```

LESSON 6
WordPerfect Block Operations

An important feature of word processing is its ability to deal with segments or "blocks" of a document (sentences, paragraphs, etc.) independent from the rest of the document. The process involves two steps: (1) the segment of text is defined and (2) a WordPerfect command is used to affect that segment of text.

In the following lesson you will create a second page for the document you have been working on that describes four townhouse apartments immediately available for occupancy. While you create the page, several WordPerfect block operations will be introduced.

Formatting Blocks of Text

The **Alt-F4** (Block) command is used to define a portion of text to be subsequently affected by another WordPerfect command. To block (define) a portion of text, you move the cursor to the beginning of the text and type **Alt-F4** (Block). A blinking "Block on" message will appear on the status line at the bottom of the screen. You then move the cursor to the end of the text. The text being blocked will be displayed on the screen in reverse video. If you decide to abort the block operation, you may type **F1** (Cancel) to turn off the block. The last step to a block operation is to type the command keystroke or keystroke combination to affect the block of text. To demonstrate, do the following.

1. Move the cursor to the immediate right of the period in the last line of text.
2. Use the **Alt-F3** (Reveal Codes) screen and the Del or Delete key to delete any text or codes that may have been inadvertently placed in the document beyond this point.

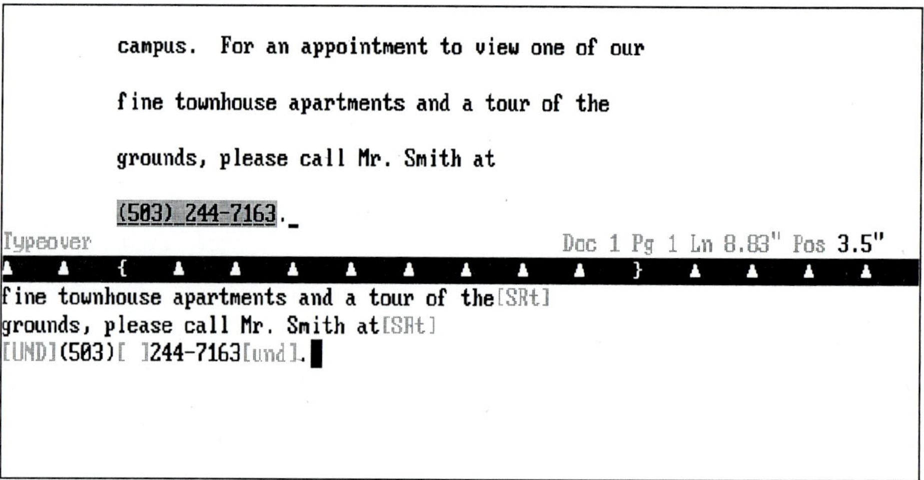
campus. For an appointment to view one of our
fine townhouse apartments and a tour of the
grounds, please call Mr. Smith at
(503) 244-7163.
Typeover
Doc 1 Pg 1 Ln 8.83" Pos 3.5"
fine townhouse apartments and a tour of the[SRt]
grounds, please call Mr. Smith at[SRt]
[UND](503)[ ]244-7163[und].

3. Exit the Reveal Codes screen by typing **Alt-F3.** Then type ‖ ↵ ‖ four times.

A dotted horizontal line should appear on the screen. The line is generated by a [SPg] (Soft Page code) which indicates that a new printed page will begin at this point.

4. With the cursor at line (Ln) 1.33″ use the **Shift-F8** (Format),**Line**,**Line Spacing** command to set the line spacing for the second page to single spacing. Before exiting the (Format),**Line** command menu screen, use the **7** (**M**argins) command to set the left and right margins to 1″ each for the second page. Finally, type ‖ ↵↵ ‖ to return from the **Shift-F8** (Format),**Line** menu to normal editing.

5. Next type

```
↵
↵
Vista Ridge Townhouses↵
======================== ↵
↵
Units Available↵
For Immediate Occupancy↵
```

6. Move the cursor to the *V* in *Vista* (Ln 1.67″ Pos 1″) and type **Alt-F4** (Block).

A blinking "Block on" message should appear at the bottom of the screen.

7. Move the cursor down five lines to Ln 2.5″.

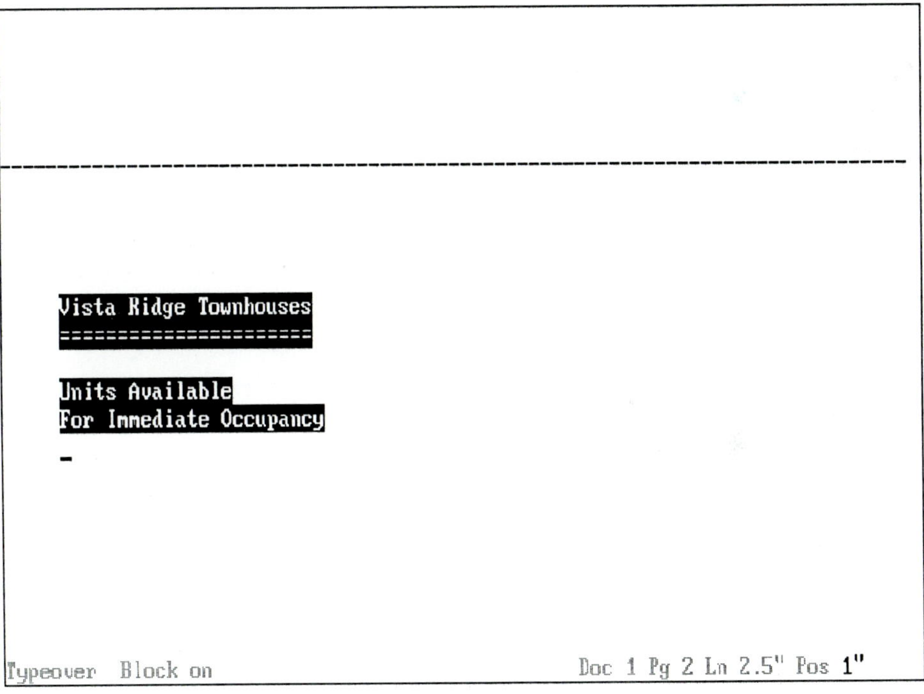

8. Now type the **Shift-F6** (Center) command.

At the bottom of the screen you should see the prompt "[Cntr]? (Y/N) No."

9. Type **Y** to center the document heading.

Since many people prefer to format their text after it has been entered, the ability to **Alt-F4** (Block) existing text and then **Shift-F6** (Center), **F8** (Underline), or **F6** (Bold) the blocked text is a useful feature.

Several other commands that may be used to format a block of text may be found on the Block/**Ctrl-F8** (Block/Font) menu of commands. To use the Block/Font commands, you block the text to be affected by the command, type **Ctrl-F8** (Font), select **1** Size or **2** Appearance, and then select from the Size or Appearance menu the formatting command to affect the blocked text. The complete Block/Font menu can be shown graphically as follows.

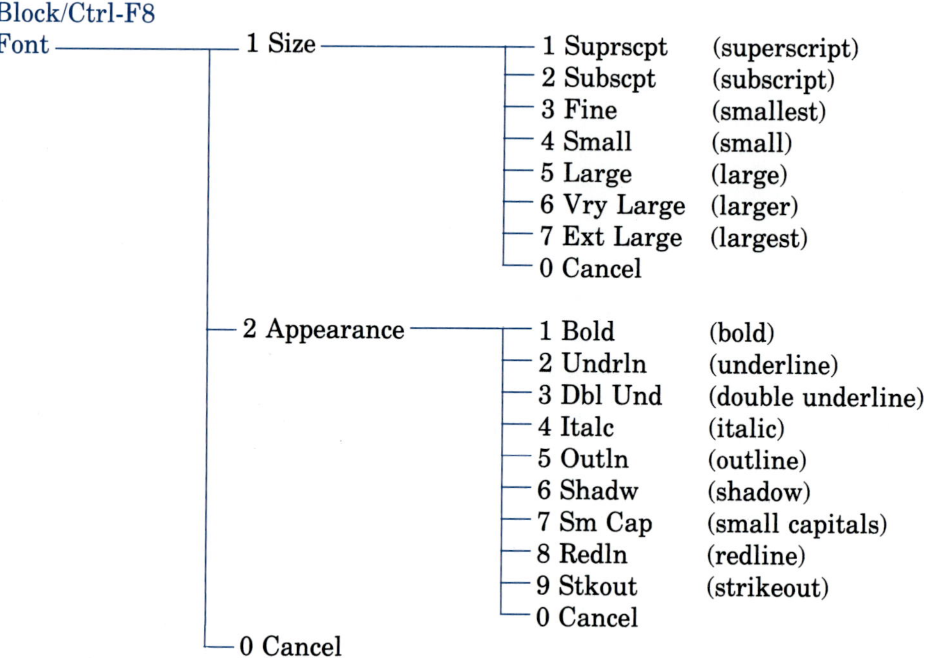

You should note, however, that printers vary in their ability to support the full range of styles and sizes for printed characters that the Font command offers.

LESSON 7
Cut-and-Paste Operations

The term *cut and paste* refers to the ability to move, copy, or delete blocks of text. WordPerfect provides several ways in which you may perform cut-and-paste operations.

1. Move the cursor to Ln 3.17″ Pos 1″ by typing ‖ ↵ ‖ three times.
2. Now type ‖ # 12 - 1850 Square Feet, 3 Bedrooms, 2 Baths ‖ .
3. Next type the **Alt-F6** (Flush Right) command.

The **Alt-F6** (Flush Right) command is used to enter text from right to left starting at the right margin.

4. Type ‖ $480.00/Month↵↵ ‖ .
5. Continue by typing in the remaining text shown in the following.

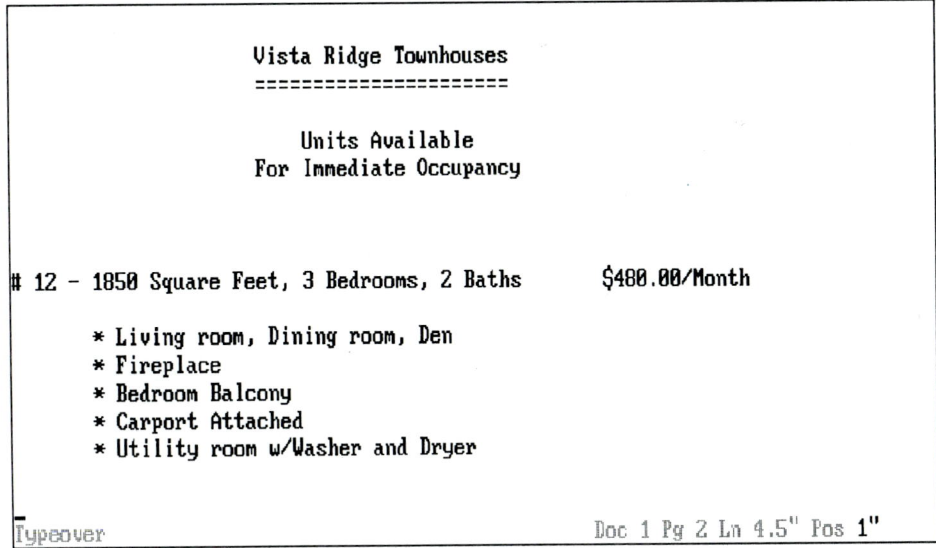

Using the Block/**Ctrl-F4** (Move) Command

The Block/Move command may be used to move, copy, or delete a block of text. When the **Ctrl-F4** (Move) command is used to perform such operations, a copy of the blocked text is made and placed into what is known as the Move Block buffer. WordPerfect then treats the copy of text in the Move Block buffer as a separate file. Once a copy of blocked text has been placed into the Move Block buffer, it remains there until another Block/Move command causes another blocked section of text to replace it.

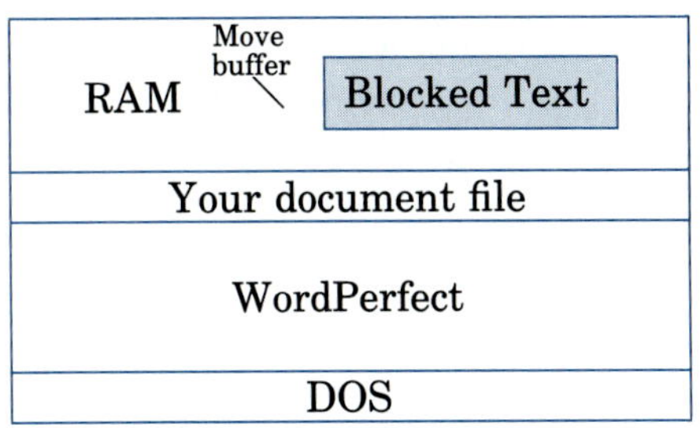

The Block/**Ctrl-F4** (Move),**B**lock,**M**ove Command

To gain experience at using the Block/Move command you will first use the command to move the last feature listed to become the second feature listed.

6. Move the cursor to Ln 3.67″ Pos 1″ (beginning of the line with * *Fireplace* on it) and type ‖ ↵ ‖ to create a blank line there.
7. Now move the cursor to the beginning of the line starting with * *Utility room* (Ln 4.33″ Pos 1″) and type **Alt-F4** (Block),Home,End to block the line of text.
8. Next type the **Ctrl-F4** (Move) command.

The following menu should appear at the bottom of the screen:

```
# 12 - 1850 Square Feet, 3 Bedrooms, 2 Baths        $480.00/Month

       * Living room, Dining room, Den

       * Fireplace
       * Bedroom Balcony
       * Carport Attached
       * Utility room w/Washer and Dryer



Move: 1 Block; 2 Tabular Column; 3 Rectangle: 0
```

9. Type **1** or **B** to specify **B**lock.

The next menu to appear is

```
1 Move; 2 Copy; 3 Delete; 4 Append: 0
```

10. Now select **1** or **M** to **M**ove.

When you selected **1** or **M** to move the block of text, WordPerfect first made a copy of the block of text and placed it into the Move Block buffer. It then erased the block of text from the screen.

The prompt at the bottom of the screen (Move cursor; press Enter to retrieve) indicates what you are to do next.

11. Move the cursor to the beginning of the blank line you created in step 6 (Ln 3.67″ Pos 1″) and type ‖ ↵ ‖ .

In the second part of executing the Block/**Ctrl-F4** (Move),**B**lock,**M**ove command, a copy of the text in the Move Block buffer is inserted (regardless of the current Typeover/Insert mode) into the document at the location of the cursor. It is important to note that a copy of the text still remains in the Move Block buffer.

12. Use the cursor down key and ↵ key (if necessary) to move the cursor to Ln 4.5″ Pos 1″.

```
# 12 - 1850 Square Feet, 3 Bedrooms, 2 Baths        $480.00/Month

       * Living room, Dining room, Den
       * Utility room w/Washer and Dryer
       * Fireplace
       * Bedroom Balcony
       * Carport Attached


_

Typeover                                    Doc 1 Pg 2 Ln 4.5" Pos 1"
```

The **Ctrl-F4** (Move),**R**etrieve,**B**lock Command

The **Ctrl-F4** (Move),**R**etrieve,**B**lock command may be used to copy the text currently in the Move Block buffer into the document at the location of the cursor.

13. Now type **Ctrl-F4** (Move), then **4** or **R** (**R**etrieve), and then **1** or **B** (**B**lock) to retrieve the Move Block buffer text.

14. Now repeat the last step (**Ctrl-F4** (Move),**4,1**) two more times.

```
# 12 - 1850 Square Feet, 3 Bedrooms, 2 Baths       $480.00/Month

        * Living room, Dining room, Den
        * Utility room w/Washer and Dryer
        * Fireplace
        * Bedroom Balcony
        * Carport Attached

_       * Utility room w/Washer and Dryer       * Utility room
w/Washer and Dryer       * Utility room w/Washer and Dryer

Typeover                                  Doc 1 Pg 2 Ln 4.5" Pos 1"
```

The Block/**Ctrl-F4** (Move),**B**lock,**C**opy Command

To copy a block of text, the Block/**Ctrl-F4** (Move),**B**lock,**C**opy command is used in the same manner as the Block/**Ctrl-F4** (Move),**B**lock,**M**ove command. The only difference between the two commands is that moving text causes the original block of text to be erased from the screen and copying text does not erase the original block of text.

The Block/**Ctrl-F4** (Move),**B**lock,**M**ove and Block/**Ctrl-F4** (Move),**B**lock,**C**opy commands both work by placing a copy of blocked text into the Move Block buffer where it can be retrieved later with the **Ctrl-F4** (Move),**R**etrieve, **B**lock command. However, only the most recently moved or copied text will be in the Move Block buffer at any point in time.

The Block/**Ctrl-F4** (Move),**B**lock,**D**elete Command

To continue, do the following.

15. Use the **Alt-F4** (Block) command and cursor keys to block the last two lines in the document, and then type **Ctrl-F4,1** (Move),**B**lock.

```
# 12 - 1850 Square Feet, 3 Bedrooms, 2 Baths       $480.00/Month

       * Living room, Dining room, Den
       * Utility room w/Washer and Dryer
       * Fireplace
       * Bedroom Balcony
       * Carport Attached

       * Utility room w/Washer and Dryer        * Utility room
w/Washer and Dryer        * Utility room w/Washer and Dryer

1 Move; 2 Copy; 3 Delete; 4 Append: 0
```

16. Now type **3** or **D** (**D**elete) to delete the block of text.
17. Next type the **F1** (Cancel) command.

The block of text just deleted with the Block/**Ctrl-F4** (Move),**B**lock,**D**elete command will appear on the screen.

As mentioned earlier, the **F1** (Cancel) command may be used to recover (Undelete) text that has been previously typed over or deleted. The **F1** (Cancel) command works in a manner similar to the Move command. The **F1** (Cancel) command maintains three buffers, called Undelete buffers, into which typed over or deleted text is automatically copied at the time the event occurs. The last typeover or deletion is kept in the first buffer; the previous two typeovers or deletions are kept in the second and third buffers.

Unlike the Block/(Move),**B**lock,**M**ove and Block/(Move),**B**lock,**C**opy commands, the Block/(Move),**B**lock,**D**elete command does not place the blocked text into the Move Block buffer. Instead, it places it in the first buffer of the three Undelete buffers.

18. Now type **F1** (Cancel) or ‖ ↵ ‖ to exit from the Cancel command and return to normal editing.

Block/Backspace or Block/Del

A much faster method to delete a block of text is to first block the text with **Alt-F4** (Block) and then simply type the Backspace or Del key. The prompt "Delete Block? (Y/N) No" will appear at the bottom of the screen. To complete the deletion, type **Y.** The end result of Block/Backspace or Block/Del is exactly the same as Block/(Move),**B**lock,**D**elete.

Using the Undelete Buffers to Perform Move and Copy Operations

It might occur to you that you could delete text and then later undelete text to perform various move and copy operations—that is, use the Undelete buffers rather than the Move Block buffer to hold the text. One advantage to this approach is that considerably fewer keystrokes are required.

In fact, using the Cancel command is another way in which one can perform cut-and-paste operations. However, to do so requires that you keep in mind that the text in the Undelete buffers is easily and automatically replaced each time a typeover or deletion occurs.

Using the Block/**F10** (Save) Command to Perform Move and Copy Operations

The last method of performing cut-and-paste operations with WordPerfect involves saving a block of text onto the disk as a separate file and then later reading the file into the current document. To give you experience performing such cut-and-paste operations, do the following.

19. Move the cursor to the # character (Ln 3.17″ Pos 1″), and then block the text which describes the available townhouse unit.

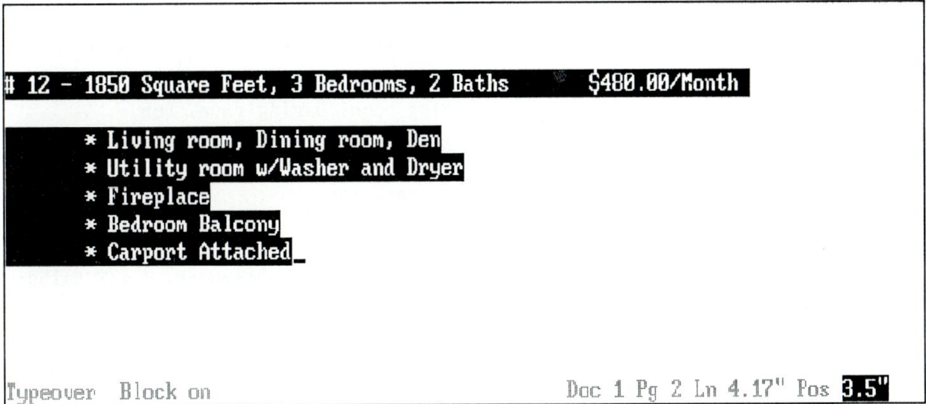

20. Now type the **F10** (Save) command. At the bottom of the screen the message "Block name:" should appear.

NOTE: In the next steps, drive *means type the letter (A, B, etc.) for the disk drive in which your files disk is kept.*

21. Type ‖ *drive*:T12↵ ‖ (for townhouse #12).
22. Next, move the cursor to Ln 4.5″ Pos 1″ and type **Shift-F10** (Retrieve). Answer the prompt "Document to be retrieved:" by typing ‖ *drive*:T12↵ ‖ .

Saving a block of text as a separate file and then reading the block into a document has several advantages over the other cut-and-paste operations discussed here. There are relatively few keystrokes involved, and the saved block will only be replaced on the disk if another block or document is saved with the same filename. The method also provides a simple means to copy blocks of text from one document file to one or more other document files. The biggest disadvantage of the approach is the possible accumulation over time of several small files on your disk.

LESSON 8 Finishing the Document

1. Use the commands of your choice to bring the second page of the document to the form shown on the following page.

```
                  Vista Ridge Townhouses
                  ======================

                      Units Available
                  For Immediate Occupancy


# 12 - 1850 Square Feet, 3 Bedrooms, 2 Baths       $480.00/Month

       * Living room, Dining room, Den
       * Utility room w/Washer and Dryer
       * Fireplace
       * Bedroom Balcony
       * Carport Attached

# 27 - 1600 Square Feet, 3 Bedrooms, 1 1/2 Baths   $430.00/Month

       * Living room, Dining room, Den
       * Utility room w/Washer and Dryer Hookups
       * Fireplace
       * Carport Attached

# 44 - 1050 Square Feet, 3 Bedrooms, 2 Baths       $465.00/Month

       * Living room, Dining room, Den
       * Utility room w/Washer and Dryer
       * Fireplace
       * Bedroom Balcony

# 53 - 1200 Square Feet, 2 Bedrooms, 1 Bath        $380.00/Month

       * Living room, Dining room
       * Utility room w/Washer and Dryer
       * Fireplace

Typeover                                  Doc 1 Pg 2 Ln 7.67" Pos 1"
```

LESSON 9 Using the **F5** (List Files) Command

The **F5** (List Files) command may be used to change the default disk drive and perform several file management operations from within WordPerfect. The screen presented by the List Files command displays the files on the current disk or directory. To demonstrate some of the List Files command features do the following.

1. Type the **F5** (List Files) command.

At the bottom of the screen you will see a message similar to

```
Dir A:\*.*                                (Type = to change default Dir)
```

Changing the Default Disk Drive/ Directory

The current default disk drive and directory appears on the left side of the status line. The information displayed there should describe where your files are currently located. To change WordPerfect's default disk drive and directory, you may type = and then enter the appropriate drive and directory.

2. If the drive and directory displayed on the left side of the message does not describe where your files are currently located, change the default disk drive and then type ‖ ↵↵ ‖ to view the List Files screen. Otherwise, type ‖ ↵ ‖ to view the List Files screen.

The **F5** (List Files) Command Screen

A screen similar to the following will appear.

```
11/09/88 09:45                Directory A:\*.*
Document size:     2588   Free:  1450496   Used:      5779          Files:  4

. <CURRENT>     <DIR>                      | .. <PARENT>      <DIR>
EXAMPLE .          1340  11/07/88 16:01    | T12      .          791  10/28/88 10:50
TESTFILE.          1068  11/07/88 12:02    | WPTUT1   .         2580  10/30/88 11:03

1 Retrieve; 2 Delete; 3 Move/Rename; 4 Print; 5 Text In;
6 Look; 7 Other Directory; 8 Copy; 9 Word Search; N Name Search: 6
```

The reverse video bar shown in the top left corner of the screen is the (List Files) cursor. The cursor may be moved about the screen with the cursor control keys. In general, to use the **F5** (List Files) commands, you first move the cursor to a file listed on the screen and then type the number or letter of the command you wish to execute, as demonstrated in the following steps.

3. Move the cursor to the file named T12 and then type **2** or **D** (**D**elete).

The message "Delete *drive*:\T12? (Y/N)" will appear at the bottom of the screen.

4. Next type **Y** to complete the Delete File operation.

The file you created for the purpose of making copies of text should now be erased from the disk.

5. Next type **F1** (Cancel) or **F7** (Exit) to leave the List Files screen and return to normal editing of the document.

LESSON 10
Saving a Document

You may save a document file onto your disk by using the **F10** (Save) command.

1. Type **F10** (Save) to begin the save operation.

The message "Document to be saved:" will appear at the bottom of the screen on the status line.

2. Now type ‖ WPTUT1↵ ‖.

WPTUT1 stands for WordPerfect tutorial #1 and is simply a filename that conforms to the rules for filenames.

Notice that when the Insert mode is on, the filename now appears on the left side of the status line. If you save the document again, the procedure will be slightly different. After typing **F10** (Save) WordPerfect will respond with the prompt "Document to be saved: *drive*:\WPTUT1." If you type ↵, WordPerfect assumes you want to save the document under the same name. The message "Replace *drive*:\WPTUT1? (Y/N) No" appears on the status line as a precaution against accidentally replacing the file on the disk with the file in memory. You must type **Y** to complete the resave operation.

While you create and edit your documents it is highly recommended that you use the **F10** (Save) command about every 15 minutes or so.

LESSON 11
Printing a Document

You are now ready to print the document. To print a document currently in memory, the **Shift-F7** (Print) command is used.

1. Make sure the printer is on, on-line, and connected to your computer. (Your lab may have a shared device control switch. You will need to select your computer as the one currently connected to the printer.)
2. Advance the paper in the printer to the top of the next page.
3. Now type **Shift-F7** (Print).

The following menu will appear on the screen.

```
Print

     1 - Full Document
     2 - Page
     3 - Document on Disk
     4 - Control Printer
     5 - Type Through
     6 - View Document
     7 - Initialize Printer

Options

     S - Select Printer                 Epson FX-86e/286e
     B - Binding                        0"
     N - Number of Copies               1
     G - Graphics Quality               Medium
     T - Text Quality                   High




Selection: 0
```

4. Type **1** or **F** to select the **Shift-F7** (Print), **F**ull Document command.

The printer should respond by printing the document complete with margins, centered text, and underlining. Notice that the printed text is left and right justified to the margins. To print text with a ragged right margin (the type of justification you see on the screen), you must turn justification off with the **Shift-F8,1,3** (Format),**L**ine,**J**ustification command.

LESSON 12 Exiting WordPerfect

The WordPerfect **F7** (Exit) command may be used to properly exit from many WordPerfect commands, or to erase your document file from memory and return to DOS (erase your document and WordPerfect from memory). The Exit command is the only proper way to quit WordPerfect. Any other method may result in lost data. To conclude the tutorial, do the following.

1. Type **F7** (Exit).
2. Answer the prompt "Save document? (Y/N) Yes" by typing **N.** You have already just saved the document with the **F10** (Save) command.
3. Answer the next prompt "Exit WP? (Y/N) No" by typing **Y.**

Vista Ridge Townhouses
~~~~~~~~~~~~~~~~~~~~~~~~

1800 S.W. Sunset View Avenue
Portland, OR 97207

Thank you for your interest in Vista Ridge Townhouses. We feel that our one and two bedroom deluxe townhouse apartments offer adult living at its finest.

Each spacious townhouse unit has wall-to-wall carpeting, drapes, private patio and sun deck. You will find the townhouse of your choice equipped with a completely modern kitchen including a self-defrosting refrigerator, self-cleaning oven, dishwasher and garbage disposal unit. In addition, every Vista Ridge tenant enjoys year-round swimming and sauna plus use of our recreation room and tennis courts.

We are located in the South West Heights area, close to shopping, city parks and University campus. For an appointment to view one of our fine townhouse apartments and a tour of the grounds, please call Mr. Smith at (503) 244-7163.
~~~~~~~~~~~~~~~~~~~~~~~~

Vista Ridge Townhouses
======================

Units Available
For Immediate Occupancy

12 - 1850 Square Feet, 3 Bedrooms, 2 Baths $480.00/Month

* Living room, Dining room, Den
* Utility room w/Washer and Dryer
* Fireplace
* Bedroom Balcony
* Carport Attached

27 - 1600 Square Feet, 3 Bedrooms, 1 1/2 Baths $430.00/Month

* Living room, Dining room, Den
* Utility room w/Washer and Dryer Hookups
* Fireplace
* Carport Attached

44 - 1850 Square Feet, 3 Bedrooms, 2 Baths $465.00/Month

* Living room, Dining room, Den
* Utility room w/Washer and Dryer
* Fireplace
* Bedroom Balcony

53 - 1200 Square Feet, 2 Bedrooms, 1 Bath $380.00/Month

* Living room, Dining room
* Utility room w/Washer and Dryer
* Fireplace

EXERCISE 1
Printer Fonts

Required Preparation

Study the use of the **Ctrl-F8** (Font), **S**ize and **A**ppearance commands and the **Shift-F7** (Print) **V**iew Document command presented in the WordPerfect Command Summary.

Exercise Steps

1. Load WordPerfect into memory.
2. Type ‖ This is an EXAMPLE ‖ , **Alt-F6** (Flush Right), ‖ of Size:↵ ‖ .
3. Next type ‖ This is an EXAMPLE ‖ , **Alt-F6** (Flush Right), ‖ of Appearance:↵ ‖ .

The two lines should appear as follows.

```
This is an EXAMPLE                                      of Size:
This is an EXAMPLE                                of Appearance:
```

4. Make six copies of the first line and eight copies of the second line, and then edit the lines so they appear as in the following.

```
This is an EXAMPLE                           of Size:Superscript
This is an EXAMPLE                             of Size:Subscript
This is an EXAMPLE                                  of Size:Fine
This is an EXAMPLE                                 of Size:Small
This is an EXAMPLE                                 of Size:Large
This is an EXAMPLE                            of Size:Very Large
This is an EXAMPLE                           of Size:Extra Large


This is an EXAMPLE                            of Appearance:Bold
This is an EXAMPLE                       of Appearance:Underline
This is an EXAMPLE                of Appearance:Double Underline
This is an EXAMPLE                          of Appearance:Italic
This is an EXAMPLE                         of Appearance:Outline
This is an EXAMPLE                          of Appearance:Shadow
This is an EXAMPLE                  of Appearance:Small Capitals
This is an EXAMPLE                         of Appearance:Redline
This is an EXAMPLE                       of Appearance:Strikeout







Typeover                            Doc 1 Pg 1 Ln 3.83" Pos 1"
```

5. On each line use the **Alt-F4** (Block) command to first block the text "This is an EXAMPLE." Then select **Ctrl-F8** (Font),**S**ize or **Ctrl-F8** (Font),**A**ppearance and select the appropriate format for that line (the appropriate format is indicated on the flush right side of the line).
6. Set the line spacing to 2 (double) for the entire document.

7. Use the **Shift-F6** (Center) command, and enter your brand of printer where "Make/Model" is indicated to the following heading:

WordPerfect Fonts
Ctrl-F8 (Font) - Size:/Appearance:
Printer - Make/Model

8. Use the **Shift-F7** (Print), **V**iew Document commands to preview the page before you print it. The screen should appear similar to the following.

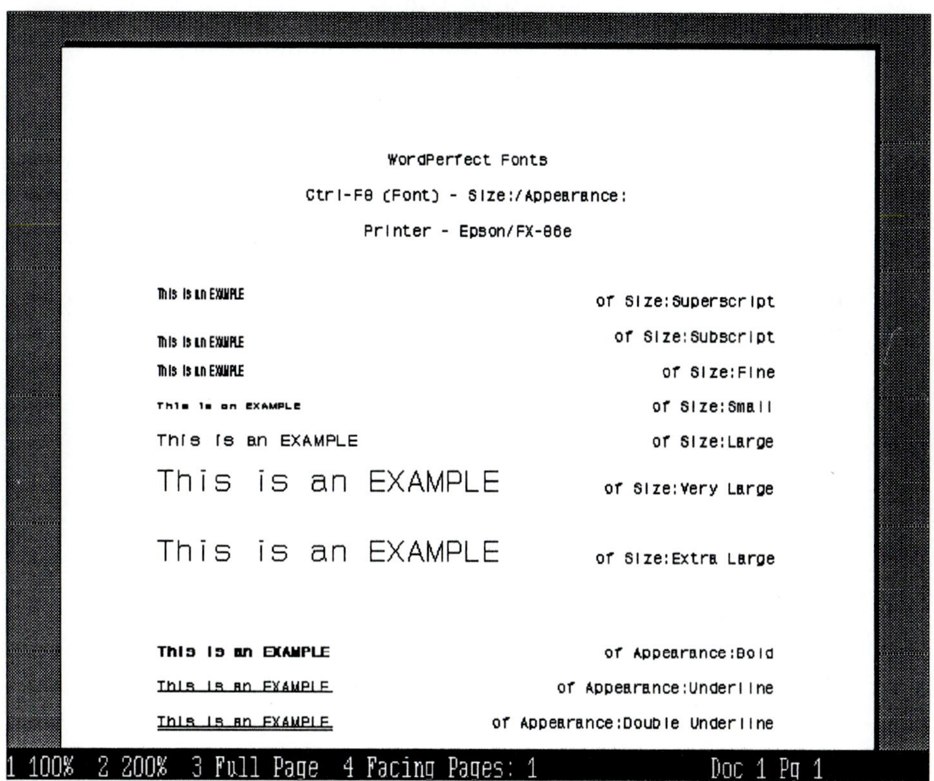

9. Print the document.

The appearance of the printed document will vary depending on the make and model of printer being used. Few printers support all of the available **Ctrl-F8** (Font) command formats.

10. Use the information obtained from the first page of the document to create a second page showing combined formats in a similar manner. For instance, show what a segment of large, bold, italic printed text looks like. Produce four such combinations.
11. Print two copies of the finished document and keep one copy with your WordPerfect documentation for future reference.
12. Save the document file under the name MYFONTS and then exit WordPerfect.

EXERCISE 2
Personal Résumé

The following is a classic exercise that uses many basic word processing skills while providing the opportunity to create an important personal document.

Required Preparation

Study the use of the **F4** (→Indent) and **Ctrl-F8** (Font) commands presented in the WordPerfect Command Summary.

Exercise Steps

1. Load WordPerfect into memory.
2. Using the following example résumé, create your own résumé (or résumé for someone else) in the same or similar form.
3. On a separate page, list the commands you used to format the document together with the codes that the commands imbedded into the résumé.
4. Print the résumé and summary of commands/codes and then save the file under the name RESUME.
5. Exit WordPerfect.

JEROME C. FAIRFAX

P.O. Box 198 Portland, OR 97207
(503) 244-8733 H (503) 229-2724 W

EDUCATION

Bachelor of Arts, Business Administration - Marketing
Bachelor of Arts, Spanish
Certificate of International Business Studies
PORTLAND STATE UNIVERSITY, Portland, OR June 1990

EXPERIENCE

Front Desk/Public Relations
Center Court Athletic club, Portland, OR. Greet and register members and guests. Conduct tours of facility and explain benefits. Attend to members needs, serve snack bar items and make reservations. Promote club programs, answer telephone inquiries, collect and process payments on accounts. (September 1988 to present)

Manager
Coffee House Juice Bar, Portland, OR. Directed set-up and closing procedures. Planned for special events. Presented and promoted product line. Screened and interviewed applicants. Oriented and trained new employees. Supervised five employees. Managed and supervised a food booth at the Artquake Festival with a crew of 20. Controlled cash flow. (June 1985 to September 1988)

Order Desk/Billing Clerk
Ruston Wholesale Glassware, Portland, OR. assisted customers with glassware selections. Handled telephone orders, explained shipping policies to customers and invoiced the previous day's orders. Represented company at Oregon Restaurant Association Convention. (September 1984 to June 1985)

ORGANIZATIONS

AIESEC Association Internationale des Etudiants en Sciences Economiques et Commerciales .. International Association of Students in Economics and Commerce.

- Chapter Vice-President, 1987 - 1988
- Chairperson, Fundraising Committee 1986 - 1988

INTERESTS

Racquetball, white-water rafting, fishing and boating.

Excellent References Available

EXERCISE 3
Search and Replace

Required Preparation

Study the use of the **F2** (→Search), **Shift-F2** (←Search), and **Alt-F2** (Replace) commands presented in the WordPerfect Command Summary.

Exercise Steps

1. Load WordPerfect and then retrieve the document you created in the introductory tutorial (WPTUT1).
2. Start at the top of the file and use the **F2** (→Search) command to find the first occurrence of *Mr. Smith.* Edit the text to read *Mr. Jennings.*
3. Type Home,Home,Up to move the cursor to the top of the file. Turn on the Reveal Codes screen and then use the **F2** (→Search) command to find the next six occurrences of a center [Cntr] code. When finished, return the screen to normal editing.
4. Type Home,Home,Up to move the cursor to the top of the file and then use the **Alt-F2** (Replace) command to replace all occurrences of *townhouse* with *condominium.* Make sure that the replace operation is performed with Confirm as **Y** for *Yes.*
5. Next use the **Alt-F2** (Replace) command to delete all occurrences of the word *apartments.* Conduct the search backwards through the file and make sure that Confirm is **Y**es.
6. Save the file under the name WPTUT1B and then print the document and exit WordPerfect.

Vista Ridge Condominiums
~~~~~~~~~~~~~~~~~~~~~~~~

1800 S.W. Sunset View Avenue
Portland, OR 97207

Thank you for your interest in Vista Ridge Condominiums. We feel that our one and two bedroom deluxe condominiums offer adult living at its finest.

Each spacious condominium unit has wall-to-wall carpeting, drapes, private patio and sun deck. You will find the condominium of your choice equipped with a completely modern kitchen including a self-defrosting refrigerator, self-cleaning oven, dishwasher and garbage disposal unit. In addition, every Vista Ridge tenant enjoys year-round swimming and sauna plus use of our recreation room and tennis courts.

We are located in the South West Heights area, close to shopping, city parks and University campus. For an appointment to view one of our fine condominiums and a tour of the grounds, please call Mr. Jennings at <u>(503) 244-7163</u>.
~~~~~~~~~~~~~~~~~~~~~~~~

EXERCISE 4
Tabular Columns

Required Preparation

Study the use of the **Shift-F8** (Format),**L**ine,**T**ab Set and Block/**Ctrl-F4** (Move) commands presented in the WordPerfect Command Summary.

Exercise Steps

1. Load WordPerfect into memory.

In this exercise, you will specify tab stop settings and use the Tab key to produce the following document.

```
Paper Product        Descr.     Units Per      Average          Cost/Case
   Items                          Case       Sales/Week

Take-Out Cups

  Paper              8 oz         250           400. . . . . . . $15.00
                     12 oz        250           800. . . . . . . $17.00
                     16 oz        150           300. . . . . . . $12.50

  Styrofoam          8 oz          75          1200. . . . . . . .$3.50
                     12 oz         75           600. . . . . . . .$4.25

Sandwich Wrap

  Wax Paper          Plain       5000          4000. . . . . . . $50.75
                     Printed     5000          2500. . . . . . . $75.30
  Aluminum           Printed     5000           900. . . . . . .$125.00

Take-Out Utensils

  Forks              Plastic      500           350. . . . . . . .$7.50
  Spoons             Plastic      500           275. . . . . . . .$6.00
  Knives             Plastic      750            75. . . . . . . .$9.00
                                                      Doc 1 Pg 1 Ln 1" Pos 1"
```

On Line 1″ at Pos 1″ you will insert a [Tab Set:] code into the document. The tabs are designed for centering the table headings to the tab stops in the first two lines of text. When you are finished specifying the appropriate tab stops, the **T**ab Set screen will appear as follows.

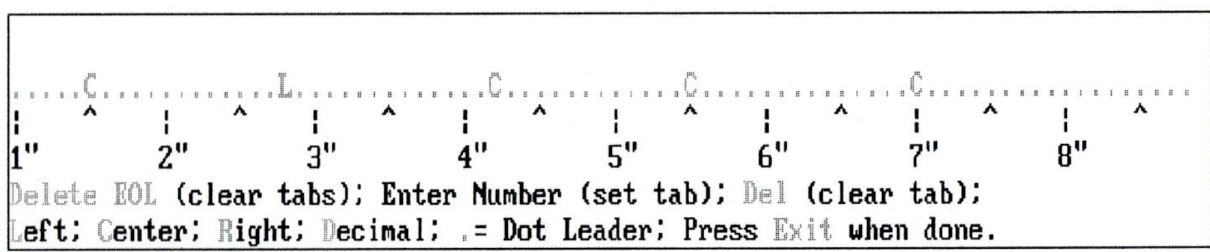

```
....C..........L............C...........C.............C..................
!    ^    !     ^    !     ^    !     ^    !     ^    !     ^    !     ^    !     ^
1"        2"         3"         4"         5"         6"         7"         8"
Delete EOL (clear tabs); Enter Number (set tab); Del (clear tab);
Left; Center; Right; Decimal; .= Dot Leader; Press Exit when done.
```

2. Move the cursor to the appropriate Ln″/Pos″ screen position and then use the **Shift-F8** (Format),**L**ine,**T**ab Set command to set the correct tab stop types at the positions shown.

3. Enter the first two lines of text, being sure to use the Tab key to move the cursor to the next heading position. End each line with a [HRt] (↵).

When finished, use the Reveal Codes screen to ensure that only text characters and [Tab] codes occur in the two lines.

On the line beneath the headings (Ln 1.5″ Pos 1″) there is another [Tab Set:] code designed to align the items in the table to their respective tab stops in a variety of ways. When you are finished specifying the appropriate tab stops for the second [Tab Set:] code, the **T**ab Set screen will appear as follows.

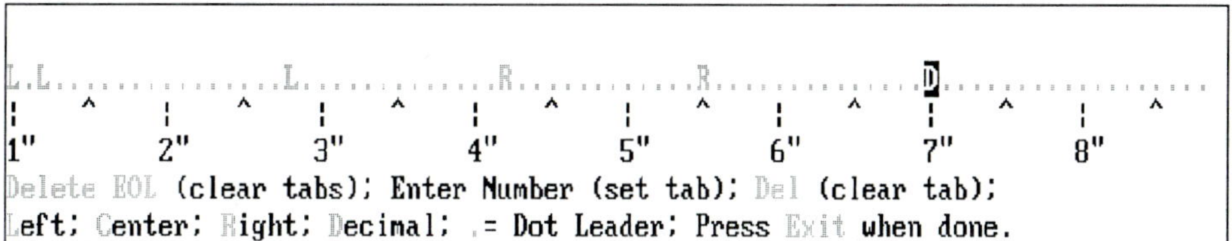

Notice that the last tab stop is **D**ecimal type with a Dot Leader.

4. Move the cursor to the appropriate Ln″/Pos″ screen position and then use the **Shift-F8** (Format),**L**ine,**T**ab Set command to set the correct tab stop types at the positions shown for the second [Tab Set:] code.
5. Enter the lines of text that comprise the table of items, numbers, and costs. Again, be sure to use the Tab key to move the cursor to the next entry position on a line and use a ↵ to end each line. Use the Reveal Codes screen to ensure that only text characters and [Tab] codes occur in the table.
6. Save the file under the name TABCOLS.

In the next steps you will move the column labeled "Average Sales/Week" one column to the left. To do so, you will need to use the Block/**Ctrl-F4** (Move),Tabular **C**olumn,**M**ove command.

7. Review the steps required to perform a Tabular **C**olumn,**M**ove operation in the WordPerfect Command Summary.

If the following does not work as expected, use the **F7** (Exit) command to clear the screen (**F7**,N,↵) and then retrieve "TABCOLS" and try again.

8. Use the command to move the "Average Sales/Week" column (with its label) one column to the left.

Paper Product Items	Descr.	Average Sales/Week	Units Per Case	Cost/Case
Take-Out Cups				
Paper	8 oz	400	250. . . . . . . $15.00	
	12 oz	800	250. . . . . . . $17.00	
	16 oz	300	150. . . . . . . $12.50	
Styrofoam	8 oz	1200	75. . . . .$3.50	
	12 oz	600	75. . . . .$4.25	
Sandwich Wrap				
Wax Paper	Plain	4000	5000. . . . . . . $50.75	
	Printed	2500	5000. . . . . . . $75.30	
Aluminum	Printed	900	5000. . . . . .$125.00	
Take-Out Utensils				
Forks	Plastic	350	500. . . . .$7.50	
Spoons	Plastic	275	500. . . . .$6.00	
Knives	Plastic	75	750. . . . .$9.00	

Doc 1 Pg 1 Ln 1" Pos 1"

9. Save the document under the name TABCOLS2 and then print the document.

To gain further experience, it is recommended that you practice copying and moving other columns in the table using the Block/**Ctrl-F4** (Move),Tabular Column commands.

10. When finished, exit WordPerfect.

EXERCISE 5 Formal Reports

Required Preparation

Study the use of the **Ctrl-2** (Spell), **Alt-F1** (Thesaurus), **Shift-F8** (Format), **P**age,**H**eader, **Shift-F7** (Print), **V**iew Document, and **Ctrl-F7** (Footnote) commands presented in the WordPerfect Command Summary.

Exercise Steps

1. Load WordPerfect into memory.
2. To begin the exercise, type the following text. The misspelled words in the text are intentional, so take care to enter the text exactly as it is shown here. Begin the heading "Introduction" six lines down from the top of the document (at Ln 2.16").

Introduction

Word Processing has longe been an intregal part of many business organizations. Webster difines Word Processing as "the production of typewriten documents (as business letters) with automated and usually computerized typing and text-editing equipment." The equipment may range from typewriters with memory, correction and mag card features to dedicated word processing equipment to general perpuse computers using specalized word processing software.

Until recently, the the expanse of word processing equipment and software made it a viable option only to document-intense businesses that could justify the cost. Many businesses with lower volume needs turned to outside service organizations specalizing in Word Processing to provide this function. With the apperance of the microcomputer, however, even small businesses could afford to computerize many business functions, and soon thereafter word processing software became available and afordable to anyone with even minimal word processing requirements.

With the recent development and proliferation of word processing software for the desktop microcomputer comes a wide array of choices. Software prices now range from under fifty to several hundred dollars, with a coresponding range of features and capapilities. Its role in business has also changed, as word processing has become recognized as a useful and versitile tool for people at various organizational levels.

3. Use the **Ctrl-F2** (Spell) command to perform a spelling check on the entire document. Correct any misspelled words and remove any unnecessary double words from the document using WordPerfect's Spell feature. The following is a list of correct spellings for the words upon which the spelling check should stop.

   long

   integral (use the **L**ook Up command to find the proper spelling for this word)

   defines

   typewritten

   purpose

   specialized

   specializing

   appearance

   affordable

   desktop (this word is spelled correctly, use the Skip command)

   corresponding

   capabilities

   versatile

Notice that the spell checker did not catch the misspelling of the word *expense,* located in the first line of the second paragraph. The misspelled word *expanse* is itself a correctly spelled word. The word was included in the exercise to demonstrate that spell checking is no substitute for proofreading.

4. Edit the word *expanse* to reflect the correct spelling of the word *expense.*

5. Next use **Alt-F1** (Thesaurus) to find suitable synonyms for the following words.

viable
justify
outside
available
useful

6. Now use **Shift-F8** (Format) to add an *A* page header to be printed on every page of the document. The header should be aligned flush right, and should include the words "Word Processing Page #" followed by the code that will print the current page number in the header.
7. Next set the line spacing to 2 for the entire document. Then use the **Shift-F7** (Print), **V**iew Document command to ensure that the header will be properly printed.
8. Now move the cursor to the right of the word *dedicated* found in the first paragraph and enter a footnote containing the following text

|| Dedicated refers to hardware designed for one specific function. ||

9. Move the cursor to the space following the second word in the first paragraph, *Processing,* and enter another footnote containing the text

|| Also referred to as Text Processing, a term deemed more appropriate by some. ||

10. Use the **Shift-F7** (Print), **V**iew Document command to see that the two footnotes will be properly printed.
11. Save the document under the name "REPORT", print the document, and then exit WordPerfect.

EXERCISE 6
Boiler Plate Contracts

Many situations require a standard form or document (general text) which needs to be filled in with specific information. When this is the case, it is often possible to automatically merge the specific information into the general text to produce the desired finished document.

This exercise is designed to demonstrate the use of merge codes used in a procedure called *boiler plating.* In boiler plating, the general text is called the *primary file* and is the document in which the merge codes are placed. The specific information is either typed in by the user or is kept in other related files. In this exercise, the following merge codes will be used.

^C Pauses the merge operation to allow text to be entered from the keyboard. The **F9** (Merge R) command is used to resume the merge operation after the pause.

^O (^Omessage^O). Two ^O codes are used to enclose a message which will be displayed on the status line during the merge operation. ^O codes are usually used in conjunction with other merge codes in the primary file.

^P (^Pfilename^P). Two ^P codes are used to enclose the filename of a file to be merged into the Primary file during the merge operation. It is most useful when combined with a ^C merge code.

Merge codes are placed into the primary file with the **Shift-F9** (Merge Codes) command. After typing **Shift-F9** (Merge Codes), type the letter of the code you want placed into the document at the current cursor location.

Required Preparation

Study the use of the **Ctrl-F9** (Merge/Sort),**M**erge commands, the **Shift-F9** (Merge Codes) command, and the **F9** (Merge R) command presented in the WordPerfect Command Summary.

Exercise Steps

To begin, you will create the primary file for a rental contract. Here the merge codes have been shaded to improve the readability of the text. The merge codes on your monitor screen will probably not be shaded.

1. Create the primary file as it is shown in the following. Be sure to use the **Shift-F9** (Merge Codes) command to generate the various merge codes included. Note that the dollar signs occur at Pos 6.1".

```
                    Vista Ridge Townhouses
                       Rental Agreement
                    ======================

This rental agreement made and entered into this ^C day of ^C 1989,
by and between Vista Ridge Townhouses hereinafter called the
lessor, and ^OEnter lessee's first and last names^O^C hereinafter
called lessee,

In consideration of the covenants and stipulations herein contained
on the part of the lessee to be paid, kept and faithfully
performed, the lessor does hereby lease, demise, and let unto said
lessee those certain premises, for the stated payments in lawful
money, known and described as follows:

^OEnter townhouse number^PT^C^P^O

Additional monthly fees:
^OLocker Storage? (Y/N) ^PLOCK^C^P^O

                                   Total Monthly Rent $

Deposits:
^OCleaning fee: 1 Small, 2 Large ^PCLEAN^C^P^O
^OPet Deposit? (Y/N) ^PPET^C^P^O

                                       Total Deposits $

                                     Payment Received $

Signed: ________________________ Lessor

        ________________________ Lessee
```

2. Save the file under the name "RNTCNT" (for rental contract) and then use the **F7** (Exit) command to clear the screen (**F7**,n,↵).

The next steps involve creating four separate *secondary files*.

3. Note that the dollar sign occurs at 6.1″ and then type the following.

```
Townhouse # 12 - 1850 Square Feet, 3 Bedrooms, 2 Baths. Includes
drapes, carpets, kitchen appliances, washer and dryer.

Address: 9110 S.W. Sunset Ave  Portland, OR 97207

Rental Fee ..................................... $480.00/Month
```

4. Now make two copies of the townhouse description and edit the copied text to the following form.

```
Townhouse # 12 - 1850 Square Feet, 3 Bedrooms, 2 Baths. Includes
drapes, carpets, kitchen appliances, washer and dryer.

Address: 9110 S.W. Sunset Ave  Portland, OR 97207

Rental Fee ..................................... $480.00/Month


Townhouse # 27 - 1600 Square Feet, 3 Bedrooms, 1 1/2 Baths.
Includes drapes, carpets, kitchen appliances, washer and dryer.

Address: 9157 S.W. Sunset Ave  Portland, OR 97207

Rental Fee ..................................... $430.00/Month


Townhouse # 44 - 1850 Square Feet, 3 Bedrooms, 2 Baths. Includes
drapes, carpets, kitchen appliances, washer and dryer.

Address: 9157 S.W. Sunset Ave  Portland, OR 97207

Rental Fee ..................................... $465.00/Month
Typeover                              Doc 1 Pg 1 Ln 4.67" Pos 1"
```

5. Use the Block/**F10** (Save) command to first block and then save each of the townhouse descriptions. Save the blocks under the filenames T12, T27, and T44 for the townhouse descriptions, top to bottom on the screen respectively.
6. Now clear the screen with the **F7** (Exit) command (**F7**,N,↵).
7. Type the following five lines of text. Note that the lines begin at Pos 1.5″ and that the dollar signs occur at 6.1″.

```
Cleaning Fee Non-refundable ................ $ 35.00

Cleaning Fee Non-refundable ................ $ 55.00

Pet Deposit ................................ $ 50.00/pet

No Pet Deposit Made

Locker Storage ............................. $ 25.00/month
```

8. Next block and save each line under the filename indicated.

CLEAN 1	Cleaning Fee Non-refundable .... $ 35.00
CLEAN 2	Cleaning Fee Non-refundable .... $ 55.00
PETY	Pet Deposit .... $ 50.00/pet
PETN	No Pet Deposit Made
LOCKY	Locker Storage .... $ 25.00/month

9. Now block a single space character and save it under the filename "LOCKN".

During a merge operation, WordPerfect must find all related files to be merged with the primary file. The file LOCKN (consisting of one space character) will be merged into the contract should the user answer N to the "Locker Storage? (Y/N) " prompt (found between the ^O codes on Ln 4.17″ of the primary file).

10. Next use the **F7** (Exit) command to clear the screen.

You now are ready to perform a boiler plate merge. The contract you will produce is for the following situation. The date is July 29th. The new renters are John and Lisa Livingston. They will be renting townhouse #27, which is a small unit requiring the $35 cleaning deposit. They have a Siamese cat and will need locker storage for their belongings.

11. Make sure the screen is clear and then type **Ctrl-F9, 1** (Merge/Sort),**M**erge.
12. Answer the "Primary file:" prompt by typing ‖ RNTCNT↵ ‖ . Answer the next prompt "Secondary file:" by typing ‖ ↵ ‖ .

Secondary files are not normally used during boiler plate merge operations.

A copy of the primary file (RNTCNT) should appear on the screen with the cursor stopped where the first ^C code occurred in the file.

13. Type ‖ 29th ‖ and then type the **F9** (Merge R) command.
14. When the cursor stops at the next ^C code type ‖ July ‖ and then type the **F9** (Merge R) command.

The next merge codes encountered

^OEnter lessee's first and last names^O^C

are combined to present a message on the status line and then pause for the user to type in an entry. Notice the message at the bottom of the screen.

15. Type || John and Lisa Livingston || and then type the **F9** (Merge R) command.

The remaining four sets of merge codes all perform similarly. They present a message at the bottom of the screen requesting a particular response from the user. The responses to the messages (27, Y, 1, etc.) then are used as the last part of the filename (T27, LOCKY, CLEAN1, etc.) to specify the particular file to be merged into the primary file.

^OEnter townhouse number^PT^C^P^O

16. Continue by typing || 27 || and then the **F9** (Merge R) command. Now answer the remaining three prompts appropriately. Be sure to end each entry by typing **F9** (Merge R).
17. Save the finished contract under the name LIVICNT and print the document. Next clear the screen with the **F7** (Exit) command, retrieve RNTCNT, and print the primary file. Finally, exit WordPerfect.

EXERCISE 7 Business Form Letters—Part A

This exercise concerns a "frequent flyers" club that rewards its members with free air travel based on the number of miles they have traveled with a particular airline. In the exercise you will create a small database (secondary) file in which information on club members will be kept. There are 13 fields of data for each member in the database. The first field contains the member's account number and the second field contains a letter code to indicate if the member is a Regular, Silver Wings, or Platinum Wings member (three different classes of members having varying club privileges). Fields three through ten contain the member's title, first name, middle initial (if any), last name, address, city, state, and ZIP code. The last three fields in the record contain the air miles logged by the member in the years 1988, 1989 and 1990, respectively.

Required Preparation

Study the **Ctrl-F9** (Merge/Sort),**M**erge commands presented in the WordPerfect Command Summary.

Exercise Steps

1. Load WordPerfect and begin the exercise by creating a secondary file that contains the following fields of record data. When finished, save the file under the name MEMDAT1.

ACCTNO	L	T	FIRST	M	LAST	ADDRESS	CITY	ST	ZIP	(Miles Traveled) 1988	1989	1990
1-00117	R	Ms.	Robin	R.	Nichols	1680 Rio Lindo	Portland	OR	97206	27,904	28,941	12,444
2-00014	R	Mr.	Richard	L.	Dehen	9215 Lincoln Drive	Portland	OR	97221	57,906	64,852	83,352
2-00021	R	Dr.	Michael	S.	Brown	1025 SW Jenkins Road	Beaverton	OR	97005	40,912	45,815	58,836
2-00037	S	Mr.	Mark	A.	Egger	1017 Molalla Avenue	Oregon City	OR	97045	119,899	110,506	112,716
2-00042	R	Mr.	Stewart		Matsura	140 South Spruce	Portland	OR	97256	50,825	68,432	10,256
2-00054	S	Ms.	Joanna	D.	Rowe	1800 River Drive	Eugene	OR	97401	98,803	110,647	142,128
2-00057	P	Mr.	John	J.	Corrida	1091 Tuckman Road	Hood River	OR	97031	285,005	263,755	255,000
2-00075	S	Dr.	Leslie	C.	Walther	1400 NW Garden Blvd	Roseburg	OR	97470	137,886	143,423	66,444
5-00110	R	Mr.	Kevin	W.	McAdams	3770 Commercial SE	Salem	OR	97302	30,126	1,012	2,598
2-00111	P	Ms.	Paula		Hartkorn	Box 2880	Portland	OR	97212	329,490	304,826	295,968

With the cursor at the top of the file, the screen should now appear as follows.

```
1-00117^R
R^R
Ms.^R
Robin^R
R.^R
Nichols^R
1680 Rio Lindo^R
Portland^R
OR^R
97206^R
27,904^R
28,941^R
12,444^R
^E
==============================================================================
2-00014^R
R^R
Mr.^R
Richard^R
L.^R
Dehen^R
9215 W. Lincoln Drive^R
Portland^R
OR^R
A:\MEMDAT1                                          Doc 1 Pg 1 Ln 1" Pos 1"
```

2. Make sure the file has been properly saved and then clear the screen.

You next will create a form letter which will serve as the primary file for the merge operation. The primary file, when merged with the secondary file, will produce the following document for the first record in the database.

```
                   Trans Continental Airways
                     Super Travellers Club

    Air England - French Airways - Asian Pacific - Bundesluft

Account No:  1-00117                          October 15, 1989

Robin R. Nichols
1680 Rio Lindo
Portland, OR 97206

Dear Ms. Nichols

It is now easier than ever to find out your current mileage balance
with our new automated phone service.  Our toll free number for
account information is 1-800-445-7036.

When calling for information, you will be instructed to press the
buttons on your touch phone to enter your account number and
request information.  Of course, if you are not at a touch phone
or would like other information, simply stay on the line and your
call will be answered by a service representative.  We hope find
this new system to be fast and convenient.

                                          Doc 1 Pg 1 Ln 1" Pos 1"
```

3. Enter the appropriate merge codes and text to create the primary file. When finished, save the file under the name FORMLET and clear the screen.
4. Now perform the merge operation that will produce a form letter for each record in the member database. After the merge operation has been completed, print the first three merged form letters, a copy of the primary file used, and the first three records in the secondary file. Then exit WordPerfect.

EXERCISE 8 Business Form Letters—Part B

This exercise uses the small database of club member information created in exercise 7.

Required Preparation

Study the **Ctrl-F9** (Merge/Sort) commands presented in the WordPerfect Command Summary.

Exercise Steps

To begin the exercise you will create a small file that contains the text and merge codes that will later serve as the *header record* for the secondary file MEMDAT1.

1. Load WordPerfect into memory and then create a header record for the database MEMDAT1 that uses the following field names.

Field 1 — ACCTNO
Field 2 — STATUS
Field 3 — TITLE
Field 4 — FIRST
Field 5 — MI
Field 6 — LAST
Field 7 — ADDRESS
Field 8 — CITY
Field 9 — STATE
Field 10 — ZIP
Field 11 — M88
Field 12 — M89
Field 13 — M90

2. When finished, save the file under the name MEMHEAD and then clear the screen.
3. Next, create the primary file that, if merged with the first record of the member database (assuming the header record is present), would produce the following form letter.

```
                    Trans Continental Airways
                      Super Travellers Club

    Air England - French Airways - Asian Pacific - Bundesluft


Account No:  1-00117                              October 15, 1989

Robin R. Nichols
1600 Rio Lindo
Portland, OR 97206

Dear Ms. Nichols

Congratulations!

Because your mileage balance is now over 100,000 miles for the
year, you have earned your Silver Wings making you one of our most
valuable customers.  Full details of the Silver Wings membership
privileges will be in your mail soon.

Super Travellers Club
Silver Wings Department
                                          Doc 1 Pg 1 Ln 1" Pos 1"
```

4. Save the document under the name SILVER and then clear the screen.
5. Now use the **Ctrl-F9** (Merge/Sort) commands to select (copy) from the disk file MEMDAT1 to the screen those member records where the 1990 air mileage is greater than 100,000 miles but less than 200,000 miles.
6. Next move the cursor to the top of the selected records file and retrieve the file named MEMHEAD (the header record file). Next, save the selected records under the name MEMSILV and then clear the screen.
7. Use the **Ctrl-F9** (Merge/Sort) commands to merge the primary file SILVER with the secondary file MEMSILV and print the two resulting form letters. Then exit WordPerfect.

EXERCISE 9
Keyboard Macros

WordPerfect's *Macro* feature may be used to save a series of frequently used keystrokes. The same keystrokes then may be executed at any time.

Required Preparation

Before beginning the exercise, read about the **Ctrl-F10** (Macro Define) and **Alt-F10** (Macro) commands in the WordPerfect Command Summary.

Exercise Steps

Before defining your own macros, you will reset the default directory for macro files with the **Shift-F1** (Setup) command. You should make a note of the currently defined directory for macro files in order to change it back upon completion of the exercise.

1. Type **Shift-F1,7,3** (Setup),**L**ocation of Auxiliary Files,**K**eyboard/Macro Files. Write down the entry displayed and then change it to the location (drive and directory) of your tutorial files disk/directory. Then use the ↵ key to return to normal editing.

Suppose that you often change from single-spaced to double-spaced text, and vice versa. You would like a macro to perform the necessary keystrokes. The steps to change line formatting to double spacing are as follows.

1. Type **Shift-F8,1,6** (Format),**L**ine,Line **S**pacing
2. Type ‖ 2↵ ‖
3. Type **F7** (Exit)

2. Define a macro named ALT-D to change to double spacing.
3. Test the macro by executing it with the **Alt-F3** (Reveal Codes) screen on.
4. Type **Ctrl-F10,**Alt-D,**2** (Macro Define),*(name)*,**E**dit to check the macro against the example that follows the exercise. With the Macro Define screen displayed, type Shift-Print Screen (Shift-PrtScr) to print the screen.

NOTE: Shift-PrtScr is a DOS function call used to output the contents of the screen to the printer and is not specific to WordPerfect. Be sure that a printer is connected to your computer and is on line before you execute this command.

The steps to change line formatting to single spacing are as follows.

1. Type **Shift-F8,1,6** (Format),**L**ine,**L**ine **S**pacing
2. Type ‖ 1↵ ‖
3. Type **F7** (Exit)

5. Define and test a macro named ALT-S to change to single spacing.

Now suppose that you often call out specific words in a document with both double underlining and bolding. With the cursor at the beginning of a word within a sentence, the steps for double underlining and bolding the word would be as follows.

1. **Alt-F4** (Block)
2. Ctrl-→ (Word right)
3. ← (Cursor left)
4. **Ctrl-F8,2,3** (Font),**A**ppearance,**D**bl Und
5. **Alt-F4** (Block)
6. Ctrl-← (Word left)
7. **F6** (Bold)

6. Define and test a macro named ALT-U to hold the keystrokes for double underlining and bolding a word.
7. The following are suggestions for relatively simple macros. Now define and test a macro to perform an operation (execute keystrokes). The macro may be based upon the suggestions here or may be a macro of your choice.
   1. Write a macro to type the headings for a memo, with lines for DATE:, TO:, FROM:, SUBJECT:, and so forth.
   2. Write a macro to set left and right margins to two inches, and to set left tabs every inch.
   3. Read about the **Shift-F5** (Date/Outline) commands in the Word-Perfect Command Summary. Then write a macro to place date text in the format: Friday, 6 January 1989, 3:02 pm.
8. Before exiting WordPerfect, use the **Shift-F1** (Setup) command to change the default drive/directory for macro files to its original drive/directory as noted in step 1.

Example Macros

```
Macro: Edit

      File              ALTD.WPM

  1 - Description       Double Space Text

  2 - Action

    {DISPLAY OFF}{Format}ls2{Enter}
    {Exit}
```

```
Macro: Edit

     File            ALTS.WPM

  1 - Description    Single Space Text

  2 - Action

      {DISPLAY OFF}{Format}ls1{Enter}
      {Exit}
```

```
Macro: Edit

     File            ALTU.WPM

  1 - Description

  2 - Action

      {DISPLAY OFF}{Block}{Word Right}{Left}{Underline}{Block}{Word Left}
      {Bold}
```

CASES

CASE 1
Los Baez, Mexican Restaurant

Burke Wilson is the new owner of the Los Baez, a Mexican restaurant located near a large university in Seattle, Washington. The restaurant's main business is serving lunch and dinner to college students and faculty. Burke bought the restaurant knowing that it had several regular customers who enjoyed the quiet hacienda atmosphere and high-quality food available there.

The restaurant seats about 85 people, with most of the tables seating four to six customers. After several months of operating the restaurant, Burke noticed that during the lunch and dinner rushes many of the tables had only one or two people seated at them. In talking with customers, he found that often there were more people who would have joined the party for lunch, but didn't because they didn't care for Mexican food.

Burke decided to offer a non-Mexican meal special during rush hours to encourage new customers to join their friends. Burke and the cook decided that a different non-menu meal special would be offered every day. After a few weeks of serving the specials, Burke noted in a conversation with the cook that the customers were taking advantage of the new special offerings: "Not only are new customers coming in, but regular customers are ordering the specials for a change of pace. The lasagna you made for today sold out before 2:00 PM. We should double the amount of meat loaf planned for tomorrow. I've noticed that very few customers can see the daily special chalkboard from their seats. What we really need is some way to include the daily special in our regular menu. If I had a nicely laid-out master copy, I could have it copied for about four cents a page. Besides making selecting from the menu more convenient for the customer, "disposable" menus might save us money over time because typesetting and laminating menus, like we do now, costs quite a bit."

The Los Baez
1939 S.W. 6th Ave
Seattle, Washington
(206) 365-7741

Regular Menu Items and Ingredients

(all nachos are topped with green onions, tomatoes and black olives—add sour cream or guacamole/$1.25 extra.)

CHEESE NACHO
cheddar cheese, white cheese, taco chips $3.95
1/2 order $2.95

NACHO GRANDE
cheddar cheese, meat sauce, spiced meat $4.95
1/2 order $3.95

THE MINI NACHO
cheddar cheese, meat sauce, spiced meat
sour cream, guacamole $3.25

CHIPS and SALSA $1.50
CHIPS and BEAN DIP $1.95
CHIPS and GUACAMOLE $2.75
Side of Guacamole . . . . $.75
Side of Sour Cream . . . . $.50

(all chili topped with cheese and onions)

CHILI CON CARNE	cup-$1.95	bowl-$2.25
ALL BEEF CHILI	cup-$2.75	bowl-$3.75
TEXICANA HOT CHILI	cup-$2.50	bowl-$3.00

DINNER SALAD (topped with cheese and tomatoes) $1.50
CHILI AND SALAD $4.00
TACO SALAD - A bed of lettuce topped with spiced meat, cheese, sour cream, guacamole, tomatoes, green onions, black olives and a ring of taco chips $3.95

SOUTH OF THE BORDER

(all served with taco chips, add rice and beans for $1.25 extra)

TACO
A soft flour tortilla, cheese, lettuce, tomatoes, spiced meat.
1 Taco $1.75
2 Tacos $2.95

CHEESE ENCHILADA
A corn tortilla, cheese, sour cream, enchilada sauce, topped with green onions $3.25

BEEF ENCHILADA
Same as cheese enchilada with spiced meat, refried beans, topped with green onions and olives $3.75

BEAN BURRITO
A flour tortilla filled with refried beans, cheese and sauce $3.25

BEEF BURRITO
Same as a bean burrito with spiced meat $3.75

BEAN TOSTADA
A corn tortilla topped with refried beans, shredded lettuce, cheese and tomatoes $3.25

BEEF TOSTADA
Same as a bean tostada with spiced meat $3.75

COMBINATION PLATTER
Choice of any two of the above dishes served with rice and beans $6.25

Side Orders	
Refried Beans	$.75
Rice	$.75
Sour Cream	$.50
Guacamole	$.75
Flour Tortilla	$.50
Corn Tortilla	$.50

Beverages	
Coffee/decaf	$.50
Assorted Teas	$.50
Hot Spiced Cider	$.50
Iced Tea	$.50
Milk	$.75
Sodas	$.50

CASE 2A
Lakeside Limousine Service—Part A

Laura Gauge is the senior operations manager for a limousine service based in Chicago, Illinois. The firm, Lakeside Limousine Service, has been in business since early 1984. In its initial years, the company acquired several regular clients. Throughout the operating year, most requests for limousine services are for transportation to and from the busy O'Hare Airport in Chicago. In reviewing past records, Laura has reached the conclusion that Lakeside's airport business is growing at a fairly constant rate of 8 percent per year and that competition in the area is quite high. She has decided that future growth for the company must come from promoting services in areas having less competitive market conditions.

During the coming holiday season, Lakeside's marketing department plans to release an advertising campaign aimed at generating new clients. The company intends to promote the use of its services for transportation to and from Christmas and New Year celebrations, emphasizing the offer of reduced rates to keep drunk drivers off the road for a safer holiday season. Part of the planned campaign involves distributing informational brochures through the local Restaurant and Bar Association.

In a recent conversation with William Blake, head of the marketing department, Laura was heard to say, "Bill, your holiday season promotion idea seems to be worth trying, but we have never tried to tap this market before. We'll have to keep advertising costs down and try this idea on a trial basis this year. If it works out the way you think, next year we'll add radio and newspaper spots to the promotion. Let's see if we can use that new microcomputer to produce a presentable brochure, and then go ahead with our plans to distribute it through the Restaurant and Bar Association."

Lakeside Limousine Service
11015 Lake Shore Drive
(312) 446-7785

Limousine Service - $55.00 per hour, plus $3.85/mile traveled
$5.00/hour for each additional passenger

Limousine Features - Cellular Phone, VCR, Color TV, AM/FM Cassette Stereo, Intercom, Sunroof, Privacy Windows

Campaign Slogan (key words) - Safe with Style

Discounts - Half Price Between 10:00 PM and 12:00 Midnight

CASE 2B
Lakeside Limousine Service—Part B

The Lakeside Limousine Service plans to institute a "Mileage Plus" program for regular clients who have been using its services for more than one year. The program will provide regular customers with a 15 percent mileage bonus for miles they have traveled in the current year.

To kick off the new program, form letters announcing the discounts and terms are to be mailed to clients who already qualify for bonus miles. The first mailing will be followed by a second mailing to new customers informing them of the program and their current mileage status. In addressing the marketing department, Laura stated, "As senior operations manager, it is my job to keep an eye on costs while maintaining a profitable operation. When the company was first getting started, it was important to keep costs as low as possible to get us on our feet. Everything from creating brochures to typing letters for our clients was done manually. With the onset of new microcomputer software, however, I have decided it is a good time to start to automate the processes."

Partial Customer Listing

Name	Address	City	ZIP	Date of First Use	Accrued Mileage
Keebler Ernie	7718 Ironwood Ct.	Glenview	60727	01/02/85	40
Chandler Michael	2500 Lakeview Ave.	Plainfield	60103	new client	18
Westward Grace	565 Naper Blvd.	Chicago	60163	11/12/88	120
Goodman Susan	11718 Roosevelt Rd.	Woodridge	60126	06/10/84	240
Martin Tad	9211 S. Lake	Villa Park	60223	new client	35
Walter Barbara	138 Woodland Ave.	Chicago	60111	09/15/89	76
Jordan Paul	6059 Drexel Rd.	Addison	60156	04/12/84	210
Baldwin Bradley	709 Briston Ave.	Glenview	60727	04/04/86	104
Cortland Lisa	820 Kimberly	Chicago	60163	11/01/85	86
Patton Walter	1800 79th Ct.	Addison	60156	new client	50
Carpetti George	561 Lorraine	Hillside	60150	commercial	NA
Smith Rose	11788 Holly Court	Northlake	60180	new client	15

CASE 3 Children's Hospital

Dr. Alan Rollins has been the Chief of Staff for over 27 years at a small, non-profit children's hospital located in New Hampshire. Over the years, the hospital has produced all of its correspondence through the use of conventional typewriters and handwritten documents.

Last year, Dr. Kyle Saunders came to the hospital to fill the position of chief cardiologist. When he arrived, he was surprised at the lack of modern office equipment available for staff and doctors to use. Without informing Dr. Rollins about his plans, Dr. Saunders wrote a grant proposal requesting $25,000 from a local businessmen's foundation. The proposal specified that the funds were to be used to purchase microcomputers and word processing software for the hospital. Dr. Saunders was not in his office the day that the check for $25,000 arrived at the hospital. The following day, however, Dr. Rollins had a few words for Dr. Saunders: "Kyle, what is this microcomputer business all about? Nobody here knows how to use them and I certainly don't know anything about computers. Now I'm expected to go out and spend $25,000, given to this hospital in good faith, without knowing what to buy. What a mess."

Dr. Saunders left the office thinking, "What Alan needs is a brief report that compares the two best-selling word processing software on the market today and a rough price schedule for the hardware we will need to purchase. The report should probably include footnotes for terms he won't understand and endnotes describing where the information in the report came from."

Potential Periodical References

Byte	*PC World*
Info World	*Personal Computing*
PC	*Software Digest*
PC Digest (hardware)	*Software News*
PC Week	

Other Sources of Information

Microcomputer Retail Stores	*Office Equipment Trade Shows*

CASE 4 Carousel Products, Inc.

John Hayes is the owner of Carousel Products, Inc., a company that distributes a variety of high-quality gifts and homeware exclusively through direct mail orders. To gain new customers, John contracts with other companies to enclose a color leaflet in their monthly billings to customers. The leaflet advertises a special product at an introductory price and includes a postage-paid order envelope. This method has proven very successful in attracting first-time buyers, and the sales generated have more than covered the expenses involved.

Unsure of why the amount of repeat business has been lower than expected, John conducted a telephone survey of these first-time buyers. He contacted them approximately six weeks after they received their introductory product. By this time they had received a form letter thanking them for their purchase, and had been added to the mailing list and been receiving regular mailings.

He found that although most customers were very happy with their purchases, they did not remember the name "Carousel," and subsequent mailings, including the form letter, had probably been discarded as junk mail. John feels that if the thank-you letter were more personalized and included a mention of the product ordered, customers would be more likely to remember the name of the company when they received further product information.

Although the data processing firm that manages John's database of customers can provide him with personalized form letters, the cost is too high and the quality is poor. John thinks that he might be able to produce the thank-you letters himself on his office microcomputer. Ideally, the letters would address the new customer by name and would somehow include a paragraph mentioning and describing the introductory product purchased. But the introductory product changes each month, and he's not sure how this can be handled.

Partial listing of recent first-time buyers

Name and Address			Month of Purchase
Beth Anderson	1218 S. Crestview	Glendale, UT 84052	January
David J. Kelly	112 W. Pine St.	Junction City, UT 84023	January
Eve Newman	2455 SE Ash	Cedar Grove, UT 84055	February
A.L. Strom	256 Windomere Way	Ogden, UT 84032	February
Judith Wendt	1645 S. Alberta Ave.	Orem, UT 84057	January

January's Introductory Product—Mini Wine Cellar

The Mini Wine Cellar is a solid oak cabinet that stores up to 40 bottles of wine under ideal conditions. The proper temperature and humidity are maintained through the exclusive design. Its classic design and fine craftsmanship make it an exquisite accessory for the dining room, living room, office, or den. Its outer door is made of beautifully molded hardwood, and its inner gate of polished stainless steel, with deadbolt lock, provides both elegance and security.

February's Introductory Product—Royale Towel and Bathroom Accessory Set

The set comes with a 16-piece towel ensemble that includes four king-size and four large bath towels, four handtowels, and four washcloths. The special weave of 100% cotton provides the ultimate in durability and softness. The accessories are in a rich wickerwood design that fits with any bathroom decor. The adjustable shelving unit is designed to make use of wall space over the toilet. Also included are a tissue holder, waste receptacle, two sizes of bathroom mats, and both a large and a small clothes hamper.

CASE 5 Westridge Paint Company

Ann Bender was recently promoted to the position of Controller for Westridge Paint Company, which manufactures and distributes a complete line of house paint. Westridge Paint is sold and delivered primarily to construction companies and contractors who buy in large quantities. As telephone orders are taken in the sales department, they are entered directly into the minicomputer and the company's accounting software generates invoices which include the appropriate pricing and quantity discounts for each client.

At the last sales meeting, Jerry Blackwell, the company's Sales Manager, said that he felt a substantial amount of sales could be realized if smaller quantities of paint could be sold to local contractors who would pick up their orders at the warehouse. Ann knew that this had been a point of contention between Jerry and Roger Kincaid, the company's previous controller and her former boss. Roger had been unbending on the issue, and she could recall his terse comments: "We tried it once. It didn't work. The invoices had to be handwritten by the warehouse employees and they were always wrong. They could never get the right pricing down. They couldn't even calculate the sales tax right! It's just not worth it!"

Although Ann knew that there was some basis to Roger's arguments, she felt that a simple invoicing system might be implemented in the warehouse. She also thought that this issue might have been one of the reasons Roger had been asked to leave the company. She suggested that sales from the warehouse could be most easily handled if a single price list could be used there. Everyone agreed that the warehouse employees should not be expected to deal with a complicated pricing structure. Jerry Blackwell said that he could come up with a price list for the warehouse, but that the 3 percent sales tax should be shown as a separate item on the invoices.

Ann called the warehouse foreman the next day and found that he had a microcomputer that he used only periodically for an inventory spreadsheet. He would be glad to make it available for invoice printing during regular business hours. Ann is sure that a simple invoice document could be designed in which only a quantity, product description, and price would need to be typed in, and the calculations for taxes, net price, and totals could be performed automatically. She hopes to present a workable solution at the next sales meeting.

Invoices should have columns for the following items, which should be presented in this order:

Quantity	Description	Unit Price	Total Price	Tax	Net Price

The Tax should be calculated as "3 percent of the Total Price" and the Net Price is equal to the Total Price plus the Tax. The columns for Total Price, Tax, and Net Price should be totalled at the bottom of the invoice. An example line of the invoice might be entered as follows.

Quantity	Description	Unit Price	Total Price	Tax	Net Price
5	5 gal Ivory	76.25	381.25	11.44	392.69

CASE 6 Steve Workman, Inventor

Steve Workman owns and operates a small electronics repair shop. In his spare time, however, he has developed a home security system which he hopes to make a commercial success. He has sold several of them already and has been able to produce enough to keep some inventory on hand. With the help of his broker, he is seeking venture capital in order to mass produce and market the product nationally.

Steve is going to attend a major electronics trade show in several weeks, and wants to have some promotional material about his security system to distribute at the show. However, it also will be several weeks before he will know whether any financing will be available for his product, and that will determine how much he can afford to spend on advertising. Because of the unknowns, Steve thinks his best strategy is to come up with a solution that will work whether or not the financing comes through.

Steve's plan is to produce a brochure that will serve two purposes. In addition to distributing them at the trade show, he will be mailing several hundred copies to potential customers. He has talked with a local advertising agency and come up with some ideas for the brochure, one being a single sheet of standard-size paper folded to produce a brochure with an address area on the outside. If he has the agency do the work, he can include a color photograph and have it printed in three colors. If, on the other hand, he must produce them on his microcomputer, he can substitute for the photo a graph representing performance comparisons of his system against other similar systems.

The advertising agency assured Steve that if he develops the layout and ad copy with a standard type size (10, 12 or 18 pitch), they will be able to produce a high-quality brochure within two days. Now he needs to decide on a name for his product and come up with the text for the brochure.

The home security system Steve has developed has many features and options that make it a superb system. The base unit is small and may be placed in any room in the house. It can be used with door sensors, window sensors, room motion detectors, and heat and smoke alarms. It may be set to turn on indoor or outdoor lights or to activate a siren or silent alarm at the first sign of intrusion.

When connected to a telephone line, it can be set to dial any telephone number and play a recorded message repeatedly as soon as the call is answered. It can store up to three telephone numbers, and if one is busy or does not answer within a specified time, it may be set to dial another. It also may be set with up to three recorded messages, using a different telephone number and message depending upon the type of emergency situation detected.

When away from home, you may program it to turn on any electric device, such as a television, radio, or room light at predetermined or random times of the day. If you have a television, VCR, or stereo system with remote control, it also may be programmed to change channels, stations, volume, and so forth.

You may preset a specific amount of time in which the system may be deactivated before alarms are issued, and it may be deactivated with a personal code known only to authorized persons. A separate backup unit system will be activated should any tampering be detected at the base unit.

HINTS AND HAZARDS

FILE OPERATIONS

HINT Save or resave your data every 15 minutes or so. You may want to purchase another disk to use as a backup disk for important files.

HAZARD Be careful about your keystrokes when saving your documents. You could easily miss a keystroke, which would result in saving a file named "Y" onto your disk. The keystrokes used to resave a file with the **F10** (Save) command are **F10**,↵,Y. The keystrokes used to resave a file during an exit from WordPerfect with the **F7** (Exit) command are **F7**,↵,↵,Y. To avoid confusion, it is suggested that you use the **F10** (Save) command liberally while editing and just prior to exiting WordPerfect. You should not use the **F7** (Exit) command to resave your file.

HAZARD Much literature about WordPerfect suggests that you use the space allocated to the *filename extension* for part of the name you give the document. For instance, you might name a memo "ACCT1887.MEM" to indicate that it is a memo concerning account #1887. This is poor advice because doing this might lead to a variety of complex problems. It is best not to use the extension space. Restrict your filenames to eight characters or less, begin the filename with a letter, and include no special characters or spaces in the filename.

HINT Files can be merged by simply retrieving one file into another. When a file is retrieved, it will be inserted into any existing text at the location of the editing cursor.

HAZARD Many applications software automatically erase the current file from RAM when another file is retrieved. As explained in the Hint above, this is not the case with WordPerfect. Experience has shown that beginning WordPerfect users, particularly ones that have used other software, become confused when they retrieve a file without first erasing the current file from RAM.

BLOCK OPERATIONS

HINT Most of the basic cut-and-paste operations can be done using the Undelete file buffer instead of the Move buffer as long as you are careful not to inadvertently delete or typeover text while doing so. Using the Undelete buffer requires fewer keystrokes and the Undelete buffers are able to hold three blocks of text.

HINT If you accidentally unblock a block of text, you can immediately restore it by typing **Alt-F4**,Ctrl-Home,Ctrl-Home ((Block),Previous position). The technique will not work correctly if the cursor has been moved after the unblocking event.

HAZARD There is only one set of Undelete buffers and one Move buffer. If you are editing two documents concurrently (see the **Shift-F3** (Switch) command), they share the buffers.

HINT Blocks of text can be copied or moved between Doc 1 and Doc 2 (see the **Shift-F3** (Switch) command for information on editing two files concurrently). If you want to copy a block of text from a file on the disk into the current file, use the Switch command to go to the other document screen, and then retrieve the disk file, block the text, and use either the Move command or Backspace key to put the block into a buffer. Then use the Switch command to return to the original document and retrieve the block from the buffer with the **Ctrl-F4,5** ((Move),**R**etrieve) or **F1,1** ((Cancel),**R**estore) command.

EDITING TEXT

HINT To produce a hanging paragraph (one in which the text resides offset to the right of a heading) type the heading and then type **F4** or **Shift-F4** (→Indent or →Indent←) and then enter the text.

HAZARD The default answer to the Replace command's "w/confirm" prompt is No. This is surprising since experience shows that global replace operations without confirmation often can have unanticipated results that are difficult to rectify. If using a text editor's Replace command is new to you, be sure to specify Y for "Yes" when the "w/confirm" prompt appears.

HINT When working on a large document over a period of time, it is often desirable to return to where you left off editing when you later retrieve a file. To do so, you may invent a place marker by using keyboard characters (such as the marker -=-) and place it in the file at the location to which you want to return. Then you save the file. When you later retrieve the file, you can use the **F2** (→Search) command to find the marker.

HINT To view the current tab stops on the screen while editing, type **Ctrl-F3,1**, ↑ ↑ ↵ ((Screen),**W**indow,Up,Up,Enter). To turn off the tab stop display, type **Ctrl-F3,1** ↓ ↓ ↵ ((Screen),**W**indow,Down, Down,Enter).

HINT The Esc key may be used to repeat a keystroke or keystroke combination *n* number of times. For instance, to produce a row of asterisks across the document (64 asterisks), move the cursor to the left margin and type Esc, 64,*.

WORDPERFECT CODES

HINT Be sure to develop the habit of deleting unnecessary codes from your document. Such codes will lead to a document file becoming cluttered and difficult to read in the Reveal Codes screen.

HINT You can quickly locate imbedded codes in your document with the →Search and ←Search commands. Type **F2** or **Shift-F2** (Search forward or Search backward) and then type the initial keystroke combinations that created the code for which you are searching. The screen will display a menu of commands that generate imbedded codes. Select the appropriate command from the menu and then type **F2** or **Shift-F2** again.

HINT You can quickly delete all occurrences of a particular code with the Replace command. Move the cursor to the top of the document and type **Alt-F2** (Replace). Answer Y to the "w/confirm" prompt and answer the "->Srch:" prompt by typing the initial keystroke combination that created the code. The screen will display a menu of commands that generate imbedded codes. Select the appropriate command from the menu and then type **Alt-F2** again. Answer the "Replace with:" prompt by typing **Alt-F2** once more.

HINT Be systematic about where you place your codes. If you often change line spacing or margins for paragraphs, consistently put the codes in the same place (just above the paragraph, just before the first letter, etc.) for each paragraph you reformat. If you have a favorite format of margins, line spacing, page numbering, and so on, create a small file of the necessary codes and save it under a filename like HEADER. Then when you are ready to create a new document, you can simply retrieve HEADER as the first step in creating the document.

HAZARD Some codes must occur at the top of a page in order to have the desired effect. Codes that set new page numbers, change headers or footers, or affect the top margin are some examples. You may want to place a hard page break in your document above such codes to keep them from being forced down on a page by rewrites occurring above them.

PRINTING FILES

HINT There are several ways in which you may print a file or portion of a file. To print the current page of the current document or the entire current document, use the **Shift-F7,1** or **2** (Print),**F**ull Document or **P**age command. To print a block of text, block the text and then type **Shift-7**,Y (Print),Yes. To print certain pages of the current file, save the file and then use the **Shift-F7,3** (Print),**D**ocument on Disk command.

HINT If your microcomputer has WordPerfect set up for printing on an Epson printer and you create a document file using the microcomputer, the file is saved with unseen data specifying that the file is to be printed with an Epson printer. If you take a disk holding such a file to another microcomputer set up for another printer, WordPerfect may present an error message when the file is loaded for editing. The error message simply indicates that WordPerfect detects a discrepancy between the file's data and the system being used. WordPerfect will correct the file for the current system's printer.

SPECIAL FEATURES

HINT To modify the text of page headers or footers midway through a document, place a new [Header] or [Footer] code. For instance, to create a new header A printed on every page, type **Shift-F8,3,3,1,2**-(Format),**P**age,**H**eaders,Header **A**,Every **P**age. The command **Shift-F8,3,3,1,5**(Format),**P**age,**H**eaders,Header **A**,**E**dit will not place a new header code, but may be used to modify the text of an existing header.

HAZARD Header A and Header B will both begin on the same line. To avoid overwriting one header with another, you may use one header on even pages and the other on odd pages. You also may use both headers on the same page if you design them so that they will not print in the same area of the page (use the Print,**V**iew Document command to test placement). The same hazard applies to footers.

HINT You can greatly speed up a spell check operation by not waiting for WordPerfect to display all of its dictionary found words when it stops on an unknown word. For instance, if you can see on the screen that the word is one which you want to skip, type 1 or 2 as soon as WordPerfect stops on the word. WordPerfect will immediately continue its search for unknown words.

HAZARD When you use WordPerfect to automatically generate tables of contents, lists, and indexes, the tables it produces are heavily formatted with [->Indent<-], [->Indent], [<-Margin Rel:], and [Flsh Rt] format codes. While the text of the table can be edited, it can be quite confusing to try to do so. Also, if the command to generate tables is executed again, any editing changes will be overwritten.

If you must edit a table after it has been generated, you may block and save the table, use the Switch command to change documents, retrieve the table, and resave it in DOS Text File Format with the Text In/Out command. The Text In/Out, Save DOS Text File Format command will leave the table intact and strip the WordPerfect codes from it. You then may use the Switch command to return to the original document and retrieve the table into the current document for editing.

HINT If you decide to insert a portion of newspaper-style columnar text into an existing document, first create the portion as a separate file and make sure it ends with a [Col Off:] code. Then, retrieve it into the document.

HAZARD When using WordPerfect's Math feature, [Align] codes are generated when the Tab key is used to move the cursor to a tab stop for entry of numbers. If you later edit the math portion of the document, you must be careful to keep the numbers properly aligned to their tab stops. It is usually easier to delete the original [Align] code and number and then retab to the appropriate tab stop to reenter the number.

STUDY QUESTIONS

1. What is the main difference between word processing and typing? What is the resulting advantage for word processing?

2. What keystrokes are used to enter WordPerfect's command mode?

3. There are places in a document where the cursor may not be moved with the cursor control keys. Describe the areas and the method that one might use to move the cursor to them.

4. If the cursor left key is tapped again and again, what path will the cursor follow?

5. How does WordPerfect define a paragraph?

6. Name the three general categories of format codes.

7. The codes generated by the **F6** (Bold) command belong to which of the three categories of format codes?

8. The codes generated by WordPerfect when it produces a page break after 54 lines belong to which of the three categories of format codes?

9. The codes generated by the **Shift-F8**,**1**,**6** (Format),**L**ine,Line **S**pacing belong to which of the three categories of format codes?

10. Describe two differences between hard returns and soft returns.

11. What keystrokes can be used to delete a soft page break?

12. What is a hard page and when would you want to use one in your document?

13. How can you keep WordPerfect from separating two or more words at the end of a line when it rewrites a paragraph?

14. If the format forward code [L/R Mar:] (left and right margins) is entered at the top of a document, will it stop affecting text when it reaches the format forward code [Ln Spacing:]?

____

15. What can be done to underline, boldface, or center text after it has been entered?

____

____

16. *Cut-and-paste* refers to your ability to perform three basic operations on a block of text. Name the three operations.

____

____

____

17. How does WordPerfect treat text held in its editing buffers, such as the Move and Undelete buffers?

____

____

18. How many blocks of text can be held in the Move buffer at one time?

____

19. How many blocks of text can be held in the Undelete buffers at one time?

____

20. If a block of text is undeleted with the **F1** (Cancel) command, does a copy of the block remain in the Undelete buffer?

____

21. Describe three ways in which text may be copied or moved in a document.

____

____

____

WORDPERFECT KEY TERMS GLOSSARY

Block operations Ability to deal with segments of a document independent from the rest of the document.

Boiler plating Procedure to automatically merge specific information into a standard form or document.

Close file All data in the document is saved to a disk using software commands.

Cut and paste Ability to move, copy, or delete blocks of text.

Document Text file created with word processing software.

Editing Either revising data by changing the written content of the text or formatting data by changing the appearance of the text.

Filename extension Composed of three characters that follow the filename; usually reserved for the applications software's use.

Format forward codes Codes which affect all of the following text until another similar code or the end of the document is reached.

Formatting Changing the appearance of text.

Hard codes Codes generated by the user.

Hard hyphens Cause a hyphenated word to remain whole.

Hard return Indicates the end of a line that was placed by the user typing the Enter key. Separates paragraphs of text.

Hard spaces Prevent two or more words from being separated from each other when text wraps to the next line.

Header record Used in a secondary file to assign names to each of the data fields; allows field references in a primary file to be designated by field name instead of field number.

Insert Any characters typed are inserted into the text to the left of the cursor.

Macro A sequence of keystrokes recorded and saved on the disk that can be executed at any time.

Open file Current file that is moved between RAM and disk storage as changes are made.

Page break A line of dashes across the computer screen that indicates a new page is about to begin. Soft page breaks are generated by WordPerfect and hard page breaks are generated by the user.

Primary file Standard document with merge codes.

Revising Changing the written content of text.

Screen rewrite Feature that automatically rewraps the lines in a paragraph when revisions are made to it.

Secondary file Contains specific information to be merged into a primary file.

Soft codes Codes WordPerfect generates and automatically inserts into a document.

Soft return Indicates the end of the line that was automatically wrapped to the next line.

Start and stop codes Only text between the codes is affected.

Status line Used to display messages about current software operations.

Typeover Any characters typed will overwrite existing characters of text.

Word wrap Feature that automatically begins a new line when the right margin of the current line is reached.

WORDPERFECT CONTROL KEYS

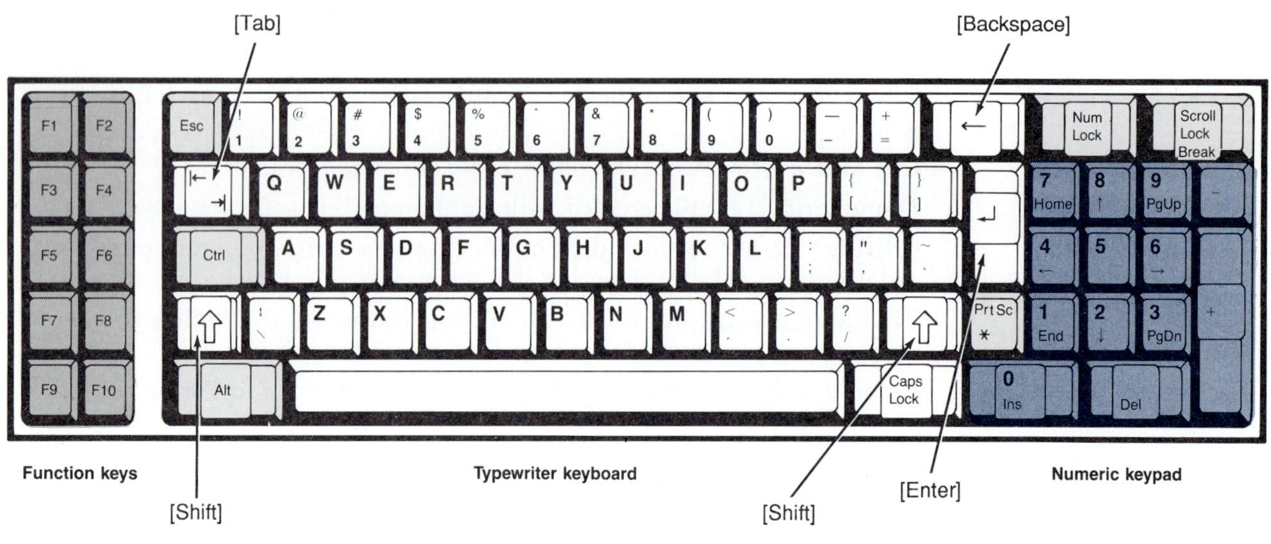

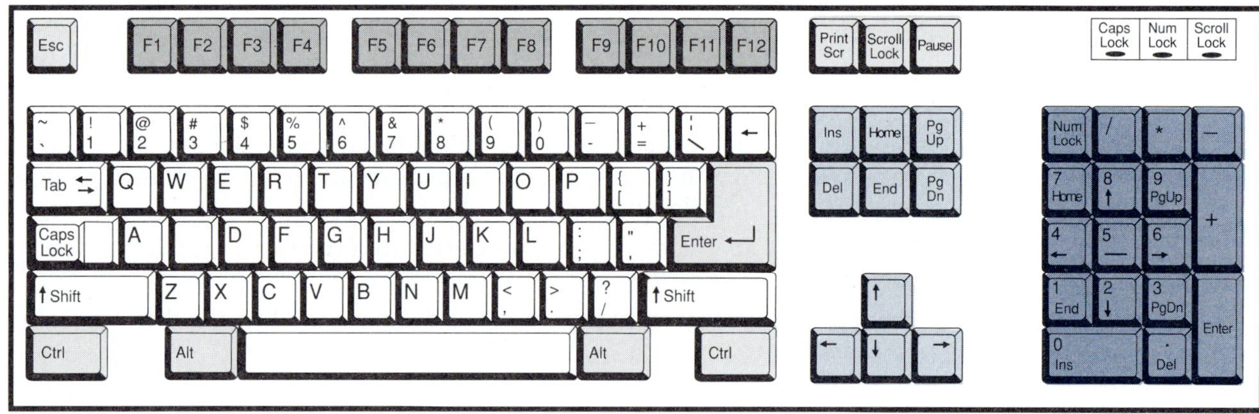

Normal Typewriter Keys

Control Keys

Function Keys

Numeric Keypad/Cursor Movement Keys

Cursor Movement Keys Only

NOTE: There are two or more keyboards in use. They are significantly different from each other.

CONTROL KEYS

Alt-letter Key Executes a keystroke macro named with the Alt key.

Ctrl-↵ Inserts a hard page break [HPg] code into the document.

Enter Key (↵) Inserts a hard return [HRt] code into the document.

Esc Key May be used to execute the following keystroke *n* number of times. Type Esc, a number, and then type the keystroke or keystroke combination to repeat.

Home,- Inserts a hard hyphen into the document.

Home, Space Inserts a hard space [ ] code into the document.

Ins Key Toggles between Insert and Typeover editing modes.

Num Lock Key Toggles ten-key numeric keypad to cursor control keys. The shift key may be used to temporarily shift this keypad to the opposite mode.

Shift-Tab Key Inserts a [←Mar Rel] code into the text, releases the left margin, and moves the cursor to the previous tab stop.

Tab Key Inserts a [TAB] code into the document and tabs the cursor to the next tab stop.

WordPerfect Cursor Control Keys

Cursor Movement	Keystroke(s)
Character Left	Left ←
Character Right	Right →
Line Up	Up ↑
Line Down	Down ↓
Word Left	Ctrl-Left
Word Right	Ctrl-Right
Forward to Character *a*	Ctrl-Home,*a*
Beginning of Line	Home,Left
End of Line	Home,Right
Top of File	Home,Home,Up
Bottom of File	Home,Home,Down
To Page *nn*	Ctrl-Home,*nn*↵
Screen Up	– (Numeric Keypad)
Screen Down	+ (Numeric Keypad)
Page Up	Page Up (PgUp)
Page Down	Page Down (PgDn)
Previous Position	Ctrl-Home,Ctrl-Home
Column Left	Ctrl-Home,Left
Column Right	Ctrl-Home,Right

WordPerfect Delete Keys

Delete Operation	Keystrokes
Current Character	Delete (Del)
Previous Character	Backspace
Current Word	Ctrl-Backspace
Current Word Left	Home,Backspace
Current Word Right	Home,Delete (Del)
End of Line	Ctrl-End
End of Page	Ctrl-Page Down (PgDn)

WORDPERFECT KEYBOARD TEMPLATE COMMANDS

Command	Keystrokes
Block	**Alt-F4**
Bold	**F6**
Cancel	**F1**
Center	**Shift-F6**
Date/Outline	**Shift-F5**
Exit	**F7**
Flush Right	**Alt-F6**
Font	**Ctrl-F8**
Footnote	**Ctrl-F7**
Format	**Shift-F8**
Graphics	**Alt-F9**
Help	**F3**
→Indent	**F4**
→Indent←	**Shift-F4**
List Files	**F5**
Macro	**Alt-10**
Macro Define	**Ctrl-F10**
Mark Text	**Alt-F5**
Math/Columns	**Alt-F7**
Merge Codes	**Shift-F9**
Merge R	**F9**
Merge Sort	**Ctrl-F9**
Move	**Ctrl-F4**
Print	**Shift-F7**
Replace	**Alt-F2**
Retrieve	**Shift-F10**
Reveal Codes	**Alt-F3**
Save	**F10**
Screen	**Ctrl-F3**
←Search	**Shift-F2**
→Search	**F2**
Setup	**Shift-F1**
Shell	**Ctrl-F1**
Spell	**Ctrl-F2**
Style	**Alt-F8**
Switch	**Shift-F3**
Tab Align	**Ctrl-F6**
Text In/Out	**Ctrl-F5**
Thesaurus	**Alt-F1**
Underline	**F8**

WORDPERFECT COMMAND INDEX

Command	Keystrokes
Align Character	**Shift-F8, 4** (Format),Other
Align Text to Tab	**Ctrl-F6** (Tab Align)
All Capitals Font	**Ctrl-F8** (Font)
Automatic References	**Alt-F5** (Mark Text)
Backup Documents	**Shift-F1** (Setup)
Base Font	**Ctrl-F8** (Font)
Block Text	**Alt-F4** (Block)
Bold Text	**F6** (Bold)
Cancel a Command	**F1** (Cancel)
Center	
Page (Top to Bottom)	**Shift-F8,2** (Format),Page
Text	**Shift-F6** (Center)
Clear Screen	**F7** (Exit)
Columnar Text Feature	**Alt-F7** (Math/Columns)
Comments in Document	**Ctrl-F5** (Text In/Out)
Compressed Font	**Ctrl-F8** (Font)
Copy	
Block of Text	**Ctrl-F4** (Move)
Rectangular Column of Text	Block/**Ctrl-F4** (Move)
Cursor Speed	**Shift-F1** (Setup)
Date	**Shift-F5** (Date/Outline)
Delete	
Block of Text	Block/BackSpace
Rectangular Column of Text	Block/**Ctrl-F4** (Move)
Directory (Change)	**F5** (List Files)
Disk Files	
Print	**Shift-F7** (Print)
Copy	**F5** (List Files)
Delete	**F5** (List Files)
Move/Rename	**F5** (List Files)
View	**F5** (List Files)
Word Search	**F5** (List Files)
Display Pitch	**Shift-F8,3** (Format),Document
Document 2	**Shift-F3** (Switch)
Endnotes	**Ctrl-F7** (Footnote)
Enlarged Font	**Ctrl-F8** (Font)
Fast Save (Unformatted)	**Shift-F1** (Setup)
Flush Right Text	**Alt-F6** (Flush Right)
Font Stop Code	**Ctrl-F8** (Font)
Footers	**Shift-F8,2** (Format),Page
Footnotes	**Ctrl-F7** (Footnote)
Force Page Number (Odd/Even)	**Shift-F8,2** (Format),Page
Graphics Boxes	**Alt-F9** (Graphics)
Headers	**Shift-F8,2** (Format),Page
Help Screens	**F3** (Help)
Hyphenation Feature	**Shift-F8,1** (Format),Line
Indent (Left and Right)	**Shift-F4** (→Indent←)
Indent (Left)	**F4** (→Indent)
Index Feature	**Alt-F5** (Mark Text)
Initial	
Codes	**Shift-F8,3** (Format),Document
Font	**Shift-F8,3** (Format),Document
Settings	**Shift-F1** (Setup)
Italic Font	**Ctrl-F8** (Font)
Justification (On/Off)	**Shift-F8,1** (Format),Line
Kerning	**Shift-F8,4** (Format),Other
Keyboard Layout	**Shift-F1** (Setup)

Command	Keystrokes
Line	
Graphics	**Alt-F9** (Graphics)
Draw	**Ctrl-F3** (Screen)
Height	**Shift-F8,1** (Format),Line
Numbering	**Shift-F8,1** (Format),Line
Spacing	**Shift-F8,1** (Format),Line
Lists Feature	**Alt-F5** (Mark Text)
Location of Auxiliary Files	**Shift-F1** (Setup)
Macro	
Create	**Ctrl-F10** (Macro Define)
Execute	**Alt-F10** (Macro)
Margins	
Left/Right	**Shift-F8,1** (Format),Line
Top/Bottom	**Shift-F8,2** (Format),Page
Master/Subdocuments Feature	**Alt-F5** (Mark Text)
Math Feature	**Alt-F7** (Math/Columns)
Merge	
Codes	**Shift-F9** (Merge Codes)
Feature	**Ctrl-F9** (Merge/Sort)
Move	
Block of Text	**Ctrl-F4** (Move)
Rectangular Column of Text	Block/**Ctrl-F4** (Move)
Outline Numbers	**Shift-F5** (Date/Outline)
Outline Font	**Ctrl-F8** (Font)
Overstrike Text	**Shift-F8,4** (Format),Other
Page Number	
New	**Shift-F8,2** (Format),Page
Placement	**Shift-F8,2** (Format),Page
Paper Size/Type	**Shift-F8,2** (Format),Page
Paragraph Numbers	**Shift-F5** (Date/Outline)
Password Protection	**Ctrl-F5** (Text In/Out)
Print	
Adjust Pitch	**Shift-F8,4** (Format),Other
Advance to Position	**Shift-F8,4** (Format),Other
Block	**Shift-F7** (Print)
Colors	**Ctrl-F8** (Font)
Current Page	**Shift-F7** (Print)
From Keyboard	**Shift-F7** (Print)
Full Document	**Shift-F7** (Print)
Multiple Copies	**Shift-F7** (Print)
Quality	**Shift-F7** (Print)
Select Printer	**Shift-F7** (Print)
Send Printer Control Code	**Shift-F8,4** (Format),Other
Stop	**Shift-F7** (Print)
View Printed Document on Screen	**Shift-F7** (Print)
Protect from Page Breaks	
Block of Text	Block/**Shift-F8** (Format)
Conditional End of Page	**Shift-F8,4** (Format),Other
Widow/Orphan	**Shift-F8,1** (Format),Line
Redline	
Add to Document (Delete Strikeout)	**Alt-F5** (Mark Text)
Method	**Shift-F8,3** (Format),Document
Text	**Ctrl-F8** (Font)
Retrieve	
ASCII File	**Ctrl-F5** (Text In/Out)
Document	**Shift-F10** (Retrieve)
File from List	**F5** (List Files)
Reveal Codes	**Alt-F4** (Reveal Codes)

Command	Keystrokes
Save	
Append Block to Disk File	Block/**Ctrl-F4** (Move)
Block of Text	Block/**F10** (Save)
Document	**F10** (Save)
Document and Exit WordPerfect	**F7** (Exit)
Document in ASCII Format	**Ctrl-F5**(Text In/Out)
Document in WordPerfect 4.2 Format	**Ctrl-F5**(Text In/Out)
Screen Displays	**Shift-F1** (Setup)
Search	
And Replace	**Alt-F2** (Replace)
Backward	**Shift-F2** (←Search)
Forward	**F2** (→Search)
Shadow Font	**Ctrl-F8** (Font)
Shell to DOS	**Ctrl-F1** (Shell)
Sort Feature	**Ctrl-F9** (Merge/Sort)
Spell Check Feature	**Ctrl-F2** (Spell)
Split Screen	**Ctrl-F3** (Screen)
Strikeout Text	**Ctrl-F8** (Font)
Style Feature	**Alt-F8** (Style)
Summary in Document	**Shift-F8,3** (Format),Document
Superscript/Subscript	**Ctrl-F8** (Font)
Suppress Formatting (Page Only)	**Shift-F8,2** (Format),Page
Tab Set	**Shift-F8,1** (Format),Line
Table of Contents Feature	**Alt-F5** (Mark Text)
Thesaurus Feature	**Alt-F1** (Thesaurus)
Undelete Text	**F1** (Cancel)
Underline	
Double	**Ctrl-F8** (Font)
Spaces and Tabs	**Shift-F8,4** (Format),Other
Text	**F8** (Underline)
Units of Measure	**Shift-F1** (Setup)
UPPER/lower Case (Convert)	Block/**Shift-F3** (Switch)

F1
Cancel——— Undelete:——— 1 - Restore
— 2 - Previous Deletion
— 0 - Cancel

F1 CANCEL

The **F1** (Cancel) command may be used to exit a WordPerfect menu or message, or recover up to three levels of deleted text from the Undelete buffers.

The **F1** (Cancel) command may be used to abort many WordPerfect menu or command operations. The command also may be used to recover any or all of the last three text deletions or typed-over text. To recover text, move the cursor to the position where you want the recovered text to appear and then type **F1** (Cancel). The most recent deletion will appear on the screen at the cursor location. The **P**revious Deletion command may be used to continuously scroll through the last three deletions, with each deletion appearing on the screen in order. When the appropriate deletion is displayed on the screen, type **1** or **R** (**R**estore) to recover it. Type **F1** (Cancel) or ↵ to abort the recovery operation.

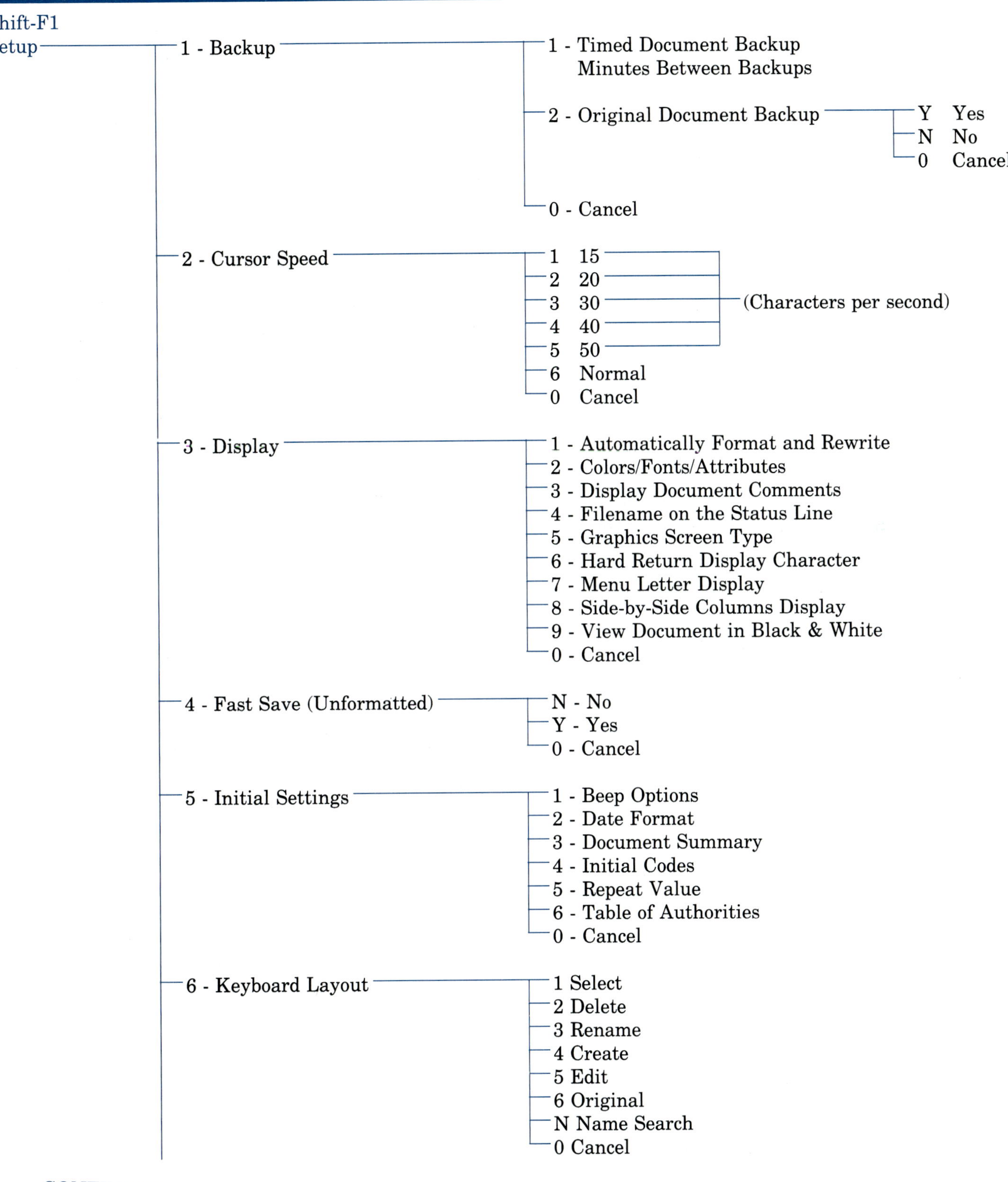

Shift-F1
Setup
1 - Backup
1 - Timed Document Backup
Minutes Between Backups
2 - Original Document Backup
Y Yes
N No
0 Cancel
0 - Cancel
2 - Cursor Speed
1 15
2 20
3 30
4 40
5 50
6 Normal
0 Cancel
(Characters per second)
3 - Display
1 - Automatically Format and Rewrite
2 - Colors/Fonts/Attributes
3 - Display Document Comments
4 - Filename on the Status Line
5 - Graphics Screen Type
6 - Hard Return Display Character
7 - Menu Letter Display
8 - Side-by-Side Columns Display
9 - View Document in Black & White
0 - Cancel
4 - Fast Save (Unformatted)
N - No
Y - Yes
0 - Cancel
5 - Initial Settings
1 - Beep Options
2 - Date Format
3 - Document Summary
4 - Initial Codes
5 - Repeat Value
6 - Table of Authorities
0 - Cancel
6 - Keyboard Layout
1 Select
2 Delete
3 Rename
4 Create
5 Edit
6 Original
N Name Search
0 Cancel

CONTINUED

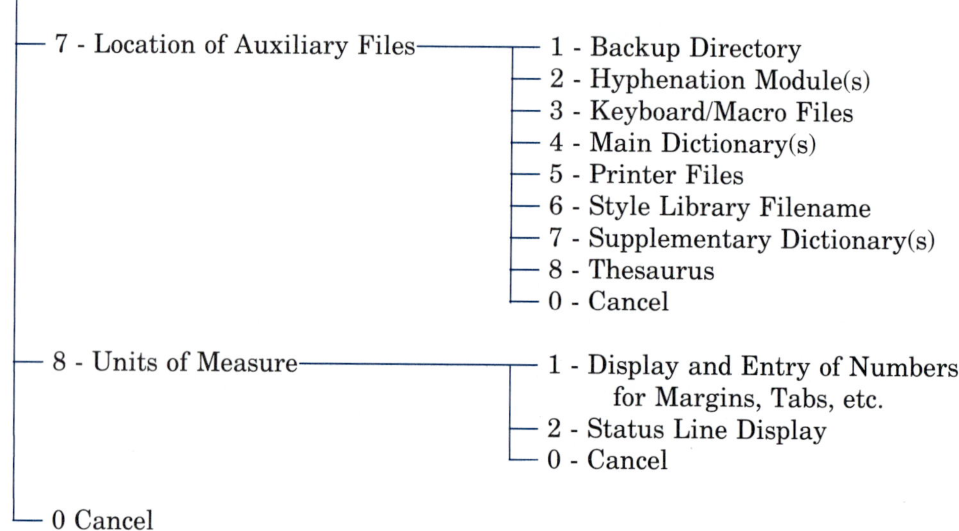

SHIFT-F1 SETUP

The **Shift-F1** (Setup) command alters or redefines the default settings for many WordPerfect commands and operations. The Setup command saves any new specifications onto the disk directory where WordPerfect resides. The specifications are kept on the disk in a file named WP{WP}.SET. WordPerfect reads the file and uses the specifications found there each time it is loaded. That is, the Setup command configures WordPerfect's environment.

*NOTE: In a microcomputing laboratory, you should never attempt to change any of the WordPerfect settings with the **Shift-F1** (Setup) command without the explicit approval of your instructor or laboratory staff.*

When a Setup command listed here has either a "Yes" or "No" setting, type Y or N, respectively, to change it.

Backup

Default—No Backup files
WordPerfect provides a backup feature to maintain backup files for your documents. The backup files may be of two types, **T**imed or **O**riginal.

Timed

Timed backup files are produced every *n* number of minutes (30 by default). When you specify **T**imed backup, you also may specify the number of minutes between the automatic backup operations. Timed backup files are given the filename and extension WP{WP}.BK1 or WP{WP}.BK2 (for Document 1 or 2, respectively. See the **Shift-F3** (Switch) command) and are kept in the directory specified with the **Shift-F1** (Setup), **L**ocation of Auxiliary Files, **B**ackup Directory command.

If the Timed Document Backup feature is being used and the system is shut off before exiting WordPerfect properly with the **F7** (Exit) command, WordPerfect will prompt "Old backup file exists **1 R**ename; **2 D**elete." At this point you may rename the WP{WP}.BK*n* file and then retrieve it for editing with the **Shift-F10** (Retrieve) command, or you may delete the Timed Backup file.

The "Old backup file exists" message does not occur until the first timed backup for the current document occurs. If the specified minutes between backups is 30, the message will not occur until 30 minutes after editing has begun.

When you have lost data from improperly exiting WordPerfect, use the **F5** (List Files) or equivalent DOS commands to access the directory where the WP{WP}.BK*n* is located, rename the backup file, and then copy it to the desired directory. Be sure to erase the old copy of the WP{WP}.BK*n* file from the backup directory.

Original

Original backups are first created the second time a document file is saved. Original backup files have the same filename, but are given a .BK! extension by WordPerfect. The document file with no extension is the last saved version; the document file with the .BK! extension is the next-to-the-last saved version. An original backup file is kept in the same directory as the file it is backing up, regardless of the directory specified in the **Shift-F1** (Setup),**L**ocation of auxiliary Files,**B**ackup Directory command.

Cursor Speed

Default—30 characters per second
Sets the speed at which any key will repeat when held down (including cursor movement keys). Options include 15, 20, 30, 40, and 50 characters per second or **N**ormal. Normal is 10 characters per second.

Display

Sets the screen display characteristics for many WordPerfect operations.

Automatically Format and Rewrite

Default—Yes
When **A**utomatic Format and Rewrite is "Yes," WordPerfect reformats the entire remaining document at the time a format forward code is inserted into it. When "No" is specified for the command, reformatting occurs as the cursor is moved through the document.

Colors/Fonts/Attributes

The **C**olors/Fonts/Attributes command is used to change the screen colors or shades for color or monochrome monitors. When the **C**olors/Fonts/Attributes command is selected, another menu will appear. At this point the procedure varies depending on the video display card and monitor being used. For instance, if your computer has an EGA or a VGA monitor card you may see the following selection appear.

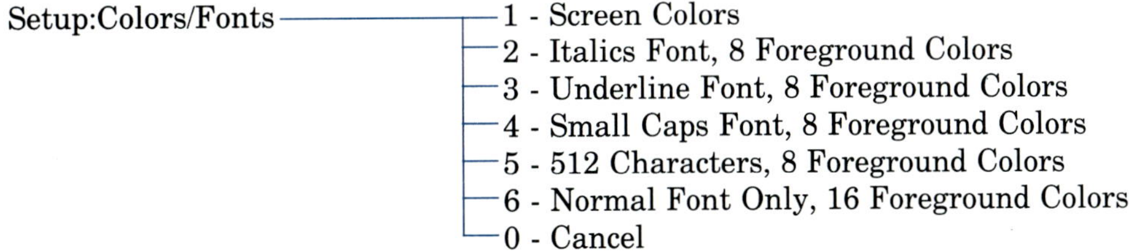

In most cases, you will select **S**creen Colors to set the display attributes for your monitor. The **S**creen Colors menu allows you to change the background/foreground colors for the various text attributes (bold, underline, etc.). The menu is largely self-explanatory.

When screen colors are changed, they affect the current document screen only (Doc 1 or Doc 2). To view the current screen colors for the other document screen, type **Shift-F3** (Switch) while viewing the **S**creen Colors menu. To copy the other document's screen colors to the current document screen, type **Ctrl-F4** (Move) while viewing the Screen Colors menu. (See **Shift-F3** (Switch) for an explanation of document screens 1 and 2.) Use **F7** (Exit) to properly exit the Screen Colors menu.

Display Document Comments

Default—Yes

You may include comments (text that will not be printed) in a document by using the **Ctrl-F5** (Text In/Out),**C**omment command. When **D**isplay Document Comments is "Yes," comments are displayed on the screen where they occur in the document. If **D**isplay Document Comments is changed to "No," the comments are not displayed on the screen.

Filename on the Status Line

Default—Yes

"Yes" causes the current document's filename to be displayed on the Status line. "No" suppresses the display of the filename on the Status line.

Graphics Screen Type

WordPerfect automatically selects the proper graphics card and monitor type when it is loaded.

Hard Return Display Character

Default—Space character

To make hard returns visible on the screen, you may use the **H**ard Return Display Character command to enter the character that you wish to be displayed on the screen where a hard return occurs in the document. The < character is often used for this purpose.

Menu Letter Display

Default—Bold

To change the screen appearance of the one letter within a WordPerfect command which may be used to execute the command, use the **M**enu Letter Display command to select (Font),**S**ize and/or (Font),**A**ppearance for the letter. The letter then will appear on the screen as its font appears in the document's screen text (see **Ctrl-F8** (Font)).

Side-by-Side Columns Display

Default—Yes

When **S**ide-by-Side Columns Display is "Yes," columns generated by the **Alt-F7** (Math/Columns) command appear on the screen as they will be printed. To speed editing of such columns, you may change **S**ide-by-Side Columns Display to "No."

View Document in Black & White

Default—No

For color monitors, selecting "Yes" or "No" alters the colors used on the **Shift-F7** (Print),**V**iew Document screen relative to print colors selected with the **Ctrl-F8** (Font),Print Color Command.

Fast Save (Unformatted)

Default—No

When **F**ast Save (Unformatted) is "Yes," WordPerfect saves the document in an unformatted manner. An unformatted document may not be printed from the disk.

Initial Settings

The **I**nitial Settings command is used to change the following elements.

Beep Options

Setup:Beep Options		Default
	1 - Beep on Error	No
	2 - Beep on Hyphenation	Yes
	3 - Beep on Search Failure	No
	0 - Cancel	

Date Format

Default—3 1, 4 (Example: December 15, 1989)

Setup:Date Format
- 1 - Day of the Month
- 2 - Month (number)
- 3 - Month (word)
- 4 - Year (all four digits)
- 5 - Year (last two digits)
- 6 - Day of the Week (word)
- 7 - Hour (24-hour clock)
- 8 - Hour (12-hour clock)
- 9 - Minute
- 0 - am / pm
- % - Leading zeros, 3 letters

See **Shift-F5** (Date/Outline).

Document Summary

Setup:Document Summary		Default
	1 - Create on Save/Exit	No
	2 - Subject Search Text	RE:
	0 - Cancel	

See **Shift-F8** (Format),**D**ocument,**S**ummary.

Initial Codes

See **Shift-F8** (Format),**D**ocument,Initial **C**odes.

Repeat Value

Default—8
Changes the repeat value for the Esc key.

Table of Authorities

Setup:Table of Authorities		Default
	1 - Dot Leaders	Yes
	2 - Underlining Allowed	No
	3 - Blank Line Between Authorities	Yes
	0 - Cancel	

Print Options

Setup:Print Options		Default
	1 - Binding	0″
	2 - Number of Copies	1
	3 - Graphics Quality	Medium
	4 - Text Quality	High
	0 - Cancel	

See **Shift-F7** (Print).

Keyboard Layout

Keyboard Layout is an advanced Setup feature which allows you to assign alternate keys for WordPerfect's commands and operations.

Location of Auxiliary Files

WordPerfect is composed of and maintains several types of files. The (Setup),**L**ocation of Auxiliary Files command is used to direct WordPerfect to the proper directories for accessing and storing each type of file.

Units of Measure

Default = ″ (inches)
Units of measure refers to the scale WordPerfect uses when it references document positions. The default scale is inches (″). The (Setup),**U**nits of

Measure command may be used to change the default scale to any one of the following:

c = centimeters

p = points (1/72 of an inch)

w = 1,200ths of an inch

u = WordPerfect 4.2 units (lines/columns)

Alt-F1
Thesaurus——[Word:<entry>] ——1 Replace Word ——Press letter for word
 ——2 View Doc
 ——3 Look Up Word ——Word:<entry>
 ——4 Clear Column
 ——0 Cancel

Alt-F1 Thesaurus

WordPerfect comes with a thesaurus feature which displays synonyms and antonyms for words. The data through which WordPerfect searches to find synonyms and antonyms are kept on a separate disk. If you are using a computer with two floppy disk drives, you will need to insert the Thesaurus disk into the B: drive each time it is needed. If you have a hard disk drive, the Thesaurus disk may be copied into the same subdirectory as WordPerfect.

To cause WordPerfect to display synonyms and antonyms for a word in your document, move the cursor under the word and then type **Alt-F1** (Thesaurus).

If the word is a headword, a word that can be looked up by WordPerfect, the screen will appear similar to the following.

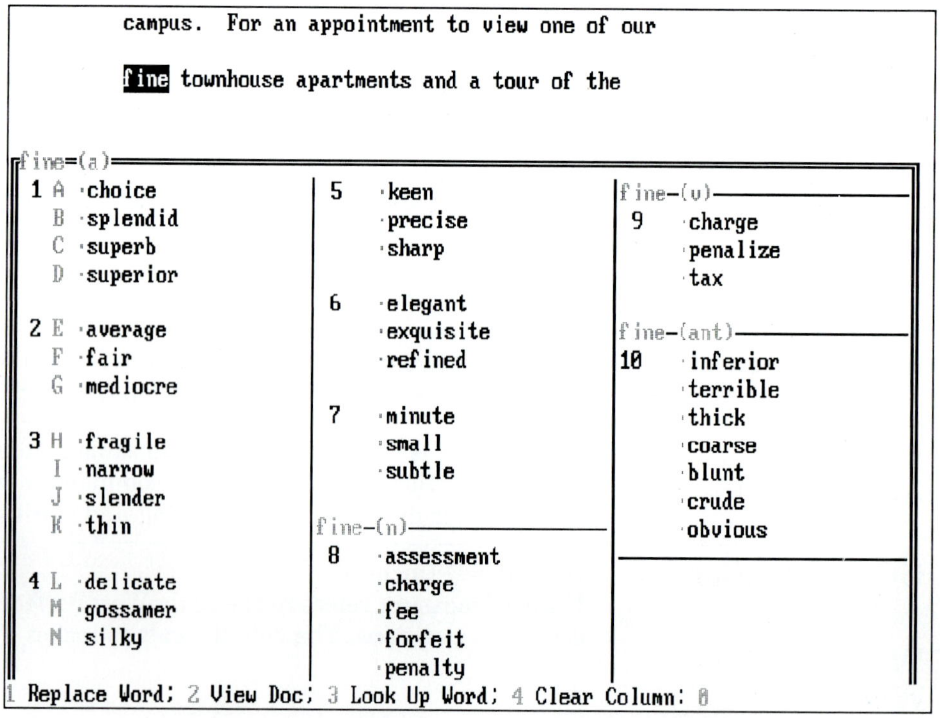

```
campus.  For an appointment to view one of our

fine townhouse apartments and a tour of the

fine=(a)
 1 A ·choice         5  ·keen            fine-(v)
   B ·splendid          ·precise          9   ·charge
   C ·superb            ·sharp                ·penalize
   D ·superior                                ·tax
                     6  ·elegant
 2 E ·average           ·exquisite       fine-(ant)
   F ·fair              ·refined          10  ·inferior
   G ·mediocre                                ·terrible
                     7  ·minute               ·thick
 3 H ·fragile           ·small                ·coarse
   I ·narrow            ·subtle               ·blunt
   J ·slender                                 ·crude
   K ·thin           fine-(n)                 ·obvious
                     8  ·assessment
 4 L ·delicate          ·charge
   M ·gossamer          ·fee
   N silky              ·forfeit
                        ·penalty
1 Replace Word; 2 View Doc; 3 Look Up Word; 4 Clear Column: 0
```

Alt-F1 (Thesaurus)

The word shown in reverse video in the text at the top of the screen is the headword for which the search was made.

Beneath the text are displayed reference words organized into word type categories: synonomous adjectives (a), nouns (n), verbs (v), and antonyms (ant). Reference words within a word type category are organized into subgroups according to connotation.

The column with capital letters next to reference words is referred to as the current column. The current column may be changed with the cursor right and cursor left keys. The reference words displayed with a bullet (small dot to the left) are themselves headwords for which other reference words may be displayed. There may be more than one headword's list of reference words displayed on the screen. If there are, the headwords and reference word lists are displayed in separate columns.

There may be more reference words found than can be displayed on the screen. If this is the case, the cursor up and cursor down keys (also PgUp and PgDn keys) may be used to scroll through them.

Note that the following commands can only be executed by typing the command number.

1 Replace Word

A reference word may be selected to replace the headword in the text. To do so, you type **1** and then the letter displayed to the left of the appropriate reference word. If a letter is not displayed next to the reference word of your choice, you may change the current column by typing the cursor left or cursor right keys before entering the Replace Word command.

2 View Doc

The View Doc command allows you to move the cursor through the text at the top of the screen without leaving the Thesaurus command. You may not edit the text; however, you may scroll through it to view text not currently displayed.

If you wish to select another headword from the text, you may move the cursor under it and type **Alt-F1** (Thesaurus) again. If you do not want to select another headword, you may type **F7** (Exit) to return to the Thesaurus.

3 Look Up Word

The Look Up Word command allows you to directly type in a headword for which WordPerfect will search.

4 Clear Column

The Clear Column command erases the current column's headword and reference word list from the screen.

Ctrl-F1
Shell ─┬─ 1 Go to DOS ── <enter DOS commands> ── {Enter 'EXIT' to return to WordPerfect}
└─ 0 Cancel

CTRL-F1 SHELL

The **F1** (Shell) command allows you to temporarily exit WordPerfect to DOS if the computer has enough RAM to accommodate the operation. To return to WordPerfect from DOS, type ||EXIT↵||.

If you choose to exit to DOS through the Shell command, you should always return to WordPerfect and exit WordPerfect properly by typing **F7** (Exit) before turning off the computer.

F2
->Search ── <entry> ─┬─ F2 ──── {If found, cursor moves to next occurrence of entry}
└─ Cancel key

F2 →SEARCH

The **F2** (→Search) command is used to move the cursor forward to occurrences of specific words, phrases, and/or WordPerfect codes. To use the →Search command, type **F2** (→Search). The prompt "->Srch:" will be displayed on the screen by the command. At this point, type the word/code pattern for which you want to search. You may type any keyboard characters, and you may include many WordPerfect codes by typing the keystroke combinations that would normally generate the command menus for the codes. For instance, to search for a line margins code [L/R Mar], you would type **F2** (→Search) and then type **Shift-F8,1,6** (Format,Line,**M**argins).

When you have finished typing the search word/code pattern, type **F2** (→Search) again and the search operation will commence. When the specified word/code pattern is found, the search will halt and the cursor will be moved to the location where the word/code pattern occurs in the document. To continue the search for the same word pattern, type **F2, F2** (→Search, →Search).

Lower-case search characters will match upper- and lower-case characters in the document. Upper-case search characters will match upper-case characters only. To search for stop codes such as [bold], type the command keystroke sequence twice and then delete the start code from the "->Srch:" entry.

An extended search (one in which headers, footers, footnotes, and endnotes are also searched) may be performed by typing the Home key before typing **F2** (→Search).

Block/→Search

The →Search command may be used to expand (contract) a blocked portion of text up to the found word/code pattern.

The **F2** (→Search), **Shift-F2** (←Search), and **Alt-F2** (Replace) commands are highly interrelated commands.

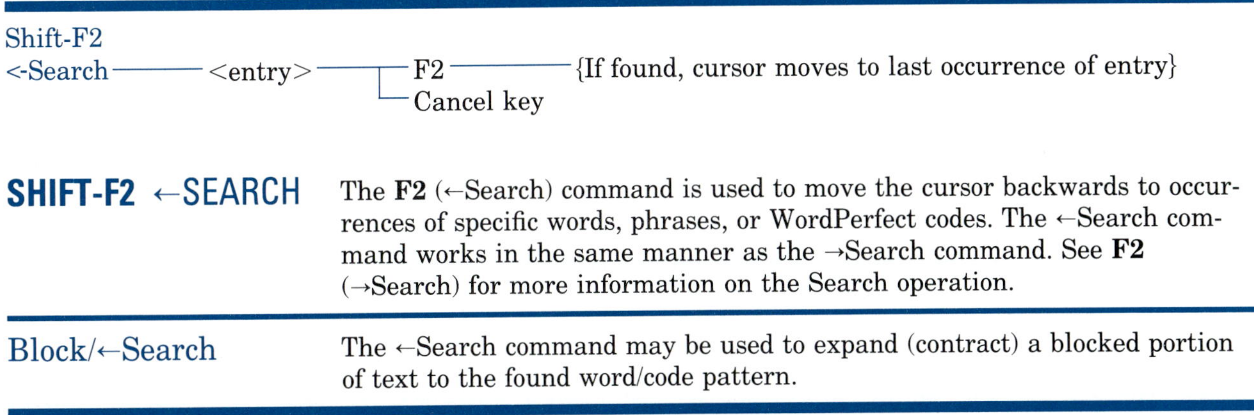

SHIFT-F2 ←SEARCH

The **F2** (←Search) command is used to move the cursor backwards to occurrences of specific words, phrases, or WordPerfect codes. The ←Search command works in the same manner as the →Search command. See **F2** (→Search) for more information on the Search operation.

Block/←Search

The ←Search command may be used to expand (contract) a blocked portion of text to the found word/code pattern.

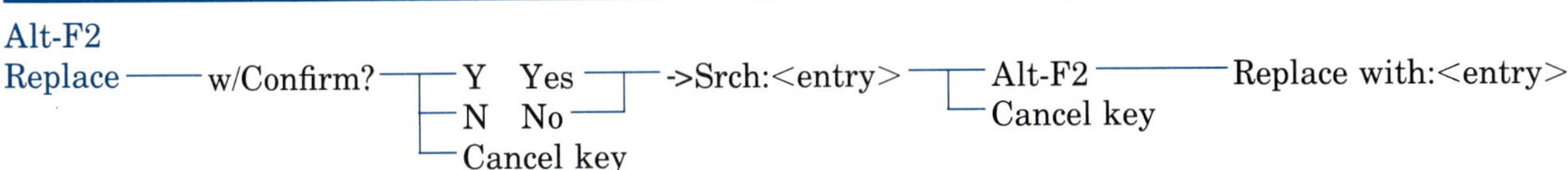

ALT-F2 REPLACE

The **Alt-F2** (Replace) command is used to search the document for occurrences of specific words, phrases, or WordPerfect codes and replace them with other words, phrases, or codes. To use the Replace command, begin by typing **Alt-F2** (Replace).

The prompt "w/Confirm? (Y/N) No" will appear on the screen. If you type Y, WordPerfect will stop on each word pattern for which it is searching and will prompt "Confirm? (Y/N) No". You then may type Y to replace the word pattern or N or ↵ to skip over the word pattern and continue searching.

It is recommended that you type Y at the initial "w/Confirm (Y/N)" prompt. If you type N or ↵ at the initial "w/Confirm (Y/N)" prompt, WordPerfect will automatically replace all of the occurrences of the word/code pattern in the document with the replacement word/code pattern.

The next prompt displayed by the Replace command is "->Srch:". WordPerfect normally searches for word/code patterns from the current cursor position forward in the document. To cause a search backwards in the document, type the cursor up key when you see the "->Srch:" prompt and the prompt will change to "<-Srch:". (Typing the cursor down key returns the search to forward.)

You next type the word pattern for which to search. You may type any keyboard characters or specify WordPerfect codes by typing the keystroke combinations that would normally generate the command menus for the codes. When finished, type the **Alt-F2** (Replace) command again.

The next prompt "Replace with:" is answered by typing the word pattern with which you want the search word pattern to be replaced. You may answer this prompt in the same manner as you answer the "->Srch:" prompt. When you have finished typing the replacement word pattern, type **Alt-F2** (Replace) once more, and the search and replace operation will commence.

Lower-case search characters will match upper- and lower-case characters in the document; upper-case search characters will only match upper-case characters. An extended search, one in which headers, footers, footnotes, and endnotes are also searched, may be done by typing the Home key before typing **Alt-F2** (Replace).

Block/Replace

The Replace command operation may be done on a block of text by blocking the text to be searched before typing **Alt-F2** (Replace).

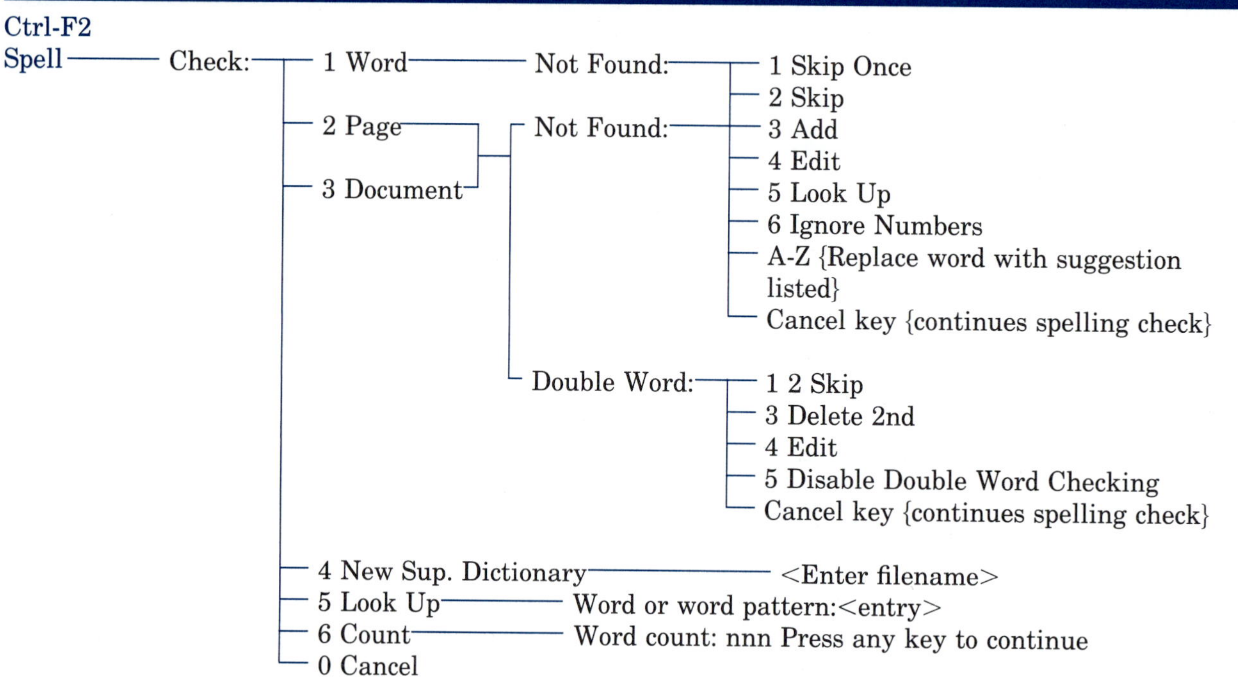

CTRL-F2 SPELL

WordPerfect comes with a spell checking feature that will search a document for words not found in its dictionary. The dictionary data are kept on a separate disk. If you are using a computer with two floppy disk drives, you will need to insert the Speller disk into the B: drive each time it is needed. If you have a hard-disk drive, the Speller diskette files may be copied into the same subdirectory as WordPerfect.

Check: **Word Page Document**

The spelling feature may be used to check the current word, page, or document. Each is similar in how WordPerfect checks for spelling errors.

WordPerfect will move to the start of the word, page, or document and begin comparing the word(s) found there with the words in its dictionary. When it finds a word not listed in its dictionary, it stops and presents a screen similar to the following.

```
        Each spacious townhouse unit has wall-to-wall

        carpeting, drapes, privite patio and sun deck.

        You will find the townhouse of your choice

        equipped with a completely modern kitchen

        including a self-defrosting refrigerator, self-

==========================================================================

  A. primite                B. private                C. privity
  D. previewed              E. privata                F. privati
  G. privet                 H. proved                 I. provide






Not Found: 1 Skip Once; 2 Skip; 3 Add; 4 Edit; 5 Look Up; 6 Ignore Numbers: 0
```

Not Found

At the top of the screen is the portion of the document where WordPerfect found an unknown word. Beneath is a list of words WordPerfect did find in its dictionary that may be the correct spelling for the unknown word. At the bottom of the screen is the Spell menu of commands.

If the correct spelling for the word appears in the middle of the screen, you may type the letter preceding it (A., B., etc.) to cause WordPerfect to replace the unknown word with a correctly spelled word. WordPerfect will automatically capitalize the replacement word if the word being replaced is capitalized.

Note that the following commands can only be executed by typing the command number.

1 Skip Once If you type **1** (Skip Once), WordPerfect will continue its search and, if it encounters the word again, it will stop for you to correct it.

2 Skip If you type **2** (Skip), WordPerfect will continue its search and ignore the word if it occurs again.

3 Add You may use the Add command to cause WordPerfect to add the current word to a supplemental dictionary.

4 Edit You may use the Edit command to edit the word. When you have finished editing, type the Enter key. If the edited word is found in the dictionary, WordPerfect will continue.

5 Look Up You may use the Look Up command to look up words that match a pattern. The pattern is described by using the wild card characters ? and *. *Ca?e* will return *cafe, cage, cake,* etc. *Ca*e* will return *cabbage, cable, caboose,* etc.

6 Ignore Numbers Use the Ignore Numbers command to cause WordPerfect to skip over all words containing a number.

Double Word

During its spelling check, WordPerfect also will stop on occurrences of double words. You are given the options to **1** or **2** Skip, **3** Delete the 2nd word, **4** Edit the text, or **5** Disable double-word checking.

New Sup. Dictionary

The New Supplemental Dictionary command may be used to create a personal dictionary for use in a spelling check.

Look Up

The (Spell),Look Up command is the same as the (Spell),Not Found,**5** Look Up command. You may use the (Spell),Look Up command to look up words without starting a spell checking operation.

Count

When it has finished spell checking the document, WordPerfect will display the total number of words it checked during the spell check operation. Use the Count command to count the number of words in a document without performing the spell checking operation.

Block/Spell

You can conduct a spell check operation on a block of text by using the Block/(Spell) command.

F3
Help ——————— {Press Enter or Space bar to exit Help}

F3 HELP

The **F3** (Help) command provides an extensive set of on-line documentation for the user. The documentation is kept on the WordPerfect 1 disk. If you are using a computer with two floppy disk drives, you will need to insert the disk into the disk drive to use the **F3** (Help) command.

To exit the Help command screens, type Space or ↵.

Shift-F3
Switch ——————— {Press Switch key to return to original document}

SHIFT-F3 SWITCH

WordPerfect allows editing of two text files at the same time. When WordPerfect is first loaded, the default file for editing is document 1 (displayed as "Doc 1" on the status line). To begin editing document 2, type **Shift-F3.** Editing and file operations are treated as separate operations between the two documents. You must exit both documents with the **F7** (Exit) command to properly exit WordPerfect.

The two documents share the same Move buffer and Undelete buffers. You may copy text from one file to the other by using these buffers and the appropriate commands.

You may view both document 1 and document 2 at the same time by using the **Ctrl-F3,1** (Screen),**W**indow command.

Block/Switch

You may use the Block/(Switch) command to convert letters in a block of text to all upper-case or all lower-case letters.

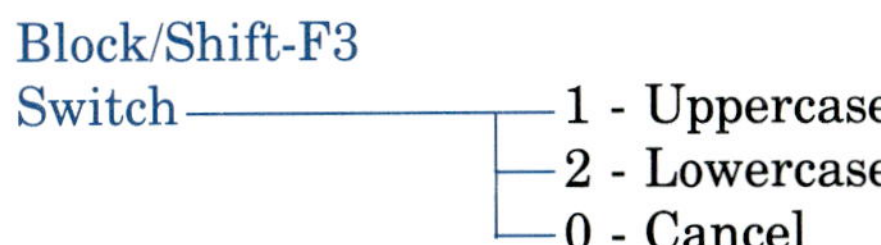

To convert lower-case letters to upper-case letters, block the text to be converted and type **Shift-F3 (Switch).** Next type **1** or **U** (**U**ppercase). To convert upper-case letters to lower-case letters, block the text to be converted and type **Shift-F3** (Switch). Next type **2** or **L** (**L**owercase).

Alt-F3
Reveal Codes —— {Press Reveal Codes key to restore screen}

ALT-F3 REVEAL CODES

The **Alt-F3** (Reveal Codes) command splits the screen and reveals imbedded WordPerfect codes. Cursor control keys synchronously move top and bottom cursors (cursors in the text and code screens). All editing and command operations are available while the Reveal Codes screen is on. Type **Alt-F3** (Reveal Codes) again to return to normal editing.

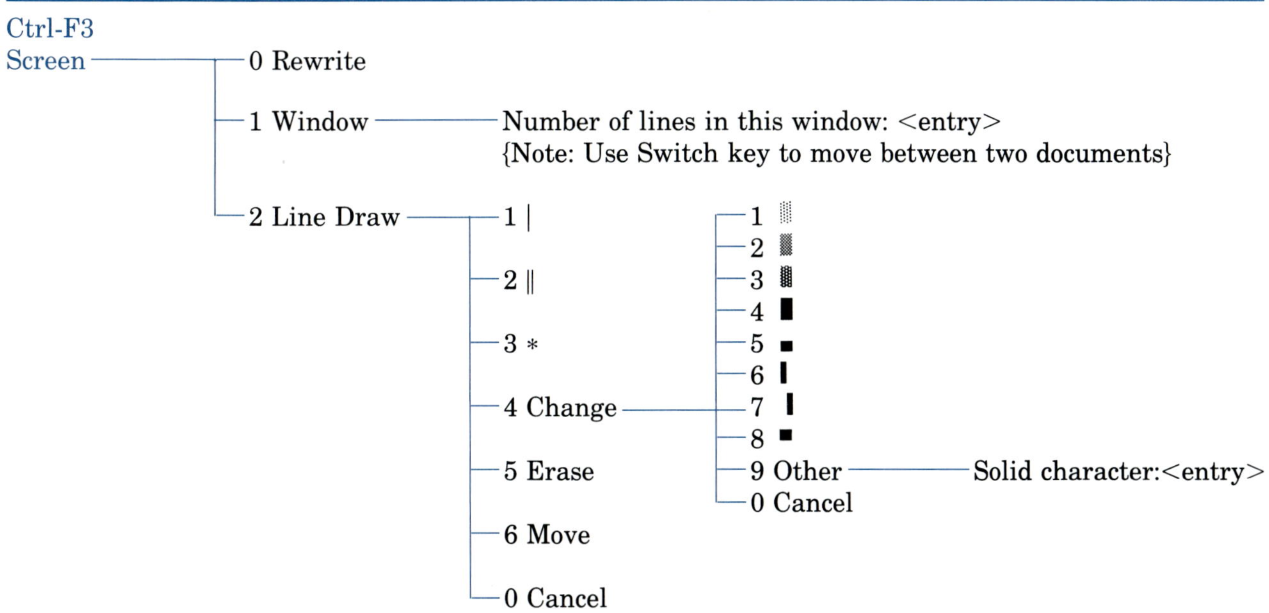

CTRL-F3 SCREEN

The **Ctrl-F3** (Screen) command may be used to rewrite the document for new margins, line spacing, split the screen in order to view documents 1 and 2 simultaneously (see the **Shift-F3** (Switch) command), or to create various lines and boxes to be included in the current document.

Rewrite

The **R**ewrite command may be used to rewrite the screen after the **Shift-F1,3,1** (Setup),**D**isplay,**A**utomatically Format and Rewrite command has been changed to "No" (see the **Shift-F1** (Setup) command). Type **Ctrl-F3,0** or **Ctrl-F3,**↵ to rewrite the screen.

Window

The **W**indow command may be used to split the screen horizontally to view documents 1 and 2 at the same time (see **Shift-F3** (Switch)). Type **Ctrl-F3,1** and then enter the number of screen lines to be displayed for the current document. Typing 11 will split the screen in half (two equal windows). Typing 24 will return the screen to the normal one-screen mode. Screens may not be split into windows of less than two lines.

Use the **Shift-F3** (Switch) command to move the cursor from one window to the other.

Line Draw

The **L**ine Draw command is used for drawing boxes and lines in the current text file. It provides screen graphic characters and commands that allow shapes to be drawn on the screen by using the cursor control keys. However, some printers do not support the screen graphics characters used by the **L**ine Draw command, and printing a file with such characters in it may lead to unpredictable results.

The **L**ine Draw command is composed of two menus. The relationship of the menus may be graphically represented as follows.

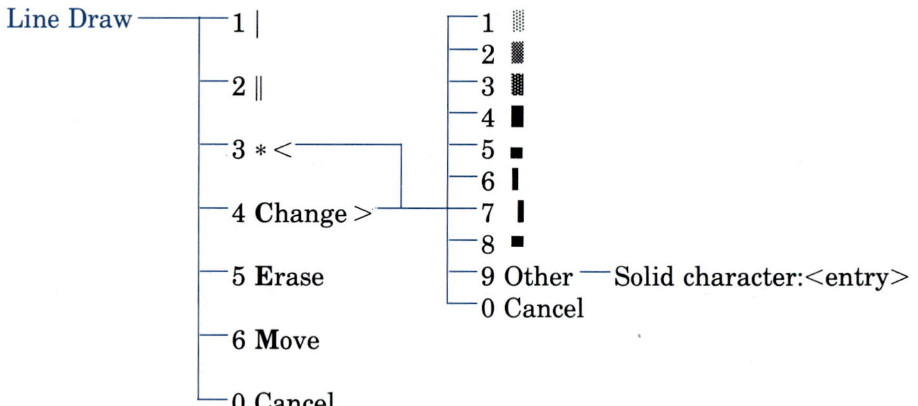

The first menu presented (left side) has six commands. Commands **1** through **3** are used to select different graphics characters with which boxes and lines will be drawn. The third character (*) may be changed with the **C**hange command. The last two commands are **E**rase and **M**ove.

To draw a line or box, first move the cursor to the point at which drawing is to begin. Next type **Ctrl-F3,2** (Screen),**L**ine Draw, and enter the number **1, 2,** or **3** to select the graphics character of your choice. You may now draw lines composed of the selected character by using the cursor control keys to move in the appropriate draw direction.

To stop drawing and move the cursor to a new location, type **6** or **M** (**M**ove). To erase characters on the screen, type **5** or **E** (**E**rase) and then move the cursor across the characters you wish to erase.

The third graphics character shown on the Line Draw menu, *, can be changed to any one of the characters shown on the right (**1** through **8**). Type **4** or **C** (**C**hange) and then type number of the desired graphics character on the second **L**ine Draw menu. **9** or **O** (**O**ther) may be used to define a keyboard character to use in drawing lines.

It is generally recommended that you enter **L**ine Draw characters into an area of document text that has single line spacing (see **Shift-F8,1,6** (Format),**L**ine,Line **S**pacing) and that no [->indent], [->indent<-], [Tab], or [←Mar Rel] codes occur within the area. It also is recommended that each line of text in the area end with a hard return [HRt] code.

F4
->Indent ———— {Places indent code [->Indent] and moves cursor to next tab stop}

F4 →INDENT

CODE = [->INDENT]

The **F4** (→Indent) command indents subsequent text in a paragraph to the next tab stop. See the **Shift-F8** (Format),**L**ine,**T**ab Set command for information on setting tab stops.

To create a "hanging" paragraph, one which is indented to the right of a heading, type the heading **F4** (→Indent) and then type the paragraph.

Heading This is an example of a "hanging" paragraph produced with the **F4** (→Indent) command.

Shift-F4
->Indent<- ———— {Places indent code [->Indent<-] and moves cursor to next tab stop}

SHIFT F4 →INDENT←

CODE = [->INDENT<-]

The **Shift-F4** (→Indent←) command causes subsequent text in a paragraph to be indented an equal number of tab stops from both the left and right margins. The next tab stop to the right of the cursor position determines the number of tab stops to be used for indentation. If the cursor position is to the right of half of the tab stops set, the [->Indent<-] code will not be placed. See the **Shift-F8** (Format), **L**ine,**T**ab Set command for information on setting tab stops.

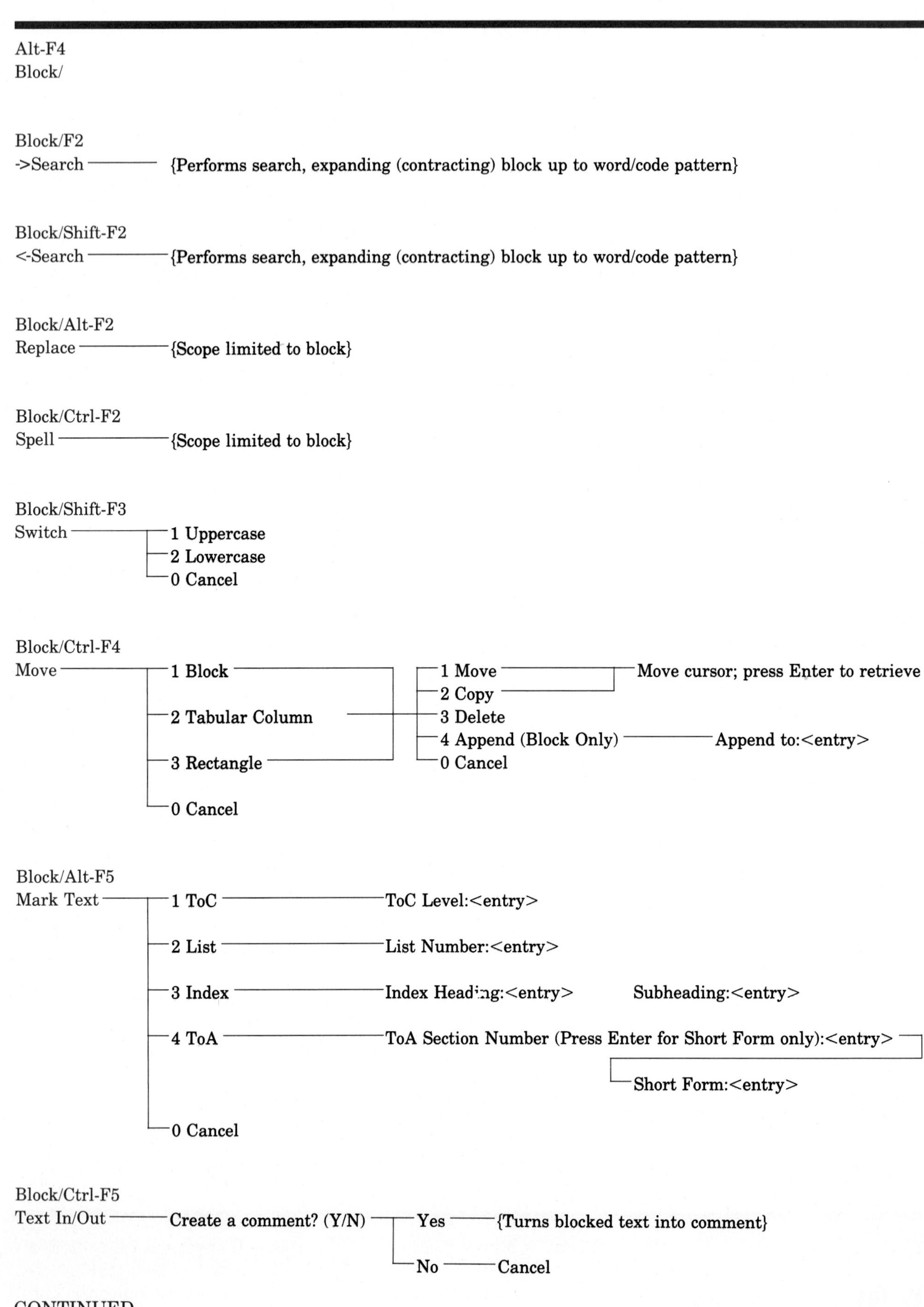
Alt-F4
Block/
Block/F2
->Search
{Performs search, expanding (contracting) block up to word/code pattern}
Block/Shift-F2
<-Search
{Performs search, expanding (contracting) block up to word/code pattern}
Block/Alt-F2
Replace
{Scope limited to block}
Block/Ctrl-F2
Spell
{Scope limited to block}
Block/Shift-F3
Switch
1 Uppercase
2 Lowercase
0 Cancel
Block/Ctrl-F4
Move
1 Block
2 Tabular Column
3 Rectangle
0 Cancel
1 Move
2 Copy
3 Delete
4 Append (Block Only)
0 Cancel
Move cursor; press Enter to retrieve
Append to:<entry>
Block/Alt-F5
Mark Text
1 ToC
ToC Level:<entry>
2 List
List Number:<entry>
3 Index
Index Heading:<entry>
Subheading:<entry>
4 ToA
ToA Section Number (Press Enter for Short Form only):<entry>
Short Form:<entry>
0 Cancel
Block/Ctrl-F5
Text In/Out
Create a comment? (Y/N)
Yes
{Turns blocked text into comment}
No
Cancel
CONTINUED

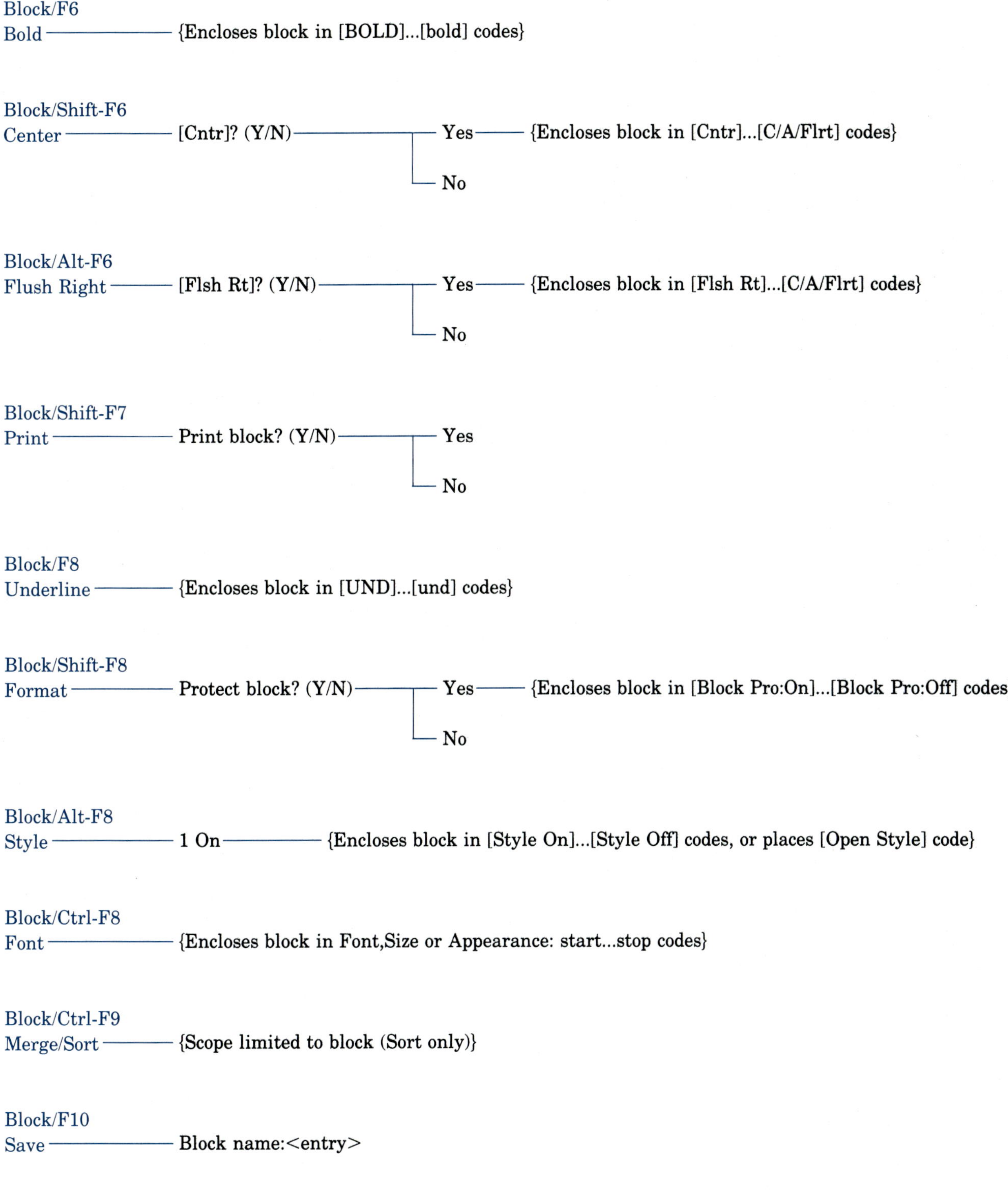

ALT-F4 BLOCK

Code = [Block]

The **Alt-F4** (Block) command is used to define a portion of text to be subsequently affected by another WordPerfect command. To block a portion of text, move the cursor to the beginning of the text to be blocked and type **Alt-F4** (Block). A blinking "Block on" message will appear at the bottom of the screen. Next, move the cursor to the end of the text to be blocked. Note that while Block is on, typing a character will automatically move the cursor forward to the character and typing ↵ will move the cursor forward to the next hard return [HRt] code. The blocked text will be displayed on the screen in reverse video.

The **Alt-F4** (Block) command trees describe which commands may be used to affect a section of blocked text. For more information on the Block command operations, refer to the appropriate command menu.

To turn a Block off, type **F1** (Cancel) or **Alt-F4** (Block).

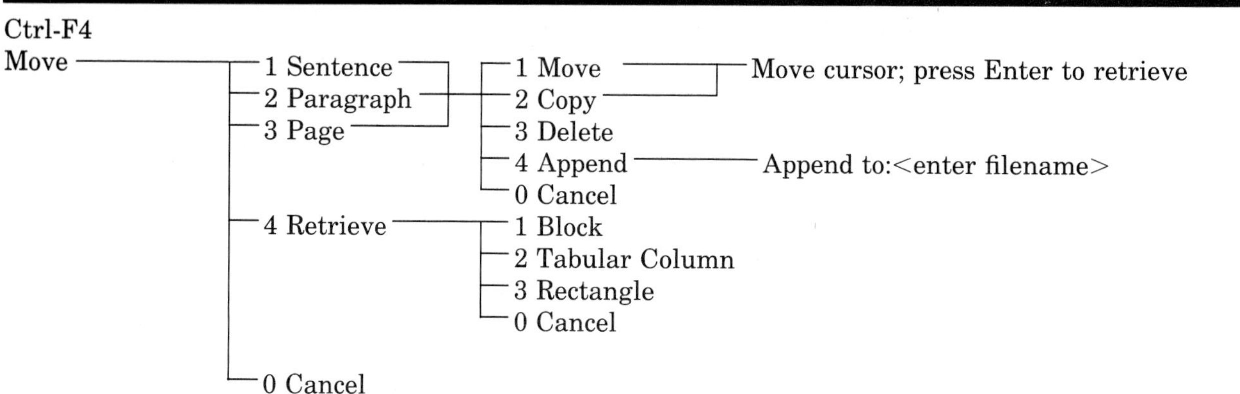

CTRL-F4 MOVE

The **Ctrl-F4** (Move) command is used to perform cut-and-paste operations. The operations include moving a section of text to another location, copying a section of text to another location, and deleting a section of text from the document.

The text being moved or copied is temporarily held during and after the operation in what is called a Move buffer. When text is deleted, it is held in an Undelete buffer. Once a cut-and-paste operation is completed, a copy of the text remains in the buffer. The copy of text in the buffer will be replaced by a subsequent Move or Delete operation. (See the introductory tutorial for more information on Move and Undelete buffers.)

The Move and Block/(Move) commands are highly related. Both are designed to facilitate the cutting and pasting of various sizes and shapes of text. The following discusses each of the commands and the type of text for which they are designed.

Move: **S**entence **P**aragraph **P**age

The (Move), **S**entence, **P**aragraph, and **P**age commands differ only in the number of lines of text they are designed to cut, copy, or delete. A sentence is defined by WordPerfect as that text which occurs between periods and/or hard returns. A paragraph is defined by WordPerfect as that text which occurs between hard returns. A page is defined by WordPerfect as that text which occurs between soft or hard page breaks.

To perform a cut-and-paste operation on such sections of text, position the cursor on the sentence, paragraph, or page to be affected and type **Ctrl-F4** (Move). Next select the appropriate text definition, **S**entence, **P**aragraph, or **P**age, by typing the command number or letter. The sentence, paragraph, or page of text will become highlighted on the screen (automatically blocked). The next menu that appears includes the options to **M**ove, **C**opy, **D**elete, or **A**ppend the blocked section of text.

Move

Use **M**ove to erase the blocked section from the screen and prepare to retrieve it from the Move buffer into another location in the text. To complete the **M**ove operation, move the cursor to where the text is to be retrieved and type ↵. You may type **F1** (Cancel) to interrupt the **M**ove operation and use the **Ctrl-F4,4,1** (Move),**R**etrieve,**B**lock command at a later time to retrieve the block of text. (See the **Ctrl-F4** (Move),**R**etrieve command.)

Copy

Use **C**opy to prepare to retrieve a copy of the blocked section of text from the Move buffer into another location in the text. To complete the **C**opy operation, move the cursor to where the copied text is to be retrieved and type ↵. You may type **F1** (Cancel) to interrupt the **C**opy operation and use the **Ctrl-F4,4,1** (Move),**R**etrieve,**B**lock command at a later time to retrieve the block of text. (See the **Ctrl-F4** (Move),**R**etrieve command.)

Delete

Use **D**elete to delete the text from the document. A copy of the deleted text will be placed into the first Undelete buffer.

Append

Use the **A**ppend command to add the blocked text to the bottom of a document file stored on the disk. When **A**ppend is used, WordPerfect will prompt "Append to:". Enter the filename for the file to which you want the blocked text appended.

Retrieve

As previously mentioned, the Move and Block/(Move) commands are highly interrelated. In fact, the (Move),**S**entence, (Move),**P**aragraph, and (Move),P**a**ge commands simply provide the feature of automatically blocking the section of text before proceeding with the cut-and-paste operation. When the Move or Block/(Move),**B**lock commands are used to perform a copy or move operation, the blocked text is copied to the Move buffer and may later be retrieved with the (Move),**R**etrieve,**B**lock command.

The (Move),**R**etrieve command, however, has two other options besides **B**lock: Tabular **C**olumn and **R**ectangle. These options are used to retrieve text from another Move buffer (the column buffer)—a buffer into which text may only be placed using the Block/(Move),Tabular **C**olumns or the Block/(Move),**R**ectangle commands.

Block/Move

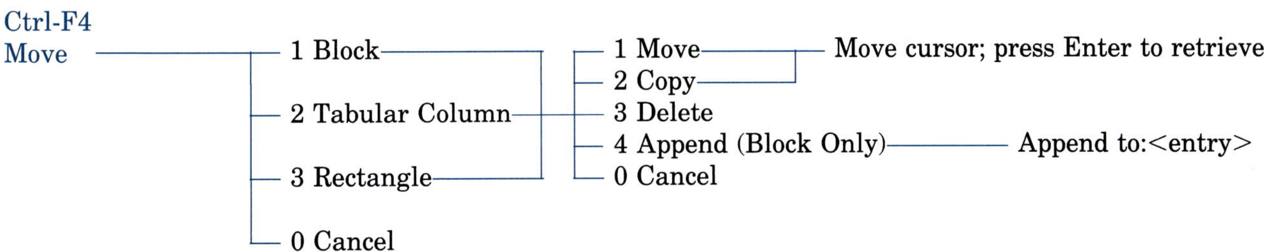

The Block/(Move) command may be used to perform cut-and-paste operations on two different shapes of text—block or column.

Block

The Block/(Move),**B**lock command is used to perform cut-and-paste operations on text that can be described as being left to right, top to bottom in nature. Sentences, paragraphs, pages, or portions thereof, are block shaped.

Block the text to be affected and type **Ctrl-F4,1** (Move),**B**lock. Next select **M**ove, **C**opy, **D**elete, or **A**ppend. Finally, if the operation is to move or copy the column of text, move the cursor to where you want the column of text to appear and type ↵. You may type **F1** (Cancel) to interrupt the copy operation and use the **Ctrl-F4** (Move),**R**etrieve,**B**lock command at a later time to retrieve the block of text.

Tabular Columns

Block/(Move),Tabular **C**olumns is used to perform cut-and-paste operations on a column of text defined by tabs, tab aligns, indents, or hard returns. Move the cursor to the top of the column of text you want to move, copy, or delete, and then turn Block on by typing **Alt-F4** (Block). Next move the cursor to the bottom of the column. The entire block will be highlighted at this point. Then type **Ctrl-F4,2** (Move), Tabular **C**olumns. Now only the column in which the cursor is located will be highlighted. Next select **M**ove, **C**opy, **D**elete, or **A**ppend. Finally, if the operation is to move or copy the column of text, move the cursor to where you want the column of text to appear and type ↵. You may type **F1** (Cancel) to interrupt the copy operation and use the **Ctrl-F4,4,2** (Move),**R**etrieve,Tabular **C**olumn command at a later time to retrieve the block of text.

Rectangle

The Block/(Move),**R**ectangle command is used to perform cut-and-paste operations on a rectangular segment of text. Move the cursor to the top left corner of the rectangle of text you want to move, copy, or delete, and then turn Block on by typing **Alt-F4** (Block). Next move the cursor to the bottom right corner of the rectangle. The entire block will be highlighted at this point. Then type **Ctrl-F4** (Move),**R**ectangle. Now only the rectangle described by its top left and bottom right corners will be highlighted. Next select **M**ove, **C**opy, **D**elete, or **A**ppend. Finally, if the operation is to move or copy the rectangle of text, move the cursor to the place you want the rectangle to appear and type ↵. You may type **F1** (Cancel) to interrupt the copy operation and use the **Ctrl-F4,4,3** (Move),**R**etrieve,**R**ectangle command at a later time to retrieve the block of text.

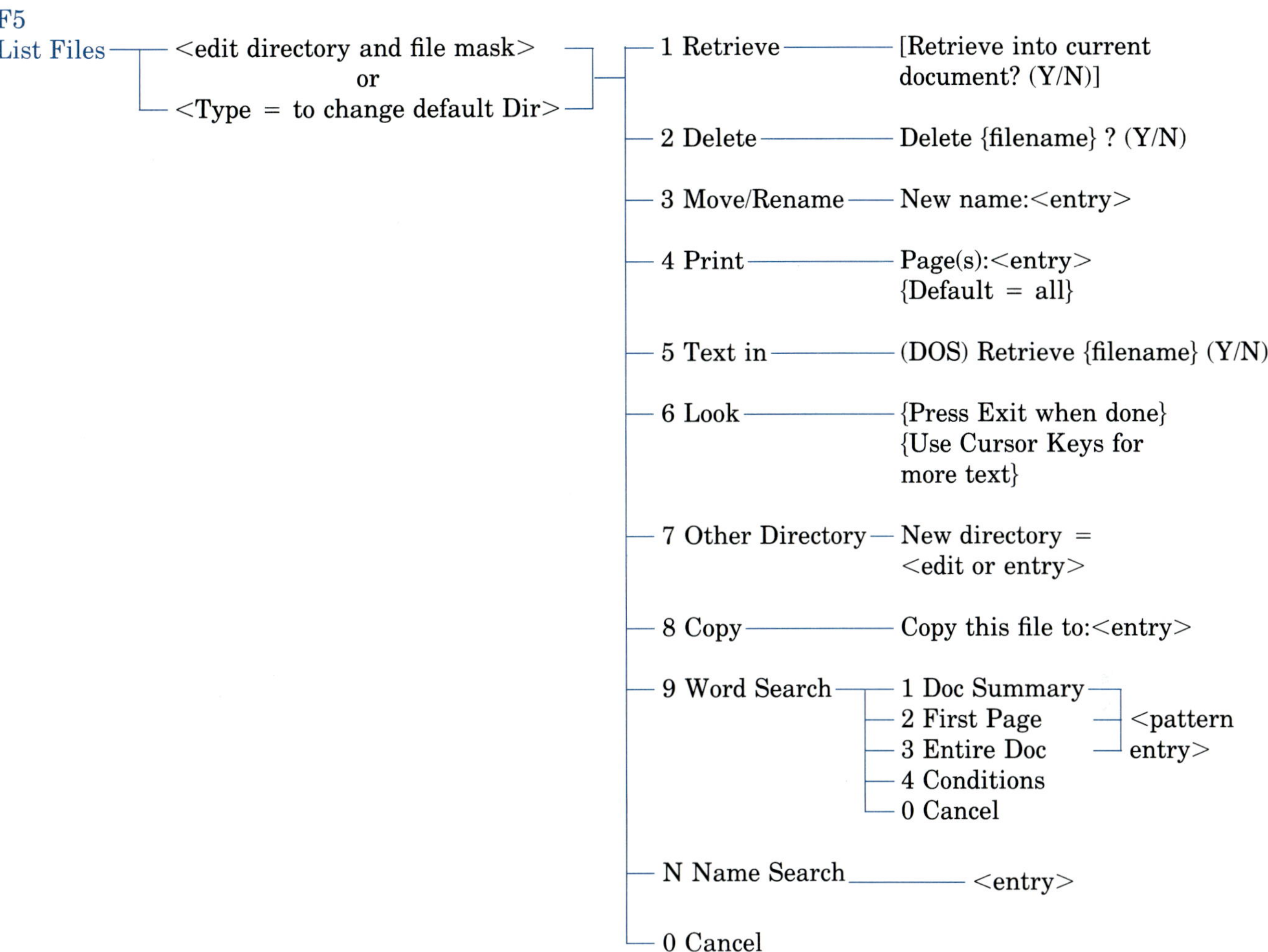

F5 LIST FILES

The **F5** (List Files) command provides commands to change the default disk drive, perform basic file maintenance operations, and search through files for word pattern occurrences.

Changing the Default Disk Drive

When the **F5** (List Files) command is typed a message

Dir A:*.*   (Type = to change default Dir)

appears on the screen. The A:*.* part of the message indicates which drive is the current drive. To cause WordPerfect to automatically look to another drive or directory for your word processing files, type =↵ and then enter the drive name and/or path for the appropriate subdirectory. (See **F5,7** (List Files),**O**ther Directory for another method of changing the default drive.)

The List Files Screen

When the correct directory is displayed, type ↵ to cause WordPerfect to display the List Files screen. The screen will appear similar to the following.

```
11/13/89  15:59              Directory A:\*.*
Document size:     2529   Free:  1415680   Used:    37185        Files:  17

. <CURRENT>     <DIR>                        .. <PARENT>      <DIR>
BRIEF    .          6640  10/26/89 08:58     CHART    .         4218  09/26/89 09:59
CLIENTS  .          1357  08/10/89 15:35     FUTURE   .         3136  10/23/89 08:18
INVOICE  .          2444  09/29/89 07:24     ITINERY  .         2257  09/19/89 06:40
LABELA   .           510  08/16/89 08:52     LABELB   .          929  08/16/89 09:52
LIST     .           518  10/13/89 14:18     MASTER   .          808  10/26/89 15:13
MEMO     .           935  09/09/89 15:24     MINUTES  .         2703  09/19/89 10:40
OUTLINE  .          1177  08/12/89 18:52     PAST     .         2875  10/12/89 14:19
PRESENT  .          4391  09/16/89 09:29     RETAILA  .         1585  08/06/89 10:52
TABLE    .           602  10/06/89 16:35

1 Retrieve; 2 Delete; 3 Move/Rename; 4 Print; 5 Text In;
6 Look; 7 Other Directory; 8 Copy; 9 Word Search; N Name Search: 6
```

The top of the screen displays a header with information about the DOS system date and time, the size of the document currently being edited, the current directory, disk space available, and number of files on the disk.

List Files File Maintenance Commands

The first eight commands on the List Files screen are commands associated with file maintenance. The inverted screen appearing at the top of the list of filenames is a cursor. The cursor may be moved with the cursor control keys to any one of the files displayed on the screen. The PgUp and PgDn keys also may be used to move the cursor. To execute the file maintenance commands, you first move the cursor to the appropriate filename and then type the number or letter of the command you wish to execute.

Retrieve

The **R**etrieve command loads a document into memory for editing or printing. The retrieved document will be inserted at the editing cursor location into any document that may already be in memory. Move the List Files cursor to the file to be retrieved and then type **1** or **R** (**R**etrieve). (See **Shift-F10** (Retrieve) for another method of retrieving document files.)

Delete

Erases a file from the disk. Move the List Files cursor to the file to be deleted and then type **2** or **D** (**D**elete). The message "Delete *filename*? (Y/N) No" will appear at the bottom of the screen. Type Y to complete the file deletion operation. When a file is deleted, it is permanently erased from the disk.

Move/Rename

May be used to move a file to another disk or directory or rename a file. Move the List Files cursor to the file to be affected and then type **3** or **M** (**M**ove/Rename). To move the file, type the full directory specification for where the file is to be moved (drive/path). To rename the file, type a new filename. To move and rename the file, type the full file directory specification followed by the new filename.

Print

Prints a file from the disk. Move the List Files cursor to the file to be printed and type **4** or **P** (**P**rint). WordPerfect will respond with the prompt "Page(s): (All)." If you want the whole document to be printed, type ↵. You may, however, specify that only certain pages be printed. To specify certain pages, you may enter one of the following.

N	Print page number *N*
N-	Print from page number *N* to end of document
N-*n*	Print pages *N* through *n* inclusive
-*N*	Print from beginning of document through page *N*
N, *n*	Print the specified pages

Page numbers must be entered in the way they appear on the printed document. To cancel a print operation, type **F1,Shift-F7,4,1** ↵ (Cancel),(Print), **C**ontrol Printer,**C**ancel Job(s). (See **Shift-F7** (Print) for another method of printing certain pages of a disk file.)

Text In

The **T**ext In command may be used to retrieve an ASCII file. Such ASCII files may include Lotus .PRN files and dBase III .TXT, .FMT, or .PRG files. (See **Ctrl-F5** (Text In/Out) for another method of retrieving ASCII files.)

Look

The **L**ook command allows you to view a file on the disk without retrieving it. **L**ook is the default command on the List Files screen. If you move the List Files cursor to a filename and type ↵, the contents of the file will be displayed on the screen, but the file will not be retrieved.

Other Directory

The **O**ther Directory command may be used to change the default disk drive and/or subdirectory after the List Files screen has been presented. (See **F5** (List Files) "Changing the Default Disk Drive" for another method of changing the default drive.)

Copy

The **C**opy command is used to make a copy of a file. Move the List Files cursor to the file to be copied and then type **8** or **C** (**C**opy). Then enter the file specification for the copied file.

List Files Search Commands

Word Search

The **F5** (List Files),**W**ord Search command is designed to search for occurrences of a word pattern in the files of the current disk and/or subdirectory. The size of the word pattern is limited to 39 characters. When the search is completed, the List Files screen will display those files having the specified word pattern within them on the screen with an asterisk next to the file size (bytes) for the file.

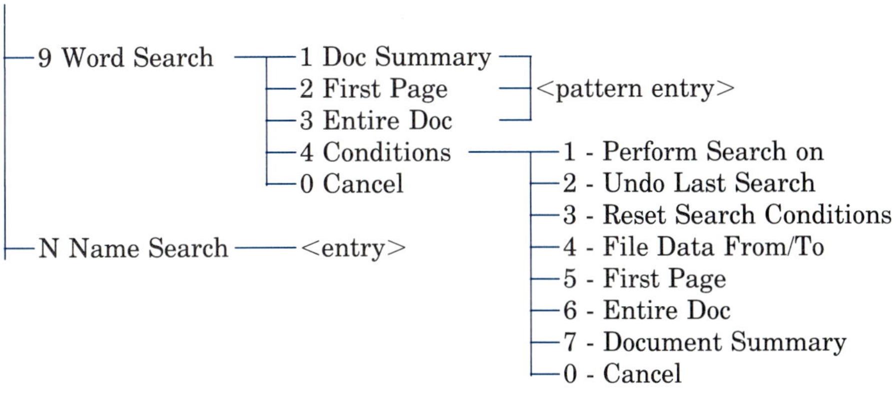

- 9 Word Search
  - 1 Doc Summary — <pattern entry>
  - 2 First Page — <pattern entry>
  - 3 Entire Doc — <pattern entry>
  - 4 Conditions
    - 1 - Perform Search on
    - 2 - Undo Last Search
    - 3 - Reset Search Conditions
    - 4 - File Data From/To
    - 5 - First Page
    - 6 - Entire Doc
    - 7 - Document Summary
    - 0 - Cancel
  - 0 Cancel
- N Name Search — <entry>

To use the **W**ord Search command, you first specify the scope of the search. The options include search **D**oc(ument) Summaries only (see **Shift-F8,3,5** (Format),**D**ocument,**S**ummary for information on Document Summaries), search **F**irst Page only (first 4,000 bytes of the file), or search the **E**ntire Doc(ument) for the word pattern. After you have selected the scope of the search, enter the word pattern for which to search.

You may use the **C**onditions command to bring up a different menu screen that may be used to set various additional criteria for the search.

Word Patterns It is recommended that you enclose the word pattern to be searched for with quotes. Upper- and lower-case characters are treated the same when a word search is performed.

The wild card characters ? and * may be used in the word pattern. The ? (question mark) has the effect of saying "accept any character here." For example, if the word pattern to search for is entered as "April ?, 1988," all files with dates entered as text that match the word pattern, except for the middle character, will be displayed on the List Files screen. That is, files dated "April 2, 1988," "April 3, 1988," and so on, will be displayed.

The * (asterisk) has the effect of saying "accept any characters from this point on." For example, if the word pattern to search for is entered as "Water*" all files having words such as "Waterville," "Waterdale," and so on, will be displayed.

Logical operators may be entered with the ; (semicolon) for AND and , (comma) for OR. The order of logical operator execution is from left to right. For example, "Bill";"product review" will display all files with the word patterns "Bill" and "product review" within them.

"Bill","Larry";"product review" will display all files with the word patterns "Bill" or "Larry" that also have the pattern "product review"—that is, ("Bill" OR "Larry") AND "product review."

Name Search

If you type **N** (**N**ame Search), the **N**ame Search command will begin execution. With **N**ame Search, you begin to type the filename of a file and the cursor will jump to the first filename with matching characters for the keystroke(s) you type. To end **N**ame Search, type **F1** (Cancel) or ↵.

Marking Files You can Delete, Print, Copy, or Word Search several files at once by marking the files with an asterisk. Move the List Files cursor to the file(s) you want to erase, copy, print, or search, and then type an * (asterisk). When all of the appropriate files are marked, select the command you want executed from the List Files menu.

To "unmark" a file, move the List Files cursor to the file and type an * (asterisk) again.

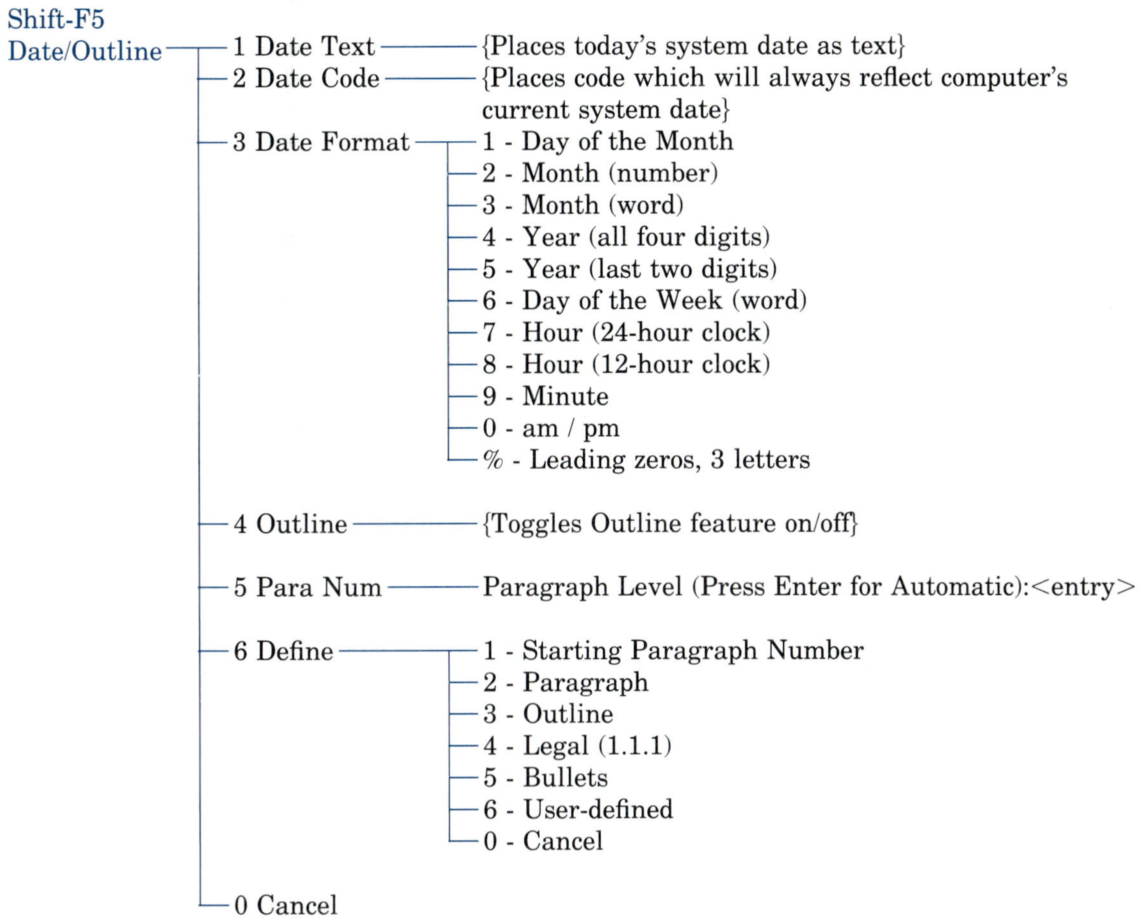

SHIFT-F5 DATE/OUTLINE

The **Shift-F5** (Date/Outline) command may be used to insert (in a variety of formats) the current DOS system date and/or time into a document or to generate automatic outline and paragraph numbering.

Date **T**ext

The Date **T**ext command inserts the system date/time as text at the current cursor location.

Date **C**ode
Code =
[Date:*format*]

Inserts the date/time as a WordPerfect code. The code will display the current DOS date and/or time each time the document is opened for editing or printing. The display will be in the current date format.

Date **F**ormat

Default—3 1, 4 Example—December 15, 1989

The Date **F**ormat command allows the date/time format to be changed for the document. The menu of format options is largely self-explanatory. When the Date **F**ormat command is used to reset the display of dates in a document, all subsequent date text or date codes inserted into the file during the editing session will reflect the changed date format. To change the date format for all subsequent editing sessions, use **Shift-F1** (Setup),**I**nitial Settings,**D**ate Format.

Outline
Code =
[Par Num:Auto]

WordPerfect provides a feature which automatically inserts and maintains outline numbers. The numbers are generated by codes that are inserted into the text when the **O**utline feature is on and the Enter key is typed. To turn the **O**utline feature on, type **Shift-F5,4** (Date/Outline),**O**utline. The message

"Outline" will appear on the status line. To turn the Outline feature off, type **Shift-F5,4** again.

The nature of the number displayed by an Outline code depends on the code's position on the screen—it changes according to the tab stop (see **Shift-F8** (Format),**L**ine,**T**ab Set) upon which the code occurs or follows.

It is generally easier to insert [TAB]s or [->Indent]s before a code to ensure that it is moved to a current tab stop. The following shows the various default number type displays and the [TAB]s required to generate them.

I.	No [TAB]s
[TAB] A.	1 [TAB]
[TAB] [TAB] 1.	2 [TAB]s
[TAB] [TAB] [TAB] a.	3 [TAB]s
[TAB] [TAB] [TAB] [TAB] (1)	4 [TAB]s
[TAB] [TAB] [TAB] [TAB] [TAB] (a)	5 [TAB]s
[TAB] [TAB] [TAB] [TAB] [TAB] [TAB] i)	6 [TAB]s

To use the **O**utline command it is recommended that you turn the **O**utline feature on and then generate several outline codes by typing Enter, Space, Enter, Space, Enter, and so on, until the screen appears:

I.
II.
III.
IV.
V.
VI.
VII.
VIII.
IX.
X.
XI.
XII.
XIII.

Next turn off the **O**utline feature and then edit the text into an outline form using the Tab key or **F4** (→Indent) command to insert [TAB]s or [->Indent] codes before the [Par Num:] outline codes. Renumbering of the displayed numbers will be automatic. The following is an example of how the text will appear after editing:

I. Introduction
    A. History of Company
        1. Founding Father
        2. Beginning Era
            a. First Product Line
            b. Number of Employees
            c. Community Response
        3. The Expansion Years
            a. New Product Lines
            b. New Markets
                (1) Foreign Sales
                    (a) Japan
                    (b) England
            c. Growth in Earnings
II.

To begin another outline in the same document, type **Shift-F5,6,1,**↵ (Date/Outline),**D**efine,**S**tarting Paragraph Number.

Para Num
Code =
[Par Num:Auto]
(Automatic)
[Par Num:*n*]
(Fixed level)

The **P**ara Num command is very similar to the **O**utline command except that only one code is inserted into the text each time the command is typed and you are able to defeat the automatic level number type.

To fix the displayed level number type, you may enter the desired level when you see the "Paragraph Level (Press Enter for Automatic):" prompt. For instance, if you type 2 when you see the message, the paragraph number will appear in the default form A. A fixed-level paragraph number will not change its form when it is indented or tabbed to the right on the screen. It will change its value, however, if preceding codes of the same level are deleted or inserted (i.e., numbering stays in effect).

To insert a [Par Num:Auto] code when the **P**ara Num command is executed, type ↵ in answer to the "Paragraph Level (Press Enter for Automatic):" prompt.

Define
Code =
[Par Num Def]

The **D**efine command is used to reset paragraph numbering within a document or change the style and punctuation used in automatic paragraph and outline numbering.

Starting Paragraph Number — Code = [Par Num:*n*]

Use the **S**tarting Paragraph Number command to reset outline/paragraph numbering within a document. A [Par Num Def] code will be inserted into the text which will affect all subsequent outline or paragraph codes.

Paragraph **O**utline **L**egal **B**ullets
User-**D**efined — Code = [Par Num Def]

At the top of the screen presented by the **D**efine command, there are four predefined numbering styles, any one of which you may select by typing **2**, **3**, **4**, **5** or **P**, **O**, **L**, **B**. The Current Definition (selection) will be displayed beneath the predefined sets. To create your own style, type **6** or **U** (**U**ser-Defined) and then edit the set of levels for the number styles and punctuation from the menu below to reflect your choices.

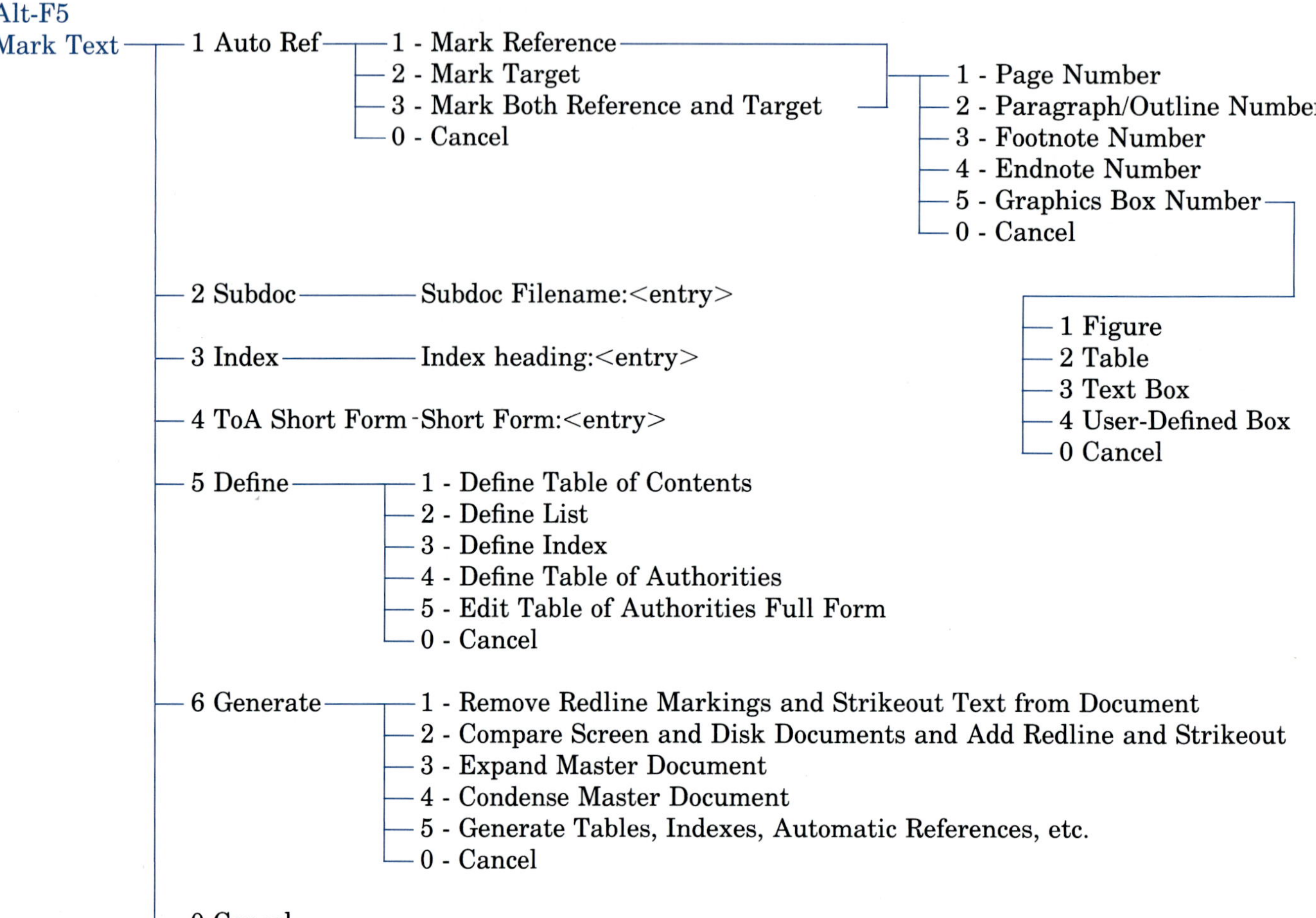

ALT-F5 MARK TEXT

The Mark Text command is used to insert automatic references to other locations in a document; to create, expand and contract a master document; and to automatically produce tables of contents, lists, and indexes. The Block/(Mark Text) command is highly related to the Mark Text command.

Auto **R**ef

The Auto **R**ef (Automatic Reference) command is used to insert a code where a reference to another part of the document is made, such as "see Contract Provisions, page 12." The reference number used, in this case the page number, will be automatically maintained for changes that may occur to the document. For instance, if page 10 in the document is later deleted, the reference to page 12 will become a reference to page 11. It is necessary, however, to use the (Mark Text),**G**enerate,**G**enerate Tables, Indexes, Automatic References, etc. command to cause automatic references to become updated for such editing changes to the document. See **Alt-F5,6** (Mark Text),**G**enerate for more information.

The place in the document where the reference is made is called the reference; the page, paragraph/outline, footnote, endnote, or graphics box being referenced is called the target. A reference and target are linked by a name that you enter when you create the automatic reference within the document.

To create a single reference to a single target, you first move to where the reference is to occur and type the reference text up to the point where the target number is to appear, for instance, "(see Contract Provisions, page 12)". You then type **Alt-F5,3** (Mark Text),Mark **B**oth Reference and Target:.

The next command menu presented allows you to select one of several different types of numbers for the reference: **P**age Number; Paragraph/**O**utline number; **F**ootnote Number; **E**ndnote Number; or **G**raphics Box Number. In the example here, you would select **P**age Number by typing **1** or **P.** The next step is to move the cursor to the target. In the case where text (a sentence, paragraph, etc.) is the target, you will want to place the cursor at the beginning of the target text. When the cursor is properly located, type ↵. The message "Target Name:" will appear on the status line. The final step in creating an automatic reference is to type and enter a name for the reference and its target.

Mark **R**eference   Code = [REF(*name*):Type #]

When you plan to later create a target for a reference, or will have many references to one target, use the Mark **R**eference command to create a reference with the intended target name. A ? will appear in the document at the reference position until a target with a matching name is created and the **Alt-F5,6** (Mark Text),**G**enerate command is used.

Mark **T**arget   Code = [Target(*name*)]

If you have a reference without a target, or intend to have one target referenced more than once, use the Mark **T**arget command to name the target with the same name as its matching reference(s).

Mark **B**oth Reference and Target   Code = [REF(*name*):Type #] [Target(*name*)]

Use the Mark **B**oth Reference and Target command to name the reference and target in one operation.

Marking Footnote Targets To mark a footnote as a target, move the cursor to where the footnote number appears in the text and type **Ctrl-F7,1,2**↵ (Footnote),**F**ootnote,**E**dit. When the editing screen appears, place the target mark in the footnote itself.

Marking Graphics Box Targets To mark a graphics box as a target (see **Alt-F9** (Graphics) for information on graphic box types) move the cursor immediately after the graphics box code to mark it as a target. A reference to a graphics box will be displayed as "*box type n*" (e.g., Figure 2).

Subdoc
Code = [Subdoc:*filename*]

The **S**ubdoc (Subdocument) command places a code in the document which includes the filename of a disk file. It is used in a boiler plate operation where subdocuments (plates) can be automatically merged into a master document (creating a boiler). See **Alt-F5** (Mark Text),**G**enerate,**E**xpand Master Document for more information.

Creating Tables of Contents, Lists, Indexes, and Tables of Authorities

Each of the following procedures produces a table of references with or without associated page numbers. The table is either alphabetized by reference (as in an index) or ordered by appearance (as in a table of contents). The sorting and generating of page numbers (if any) are both done automatically by WordPerfect. The overall process for producing any of the tables involves the following steps.

1. Mark the words, phrases, or topics within the document to which the table will refer.
2. Select the page position and format for the table.
3. Generate the table.

Marking Text for Tables

The following discusses the various table types and how you may mark text to be included in them. For information on how to position, format, and generate the various tables, refer to the Mark Text command section "Defining and Generating Tables." Note that the Block/(Mark Text) commands are necessary for marking certain text for tables and are discussed here rather than at the end of the command explanations. The remaining Mark Text commands are discussed later.

BLOCK/MARK TEXT

To mark text to be included in a Table of Contents (ToC), List, Index or Table of Authorities (ToA) the Block/(Mark Text) command is used.

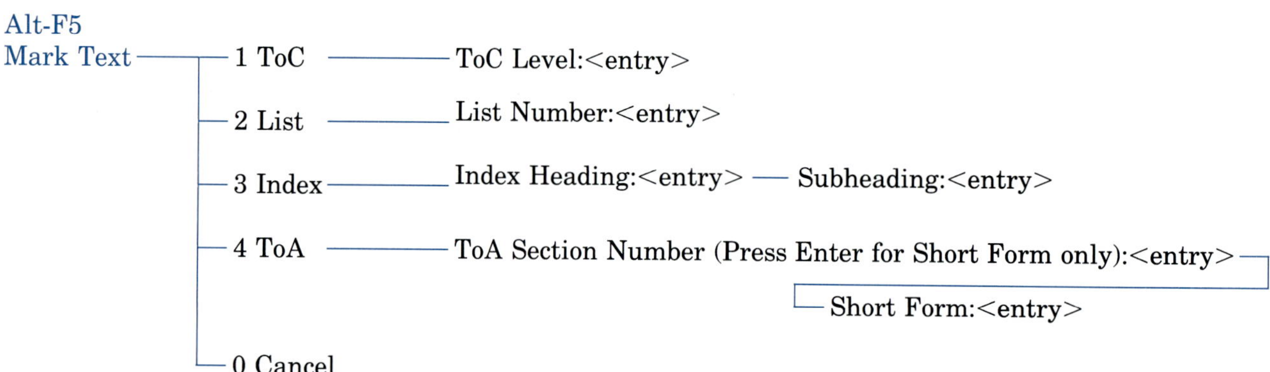

Block/Mark Text: ToC

Code = [Mark: ToC,*n*] *heading text* [EndMark:ToC,*n*]

The Block/(Mark Text), ToC command is used to mark text to be included in a table of contents. To mark the text, block the topic heading to be included in the table of contents and type **Alt-F5,1** (Block/Mark Text),**ToC.**

Up to five levels of headings may be included in a table of contents. When you mark a portion of text to be included in a table of contents, you must specify which ToC level (1 to 5) the heading is to be. The headings in the finished table of contents will appear indented to their appropriate level.

First Level .... nn
    Second Level .... nn
    Second Level .... nn
    Second Level .... nn
        Third Level .... nn
        Third Level .... nn
    Second Level .... nn
First Level .... nn

Block/Mark Text:List

Code = [Mark:List,*n*] *list text* [EndMark:List,*n*]

The Block/(Mark Text),**List** command is used to mark text to be included in a list. To mark the text, block the word, phrase, or heading and then type **Alt-F5,2** Block/(Mark Text),**List**.

Up to nine lists (1 to 9) may be generated per document. When you mark a block of text to be included in a list, you must specify in which list (1 to 9) the text is to be included. All entries must be blocked and marked for lists 1 through 5. However, if graphics boxes are included in the document, some entries for lists 6 through 9 may be defined automatically by WordPerfect as follows: list 6 will include captions of figures; list 7 will include captions of tables; list 8 will include captions of text boxes; and list 9 will include captions of user-defined boxes. (See **Alt-F9** (Graphics) for more information on graphics boxes.)

Mark Text: **Index**
Code =
[Index:*heading*]

There are several ways in which you may mark words or phrases to be included in an index. The general procedure is to move the cursor to the location in the text where the desired subject for the index occurs. You next type **Alt-F5,3** (Mark Text),**Index**. At this point you will be prompted to enter a heading.

Index Headings Items marked for inclusion in an index may have one or two headings (a heading and/or a subheading) which are entered at the time the item is marked. If only a heading is entered, the item appears in the index by itself. If a heading and a subheading are entered, all items having the same heading will appear under the heading with their own subheading, as shown in the following example.

```
Almond..........................................15
Apples
   Crab.........................................23
   Delicious....................................34
   Gravenstein.................................. 5
   McIntosh ....................................12
   Newton ......................................16
Artichoke ......................................36
```

Here, the subjects Almond and Artichoke were marked in the text with only a heading. The varieties of apples were all marked with the heading "Apples" and the appropriate variety type subheading.

Methods of Entering Index Headings To enter the index heading(s) for a subject do one of the following.

1. Move the cursor to a key word in the text and type **Alt-F5,3** (Mark Text),**Index**. The word at the cursor location will be displayed with the heading prompt at the bottom of the screen, and typing ↵ will cause the word to become the heading. If the word does not appear how you want the heading to appear, you may type and enter a different heading.
2. Block the word or phrase in the text and type **Alt-F5,3** Block/(Mark Text),**Index**. The blocked text will be displayed with the heading prompt, and typing ↵ will cause it to become the heading.
3. Create a Concordance file. A Concordance file may be used to save time when an index reference is made to a subject that occurs in several places.

   Creating a Concordance File A Concordance file is simply a WordPerfect document that you create that contains a list of words or phrases separated by hard returns [HRt]s. The file is used by WordPerfect to search the document for the words and phrases and to generate index references for them. The words and phrases within a Concordance file may be used in conjunction with words or phrases marked otherwise throughout the text to generate the index. The generation of an index will take less time if the words and phrases within the Concordance file are sorted.

Mark Text:To**A** and
Block/Mark
Text:To**A**

These two commands are used to mark text for a table of authorities. A table of authorities is a list of citations for a legal brief. See the WordPerfect manual or Help screens for more information on the subject.

Defining and Generating Tables

The final two Mark Text commands are **D**efine and **G**enerate.

Define

The (Mark Text),**D**efine command is used to define the location and format for tables.

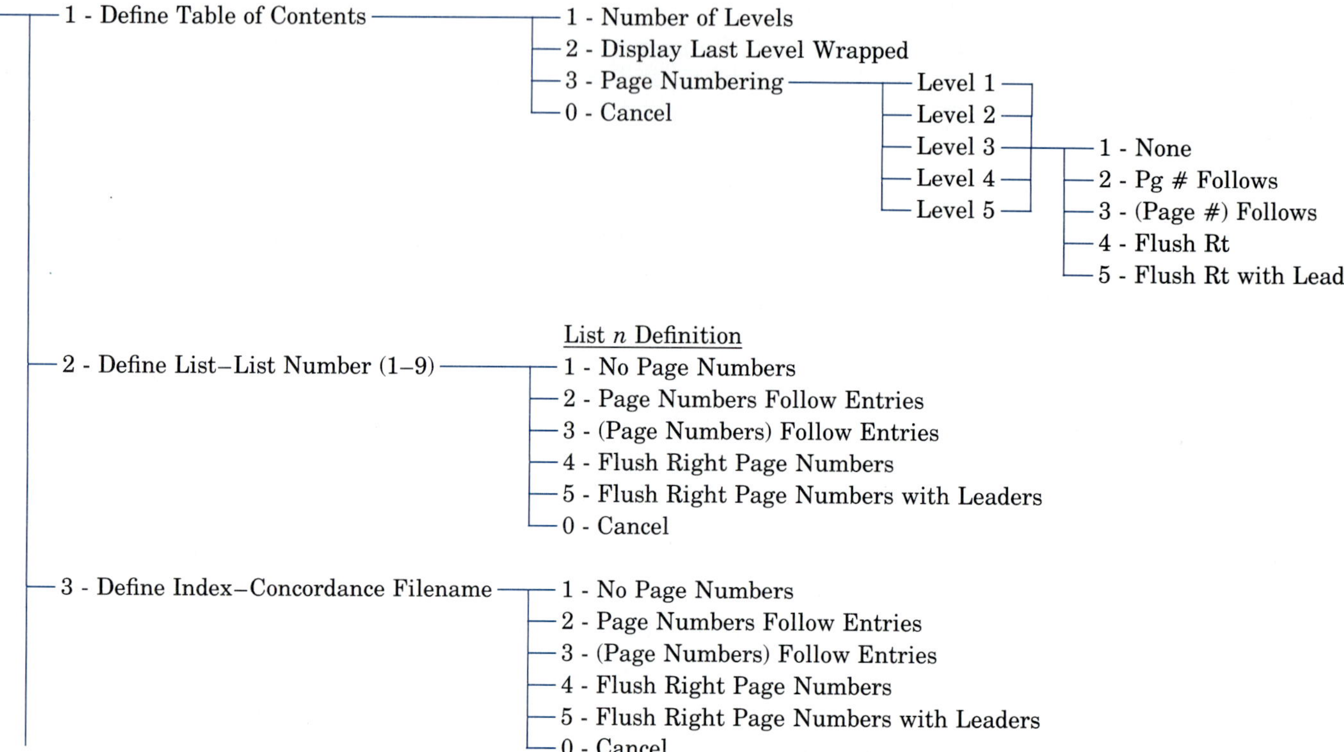

Define Table of **C**ontents   Define **L**ist   Define **I**ndex

The three commands discussed here are used to determine the position and format of the tables that will be subsequently generated. The commands here differ only slightly in their form. The Define Table of **C**ontents command will prompt for the number of heading levels you desire; the Define **L**ist command will prompt for the number (1 to 9) of the list you are currently defining; and the Define **I**ndex command will prompt you for a Concordance file filename (if any).

To define a table of contents, list, or index, first move the cursor to the page and location where you want the table to appear when it is generated. Next, type **Alt-F5,5** (Mark Text),**D**efine and select the number for the type of table you are defining. After answering the initial prompts, you must specify the format for the table. The options and examples of each follow.

1	No Page Numbers	Example
2	Page Numbers Follow Entries	Example 47
3	(Page Numbers) Follow Entries	Example (47)
4	Flush Right Page Numbers	Example 47
5	Flush Right Page Numbers with Leaders	Example.........47

After defining the table, a [DefMark:ToC], [DefMark:List*n*], or [DefMark:Index] code will be inserted into the document at the cursor location. If you later wish to reposition, redefine, or regenerate a table, you first should remove the existing [DefMark] code from the document.

Define/Edit Table of Authorities

These two commands are used to define location and format for a table of authorities. A table of authorities is a list of citations for a legal brief. See the WordPerfect manual or Help screens for more information on the subject.

Generate

The (Mark Text),**G**enerate command is used to remove all redline markings and strikeout text from the document; expand and condense master documents; generate tables of contents, lists, and indexes; and update automatic references for the document.

Remove Redline Markings and Strikeout Text from Document

This command removes all [RedLn][r] codes from the document and deletes all text currently marked as Font,Strikeout. See **Ctrl-F8,2,8** and **9** (Font),**A**ppearance,**R**edln and **S**tkout for more information.

Compare Screen and Disk Documents and Add Redline and Strikeout

This command compares a document on the disk with the document in memory. The comparison is made phrase by phrase. A phrase is defined by WordPerfect as text occurring between phrase markers which may be periods, hard returns, and so forth. Differences between the two files are marked in the current file (the file in memory). Text existing in the disk file but not in the current file is added to the current file formatted as Strikeout. Text existing in the current file but not in the disk file is formatted as Redline in the current file. Text that has been moved in the current file is displayed with a message "Text Moved." See **Ctrl-F8,2,8** and **9** (Font),**A**ppearance,**R**edln and **S**tkout for more information.

Expand Master Document

A master document is a document in which subdocument codes have been placed by the (Mark Text),**S**ubdoc command. Subdocuments are disk files to be included in a master document. To place a subdocument code into a master document type **Alt-F5,2***filename*↵(Mark Text),**S**ubdoc. A nonprinting message similar to the following will appear on the screen.

```
Subdoc: CHAPT11
```

When the **E**xpand Master Document command is used, the files referenced by the subdocument codes are retrieved and inserted into the master document.

Condense Master Document

The C**o**ndense Master Document command deletes subdocument text from a master document. See **E**xpand Master Document above.

Generate Tables, Indexes, Automatic References, etc.

The **G**enerate Tables, Indexes, Automatic References, etc. command is used to generate tables of contents, lists, and indexes as well as to update automatic references within the document. For tables with [MarkDef] codes in the document, the command inserts an [EndDef] code at the bottom of the generated table.

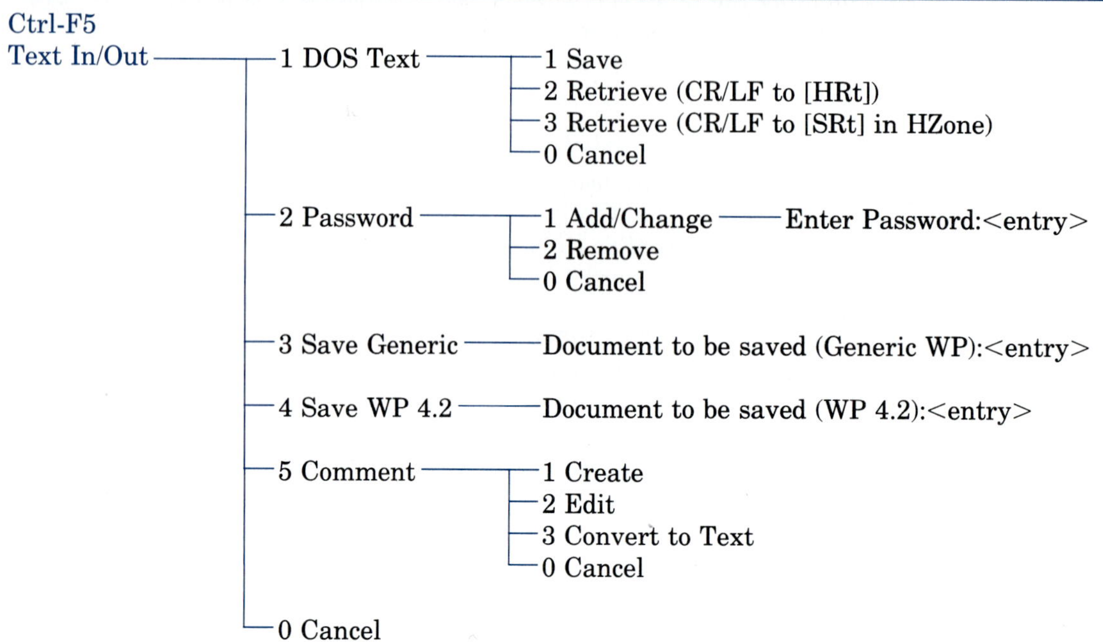

CTRL-F5 TEXT IN/OUT

The Text In/Out command is used to convert file formats for transfer between different software, to protect files from being viewed or printed by others, and to create or edit text comments.

DOS Text

WordPerfect refers to ASCII files as being DOS text. When you intend to transfer a file into another software such as Lotus 1-2-3 or WordStar, you will first need to convert the file to ASCII using the DOS **T**ext,**S**ave command.

Save

The DOS **T**ext,**S**ave command saves the current document in ASCII format and removes all imbedded WordPerfect codes. All soft returns are converted to hard returns. CHR(13)s and [TAB]s are converted to spaces, CHR(32)s. Spaces are used to pad Center, Indent, and Flush Right text. See **Shift-F7** (Print), **S**elect Printers for information on creating DOS text (ASCII) files that include the printer control codes such as bold, underline, and so forth.

Retrieve (CR/LF becomes [HRt])

The **R**etrieve command may be used to retrieve an ASCII file created by another software. Hard returns and line feeds in the file become hard returns in WordPerfect. See **F5** (List Files) for another method of retrieving ASCII files.

Retrieve (CR/LF to [Srt] in H-Zone)

If Retrieve is used, hard returns in the file become soft returns in WordPerfect if they occur between the current left and right margins. Two or more sequential hard returns in the file become hard returns in WordPerfect. See **F5** (List Files) for another method of retrieving ASCII files.

Password

WordPerfect allows a document to be locked with a password. If you forget the password, however, you will not be able to retrieve the file.

Add/Change

To lock the current text file, type **Ctrl-F5,2** (Text In/Out),**P**assword,**A**dd/Change. WordPerfect will respond with the message "Enter password:." The password you type will not be displayed on the screen. Instead, WordPerfect will prompt you to "Re-Enter Password:" so it may check for correct duplication of keystrokes. A password may be up to 24 characters long.

Once the password has been verified, you may save the document. From that point on, the password will be needed to retrieve the file.

Remove

To unlock a locked document, it is necessary to use the **Ctrl-F5,2,2** (Text In/Out),**P**assword,**R**emove command. Retrieve the file and then type **Ctrl-F5,2,2** (Text In/Out),**P**assword,**R**emove to remove the password. Then save the file under its original name.

Save Generic

Saving the current document in a generic word processor format removes all imbedded WordPerfect codes from within the file and replaces soft return [SRt] codes with spaces, CHR(32)s. Spaces are used to pad Center, Indent, and Flush Right text.

Save WP 4.2

Removes all control codes specific to WordPerfect's Version 5.0 before saving the document.

Comment Code = [Comment]

WordPerfect has a means for you to provide documentation for your documents by inserting comments into them which will not be printed. Such internal documentation is done through the **Ctrl-F5** (Text In/Out),**C**omment command.

Create

The **C**reate comment command provides room for characters to be entered into the text at the current cursor location. Text formatting within the Comments screen is limited. The comment will be displayed on the screen enclosed in a double-line box, as shown in the example below.

The following information should be revised each spring.

To remove the display of comments on the screen, use the **Shift-F1,3,3** (Setup),**D**isplay,**D**isplay Document Comments command. To delete a comment, move the cursor to the place where the comment occurs and use **Alt-F3** (Reveal Codes) to find the imbedded [Comment] code. Then, use the Backspace or Del key to erase it.

Edit

The **E**dit command may be used to modify an existing comment. Type **Ctrl-F5,5,2** (Text In/Out),**C**omment,**E**dit to begin editing. WordPerfect will find the comment for editing by searching backwards through the file. If there is more than one comment in the file, you must move the cursor past the comment you wish to edit and then execute the **E**dit command.

Convert to Text

To convert a comment into text, move the cursor past the comment and then type **Ctrl-F5,5,3** (Text In/Out),**C**omment,Convert to **T**ext.

Block/Text In/Out

To convert a section of text into a comment, first block the text and then type **Ctrl-F5** (Text In/Out). Next type Y in response to the "Create a comment? (Y/N)" prompt.

F6
Bold —— {Places Bold Start Code [BOLD]} —— <enter text> —— Bold key {Places Bold Stop Code [bold]}

F6 BOLD

Code = [BOLD] *bold text* [bold]

The Bold command is used to print text in boldface type (darker than normal). Typing **F6** (Bold) inserts [BOLD] and [bold] codes into text. Text typed afterwards is entered between the codes and is displayed on the screen in highlight. To stop bolding text, type **F6** (Bold) again.

Block/Bold	To boldface existing text, block the text and then type **F6** (Bold).

Shift-F6
Center —— {Places Center Start Code [Cntr]} —— <enter text> —— Center key {Places Center Stop Code [C/A/Flrt]}

SHIFT-F6 CENTER

Code = [Cntr] *centered text* [C/A/Flrt]

The Center command is used to center text between the current left and right margins. To assure proper centering, move the cursor to the left margin before using the Center command. Typing **Shift-F6** (Center) inserts [Cntr] and [C/A/Flrt] codes into the text. Text typed afterwards is entered between the codes and appears centered as it is typed. Centering of text is stopped when the ↵, ↑, or ↓ (Enter, cursor up, or cursor down, respectively) keys are typed.

You can center an existing line of text by moving the cursor to the left margin on the line and typing **Shift-F6,** ↓ (Center),Cursor Down.

Block/Center	To center one or more lines of existing text, block the text and then type **Shift-F6** (Center). Next type Y to the "[Cntr]? (Y/N)" prompt.

Alt-F6
Flush Right —— {Places Flush Right Start Code [Flsh Rt]} —— <enter text> —— Flush Right key {Places Flush Right Stop Code [C/A/Flrt]}

ALT-F6 FLUSH RIGHT

Code = [Flsh Rt] *text* [C/A/Flrt]

The Flush Right command is used to align text flush against the right margin. Typing **Alt-F6** (Flush Right) inserts [Flsh Rt] and [C/A/Flrt] codes into the text and moves the cursor to the right margin. Text typed afterwards is entered between the codes and appears right justified as it is typed. Right justifying of text is stopped when the ↵, ↑, or ↓ (Enter, cursor up, or cursor down, respectively) keys are typed. (To right justify text at tab stops, see the **Ctrl-F6** (Tab Align) command.)

Block/Flush Right — To right justify one or more lines of existing text, block the text and then type **Alt-F6** (Flush Right).

Ctrl-F6
Tab Align —— {Places Tab Align Start Code [Align]} —— <enter text> —— Tab Align key {Places Tab Align Stop Code [C/A/Flrt]}

CTRL-F6 TAB ALIGN

Code = [Align] *aligned text* [C/A/Flrt]

The Tab Align command is used to tab the cursor to the next tab stop and align the text typed afterwards flush right to the tab stop. See **Shift-F8** (Format),**L**ine,**T**ab Set for information on setting tab stops. The text typed after the Tab Align command is entered between [Align] and [C/A/Flrt] codes imbedded in the text. The Enter, Tab, or the Tab Align command will stop the flush right formatting of the text.

The Enter key may be used to produce right aligned columns of text. In the following example, the Tab Align command was used to move the cursor to the tab stop, the name was typed, and then the Enter key was pressed.

tab stop

Richard Alden
Kathey Dole
Jerry Calvin
Jo Hays

The Tab key and Tab Align command may be used together to produce right and left justified columns of text. In the following example, the Tab key was used to move the cursor to the first tab stop, the role was entered, and then the Tab Align command was used to move the cursor to the second tab stop where the name was entered. The Enter key was used to move to the next line.

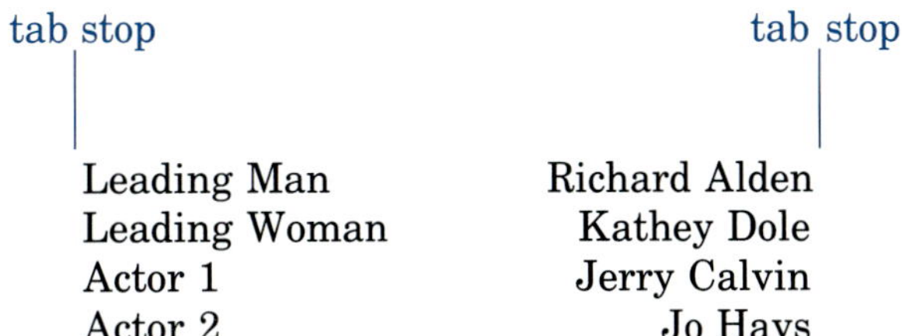

tab stop
tab stop
Leading Man
Richard Alden
Leading Woman
Kathey Dole
Actor 1
Jerry Calvin
Actor 2
Jo Hays

The default Align Character is the period (.). The Align Character may be changed with the **Shift-F8** (Format),**O**ther,**D**ecimal/Align Character command. With the Align Character key, the text is right justified until the current Align Character is typed. Then the text entered becomes left justified. The feature is most useful for entering dollar amounts. In the following example, the Tab Align command was used to move the cursor to the tab stop. The dollar amounts were typed and then the period key (the current Align Character key) was typed. Finally the cent amount was entered and the Enter key was typed to move to the next line.

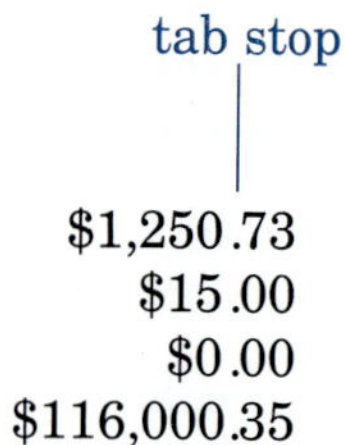

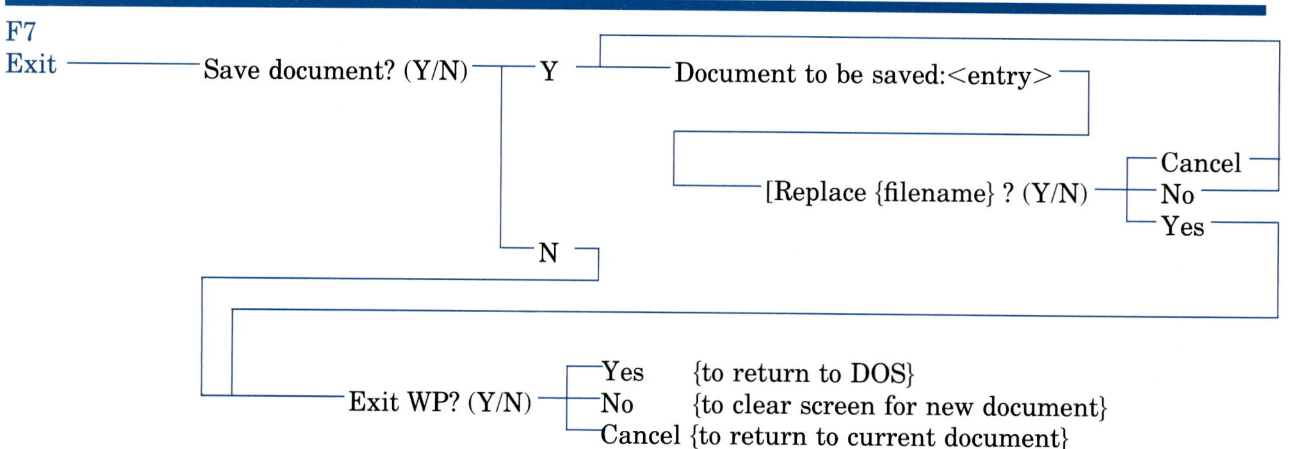

F7 EXIT

The Exit command is used to save the current document and exit WordPerfect. It also is used to exit many WordPerfect commands or operations.

In order to assure that your documents are saved correctly, you should always quit WordPerfect with the **F7** (Exit) command. Type **F7** (Exit), and then either save or do not save your file (type Y or N, respectively). Next type Y in answer to the "Exit WP? (Y/N)" prompt.

To remove the current document from RAM without leaving WordPerfect, you type N in answer to the "Exit WP? (Y/N)" prompt.

If you are editing two documents (see the **Shift-F3** (Switch) command), you will need to exit from each before returning to DOS.

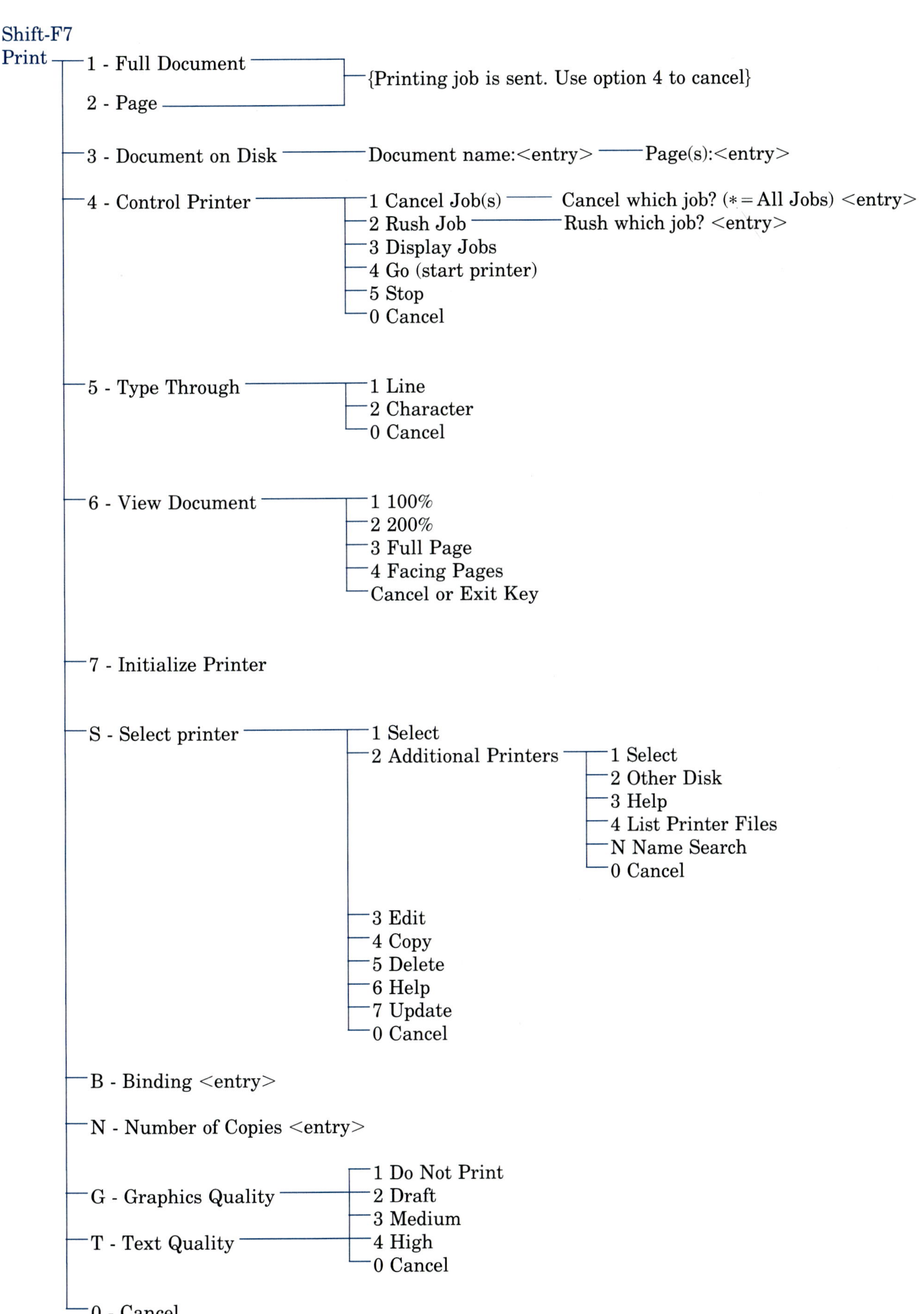
Shift-F7
Print
1 - Full Document
2 - Page
{Printing job is sent. Use option 4 to cancel}
3 - Document on Disk
Document name:<entry>
Page(s):<entry>
4 - Control Printer
1 Cancel Job(s)
Cancel which job? (* = All Jobs) <entry>
2 Rush Job
Rush which job? <entry>
3 Display Jobs
4 Go (start printer)
5 Stop
0 Cancel
5 - Type Through
1 Line
2 Character
0 Cancel
6 - View Document
1 100%
2 200%
3 Full Page
4 Facing Pages
Cancel or Exit Key
7 - Initialize Printer
S - Select printer
1 Select
2 Additional Printers
1 Select
2 Other Disk
3 Help
4 List Printer Files
N Name Search
0 Cancel
3 Edit
4 Copy
5 Delete
6 Help
7 Update
0 Cancel
B - Binding <entry>
N - Number of Copies <entry>
G - Graphics Quality
T - Text Quality
1 Do Not Print
2 Draft
3 Medium
4 High
0 Cancel
0 - Cancel

SHIFT-F7 PRINT

The **Shift-F7** (Print) command is used to print a document either in full or by page; control the current print operation; print directly from the keyboard; preview the printed page(s) of a document on the screen; select printer types; and select certain print options.

Full Document

Type **Shift-F7,1** (Print),**F**ull Document to print the entire current document. To print a document from the disk, see the **Shift-F7** (Print),**D**ocument on Disk command or the **F5** (List Files),**P**rint command. To cancel a print operation, see the **Shift-F7** (Print),**C**ontrol Printer,**C**ancel Job(s) command.

Page

Type **Shift-F7,2** (Print),**P**age to print the current page (the page upon which the cursor is located). To print page(s) from a document on a disk, see the **Shift-F7** (Print),**D**ocument on Disk command or the **F5** (List Files),**P**rint command.

Document on Disk

Use the **D**ocument on Disk command to print all or part of a document on the disk. Type **Shift-F7,3** (Print),**D**ocument on Disk. WordPerfect will prompt "Document name:." Enter the name of the document to print. WordPerfect next will respond with the prompt "Page(s): (All)." If you want the whole document to be printed, type ↵. You may, however, specify that only certain pages be printed. To specify certain pages, you may enter one of the following.

N	Print page number *N*
N-	Print from page number *N* to end of document
N-*n*	Print pages *N* through *n,* inclusive
-*N*	Print from beginning of document through page *N*
N,*n*	Print the specified pages

Page numbers must be entered in the way they appear in the printed document.

Control Printer

The **C**ontrol Printer command is used to monitor and control ongoing print operations. The **C**ontrol Printer command screen appears as follows.

```
Print: Control Printer

Current Job

Job Number: 1                                  Page Number:  3
Status:     Printing                           Current Copy: 1 of 1
Message:    None
Paper:      Standard 8.5" x 11"
Location:   Continuous feed
Action:     None


Job List

Job  Document          Destination          Print Options
 1   A:\RNTCNT         LPT 1


Additional Jobs Not Shown: 0



1 Cancel Job(s); 2 Rush Job; 3 Display Jobs; 4 Go (start printer); 5 Stop: 0
```

In this example, there is one file (A:\RNTCNT) currently being printed. It is listed as Job 1. When the current document is being printed, "(Screen)" is displayed in place of the filename. At the bottom of the screen appears the (Print),Control Printer menu.

Cancel Job(s)

The **C**ancel Job(s) command may be used to stop printing. Type **Shift-F7,4,1** (Print),Control Printer,**C**ancel Job(s). WordPerfect will respond with the message "Cancel which job? (* = All Jobs)." To cancel all print jobs, type * and then answer Y to the "Cancel all print jobs? (Y/N)" prompt. To cancel the current print job, type ↵ instead of *.

Rush Job

When more than one print job is being sent to the printer, the **R**ush Job command may be used to move a document waiting to be printed to the head of the printing queue.

Display Jobs

The **D**isplay Jobs command may be used to produce a list of all documents waiting to be printed. The Control Printer screen will normally display only the next three jobs.

Go (start printer)

Resumes printing a document after the printer has been stopped.

Stop

Stops the printer without cancelling the print jobs. Use (Print),Control Printer,**G**o (start printer) to resume printing.

Type Through

The **Ty**pe Through command allows the printer to be used as a typewriter. Options include sending each character to the printer as it is typed or sending a line of text to the printer after it has been typed and edited on the screen.

View Document

The **V**iew Document command creates a temporary file for you to view on the screen. The file is designed to most closely resemble the document as it will be printed, and includes footnotes, headers, page numbers, and so forth. The command is useful for discovering formatting problems caused by errant codes.

To preview a document, type **Shift-F7,6** (Print),**V**iew Document. In a few moments the screen will display the current page of the document as it will appear when printed. You cannot edit the text displayed by the **V**iew Document screen. You may, however, view different portions of the text by using the cursor control keys ↑, ↓, PgUp, and PgDn. The options of the **V**iew Document command include: (1) 100% (actual size); (2) 200% (enlarge the text on the screen); (3) Full page (reduce the text to fit a full page on the screen, the default size for the text on the screen); and (4) Facing Pages (display two full pages on the screen at once). Note that there is no command letter available for these commands. When you are finished with viewing the file, type **F7** (Exit).

Initialize Printer

This command is used to download soft fonts to the printer. See the WordPerfect Help screens or manual for more information.

Options

The following commands are listed under the heading "Options" on the **Shift-F7** (Print) screen.

Select Printer

Printers vary in their capabilities and in the ASCII codes that cause them to do what they do. Therefore, WordPerfect needs to know what printer(s) it will be using. WordPerfect comes with four standard 5¼″ disks labeled Printer Disk 1 through 4. These disks contain small files, each of which describes a particular printer. When printers are selected (using the **S**elect Printer,**A**dditional Printers command), these printer disks must be available. However, after the printer(s) have been selected, the specific printer information for the selected printer(s) is saved with the WordPerfect software and need not be specified again. When one, two, or more printers are selected, the selected printers can be thought of as "available" printers for WordPerfect.

Select

The **S**elect command is used to choose one of the available printers for use in printing a document. Information on the selected printer is saved with the current document file. The default printer for the **S**elect command is the first available printer specified or the last available printer selected. To select a printer, move the Select Printer cursor to the appropriate printer and type **1** or **S** (**S**elect).

Additional Printers

The **A**dditional Printers command is used to add to the list of available printers and is the command which requires that the Printer Disks 1 through 4 be available. To add an additional printer to the available printers, type **Shift-F7,S,2** (Print),**S**elect Printer,**A**dditional Printers. WordPerfect will present a list of all the printers it is capable of supporting. Move the **A**dditional Printers cursor to the desired printer and type **1** or **S** (**S**elect). WordPerfect will display the filename for the file that contains the specific information for the printer you have selected. In most cases you will type ↵ at this point. If WordPerfect is able to access the file, it will respond by presenting a screen labeled "Helps and Hints" which provides information about the printer being selected. The next screen presented will be a screen which allows you to edit the printer information (see **E**dit below). In most cases you will simply type ↵ to exit this screen. The final screen presented will be the **S**elect Printer screen.

Edit

The **E**dit command allows you to edit information about the available printer upon which the **S**elect Printer cursor is currently located (the current printer). The command has the following extended tree structure.

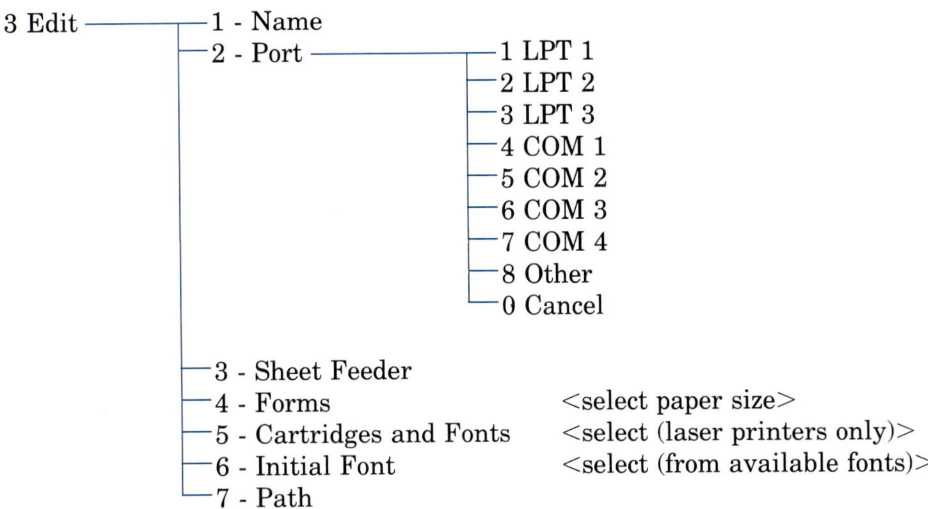

While an explanation of all menu commands found here is beyond the scope of this text, there is one important procedure associated with the **E**dit command which involves creating an ASCII text file which has printer control codes included in it.

To create such a file, type **Shift-F7,S** (Print),**S**elect Printer. Next move the Select Printer cursor to the appropriate printer listed and if necessary, type **1** or **S** (**S**elect) to make it the current printer. Then type **3** or **E** to present the **E**dit menu. Next type **2** or **P** (**P**ort) and make a note as to what the current port is. Type **8** or **O** (**O**ther) and then enter a path and filename for the ASCII file. Next return to the **Shift-F7** (Print) menu by typing the **F7** (Exit) key twice and then print the full document or page(s) desired. You will need to use the **S**elect Printer,**E**dit command to reset the original port for the printer when finished.

Copy Delete Help Update

These four commands are used to perform maintenance routines on the available printers. The **C**opy command makes a copy of the current printer file making two of them available, one of which you may want to edit. **D**elete deletes the current printer. **H**elp provides the "Helps and Hints" screen for the current printer. **U**pdate saves any editing changes made to the available printers.

Binding

The **B**inding width command offsets printing by the specified inches on odd and even pages for binding two-sided copies. Text is shifted to the right on odd-numbered pages and to the left on even-numbered pages.

Number of Copies

The **N**umber of Copies command is used to print multiple copies of a file. Type **Shift-F7,N** (Print),**N**umber of Copies, enter the number desired, and then continue with the print command operation.

Graphics Quality/ Text Quality

The two Quality commands, **G**raphics and **T**ext may be used to speed up printing of a rough draft by reducing the quality of either the graphics or text included in the document. The selections for both commands include Do **N**ot Print, **D**raft, **M**edium, and **H**igh.

Block/Print

To print a block of text, block the text to be printed and then type **Shift-F7** (Print).

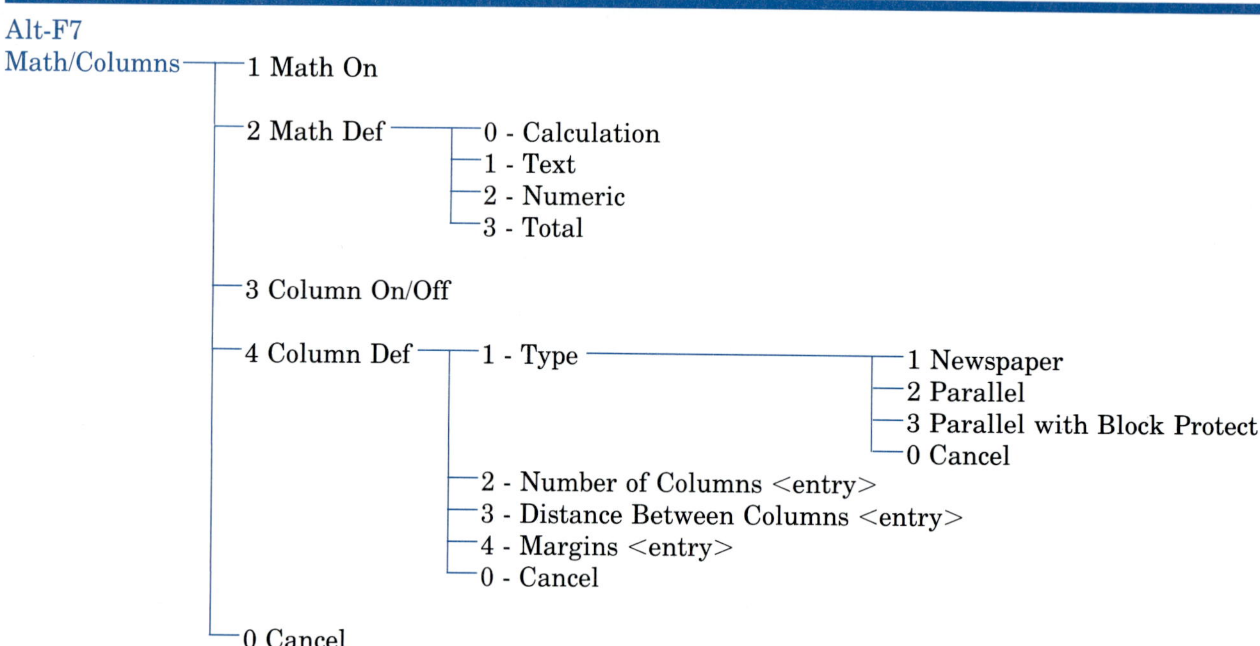

ALT-F7 MATH/ COLUMNS

The Math/Columns command is used to deal with two separate types of operations: inserting math codes into a document with the math feature of WordPerfect and typing columnar text to produce text in a newspaper-style column or table format with WordPerfect's text columns feature.

Using the Math Feature

WordPerfect provides a math feature for doing automatic calculations within a document. There are several steps involved in preparing a document to include math calculations. When the steps are completed, the document will include a portion of text that has been structured for doing math calculations. The structured portion of text may be represented as follows.

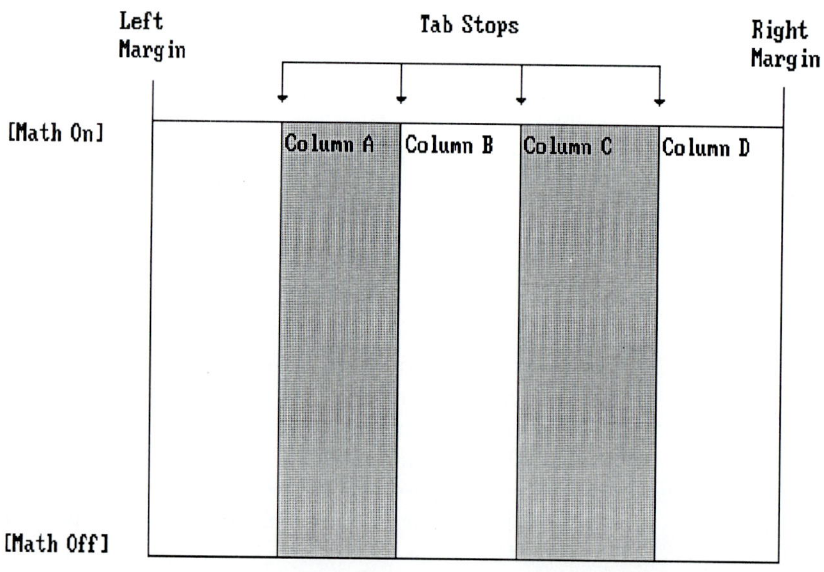

The text defined for math operations is set apart with [Math On] and [Math Off] codes imbedded into the text. Within the math portion of text various columns are defined by the current tab stops (see **Shift-F8** (Format),**L**ine,**T**ab Set for information on setting tab stops).

The area between the left margin and the first tab stop to the right of the left margin may be used to enter text. The columns labeled A, B, C, and so on, may be defined for one of four different data types. If you want the column to contain subtotals, totals, and grand totals, specify the column to be Numeric. Numeric is the default definition of all columns. If you want the column to contain text, specify the column to be Text. If you want the column to display totals obtained from the column to the immediate left, specify the column to be Total. Finally, if you want the column to display the results of formulas referring to values obtained from other columns, specify the column to be Calculation.

Steps in Creating a Math Document

There are five basic steps in creating a math area within a document.

1. Set the appropriate tab stops.
2. Define the columns for math data type.
3. Create a math area using Math On and Math Off.
4. Enter the math data.
5. Calculate.

The following discusses the various Math commands in conjunction with other steps required to create such a document.

Set the Tab Stops

The first step in creating a math area within a document is to set tab stops for the math portion that coincide with the planned format. Note that a [Tab Set:] code will be imbedded in the text at the current cursor location and will affect only the text following it.

Define the Columns

To define the columns for the type of math data they will be holding, the Math **D**ef command is used.

Math Def
Code = [Math Def]

The next step is to define the columns for the particular type of data they will contain. When the Math **D**ef command is executed, the screen appears as follows.

```
Math Definition            Use arrow keys to position cursor

Columns                    A B C D E F G H I J K L M N O P Q R S T U V W X

Type                       2 2 2 2 2 2 2 2 2 2 2 2 2 2 2 2 2 2 2 2 2 2 2 2

Negative Numbers           ( ( ( ( ( ( ( ( ( ( ( ( ( ( ( ( ( ( ( ( ( ( ( (

Number of Digits to        2 2 2 2 2 2 2 2 2 2 2 2 2 2 2 2 2 2 2 2 2 2 2 2
  the Right (0-4)

Calculation   1
  Formulas    2
              3
              4

Type of Column:
      0 = Calculation     1 = Text      2 = Numeric      3 = Total

Negative Numbers
      ( = Parentheses (50.00)         - = Minus Sign  -50.00



Press Exit when done
```

The various columns (A through X) are displayed at the top of the screen. "A" corresponds to the first tab stop, "B" to the second, and so on. Beneath each column letter are three specifications that can be changed for the column using the Math Definition screen: the column type; how negative numbers will be displayed (in parentheses or with negative signs); and how many digits to display to the right of the decimal. Initially, all columns are set to Numeric type, negatives in parentheses, and a display of two digits to the right of the decimal. The following briefly discusses the different column types available and the operations associated with them.

(1) Text

Defining a column for text allows you to enter labels, headings, descriptions, and so on, into the column. The area from the left margin to the first tab stop is always Text in nature. Columns after the first tab stop should be defined for text if they are to contain text.

(2) Numeric

Columns defined as Numeric are designed to contain numbers and WordPerfect operators for subtotals, extra subtotals, totals, extra totals, and grand totals. The following table describes the operators used by WordPerfect and the order in which they should appear within a column.

Order	Operator	Meaning
1st	+	Subtotal (totals the numbers up to the last subtotal above it)
2nd	t	Extra subtotal (used for a single entry subtotal)
3rd	=	Total (totals the subtotals up to the last total above it)
4th	T	Extra total (used for a single entry total)
5th	*	Grand total (totals the totals up to the last grand total above it)

A sixth operator, *N*, may be used in conjunction with the other operators listed to produce a negative subtotal. For instance, the operator *N*+ will produce a subtotal that will be subtracted, rather than added, in a subsequent total or grand total.

(3) Total

Columns defined as Total are most often used to display totals obtained from the column to the immediate left. The operators used in Total columns are the same as those used in Numeric columns.

It is important to note that subtotals, totals, and grand totals in a Total column will obtain their displayed values from both the column to the left and from the same column. That is, a Total (=) entered into a Total column will display the sum amount for all subtotals occurring above it in both the Total column and in the column to the left.

(0) Calculation

A column defined as Calculation may be used to enter formulas into the document. A maximum of four columns may be defined as Calculation in nature. One formula may be entered into a Calculation column. The formula then is used to compute values from numbers found across the rows in the math area. When you tab the cursor to a Calculation column, WordPerfect displays an exclamation point (!) at the cursor location. The ! indicates that the formula will be used to compute a value for that row (line).

Enter a Calculation formula into the Math Definition screen at the time you specify the column to be Calculation type. An example of a formula designed to display 20% of the value found on the same line in the A column would be .2*A. Totals across rows in the A, B, and C columns could be obtained with the formula A+B+C.

All formulas are evaluated from left to right (there is no operator precedence), and nested parentheses are not allowed.

Four WordPerfect specific operators are available; however, they must be used independently of one another and other formulas. The operators are as follows.

+	Add numbers in the Numeric columns
+/	Average numbers in the Numeric columns
=	Add numbers in the Total columns
=/	Average numbers in the Total columns

Turn Math On and Math Off

The next step in creating a math area in the document is to insert a [Math On] code at the top of the area and a [Math Off] code at the bottom of the area.

Math On
Code =
[Math On]
[Math Off]

To insert a [Math On] code into the document move the cursor to the top of the math area and type **Alt-F7,1** (Math/Columns),**M**ath On. Executing the **M**ath On command inserts a [Math On] code into the document. When the cursor is moved past a [Math On] code, the message "Math" appears on the status line. As long as the message appears on the screen, the Math/Columns menu changes. **M**ath On becomes **M**ath Off, and **M**ath Def becomes **C**alculate. To insert a [Math Off] code into the document, move the cursor to the bottom of the math area and type **Alt-F7,1** (Math/Columns),**M**ath Off.

Enter the Math Data

The next step involves entering the text and math data for the math area. To do this, enter text into the columns defined as text and use the tab key to move the cursor to the appropriate places in other type columns to enter numbers and appropriate WordPerfect operators.

A typical math portion having one Numeric column and using the area between the left margin and first tab stop for labels might appear as follows.

```
April 1989
                          Sales
Purchases
    Item A               100.00
    Item B               200.00
    Item C               300.00
        Subtotal            +

    Item 1                50.00
    Item 2               100.00
    Item 3               150.00
        Subtotal            +

     Other              t200.00

Returns
    Item A                10.00
    Item B                20.00
    Item C                30.00
        Subtotal           N+


Month End Total             =

Math                                       Doc 1 Pg 1 Ln 4.85" Pos 1"
```

As you enter the math data, numbers will align flush right to their tab stops and the period (.) key is used for alignment. Numbers that overlap into the previous column will cause incorrect calculations. Reset the tab stops for the math portion to widen the column if this problem occurs.

Calculate the Math Area

The final step in creating a math document is to calculate the math area. Calculations or recalculation may only be done while the "Math" message is displayed at the bottom of the screen. Therefore, the cursor must be somewhere between the imbedded [Math On] and [Math Off] codes. Type **Alt-F7,2** (Math/Columns),Calculate to calculate the math area. In the example, the calculated portion of the document would appear as follows.

```
April 1989
                    Sales
Purchases
   Item A          100.00
   Item B          200.00
   Item C          300.00
      Subtotal     600.00+

   Item 1           50.00
   Item 2          100.00
   Item 3          150.00
      Subtotal     300.00+

    Other         t200.00

Returns
   Item A           10.00
   Item B           20.00
   Item C           30.00
      Subtotal     N60.00+


Month End Total  1,040.00=

Math                                    Doc 1 Pg 1 Ln 1" Pos 1"
```

Although the screen displays the WordPerfect math operators next to the calculated values, they will not be printed.

Once a math portion of a document has been created, you may move the cursor to the area and change the numbers within it. Care must be taken to maintain the original alignment of numbers to their tab stops. It is generally easier to delete a number and its preceding alignment codes with the Backspace key and then to retab to the column and enter a new number. You then must use the **Alt-F7** (Math/Columns),**C**alculate command to recalculate the area for the new values.

Using the Columns Feature

The Columns feature is used to produce text that is columnar in format. The two basic styles of columnar text are Newspaper Type (text continuously runs through columns on a page) and Parallel Type (text is in table format).

Steps in Creating Text Columns

There are four basic steps in creating a document with columnar text.

1. Define the type and left/right margins for the columns.
2. Turn Columns On.
3. Enter the text.
4. Turn Columns Off.

The following discusses the various column commands in conjunction with other steps required to create text columns.

Define the Columns

Column **D**ef
Code = [Col Def:]

The Text Column Definition screen is used to define the style and margins for text columns. When the definition screen is exited, a [Col Def:] code is inserted into the text at the cursor location. The style and margins for columns stay in effect for the rest of the document or until another [Col Def:]

code is encountered. When the Columns **D**ef command is executed, the following screen appears.

```
Text Column Definition

     1 - Type                                      Newspaper

     2 - Number of Columns                         2

     3 - Distance Between Columns

     4 - Margins

     Column     Left       Right      Column     Left       Right
      1:        1"         4"         13:
      2:        4.5"       7.5"       14:
      3:                              15:
      4:                              16:
      5:                              17:
      6:                              18:
      7:                              19:
      8:                              20:
      9:                              21:
     10:                              22:
     11:                              23:
     12:                              24:

Selection: 0
```

Type

The **T**ype command is used to specify either Newspaper or Parallel column style.

Newspaper Newspaper style produces columns through which text flows from the last line in a column on a page to the first line of the next column on the page. The following screen shows an example of Newspaper style.

```
                        Vista Ridge June Newsletter

- Rec Room Remodeled -        toddlers area, a new          social events, see Mr.
The recreation room in        indoor propane gas bar-       Smith in the manager's
Harris Commons will be        b-que (with all the           office, Building A.
closed for remodeling         accessories), and a
until July 17th.              spacious cedar sun deck       - Welcome Newcomers -
                              facing the pool.              Vista Ridge is pleased
When completed, the                                         to welcome two new
newly remodeled facility      To reserve rental time        families this month.
will provide a large          for your late summer
```

Parallel Parallel style produces columns into which text is entered in a horizontal fashion. It is used when the text is record-like in structure and where items within the records have varying line lengths. The following screen shows an example of Parallel style.

```
                    Vista Ridge Cleaning/Occupancy Journal
                    ______________________________________

Unit                      Style                       Comments
----                      -----                       --------
Apartment #14             3 bedroom, 2 floors, 1      Available for occupancy
                          and 1/2 baths.              August 23rd.  Replace
                                                      living room carpet, paint
                                                      throughout.

Apartment #32             1 bedroom studio            Vacant, Repaper walls in
                                                      kitchen, repair front
                                                      steps.
```

Parallel with Block Protect A third column style, Parallel with Block Protect, may be specified to create parallel columns in which the records of data are protected against being separated by soft page breaks. See Block/(Format) (Block/**Shift-F8**) for more information on protecting blocks of text.

Number of Columns

The Number of Columns command is used to specify the number of columns you want to appear on a page. In the examples above, three columns were specified.

Distance Between Columns

The Distance Between Columns command is used by WordPerfect when it sets automatic left and right margins for each column. However, the margins may be changed after they are generated.

Margins

The last specifications made to define columns are the left and right margins for each column. WordPerfect will compute a set of margins and allow you to edit them. When the margins are all correctly specified, type **F7** (Exit) to exit the Text Column Definition.

Turn Columns On

Column On/Off Code = [Col On][Col Off]

The next step in creating text columns is to define the portion of the document in which the columnar format is to occur. A note of caution is in order here. When you turn columns on within a document, the remainder of the document becomes formatted into the defined columns. If you are creating a columnar portion of text anywhere other than at the end of a document, it is recommended that you create the columnar portion in Document 2 (see **Shift-F3** (Switch)) and then copy the portion (including the [Col Def:], [Col On], and [Col Off] codes) into Document 1.

To format a portion of text into Text Columns, move the cursor to where the columns are to begin and type **Alt-F7,3** (Math/Columns),Columns On/Off. The command will insert a [Col On] code into the text.

Enter the Text

Newspaper Style If the style of columns is Newspaper, you simply enter the text as you would during normal editing. When the first column on a page is filled (the bottom of the page is reached), WordPerfect will move to the top of the second column and you may continue entering text.

If you want to begin the next column before the bottom of the page is reached, you may do so by entering a hard page (Ctrl-↵) in front of the line that you want moved to the next column.

Parallel Style If the style of columns is Parallel, you begin by entering the text for the first record item into the first column. When done, you type Ctrl-↵ (hard page) to move the cursor to the second column to enter the second item for the record.

The Hard Page keystroke in Parallel column text mode causes [Col Off] and [Col On] codes to be imbedded in the document at the end of each record's data (after the last column). The codes are used by WordPerfect to maintain the horizontal structure of the record-type data. Care must be taken to avoid deleting these codes.

Editing in Columnar Text Modes To move from one column to the next, the following keystrokes may be used.

Ctrl-Home,→	Jump one column right
Ctrl-Home,←	Jump one column left
Ctrl-Home,Home,→	Jump to last column
Ctrl-Home,Home,←	Jump to first column

You must block text to cut or copy it within a column. You may speed up scrolling and screen rewriting by using the **Shift-F1,3,8** (Setup),**D**isplay, **S**ide-by-Side Columns Display command to display each column on a separate page while editing.

Turn Column Off

The final step in creating text columns is to turn Columns Off. Move the cursor to where columnar text is to end and type **Alt-F7,3** (Math/Columns),**C**olumns On/Off again. When the command is issued forward of a [Col On] code, it inserts a [Col Off] code into the text.

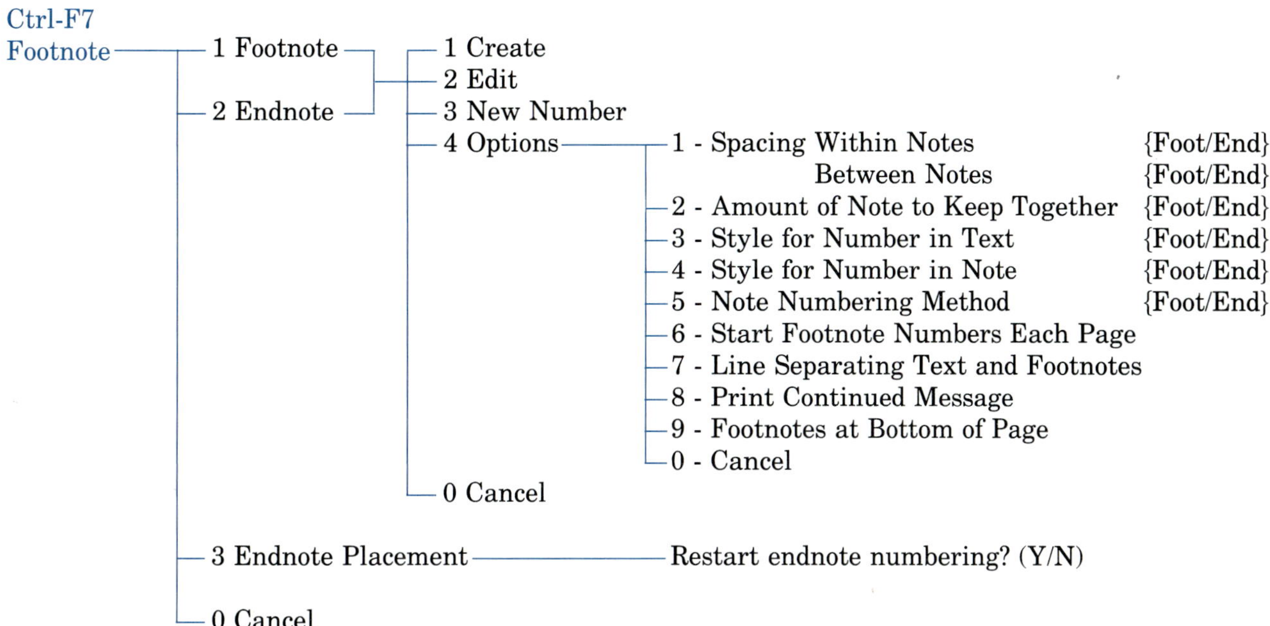

CTRL-F7 FOOTNOTE

WordPerfect provides for footnotes and endnotes to be included in a document in a variety of standard formats. The numbering of the notes is maintained automatically by WordPerfect.

Footnote and Endnote

The procedure for creating footnotes or endnotes is straightforward. Move the cursor to the word, sentence, or paragraph that the footnote will reference, and where you want the note number to appear in the text. Then type **Ctrl-F7** (Footnote) and select either the **F**ootnote or **E**ndnote command from the menu. Next, enter the note text on a blank screen provided by the command. When finished, type **F7** (Exit) and a note number appears on the document screen at the cursor position.

Footnotes will be printed at the bottom of the page containing the text they reference, while endnotes will be printed on pages where endnote placement codes occur in the document. Endnotes must be generated with the **Alt-F5** (Mark Text),**G**enerate,**G**enerate Tables, Indexes, Automatic References, etc. command before they may be printed. **Alt-F3** (Reveal Codes) may be used to view the first 50 characters of a note imbedded in a document.

Create — Code = [Footnote:*text*][Endnote:*text*]

The **C**reate command is used to create footnotes and endnotes. Move the cursor to the place where the note number is to appear and type **Ctrl-F7,1** or **2,1** (Footnote),**F**ootnote or **E**ndnote,**C**reate. Next, enter the text for the footnote on the blank screen provided by the command and then type **F7** (Exit).

Edit

The **E**dit command is used to edit existing footnotes or endnotes. Type **Ctrl-F7,1** or **2,2** (Footnote),**F**ootnote or **E**ndnote,**E**dit and then enter the number of the note you want to edit. Type **F7** (Exit) when done.

New Number — Code = [New Ftn Number:*n*][New End Num:*n*]

The **N**ew Number command is most useful when one document is divided into two or more files. To resume proper footnote or endnote numbering in the next file, move the cursor to the left of the first note number in the file and type **Ctrl-F7,1** or **2,3** (Footnote),**F**ootnote or **E**ndnote,**N**ew Number. Then, enter the appropriate starting number for the footnotes or endnotes in the file. All subsequent notes in the file will be automatically renumbered.

Options Code = [Ftn Opt][End Opt]

The **O**ptions command provides several formatting styles for footnotes and endnotes. When a default option setting is changed with the **O**ptions command, a [Ftn Opt] or [End Opt] code is inserted into the text at the cursor location. The formatting change then affects the footnotes or endnotes in the subsequent text. The **O**ptions menu screen differs slightly for footnotes and endnotes. The first five options discussed here may be selected for footnotes and/or endnotes; the remaining four options are for footnotes only.

The following are brief descriptions of the format styles and their default values.

Spacing Within Notes/Between Notes Default—1 line/0.17″ (inches, normally 1 line)
Sets the line spacing for text within footnotes or endnotes at 1, 1.5, 2 lines, and so forth, and/or the spacing between separate footnotes or endnotes. Enter the "Between Notes" number as the number of inches that you desire between notes.

Amount of Note to Keep Together Default—0.5″ (normally 3 lines)
Forces WordPerfect to keep *n* inches of footnote and/or endnote text within a note together if the note needs to be split onto two pages.

Style for Number in Text Default—[SUPRSCPT][Note Num][suprscpt]
You may redefine the display of a number by including characters, or any of the Font,**S**ize or **A**ppearance attributes (see **Ctrl-F8** (Font)). The codes necessary for the new display are obtained from typing command keys. For instance, to add parentheses to the footnote numbers appearing in the text, you would type **Ctrl-F7,1,4** (Footnote),**F**ootnote, **O**ptions and type **3** or **T** (Style for Number in **T**ext).

The message "Replace with: [SUPRSCPT][Note Num][suprscpt]" will appear on the screen. You then type **Ctrl-F8,1,1(,Ctrl-F7,1,2,),Ctrl-F8,1,1**↵ which reads **S**ize,**Sup**erscript, Left parenthesis, **F**ootnote, Number **C**ode, Right parenthesis, **S**ize,**Sup**erscript(end). The status line will display [SUPRSCPT]([Note Num])[suprscpt] and the number appearing in the text for a footnote will be displayed as $^{(2)}$.

Style for Number in Note Default— [SUPRSCPT][Note Num][suprscpt] (five preceding spaces)
This command is the same as Style for Number in **T**ext except it affects the display of the number in the note itself rather than how the number appears in the text.

Note Numbering Method Default—Numbers
Options include **1 N**umbers (1, 2, 3, etc.)
2 Letters (a, b, c, etc.)
3 Characters (*, **, ***, etc.)

The following four commands appear on the Footnote,Options screen only.

Start Footnote Number Each Page Default—No
Y causes footnote numbers to start at 1, a, or * for each page.

Line Separating Text and Footnotes Default—2-inch Line
Before printing footnotes on a page, WordPerfect prints a solid line to sepa-

rate them from the text. This option is used to define what type of line will be printed. The choices are

1 **N**o Line
2 **2**-inch Line
3 **M**argin to Margin

Print **C**ontinued Message   Default—No
Y causes the message "(Continued)" to be printed if the footnote is broken up by a soft page break.

Footnotes at **B**ottom of Page   Default—Yes
N causes footnotes to immediately follow the text on a page.

Endnote Placement Code = [Endnote Placement]

The Endnote **P**lacement command inserts a code into the text that will cause WordPerfect to print the endnotes at the code's location. While placing the code, the message "Restart endnote numbering? (Y/N)" will appear. To restart numbering after the placement code type Y. WordPerfect will place the [Endnote Placement] code followed by a hard page [HPg] code into the text. The following message will appear on the screen.

> Endnote Placement
> It is not known how much space endnotes will occupy here.
> Generate to determine.

= =

To determine the amount of space the endnotes will occupy, type **Alt-F5,6,5** (Mark Text),**G**enerate,**G**enerate Tables, Indexes, Automatic References, etc. The endnote placement message will indicate the area to be occupied by endnotes when the document is printed.

F8
Underline ——— {Places Underline Start Code [UND]} ——— <enter text> ——— Underline key {Places Underline Stop Code [und]}

F8 UNDERLINE   Code = [UND][und]

The Underline command is used to underline printed text. Typing **F8** (Underline) inserts [UND] and [und] codes into the text. Text typed afterwards is entered between the codes and is displayed on the screen as underlined. To stop underlining text, type **F8** (Underline) again.

To double underline text see **Ctrl-F8,2** (Font),**A**ppearance. To stop underlining spaces or to underline tabs, see **Shift-F8,4**(Format),**O**ther.

Block/Underline

To underline a block of text, block the text and then type **F8** (Underline).

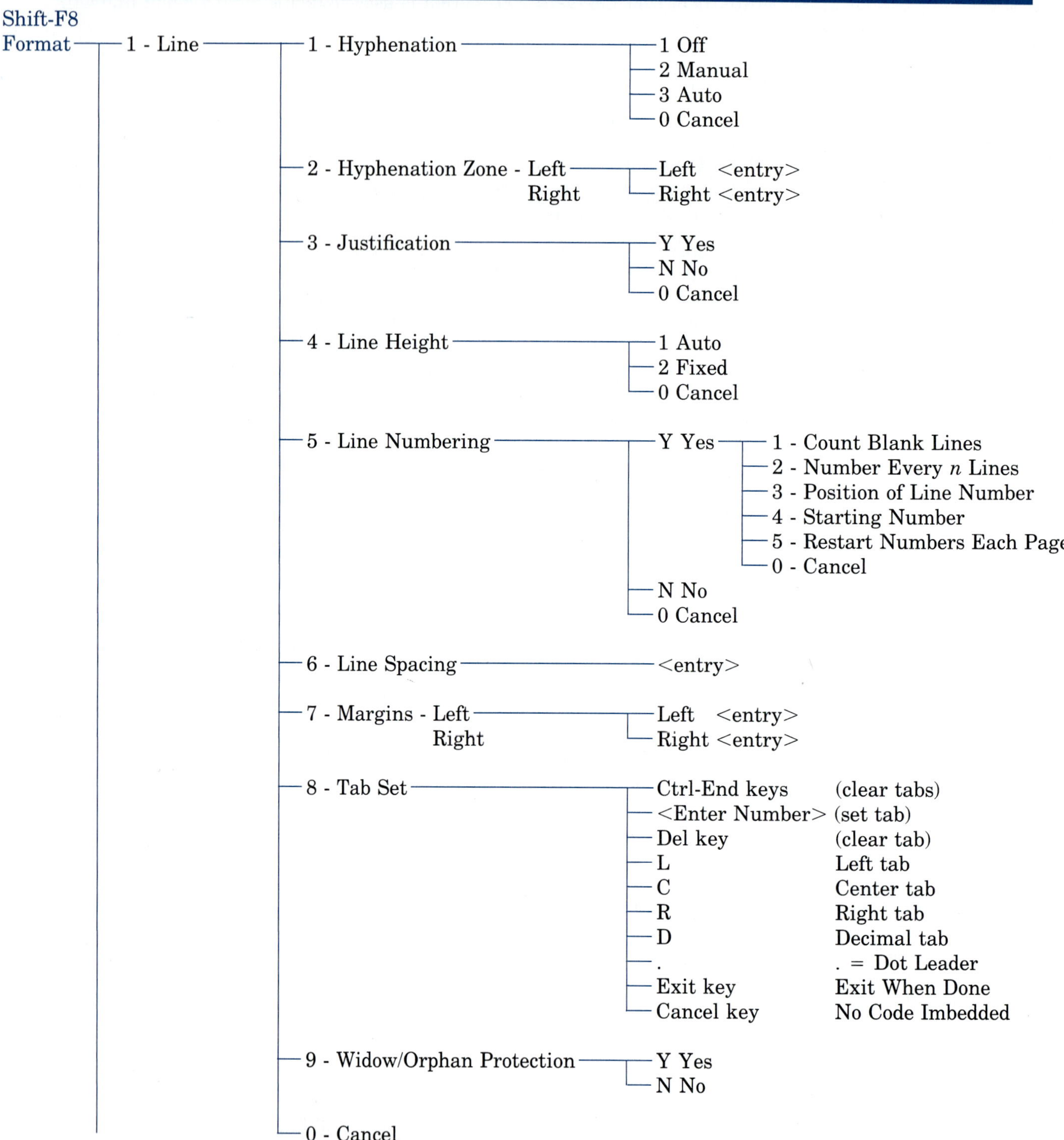
Shift-F8
Format
1 - Line
1 - Hyphenation
1 Off
2 Manual
3 Auto
0 Cancel
2 - Hyphenation Zone - Left
Right
Left <entry>
Right <entry>
3 - Justification
Y Yes
N No
0 Cancel
4 - Line Height
1 Auto
2 Fixed
0 Cancel
5 - Line Numbering
Y Yes
1 - Count Blank Lines
2 - Number Every n Lines
3 - Position of Line Number
4 - Starting Number
5 - Restart Numbers Each Page
0 - Cancel
N No
0 Cancel
6 - Line Spacing
<entry>
7 - Margins - Left
Right
Left <entry>
Right <entry>
8 - Tab Set
Ctrl-End keys (clear tabs)
<Enter Number> (set tab)
Del key (clear tab)
L Left tab
C Center tab
R Right tab
D Decimal tab
. . = Dot Leader
Exit key Exit When Done
Cancel key No Code Imbedded
9 - Widow/Orphan Protection
Y Yes
N No
0 - Cancel

CONTINUED

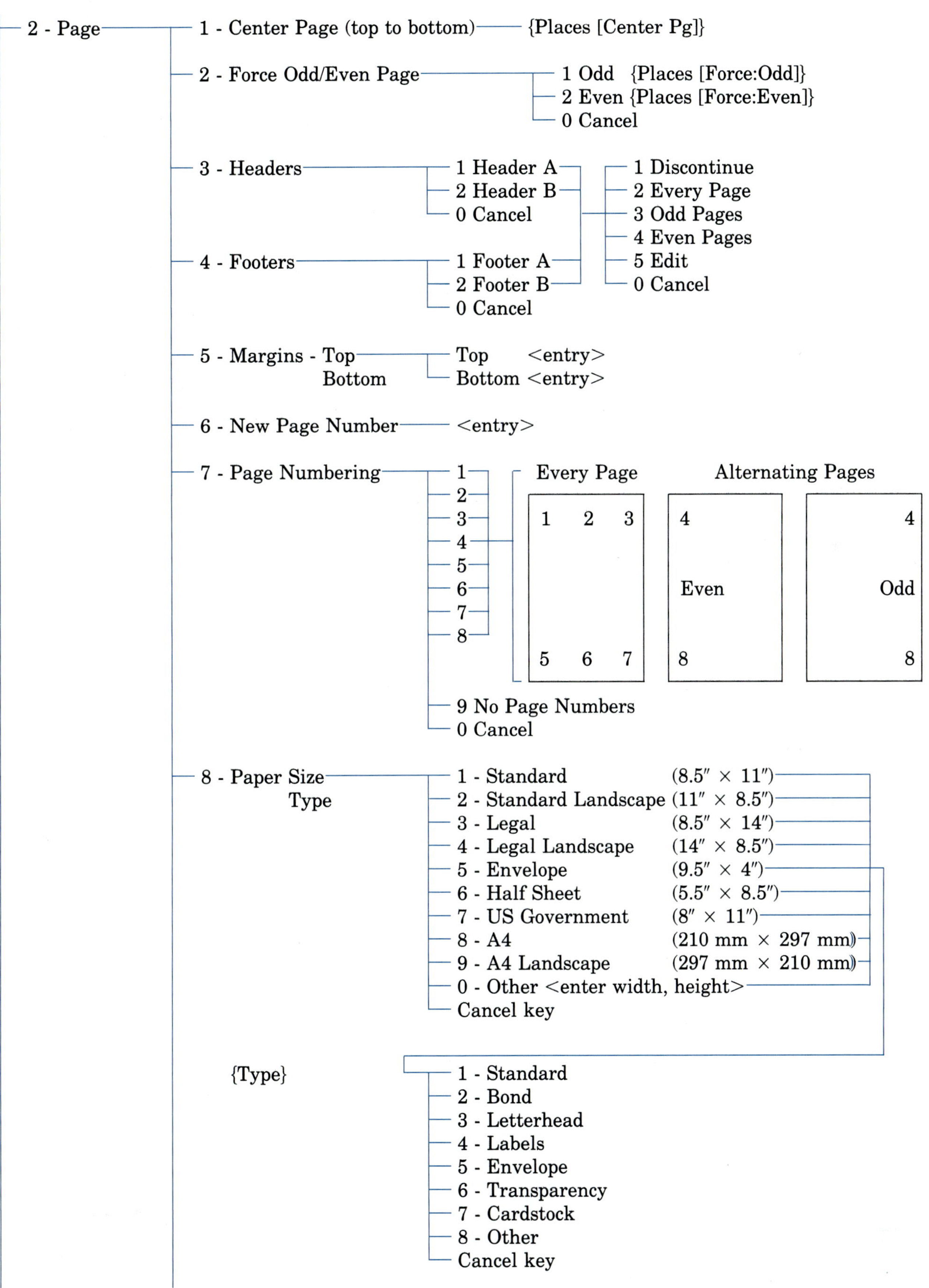

W-143 CONTINUED

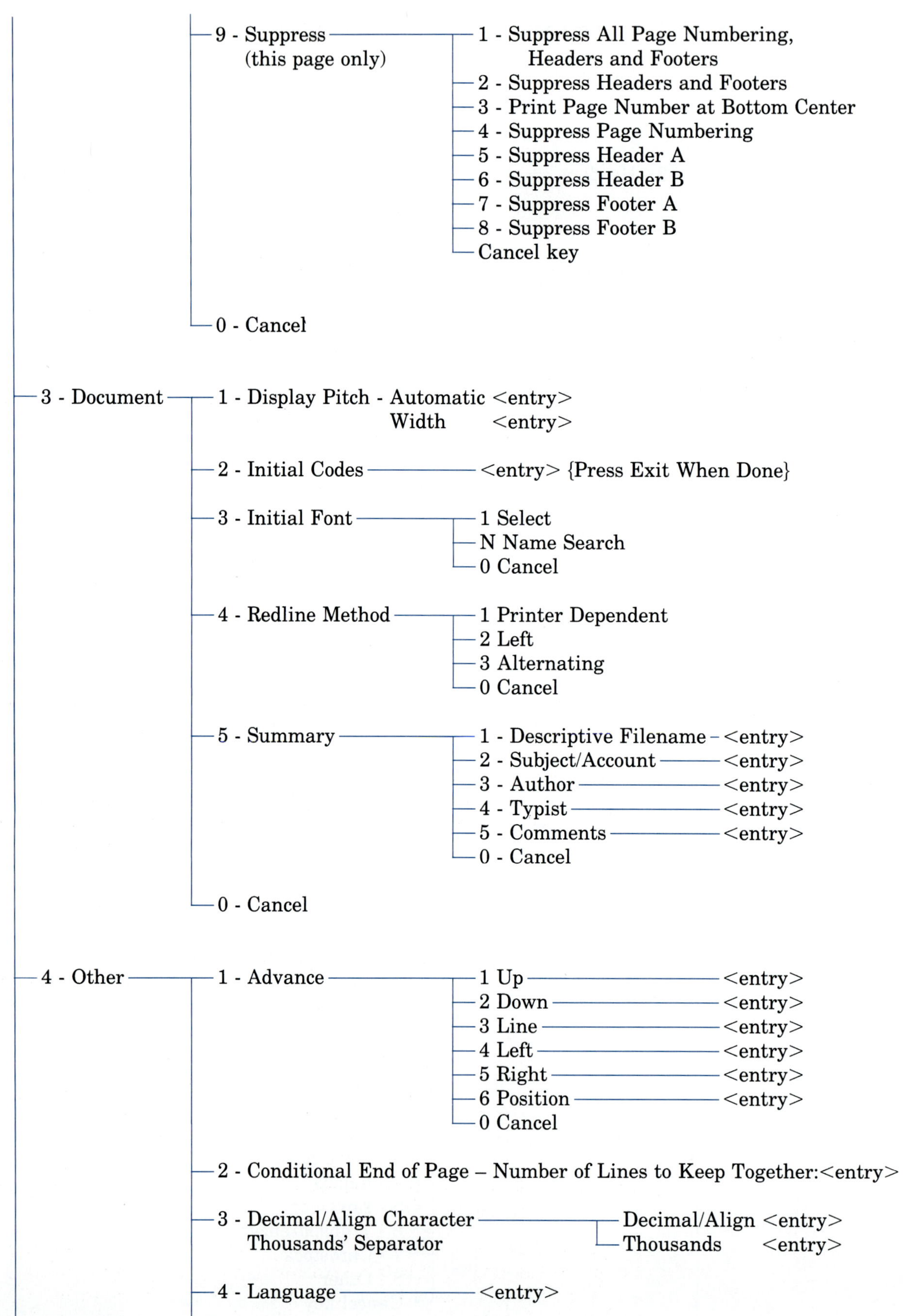
9 - Suppress (this page only)
1 - Suppress All Page Numbering, Headers and Footers
2 - Suppress Headers and Footers
3 - Print Page Number at Bottom Center
4 - Suppress Page Numbering
5 - Suppress Header A
6 - Suppress Header B
7 - Suppress Footer A
8 - Suppress Footer B
Cancel key
0 - Cancel
3 - Document
1 - Display Pitch - Automatic <entry>
Width <entry>
2 - Initial Codes
<entry> {Press Exit When Done}
3 - Initial Font
1 Select
N Name Search
0 Cancel
4 - Redline Method
1 Printer Dependent
2 Left
3 Alternating
0 Cancel
5 - Summary
1 - Descriptive Filename - <entry>
2 - Subject/Account <entry>
3 - Author <entry>
4 - Typist <entry>
5 - Comments <entry>
0 - Cancel
0 - Cancel
4 - Other
1 - Advance
1 Up <entry>
2 Down <entry>
3 Line <entry>
4 Left <entry>
5 Right <entry>
6 Position <entry>
0 Cancel
2 - Conditional End of Page – Number of Lines to Keep Together:<entry>
3 - Decimal/Align Character Thousands' Separator
Decimal/Align <entry>
Thousands <entry>
4 - Language <entry>

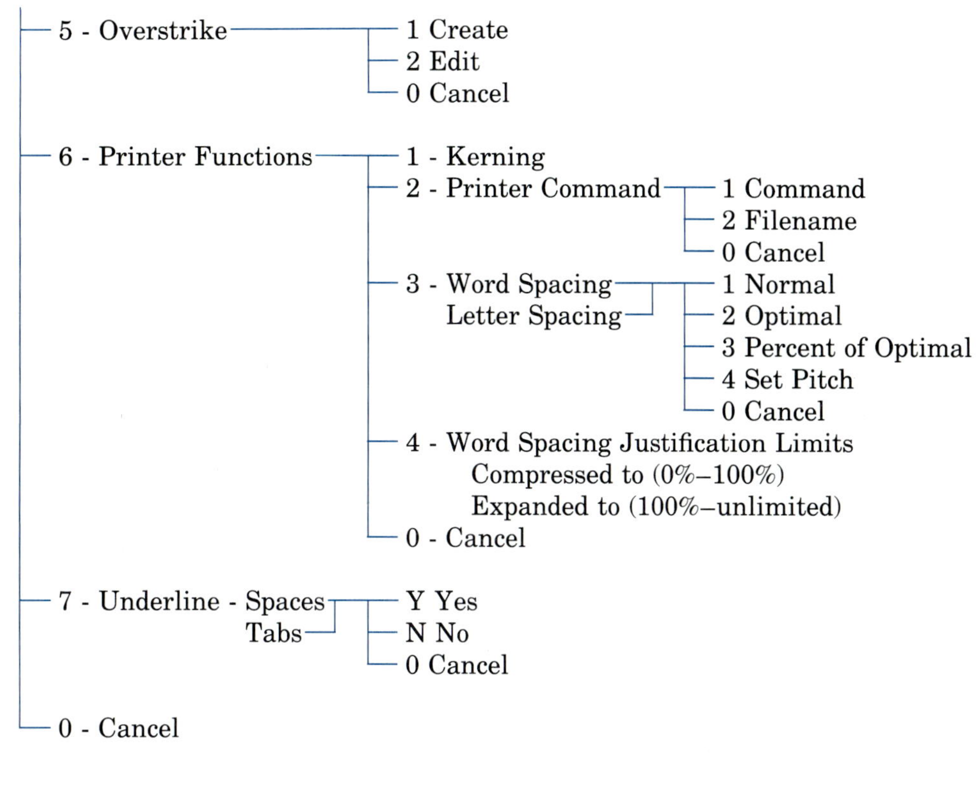

SHIFT-F8 FORMAT

The **Shift-F8** (Format) command has a rather extensive command tree associated with it. In general, the Format commands are designed to control the appearance of the finished document. The various Format commands are categorized by the relative size of document text they are designed to affect: **L**ine, **P**age, **D**ocument, and **O**ther.

Line

The **L**ine commands affect the appearance and/or WordPerfect's treatment of the lines of text within a document. The following discusses the default values and uses for each **Shift-F8,1** (Format),**L**ine command.

Hyphenation

Default—Off

Word wrapping occurs in a paragraph when the last word of a line is wrapped to the next line in the document. By default, if a word begins before the right margin and ends after the right margin, the entire word is automatically wrapped to the next line.

The **Hy**phenation command may be used to cause WordPerfect to either automatically hyphenate a word or pause and allow you to hyphenate a word before wrapping the hyphenated portion to the next line. The hyphenation feature only hyphenates words that meet certain criteria. The criteria for such words may be changed with the Hyphenation **Z**one command. See **Shift-F8,1,2** (Format),Line,Hyphenation **Z**one command. The H**y**phenation commands insert codes into the document that affect the remaining text.

Hyphens inserted into a word by the Hyphenation feature are soft hyphens, hyphens that will only be displayed or printed when they occur at the end of a line. Undisplayed soft hyphens may be viewed with the Reveal Codes command. You may enter soft hyphens into a document without the Hyphenation feature by typing Ctrl- -(press and hold the Ctrl key and then type the hyphen (-) key).

Off Code = [Hyph Off] The **Off** command turns hyphenation off, the default hyphenation status for WordPerfect.

Manual Code = [Hyph On] When hyphenation is **M**anual, WordPerfect will stop the word wrap operation on a word to be hyphenated and allow you to select where to hyphenate the word. To hyphenate such a word, use the ← → keys to move the cursor to where hyphenation is to occur and type the Esc key. If hyphenation is not desired, type the **F1** (Cancel) command. If **F1** (Cancel) is typed, a [/] (Cancel hyphenation code) is inserted into the document at the beginning of the word. The [/] code prevents WordPerfect's hyphenation feature from stopping on the word in the future. To produce your own [/] code in a document type Home,/.

Auto Code = [Hyph On] When hyphenation is **A**uto (automatic), WordPerfect will automatically hyphenate words according to its internal set of rules. If automatic hyphenation is in effect and WordPerfect encounters a word not covered by its internal rules, it will temporarily shift to manual hyphenation.

Hyphenation **Z**one

Default—Left = 10%, Right = 4 %

The hyphenation zone is what determines which words will be hyphenated when the hyphenation feature is on. The zone is an area measured in inches to the left and right of the current right margin. The default zone used by WordPerfect is 10 percent of the current line length (the distance between the left and right margins) to the left of the right margin, and 4 percent of the current line length to the right of the right margin. The setting causes the hyphenation feature to stop on words which begin at a position equal to or greater than 90 percent of the current line length, and extend 4 percent or more of the current line length to the right of the right margin. You may use the Hyphenation **Z**one command to change the percentages.

Justification Code = [Just Off][Just On]

Default—Yes (On)

Text may be justified to both the left and right margins when it is printed. To view justified text on the screen, you must use the **Shift-F7,6** (Print),**V**iew Document command.

To stop left/right justification, move the cursor to where you want the justification to end and type **Shift-F8,1,3,**N (Format),**L**ine,**J**ustification,*No*. A [Just Off] code will be imbedded in the text. To begin left and right justification of text, move the cursor to the place where left/right justification is to begin and type **Shift-F8,1,3,**Y (Format),**L**ine,**J**ustification,*Yes*. A [Just On] code will be imbedded in the document and will affect the following text.

Line **H**eight Code = [Ln Height:*nn*"] [Ln Height:Auto]

Default—Auto

The Line **H**eight command is used to change the number of lines printed in a vertical inch on the page. The two possible settings are **A**uto and **F**ixed. With **A**uto, WordPerfect automatically maintains the appropriate line height for the font in use (see **Ctrl-F8,1** (Font),**S**ize for more information on fonts). Specifying **F**ixed allows you to enter a fixed height in inches for the printed lines. However, specifying **F**ixed for any line height other than 0.17" (six lines per inch) may cause problems with some printers. See **Shift-F8,1,6** (Format),**L**ine,Line **S**pacing for information on changing line spacing.

Line Numbering Code = [Ln Num:On] [Ln Num:Off]

Default—No (Off)

The Line **N**umbering command is used to automatically number each line in a document. Move the cursor to where you want line numbering to begin and then type **Shift-F8,1,5,**Y (Format),**L**ine,Line **N**umbering,*Yes*. A small, self-explanatory menu concerning ways of numbering will be presented on the screen. To turn off the line numbering, move the cursor to the place where numbering is to end and type **Shift-F8,1,5,**N (Format),**L**ine,Line **N**umbering,*No*.

Line Spacing Code = [Ln Spacing:*n.n*]

Default—1 (single spacing)

The Line **S**pacing command is used to set the spacing between lines in the document. When the command is executed, a [Ln Spacing:] code is inserted into the document. Line spacing then will stay in effect for the rest of the document or until another [Ln Spacing:] code is encountered.

Spacing may be set at line and half-line intervals. For instance, 2 specifies double spacing and 1.5 specifies one-and-a-half lines between text lines. Finer adjustments may be made by entering values such as 1.1, 1.05, etc.; however, not all printers are able to support the finer adjustments. The screen will display the nearest whole number of line spaces for the current line spacing.

Margins Left/Right Code = [L/R Mar:*n.nn″*,*n.nn″*]

Default—Left = 1″, Right = 1″

The **M**argins command is used to set the left and right margins within a document. When the **M**argins command is executed, a [L/R Mar:] code is inserted into the document and the margins will stay in effect for the rest of the document or until another [L/R Mar:] code is encountered. To change margins, type **Shift-F8,1,7** (Format),**L**ine,**M**argins and then enter the new left and right margins in inches. To set top/bottom page margins, see **Shift-F8,2,5** (Format),**P**age,**M**argins.

Tab Set Code = [Tab Set:]

Default—0″, every 0.5″

The **T**ab Set command is used to set tab stops within a document. When tab stops are set with the **T**ab Set command, a [Tab Set:] code is inserted into the text. It stays in effect for the rest of the document or until another [Tab Set:] code is encountered.

When the **T**ab Set command is executed, the following lines appear at the bottom of the screen.

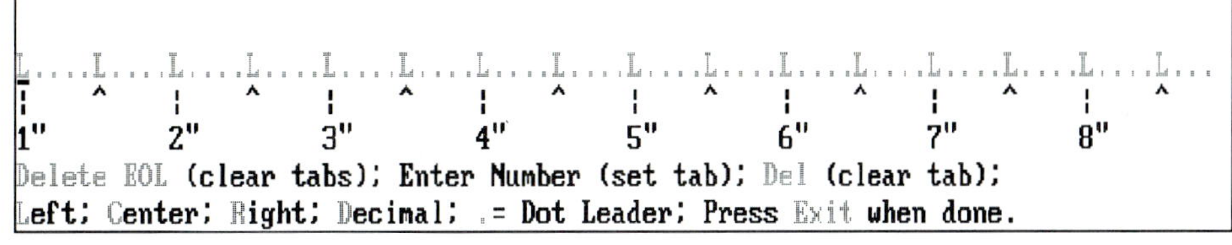

```
L....L....L....L....L....L....L....L....L....L....L....L....L....L....L....L...
1"        2"        3"        4"        5"        6"        7"        8"
Delete EOL (clear tabs); Enter Number (set tab); Del (clear tab);
Left; Center; Right; Decimal; .= Dot Leader; Press Exit when done.
```

The top line indicates the tab position of the current tab stops. By default, WordPerfect automatically sets L (Left justified) tabs every 0.5 inch. A cursor will be displayed on the line. The cursor may be moved left and right with the cursor control keys.

Types of Tab Stops There are seven different types of tab stops you may specify with the **T**ab Set command. Each type affects the manner in which data will be oriented to the tab stop when it is typed after the Tab key is used to move the cursor to the tab stop. The following describes the tab stop types and provides examples of how they affect text.

		Tab Stop
L	Left justify	Left justify
C	Center	Center text
R	Right justify	Right justify
D	Decimal align	123.00
L.	Left justify w/dot leader	.........................Left w/leader
R.	Right justify w/dot leader	...... Right w/leader
D.	Decimal align w/dot leader	.................123.00

Deleting Tab Stops To delete an existing tab stop, you may move the cursor to the tab position and type the Del key. To delete all tab stops to the right of the cursor, you may type Ctrl-End.

Setting Tab Stops There are two ways in which you may set new tab stops. One is to enter the position number for the tab stop. When a number is typed and entered, WordPerfect automatically puts an L (Left tab stop) at the position number. You also may set multiple tab stops in this way by typing the first tab stop position, a comma, and then the interval between tab stops that you desire. For instance, 0,0.5↵ will return the tabs to WordPerfect's default tab setting of *L*s occurring every 0.5 inches.

The other method of setting tab stops is to move the cursor to the appropriate place on the tab line and enter the letter of the type of tab stop you want to occur there. If you want the tab stop to have a preceding dot leader, you type the letter and then a period (.).

When finished specifying tab stops, you type **F7** (Exit) to quit the **T**ab Set command.

Widow/Orphan Protection Code = [W/O On] [W/O Off]

Default—No (Off)

A widow is the last line of a paragraph appearing on the first line of a page and an orphan is the first line of a paragraph appearing on the last line of a page. To prevent such last and first lines from being separated from their paragraphs, type **Shift-F8,1,9,**Y (Format),**L**ine,**W**idow/Orphan Protection, *Yes.* A [W/O On] code will be inserted at the cursor location and the following text will be protected against widows and orphans. To turn off widow/orphan protection, move the cursor to where protection is to end and type **Shift-F8,1,9,**N (Format),**L**ine,**W**idow/Orphan Protection,*No.*

Page

The (Format),**P**age commands affect the appearance of and/or WordPerfect's treatment of the pages within a document. The following discusses the default values (if any) and uses for each **Shift-F8,2** (Format),**P**age command.

Center Page (top to bottom) Code = [Center Pg]

The **C**enter Page command is used to vertically center a page of text. Move the cursor to the top of the page (before any imbedded codes) and type **Shift-F8,2,1** (Format),**P**age,**C**enter Page.

Force Odd/Even Page Code = [Force:Odd] [Force:Even]

The F**o**rce Odd/Even Page command forces the page number for a page to be either odd or even. If the page number does not need to be changed, it will remain the same. If the page number needs to be changed, it will be increased by 1.

Headers and Footers Codes = [Header:*text*] and [Footer:*text*]

Headers or footers may be included in a document by using the **P**age,**H**eaders or **P**age,**F**ooters command. Up to two headers (A and B) and two footers (A and B) may be included on the pages in a document.

To create a header or footer, move the cursor to the beginning of the page and type **Shift-F8,2,3** or **4** (Format),**P**age,**H**eaders or **F**ooters. Next, select the header or footer you want to create (A or B). The next menu to appear allows you to **D**iscontinue header/footer displays in the document, or to specify the pages upon which you want the header or footer to appear. Your page choices are Every **P**age, **O**dd Pages, or E**v**en Pages. The final option on the menu allows you to **E**dit a header or footer.

Continue by selecting the page display format (every, odd, or even) and an editing screen will appear for you to enter the header or footer text. Most of WordPerfect's Font commands (underline, flush right, bold, etc.) are available when entering the text for a header or footer. When finished, type **F7** (Exit) to save the data and return to the (Format),**P**age menu.

A [Header:] or [Footer:] code will be inserted into the text. To edit a header or footer, move the cursor past the location of the header/footer code and type **Shift-F8,2,3** or **4, 1** or **2** (Format),**P**age,**H**eaders or **F**ooters, **A** or **B,** and then type **5** (**E**dit). WordPerfect will search backwards through the file for the most recent A or B header or footer definition to be edited.

You may include a page number in a header or footer by typing Ctrl-B at the location within the header or footer where you want the page number to occur.

Margins Top/Bottom Code = [T/B Mar]

Default—Top = 1″ Bottom = 1″

The **P**age,**M**argins command is used to set the top and bottom page margins within a document. When the **M**argins command is executed, a [T/B Mar:] code is inserted into the document and the margins will stay in effect for the rest of the document or until another [T/B Mar:] code is encountered. To change margins, move the cursor to the top of the page and type **Shift-F8,2,5** (Format),**P**age,**M**argins. Then enter the new left and right margins in inches. To set left/right margins see the **Shift-F8,1,7** (Format),**L**ine, **M**argins command.

New Page Number Code = [Pg Num:*n*]

The **N**ew Page Number command may be used to set a new beginning page number within a document. Type **Shift-F8,2,6** (Format),**P**age,**N**ew Page Number) and then enter the beginning page number. Page numbers may be printed in Arabic (1,2,3, . . .) or lower-case Roman (i,ii,iii, . . .) number style.

Page Numbering Code = [Pg Numbering:*placement*]

Default—No page numbering

The **P**age Numbering command may be used to begin or discontinue printed page numbering and to specify printing of page numbers in one of eight different page positions. The page number placements include: (1) Top Left of every page; (2) Top Center of every page; (3) Top Right of every page; (4) Top Alternating left and right pages; (5) Bottom Left of every page; (6) Bottom Center of every page; (7) Bottom Right of every page; and (8) Bottom Alternating left and right pages. Option (9) **N**o Page numbers may be used to discontinue printing of page numbers.

To include a page number in a header or footer, enter Ctrl-B (^B) into the header or footer text at the location where the page number is to be printed.

Paper **S**ize/Type — Code = [Paper Sz/Typ:]

Default—8.5″ × 11″/Standard
This command may be used when printing with a printer which has more than one location for forms (different sizes of paper or orientations of text). The various forms that the printer supports are defined for WordPerfect using the **Shift-F7,S,3** (Print),**S**elect Printer,**E**dit command. For more information on these commands, see the WordPerfect manual or **F3** (Help) screens.

S**u**ppress (this page only)

The S**u**ppress command is used to suppress various page format options for the current page. The command is self-explanatory.

Document

The **D**ocument commands affect the appearance and/or WordPerfect's treatment of the entire document. The following discusses the default values (if any) and uses for each **Shift-F8,3** (Format),**D**ocument command.

Display Pitch

Default—Automatic = Yes/Width = 0.1″
The **D**isplay Pitch command may be used to expand or contract the screen display widths of absolute measured characters such as tabs, indents, and so forth, etc. The higher the Width setting, the less screen space is displayed for such characters.

Initial **C**odes

The Initial **C**odes command provides a method to override many of WordPerfect's default command settings for a document. The command presents a screen similar to the **Alt-F3** (Reveal Codes) screen. To change the default setting for a document, type **Shift-F8,3,2** (Format),**D**ocument,Initial **C**odes. When the Initial **C**odes screen is presented, you next type the keystrokes which would normally change a command's default setting. For instance, to change the default line spacing from one to two (double spacing) you would type **Shift-F8,1,6,2** (Format),**L**ine,Line **S**pacing,2. A [Ln Spacing:2] code will appear in the bottom portion of the Initial **C**odes screen. You may continue to enter such codes into the Initial **C**odes screen until all of the default settings you desire are made. You next type **F7** (Exit) to properly exit the command.

The Initial **C**odes command does not place a visible code into the document; however, the Initial **C**odes settings are saved with the document. You may edit a document's initial codes by again executing the Initial **C**odes command and using the same editing keystrokes that are used in the Reveal Codes screen. To change the initial codes for all documents, see **Shift-F1,5,4** (Setup), **I**nitial Settings,**I**nitial Codes.

Initial **F**ont

Most printers are capable of printing in more than one font. When the **Shift-F7,S,2** (Print),**S**elect Printer,**A**dditional printers command is used, WordPerfect automatically selects one of the printer's fonts as the default font. You may use the Initial **F**ont command to change the default printer font for a document. See **Ctrl-F8,4** (Font),Base **F**ont for another method to change the default printer font for a document.

Redline Method

Default—Printer Dependent
The **R**edline Method command is used to select how redlined text is printed. The choices include **P**rinter Dependent (determined by WordPerfect's printer definition file), **L**eft (prints redline text with a horizontal bar printed in the left margin, and **A**lternating (prints redlined text with horizontal bars alternating between left and right margins for facing pages). See **Ctrl-F8,2,8** (Font),**A**ppearance,**R**edln for more information on redlined text.

Summary

WordPerfect has a means for you to provide documentation for your documents. In other words, you are able to insert text into a document that will not be printed. Such internal documentation may be done through the **S**ummary command.

The command provides a screen for entry of the following information: **D**escriptive Filename (an extended name); **S**ubject/Account (further description of the file); and **A**uthor and **T**ypist name. In addition, up to 780 characters of text may be included in an area labeled "Comments." Text formatting within the summary screen is limited. Also displayed on the Document Summary screen are the system filename (the same name under which the file is saved) and the date of creation (obtained by WordPerfect from the current DOS system date).

Other

The **O**ther commands are the final group of **Shift-F8** (Format) commands. The following discusses the default values (if any) and uses for each **Shift-F8,4** (Format),**O**ther command.

Advance — Code = [Adv]

The **A**dvance command imbeds a code that causes the printer to adjust its printing position for the text following the code. The options of the **A**dvance command include **U**p, **D**own, **Li**ne, **L**eft, **R**ight, and **P**osition.

To cause all following characters to be printed above or below the normal line, use the **U**p or **D**own commands. To cause all following characters to be printed to the left or right of the normal position, use the **L**eft or **R**ight commands. The **U**p, **D**own, **L**eft, and **R**ight commands all require a relative position in inches to be entered. For example, to cause the following text to be printed one-half line higher than the preceding text, you would use the **U**p command and enter the distance as being 0.08 (assuming 6 lines per inch, 0.167″ per line). The **Li**ne and **P**osition command require that an absolute position be entered, the same position you would see on the status line (Ln ″ or Pos ″) if you were to move the cursor there.

To readjust printing to the previous position, use the **A**dvance command to move in the opposite direction for the same distance.

*NOTE: Many printers do not support the **A**dvance feature.*

Conditional End of Page — Code = [CndlEOP:*n*]

The **C**onditional End of Page command is used to keep a certain number of lines in a document from being separated by a soft page break.

Move the cursor to the line above the first line in the document to be protected and type **Shift-F8,4,2** (Format),**O**ther,**C**onditional End of Page and then enter the number of lines to protect.

Decimal Align Character Code = [Decml/Align Char:]

Default—./,
The **D**ecimal Align Character command is used to change the character that WordPerfect uses to align text at tab stops. The default Align Character is the period (.). The command also is used to change the character that WordPerfect uses to separate the thousands used in numbers within a math portion of text. The default Thousands' separator is the comma (,).

Language Code = [Lang:]

Default—US
The **L**anguage command is used to change the language used with the spell Check, Thesaurus, and Hyphenation features. Separate disks must be purchased to perform the other language operations.

Overstrike Code = [Ovrstk:]

The **O**verstrike command causes one character to be overstruck by one or more following characters. To overstrike characters, type **Shift-F8,4,5** (Format),**O**ther,**O**verstrike. The Overstrike options include **C**reate and **E**dit. You next select the **C**reate command and enter the text to be overstruck. For instance, to produce a not-equal sign, type **Shift-F8,4,5,1** =/↵. The screen will display only the /; however, the printer will print ≠. In the example, the Reveal Codes screen would show the code [Ovrstk: =/]. To edit an overstrike code, type **Shift-F8,4,5,2** (Format),**O**ther,**O**verstrike,**E**dit.

Printer Functions

The **P**rinter Functions command is used for specialized control over the printing of a document.

Kerning Code = [Kern:On] [Kern:Off] Default—No (Off)

Kerning reduces the space between the letters in a word by eliminating unneeded space for certain letter combinations. For instance, the letters WA will be printed closer together since they "fit" each other. Not all printers or fonts support the kerning feature.

Printer Command Code = [Ptr Cmd:]

Printer Command is used to insert a printer control code into a document. Control codes must be obtained from the printer's manual. When entering the control code into a document, characters less than ASCII 32 or greater than ASCII 126 must be entered as decimal numbers in angle brackets (for example, <27> = Esc). All keyboard characters may be entered directly or as decimal numbers in angle brackets (for example, M or <77>).

Command

Use the **C**ommand command to enter a printer code that will reside within the document.

Filename

Use the **F**ilename command to specify a file in which the desired printer codes reside.

Word Spacing/Letter Spacing Code = [Wrd/Ltr Spacing:]

Default—Optimal/Optimal
The **W**ord Spacing/Letter Spacing command is used to change the printed spacing of the letters and words within a document. The choices include **N**ormal (the printer manufacturer's settings), **O**ptimal (WordPerfect's settings), **P**ercent of Optimal (user-defined setting), and **S**et Pitch (user-defined characters per inch).

Word Spacing Justification Limits Code = [Just Lim:]

Default—Compressed 60%/Expanded 400%

When right justification is on (the default mode), WordPerfect expands and compresses spaces between words to right justify lines of text when it prints a document. The Word Spacing **J**ustification Limits command may be used to alter the way in which WordPerfect treats the expansion/contraction of spaces. See the WordPerfect manual or **F3** (Help) screens for more information.

Underline — Code = [Underln:Spaces/Tabs]

Default—Spaces Yes/Tabs No
The **U**nderline command may be used to stop WordPerfect from underlining spaces or to cause WordPerfect to start underlining tabs in a document.

Block/Format
Code =
[BlockPro:On]
[BlockPro:Off]

To protect a block of text from being separated by soft page breaks, first block the text to be protected and then type **Shift-F8** (Format). Next answer Y to the "Protect block? (Y/N)" prompt.

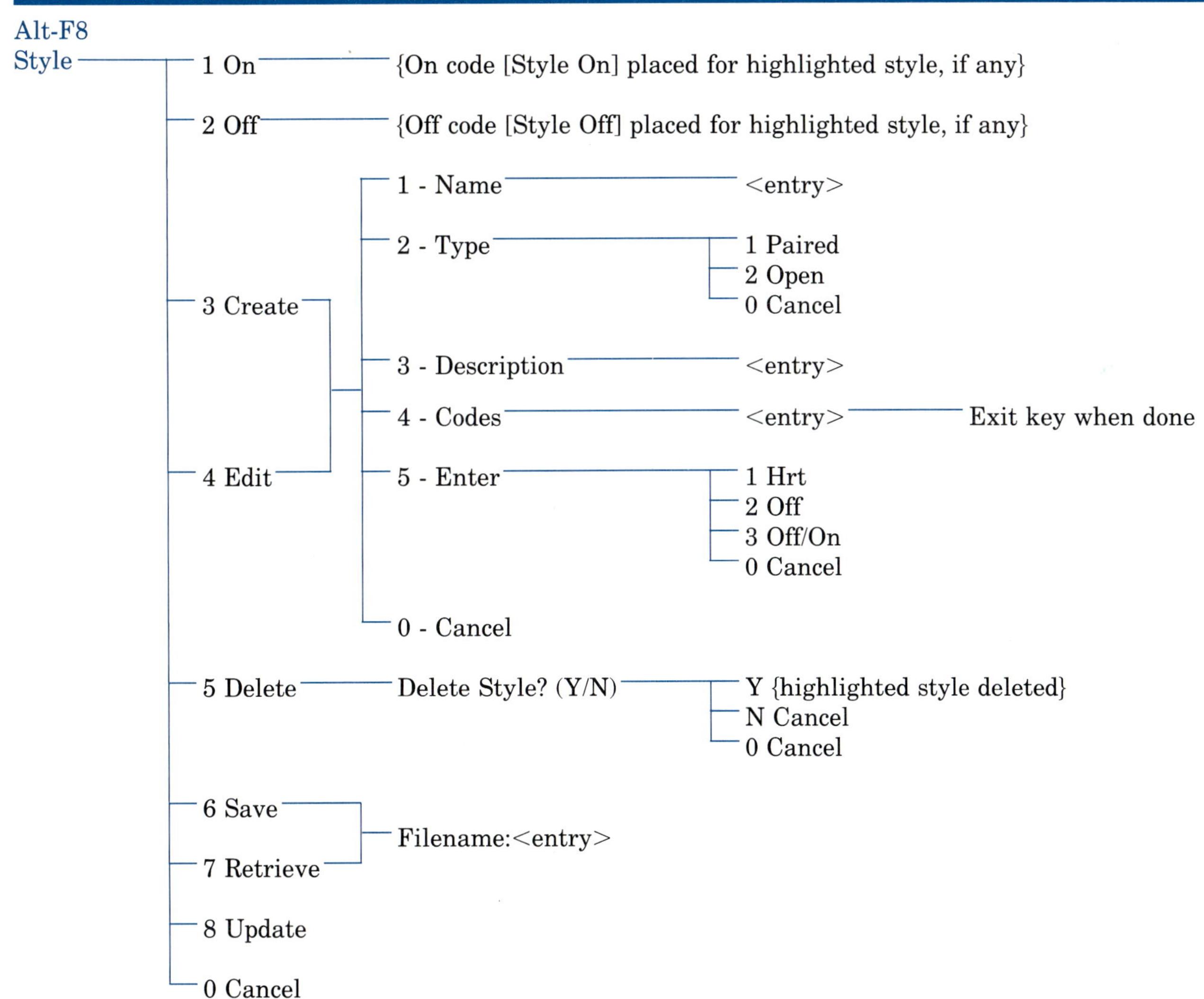

During the creation and editing of a document, you often will find that certain combinations of codes and/or text are repeated throughout the text. When this occurs, a Style containing the combination of codes/text may be created once using the **Alt-F8** (Style) command. The Style then can be inserted into the text at the appropriate places. The **Alt-F8** (Style) command is most useful when code combinations are included in the recurring event.

There are two types of Styles, Paired and Open. A Paired Style type contains codes that are start and stop in nature (such as [BOLD] [bold]). A Paired Style type inserts a [Style On:] and [Style Off:] code into the document. Text typed afterwards is inserted between the two codes and becomes affected by the start and stop codes included in the Style. To stop the Style from affecting subsequent text being entered, the **Alt-F8** (Style) command is executed again.

An Open Style may or may not contain start and stop codes; however, it does not pause for the user to enter text between them if it does have such codes. An Open Style is used primarily to contain codes that are format forward in nature (such as [L/R Mar:]). An Open Style inserts a [Open Style:] code into the document which contains the Style's codes and text. Format forward codes in an Open Style stay in effect until another code of the same type is encountered (in another [Open Style:] code or singularly).

Styles created with the **Alt-F8** (Style) command are saved with the document. You may, however, save Styles in their own files in order to later retrieve them into another document.

The Style Command Screen

When the **Alt-F8** (Style) command is executed a screen similar to the following appears.

```
Styles

 Name          Type   Description

 BLDUND        Paired Bold and Double underline
 HEADINGS      Paired Very large, bold for title headings
 QUOTE         Open   Single spaced, indented margins for citations
 TEXT          Open   Double spaced, normal margins for text
 TITLE         Open   Centered, term paper title page










1 On; 2 Off; 3 Create; 4 Edit; 5 Delete; 6 Save; 7 Retrieve; 8 Update: 1
```

Here, five Styles (two Paired and three Open) have been previously created. The reverse video bar across the screen is the Style screen cursor. The cursor may be moved up and down with the cursor controls keys ↑ and ↓.

At the bottom of the screen appears the Style menu of commands. In general, the procedure used to execute a command is first to move the cursor to the appropriate Style shown on the screen and then type the number or letter of a command. For instance, to delete the Style named TITLE, you would move the cursor to the last Style shown on the screen and then type **5** (**D**elete).

On and **O**ff Codes = [Style On:] [Style Off:]

Once a Style has been created (see **Alt-F8** (Style),**C**reate), the **O**n and **O**ff commands are used to insert the Style codes into the document for the current Style (the Style upon which the Style cursor is currently located).

If the Style is Paired, the **O**n command is used to begin the insert operation. After the text to be affected has been entered, the **Alt-F8,2** (Style),**O**ff command is executed to end the operation. A set of Paired Style codes (On/Off) also may be placed around existing text by first blocking the text in the document and then typing **Alt-F8,1** (Style),**O**n. The [Style On:] code will be placed at the beginning of the block and the [Style Off:] code will be placed at the end. If the Style is Open, only the **O**n command is used.

Create and **E**dit

The **C**reate command is used to create a new Style and the **E**dit command is used to edit the current Style. Both commands present the same screens. The first screen presented allows you to enter the following information.

Name

A name for the Style, preferably eight characters or less in length.

Type

Selected from a menu, the type is either **P**aired or **O**pen.

Description

Room is available for you to enter a full description of what the Style is intended for (approximately 50 characters).

Codes

The **C**odes command presents a screen similar to the **Alt-F3** (Reveal Codes) screen. When the (Style),**C**odes screen is presented, you type the keystrokes which would normally cause a command code to be generated. For instance, to change the line spacing from one to two (double spacing) you would type **Shift-F8,1,6**,2↵ (Format),**L**ine,Line **S**pacing 2. A [Ln Spacing:2] code will appear in the bottom portion of the (Style),**C**odes screen. You may continue to enter such codes or text into the (Style),**C**odes screen until all of the desired codes/text appear there. You next type **F7** (Exit) to properly exit the Style editing screen.

Enter

The **E**nter command is used for Paired Styles only. The command may be used to define the use of the Enter key during the text entering portion of the insert [Style:] code operation. The choices are **H**rt (hard return, the normal use), **O**ff (have the keystroke turn the Style off), Off/**O**n (have the keystroke turn the Style off and then back on again).

Delete

The **D**elete command may be used to delete a Style definition. Move the Style screen cursor to the Style you want to delete and type **5** or **D.** Next answer Y to the "Delete Style? (Y/N)" prompt. Deleting a Style from the

Style screen does not delete any of the Style codes already in the document for the deleted Style.

Save	The **S**ave command may be used to save the current Style to a file of its own. Move the Style screen cursor to the appropriate Style and type **6** or **S** (Save) and then enter a filename to save the Style.
Retrieve	The **R**etrieve command may be used to retrieve a Style that has been saved to its own file.
Update	You can create a library of Styles (a file of Styles that may be retrieved into the Style screen). If a Style library has been created, the **U**pdate command may be used to retrieve the file into the Style screen. See the WordPerfect manual or **F3** (Help) screens for more information.
Block/Style	A set of Paired Style codes (On/Off) can be placed around existing text by first blocking the text in the document and then typing **Alt-F8,1** (Style),**O**n. The [Style On:] code will be placed at the beginning of the block, and the [Style Off:] code will be placed at the end.

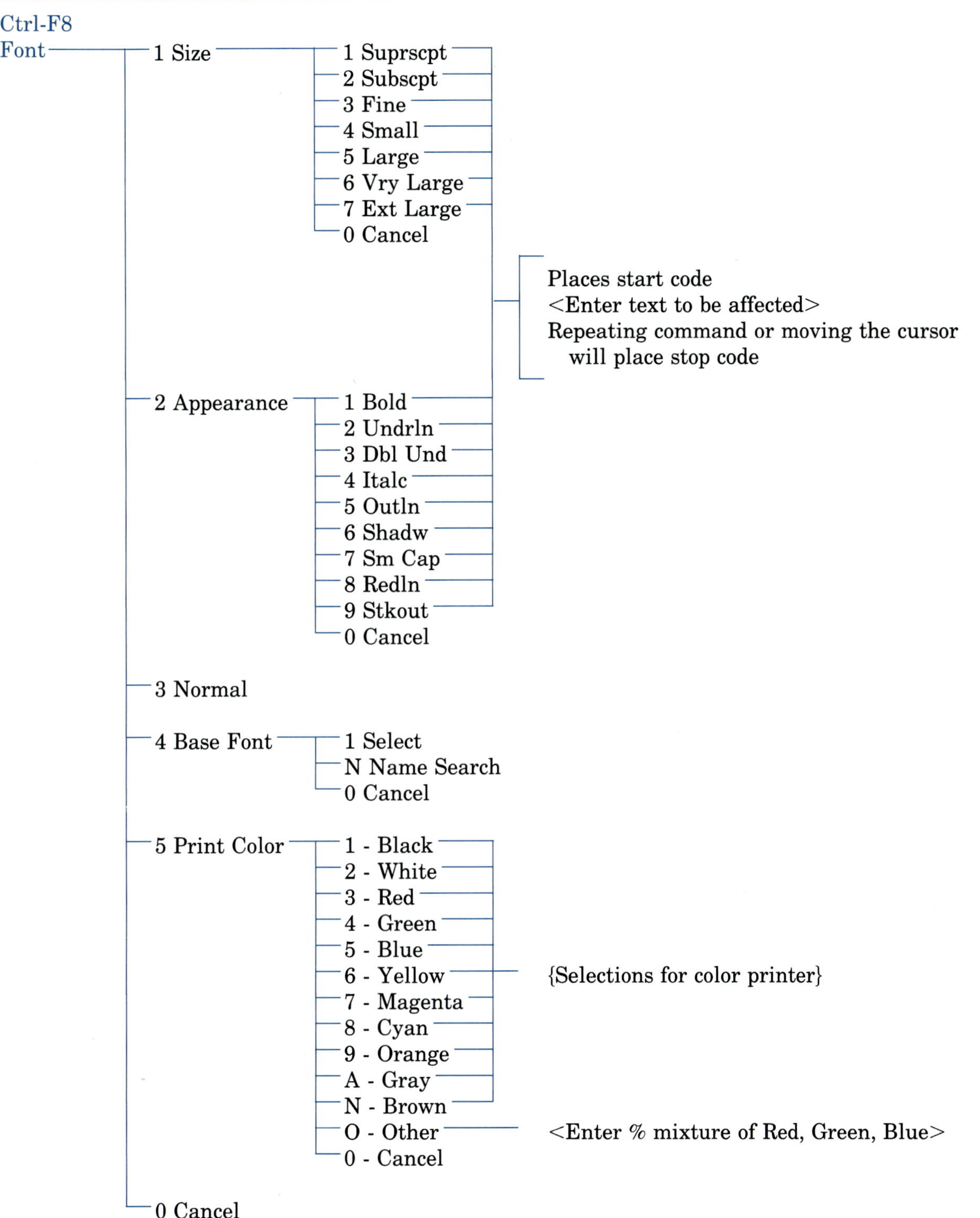

CTRL-F8 FONT

W-157

The **Ctrl-F8** (Font) command is used to select various sizes and styles of printed characters. *Font* is a term that describes a set of printed characters that have the same size and style.

Size refers to the height and width of the characters within a font. Two terms used to describe different sizes of types are *point* and *pitch.* Point is a measurement of height for characters in a font. One point is approximately

1/72 of an inch in height. Pitch is a measurement of width for characters in a font. Pitch describes the number of characters that occur in a printed inch of text. In other words, 10 pitch equals ten characters per inch (CPI).

Proportional is a term that describes a font which has no pitch. In a proportional font, the distance separating printed characters is dependant on the width of the characters. That is, the characters *il* will be printed closer together than the characters *LO* in a proportional font.

Style refers to the appearance of the printed character. Italic, Roman, and Helvetica are all proper names for different styles of type. The proper name for a style is often used with other terms (such as *Bold*) to further describe the style.

In many cases, the printer you are using will print in the default font San Serif or Pica, 12 point, 10 pitch.

The following **Ctrl-F8** (Font) commands all deal with changing the size and appearance of printed characters in a document. The commands, however, are highly printer dependent and you should test them before including them in your documents.

Size

In general, the **S**ize commands are used to alter the point and pitch for printed characters. The **S**ize commands all generate start and stop codes to effect the change in font. To use the commands, you may begin by typing the appropriate **S**ize command and then entering the text to be affected by the command. To stop the **S**ize affect on text being entered, move the cursor ↑, ↓, or → past the stop code in the document, or type **Ctrl-F8,3** (Font), **N**ormal to insert a new code into the document to the left of the cursor location. To change the size of existing text, block the text and then type the appropriate **S**ize command.

Su**p**rscpt — Code = [SUPRSCPT] [suprscpt]

The Su**p**rscpt (Superscript) command causes characters of text to be printed above the normal line or to be reduced to Fine size and printed at the top margin of the current line.

Su**b**scpt — Code = [SUBSCPT] [subscpt]

The Su**b**scpt (Subscript) command causes characters of text to be printed below the normal line or to be reduced to Fine size and printed at the bottom margin of the current line.

Fine — Code = [FINE] [fine]

The **F**ine command reduces the size of print to the smallest size available with the **S**ize commands (often to 17 pitch).

Small — Code = [SMALL] [small]

The **S**mall command reduces the size of print (often to 12 pitch).

Large — Code = [LARGE] [large]

The **L**arge command enlarges the print (often to 8.5 pitch).

Vry Large — Code = [VRY LARGE] [vry large]

The **V**ry Large (Very Large) command enlarges the print (often to 5 pitch).

Ext Large — Code = [EXT LARGE] [ext large]

The **E**xt Large (Extra Large) command enlarges the print (often the same as Very Large).

Appearance

The **Appearance** commands are used to alter the style for printed characters. The **Appearance** commands all generate start and stop codes and insert them into the text in order to effect the change in font. To use the commands, you may begin by typing the appropriate **Appearance** command, and then enter the text to be affected by the command. To stop the **Size** effect on text being entered, move the cursor ↑, ↓, or → past the stop code in the document, or type **Ctrl-F8,3** (Font),**N**ormal to insert a new stop code into the document to the left of the cursor location. To change the style of existing text, block the text and then type the appropriate **Appearance** command.

Bold and **U**ndrln — Codes = [BOLD] [bold]/[UND] [und]

The **Crtl-F8** (Font),**A**ppearance,**B**old command is the same as the **F6** (Bold) command. The **Ctrl-F8** (Font),**A**ppearance,**U**ndrln command is the same as the **F8** (Underline) command.

Dbl Und — Code = [DBL UND] [dbl und]

The **D**bl Und (Double Underline) command produces a double underline for text in a document.

Italic — Code = [ITALC] [italc]

The **I**talic command changes the font to italic for text in a document.

Outln and **S**hadw — Codes = [OUTLN] [outln]/[SHADW] [shadw]

The **O**utln (Outline) and **S**hadw (Shadow) commands offset and reprint text to create a double image effect.

Sm **C**ap — Code = [SM CAP] [sm cap]

The Sm **C**ap (Small Capitals) command prints lower-case letters as smaller upper-case letters.

Redln and **S**tkout — Codes = [REDLN] [redln]/[STKOUT] [stkout]

When two or more people are involved in revising text, it is often desirable to "call out" or identify certain segments of text as being text for proposed changes. The **R**edln (Redline) command is designed to help identify text being suggested for addition to a document. The **S**tkout (Strikeout) command is designed to help identify text being suggested for deletion from a document. Different printers mark such text in different ways. See **Shift-F8,3,4** (Format),**D**ocument,**R**edline Method for information on changing the way in which redlined text is marked.

To remove all redline codes and delete all strikeout text from a document, use the **Alt-F5,6,1** (Mark Text),**G**enerate,**R**emove Redline Markings and Strikeout Text From Document command.

Normal

The **N**ormal command may be used to insert **Ctrl-F8** (Font) stop code(s) into a document. The command may be used to exit the Font code procedure used to change the size or appearance of text, or to edit previously formatted text. The **N**ormal command generates stop codes for all unmatched Font start codes preceding the current cursor location.

Base **F**ont
Code = [Font:]

The Base **F**ont command may be used to change the normal printer font used in printing a document. The command presents a screen of all fonts your printer supports. To select a different printer font, move the screen's cursor to the appropriate font and type ↵.

Print Color Code = [Color:]

The Print Color command is used to change the colors for text printed on a printer capable of printing colors. See the WordPerfect manual or **F3** (Help) screens for more information.

F9
Merge R —————— {End-of-field marker in secondary file}
{Ends keyboard entry when merging}

F9 MERGE R

The Merge R command inserts a ^R merge code and a hard return [HRt] into a document. The command may be used to separate fields within records in a secondary merge file. The command also is used to end keyboard input during a merge operation. (For more information on merge text operations, see **Ctrl-F9** (Merge/Sort)).

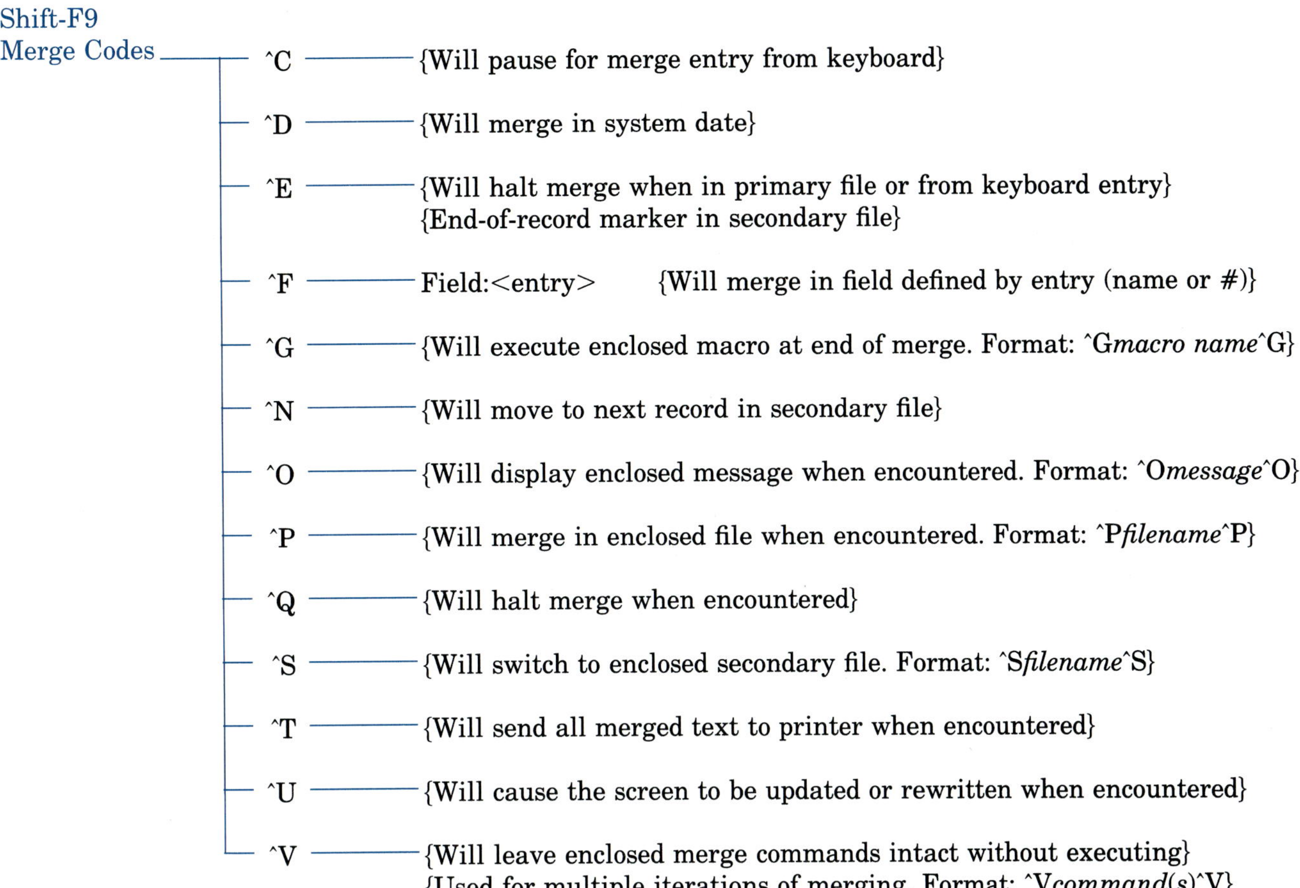

Shift-F9
Merge Codes
^C {Will pause for merge entry from keyboard}
^D {Will merge in system date}
^E {Will halt merge when in primary file or from keyboard entry}
{End-of-record marker in secondary file}
^F Field:<entry> {Will merge in field defined by entry (name or #)}
^G {Will execute enclosed macro at end of merge. Format: ^G*macro name*^G}
^N {Will move to next record in secondary file}
^O {Will display enclosed message when encountered. Format: ^O*message*^O}
^P {Will merge in enclosed file when encountered. Format: ^P*filename*^P}
^Q {Will halt merge when encountered}
^S {Will switch to enclosed secondary file. Format: ^S*filename*^S}
^T {Will send all merged text to printer when encountered}
^U {Will cause the screen to be updated or rewritten when encountered}
^V {Will leave enclosed merge commands intact without executing}
{Used for multiple iterations of merging. Format: ^V*command(s)*^V}

SHIFT-F9 MERGE CODES

The **Shift-F9** (Merge Codes) command provides a menu of merge codes used in merge text operations. A merge code selected from the menu is inserted into the document at the current cursor location. Unlike most of WordPerfect's codes, the codes are not hidden but instead appear on the screen during normal editing. To select a code from the menu, type **Shift-F9** (Merge Codes) and then type the letter of the merge code you wish to insert into the document. (For more information on merge text operations, see the **Ctrl-F9** (Merge/Sort) command).

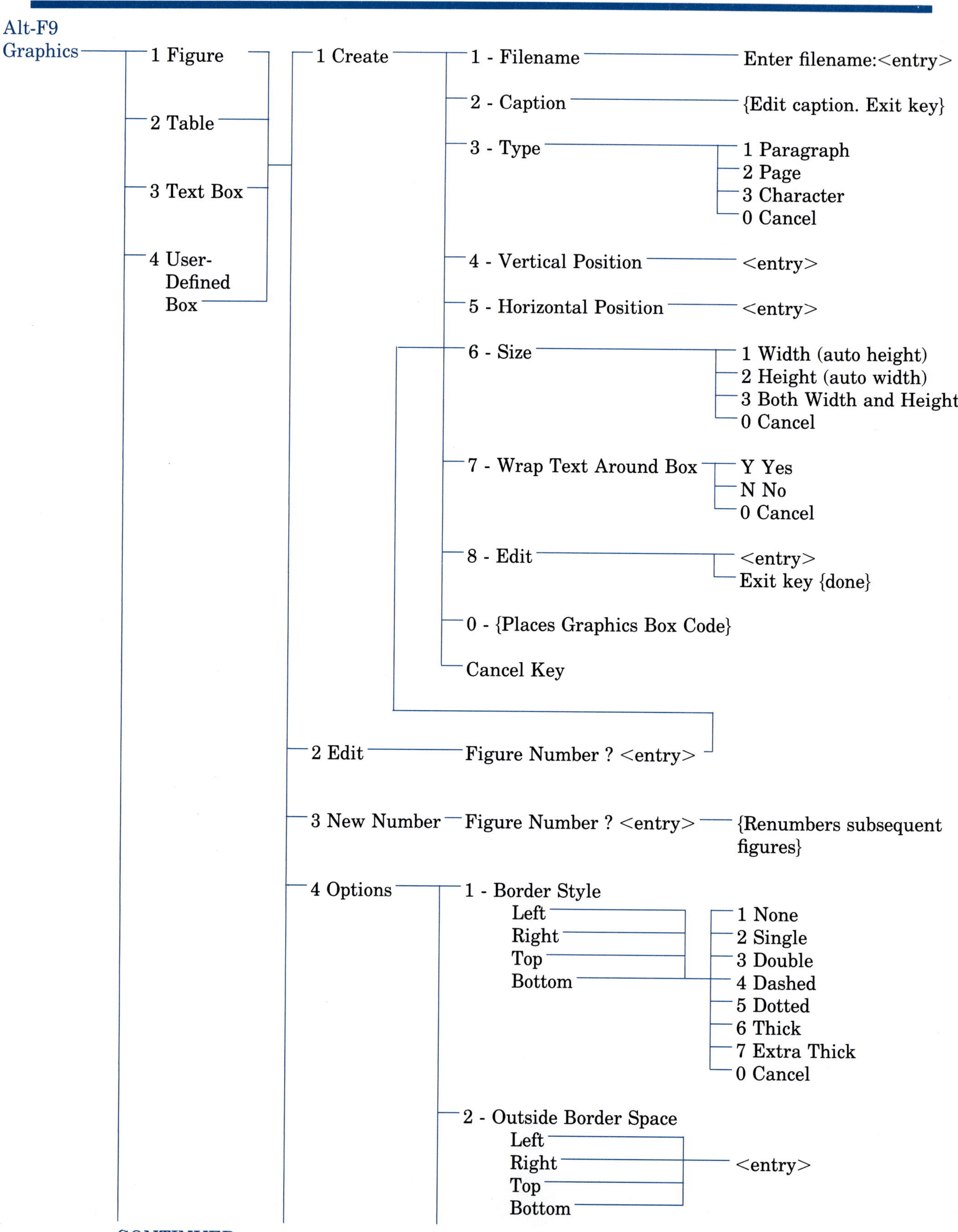
Alt-F9
Graphics
1 Figure
2 Table
3 Text Box
4 User-Defined Box
1 Create
1 - Filename
Enter filename:<entry>
2 - Caption
{Edit caption. Exit key}
3 - Type
1 Paragraph
2 Page
3 Character
0 Cancel
4 - Vertical Position
<entry>
5 - Horizontal Position
<entry>
6 - Size
1 Width (auto height)
2 Height (auto width)
3 Both Width and Height
0 Cancel
7 - Wrap Text Around Box
Y Yes
N No
0 Cancel
8 - Edit
<entry>
Exit key {done}
0 - {Places Graphics Box Code}
Cancel Key
2 Edit
Figure Number ? <entry>
3 New Number
Figure Number ? <entry>
{Renumbers subsequent figures}
4 Options
1 - Border Style
Left
Right
Top
Bottom
1 None
2 Single
3 Double
4 Dashed
5 Dotted
6 Thick
7 Extra Thick
0 Cancel
2 - Outside Border Space
Left
Right
Top
Bottom
<entry>
CONTINUED

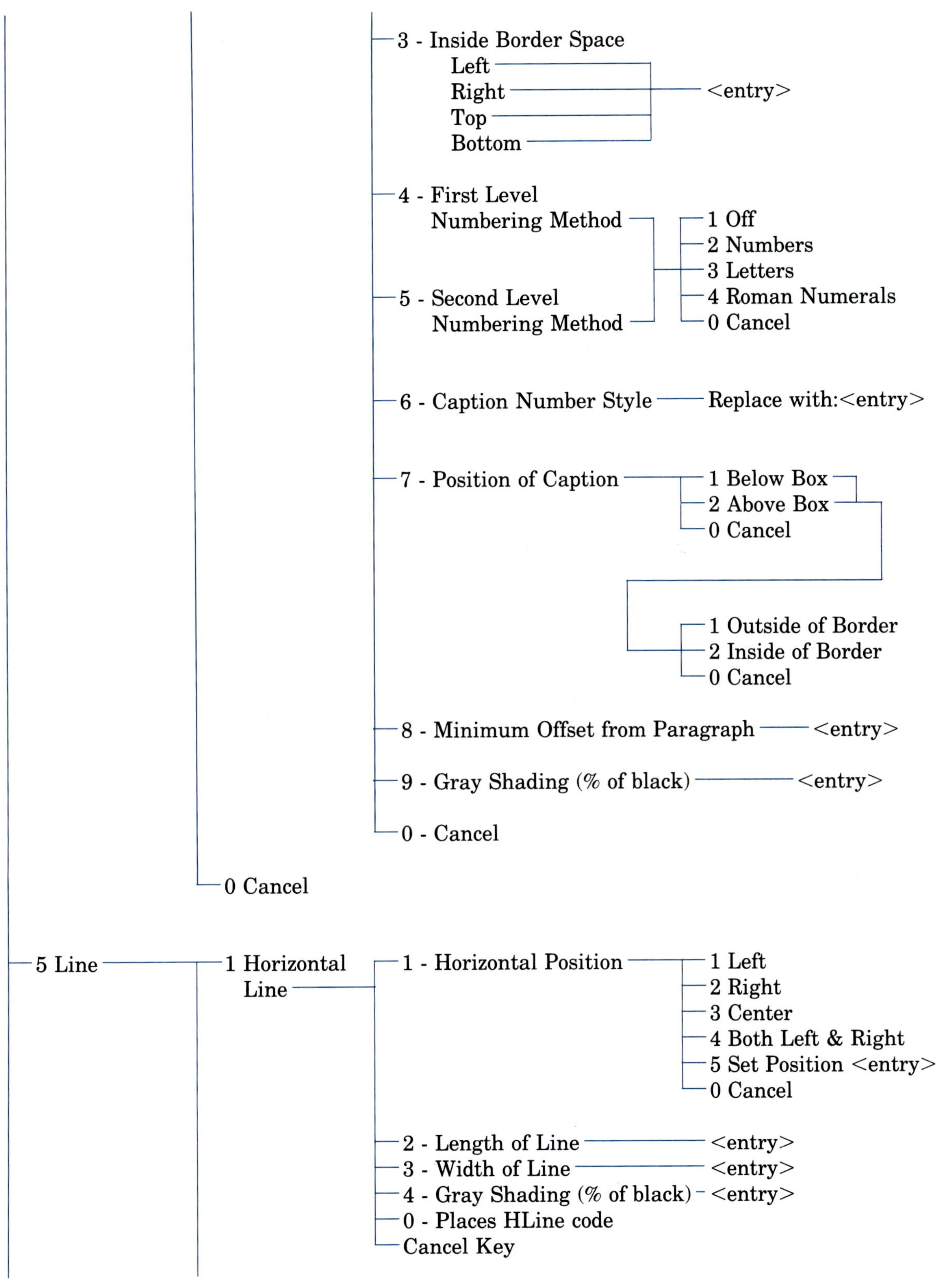
3 - Inside Border Space
Left
Right
Top
Bottom
<entry>
4 - First Level
Numbering Method
5 - Second Level
Numbering Method
1 Off
2 Numbers
3 Letters
4 Roman Numerals
0 Cancel
6 - Caption Number Style
Replace with:<entry>
7 - Position of Caption
1 Below Box
2 Above Box
0 Cancel
1 Outside of Border
2 Inside of Border
0 Cancel
8 - Minimum Offset from Paragraph
<entry>
9 - Gray Shading (% of black)
<entry>
0 - Cancel
0 Cancel
5 Line
1 Horizontal
Line
1 - Horizontal Position
1 Left
2 Right
3 Center
4 Both Left & Right
5 Set Position <entry>
0 Cancel
2 - Length of Line
<entry>
3 - Width of Line
<entry>
4 - Gray Shading (% of black)
<entry>
0 - Places HLine code
Cancel Key

CONTINUED

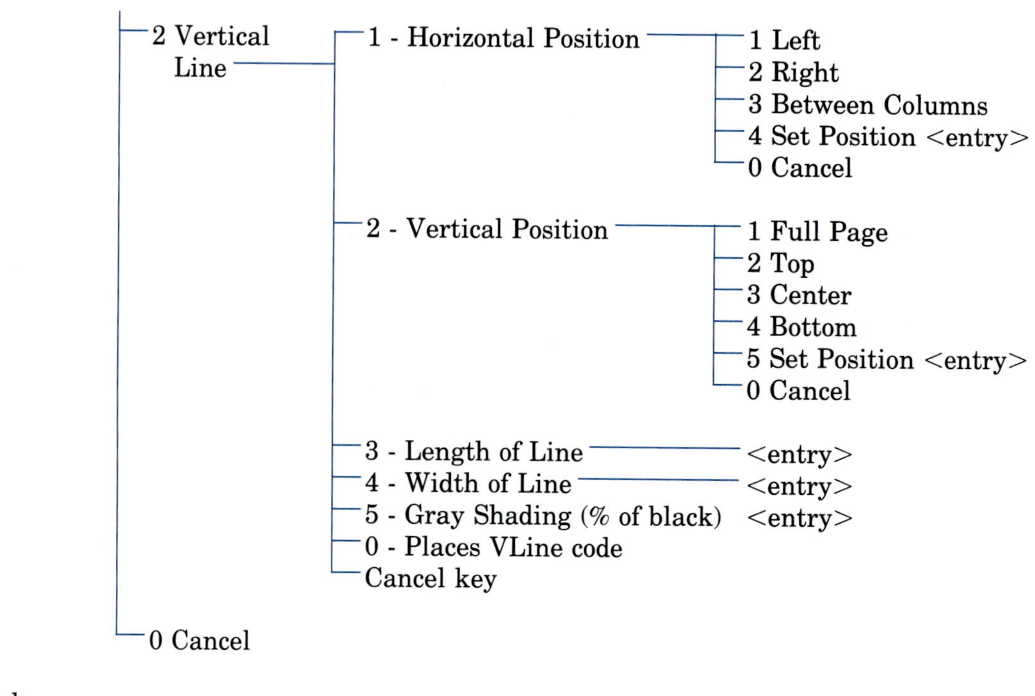

ALT-F9 GRAPHICS

The **Alt-F9** (Graphics) command allows you to present "boxes" of data (often obtained from other files) on the printed pages of a document file and to print various types of lines in a document. The four categories of boxes are Figure, Table, Text and User-Defined.

Figure Boxes

Figure boxes may be used to display graphics obtained from files generated by software other than WordPerfect. Lotus 1-2-3 .PIC files are one such type of file. Other well-known software graphics directly supported by WordPerfect are Dr. Halo, GEM, Enable, PC Paint Plus, PC Paintbrush, and Symphony.

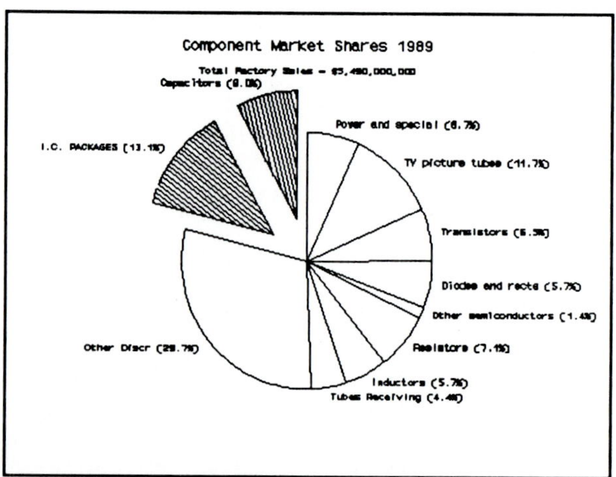

Figure 1 Western States

Table Boxes

Table boxes may be used to place tables of numbers, statistics, and other data into a document. Tables may be obtained from files created by WordPerfect or from ASCII files generated by other software and subsequently edited by WordPerfect. Edited Lotus .PRN files are a type of ASCII files.

Table I Western States

Capacitor Markets by Material Type	1989	1990
Aluminum	19.60%	16.90%
All other, fixed	2.90%	1.80%
Ceramic	16.00%	15.40%
Mica	4.90%	4.10%
Variable	4.60%	2.40%
Paper & film	32.10%	30.50%
Tantalum	21.20%	20.90%

Text Boxes

Text boxes may be used to display cameos, side bars, quotes, or other special text that you want set off from the rest of the document. The text for a Text box may be obtained from files created by WordPerfect or from ASCII files generated by other software and subsequently edited by WordPerfect.

Historical Note

The advent of Integrated Circuits occurring in the early 1970s began to impact capacitor industry sales by the mid 1980s. Market shares for paper, film, and aluminum material capacitors dropped sharply, while mica capacitors maintained a constant 5% of total market share in units.

1 Industry Cameo

User-Defined Boxes

User-defined boxes may be used to present data that is not figure, table or text in nature.

Box Labels and Numbers

The different box types have nothing to do with the data displayed within them. Table boxes may be used to display graphics and Figure boxes may be used to display tables. The box types are used by WordPerfect when it automatically labels and numbers the boxes in a document. Figure boxes are automatically labeled “Figure 1,” “Figure 2,” and so forth, and Table boxes are automatically labeled “Table I,” “Table II,” and so forth. Specifying certain boxes as Figure and other boxes as Table allows for such events as having box Figure 6 displayed on the same page as box Table IV.

The graphics box number may be referenced with an Automatic Reference within the document (see **Alt-F5,1** (Mark Text),Auto **R**ef).

Creating a Graphics Box

There are four basic steps involved in creating a graphics box.

1. Select the box type—Figure, Table, Text or User-Defined.
2. Use the **C**reate command to specify the filename for the data to be included in the box, and also to specify various settings such as size, position, labels, etc.
3. Exit the Graphics command with the **F7** (Exit) command and use the **Shift-F7,6** (Print),**V**iew Document command to preview the page.
4. Continue by editing the graphics box and/or graphics box file and viewing the document page until the desired result is achieved.

Figure
Table
Text **B**ox
User-Defined Box

The first four **Alt-F9** (Graphics) commands allow you to specify the type of graphics box that you want to create or edit.

Create   Code = [*Box Type*:*n*:*filename*;[Box Num]]

The **C**reate command produces a screen of commands used to set various specifications for the graphics box being created. Once a graphics box has been created, a graphics box code is inserted into the document. A graphics box outline (screen display) that indicates where the box will be printed can be viewed on the screen during normal editing. To view the appearance of the page without printing it, you may use the **Shift-F7,6** (Print),**V**iew Document command. To change the box type of a graphics box (Figure, Table, etc.), you can type **Alt-F9** while the **C**reate menu is on the screen, and then reenter the box type specification. To properly exit the **C**reate command you should type ↵ or **F7** (Exit). Typing **F1** (Cancel) aborts the (Graphics),**C**reate operation. The following options are available on the **C**reate menu.

Filename Use the **F**ilename command to specify the file in which the graphics box's data resides (the source file). Be sure to specify the filename extension, if any. When the **F**ilename command is used, the data in the source file is copied into the document's graphics box. If you later edit or change the data in the source file, you will need to edit the graphics box and again enter the filename to ensure that the last edited version of the source file is displayed in the document. You may create an empty graphics box by not specifying a filename. An empty graphics box can have text directly entered into it by using the **Alt-F9** (Graphics),**C**reate,**E**dit command. It is generally easier to directly enter text into the graphics box when the type is Text in nature.

Caption The **C**aption command is used to provide a label for the graphics box. The label will automatically include the box type and the number, which is generated by a [Box Num] code. You may add to the label by typing text onto the screen presented by the **C**aption command and/or delete the automatic label by backspacing over the [Box Num] code.

The position of the label relative to the graphics box is determined by the type of graphics box being created. To change the position of the label, use the (Graphics),**O**ptions,**P**osition of Caption command.

Type Default—Paragraph
The **T**ype command is used to determine how the graphics box will maintain its position in the document.

If **P**aragraph is selected, the graphics box code is placed at the beginning of the current paragraph (the paragraph in which the editing cursor is currently located). The normal editing screen will display a box outline showing the box's top side located at the line position where the editing cursor was located when the box was created. A Paragraph-type graphics box will move up and down in the document along with its associated text (the text in the paragraph that begins with the graphics box code).

If **Page** is selected, the graphics box code is inserted at the current cursor location. A Page-type graphics box will remain fixed in its position when the text around it is moved up or down. The **Page** command should be executed before any text has been entered around the graphics box.

If **Character** is selected, a graphics box code is inserted at the current cursor location; however, the graphics box outline displayed on the screen will only be one character in size (regardless of the actual size of the graphics box). A Character-type graphics box moves about in a text as its box code moves. (During normal editing, the code is treated like a single character of data.)

Vertical Position   The **V**ertical Position command is used to adjust the placement of the graphics box vertically on the page. The options for the command depend on the type (Paragraph, Page, or Character) currently specified for the graphics box.

Vertical position (Paragraph)——Offset from top of paragraph: <entry in inches>

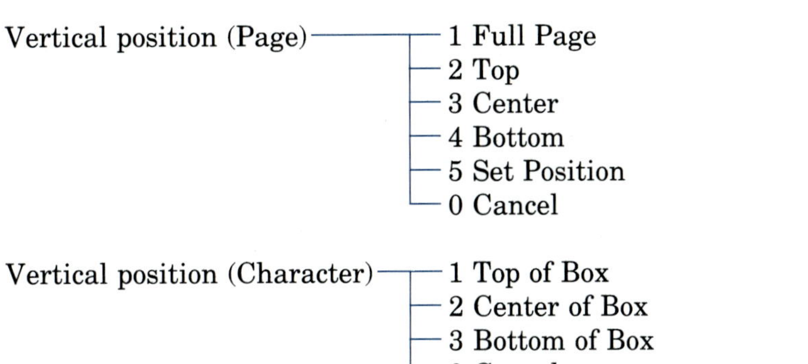

If the graphics box type is Paragraph, you may enter a positive number of inches to position the box below the line on which the graphics box code resides. 0" positions the top of the graphics box on the same line as its code.

If the graphics box type is Page, you can align the graphics box against the **T**op line of the page of text, **B**ottom of the page, **C**enter of the page, or you can **S**et Position as being *n*" below the top of the page. The option "**F**ull Page" produces a graphics box that fills the page area within the current margins. A Full Page position box code should be placed on a page by itself.

If the graphics box type is Character, you can position the box so that the text of the line on which the code resides aligns to the **T**op of Box, **C**enter of Box, or **B**ottom of Box.

Horizontal Position   The **H**orizontal Position command is used to adjust the placement of the graphics box horizontally on the page. The options for the command depend on the type (Paragraph or Page) that has been specified for the graphics box. Character-type boxes may not be positioned with the **H**orizontal Position command.

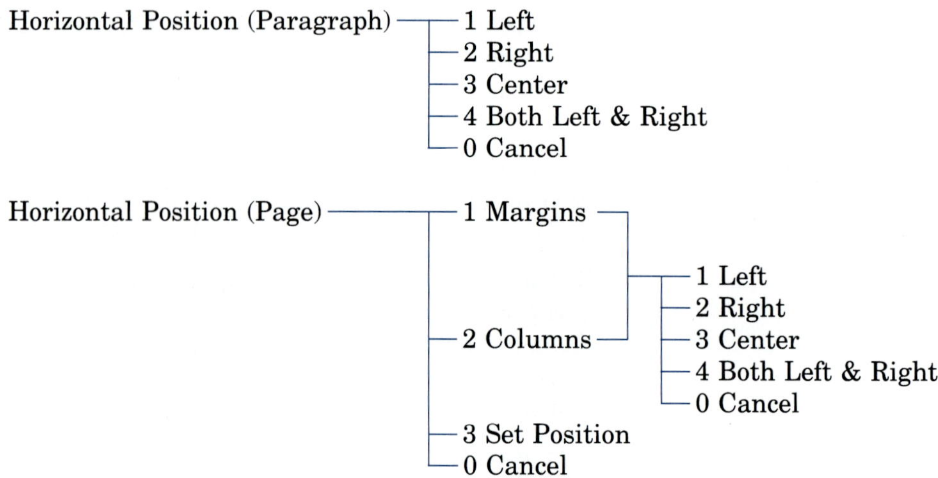

If the graphics box type is Paragraph, the **H**orizontal Position command may be used to align the box with the current **L**eft or **R**ight margins or horizontally **C**enter the box between the current left and right margins. The option **B**oth Left & Right expands the box to fill the area between the left and right margins.

If the graphics box type is Page, the **H**orizontal Position command may be used to align the box with the current **M**argins in the same manner as a Paragraph-type box is aligned. The **C**olumns command may be used to align the box (**L**eft, **R**ight, **C**enter, or **B**oth) inside of a column included in a columnar portion of text (see **Alt-F7** (Math/Columns) for more information on creating columnar text). The **S**et Position command may be used to offset the box from the left edge of the form by *n* number of inches.

Size The **S**ize command may be used to enlarge or contract a graphics box by specifying the box's dimensions (in inches). The **S**ize options include **W**idth (auto height), **H**eight (auto width), and **B**oth Width and Height. With graphic boxes containing graphics data, the first two options (**W**idth and **H**eight) allow you to change the size of the box without altering the aspect (shape) of the graphics in the box. In other words, if the **W**idth (auto height) command is used to change the width of the graphics box, WordPerfect will automatically compute the height necessary to maintain the original shape of the graphics in the box. If the box contains only text, the lines of text will be rewrapped within the box to conform to the box's new dimensions. You may use only the **W**idth (auto height) and **B**oth Width and Height commands to change the size of the graphics box containing text.

Wrap Text Around Box Default—Yes
When the **W**rap Text Around Box command is changed to "No," the text in the document overwrites the data in the graphics box when the document is printed. The box outline screen display is turned off when the command is changed to "No."

Edit

The **E**dit command may be used to alter the appearance of the data in a graphics box. If the data in the box are Text in nature or if no filename has been entered with the **C**reate command, the screen presented by the **E**dit command allows you to enter and/or edit the text in the box. You also are allowed to rotate the graphics box relative to the page on which it will be printed. To rotate a graphics box, type **Alt-F9** (Graphics) while in the **E**dit command's screen. The Rotate options include 0°, 90°, 180°, and 270°. It should be noted, however, that the printer used must support the rotated orientation of the current font or the text will not be printed.

If the data in the graphics box is Graphic in nature, an **E**dit screen similar to the following will be presented.

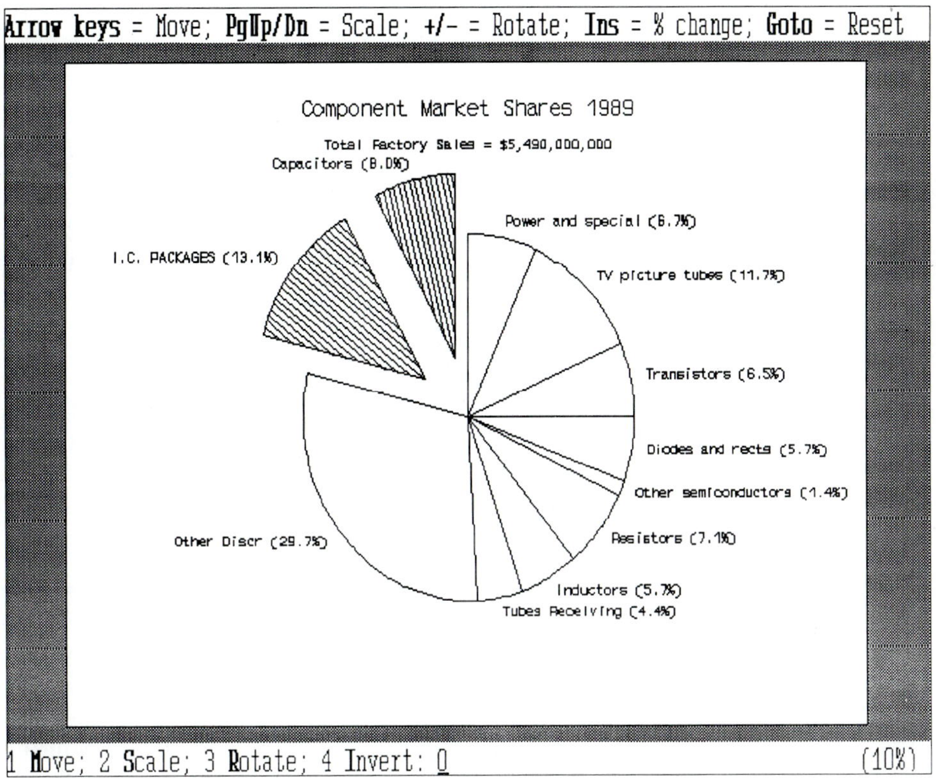

Two menus appear on the screen: one displayed across the top of the screen and one displayed across the bottom of the screen. The menus have similar functions.

The message "Arrow keys = Move" appears on the top menu. To move the graphics within the box, you may type the cursor keys ↑, ↓, →, or ←. By default, typing a direction key will move the graphics image approximately 1/6th of the graphics box's horizontal or vertical dimension. The command option "**M**ove" appears at the bottom of the screen. The **M**ove command may be used to enter the precise distance in inches (positive or negative) you want to move the graphics image horizontally and/or vertically within the graphics box.

The message "PgUp/Dn = Scale" appears on the top menu. To expand the graphics image in the box, you may type the PgUp key. To contract the size of the graphics image in the box, you may type the PgDn key. By default, typing the PgUp or PgDn keys adjusts the size of the image by 10%. The command option "**S**cale" appears at the bottom of the screen. The **S**cale command may be used to expand the image horizontally (Scale X) and/or vertically (Scale Y) by entering a precise percentage of the original size for each dimension.

The message "+/− = Rotate" appears on the top menu. To rotate the graphics image 36° counterclockwise, you may type the + (plus) key. Typing the − (minus) key rotates the image 36° in the opposite direction. The command option "**R**otate" appears at the bottom of the screen. The **R**otate command may be used to rotate the image to an absolute orientation ranging in degrees from 0° to 360°.

The message "Ins = % change" appears on the top menu. You may change the default placement values of the top menu by typing the Ins key. The current value (10% by default) is shown in the bottom right-hand corner of the **Edit** screen. Typing the Ins key presents (in order) the other possible percentage options: 5%, 1%, and 25%. Type the Ins key until the desired percentage is displayed.

The message "Goto = Reset" appears also on the top menu. Typing the Ctrl-Home (Goto) keys while in the (Graphics),**Edit** screen causes the image to be returned to its original form.

The last command, **I**nvert, occurs only on the bottom menu. The **I**nvert command may be used to reverse the colors (black and white) for the image in the graphics box.

New Number — Code = [New *box type* Num:*n*]

The **N**ew Number command is used to restart graphics box numbering within a document. To use the command, first move the cursor to where renumbering is to begin and type **Alt-F9** (Graphics). Next select the type box (Figure, Table, Text, or User-Defined) for the new numbering to affect and then enter the beginning number to use in the renumbering.

Options — Code = [*Box type* Opt]

The **O**ptions commands are designed to customize the appearance of the graphics box borders and captions for the Figure, Table, Text or User-Defined boxes occurring in the text. The **O**ptions command inserts [Fig Opt], [Tbl Opt], [Txt Opt], or [Usr Opt] codes into the document which affect the four types of graphic boxes occurring in the rest of the document. To use the **O**ptions command, first type **Alt-F9** (Graphics) and then select the type of graphics box (Figure, Table, Text, or User-Defined) for which your intended changes will be made. You then type **4** or **O** (**O**ptions). When the **O**ptions command is selected, a screen menu similar to the following is presented.

```
Options:    Figure

     1 - Border Style
              Left                             Single
              Right                            Single
              Top                              Single
              Bottom                           Single
     2 - Outside Border Space
              Left                             0.17"
              Right                            0.17"
              Top                              0.17"
              Bottom                           0.17"
     3 - Inside Border Space
              Left                             0"
              Right                            0"
              Top                              0"
              Bottom                           0"
     4 - First Level Numbering Method          Numbers
     5 - Second Level Numbering Method         Off
     6 - Caption Number Style                  [BOLD]Figure 1[bold]
     7 - Position of Caption                   Below box, Outside borders
     8 - Minimum Offset from Paragraph         0"
     9 - Gray Shading (% of black)             0%

Selection: 0
```

Border Style The **B**order Style command allows you to change the appearance of the left, right, top, and/or bottom sides of the box surrounding the Figure, Table, Text, or User-Defined graphics data. The Border Style options include **N**one or any of the following.

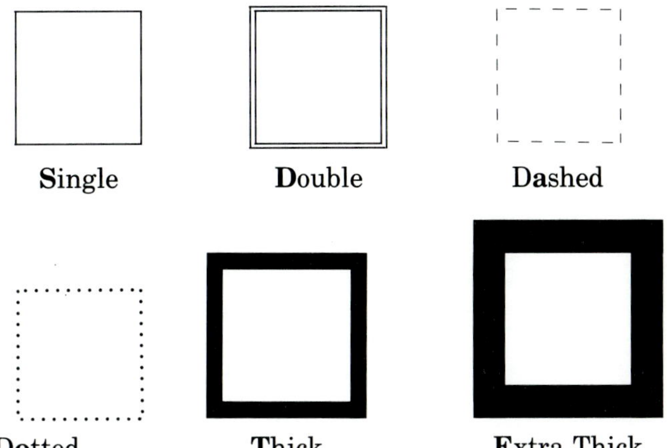

To change the border style, type **1** or **B** and then enter the appropriate command number or letter to set the border style for each side of the graphics box.

Outside Border Space The **O**utside Border Space command allows you to adjust the amount of space (margin) that occurs between text wrapped around a box and the box's left, right, top, and bottom sides.

Inside Border Space The **I**nside Border Space command allows you to adjust the amount of space (margin) that occurs between the graphics data within a graphics box and the box's left, right, top, and bottom sides.

First Level Numbering Method The **F**irst Level Number Method command may be used to change the appearance of the graphics box number generated by the **C**aption command's [Box Num] code. The choices include O**ff** (no number), **N**umbers (1, 2, 3), **L**etters (A, B, C), and **R**oman Numerals (I, II, III).

Second Level Numbering Method A second level of caption numbering may be used to allow for automatic box numbers such as "Figure 1a." To print the extended box number with the graphics box, you will need to use the **C**aption Number Style command below. The **S**econd Level Numbering Method command may be used in the same manner as the **F**irst Level Numbering Method command. Letters and Roman numerals in the second level are lower case (a, b, c, and i, ii, iii).

Caption Number Style The **C**aption Number Style command allows you to change the printed appearance of the caption generated by the **C**aption command's [Box Num] code. When the **C**aption Number Style command is used, the current style is placed on the status line for you to edit. You may change the label used (for instance, change "Figure" to "Graph" or change "Table" to "Chart"). Format codes from the (Font),**A**ppearance menu (Bold, Underline, Italic, etc.) may be included in the caption by typing the command keystrokes that would normally produce the codes. To produce a stop code for such format codes, move the editing cursor to where the stop code is to be inserted and type the appropriate command keystrokes again. To print the first level number, type a 1 where you want the automatic number to appear. To print a second level number, type a 2 where you want the number to appear.

Position of Caption The **P**osition of Caption command may be used to locate the graphic box's caption: **B**elow Box or **A**bove Box, then **O**utside of Border or **I**nside of Border.

Minimum Offset from Paragraph For Paragraph-type boxes, WordPerfect will reduce the offset from the top line (see Graphics,Create,Vertical Position) if the paragraph is too close to the bottom of the form for the box to fit on the page. The **M**inimum Offset from Paragraph command may be used to set a minimum distance from the top of the paragraph for WordPerfect to use when it starts to reduce the offset amount.

Gray Shading (% of black) The **G**ray Shading command may be used to shade the contents of graphics boxes in the document. The shading factor is entered as a percentage of black (100% = totally black, 0% = no shading).

Line

The **Alt-F9,5** (Graphics),**L**ine command allows you to create horizontal and vertical lines that will be printed with your document. The lines cannot be viewed on the screen during normal editing; however, they may be viewed on the screen using the **Shift-F7,6** (Print),**V**iew Document command.

Horizontal Line Code = [Hline:]

The **H**orizontal Line command is used to produce horizontal lines in the document. To use the command, you first move the editing cursor to where the line is to appear and then type **Alt-F9,5,1** (Graphics),**L**ine,**H**orizontal Line.

Horizontal Position Default—Left & Right
The **H**orizontal Position command may be used to position the line: **L**eft (against the left margin); **R**ight (against the right margin); **C**enter (centered between the left and right margins); **B**oth Left and Right (extending from the left margin to the right margin); or **S**et position (starting at a specified number of inches in from the left of the page and extending right).

Length of Line If the horizontal position is anything other than Left & Right you may use the **L**ength of Line command to enter the length of the line in inches.

Width of Line The **W**idth of Line command may be used to set the thickness of the line. The default value is 0.01″ wide.

Gray Shading (% of black) Default—100%
The **G**ray Shading command may be used to shade the line in the document. The shading factor is entered as a percentage of black: 100% = totally black, 0% = no shading.

Vertical Line Code = [Vline:]

The **V**ertical Line command is used to produce vertical lines in the document. With a vertical line, both the horizontal and vertical positions on the page are specified.

Horizontal Position Default—Left Margin
The **H**orizontal Position command may be used to position the line: **L**eft (against the left margin); **R**ight (against the right margin); **B**etween Columns (centered between columns in columnar text) (see **Alt-F7** (Math/Columns) for more information on columnar text); or **S**et position (a specified number of inches in from the left of the page).

Vertical Position Default—Full Page
The **V**ertical Position command may be used to position the line: **F**ull Page (extending from the top margin to the bottom margin); **T**op (against the top margin); **C**enter (centered between the top and bottom margins); **B**ottom

(against the bottom margin); and **S**et position (a specified number of inches down from the top margin).

Length of Line If the vertical position is anything other than Full Page you may use the **L**ength of Line command to enter the length of the line in inches.

Width of Line The **W**idth of Line command may be used to set the thickness of the line. The default value is 0.01″ wide.

Gray Shading (% of black) Default—100%
The **G**ray Shading command may be used to shade the line in the document. The shading factor is entered as a percentage of black: 100% = totally black, 0% = no shading.

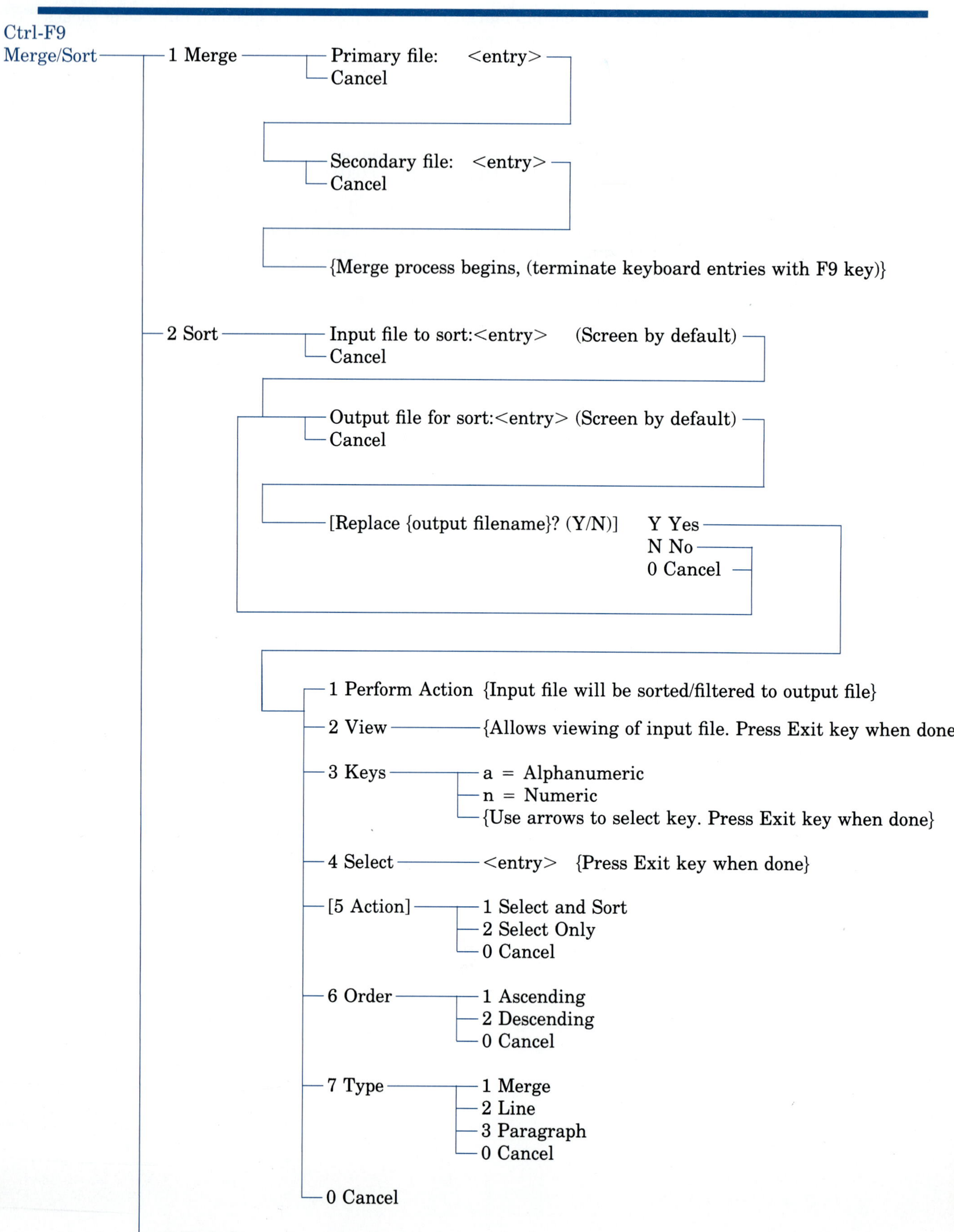

Ctrl-F9 (Merge/Sort)

CTRL-F9 MERGE/SORT

The **Ctrl-F9** (Merge/Sort) command provides two WordPerfect features that are similar to those found in database management system software. The merge feature includes operations which combine text from two or more files to produce form letters, mailing labels, contracts, and so on. The sort operations may be used to sort text within a document and conditionally select and extract text from a document.

Merge

Certain situations exist where a standard form or document (general text) needs to be filled in with specific information. When this is the case, it is possible to automatically merge the specific information into the general text to produce the desired finished document.

All merge operations require a primary file (the file containing the general text) and may require a secondary file (a file containing specific information). Specific information may be entered from the keyboard or obtained from document files during the merge operation. Merge codes are placed into the primary file. It is the merge codes that cause WordPerfect to look to the secondary file, keyboard, or document file for specific information. When a merge is completed, the appropriate specific information will be merged with the general text and the finished document(s) will be ready to print.

The following discusses the steps and merge codes involved in completing a merge operation. It begins with an example of a simple merge used to create a form letter.

Simple Merges The most common use of merge operations is to provide inside addresses and salutations for form letters. In this case, the general text (primary file) is the letter and the specific information (names and addresses of people to be included in the letter) is kept in a secondary file.

Creating a Secondary File In the example, the first step will be to create the secondary file. The information in the secondary file will include the first names, last names, phone numbers, and complete addresses of three people.

Records in a Secondary File The information in the secondary file is organized like data in a database. Together, the four separate information items for each person (first and last names, phone number, and address) constitute a record of data. Records in a secondary file are separated from each other with a ^E merge code and a hard page code [HPg]. The **Shift-F9,E** (Merge Codes),**^E** command inserts a ^E code and a [HPg] code into the file.

Fields in a Secondary File The separate information items for each record (first and last names, phone number, etc.) are entered into fields within the record and are separated from each other with a ^R merge code and a hard return [HRt]. The **F9** (Merge R) command inserts a ^R merge code and a hard return into the file.

The finished secondary file has the following form.

```
Mr.^R                          <---- Field #1
David^R                        <---- Field #2
Cupra^R                        <---- Field #3
(503) 229-3767^R               <---- Field #4
9100 S.W. Alder Street^R       <---- Field #5
Portland, OR 97221^R           <---- Field #6
^E                        <--------- End of record #1
=========================================================
Ms.^R                          <---- Field #1
Sharon^R                       <---- Field #2
Colson^R                       <---- Field #3
^R                             <---- Field #4
8766 N.W. Everett^R            <---- Field #5
Portland, OR 97207^R           <---- Field #6
^E                        <--------- End of record #2
=========================================================
Dr.^R                          <---- Field #1
Michael^R                      <---- Field #2
Jerich^R                       <---- Field #3
(503) 244-7163^R               <---- Field #4
178 S.W. 4th Ave               <---- Field #5
Apartment 27G^R
Portland, OR 97001^R           <---- Field #6
^E                        <--------- End of record #3
=========================================================
```

The fields in the secondary file may be referred to by their number. Notice that Field #3 is the field that holds the last name for every person (each record) in the file. The field#/item relationship must be maintained in the secondary file. If an item is not available for a given record, as is the case with Ms. Colson's phone number (Field #4, record #2), an empty field must be entered there. However, the fields may be variable in length, as is the case with the address (Field #5) for Dr. Jerich (record #3).

The next step in the example is to save the file under the filename PROSPCTS and clear the document from RAM with the Exit command.

Creating a Primary File The primary file in the example will be the form letter into which the names and addresses from the secondary file will be merged. Fields of data from the secondary file are inserted into the primary file at the locations where ^F*n*^ merge codes appear. The ^F indicates Field and the *n*^ indicates the Field number. For instance, putting the merge code ^F3^ into the primary file will cause the last names in the example secondary file to be inserted at the position where the ^F3^ merge code occurs.

The ^F*n*^ codes may be generated by moving the cursor to the appropriate location in the primary file and typing **Shift-F9,F** (Merge Codes),**^F**. You then answer the "Field:" prompt by entering the appropriate field number.

If you want to avoid blank lines in the finished document caused by empty fields in the secondary file, you may enter the ^F code as ^F*n*?^.

When the primary file is finished it might appear something like the following.

```
                    Vista Ridge Townhouses

^F1^ ^F2^ ^F3^
^F5^
^F6^

Dear ^F2^,

Thank you, ^F2^, for your recent visit and tour of the grounds at
Vista Ridge Townhouses.

We have reviewed your references and are pleased to inform you that
we are able to offer any of our available units for your immediate
occupancy.

We appreciate your patience and look forward to meeting you again.
If you have any questions we can answer at this time, please call
me.

Sincerely,


Jerome Smith
Manager
                                           Doc 1 Pg 1 Ln 1" Pos 1"
```

Once the primary file is created, it is saved onto the disk (under the filename ACCEPTED in this example) and the document screen is cleared with the Exit command.

The final step in completing the simple merge is to type **Ctrl-F9,1** (Merge/Sort),**M**erge and then answer the "Primary file:" prompt by entering ACCEPTED and the "Secondary file:" prompt by entering PROSPCTS.

When the merge operation is completed, a document will appear on the screen consisting of three form letters, each separated by hard page codes automatically inserted by the merge feature. Each letter will have a different inside address and salutation. The first such letter appears as follows.

```
                    Vista Ridge Townhouses

Mr. David Cupra
9100 S.W. Alder Street
Portland, OR 97221

Dear David,

Thank you, David, for your recent visit and tour of the grounds at
Vista Ridge Townhouses.

We have reviewed your references and are pleased to inform you that
we are able to offer any of our available units for your immediate
occupancy.

We appreciate your patience and look forward to meeting you again.
If you have any questions we can answer at this time, please call
me.

Sincerely,


Jerome Smith
Manager
                                          Doc 1 Pg 1 Ln 1" Pos 1"
```

The file may then be printed.

Other Merge Codes There are several merge codes available with WordPerfect. For a complete list and brief description of merge codes, see **Shift-F9** (Merge Codes). The following discusses some of the more important merge codes and how they may be used.

^C

The **^C** code pauses the merge to allow text to be entered from the keyboard. It may be used to customize certain portions of a document or, in conjunction with other codes, to direct the merge process. After entering the text from the keyboard, type **F9** (Merge R) to continue the merge.

^D

The **^D** merge code may be placed in the primary file to automatically insert the current DOS system date into the text. The date will be inserted as text in the current date format (see **Shift-F5** (Date/Outline) for information on setting date formats).

^N

The **^N** code is used to create a unique record (called a *header* record) in a secondary file. The header record assigns names to the fields in the database. The header record must be the first record in the file, and must begin with a **^N** merge code and end with a **^R** and then **^E** merge code. The fields in the header record hold the names for the fields in the database. Each field in the header record must be individually bolded and end with a hard return [HRt] code. A header record for the example database might appear as follows.

Including a header record in the secondary file allows you to reference fields from the primary file by using field names instead of field numbers. For example, the text in a primary file may have the inside address and salutation

^Ftitle^F ^Ffstname^F ^Flstname^F
^Faddress^F
^Fcity^F

Dear ^Ffstname^

^O*message*^O

The **^O** merge code is generally used with other merge codes in the primary file. It displays a message on the status line at the bottom of the screen. Examples of how **^O** may be used with other codes include the following.

^O Enter tenant's name ^O^C   Displays the "Enter tenant's name" message at the bottom of the screen and then pauses the merge at the position of the ^C merge code to allow text to be entered from the keyboard.

^O Enter filename to merge ^P^C^P^O   Displays the "Enter filename to merge" message at the bottom of the screen and then pauses between two ^P codes for the filename to be entered from the keyboard.

^P*filename*^P

The **^P** merge code is used to insert a document file into the text. The code is most useful when used in conjunction with a **^C** merge code (^P^C^P) to allow the filename to be entered from the keyboard during the merge.

^Q

The **^Q** merge code stops the merge at the point where the code occurs. A **^Q** code may be placed in the primary or secondary file.

^S*filename*^S

Placed in a primary file, the **^S** merge code may be used to switch to a different secondary file during the merge.

^T

Used in the primary file, the **^T** merge code sends all previously merged text to the printer.

Sort

The **Ctrl-F9** (Merge/Sort) command may be used to sort text or conditionally extract (Select) text from a document. When text is sorted, it appears ascending or descending in alphabetical or numeric order. When text is selected, only certain text (text which passes a condition) will appear.

Input/Output Files When sorting or selecting text, WordPerfect uses the following approach.

input file ⟶ process ⟶ output file

The text to be sorted or selected from exists in the input file. During the sort or select operation, a copy of the data in the input file is made first. The copy then is sorted and/or selected (processed), and the processed data next are written to the output file. If the output file is specified as being the same as the input file, the original data in the input file will be overwritten by the processed data.

When the data to be processed exists as a portion of text within a larger document, the recommended procedure is as follows: (1) retrieve the file; (2) block the portion of text to be processed; (3) type **Ctrl-F9,2** (Merge/Sort),**S**ort to begin the sort or select operation. The block of text is treated as both the input and output file by the **S**ort command.

Because of the overwriting nature of the process, it is highly recommended that you save or back up your files before attempting to complete a sort or select operation.

Sort/Select Keys Keys are the data items upon which WordPerfect sorts text, or they are the data items used in logical expressions upon which WordPerfect selects text. Keys are specified by their location in the text and by their data type, string or numeric (WordPerfect refers to string data as being "alphanumeric").

There are three different text formats that may be sorted or selected: Line, Merge, or Paragraph. In each case, the text is organized into records (the units of text which will be sorted or selected).

Line Format In Line format text, the records to sort or select are arranged on lines with fields of data (data items) occurring at tab stops (see **Shift-F8,1,8** (Format),**L**ine,**T**ab Stops for more information on setting tab stops). Each line of data is considered to be a record, and each data item is considered to be a field of data. The data items are entered by using the Tab key or **F4** (Indent) command to separate them from each other, as shown in the following example.

Field 1	Field 2	Field 3	Field 4	Field 5	Field 6
Pratt John	225-1234	M	06/22/82	1949.00	200.00
Smoler Ellen	225-3212	F	09/15/83	1650.00	300.00
Jones David	292-3832	M	06/15/82	1550.00	25.00
Sill Sally	224-4321	F	02/15/84	1507.00	0.00
	↑	↑	↑	↑	↑
	L	**L**	**L**	**D**	**D**

In the example above, Left and Decimal tab stops were set, and the data items for name, phone, gender, date, salary, and account were entered, with the Tab key used to align the data items at the appropriate tab stops.

The keys for Line format text are defined by data type (string or numeric), the field number where they occur, and the word number within the field where they occur. For instance, if you wanted to sort or select the example text by salary, you would define the appropriate key as numeric, field #5, word #1. If you wanted to sort or select the text by first names, you would specify the key as alphanumeric, field #1, word #2.

Merge Format With Merge format text, records exist in a secondary file and are separated by ^E merge codes. Fields are separated by ^R merge codes. See **Ctrl-F9** (Merge/Sort),Merge Operations for more information on secondary merge files. The following is an example of the use of ^E merge codes.

```
Mr. ^R                          <------ Field #1
David ^R                        <------ Field #2
Cupra^R                         <------ Field #3
(503) 229-3767^R                <------ Field #4
9100 S.W. Alder Street^R        <------ Field #5
Portland, OR 97221^R            <------ Field #6
^E                   <---------------- End of record #1
==========================================================
Ms. ^R                          <------ Field #1
Sharon^R                        <------ Field #2
Colson^R                        <------ Field #3
^R                              <------ Field #4
8766 N.W. Everett^R             <------ Field #5
Portland, OR 97207^R            <------ Field #6
^E                   <---------------- End of record #2
==========================================================
```

The keys for Merge format text are defined by data type (string or numeric), the field number where they occur, and the word number within the field where they occur. For instance, if you wanted to sort or select the example merge text by last name, you would define the appropriate key as alphanumeric, field #3, word #1. If you wanted to sort or select the merge text by ZIP codes, you would specify the key as alphanumeric, field #6, word #3.

Paragraph Format In Paragraph format, the record is considered to be the text occurring between two or more hard returns [HRt]s. The keys used to sort or select paragraphs are defined by the line in which they occur, the field in which they occur (if Tabs or Indents are used they define fields such as Field #1 at [TAB] or [Indent] #1, and so on), and the word number in the line or field of the paragraph where they occur. For instance, if you wanted to sort or select paragraphs by the first word of the first line in each paragraph, and the first line of each paragraph is indented, you would specify the key as alphanumeric, line #1, field #2, word #1.

Sorting/Selecting Text You begin to sort or select text by making sure that there are current backup copies of the text available. You next decide if the text needs to be blocked. If so, you block the text. You then type **Ctrl-F9** (Merge/Sort). If text is blocked, the Sort command menu screen will appear next.

If text is not blocked, you will need to type **2** or **S** (**S**ort) and then answer the Input file/Output file prompts by entering the filenames or typing ↵ for Screen. Selecting Screen is the same as specifying the current document as the input and/or output file. After completing the steps, the Sort command menu screen will appear. In the following examples, a line format blocked portion of text will be used. The records to sort and/or select from concern employees, and the fields within the records are last name/first name, phone number, date hired, salary, and amount on personal account with the company. The Sort command menu screen appears as follows.

```
Smoler Ellen   225-3212  F   09/15/83   1650.00    300.00
Pratt John     225-1238  M   06/22/84   1949.00    200.00
Jones David    292-3832  M   06/15/82   1550.00     25.00
Sill Sally     224-4321  F   02/15/84   1507.00      0.00
Knat Michael   221-1235  M   09/15/80   1800.00    125.00
Smith Paul     223-8251  M   11/15/81   1700.00    350.00
Martins Mary   222-2123  F   11/01/85   1600.00    200.50
Beam Sandy     22-6912   F   02/15/86   1450.00    175.00
Johnson Frank  223-7928  M   03/20/86   1500.00      0.00

                                     Doc 2 Pg 1 Ln 1" Pos 1"
[          ▲         ▲   ▲           ▲         ▲        ]
------------------------------ Sort by Line ------------------------------

Key Typ Field Word          Key Typ Field Word          Key Typ Field Word
 1   a    1     1            2                           3
 4                           5                           6
 7                           8                           9
Select


Action                      Order                      Type
Sort                        Ascending                  Line sort

1 Perform Action; 2 View; 3 Keys; 4 Select; 5 Action; 6 Order; 7 Type: 0
```

A portion of the blocked text is displayed at the top of the screen. The Sort command menu screen begins with a ruler line which displays the current tab stops. Beneath the ruler line is an area used to define keys and give descriptions of the four current Sort screen settings: Select, Action, Order, and Type (of Sort). The Sort command menu appears at the bottom of the screen.

Perform Action

The **P**erform Action command is used to execute the sort or select operation after all of the appropriate sort/select settings have been made.

View

The **V**iew command may be used to scroll through the text at the top of the screen without leaving the Sort menu screen. The **F7** (Exit) command is used to exit the **V**iew command.

Keys

The **K**eys command is used to define the keys to be used in a sort or select operation. When the **K**eys command is executed, the cursor jumps to the key definition area of the Sort menu screen and you are allowed to edit the key definition displayed there. The first Sort key is defined, by default, as alphanumeric, field #1, word #1.

There are nine key definitions available. If the action for which the keys are being defined is Sort, the sort order will be primary sort on key #1, secondary sort on key #2, and so on. In the example above, if you wanted the records to be sorted first by male/female and then by salary amounts within those two categories, you would set key #1 to a, 3, 1 (alphanumeric, field #3, word #1) and key #2 to n, 5, 1 (numeric, field #5, word #1).

Select

The **S**elect command is used to extract records of text that meet certain criteria. When the select process is over, only those records meeting the criteria will appear in the output file or on the screen. To select records, you must first define all keys that will be used in the criteria. You then type **4** or **S** (**S**elect) and enter the logical expression to be used as the select criteria. The WordPerfect operators for such expressions include the following.

Relational		Logical	
=	Equal	+	OR
<	Less than	*	AND
>	Greater than		
<=	Less than or equal to		
>=	Greater than or equal to		
<>	Not equal to		

In the example, if you wanted to extract those records for men with salaries greater than or equal to $1,650.00, you would first define the two keys for gender and salary. Here, key #8 will be defined for gender as a, 3, 1 (alphanumeric, field #3, word #1) and key #9 will be defined for salary as n, 5, 1 (numeric, field #5, word #1).

You then may type **4** or **S** (**S**elect) and the cursor will jump to the Select description area on the screen for you to enter the criteria. The criteria is entered in the form

key8=M * key9>=1650

Once the **S**elect command has been used to enter the criteria, the action to perform automatically becomes Select rather than Sort. To return to sorting, you must type **4** or **S** (**S**elect) and delete the criteria shown on the screen (use the Del, Backspace key, or Ctrl-End keys to complete the deletion).

Action

When a select criteria exists, the **A**ction command may be used to **S**elect and Sort or Select **O**nly. With **S**elect and Sort, the extracted records are sorted on the currently defined keys. With Select **O**nly, the records are only extracted.

Order

The **O**rder command may be used to set the sort order to **A**scending or **D**escending.

Type

The **T**ype command is used to specify the format type, **M**erge, **L**ine, or **P**aragraph, for the data being sorted or selected. The current type is displayed under the ruler line of the Sort menu screen.

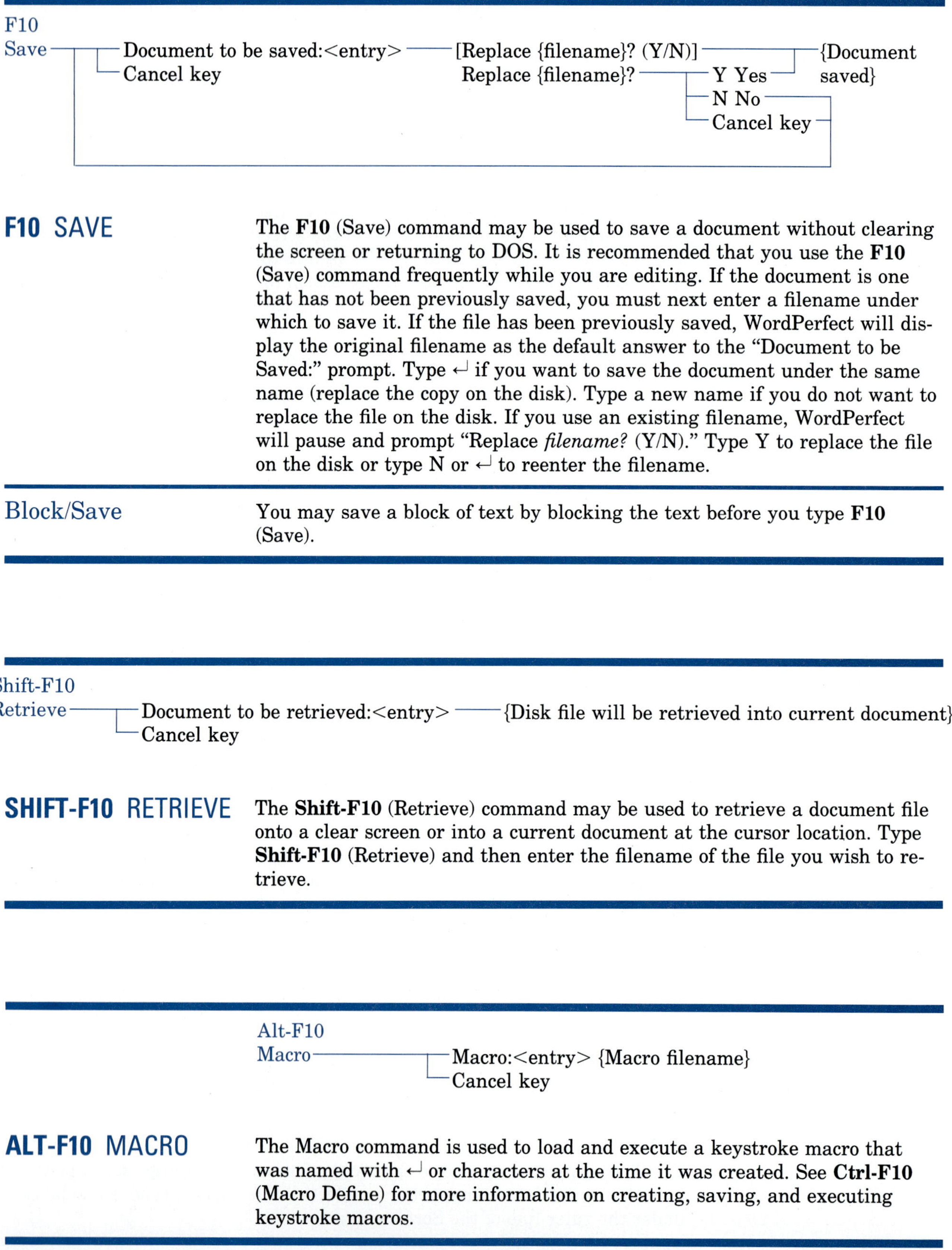

F10
Save
- Document to be saved:<entry> — [Replace {filename}? (Y/N)] / Replace {filename}?
  - Y Yes — {Document saved}
  - N No
  - Cancel key
- Cancel key

F10 SAVE

The **F10** (Save) command may be used to save a document without clearing the screen or returning to DOS. It is recommended that you use the **F10** (Save) command frequently while you are editing. If the document is one that has not been previously saved, you must next enter a filename under which to save it. If the file has been previously saved, WordPerfect will display the original filename as the default answer to the "Document to be Saved:" prompt. Type ↵ if you want to save the document under the same name (replace the copy on the disk). Type a new name if you do not want to replace the file on the disk. If you use an existing filename, WordPerfect will pause and prompt "Replace *filename?* (Y/N)." Type Y to replace the file on the disk or type N or ↵ to reenter the filename.

Block/Save

You may save a block of text by blocking the text before you type **F10** (Save).

Shift-F10
Retrieve
- Document to be retrieved:<entry> — {Disk file will be retrieved into current document}
- Cancel key

SHIFT-F10 RETRIEVE

The **Shift-F10** (Retrieve) command may be used to retrieve a document file onto a clear screen or into a current document at the cursor location. Type **Shift-F10** (Retrieve) and then enter the filename of the file you wish to retrieve.

Alt-F10
Macro
- Macro:<entry> {Macro filename}
- Cancel key

ALT-F10 MACRO

The Macro command is used to load and execute a keystroke macro that was named with ↵ or characters at the time it was created. See **Ctrl-F10** (Macro Define) for more information on creating, saving, and executing keystroke macros.

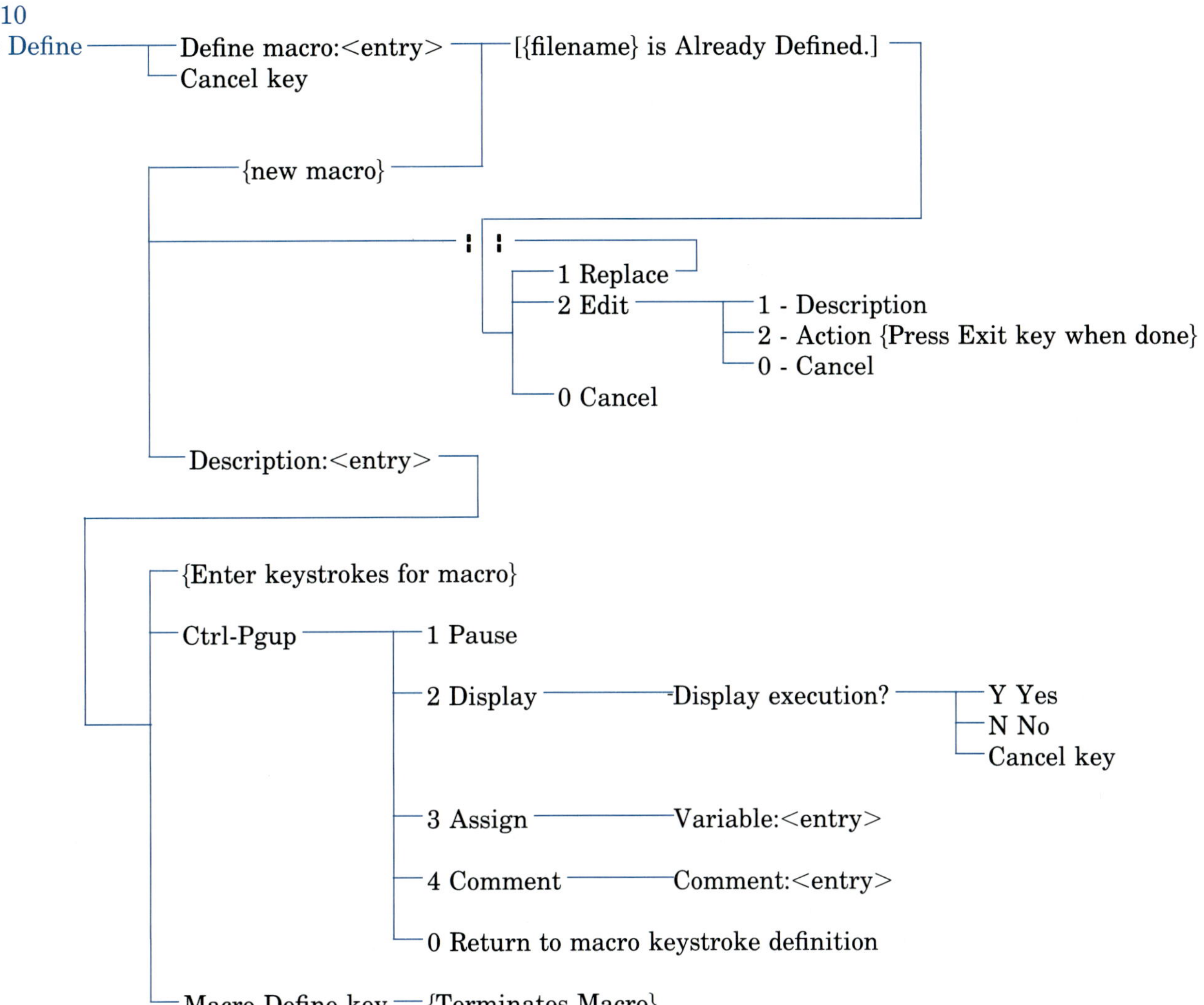

CTRL-F10 MACRO DEFINE

When using WordPerfect, you use three basic types of keystrokes: character keystrokes, which enter text into the document; keystroke commands, which perform certain operations (such as Ctrl-End to delete the line right); and menu keystrokes, which invoke WordPerfect's command mode.

Macros are a time-saving feature of WordPerfect. A macro is a collection of keystrokes, saved by WordPerfect, that may be executed (automatically re-typed) at any time. The keystrokes in the macro may be character, key-stroke command, and/or command menu in nature.

To explain how keystroke macros may be created, suppose that you have created a document within which there are several key words you now wish to italicize. To italicize the words in the document you use the following steps.

1. Move the cursor to the beginning of the word and type **Alt-F4** (Block).
2. Type Ctrl-Right (to jump the cursor to the other side of the word, thus blocking the word).
3. Type **Ctrl-F8,2,4** (Font),**A**ppearance,**I**talc (the set of keystrokes used to insert the start and stop codes for italics ([ITALC] and [italc]).

Notice that, except for the keystrokes used to move the cursor to the word in step 1, all other keystrokes are exactly the same for any word you may want to italicize. In other words, the remaining keystrokes are systematic. Large groups of systematic keystrokes are prime candidates for becoming keystroke macros.

Steps in Creating and Using Keystroke Macros

There are five basic steps required to create a keystroke macro.

1. Begin defining the macro by typing **Ctrl-F10** (Macro Define).
2. Enter a name and description for the macro.
3. Type the keystrokes you want saved in the macro.
4. End defining the macro by typing **Ctrl-F10** (Macro Define) again.
5. Edit the macro, if necessary.

How you execute a macro (cause WordPerfect to automatically retype the keystrokes within it) depends on the name you give the macro in step 2 above.

Naming and Using a Macro

If you enter a name consisting of up to eight characters, the macro is saved on the disk in the Keyboard/Macro Files subdirectory with a .WPM filename extension (see **Shift-F1,7** (Setup),Location of Auxiliary Files for more information). To execute the macro, type **Alt-F10** (Macro) and then enter the filename of the macro.

Alt-letter

If you name the macro by holding down the Alt key and typing a letter key (A to Z), the macro is saved on the disk in the Keyboard/Macro Files subdirectory under the filename ALT*letter* with a .WPM extension. To execute the macro you simply type Alt-*letter*. For instance, if you named the macro Alt-A (filename is ALTA.WPM), you would later type **Alt-A** to execute it.

Enter Key

If you name the macro by typing ↵, the macro is saved on the disk in the Keyboard/Macro Files subdirectory under the filename and extension WP{WP}.WPM. Only one such macro may be in the current Keyboard/Macro Files subdirectory at one time. To execute the macro, you type **Alt-F10** (Macro) and then ↵.

Defining a Macro

To begin defining a macro type **Ctr1-F10** (Macro Define). A "Define macro:" prompt will appear on the status line. At this point enter the macro name of your choice. If the macro name entered is not the current name for another macro, the prompt "Description:" will next appear on the status line. Here you are allowed to enter a short (39-character) description (documentation) for the macro. After the description is entered, a blinking "Macro Def" prompt appears on the status line. At this point, the keystrokes made after the prompt become the content of the macro.

Entering the Keystrokes for a Macro

To enter the keystrokes for a macro simply type them as you would during normal editing. For instance, to enter the keystrokes to italicize the current word you would type **Alt-F4,**Ctrl-Left,**Ctrl-F8,2,4** ((Block),Word Left,(Font),**A**ppearance,**I**talc).

The Ctrl-PgUp Keystroke

While entering the keystrokes for a macro in the fashion described above, the Ctrl-PgUp keystroke may be used to present a menu of optional changes that may be made to the macro. If you are in the normal editing mode, the Ctrl-PgUp keystroke presents a menu consisting of **P**ause, **D**isplay, **A**ssign, and **C**omment. If you are in a command mode, the menu consists of **P**ause and **D**isplay.

Pause

The **P**ause command may be used to cause the macro to temporarily stop its execution so that you may enter text or move the cursor. A pause in a macro is ended when the user types ↵.

In the example, if you wanted to create a macro that could be used to italicize either a word, letter in a word, or paragraph, you could enter a pause after the **Alt-F4** (Block) keystroke in the macro. That is, the keystrokes to enter into the macro would become **Alt-F4**,Ctrl-PgUp,**1**,↵,**Ctrl-F8,2,4** ((Block),Pause,(Font),**A**ppearance,**I**talc).

To use the macro first move the cursor to the beginning of the text you want to italicize and then begin the execution of the macro. After the macro starts the block operation (types **Alt-F4** (Block)) it pauses for you to move the cursor, thus expanding the block to cover whatever text you want to italicize. When the appropriate text is blocked, you type ↵, and the remaining keystrokes in the macro are executed.

Display

Default—No (Off)
The **D**isplay command may be used to cause WordPerfect to display all menus, and other items that would normally be displayed during the execution of the macro's keystrokes.

Assign

The **A**ssign command may be used to pause the macro for the user to assign a value to a WordPerfect variable. The command is related to a group of commands collectively referred to by WordPerfect as being Advanced Macro commands. See the WordPerfect manual or Help screens for more information.

Comment

The **C**omment command allows keystrokes which you do not want to be executed to be included in the macro. The command is most useful for entering short sections of documentation into the macro.

Finishing the Macro's Definition

Once all of the keystrokes have been entered into the macro, type **Ctrl-F10** (Macro Define) again to stop defining the macro.

Editing a Macro

WordPerfect provides a means to edit the keystrokes in a macro. To edit a macro, type **Ctrl-F10** (Macro Define) and then enter the name of the macro you wish to edit. When the Macro Define command is used to define a macro that already exists, WordPerfect will prompt "*macro name*.WPM is Already Defined. 1 **R**eplace; 2 **E**dit:." To edit the macro, you type **2** or **E** (**E**dit). The

Ctrl-F10 (Macro Define),**E**dit command will present a screen similar to the following.

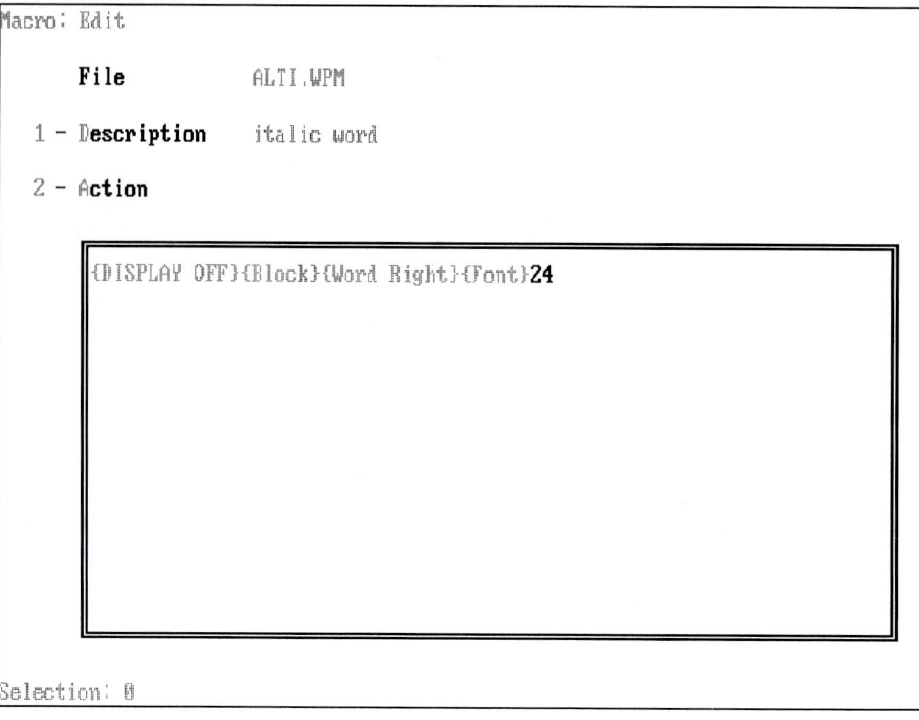

The two options of the **Ctrl-F10** (Macro Define),**E**dit command include **D**escription and **A**ction.

Description

The **D**escription command may be used to edit the macro's description. Type **1** or **D** (**D**escription) and edit the 39-character space allocated for the description. When finished, type ↵.

Action

The **A**ction command may be used to edit the keystrokes in the macro. Type **2** or **A** (**A**ction) and an editing cursor will appear in the box holding the macro keystrokes. To delete a keystroke you may use the Backspace or Del keys in the same manner as during normal editing. To insert keyboard characters such as "1" or "F" you may move the cursor to where the characters are to be inserted and then type the characters. To insert nonprintable keystrokes such as {Left} and {Enter} (← and ↵) first move the cursor to where the keystrokes are to appear in the macro and then type **Ctrl-F10.** Next, type the keystrokes to be inserted in the macro. When finished, type **Ctrl-10** again to return to normal editing of the macro. When finished editing the macro you type **F7** (Exit) and then ↵ to return to normal document editing.

WORDPERFECT CODES

The following is a list of the WordPerfect codes that may appear on the Reveal Codes screen.

Code	Meaning
[ ]	Hard Space
[-]	Hyphen
-	Soft Hyphen
/	Cancel Hyphenation
[Adv]	Advance
[Align]	Tab Align
[Block]	Beginning of Block
[Block Pro]	Block Protection
[Bold]	Bold
[Box Num]	Caption in Graphics Box
[C/A/FLRt]	End of Tab Align or Flush Right
[Center Pg]	Center Page Top to Bottom
[Cntr]	Center Line
[Cndl EOP]	Conditional End of Page
[Col Def]	Column Definition
[Col Off]	End of Text Columns
[Col On]	Beginning of Text Columns
[Comment]	Document Comment
[Color]	Print Color
[Date]	Date/Time function
[Dbl Und]	Double Underline
[Decml Char]	Decimal Character/Thousands Separator
[Def Mark:Index]	Index Definition
[Def Mark:Listn]	List Definition
[Def Mark:ToC]	Table of Contents Definition
[End Def]	End of Index, List, or Table of Contents
[End Opt]	Endnote Options
[Endnote]	Endnote
[Endnote Placement]	Endnote Placement
[Ext Large]	Extra Large Print
[Figure]	Figure Box
[Fig Opt]	Figure Box Options
[Fine]	Fine Print
[Flsh Rt]	Flush Right
[Footnote]	Footnote
[Font]	Base Font
[Footer]	Footer
[Force]	Force Odd/Even Page
[Form]	Form (Printer Selection)
[Ftn Opt]	Footnote/Endnote Options
[Full Form]	Table of Authorities, Full Form
[HLine]	Horizontal Line
[Header]	Header
[HPg]	Hard Page
[HRt]	Hard Return
[Hyph]	Hyphenation
[HZone]	Hyphenation Zone
[>Indent]	Indent
[>Indent<]	Left/Right Indent
[Index]	Index Entry

[ISRt]	Invisible Soft Return
[Italc]	Italics
[Just]	Right Justification
[Just Lim]	Word/Letter Spacing Justification Limits
[Kern]	Kerning
[L/R Mar]	Left and Right Margins
[Lang]	Language
[Large]	Large Print
[Line Height]	Line Height
[Ln Num]	Line Numbering
[<Mar Rel]	Left Margin Release
[Mark:List]	List Entry
[Mark:ToC]	Table of Contents Entry
[Math Def]	Definition of Math Columns
[Math Off]	End of Math
[Math On]	Beginning of Math
!	Formula Calculation
t	Subtotal Entry
+	Calculate Subtotal
T	Total Entry
=	Calculate Total
*	Calculate Grand Total
[Note Num]	Footnote/Endnote Reference
[Outln]	Outline (attribute)
[Ovrstk]	Overstrike
[Paper Sz/Typ]	Paper Size and Type
[Par Num]	Paragraph Number
[Par Num Def]	Paragraph Numbering Definition
[Pg Num]	New Page Number
[Pg Numbering]	Page Number Position
[Ptr Cmnd]	Printer Command
[RedLn]	Redline
[Ref]	Reference (Automatic Reference)
[Set End Num]	Set New Endnote Number
[Set Fig Num]	Set New Figure Box Number
[Set Ftn Num]	Set New Footnote Number
[Set Tab Num]	Set New Table Box Number
[Set Txt Num]	Set New Text Box Number
[Set Usr Num]	Set New User-Defined Box Number
[Shadw]	Shadow
[Sm Cap]	Small Caps
[Small]	Small Print
[SPg]	Soft New Page
[SRt]	Soft Return
[StkOut]	Strikeout
[Style]	Styles
[Subdoc]	Subdocument (Master Documents)
[SubScrpt]	Subscript
[SuprScrpt]	Superscript
[Suppress]	Suppress Page Format
[T/B Mar]	Top and Bottom Margins
[Tab]	Tab

[Tab Opt]	Table Box Options
[Tab Set]	Tab Set
[Table]	Table Box
[Target]	Target (Auto Reference)
[Text Box]	Text Box
[Txt Opt]	Text Box Options
[Und]	Underlining
[Undrln]	Underline Spaces/Tabs
[Usr Box]	User-Defined Box
[Usr Opt]	User-Defined Box Options
[VLine]	Vertical Line
[Vry Large]	Very Large Print
[W/O]	Widow/Orphan
[Wrd/Ltr Spacing]	Word and Letter Spacing

Lotus 1-2-3
Version 2.01

INTRODUCTION

Lotus 1-2-3® is an applications software designed for creating formula-based models called *spreadsheets*. In addition to its spreadsheet features, Lotus 1-2-3 has features that provide the user with the ability to create graphs and perform basic database management operations. It also has software that incorporates a built-in programming language whose programs are called *macros*. Lotus 1-2-3 has some word processing capabilities.

This module begins with a brief discussion of Lotus 1-2-3's basic spreadsheet concepts. It continues with a set of introductory tutorial lessons that present the basic operations used to create, format, and print a Lotus spreadsheet. The initial tutorial lessons focus on the essential concepts and operations involved in creating and using an electronic spreadsheet. The remaining tutorial lessons expose you to techniques, commands, and operations that will enhance your spreadsheet skills.

The introductory tutorial lessons are followed by discussions of spreadsheet design, mixed cell references, and Lotus 1-2-3 functions. These discussions conclude the module's materials that relate directly to Lotus 1-2-3's spreadsheet feature. Three remaining discussions address other Lotus features—graphics, databases, and macros. Each discussion includes several specific examples of how to perform the various operations.

The discussions of Lotus features are followed by several short exercises and cases designed to introduce and reinforce the use of additional Lotus 1-2-3 features, commands, and operations.

At the end of the module you will find a Lotus 1-2-3 operation and command summary that briefly describes the full range of commands and control keys available with Lotus 1-2-3. Each major set of command descriptions is prefaced with a tree-style graphic representation of the command's structure. Here you also will find a quick reference command index that may be used to initiate several common spreadsheet operations.

SPREADSHEET BASICS

Spreadsheet Layout

In the Lotus 1-2-3 spreadsheet, letters are used to designate columns and numbers are used to designate rows. You specify a particular position (or cell) in the spreadsheet by column letter and row number. For example, the cell G3 is located in column G, row 3. Lotus calls this combination of letter and number the *cell address*. (Note that the actual Lotus spreadsheet does not display the lines that designate cell locations as they are shown here.)

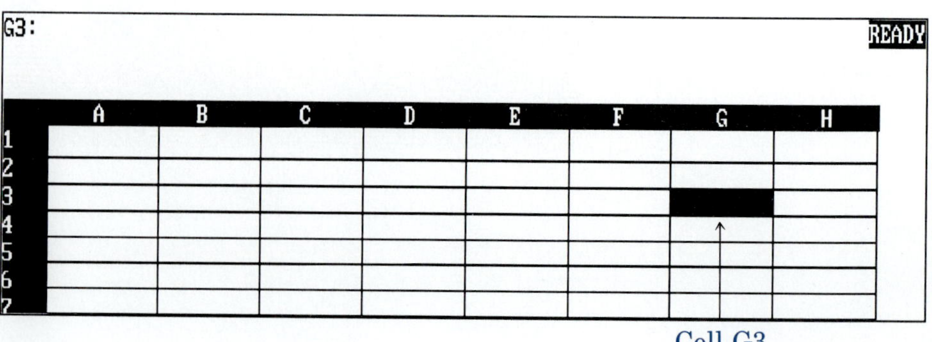

Cell G3

Entering Data into a Spreadsheet

The reverse video screen display shown at cell position G3 is called the *spreadsheet pointer.* The pointer may be moved about the spreadsheet by typing the keyboard cursor control keys. To directly enter data into a spreadsheet cell, you first move the pointer to the appropriate cell and then type your entry. When entering data in this manner, you normally have the option of entering either a string expression or a numeric expression into the cell. Lotus refers to string expressions as being *labels* and numeric expressions as being *values*. Here, a cell entry that must be string data is referred to as being a label, string value, or simply *string*. An entry that must be numeric data is referred to as being a numeric value or simply *numeric*. On occasions where the entry may be either string or numeric, it is referred to here as being simply a value.

When you make a cell entry, Lotus 1-2-3 automatically determines which of the two data types (string or numeric) is being entered into a cell at the first keystroke of the data entry operation. If the first keystroke is any of the following, Lotus 1-2-3 assumes you are entering a numeric value into the cell.

0 1 2 3 4 5 6 7 8 9 + − . (@ # $

If the first keystroke is any other keyboard character, Lotus 1-2-3 assumes you are entering a string value (label) into the cell.

The following example spreadsheet shows some string and numeric values that have been entered into cells. Notice that labels automatically justify to the left side of the cell and that numeric values automatically justify to the right side. The numerics in this case are constants, the number 1200. Numeric values also may take the more complex form of spreadsheet formulas.

A10: READY

	A	B	C	D	E	F	G	H
1		JAN	FEB	MARCH	APRIL			
2	INCOME	1200	1200	1200	1200			
3	TAXES							
4	NET PAY							
5								
6								
7								

Spreadsheet Formulas

To determine taxes and net pay in the example, the user may enter formulas into each of the cells within rows 3 and 4. For instance, if a 28% tax rate is assumed, the formula .28*B2 may be entered as the numeric value for January's tax amount (into cell B3) and the formula +B2−B3 may be entered into cell B4 for January's net pay.

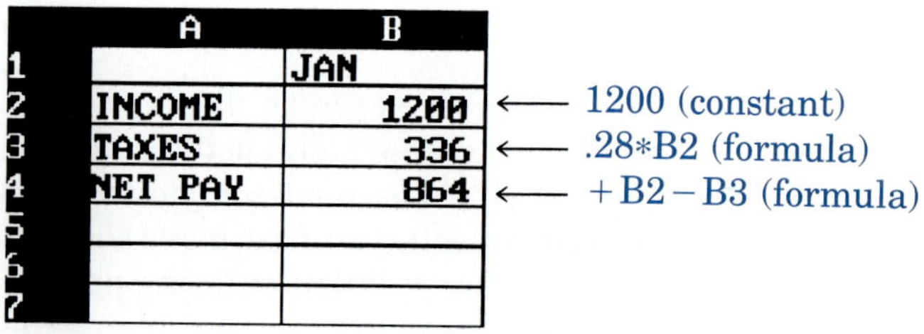

	A	B	
1		JAN	
2	INCOME	1200	← 1200 (constant)
3	TAXES	336	← .28*B2 (formula)
4	NET PAY	864	← +B2−B3 (formula)
5			
6			
7			

Although formulas become the contents of cells B3 and B4, Lotus 1-2-3 will display 336 and 864 (the evaluations of the expressions). If you later change January's income (cell B2), the values displayed for January's taxes (cell B3) and net pay (cell B4) will change automatically.

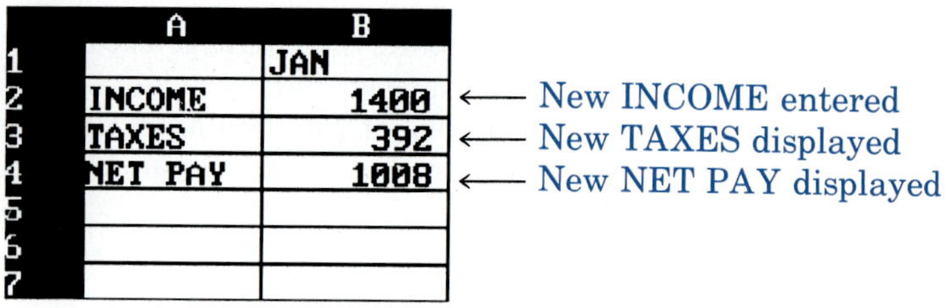

	A	B	
1		JAN	
2	INCOME	1400	← New INCOME entered
3	TAXES	392	← New TAXES displayed
4	NET PAY	1008	← New NET PAY displayed
5			
6			
7			

Window Lines

Lotus 1-2-3 reserves three lines (called *window lines* or, collectively, the *control panel*) at the top of the monitor screen to display information about current operations. The lines indicate the cell where the spreadsheet pointer is currently located (called the current cell). The area to the right of the current cell display indicates the cell's actual contents (as opposed to its displayed contents). The lines also are used to display command menu options, messages, and prompts for the various Lotus command operations.

Lotus Command Structure

When you use Lotus 1-2-3, you are either directly entering data (labels or numeric values) into the spreadsheet's cells or you are executing a Lotus 1-2-3 command.

To manipulate the data in a spreadsheet, Lotus 1-2-3 provides *menus* from which you may select commands. The menus often are connected in a layered fashion: one menu command providing (calling) another submenu of commands. Sometimes a final command operation will require that you pass through several preliminary menus to reach the desired one.

Calling the Main Menu

When you type the Slash key (/), you enter Lotus 1-2-3's command mode by calling the Main menu.

```
B2: 1400                                                                   MENU
Worksheet  Range  Copy  Move  File  Print  Graph  Data  System  Quit
```

The menu is displayed on the middle line of the control panel at the top of the screen. To select a Lotus command, you may either type the first letter of the command word or move the *command pointer* (shown here located on **W**orksheet) to the desired command and press the Enter key. (When a Lotus command is referred to in this module, the first letter of the command—the portion you would need to type to execute the command—appears in bold type.)

The bottom window line displays a listing of the submenu (or a brief explanation) for the command upon which the command pointer is currently located (the current command). In this example, with the command pointer on **W**orksheet, its submenu of commands would appear on the screen as follows.

```
B2: 1400                                                                  MENU
Worksheet  Range  Copy  Move  File  Print  Graph  Data  System  Quit
Global, Insert, Delete, Column, Erase, Titles, Window, Status, Page
        A         B         C         D         E         F         G         H
1              JAN       FEB       MARCH     APRIL
2  INCOME         1400      1200      1200      1200
3  TAXES           392
4  NET PAY        1008
```

Working through Command Submenus

If you select **W**orksheet from the Main menu, the submenu for the command moves to the middle (menu) line and becomes the menu from which to select. An explanation for the current submenu command is displayed on the bottom line.

```
B2: 1400                                                                  MENU
Global  Insert  Delete  Column  Erase  Titles  Window  Status  Page
Set worksheet settings
        A         B         C         D         E         F         G         H
1              JAN       FEB       MARCH     APRIL
2  INCOME         1400      1200      1200      1200
3  TAXES           392
4  NET PAY        1008
```

If the command pointer is next moved one command to the right, the explanation on the bottom line changes.

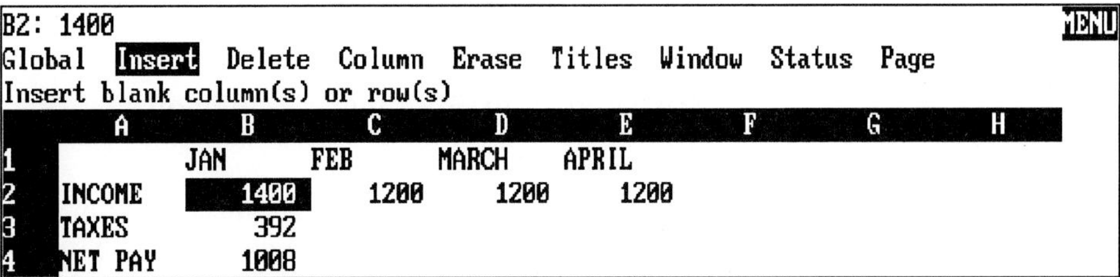

If you now select the **I**nsert command, a third menu that allows you the option of inserting a column or a row into the spreadsheet appears on the menu line and becomes the menu from which to select.

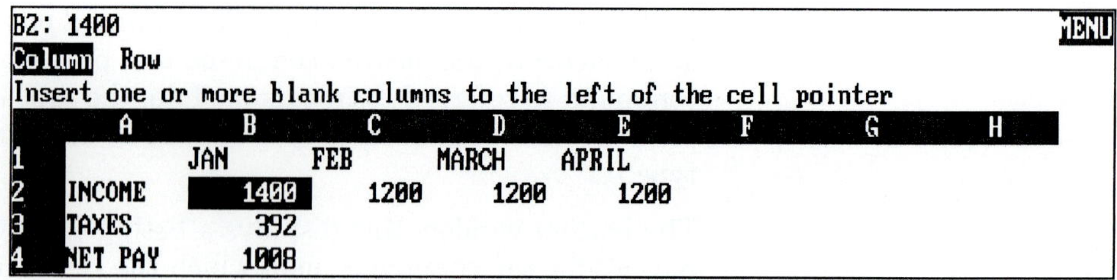

Finally, if you elect to insert a row into the spreadsheet, the row is inserted and you are left in the data entry (READY) mode.

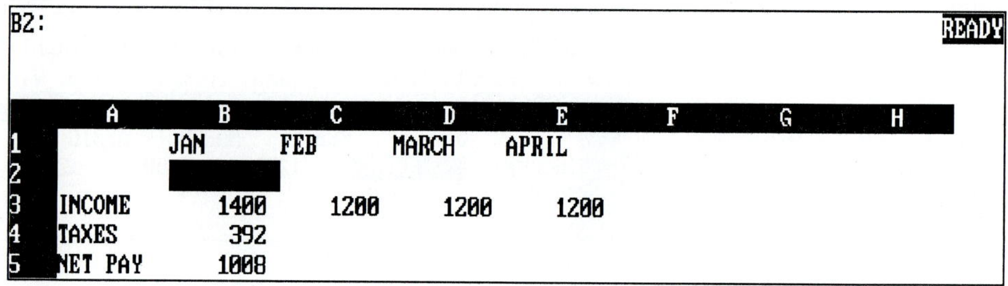

This process of working through submenus often requires a series of steps progressing toward the end command operation. The series of steps may be viewed in a tree structure format as follows.

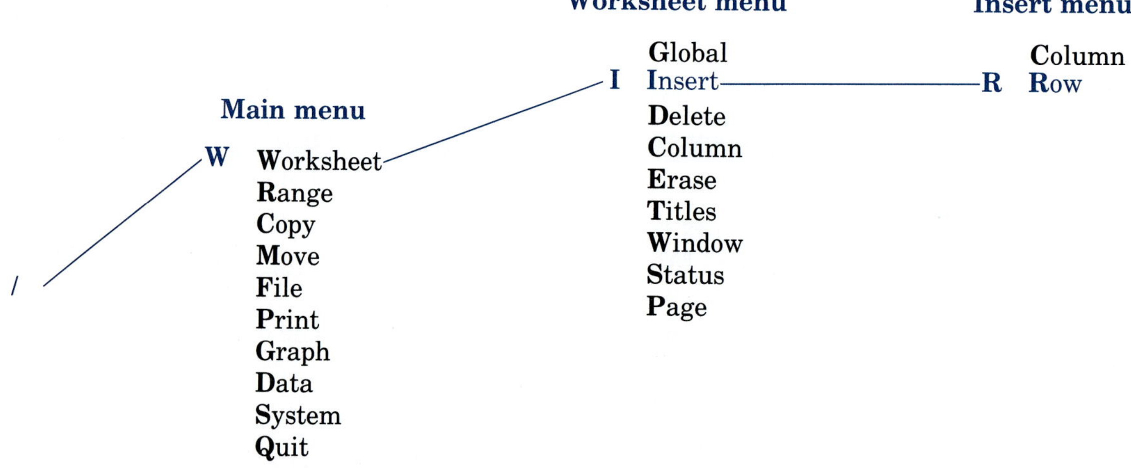

Backing Up or Aborting a Command Operation

When executing a final command operation involves several steps, it is useful to know that typing the Esc key will cause Lotus 1-2-3 to back up one menu or command operation. Pressing the key marked Ctrl and then typing the key marked Scroll Lock (or Break) will abort a command operation and return you to the data entry (READY) mode.

Learning Lotus 1-2-3

Lotus 1-2-3 often requires the completion of a number of steps in specific order to perform a particular command operation. As you use this applications software, you will become familiar with the steps involved. Careful study of the tree diagrams and command summaries will help you master the command sequences.

Getting Help

Lotus 1-2-3 also has an on-line help facility that tries to anticipate your questions and provides a screen of information about the command(s) you are trying to use. You can gain access to a *help screen* at any time by typing the F1 Function key. Each help screen provides information and a selection of other help screens from which to choose. You can select other help screens by using the pointer control keys to move the pointer to highlight the subject of your choice. You then type the Enter key to view that help screen. Typing the Esc key exits you from the help screen mode and returns you to where you left off.

REQUIRED PREPARATION

The tutorial lessons and exercises in this module will give you experience using the commands and features of Lotus 1-2-3. Before you begin the "hands-on" learning experience, however, you will need to complete a few initial steps and gain some preliminary information in order to be adequately prepared.

Initial Steps

1. Obtain a floppy disk appropriate for the microcomputer you will be using to complete your course assignments. Your instructor or laboratory staff will be able to tell you which kind of disk to purchase.

   Size: ______________________

   Sides: ______________________

   Density: ______________________

2. Format your disk to the specifications of the DOS and microcomputer hardware you will be using to complete your course assignments. Your instructor or laboratory staff will be able to tell you the steps to follow. ***Caution: Formatting a disk will erase all files that may exist on that disk.***

   Steps to Format a Disk: ______________________________

   ____

   ____

   ____

   ____

   ____

   ____

3. Each time you use the Lotus 1-2-3 software, you will want to be sure that your spreadsheet files are saved on your disk. There will be certain steps to follow, either when you first load Lotus into RAM or immediately afterwards, to ensure that your files are automatically saved on your disk. Your instructor or laboratory staff will be able to tell you the steps to follow.

Starting a Lotus 1-2-3 Spreadsheet Session: ______________________

REQUIRED MATERIALS

1. An IBM DOS floppy disk (or hard-disk directory containing the DOS software).
2. A Lotus system disk (or hard-disk directory containing the software).
3. A formatted disk (your files disk).
4. This manual.
5. Other ______________________________

TUTORIAL CONVENTIONS

During the introductory Lotus tutorial you will create a spreadsheet file using various Lotus 1-2-3 commands. The following are the conventions the tutorial's instructions will use.

↵	The bent arrow means to type the Enter key located on the right side of the keyboard.
Key-Key	Key combinations using a hyphen indicate that you should press and hold the first key and then type the next key shown.
Key,Key	Key combinations using a comma indicate that you should type the first key and then type the second key.
‖ ‖	Do not type the double lines; type only what is inside them.

HOW TO GET OUT OF TROUBLE

If you want to:	*Then:*
▪ Erase characters before you have entered them into a cell. . .	▪ Type the Backspace key located on the right top side of keyboard.
▪ Erase the existing contents of a cell. . .	▪ Move the pointer to the cell to be erased and type ‖ **/R,E,** ↵ ‖ .
▪ Back up one command operation or menu. . .	▪ Type the Esc key once (the Esc key is located on the top row, far left side).
▪ Stop any command operation and return to the data entry mode. . .	▪ Press and hold the Ctrl key (left side) and then type the Break key (top right side).
▪ Stop the tutorial to continue later. . .	▪ Type ‖ **/F,S,***filename,* ↵ ‖ . Watch the disk drive light to make sure the spreadsheet has been saved. Then type ‖ **/Q,Y** ‖ to quit Lotus 1-2-3.
▪ Continue with the tutorial after stopping. . .	▪ Load Lotus 1-2-3 into memory and then type ‖ **/F,R,***filename,* ↵ ‖ .

Throughout the tutorial lessons you will see the following symbol.

It indicates an opportune time to save your file(s) and quit the microcomputer session if you so desire.

GETTING STARTED

The proper "getting started" procedures require information specific to the hardware and software you are using. Refer to your notes in the preceding Required Preparation section for the specific information. The following is a general procedure for getting started; however, you may need to refer to Appendix A, "The Basics of DOS," to understand some of the terminology used here.

You will need to know in which disk drive (A: or B:) your files disk will be and where (disk drive and path) the Lotus 1-2-3 software will be.

NOTE: Here drive *means type the letter (A, B, etc.) for the disk drive in which your files disk is kept.*

1. Load DOS from a floppy disk or hard disk, or return to the DOS operating level from the current software operating level.
2. Put your files disk into the proper disk drive (drive name ______:).
3. If necessary, put the Lotus System disk in the proper disk drive (drive name ______:).
4. Now make the drive\directory for the Lotus software the current directory by typing *drive:*,**CD***path*↵.
5. Type ‖ LOTUS↵ ‖ .

The Lotus Access System

Lotus 1-2-3 is comprised of several different programs which come on different disks when the software is purchased. LOTUS is the filename for the 1-2-3 Access System, the software selection program that helps the user select which Lotus program to load into RAM.

You should now see the Access System commands at the top of the monitor screen.

```
1-2-3  PrintGraph  Translate  Install  View  Exit
Enter 1-2-3 -- Lotus Worksheet/Graphics/Database program

                       1-2-3 Access System
                     Copyright (C) 1986, 1987
                   Lotus Development Corporation
                        All Rights Reserved
                           Release 2.01

The Access System lets you choose 1-2-3, PrintGraph, the Translate utility,
the Install program, and A View of 1-2-3 from the menu at the top of this
screen.  If you're using a diskette system, the Access System may prompt
you to change disks.  Follow the instructions below to start a program.

o  Use [RIGHT] or [LEFT] to move the menu pointer (the highlight bar at
   the top of the screen) to the program you want to use.

o  Press [RETURN] to start the program.

You can also start a program by typing the first letter of the menu
choice.  Press [HELP] for more information.
```

Different versions of Lotus have different commands and screens associated with the Access System. Take a moment to note which version of Lotus 1-2-3 you are using.

LESSON 1 Loading the Lotus 1-2-3 Spreadsheet Software

Using the Command Pointer

The reverse video display around the command 1-2-3 is Lotus 1-2-3's command pointer. On the far right side of the keyboard is a numeric keypad which contains four keys with arrows on them. Lotus 1-2-3 has programmed the arrow keys to move its pointers.

1. Use the → and ← arrow keys to move the pointer across the command menu.

A short explanation of each menu command appears below the menu of commands as the pointer moves across it. Two methods allow you to select a command from a Lotus menu. You can move the pointer to the desired command and then type the Enter key, or you can type the first letter or character of the desired command. 1-2-3 is the command that will erase the Access System program from RAM and then load the Lotus spreadsheet software into memory.

2. Move the pointer to the 1-2-3 command and type ↵. Depending on the version of Lotus you are using, you next may need to type a keyboard key to remove the Lotus copyright notice or emblem from the screen.

The screen should now appear similar to the following.

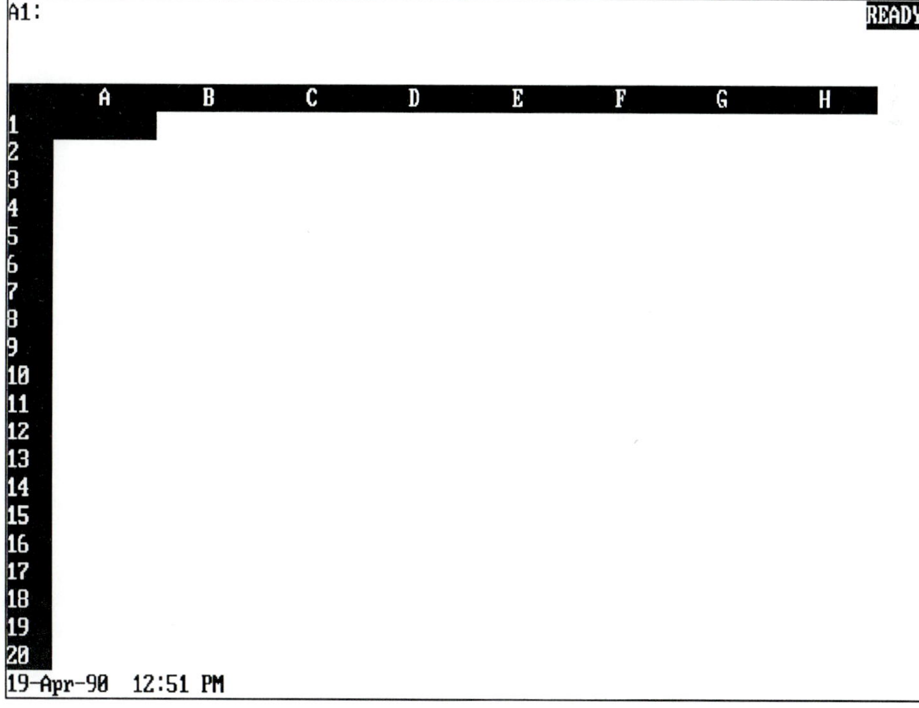

LESSON 2
Viewing the Spreadsheet

What you now see on the screen is one small part of a large matrix or spreadsheet.

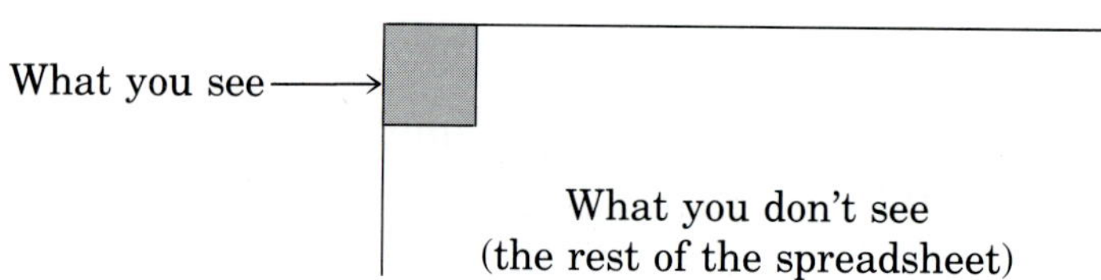

The reverse video display at cell A1 is the Lotus spreadsheet pointer.

1. Move the spreadsheet pointer by using the four arrow (pointer control) keys to your right. If, instead of moving the pointer, the arrowed keys cause numbers to appear at the top left of the screen, type the Esc key and then the Num Lock key.

What happens when you keep moving the pointer to the right or keep moving the pointer down? Notice that the pointer may be used to "push" the monitor screen around on the spreadsheet.

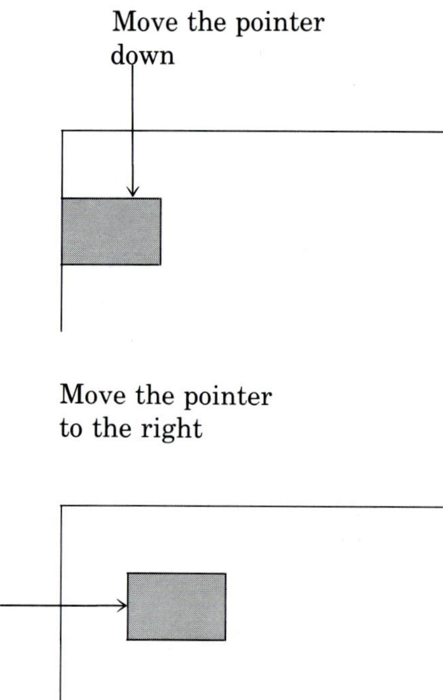

Typing the Home key (found on the numeric keypad) will send the spreadsheet pointer to the A1 (top left) cell.

2. Type the Home key.

On the far left of the keyboard (or across the top) are ten keys marked F1 through F10. These are Function keys. Each is programmed to perform a particular operation.

3. Type the key marked F5 and read the prompt shown at the top of the screen.

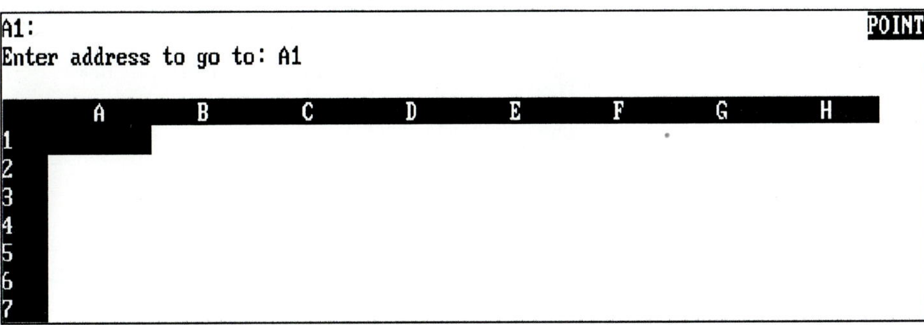

4. Now type ‖G57↵‖.

Notice where the pointer is located now. The F5 key may be used to send the pointer wherever you wish on the spreadsheet.

5. Press the Home key to return the pointer to cell A1.

LESSON 3
Entering Labels into a Spreadsheet

1. Move the pointer to cell B2.

In the upper left corner of the screen you will see the letter-number coordinate for the current pointer position.

2. Type ‖JAN‖ and then move the pointer to the right one cell (C2).
3. Type ‖FEB‖. Keep going until you reach ‖DEC‖ (M2).
4. Type the Home key.

The screen should appear as follows.

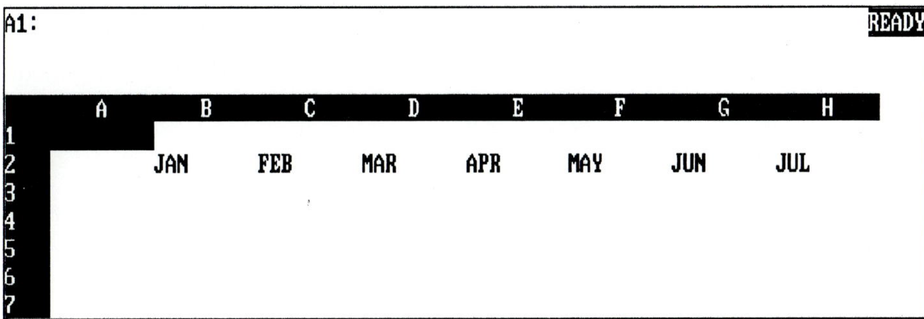

You have just labeled the spreadsheet's columns and now you are going to label its rows. As you continue, watch the control panel at the top of the monitor screen to keep track of what Lotus 1-2-3 is doing.

5. Move the pointer to cell A4 and type ‖GROSS PAY AMOUNT‖.
6. Move the pointer to cell A5 and type ‖TAX RATE‖.
7. Move the pointer to cell A7 (two cells down) and type ‖FED & STATE TAXES ↵‖.

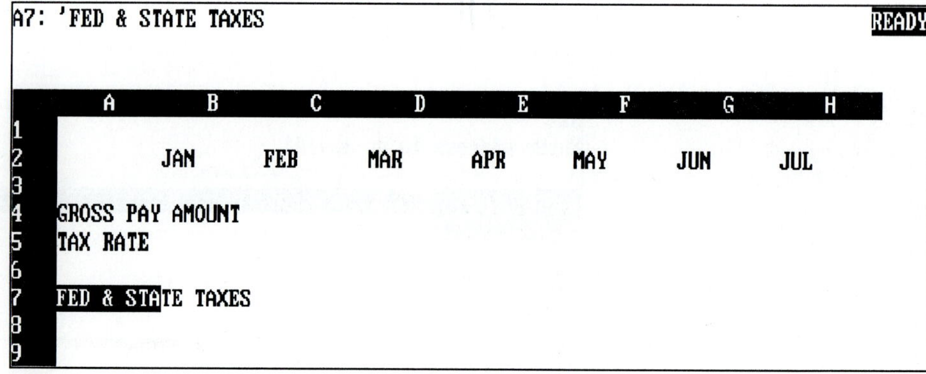

Editing the Contents of a Cell

Once a cell entry has been made, you may edit the entry by using the F2 (EDIT) Function key.

8. Move the pointer to cell A4 and then type the F2 Function key.

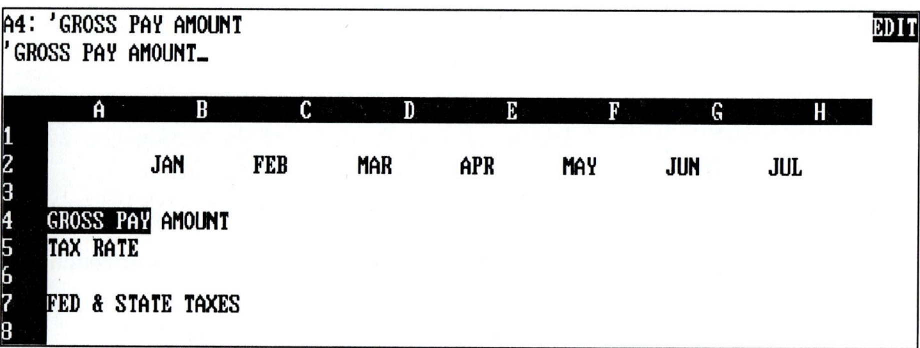

On the middle line of the control panel at the top of the screen you will see a blinking *edit cue* or cursor. To the right you will see the message "EDIT" which indicates you are now in an editing mode. While in the editing mode, the keystrokes listed in the following tables may be used to change the contents of the current cell.

Cursor Movement	Keystrokes
Character Left	Left ←
Character Right	Right →
Beginning of Cell	Home
End of Cell	End

Delete Operation	Keystrokes
Current Character	Del
Preceding Character	Backspace
Typeover Text	Ins (toggles between Insert and Typeover modes)

9. Use the available editing keystrokes to change the label in A4 to read GROSS INCOME and then type Enter.

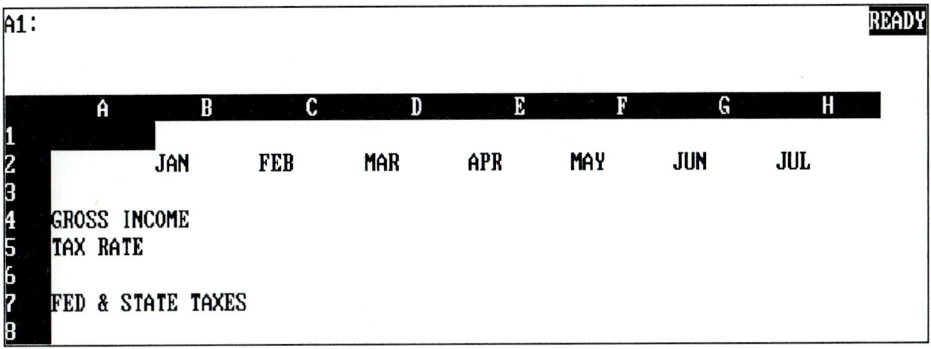

Using Label Prefixes

To make the next label entry into the spreadsheet you will use one of Lotus 1-2-3's label-prefixes. The prefixes are used to format labels in their cells. The following table lists each prefix and its effect.

Character	Effect
Single quote (')	Left justifies label (default)
Caret (^)	Centers label
Double quote (")	Right justifies label
Backslash (\)	Repeats label in cell

The label prefix you will use is \, the *repeating label* prefix, which is most useful for creating underlines in spreadsheets.

10. Move the pointer to cell A8 and then type ‖ \-↵ ‖. (Be sure to use the backslash key.)

Cell A8 now should be filled with dashes.

Finishing the Row Labels

Enter the rest of the spreadsheet's row labels. After you have typed row labels A4 through A22 your spreadsheet should appear as follows.

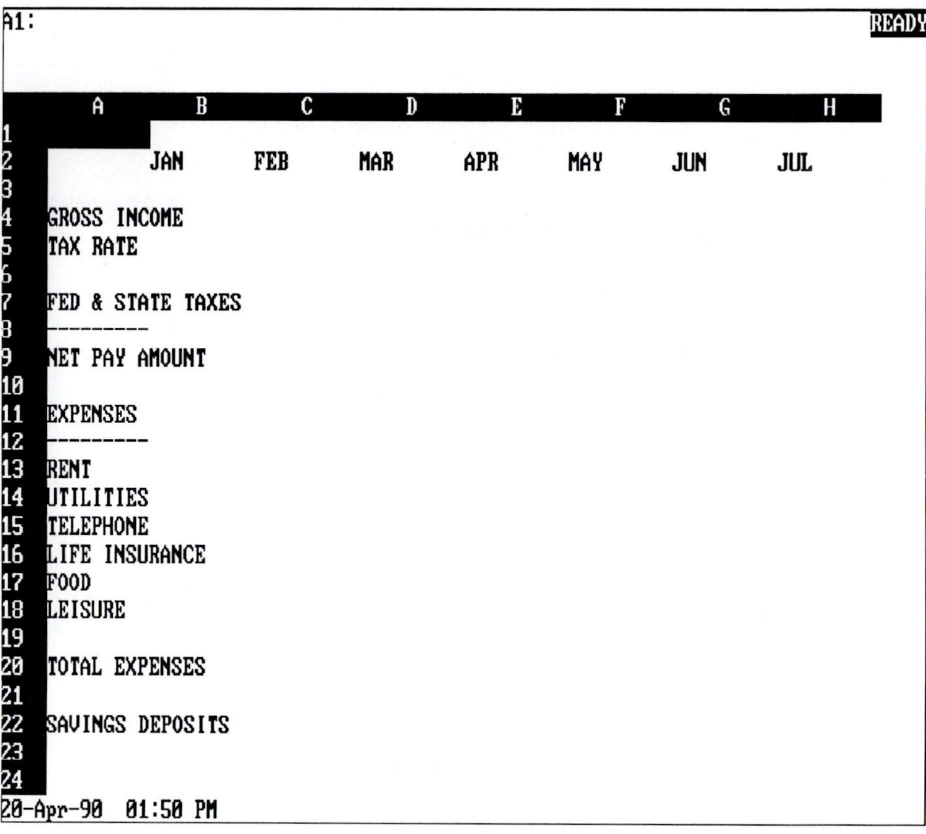

LESSON 4
Introduction to Lotus 1-2-3 Commands

Changing a Column's Width

Many of the row labels you have entered extend into column B. Lotus 1-2-3 allows a label to extend into the next cell if the cell into which it is extending is blank. The default column width setting is 9.

1. Move the pointer to column A (the pointer needs to be in the column whose width you are changing).
2. Type ‖ / ‖.

The / keystroke will call Lotus 1-2-3's Main menu. In the row of submenu commands for the current Main menu command (/**W**orksheet), you should see the command **C**olumn. This is the command you want to use. To access this submenu command you first must select the /**W**orksheet command of the Main menu.

Calling the /Worksheet Submenu

3. Type ‖ **W** ‖ (or ↵) to select the /**W**orksheet commands.

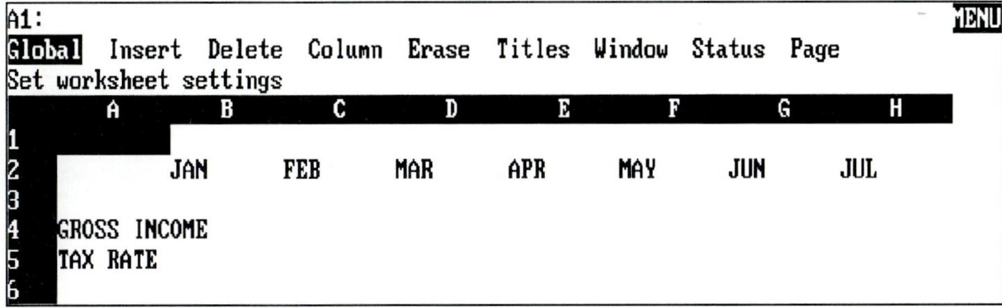

Now the /**W**orksheet submenu has become the menu from which you are choosing, and the line under the submenu provides a short explanation of the current submenu command.

4. Move the menu pointer to the command **C**olumn and read the message line.

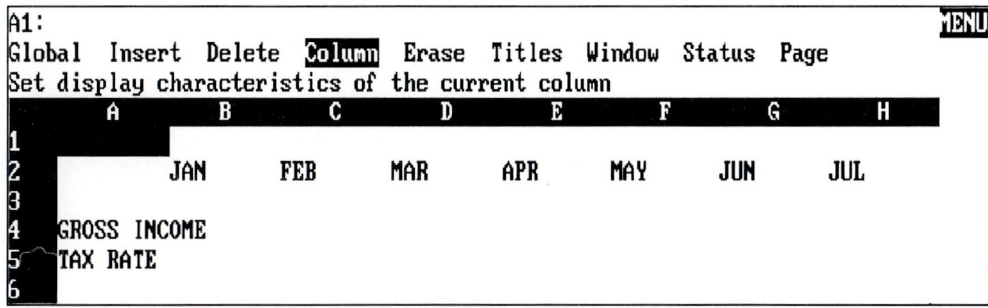

5. Type ↵ to select the **C**olumn command.

Setting the New Column Width

You should now see the following commands.

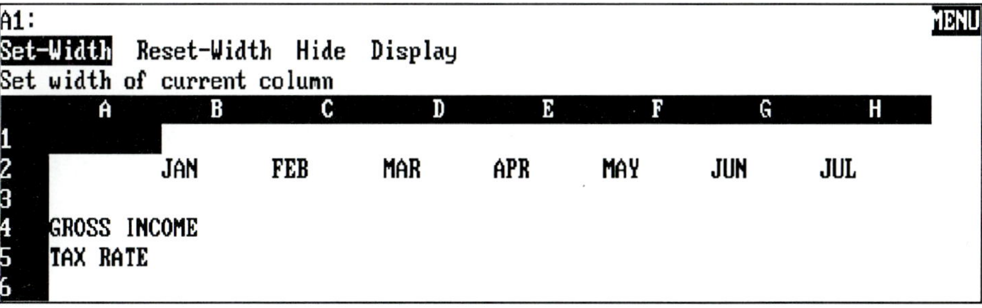

6. Select the command to Set-Width and answer the next prompt

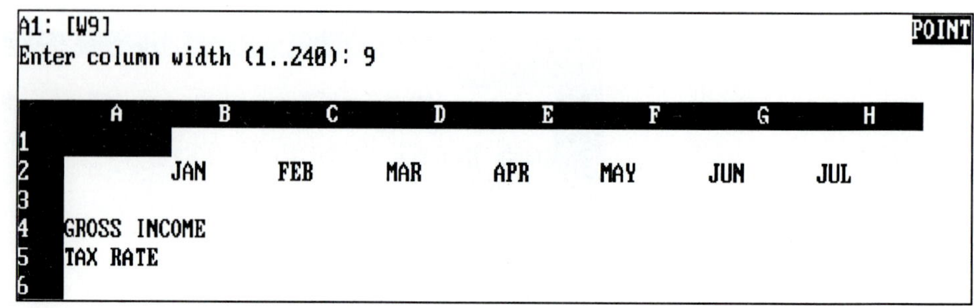
```
A1: [W9]                                                              POINT
Enter column width (1..240): 9

      A        B        C        D        E        F        G        H
1
2            JAN      FEB      MAR      APR      MAY      JUN      JUL
3
4  GROSS INCOME
5  TAX RATE
6
```

by typing || 18↵ || .

Column A should now be twice as wide as the other columns in the spreadsheet. Notice that the column width indicator at the top left of the screen has changed to [W18].

Changing the Default Disk Directory

Another Lotus command may be used to change the current default directory where Lotus will automatically look to read and write spreadsheet files. The sequence of the commands is /**F**ile,**D**irectory.

7. Use the proper command sequence to reach the point where the top of the screen appears similar to the following.

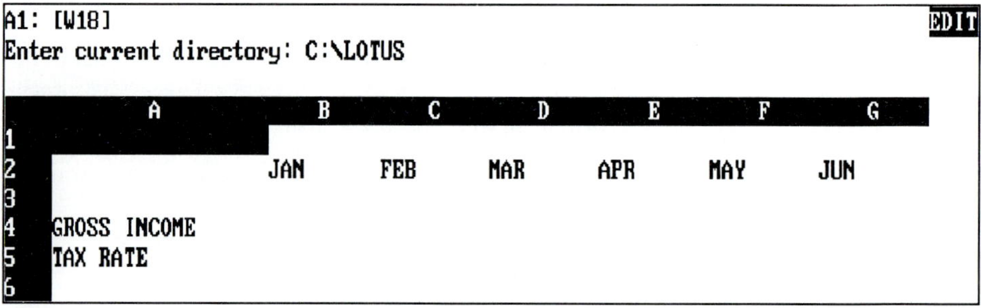
```
A1: [W18]                                                             EDIT
Enter current directory: C:\LOTUS

           A              B        C        D        E        F        G
1
2                       JAN      FEB      MAR      APR      MAY      JUN
3
4  GROSS INCOME
5  TAX RATE
6
```

8. If the current default drive and directory (shown here as C:\LOTUS) is not the same as the location of your files disk, enter the drive and directory describing where your files disk is located. (In many cases, A:↵ or B:↵ will be the appropriate entry.) If the default directory does not need to be changed, simply type ↵.

If the Lotus software you are using does not automatically save its spreadsheet files to the location of your files disk, you will want to use the /**F**ile,**D**irectory command in this manner each time you begin a spreadsheet session.

Using the /File,Save Command

The next command presented here will be used to save a copy of the spreadsheet work you have completed so far. The sequence of the commands is /**F**ile,**S**ave.

9. Use the proper command sequence to reach the point where the top of the screen appears similar to the following.

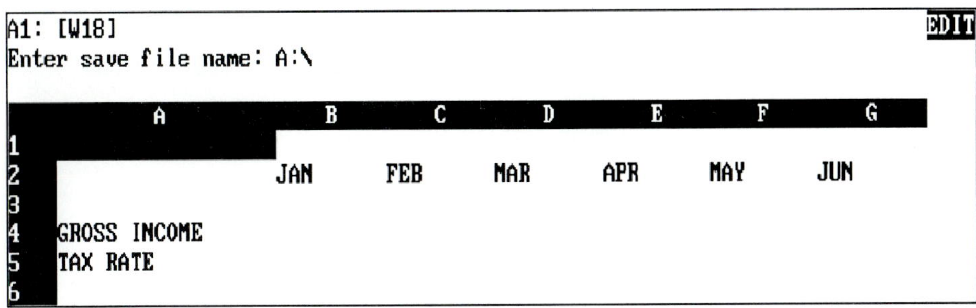

10. Next type ||LOTUT↵ || to cause Lotus to save the partially completed spreadsheet under the name LOTUT (for Lotus Tutorial).

LESSON 5
Ranges of Cells

A *range* of cells may be a single cell, a row of cells, a column of cells, or any rectangular block of cells. In this section of the tutorial lessons you will be dealing with ranges composed of single cells or rows of cells. Many of Lotus's commands act on ranges of cells, so you should develop a thorough understanding of their use. This lesson will introduce you to ranges by using the /Copy command.

Specifying Ranges in the /**C**opy Command

You now will use the Main menu command /Copy, which is designed to copy the contents of a cell or group of cells into another cell or group of cells. The cells from which data are copied are referred to as the "FROM range" of cells; the cells into which data are copied are referred to as the "TO range" of cells.

1. Move the pointer to A8 (------------------) and type || / || to call the Main menu.
2. Now select the Copy command from this menu.

Default Range Specifications

When you look at the top of the screen you will see that Lotus 1-2-3 is asking for the FROM range. Your object is to copy the set of dashes (in cell A8) into the rest of the cells in that row.

Since you will copy from cell A8, that single cell is the FROM range. Lotus 1-2-3 anticipates that this may be the case and has put the range A8..A8 (cell A8 to cell A8) as the default answer to its own prompt.

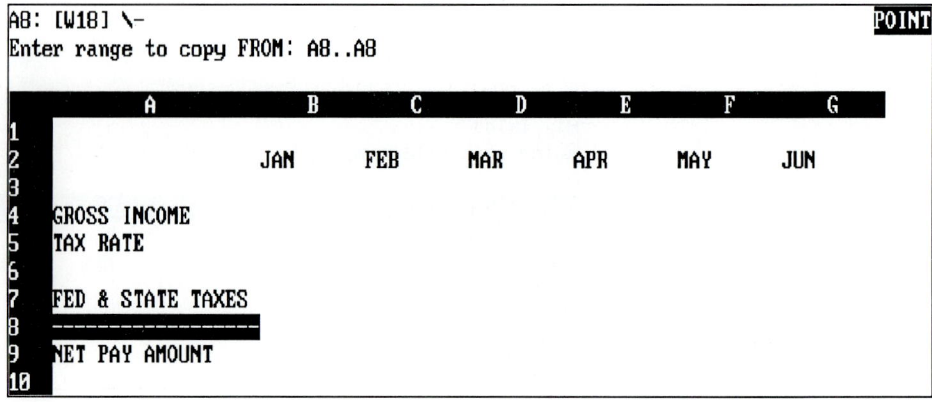

3. Type ↵ to accept cells A8..A8 as the range from which you want to copy.

Now Lotus 1-2-3 wants to know the range of cells into which you want the data copied. Since you are going to underline across the rest of the spreadsheet (up to cell M8), the TO range is the row of cells from B8 through M8 (B8..M8). The default answer (now cell A8), however, is not the correct TO range.

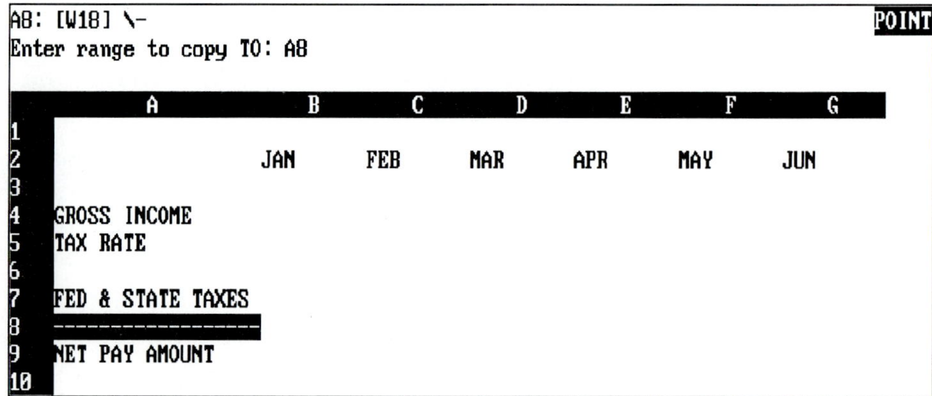

Typing in a Range Specification

You can change a default range specification by typing and entering the desired range from the keyboard. When typing in a range specification, the entry is made in the following order: top left cell, period, bottom right cell.

4. Type ‖ B8.M8 ↵ ‖ . Then make sure that this row has indeed been copied as you directed.

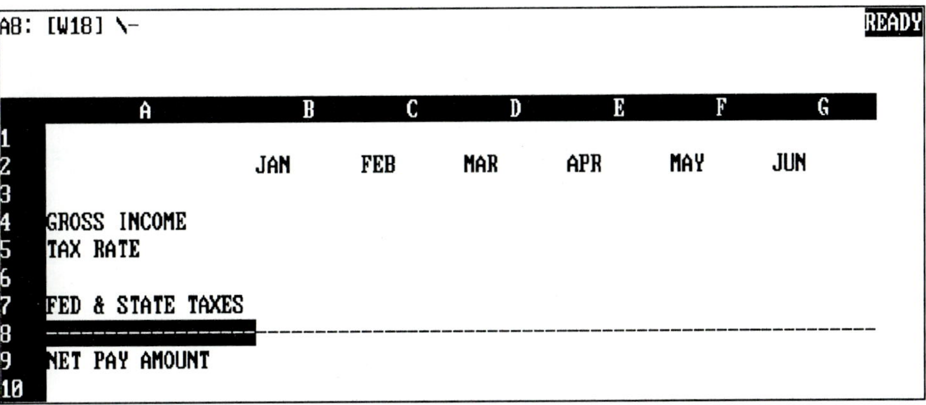

Pointing to a Range Specification

Another very useful way to specify a range while using a command such as /Copy is to point to the range with the spreadsheet pointer. When you use the pointer to specify a range of cells, you first move the pointer to the beginning cell of that range, type the period key to *anchor* the pointer to that cell, and then move the pointer to the ending cell of the range and press the Enter key. You may use the Esc key to "unanchor" the pointer at any time.

To give you experience in pointing to a range, you will use the /Copy command to copy the contents of cell A12 into the rest of the cells in that row (B12..M12).

5. Move the pointer to cell A12 and type ‖ /C ‖ to call the Main menu and select the /Copy command.

The top of the screen should appear as follows.

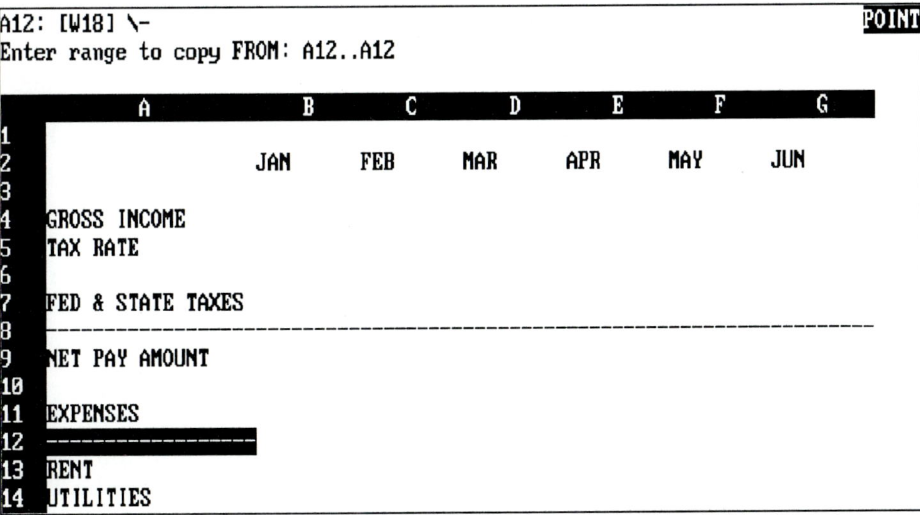

6. Type the Enter key to accept the current default FROM range.
7. Now move the pointer around on the spreadsheet and watch the "Enter range to copy TO:" prompt's default answer change.

The default answer changes with every move of the pointer. Lotus is waiting for you to move to the beginning of the TO range.

8. Move the pointer to cell B12 and then type the period key.

You have just anchored the pointer so that you may now point to the range you are specifying.

9. Start moving the pointer to the right along row 12.

Notice that with each move of the pointer, the TO range specification at the top of the screen changes, and that the range being pointed to on the spreadsheet is displayed in reverse video.

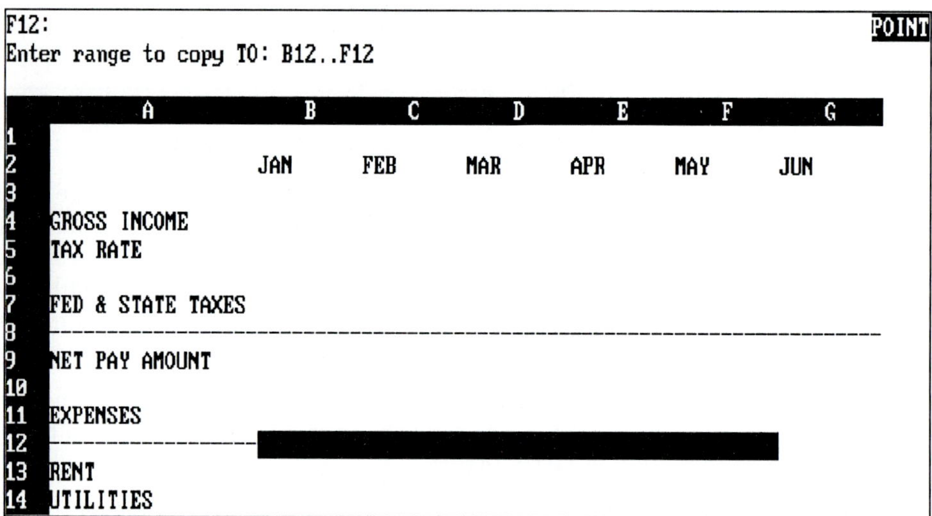

10. Move the pointer to cell M12; again look at the TO range prompt at the top of the screen (B12..M12). Then type the Enter key to accept the range B12..M12 as the appropriate TO range for the copy operation.

Pointing to a range rather than typing it is most useful when you are not sure how far the range goes or how large it is. When you need to see what the range includes, simply anchor the pointer to the top left corner of the range and then move it to the other side, the bottom right corner. You type the Enter key to specify the range as the area displayed in reverse video.

Naming a Specified Range

A third method of specifying a range uses Lotus 1-2-3's ability to name a range and later specify the range by using its name.

In completing the next steps, it is useful to know that when the FROM range is larger than one cell, the TO range may be specified as the single cell located in the upper left corner of the TO range. The FROM range then will be copied to the TO range with the upper left cell of the FROM range corresponding to the upper left cell of the TO range.

*The /**R**ange,**N**ame,**C**reate Command*

11. Type ‖ / ‖ to call the Main menu. Then progress through the sequence of commands **R**ange,**N**ame,**C**reate.

The prompt "Enter name:" will appear at the top of the screen. Lotus 1-2-3 is waiting for you to name the range you will specify in the next step of using this command. Range names may be up to 14 characters long and must not have spaces or special characters in them.

12. Name the range by typing ‖ undrl ↵ ‖ (for underline).

Next, Lotus 1-2-3 will prompt for the range specification of cells you want named "undrl."

13. Answer the "Enter range:" prompt by typing ‖ A8.M8 ↵ ‖.

Now that you have named the range of cells (the row of underlines from cell A8 through cell M8) you may refer to the range by its name in any Lotus command requesting a range specification.

Using a Named Range in a Command

14. Move the pointer to cell A19 and type ‖ /**C** ‖ to begin executing the /**C**opy command.
15. This time answer the FROM range prompt by typing ‖ undrl ↵ ‖ .

The TO range begins at cell A19 and goes through cell M19. Using the rule for copying more than one cell to a range, the uppermost left cell of the TO range is cell A19. The default destination displayed is A19. If you press the period key the default destination will change to A19..A19. Either A19 or A19..A19 will work.

16. Answer the "TO" prompt by typing ↵.
17. Finally, repeat this last process to underline the last row in the spreadsheet (under SAVINGS DEPOSITS).

Summary on Ranges and Using the /**C**opy Command

Your understanding of the concept of ranges and their use may be highly instrumental in determining how you can best design your spreadsheets. Ranges always have the form of a rectangle. They may be defined by: a) pointing to them; b) typing in their coordinates; or 3) using a name you have previously given them. Your choice of range specification method will depend on how you plan to use the range.

The rule for copying ranges of more than one cell into other ranges illustrates how experimentation can teach you a great deal about how Lotus 1-2-3 behaves. Try copying a row of cells into a column of cells, or vice versa. Although you may not get what you expect, you will learn something that could be useful later.

Resaving a Spreadsheet

Now is a good time to update the copy of LOTUT on your disk with the copy in RAM. The process of resaving a spreadsheet is slightly different than that of saving one.

18. Start the resave operation by typing the /**F**ile,**S**ave command. The top of the screen should appear similar to the following.

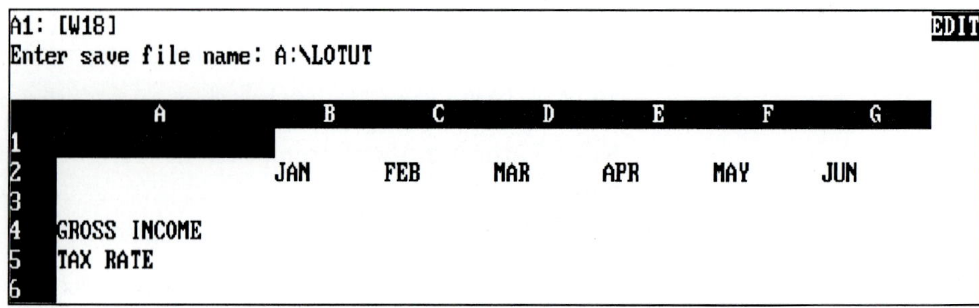

When a spreadsheet is being resaved, Lotus places its original name after the "Enter save file name:" prompt as a default answer.

19. Type ↵ to save the spreadsheet under the same name used previously.

The next prompt displayed is a precautionary step to help prevent you from accidentally replacing a spreadsheet file having the same name on the disk with the file currently in RAM.

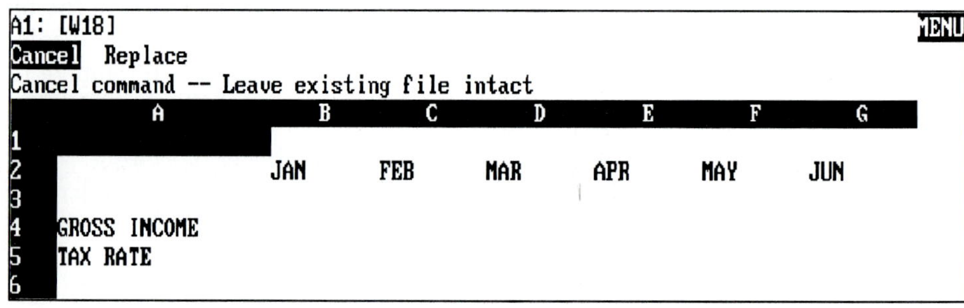

20. Select the **R**eplace command to complete the resave operation.

LESSON 6
Relative vs. Absolute Cell References

Copying Formulas

When the /**C**opy command is used to copy formulas, a new dimension of spreadsheet design is introduced. To show you how the /**C**opy command affects how you enter formulas into the spreadsheet, and how those formulas later derive their values, you will begin to fill in the spreadsheet's numeric data.

Entering and Copying a Simple Formula

1. Move the pointer to January's gross income (B4) and type ‖ 1855 ‖ .
2. Now move to cell C4 and type ‖ +B4 ↵ ‖ .

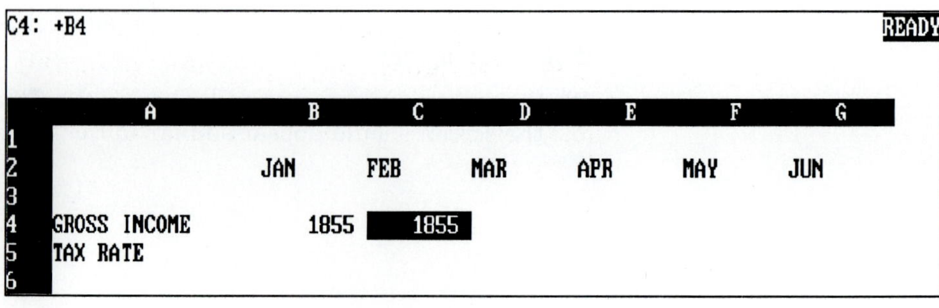

For copying purposes, this simple formula effectively says "the value in cell C4 is to be the same value found one cell to the left (cell B4)."

3. With the pointer on cell C4, type ‖ /C ‖ to call the /Copy command.

You next will copy the formula into the entire year's gross income amounts.

4. Specify the single cell C4..C4 as the FROM range by typing ↵.
5. Specify the TO range as cells D4 through M4, ‖ D4.M4 ↵ ‖ .

The formula will be copied into the appropriate range of cells, and all months should show a gross income of 1855.

Relative References

Move the pointer along the row labeled GROSS INCOME and watch the window line with the current cell information at the top of the screen. Notice that the formula was copied in a *relative* fashion. That is, each cell formula says "the value in this cell is to be the same value found one cell to the left."

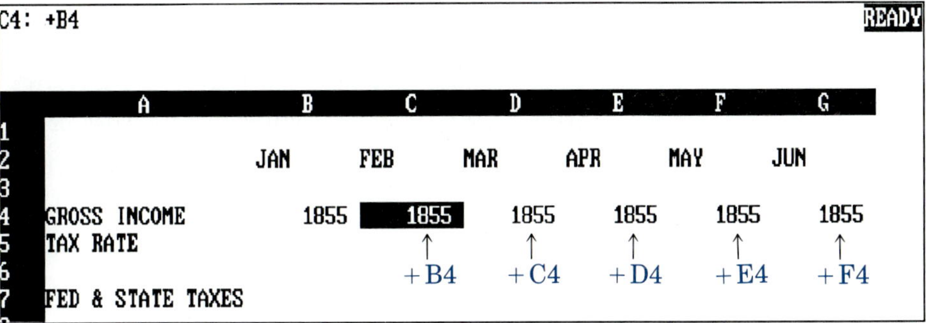

When you use a formula to compute a value for a cell to display, the formula will usually contain *cell references* (Lotus refers to them as cell addresses). The single cell reference in the original formula for this example was +B4.

When the formula was copied, it was copied in a relative fashion. That is, as the cell into which the formula was being copied moved to the right one position, the cell reference in the formula shifted to the right one position.

Absolute References

It is possible, and often desirable, to have one or more cell references in a formula remain the same (not change) when the formula is copied into one or more cells. Lotus refers to such a reference as an *absolute cell address* or absolute cell reference. To produce an absolute cell reference within a formula, you include a dollar sign ($) before the column letter and row number in the cell reference. For instance, if you wanted all of the copied formulas in cells C4 through M4 to reference the starting gross income amount, you would enter the original formula as +$B$4. The result of copying the absolute formula into the same range as before would be as shown in the following screen.

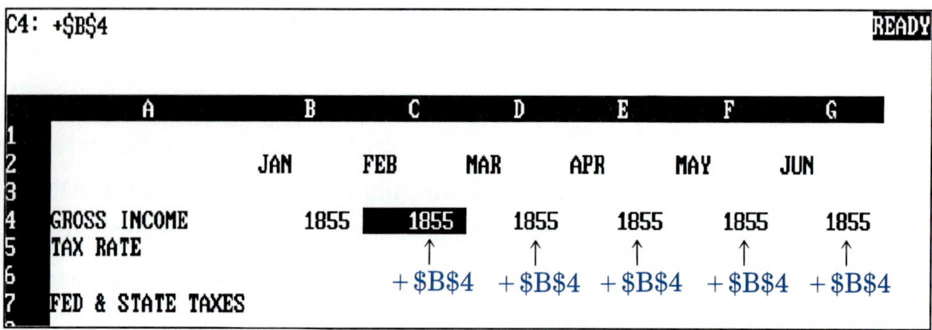

Although the cells would still display the number 1855, the amount would be derived in a different manner. The copied formulas now all say, in effect, "display the same value here as is displayed in cell B4" (the month of January).

The Difference between Relative and Absolute References

To demonstrate the difference between copying a formula with a relative reference and copying a formula with an absolute reference into a range of cells, assume that the year's gross income will be the same for four months. After four months you will receive a raise of $200 per month.

6. Move the pointer to May's gross income (F4) and type F2 (EDIT). Then type ‖ +200 ↵ ‖ . The formula in cell F4 should now read +E4+200.

If you received a raise in May, that raise probably would stay in effect for the rest of the year. When you create an original formula to be copied into other cells, whether you enter the cell references for that formula as relative or absolute determines an important element of your spreadsheet's design.

Entering and Copying a Formula with an Absolute Reference

In the following steps you will create a formula that must have one of its cell references remain absolute when it is copied into the rest of the row's cells. This formula will be used to compute the federal and state taxes for the spreadsheet.

7. Move the pointer to cell A6 and type ‖ .23 ↵ ‖ .

This figure represents the effective yearly tax rate you expect to pay. The formula to compute your federal and state taxes will multiply the tax rate (23%) times your gross pay amount for each month. The formula for the month of January could be typed as +A6*B4.

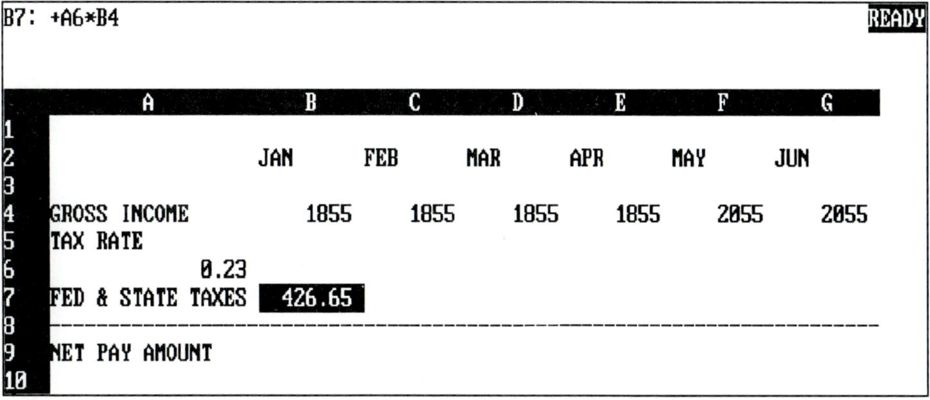

If this formula then was copied into the rest of the cells in the row, the results would be as follows.

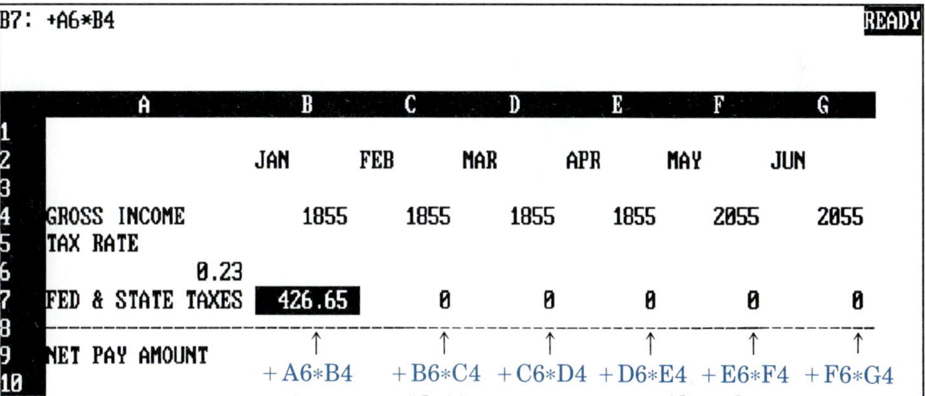

The formulas are copied with both cell references adjusting relative to the cell into which the formula is being copied.

Although the formula works for January's federal and state taxes, it has not been entered to copy correctly to the rest of the cells in the row. To make each formula in the row refer to cell A6 for the tax rate by which that month's pay amount will be multiplied, the original formula should be entered as either $A6*B4 or $A$6*B4. That is, the cell reference for the tax rate in this formula must be kept absolute.

8. Enter the correct formula for cell B7 and then copy that formula into the range of cells for the row.
9. Now move the pointer along the row and observe how the formulas differ from each other.

LESSON 7 Using the Pointer to Enter a Formula

When you enter a formula you can use the pointer to identify cell references for that formula. You may use this feature to reduce the chance of incorrect cell references being entered into a formula.

The formula for the net pay amount in the month of January is +B4−B7. To enter this formula, do the following.

1. Move the pointer to cell B9 (the cell in which to enter the formula) and type ‖ + ‖.
2. Move the pointer to cell B4 (January's GROSS INCOME). Look at the control panel at the top of the screen. It indicates the formula you are entering into cell B9.
3. Type ‖ − ‖ and move the pointer to cell B7. The finished formula should appear on the edit line as +B4−B7.
4. Type ↵ to finish entering the formula.
5. Copy the formula into the range of cells C9 through M9.
6. Once more, move the pointer along the ninth row and look at the window line at the top of the screen to see how the cell references changed for each cell when the formula was copied.

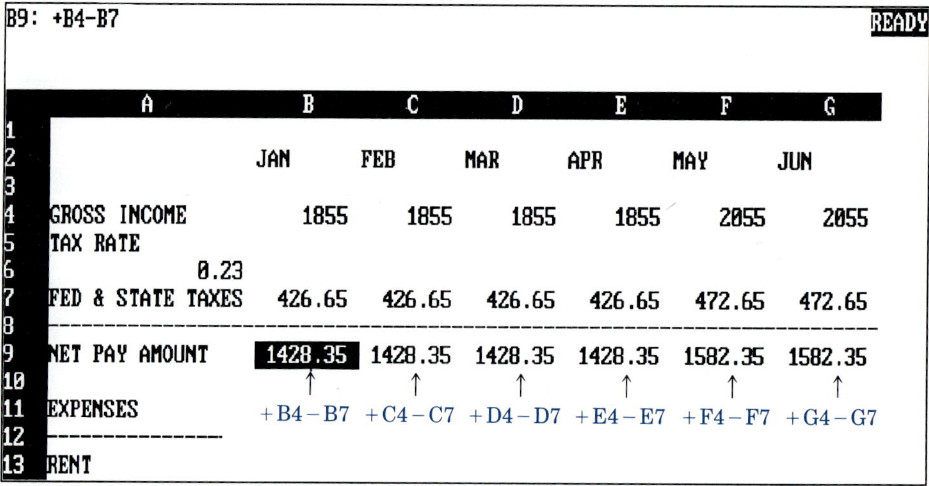

B9: +B4-B7 READY

	A	B	C	D	E	F	G
1							
2		JAN	FEB	MAR	APR	MAY	JUN
3							
4	GROSS INCOME	1855	1855	1855	1855	2055	2055
5	TAX RATE						
6	0.23						
7	FED & STATE TAXES	426.65	426.65	426.65	426.65	472.65	472.65
8	------------------	----------	----------	----------	----------	----------	----------
9	NET PAY AMOUNT	1428.35	1428.35	1428.35	1428.35	1582.35	1582.35
10		↑	↑	↑	↑	↑	↑
11	EXPENSES	+B4−B7	+C4−C7	+D4−D7	+E4−E7	+F4−F7	+G4−G7
12	---------------						
13	RENT						

Both cell references were copied as relative references, as they should have been.

LESSON 8
Rejustifying a Range of Labels

You may have noticed that the month labels are not lined up very well with the numeric values you are entering into the spreadsheet. To demonstrate one of the /**R**ange commands and to make the spreadsheet more readable, do the following.

Using the /**R**ange,**L**abel Command

1. Type ‖ /**R**‖ to call the /**R**ange commands, and then select the command **L**abel.
2. Choose the command that will "Align labels with right edges of cells." Then define the range of label cells to align flush right as B2..M2 (the row of month labels).
3. Type the Home key. The following shows what you should see.

```
A1: [W18]                                                            READY

            A              B        C        D        E        F        G
1
2                         JAN      FEB      MAR      APR      MAY      JUN
3
4  GROSS INCOME          1855     1855     1855     1855     2055     2055
5  TAX RATE
6                0.23
7  FED & STATE TAXES   426.65   426.65   426.65   426.65   472.65   472.65
8  ----------------------------------------------------------------------
9  NET PAY AMOUNT     1428.35  1428.35  1428.35  1428.35  1582.35  1582.35
10
11 EXPENSES
12 ----------------------------------------------------------------------
13 RENT
14 UTILITIES
15 TELEPHONE
16 LIFE INSURANCE
17 FOOD
18 LEISURE
19 ----------------------------------------------------------------------
20 TOTAL EXPENSES
22-Apr-90  05:08 PM
```

LESSON 9
Adding Data to the Spreadsheet

Finish the next expense amounts in the spreadsheet by entering the following numeric values in the same manner as you entered the year's gross income amounts. For instance, for the first item, RENT, enter the number 375 into cell B13 and the formula +B13 into cell C13, and then copy the formula into the rest of the year's rent row.

1. RENT is 375 per month all year.
2. UTILITIES are 100 per month all year.
3. TELEPHONE is 18 per month all year.
4. LIFE INSURANCE is 28.65 per month all year.

Enter the remaining expense items by using a formula to compute the amounts. For instance, the formula to enter into cell B17 (JAN's FOOD expense) is .30*B9.

5. FOOD is 30% of NET PAY AMOUNT all year.
6. LEISURE is 15% of NET PAY AMOUNT all year.

This is what your spreadsheet should look like at this point.

A1: [W18] READY

	A	B	C	D	E	F	G
1							
2		JAN	FEB	MAR	APR	MAY	JUN
3							
4	GROSS INCOME	1855	1855	1855	1855	2055	2055
5	TAX RATE						
6	0.23						
7	FED & STATE TAXES	426.65	426.65	426.65	426.65	472.65	472.65
8	------------------	---------	---------	---------	---------	---------	---------
9	NET PAY AMOUNT	1428.35	1428.35	1428.35	1428.35	1582.35	1582.35
10							
11	EXPENSES						
12	------------------	---------	---------	---------	---------	---------	---------
13	RENT	375	375	375	375	375	375
14	UTILITIES	100	100	100	100	100	100
15	TELEPHONE	18	18	18	18	18	18
16	LIFE INSURANCE	28.65	28.65	28.65	28.65	28.65	28.65
17	FOOD	428.505	428.505	428.505	428.505	474.705	474.705
18	LEISURE	214.2525	214.2525	214.2525	214.2525	237.3525	237.3525
19	------------------	---------	---------	---------	---------	---------	---------
20	TOTAL EXPENSES						

23-Apr-90 08:35 AM

LESSON 10 Introduction to Functions

Total expenses could be expressed in a formula as +B13+B14+B15+B16+B17+B18 for the month of January. Instead, you will use one of Lotus 1-2-3's spreadsheet functions. The general form of a *function* is @**XYZ** (argument). The @ sign tells Lotus 1-2-3 that you are entering a function into a cell. The XYZ represents the function's name, and the *arguments* in the parentheses are composed of cell references, ranges, values, or formulas for the function to act upon.

Using the @SUM Function

1. Move the pointer to cell B20 and type ‖ @**SUM**(B13.B18) ↵ ‖ .

The formula @**SUM**(B13..B18) will sum the cell contents of the cells in the range specified in the function's argument.

2. Now copy the function into cells C20 through M20. Notice that the cell references in the function also were copied in a relative fashion.

LESSON 11 Finishing the Spreadsheet

Entering Savings Deposits

The label SAVINGS DEPOSITS represents money left to deposit in your bank account.

1. Enter the appropriate formula into cell B22 and copy it into the rest of the cells in the spreadsheet row.

Now the bottom lines of your spreadsheet should look like this.

```
20 TOTAL EXPENSES    1164.407 1164.407 1164.407 1164.407 1233.707 1233.707
21
22 SAVINGS DEPOSITS  263.9425 263.9425 263.9425 263.9425 348.6425 348.6425
23 ------------------------------------------------------------------------
24
23-Apr-90  08:50 AM
```

A Running Savings Account Balance

You have one more row of values to add to the spreadsheet. This row will be labeled SAVINGS ACCOUNT and will reflect the total savings you expect after each month's deposit, with *x* amount of yearly interest, compounded monthly.

2. Move the pointer to cell A24 and type ‖ SAVINGS ACCOUNT ‖ .
3. Now move to cell A25 and type ‖ INTEREST RATE = ‖ .
4. Move to cell B25 and type ‖ .0525 ‖ (the yearly rate of interest, 5 1/4%).
5. Move to cell A26. Type ‖ \= ↵ ‖ . Now copy this repeating label underline through to DEC (M26).
6. Move the pointer to cell A27 and type ‖ BEGINNING BALANCE ‖ .
7. Move to cell B27 and type in ‖ 0 ↵ ‖ (zero), the beginning balance for the savings account.

Entering a More Complicated Formula

You are ready to enter the formula for computing a running total of the savings account for the year. The formula will multiply the previous month's balance by 1 plus the monthly interest rate (add that month's interest earned). Then it will add the deposit made at the end of the previous month to derive the beginning balance for the current month. The general form of the formula for the month of FEB is +B27*(1+B25/12)+B22. The order in which the formula will be computed is as follows.

1. Take the yearly interest rate, B25, and divide it by 12 to determine the monthly interest rate.

   B25/12

2. Add 1 to this, giving the correct multiplier for determining the balance with interest added to it.

   (1+B25/12)

3. Take what you already have in the bank, B27, and multiply it by the multiplier to give principal plus interest earned for the month.

   +B27*(1+B25/12)

4. Finally, add the deposit you will make from the money you had (after expenses) from the month before.

   +B27*(1+B25/12)+B22

After entering this formula into February's beginning balance, you will copy it into the appropriate cells for the rest of the year. However, one of the cell references in the formula must be copied with an absolute cell reference. All cells in the row will refer to this specific cell in their formulas. This cell reference will need to be typed with a $ sign preceding its column letter. The other two references in the formula will be relative to the particular month into which they are being copied.

To test your understanding of relative and absolute cell addresses, the following step requires you to decide which cell addresses to enter as relative and which as absolute. Refer to the previous discussions on relative and absolute cell addresses of formulas if necessary.

8. Type the correct formula for the month of FEB and copy it into the range of cells for BEGINNING BALANCE (set the TO range as D27..M27).

The bottom lines of your spreadsheet should look like the following if you have typed the original formula correctly.

```
19 -----------------------------------------------------------------------
20 TOTAL EXPENSES     1164.407 1164.407 1164.407 1164.407 1233.707 1233.707
21
22 SAVINGS DEPOSITS   263.9425 263.9425 263.9425 263.9425 348.6425 348.6425
23 -----------------------------------------------------------------------
24 SAVINGS ACCOUNT
25 INTEREST RATE =      0.0525
26 =======================================================================
27 BEGINNING BALANCE          0 263.9425 529.0397 795.2967 1062.718 1416.010
28
23-Apr-90  09:14 AM
```

Causing the Spreadsheet to Recalculate

Now that the spreadsheet is functionally complete, you can test its ability to recalculate automatically for any changes you enter into it.

Assume your boss gives you a $100.00 raise immediately (in January) and another $150.00 raise in May in lieu of the $200.00 raise in May.

9. Change your spreadsheet to accommodate the changed salary.

Assume that taxes are cut this year and your estimated effective federal and state tax rate will drop to 18%.

10. Enter the new tax rate to see how it affects your home budget spreadsheet.

Suppose you receive a notice from your landlord informing you rent will be increased $20.00 per month beginning in March.

11. Enter the change into your spreadsheet.

Assume UTILITIES will be $125.00 JAN through MAR; $100.00 APRIL through AUGUST; $130.00 SEPT through DEC.

12. Change your spreadsheet to accommodate these expectations.

Your spreadsheet should look like this.

A1: [W18] READY

	A	B	C	D	E	F	G
1							
2		JAN	FEB	MAR	APR	MAY	JUN
3							
4	GROSS INCOME	1955	1955	1955	1955	2105	2105
5	TAX RATE						
6	0.18						
7	FED & STATE TAXES	351.9	351.9	351.9	351.9	378.9	378.9
8	----------	----------	----------	----------	----------	----------	----------
9	NET PAY AMOUNT	1603.1	1603.1	1603.1	1603.1	1726.1	1726.1
10							
11	EXPENSES						
12	----------	----------	----------	----------	----------	----------	----------
13	RENT	375	375	395	395	395	395
14	UTILITIES	125	125	125	100	100	100
15	TELEPHONE	18	18	18	18	18	18
16	LIFE INSURANCE	28.65	28.65	28.65	28.65	28.65	28.65
17	FOOD	480.93	480.93	480.93	480.93	517.83	517.83
18	LEISURE	240.465	240.465	240.465	240.465	258.915	258.915
19	----------	----------	----------	----------	----------	----------	----------
20	TOTAL EXPENSES	1268.045	1268.045	1288.045	1263.045	1318.395	1318.395
21							
22	SAVINGS DEPOSITS	335.055	335.055	315.055	340.055	407.705	407.705
23	----------	----------	----------	----------	----------	----------	----------
24	SAVINGS ACCOUNT						
25	INTEREST RATE =	0.0525					
26	==========	==========	==========	==========	==========	==========	==========
27	BEGINNING BALANCE	0	335.055	671.5758	989.5690	1333.953	1747.494
28							

READY

	H	I	J	K	L	M	N	O
1								
2	JUL	AUG	SEP	OCT	NOV	DEC		
3								
4	2105	2105	2105	2105	2105	2105		
5								
6								
7	378.9	378.9	378.9	378.9	378.9	378.9		
8	----------	----------	----------	----------	----------	----------		
9	1726.1	1726.1	1726.1	1726.1	1726.1	1726.1		
10								
11								
12	----------	----------	----------	----------	----------	----------		
13	395	395	395	395	395	395		
14	100	100	130	130	130	130		
15	18	18	18	18	18	18		
16	28.65	28.65	28.65	28.65	28.65	28.65		
17	517.83	517.83	517.83	517.83	517.83	517.83		
18	258.915	258.915	258.915	258.915	258.915	258.915		
19	----------	----------	----------	----------	----------	----------		
20	1318.395	1318.395	1348.395	1348.395	1348.395	1348.395		
21								
22	407.705	407.705	377.705	377.705	377.705	377.705		
23	----------	----------	----------	----------	----------	----------		
24								
25								
26	==========	==========	==========	==========	==========	==========		
27	2162.844	2580.012	2999.004	3389.830	3782.365	4176.618		
28								

13. Now is a good time to resave your work. Use the /**F**ile,**S**ave command to update the copy of LOTUT on the disk.

LESSON 12 Stopping and Restarting a Lotus Session

This lesson marks the halfway point in the tutorial lessons. To give you experience in using two important commands, and to provide an opportunity to quit the tutorial and resume later, do the following.

Erasing a Spreadsheet from RAM

1. Make sure the spreadsheet is saved on your disk and then type the /**W**orksheet,**E**rase command.

The /**W**orksheet,**E**rase command is used to erase the current spreadsheet from RAM, which allows you to begin creating a new spreadsheet. The prompt at the top of the screen is a precautionary step designed to prevent you from erasing the spreadsheet from RAM before you have saved it on the disk.

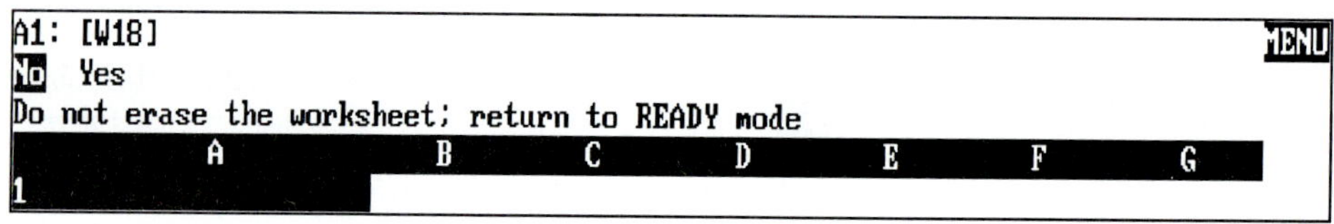

2. Answer **Y**es to the prompt. The screen should now be cleared.

The /Quit Command

The /**Q**uit command is used to erase the Lotus spreadsheet software from RAM. If it is your intention to stop the tutorial now and continue at a later time, do the following.

3. Type the /**Q**uit command and answer **Y**es to the precautionary **N**o **Y**es prompt that appears.
4. Use the **E**xit command of the Access System to return to the DOS operating level. You will need to repeat the Getting Started section of the tutorial lessons when you are ready to resume.

The /File,Retrieve Command

When you are ready to resume work on a spreadsheet file you have previously saved on your disk, the /**F**ile,**R**etrieve command is used to copy the file from the disk into RAM.

5. Type the /**F**ile,**R**etrieve command. A screen similar to the following should appear.

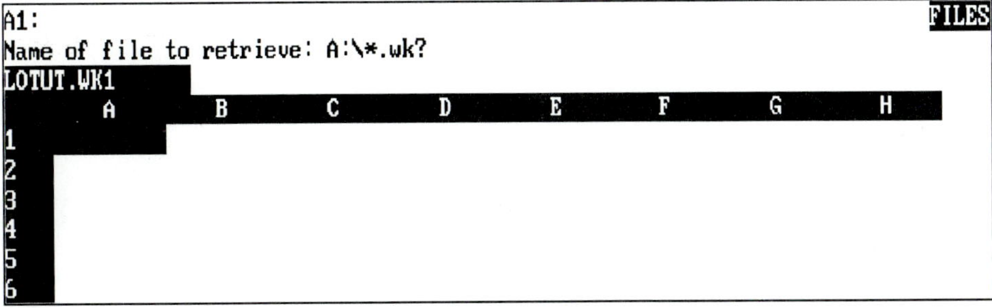

Lotus begins the process of retrieving a spreadsheet file by reading the current disk directory and placing the names of all spreadsheet files (files having a WK1 extension) on the bottom line of the control panel. You then may retrieve a particular spreadsheet by moving the pointer on that line to the appropriate spreadsheet filename and typing ↵.

6. Retrieve the LOTUT spreadsheet into RAM.

LESSON 13 Formatting a Spreadsheet

Formatting Ranges of Cells

The command to call a set of /**R**ange commands is on the Main menu. You used one of these commands to assign a label prefix (/**R**ange,**L**abel) for the row of month labels to align them more precisely with the numeric values in the spreadsheet. You also used the /**R**ange commands to name a range, and then later used the name to specify the range. The /**R**ange commands include the following.

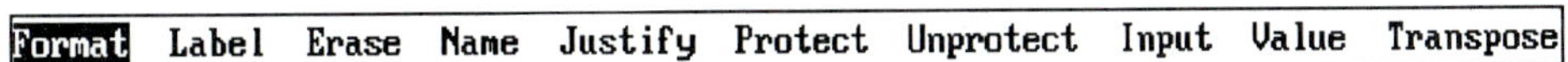

The first item in the /**R**ange submenu is the **F**ormat command, which is used for formatting ranges of cells. The submenu of /**R**ange,**F**ormat commands includes

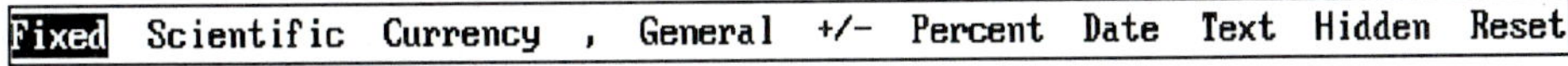

1. Move the pointer to cell B25 (the yearly interest rate on savings).

You will use the /**R**ange,**F**ormat commands to format this single cell to display its data in percent notation.

2. Type the /**R**ange,**F**ormat command, and then find and select the command to format as a **P**ercent.

The number of decimal places will be two (2). Since 2 is the default value shown with the prompt, you can simply type ↵.

3. Type ↵.

4. Type ↵ to enter B25..B25 as the appropriate range to format.

BEFORE:

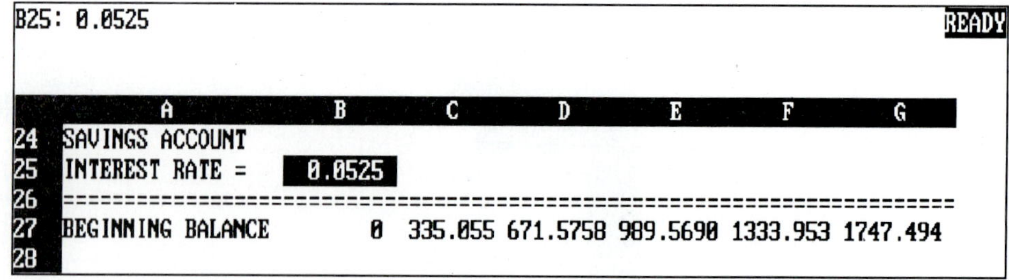

STEPS: **/RFP** (/**R**ange,**F**ormat,**P**ercent)
Enter number of decimal places (0..15): 2↵
Enter range to format: B25..B25↵

AFTER:

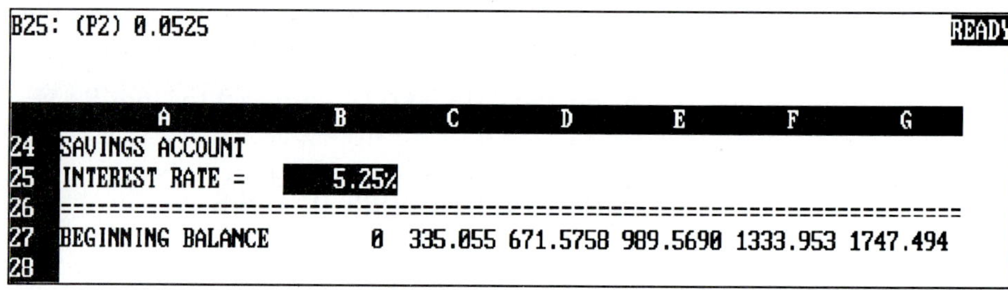

Notice that the value shown at the top of the screen remains 0.0525; however, for purposes of viewing the spreadsheet, the value in the cell B25 now is shown as 5.25%. The (P2) shown at the top of the screen with the cell's value indicates the cell now is formatted to display as a percentage with two decimal places.

5. Repeat the last step to format the tax rate (the 0.18 in cell A6) to display as a percent with zero decimal places.
6. Move the pointer to B22 (SAVINGS DEPOSITS row) and type the /**R**ange,**F**ormat. Select **C**urrency with 2 decimal places. Set the range to format as B22 through M22.

BEFORE:

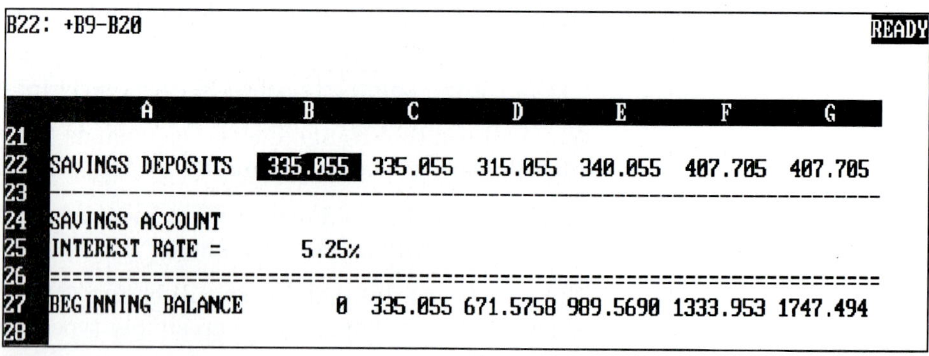

STEPS: **/RFC** (/**R**ange,**F**ormat,**C**urrency)
Enter number of decimal places (0..15): 2 ↵
Enter range to format: B22..M22 ↵

AFTER:

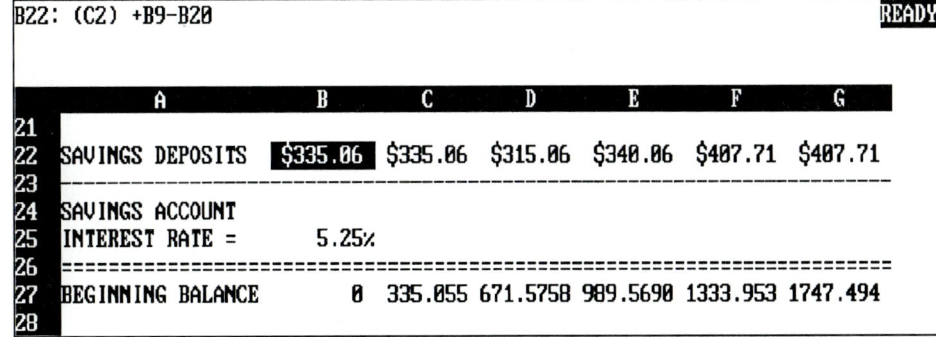

If you use the **C**urrency format, cells with values in them display their values in standard currency notation. The partial cents that were shown before have been rounded just for display purposes. They remain part of the value held in the cell and will be used in any formula referring to that cell.

7. Repeat the last step selecting the **T**ext command instead of the **C**urrency command for this range of cells.

BEFORE:

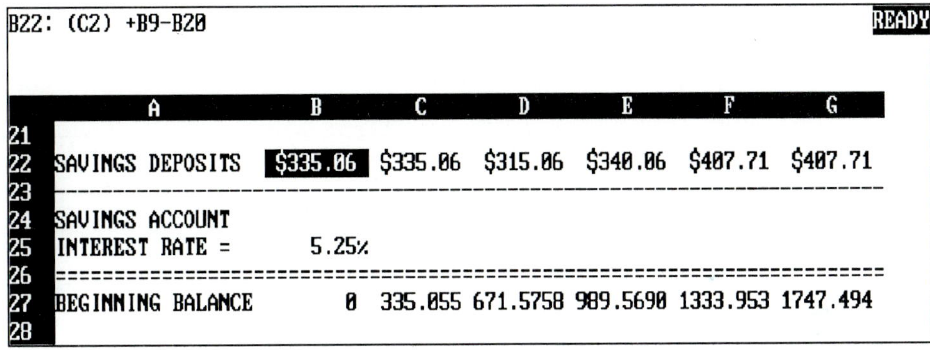

STEPS: **/RFT** (/**R**ange,**F**ormat,**T**ext)
Enter range to format: B22..M22 ↵

AFTER:

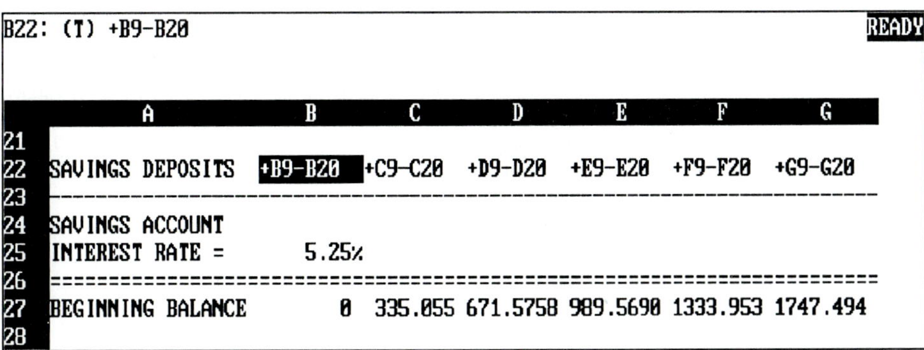

The **T**ext formatting command will display the formulas used in a range of cells.

8. Finally, use the /**R**ange,**F**ormat,**R**eset command to return the row of cells B22..M22 back to the default spreadsheet format (General).

Global Formatting Commands

When the term *global* is used in computers, it generally means "in effect or affecting the entire set of data." The term *default* means "automatically in effect." For instance, the default global label-prefix for Lotus 1-2-3 is the single quote (') (left justified). Unless you specify otherwise, any label you enter into a cell will automatically be justified to the left in that cell. When you do specify otherwise, such as when you used the /**R**ange,**L**abel,**R**ight command to right justify the month labels in their cells, you are overriding the default global setting.

Lotus 1-2-3 allows you to change certain global settings through the /**W**orksheet,**G**lobal commands. These commands are as follows.

```
Format  Label-Prefix  Column-Width  Recalculation  Protection  Default  Zero
```

Lotus 1-2-3 allows you to define a global format for the entire spreadsheet through the /**W**orksheet,**G**lobal,**F**ormat commands. The available formatting commands are the same as in the /**R**ange,**F**ormat commands, except that the entire spreadsheet rather than just a specified range is affected.

9. Type the /**W**orksheet,**G**lobal,**F**ormat command and then select the **T**ext command.

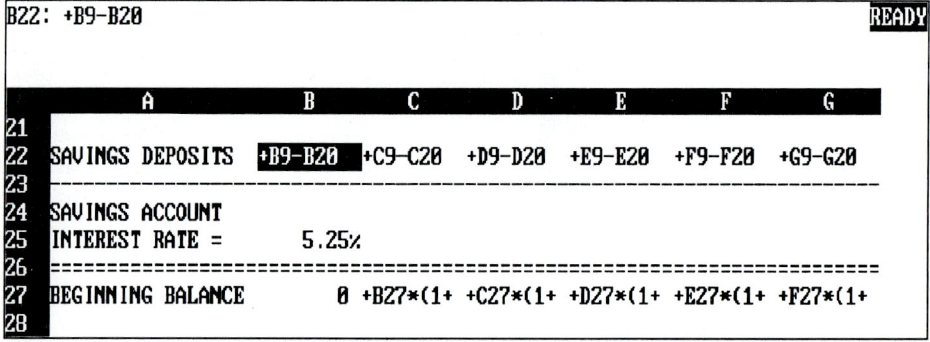

10. Type the /**W**orksheet, **G**lobal,**F**ormat command and select the **C**urrency command (two decimal places).

```
B22: +B9-B20                                                               READY

                      A              B        C        D        E        F        G
10
11 EXPENSES
12 ---------------------------------------------------------------------------------
13 RENT                         $375.00  $375.00  $395.00  $395.00  $395.00  $395.00
14 UTILITIES                    $125.00  $125.00  $125.00  $100.00  $100.00  $100.00
15 TELEPHONE                     $18.00   $18.00   $18.00   $18.00   $18.00   $18.00
16 LIFE INSURANCE                $28.65   $28.65   $28.65   $28.65   $28.65   $28.65
17 FOOD                         $480.93  $480.93  $480.93  $480.93  $517.83  $517.83
18 LEISURE                      $240.47  $240.47  $240.47  $240.47  $258.92  $258.92
19 ---------------------------------------------------------------------------------
20 TOTAL EXPENSES              ******************************************************
21
22 SAVINGS DEPOSITS             $335.06  $335.06  $315.06  $340.06  $407.71  $407.71
23 ---------------------------------------------------------------------------------
24 SAVINGS ACCOUNT
25 INTEREST RATE =                5.25%
26 =================================================================================
27 BEGINNING BALANCE              $0.00  $335.06  $671.58  $989.57 ******************
28
29
24-Apr-90  09:31 AM
```

Notice that when a value becomes too large to display in a cell (in this case because of the addition of $ signs and commas), Lotus 1-2-3 indicates the situation by putting asterisks in the affected cell.

LESSON 14
Global Change of Column Widths

One solution to the problem of numeric entries that are too large to display in their cells is to enlarge the display width of the cell. One /**W**orksheet,**G**lobal command allows you to change the default global column width of nine characters to any width size between 1 and 240 characters.

1. Type the /**W**orksheet,**G**lobal,**C**olumn-Width command and enter the new global column width as 12.

```
A28: [W18]                                                          READY

                      A              B           C           D           E
19 ------------------------------------------------------------------------
20 TOTAL EXPENSES           $1,268.05   $1,268.05   $1,288.05   $1,263.05
21
22 SAVINGS DEPOSITS           $335.06     $335.06     $315.06     $340.06
23 ------------------------------------------------------------------------
24 SAVINGS ACCOUNT
25 INTEREST RATE =              5.25%
26 ========================================================================
27 BEGINNING BALANCE            $0.00     $335.06     $671.58     $989.57
28
```

LESSON 15 Altering the Spreadsheet

Suppose you neglected an expense item (or acquired a new one) and needed to include it in your spreadsheet. The following steps will show you how to add it to your spreadsheet.

Inserting a Spreadsheet Row or Column

1. Move the pointer to anywhere in row 14 (UTILITIES) and type the /**W**orksheet,**I**nsert,**R**ow command.

The command to insert rows allows you to insert one row or more at once by specifying a range of rows to insert. In this case you will insert only one row, so the default range shown is correct.

2. Type ↵ to insert the single row.
3. Move the pointer to any month's total expense amount.

Notice that Lotus automatically adjusts existing cell references in its formulas and functions to accommodate an alteration (such as an inserted or deleted row) of the spreadsheet. For instance, the formula for January's total expenses @**SUM**(B13..B18) in row 21 automatically has been changed to @**SUM**(B13..B19) to accommodate the row inserted into the range. Similarly, the formula +B9−B20 for January's savings deposits has been changed to +B9−B21.

4. Move the spreadsheet pointer to A14 and label the new row PARKING since it will be the row for parking fees paid for three-month parking permits.
5. Now move to the months January, April, July, and October to enter the amount of $75.00 into these cells for the PARKING spreadsheet row.

Moving a Spreadsheet Row or Column

What if you decide parking expenses should be located below utilities rather than below rent?

6. Move the pointer to row 16 for telephone expenses and insert a single row there.
7. Move the pointer to A14 and type the /**M**ove command.
8. Enter the range to /**M**ove FROM as A14..M14 and the TO range as A16 (the uppermost left cell of the row you just inserted).

Deleting a Spreadsheet Row or Column

9. Move the pointer back to row 14, where PARKING used to be. Type the /**W**orksheet commands, find the **D**elete command, and then use the command to delete that single row.

LESSON 16 More on Viewing the Spreadsheet

The spreadsheet you have created is so large that only a portion of it may be viewed on the screen at a time. The portion to the top left should appear as follows.

```
A1: [W18]                                                   READY

           A              B          C          D          E
1
2                        JAN        FEB        MAR        APR
3
4  GROSS INCOME     $1,955.00  $1,955.00  $1,955.00  $1,955.00
5  TAX RATE
6                18%
7  FED & STATE TAXES  $351.90    $351.90    $351.90    $351.90
8  ---------------------------------------------------------------
9  NET PAY AMOUNT   $1,603.10  $1,603.10  $1,603.10  $1,603.10
10
11 EXPENSES
12 ---------------------------------------------------------------
13 RENT                $375.00    $375.00    $395.00    $395.00
14 UTILITIES           $125.00    $125.00    $125.00    $100.00
15 PARKING              $75.00                           $75.00
16 TELEPHONE            $18.00     $18.00     $18.00     $18.00
17 LIFE INSURANCE       $28.65     $28.65     $28.65     $28.65
18 FOOD                $480.93    $480.93    $480.93    $480.93
19 LEISURE             $240.47    $240.47    $240.47    $240.47
20 ---------------------------------------------------------------
24-Apr-90  10:07 AM
```

To view the last eight columns of the spreadsheet you need to use the pointer to "push" or *scroll* the screen across. Lotus 1-2-3 provides several ways to use the pointer to move the screen about on a large spreadsheet.

Moving Quickly about the Spreadsheet

You already have used Function key F5 to "GOTO" a particular cell and have used the Home key to move quickly back to cell A1. To see the other ways that you can move quickly about the spreadsheet, do the following.

1. Type the Home key to send the pointer to cell A1. Next type the PgDn key on the numeric keypad. Then type the PgUp key found on the same keypad.

The PgDn and PgUp keys move the pointer and the screen one "page" (one screen's worth of spreadsheet) up or down at a time.

Next, find the Tab key on the left side of the keyboard marked with two arrows. It is just above the key marked Ctrl.

2. Type the Tab key once or twice.

The lower case of this key moves the pointer and the screen one page (one screen) to the right. Shift to the upper case of the key to move the pointer and screen one page to the left.

3. Type the Home key to send the pointer to cell A1.
4. Now move the pointer to A8 and type the key marked End on the numeric keypad.

Notice the indicator at the bottom of the spreadsheet showing the END mode is turned on.

5. Type the Pointer Right key (→).
6. Type the End key. Then type the Pointer Left key (←).
7. Now type the End key/Pointer Down key (↓) combination three times in a row.
8. Type the End key/Pointer Up key (↑) combination four times in a row.

The End key turns on a mode that, when used with the pointer control keys, moves in the direction indicated by the pointer control key until the pointer reaches the last nonblank cell in the spreadsheet, if the pointer was originally on a nonblank cell. The pointer will move to the cell following the last blank cell if it was originally on a blank cell.

9. Type the End key and then the Home key.

This End key combination sends the pointer to the lowest right cell of the rectangle defined by the spreadsheet (the effective opposite of Home).

These methods of moving the pointer are extremely useful when pointing to ranges at the time they are being specified, or when pointing to cell references in a formula when a formula is being created.

Freezing Titles

Lotus 1-2-3 has the ability to let you "freeze" rows, columns, or both when viewing large spreadsheets. This is particularly useful when row or column labels disappear from view because the screen is pushed to another section of the spreadsheet. For instance, when you want to view the row labeled BEGINNING BALANCE, the month labels for the row disappear off the top of the screen.

10. Move the pointer to row 4. Type the /**W**orksheet command and select the **T**itles command.

You want to freeze the row of month labels that is horizontal in the spreadsheet.

11. Select the **H**orizontal command of this menu.
12. Now use the pointer to push the screen down the spreadsheet until the last rows appear for viewing.

Notice that the rows above the pointer's position at the time the titles were frozen do not scroll off the screen.

13. Use the pointer to push the screen to the right until the month of December is showing.

The month labels scroll with the rest of the spreadsheet, but now the row labels have disappeared.

14. Type the Home key, move the pointer to cell B4, and then use the **T**itles command to set both horizontal and vertical title freeze.
15. Scroll the screen to the right and then down. Both the row labels and column labels now are frozen.
16. Type the Home key.

Notice that when titles are frozen you are unable to move the pointer to them with the pointer control keys. Home now is defined as the upper left corner of the unfrozen spreadsheet. To move the pointer into a frozen area, press Function key F5 (GOTO) and then the address of a cell within the frozen area.

The /**W**orksheet,**T**itles,**C**lear command unfreezes all fixed titles.

17. Use this command to unfreeze the titles on your spreadsheet.

The next portion of the tutorial introduces a concept called modeling and also will demonstrate techniques for dealing with large spreadsheets.

LESSON 17 Modeling with a Spreadsheet

Modeling allows you to ask "What if?" and then use the rapid recalculation power of the spreadsheet to obtain the answer quickly. To take you through a lesson on how you can model with the spreadsheet, you will add another value to the spreadsheet.

Adding a Summary for Interest Earned

1. Move to cell L30 and type ‖   INTEREST EARNED = ‖ .

5 spaces

2. Next move to cell N26 and type ‖ ENDING BALANCE ‖ .

3. Copy the formula in cell M28 to cell N28.

This area of the spreadsheet should now look like the following.

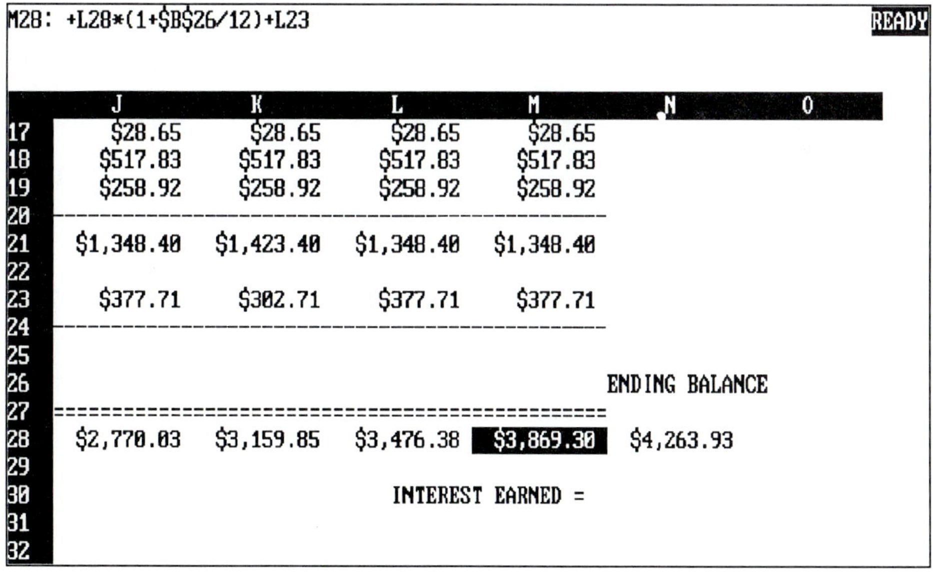
M28: +L28*(1+$B$26/12)+L23 READY

	J	K	L	M	N	O
17	$28.65	$28.65	$28.65	$28.65		
18	$517.83	$517.83	$517.83	$517.83		
19	$258.92	$258.92	$258.92	$258.92		
20	----------	----------	----------	----------		
21	$1,348.40	$1,423.40	$1,348.40	$1,348.40		
22						
23	$377.71	$302.71	$377.71	$377.71		
24	----------	----------	----------	----------		
25						
26					ENDING BALANCE	
27	==========	==========	==========	==========		
28	$2,770.03	$3,159.85	$3,476.38	$3,869.30	$4,263.93	
29						
30			INTEREST EARNED =			
31						
32						

Advantages of Pointing to Enter a Formula

In cell N30 you will enter the formula that will give the total interest earned on your savings for the year. The formula will subtract the beginning balance and all deposits from the ending balance to determine its answer. Since cell references for the formula are located in several areas of the spreadsheet, you will use the pointing method to enter the formula into the appropriate spreadsheet cell. As you move about the spreadsheet to point to various cell references, try using the rapid methods of moving the pointer.

4. With the pointer on cell N30 type ‖ + ‖ to indicate that you are starting to enter a numeric value into this cell.
5. Move the pointer to the year's ending balance amount. Look at the edit line at the top of the screen to see that the formula is being entered.
6. Type ‖ – ‖ (minus).

The pointer will return to N30 and the edit line should show +N28–.

7. Move the pointer to the beginning balance amount for January and type ‖ – ‖ again.

The pointer will return again to N30 and the formula continues to grow.

8. Now type ‖ **@SUM**(‖ and then move the pointer to the beginning of the savings deposits values.
9. Press the period key to set the anchor for the range you are going to sum.
10. Move the pointer to the end of the savings deposits row and type ‖) ‖ .

The formula is complete: +N28 – B28 – **@SUM**(B23..M23).

11. Now type ↵ to enter the formula.

```
N30: +N28-B28-@SUM(B23..M23)                                          READY

         J            K            L            M            N            O
17     $28.65       $28.65       $28.65       $28.65
18    $517.83      $517.83      $517.83      $517.83
19    $258.92      $258.92      $258.92      $258.92
20 ------------------------------------------------
21  $1,348.40    $1,423.40    $1,348.40    $1,348.40
22
23    $377.71      $302.71      $377.71      $377.71
24 ------------------------------------------------
25
26                                                  ENDING BALANCE
27 ================================================
28  $2,770.03    $3,159.85    $3,476.38    $3,869.30    $4,263.93
29
30                               INTEREST EARNED =        $97.07
31
32
```

Splitting the Window on the Spreadsheet

With deposits given, two factors will affect interest earned—the interest rate and the beginning balance. You can find both values in the B column, and you can find the interest earned to the far right (out of view) in the N column. To view these columns at the same time and access them with the pointer, you may use the /**W**orksheet,**W**indow set of commands.

12. Move the pointer anywhere in the C column and type the /**W**orksheet,**W**indow,**V**ertical command.

B1: READY

	A	B		C	D	E
1			1			
2		JAN	2	FEB	MAR	APR
3			3			
4	GROSS INCOME	$1,955.00	4	$1,955.00	$1,955.00	$1,955.00
5	TAX RATE		5			
6	18%		6			
7	FED & STATE TAXES	$351.90	7	$351.90	$351.90	$351.90
8	------------------	----------	8	----------	----------	----------
9	NET PAY AMOUNT	$1,603.10	9	$1,603.10	$1,603.10	$1,603.10
10			10			
11	EXPENSES		11			
12	------------------	----------	12	----------	----------	----------
13	RENT	$375.00	13	$375.00	$395.00	$395.00
14	UTILITIES	$125.00	14	$125.00	$125.00	$100.00
15	PARKING	$75.00	15			$75.00
16	TELEPHONE	$18.00	16	$18.00	$18.00	$18.00
17	LIFE INSURANCE	$28.65	17	$28.65	$28.65	$28.65
18	FOOD	$480.93	18	$480.93	$480.93	$480.93
19	LEISURE	$240.47	19	$240.47	$240.47	$240.47
20	------------------	----------	20	----------	----------	----------

24-Apr-90 11:44 AM

The **W**indow commands **H**orizontal and **V**ertical split the screen into separate windows through which you can view the spreadsheet. Each window may be used to scroll the spreadsheet.

The pointer can reside in only one window at any given time, but it may be moved from one window to the other by typing Function key F6.

13. Type Function key F6 several times. Then move the pointer to the window on the left.

14. Try moving the pointer to the right six columns.

You can scroll the spreadsheet in this window with the pointer in the same manner as you previously scrolled the spreadsheet.

15. Type the Home key and then use the pointer to scroll up the spreadsheet until the bottom three rows are located in about the middle of the screen.

Notice that the spreadsheet on the right also scrolls. The term for such scrolling is *synchronized scrolling* and the /**W**orksheet,**W**indow commands include the commands to **S**ynchronize and **U**nsynchronize the scrolling of spreadsheets being viewed through the windows.

16. Type the F6 key to move to the right window and scroll it to the left until you can see the last three columns (L, M, and N).

17. Now move to the left window by typing F6.

```
B36:                                                                 READY

            A                  B                 L          M           N
17 LIFE INSURANCE          $28.65  17       $28.65     $28.65
18 FOOD                   $480.93  18      $517.83    $517.83
19 LEISURE                $240.47  19      $258.92    $258.92
20 ------------------------------- 20 ----------------------
21 TOTAL EXPENSES       $1,343.05  21    $1,348.40  $1,348.40
22                                 22
23 SAVINGS DEPOSITS       $260.06  23      $377.71    $377.71
24 ------------------------------- 24 ----------------------
25 SAVINGS ACCOUNT                 25
26 INTEREST RATE =          5.25%  26                          ENDING BALANCE
27 =============================== 27 ======================
28 BEGINNING BALANCE        $0.00  28    $3,476.38  $3,869.30  $4,263.93
29                                 29
30                                 30     INTEREST EARNED =        $97.07
31                                 31
32                                 32
33                                 33
34                                 34
35                                 35
36                                 36
24-Apr-90  03:54 AM
```

You may move the pointer in the left window to change the interest rate, beginning balance, or both, and you can see the effect the changes have on interest earned for the year in the window to the right.

Test Your Understanding: Using the Spreadsheet to Model

Suppose you actually had $1500.00 in the account at the beginning of the year. Where would you enter this figure in your spreadsheet and by how much does this change affect the year's interest earned?

18. Make the change to the spreadsheet.

Assume you hear about a "sure thing" investment and are considering it as an alternative to putting your money in the savings and loan. The investment offers a 28% return instead of the 5.25% you currently receive. What effect would this investment have on the year's interest earned?

19. Enter the change in interest rate and observe the effect on interest earned.

Removing a Split Screen Display

20. Type the /**W**orksheet,**W**indow command and select the command to **C**lear.

The **C**lear command returns the screen to one window and to its normal appearance.

LESSON 18 Other Yearly Summaries

To complete the spreadsheet you will add a final column of summary information of total amounts for various income and expense items.

1. Move to cell N2 and type ‖ "TOTALS↵ ‖ .

NOTE: We've used the label prefix " to right justify the label in the cell.

2. Move to cell N4 and type ‖ @**SUM**(B4.M4)↵ ‖ .
3. Now copy the formula into the range N5..N23.

Notice that several cells in this column now display $0.00. It is important to note that cells containing labels, when included in a numeric entry such as an @**SUM** function, are assigned a numeric value of zero.

4. Use the /**R**ange,**E**rase command to erase the cells that tried to sum a range holding nothing except labels.

Turning Off Automatic Recalculation

Depending on the type of hardware you are using, you may note an increasing wait (the pointer disappears) after you make a cell entry or change a cell's contents. This is because Lotus 1-2-3 (by default) automatically recalculates the entire spreadsheet every time a cell's contents are changed. The larger the spreadsheet is, the longer the wait becomes. To stop automatic recalculation you may use the /**W**orksheet,**G**lobal,**R**ecalculation,**M**anual command. To turn automatic calculation back on, you use the /**W**orksheet,**G**lobal,**R**ecalculation,**A**utomatic command.

While **R**ecalculation is in the **M**anual mode, you need to type the F9 (CALCULATE) Function key to cause a recalculation of the spreadsheet.

LESSON 19 Printing a Spreadsheet

Using the /**P**rint Commands

You now are ready to set up the spreadsheet to be printed. It is far too wide to fit on an 8½″ × 11″ piece of paper; however, Lotus 1-2-3 compensates by printing it on additional pieces of paper. You also can choose to condense the spreadsheet as it is printed if your printer has that feature.

1. To begin, type the /**P**rint,**P**rinter command.

Your first set-up operation will be to define the range of cells you want printed.

2. Select the **R**ange command and set the range for printing to be the entire year's budget spreadsheet (A1..030).

Sticky Menus

Notice that you were not returned to the data entry mode after the **R**ange command was finished. Instead, the /**P**rint,**P**rinter submenu still appeared on the screen. Lotus refers to command menus that do not immediately return you to the data entry mode as being "*sticky menus.*" Such menus often have the option to **Q**uit included in them. The **Q**uit command usually may be used to return to the data entry mode.

Completing the Print Operation

Once you have specified the range to print, the specification becomes part of the spreadsheet's data (as do all of the options and specifications you select for a particular spreadsheet). So, if you save the spreadsheet after you have set your print range, you need not specify that range again in order to print the same portion of the spreadsheet later.

3. Make sure the printer is turned on, on-line, and connected to your computer.

NOTE: Your lab may have a shared device control switch. You will need to select your computer as the one currently connected to the printer.

4. Advance the paper in the printer to the top of the next page.
5. Select and enter the **A**lign command of the /**P**rint,**P**rinter menu to tell Lotus 1-2-3 that the printer is at the top of a page.

*NOTE: Selecting **A**lign does not produce a visible reaction from Lotus 1-2-3.*

6. Now select the **G**o command of the menu.

Notice that Lotus 1-2-3 will print (by default) the number of columns it can fit in 72 characters across the page, and then advance a page and begin printing columns where it left off. Lotus 1-2-3 also will automatically "page" its printing for spreadsheets that have too many rows to fit in its default page length of 66 lines per page.

Default widths and lengths for printing (as well as several other default settings) can be changed by using the /**P**rint,**P**rinter,**O**ptions commands.

```
Header  Footer  Margins  Borders  Setup  Pg-Length  Other  Quit
```

Using Print Options

To gain experience using three very useful print **O**ptions available, do the following.

7. Select the **O**ptions command of the /**P**rint,**P**rinter menu.
8. Set the **B**orders to be "**C**olumns" A1.

With Lotus 1-2-3 you may choose certain columns and/or rows to be automatically included in each page of the printed spreadsheet.

9. Next select the **S**etup command.

The **S**etup command sends special control codes to the printer to alter its normal printing. One of the most useful control codes with spreadsheet applications causes the printer to print in condensed mode. If your printer is able to print in this mode, you must send it the correct code. Since the correct codes vary from printer to printer, your answer to the "Enter Setup String:" prompt on the screen will vary depending on the brand of printer you are using. However, with such major manufacturers as Epson, Gemini, IBM, and Okidata, the code is \027\015.

10. Type and enter the appropriate code for your printer.
11. Now select the **M**argins command and set the **R**ight margin to 132.

With condensed print, the number of characters you can fit across a standard 8½″ × 11″ sheet of paper is 132. You do, however, need to extend the right margin setting to tell Lotus 1-2-3 to start paging its spreadsheet at 132 characters rather than 72.

12. Select the **Q**uit command of the **O**ption commands to return you to the /**P**rint, **P**rinter commands.
13. Finally, respecify the **R**ange to be printed as B1..030.

The A column in the spreadsheet has been specified as a border and will be printed automatically with each page printed.

14. Make sure the paper is advanced to its top. Now select the **A**lign command and then tell Lotus 1-2-3 to **G**o ahead and print the spreadsheet.
15. After the printer has finished printing your spreadsheet, turn the printer off and then back on again to return it to its default print settings.
16. When you return to your computer, type the **Q**uit command to exit the /**P**rint,**P**rinter commands.

LESSON 20 Finishing the Tutorial Lessons

To conclude the tutorial lessons, do the following.

1. Use the /**F**ile command to resave the spreadsheet under its original name LOTUT.
2. Use the /**Q**uit command to exit the spreadsheet software, and then use the Access System's **E**xit command to return to the DOS operating level.

Only a few specific rules exist to help you design your spreadsheet. These rules may, however, prove useful in helping you design spreadsheets that avoid the problems that beginning users are likely to experience.

SEPARATE KINDS OF DATA IN SEPARATE SPREADSHEET AREAS

The Spreadsheet's Keys

In the introductory tutorial you created a spreadsheet that incorporated elements of poor spreadsheet design. The most serious design flaw was the way in which constants (real numbers) were included within the calculating body of the spreadsheet. Below is a portion of the spreadsheet you created in the tutorial section with the contents of the cells shown. The constants are shown in gray.

```
A1: [W18]

            A                B          C          D          E
1
2                           JAN        FEB        MAR        APR
3
4  GROSS INCOME            1955        +B4        +C4        +D4
5  TAX RATE
6                  0.18
7  FED & STATE TAXES   +$A$6*B4   +$A$6*C4   +$A$6*D4   +$A$6*E4
8  ------------------------------------------------------------
9  NET PAY AMOUNT        +B4-B7     +C4-C7     +D4-D7     +E4-E7
10
11 EXPENSES
12 ------------------------------------------------------------
13 RENT                     375       +B13    +C13+20       +D13
14 UTILITIES                125       +B14       +C14        100
15 PARKING                   75                               75
16 TELEPHONE                 18       +B16       +C16       +D16
17 LIFE INSURANCE         28.65       +B17       +C17       +D17
18 FOOD                  0.3*B9     0.3*C9     0.3*D9     0.3*E9
19 LEISURE              0.15*B9    0.15*C9    0.15*D9    0.15*E9
20 ------------------------------------------------------------
29-Apr-90  03:02 AM
```

Such constants are called the *spreadsheet's keys*. They are the primary source of all values displayed in the spreadsheet. If you retrace the references of the formulas you will find that they ultimately refer to a cell holding a spreadsheet key.

As you look at the spreadsheet on the screen, however, it is difficult to tell which cells are holding formulas and which are holding keys. Even using the /**W**orksheet,**G**lobal,**F**ormat,**T**ext command will not always result in the display of a formula where a formula actually exists (such as when a cell has previously been /**R**ange,**F**ormatted).

Keys in Their Own Area

It is an accepted rule of spreadsheet design that, whenever possible, all keys should be kept in a separate, identifiable area of the spreadsheet. The calculating area should contain either formulas referring *directly* to the keys or referring *back* to them through a series of formulas. The spreadsheet should have been initially designed in two parts.

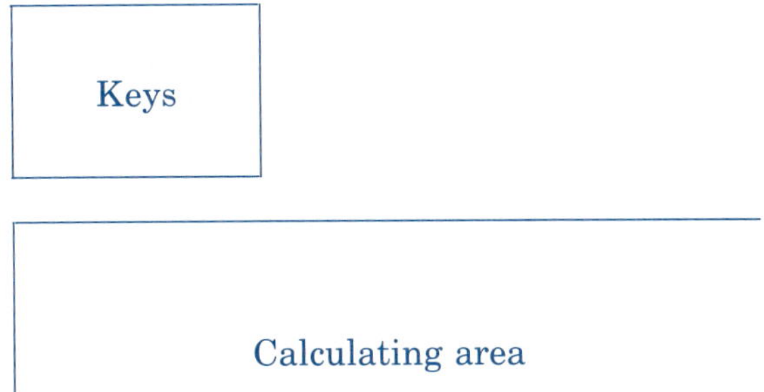

Cell references should refer directly to a given key

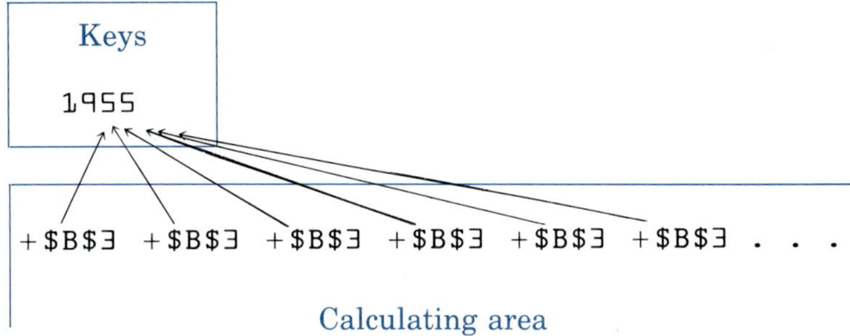

or, they should refer to a key indirectly through a series of formulas.

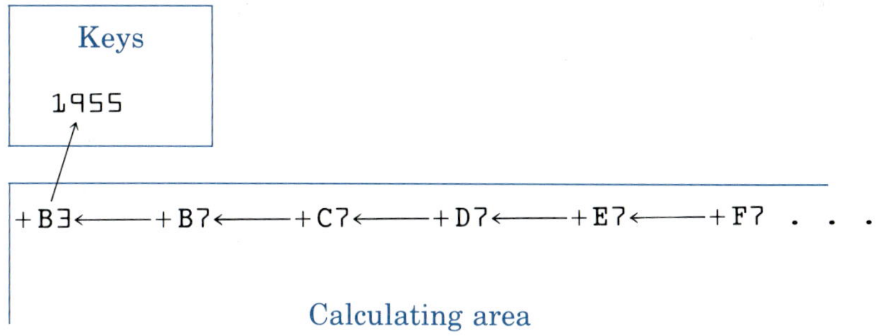

They also might use a variation.

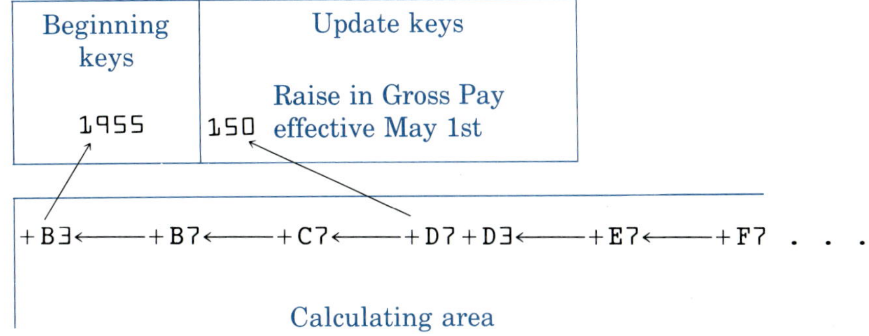

In the last example the keys have been separated into two types, beginning amounts and updates. In this spreadsheet a third type of key, percentage rates, could be included in a separate area within the spreadsheet's keys area.

SPREADSHEET DOCUMENTATION

Each key value in the spreadsheet should have its own label to explain its use and relevance to the calculating portion of the spreadsheet. That is, the key should be documented.

Along with separating the keys into their own area(s) and thoroughly documenting them, you should have an area set aside for additional documentation of the spreadsheet. This area could include things such as remarks and comments about the assumptions and relationships built into the spreadsheet, the date it was last updated, its filename, current print settings and more.

MAPPING OUT THE SPREADSHEET

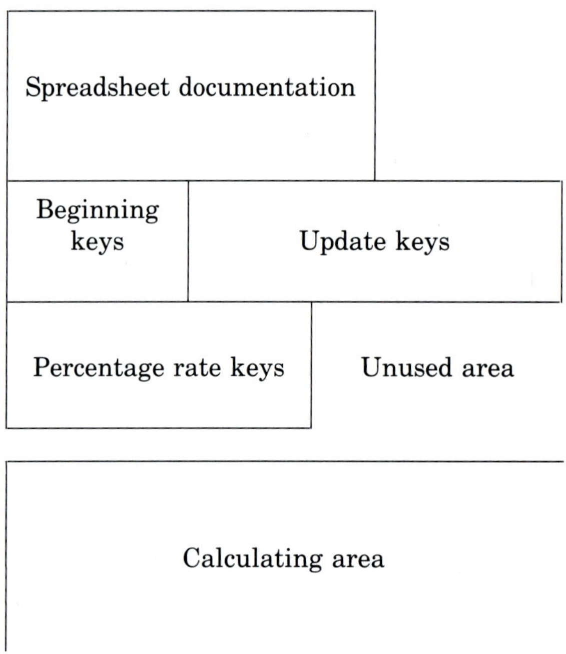

As you create more complex spreadsheets using more advanced features of Lotus 1-2-3, you will recognize that the spreadsheet should be mapped out with a pencil and piece of paper before it is created on the computer. A question such as "What happens to my key area if I need to use the /**W**orksheet command to insert a column or a row into my calculating area?" may lead you initially to map your spreadsheet as follows.

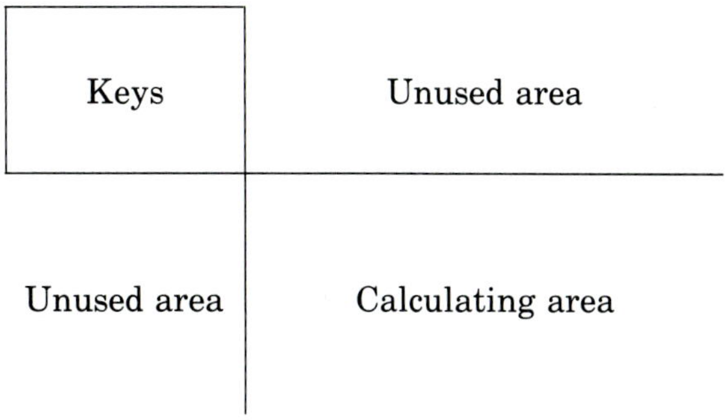

Keys	Unused area
Unused area	Calculating area

Such a plan may help you avoid disruption of spreadsheet areas later.

SPREADSHEET TEMPLATES

You may want to design a spreadsheet that is to be used more than once. For example, a spreadsheet designed to track expenditures against a departmental budget may be needed periodically. In a case like this, you can create a spreadsheet that acts as a master copy, or in spreadsheet jargon, as a *template*. The purpose of having a spreadsheet template is to avoid having to recreate the spreadsheet each time it is needed. The procedure for creating a spreadsheet template is as follows.

Once you have mapped out the spreadsheet, enter and test the labels, formulas, and keys to ensure the spreadsheet is reliable in its answers. Add any necessary documentation.

After the spreadsheet is operationally complete, set all relevant keys (those constants that may change from period to period) to zero by entering zeros in the cells that contain them. Save the spreadsheet on the diskette in its template form. To save a template it is customary to use a name such as "Master" to indicate that it is the master copy.

Once you have created and saved the template, you need to: a) load that spreadsheet into RAM; b) enter the appropriate key values for that period; and c) save that period's finished spreadsheet on the diskette under a different name. The original template remains on the diskette in its original form for the next time it is needed.

MIXED CELL REFERENCES

The cell references you have used so far have been either totally relative (as in +A5) or totally absolute (as in +$A$5). These are the two most common forms of cell references used in formulas destined to be copied into other cells.

Lotus 1-2-3 calls variations from these two forms *mixed references*. Although they are used less frequently, mixed references can be the desirable form for copying formulas into other cells. Using the example reference of cell A5, the variations are

+$A5 copies the formula with the references to the A column as absolute, but with the references to the fifth row as relative.

+A$5 copies the formula with the references to the A column as relative, but with the references to the fifth row as absolute.

Example of Using Mixed Cell References

To demonstrate the use of mixed references and their implication for spreadsheet design, consider the following situation.

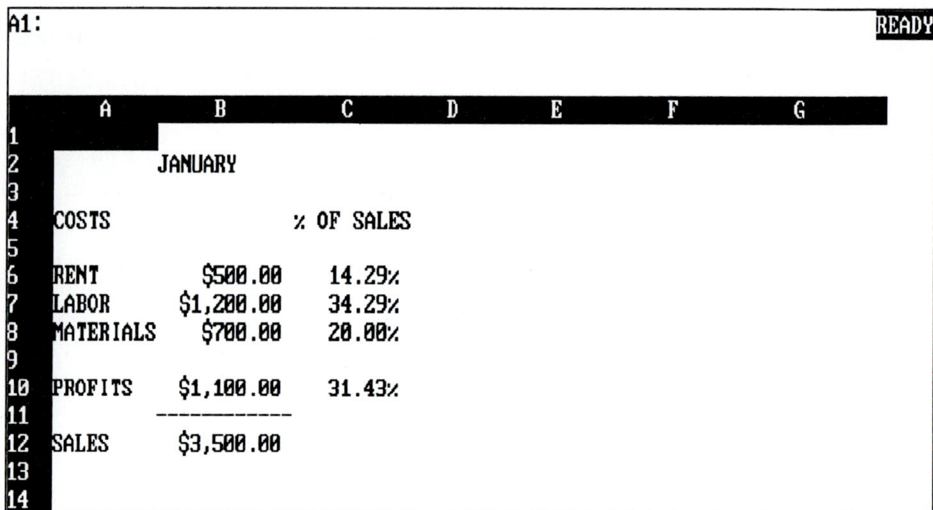

A1: READY

	A	B	C	D	E	F	G
1							
2		JANUARY					
3							
4	COSTS		% OF SALES				
5							
6	RENT	$500.00	14.29%				
7	LABOR	$1,200.00	34.29%				
8	MATERIALS	$700.00	20.00%				
9							
10	PROFITS	$1,100.00	31.43%				
11		------------					
12	SALES	$3,500.00					
13							
14							

In this spreadsheet all values in the B column (the dollar figures) are spreadsheet keys. Values in the C column are derived by formulas.

The designer of this spreadsheet intended to copy the rectangular range of labels, keys, and formulas of the spreadsheet into the area on the right side for the next month's figures.

	A	B	C	D	E	F	G
1							
2		JANUARY				JANUARY	
3							
4	COSTS		% OF SALES		COSTS		% OF SALES
5							
6	RENT	$500.00	14.29%		RENT	$500.00	14.29%
7	LABOR	$1,200.00	34.29%		LABOR	$1,200.00	34.29%
8	MATERIALS	$700.00	20.00%		MATERIALS	$700.00	20.00%
9							
10	PROFITS	$1,100.00	31.43%		PROFITS	$1,100.00	31.43%
11		------------				------------	
12	SALES	$3,500.00			SALES	$3,500.00	
13							
14		FROM : range				TO : range	
15							

After copying the range of cells the designer can change the label JANUARY to FEBRUARY, enter new keys, and have the formulas compute the correct percent of sales figures for that month.

In constructing the original portion of the spreadsheet the formula for rent as a percent of sales would be entered and copied into the rest of the appropriate cells for that column. To be copied correctly during this first copy operation, the formula would need to keep the reference to sales (B12) as absolute. But, for the next copy operation (creating February's report) the reference for the cell must be able to shift to the right in a relative fashion (to cell F12).

The solution to the problem is to keep the reference to the SALES row absolute so it does not shift down (in a relative fashion) in the first copy operation, and leave the reference to the SALES column as relative so it will shift to the right in the second copy operation. To do this, the original formula would be entered as

+B6/B$12

First: The original formula is entered.

```
       A           B            C          D       E       F       G
1
2              JANUARY
3
4   COSTS                    % OF SALES
5
6   RENT          $500.00   +B6/B$12
7   LABOR       $1,200.00
8   MATERIALS     $700.00
9
10  PROFITS     $1,100.00
11             -------------
12  SALES       $3,500.00
13
14
```

Second: The formula is copied into that column.

```
       A           B            C          D       E       F       G
1
2              JANUARY
3
4   COSTS                    % OF SALES
5
6   RENT          $500.00   +B6/B$12
7   LABOR       $1,200.00   +B7/B$12
8   MATERIALS     $700.00   +B8/B$12
9
10  PROFITS     $1,100.00   +B10/B$12
11             -------------
12  SALES       $3,500.00
13
14
```

Third: The second copy operation is completed.

	A	B	C	D	E	F	G
1							
2		JANUARY				JANUARY	
3							
4	COSTS		% OF SALES		COSTS		% OF SALES
5							
6	RENT	$500.00	+B6/B$12		RENT	$500.00	+F6/F$12
7	LABOR	$1,200.00	+B7/B$12		LABOR	$1,200.00	+F7/F$12
8	MATERIALS	$700.00	+B8/B$12		MATERIALS	$700.00	+F8/F$12
9							
10	PROFITS	$1,100.00	+B10/B$12		PROFITS	$1,100.00	+F10/F$12
11		------------				------------	
12	SALES	$3,500.00			SALES	$3,500.00	
13							
14							

Fourth: The month label and keys are changed, and the spreadsheet computes the correct figures for FEBRUARY.

	A	B	C	D	E	F	G
1							
2		JANUARY				FEBRUARY	
3							
4	COSTS		% OF SALES		COSTS		% OF SALES
5							
6	RENT	$500.00	14.29%		RENT	$500.00	11.76%
7	LABOR	$1,200.00	34.29%		LABOR	$1,500.00	35.29%
8	MATERIALS	$700.00	20.00%		MATERIALS	$950.00	22.35%
9							
10	PROFITS	$1,100.00	31.43%		PROFITS	$1,300.00	30.59%
11		------------				------------	
12	SALES	$3,500.00			SALES	$4,250.00	
13							
14							

LOTUS 1-2-3 FUNCTIONS

A *spreadsheet function* can be described as a shorthand method of accomplishing a specific task. The general formats for Lotus functions are

@**XYZ**(argument)
@**XYZ**(argument1,argument2,..argumentN)
@**XYZ**

Functions always begin with the @ sign and the function name. Arguments then are placed within parentheses. Some functions require only one argument, some require several arguments, and some require no arguments at all. When more than one argument is specified, the arguments must be separated by commas.

When referring to a function, one says that the function returns a value based upon the function's argument(s), if any. For example, the @**SUM** function returns the sum of the cells specified by its argument(s). If entered as @**SUM**(B13..B18), all cells within the range B13..B18 will be summed. If entered as @**SUM**(B13..B18,G12..J12), all cells within both ranges B13..B18 and G12..J12 will be summed.

Depending upon the function, arguments may be specified as follows.

Specification	Example
A single cell	@**ABS**(G12)
A range of cells (with coordinates)	@**SUM**(B13..B18)
A named range	@**SUM**(totals)
A constant numeric value	@**SQRT**(1250)
A constant string value	@**LENGTH**("Net Pay")
A condition or formula	@**IF**(A6>7,A6*1000,A6*B2)

Lotus 1-2-3 functions may be divided into the following basic categories.

1. Mathematical functions
2. Statistical functions
3. Financial functions
4. Date and Time functions
5. String functions
6. Logical and Special functions
7. Engineering functions

In the subsequent discussions, the most important or most often used functions in each of these categories are covered.

MATHEMATICAL FUNCTIONS

@**ABS**(value)	Returns the absolute value of the value argument.
@**INT**(value)	Returns the integer portion of a value.
@**MOD**(value, modulo)	Returns the remainder of a division operation. The value is divided by the modulo and the function returns the remainder (the modulus).

@**RAND**	Generates a random number. The function has no argument and the value returned changes each time the spreadsheet is recalculated.
@**ROUND**(value,places)	Returns the value rounded to the specified number of decimal places.
@**SQRT**(value)	Returns the square root of the value.

Most mathematical functions are fairly straightforward. Their arguments consist of single values, such as constants, cell references, or the computed results of formulas.

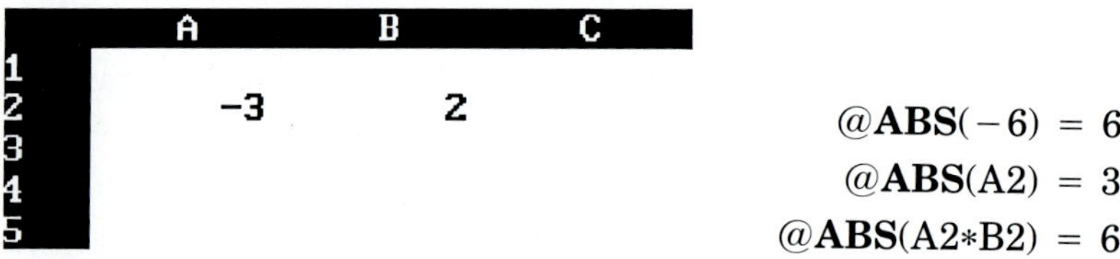

@**ABS**(−6) = 6

@**ABS**(A2) = 3

@**ABS**(A2*B2) = 6

@ROUND(value,places)

The @**ROUND** function is important for financial and other business-related spreadsheets. It is important because the values you see displayed on the monitor screen are formatted for display purposes only. All values are actually stored in RAM and are accurate to about 15 decimal places. The stored values are used in all of Lotus's computations. The results of the computations can often be confusing to beginning users who are trying to figure out why the spreadsheet does not agree with their calculators.

A solution for avoiding discrepancies in accuracy is to use the @**ROUND** function to return the rounded value (to the desired number of decimal places) for all values of concern. As an example, the internal results become

10/3 = 3.333333333333333

@**ROUND**(10/3,2) = 3.330000000000000

(Actually, the last two or three decimal places are undependable; however, this seldom interferes with the practical use of a spreadsheet.)

Negative "places" may be used in the @**ROUND** function to round numbers to the left of the decimal.

@**ROUND**(10000/3,2) = 3333.33

@**ROUND**(10000/3,−2) = 3300

@INT(value)

The Integer function is useful when decimal parts of a value are not desired and rounding is unnecessary, such as in some production models where a fraction of a unit will not be produced. With Lotus the value returned is the true integer portion of the argument with the remainder truncated for both positive and negative numbers.

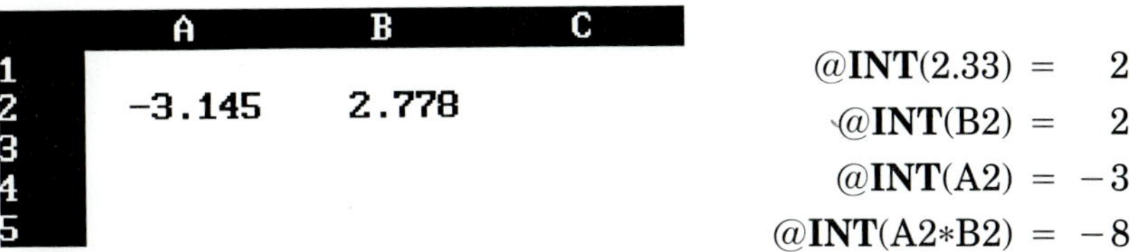

@**MOD**(value,modulo)

The @**MOD** function returns the modulus of the value divided by the modulo. In longhand division it looks like this:

```
                12
Modulo ——→ 3)38 ←—— Value
                30
                08
                 6
                 2 ←—— Modulus
```

The modulus is the numerator of the fractional remainder, 2/3, to the answer for this problem, 12 ⅔. The @**MOD** function can be useful in determining if partial batches or even/odd situations exist.

STATISTICAL FUNCTIONS

@**AVG**(list)	Returns the average value of all nonblank cells specified.
@**COUNT**(list)	Returns the number of nonblank cells in the specified list.
@**MAX**(list)	Returns the highest single value found in the specified list.
@**MIN**(list)	Returns the lowest single value found in the specified list.
@**STD**(list)	Returns the standard deviation from the mean for the nonblank cells in the specified list.
@**SUM**(list)	Returns the sum of all cells in the specified list.
@**VAR**(list)	Returns the variance of the values for the nonblank cells in the specified list.

Since all of these functions are important in business and are similar in form, they will be discussed as a group. The statistical functions are fairly straightforward, but are designed to deal with several values rather than the single value used by the mathematical functions.

The values may be cell references, ranges of cells, constants, or any combination of these, separated by commas in a list.

	A	B	C
1			
2	2	5	7
3	4		
4	6		
5	8	12	

@**SUM**(6,8,1) = 15
@**SUM**(A2..A5) = 20
@**SUM**(A2..A5,B2) = 25
@**SUM**(A2..A5,A2..C2,B5,10) = 56

Note that Lotus assigns all labels the value of 0 (zero) and uses the zeros in computing the value returned by a function. Lotus does not, however, use blank (empty) cells in computing the value returned. With most of the statistical functions, if cells with labels in them are included in the function's argument(s), an incorrect value will be returned by the function for the group of values of concern. Blank cells are ignored in calculations, and thus do not interfere with the results.

In the following example, for instance, within the range A1..A6 are the values of concern 2, 4, and 6; two cells with labels in them (A3 and A5); and the blank cell A1. Notice the results of using this range as the argument for the statistical functions.

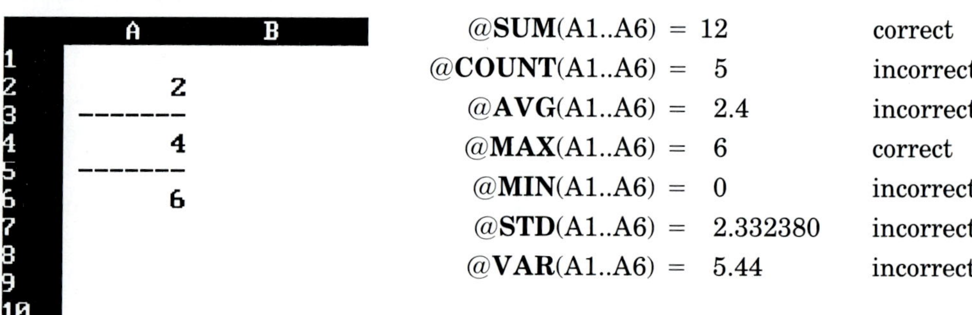

	A	B
1		
2	2	
3	-------	
4	4	
5	-------	
6	6	
7		
8		
9		
10		

Function	Result	
@**SUM**(A1..A6) =	12	correct
@**COUNT**(A1..A6) =	5	incorrect
@**AVG**(A1..A6) =	2.4	incorrect
@**MAX**(A1..A6) =	6	correct
@**MIN**(A1..A6) =	0	incorrect
@**STD**(A1..A6) =	2.332380	incorrect
@**VAR**(A1..A6) =	5.44	incorrect

To illustrate how statistical functions may be used, study the following example spreadsheet and the table below it.

	A	B	C	D
1				
2	SALES	1984	1985	1986
3		----------	----------	----------
4	JAN	1250	1310	1340
5	FEB	1115	1170	1195
6	MAR	1320	1390	1420
7	APR	1405	1485	1515
8	MAY	1380	1450	1480
9	JUN	1550	1630	
10	JUL	1575	1655	
11	AUG	1525	1600	
12	SEP	1515	1590	
13	OCT	1490	1565	
14	NOV	1385	1450	
15	DEC	1320	1390	
16				

Measurement	Function Used	Returned Value
Total 1985 sales	@**SUM**(C4..C15)	17685
1984 top month's sales	@**MAX**(B4..B15)	1575
1985 low month's sales	@**MIN**(C4..C15)	1170
Average January sales	@**AVG**(B4..D4)	1300
Average 1st quarter sales	@**AVG**(B4..D6)	1278.888
Average 1st & last quarter sales	@**AVG**(B4..D6,B13..D15)	1340.666
Total sales entered to date	@**SUM**(B4..B15,C4..C15, D4..D15) or @**SUM**(B4..D15)	41465
Total data entries to date	@**COUNT**(B4..D15)	29
Standard Deviation of total monthly sales	@**STD**(B4..D15)	136.6816
Variance of total monthly sales	@**VAR**(B4..D15)	18681.86

FINANCIAL FUNCTIONS

@**CTERM**(int,fv,pv)	Returns the number of periods needed for a present value investment (pv) to grow to a given future value (fv) at a given periodic interest rate (int).
@**DDB**(cost,salvage, life,period)	Returns the calculated depreciation on an asset using the double-declining balance method.
@**FV**(pmt,int,n)	Returns the future value of a stream of equal annuity payments (pmt) at a given periodic interest rate (int) over a given number of periods (n).
@**IRR**(guess, range)	Returns the approximate internal rate of return for a range of cash flows, given the help of a guess to start the computation.
@**NPV**(rate,range)	Returns the net present value of a stream of cash flows at a given discount rate.
@**PMT**(pv,int,n)	Returns the amount of a stream of equal annuity payments given a present value investment (pv), an interest rate (int), and number of periods (n).
@**PV**(pmt,int,n)	Returns the present value of a stream of equal annuity payments (pmt) for a given number of periods (n) at a given periodic interest rate (int).
@**RATE**(fv,pv,n)	Returns the required rate of interest for a present value investment (pv) to grow to a specified future value (fv) in a given number of periods (n).
@**SLN**(cost, salvage,life)	Returns the depreciation on an asset for a single period using the straight-line method.

@**SYD**(cost,salvage, life,period)	Returns the depreciation on an asset for a specified period using the sum-of-the-years'-digits method.
@**TERM**(pmt,int,fv)	Returns the number of periods required for a stream of equal annuity payments (pmt) to grow to a given future value (fv) at a given interest rate (int).

The financial functions are related to the time value of money and depreciation of assets. The time value of money functions, which will be covered in this section, are frequently used in business applications. Each function requires more than one argument in order to return the correct answer.

Compounding Interest Formula

When an investment is made at a fixed interest rate, the interest is compounded over the time of the investment. For instance, if $1,000 is invested for three years, earning 10% interest compounded annually, the balance at the end of the three years (fv) would be $1,331, which could be calculated as follows.

	Year 1	Year 2	Year 3
Beginning Balance	$1,000	$1,100	$1,210
+Interest Earned	$ 100	$ 110	$ 121
Ending Balance	$1,100	$1,210	$1,331

If you are interested in only the balance at the end of the last period (fv), you could use a formula to calculate the future value. The formula for computing this future value (fv) for any present value investment (pv), periodic interest rate (int), and number of periods (n) is

fv = pv * (1+int)^n

Thus, if you wanted to know the future value of $5,000 invested for 7 years at 5.25% (.0525) interest compounded annually, you could enter the formula into a spreadsheet as follows.

```
      A            B                        C              D          E
1
2        Present Value (pv)             $5,000
3
4        Interest Rate (int)            0.0525
5
6        Number of Periods (n)               7
7        ----------------------------------------------------------------
8        Future Value (fv) =         +C2*(1+C4)^C6   =   $7,153.601
9
```

On the other hand, if you knew the future value you wished to earn, but needed the present value investment required given the interest rate and number of periods, the formula for present value would be used.

$$pv = fv * 1/(1+int)^n$$

For example, if you wanted to know the investment needed today (pv) to earn $7,500 (fv) in 7 years at 5.25% interest compounded annually, you could enter the formula into a spreadsheet as follows.

```
      A            B                        C           D          E
 1
 2          Future Value (fv)          $7,500
 3
 4          Interest Rate (int)        0.0525
 5
 6          Number of Periods (n)           7
 7          ---------------------------------------------------------
 8          Present Value (pv) =     +C2*1/(1+C4)^C6   =   $5,242.114
 9
```

All of the Lotus functions concerned with the time value of money derive their computations from these basic interest compounding formulas. Note, however, that interest is often compounded for periods other than a year. When this is the case, you must specify both interest rate (int) and number of periods (n) using the same type of time period. For instance, if interest were to be compounded monthly in the last example, the interest should be entered as .004375 (.0525/12) and the number of periods should be entered as 84 (7*12).

@**CTERM**(int,fv,pv) and @**RATE**(fv,pv,n)

The @**CTERM** and @**RATE** functions are designed to provide either the number of periods (n) or the periodic interest rate (int) when the other variables in the equation are given. In the following example, a present value of $5,000 and a future value of $7,500 are used. When the interest rate (.0525) is given, @**CTERM** returns the exact number of periods required. When the number of periods (5) is given, @**RATE** returns the exact interest rate required.

```
      A            B                        C           D          E
 1
 2          Present Value (pv)               5,000
 3          Future Value (fv)                7,500
 4
 5          ---------------------------------------------------------
 6          Interest Rate (int)            0.0525
 7          Number of Periods (n) =   @CTERM(C6,C3,C2) = 7.924148
 8          ---------------------------------------------------------
 9
10          ---------------------------------------------------------
11          Number of Periods (n)                  5
12          Interest Rate (int) =     @RATE(C3,C2,C11) = .084471
13          ---------------------------------------------------------
```

Annuity Functions @**FV**, @**PV**, @ **PMT**, and @**TERM**

The functions discussed in the previous section deal with a lump sum investment earning compounded interest. When an investment involves equal payments to be made or received for every period involved, it is called an annuity. Annuities may be viewed in terms of the future value that will be produced by some number of equal annuity payments, or in terms of the present value required to produce a stream of equal annuity payments.

@**FV**(pmt,int,n)

The @**FV** function returns the future value, given an annuity payment (pmt), interest rate (int), and number of periods (n). For example, if you wanted to know the future value of $125 annuity payments invested every month for 3 years (36 periods), and earning .4375% (.004375) interest compounded monthly (5.25% annual percentage rate/12 months), you could use the @**FV** function.

```
     A            B                    C          D         E
1
2       Payment (pmt)                 $125
3       Interest (int)            0.004375
4       Number of Periods (n)           36
5       ----------------------------------------------------------
6       Future Value (fv) =      @FV(C2,C3,C4)  =  $4,862.248
7
```

@**PV**(pmt,int,n)

The @**PV** function returns the present value (pv) of a stream of annuity payments (pmt), given the interest rate (int) and number of periods (n). If the above example were restated so that you wanted to know how much to invest today in order to provide an annuity of $125 per month for 36 months (given the same monthly interest rate of .4375% compounded monthly) you could use the @**PV** function.

```
     A            B                    C          D         E
1
2       Payment (pmt)                 $125
3       Interest (int)            0.004375
4       Number of Periods (n)           36
5       ----------------------------------------------------------
6       Present Value (pv) =     @PV(C2,C3,C4)  =  $4,155.133
7
```

@**PMT**(pv,int,n)

The @**PMT** function returns the amount of an annuity payment, given a present value (pv), interest rate (int) and number of periods (n). For instance, if you wanted to make a $3,000 purchase today financing it by obtaining a loan to be repaid over three years at a 1.25% monthly percentage rate, you could determine the amount of your installment payments as shown in the following example.

	A	B	C	D	E
1					
2		Present Value (pv)	$3,000		
3		Interest (int)	0.0125		
4		Number of Periods (n)	36		
5		------------------------------------			
6		Payment (pmt) =	@PMT(C2,C3,C4)	=	$103.9959
7					

@**TERM**(pmt,int,fv)

The @**TERM** function returns the number of periods (n) required to reach a given future value (fv), given the amount of annuity payments (pmt) and the interest rate (int). For example, if you wanted to know the length of time it would take to accumulate $50,000 (fv), given annuity payments of $6,500 per year earning an annual percentage rate of 7.5% (.075), you could use the @**TERM** function.

	A	B	C	D	E
1					
2		Future Value (fv)	$50,000		
3		Interest (int)	0.075		
4		Payment (pmt)	$6,500		
5		------------------------------------			
6		Number of Periods (n) =	@TERM(C4,C3,C2)	=	6.298
7					

@**NPV**(rate,range) and @**IRR**(guess,range)

While the annuity functions deal with streams of equal payments, the @**NPV** and @**IRR** functions deal with streams of unequal cash flows. The stream of cash flows is represented by a range of values entered in the spreadsheet. Negative values are treated as cash outflows and positive values as cash inflows.

The net present value function @**NPV** returns the present value of a range of cash flows discounted at an opportunity cost determined at an alternate rate (called the discount rate) for the same flows. The periods are assumed to be equal in time and the rate used is a periodic discount rate. Note that with the @**NPV** function, the first cash flow in the range of cash flows is treated as occurring at the end of the first period. Subsequent cash flows are treated as occurring at the end of their periods.

The range in the argument must be a single row or column of cells. Blank cells and cells with labels within the range are counted as cash flows of 0 for the period. The rate argument used in the function is the periodic discount rate. Since it is usually the case (for valuation purposes) that the first cash flow is to occur at time 0 (zero), the use of the @**NPV** function often takes the following form.

First cash flow + @**NPV**(discount rate,subsequent cash flows)

The following example uses this formula with a periodic discount rate of 5.25%, an initial cash outflow of $500, and subsequent cash inflows of $200, $175, $150, and $125.

```
     A       B       C       D       E       F       G       H
1
2                       Periodic Cash Flows
3            0       1       2       3       4
4         -500     200     175     150     125
5
6        Discount Rate (rate)        0.0525
7        ---------------------------------------------------------
8        Net Present Value (npv) =  +B4+@NPV(E6,C4..F4)  =  $78.51943
9
```

The @**IRR** function returns an approximate internal rate of return for a series of cash flows in which the IRR is defined as the rate at which those cash flows have a zero net present value. The periods are assumed to be equal in time. The guess argument of the @**IRR** function serves as a starting point for the iterative process that the function uses to determine the IRR. If the guess is too far off the actual IRR, the function will return ERR. Guesses between 0.0 and 1.0 usually will yield a calculated IRR. Sometimes there is more than one IRR possible for a series of cash flows, so different guesses may result in different values.

The guess rate is entered as a decimal and the range in the argument must be a single row or column of cells. Blank cells and cells with labels within the range are counted as cash flows of 0 for that period. Note also that the IRR is a periodic rate, so if the cash flows are yearly, the value returned by the function will be an annual rate. The following example calculates an IRR using 14% (.14) as the guess, an initial cash outflow of $500, and subsequent cash inflows of $200, $175, $150, and $125.

```
     A       B       C       D       E       F       G       H
1
2                       Periodic Cash Flows
3            0       1       2       3       4
4         -500     200     175     150     125
5
6        Estimated Rate (guess)       0.14
7        ---------------------------------------------------------
8        Internal Rate of Return =  @IRR(E6,B4..F4)  =  0.124414
9
```

DATE AND TIME FUNCTIONS

@**DATE**(year, month, day)	Returns the serial number date value for the year, month, and day.
@**DATEVALUE**(date string)	Returns the serial number date value for a date string that is in a valid Lotus date format.
@**DAY**(serial date value)	Returns the day of the month (1–31) for a serial date value.
@**HOUR**(serial date value)	Returns the hour (0–23) for the fractional portion (time value) of a serial date value.
@**MINUTE**(serial date value)	Returns the minute (0–59) for the fractional portion (time value) of a serial date value.

@**MONTH**(serial date value)	Returns the month number (1–12) for a serial date value.
@**NOW**	Returns the current date and time as a serial date/time value.
@**SECOND**(serial date value)	Returns the seconds (0–59) for the fractional portion (time value) of a serial date value.
@**TIME**(hr,min,sec)	Returns the fractional portion (time value) of a serial date value for the specified hour, minute, and second value arguments.
@**TIMEVALUE**(time string)	Returns the fractional portion (time value) for a time string that is in a valid Lotus time format.
@**TODAY**	Returns @**INT**(@**NOW**), the integer portion of the function @**NOW.**
@**YEAR**(serial date value)	Returns the year for a serial date value.

Date and Time functions have many business-related spreadsheet applications. Lotus 1-2-3 maintains an internal calendar that extends from January 1, 1900 to December 31, 2099. Lotus has assigned a number to each day in this period. The numbers are serial: the date January 1, 1900 has been assigned the value 1; January 2, 1900 the number 2; and so on up to December 31, 2099, which has been assigned the value 73050.

With each date assigned a serial number in this manner, the computer can perform "date arithmetic."

	Date	Serial Number	Arithmetic	
Date #1	4/17/91	33345	−33345	
Date #2	12/25/91	33597	+33597	
			252	Shopping days until Christmas

If a decimal portion is added to a serial date value, it is used to represent a fractional part of a day and may be used as a Lotus time value. For example, .25 represents 1/4 of a day or 6 hours. Therefore, the serial date value 33597.25 would represent both the date 12/25/91 and the time 6:00 AM.

@**DATE**(year,month,day) and @**TIME**(hr,min,sec)

The @**DATE** and @**TIME** functions allow you to enter dates and times in a format to which you are accustomed, returning the appropriate serial date/time value.

	A	B	C
1			
2		@DATE(91,4,17) =	33345
3			
4		@TIME(8,30,0) =	0.3541666667
5			
6		@DATE(91,4,17)+@TIME(8,30,0) =	33345.354167
7			

If a year beyond 1999 is to be used in the @**DATE** function, it must be specified by adding 100 to the last two digits of the year. For example, April 17, 2000 would be entered as @**DATE**(100,4,17) and April 17, 2010 as @**DATE**(110,4,17)

Once a serial date/time value has been entered, either directly or with the @**DATE** or @**TIME** functions, the /**R**ange,**F**ormat,**D**ate command may be used to format the cell to display the value in a date or time format.

	A	B	C	D	E
1					
2		@DATE(91,4,17)+@TIME(8,30,0) =	33345.354167	<-- Format General	
3					
4		@DATE(91,4,17)+@TIME(8,30,0) =	17-Apr-91	<-- Format D1	
5		@DATE(91,4,17)+@TIME(8,30,0) =	17-Apr	<-- Format D2	
6		@DATE(91,4,17)+@TIME(8,30,0) =	Apr-91	<-- Format D3	
7		@DATE(91,4,17)+@TIME(8,30,0) =	04/17/91	<-- Format D4	
8		@DATE(91,4,17)+@TIME(8,30,0) =	04/17	<-- Format D5	
9		@DATE(91,4,17)+@TIME(8,30,0) =	08:30:00 AM	<-- Format D6	
10		@DATE(91,4,17)+@TIME(8,30,0) =	08:30 AM	<-- Format D7	
11		@DATE(91,4,17)+@TIME(8,30,0) =	08:30:00	<-- Format D8	
12		@DATE(91,4,17)+@TIME(8,30,0) =	08:30	<-- Format D9	
13					

Remember that the displayed contents of a cell formatted with /**R**ange,**F**ormat,**D**ate are not the actual contents of the cell. The cell holds, or has returned, a number that can be used in, or derived by, a formula.

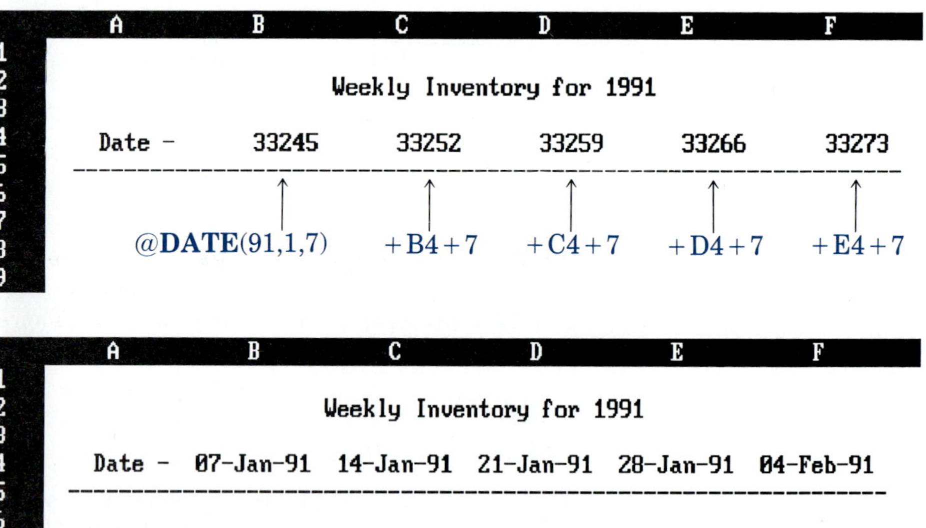

Weekly Inventory for 1991

	A	B	C	D	E	F
4	Date -	33245	33252	33259	33266	33273
8		@**DATE**(91,1,7)	+B4+7	+C4+7	+D4+7	+E4+7

Weekly Inventory for 1991

	A	B	C	D	E	F
4	Date -	07-Jan-91	14-Jan-91	21-Jan-91	28-Jan-91	04-Feb-91

@DAY @MONTH @YEAR @HOUR @MINUTE @SECOND

Once a serial date/time value has been entered into the spreadsheet, certain elements of the date or time such as the month number (1–12) or the hour number (0–23) may be returned by a function that uses a serial date value as its argument.

	A	B	C	D	E	F
1						
2		@DATE(91,4,17) =	33345		@DAY(C6) =	17
3					@MONTH(C6) =	4
4		@TIME(8,30,0) =	0.3541666667		@YEAR(C6) =	91
5						
6		+B2+B4 =	33345.354167		@HOUR(C6) =	8
7					@MINUTE(C6) =	30
8					@SECOND(C6) =	0
9						

STRING FUNCTIONS

@**CHAR**(number)	Returns the corresponding ASCII character. The number argument must be between 1 and 255; otherwise, the function will return ERR.
@**CLEAN**(string)	Removes nonprintable characters from strings imported with the /**F**ile,**I**mport command.
@**CODE**(string)	Returns a number representing the ASCII value of the first character in the string. If the argument is an empty cell or a cell containing a value, @**CODE** will return ERR.
@**EXACT**(string1, string2)	Compares two strings to test if the strings are exactly the same. Returns 1 (true) if the strings match exactly and 0 (false) if the strings do not match exactly.
@**FIND**(string1,string2, n)	Returns the location of string1 (substring) in string2, with the search beginning at the *n*th position of string2. The first character of string2 is considered position 0.
@**LEFT**(string,n)	Returns the left-most n characters in a string.
@**LENGTH**(string)	Returns the number of characters in a string.
@**LOWER**(string)	Returns the same string, with all letters converted to lower case.
@**MID**(string,start,n)	Returns an extracted substring from a larger string. The start argument determines the position in the string where the substring is to begin (the first character is position 0), and the n argument determines the length of the substring.
@**N**(range)	Returns the value of a number or a formula found in the top left cell of the specified range. If the cell is empty or contains a label, @**N** returns the value 0. @**N** always returns a numeric value.
@**PROPER**(string)	Returns the same string, with all first letters of words converted to upper case and subsequent letters converted to lower case.
@**REPEAT**(string,n)	Returns a string with the specified string argument repeated n times.

@**REPLACE**(string1, start,n,string2)	Returns a string in which a certain portion of string1 has been replaced by string2. The start argument specifies the position in string1 to begin the replacement (first position is 0), and the n argument determines how many characters will be replaced in string1. The entire string2 will be inserted into string1, regardless of the n argument.
@**RIGHT**(string,n)	Returns the right-most n characters in a string.
@**S**(range)	Returns the string value of the top left cell of the range. If the cell is empty or contains a numeric value, @**S** returns an empty (null) string. @**S** always returns a string value.
@**STRING**(n,decimals)	Returns the string of a numeric value n, rounded to the number of places specified by the decimal's argument.
@**TRIM**(string)	Removes trailing spaces from a string. Will change the value returned by the @**LENGTH** function.
@**UPPER**(string)	Returns the same string, with all letters converted to upper case.
@**VALUE**(string)	Returns a numeric value from a number that has been entered as a label or string value. The string may contain only number characters (0–9), a currency sign ($), thousand's separators (,), a decimal indicator (.), and leading or trailing spaces; otherwise, the function will return ERR.

The Lotus String functions provide a method of performing a number of common string manipulations. These functions may be useful when data has been imported with the /**F**ile,**I**mport command, when a spreadsheet contains much text, and when macros are being executed. The following is an example of the values returned by some of the String functions.

```
   A    B     C     D     E     F     G     H
1
2    Trouble brings experience, and experience brings wisdom.
3 ------------------------------------------------------------------
4 @FIND("experience",B2,0)  =          15
5 @FIND("experience",B2,16) =          31
6 @LENGTH(B2)               =          56
7
8 @LEFT(B2,14) =        Trouble brings
9 @RIGHT(B2,7) =        wisdom.
10 @MID(B2,8,5) =       bring
11
12 @LOWER(B2)  = trouble brings experience, and experience brings wisdom.
13 @PROPER(B2) = Trouble Brings Experience, And Experience Brings Wisdom.
14 @UPPER(B2)  = TROUBLE BRINGS EXPERIENCE, AND EXPERIENCE BRINGS WISDOM.
15
16 @REPLACE(B2,0,7,"Adversity") = ─┐
17   ┌─────────────────────────────┘
18   └→Adversity brings experience, and experience brings wisdom.
19
```

LOGICAL AND SPECIAL FUNCTIONS

@@(cell address)	When the cell address argument specifies a cell containing a label which, in turn, is another cell's address (e.g., A1), the function returns the contents of the cell referenced by the label. For example, if cell A1 = 15 and cell B2 = A1, then @@(B2) returns 15.
@**CELL**(attribute, range)	Returns the specified attribute of the cell in the upper left corner of the specified range. The result of the function is updated whenever the spreadsheet is recalculated.
@**CELLPOINTER** (attribute)	Returns the specified attribute of the cell in which the pointer is located. @**CELLPOINTER** functions will only display new values when the spreadsheet is recalculated.
@**CHOOSE**(valueX, value0, value1, ...valueN)	Returns one value from a list of possible values, based on the index (valueX). If valueX = 0, then value0 is returned; if valueX = 1, value1 is returned, and so forth. If valueX is not within the range of choices (value0...valueN), the function will return ERR.
@**COLS**(range)	Returns the number of columns in a range.
@**ERR**	Returns ERR (error).
@**FALSE**	Returns the value 0 (false).
@**HLOOKUP**(valueX, range,offset)	Returns the contents of some cell in a table. The location of the table is specified by the range argument. The column of the lookup cell is determined by comparing the valueX argument to ascending values found in the top row of the table. The row of the lookup cell is determined by the offset argument, which speci-

	fies some number of rows below the top row of the table.
@**IF**(condition,true value,false value)	Returns one of two values—the true value if the condition tests true or the false value if the condition tests false.
@**INDEX**(range,column, row)	Returns the contents of the cell found in the specified range at the intersection of the column and row arguments specified. The first column is column 0 and the first row is row 0. If the column or row specified does not fall within the specified range, the function will return ERR.
@**ISERR**(cell address)	Returns 1 (true) if the cell specified by the cell address argument contains ERR; otherwise, returns 0 (false).
@**ISNA**(cell address)	Returns 1 (true) if the cell specified by the cell address argument contains NA; otherwise, returns 0 (false).
@**ISNUMBER**(cell address)	Returns 1 (true) if the cell specified by the cell address argument contains a numeric value or is empty; otherwise, returns 0 (false).
@**ISSTRING**(cell address)	Returns 1 (true) if the cell specified by the cell address argument contains a label (string); otherwise, returns 0 (false).
@**NA**	Returns NA (not available).
@**ROWS**(range)	Returns the number of rows in a range.
@**TRUE**	Returns the value 1 (true).
@**VLOOKUP**(valueX, range,offset)	Returns the contents of some cell in a table. The location of the table is specified by the range argument. The row of the lookup cell is determined by comparing the valueX argument to ascending values found in the left-most column of the table. The column of the lookup cell is determined by the offset argument, which specifies some number of columns to the right of the left-most column of the table.

The Logical and Special functions allow the spreadsheet designer to incorporate some decision-making capabilities into a spreadsheet, and to trap for some possible error occurrences when building a spreadsheet template.

@IF(condition,true value,false value)

@**IF** is the true conditional function of Lotus. The first part of its argument is a logical expression using the relational operators <, >, and =. It also may include the logical operators #NOT#, #AND#, and #OR#. The computer evaluates the condition as either TRUE (equal to 1) or FALSE (equal to 0). Based on this evaluation, the @**IF** function returns either the true value or the false value argument. The following example spreadsheets demonstrate the use of the @**IF** function. Some rules of spreadsheet design will be set aside in order to help make the example easier to read and more understandable.

Simple Condition, Single @IF

The following spreadsheet computes the gross pay for salespersons working for a particular firm. Each salesperson receives a base pay per month of $1200.00 and an additional 10% commission on sales greater than $10000.

	A	B	C	D	E
1					GROSS
2	DATE HIRED	SALESPERSON	TERR	SALES	PAY
3					
4	05-Dec-79	Speakerman, Larry	1	15050	1705
5	15-Feb-76	Adams, Deborah	1	9050	1200
6	10-Jun-82	Edwards, Carl	1	7500	1200
7	25-Apr-84	Parsons, Shelly	2	16050	1805
8	01-Aug-67	Russell, Bob	2	14000	1600
9	31-Oct-77	Carlson, Richard	2	9050	1200
10	20-Mar-84	Hart, Nelson	3	11000	1300
11	05-May-84	Martin, Cathy	3	8750	1200
12	01-Jan-85	Hunter, Carol	3	7800	1200
13	25-Aug-78	Jackson, Steve	3	7650	1200
14					

The function originally entered into cell E4 (Larry Speakerman's gross pay) was

@**IF**(D4>10000,1200+0.1*(D4−10000),1200)

The function says

If the value in cell D4 is greater than 10000
return the value 1200 + 10% of the difference between the value in cell D4 and 10000.
Otherwise, return the value 1200.

The @**IF** function then was copied into the other cells in that column.

Simple Condition, Nested @IFs

Each salesperson is to receive a bonus based on the performance of all salespersons in their territory. Salespersons in territory #1 will receive a $50.00 bonus; those in territory #2, a $75.00 bonus; and those in territory #3, a $25.00 bonus.

	A	B	C	D	E	F
1					GROSS	
2	DATE HIRED	SALESPERSON	TERR	SALES	PAY	BONUS
3						
4	05-Dec-79	Speakerman, Larry	1	15050	1705	50
5	15-Feb-76	Adams, Deborah	1	9050	1200	50
6	10-Jun-82	Edwards, Carl	1	7500	1200	50
7	25-Apr-84	Parsons, Shelly	2	16050	1805	75
8	01-Aug-67	Russell, Bob	2	14000	1600	75
9	31-Oct-77	Carlson, Richard	2	9050	1200	75
10	20-Mar-84	Hart, Nelson	3	11000	1300	25
11	05-May-84	Martin, Cathy	3	8750	1200	25
12	01-Jan-85	Hunter, Carol	3	7800	1200	25
13	25-Aug-78	Jackson, Steve	3	7650	1200	25
14						

The function originally entered into cell F4 (Larry Speakerman's bonus) was

@**IF**(C4 = 1,50,@**IF**(C4 = 2,75,25))

In the example, the false value of the first @**IF** is another @**IF** function.

@**IF**(cond,true value,@**IF**(cond,true value,false value))

The total nested function says:

If the value in C4 equals 1,
  return the value 50.
Otherwise,
  if the value in C4 equals 2,
    return the value 75.
  Otherwise, return the value 25.

Complex Condition, Single @IF

In the final example, complex conditions using logical operators will be used in a single @**IF** function.

In addition to receiving gross pay with commissions and the territory performance bonus, any salesperson who was hired after May 1, 1984 and has sales greater than $7,500, or any salesperson who was hired after May 1, 1982 and has sales greater than $10,000, will receive an additional bonus of $15.00.

	A	B	C	D	E	F	G
1					GROSS		ADDED
2	DATE HIRED	SALESPERSON	TERR	SALES	PAY	BONUS	BONUS
3							
4	05-Dec-79	Speakerman, Larry	1	15050	1705	50	0
5	15-Feb-76	Adams, Deborah	1	9050	1200	50	0
6	10-Jun-82	Edwards, Carl	1	7500	1200	50	0
7	25-Apr-84	Parsons, Shelly	2	16050	1805	75	15
8	01-Aug-67	Russell, Bob	2	14000	1600	75	0
9	31-Oct-77	Carlson, Richard	2	9050	1200	75	0
10	20-Mar-84	Hart, Nelson	3	11000	1300	25	15
11	05-May-84	Martin, Cathy	3	8750	1200	25	15
12	01-Jan-85	Hunter, Carol	3	7800	1200	25	15
13	25-Aug-78	Jackson, Steve	3	7650	1200	25	0
14							

The @**IF** function originally entered into cell G4 was

@**IF**((A4>@**DATE**(84,5,1)#AND#D4>7500)#OR#(A4>@**DATE**(82,5,1)
#AND#D4>10000),15,0)

Here Lotus's normal order of precedence for logical operators #AND# and #OR# (evaluation left to right) is overridden by including parentheses in the complex condition of the form

(cond AND cond)   or   (cond AND cond)

If the total condition is evaluated as being true, this @**IF** function will return the value 15; if false, the value 0 will be returned.

@**CHOOSE**(valueX,value0,value1,value2,...valueN)

The @**CHOOSE** function uses an index (the integer valueX) to select a value to return from a list of values (value0...valueN). For example, if valueX equals 0, the first value of the list is returned; if valueX equals 1, the second value of the list is returned. If valueX is greater than the number of values in the list, the value ERR is returned.

In the following example, the @**CHOOSE** function is used to return values for a summary report for any one of three different divisions within a firm. The Summary Report area of the spreadsheet uses the value held in cell D3 as the index for its two @**CHOOSE** functions. To change the Summary Report, the user need only change the value in the cell D3.

```
   A       B             C          D         E          F          G
1
2    ------------------------------------------------------------
3    SUMMARY REPORT  Division #       3
4
5    Sales/Salesperson  $9,680 ←— @CHOOSE(D3,@NA,C12/C14,E12/E14,G12/G14)
6
7    Sales/Advertising   10.24 ←— @CHOOSE(D3,@NA,C12/C16,E12/E16,G12/G16)
8    dollar
9    ============================================================
10                Divison #1        Division #2        Division #3
11
12   SALES............$150,900          $135,500           $96,800
13
14   # Salespersons...        12                16                10
15
16   Advertising cost. $13,240           $21,275            $9,450
17
```

Based on the value in cell D3, the @**CHOOSE** functions will return the appropriate values for Sales/Salesperson and Sales/Advertising dollar for divisions 1, 2, or 3. Notice that the @**NA** function is listed as the zero index list value. This is one method of compensating for the awkward zero index that Lotus uses in this function.

@**VLOOKUP**(valueX,range,offset)

The @**VLOOKUP** function uses a table of values through which to search and from which to return an appropriate value. The search is based on the valueX argument. A classic example of the usefulness of the @**VLOOKUP** function is in looking up the appropriate tax amount for a given individual. The search through the table is based on the individual's taxable income and the value returned from the table is based on the filing status of the individual.

Using a small portion of the actual tax table that would be used, the following spreadsheet lets the user enter the taxable amount (from $24,000 to $24,400) into cell G2 and his or her filing status (1 through 4) into cell G4. The spreadsheet then uses an @**VLOOKUP** function in cell G7 to return the appropriate tax amount from the table found in range A12..E20.

```
      A        B        C        D        E        F        G
1          Filing Status
2   Single.......................1   TAXABLE INCOME -->   24,256
3   Married, filing jointly.......2
4   Married, filing separately....3   FILING STATUS  -->        2
5   Head of household............4
6                                    TAX AMOUNT
7                                    FROM TAX TABLE -->    3,394
8                                                              ↑
9   Taxable          Married  Married   Head of                |
10   Income  Single    Joint  Separate    House  @VLOOKUP(G2,$TAXTABLE,G4)
11  -------  -------  -------  -------  -------
12   24,000   4,273    3,339    5,314    3,953
13   24,050   4,288    3,350    5,333    3,967
14   24,100   4,303    3,361    5,352    3,981
15   24,150   4,318    3,372    5,371    3,995
16   24,200   4,333    3,383    5,390    4,009
17   24,250   4,348    3,394    5,409    4,023
18   24,300   4,363    3,405    5,428    4,037
19   24,350   4,378    3,416    5,447    4,051
20   24,400   4,393    3,427    5,466    4,065
```

The @**VLOOKUP** function in cell G7 was entered as @**VLOOKUP** (G2,$TAXTABLE,G4). Before the function can be evaluated, the range of cells A12..E20 must have been named TAXTABLE. The $ sign keeps the range reference absolute if the function is copied into other cells at a later time.

When the computer evaluates the @**VLOOKUP** function it moves to the top left cell of the range named TAXTABLE (cell A12) and compares the value there (24,000) to the first value in its argument (24,256). It then continues down that column, comparing each value with 24,256 (in this case until it reaches cell A18, 24,300). It then backs up one cell (to A17) and uses the offset argument (in this case, 2) to move that number of cells (2) to the right. There it finds the value 3,394 and returns it as the appropriate value for the function.

The values in the first column of the table (the values used to look up) must be in ascending order with no duplicates. If the first value in this column is larger than the value being looked up, or if the offset (the third argument) is greater than the width of the table range in columns, the result will be ERR. The offset for the first column is 0 (zero).

The @**VLOOKUP** function gets its name from the direction in which it looks up values—(V)ertically down the first column on the left side of a table. The @**HLOOKUP** function performs the same operations, but looks up its values (H)orizontally across the top row of a table, with its offset being the number of rows down from the first row.

@**CELL**(attribute,range) and @**CELLPOINTER**

The functions @**CELL** and @**CELLPOINTER** return information about an attribute of a cell in the spreadsheet. The attributes that may be returned are listed in the following table.

Attribute	**Return Value**	**Example**	
Address	Cell Address	$B$3	
Row	Row Number	3	
Col	Column Number	2	(column B)
Contents	Cell Contents	1225	
Type	Type of data 1,v,b	v	(label, value, blank)
Prefix	Label Prefix ',",^, none	'	
Protect	Protection Status 1,0	1	(1 = Protected)
Width	Column Width	12	
Format	Cell Format Abbreviation	C2	(currency, 2 decimals)

The returned value for the specified attribute will be updated whenever the spreadsheet is recalculated, either automatically or manually with the F9 (CALC) key. The @**CELL** function returns the specified attribute of the top left cell in the specified range. The @**CELLPOINTER** function returns the specified attribute of the cell in which the pointer is located when a spreadsheet recalculation occurs.

The following is an example of each of the attributes that may be returned by the @**CELL** and @**CELLPOINTER** functions. In the @**CELL** function, the range was specified as NET, which is the named range B5..B5, and the pointer was located at cell A3 when the CALC key (F9) was pressed.

A3: [W24] 'Taxes 

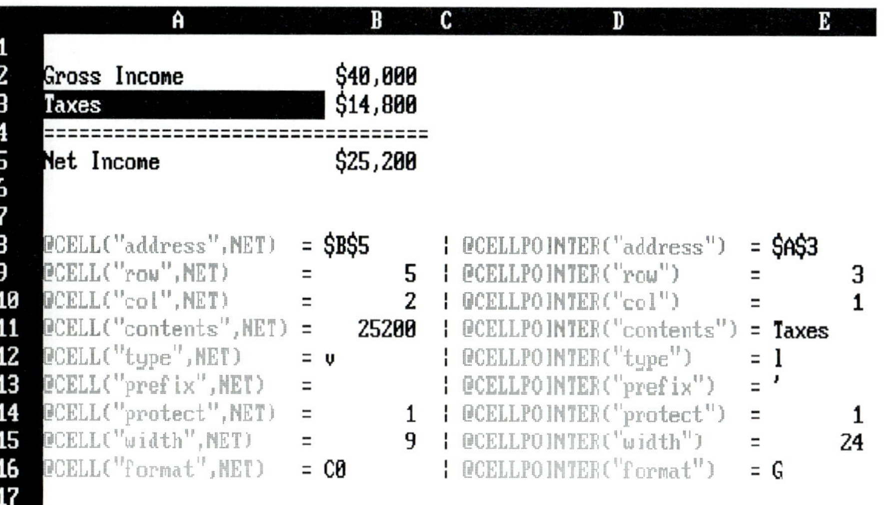

	A	B	C	D	E
1					
2	Gross Income	$40,000			
3	Taxes	$14,800			
4	================================				
5	Net Income	$25,200			
6					
7					
8	@CELL("address",NET) =	$B$5	¦	@CELLPOINTER("address") =	$A$3
9	@CELL("row",NET) =	5	¦	@CELLPOINTER("row") =	3
10	@CELL("col",NET) =	2	¦	@CELLPOINTER("col") =	1
11	@CELL("contents",NET) =	25200	¦	@CELLPOINTER("contents") =	Taxes
12	@CELL("type",NET) =	v	¦	@CELLPOINTER("type") =	l
13	@CELL("prefix",NET) =		¦	@CELLPOINTER("prefix") =	'
14	@CELL("protect",NET) =	1	¦	@CELLPOINTER("protect") =	1
15	@CELL("width",NET) =	9	¦	@CELLPOINTER("width") =	24
16	@CELL("format",NET) =	C0	¦	@CELLPOINTER("format") =	G
17					

ENGINEERING FUNCTIONS

Function	Description
@**ACOS**(value)	Returns the arc cosine.
@**ASIN**(value)	Returns the arc sine.
@**ATAN**(value)	Returns the arc tangent.
@**ATAN2**(value1,value2)	Returns the 4-quadrant arc tangent.
@**COS**(value)	Returns the cosine.
@**EXP**(value)	Returns the exponential.
@**LN**(value)	Returns the log base e.
@**LOG**(value)	Returns the log base 10.
@**PI**	Returns pi (3.141592653589794).
@**SIN**(value)	Returns the sine.
@**TAN**(value)	Returns the tangent.

Engineering functions actually are mathematical functions, but are treated separately because they are used less often in business-related spreadsheets.

LOTUS 1-2-3 GRAPHICS

Businesses frequently use graphics to aid in understanding data. Lotus 1-2-3 gives you the capability of presenting your spreadsheet's data in a variety of graphic forms.

LOTUS GRAPHICS OVERVIEW

To create a graph using Lotus, use the Main menu's /Graph commands. They are as follows.

```
Type  X  A  B  C  D  E  F  Reset  View  Save  Options  Name  Quit
```

Types of Graphs

You usually begin the process of creating a graph by selecting the type of graph to produce. Your options are **L**ine graph, **B**ar graph, **XY** graph, **S**tacked-Bar graph, and **P**ie chart.

```
         Type  X  A  B  C  D  E  F  Reset  View  Save  Options  Name  Quit
          ↑
 Line  Bar  XY  Stacked-Bar  Pie
```

Specifying Data to be Graphed

After selecting the type of graph, you may select the range(s) of numeric data you want graphically represented. As many as six different ranges of data may be graphically displayed. The ranges are specified as the **A** (first), **B** (second), **C** (third), **D** (fourth), **E** (fifth), and **F** (sixth) data ranges of the /**G**raph commands. Sometimes an additional data range (the **X** range) is required to produce the graph.

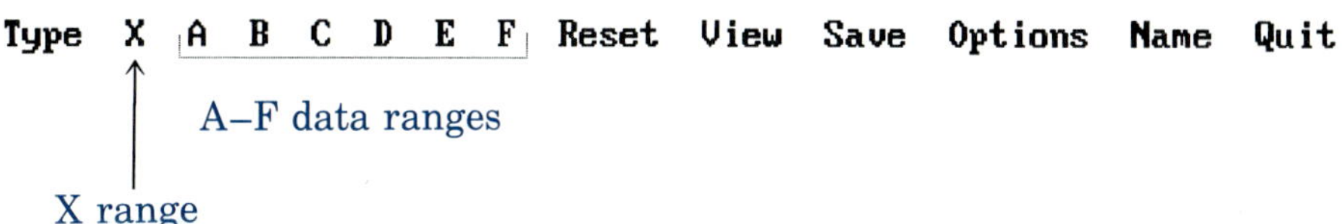

Viewing the Graph

After you have specified the data ranges, you may view the graph on the monitor screen by selecting the **V**iew command of the /**G**raph commands. The graph will be displayed in its basic form.

```
Type  X  A  B  C  D  E  F  Reset  View  Save  Options  Name  Quit
                                   ↑
```

View the graph on the monitor screen

Adding Options

Typing any key will return you from viewing the graph to the /**G**raph menu of commands. There you may use the **O**ptions command to add **T**itles, **L**egends, **D**ata-Labels, **G**rids, and more to the graphics display. As you make changes or additions, you may use the **V**iew command to again look at the graph.

```
Type  X  A  B  C  D  E  F  Reset  View  Save  Options  Name  Quit
```

Options: Add labels and format the graph

Using the GRAPH (F10) Function Key

When you are satisfied with the appearance of the graph, you may exit the /**G**raph commands by using the /**G**raph,**Q**uit command. You then can change the data in your spreadsheet and observe how those changes affect the graph by tapping the F10 (GRAPH) Function key. This key serves as a substitute for typing the command key sequence /**G**raph,**V**iew,any key,**Q**uit that would otherwise be necessary to accomplish the same operation. After you use the F10 key to view the graph, tap any key to return to the spreadsheet display (READY mode).

Erasing the Graph Settings

When you are ready to create another graph for the spreadsheet, you may use the **R**eset command of the /**G**raph commands to erase all or some of the settings for the current graph.

```
Type  X  A  B  C  D  E  F  Reset  View  Save  Options  Name  Quit
```

Reset: Erases all or some of the graph settings

Naming a Graph

If you want to produce another graph for the same spreadsheet and do not want to lose the current graph's settings (data ranges, titles, etc.) you must use the /**G**raph,**N**ame,**C**reate command to name the current graph. When you name the graph, its settings are stored with the spreadsheet's data under the name you have given them. You then may make specifications for another graph and view them as you set it up.

```
Type  X  A  B  C  D  E  F  Reset  View  Save  Options  Name  Quit
```

Name: Makes current /**G**raph settings a permanent part of the spreadsheet's data

Printing a Graph

When you are ready to print the current graph on the printer, you must first use the **S**ave command of the /**G**raph commands to save the screen output of the current graph to its own file on the diskette. The file is given a .PIC extension by Lotus to identify it as a Lotus "Picture" file.

```
Type  X  A  B  C  D  E  F  Reset  View  Save  Options  Name  Quit
                                         ↑
```

Saves the current graph's screen output to a separate file

The next step in printing a graph is to /**Q**uit the Lotus spreadsheet program and use the PrintGraph program to print the finished graph on the printer. The PrintGraph program is available on a separate diskette or as a separate program file on a hard-disk system.

CREATING THE FIVE BASIC GRAPH TYPES

The following spreadsheet will be used to illustrate how each of the five basic graph types may be produced.

	A	B	C	D	E	F	G	H
1								
2		* * Quarterly Sales Figures * *				Totals	Adv $/	
3						1990	Sales	
4	SALES REGION	#1	#2	#3	#4	-------	-----	
5								
6	California	20,769	25,487	16,037	36,043	98,336	7.8%	
7	Washington	18,753	23,065	19,250	29,610	90,678	5.1%	
8	Oregon	19,250	22,400	17,374	28,525	87,549	4.2%	
9	Idaho	14,070	19,376	14,126	25,200	72,772	2.9%	
10	Alaska	13,230	14,070	10,780	14,000	52,080	2.1%	
11								

Pie Charts

In many ways, a Lotus pie chart is the simplest form of graph to produce. A pie chart uses only one data range whose sum constitutes the pie to be divided among the data elements of the range. Each slice of the pie is displayed graphically as a computed percent of the whole. Labels describing each piece of the pie may be specified in an X range. The labels in the X range should correspond to the data elements in the A data range.

	A	B	C	D	E	F	G	H
1								
2		* * Quarterly	Sales	Figures	* *	Totals	Adv $/	
3						1990	Sales	
4	SALES REGION	#1	#2	#3	#4	-------	-----	
5								
6	California	20,769	25,487	16,037	36,043	98,336	7.8%	
7	Washington	18,753	23,065	19,250	29,610	90,678	5.1%	
8	Oregon	19,250	22,400	17,374	28,525	87,549	4.2%	
9	Idaho	14,070	19,376	14,126	25,200	72,772	2.9%	
10	Alaska	13,230	14,070	10,780	14,000	52,080	2.1%	
11								
12								
13								

X range A6..A10

A data range F6..F10

```
Type          = Pie
A data range  = F6..F10
X range       = A6..A10
View
```

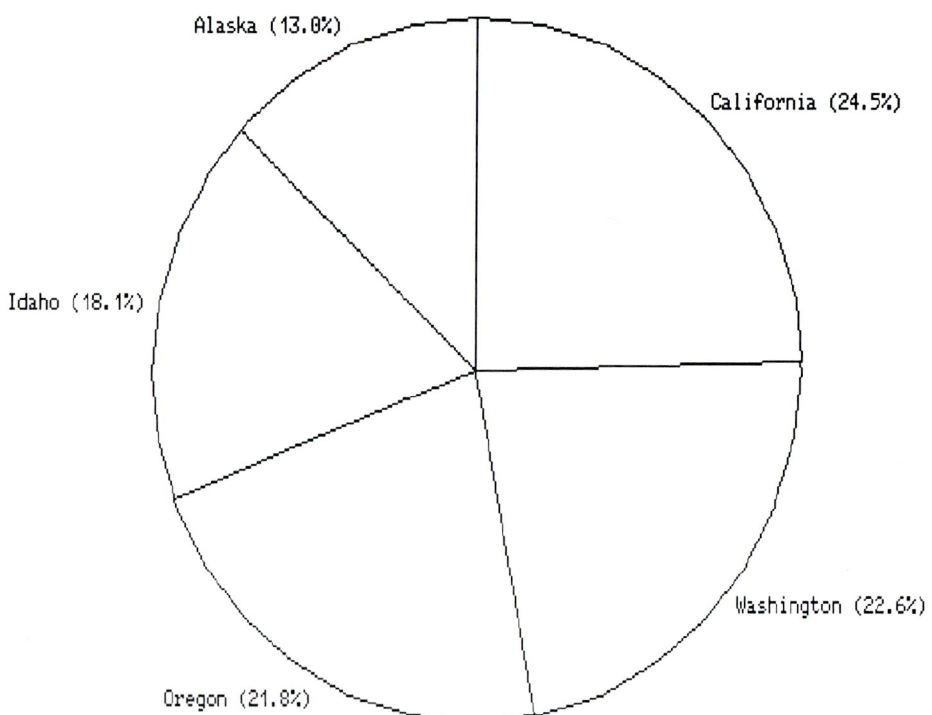

While the pie chart uses only a single data range (the A range) to create the graph, a second data range (the B range) may be used to effect shading patterns and to "explode" the pie by offsetting one or more slices. The numeric values 1–7 may be used to designate shading patterns, and the numeric values used 0 or 8 to designate no shading. Adding 100 to any of these values will cause the corresponding pie slice to be offset from the rest of the pie. Like the X range for labels, the B data range for shading should be set to correspond to the A data range.

	A	B	C	D	E	F	G	H
1								
2		* * Quarterly Sales Figures * *				Totals	Adv $/	
3						1990	Sales	
4	SALES REGION	#1	#2	#3	#4	-------	-----	
5								
6	California	20,769	25,487	16,037	36,043	98,336	7.8%	1
7	Washington	18,753	23,065	19,250	29,610	90,678	5.1%	2
8	Oregon	19,250	22,400	17,374	28,525	87,549	4.2%	3
9	Idaho	14,070	19,376	14,126	25,200	72,772	2.9%	4
10	Alaska	13,230	14,070	10,700	14,000	52,000	2.1%	105
11								
12								
13								
14								

X range A6..A10

A data range F6..F10

B data range H6..H10

```
Type          = Pie
A data range  = F6..F10
B data range  = H6..H10
X range       = A6..A10
View
```

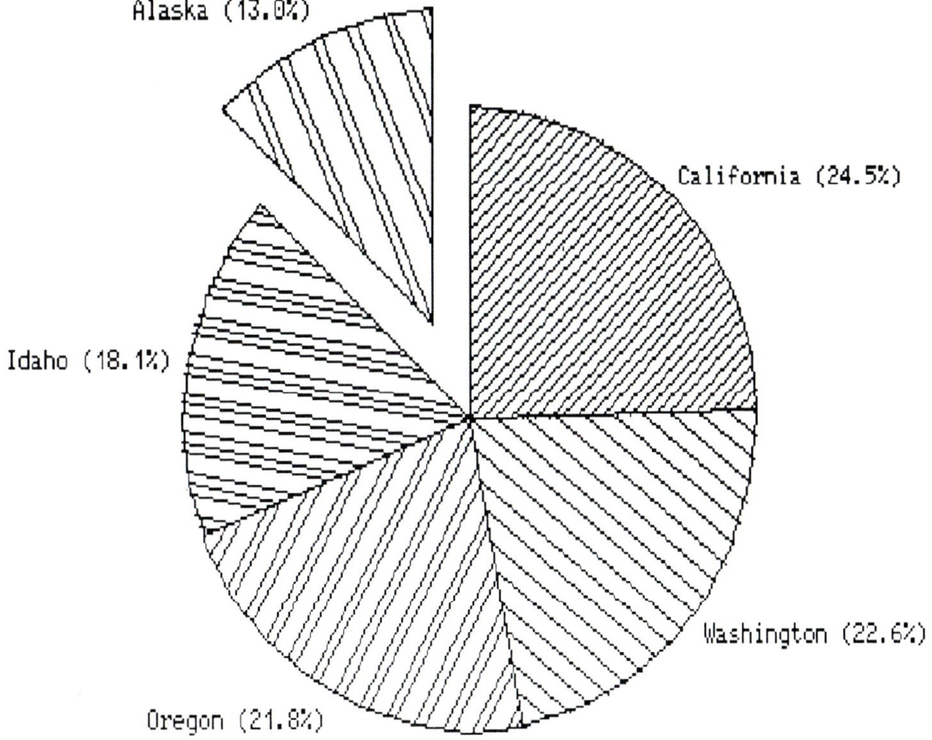

Line Graphs

Line graphs may include up to six data ranges that are plotted with the X range used to label the X axis of the graph. The first example plots quarterly sales for the California sales region.

	A	B	C	D	E	F	G
1							
2		* * Quarterly	Sales Figures	* *		Totals	Adv $/
3						1990	Sales
4	SALES REGION	#1	#2	#3	#4	-------	-------
5							
6	California	20,769	25,487	16,037	36,043	98,336	7.8%
7	Washington	18,753	23,065	19,250	29,610	90,678	5.1%
8	Oregon	19,250	22,400	17,374	28,525	87,549	4.2%
9	Idaho	14,070	19,376	14,126	25,200	72,772	2.9%
10	Alaska	13,230	14,070	10,780	14,000	52,080	2.1%
11							
12	X-range	A data range					

```
Type          = Line
A data range  = B6..E6
X range       = B4..E4
View
```

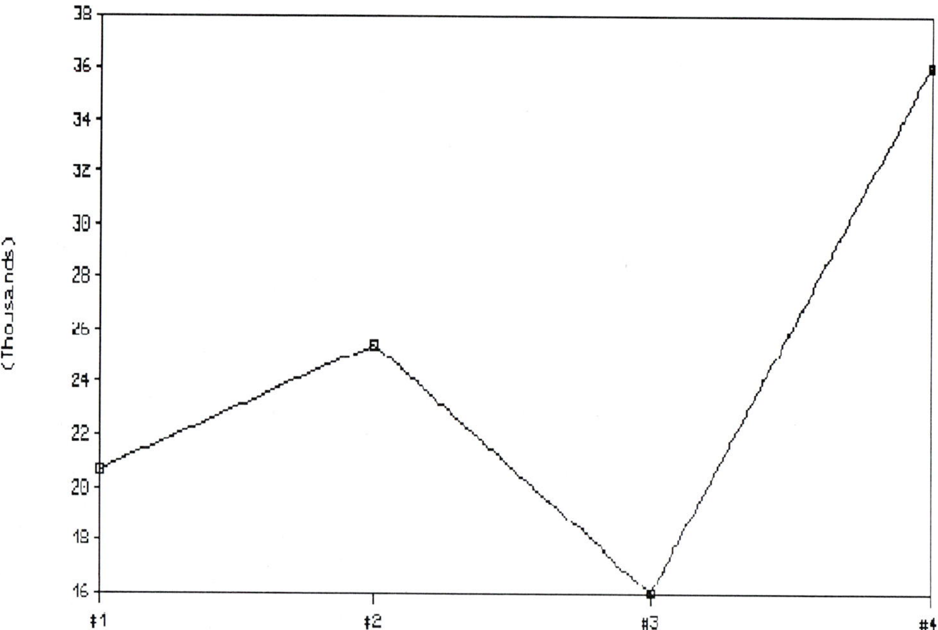

The next example uses several data ranges (A through E) to produce a line graph.

	A	B	C	D	E	F	G
1							
2		* * Quarterly	Sales Figures	* *		Totals	Adv $/
3						1990	Sales
4	SAL X range →	#1	#2	#3	#4	-------	-------
5							
6	Cal A range →	20,769	25,487	16,037	36,043	98,336	7.8%
7	Was B range →	18,753	23,065	19,250	29,610	90,678	5.1%
8	Ore C range →	19,250	22,400	17,374	28,525	87,549	4.2%
9	Ida D range →	14,070	19,376	14,126	25,200	72,772	2.9%
10	Ala E range →	13,230	14,070	10,780	14,000	52,080	2.1%
11							

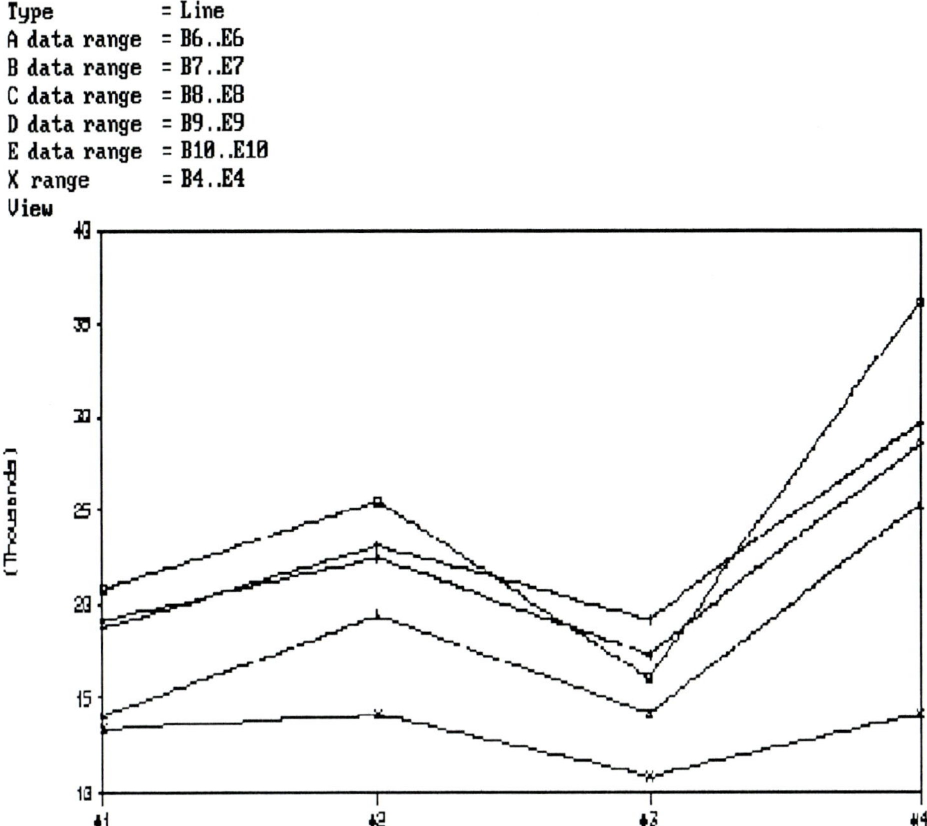

Bar Graphs

The following examples change the two preceding line graphs to bar graphs (/**G**raph,**T**ype,**B**ar). All other settings for the graphs remain the same.

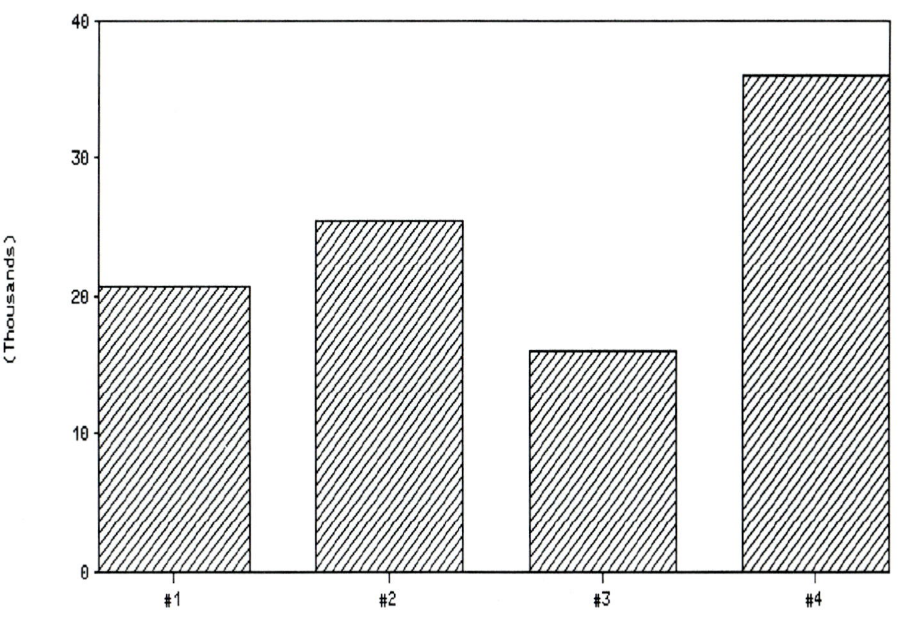

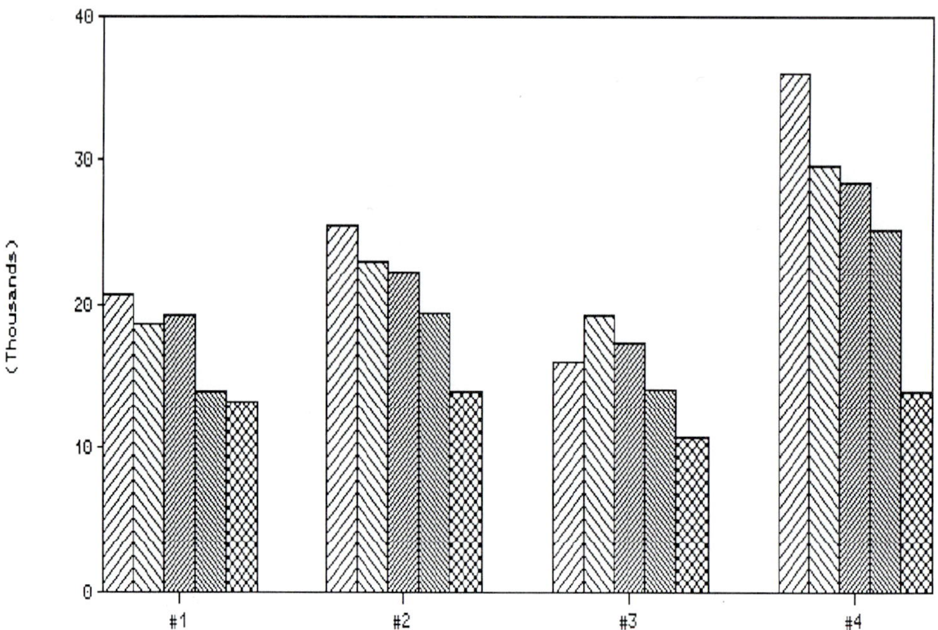

Notice that the bars for each data range are automatically assigned a different shading pattern.

Stacked Bar Graphs

Stacked bar graphs vary from bar graphs in that they show the elements in the data ranges as distinct contributors to the total height of a bar. All settings except **Type** (used in the preceding bar graph) are the same for the stacked bar graph.

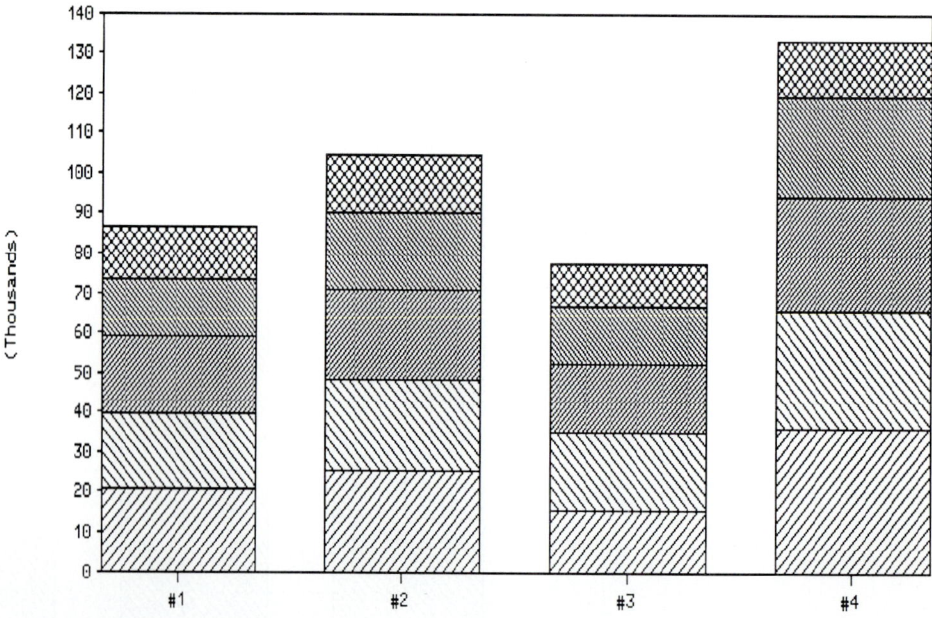

XY Graphs

XY graphs differ from the other types of graphs in that the X range is used not for labels, but for a data range containing values to be used as the X axis scale. The Y axis scale reflects values in the A–F data ranges. For each value in the A–F ranges, a data point appears on the graph at the appropriate intersection of the two axes. This type of graph may be used to show correlations or relationships between two types of data.

In the following example, the X range is specified as the range of cells containing the advertising-dollars-to-sales-dollars ratio expressed as a percent. The single A data range is specified as the total yearly sales for each region. The resulting XY graph indicates that sales increase with an increase in advertising expenditures, but that the rate of increase diminishes as advertising expenditures continue to rise.

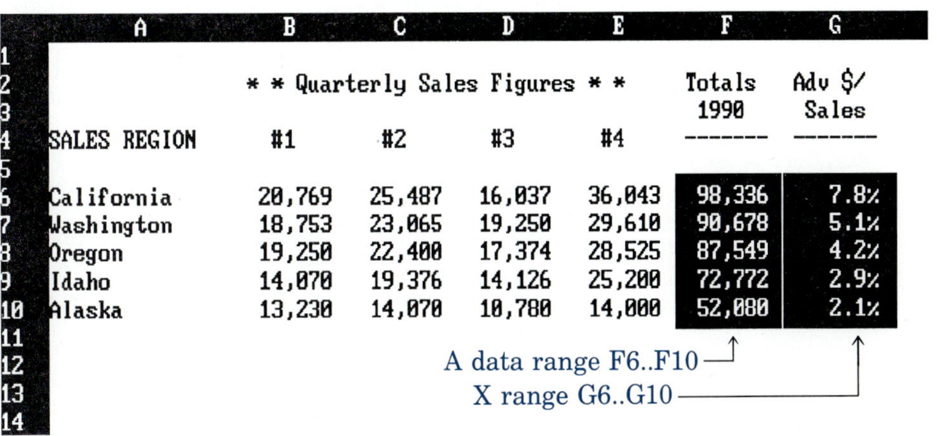

	A	B	C	D	E	F	G
1							
2		* * Quarterly Sales Figures * *				Totals	Adv $/
3						1990	Sales
4	SALES REGION	#1	#2	#3	#4	-------	-------
5							
6	California	20,769	25,487	16,037	36,043	98,336	7.8%
7	Washington	18,753	23,065	19,250	29,610	90,678	5.1%
8	Oregon	19,250	22,400	17,374	28,525	87,549	4.2%
9	Idaho	14,070	19,376	14,126	25,200	72,772	2.9%
10	Alaska	13,230	14,070	10,780	14,000	52,080	2.1%
11							
12							
13							
14							

A data range F6..F10

X range G6..G10

```
Type           = XY
A data range   = F6..F10
X range        = G6..G10
View
```

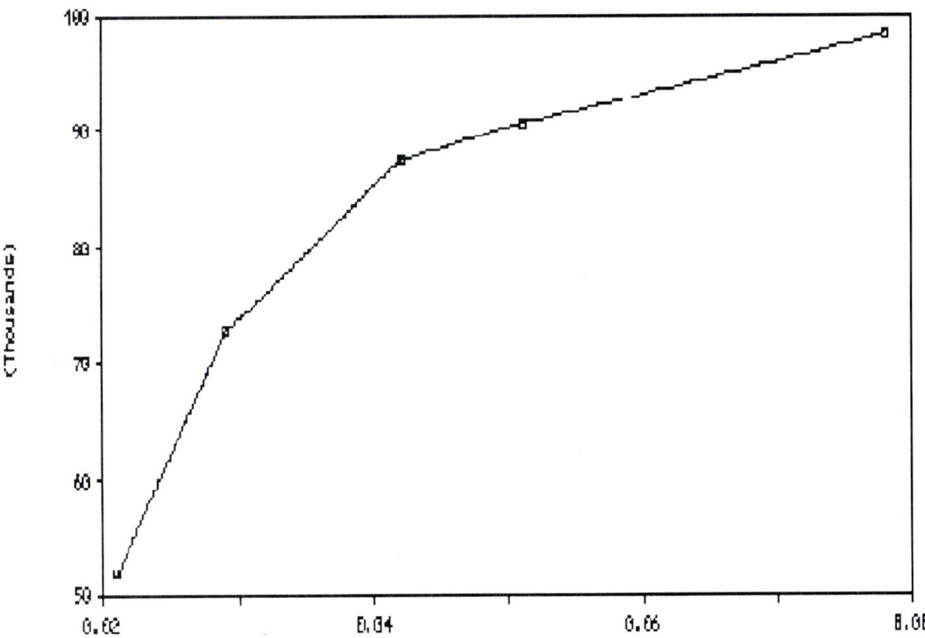

The line connecting the data points may or may not be displayed with the graph.

ADDING OPTIONS TO A GRAPH

Several **O**ptions commands are available with the /**G**raph commands. They may be used to enhance and/or alter the appearance of a graph. The options tend to fall into two general categories: those used to add labels to the graph and those used to change the display format of the graph.

Adding Labeling Options

The **L**egend, **T**itles, and **D**ata-Labels commands of the **O**ptions commands are all used to add labeling to the current graph.

Legends

A legend identifies the various lines on a line graph, the bars on a bar graph, or the points on an XY graph. Legend labels are entered for the data ranges used to produce a graph. The legend is displayed at the bottom of the graph with the symbols, shading, or color used in the line, XY point, or bar displayed for the data range.

Titles

The **T**itles command labels an entire graph with a first graph title line and a second graph title line. These two titles are centered and displayed at the top of the graph. Titles also may be put on the X axis and the Y axis of graphs having these two axes.

Data-Labels

Data-Labels are entered as a range of labels corresponding to the data elements in a data range. The specification of Data-Labels is very similar to the specification of an X range used to label an X axis. Specified Data-Labels, however, are displayed within the graph. They may be centered, or may be to the left, right, above, or below the corresponding data point in the graph. Data-Labels are always centered when they are used in bar graphs.

The following graph demonstrates how legends, titles, and Data-Labels may be included in a graph.

```
Type           = Bar
A data range   = B6..E6
B data range   = B7..E7
C data range   = B8..E8
D data range   = B9..E9
E data range   = B10..E10
X range        = B4..E4
Options
  Legend
    A range = California
    B range = Washington
    C range = Oregon
    D range = Idaho
    E range = Alaska
  Titles
    First  = Comparative Quarterly Sales
    Second = California Sales Figures Displayed
    X-Axis = QUARTERS
    Y-Axis = DOLLAR SALES
  Data-Labels
    A range = B6..E6
    Center
View
```

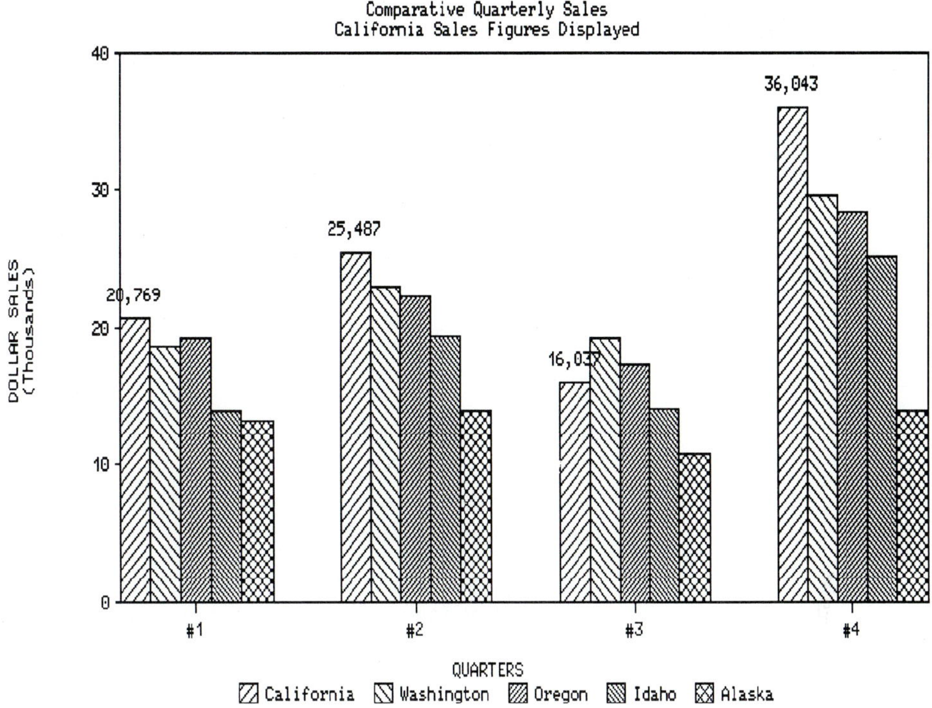

Changing Graph Formats

The **Format**, **Grid**, **Scale**, **Color**, and **B&W** commands of the **Options** commands are used to format the display of the current graph.

Format Commands

The **Format** command is used for line and XY graphs. It allows the graph to display only lines, only symbols, both lines and symbols (the default setting), or neither lines nor symbols. The display can be for the entire graph or for any of the data ranges A through F.

Grid Commands

A **Grid** within a graph may be displayed as horizontal lines corresponding to the ticks (perpendicular hash marks) on the Y axis, vertical lines corresponding to the ticks on the X axis, both (a true grid display), or cleared from the graph after having been set. The default setting is **Clear** (no grid lines).

Scale Commands

The **Scale** command may be used to override Lotus's automatic scaling of the Y axis or the X axis, or to skip the display of every *n*th label in an X range used to label the X axis. If **Scale Y** axis or **Scale X** axis is the command you select, the options become as follows.

Automatic Manual Lower Upper Format Indicator Quit

Manual turns off the automatic scaling and must be selected before you view a graph with upper and/or lower limits set with the **Upper** or **Lower**

commands of this menu. The **A**utomatic command returns Lotus to automatic scaling (its default setting). The **I**ndicator command allows you to suppress the display of the scale indicator on the graph.

If you select the **F**ormat command, the next menu presented will be similar to those used to format a range of cells or to globally format the spreadsheet.

```
Fixed  Scientific  Currency  ,  General  +/-  Percent  Date  Text  Hidden
```

Here it is used to format the axis scale numbers.

Color and **B**&W Commands

The **C**olor and **B**&W commands are mutually exclusive and, when selected, provide no further menus. If you select the **C**olor command, the graph will be displayed in color. If you select **B**&W (the default setting), the graph will be displayed in black and white.

The last bar graph example will now be further enhanced to demonstrate some of the formatting **O**ption commands. The following settings have been added to it.

```
Grid          = Horizontal
Scale
   Skip       = 2
   Y Scale
      Manual
      Upper   = 60000
      Format  = Currency, 0 decimals
```

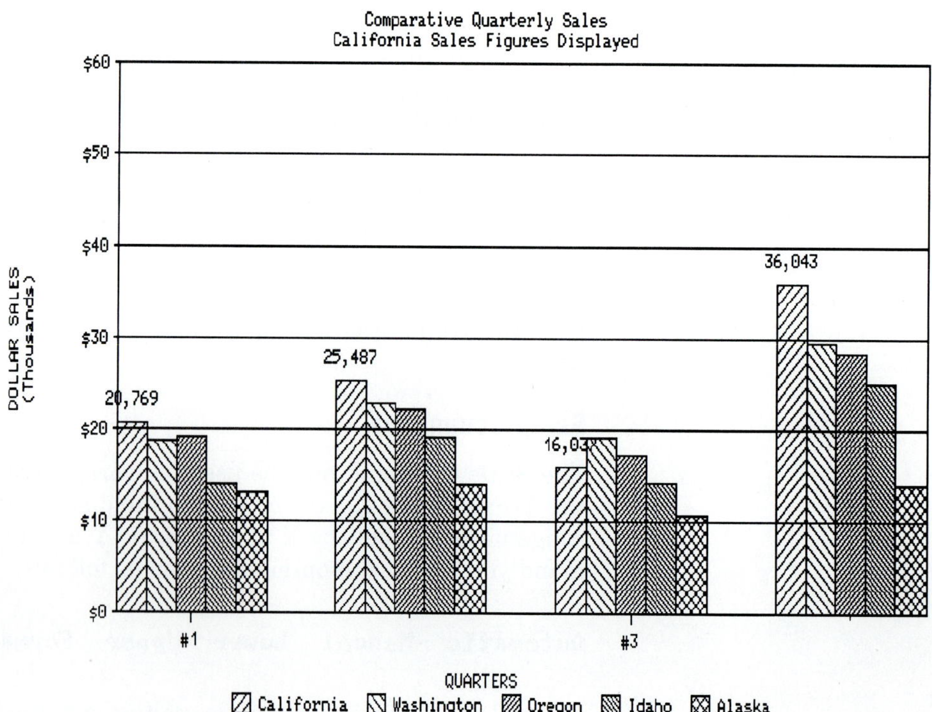

PRINTING A GRAPH

Saving a Picture File

Before you print a Lotus 1-2-3 graph, you must save the screen output of that graph to its own file on the diskette by using Lotus's /**G**raph,**S**ave command. Once you have saved it, you must exit the spreadsheet with the /**Q**uit command, returning to the Lotus Access System or to DOS.

Accessing the PrintGraph Program

You may either select the **P**rintGraph command of the Lotus Access System, or you may load this software directly from the DOS operating level by typing in its filename PGRAPH.EXE (or simply PGRAPH). First be sure that the diskette with the PGRAPH.EXE file on it is in the current default disk drive or that it is available and will be accessed on your network or hard drive.

After the software has been loaded into RAM, the following screen will be displayed with the menu of **P**rintGraph commands at the top of the screen and current settings at the bottom.

```
Copyright 1986, 1987 Lotus Development Corp.  All Rights Reserved. V2.01    MENU

Select graphs for printing
Image-Select  Settings  Go  Align  Page  Exit

 GRAPH      IMAGE OPTIONS                    HARDWARE SETUP
 IMAGES      Size           Range Colors      Graphs Directory:
 SELECTED     Top      .395  X                  A:\
              Left     .750  A                Fonts Directory:
              Width   6.500  B                  A:\
              Height  4.691  C                Interface:
              Rotate   .000  D                  Parallel 1
                             E                Printer Type:
             Font            F
              1  BLOCK1                       Paper Size
              2  BLOCK1                         Width      8.500
                                                Length    11.000

                                             ACTION OPTIONS
                                              Pause: No   Eject: No
```

The tree structure of the **PrintGraph** command menus and explanations of the **PrintGraph** commands follow.

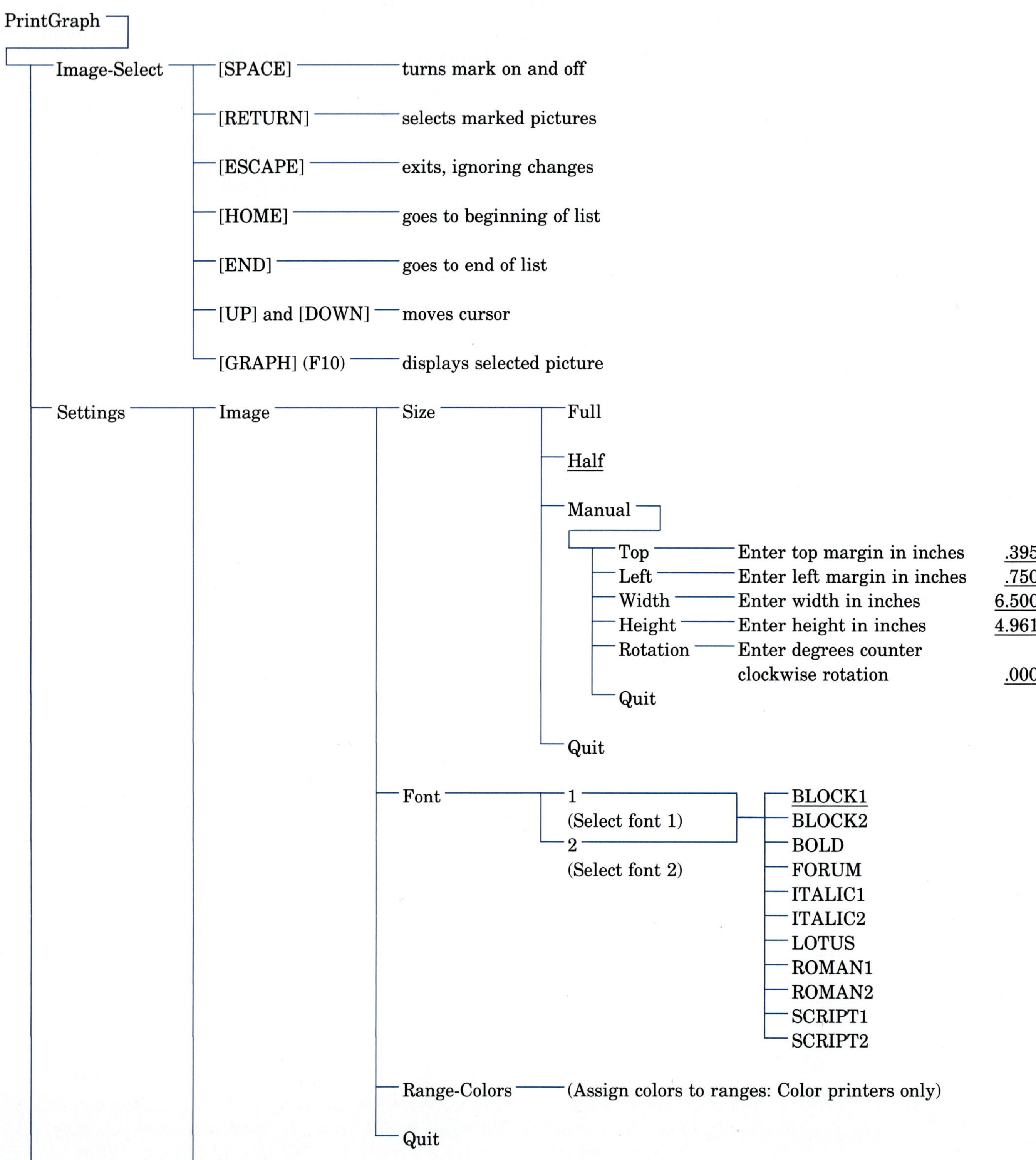

CONTINUED

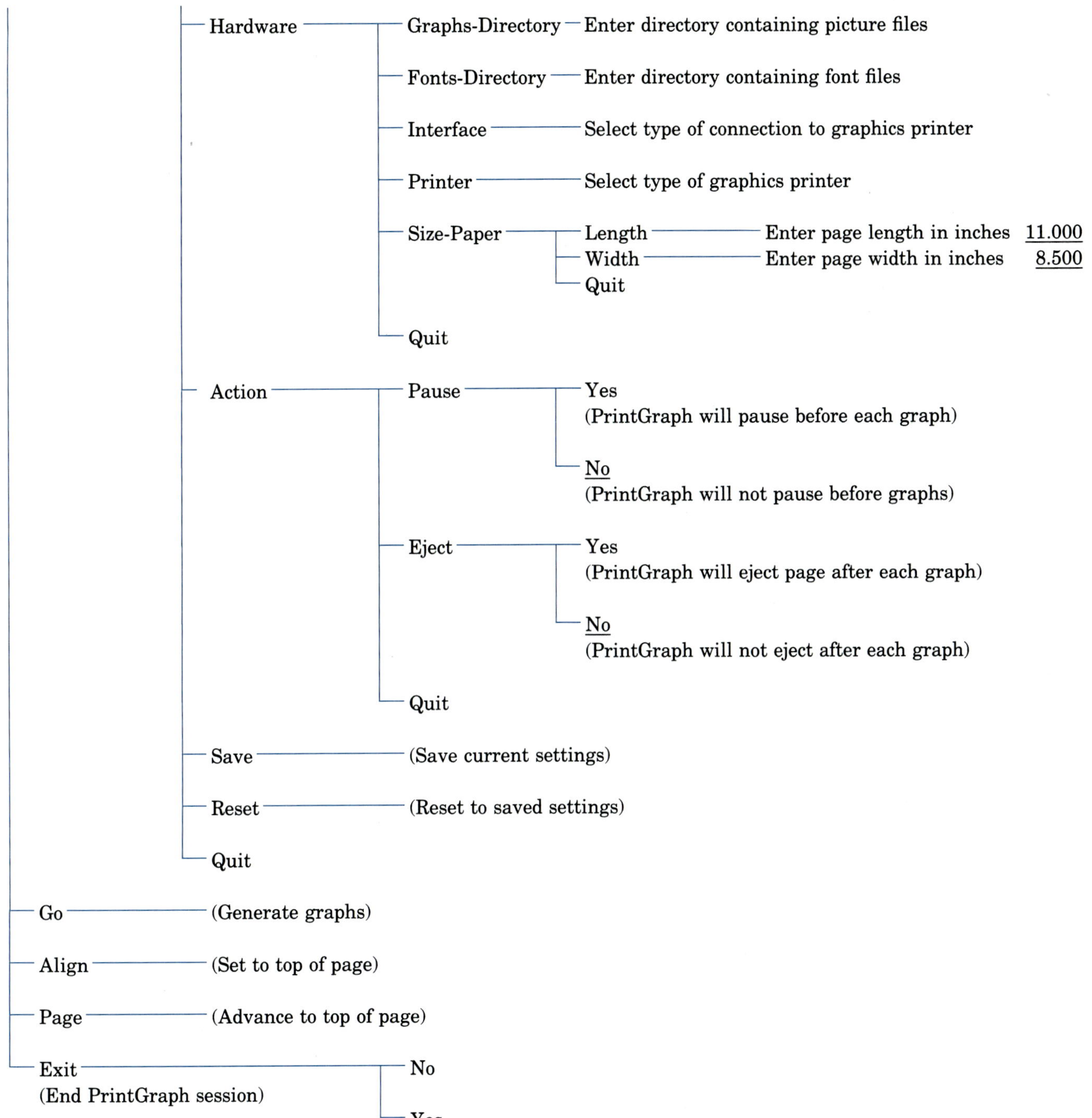

The Image-Select Command

The graph(s) to be printed must first be selected by using the **I**mage-Select command of the **P**rintGraph menu. When the command is used, the screen displays a listing of the .PIC files on your disk. If no files appear, you may need to designate another drive/directory for .PIC files (see the **S**ettings command). A pointer used to highlight files in the list may be moved up and down with the cursor control keys. The space bar marks (or unmarks) the highlighted file. The F10 (GRAPH) function key may be used to view the highlighted graph on the screen. After one or more files have been selected, the Enter key may be used to end the selection process and return to the **P**rintGraph menu.

The **S**ettings Command

Before your graph can be printed, you must specify the type of printer hardware being used and the disk drive/directories where the needed files may be found. You also may specify various options concerning how graphs are to be printed, such as margins and placement on the page. Once you have specified this information, it may be saved in its own file. The **P**rintGraph program will use these settings each time the program is loaded.

The **G**o Command

Once you have selected the appropriate printer, directories, and options with the **S**ettings command and have selected the .PIC file(s) to be printed with the **I**mage-Select command, the **G**o command may be used to begin printing the graph(s).

The **A**lign and **P**age Commands

The **A**lign and **P**age commands work in the same way as their counterparts in the spreadsheet /**P**rint commands. **A**lign tells the computer that the paper in the printer is at the top of a page; **P**age causes the computer to advance the paper in the printer to the top of the next page.

Configuring PrintGraph with the Settings Command

The **S**ettings commands of the PrintGraph program provide Lotus with information about how graphs are to be printed. After the **S**ettings command is selected, the following options are available.

```
Image  Hardware  Action  Save  Reset  Quit
```

Image Commands

The **S**ettings,**I**mage,**S**ize command is used to select automatic or manual placement of the graph on the page when printed. Automatic placement selections are **F**ull to print the graph on a full page and rotated 90 degrees or **H**alf to print the graph on the top half of a page with no rotation. **H**alf is the default setting. Manual placement may be selected to change the **T**op margin, **L**eft margin, **W**idth, **H**eight, and **R**otation of the graph.

The **S**ettings,**I**mage,**F**ont command may be used to select one of several PrintGraph fonts (styles of lettering) to be used for titles and labels on the printed graph. Two different fonts may be used on the graph. Font **1** is used for the first title line. Font **2** is used for all other titles and labels on the graph. The directory where font files are located must be selected with the **S**ettings,**H**ardware,**F**onts-Directory command before fonts may be selected.

The **S**ettings,**I**mage,**R**ange-Colors command is used only in conjunction with a color printer. The colors for the graph's X range and A–F data ranges may be set to the desired colors.

Hardware Commands

The Settings,**H**ardware commands are used to specify directories where files needed by PrintGraph are located, the printer being used, and how commands should be sent to the printer. In a microlab, the hardware specifications will probably have been set and saved previously, and you will not need to change them. If they have not, you may need to use the following **H**ardware commands.

The Settings,**H**ardware,**G**raphs-Directory command is used to specify the location of your .PIC files. The Settings,**H**ardware,**F**onts-Directory command is used to specify the location of PrintGraph font files. These directories must be set before .PIC files or fonts may be selected.

The Settings,**H**ardware,**I**nterface command is used to specify the printer port to which your graphics printer is connected. The interface may be either a parallel or serial port on your computer.

The Settings,**H**ardware,**P**rinter command is used to select the type of printer you have and the density (high or low) in which graphs are to be printed. If high density is selected, the graph quality will be higher, but the graph will take longer to print. The printers that appear on the list for selection will include only those previously selected through the Lotus Install program.

The Settings,**H**ardware,**S**ize-Paper command may be used to specify the height and width of your printer's paper. Default settings are for standard size 8½″ by 11″ paper.

Action Commands

The Settings,**A**ction,Pause command may be used to cause PrintGraph to pause before printing each graph selected. **P**ause may be set to **Y**es or **N**o. **N**o is the default, but **Y**es may be selected if you are using your printer's single sheet feed option.

The Settings,**A**ction,**E**ject command is used to determine whether or not the printer should advance to the top of a new page automatically after each graph is printed. The default is **N**o eject.

Save and Reset Commands

The Settings,**S**ave command is used to save the currently defined settings in a configuration file so that these settings will become the defaults the next time PrintGraph is used. The Settings,**R**eset command may be used to restore all settings to the default values found in the configuration file.

/DATA,SORT, /DATA,QUERY, AND DATABASE FUNCTIONS

Lotus 1-2-3 has two specialized commands for database operations, /**D**ata,**S**ort and /**D**ata,**Q**uery, as well as some special database functions. These data commands and functions are designed to deal with spreadsheet data similar to the way a database management system (DBMS) deals with data. Although Lotus is not a DBMS, some of the terminology and concepts of database management will be used in discussing how the spreadsheet database commands and functions work.

DATABASE STRUCTURE AND TERMINOLOGY

The /**D**ata,**S**ort commands are used to sort data and the /**D**ata,**Q**uery commands are used to search through data and find cases evaluated as true for a given condition. Like the /**D**ata,**Q**uery commands, the database functions search for occurrences of a condition in a set of data and then return summary values based upon only instances for which the condition is true. The spreadsheet's data must be organized in a particular way for these commands and functions.

Related data items are entered in adjacent cells of a row in the spreadsheet. Each data item is called a *field* of data. A single row of related data is called a *record,* and the rectangular range of records is called the *database.* When you use the /**D**ata,**Q**uery commands or data functions, you must have an additional row of *field names* occupying the top row of the database.

	A	B	C	D	E	F	G	H	I
1									
2		LAST	FIRST	SEX	AGE	SALARY			
3		Nichols	Sandy	F	40	$31,090			
4		Barons	Harold	M	21	$18,200			
5		Able	Richard	M	25	$18,450			
6		Samson	Carol	F	24	$19,380			
7		Jackson	Julie	F	32	$22,280			
8		Trember	Nick	M	30	$20,520			
9		Coneal	Rachael	F	20	$19,210			
10		Brown	Scott	M	23	$18,400			
11		Sheradon	Leslie	F	22	$19,230			
12		Shackley	Suzanne	F	35	$23,850			
13		Wertz	Herbert	M	55	$31,300			
14		Ralston	Sherry	F	24	$18,170			
15		Brusky	Wayne	M	27	$20,930			
16		Austin	Chip	M	22	$18,380			
17		Drexler	Anne	F	26	$20,910			

Field names (row 2) — Database (rows 3–17) — Field (one column) — Record for Anne Drexler (row 17)

THE /DATA,SORT COMMANDS

The /**D**ata,**S**ort commands are straightforward and require only three steps to sort spreadsheet data which are organized in a database form. The menu of /**D**ata,**S**ort commands consists of the following.

Data-Range Primary-Key Secondary-Key Reset Go Quit

Setting the Data-Range to Sort

The first step in sorting spreadsheet data is to define the range of data to be sorted by using the **D**ata-Range command. The range includes only the actual records of the database to be sorted. Using the previous example, an appropriate range to sort would be B3..F17.

	A	B	C	D	E	F	G	H	I
1									
2		LAST	FIRST	SEX	AGE	SALARY			
3		Nichols	Sandy	F	40	$31,090			
4		Barons	Harold	M	21	$18,200			
5		Able	Richard	M	25	$18,450			
6		Samson	Carol	F	24	$19,380			
7		Jackson	Julie	F	32	$22,280			
8		Trember	Nick	M	30	$20,520			
9		Coneal	Rachael	F	20	$19,210			
10		Brown	Scott	M	23	$18,400			
11		Sheradon	Leslie	F	22	$19,230			
12		Shackley	Suzanne	F	35	$23,850			
13		Wertz	Herbert	M	55	$31,300			
14		Ralston	Sherry	F	24	$18,170			
15		Brusky	Wayne	M	27	$20,930			
16		Austin	Chip	M	22	$18,380			
17		Drexler	Anne	F	26	$20,910			

Data-Range

Setting Sort Keys

The next step is to define the sort key(s). A key is any cell address in the column of data on which the database is to be sorted. Up to two fields may be specified as keys on which to sort: one is called the Primary-Key and the other is called the Secondary-Key.

The field specified as the Primary-Key has the highest precedence for sorting. The Primary-Key is the only sort key required. If a Secondary-Key is specified, the database also will be sorted on that field, but it will take a lower precedence. When a sort key is selected, you are provided a choice of either ascending or descending sort order.

Sorting the Database

Once the data range, sort key(s), and the sort order for each key have been specified, the **G**o command of the /**D**ata,**S**ort commands causes the data in the data range to be sorted. The following example uses the field named SEX as the Primary-Key and the field named SALARY as the Secondary-Key for a data sort operation.

```
/Data,Sort,Data-Range      - Enter Data-Range: B3..F17
           Primary-Key     - Primary sort key: D2
                             Sort order (A or D): A
           Secondary-Key   - Secondary sort key: F2
                             Sort order (A or D): D
           Go
```

	A	B	C	D	E	F	G	H	I
1									
2		LAST	FIRST	SEX	AGE	SALARY			
3		Nichols	Sandy	F	40	$31,090			
4		Shackley	Suzanne	F	35	$23,850			
5		Jackson	Julie	F	32	$22,280			
6		Drexler	Anne	F	26	$20,910			
7		Samson	Carol	F	24	$19,380			
8		Sheradon	Leslie	F	22	$19,230			
9		Coneal	Rachael	F	20	$19,210			
10		Ralston	Sherry	F	24	$18,170			
11		Wertz	Herbert	M	55	$31,300			
12		Brusky	Wayne	M	27	$20,930			
13		Trember	Nick	M	30	$20,520			
14		Able	Richard	M	25	$18,450			
15		Brown	Scott	M	23	$18,400			
16		Austin	Chip	M	22	$18,380			
17		Barons	Harold	M	21	$18,200			

THE /DATA,QUERY COMMANDS

The /**D**ata,**Q**uery commands locate records in the database. The variation of /**D**ata,**Q**uery discussed here searches the database for records that meet certain conditions (criteria). It also copies the data in certain fields of the records to another place in the spreadsheet. This process is called *extracting data from the database.*

The Three Ranges Required to Extract Data

1. The Input range includes the database and its row of field names. It is the range in which Lotus searches for records. It is specified with the **I**nput command of the /**D**ata,**Q**uery commands.
2. The Criterion range holds logical expressions that determine which records will be extracted from the Input range. It is usually a small range and is specified by using the **C**riterion command of the /**D**ata,**Q**uery commands.
3. The Output range, specified with the **O**utput command of the /**D**ata,**Q**uery commands, determines which fields of the records will be extracted and the location of the copied data. Data from records in the Input range that meet the condition(s) in the Criterion range will be copied to the Output range only for those fields included in the Output range.

To use the /**D**ata,**Q**uery commands effectively, you need to understand how the three ranges relate to each other and how the conditions in the criterion range work. The following example will show how the ranges are defined for an extract operation.

An Example of Extracting Data

Using the same database used in the /**D**ata,**S**ort example, you want to extract the last names, ages, and salaries of all employees over age 30.

The first step is to define the Input range as B2..F17, which includes the row of field names and all records in the database. The field names must be included in the Input range; however, if you were only interested in searching through the first ten records, you should define the Input range to include only the row of field names and those ten records.

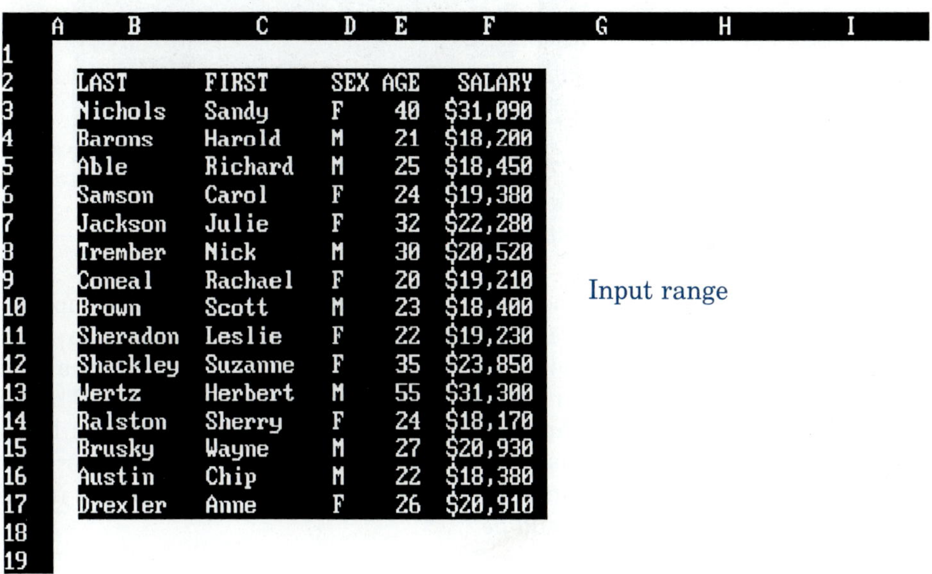

	A	B	C	D	E	F	G	H	I
1									
2		LAST	FIRST	SEX	AGE	SALARY			
3		Nichols	Sandy	F	40	$31,090			
4		Barons	Harold	M	21	$18,200			
5		Able	Richard	M	25	$18,450			
6		Samson	Carol	F	24	$19,380			
7		Jackson	Julie	F	32	$22,280			
8		Tremher	Nick	M	30	$20,520			
9		Coneal	Rachael	F	20	$19,210			
10		Brown	Scott	M	23	$18,400			
11		Sheradon	Leslie	F	22	$19,230			
12		Shackley	Suzanne	F	35	$23,850			
13		Wertz	Herbert	M	55	$31,300			
14		Ralston	Sherry	F	24	$18,170			
15		Brusky	Wayne	M	27	$20,930			
16		Austin	Chip	M	22	$18,380			
17		Drexler	Anne	F	26	$20,910			
18									
19									

The next step is to define the Output range, the area into which the records meeting the criteria will be copied. The first row of the Output range contains the field names for the fields to be copied from the Input range. Since you want to copy into the Output range only the last names, ages, and salaries for records meeting the criterion (all employees over age 30), the corresponding field names should be entered into another area of the spreadsheet, which will then be defined as the Output range. The **O**utput command of the /**D**ata,**Q**uery commands then is used to specify the range by its location. Here it would be H2..J17.

NOTE: The field names used in the Output range must exactly match the spelling of the field names in the Input range; however, case (upper or lower) and label prefixes used may be different.

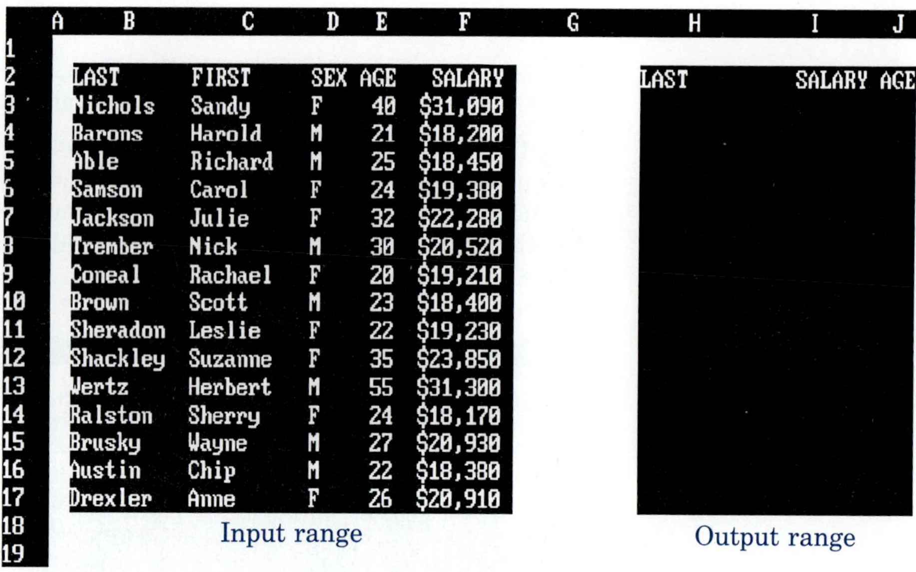

	LAST	FIRST	SEX	AGE	SALARY
3	Nichols	Sandy	F	40	$31,090
4	Barons	Harold	M	21	$18,200
5	Able	Richard	M	25	$18,450
6	Samson	Carol	F	24	$19,380
7	Jackson	Julie	F	32	$22,280
8	Tremblr	Nick	M	30	$20,520
9	Coneal	Rachael	F	20	$19,210
10	Brown	Scott	M	23	$18,400
11	Sheradon	Leslie	F	22	$19,230
12	Shackley	Suzanne	F	35	$23,850
13	Wertz	Herbert	M	55	$31,300
14	Ralston	Sherry	F	24	$18,170
15	Brusky	Wayne	M	27	$20,930
16	Austin	Chip	M	22	$18,380
17	Drexler	Anne	F	26	$20,910

LAST	SALARY	AGE

The last range that must be defined to complete a /**D**ata,**Q**uery,**E**xtract operation is the Criterion range. This is where the logical expression equivalent to "Age > 30" will be entered. The smallest possible Criterion range consists of two cells, one above the other. The top cell must hold a field name and the bottom cell normally holds a logical expression. The expression should reference a cell in the first record of the database, normally the same field as the field name entered above it. Here an appropriate criterion would be

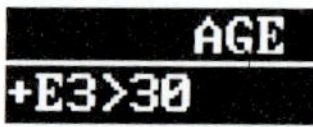

AGE
+E3>30

The next step is to move to a third area of the spreadsheet and enter into one cell the label AGE and to enter into the cell below it the expression +E3>30. The two cells into which this data is entered will display

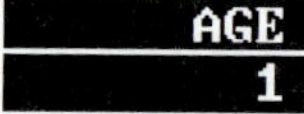

AGE
1

The 1 displayed in the second cell is the result of the computer's evaluation of the logical expression +E3>30. The value in E3 is greater than 30, so the computer evaluates it as true and displays the numeric value 1 (true). If the value in E3 were not greater than 30, the numeric value displayed would be 0 (false). To make the expressions in a Criterion range readable, cells holding logical expressions often are formatted as Text with the /**R**ange,**F**ormat,**T**ext command.

Once the Criterion range data have been entered into cells, the **C**riterion command of the /**D**ata,**Q**uery commands is used to specify the cells comprising the Criterion range.

The final step in the extract operation is to use the **E**xtract command of the /**D**ata,**Q**uery commands to begin the data extraction. When this is done, the last names, salaries, and ages of every Input range record for a person over age 30 will appear in the Output range.

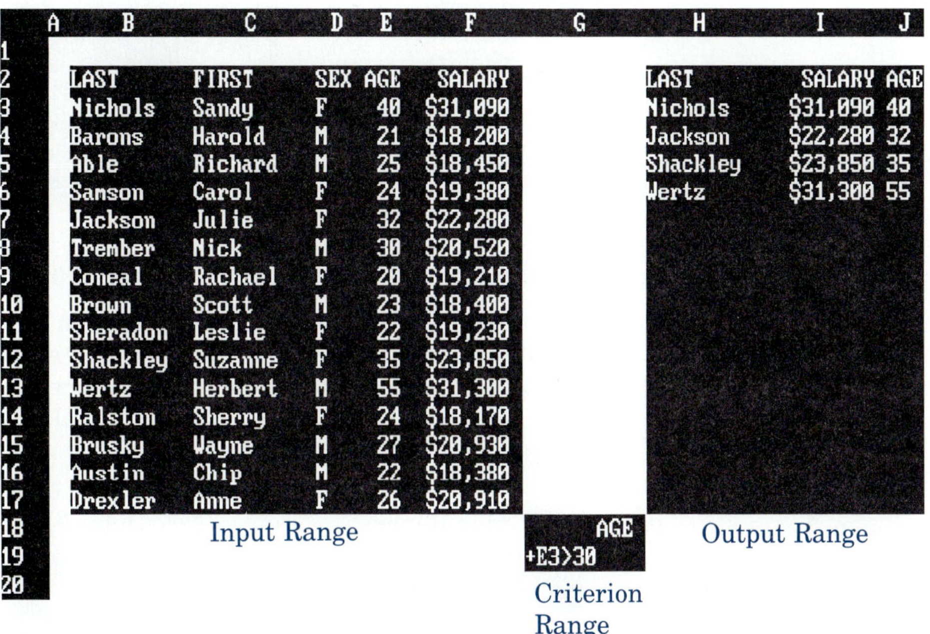

	A	B	C	D	E	F
1						
2		LAST	FIRST	SEX	AGE	SALARY
3		Nichols	Sandy	F	40	$31,090
4		Barons	Harold	M	21	$18,200
5		Able	Richard	M	25	$18,450
6		Samson	Carol	F	24	$19,380
7		Jackson	Julie	F	32	$22,280
8		Tremper	Nick	M	30	$20,520
9		Coneal	Rachael	F	20	$19,210
10		Brown	Scott	M	23	$18,400
11		Sheradon	Leslie	F	22	$19,230
12		Shackley	Suzanne	F	35	$23,850
13		Wertz	Herbert	M	55	$31,300
14		Ralston	Sherry	F	24	$18,170
15		Brusky	Wayne	M	27	$20,930
16		Austin	Chip	M	22	$18,380
17		Drexler	Anne	F	26	$20,910

	G
18	AGE
19	+E3>30

	H	I	J
2	LAST	SALARY	AGE
3	Nichols	$31,090	40
4	Jackson	$22,280	32
5	Shackley	$23,850	35
6	Wertz	$31,300	55

Criterion Range Conditions

The way that you structure your field name labels and logical expressions within a Criterion range determines the character of the records evaluated as true for the criteria (conditions) in the range. To demonstrate the alternatives, several different Criterion ranges relating to this database will be discussed.

A Criterion Range with No Condition

The simplest criterion is no criterion at all. If two blank cells are defined as the Criterion range, all records are evaluated as true for the criterion, and the appropriate fields will be copied to the Output range.

Simple Criterion Range/Simple Condition

The example used to extract records for employees older than age 30 showed a simple Criterion range (two cells) and a simple numeric condition. A simple Criterion range also could hold a string condition using the relational operators =, >, <, >=, <=, and < >. For example, to extract all records for employees whose last name begins with *M* or greater, the condition *last name* >= *"M"* would be entered in the Criterion range.

Criterion Range

LAST
+B3>"M"

Output Range

LAST	SALARY	AGE
Nichols	$31,090	40
Samson	$19,380	24
Tremher	$20,520	30
Sheradon	$19,230	22
Shackley	$23,850	35
Wertz	$31,300	55
Ralston	$18,170	24

Simple Criterion Range/Complex Condition

It is possible to include a complex condition in a simple Criterion range (two cells) by using the logical operators #AND# and #OR#. For example, if you want to extract records for employees who are both over age 30 *and* who are female, the complex condition would be entered using the #AND# operator.

Criterion Range

LAST
+E3>30#AND#D3="F"

Output Range

LAST	SALARY	AGE
Nichols	$31,090	40
Jackson	$22,280	32
Shackley	$23,850	35

If you want to extract records for employees who are either over age 30 *or* who are female, the complex condition would be entered using the #OR# operator.

Criterion Range

LAST
+E3>30#OR#D3="F"

Output Range

LAST	SALARY	AGE
Nichols	$31,090	40
Samson	$19,380	24
Jackson	$22,280	32
Coneal	$19,210	20
Sheradon	$19,230	22
Shackley	$23,850	35
Wertz	$31,300	55
Ralston	$18,170	24
Drexler	$20,910	26

Notice that when cell references are used to enter the condition expression, the actual field name used in the Criterion range need not be related to the condition. It must, however, be a valid field name from the Input range. For instance, in the last two examples the field name LAST was used; however, the condition +E3>30 references the field AGE and the condition D3="F" references the field SEX.

Wild Card Characters

Special string expressions in the Criterion range also may produce partial comparisons in a data search by including "wild card" characters in the expression. The two wild card characters are the asterisk (*), which means "any other characters remaining," and the question mark (?), which means "any character located here."

When wild card characters are used, no cell references or relational operators are included in the condition expression. In this case, therefore, the field name used in the Criterion range must be that field for which the comparison is to be made.

For example, the following Criterion ranges will produce the output shown in the Output ranges, given the same Input range used in the preceding examples.

Criterion Ranges / Output Range

LAST
Sh*

LAST	SALARY	AGE
Sheradon	$19,230	22
Shackley	$23,850	35

LAST
S*

LAST	SALARY	AGE
Samson	$19,380	24
Sheradon	$19,230	22
Shackley	$23,850	35

LAST
?r*

LAST	SALARY	AGE
Trember	$20,520	30
Brown	$18,400	23
Brusky	$20,930	27
Drexler	$20,910	26

LAST
?r???er

LAST	SALARY	AGE
Trember	$20,520	30
Drexler	$20,910	26

Complex Criterion Range/Simple Conditions

When you need to combine string conditions that include wild card characters with other numeric or string conditions, the Criterion range needs to be enlarged. The logical operators connecting the different conditions become implicit by the expressions' positioning in the Criterion range.

For example, if you want to extract records for all employees whose last name begins with *S and* whose salary is less than $20,000, the appropriate logical operator would be AND. The equivalent of the logical operator #AND# in a complex Criterion range is achieved by entering field names and condition expressions side by side in the Criterion range.

LAST	SALARY
S*	+F3<20000

If, on the other hand, you want to extract records for all employees whose last name begins with *S or* whose salary is less than $20,000, the appropriate logical operator would be OR. The equivalent of the logical operator #OR# in a complex Criterion range is achieved by entering field names side by side, but entering the condition expressions in separate rows in the Criterion range.

LAST	SALARY
S*	
	+F3<20000

When complex Criterion ranges are used to extract data, it is useful to think of the Criterion range as a filter through which the record must pass to reach the Output range. Records can be thought of as starting at the left of the Criterion range and attempting to move through the filter to the Output range on the right.

In a complex Criterion range with an implicit AND (condition AND condition), conditions are located side by side in the same row. Records are first tested against the left-most condition. Those that fail the condition drop out. Those that pass the condition then are tested against the next condition to the right. Only records evaluated as true for all conditions pass to the Output range.

In the preceding example of the complex Criterion range with the implicit AND, the records would attempt to pass the two conditions as shown in the following. Notice that only records for Samson, Sheradon, and Shackley pass the first condition, and of those, only records for Samson and Sheradon pass the second condition.

LAST	SALARY
S*	+F3<20000

LAST	FIRST	SEX	AGE	SALARY
Nichols	Sandy	F	40	$31,090
Barons	Harold	M	21	$18,200
Able	Richard	M	25	$18,450
Samson	Carol	F	24	$19,380
Jackson	Julie	F	32	$22,280
Tremper	Nick	M	30	$20,520
Coneal	Rachael	F	20	$19,210
Brown	Scott	M	23	$18,400
Sheradon	Leslie	F	22	$19,230
Shackley	Suzanne	F	35	$23,850
Wertz	Herbert	M	55	$31,300

When a complex Criterion range has condition expressions entered into separate rows (condition OR condition), the record may pass through the Criterion range via any of the condition rows. Records that pass the condition(s) in the upper-most condition row pass directly to the Output range. Those that fail drop to the next condition row down and are tested against the condition(s) there. Only records that fail to pass all condition rows drop out. All others are copied to the Output range.

In the preceding example of the complex Criterion range with the implicit OR, the records would attempt to pass the Criterion range conditions as shown. Notice that while the records for Barons and Able fail the first condition, they pass the second. Since the record for Samson passes the first condition, it is not even tested against the second condition, but passes directly to the Output range.

LAST	SALARY
S*	
	+F3<20000

LAST	FIRST	SEX	AGE	SALARY
Nichols	Sandy	F	40	$31,090
Barons	Harold	M	21	$18,200
Able	Richard	M	25	$18,450
Samson	Carol	F	24	$19,380
Jackson	Julie	F	32	$22,280

Database Functions

The statistical functions of Lotus have counterparts designed specifically for dealing with database spreadsheet data. These functions are as follows.

@**DCOUNT**	@**DMIN**	@**DSTD**	@**DAVG**
@**DSUM**	@**DMAX**	@**DVAR**	

The purpose of database functions is to return a computed value (such as an average) from a range of cells (such as the column of salaries in a database) based only upon records that meet a Criterion (such as all males in the database). A database function's general form is

@**DFUNCT**(Input range,offset,Criterion range)

The Input range and Criterion range arguments are specified in the same way as specified for the /**D**ata,**Q**uery commands. The offset argument is used to specify the column (field) in the database for which the computation is to be made. Since offset means "how many columns to the right of the first column," an offset value of 0 specifies the first column, an offset value of 1 specifies the second column, and so forth.

Example of Using Database Functions

Like the statistical functions, the database functions are very similar to each other in form and use. To demonstrate how the data functions may be used, in the following example two @**DAVG** functions are used to return the average salaries for all males and females in the employee database.

	A	B	C	D	E	F	G	H	I	J
1										
2		LAST	FIRST	SEX	AGE	SALARY		Averages		
3		Nichols	Sandy	F	40	$31,090		------------------------------		
4		Barons	Harold	M	21	$18,200		Male Salaries	=	$20,883
5		Able	Richard	M	25	$18,450				
6		Samson	Carol	F	24	$19,380		@DAVG(B2..F17,4,H18..H19)		
7		Jackson	Julie	F	32	$22,280				
8		Trember	Nick	M	30	$20,520				
9		Coneal	Rachael	F	20	$19,210		Female Salaries	=	$21,765
10		Brown	Scott	M	23	$18,400				
11		Sheradon	Leslie	F	22	$19,230		@DAVG(B2..F17,4,I18..I19)		
12		Shackley	Suzanne	F	35	$23,850				
13		Wertz	Herbert	M	55	$31,300				
14		Ralston	Sherry	F	24	$18,170				
15		Brusky	Wayne	M	27	$20,930				
16		Austin	Chip	M	22	$18,380		Criterion Ranges		
17		Drexler	Anne	F	26	$20,910		------------------------------		
18								SEX	SEX	
19			Input Range					M	F	
20										

WHAT IS A MACRO?

In its simplest form, a macro is a collection of keystrokes entered as labels into a cell or range of cells. The top cell of the range is then named using the /**R**ange,**N**ame,**C**reate command. The name given to a range that holds a macro must begin with a backslash (\) followed by a single letter of the alphabet. Once the macro has been entered and named, Lotus will sequentially execute the keystrokes represented in it whenever the Alt key is held down and the letter of the macro's name is typed.

STEPS REQUIRED TO CREATE A MACRO

The following example will show the steps involved in creating a macro.

Assessing the Problem

Macros are created to solve problems or to save time. Let's suppose that you have a spreadsheet file that you have been working on for several days. Your routine is always the same. After each session you save the spreadsheet under its original name to update the file on the disk, and you then exit 1-2-3. Eight keystrokes are required to accomplish your save-and-exit routine. A macro can accomplish the task faster and in one keystroke combination.

Coding the Macro

To create a macro you record the exact sequence of keystrokes required for your regular routine. With paper and a pencil you write down the keys that you press when you complete the save-and-exit steps manually. The keystrokes and commands that you use are as follows.

Keystrokes	Actions and Prompts
/	Call the Main Menu.
F	Select the **F**ile command.
S	Select the **S**ave command.
	Lotus presents the prompt
	`Enter save file name: A:\ASSGN1.WK1`
	The name shown is the one with which you loaded the file (its original name) and is the default prompt of the /**F**ile,**S**ave command.
↵	Type the Enter key to enter this as the correct filename.
	Next you see the prompt
	`Cancel  Replace`
R	Select **R**eplace to update the file.
	Lotus returns to the READY mode.
/	Call the Main Menu again.
Q	Select the **Q**uit command.
	Next you see the prompt
	`No  Yes`
Y	Select **Y**es to complete the Quit operation.

After you systematically record the keystrokes as **/FS↵ R/QY** on a piece of paper, you are ready to create the macro that, when executed, will complete these eight keystrokes.

Locating the Macro

Following the rules of spreadsheet design, you move the pointer to an area set off from any current or foreseeable spreadsheet overlap or interference. You next document the area by entering the label "Spreadsheet Macros." You then are ready to type in the macro. Note this very important fact, however—the keystroke ↵ (Enter) is represented in a macro with a tilde (~) character.

Entering the Macro

You begin entering into a cell the keystrokes you have written down for the macro. Since your keystrokes must be entered as labels, you begin your entry by typing in a label prefix (', ", or ^). When it is complete, your macro should look like this.

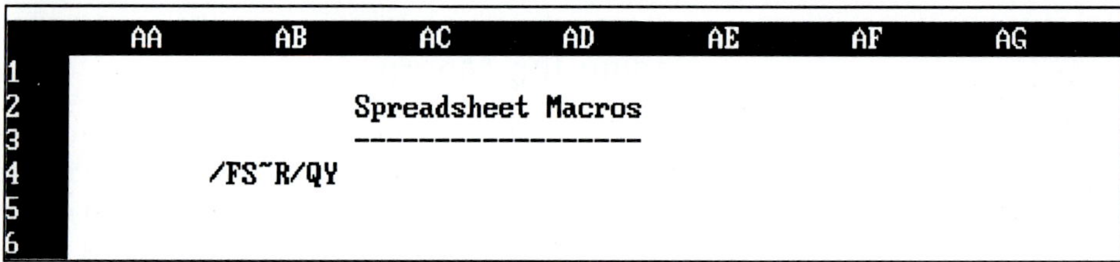

Naming a Macro

Your next step is to use the /**R**ange,**N**ame,**C**reate command to name the single cell AB4..AB4 with an appropriate macro name. Since "D" might be a good name for "Done," you specify the range name as \D.

Enter name: \D

Lotus recognizes a named range as being a macro by the backslash in its name. To complete documentation of the macro, you enter the macro name as a label into the AA column and a short description of the macro's function into the AC column.

Invoking a Macro

Now that the macro has been entered and named, the next time you are ready to save-and-exit you simply press and hold the Alt key and then type the D key. Lotus then will begin to execute, in order, the keystrokes in the macro named \D. The result is that the save-and-exit routine is completed with one keystroke combination rather than eight keystrokes, saving you valuable time.

CAUTIONS ABOUT MACROS

Although macros can be useful, they also have some drawbacks. The keystrokes in them are executed so fast that there is seldom time to stop a rampaging macro before it has done substantial damage to your spreadsheet.

Even in the very simple macro used in the example, if a C or ~ character is accidentally placed where the R character should be (/**FS~R/QY**), the macro would not replace the file on the disk. It would, however, execute the /**Q**uit,**Y**es command, causing you to lose all of the work you had completed during the current editing session.

Safeguards Against Macro Catastrophes

1. Always save your spreadsheet prior to testing a new macro.
2. The Alt-F2 key combination turns on and off (toggles) a STEP mode. When the STEP mode is on, Lotus executes each keystroke in the macro only after you have typed a keyboard key. Thus, execution of the macro is slowed down, allowing you to observe the results of each keystroke in it.
3. While a macro is being executed, an indicator at the bottom of the screen will show CMD. If you want to stop the execution of the macro before it is completed, the Ctrl-Break key combination will interrupt the execution of the macro.

REPRESENTING SPECIAL KEYSTROKES IN A MACRO

As you will recall, the tilde character (~) is used in macros to represent the Enter key keystroke. This is one example of how a substitute entry may be used in a macro to represent the actual keystroke used. Other special keystrokes are represented in a macro by entering the key's name or function enclosed in braces. For instance, if you want to create a macro to copy a single cell into the cell below it, your macro would look like /**C**~{**DOWN**}~. The macro duplicates the following steps.

1. After you have moved to the cell from which to copy you would type /**C** to call the **C**opy command.
2. The default FROM range shown would be that single cell, so the Enter key would be pressed (~).
3. The default TO range next shown also would be that cell, but it can be changed by pointing to the appropriate TO range. To do so you would type the "down" pointer control key once. To represent the keystroke in a macro, you enter {**DOWN**}.
4. The default TO range shown then would be the cell that the pointer indicates (the cell below the original cell), so the Enter key would be pressed (~).

The following table lists the macro commands for special keystrokes and the keyboard equivalents which they represent within a macro. The pointer movement commands and editing commands also may include a number indicating that the command is to be repeated several times. For example, {**DOWN 3**} would be equivalent to {**DOWN**} {**DOWN**} {**DOWN**}.

Macro Keyboard Equivalent Commands

Command	Keyboard Equivalent
Function Keys	
{**EDIT**}	F2
{**NAME**}	F3
{**ABS**}	F4
{**GOTO**}	F5
{**WINDOW**}	F6
{**QUERY**}	F7
{**TABLE**}	F8
{**CALC**}	F9
{**GRAPH**}	F10
Pointer Movement Keys	
{**UP**}	↑
{**DOWN**}	↓
{**LEFT**}	←
{**RIGHT**}	→
{**PGUP**}	PgUp
{**PGDN**}	PgDn
{**BIGLEFT**}	Shift-Tab
{**BIGRIGHT**}	Tab
{**HOME**}	Home
{**END**}	End
Editing Keys	
{**DEL**} or {**DELETE**}	Del
{**ESC**} or {**ESCAPE**}	Esc
{**BS**} or {**BACKSPACE**}	Backspace key
~	Enter key ↵
{~}	Tilde character
{{ } and { }}	Brace characters

Interactive Macros

{**?**} is a unique macro command. It may be used to suspend the execution of a macro in order to allow the user to type in spreadsheet data, to answer command prompts, or to move the spreadsheet pointer. In the following example, a macro has been designed to /**R**ange,**F**ormat any range of cells to display Currency format with two decimal places.

```
/RFC2~{?}~
```

To use the macro you first move to the beginning of the range to be formatted, and then invoke the macro with the Alt-letter key combination. The macro calls the /**R**ange,**F**ormat,**C**urrency command and specifies 2 decimal places. The pointer is automatically anchored. The {**?**} command then suspends the execution of the macro to let you move the pointer to the end of the range to be formatted (point to the range). When you are finished, you type the Enter key to signal your completion. The macro will continue executing where it left off. The final ~ in the macro is used to Enter the range you have pointed to.

BUILDING A MACRO LIBRARY

The macros discussed here so far are simple, general purpose macros that could be useful in any spreadsheet. As you continue to use Lotus you will identify sets of keystrokes that you use often, and you may want to create a library or collection of macros to use in each of your spreadsheets. The following procedure may be used to create a single set of general purpose macros, which may then be combined into any of your spreadsheets.

You begin by creating and testing your set of macros within an existing spreadsheet. In the following example, five macros have been put in a well-documented area of a spreadsheet.

```
     AA          AB                   AC       AD       AE       AF
1
2         Spreadsheet Macros
3    ------------------------------------------------------------------
4    Name Macro                  Description
5
6     \D  /FS~R/QY               Save/update spreadsheet and exit 1-2-3
7
8     \C  /C~{?}~                Copy current cell into any cell by
9                                pointing
10
11    \M  /RFC2~{?}~             Format $xx,xxx.xx range beginning
12                               at current cell
13
14    \B  /RE~                   Erase the current cell
15
16    \P  /PPOML10~~R132~S\015~QQ Print macro -
17                               Set Margins Left = 10, Right = 132
18                               Setup string - condensed (Epson)
19
```

The macro names have been entered as labels into the AA column; the actual macros have been entered into the AB column; and a short description of each macro has been entered in the AC column. The macros in the AB column must be separated from each other by blank cells.

Using the /File,Xtract Command

Once you have entered and documented this area of the spreadsheet (AA2..AC18), it may be saved as its own file by using the /File,**X**tract command. In the example, the spreadsheet macro area might be saved under the name MACLIB. The command would be

/**F**ile,**X**tract,**F**ormulas or **V**alues
Enter xtract file name: A:\MACLIB
Enter xtract range: AA2..AC18

NOTE: An Xtracted file may have its formulas converted to constants (Values) or left intact (Formulas). Since this area of the spreadsheet is all labels, it doesn't matter which option is selected.

When the **X**tract operation is complete, the macro area of the spreadsheet will be saved on the disk in its own .WK1 file.

Using the /**F**ile,**C**ombine Command

When you start a new spreadsheet or when you want to have your library of macros available within an existing spreadsheet, you may use the /**F**ile,**C**ombine command to read the macro library file (MACLIB.WK1) into the current spreadsheet. The command will copy it into any location you desire. Here the macros will be read into the current spreadsheet at the cell address A100.

The first step in combining a .WK1 file from the disk into a current file is to move the spreadsheet pointer to the upper left corner of the desired range location for the incoming spreadsheet data. In the example the pointer would be moved to cell A100. The command then would be

/**F**ile,**C**ombine,**C**opy,**E**ntire-File
Enter name of file to combine: A:\MACLIB

When the operation is complete, the MACLIB spreadsheet will be combined with the current spreadsheet and its location will be A100..C116.

```
     A        B        C        D        E        F        G        H
99
100           Spreadsheet Macros
101  ------------------------
102  Name   Macro    Description
103
104   \D    /FS~R/QY Save/update spreadsheet and exit 1-2-3
105
106   \C    /C~{?}~  Copy current cell into any cell by
107                  pointing
108
109   \M    /RFC2~{?}Format $xx,xxx.xx range beginning
110                  at current cell
111
112   \B    /RE~     Erase the current cell
113
114   \P    /PPOML10~Print macro -
115                  Set Margins Left = 10, Right = 132
116                  Setup string - condensed (Epson)
117
```

Any range names that may have existed in the file being combined no longer exist after the **C**ombine operation. After combining your macro library into a spreadsheet, you need to again name each macro range in order for it to be used in the new spreadsheet.

Using the /**R**ange,**N**ame,**L**abels,**R**ight Command

If the macro names have been entered as labels into cells to the left of all macros, as in this example, the /**R**ange,**N**ame,**L**abels,**R**ight command may be used to name the macro cells. With the pointer located at cell A104, the top label, the command would be executed as follows.

/**R**ange,**N**ame,**L**abels,**R**ight
Enter label range: A104..A114

After this command has been executed, each of the labels in the range A104..A114 will be used to name the cell to its right.

A Macro to Name Macros

If the macros in your library are laid out differently, you may find it more convenient to include in your macro library a macro that, when executed, will name each of the other macros. You will still need to name this macro before it may be executed.

Several different designs for this macro exist. The macro shown at the bottom of this macro library works if the spreadsheet pointer is on the cell indicated when the macro is invoked. The manual steps required to name and then execute the macro have been included in the description area.

```
       A       B         C         D         E         F         G         H
102  Name    Macro     Description
103
104   \D     /FS~R/QY  Save/update spreadsheet and exit 1-2-3
105
106   \C     /C~{?}~   Copy current cell into any cell by pointing
107
108   \M     /RFC2~{?}Format $xx,xxx.xx range beginning at current cell
109
110   \B     /RE~      Erase the current cell
111
112   \P     /PPOML10~~R132~S\015~QQ
113                    Print macro -
114                    Set Margins Left = 10, Right = 132
115                    Setup string - condensed (Epson)
116 pointer->  HERE
117   \S     {UP 4}/RNC\P~~      Macro to Name Ranges for Macros in Library
118          {UP 2}/RNC\B~~      1) Name the first cell in this macro \S
119          {UP 2}/RNC\M~~      2) Move the pointer to the cell marked HERE
120          {UP 2}/RNC\C~~      3) Type Alt-S
121          {UP 2}/RNC\D~~
```

HOW LOTUS EXECUTES A MACRO

Notice that the macro to name macros is several cells deep and that its range name names only the top cell of the macro. When a macro is invoked, Lotus begins executing the keystrokes in the named cell from left to right. When all the keystrokes in a cell have been executed, Lotus looks to the next cell down for further macro keystrokes. This continues until a blank cell (or the {**QUIT**} command) is encountered, causing execution of the macro to stop. An interesting implication of this is that a cell within a macro can also be named as a different macro, which can then be used to execute only the portion of the larger macro from that cell down (a macro within a macro).

A MENU OF MACROS—THE {**MENUBRANCH**} COMMAND

One of Lotus's special macro commands, the {**MENUBRANCH**} command, allows one macro to display a menu of eight different macros. Any of the macros in the menu then may be invoked through a menu selection process almost identical to Lotus's command selection process. To demonstrate the use of the {**MENUBRANCH**} command, the separate macros used so far will be incorporated into a menu.

The Structure of a Menu Range

The overall design of a menu range is as follows.

row 1 →	first selection	second selection	third selection
row 2 →	first description	second description	third description
row 3 →	commands	commands	commands

The menu range may be defined to include all selections, descriptions, and commands. It also may be defined as only the cell containing the first selection. Lotus then will automatically use up to seven additional cells to the right of the first until a blank cell is encountered. The cell immediately below each menu selection is used for a longer label describing the menu selection. The cell below each description is where the commands for that selection begin.

An Example of a Menu Macro

To demonstrate the basic menu range structure, a macro named \M (cell B103) will hold the single command {**MENUBRANCH** MENU1} which tells Lotus to present the menu located at the range named MENU1 (cell B107).

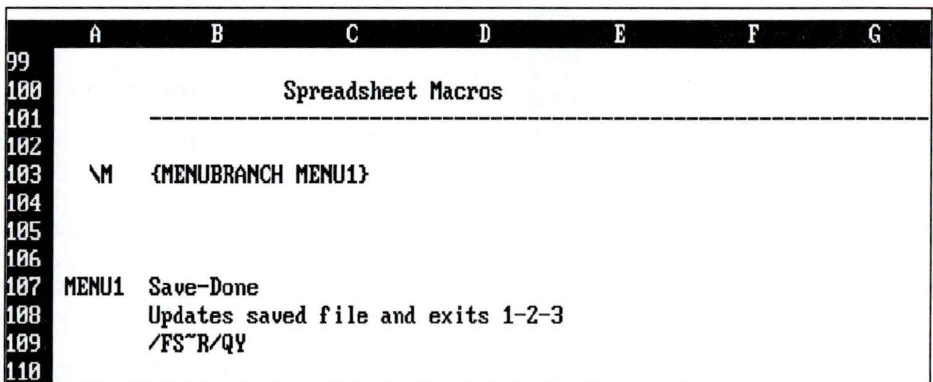

Invoking the Menu Macro

When the \M macro is executed from anywhere in the spreadsheet, the top of the screen now will display the Macro Menu named MENU1 as follows.

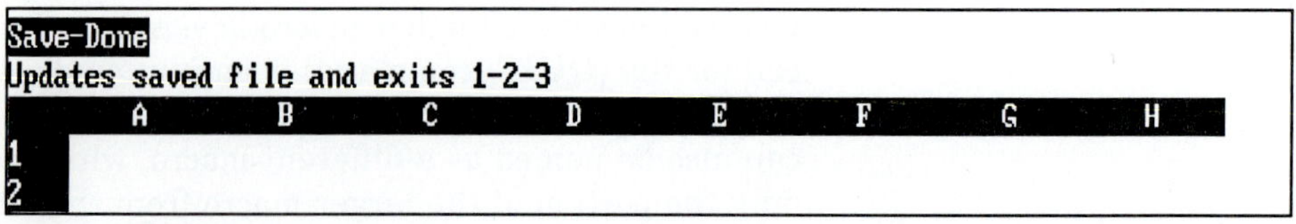

If you press the Enter key or the first letter of the menu selection, **S,** the macro keystrokes /**FS**~**R**/**QY** will be executed.

Adding Menu Options

To expand the example, the macro commands to copy a single cell into any location (previously \C) will be added to the menu range.

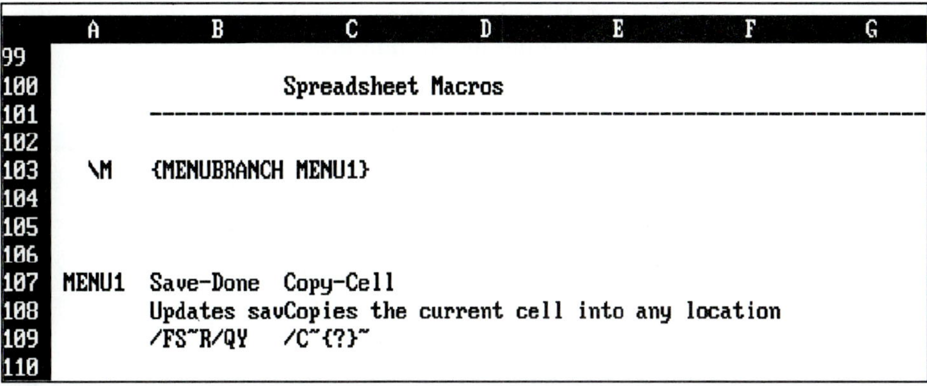

Entering the description for the new command stops the description for the first command from extending into that cell's area. If you wanted to view the first description again, you could move the pointer to that cell and the description would be displayed at the top of the screen.

Now when the \M macro is invoked, the first and second prompt lines of the spreadsheet will display

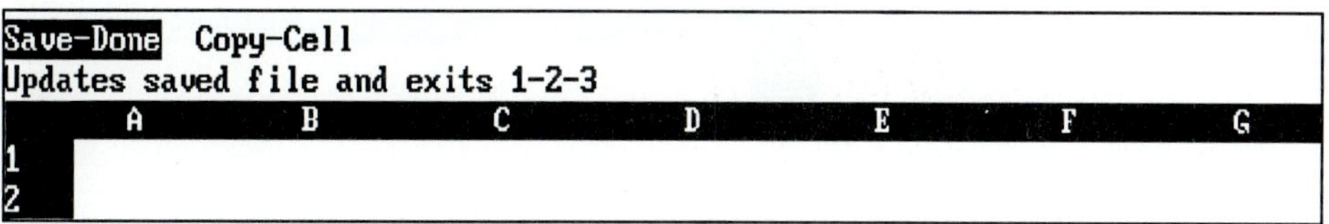

If you move the command pointer to the right it will display

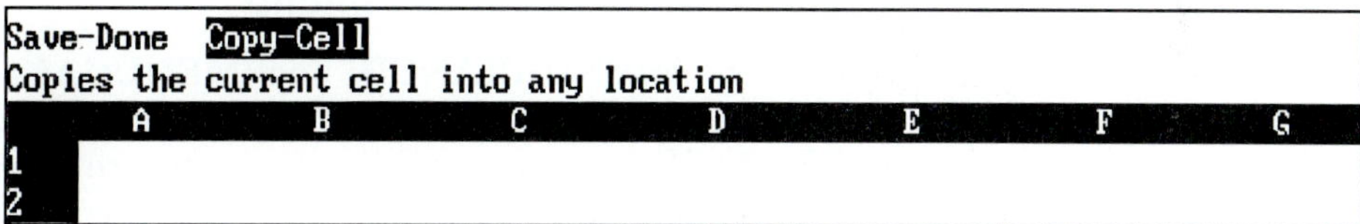

You now may select from the menu the macro commands to execute—either those to save and exit or those to copy a cell into any location. To select, either use the pointer and type the Enter key, or type the first character (**S** or **C**) of a selection. Since the first character may be typed, each menu selection should begin with a different character. The Ctrl-Break key combination may be used to return to the READY mode.

To complete the example, the entire macro library will be put into the following menu macro.

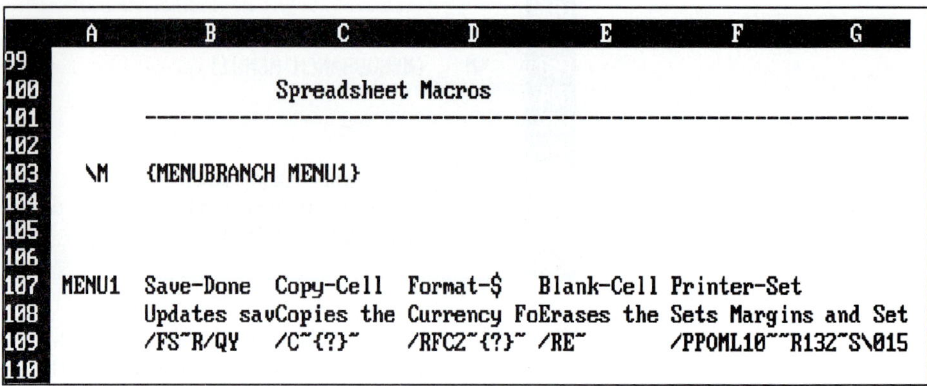

Now when the Alt-M keys are typed, the screen displays

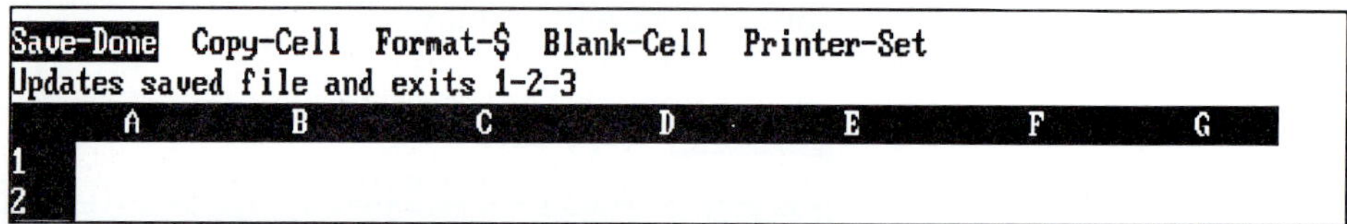

You have created your own Lotus menu, complete with explanations for each command in it. It operates just like a spreadsheet menu of commands: each command shown invokes a macro you have written.

The {**MENUCALL**} Command

Both the {**MENUBRANCH**} and {**MENUCALL**} commands pass control to the menu found in the location specified by the command. If {**MENUBRANCH**} is used to call the menu, macro execution will not return to the calling macro unless another command directs it to do so. However, if {**MENUCALL**} is used to call a menu, after the menu selection is made and its commands have been executed, macro execution will return to the macro that called the menu, beginning with the command following the {**MENUCALL**} command.

The following is an example of using {**MENUCALL**} for the same menu as in the previous example.

```
      A      B          C          D          E          F          G
99
100                     Spreadsheet Macros
101          ---------------------------------------------------------------
102
103   \M     {INDICATE UTIL}{MENUCALL MENU1}{INDICATE}
104
105
106
107   MENU1  Save-Done  Copy-Cell  Format-$   Blank-Cell Printer-Set
108          Updates savCopies the Currency FoErases the Sets Margins and Set
109          /FS~R/QY   /C~{?}~    /RFC2~{?}~ /RE~       /PPOML10~~R132~S\015
110
```

In the macro shown here, the {**INDICATE** UTIL} command is used before executing the menu to cause the indicator in the top right corner of the screen to display UTIL (for utilities) while the menu is being displayed. This might be useful to differentiate menus you have created from the normal Lotus menus. However, once executed, the indicator will continue to display UTIL until another command is executed to change it.

To return the indicator to its normal displays (READY, MENU, POINT, etc.), the {**INDICATE**} command must be executed without a string argument. As an alternative to placing this command at the end of each set of macro commands in the menu, it is placed after the {**MENUCALL**} command. This causes the command to be executed after the menu has been called, regardless of which menu option is selected.

ADVANCED MACRO COMMANDS

If you have computer programming experience, you may have noticed similarities between the macros discussed so far and writing programs using a programming language such as BASIC. In fact, macros are a type of spreadsheet programming language and the similarities become more apparent when advanced macro commands are discussed.

The macro commands discussed in this section are treated as advanced commands since their use requires some understanding of the principles of programming. The commands will be presented by using an example macro that will be built up as new commands are discussed. The macro will be designed to assist in data entry for the following spreadsheet area.

```
      A        B        C          D           E           F        G
1
2           -- -- -- -- -- -- -- -- -- -- -- -- -- -- -- -- --
3          ¦ Purchase Item =                                    ¦
4          ¦ -------------------------------------------------- ¦
5          ¦ Purchase Price =                                   ¦
6          ¦                                                    ¦
7          ¦ Down Payment =                                     ¦
8          ¦                                                    ¦
9          ¦ Terms                                              ¦
10         ¦ -----      Interest Rate     =                     ¦
11         ¦            Periods in Years =                      ¦
12         ¦                                                    ¦
13         ¦                                                    ¦
14         ¦            Monthly Payments =                      ¦
15         ¦                                                    ¦
16          -- -- -- -- -- -- -- -- -- -- -- -- -- -- -- -- --
17
```

In a separate portion of the spreadsheet, the following macro will be created.

```
      AA          AB                  AC                  AD
2           Spreadsheet Macros
3           ------------------------------------
4           {HOME}{BLANK D3}{BLANK D5..D7}{BLANK E10..E14}{CALC}
5           {GETLABEL "Type in Item Description:  ",D3}{CALC}
6           {GETNUMBER "Enter Purchase Price: ",D5}{CALC}
7           {GETNUMBER "Enter Down Payment: ",D7}{CALC}
8           {GETNUMBER "Yearly Interest Rate as a Decimal: ",E10}{CALC}
9           {GETNUMBER "Number of Periods in Years: ",E11}{CALC}
10          {GOTO}E14~
11          @PMT(D5-D7,E10/12,E11*12)~
12          {HOME}{QUIT}
13
```

The {**BLANK**} Command

The macro begins by moving the pointer to the Home position and erasing all of the data entry cells it will use when it is executed (which is essentially the same as initializing variables in a BASIC program). The {**BLANK**} command is used to perform a /**R**ange,**E**rase without having to move the cursor. After the {**HOME**} command is used to move the pointer to the Home position, the {**BLANK** range} command is used to erase the ranges where new data is to be entered.

The {**GETNUMBER**} and {**GETLABEL**} Commands

The {**GETNUMBER** "message",range} and {**GETLABEL** "message",range} commands are used to display a message (prompt) on the first prompt line of the spreadsheet. They then wait for the user to enter a response, and the response is copied into the cell at the upper left corner of the range specified in the command. If the response is intended to be a string value, the {**GET-LABEL**} command is used; if it is intended to be a numeric value, the {**GETNUMBER**} command is used.

When the {**GETLABEL**} command is executed, its prompt is presented at the top prompt line of the spreadsheet.

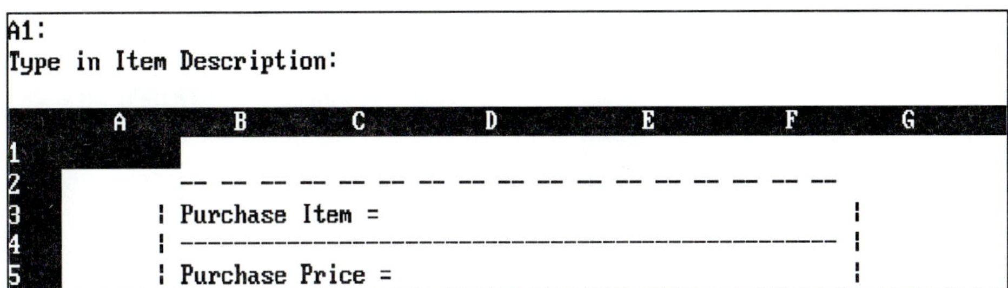

A label describing the item being considered for purchase is then typed in. After the Enter key is pressed, the label is copied into the cell D3. The commands {**GETLABEL**} and {**GETNUMBER**} must be followed by the {**CALC**} command in order for entries to appear while the macro is being executed. The next command, {**GETNUMBER** "Enter Purchase Price: ",D5}, is then executed.

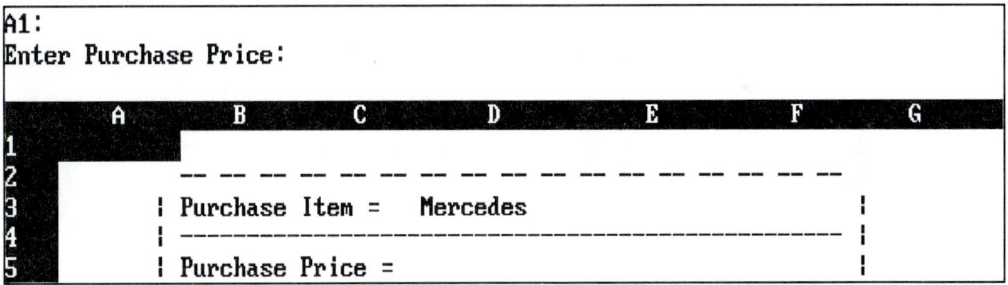

The macro continues to present prompts, accept data, and copy that data to the appropriate cells until the command {**GOTO**}E14~@**PMT**(D5-D7,E10/12,E11*12)~ is reached. This command causes the pointer to move to cell E14 and enter the @**PMT** function to calculate monthly payments, given the data provided by the user.

The {**QUIT**} Command

The {**QUIT**} command is used to stop execution of a macro. This command will be included in the example at various points in the macro's development.

When execution of the macro is completed, the spreadsheet will appear similar to the following.

```
       A        B        C          D               E          F        G
1
2              -- -- -- -- -- -- -- -- -- -- -- -- -- -- -- -- --
3            ! Purchase Item =   Mercedes                          !
4            ! ------------------------------------------------ !
5            ! Purchase Price =    $45,000.00                      !
6            !                                                     !
7            ! Down Payment =      $10,000.00                      !
8            !                                                     !
9            ! Terms                                               !
10           ! -----      Interest Rate     =          18.00%      !
11           !            Periods in Years =              4        !
12           !                                                     !
13           !                                                     !
14           !            Monthly Payments =      $1,028.12        !
15           !                                                     !
16             -- -- -- -- -- -- -- -- -- -- -- -- -- -- -- -- --
17
```

The example macro now will be expanded to include conditional execution of a subroutine if the monthly payment calculated is greater than $200. The modified macro is shown here.

```
        AA          AB                   AC                     AD
2              Spreadsheet Macros
3              ----------------------------------------
4              {HOME}{BLANK D3}{BLANK D5..D7}{BLANK E10..E14}{CALC}
5              {GETLABEL "Type in Item Description:  ",D3}{CALC}
6              {GETNUMBER "Enter Purchase Price: ",D5}{CALC}
7              {GETNUMBER "Enter Down Payment: ",D7}{CALC}
8              {GETNUMBER "Yearly Interest Rate as a Decimal: ",E10}{CALC}
9              {GETNUMBER "Number of Periods in Years: ",E11}{CALC}
10             {GOTO}E14~
11             @PMT(D5-D7,E10/12,E11*12)~
12             {IF E14>200}{EXCESS}
13             {HOME}{QUIT}
14
15   EXCESS    {GOTO}C17~EXCESSIVE PAYMENT~
16             {GETLABEL "Press Enter to continue",C17}{BLANK C17}
17
```

The {IF} Command

The {**IF** condition} command is the conditional macro command. When Lotus encounters the {**IF**} command, it evaluates the logical expression specified as the command's condition. If the condition is evaluated as true, the rest of the commands in the same cell are executed. If the condition is evaluated as false, execution of the macro resumes at the next cell down.

In the example, cell AB12 holds the command {**IF** E14>200}. When the command is executed, if the expression E14>200 is evaluated as true, the subroutine EXCESS is called with the {routine-name} command found in the same cell; otherwise, execution continues with the {**HOME**} {**QUIT**} commands in the next cell down.

The {routine-name} Command

The {routine-name} command is used to execute a subroutine. A subroutine is simply another range where macro commands are located. The range is named with the /**R**ange,**N**ame,**C**reate command. During macro execution, when the range name is encountered in a {routine-name} command, the commands in the subroutine will be executed before subsequent commands in the calling macro are executed.

In the example, cell AB15 has been given the range name EXCESS, and the commands beginning there are executed if the {**IF** condition} in the calling macro is evaluated as true. The subroutine displays a message indicating that the payment is too high and then erases the message when the Enter key is pressed. Now if the same values used in the previous example are entered, the screen will appear as follows after the payment is calculated.

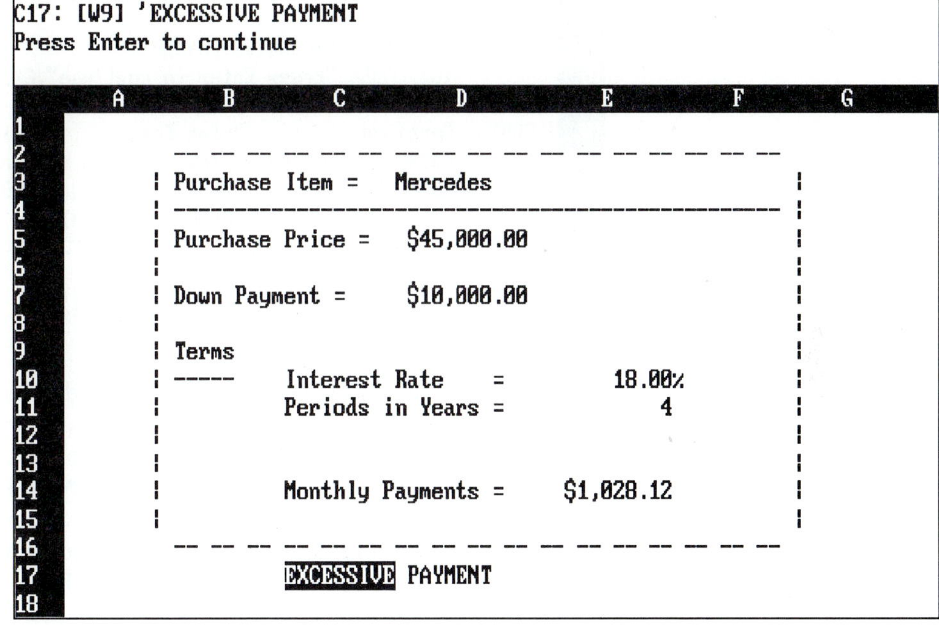

The last modification to the macro will be to include options to repeat the process for another set of values, to print the form, or to quit. The modified macro appears as follows.

```
AD13:                                                                    READY

        AA          AB                  AC                  AD
2                   Spreadsheet Macros
3                   ------------------------------------
4                   {HOME}{BLANK D3}{BLANK D5..D7}{BLANK E10..E14}{CALC}
5                   {GETLABEL "Type in Item Description:  ",D3}{CALC}
6                   {GETNUMBER "Enter Purchase Price: ",D5}{CALC}
7                   {GETNUMBER "Enter Down Payment: ",D7}{CALC}
8                   {GETNUMBER "Yearly Interest Rate as a Decimal: ",E10}{CALC}
9                   {GETNUMBER "Number of Periods in Years: ",E11}{CALC}
10                  {GOTO}E14~
11                  @PMT(D5-D7,E10/12,E11*12)~
12                  {IF E14>200}{EXCESS}
13                  {MENUBRANCH CONT}
14
15     EXCESS       {GOTO}C17~EXCESSIVE PAYMENT~
16                  {GETLABEL "Press Enter to continue",C17}{BLANK C17}
17
18      CONT        Continue            Print form          Quit
19                  Enter another set   Print the form shoDone entering data
20                  {BRANCH AB4}        /PPRA1..G17~AGQ     {HOME}{QUIT}
21                                      {MENUBRANCH CONT}
```

The {**BRANCH**} and {**MENUBRANCH**} Commands

The {**MENUBRANCH**} command at the end of the original macro (cell AB13) is used to send macro execution to the menu located at cell AB18 (range name CONT). The menu has three options: Continue, Print form, and Quit. If Continue is selected, the {**BRANCH**} command is used to send control back to the beginning of the original macro (cell AB4). If Print form is selected, keystrokes to print the range comprising the data entry form are executed and then another {**MENUBRANCH**} command is executed to repeat the same menu. If the Quit option is selected, the commands to end the macro are executed.

When the macro is executed, and all the values have been entered, the screen will appear as follows.

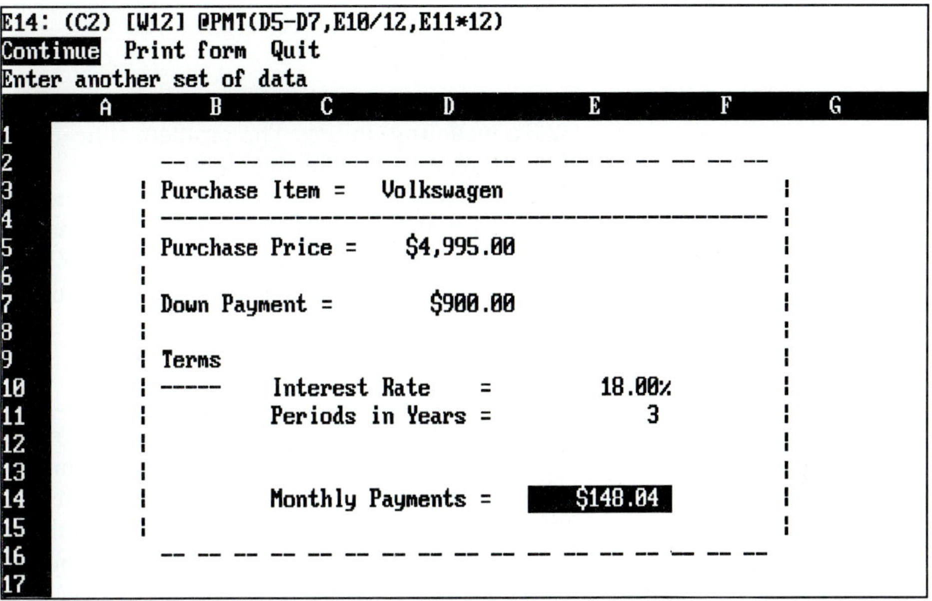

EXERCISES

EXERCISE 1
What If?

Required Preparation

Study the section titled *Spreadsheet Design* (pages L-50–L-56).

Exercise Steps

A classic management problem will be used here to demonstrate Lotus 1-2-3's modeling ability. The problem concerns a factory that produces tables and chairs. The factory makes a profit of $8.00 for every table and $6.00 for every chair it produces. The production process involves two operations—assembly and finishing. Each table takes 4 hours to assemble and 2 hours to finish. Each chair takes 2 hours to assemble and 4 hours to finish. There are 60 total assembly hours and 48 total finishing hours available per week in the factory.

1. Design a spreadsheet to determine how many tables and chairs per week the company should make to maximize profits. The spreadsheet should contain two cells (one for tables and one for chairs) into which you will enter "best guess" numbers (the number of tables and number of chairs, respectively, that should be produced each week). The rest of the spreadsheet should display the number of assembly and finishing hours left available in the week, and the dollar profits expected, based on the two current best guess numbers. Be sure to separate all key values from formulas in the spreadsheet.
2. Load Lotus 1-2-3 and then create the spreadsheet to determine the solution to the problem posed in part 1. Note that the number of assembly and/or finishing hours left available in the week cannot be negative.

Management is considering a change in production of its tables that would increase the assembly time to 6 hours per table. However, the change also would increase profits to $10.00 per table. Write down the answers to the following questions.

3. To maximize profits, should management make the change to the production of its tables?
4. How much profit must management make per table to achieve the same profits as before?
5. What impact would the change have on the efficient use of the available assembly and finishing times per week?
6. Return the spreadsheet to the original set of assumptions (4 hours assembly, $8.00 profit per table).

Another suggestion has been made that would increase the total assembly time to 68 hours and the total finishing time to 58 hours per week. However, the changes would cost $.50 in profits for both tables and chairs (profits/table = $7.50, profits/chair = $5.50).

7. Under the assumptions above, how many tables and chairs should be manufactured per week in order to maximize profits?
8. Do the changes to assembly and finishing times increase net profits for the factory?
9. What impact would the change have on the efficient use of the available assembly and finishing times per week?

10. Save the spreadsheet under the name PRODMOD (production model), print the spreadsheet, and then exit the spreadsheet software with the /**Q**uit command.

EXERCISE 2
Meat and Cheese Portions

Required Preparation

Study the section titled *Spreadsheet Design* (pages L-50–L-56).

Exercise Steps

This exercise concerns a fast-food restaurant that specializes in Mexican-American food. One element of cost/quality control in such a restaurant involves the amount of meat and cheese used when a food item is assembled by kitchen employees (food portioning). The following table describes the various food items and the amounts of meat and cheese that should be included in them.

Item	**Meat**	**Cheese**	**Price**
Taco	2 oz	.5 oz	.89
Burrito	4 oz	1.0 oz	1.89
Enchilada	3 oz	.75 oz	1.29
Tostado	2 oz	.5 oz	.89
Tamale	3 oz	.75 oz	1.39

The restaurant uses a point-of-sale cash register that produces a tape at the end of the week listing the total units sold of each item. Management takes a physical inventory at the beginning of each week and keeps track of any meat or cheese shipments that arrive during the week. By comparing the weekly inventories, management is able to determine how much meat and cheese were actually used. The register tape and portion tables are used to determine how much meat and cheese should have been used. The management wants the total cost of the meat used in a week to amount to 16.5% of item sales for the week. Similarly, it wants the cost of cheese to be close to 6.5% of sales. At the end of each week, management wants a report that shows the actual pounds of meat and cheese used compared against the amounts that should have been used, with the difference (variance) in pounds shown. It also wants the report to include the actual meat/cheese cost percentages for the week shown. The following information may be used to create and test the spreadsheet.

Meat Information

Cost	$1.19/lb
Beginning Amount	550 lbs
Shipments:	
Tuesday	350 lbs
Thursday	295 lbs
Ending Amount	500 lbs

Cheese Information

Cost	$1.87/lb
Beginning Amount	215 lb
Shipments:	
Wednesday	290 lbs
Ending Amount	305 lbs

Sales Information

Item	Units Sold
Tacos	2067
Burritos	789
Enchiladas	507
Tostados	456
Tamales	308

1. Use paper and pencil to map out (design) a spreadsheet template for the restaurant.
2. Load Lotus 1-2-3 and then enter the data and commands necessary to create the spreadsheet template.
3. Save the template under the name "FOODCOST" and then print the spreadsheet.
4. Enter the week's sample data and then print the spreadsheet again.
5. Save the spreadsheet again under the name "WEEK1" and then exit the spreadsheet software with the /**Q**uit command.

EXERCISE 3 Payment Schedules

Required Preparation

Study the @**PMT** function in the section on Financial functions (pages L-61–L-64) and the @**CHOOSE** function in the section on Logical and Special functions (page L-75). See also the explanation of mixed references on page L-53, and the /**D**ata,**F**ill command in the Lotus Command Summary.

Exercise Steps

In this exercise you will create a table of monthly payments for a retail store that offers financing to its customers. The salespeople would like to have a printed copy of the tables to carry with them as they help customers in the showroom. Although they will have to calculate the payment for the exact price of an item, they would like a quick reference that gives the monthly payments their customers could expect, given a ballpark price within $50 to $100 of the actual price. Prices of merchandise that may be financed range from $200 to $10,000. Since the company changes its interest rates based upon a fluctuating prime rate, these schedules will have to be updated and reprinted periodically.

1. Leaving several rows for key entries at the top of a new spreadsheet, enter labels for the payment table with columns for financing periods of 12 months, 24 months, 36 months, and 48 months.

The table area should look similar to the following.

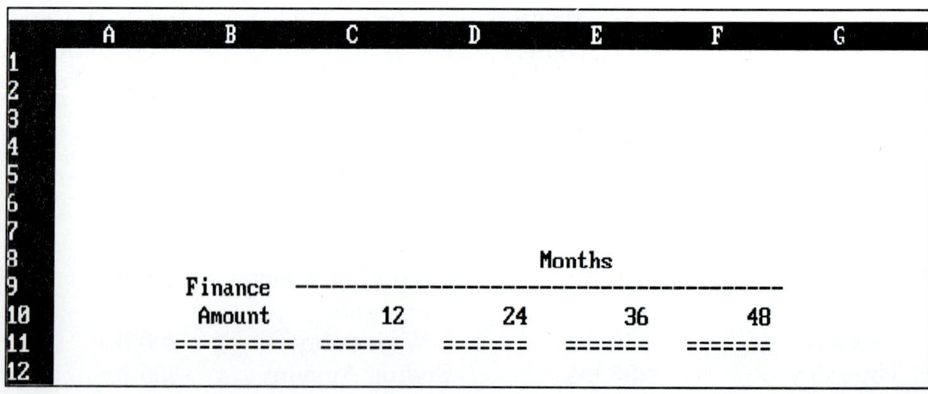

2. Use the /**D**ata,**F**ill command to create a list of finance amounts in the appropriately labeled column of the spreadsheet. The amounts from $200 to $1,000 should be listed at $50 intervals and those from $1,000 to $10,000 at $100 intervals.
3. Format the finance amounts to display as currency with 0 decimal places.
4. In the key area above the table, enter labels for the interest rate, stated as a monthly rate and an annual rate.
5. Enter the annual rate as 18% (.18) and the monthly rate as 1.5% (.015), and format these cells to display percentages with 2 decimal places.

The spreadsheet now should appear similar to the following.

```
      A        B          C          D          E          F        G
1
2          Interest Rate
3          ====================
4            Monthly    Annual
5               1.50%    18.00%
6
7
8                                       Months
9           Finance   ---------------------------------------
10           Amount         12         24         36         48
11         ==========  =======    =======    =======    =======
12              $200
13              $250
14              $300
15              $350
16              $400
17              $450
18              $500
19              $550
20              $600
```

By using an absolute reference and two mixed references in the arguments of the @**PMT** function, you should be able to enter the function into one cell in such a way that it then may be copied to all other cells in the table.

6. Now enter the @**PMT** function to calculate the payment for the upper left corner of the table ($200 financed for 12 months) using the appropriate interest rate.
7. Copy the cell with the @**PMT** function to all cells in the table area, and then format these cells to display currency with 2 decimal places.

The last two steps should result in a table displaying the following payment values.

	A	B	C	D	E	F	G
1							
2		Interest Rate					
3		==========	==========				
4		Monthly	Annual				
5		1.50%	18.00%				
6							
7							
8					Months		
9		Finance	-----------	-----------	-----------	-----------	
10		Amount	12	24	36	48	
11		==========	=======	=======	=======	=======	
12		$200	$18.34	$9.98	$7.23	$5.87	
13		$250	$22.92	$12.48	$9.04	$7.34	
14		$300	$27.50	$14.98	$10.85	$8.81	
15		$350	$32.09	$17.47	$12.65	$10.28	
16		$400	$36.67	$19.97	$14.46	$11.75	
17		$450	$41.26	$22.47	$16.27	$13.22	
18		$500	$45.84	$24.96	$18.08	$14.69	
19		$550	$50.42	$27.46	$19.88	$16.16	
20		$600	$55.01	$29.95	$21.69	$17.62	

The key area now will be modified so that one of four different interest rates may be selected for the table. The annual interest rates are 15%, 18%, 21% and 24%. Someone using this spreadsheet should be able to enter a number from 1 to 4, respectively, to select one of these interest rates and then print a new rate schedule.

8. Modify the key area to include an @**CHOOSE** function so that one of the four interest rates may be selected.
9. Set the appropriate print range, add any special print formatting desired such as border rows or columns, and print the spreadsheet.
10. Save the spreadsheet under the name PMTSCHED.

EXERCISE 4 Employees Payroll

Required Preparation

Study the section titled Lotus 1-2-3 Functions (pages L-57–L-78).

Exercise Steps

In the following exercise several of the more commonly used functions will be introduced. The exercise concerns a small group of half-time and full-time employees who work at varying rates of pay.

1. Begin the exercise by entering the following data into the spreadsheet. Note that the labels across the top have been centered with the /**R**ange,**L**abel,**C**enter command, and that the dollar amounts in column E are formatted as currency with two decimal places. Also, use the

/**W**orksheet,**C**olumn,**S**et-Width command to make column D six characters wide and column E 11 characters wide.

```
A1:                                                         READY

     A         B         C        D          E         F         G         H
1
2
3  EMPLOYEE   LAST      FIRST   ALLOW       PAY
4   STATUS    NAME      NAME    ANCES      RATES
5
6  HALF      Adams    Eric          0       $7.00
7  FULL      Edwards  Carol         2      $12.65
8  FULL      Hill     Bob           0       $7.50
9  HALF      Johnson  Janet         1      $17.52
10 FULL      Martin   Rebecca       0       $8.29
11 FULL      Miller   Nancy         1       $8.01
12 HALF      Parkison Mark                  $9.50
13 FULL      Parsons  Larry         2       $7.86
14 HALF      Randall  Cathy         1      $21.52
15 HALF      Russell  Wesley        0      $16.83
16 HALF      Smith    Jennie               $12.35
17 FULL      Williams Laurie        1       $8.90
18
19
20
17-May-90  09:51 PM
```

2. Now move the pointer to row 6 and fix the horizontal titles using the /**W**orksheet,**T**itles,**H**orizontal command.
3. Move the pointer to cell A20 and enter the following labels.

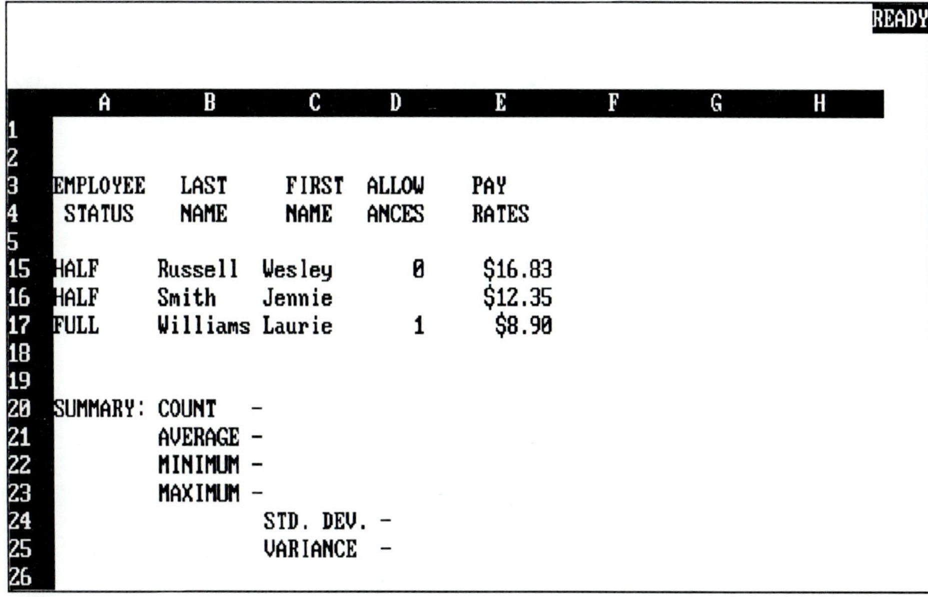

```
                                                            READY

     A         B         C        D          E         F         G         H
1
2
3  EMPLOYEE   LAST      FIRST   ALLOW       PAY
4   STATUS    NAME      NAME    ANCES      RATES
5
15 HALF      Russell  Wesley        0      $16.83
16 HALF      Smith    Jennie               $12.35
17 FULL      Williams Laurie        1       $8.90
18
19
20 SUMMARY:  COUNT   -
21           AVERAGE -
22           MINIMUM -
23           MAXIMUM -
24                    STD. DEV. -
25                    VARIANCE  -
26
```

4. Move the pointer to cell C20 and enter an @**COUNT** function to count the number of employees (first names) contained in that column. Next copy the function into the next two cells to the right.

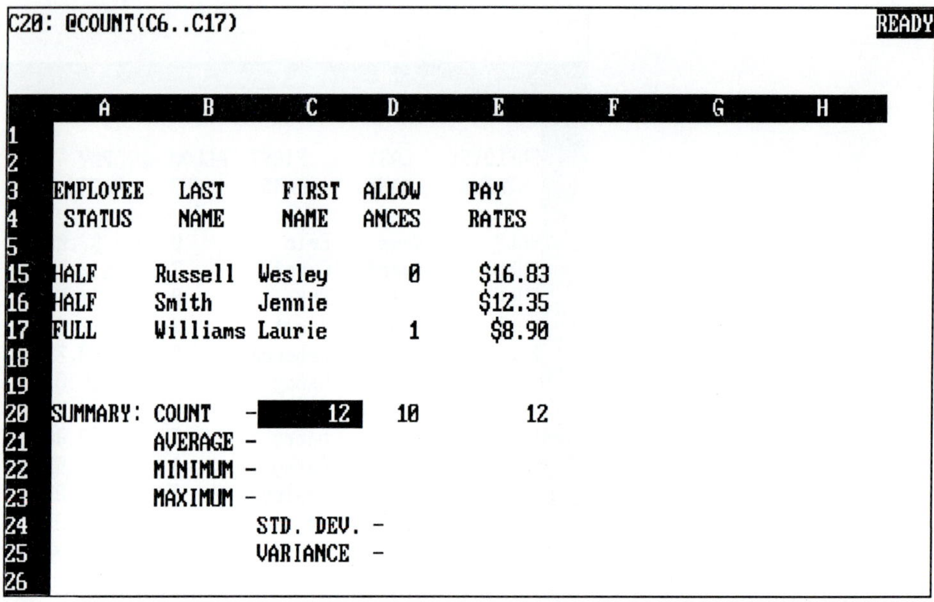

Notice that the ALLOWANCES column shows a total of 10 entries, while the others show 12 each. The @**COUNT** function counts only the nonblank cells in the specified range.

5. Move to the lower of the two blank cells in the ALLOWANCES column and type ||@**NA**←||.

Notice that the count for this column is now 11 and that cell D16 now contains the letters NA—which stands for "not available." The @**NA** function is an example of a function that uses no argument. This type of function is useful where a lack of information should be noted whenever the cell is referenced by a spreadsheet formula.

6. Move to the other blank cell in this column across from the name Mark Parkison and enter another @**NA** function. The SUMMARY area of the spreadsheet should now appear as follows.

```
D12: (G) [W6] @NA                                                    READY

        A         B         C       D        E         F         G         H
1
2
3  EMPLOYEE    LAST      FIRST   ALLOW    PAY
4   STATUS     NAME      NAME    ANCES    RATES
5
12 HALF      Parkison Mark         NA      $9.50
13 FULL      Parsons  Larry         2      $7.86
14 HALF      Randall  Cathy         1     $21.52
15 HALF      Russell  Wesley        0     $16.83
16 HALF      Smith    Jennie       NA     $12.35
17 FULL      Williams Laurie        1      $8.90
18
19
20 SUMMARY:  COUNT   -      12     12         12
21           AVERAGE -
22           MINIMUM -
23           MAXIMUM -
24                    STD. DEV. -
25                    VARIANCE  -
26
17-May-90  10:50 PM
```

You will be entering a number of functions which will use the pay rates found in column E, so it will save time if you now name that range.

7. Use the /**R**ange,**N**ame,**C**reate command to name this range (E6..E17) RATES, and then move to cell E21 and type ||@**AVG**(RATES)↵||.

The average pay rate of 11.4941666 should now appear in this cell.

8. To keep the spreadsheet easy to read, format the range D21..E25 to be fixed with 2 decimal places.

9. Now copy the @**AVG** function in cell E21 to cell D21.

You need to take note of two things: (1) when copied, the formula changed to read @**AVG**(D6..D17) (was copied in a relative fashion), and (2) the cell for average allowances now displays NA. Since one or more cells in the referenced range (D6..D17) contain an @**NA** function, the cell making the reference will display NA. This prevents the referencing cell from displaying possibly inaccurate information.

10. Now use the @**MIN**, @**MAX**, @**STD**, and @**VAR** functions to complete the SUMMARY portion of the spreadsheet. When finished, the area should appear as follows.

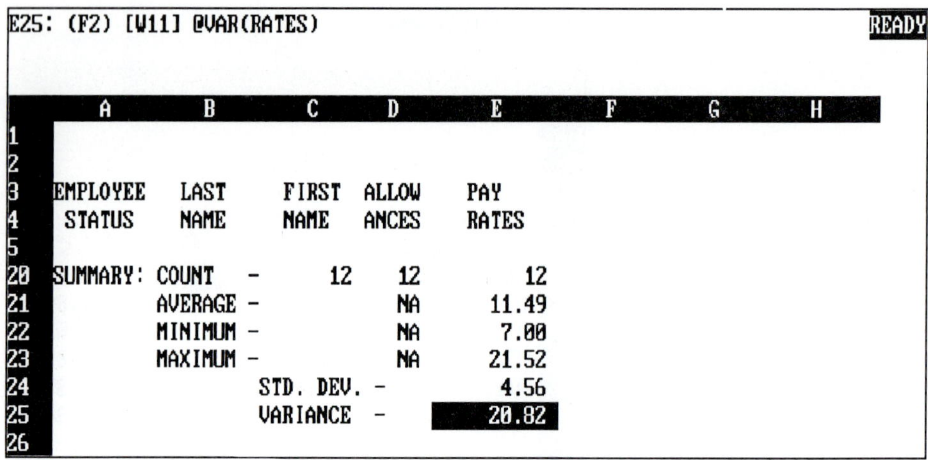

11. Type the Home key and remove (clear) the titles fix. Next move the pointer to cell F4 and complete the following column labels. Note that the labels all use the **^** (Center) label prefix.

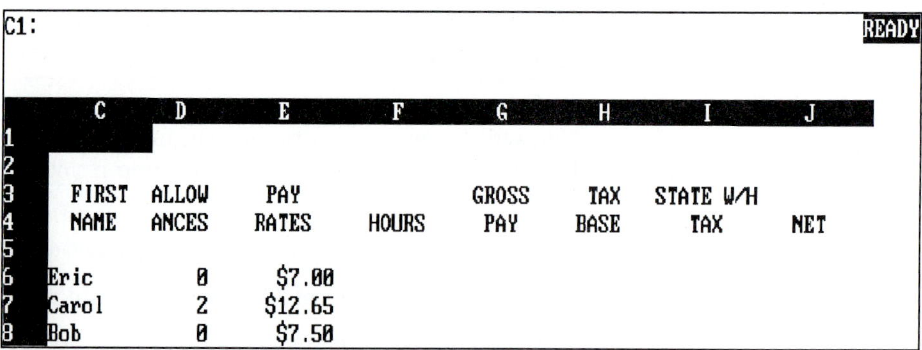

Here all employees with a STATUS of HALF are half-time employees, and all others are full-time. A two-week payroll is being prepared, and all full-time employees have worked 80 hours, while half-time employees have worked 40 hours. To complete the HOURS column in the spreadsheet, the @**IF** function will be used.

The @**IF** function is used to evaluate a condition, and then return one value in the cell if the condition is true and another value if the condition is false. The @**IF** function has the form

@**IF**(condition, true value, false value)

The condition in the function may be any expression which can be evaluated as either true or false. An expression might be D6>1, D6=D10, or C3="FIRST". If the expression is evaluated as true, the true value will be displayed in the cell. If it is evaluated as false, the false value will appear in the cell.

12. Move to cell F6 and enter the @**IF** function that will test if the employee is half-time or not, and then return the number 40 if the em-

ployee is half-time or the number 80 if not. Next copy the formula into the remaining rows of the HOURS column.

A1: READY

	A	B	C	D	E	F	G	H
1								
2								
3	EMPLOYEE	LAST	FIRST	ALLOW	PAY		GROSS	TAX
4	STATUS	NAME	NAME	ANCES	RATES	HOURS	PAY	BASE
5								
6	HALF	Adams	Eric	0	$7.00	40		
7	FULL	Edwards	Carol	2	$12.65	80		
8	FULL	Hill	Bob	0	$7.50	80		
9	HALF	Johnson	Janet	1	$17.52	40		
10	FULL	Martin	Rebecca	0	$8.29	80		
11	FULL	Miller	Nancy	1	$8.01	80		
12	HALF	Parkison	Mark	NA	$9.50	40		
13	FULL	Parsons	Larry	2	$7.86	80		
14	HALF	Randall	Cathy	1	$21.52	40		
15	HALF	Russell	Wesley	0	$16.83	40		
16	HALF	Smith	Jennie	NA	$12.35	40		
17	FULL	Williams	Laurie	1	$8.90	80		
18								

13. Move to column G under the title GROSS PAY. Calculate the gross pay for the first employee and copy this formula (rate∗hours) for the rest of the employees.

The next column (TAX BASE) will be calculated by using the following formula

tax base = gross pay − (42 ∗ number of allowances)

14. Move to cell H6 and enter the appropriate formula. Then copy it to the rest of the cells in the column.

A1: READY

	A	B	C	D	E	F	G	H
1								
2								
3	EMPLOYEE	LAST	FIRST	ALLOW	PAY		GROSS	TAX
4	STATUS	NAME	NAME	ANCES	RATES	HOURS	PAY	BASE
5								
6	HALF	Adams	Eric	0	$7.00	40	280	280
7	FULL	Edwards	Carol	2	$12.65	80	1012	928
8	FULL	Hill	Bob	0	$7.50	80	600	600
9	HALF	Johnson	Janet	1	$17.52	40	700.8	658.8
10	FULL	Martin	Rebecca	0	$8.29	80	663.2	663.2
11	FULL	Miller	Nancy	1	$8.01	80	640.8	598.8
12	HALF	Parkison	Mark	NA	$9.50	40	380	NA
13	FULL	Parsons	Larry	2	$7.86	80	628.8	544.8
14	HALF	Randall	Cathy	1	$21.52	40	860.8	818.8
15	HALF	Russell	Wesley	0	$16.83	40	673.2	673.2
16	HALF	Smith	Jennie	NA	$12.35	40	494	NA
17	FULL	Williams	Laurie	1	$8.90	80	712	670
18								

You next will use one of the LOOKUP functions, which are used for looking up values in a table. The function you will be using is @**VLOOKUP,** the vertical LOOKUP function. The format is

@**VLOOKUP**(valueX,range,offset)

where valueX is a number or string to be looked up in the first column of a table, the range is the location of the table itself, and the offset is the number of columns to the right of the first column in the table where the function finds the value to return.

15. Move to cell A34 and enter the appropriate labels and numbers for the area. Note that the values in column C have been formatted to display percentage notation with one decimal place.

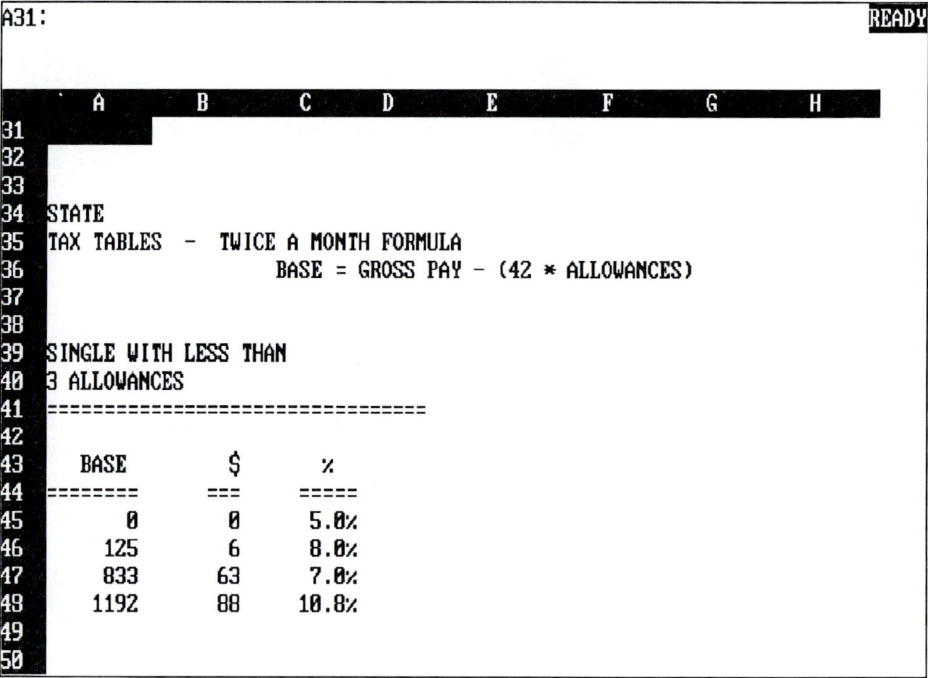
```
A31:                                                            READY

      A         B         C         D         E         F         G         H
31
32
33
34 STATE
35 TAX TABLES  -   TWICE A MONTH FORMULA
36                         BASE = GROSS PAY - (42 * ALLOWANCES)
37
38
39 SINGLE WITH LESS THAN
40 3 ALLOWANCES
41 ===================================
42
43    BASE        $        %
44 ========     ===     =====
45        0       0      5.0%
46      125       6      8.0%
47      833      63      7.0%
48     1192      88     10.0%
49
50
```

16. Use the /**R**ange,**N**ame,**C**reate command to give the range A45..C48 the name TABLE.

The formula for computing an employee's state withholding tax will use the values from this table, based upon the tax base.

Consider the following example

@**VLOOKUP**(130,$TABLE,2)

There the @**VLOOKUP** function begins by looking up the value 130 in the right-most column of TABLE. Since the formula ultimately will be copied into other cells, the reference to TABLE has been made absolute by preceding the name with a dollar sign. The look up operation results in row 46 being identified as the appropriate row in the table from which to return a value. The final argument in the function (2) tells it to move 2 columns to the right and return the value found there. The displayed value of the example function here will be 8.0%.

The general formula for calculating the state withholding tax in this spreadsheet is

$ column + % column * (TAX BASE − BASE column)

You will use the @**VLOOKUP** function to return the appropriate values from the table in this formula, so the actual formula in your spreadsheet will have the following format.

@**VLOOKUP**(x,range,offset) + @**VLOOKUP**(x,range,offset)*(x − @**VLOOKUP**(x,range,offset))

In this formula the x value and the range will remain the same for all three functions. The offset, however, will change with each function. The x value you will be using is the employee's TAX BASE. The range will be $TABLE, where the $ designates the range as an absolute range so that it may be copied. The offsets must be entered so that the appropriate values from the table are placed in the formula.

17. Move to cell I6 under the label STATE W/H TAX. Type in the formula to calculate tax, according to the model above. (It may be helpful to split the screen into 2 windows with the /**W**orksheet,**W**indow,**H**orizontal command, and to set the windows to unsynchronized scrolling.)

The tax for the first employee should come to 18.4. If you don't get this answer, check your offset values against the table again. Once the formula has been correctly entered, copy it to the rest of the cells in this column.

C1: READY

	C	D	E	F	G	H	I	J
1								
2								
3	FIRST	ALLOW	PAY		GROSS	TAX	STATE W/H	
4	NAME	ANCES	RATES	HOURS	PAY	BASE	TAX	NET
5								
6	Eric	0	$7.00	40	280	280	18.4	
7	Carol	2	$12.65	80	1012	928	69.65	
8	Bob	0	$7.50	80	600	600	44	
9	Janet	1	$17.52	40	700.8	658.8	48.704	
10	Rebecca	0	$8.29	80	663.2	663.2	49.056	
11	Nancy	1	$8.01	80	640.8	598.8	43.904	
12	Mark	NA	$9.50	40	380	NA	NA	
13	Larry	2	$7.86	80	628.8	544.8	39.584	
14	Cathy	1	$21.52	40	860.8	818.8	61.504	
15	Wesley	0	$16.83	40	673.2	673.2	49.856	
16	Jennie	NA	$12.35	40	494	NA	NA	
17	Laurie	1	$8.90	80	712	670	49.6	
18								

The last column to be added to this worksheet will be the net pay amount. For the purposes of this example, the state tax will be the only deduction from gross pay. You may have noticed that some of the tax figures came out to three decimal places. When deducting this from gross pay, however, you will want to have this rounded off to a dollars and cents figure with just two decimal places. You will use the @**ROUND** function to do this. Its format is

@**ROUND**(value,places)

18. Move to cell J6 and enter a formula which will subtract the rounded tax figure from the gross pay. Copy this formula to the rest of the cells in the J column.

The final addition to this spreadsheet will be to add some dates. The function for entering a date value has the following format

@**DATE**(year,month,day)

For example, the date December 25, 1990 would be entered as @**DATE**(90,12,25)

19. Move the pointer to cell A1 and enter the label DATE:. Move to cell B1 and enter the @**DATE** function with the year, month, and date values for today's date.

A number should now appear in this cell; however, it will not look much like a date. The number is called a serial date and represents the number of days from December 31, 1899.

20. Change the format for this cell with the /**R**ange,**F**ormat,**D**ate command, and select the (DD-MMM) date format.
21. Move to cell D1 and type ||WEEK 1 ENDING:||, and then move to cell D2 and enter the label ||WEEK 2 ENDING:||. (Assume that the week-ending dates are always Fridays.)
22. In cell F2 enter a formula to calculate the date for the most recent Friday. This should be the value in cell B1 minus some number of days. After doing that, enter a formula in cell F1 that subtracts 7 days from the value in cell F2. Then use the /**R**ange,**F**ormat,**D**ate command to format both cells as (DD-MMM).
23. Save the spreadsheet under the name "PAYROLL," and then print the spreadsheet using condensed print. Then exit the spreadsheet software using the /**Q**uit command.

EXERCISE 5
Bar Graphs and Pie Charts

Required Preparation

Study the section titled Lotus 1-2-3 Graphics (pages L-79–L-95) and the /**G**raph commands presented in the Lotus 1-2-3 Command Summary.

Exercise Steps

1. Load Lotus 1-2-3, and then enter the data and commands necessary to create the following spreadsheet.

A1: [W12] READY

	A	B	C	D	E	F	G
1							
2		WESTERN REGIONAL SALES (Dollars in '000s)					
3							
4			1986	1987	1988	1989	1990
5							
6	TRUCKS	Units	362	420	504	601	632
7		Dollars	$5,068	$6,510	$8,568	$12,020	$13,904
8							
9	VANS	Units	120	166	132	110	94
10		Dollars	$1,680	$2,407	$1,980	$1,733	$1,551
11							
12	FULL SIZE	Units	140	231	350	475	550
13		Dollars	$2,030	$3,581	$6,300	$9,500	$12,650
14							
15	MID SIZE	Units	675	800	1,104	1,307	1,445
16		Dollars	$683	$7,600	$13,248	$18,298	$22,398
17							
18	COMPACTS	Units	1,685	1,469	1,046	918	1,005
19		Dollars	$7,583	$8,080	$6,276	$6,059	$7,035
20							

26-Apr-90 05:27 AM

You will next create a bar graph that displays the number of vehicle units sold for each category (TRUCKS through COMPACTS) over the years 1986 to 1990.

2. Use Lotus to create the following graph.

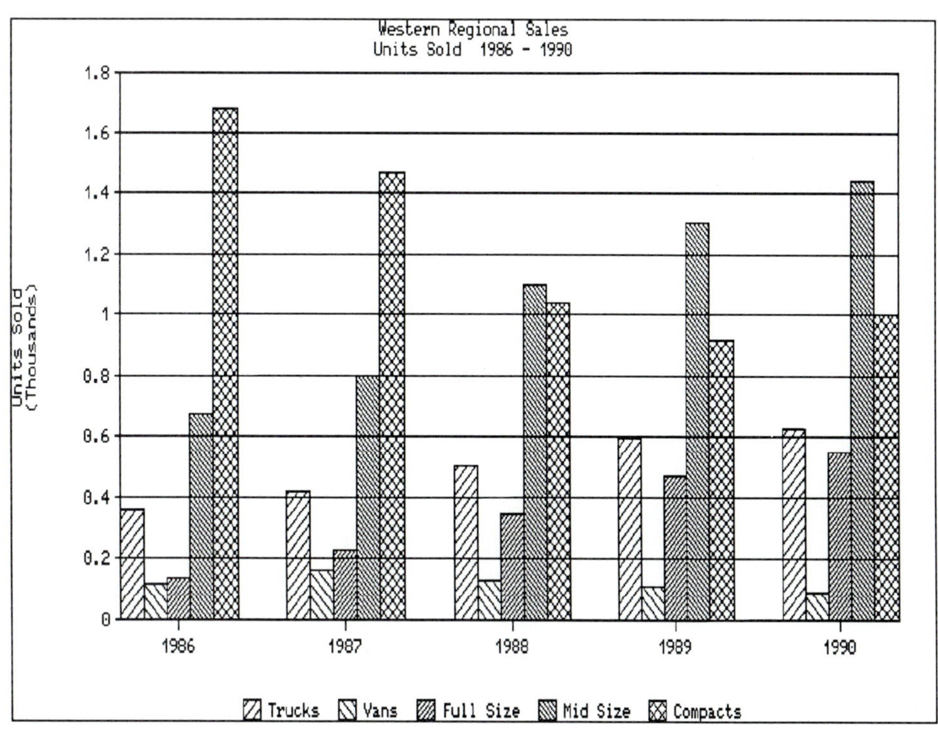

3. Use the /**G**raph,**N**ame command to create the name "UNITS" for the graph. Then use the /**G**raph,**R**eset command to reset all graph settings.

You next will create two pie charts designed to demonstrate the increase in sales for mid-size passenger automobiles for the period from 1986 to 1990. Before you set the data ranges to graph, however, you will need to modify the spreadsheet. Copy the necessary ranges of data to another place in the spreadsheet and make your modifications to the copied data.

4. Use Lotus to create the following pie chart.

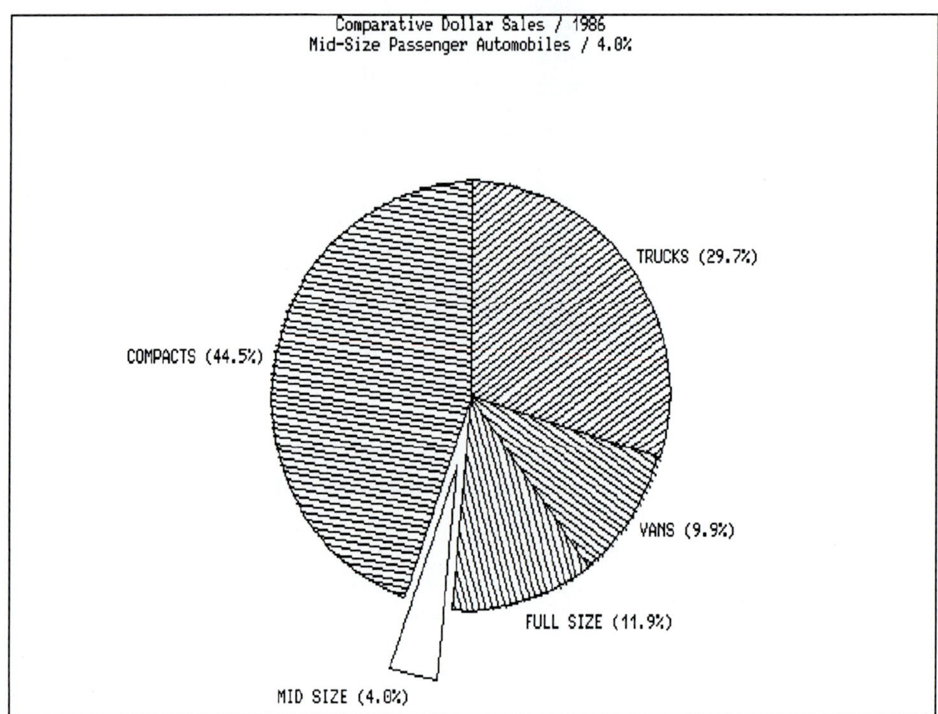

5. Name the graph "PIE1" and then create the next pie chart as shown here.

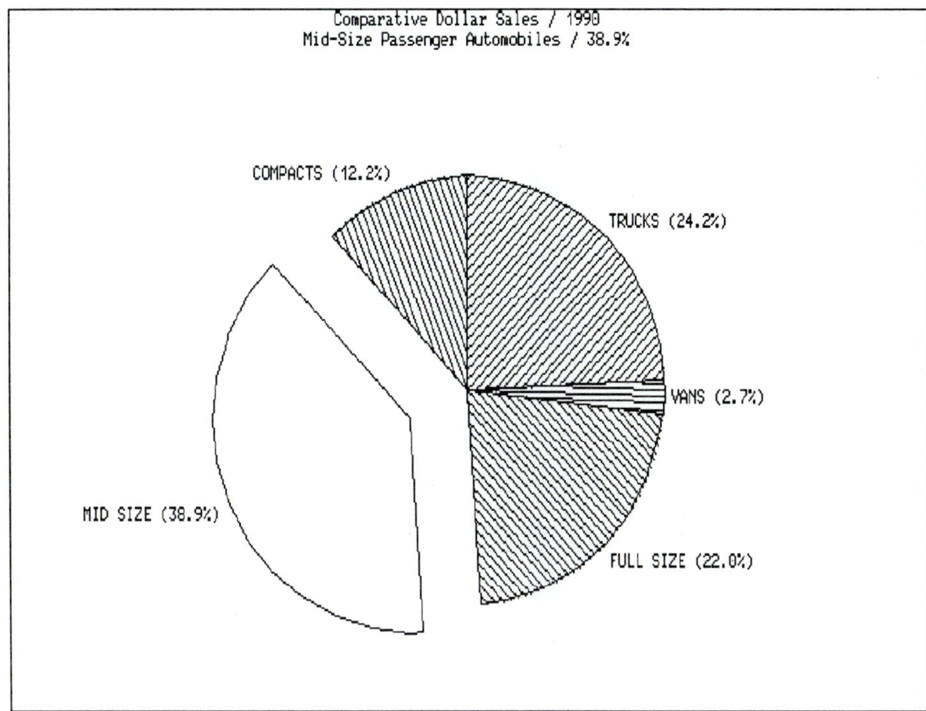

6. Name the second pie chart "PIE2" and then use the /**G**raph,**S**ave command to save each graph under the same name you used when you previously named them.
7. Save the spreadsheet under the name "GRAPH1" and then use the /**Q**uit command to exit the spreadsheet software.
8. Load the PGRAPH (PrintGraph) software and use its commands to print out each graph.

EXERCISE 6 Monthly Sales Projections

Required Preparation

Study the /**F**ile,**X**tract and /**F**ile,**C**ombine commands in the Lotus Command Summary. Also review the /**R**ange,**N**ame,**C**reate and /**R**ange,**N**ame,**D**elete commands.

Exercise Steps

In this exercise you will gain experience using Lotus's /**F**ile commands to extract and combine portions of a spreadsheet. This exercise involves a department store that projects sales on a monthly basis, and then compares the projected sales to actual sales. Management is concerned with the wide variances that occur monthly using their current method of projecting sales. It would like to review the figures for January, February, and March, as well as year-to-date figures for the end of February and March.

The following spreadsheet layout will be used for calculating variances for the three months for each of the five departments shown.

	A	B	C	D	E	F
1			Actual Sales	Projected	Variance ($)	Variance (%)
2	JANUARY					
3		Automotive	$101,519	$120,506		
4		General	$354,660	$326,417		
5		Hardware	$74,827	$76,250		
6		Housewares	$506,125	$575,064		
7		Plant & Garden	$55,965	$34,700		
8			----------	----------	----------	----------
9						
10	FEBRUARY					
11		Automotive	$126,898	$140,995		
12		General	$336,927	$408,021		
13		Hardware	$66,596	$70,912		
14		Housewares	$683,268	$661,319		
15		Plant & Garden	$41,973	$41,640		
16			----------	----------	----------	----------
17						
18	MARCH					
19		Automotive	$184,002	$184,278		
20		General	$411,405	$396,596		
21		Hardware	$87,906	$83,906		
22		Housewares	$611,524	$550,548		
23		Plant & Garden	$39,033	$48,580		
24			----------	----------	----------	----------

1. Begin by setting a global column width of 14 for the spreadsheet and a global format of Currency with 0 decimal places.
2. Set the width of column A to 2 characters.
3. Type in the labels and numeric sales figures as shown in the example.

The formulas for the two variance columns are as follows.

Dollar Variance = Actual Sales − Projected Sales
Percent Variance = Dollar Variance/Actual Sales

4. Enter the appropriate formulas to calculate the two variance values for the January automotive department sales figures. Then copy these formulas for all departments and months.
5. Now change the format for cells holding a percent variance to display as a percentage with 2 decimal places.
6. Enter the word "Total" as a right-aligned label in cells B9, B17, and B25.
7. Enter the appropriate function to calculate monthly totals of actual sales, projected sales, and dollar variances for all departments.

The total percentage variance for all departments is not a sum of the individual departments' percentage variances, but is calculated using the same formula that was used for the individual departments.

8. Enter or copy the appropriate formula for the monthly total percentage variances.

The spreadsheet should now appear as follows.

	A	B	C	D	E	F
1			Actual Sales	Projected	Variance ($)	Variance (%)
2	JANUARY					
3		Automotive	$101,519	$120,506	($18,987)	-18.70%
4		General	$354,660	$326,417	$28,243	7.96%
5		Hardware	$74,827	$76,250	($1,423)	-1.90%
6		Housewares	$506,125	$575,064	($68,939)	-13.62%
7		Plant & Garden	$55,965	$34,700	$21,265	38.00%
8			----------	----------	----------	----------
9		Total	$1,093,096	$1,132,937	($39,841)	-3.64%
10	FEBRUARY					
11		Automotive	$126,898	$140,995	($14,097)	-11.11%
12		General	$336,927	$408,021	($71,094)	-21.10%
13		Hardware	$66,596	$70,912	($4,316)	-6.48%
14		Housewares	$683,268	$661,319	$21,949	3.21%
15		Plant & Garden	$41,973	$41,640	$333	0.79%
16			----------	----------	----------	----------
17		Total	$1,255,662	$1,322,887	($67,225)	-5.35%
18	MARCH					
19		Automotive	$184,002	$184,278	($276)	-0.15%
20		General	$411,405	$396,596	$14,809	3.60%
21		Hardware	$87,906	$83,906	$4,000	4.55%
22		Housewares	$611,524	$550,548	$60,976	9.97%
23		Plant & Garden	$39,033	$48,580	($9,547)	-24.46%
24			----------	----------	----------	----------
25		Total	$1,333,870	$1,263,908	$69,962	5.25%
26						

9. Make any corrections necessary in your spreadsheet. Then save it under the filename PROJQTR1.

In the next steps you will extract the data for each of the three months, creating three new spreadsheet files. Before extracting the data, you will name the three data ranges for the monthly sales and the range of titles in row 1 of the spreadsheet.

10. Use the /**R**ange,**N**ame,**C**reate command to name ranges as follows: range A2..F9 JANUARY; range A10..F17 FEBRUARY; the range A18..F25 MARCH; and the range C1..F1 TITLES.
11. Save the file again under the name PROJQTR1 so that the saved copy will include the range names.

The /**F**ile,**X**tract command is used to save a portion of a spreadsheet file to another spreadsheet file (extension .WK1). The extracted portion may be saved with all of its formulas kept intact, or with all cells converted into their numeric or string values in the new spreadsheet file.

12. With the cursor located at cell A1, type the /**F**ile,**X**tract,**F**ormulas command and at the prompt "Enter xtract file name:," type ||JANPROJ←||.
13. When the prompt "Enter xtract range: A1..A1" appears, use the pointer control keys to expand the range to include cells A1..F9. Then type the Enter key.

When the ranges to be extracted have been named, you may use the range name instead of pointing to the range to be extracted with the /**F**ile,**X**tract command.

14. Leaving the cursor at cell A1, repeat the /**F**ile,**X**tract,**F**ormulas command. At the prompt "Enter xtract file name:," type ||FEBPROJ←|| and at the prompt "Enter xtract range: A1..A1," type ||FEBRUARY←|| to specify the range named FEBRUARY as the range to be extracted.
15. Repeat the /**F**ile,**X**tract,**F**ormulas command again. At the prompt "Enter xtract file name:," type ||MARPROJ←||. This time at the prompt "Enter xtract range: A1..A1," type the F3 (NAME) key to see a list of named ranges at the top of the screen. Use the pointer control keys to point to the name MARCH, and then type the Enter key.
16. Use the /**F**ile,**R**etrieve command to retrieve the first extracted file JANPROJ.

The screen should now appear as follows.

	A B	C	D	E	F
1		Actual Sales	Projected	Variance ($)	Variance (%)
2	JANUARY				
3	Automotive	$101,519	$120,506	($18,987)	-18.70%
4	General	$354,660	$326,417	$28,243	7.96%
5	Hardware	$74,827	$76,250	($1,423)	-1.90%
6	Housewares	$506,125	$575,064	($68,939)	-13.62%
7	Plant & Garden	$55,965	$34,700	$21,265	38.00%
8		----------	----------	----------	----------
9	Total	$1,093,096	$1,132,937	($39,841)	-3.64%
10					

17. Type the F5 (GOTO) key, and then type the F3 (NAME) key to see a list of named ranges in this extracted spreadsheet. Move the pointer to select MARCH as the named range to go to. Then type the Enter key.

Notice that although the range extracted from the PROJQTR1 file only included the ranges named JANUARY and TITLES, all range name definitions were kept in the extracted file. Since the ranges named FEBRUARY and MARCH have no data in this spreadsheet, these names should be deleted.

18. Use the /**R**ange,**N**ame,**D**elete command to delete the range names FEBRUARY and MARCH.
19. Print the spreadsheet, and then resave the file under the name JANPROJ and retrieve the file FEBPROJ.

The screen should now appear as follows.

	A B	C	D	E	F
1	FEBRUARY				
2	Automotive	$126,898	$140,995	($14,097)	-11.11%
3	General	$336,927	$408,021	($71,094)	-21.10%
4	Hardware	$66,596	$70,912	($4,316)	-6.48%
5	Housewares	$683,268	$661,319	$21,949	3.21%
6	Plant & Garden	$41,973	$41,640	$333	0.79%
7		----------	----------	----------	----------
8	Total	$1,255,662	$1,322,887	($67,225)	-5.35%
9					

Notice that although February data extracted from the file PROJQTR1 was in the range A10..F17 in the original file, it begins at cell A1 in the extracted file.

20. Use the F5 (GOTO) and F3 (NAME) keys to move the pointer to the various named ranges and see how Lotus has adjusted the location of the ranges in this file.
21. Delete the unnecessary range names, and then resave the file under the name FEBPROJ.

The /**F**ile,**C**ombine command is used to combine data from a file saved on the disk with the file currently in RAM (on the screen). It includes options to copy, add, or subtract the incoming data, and to include the entire file specified or only a range of data from that file.

You will first use the **C**opy option to add titles to the current spreadsheet. The incoming data is copied into the spreadsheet beginning at the current pointer location and overwrites any data located there.

22. Move the pointer to row 1 and use the /**W**orksheet,**I**nsert,**R**ow command to insert a blank row at the top of the spreadsheet for titles.
23. Move the cursor to cell C1 and execute the command /**F**ile,**C**ombine,**C**opy,**N**amed/Specified-Range. At the prompt "Enter range name or coordinates:," type ||TITLES↵||.
24. Then at the prompt "Name of file to combine:," either point to the file PROJQTR1 and type the Enter key or type ||PROJQTR1↵||.
25. Resave this file under the name FEBPROJ.

The **A**dd option of the /**F**ile,**C**ombine command is used to add incoming values to the values in the current spreadsheet. Labels and cells containing formulas are not overwritten by incoming data; only cells containing values or blank cells will have incoming values added. You now will use this command to add the January values in the JANPROJ file to the February values on the screen, resulting in cumulative year-to-date figures for the end of February.

26. Change the label in cell A2 to "FEBRUARY YTD."
27. With the pointer still located at cell A2, execute the command /**F**ile,**C**ombine,**A**dd,**N**amed/Specified-Range. Specify JANUARY as the range name and JANPROJ as the filename.

The spreadsheet on the screen should now display as follows.

	A	B	C	D	E	F
1			Actual Sales	Projected	Variance ($)	Variance (%)
2	FEBRUARY YTD					
3	Automotive		$228,417	$261,501	($33,084)	-14.48%
4	General		$691,587	$734,438	($42,851)	-6.20%
5	Hardware		$141,423	$147,162	($5,739)	-4.06%
6	Housewares		$1,189,393	$1,236,383	($46,990)	-3.95%
7	Plant & Garden		$97,938	$76,340	$21,598	22.05%
8			----------	----------	----------	----------
9		Total	$2,348,758	$2,455,824	($107,066)	-4.56%
10						

28. Print the spreadsheet, and then save it under the filename FEBYTD.

29. Now change the label in cell A2 to read MARCH YTD. Then execute the appropriate command to add the March values to the spreadsheet.

The March year-to-date values should appear as follows.

	A B	C	D	E	F
1		Actual Sales	Projected	Variance ($)	Variance (%)
2	MARCH YTD				
3	Automotive	$412,419	$445,779	($33,360)	-8.09%
4	General	$1,102,992	$1,131,034	($28,042)	-2.54%
5	Hardware	$229,329	$231,068	($1,739)	-0.76%
6	Housewares	$1,800,917	$1,786,931	$13,986	0.78%
7	Plant & Garden	$136,971	$124,920	$12,051	8.80%
8		----------	----------	----------	----------
9	Total	$3,682,628	$3,719,732	($37,104)	-1.01%
10					

30. Print the spreadsheet. Then save it under the name MARYTD and exit Lotus.

EXERCISE 7 Customer Information

Required Preparation

Study the section titled /**D**ata,**S**ort, /**D**ata,**Q**uery, and Database Functions, (pages L-96–L-106), the @**DATE** function found in the section titled Lotus 1-2-3 Functions (pages L-66), and the /**D**ata commands presented in the Lotus 1-2-3 Command Summary.

Exercise Steps

1. Load Lotus 1-2-3 and then change the spreadsheet's column widths to the following: Column A—18 characters; column E—3 characters; and columns F and G—both 11 characters.

2. Enter the following data. Note the following: (1) the column labels all begin with the **^** (Center) label prefix (except TERRITORY); (2) column F is formatted as currency with 2 decimal places; (3) and the dates in column G are entered with @**DATE** functions and are formatted as (DD-MMM-YY).

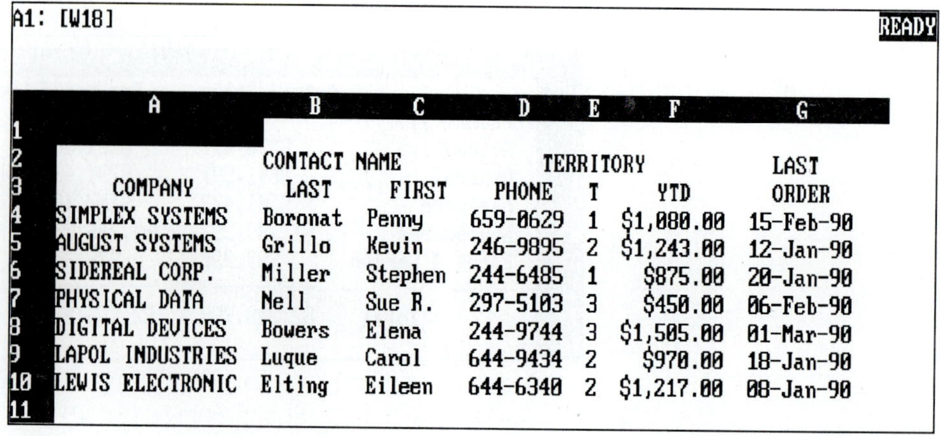

A1: [W18] READY

	A	B	C	D	E	F	G
1							
2		CONTACT NAME		TERRITORY			LAST
3	COMPANY	LAST	FIRST	PHONE	T	YTD	ORDER
4	SIMPLEX SYSTEMS	Boronat	Penny	659-0629	1	$1,080.00	15-Feb-90
5	AUGUST SYSTEMS	Grillo	Kevin	246-9895	2	$1,243.00	12-Jan-90
6	SIDEREAL CORP.	Miller	Stephen	244-6485	1	$875.00	20-Jan-90
7	PHYSICAL DATA	Nell	Sue R.	297-5103	3	$450.00	06-Feb-90
8	DIGITAL DEVICES	Bowers	Elena	244-9744	3	$1,505.00	01-Mar-90
9	LAPOL INDUSTRIES	Luque	Carol	644-9434	2	$970.00	18-Jan-90
10	LEWIS ELECTRONIC	Elting	Eileen	644-6340	2	$1,217.00	08-Jan-90
11							

The database here is meant to represent a partial list of corporate customers who make purchases throughout the year. The field names and their descriptions are as follows.

Field Names	Explanation
COMPANY	The name of the customer
LAST	Purchasing individual's last name
FIRST	Purchasing individual's first name
PHONE	Telephone number
T	Customer's sales territory
YTD	Customer purchases for the year-to-date
ORDER	Date of the last order made by the customer

3. Sort the range of records in ascending order on the company's name.

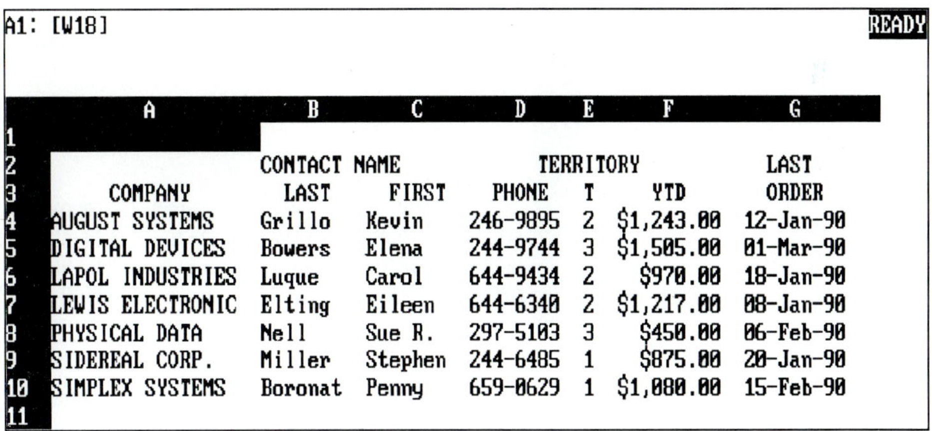

A1: [W18] READY

	A	B	C	D	E	F	G
1							
2		CONTACT NAME		TERRITORY			LAST
3	COMPANY	LAST	FIRST	PHONE	T	YTD	ORDER
4	AUGUST SYSTEMS	Grillo	Kevin	246-9895	2	$1,243.00	12-Jan-90
5	DIGITAL DEVICES	Bowers	Elena	244-9744	3	$1,505.00	01-Mar-90
6	LAPOL INDUSTRIES	Luque	Carol	644-9434	2	$970.00	18-Jan-90
7	LEWIS ELECTRONIC	Elting	Eileen	644-6340	2	$1,217.00	08-Jan-90
8	PHYSICAL DATA	Nell	Sue R.	297-5103	3	$450.00	06-Feb-90
9	SIDEREAL CORP.	Miller	Stephen	244-6485	1	$875.00	20-Jan-90
10	SIMPLEX SYSTEMS	Boronat	Penny	659-0629	1	$1,080.00	15-Feb-90
11							

4. Print the sorted database.
5. Sort the records according to territory (ascending) and year-to-date sales within each territory (descending). Then print the database again.

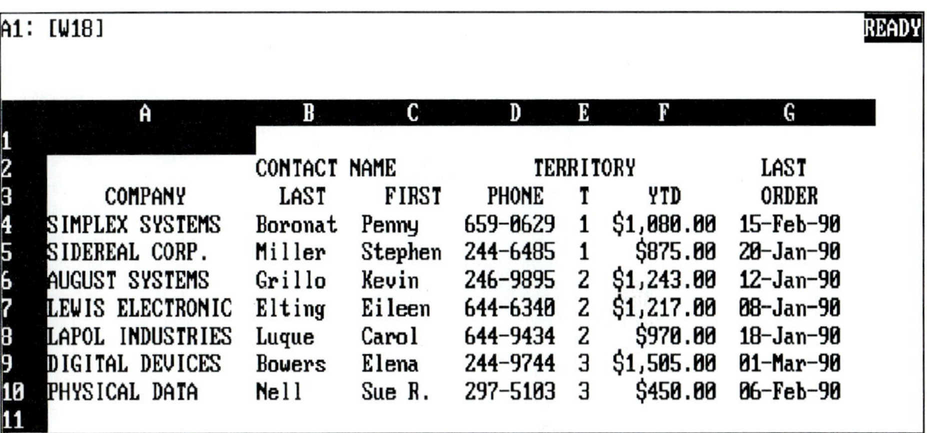

A1: [W18] READY

	A	B	C	D	E	F	G
1							
2		CONTACT NAME		TERRITORY			LAST
3	COMPANY	LAST	FIRST	PHONE	T	YTD	ORDER
4	SIMPLEX SYSTEMS	Boronat	Penny	659-0629	1	$1,080.00	15-Feb-90
5	SIDEREAL CORP.	Miller	Stephen	244-6485	1	$875.00	20-Jan-90
6	AUGUST SYSTEMS	Grillo	Kevin	246-9895	2	$1,243.00	12-Jan-90
7	LEWIS ELECTRONIC	Elting	Eileen	644-6340	2	$1,217.00	08-Jan-90
8	LAPOL INDUSTRIES	Luque	Carol	644-9434	2	$970.00	18-Jan-90
9	DIGITAL DEVICES	Bowers	Elena	244-9744	3	$1,505.00	01-Mar-90
10	PHYSICAL DATA	Nell	Sue R.	297-5103	3	$450.00	06-Feb-90
11							

6. Use the /**D**ata,**Q**uery commands to specify the database (with field names included) as being the Input range, the cells A13..A14 as the Criterion range (format cell A14 to display Text), and cells A16..E16 as the Output range.

7. Finish the necessary steps to extract the company name, first and last names of the purchaser, phone number, and territory number for all records in territory 2. Organize the Input range so that the extracted data is sorted by the last name of the purchaser.

```
A1: [W18]                                                          READY

            A           B        C         D     E     F          G
1
2                  CONTACT NAME             TERRITORY            LAST
3         COMPANY     LAST     FIRST     PHONE   T    YTD        ORDER
4  SIMPLEX SYSTEMS   Boronat  Penny    659-0629  1 $1,080.00  15-Feb-90
5  DIGITAL DEVICES   Bowers   Elena    244-9744  3 $1,505.00  01-Mar-90
6  LEWIS ELECTRONIC  Elting   Eileen   644-6340  2 $1,217.00  08-Jan-90
7  AUGUST SYSTEMS    Grillo   Kevin    246-9895  2 $1,243.00  12-Jan-90
8  LAPOL INDUSTRIES  Luque    Carol    644-9434  2   $970.00  18-Jan-90
9  SIDEREAL CORP.    Miller   Stephen  244-6485  1   $875.00  20-Jan-90
10 PHYSICAL DATA     Nell     Sue R.   297-5103  3   $450.00  06-Feb-90
11
12 Criterion Range
13         T
14 +E4=2
15
16        COMPANY     FIRST    LAST      PHONE   T
17 LEWIS ELECTRONIC  Eileen   Elting   644-6340  2
18 AUGUST SYSTEMS    Kevin    Grillo   246-9895  2
19 LAPOL INDUSTRIES  Carol    Luque    644-9434  2
20
```

8. Change the Output range to include the company name, year-to-date sales, last order date, and territory number. Then perform a /**D**ata,**Q**uery,**E**xtract again.

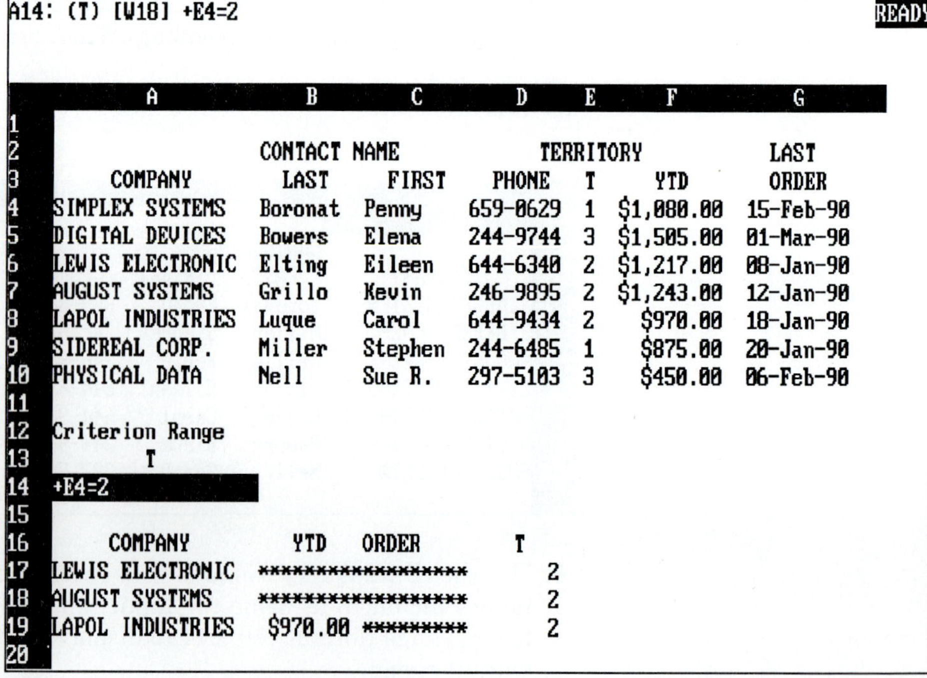

```
A14: (T) [W18] +E4=2                                               READY

            A           B        C         D     E     F          G
1
2                  CONTACT NAME             TERRITORY            LAST
3         COMPANY     LAST     FIRST     PHONE   T    YTD        ORDER
4  SIMPLEX SYSTEMS   Boronat  Penny    659-0629  1 $1,080.00  15-Feb-90
5  DIGITAL DEVICES   Bowers   Elena    244-9744  3 $1,505.00  01-Mar-90
6  LEWIS ELECTRONIC  Elting   Eileen   644-6340  2 $1,217.00  08-Jan-90
7  AUGUST SYSTEMS    Grillo   Kevin    246-9895  2 $1,243.00  12-Jan-90
8  LAPOL INDUSTRIES  Luque    Carol    644-9434  2   $970.00  18-Jan-90
9  SIDEREAL CORP.    Miller   Stephen  244-6485  1   $875.00  20-Jan-90
10 PHYSICAL DATA     Nell     Sue R.   297-5103  3   $450.00  06-Feb-90
11
12 Criterion Range
13         T
14 +E4=2
15
16        COMPANY       YTD    ORDER            T
17 LEWIS ELECTRONIC  ******************            2
18 AUGUST SYSTEMS    ******************            2
19 LAPOL INDUSTRIES   $970.00 *********            2
20
```

Notice that the column widths here are not wide enough to display the numeric values that were extracted. You can increase the widths of the two columns to view or print the extracted data.

In completing the next steps, you will find the following information helpful. The order of the field names occurring in the Output range does not have to be the same order that they occur in the Input range. However, you may need to increase the width of columns in order to print the extracted data in the spreadsheet. You may include columns in an Output range that have no field name at the top. In such cases the column will be left blank. If you increase (lengthen) an Output range by adding a field name to it, you must respecify the size of the Output range by using the /**D**ata,**Q**uery,**O**utput command.

9. Change the Output range to include the company name, first and last names of the purchaser, and the phone number. Next change the Criterion range to extract the data for all companies whose name begins with "LAPO." Extract the data and print the entire spreadsheet.
10. Change the Output range to include the company name, territory number, and year-to-date sales. Then change the Criterion range to extract the data for all companies in territory 2 with sales greater than $1000.00. Extract the data and print the entire spreadsheet.
11. Change the Output range to include the company name, last order date and year-to-date sales. Then change the Criterion range to extract the data for all companies in territory 1 whose last order was in January. Extract the data and then move the pointer to cell A14. Type F2 (EDIT) and then type the Home key. Next type a label prefix (′,″ or ^) and then type ↵. (The last steps simply change the condition into a label so that it can be entirely printed). Print the entire spreadsheet.
12. Erase the data in the Criterion range and then use the @**DSUM** and @**DAVG** functions (in cells F13 and F14) along with the appropriate labels to produce the following summary added to the spreadsheet. Note that the Criterion range for the functions is found in cells B13 and B14, and that the criterion references a cell (E12) for the territory number. When such a reference is made in a criterion, it must be entered as absolute.

```
B14: (T) [W11] +E4=$E$12                                           POINT

          A             B          C        D     E      F          G
1
2                   CONTACT NAME                TERRITORY           LAST
3          COMPANY      LAST       FIRST    PHONE    T     YTD        ORDER
4  SIMPLEX SYSTEMS  Boronat    Penny    659-0629  1  $1,080.00  15-Feb-90
5  DIGITAL DEVICES  Bowers     Elena    244-9744  3  $1,505.00  01-Mar-90
6  LEWIS ELECTRONIC Elting     Eileen   644-6340  2  $1,217.00  08-Jan-90
7  AUGUST SYSTEMS   Grillo     Kevin    246-9895  2  $1,243.00  12-Jan-90
8  LAPOL INDUSTRIES Luque      Carol    644-9434  2    $970.00  18-Jan-90
9  SIDEREAL CORP.   Miller     Stephen  244-6485  1    $875.00  20-Jan-90
10 PHYSICAL DATA    Nell       Sue R.   297-5103  3    $450.00  06-Feb-90
11
12 Criterion Range             Territory -----> 2   Summary YTD
13                     T                Total ....       3430
14                  +E4=$E$12           Average ..  1143.33333
15
16         COMPANY                                    ORDER        YTD
17 SIDEREAL CORP.                                   20-Jan-90    $875.00
18
19
20
```

13. Save the spreadsheet under the name CUSTOMER and then print the spreadsheet. Next exit the spreadsheet software by using the /**Q**uit command.

EXERCISE 8
A Basic Macro Library

Required Preparation

Study the section titled Lotus 1-2-3 Macros up to the section titled *Advanced Macros* (pages L-107–L-117). Also review the @**ROUND,** @**UPPER** , @**LOWER,** and @**PROPER** functions found in the section titled Lotus 1-2-3 Functions (pages L-57–L-105), and the /**R**ange,**N**ame,**L**abels command presented in the Lotus 1-2-3 Command Summary.

Exercise Steps

The @**ROUND** function forces Lotus to keep a cell's value at a certain level of accuracy. In the following steps you will create a macro that will both edit a cell containing a value and properly insert an @**ROUND** function into it.

1. Load Lotus 1-2-3 and then move the pointer to any cell and enter the formula 10/3.

The value 3.333333 should be displayed in the cell.

2. With the pointer on the cell, type the following keystrokes: F2,Home. Then type ‖ @**ROUND**(‖ . Next type the keys End,comma,2,),↵.

The contents of the cell should appear as @**ROUND**(10/3,2) and the cell should display the value 3.33. You should note that the keystrokes used in this example were general purpose in nature. That is, the same keystrokes will produce the same results when used on any cell containing a value.

3. Use the /**R**ange,**E**rase command to erase the cell containing the @**ROUND** function. Then use the /**W**orksheet,**G**lobal,**C**olumn-Width command to set all columns in the spreadsheet to a width of 12. Next use the /**W**orksheet,**C**olumn command to set the A column to a width of 4.
4. Move to cell A7 and type ‖ '\R↵ ‖ . The label "\R" should now appear in the cell. Next move to cell B7 and enter the following label: {EDIT}{HOME}@**ROUND**({END},2)~{QUIT}

The {QUIT} command is used to end the execution of a macro and should be the final command that occurs in a macro.

5. Now use the /**R**ange,**N**ame command to give the name \R to the cell containing the macro.
6. Save the spreadsheet under the name MACLIB. Then enter a fraction, such as 4/7, into a blank cell in the spreadsheet. With the pointer on the cell containing the fraction, type Alt-R to test the macro you have just created.

The @**LOWER,** @**PROPER,** and @**UPPER** functions are used to change the displayed case of the string (Label) contents of a spreadsheet cell. The set of keystrokes used to insert any one of these String functions into a cell are very similar to those used to insert an @**ROUND** function into a cell.

To create the next three macros, use the following procedure.

a. Enter into column A the label that describes the macro's name. Be sure to start the entry with the left justify Label-Prefix (').

b. Into a blank cell enter an appropriate label from which the intended function will return a value (this will be a test cell).

c. Type the keystrokes necessary to insert the function into the test cell. Record (write down) the keystrokes used.

d. Into the cell to the immediate right of the cell containing the macro's name, enter the keystrokes recorded above in their proper order and macro syntax. Be sure to end the macro with a {QUIT} command.

e. When finished entering the macro, use the /**R**ange,**N**ame command to name the cell containing the macro the same name that appears to its left (the name in column A).

f. Save the spreadsheet and then test the macro on a test cell.

7. Into cell A8 enter the label "\L." Then enter a macro into cell B8 that will insert an @**LOWER** function into the current spreadsheet cell.
8. Into cell A9 enter the label "\P." Then enter a macro into cell B9 that will insert an @**PROPER** function into the current spreadsheet cell.
9. Into cell A10 enter the label "\U." Then enter a macro into cell B10 that will insert an @**UPPER** function into the current spreadsheet cell.

In the next steps you will create macros designed to remove @**ROUND,** @**LOWER,** @**PROPER,** and @**UPPER** functions from a spreadsheet cell without removing their data arguments.

10. Move the pointer to a blank cell in the spreadsheet and enter the formula 10/3.

The value 3.333333 should be displayed in the cell.

11. Use the Alt-R macro to insert an @**ROUND** function into the cell.
12. With the pointer on the cell, type the keystrokes F2,Home. Then type the Del key 7 times. Next type the End key and then type the Backspace key 3 times. Typing ↵ will finish the editing of the cell.
13. Move to cell A17 and type ‖ '\X↵ ‖ . The label "\X" should now appear in the cell. Next move to cell B17 and enter the following label: {EDIT} {HOME} {DEL 7} {END} {BS 3}~{QUIT}.
14. Use the /**R**ange,**N**ame command to give the name \X to the cell containing the macro designed to remove an @**ROUND** function from a cell.

To create the next two macros, use the same procedures as you used before.

15. Into cell A18 enter the label "\Y." Then enter a macro into cell B18 that will remove an @**LOWER** or @**UPPER** function from the current spreadsheet cell.
16. Into cell A19 enter the label "\Z." Then enter a macro into cell B19 that will remove an @**PROPER** function from the current spreadsheet cell.

You next will create a menu macro designed to access the three macros contained in cells B17 through B19.

17. Move to cell A12 and enter the label "\E." Then move to cell B12 and enter the label {MENUBRANCH B13}. Next give the range name \E to the cell B12.
18. Now enter the following labels into the range B13..D15.

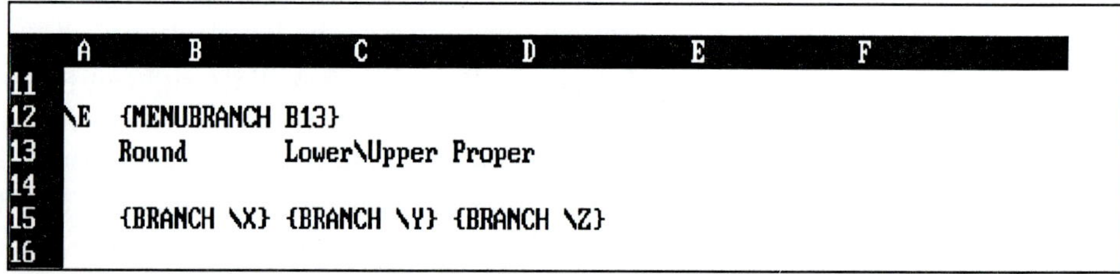

19. Now enter the following labels into the cells in row 14.

B14	Erase @**ROUND** function
C14	Erase @**LOWER** or @**UPPER** function
D14	Erase @**PROPER** function

The screen should now appear as follows.

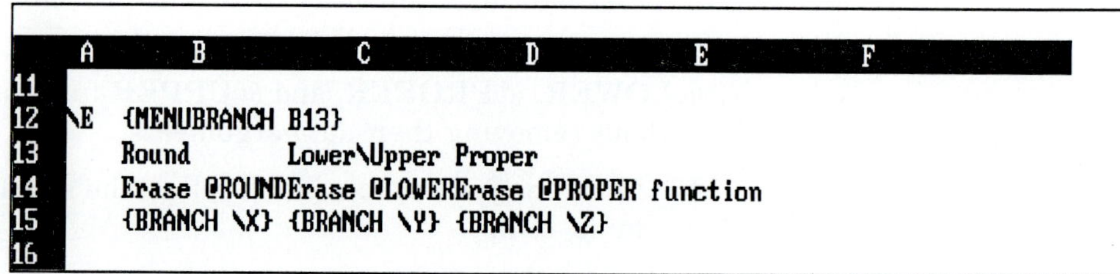

20. Save the spreadsheet. Then create three or four test cells to test the menu macro. Next test the macro by moving the pointer to one of the test cells and typing Alt-E.

In the final steps of the exercise you will create another menu macro named \M that will access the macros to insert functions into cells and access the \E menu macro if desired.

21. Move to cell A2 and enter the following labels into the range A2..F3.

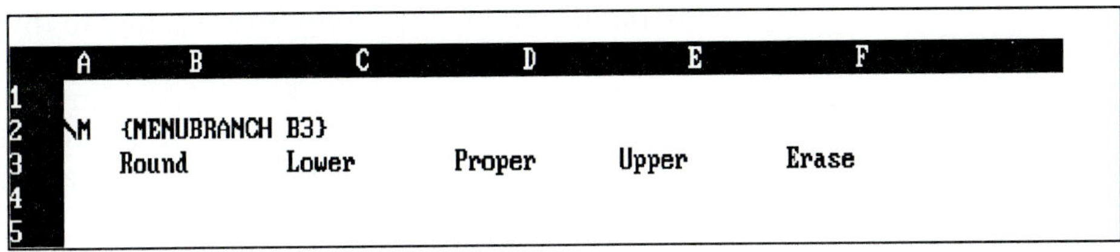

	A	B	C	D	E	F
1						
2	\M	{MENUBRANCH B3}				
3		Round	Lower	Proper	Upper	Erase
4						
5						

22. Complete the menu macro by entering suitable descriptions for each macro into row 4 and by entering the appropriate {BRANCH} commands into row 5.

23. Name the new menu macro. Then save the spreadsheet and thoroughly test the Alt-M menu macro. Print the spreadsheet and then exit Lotus 1-2-3 by using the /**Q**uit command.

CASES

CASE 1
SIMS, Inc.

Sharon Albright is a project manager for Specialized Inventory Management Systems, Inc. (SIMS), a company that does customized software installations throughout the world. She manages about ten teams of two to eight analysts each, who are sent to client organizations to install systems. Although the people under her direction submit progress reports weekly, they submit their expense reports whenever they get around to it, and many times she has found it hard to read the handwritten entries. This has been a constant source of annoyance for Sharon, since she must take time to decipher and double check the reports before submitting the information to accounting.

Sharon has tried everything from cajoling to threatening not to pay expenses in order to get her employees to submit their reports weekly and to type them or at least print them legibly. But the Vice-President in charge of Operations, Roger Anderson, is one of the worst offenders. Because the analysts know this, they haven't paid much attention to Sharon's requests. But now Sharon thinks she may be able to solve this problem.

About nine months ago Roger Anderson talked the company into purchasing personal laptop computers for every analyst in the company. Top management disagreed about whether having these laptop computers would really be useful. Knowing that Roger now must prove that his suggestion is benefitting the company, Sharon approached him with the idea of having expense reports entered on the laptop computers, to be submitted weekly from anywhere in the world by using the computers' modems. Roger jumped at the idea and asked her to design a spreadsheet for this purpose as soon as possible.

Sharon feels that the existing expense report form needs revision since no one seems to fill it out in the same way. She would design it so that the beginning and ending date for the one-week period (Sunday through Saturday) would appear at the top of the form. Also, a place for the name of the person submitting the report and a mailing address to which the check is to be sent would appear near the top of the form. Below it would give space for daily expenses, including hotel room charges and a per diem of $30–$55 depending on the country. Also included in the report would be car rental expenses or a $0.32 per mile auto allowance if a personal car is used, in which case beginning and ending odometer readings would be given. If other transportation expenses such as round-trip airfare, cab fares and road tolls were incurred, they would also be listed in the report. All other expenses would be treated as miscellaneous expenses, but ample space would be provided for a description.

CASE 2
Westport Pet Supplies

Jim Southland has founded a new company called Westport Pet Supplies. The company's main business will be mixing and packaging a variety of premium canned pet foods. Jim's initial plans are to produce two product lines of cat food, adult and kitten mixes. The adult mix will provide $0.16 profit per 7 oz. can, while the kitten mix will provide $0.07 profit per 4 oz. can. Both mixes are made from the same ingredients—meat by-products that provide protein and a moist premixed cereal blend that provides fiber, carbohydrates, and nine essential vitamins. Both ingredients must be constantly and individually refrigerated prior to the mixing/canning process.

When building the production facility, Jim installed two large refrigeration units, one which holds 700 lbs. of meat by-products and one which holds 500 lbs. of premixed cereal. In the production process the refrigerated bins must be completely emptied and then sanitized before they can be refilled with new ingredients.

A can of adult cat food contains 4 oz. of meat by-products and 3 oz. of cereal. The kitten mix requires 3 oz. of meat by-products and 1 oz. of cereal per can.

In a recent conversation with his soon-to-be production manager, Stan Thomas, Jim was overheard to say, "Look, Stan, this thing is complicated. In order to get the price break we need to stay in business, I had to guarantee the supplier that we would order 700 lbs. of meat and 500 lbs. of cereal in the same shipment twice a week. That means we need to produce just the right number of cans of each cat food from each shipment so that we aren't wasting ingredients and are maximizing our profits. You know we need to make at least $375 on each shipment of ingredients to cover our operating costs. I'm not certain, but I'm beginning to think we may need to raise our prices or build larger refrigeration units to make a reasonable profit. I wish there was some way to put all these factors together in one place so that we could see how these kinds of changes would affect our operation."

CASE 3
Paint Contract Bids

Larry Scott is a self-employed house painter who has become quite successful through word-of-mouth advertising and referrals from several local paint stores. Larry's typical job begins with a visit to a house to interview the homeowner. The visit provides Larry with information about the size of the job, type and color of paint desired, the amount of trim work involved, and the extent of preparation (washing and/or scraping) required before painting can begin.

Following the visit, Larry returns home to prepare a bid for the job. The bid takes into account the cost of paint used, the estimated number of hours of labor involved (Larry employs two assistants to help him on the job), and any incidentals that may need to be included (such as replacing broken panes of glass). Normally the bid is itemized so the potential customer can see what he/she is paying for.

In a recent conversation with one of his assistants, Larry was heard to say, "Kevin, how are your evening classes going at the college? Robin tells me the two of you are taking a computer course. I don't know anything about computers, but it sounds like I might be able to use one to help me prepare the bids for our jobs. Business has gotten to the point where I'm spending hours in the evening doing calculations and paperwork. If I could see exactly how the computer could help, I might be tempted to take some of this summer's profits and buy one."

Note that several of the prices here are calculated prices based on the square footage of the area to paint.

Preparation	Bid Price
Pressure Washing	$150.00 per house
Scraping	$100.00 per day (each man working)
Priming	$0.25/1 sq. ft.
Materials	10% of total preparation price

Painting	Bid Price
If Latex	$15.00/400 sq. ft.
If Stain	$12.00/450 sq. ft.
If Oil	$22.00/400 sq. ft.
Painting Labor	$0.25/1 sq. ft.
If second coat	65% of total first coat price

Finishing

Trim Openings (doors, windows, etc.) $30.00 each

Other

Add 15% for three story (or otherwise difficult) structure

CASE 4 College Financial Plan

Jake Williams is a sophomore at Mt. Scott Community College. He plans to transfer to the nearby state university next year, and is in the process of determining how he will finance next year's tuition since it is higher at the university than at the community college. So far, he's been able to work part time to pay most of his college expenses, and financial aid has helped pay for the rest. He will be eligible to receive more aid next year since he is now independent of his parents.

Jake has obtained the information he needs to start planning his budget for next year, but there are a few things he hasn't decided. For instance, he's not sure whether he wants to live on campus or remain in his present apartment, which requires a 30-minute commute to the university. If he stays where he is, his rent will be $320 per month, his board (food and sundry items) will be $160 per month, and his transportation costs will be $70 per month. The university is located downtown, where prices are much higher. If he moves on campus, his board will be $200 per month, but his rent will be only $275 per month and transportation only $25 per month.

Jake's also not sure whether he wants to work next year, because he expects his courses at the university to require more time than he puts in now. If he doesn't work, he will have to obtain more money in loans, and he's concerned about how much debt he should incur during his college years. If he stays in his apartment off campus, he can keep his current job and net about $400 per month. On campus jobs are extremely scarce, and he would have to take a work-study position as part of his financial aid package if he wants to work on campus. The work-study job would net him only $200 per month. If he lives on campus he cannot keep his current job, and if he lives off campus he cannot take a work-study job. His other option is to not work at all, but he doesn't know if this is even feasible.

He can obtain three types of financial aid: a grant, which does not have to be paid back; a university loan at 5% interest; and a bank loan at 8% interest. Loan interest does not begin accruing until he graduates. He may repay the university loan over 10 years, and interest on the bank loan will go up to 10% after the first four years of repayment.

Since the grant is dependent on the amount of money he earns during the year, he will receive nothing if he works off campus, $300 each term if he takes the work-study job, and $600 each term if he doesn't work at all. The amount available as a lower interest university loan also will depend upon his income. He may receive $800 per term if he works off campus, $1,000 each term if he takes the work-study job, and $1,335 per term if he doesn't work at all. The 8% bank loan may be used to pay the rest of his expenses up to a limit of $2,000 for the year (not $2,000 per term). The 8% bank loan amount may not exceed the amount needed to meet his total expenses after any earned income, grant, and university loan monies have been determined.

Aside from his room, board, and transportation expenses, Jake's cost of attending the university will be $561 per term, which will cover his tuition, fees, and books. The tuition expenses and financial aid payments occur in October, January, and April. His income from an off-campus job or a work-study job, as well as his room, board, and transportation expenses, occur on a monthly basis for the full year, October to September, even though he will not be attending summer term (July through September).

Jake wants to determine what his full year's budget (October to September) will be given his various alternatives. He needs to know what alternatives are possible in terms of living on campus or off campus and working or not working, and the impact each would have on the amount of grant money he may receive and the amount he would have to borrow under the two loan programs. He also would like to determine his expected monthly cash flow situation given the expenses and income for the various alternatives. Jake has heard a friend talk about a spreadsheet program that is useful for "what if?" situations like his, and he wonders if it could be used to help him sort out his alternatives.

CASE 5
C & B Foods Company

C & B Foods is a food processing company that produces a line of freeze-dried camping and backpacking products. As product manager, Steve McGrath has been asked to research and evaluate the feasibility of adding a new product. Steve has identified freeze-dried eggs with chili peppers as a likely new product. This new product could be used to make Mexican omelets and other spicy egg dishes. The company does not produce any freeze-dried egg products because of poor consumer acceptance. However, Steve thinks the added flavor of chili peppers could help eliminate the usual complaint that freeze-dried eggs taste like sulfur.

Steve had some initial market research done and found that in addition to the expected market of campers and backpackers, there is also a potential market among busy consumers who want a quick and easy breakfast product. The new freeze-dried egg product will be sold in eight ounce packages. Steve has developed the following estimates from the market research figures concerning potential sales for the new product and the probability of achieving different sales levels.

First Year Sales:	250,000 units	20% chance (worst case)
	500,000 units	50% chance (likely case)
	750,000 units	30% chance (best case)

To determine the feasibility of introducing the new product, Steve decided to forecast potential sales for 15 periods (years). Steve predicts that the sales growth rate will be approximately 10 percent per year for years one through three, 15 percent per year for the next five years, and about 8 percent per year thereafter. Market indicators show that the total market for freeze-dried egg products of all types should be about 5 million units annually by the beginning of year six.

Steve must develop a sales forecast for each of the potential first-year sales levels (worst case, likely case, and best case scenarios). Since the first year's sales, the sales growth rates, and the total market size are predictions, Steve wants a model that will allow him to change these factors as new information becomes available.

Bob Kane, the sales manager, will want to know potential sales levels and the market share the company can expect given each scenario. Steve will make a formal presentation of his product idea and research findings at the next product development meeting, and he hopes to use graphs to make his information easy to understand. He plans to use a microcomputer during his presentation, with his spreadsheet model projected onto a screen so that he can easily respond to comments and opinions of the people in the meeting by adjusting the key values in his model, if necessary.

CASE 6
Prescott Stoneware, Inc.

Mark Prescott is a craftsman who makes and sells stoneware planters, lamps, and various other items. He has earned a good reputation at art festivals and craft shows where he displays and sells his products. He also has begun selling his stoneware items to a few giftware shops in the area, and demand for his products is growing. A few months ago he built on to his home, adding a small retail shop, office, and inventory storage room. About a year ago he purchased a microcomputer, and he does some of the accounting for his business using a spreadsheet program.

Sales from his home shop have been good, and he thinks that they will continue to grow. He has developed a spreadsheet for entering and printing invoices as orders are taken. The invoice portion of his spreadsheet, with a sample invoice entered, follows.

	A	B	C	D	E	F	G	H	I
1									
2	SOLD TO:		Adams Gift Gallery			SHIP TO:	Adams Gift Gallery		
3			1202 SW Fifth Ave.				1202 SW Fifth Ave.		
4			James Lake, MA 02156				James Lake, MA 02156		
5									
6		QTY	PROD NO	DESCRIPTION		PRICE	TOTAL	DSCNT	NET
7	1	6	L2015	Lamp 15", 2-tone		$5.50	$33.00	8.50%	$30.20
8	2	10	P2010	Planter 10"		$6.00	$60.00	7.50%	$55.50
9	3	4	P2014	Planter 14"		$12.00	$48.00		$48.00
10	4								
11	5								
12	6								
13	7								
14	8								
15	9								
16	10								
17								SUBTOTAL	$133.70
18								3% SALES TAX	$4.01
19								FREIGHT	$25.00
20								INVOICE TOTAL	$162.71

The name and address next to the label SOLD TO: indicates where the invoice is to be sent. This is usually the same as the SHIP TO: name and address, though sometimes it is different. Mark's invoice has space for ten products, and he has decided that, for now, if anyone should order more than that, he will simply create another invoice. He has developed a set of product codes with associated descriptions, prices, and discount percentages for orders of more than five products. He maintains his product list in another portion of the spreadsheet, as follows.

	J	K	L	M	N	O
1						
2						
3						
4		PROD	DESCRIPTION	PRICE	DSCNT	
5		L2015	Lamp 15", 2-tone	$5.50	8.50%	
6		L2024	Lamp 24", 2-tone	$7.50	8.50%	
7		L2036	Lamp 36", 2-tone	$10.00	10.00%	
8		L3015	Lamp 15", designed	$7.00	7.50%	
9		L3024	Lamp 24", designed	$10.00	7.50%	
10		L3030	Lamp 30", designed	$15.50	8.00%	
11		L3036	Lamp 36", designed	$18.00	8.00%	
12		P2004	Planter 4"	$2.00	6.50%	
13		P2006	Planter 6"	$3.00	6.50%	
14		P2008	Planter 8"	$4.50	7.50%	
15		P2010	Planter 10"	$6.00	7.50%	
16		P2012	Planter 12"	$9.00	8.50%	
17		P2014	Planter 14"	$12.00	8.50%	
18						

Mark has found that he can use the @**VLOOKUP** function to automatically enter the description, unit price, and discount percentage into the invoice after the product code has been entered. To do this, he first named the range that holds his product list PRODUCTS. He specified the range as K5..N18 to include one row beyond the last product so that a blank invoice line would look up the blank cells K18..N18. He also used the global zero suppression feature of the spreadsheet software so that the @**VLOOKUP** functions could be entered into his invoice template without displaying a full invoice of zeros.

The function he used for the first description entry was

@**VLOOKUP**(C7,$PRODUCTS,1)

He copied this function to all the cells in the D column, and entered and copied similar functions in the F and H columns. The total column is calculated as quantity * price, and the net column subtracts the discount percentage if the quantity was over five. The subtotal and sales tax cells hold formulas, but the freight cell is a manual entry because the amount depends on how each customer wants his/her order shipped.

So far, Mark is the only one who has been entering and printing invoices, so he's very familiar with the operation of his spreadsheet. He would like to turn over more of these responsibilities to his wife, Sally, who has been helping run the business. Sally, however, is not very familiar with the computer and is somewhat apprehensive about taking on this responsibility. She told Mark that he has to make it "idiot-proof," so that she can enter and print the invoices without having to type much or make a lot of calculations. The last time she tried to enter an invoice, she accidentally typed over some of the formulas he had in the spreadsheet.

Mark knows that there is a way of protecting cells so that they cannot be overwritten, but he's never used this feature before. He has to decide which areas of the spreadsheet he would leave unprotected for Sally to enter invoice information. He also would like to make certain procedures more automatic, such as copying the SOLD TO: name and address to the SHIP TO: area when it is the same, printing the invoice, and blanking out the invoice after it has been printed and saved. He wants to modify the invoice spreadsheet to make it an easy to use template.

HINTS AND HAZARDS

DATA ENTRY

HINT When you enter data into cells, watch the LABEL/VALUE indicator at the top right of the screen. Based on your first keystroke, Lotus makes an assumption about the type of data you are entering into a cell. String data beginning with a numeric character, such as 4th Street, must be entered by first typing a label prefix ', ", or ^. Numeric data beginning with an alphabetic character, such as a cell reference, must be preceded by a numeric character 0 through 9, +, −, ., (, @, #, or $.

HAZARD If a formula displays an incorrect value that could be attributable to a cell reference value equal to zero (0), check the cells to which the formula refers to see if a number accidentally was entered as a label. If one of the cells has its data left-justified, it may well be an incorrectly entered cell. Remember that, by default, values are automatically justified to the right and labels are automatically justified to the left.

HINT Use the pointing method of entering formulas for faster and more accurate results.

HINT The keys on the numeric keypad at the right side of the keyboard toggle between a numeric mode and a pointer control mode when you type the Num Lock key. However, they also shift to the opposite mode if you hold down the Shift key. When you are entering several cells worth of numeric data, it is useful to leave the keypad in the pointer control mode. When you are ready to enter data into a cell, shift with your left hand and enter the data with the ten-key pad. When you are done, release the Shift key and move the pointer to the next cell.

HINT You may use the F2 (EDIT) key to edit the current cell. In the EDIT mode, the cell's data are displayed at the second prompt line. You can use the pointer control keys (←, →) to move a cursor across the data. The Home key jumps the cursor to the far left of the data; the End key jumps the cursor to the far right of the data.

Any characters that you type are inserted to the left of the cursor. The Ins key may be used to toggle the overwrite mode (indicator OVR) on or off. The Del or Backspace keys delete characters. When you are done editing, press the Enter key.

HINT Formulas and numbers may be converted to string data by using the EDIT mode to insert a label prefix as the first character.

HINT Pressing the F2 key (EDIT) and then the F9 key (CALC) converts the contents of the current cell from a formula or string expression into a constant value on the editing line. If the Enter key is typed, the change becomes permanent; if the Esc key is typed, the cell will retain its original contents. To convert several cells to constant values, use the /**R**ange,**V**alue command.

HAZARD Beginners often find that the spreadsheet's computed answers do not agree with answers they have gotten on a calculator or by hand. The reason is that Lotus holds all numeric data to fifteen places of accuracy. To control Lotus's level of accuracy, use the **@INT** or **@ROUND** functions. For more information, refer to **@ROUND** in the "Spreadsheet Functions" section and see the next Hint.

HINT The following macro, when invoked, will edit the current cell to include the @**ROUND** function, with two decimal places of accuracy for the value that the cell computes or holds.

{**EDIT**} {**HOME**}@**ROUND**({**END**},2)~

HINT In larger spreadsheets, automatic recalculation of the entire spreadsheet will slow down data entry. You may turn off the automatic recalculation with the /**W**orksheet,**G**lobal,**R**ecalculation,**M**anual command. When you turn it off, the spreadsheet only recalculates when the F9 (CALC) key is pressed. (See next Hazard.)

HAZARD When recalculation is manual, a CALC indicator at the bottom of the screen will tell you that your spreadsheet needs to be recalculated. Even so, it is an easy point to forget. To return Lotus to automatic recalculation, use the /**W**orksheet,**G**lobal,**R**ecalculation,**A**utomatic command.

RANGES

HINT When specifying a range by pointing to it, the period key may be used to shift the pointer's anchor from corner to corner. The blinking cursor indicates the free cell, the cell at the corner opposite the anchored cell. The anchor cell and free cell will shift each time the period key is pressed.

HINT You can use the /**R**ange,**N**ame,**C**reate command to name areas of the spreadsheet to facilitate rapid movement about the spreadsheet with the F5 (GOTO) key. First, name a cell in a specified area of the spreadsheet with a range name. When you are ready to move to the area, type the F5 (GOTO) key and answer its "Enter address to go to:" prompt by typing the F3 (NAME) key. The named ranges in the spreadsheet will be displayed in a menu at the top of the screen. You may use the pointer control keys to enter the name of your choice as the answer to the prompt.

HAZARD When naming ranges, you often may want to use abbreviated names to identify the ranges. Care must be taken, however, not to use a legal cell address as a range name. For example, a range holding an income statement for the 4th quarter might be named INC4, but should not be named IS4 since this is also a cell address. In such a case, Lotus always would recognize the name as a cell address, even if selected from a list of range names as described in the previous Hint.

HINT The top left cell of any range is the key cell for the range. The F5 (GOTO) key will send the pointer to the top left cell of a named range as the address to GOTO. The top left cell is specified as the TO range for a copy or move operation.

HINT If a range has been named, both the top left and bottom right corner cells are key cells for identifying the range by name. If either of these cells is deleted with the /**W**orksheet,**D**elete command, or if either is replaced with the /**M**ove command, the range becomes undefined even though its name remains intact. Any formulas referencing the range name will display ERR.

CELL REFERENCES

HINT When pointing to cells while entering a formula, the F4 (ABS) key may be used to automatically insert dollar signs ($) into the cell reference for the cell that the pointer is currently pointing to.

HINT Moving a cell or range of cells with the /**M**ove command does not cause a change in cell references in the same manner as copying a cell or range of cells with the /**C**opy command. With the /**M**ove command, all cells with references to cells in the moved range have their references updated in a relative fashion. The updating occurs even if the references were originally entered as absolute. References in the moved range are updated only if they are references to other cells in the moved range.

HINT You may keep a reference to a named range absolute by inserting a dollar sign ($) in front of the range's name. For example, if the range B5..B20 were named EXPENSES, the name in a function such as @**SUM**($EXPENSES) would be interpreted by Lotus as @**SUM**($B$5..$B$20). If range names are specified in a formula without the dollar sign, any copy operation involving the range reference will adjust the range's location in a relative fashion.

HAZARD It is possible to create a cell reference that is circular. By tracking the cell references, you find that they lead back to the original cell, thus forming a circle of references with every cell's displayed value dependent on that of the next. In a few esoteric applications, you may do this intentionally. Usually, however, it indicates that an error has been made. Circular references are detected by Lotus and when one occurs, a CIRC indicator is displayed at the bottom of the screen.

ALTERING THE SPREADSHEET

HAZARD Avoid using the commands /**W**orksheet,**I**nsert and /**W**orksheet,**D**elete to expand or contract areas of the spreadsheet by inserting and deleting rows and columns. When possible, use the /**M**ove command instead to avoid accidentally inserting or deleting rows or columns important to other areas of the spreadsheet. For instance, when a row is deleted, it is deleted from the entire spreadsheet.

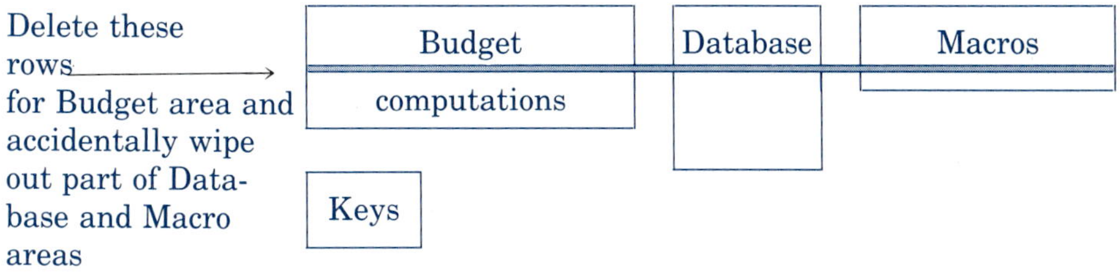

By using the /**M**ove command, you overcome the problem. Here you would move the FROM range indicated to the TO range indicated.

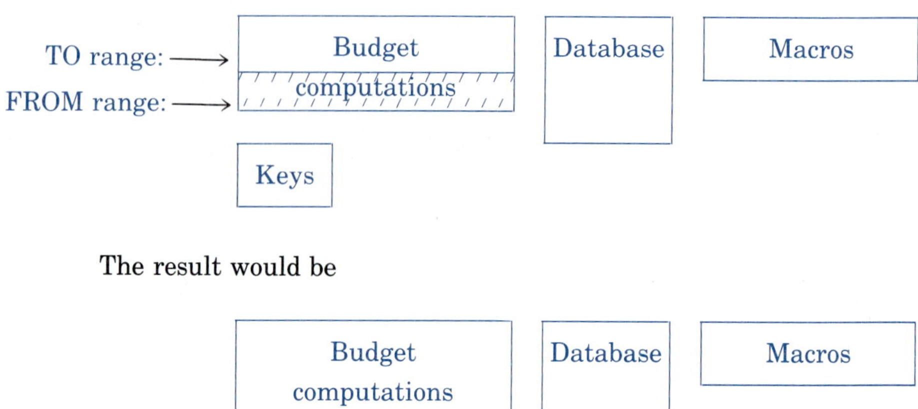

The result would be

Budget computations
Database
Macros
Keys

HINT Any spreadsheet data that are arranged in columns may be sorted with the /**D**ata,**S**ort command. This can be useful for setting up or restructuring @**VLOOKUP** tables.

HAZARD When you use the /**D**ata,**S**ort commands, if one or more columns are accidentally omitted from the data range to sort, the entire set of data will probably be irreparably altered. When several sorting operations must be done on the same data range, it is a good idea to use the /**R**ange,**N**ame,**C**reate command to name the range, and then use its range name to specify it as the range to sort with the /**D**ata,**S**ort,**D**ata-Range command.

SPREADSHEET DESIGN

HINT The amount of RAM that a spreadsheet uses is dependent on the size of its active area. The active area is defined as the rectangle encompassing all of the cells into which data have been entered. For example:

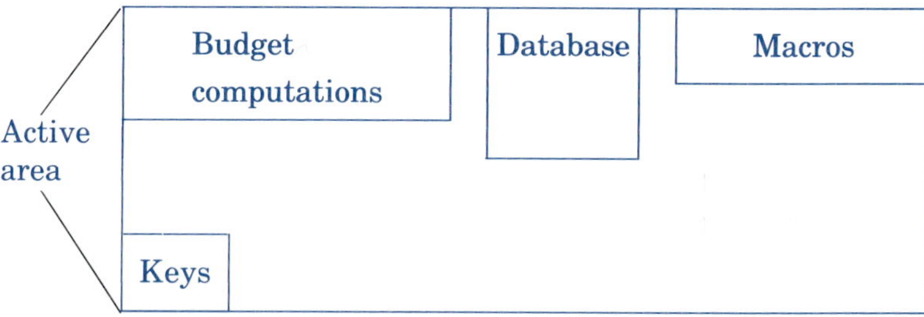

Here the active area is much larger than the area necessary to hold the spreadsheet's data, and the difference in size uses up RAM. Although rules of good spreadsheet design may require that some areas of the spreadsheet be left blank, you also will want to consider RAM limitations when you map out a large spreadsheet.

HINT If you move data, delete rows and/or columns, or erase a range of cells in a spreadsheet to make more RAM available, the active area of the current spreadsheet remains the same and you have no immediate gain. The End,Home keystroke sequence may be used to verify the position of the right-most and bottom-most cell in the active area. To decrease the active area and make more RAM available, use the /**F**ile,**X**tract,**F**ormulas command to save the range that now encompasses all spreadsheet entries to disk. Then retrieve the Xtracted file with the /**F**ile,**R**etrieve command.

PHANTOM SPACE CHARACTERS

HAZARD

When a space character is inadvertently added to the end of a character string, you may experience errors that are difficult to detect. When entering range names, field names for a database, or macro keystroke cells, use particular care that unwanted spaces do not occur at the end of an entry. For example, if a macro that is supposed to round the contents of a cell to two decimal places is entered as

‖ {**EDIT**} {**HOME**}@**ROUND**({**END**},2)~ ↵ ‖

when the macro is executed a space will be entered into the current cell as soon as the pointer is moved upon completion of the macro, and the original cell entry will be lost.

A database field name or range name with a trailing space will not match the same name without the trailing space. If a /**D**ata,**Q**uery operation is not working properly, check for phantom spaces at the end of field names in the Input, Output, and Criterion ranges. If an error message occurs indicating that a range name you have used does not exist, check that you have not added a trailing space.

STUDY QUESTIONS

1. With the spreadsheet pointer on cell D2, the screen appears as

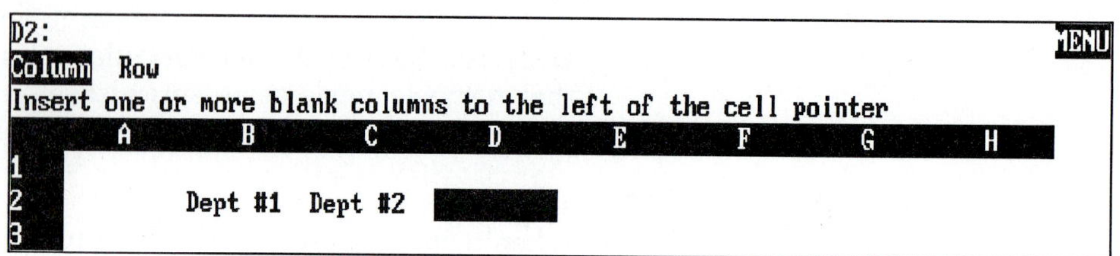

You try entering "Dept #3" into cell D2, but instead of seeing the date being entered you hear several beeps. What is the problem?

____

2. The spreadsheet pointer is on cell B2. You are trying to enter a row of column labels. You type ‖1st Quarter‖ to enter the first cell's data and the screen appears as

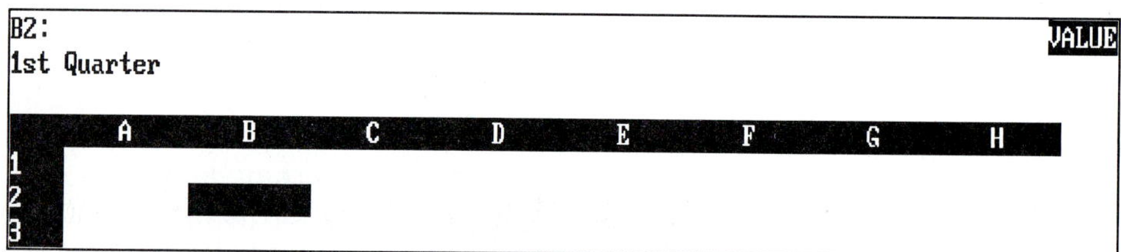

When you type the Enter key to enter the data into B2, the computer beeps. What is the problem and how can it be solved?

____

____

____

3. The following spreadsheet is used for a simple break-even model.

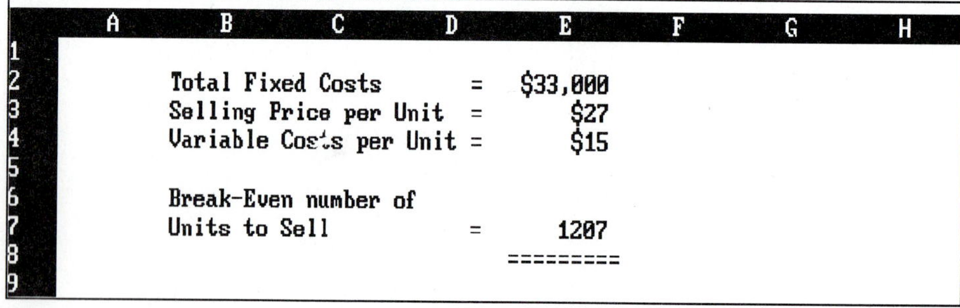

a. The difference between a unit's selling price and its variable cost is the contribution margin. You determine break-even sales in units by dividing total fixed costs by a unit's contribution margin. The formula in cell E7 has been entered as +E2/E3−E4. The resulting answer of 1207, however, is incorrect. The actual answer should be derived by Price − Variable Cost = $12, and $33,000/$12 = $2750. What is the problem and how can it be solved?

____

____

____

b. Another way of mathematically "saying" the same thing as the formula in the last question is "the reciprocal of the contribution margin times fixed cost, or 1/contribution margin * fixed cost." What would be an appropriate formula, using this alternate form of the equation, to enter into cell E7?

____

4. The following spreadsheet is designed to provide a simple financial forecast. The keys for the spreadsheet are a beginning sales figure of $65,000 for January; an expected growth in sales of 1.00% per month for the year; and the cost of goods sold as a percent of sales equal to 65.00%. The cells showing percent figures hold numeric constants formatted with the /**R**ange,**F**ormat,**P**ercent command. All other cells holding numeric data have been formatted with the /**R**ange,**F**ormat,**C**urrency command (0 decimal places).

```
     A        B        C        D        E        F        G        H
1
2          199x  FINANCIAL FORECAST
3
4          January Sales    = $65,000           COGS/SALES       =   65.00%
5          Sales Growth Rate=     1.00%
6
7
8                     SALES      COGS       NET
9
10         JAN
11         FEB
12         MAR
13         APR
14         MAY
15         JUN
16         JUL
17         AUG
18         SEP
19         OCT
20         NOV
21         DEC
22
23         TOTALS
24                   -------   -------   -------
```

a. The first formula you enter will be the formula to display January's sales figure. What would be an appropriate formula to enter into cell C10?

____

b. You will enter the next formula into C11. It will be the formula to display February's sales figure. The formula will be copied into the rest of the month cells in column C (C12..C21) with the /Copy command. What would be an appropriate formula to enter into cell C11?

____

```
     A      B       C         D         E         F         G         H
1
2           199x  FINANCIAL FORECAST
3
4           January Sales    = $65,000            COGS/SALES        =    65.00%
5           Sales Growth Rate=     1.00%
6
7
8                           SALES     COGS      NET
9
10          JAN           $65,000
11          FEB           $65,650
12          MAR           $66,307
13          APR           $66,970
14          MAY           $67,639
15          JUN           $68,316
16          JUL           $68,999
17          AUG           $69,689
18          SEP           $70,386
19          OCT           $71,090
20          NOV           $71,800
21          DEC           $72,518
22
23          TOTALS
24                        -------   -------   -------
```

c. Next enter the formula to total the C column into cell C23. Use a spreadsheet function. Once you enter the function, it will be copied into the two cells in row 23 (D23 and E23). What would be an appropriate entry for cell C23?

____

d. Next enter the formula for January's COGS into D10. The formula will be copied into the remaining cells in the column (D11..D21). What would be an appropriate formula to enter into cell D10?

____

e. NET is the difference between SALES and COGS for each month. The next steps in creating this forecasting spreadsheet are to enter a formula into January's NET (E10) and to copy that formula into the rest of the months' NET cells (E11..E21). What would be an appropriate formula to enter into E10?

____

f. Checking the spreadsheet with your calculator, you find the SALES TOTALS (C23) to be off by a dollar. Why the discrepancy? How can it be remedied?

____

____

5. The next five questions refer to the following spreadsheet. The constants and formulas that are entered in column D are shown here documented to the right on the same row in which they occur.

```
     A    B       C         D         E        F        G       H
 1
 2         Invoice Discount =   15.00%   <----- 0.15
 3
 4         Product #1
 5         -------------------
 6         Quantity Ordered =       30   <----- 30
 7         Suggested Retail =   $21.95   <----- 21.95
 8
 9         Invoice Total     = $658.50   <----- +D6*D7
10         Less Discount        $98.78   <----- +$D$2*D9
11
12         Invoice Billing   = $559.73   <----- +D9-D10
13
```

a. If the formula in cell D10 were copied into the second cell to its right, F10, what would be the formula in cell F10 after the copy operation?

____

b. If the formula in cell D12 were copied into cell D14, what would be the formula in cell D14 after the copy operation?

____

c. If the formula in cell D12 were copied into cell F9, what would be the formula in cell F9 after the copy operation?

____

d. If the /**M**ove command were used to move the formula in cell D9 to the right two cells (to F9), what would be the formulas in cells D10, D12, and F9 after the move operation?

____

____

____

e. If a single row were inserted with the pointer on the seventh row, as shown in the following screen, what would be the formulas in cells D10, D11, and D13 after the insertion?

____

____

____

```
       A        B        C        D        E        F        G        H
 1
 2              Invoice Discount =   15.00%
 3
 4              Product #1
 5              ----------------
 6              Quantity Ordered =      30
 7
 8              Suggested Retail =  $21.95
 9
10              Invoice Total    = $658.50
11              Less Discount       $98.78
12
13              Invoice Billing  = $559.73
14
```

6. The default global column width for a spreadsheet is nine characters. If you use the /**W**orksheet,**C**olumn,**S**et-Width command to set column C to 12 characters wide, and then use the /**W**orksheet,**G**lobal,**C**olumn-Width command to set the spreadsheet's columns one character wider (ten characters each), what is the effect on the width of column C?

____

7. A range of cells is formatted to display currency format with zero (0) decimal places with the /**R**ange,**F**ormat,**C**urrency command. The spreadsheet then is globally formatted to display currency format with two decimal places with the /**W**orksheet,**G**lobal,**F**ormat,**C**urrency command. What is the effect on the previously formatted range?

____

8. The following spreadsheet is designed to provide budget information for a monthly period. Projected sales are compared to actual sales. A budgeted labor cost based on 17.5% of actual sales is compared to an actual labor cost, and a budgeted cost of goods sold based on 55% of actual sales is compared against actual COGS. The formulas and constants used in the spreadsheet are documented on the same line in which they occur. How might the spreadsheet have been better designed?

____

____

```
       A        B        C        D        E        F        G        H
 1
 2              Monthly Report    DECEMBER              1990
 3              ------------------------------------------------
 4              Projected Sales          =    4,500 <----- 4500
 5              Actual Sales             =    5,200 <----- 5200
 6              Over (Under) Projected   =      700 <----- +E5-E4
 7              Budgeted Labor Cost      =      910 <----- 0.175*E5
 8              Actual Labor Cost        =    1,200 <----- 1200
 9              Over (Under) Budget      =      290 <----- +E8-E7
10              Budgeted COGS            =    2,860 <----- 0.55*E5
11              Actual COGS              =    2,750 <----- 2750
12              Over (Under) Budget      =    (110) <----- +E11-E10
13
```

9. Describe the steps involved in making the preceding example a spreadsheet template to be used each month.

10. Use the following inventory spreadsheet for the next five questions.

	A	B	C	D	E	F	G
1		Item Part	Quantity	Per Unit		Extensions	
2		Number	On Hand	Cost	Price	Cost	Price
3		19165	35	$1.21	$1.65	$42.35	$57.75
4		19166	46	$0.35	$0.49	$16.10	$22.54
5		19167	89	$3.55	$4.80	$315.95	$427.20
6		19168	12	$2.67	$3.60	$32.04	$43.20
7		19169	53	$2.25	$3.00	$119.25	$159.00
8		19170	6	$1.95	$2.65	$11.70	$15.90
9		19171	22	$1.55	$2.10	$34.10	$46.20
10		19172	31	$5.50	$7.45	$170.50	$230.95
11		19173	100	$3.95	$5.35	$395.00	$535.00
12		19174	19	$4.25	$5.75	$80.75	$109.25
13		19175	77	$0.65	$0.85	$50.05	$65.45
14		19176	33	$1.19	$1.60	$39.27	$52.80
15							
16		INVENTORY LEVELS					
17		Maximum Quantity =		100			
18		Minimum Quantity =		6			
19		Average Quantity =		44			
20							
21		INVENTORY VALUATION					
22		Total Value of Inventory (Cost)				$1,307.06	
23		Avg. Value of Inventory per Item (Cost)				$108.92	
24							

a. In cell D17 a formula using a spreadsheet function has been entered. It returns the highest value found in its argument(s) and is used here to indicate the highest inventory quantity on hand for a single item. What is an appropriate form for the function entered into cell D17?

b. A similar formula has been entered into cell D18. It returns the lowest value found in its argument(s) and is used here to indicate the lowest inventory quantity on hand for a single item. What is an appropriate form for the function entered into cell D18?

c. The next cell entry (D19) is a formula using a function to return the mean average quantity on hand. This value (43.583333) has, in turn, been rounded by another function in the formula to return the final value of 44. What is an appropriate form for the functions entered in cell D19?

d. The extensions shown are dollar values of inventory based on per unit cost or selling price times quantity on hand. Cell F22, under the label INVENTORY VALUATION, contains a function returning the total inventory dollar amount of the cost extensions. What would be an appropriate formula for cell F22?

____

e. The final formula, in cell F23, computes the average inventory value for all items inventoried. What would be an appropriate formula to enter into cell F22?

____

LOTUS 1-2-3 KEY TERM GLOSSARY

Absolute Cell Reference A form of cell reference in a formula that keeps the referenced cell the same regardless of the location to which the formula is copied.

Anchor To specify the first cell of a range when pointing to a range.

Arguments References, ranges, values, or formulas for a function to act upon.

Cell Address The location of a cell in the spreadsheet, expressed as a combination of a letter (column) and a number (row).

Cell Reference See *Cell Address.*

Command Pointer Highlighted area of the control panel which displays the current choice in a menu.

Control Panel The top three lines of the monitor where Lotus displays menus, prompts, and commands.

Database Data arranged in groups of records, each record consisting of one or more fields.

Default A term used to define a setting that is used by Lotus when not specified by the user.

Edit Cue Blinking highlighted word EDIT which appears at the upper right corner of the monitor to indicate Lotus is in its edit mode.

Extracting Data from the Database Copying selected information from the database to another part of the spreadsheet based upon criteria designated by the user.

Field Name The name of a column where similar information is stored in each record of a database.

Function Precoded routines that perform a series of operations or calculations quickly. Functions are often shortcuts to accomplish what would otherwise require long numeric expressions.

Global An operation that is performed throughout the spreadsheet in all applicable cases.

Help Screen A screen containing information about a command, operation, and so forth, which is accessed by typing the **F1** (Help) key.

Label A string expression that is entered into a cell.

Macro A collection of keystrokes that is automatically executed when the macro is invoked.

Menus Displays of commands on the control panel at the top of the screen from which you may select.

Mixed References Cell references that are partly relative and partly absolute.

Numeric A cell entry that evaluates numeric data.

Range One cell, or any rectangular group of cells.

Record A set of related information in a database, comprised of one or more fields.

Relative A form of cell reference in a formula that allows the referenced cell to change when the formula is copied to another location.

Repeating Label Prefix The backslash (\) symbol which will cause the next characters entered in a cell to be repeated for the entire width of the cell.

Scroll To move the area of the spreadsheet visible on the monitor to another section of the spreadsheet.

Spreadsheet A software designed for entering data and performing calculations using columns and rows.

Spreadsheet Keys Constants that are the source of all values displayed in the spreadsheet.

Spreadsheet Pointer A highlighted indicator which shows which cell, or group of cells, is currently being referenced.

Sticky Menus Menus that do not immediately return the user to the data entry mode.

String A cell entry that must be a label (i.e., non-numeric expression).

Synchronized Scrolling Scrolling two separate spreadsheets as they appear in two different windows.

Template A master copy of a spreadsheet that is designed to be used more than once with new data entered and with formulas that obtain values.

Value A cell entry that may be either numeric or a string.

Window Lines The top three lines of the monitor which Lotus reserves for the Control Panel.

LOTUS 1-2-3 OPERATION AND COMMAND SUMMARY

LOTUS CONTROL KEYS

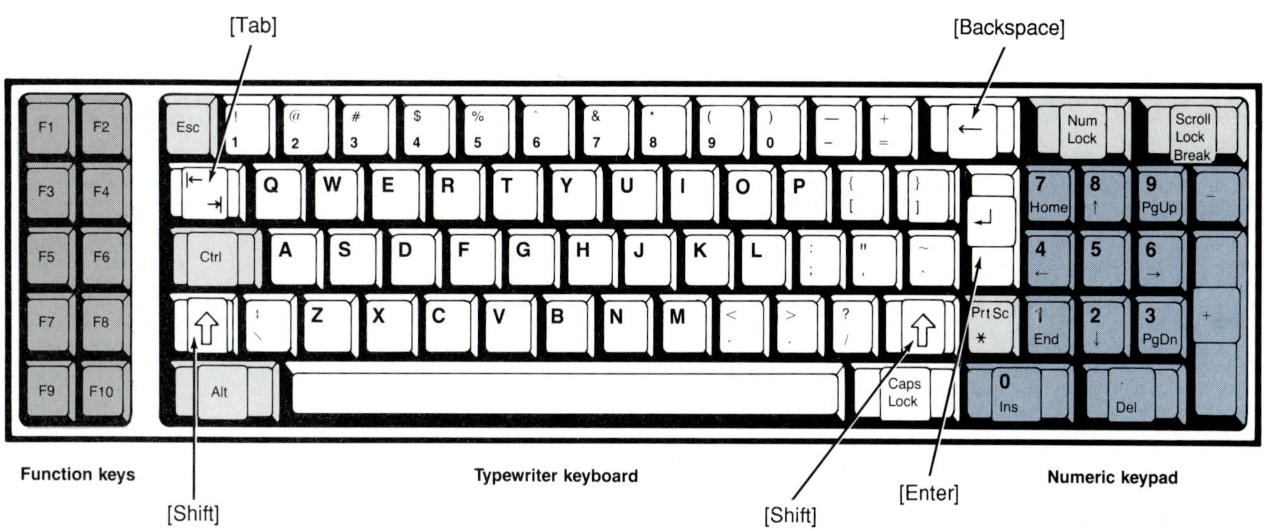

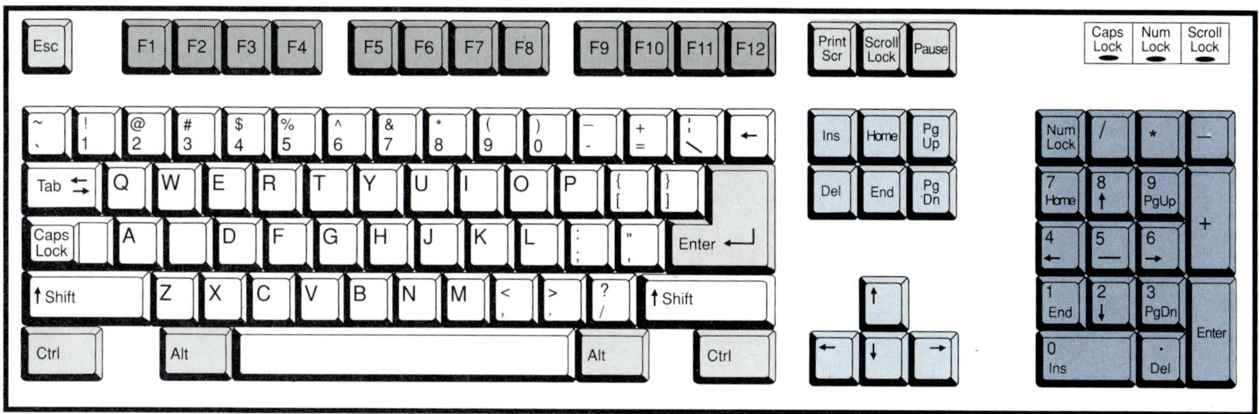

Normal Typewriter Keys

Control Keys

Function Keys

Numeric Keypad/Cursor Movement Keys

Cursor Movement Keys Only

KEY COMBINATIONS

Ctrl-Break Cancels any Lotus 1-2-3 command operation. Returns the spreadsheet to the READY mode.

Alt-Alpha Key Used with alphabetic keys to invoke keyboard macros.

Alt-F1 COMPOSE Used to compose international characters by entering a combination of standard keyboard characters.

Alt-F2 STEP Turns STEP mode on/off. The STEP mode is used during execution of macros. Lotus waits for a keystroke before executing each step of the macro.

OTHER CONTROL KEYS

Slash Key (/) Calls the spreadsheet's Main menu of commands.

Enter Key ↵ Enters the current line into memory for Lotus to act upon.

Escape Key Cancels an operation when editing a cell. In the MENU mode, backs up to previous menu level.

Num Lock Key Toggles ten-key numeric keypad to pointer control keys. The Shift key may be used to shift this keypad temporarily to the opposite mode.

FUNCTION KEYS 1–10

F1 HELP Accesses Lotus's on-line help facility. Help screens appear in context of the current operation.

F2 EDIT Allows contents of the current cell to be edited.

F3 NAME Displays the list of current range names while in the POINT mode.

F4 ABS Facilitates defining cell references as absolute or relative when in the POINT, VALUE, or EDIT mode.

F5 GOTO Moves the pointer to the specified cell or range name.

F6 WINDOW Moves the pointer from one window to the other.

F7 QUERY Repeats the last /**D**ata,**Q**uery operation.

F8 TABLE Repeats the last /**D**ata,**T**able operation.

F9 CALC Recalculates the spreadsheet.

F10 GRAPH Displays the currently defined graph.

POINTER CONTROL KEYS

Arrow Keys Move pointer one cell at a time in the direction of the arrows.

Home Key Moves pointer to top left corner of spreadsheet (A1) in the READY or POINT modes. In EDIT mode, moves cursor to beginning of cell entry.

PgUp Key Shifts screen and pointer up one page at a time.

PgDn Key Shifts screen and pointer down one page at a time.

Tab Key Shifts screen to the right one page at a time (same as Ctrl-Right). Shift-Tab shifts screen to the left one page at a time (same as Ctrl-Left).

Scroll Lock Key Toggles SCROLL indicator on/off. When SCROLL is on, scrolling of the spreadsheet occurs one row or column at a time.

Period Key Anchors current cell as one corner of a range, allowing the range to be expanded. When the range is highlighted, shifts anchor cell and free cell to allow the range to be expanded or contracted from another corner.

POINTER KEY COMBINATIONS

End-Arrow Key Causes the pointer to move in the direction of the arrow until it reaches the last nonblank cell if the pointer was originally on a nonblank cell. If the pointer was originally on a blank cell, the pointer will move to the cell following the last blank cell.

End-Home Key Moves the pointer to the bottom right cell in the spreadsheet's active area.

EDITING KEYS

Backspace Key Backspaces and erases the character to the left of the cursor when entering data into a cell or when editing a cell or command parameter.

Del Key Erases the character at the cursor location when editing a cell or command parameter.

Ins Key Toggles OVR indicator (overwrite) on and off. When in the EDIT mode, characters are inserted unless OVR is toggled on. At completion of the entry, OVR is turned off automatically.

LOTUS 1-2-3 COMMAND INDEX

Command	Keystroke
Absolute References	F4 (ABS)
Absolute Value	@**ABS**
Clear Graph Settings	/**G**raph,**R**eset
Clear Print Settings	/**P**rint,**P**rinter,**C**lear
Clear Titles	/**W**orksheet,**T**itles,**C**lear
Clear Window	/**W**orksheet,**W**indow,**C**lear
Clear Worksheet	/**W**orksheet,**E**rase
Date Calculations	@**DAY**, @**MONTH**, @**YEAR**

Date Display	/**R**ange,**F**ormat,**D**ate
Date Entry Function	**@DATE**
Date System Date/Time	**@NOW**
Decimal Places Calculation	**@ROUND**, **@INT**
Decimal Places Display	/**R**ange,**F**ormat
Delete Cell Contents	/**R**ange,**E**rase
Delete Character	F2 (EDIT)
Delete Column or Row	/**W**orksheet,**D**elete
Delete File	/**F**ile,**E**rase
Delete Range Name, single	/**R**ange,**N**ame,**D**elete
Delete Range Names, all	/**R**ange,**N**ame,**R**eset
Delete Records	/**D**ata,**Q**uery,**D**elete
Erase	See Delete
Format, Default	/**W**orksheet,**G**lobal,**F**ormat
Format, Range	/**R**ange,**F**ormat
Formulas, Removing	/**R**ange,**V**alue
Formulas, Displaying on Screen	/**R**ange,**F**ormat,**T**ext
Formulas, Printing	/**P**rint,**P**rinter,**O**ptions,**O**ther,**C**ell-Formulas
Hide Cell	/**R**ange,**F**ormat,**H**idden
Hide Column	/**W**orksheet,**C**olumn,**H**ide
Insert Character	F2 (EDIT)
Insert Column or Row	/**W**orksheet,**I**nsert
Justify Labels, Default	/**W**orksheet,**G**lobal,**L**abel-Prefix
Justify Labels in Range	/**R**ange,**L**abel
Justify Text	/**R**ange,**J**ustify
Move Range	/**M**ove
Numbering, Automatic	/**D**ata,**F**ill
Page Breaks, Printing	/**W**orksheet,**P**age
Password, File Protection	/**F**ile,**S**ave
Print Graphs	/**G**raph,**S**ave; PrintGraph
Printer Control Codes	/**P**rint,**P**rinter,**O**ptions,**S**etup
Printer Control Codes	/**W**orksheet,**G**lobal,**D**efault,**P**rinter,**S**etup
Printer Selection	/**W**orksheet,**G**lobal,**D**efault,**P**rinter,**N**ame
Protect Range of Cells On/Off	/**R**ange,**P**rotect; /**R**ange,**U**nprotect
Protection of Cells On/Off	/**W**orksheet,**G**lobal,**P**rotection
Protection On, Data Entry	/**R**ange,**I**nput
Ranges, Listing Named Ranges	/**R**ange,**N**ame,**T**able
Ranges, Locating Named Ranges	F5 (GOTO); F3 (NAME)
Ranges, Naming	/**R**ange,**N**ame,**C**reate
Recalculation Method	/**W**orksheet,**G**lobal,**R**ecalculation
Recalculation, Manual	F9 (CALC)
Regression Analysis	/**D**ata,**R**egression
Save Graph for Printing	/**G**raph,**S**ave
Save Graph Settings	/**G**raph,**N**ame
Save Range as File	/**F**ile,**X**tract
Save Worksheet	/**F**ile,**S**ave
Sorting	/**D**ata,**S**ort
Table, Listing Named Ranges	/**R**ange,**N**ame,**T**able
Tables, Transpose Columns and Rows	/**R**ange,**T**ranspose
Time Calculation	**@HOUR**, **@MINUTE**, **@SECOND**
Time Entry	**@TIME**
Time Format	/**R**ange,**F**ormat,**D**ate,**T**ime
Width of Column, single	/**W**orksheet,**C**olumn,**S**et-Width
Width of Columns, default	/**W**orksheet,**G**lobal,**C**olumn-Width
Windows, Moving Cursor	F6 (WINDOW)
Zero Display	/**W**orksheet,**G**lobal,**Z**ero

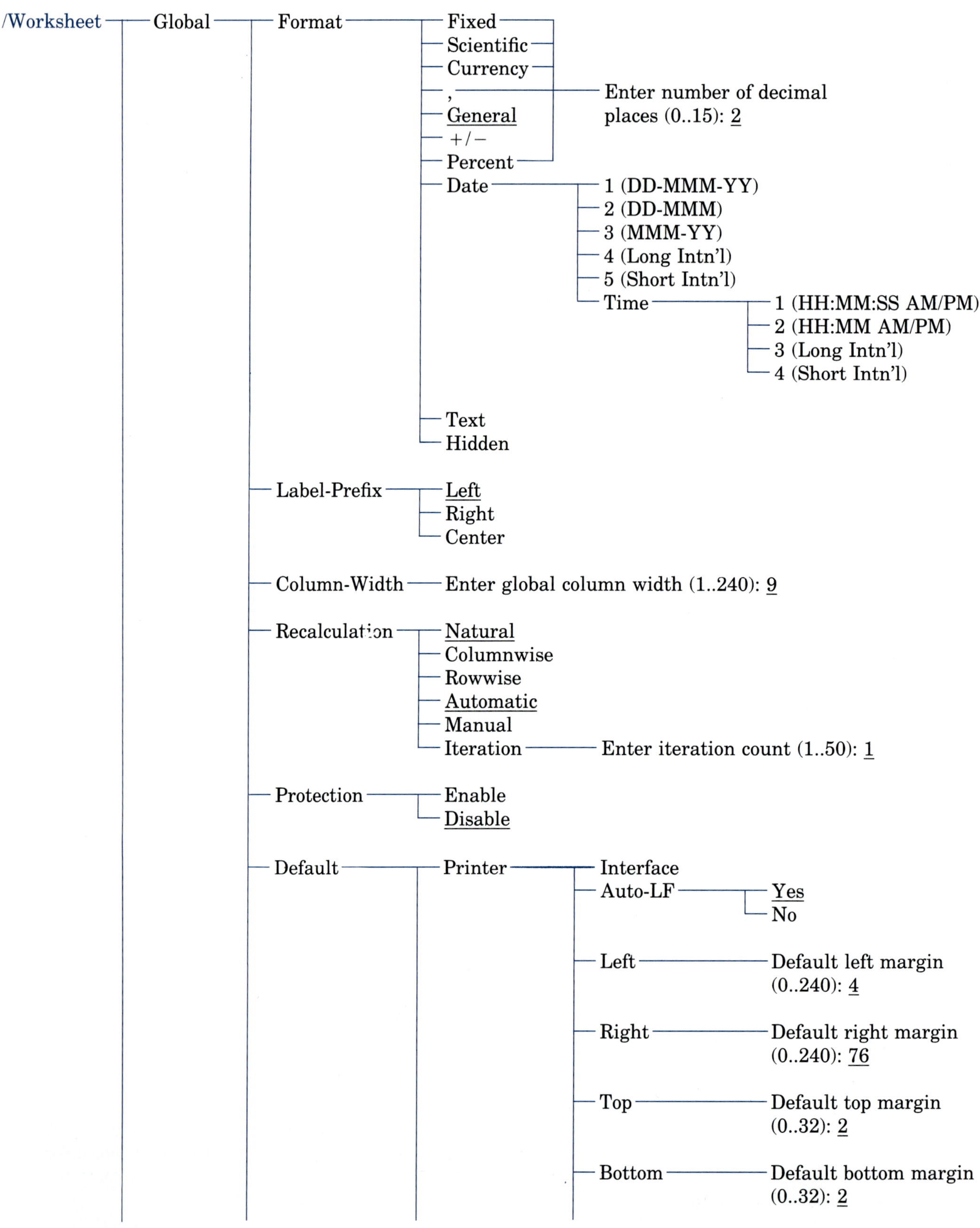
/Worksheet
Global
Format
Fixed
Scientific
Currency
,
General
+/−
Percent
Enter number of decimal places (0..15): 2
Date
1 (DD-MMM-YY)
2 (DD-MMM)
3 (MMM-YY)
4 (Long Intn'l)
5 (Short Intn'l)
Time
1 (HH:MM:SS AM/PM)
2 (HH:MM AM/PM)
3 (Long Intn'l)
4 (Short Intn'l)
Text
Hidden
Label-Prefix
Left
Right
Center
Column-Width
Enter global column width (1..240): 9
Recalculation
Natural
Columnwise
Rowwise
Automatic
Manual
Iteration
Enter iteration count (1..50): 1
Protection
Enable
Disable
Default
Printer
Interface
Auto-LF
Yes
No
Left
Default left margin (0..240): 4
Right
Default right margin (0..240): 76
Top
Default top margin (0..32): 2
Bottom
Default bottom margin (0..32): 2

CONTINUED

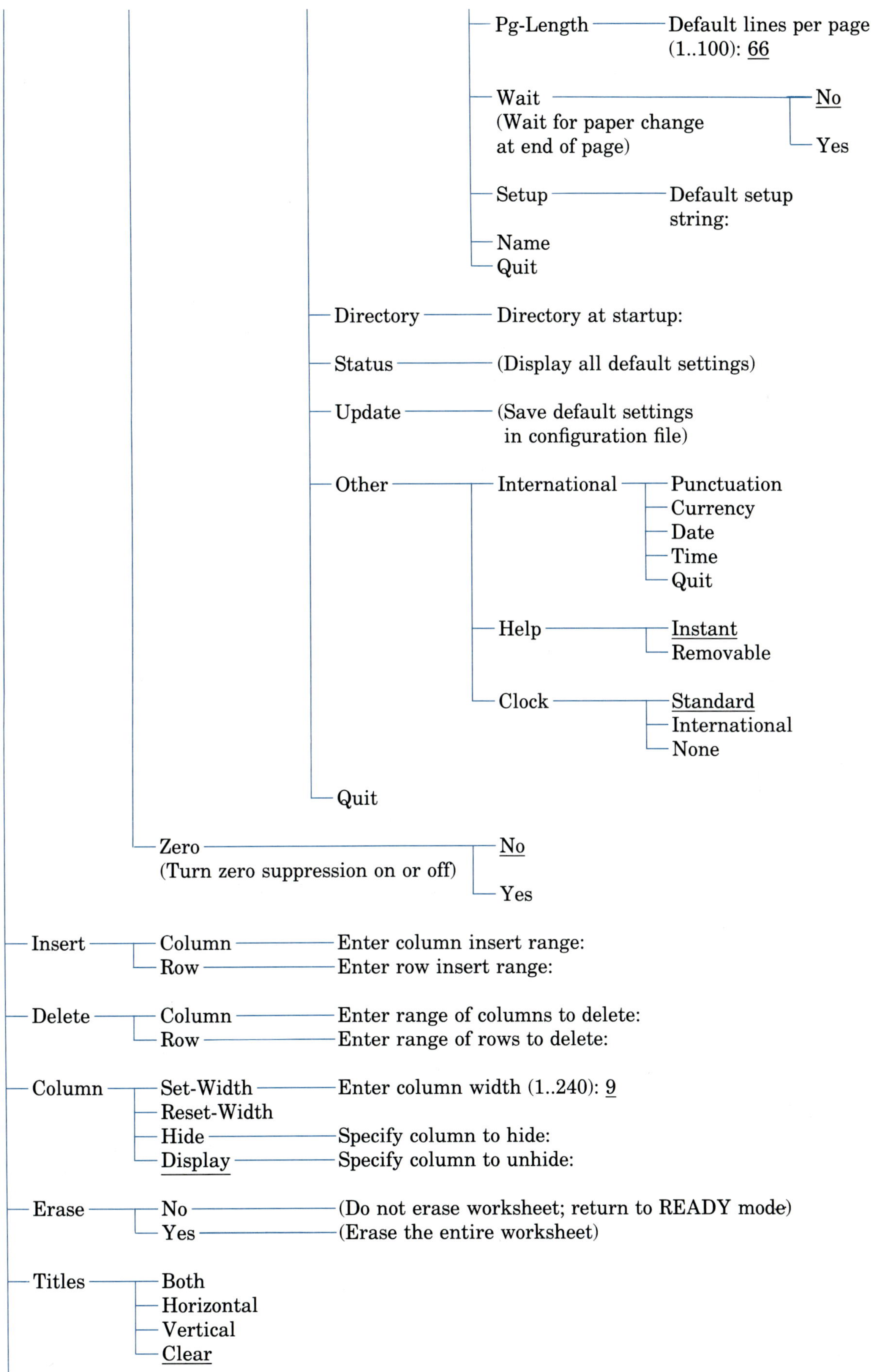
Pg-Length
Default lines per page (1..100): 66
Wait
(Wait for paper change at end of page)
No
Yes
Setup
Default setup string:
Name
Quit
Directory
Directory at startup:
Status
(Display all default settings)
Update
(Save default settings in configuration file)
Other
International
Punctuation
Currency
Date
Time
Quit
Help
Instant
Removable
Clock
Standard
International
None
Quit
Zero
(Turn zero suppression on or off)
No
Yes
Insert
Column
Enter column insert range:
Row
Enter row insert range:
Delete
Column
Enter range of columns to delete:
Row
Enter range of rows to delete:
Column
Set-Width
Enter column width (1..240): 9
Reset-Width
Hide
Specify column to hide:
Display
Specify column to unhide:
Erase
No
(Do not erase worksheet; return to READY mode)
Yes
(Erase the entire worksheet)
Titles
Both
Horizontal
Vertical
Clear

CONTINUED

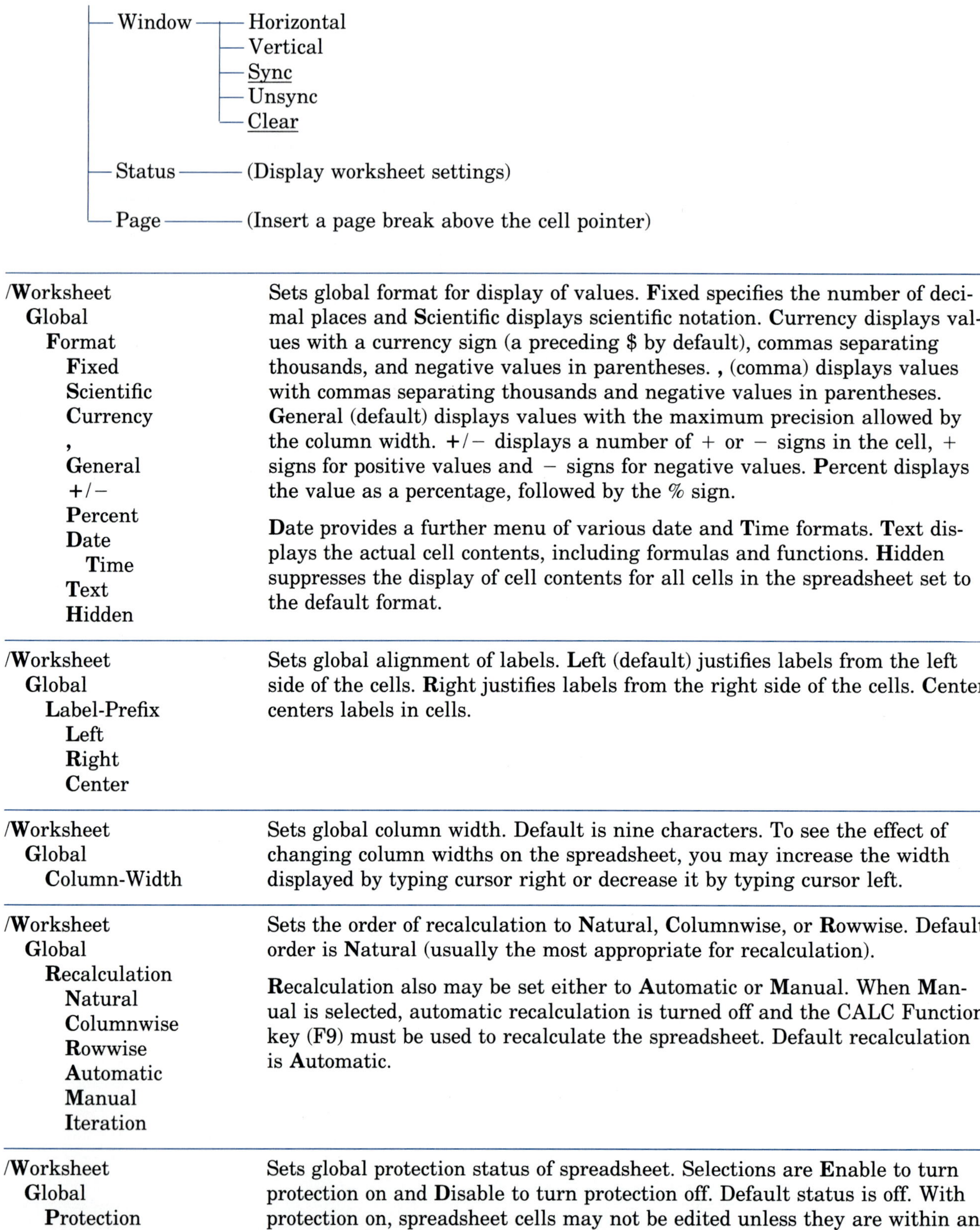

- Window
  - Horizontal
  - Vertical
  - Sync
  - Unsync
  - Clear
- Status — (Display worksheet settings)
- Page — (Insert a page break above the cell pointer)

/**W**orksheet **G**lobal **F**ormat **F**ixed **S**cientific **C**urrency **,** **G**eneral **+/−** **P**ercent **D**ate **T**ime **T**ext **H**idden	Sets global format for display of values. **F**ixed specifies the number of decimal places and **S**cientific displays scientific notation. **C**urrency displays values with a currency sign (a preceding $ by default), commas separating thousands, and negative values in parentheses. **,** (comma) displays values with commas separating thousands and negative values in parentheses. **G**eneral (default) displays values with the maximum precision allowed by the column width. **+/−** displays a number of + or − signs in the cell, + signs for positive values and − signs for negative values. **P**ercent displays the value as a percentage, followed by the % sign. **D**ate provides a further menu of various date and **T**ime formats. **T**ext displays the actual cell contents, including formulas and functions. **H**idden suppresses the display of cell contents for all cells in the spreadsheet set to the default format.
/**W**orksheet **G**lobal **L**abel-Prefix **L**eft **R**ight **C**enter	Sets global alignment of labels. **L**eft (default) justifies labels from the left side of the cells. **R**ight justifies labels from the right side of the cells. **C**enter centers labels in cells.
/**W**orksheet **G**lobal **C**olumn-Width	Sets global column width. Default is nine characters. To see the effect of changing column widths on the spreadsheet, you may increase the width displayed by typing cursor right or decrease it by typing cursor left.
/**W**orksheet **G**lobal **R**ecalculation **N**atural **C**olumnwise **R**owwise **A**utomatic **M**anual **I**teration	Sets the order of recalculation to **N**atural, **C**olumnwise, or **R**owwise. Default order is **N**atural (usually the most appropriate for recalculation). **R**ecalculation also may be set either to **A**utomatic or **M**anual. When **M**anual is selected, automatic recalculation is turned off and the CALC Function key (F9) must be used to recalculate the spreadsheet. Default recalculation is **A**utomatic.
/**W**orksheet **G**lobal **P**rotection **E**nable **D**isable	Sets global protection status of spreadsheet. Selections are **E**nable to turn protection on and **D**isable to turn protection off. Default status is off. With protection on, spreadsheet cells may not be edited unless they are within an unprotected range. (See **R**ange commands /**R,P** and /**R,U**.)

/Worksheet Global Default Printer Directory Status Update Other Intn'l Help Clock	May be used to redefine default printer, default disk drive, and directory. **S**tatus displays current default settings. Default settings are held in a configuration file on the system disk and **U**pdate causes any changes made to be written to the file. **O**ther,**I**nternational allows you to redefine the punctuation used in entry and display of decimal places, thousands separators, function argument separators, currency, dates, and times. **O**ther,**H**elp determines access to the Lotus Help feature. **I**nstant causes the Help file to remain open during the entire session. The disk containing the Help file may not be removed. Use **I**nstant when Help is on a fixed disk. When **R**emovable is selected, the Help file is closed when you exit the Help feature. The disk may be removed. Use **R**emovable when the Help file is on a removable disk. **O**ther,**C**lock determines the date and time formats used for the time indicator in the lower left corner of the screen. **S**tandard sets the date format to Lotus standard long format and the time format to Lotus standard short format. **I**nternational sets the formats to those selected with the **/W,G,D,O**ther,**I**nternational command. **N**one suppresses display of the date and time indicator.
/Worksheet Global Zero	Determines whether cells containing values equal to zero are displayed. **Y**es suppresses display of zero values. **N**o, the default setting, displays zero values.
/Worksheet Insert Row Column	Inserts one or more rows or columns in the spreadsheet. Rows are inserted just above the pointer; columns are inserted just to the left of the pointer. To insert more than one row or column, define the range of rows or columns to be inserted.
/Worksheet Delete Row Column	Deletes one or more rows or columns in the spreadsheet. A single row or column is deleted where the pointer is located. To delete more than one row or column, define the range of rows or columns to be deleted.
/Worksheet Column Set-Width Reset-Width Hide Display	**S**et-Width and **R**eset-Width are used to change the width of the column in which the pointer is currently located. **S**et-Width allows you to enter a new column width. To see the effect of the changing column width on the spreadsheet, you may increase the width by typing cursor right, or decrease it by typing cursor left. **R**eset-Width sets the column width to the current **G**lobal,**C**olumn-Width. **H**ide suppresses the display of columns while retaining the data contained in hidden columns. **D**isplay redisplays hidden columns. Columns that were hidden are marked with asterisks.
/Worksheet Erase Yes No	Erases the current spreadsheet from the computer's RAM and displays a blank spreadsheet. Before the spreadsheet is erased, you must select **Y**es. Selecting **N**o will cancel the **E**rase command. This precaution ensures that the spreadsheet is not inadvertently erased without being saved.

/**W**orksheet **T**itles **B**oth **H**orizontal **V**ertical **C**lear	Freezes either rows, columns, or both as titles that will remain on the screen even if the pointer is moved to other locations on the spreadsheet. If **H**orizontal is selected, rows just above the pointer become titles. If **V**ertical is selected, columns just to the left of the pointer become titles. **B**oth will produce both title rows and columns. **C**lear will unfreeze all titles. When titles are in use, the title rows and/or columns may only be accessed when in the POINT mode.
/**W**orksheet **W**indow **H**orizontal **V**ertical **S**ync **U**nsync **C**lear	Creates two windows on the spreadsheet by splitting the screen either horizontally or vertically, allowing two separate portions of the spreadsheet to be viewed at the same time. Either area may be accessed, and the WINDOW Function key (F6) is used to move from one window to the other. Spreadsheet settings such as Formats and Titles may be defined differently for the two windows. Scrolling may be **S**ynchronized or **U**nsynchronized. **C**lear will return the screen to just one window; the settings from the upper or left window will be retained.
/**W**orksheet **S**tatus	Displays current global settings, protection status, and amount of system memory (RAM) still available.
/**W**orksheet **P**age	Inserts a new row into the spreadsheet with a double colon (::) marking the page break in the current column of the new row. A new printed page will begin at the row below the page break row. Nothing else entered in the page break row will be printed.

/RANGE COMMANDS

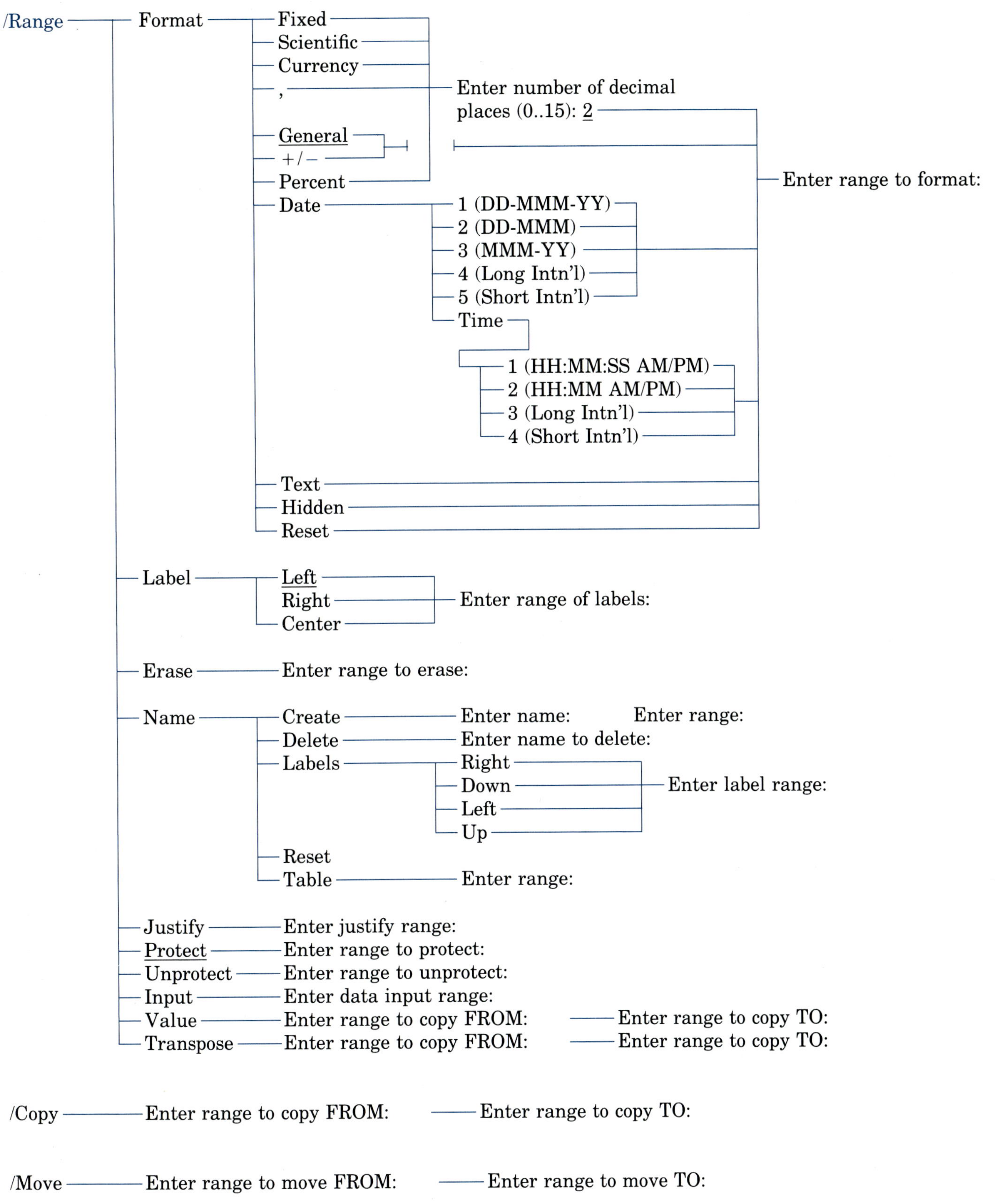

/**R**ange **F**ormat **F**ixed **S**cientific **C**urrency , **G**eneral +/− **P**ercent **D**ate **T**ime **T**ext **H**idden **R**eset	Sets format for display of values in specified range. **F**ixed specifies the number of decimal places and **S**cientific displays scientific notation. **C**urrency displays values with a currency sign (a preceding $ by default), commas separating thousands, and negative values in parentheses. **,** (comma) displays values with commas separating thousands and negative values in parentheses. **G**eneral (default) displays values with the maximum precision allowed by the column width. **+**/− displays a number of + or − signs in the cell, + signs for positive values and − signs for negative values. **P**ercent displays the value as a percentage, followed by the % sign. **D**ate provides a further menu of various date and **T**ime formats. **T**ext displays the actual cell contents, including formulas and functions. **H**idden suppresses the display of cell contents in the range. **R**eset sets format to the currently selected **G**lobal,**D**efault,**F**ormat.
/**R**ange **L**abel **L**eft **R**ight **C**enter	Sets alignment of labels in the specified range. **L**eft (default) justifies labels from the left side of the cells. **R**ight justifies labels from the right side of the cells. **C**enter centers labels in cells.
/**R**ange **E**rase	Erases the contents of all cells in the specified range.
/**R**ange **N**ame **C**reate **D**elete **L**abels **R**ight **D**own **L**eft **U**p **R**eset **T**able	**C**reate allows a range to be named. Range names may be up to fifteen characters long. The name then may be used to specify the range in any function or command calling for a range. **D**elete is used to delete a single range name. **R**eset will delete all range names. Deleting cells at the upper left or lower right corner of a named range by deleting rows or columns (/**W**,**D**) will cause the range name to become undefined, and any cells referencing that range will display ERR. **L**abels may be used to automatically name ranges from cells containing labels. Options are **R**ight, **D**own, **L**eft, and **U**p to name, respectively, the single cell ranges to the right, below, to the left, or above a range of cells containing labels. **T**able alphabetically lists all existing range names and corresponding addresses in a two-column table. Locate the **T**able in an empty portion of the spreadsheet to avoid writing over existing data.
/**R**ange **J**ustify	Rearranges the contents of cells containing labels to fit within margins set by the specified range.
/**R**ange **P**rotect **U**nprotect **I**nput	**P**rotect prevents changes to cells within the specified range when Global Protection is on. **U**nprotect allows cells to be changed. **I**nput is used to allow changes to any unprotected cell in a specified range. Pointer movement will be restricted to unprotected cells in the **I**nput range unless the Enter key is pressed before making any changes to the current cell.
/**R**ange **V**alue	Copies a range of cells, converting formulas in the FROM range to values in the TO range. Locate TO range in an empty portion of the spreadsheet if you do not want the values to replace existing data in your spreadsheet.

Command	Description
/**R**ange **T**ranspose	Copies a range of cells, transposing columns and rows. For example, a range of 2 rows by 5 columns specified as the FROM range will be copied to the TO range occupying 5 rows by 2 columns.
/**C**opy	Copies the contents of a cell or range of cells to another cell or range of cells. Cell references in formulas will be adjusted unless they are specified as absolute references before the **C**opy command is issued. The TO range coordinate is specified as the uppermost left corner of the range.
/**M**ove	While the **C**opy command causes duplication of a cell or range, the **M**ove command is used to physically move a cell or range of cells to another location on the spreadsheet. After defining the range to be moved, place the pointer at the upper left corner of the area to which the range is to be moved. All formulas referencing cells in a moved range are changed to reflect the new positions of those cells. Formulas within the moved range change only if their references are to other cells in the range.

/FILE COMMANDS

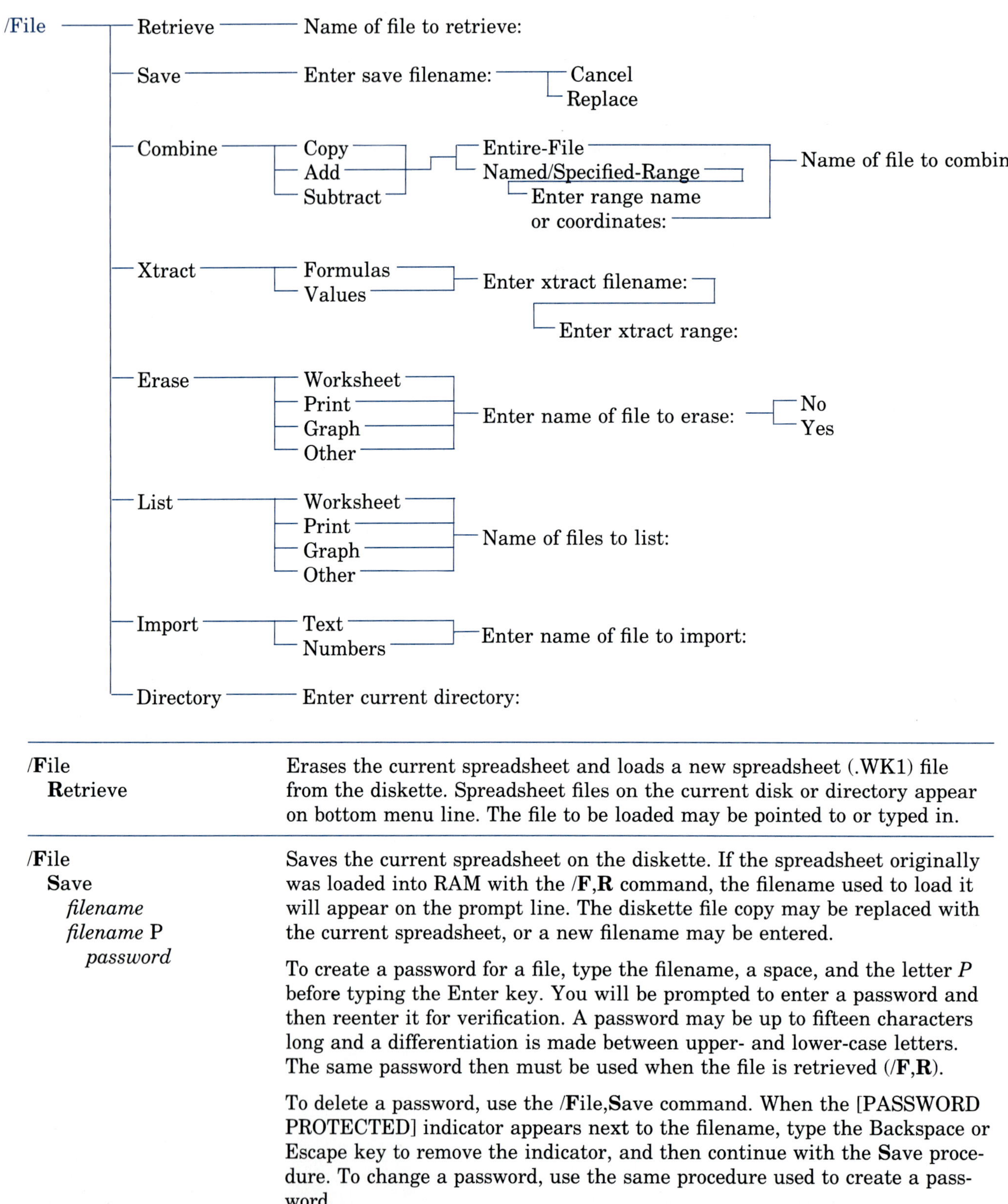

/**F**ile **R**etrieve	Erases the current spreadsheet and loads a new spreadsheet (.WK1) file from the diskette. Spreadsheet files on the current disk or directory appear on bottom menu line. The file to be loaded may be pointed to or typed in.
/**F**ile **S**ave *filename* *filename* P *password*	Saves the current spreadsheet on the diskette. If the spreadsheet originally was loaded into RAM with the /**F**,**R** command, the filename used to load it will appear on the prompt line. The diskette file copy may be replaced with the current spreadsheet, or a new filename may be entered. To create a password for a file, type the filename, a space, and the letter *P* before typing the Enter key. You will be prompted to enter a password and then reenter it for verification. A password may be up to fifteen characters long and a differentiation is made between upper- and lower-case letters. The same password then must be used when the file is retrieved (/**F**,**R**). To delete a password, use the /**F**ile,**S**ave command. When the [PASSWORD PROTECTED] indicator appears next to the filename, type the Backspace or Escape key to remove the indicator, and then continue with the **S**ave procedure. To change a password, use the same procedure used to create a password.

/**F**ile **C**ombine **C**opy **A**dd **S**ubtract	Combines all (Entire File) or part (Named Range) of a spreadsheet file on the diskette with the current spreadsheet. The position of the pointer in the current spreadsheet determines where incoming cells will be placed. Any overlaid cells below and to the right of the pointer will be replaced by the incoming cells. If the options **A**dd or **S**ubtract are selected, the combined spreadsheet will add to or subtract from the overlaid cells holding values.
/**F**ile **X**tract **F**ormulas **V**alues	Writes a portion of the current spreadsheet to a diskette file. If the option **F**ormulas is selected, the new spreadsheet file will retain the same formulas used in the current spreadsheet. Selecting **V**alues will cause only the currently displayed values of all formulas to be saved in the new spreadsheet file as constants.
/**F**ile **E**rase **W**orksheet **P**rint **G**raph **O**ther	Allows files to be erased from the diskette without exiting from the spreadsheet program. Selecting **W**orksheet, **P**rint, or **G**raph determines the type of files that will appear on the bottom menu line for selection. If **O**ther is selected, all files in the default directory will be displayed on the bottom menu line. The filename to be erased may be selected from the menu displayed or may be entered on the keyboard.
/**F**ile **L**ist **W**orksheet **P**rint **G**raph **O**ther	Temporarily replaces the spreadsheet display with a display of files and the amount of space left on the diskette. Selecting **W**orksheet, **P**rint, or **G**raph determines the type of files that will be displayed. If **O**ther is selected, all files in the default directory will be displayed.
/**F**ile **I**mport **T**ext **N**umbers	Reads data from any ASCII file into the current spreadsheet. Unless specified otherwise, only files with a .PRN extension will be displayed for selection. If **T**ext is selected, each line of the imported file will be entered into a single cell of the current spreadsheet, beginning with the current cell and moving down. If **N**umbers is selected, only values and strings delimited with legal **L**abel-Prefix characters (on both sides) in the ASCII file will be read into the current spreadsheet.
/**F**ile **D**irectory	Allows current disk drive and directory to be changed.

/PRINT COMMANDS

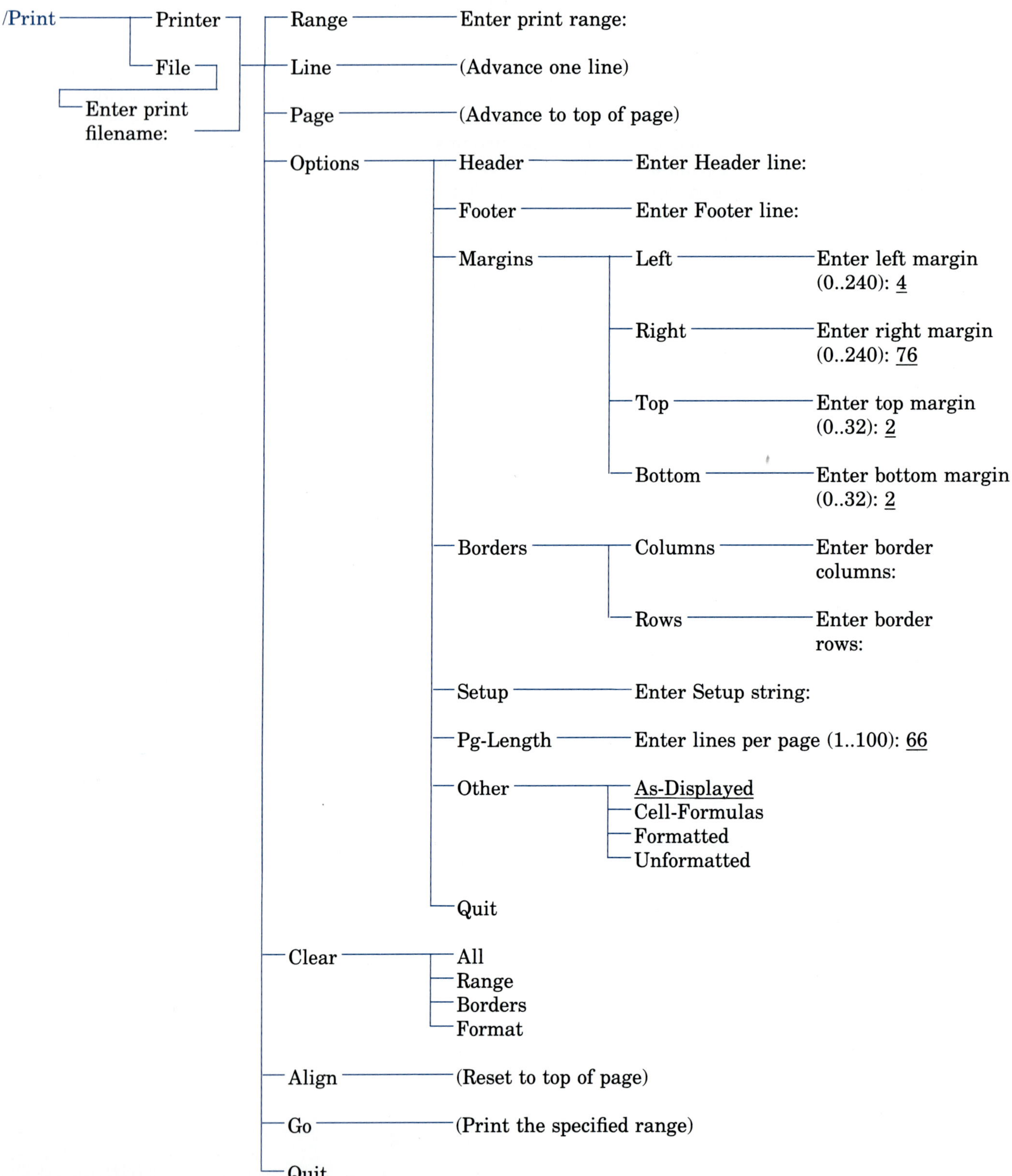

Command	Description
/**P**rint **P**rinter **R**ange	Defines the range of the current spreadsheet to be printed. If print range previously has been defined, it will be displayed and may be undefined by using the Esc or Backspace key. When the /**P**rint,**P**rinter,**G**o command is given, the currently defined range is printed.
/**P**rint **P**rinter **L**ine **P**age	**L**ine advances the paper in the printer one line. **P**age advances paper to the top of the next page. After printing, paper will not advance to the top of next page unless **P**age is selected.
/**P**rint **P**rinter **O**ptions **H**eader **F**ooter **M**argins **B**orders **S**etup **P**age-Length **O**ther **Q**uit	**O**ptions is used to set various print parameters. **H**eaders and **F**ooters (top and bottom page labels) may be added to each page of printed output. **M**argins may be adjusted from their default settings. **B**orders for each page of printed output may be specified as particular columns or rows from within the spreadsheet. Printer control codes used to invoke such options as condensed printing and line spacing may be sent to the printer through the **S**etup command. **P**age-Length also may be adjusted. The **O**ther command allows the spreadsheet's cell-formulas and labels to be printed one per line, which is useful for hard-copy documentation of a spreadsheet.
/**P**rint **P**rinter **C**lear **A**ll **R**ange **B**orders **F**ormat	Clears defined print settings or returns them to their default values. Options to **C**lear are **A**ll, **R**ange, **B**orders, and **F**ormat. **R**ange clears only the print range setting. **B**orders clears border columns and rows. **F**ormat returns margins, page length, and setup string to their default values. **A**ll clears the **R**ange, **B**orders, and **F**ormat.
/**P**rint **P**rinter **A**lign	**A**lign is selected to define the current printer position as the top of a page. Adjust paper in printer, and then select **A**lign.
/**P**rint **P**rinter **G**o	Begins printing of the spreadsheet. Before issuing the **G**o command, the print range must be defined. To assure proper pagination, use the **A**lign command to reset the top of page before printing.
/**P**rint **F**ile	Printing to a **F**ile uses the same commands as printing to the **P**rinter. In this case, however, all output is sent to a text file. Unless otherwise specified, the file is given the Lotus extension .PRN. .PRN files may be printed at a later time using other software or may be used to transfer spreadsheet data to other applications software.

/GRAPH COMMANDS

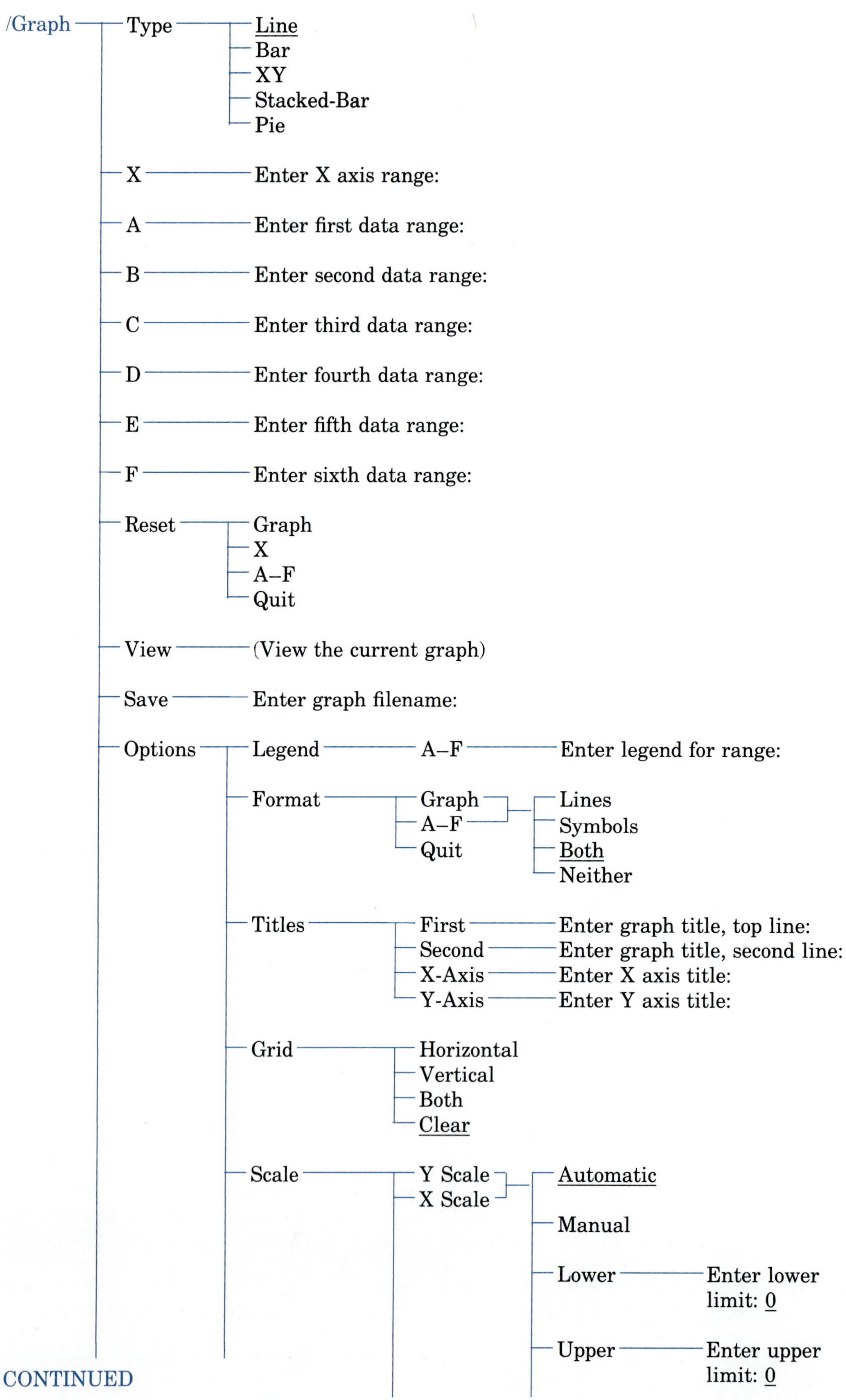
/Graph
Type
Line
Bar
XY
Stacked-Bar
Pie
X
Enter X axis range:
A
Enter first data range:
B
Enter second data range:
C
Enter third data range:
D
Enter fourth data range:
E
Enter fifth data range:
F
Enter sixth data range:
Reset
Graph
X
A–F
Quit
View
(View the current graph)
Save
Enter graph filename:
Options
Legend
A–F
Enter legend for range:
Format
Graph
A–F
Quit
Lines
Symbols
Both
Neither
Titles
First
Enter graph title, top line:
Second
Enter graph title, second line:
X-Axis
Enter X axis title:
Y-Axis
Enter Y axis title:
Grid
Horizontal
Vertical
Both
Clear
Scale
Y Scale
X Scale
Automatic
Manual
Lower
Enter lower limit: 0
Upper
Enter upper limit: 0

CONTINUED

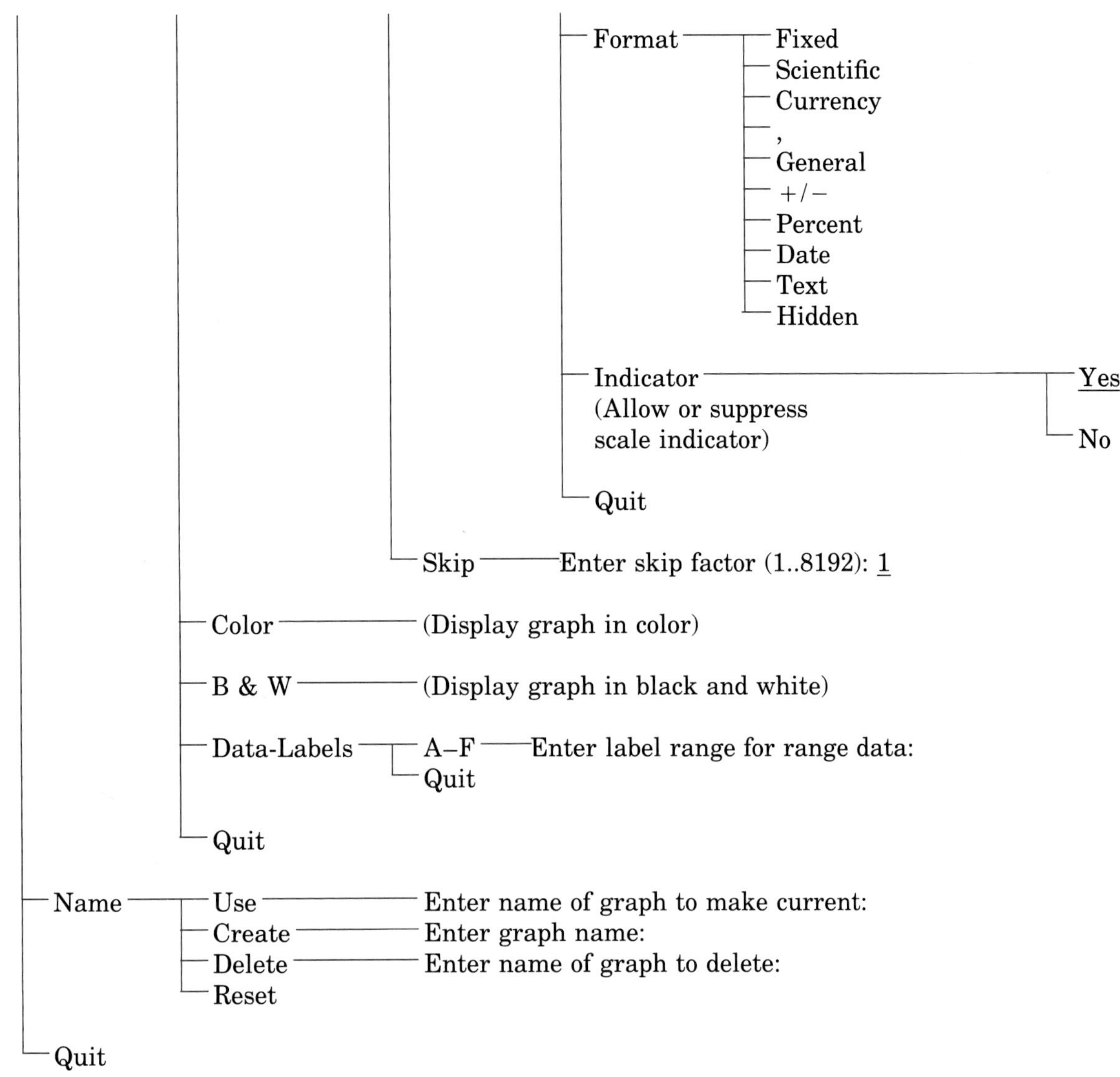

/**G**raph **T**ype **L**ine **B**ar **XY** **S**tacked-Bar **P**ie	Selects one of the five graph types: **L**ine graph, **B**ar graph, **XY** graph, **S**tacked-Bar graph, or **P**ie chart. Each type requires certain definitions of the spreadsheet data ranges to be used in creating the graph. The **B**ar, **S**tacked-Bar, and **L**ine graphs all require at least one data range to graph, and will accept up to six data ranges. These ranges are identified as the /Graph data ranges **A–F**. An **X** range may also be defined. Values or labels in the **X** range appear as labels on the graph's X axis. Only the **A** data range is required to create a **P**ie chart, but the **B** data range and **X** range also may be defined. If defined, the **B** data range is used to determine coloring or shading patterns for the slices of the pie, and the **X** range is used to label the slices of the pie. The **XY** graph is somewhat different than any of the other graph types in that the **X** range must hold values. These values are scaled and placed along the X axis. Up to six data ranges (**A–F**) may be used, and at least one is required.
/**G**raph **X**	Sets the **X** range values for the **XY** graph, and also sets labels for all other graph types.

/Graph **A–F**	Sets each of the six data ranges to be graphed.
/Graph **R**eset **G**raph **X** **A–F** **Q**uit	Cancels some or all of the currently defined graph settings. To cancel all, select **G**raph. Selecting each setting individually will cancel only that setting. Select **Q**uit when finished cancelling settings.
/Graph **V**iew	Displays the currently defined graph on the monitor screen. If the appropriate data ranges for the graph have not been defined, the screen may be blank. Pressing any key will return the display of the spreadsheet with the /**G**raph commands as the current menu.
/Graph **S**ave	Saves the current graph in a file on the diskette (.PIC) to be printed later with the Lotus PrintGraph program.
/Graph **O**ptions **L**egend **F**ormat **T**itles **G**rid **S**cale **C**olor **B**&W **D**ata-Labels **Q**uit	Sets a number of options to enhance the display of the graph. **O**ptions include adding the following to a graph: a **L**egend to identify the data ranges; a **F**ormat for **L**ine and **XY**-type graphs; **T**itles for the graph and its X and Y axes; horizontal and/or vertical **G**rid lines; and data range **D**ata-Labels. The **S**cale option may be used to change the scale used on the X and Y axes and to set a format for the numeric values displayed on the axes. **C**olor or **B&W** (Black and White) may be selected for screen display of the graph. When done setting **O**ptions for the graph, select **Q**uit.
/Graph **N**ame **U**se **C**reate **D**elete **R**eset	This command, which is similar to using range names, allows you to give the current graph settings a name. **C**reate is used to name the settings. Selecting **U**se and entering a graph name will cause the named graph to become the current graph. **D**elete is used to delete a single graph name and **R**eset deletes all graph names. Named graph settings are saved along with the spreadsheet file.

/DATA COMMANDS

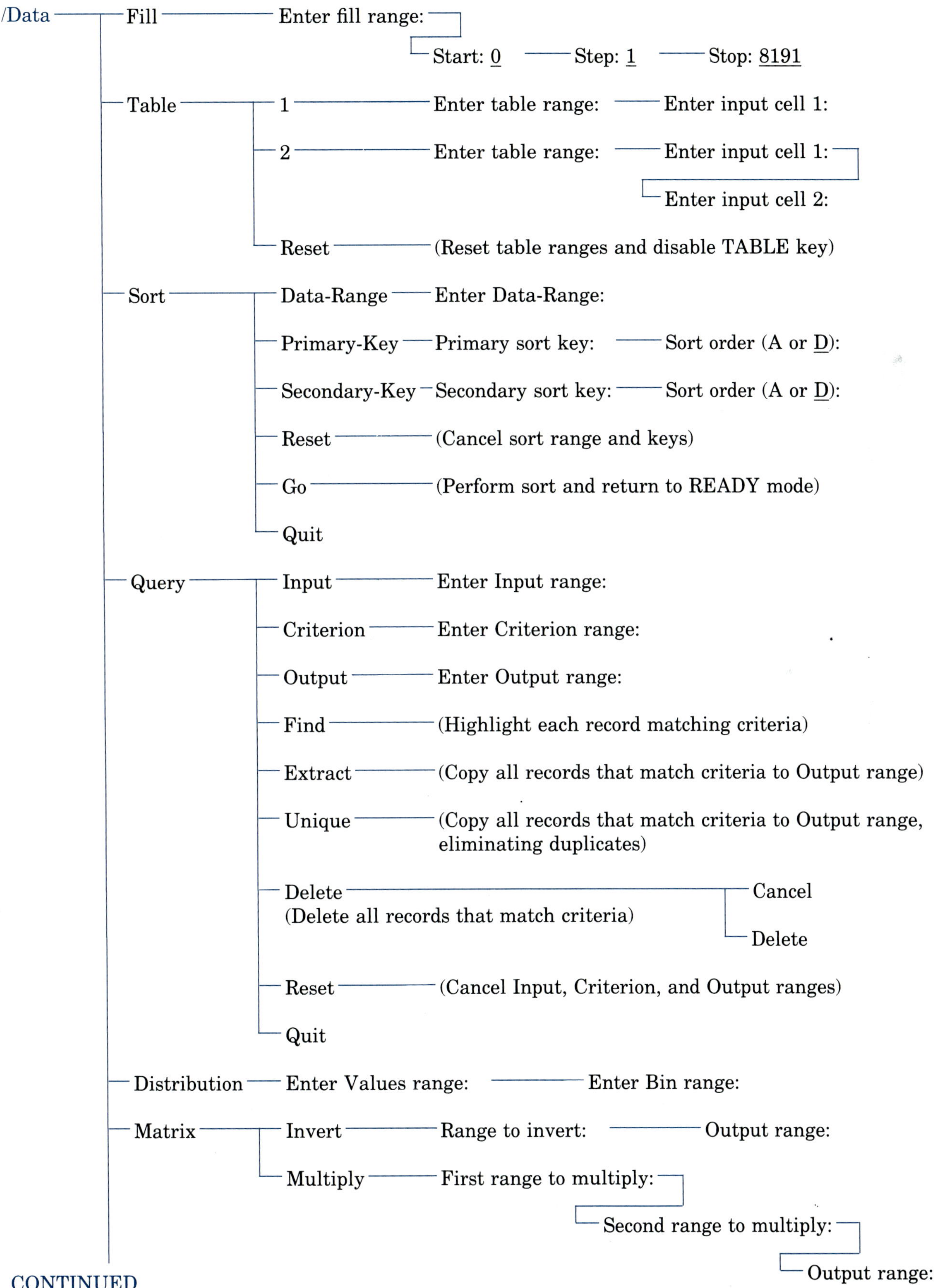

CONTINUED

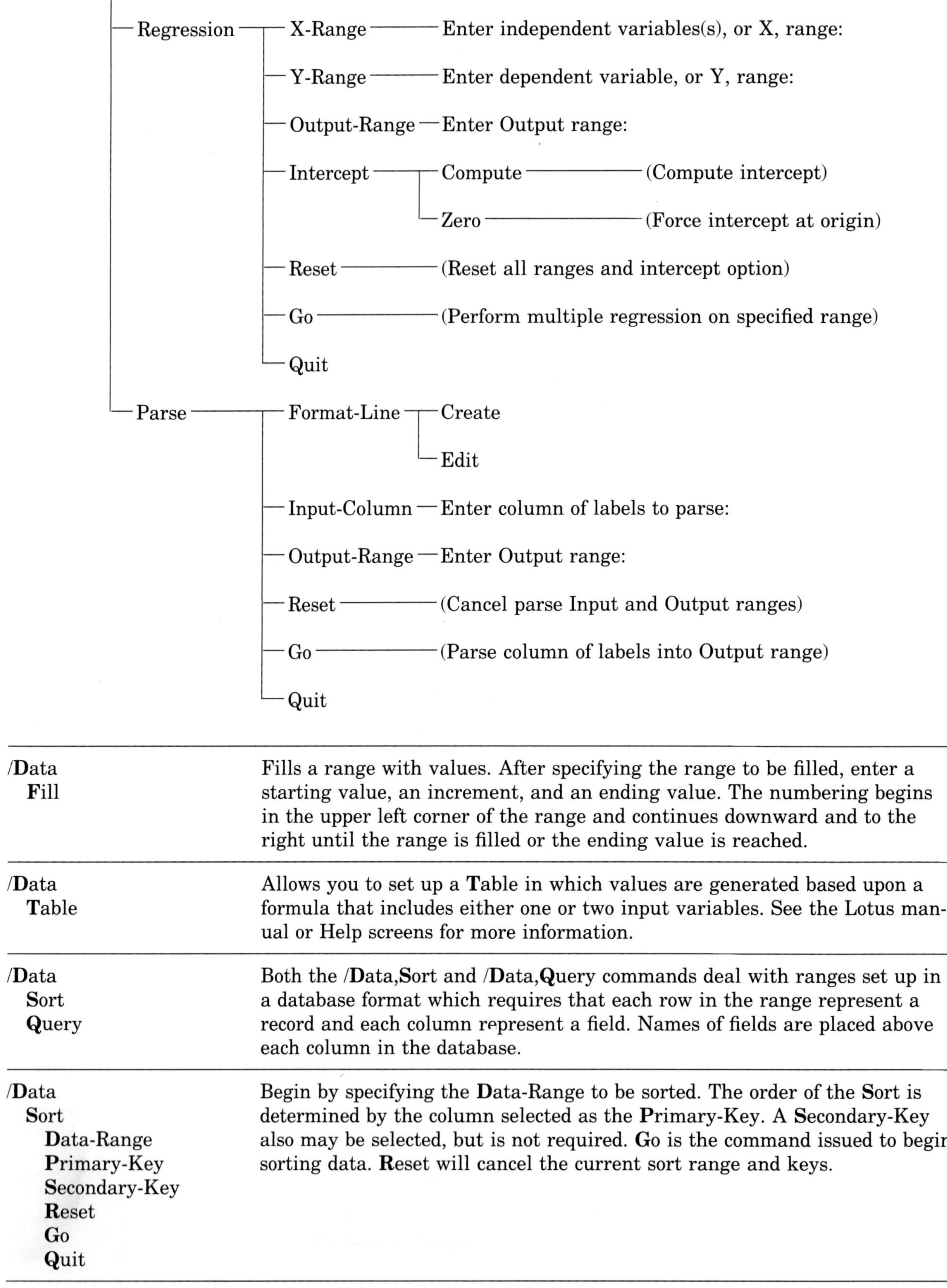

/**D**ata **F**ill	Fills a range with values. After specifying the range to be filled, enter a starting value, an increment, and an ending value. The numbering begins in the upper left corner of the range and continues downward and to the right until the range is filled or the ending value is reached.
/**D**ata **T**able	Allows you to set up a **T**able in which values are generated based upon a formula that includes either one or two input variables. See the Lotus manual or Help screens for more information.
/**D**ata **S**ort **Q**uery	Both the /**D**ata,**S**ort and /**D**ata,**Q**uery commands deal with ranges set up in a database format which requires that each row in the range represent a record and each column represent a field. Names of fields are placed above each column in the database.
/**D**ata **S**ort **D**ata-Range **P**rimary-Key **S**econdary-Key **R**eset **G**o **Q**uit	Begin by specifying the **D**ata-Range to be sorted. The order of the **S**ort is determined by the column selected as the **P**rimary-Key. A **S**econdary-Key also may be selected, but is not required. **G**o is the command issued to begin sorting data. **R**eset will cancel the current sort range and keys.

/**D**ata **Q**uery **I**nput **C**riterion **O**utput **F**ind **E**xtract **U**nique **D**elete **R**eset **Q**uit	This command is used to search a database range for records meeting given criteria. Records found in the search may be highlighted (**F**ind), copied to another area of the spreadsheet (**E**xtract and **U**nique), or deleted from the spreadsheet (**D**elete). **D**elete and **F**ind require only **I**nput and **C**riterion range specifications. **E**xtract and **U**nique require specification of an **O**utput range as well. The field names at the top of each column must be included in these ranges. **R**eset cancels the **I**nput, **C**riterion, and **O**utput range specifications.
/**D**ata **D**istribution	Calculates a frequency distribution for the values in a specified range.
/**D**ata **M**atrix **I**nvert **M**ultiply	Multiplies or inverts matrices and copies resulting matrix into another portion of the spreadsheet. Matrices have a maximum size of 90 by 90. **I**nvert converts matrix to its inverse. The matrix to be inverted must be a square matrix. **M**ultiply is used to multiply two matrices, resulting in a product matrix. The number of columns in the first range and the number of rows in the second range must be equal. Locate the Output range in an empty portion of the spreadsheet if you do not want the values to replace existing data in your spreadsheet.
/**D**ata **R**egression **X**-Range **Y**-Range **O**utput-Range **I**ntercept **C**ompute **Z**ero **R**eset **G**o **Q**uit	Determines the relationship between a set of dependent variables and one or more sets of independent variables. The **X**-Range is used to specify the range of independent variables. Data in the **X**-Range must be arranged in columns and a maximum of 16 independent variables may be specified. The **Y**-Range is used to specify the range of the dependent variable. Data in the **Y**-Range must be arranged in a single column. The number of rows in the X and Y ranges must be equal. The **O**utput-Range specifies where the results of the regression analysis will be placed. Locate the **O**utput-Range in an empty portion of the spreadsheet if you do not want the information to replace existing data in your spreadsheet. **I**ntercept is used to calculate the intercept as a constant or to set the intercept at zero. **C**ompute is the default setting. **R**eset cancels all ranges and the zero intercept option. **G**o calculates the regression results and copies them to the **O**utput-Range. The results of a regression analysis are Constant Std Err of Y Est R Squared No. of Observations Degrees of Freedom X Coefficients Std Err of Coef.

/**D**ata
  Parse
    Format-Line
      Create
      Edit
    Input-Column
    Output-Range
    Reset
    Go
    Quit

Converts an imported ASCII text file into standard spreadsheet format by treating the text as a column of long labels and entering them into a single column of the spreadsheet which overflows into the adjacent columns. The data then may be parsed or decoded into individual cell entries.

Format-Line determines the decoding pattern for rows of labels below it and how that data will be parsed into cells. Format symbols are

L first character of block = label
V first character of block = value
D first character of block = date
T first character of block = time
S skip the character for parse
> continuation of block
* undefined or blank space, may be used as wild card

Input-Column is used to specify the column of labels to be parsed plus the **F**ormat-Line. **O**utput-Range is used to specify the area in the spreadsheet where the parsed data will be copied (this may include the **I**nput-Column range or be a separate portion of the spreadsheet).

Reset cancels **I**nput-Column and **O**utput-Range settings. **G**o parses the data and copies the results to **O**utput-Range. Before parsing data, be sure the columns in the **O**utput-Range are wide enough to hold the entire block. Otherwise, the incoming data may be truncated.

/SYSTEM AND /QUIT COMMANDS

/System ———— (Type EXIT and press [RETURN] to return to Lotus)

/Quit ——┬— No ———— (Do not end 1-2-3 session; return to READY mode)
        └— Yes ———— (End 1-2-3 session; remember to save your worksheet first)

/**S**ystem	Allows you to temporarily access the DOS level of operation while leaving the Lotus spreadsheet software in memory. At the DOS level, type EXIT to return to the spreadsheet.
/**Q**uit **N**o **Y**es	Exits the Lotus spreadsheet software and removes it from memory, returning to the Lotus Access Menu or to the DOS level of operation. **Y**es must be selected to complete the command. If you have not saved your work, you may select **N**o and then use the /**F**ile,**S**ave command before exiting.

LOTUS 1-2-3 SPREADSHEET FUNCTIONS

@@(cell address) When the cell address argument specifies a cell containing a label which, in turn, is another cell's address (e.g., A1), the function returns the contents of the cell referenced by the label. For example, if cell A1 = 15 and cell B2 = "A1", then @@(B2) returns 15.

@**ABS**(value) Returns the absolute value.

@**ACOS**(value) Returns the arc cosine.

@**ASIN**(value) Returns the arc sine.

@**ATAN**(value) Returns the arc tangent.

@**ATAN2**(value1,value2) Returns the 4-quadrant arc tangent.

@**AVG**(list) Returns the average value of all cells in the specified list.

@**CELL**(attribute, range) Returns the specified attribute of the cell in the upper left corner of the specified range. The attribute to be returned by the function may be specified as "address," "row," "col," "contents," "type," "prefix," "protect," "width," or "format." The result of the function is updated only when the spreadsheet is recalculated either automatically or by pressing the CALC (F9) key.

@**CELLPOINTER**(attribute) Returns the specified attribute of the cell in which the pointer is located. @**CELLPOINTER** functions will only display new values when the spreadsheet is recalculated either automatically or by pressing the CALC (F9) key.

@**CHAR**(value) Returns the corresponding ASCII character. The value argument must be between 1 and 255 or the function will return ERR.

@**CHOOSE**(valueX,value0,value1,value2, . . . valueN) Returns one value from a list of possible values based on the index (valueX). If valueX = 0, then value0 is returned; if valueX = 1, value1 is returned, and so forth. If valueX is not within the range of choices (value1..valueN), the function will return ERR.

@**CLEAN**(string) Removes nonprintable characters from strings imported with the /**F**ile,**I**mport command.

@**CODE**(string) Returns a number representing the ASCII value of the first character in the string. If the argument is an empty cell or a cell containing a value, @**CODE** will return ERR.

@**COLS**(range) Returns the number of columns in a range.

@**COS**(value) Returns the cosine.

@**COUNT**(list) Returns the number of nonblank cells in the specified list.

@**CTERM**(int,fv,pv) Returns the number of periods needed for a present value investment (pv) to grow to a specified future value (fv) at a given periodic interest rate (int).

@DATE(year,month,day) Returns the serial number representing the date specified by the three arguments year, month, and day. For example, **@DATE**(90,12,25) = 33232. When formatted with the date format D1, this number displays as 25-Dec-90.

@DATEVALUE(date string) Returns the serial number representing the date of the date string argument. The date string must conform to one of the five date formats:

(D1) DD-MMM-YY	12-Dec-90
(D2) DD-MMM	12-Dec
(D3) MMM-YY	Dec-90
(D4) Long Intn'l	(as currently configured)
(D5) Short Intn'l	(as currently configured)

@DAY(serial date value) Returns the day of the month (1-31) for a serial date value.

@DDB(cost,salvage,life,period) Returns the calculated depreciation on an asset using the double-declining balance method.

@ERR Returns ERR (error).

@EXACT(string1,string2) Compares two strings to test if the strings are exactly the same. Returns 1 (true) if the strings match exactly. Returns 0 (false) if the strings do not match exactly.

@EXP(value) Returns the exponential.

@FALSE Returns the value 0 (false).

@FIND(string1,string2,n) Returns the location of stringl (substring) in string2, with the search beginning at the *n*th position of string2. The first character of string2 is considered position 0.

@FV(pmt,int,n) Returns the future value of a stream of annuity payments (pmt) at a periodic interest rate (int) over a specified number of periods (n).

@HLOOKUP(valueX,range,offset) Returns the contents of some cell in a table. The location of the table is specified by the range argument. The column of the lookup cell is determined by comparing the valueX argument to ascending values found in the top row of the table. The row of the lookup cell is determined by the offset argument, which specifies some number of rows below the top row of the table.

@HOUR(serial date/time value) Returns the hour value (0–23) from the fractional portion (time value) of a serial date value.

@IF(condition, true value,false value) Returns one of two values, the true value if the condition tests true, the false value if the condition tests false.

@INDEX(range,column,row) Returns the contents of the cell found in the specified range at the intersection of the column and row arguments specified. The first column is considered column 0 and the first row is considered row 0. If the column or row specified does not fall within the specified range, the function will return ERR.

@INT(value) Returns the integer portion of a value.

@IRR(guess,range) Returns the approximate internal rate of return for a range of cash flows, given the help of a guess to start the computation.

@ISERR(cell address) Returns 1 (true) if the cell specified by the cell address argument contains ERR; otherwise, returns 0 (false).

@ISNA(cell address) Returns 1 (true) if the cell specified by the cell address argument contains NA; otherwise, returns 0 (false).

@ISNUMBER(cell address) Returns 1 (true) if the cell specified by the cell address argument contains a numeric value or is empty; otherwise, returns 0 (false).

@ISSTRING(cell address) Returns 1 (true) if the cell specified by the cell address argument contains a label (string); otherwise, returns 0 (false).

@LEFT(string,n) Returns the left-most n characters in a string.

@LENGTH(string) Returns the number of characters in a string.

@LN(value) Returns the log base e.

@LOG(value) Returns the log base 10.

@LOWER(string) Returns the same string, with all letters converted to lower case.

@MAX(list) Returns the highest single value found in the specified list.

@MID(string,start,n) Returns an extracted substring from a larger string. The start argument determines the position in the string where the substring is to begin (the first character is position 0), and the n argument determines the length of the substring.

@MIN(list) Returns the lowest single value found in the specified list.

@MINUTE(serial date/time value) Returns the minute (0–59) value from the fractional portion (time value) of a serial date value.

@MOD(value,modulo) Returns the remainder of a division operation. The value is divided by the modulo and the function returns the remainder (the modulus).

@MONTH(serial date value) Returns the month number (1–12) for a serial date value.

@N(range) Returns the value of a number or a formula found in the top left cell of the specified range. If the cell is empty or contains a label, @**N** returns the value 0. @**N** always returns a numeric value.

@NA Returns NA (not available).

@NOW Returns the current date and time as a serial date/time value.

@NPV(rate,range) Returns the net present value of a stream of cash flows at a given discount rate.

@PI Returns pi (3.141592653589794).

@PMT(pv,int,n) Returns the amount of a stream of annuity payments given a present value investment (pv), an interest rate (int), and the number of periods (n).

@PROPER(string) Returns the same string, with all first letters of words converted to upper case and subsequent letters converted to lower case.

@PV(pmt,int,n) Returns the present value of a stream of equal annuity payments (pmt) for a given number of periods (n) at a given periodic interest rate (int).

@RAND Generates a random number. The function has no argument and the value returned changes each time the spreadsheet is recalculated.

@RATE(fv,pv,n) Returns the required rate of interest for a present value investment (pv) to grow to a specified future value (fv) in a given number of periods (n).

@REPEAT(string,n) Returns a string with the specified string argument repeated n times.

@REPLACE(string1,start,n,string2) Returns a string in which a certain portion of string1 has been replaced by string2. The start argument specifies the position in string1 to begin the replacement (first position is 0), and the n argument determines how many characters will be replaced in string1.

@RIGHT(string,n) Returns the right-most n characters in a string.

@ROUND(value,places) Returns the value rounded to the specified number of decimal places.

@ROWS(range) Returns the number of rows in a range.

@S(range) Returns the string value of the top left cell of the range. If the cell is empty or contains a numeric value, @**S** returns an empty (null) string. @**S** always returns a string value.

@SECOND(serial date/time value) Returns the seconds (0–59) from the fractional portion (time value) of a serial date value.

@SIN(value) Returns the sine.

@SLN(cost,salvage,life) Returns the depreciation on an asset for a single period using the straight-line method.

@SQRT(value) Returns the square root of the value.

@STD(list) Returns the standard deviation from the mean for the nonblank cells in the specified list.

@STRING(n,decimals) Returns the string of a numeric value n, rounded to the number of places specified by the decimals argument.

@SUM(list) Returns the sum of all cells in the specified list.

@SYD(cost,salvage,life,period) Returns the depreciation on an asset for a specified period using the sum-of-the-years'-digits method.

@TAN(value) Returns the tangent.

@TERM(pmt,int,fv) Returns the number of periods required for a stream of annuity payments (pmt) to grow to a given future value (fv) at a given interest rate (int).

@TIME(hr,min,sec) Returns the fractional portion (time value) of a serial date value for the specified hour, minute, and second value arguments.

@TIMEVALUE(time string) Returns the fractional portion (time value) for a time string that is in a valid Lotus time format.

@TODAY Returns **@INT**(**@NOW**), the integer portion of the function **@NOW**.

@TRIM(string) Removes trailing spaces from a string. Will change the value returned by the **@LENGTH** function.

@TRUE Returns the value 1 (true).

@UPPER(string) Returns the same string, with all letters converted to upper case.

@VALUE(string) Returns a numeric value from a number that has been entered as a label or string value. The string may contain only number characters (0–9), a currency sign ($), thousand's separators (,), a decimal indicator (.), and leading or trailing spaces; otherwise, the function will return ERR.

@VAR(list) Returns the variance of the values for the nonblank cells in the specified list.

@VLOOKUP(valueX,range,offset) Returns the contents of some cell in a table. The location of the table is specified by the range argument. The row of the lookup cell is determined by comparing the valueX argument to ascending values found in the left-most column of the table. The column of the lookup cell is determined by the offset argument, which specifies some number of columns to the right of the left-most column of the table.

@YEAR(serial date value) Returns the year for a serial date value.

LOTUS 1-2-3 MACRO COMMANDS QUICK REFERENCE

Macro Keyboard Equivalent Commands

Command	Keyboard Equivalent
Function Keys	
{EDIT}	F2
{NAME}	F3
{ABS}	F4
{GOTO}	F5
{WINDOW}	F6
{QUERY}	F7
{TABLE}	F8
{CALC}	F9
{GRAPH}	F10
Pointer Movement Keys	
{UP}	↑
{DOWN}	↓
{LEFT}	←
{RIGHT}	→
{PGUP}	PgUp
{PGDN}	PgDn
{BIGLEFT}	Shift-Tab
{BIGRIGHT}	Tab
{HOME}	Home
{END}	End
Editing Keys	
{DEL} or {DELETE}	Del
{ESC} or {ESCAPE}	Esc
{BS} or {BACKSPACE}	Backspace key
~	Enter key ↵
{~}	Tilde character
{ { } and { } }	Brace characters

Macro Programming Commands

Macros may be used to develop programs or routines that will be used repeatedly, or to accomplish tasks that are program-like in nature. The following are the most commonly used commands for controlling program flow in a macro. For those with a knowledge of BASIC programming, the equivalent BASIC commands are shown as a reference.

Lotus Macro Command	BASIC Equivalent
{**IF** condition}	**IF...THEN**
{**BRANCH** range}	**GOTO**
{routine-name}	**GOSUB**
{**RETURN**}	**RETURN**
{**QUIT**}	**END**
{**GETLABEL** message,range}~	**INPUT** "prompt" A$
{**GETNUMBER** message,range}~	**INPUT** "prompt" A
{**MENUBRANCH** range}	none

Additional Macro Commands

Controlling Output

{**BEEP**}	Causes computer to sound a beep.
{**INDICATE** string}	Changes the mode indicator in the upper right corner to display the specified string (up to five characters only). A cell reference or range may not be used. To return to standard mode indicators, use {**INDICATE**}. To remove display of indicator mode, use {**INDICATE** ""}.
{**PANELOFF**}	Used to suppress output of the window lines (top 3 lines) to speed up execution of a macro.
{**PANELON**}	Restores the output of the window lines during macro execution.
{**WINDOWSOFF**}	Used to suppress output of the spreadsheet display to speed up execution of a macro and decrease user confusion.
{**WINDOWSON**}	Restores the output of the spreadsheet during macro execution.

Controlling Program Flow

{**BRANCH** range}	Passes control of macro execution to commands located in the specified range. Equivalent to BASIC's **GOTO** or **GO TO** command.
{**DEFINE** argument1:type, argument2:type, . . . argument N:type}	{**DEFINE**} is the first command in a subroutine that is to be called with arguments. The {**DEFINE**} command specifies where and how to store data being passed. Arguments 1 through N are cell references for the cells in which the passed values will be stored. Type refers to how Lotus will treat the cell contents, either as a **VALUE** or a **STRING**. Default type is **STRING**. When using **VALUE** as the type, a string, invalid number, or invalid formula will result in an error.
{**DISPATCH** location}	Indirect branch command. Will pass control to a destination contained in the location cell. When using a range name as the specified location, the named range must contain only one cell. {**DISPATCH**} works in essentially

	the same manner as BASIC's **GO TO** command when using a variable to specify the program line number (i.e., **GO TO** *n*).
{**FOR** counter-location, start-number,stop-number, step-number, start-location}	Controls looping process. Counter-location is where the value being incremented is stored. Start-location is the cell containing the first command of the macro subroutine containing the loop commands. Start, stop, and step numbers determine the number of executions in the loop. {**FOR**} is the macro equivalent to BASIC's **FOR/NEXT** loop structure.
{**FORBREAK**}	Interrupts the current {**FOR**} loop and continues execution of the macro with the command following the {**FOR**} command. {**FORBREAK**} may be used only in a subroutine called by a {**FOR**} command.
{**IF** condition} true command	Executes the commands on the same line and following the {**IF**} command if the condition evaluates as true. Equivalent to BASIC's **IF THEN** command.
{**ONERROR** branch-location, message-location}	If an error occurs during macro execution, control is passed to the specified branch location, and the optional error message is displayed in the message location cell. The {**ONERROR**} command should be located above the most likely place for the error to occur. Only one {**ONERROR**} command is in effect at one time. {**ONERROR**} will be activated if the CTRL-BREAK keys are pressed unless the {**BREAKOFF**} command has been executed.
{**QUIT**}	Ends macro execution and returns to READY mode.
{**RESTART**}	Used only in subroutines. When {**RESTART**} is encountered, the subroutine stack is eliminated. The subsequent commands in the current subroutine will be executed; however, when the {**RETURN**} command is encountered, instead of returning control to the calling routine, macro execution ends.
{**RETURN**}	Used in subroutines called with {routine-name} and {**MENUCALL**} commands. Returns control to the calling routine, beginning with the command immediately after the command that called the subroutine.
{routine-name}	Passes control to macro commands found in the named range specified as routine-name (subroutine). Control will be passed back to calling routine when {**RETURN**} command is encountered in subroutine. If subroutine begins with {**DEFINE**} command, the {routine-name} command must include argument specifications following the range name.

{**BREAKOFF**}	Disables the CTRL-BREAK key combination, preventing the user from being able to interrupt macro execution before its completion.
{**BREAKON**}	Reenables use of the CTRL-BREAK key combination to interrupt macro execution.
{**GET** location}	Pauses during macro execution to allow a single keystroke entry, and stores that entry in the specified location. The single keystroke may be any standard keyboard character, a Lotus function key, or pointer control key. {**GET**} does not provide for a control panel prompt. An alternative command is {**?**}.
{**GETLABEL** message, range}	Displays the message on the second window line, pauses for a user entry, and stores the entry as a label in the cell specified by range.
{**GETNUMBER** message,range}	Displays the message on the second window line, pauses for a user entry, and stores the entry as a number in the cell specified by range. If the entry is not a valid numeric entry, ERR will appear in the cell specified by range.
{**LOOK** location}	Allows test of the type-ahead buffer to see if any characters have been typed during macro execution. Any characters in the buffer are copied into the specified location. Macro execution is not suspended. Characters are left in the buffer for use in the {**GET**}, {**GETLABEL**}, or {**GETNUMBER**} commands.
{**MENUBRANCH** range} and {**MENUCALL** range}	Pass macro execution to macro menu commands located in specified range. After user makes menu selection, the appropriate commands as defined in the menu will be executed. After all commands for a menu selection have been executed, control will pass back to the command following {**MENUCALL**} in the calling routine if {**MENUCALL**} was used. If {**MENUBRANCH**} was used, macro execution will end unless control is passed explicitly to another routine by a {**BRANCH**} command. If Esc is passed instead of making a menu selection, control passes back to the calling routine, regardless of which command was used to call the menu. {**MENUBRANCH**} and {**MENUCALL**} override the {**PANELOFF**} command.
{**WAIT** serial date/time value}	Interrupts execution of the macro, displays the **WAIT** indicator until the specified time, and then continues with the macro execution. The serial date/time value must contain both the date (integer portion) and time (decimal portion). CTRL-BREAK will interrupt the {**WAIT**} command unless the {**BREAKOFF**} command has been executed.

{**BLANK** range}	Erases cell contents in the specified range. Performs the same function as the /**R**ange,**E**rase command. Format and protection settings are unaffected.
{**CONTENTS** destination, source,width, format-code}	Copies string or numeric data from the source cell, converts in to string data, and enters it into the destination cell. If the specified destination or source location is a range, only the upper left cell of the range will be used. The optional width number causes Lotus to treat the source cell as if it had the specified column width, but does not actually change the column width. The optional format number causes Lotus to treat the source cell as if it had the corresponding format, but does not actually change the source cell's format. As a result, the destination cell may contain a left-aligned label that looks like a number having a different format and width than the numeric data contained in the source cell. The following table describes the various format codes available.

Code	Format	Decimals
0–15	Fixed	0–15
16–32	Scientific	0–15
33–47	Currency	0–15
48–63	Percentage	0–15
64–79	Comma	0–15
112	+/− Bar Graph	
113	General	
114	D1 (DD-MMM-YY)	
115	D2 (DD-MMM)	
116	D3 (MMM-YY)	
121	D4 (Long Intn'l)	
122	D5 (Short Intn'l)	
119	D6 (HH:MM:SS AM/PM)	
120	D7 (HH:MM AM/PM)	
123	D8 (Long Intn'l)	
124	D9 (Short Intn'l)	
117	Text Format	
118	Hidden Format	
127	Current Default Format	

{**LET** location:**VALUE**} and {**LET** location:**STRING**}	Stores an entry in a specified cell. If the specified location is a range name, only the upper left cell is used. **VALUE** or **STRING** determines the type of data that will be accepted into the location cell.

Command	Description
{**PUT** range,column-number, row-number,**NUMBER**} *and* {**PUT** range,column-number, row-number,**STRING**}	Stores an entry in a location that is specified by a row and column offset in the range. If the specified location is a single cell, an error will result unless row-number and column-number are specified as 0. A column or row number located outside the range results in an error that cannot be trapped with the {**ONERROR**} command. **NUMBER** or **STRING** determines the type of data that will be accepted into the location cell.
{**RECALCCOL** range,condition, iteration-number}	Recalculates the formulas in the specified range by columns. The optional condition will cause the range to be recalculated until the condition is true. The condition must be a logical expression or reference a cell in the range which contains a logical expression. The optional iteration argument specifies the number of recalculations performed on the range. Recalculations will be repeated until the condition is true or the iteration count is reached, whichever occurs first. The {**CALC**} command recalculates the entire spreadsheet. Use {**CALC**} at the end of a macro using {**RECALC**} to be sure that the current data is accurate.

Accessing Files

Command	Description
{**CLOSE**}	Closes a currently open file. If no file is open, the {**CLOSE**} command will be ignored and the next command in the macro will be executed. {**CLOSE**} should always be used before completion of a macro in which the {**OPEN**} command was used.
{**FILESIZE** location}	Determines the length of the currently open file in bytes and displays the value in the specified cell location. If no file is open, the {**FILESIZE**} command will be ignored.
{**GETPOS** range}	Records file pointer position in currently open file and displays the value in the upper left cell of the range. The first position in a file is 0. If no file is open, the {**GETPOS**} command will be ignored.
{**OPEN** filename, access-mode}	Opens an external file to read, write, or both. The filename specification must be a string that is a valid DOS filename (specification may include a path) or a cell containing a valid file specification string. The access-mode is a single character that specifies the type of file access. **R** Read only access to existing file. Use the {**READ**} and {**READLN**} commands. **W** Opens new file to access with {**WRITE**} and {**WRITELN**} commands. An existing

file with the same filename will be erased and replaced with the new file.

M Opens existing file for read/write access. Allows {**READ**}, {**READLN**}, {**WRITE**}, and {**WRITELN**} commands to be used.

{**READ** byte-count,range}

Reads a specified number of characters from the currently open file, beginning with the current file pointer location. The characters then are displayed as a long label in the first cell of the specified range. {**READ**} copies characters from a file to the spreadsheet. Byte-count must be a number between 0 and 240. {**READ**} should not be used with ASCII text files; use {**READLN**} for ASCII text files.

{**READLN** range}

Reads characters from the currently open file, beginning with the current file pointer location in the file. Characters are read and displayed in the specified range until the end of the line is encountered or 240 characters have been read.

{**SETPOS** file-position}

Sets position of the file pointer in the currently open file. The file-position specifies the number of bytes from the beginning of the file (byte 0). A pointer may inadvertently be set past the end of the file. The {**FILESIZE**} command will help determine the position of the last character in the file. If no file is open, the {**SETPOS**} command will be ignored.

{**WRITE** string}

Copies a string of characters from the spreadsheet to the currently open file, beginning at the current file pointer position, if a file has been opened with the {**OPEN**} command and either the **W**(rite) or **M**(odify) access mode. The string argument may be a string, a cell reference, a named range of a single cell, or an expression evaluating to a string value. {**WRITE**} may be used to concatenate characters on a line. If the file pointer is not at the end of the open file, the existing characters in the file will be overwritten. If the pointer is at the end of the file, the length of the file will be increased by the number of incoming characters. If the pointer is past the end of the file, the file length is increased to the sum of the current file pointer position plus the number of incoming characters.

{**WRITELN** string}

Copies a string of characters from the spreadsheet to the current file pointer location, if a file has been opened with the {**OPEN**} command and either the **W**(rite) or **M**(odify) access mode, adding a carriage return and line feed after the last character in the string. The string argument may be a string, a cell reference, a named range of a single cell, or an expression evaluating to a string value. {**WRITELN**} may be used with an empty string to add a carriage return and line feed to the end of a line in the open file. If the pointer is not at the end of the open file, the existing characters in the file will be overwritten. If the pointer is at the end of the file, the length of the file will be increased by the number of incoming characters. If the pointer is past the end of the file, the file length is increased to the sum of the current file pointer position plus the number of incoming characters.

dBASE III Plus
Version 1.1

INTRODUCTION

dBASE III Plus® is a database management system (DBMS) software, the type of applications software that allows the user to create, maintain, and manipulate records of data. You may use dBASE III Plus commands in two separate ways: you may use one command at a time that dBASE executes in a direct mode as it is entered; or you may use several (a batch of) commands, held in a file that you create, that dBASE will execute as a group when you type the appropriate command.

The following section begins with a brief discussion of dBASE basics and dBASE III Plus file handling. It continues with a set of tutorial lessons that focuses on the fundamentals of using dBASE commands while in the direct mode. In the tutorial lessons you will create a database file of records; learn how to edit, append, and delete records from the database; sort and index records; search for particular records in the database; and produce dBASE reports. The tutorial lessons are followed by an extended discussion about how dBASE commands may be assembled in a file and then executed as a group. Several examples are presented in a step-by-step sequence, presenting new dBASE III Plus commands and concepts, using the database file created in the tutorial lessons. After this, several exercises and cases designed to introduce and reinforce the use of additional dBASE III Plus features, commands and operations are presented. At the end of the module, a dBASE III Plus operation and command summary briefly describes the full range of commands and control key operations available with dBASE III Plus.

DATABASE BASICS

The term *database* describes data organized in a manner that makes it possible to access specific information. In many computer applications, data in a database file are organized in records with fields holding related data items. When the data are arranged in this manner, the database is known as a *relational database*. In the following example, checkbook data are shown arranged as a small relational database file.

2160	03/03/90	Payless Drug Store	13.60	Medicine
2161	03/05/90	Vista Ridge Properties	325.00	Rent
2162	03&05/90	AT&T	13.50	Phone
2163	03/11/90	Albertson's Food	35.15	Grocery
2164	03/15/90	First Federal	160.00	Car payment

In this example, each record contains data on a check written against a personal checking account. The five fields of each record hold a check number, date, payee, amount, and purchase description, respectively.

Record Structure

Before data items such as those shown above can be entered into a database file, the structure of the records for the database must be defined. The record structure describes each field with a field name, the type of data it will hold, and the length of the field measured in characters. Once the record structure has been defined, all records entered or later added to the database file will have the same number of fields with the same lengths, and each field will hold the same type of data for that record.

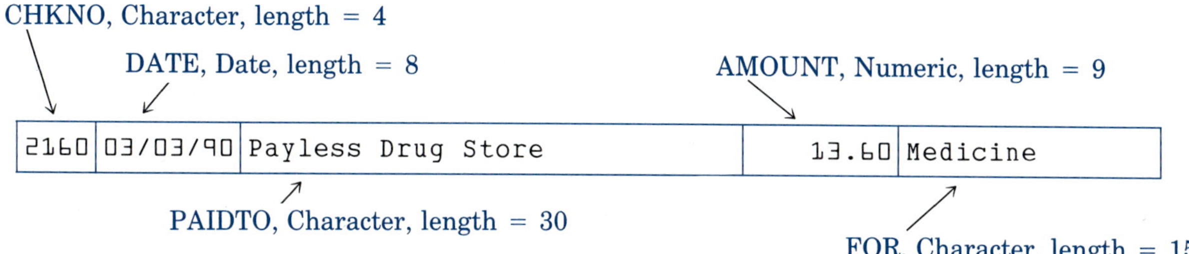

Here each field has been given a name (shown in capitals) and has been described by data type and length.

dBASE III Plus Data Types

In addition to the standard data types, string and numeric, dBASE III Plus allows date and logical data types to be entered into its variables and fields.

Date-Type Data

Date-type data are entered either into record fields whose structures have been prespecified to hold date-type data, or into variables by converting string-type data into date-type data with a dBASE function. All fields or variables holding date-type data are automatically eight characters long, and the default order of date-type data held in them is month/day/year.

03/15/90

Month Day Year

Logical-Type Data

Fields or variables holding logical-type data are automatically one character long. They hold a logical True or a logical False value. These can be directly entered into fields as T, t, Y, or y for True and F, f, N, or n for False, or entered indirectly into fields or variables as .T. or .t. for True and .F. or .f. for False. Once a logical field or variable has had data assigned to it, it may (as a single item) be used as a condition in an expression.

dBASE III Plus Command Structure

Command-Driven Software

dBASE III Plus may be used as either a menu-driven or command-driven software. *Menu-driven software* provide menus of commands from which the user selects. WordPerfect and Lotus 1-2-3 can be described as menu-driven software. *Command-driven software* respond to command words which are typed and entered. DOS, the software covered in appendix A, can be described as a command-driven software. In the following tutorial lessons, you will be given the steps to ensure you are left in dBASE's command mode, the primary use of dBASE III Plus. Entering the command **ASSIST** will put you into dBASE's menu-driven mode. While dBASE III Plus's menu-driven mode may help beginning users learn command syntax, its slow speed and limited uses make dBASE III Plus's command mode preferable.

Using dBASE's command mode requires that you memorize the dBASE command words. Fortunately, consistencies between dBASE commands make them relatively easy to memorize, and they tend to resemble standard

English terminology. For instance, to display all checks written to First Federal in the example database, you could type

DISPLAY ALL FOR paidto = "First Federal"

To display only the amounts of the checks written to First Federal, you could type

DISPLAY ALL amount **FOR** paidto = "First Federal"

dBASE III Plus Editing and Command Modes

Like other software, dBASE allows the direct entry of data while in an editing mode, and access to its commands while in a command mode. Unlike other software, however, dBASE has multiple editing and command modes.

dBASE Command Modes

The Dot (.) Prompt Command Mode

The most common method of entering dBASE commands is while in the dot (.) prompt mode. The dot (.) prompt mode is indicated when a period appears to the left of a cursor at the bottom of the screen.

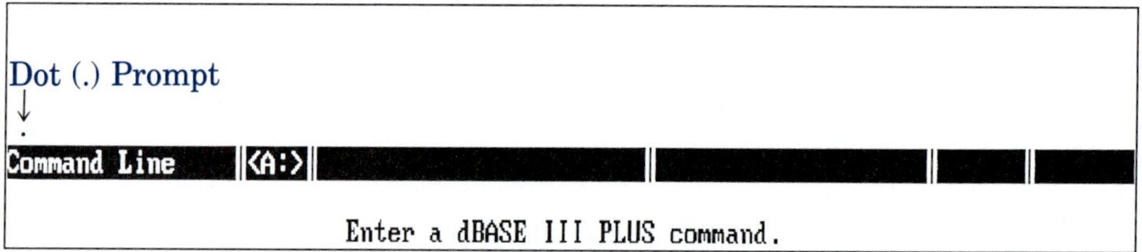

In the dot (.) prompt mode, you type and enter the dBASE command.

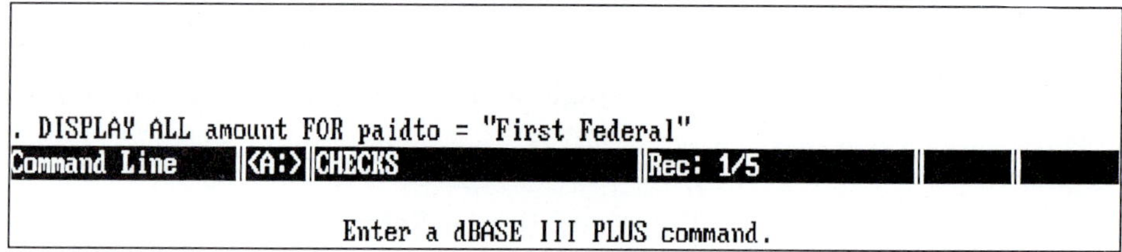

*The **ASSIST** Command Mode*

Another method of entering dBASE commands is through the use of command menus called *pull-down menus*. With such menus, the user moves a cursor across various menu options and selects a menu item by typing ↵. As menu items are selected, additional submenus often appear in order to complete a command operation. In the screen below, the **ASSIST** mode is being used to complete the same command previously entered in the dot (.) prompt mode. Notice that the dBASE command being entered appears at the bottom of the screen as the user constructs it from the pull-down menus.

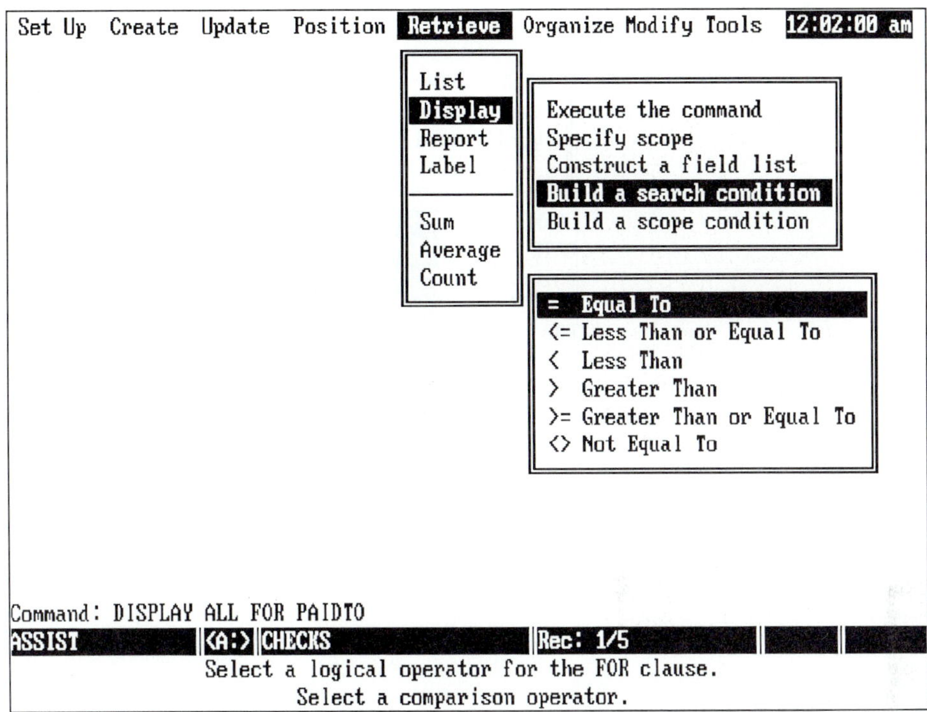

Some dBASE III Plus features provide only the pull-down menu mode for entering commands.

dBASE Editing Modes

Full-Screen Editing Mode

The full-screen editing mode is used when data held in fields or variables are to be directly entered or edited. The full-screen mode is indicated by a reverse video display of the fields or variables placed on the screen. A blinking cursor, located in one of the reverse video areas, indicates the data item currently being edited. In the following screen, the fields of the first record in the example database file have been placed on the screen in a full-screen editing mode. Notice that a menu of editing keystrokes appears at the top of the screen.

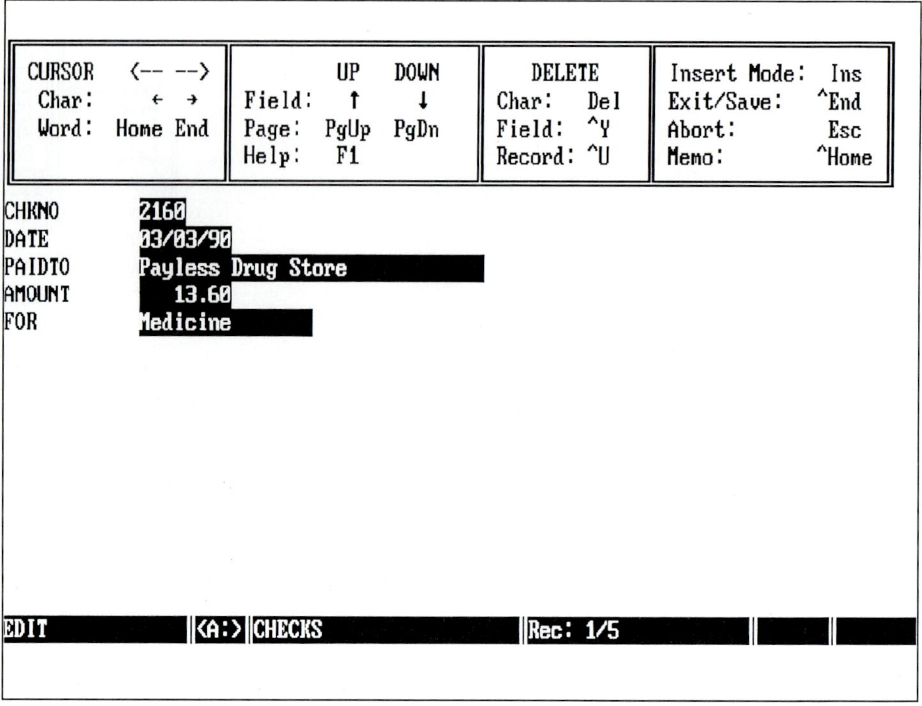

Text Editing Mode

Another dBASE editing mode is used to create the command files mentioned previously and to enter data into a .DBT file (see "dBASE's Other Files," page D-7–D-8, for more information on .DBT files). In this mode the screen appears much like a word processing screen, and keystrokes similar to those used in word processing are used to create the batch of dBASE commands contained in the file. For this reason, the editing mode is referred to here as being a text editing mode.

dBASE III Plus's File Handling

dBASE III Plus is a relatively large software which in its entirety would use up a considerable amount of RAM. In addition, as databases become several hundred records long, they would use up RAM rapidly. dBASE circumvents the RAM size limitations by keeping only data currently needed in RAM at any time. It maintains the rest of the data on the disk, bringing it into RAM as necessary.

How dBASE is Loaded into RAM

The set of instructions that makes up the dBASE III Plus software is kept in several separate program files. Using certain dBASE commands causes the disk drive holding the dBASE software to activate because such commands are not covered by the instructions currently in RAM, and the program file to execute the command needs to be read into RAM. Through software segmentation, dBASE is able to use less RAM space to accomplish its database operations. However, you must keep the appropriate dBASE programs available (in a disk drive or on a hard disk) at all times while you are using the software.

How a Database is Loaded and Saved

The first step in creating a database is to name the disk file that will hold the records of data. dBASE then creates a file on the disk, leaving it empty but structured so that data may be saved (copied) to it. A file left in this condition is said to be *open*.

dBASE then provides space in RAM to hold database record data. When you enter the data, it uses up the available RAM. When the space fills, dBASE begins to save parts (blocks) of the data into the file on the disk. Once a block of data is copied to the disk, the space it occupied in RAM may be erased to make room for new records to be entered.

When dBASE needs to process database data stored on the disk, the data are read into RAM, processed, and then written back out onto the disk file in processed form.

When you are done using dBASE, you type and enter dBASE's **QUIT** command, which causes any data left in RAM to be copied onto the disk file(s) so that all data are saved. **QUIT** is always the last command you type when using dBASE. It closes all dBASE files.

dBASE's Other Files

dBASE is able to create and maintain several types of files other than database files. These other files are typically used by dBASE to modify or support its processing of data in a database. dBASE III Plus may have several such files loaded into RAM or open at the same time. The following briefly describes the types of files dBASE III Plus can create and provides the filename extension that dBASE gives them.

.CAT — *Catalog files* are created with the **SET CATALOG TO** command. A catalog file maintains an active list of related files which dBASE will treat as belonging to a particular group or set of files.

.DBF — *Database files* are created in a full-screen editing mode. They hold the records and the record structure of a database.

.DBT — *Database memo files* are used with a .DBF database file when the database file has fields in its record structure specified for memo-type data. A memo-type field in a .DBF file is used to store up to 4,000 characters of text related to the record. The memo text is actually stored in a .DBT file and the memo-type field in the .DBF file contains a ten-character address that tells dBASE where in the associated .DBT file the memo text may be found.

.FMT — *Format files* contain dBASE commands used to customize the full-screen editing presentation of fields and/or variables.

.FRM — *Report form files* are created with the **MODIFY REPORT** command (using pull-down menus). The report form files contain user-defined specifications for producing columnar-type reports from the data in a database.

.LBL — *Label form files* are created with the **MODIFY LABEL** command (using pull-down menus). The label form files contain user-defined specifications for producing mailing or identification labels from the data in a database.

.MEM — *Memory variable files* are created with the **SAVE TO** command. They hold the variable names and contents for variables current at the time the command was executed.

.NDX *Index files* are created with the **INDEX** command. .NDX files are used concurrently with a .DBF (database) file to cause dBASE to treat the database as though its records are sorted.

.PRG *Program files* (called *command files*) are created in a text editing mode with the **MODIFY COMMAND** command. Program files contain dBASE commands to be executed in sequence when the **DO** command is used. A dBASE .PRG file can be very similar to a program written in a programming language.

.QRY *Query files* are created with the **MODIFY QUERY** command (using pull-down menus). Query files contain user-defined conditions that cause dBASE to affect only certain records during its processing of a database.

.SCR *Screen files* are produced with the **MODIFY SCREEN** command (using pull-down menus). Screen files are source files used by dBASE to produce .FMT (format) files.

.TXT *Text files* may be created with several dBASE III Plus commands. They are ASCII data format files that can be processed by other software.

.VUE *View files* are created with the **MODIFY VIEW** command (using pull-down menus). View files contain the set of working relationships that exist between a group of related files.

LEARNING dBASE III PLUS

The dBASE III Plus commands for creation, maintenance, and basic processing of a database are fairly straightforward; however, the full range of commands available in dBASE makes it closer to being a programming language than an applications software. A knowledge of another programming language such as BASIC, COBOL, or Pascal is perhaps the greatest aid in learning to use dBASE III Plus to its fullest extent.

If you have not done so already, it is highly recommended that you study appendix C “Using Expressions” before continuing with the dBASE tutorial lessons.

As you progress through the material in this manual, you may notice slight differences between the screens displayed here and those on your monitor. These differences are due to minor changes made to the different versions of dBASE III Plus.

Getting Help

dBASE has a command, **HELP,** which will present information about specific dBASE commands and operations. To use the command, you type the command word **HELP** followed by a space, and then the command or operation for which you want information. If dBASE has the information, it will display it on the monitor screen.

REQUIRED PREPARATION

The tutorial lessons and exercises in this module will give you experience using the commands and features of dBASE III Plus. Before you begin the “hands-on” learning experience, however, you will need to complete a few initial steps and gain some preliminary information in order to be adequately prepared.

Initial Steps

1. Obtain a floppy disk appropriate for the microcomputer you will be using to complete your course assignments. Your instructor or laboratory staff will be able to tell you which kind of disk to purchase.

   Size: ____________________

   Sides: ____________________

   Density: ____________________

2. Format your disk to the specifications of the DOS and microcomputer hardware that you will be using to complete your course assignments. Your instructor or laboratory staff will be able to tell you the steps to follow. ***Caution:*** **Formatting a disk erases all files that may exist on the disk.**

   Steps to Format a Disk: ____________________

3. Each time you use the dBASE software, you will want to be sure that your data files are saved on your disk. There will be certain steps to follow, either when you first load dBASE into RAM or immediately afterwards to ensure that your files are automatically saved on your disk. Your instructor or laboratory staff will be able to tell you the steps to follow.

   Starting a dBASE Session: ____________________

REQUIRED MATERIALS

1. An IBM DOS floppy disk (or hard-disk containing the DOS software).
2. A dBASE System 1 and a dBASE System 2 floppy disk (or hard-disk containing the software).
3. A formatted floppy disk (your files disk).
4. This manual.
5. Other ______________________________

TUTORIAL CONVENTIONS

During the introductory dBASE III Plus tutorial you will create various files using dBASE commands. The following are the conventions the tutorial's instructions will use.

↵	The bent arrow means to type the Enter key located on the right side of the keyboard.
^Key	Keys preceded by the ^ sign indicate that you should press and hold the Ctrl key and then type the next key shown.
Key,Key	Key combinations using a comma indicate that you should type the first key and then type the second key.
‖ ‖	Do not type the double lines; type only what is inside them.

HOW TO GET OUT OF TROUBLE

If you want to:	*Then:*
■ Erase characters being entered as a dBASE command or data. . .	■ Type the Backspace key located on the right top side of keyboard.
■ Stop any command operation and return to the dot (.) prompt. . .	■ Type the Esc key located on the top far-left side of the keyboard.
■ Stop any editing operation and return to the dot (.) prompt. . .	■ Press and hold the Ctrl key and then type the End key (convention is **^**End).
■ Stop the tutorial to continue later. . .	■ Type ‖**QUIT**↵‖ at the dot (.) prompt.
■ Continue with the tutorial after stopping. . .	■ After loading dBASE into RAM, type ‖**SET DEFAULT TO** *drive:* ↵ **USE** empfile↵‖.

NOTE: Here drive *means type the letter (A, B, etc.) for the disk drive in which your files disk is kept.*

Throughout the tutorial lessons you will see the following symbol.

It indicates an opportune time to save your file(s) and quit the microcomputer session, if you so desire.

GETTING STARTED

The proper "getting started" procedures require information specific to the hardware and software you are using. Refer to your notes in the preceding Required Preparation section for the specific information. The following is a general procedure for getting started; however, you may need to refer to Appendix A, "The Basics of DOS," to understand some of the terminology used here.

You will need to know in which disk drive (A: or B:) your files disk will be, and where (disk drive and path) the dBASE III Plus software will be.

1. Load DOS from a floppy disk or hard disk, or return to the DOS operating level from the current software operating level.
2. Put your files floppy disk into the proper disk drive (drive name ________:).
3. If necessary, put the dBASE System disk 1 in the proper disk drive (drive name ________:).
4. When you see DOS's *drive*:\> prompt on the screen, change the current disk drive and path to where the dBASE III Plus software resides by typing ||*drive:*↵ **CD***path*↵||.
5. Now begin to load the dBASE software by typing ||dBASE↵||.
6. If necessary, follow dBASE's instructions to insert the System disk 2, and type ↵ when ready.

In a few moments dBASE III Plus will load into RAM. You will know dBASE is loaded when you see a dot (.) prompt appear next to a blinking cursor at the bottom of the screen.

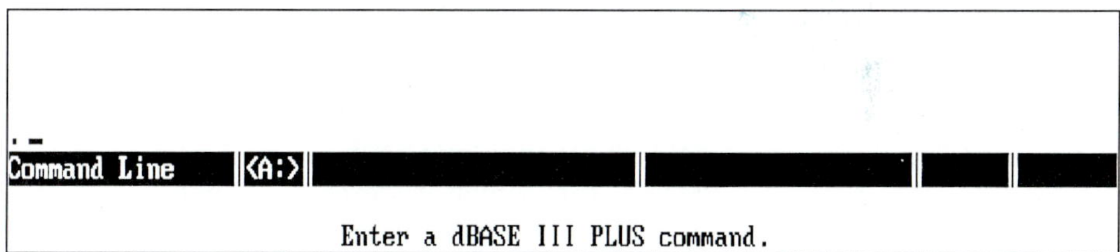

7. If you do not see the dot (.) prompt as shown here, type the Esc key.

In the next step, enter the drive letter for the drive where your files disk resides.

8. Now type ||**SET DEFAULT TO** *drive:*↵||.

This dBASE command causes dBASE to automatically address the specified drive for any file to which you later refer.

LESSON 1 Entering Commands in the Dot (.) Prompt Mode

The dot (.) appearing on the screen indicates that you are in a dBASE command mode. When the dot appears with the cursor next to it, anything that you type and enter is evaluated as a command by dBASE III Plus.

Syntax Errors

If you type an incorrect form of a dBASE command while you are in the command mode, dBASE will display a "syntax error" message, or, if the mistake is in the first word of the command, an "***Unrecognized command verb" message.

When dBASE III Plus detects a syntax error, it displays its error message and the command it was evaluating at the time on the screen with a question mark over the area where it stopped evaluating the command. For example, if in the last step of Getting Started you had typed

SET DFEAULT TO A:

dBASE would respond

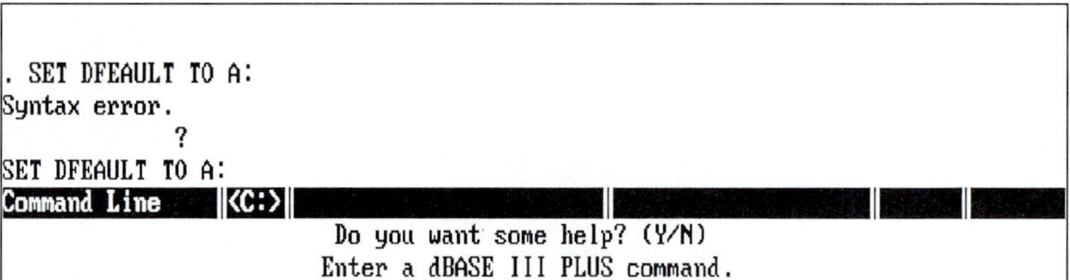

The message "Do you want some help? (Y/N)" appears at the bottom of the screen. Typing Y at this point will cause dBASE to display its **HELP** screen for the **SET** command.

Recovering from Syntax Errors

To recover from a command with a syntax error it is usually recommended that you first type any key except Y to answer the "Do you want some help?" message and then enter the command again, making sure the word **DEFAULT** and all other words are spelled correctly. However, to reenter the command, you do not need to type the entire command again.

The HISTORY Buffer

dBASE III Plus sets aside a small portion of RAM (a *buffer*) called HISTORY, into which it stores previously typed commands. The default number of commands stored in HISTORY is 20 commands. The buffer allows the user to back up, and then edit and reenter a previous command.

To display a previous command entered in the dot (.) prompt mode, the cursor up (↑) key is typed. Each time the key is typed, dBASE displays the last previous command (scrolls back through the commands in HISTORY). To scroll forward, the cursor down (↓) key is typed. When the desired command is displayed, the following keystrokes may be used to edit the command in a dBASE text editing mode.

Editing Operation	Keystrokes
Cursor Movement	
Character Left	Left ←
Character Right	Right →
Word Left	Home
Word Right	End
Insert/Overwrite	Ins
Delete Characters	
Current Character	Delete (Del)
Previous Character	Backspace
Word Right of Cursor	^T
Line Right of Cursor	^Y
Abort editing changes	Esc

When editing is completed, ↵ may be typed to reenter the command.

LESSON 2
Creating a Database

To continue the tutorial, you will create a small database of records. Each record's data concern an employee of a small retail shop where policy allows personal store purchases to be charged against the employee's store account.

Using the **CREATE** Command

To begin building the database, you will use the **CREATE** command. This command has the form **CREATE** [<filename>]. The filename you specify is used to name the database (.DBF) file.

1. Type ||**CREATE** empfile ↵||. (Empfile stands for employee file.)

The **CREATE** command causes dBASE to leave the dot (.) prompt mode and enter one of its full-screen editing modes. You can tell that you are in such a mode when the area of the screen at the cursor's location is displayed in reverse video. When you are in one of dBASE's editing modes, you do not enter dBASE commands since all characters that you type will be treated as data by dBASE. To save the data you have entered and exit from dBASE's editing modes (return to the dot (.) prompt command mode), you may type ^END.

Specifying a Database Record Structure

The following will appear on the screen.

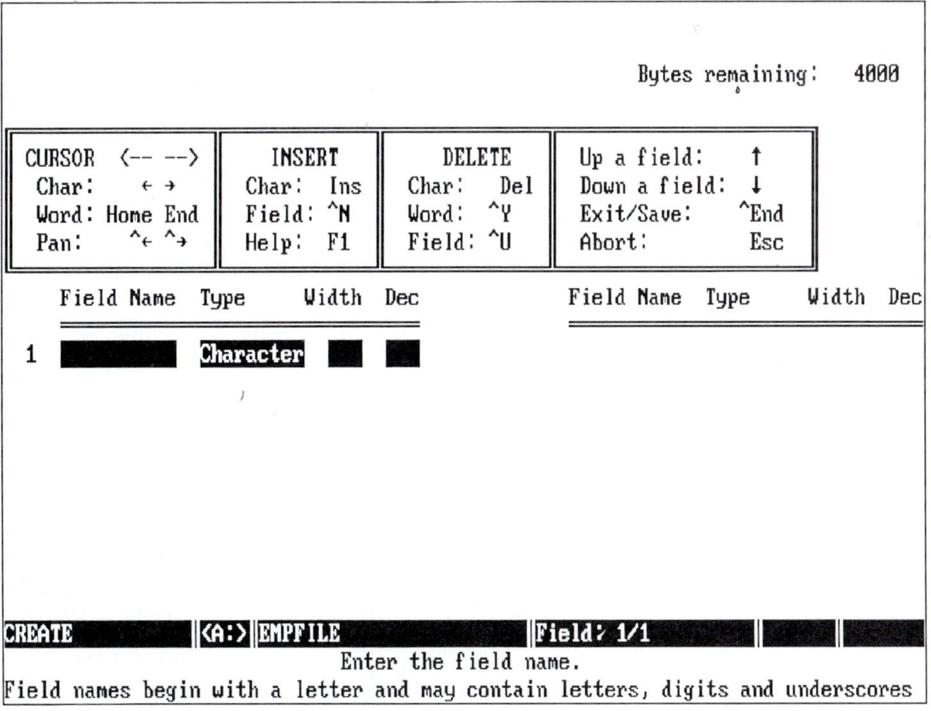

To specify the record structure, each field needs to be specified by field name; the type of data (Character, Numeric, or Date) it will hold; how many characters in width it will be; and finally, if the field is numeric, how many decimal places will be displayed.

2. Begin to specify the record structure by typing ||employee←|| into the area under Field Name.

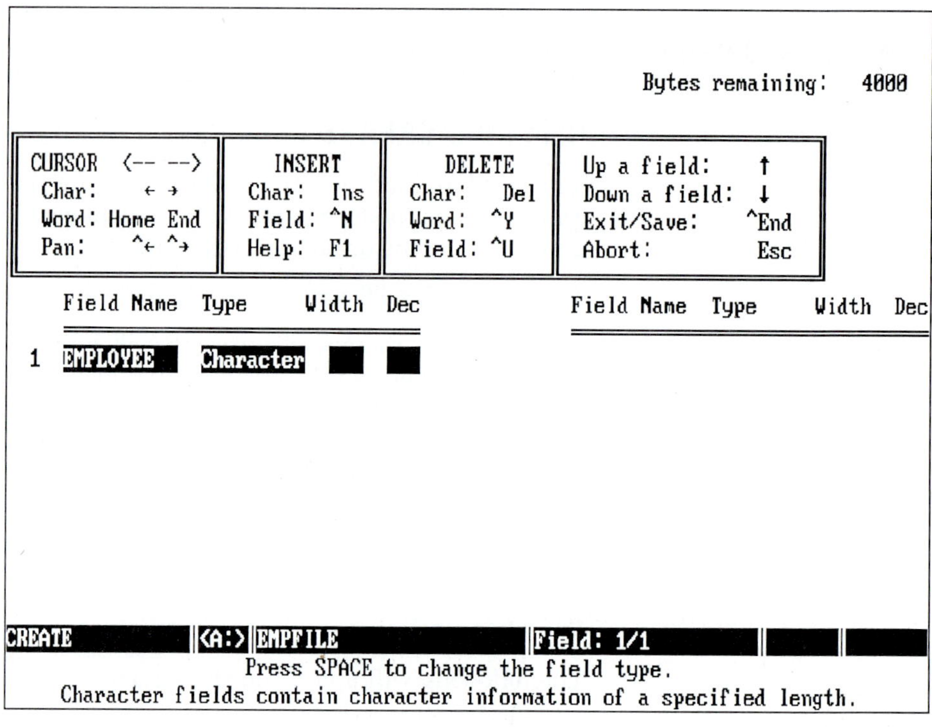

Next, you will enter the data type for the field named "EMPLOYEE." There are a total of five data types available, three of which are used in the tutorial. To select a data type for a field, you may either enter the first letter of the data type description (C = Character, N = Numeric, D = Date) or you may type the space bar to cause dBASE to display different data types in the area, and then tap the Enter key when the appropriate type is displayed.

3. Type the space bar several times to see the different data types displayed, and then type ||C|| to specify Character-type data.
4. Next type ||20←|| into the area under Width to specify that the field named "EMPLOYEE" is to be 20 characters wide.

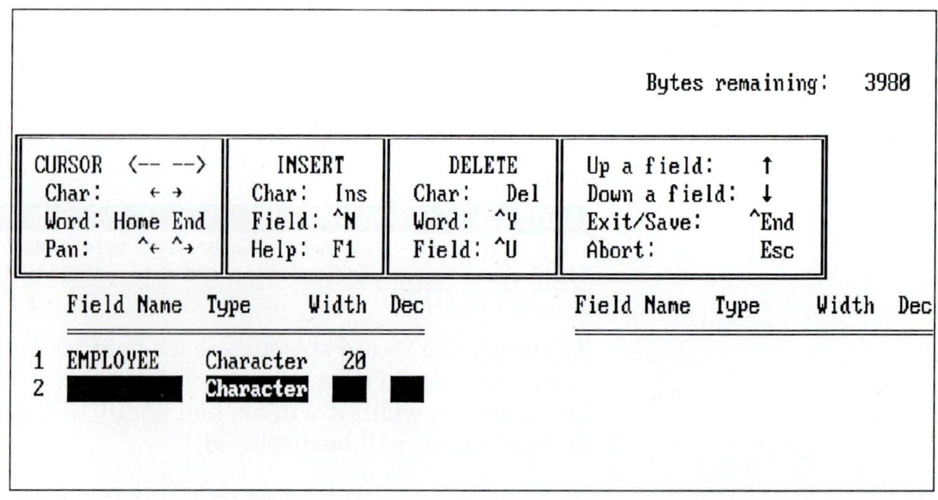

Notice that dBASE skipped over the decimal places (Dec), and the areas to specify the next field are presented. Two rules of field specification to remember are (1) only numeric fields have their decimal places specified and (2) all date fields have a width of eight characters.

In the next steps, you will finish specifying the record structure for the database empfile. Take care to enter all data exactly as shown. If you make an error entering data, try using the editing keystroke menu at the top of the screen to make your corrections. If you are unsuccessful editing the mistakes, type the Esc key twice to abort, and then start over by typing **CREATE** empfile↵.

5. Now finish specifying the record structure by entering the following data.

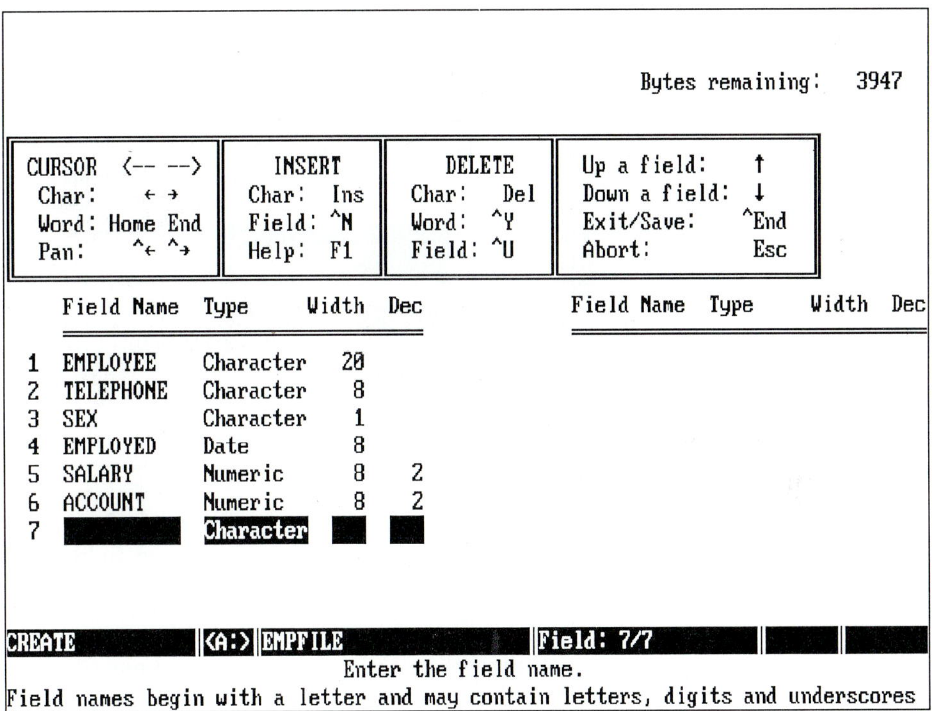

```
                                                 Bytes remaining:   3947

CURSOR  <-- -->  |    INSERT    |    DELETE    | Up a field:    ↑
 Char:    ← →    | Char:  Ins   | Char:   Del  | Down a field:  ↓
 Word: Home End  | Field: ^N    | Word:   ^Y   | Exit/Save:     ^End
 Pan:    ^← ^→   | Help:  F1    | Field:  ^U   | Abort:         Esc

    Field Name  Type      Width  Dec          Field Name  Type     Width  Dec

 1  EMPLOYEE    Character   20
 2  TELEPHONE   Character    8
 3  SEX         Character    1
 4  EMPLOYED    Date         8
 5  SALARY      Numeric      8    2
 6  ACCOUNT     Numeric      8    2
 7              Character

CREATE          |<A:>|EMPFILE               |Field: 7/7
                          Enter the field name.
Field names begin with a letter and may contain letters, digits and underscores
```

6. When dBASE presents field 7, type ↵ or ||^End||.

Typing ↵ when the last field is presented, or typing ^End, signals dBASE that you are ready to end specifying the record structure. The following message will appear at the bottom of the screen.

```
Press ENTER to confirm.  Any other key to resume.
```

7. Type the Enter key.

Each Record's Structure

The record structure you have defined for the database named empfile includes six fields, three of which will hold characters, two of which will hold numeric data, and one of which will hold date-type data. Each field's length has been specified, so the total length of each record is known.

LESSON 3
Entering Records into a Database

NOTE: If you are continuing the tutorial after having used the **QUIT** *command, type* ||**USE** empfile↵ **APPEND**↵|| *to view the following record entry screen.*

Your next steps involve entering data into the records of the database. As you enter data into records, you will be in another dBASE full-screen editing mode. On the screen, you should now see the prompt

```
Input data records now? (Y/N)
```

1. Type ||Y||.

dBASE will begin by displaying the first record with empty fields (shown in reverse video) into which you can now enter data.

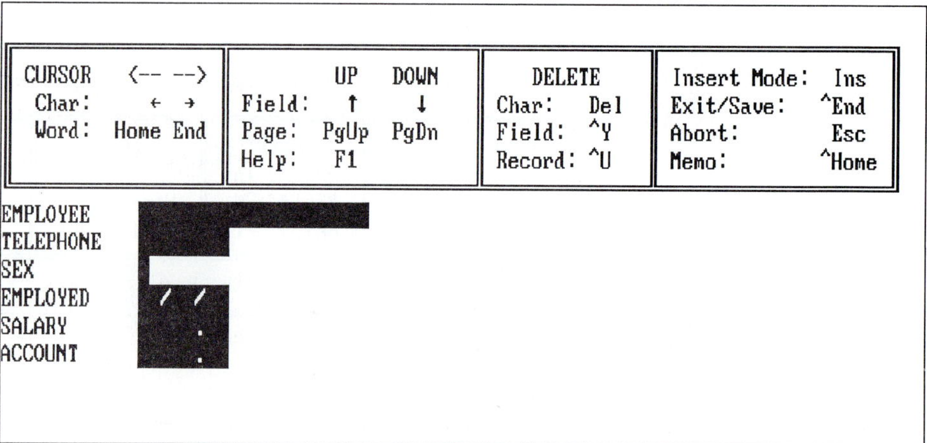

Each field's name is displayed to the left of the field. A cursor will be located at the first character of the first field to indicate where the data typed will be entered.

On the right side of the keyboard is a numeric keypad containing four keys with arrows on them. The arrowed keys *(cursor control keys)* may be used to move the cursor from field to field (↑ and ↓ keys) or from character to character within a field (← and → keys). If an attempt is made to move the cursor past the top field of the current record, the previous record is displayed.

dBASE presents the next record for data entry once the last field of the previous record has had data entered into it, or once an attempt has been made to move the cursor past the last field of the previous record.

Entering the Records Data

1. Enter the following data into each field of each record, 1 through 8, after you have read the following notes.

NOTE: (1) Make sure that you enter the upper-case/lower-case characters for the data, exactly as shown. (2) Type ||USE empfile↵ APPEND↵|| if you accidentally return to the dot (.) prompt before you are finished entering the record data. (3) If you make an error when you are entering data, don't worry. You will see later how to edit records, delete records, and make other changes. (4) A prompt that indicates which record is currently being entered appears at the bottom of the screen. It does so, however, by displaying the record number for the next previous record. That is, while the first record is being entered the prompt displays "Rec: None," while the second record is being entered the prompt displays "Rec: EOF/1." (The prompt means you are at the "End Of File" in empfile.DBF and that there is one record entered into the database file so far.)

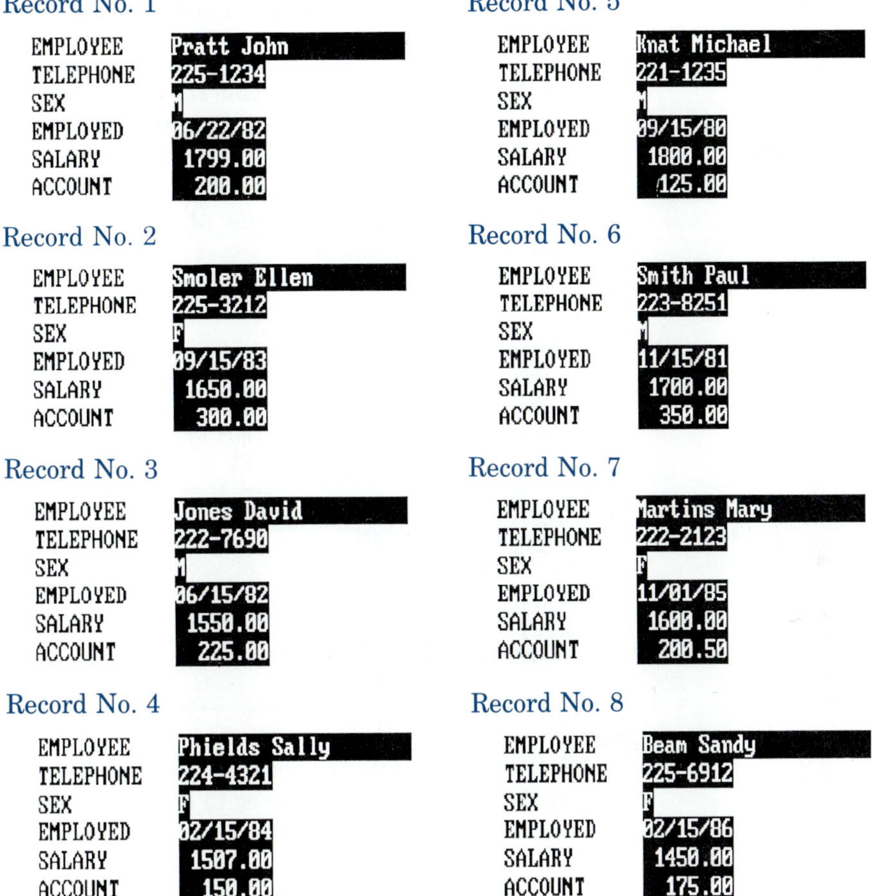

Record No. 1

EMPLOYEE	Pratt John
TELEPHONE	225-1234
SEX	M
EMPLOYED	06/22/82
SALARY	1799.00
ACCOUNT	200.00

Record No. 2

EMPLOYEE	Smoler Ellen
TELEPHONE	225-3212
SEX	F
EMPLOYED	09/15/83
SALARY	1650.00
ACCOUNT	300.00

Record No. 3

EMPLOYEE	Jones David
TELEPHONE	222-7690
SEX	M
EMPLOYED	06/15/82
SALARY	1550.00
ACCOUNT	225.00

Record No. 4

EMPLOYEE	Phields Sally
TELEPHONE	224-4321
SEX	F
EMPLOYED	02/15/84
SALARY	1507.00
ACCOUNT	150.00

Record No. 5

EMPLOYEE	Knat Michael
TELEPHONE	221-1235
SEX	M
EMPLOYED	09/15/80
SALARY	1800.00
ACCOUNT	125.00

Record No. 6

EMPLOYEE	Smith Paul
TELEPHONE	223-8251
SEX	M
EMPLOYED	11/15/81
SALARY	1700.00
ACCOUNT	350.00

Record No. 7

EMPLOYEE	Martins Mary
TELEPHONE	222-2123
SEX	F
EMPLOYED	11/01/85
SALARY	1600.00
ACCOUNT	200.50

Record No. 8

EMPLOYEE	Beam Sandy
TELEPHONE	225-6912
SEX	F
EMPLOYED	02/15/86
SALARY	1450.00
ACCOUNT	175.00

Ending Data Entry

2. When you are done entering the record data, type ↵ on the first field of the next blank record presented to save the data and return to dBASE's dot (.) prompt. When adding records to a database, the ↵ keystroke typed when a new record is presented signals dBASE to end the editing operation.

LESSON 4
Putting a Database into Use

The **USE** Command

Before you can process the records in a database with dBASE's commands, you first must specify the database file to use by typing the **USE** command.

1. Type ||**USE** empfile↵|| to cause dBASE to access (open) the database file you have created.

When a database is in use, the data in it are not constantly displayed on the screen as are other types of data with other applications software. Nonetheless, the entire database is present in RAM (or on the disk) and is now accessible to you through the commands of dBASE III Plus.

LESSON 5
Altering the Database

The **EDIT** and **BROWSE** Commands

To edit records in a database, you may use either the **EDIT** command or the **BROWSE** command of dBASE III Plus. Both commands cause dBASE to enter a full-screen editing mode where you can move to different fields of different records to change the data in them. **EDIT** and **BROWSE** differ only in the way that they present the records on the screen for viewing. **EDIT** presents the records one at a time in the same format as records are entered into a database.

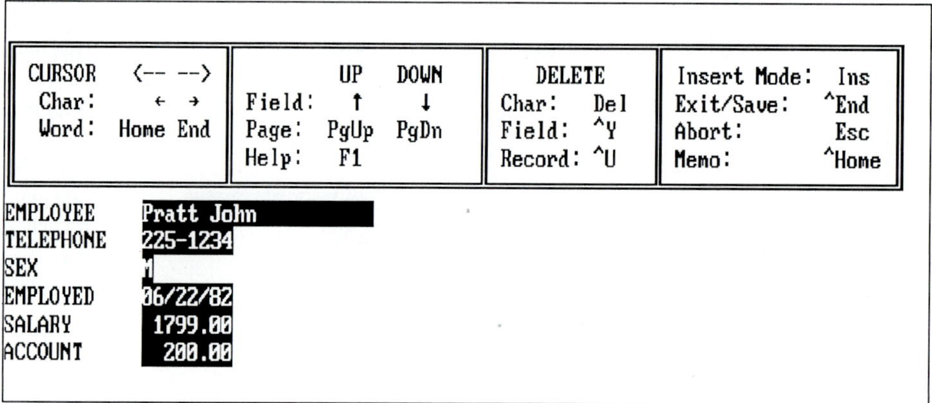

BROWSE presents the records horizontally in groups (one screen's worth at a time) in a form much closer to how you can visualize them represented in memory while dBASE is working with them.

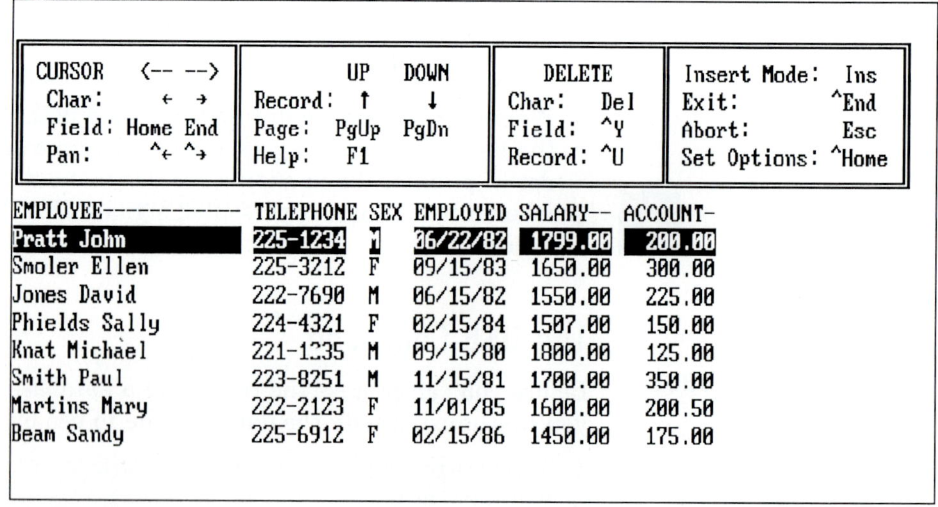

EMPLOYEE-----------	TELEPHONE	SEX	EMPLOYED	SALARY--	ACCOUNT-
Pratt John	225-1234	M	06/22/82	1799.00	200.00
Smoler Ellen	225-3212	F	09/15/83	1650.00	300.00
Jones David	222-7690	M	06/15/82	1550.00	225.00
Phields Sally	224-4321	F	02/15/84	1507.00	150.00
Knat Michael	221-1235	M	09/15/80	1800.00	125.00
Smith Paul	223-8251	M	11/15/81	1700.00	350.00
Martins Mary	222-2123	F	11/01/85	1600.00	200.50
Beam Sandy	225-6912	F	02/15/86	1450.00	175.00

Editing Keystrokes

When using either **EDIT** or **BROWSE,** you may use keystrokes for such things as moving the cursor, scrolling the database, or deleting a record. The keystroke commands are executed by tapping keys found on the numeric keypad or by typing Ctrl-keystroke combinations. The following table gives a brief summary of the keystrokes to which you may refer while you complete the following steps.

Action Desired	Keystrokes
Cursor Movement	
Character Left	Left ←
Character Right	Right →
Field Right	End
Field Left	Home
Next Record	Down ↓
Previous Record	Up ↑
Scroll 18 Records Up	PgUp
Scroll 18 Records Down	PgDn
Insert/Overwrite	Ins
Delete Characters	
Current Character	Delete (Del)
Previous Character	Backspace
Word Right of Cursor	^T
Line Right of Cursor	^Y
Delete Current Record	^U
Save Updates and Exit	^End

Using **BROWSE** to Edit Records

1. Type ||**BROWSE**←||.

dBASE will display the small database on the screen. Notice that the first record in the database is displayed in reverse video.

Moving from One Record to Another

2. Type the cursor down key several times, and then type the cursor up key several times.

The cursor up and down keystroke commands move the reverse video display from one record to another. The keystrokes demonstrate an important fundamental of database operations when they are used to move the reverse video display up and down through the database.

Introduction to the Database Record Pointer

While a database is in use, an unseen *record pointer* exists at all times. At any given moment the record pointer points to one particular record in the database, called the *current record.*

While in the **BROWSE** editing mode, the keys ↓ and ↑ move the record pointer one record down or up, and dBASE displays the current record in reverse video. In the command dot (.) prompt mode, there are commands that move the record pointer from one record to another, but it is seldom visually apparent that the pointer in fact has been moved.

Other Editing Keystroke Commands

Once you have moved the record pointer to the record to edit, you may move the cursor to the field to edit by typing the End key (forward one field) or Home key (back one field). When you have reached the field of concern, the ← and → keys may be used to move the cursor within the field. Any characters that you type will be written over the characters that exist in the field unless the Ins key is used to turn on the Insert mode. When the Insert mode is on, any characters that you type will be inserted into the field. The Del key may be used to delete the character above the cursor.

Updating the Records

3. Use the editing features of **BROWSE** to modify the database to reflect the following changes.
   a. David Jones has moved and his new phone number is 292-3832.
   b. Sally Phields is now married and her new last name is Sill.
   c. John Pratt has received a raise of $150.00 per month to bring his monthly salary to $1,949.00.
4. Correct any incorrect data that may have been entered when you created the database.

When you are finished the database should appear as follows.

```
CURSOR    <-- -->   |        UP    DOWN  |    DELETE     | Insert Mode:   Ins
 Char:      ←  →    | Record:  ↑     ↓   | Char:    Del  | Exit:         ^End
 Field: Home End    | Page:  PgUp  PgDn  | Field:  ^Y    | Abort:         Esc
 Pan:      ^←  ^→   | Help:    F1        | Record: ^U    | Set Options: ^Home

EMPLOYEE------------  TELEPHONE SEX EMPLOYED SALARY-- ACCOUNT-
Pratt John            225-1234  M   06/22/82 1949.00   200.00
Smoler Ellen          225-3212  F   09/15/83 1650.00   300.00
Jones David           292-3832  M   06/15/82 1550.00   225.00
Sill Sally            224-4321  F   02/15/84 1507.00   150.00
Knat Michael          221-1235  M   09/15/80 1800.00   125.00
Smith Paul            223-8251  M   11/15/81 1700.00   350.00
Martins Mary          222-2123  F   11/01/85 1600.00   200.50
Beam Sandy            225-6912  F   02/15/86 1450.00   175.00
```

Marking a Record for Deletion

In order to delete a record from the database, you must complete two steps. First, you mark the record for deletion. Then, you execute the dot (.) prompt command **PACK.** The **PACK** command physically removes the record from the database.

You may mark a record for deletion either in an editing mode or in the dot (.) prompt command mode. To execute the **PACK** command, you must be in the dot (.) prompt mode.

When you are in an editing mode, you mark a record for deletion by moving the record pointer to the appropriate record and typing ^U. The record still appears on the screen, but the message DEL is displayed at the bottom of the screen whenever that record becomes the current record. You may "un-mark" such a record by moving the record pointer to it and typing ^U again.

Finishing the Editing Session

5. If you have any unwanted records in the database, mark them for deletion now.

6. Type ||^End|| to save the changes made, end the editing session, and return to the dot (.) prompt command mode.
7. If you marked any records for deletion, type ||**PACK**↵|| to physically erase them from the database.

Adding Records to the Database

When you need to add records to an existing database, you may use the dBASE III Plus **APPEND** command. After you type **APPEND,** dBASE puts you in the same editing mode you were in when you last entered records. The **APPEND** command lets you add records, starting at the next available record number, until you execute the ^End (save and exit) keystroke command.

8. Type ||**APPEND**↵|| and add the following information into the blank record that dBASE will present.

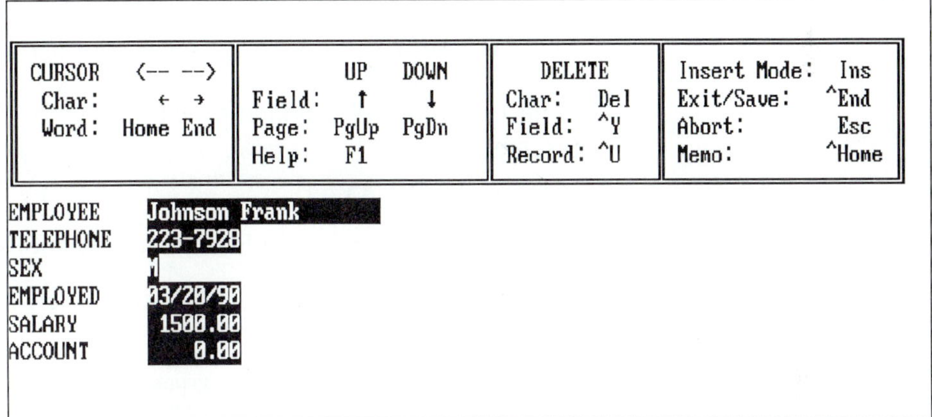

9. Type ↵ on the first field of the next record presented to quit appending records.

LESSON 6 dBASE III Plus Dot (.) Prompt Command Fundamentals

dBASE Command Conventions and Terminology

When you refer to the dBASE Operation and Command Summary in this manual or to the dBASE user's manual published by the software's developer, Ashton-Tate, you often will see the commands described in a form similar to

COMMAND [<scope>] [<expression list>] [**FOR** <condition>]

When commands are presented in the form shown above, the word(s) shown in upper case are dBASE command word(s). Although the convention uses upper case to indicate the word is a dBASE command, you may type the command in upper case or lower case when you are using it.

Command Parameters

The items following the command word(s) are called *command parameters.* Parameters may be defined as "additions to a command that affect the way the command will be executed." The types of parameters that are allowed for any particular command are described with lower-case words such as "scope." The < >s surrounding a parameter indicate that the data entered are user supplied. When a command's parameters are shown in brackets, e.g. [<scope>], they are optional—the command will work without them.

Using the **DISPLAY** Command to Explain Command Terminology

The next several steps are designed to illustrate the most important points of the command descriptions and the fundamentals of processing data using dBASE III Plus commands.

The Purpose and Form of the **DISPLAY** Command

The **DISPLAY** command may be used to display records of the database in a variety of ways. When you see the command listed in a reference, its form will be similar to

DISPLAY [<scope>] [<expression list>] [**FOR** <condition>]

Using the **DISPLAY** Command with No Parameters

1. Type ||**DISPLAY**↵||.

dBASE will respond by displaying a single record of the database.

When the **DISPLAY** command is used with no parameters, it displays all of the fields of data for a single record. The record displayed will be the one to which the record pointer is pointing at the moment.

More on the Database Record Pointer

The **APPEND** command that you executed previously moved the record pointer to the last record in the database so that you could enter data into the record. Since then, the record pointer has not been moved. It can be considered as existing alongside the records in the database.

```
          Record#  EMPLOYEE              TELEPHONE SEX EMPLOYED  SALARY  ACCOUNT
                1  Pratt John            225-1234  M   06/22/82  1949.00  200.00
                2  Smoler Ellen          225-3212  F   09/15/83  1650.00  300.00
                3  Jones David           292-3832  M   06/15/82  1550.00  225.00
                4  Sill Sally            224-4321  F   02/15/84  1507.00  150.00
                5  Knat Michael          221-1235  M   09/15/80  1800.00  125.00
                6  Smith Paul            223-8251  M   11/15/81  1700.00  350.00
                7  Martins Mary          222-2123  F   11/01/85  1600.00  200.50
Record          8  Beam Sandy            225-6912  F   02/15/86  1450.00  175.00
pointer →       9  Johnson Frank         223-7928  M   03/20/90  1500.00    0.00
```

Moving the Record Pointer Several dBASE commands move the record pointer when they are executed, and some commands are designed specifically to move the pointer. The dBASE commands **SKIP** [<n>], **GO TOP, GO BOTTOM,** and **GOTO** <n> (where n is the number of records to skip or the record number to go to) are used to move the record pointer.

2. Type and enter the following commands (shown in gray). See how the record pointer is moved as you view the record displayed (shown in black type) by the **DISPLAY** command.

NOTE: dBASE commands may be typed in upper case or lower case. You need only type the first four letters of a dBASE command. For example, typing ||disp↵|| works as well as ||DISPLAY↵||.

```
. GO TOP
. DISPLAY
Record#  EMPLOYEE              TELEPHONE SEX EMPLOYED   SALARY  ACCOUNT
      1  Pratt John            225-1234  M   06/22/82  1949.00   200.00

. SKIP
Record No.       2
. DISPLAY
Record#  EMPLOYEE              TELEPHONE SEX EMPLOYED   SALARY  ACCOUNT
      2  Smoler Ellen          225-3212  F   09/15/83  1650.00   300.00

. SKIP 3
Record No.       5
. DISPLAY
Record#  EMPLOYEE              TELEPHONE SEX EMPLOYED   SALARY  ACCOUNT
      5  Knat Michael          221-1235  M   09/15/80  1800.00   125.00

. GO BOTTOM
. DISPLAY
Record#  EMPLOYEE              TELEPHONE SEX EMPLOYED   SALARY  ACCOUNT
      9  Johnson Frank         223-7928  M   03/20/90  1500.00     0.00

. GOTO 3
. DISPLAY
Record#  EMPLOYEE              TELEPHONE SEX EMPLOYED   SALARY  ACCOUNT
      3  Jones David           292-3832  M   06/15/82  1550.00   225.00
```

Using the **DISPLAY** Command with the <scope> Parameter

*The Four Possible Scopes: **ALL, RECORD** <n>, **NEXT** <n>, and **REST***

The first listed user-supplied parameter of the **DISPLAY** command is <scope>. The parameter is found in several dBASE commands and it affects the record pointer when it is used. The four possible <scope>s are **ALL, REST, NEXT** <n>, and **RECORD** <n>. The <n> describes a number of records or a specific record number that you supply.

3. Type ||**DISPLAY ALL**↵||.

dBASE will respond by displaying the following.

```
. DISPLAY ALL
Record#  EMPLOYEE              TELEPHONE SEX EMPLOYED   SALARY  ACCOUNT
      1  Pratt John            225-1234  M   06/22/82  1949.00   200.00
      2  Smoler Ellen          225-3212  F   09/15/83  1650.00   300.00
      3  Jones David           292-3832  M   06/15/82  1550.00   225.00
      4  Sill Sally            224-4321  F   02/15/84  1507.00   150.00
      5  Knat Michael          221-1235  M   09/15/80  1800.00   125.00
      6  Smith Paul            223-8251  M   11/15/81  1700.00   350.00
      7  Martins Mary          222-2123  F   11/01/85  1600.00   200.50
      8  Beam Sandy            225-6912  F   02/15/86  1450.00   175.00
      9  Johnson Frank         223-7928  M   03/20/90  1500.00     0.00

.
Command Line     ||<A:>||EMPFILE            ||Rec: EOF/9         ||Ins ||

                       Enter a dBASE III PLUS command.
```

A <scope> of **ALL** changes the way in which the **DISPLAY** command is executed. It has the same effect as typing **GO TOP, DISPLAY, SKIP, DISPLAY, SKIP, DISPLAY,** continuing until you reach the end of the database.

4. Now type ||**DISPLAY**↵||.

dBASE will display the following.

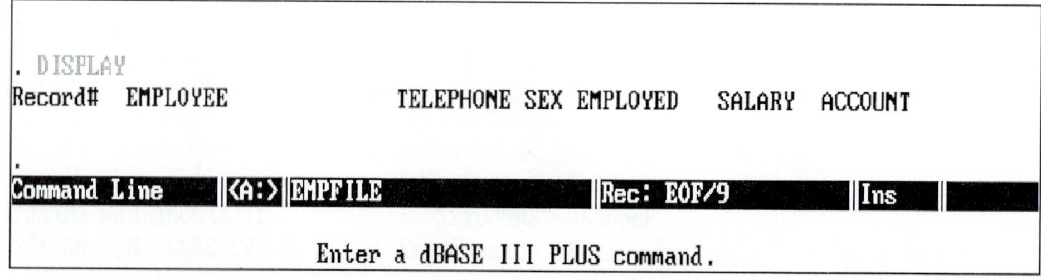

```
. DISPLAY
Record#  EMPLOYEE              TELEPHONE SEX EMPLOYED   SALARY  ACCOUNT

.
Command Line     ||<A:>||EMPFILE            ||Rec: EOF/9         ||Ins ||

                       Enter a dBASE III PLUS command.
```

The fact that no record data are displayed (including Record#) indicates that the record pointer currently resides past the bottom of the database (EOF/9).

5. Type ||**DISPLAY RECORD** 2←┘||.

dBASE will display the following.

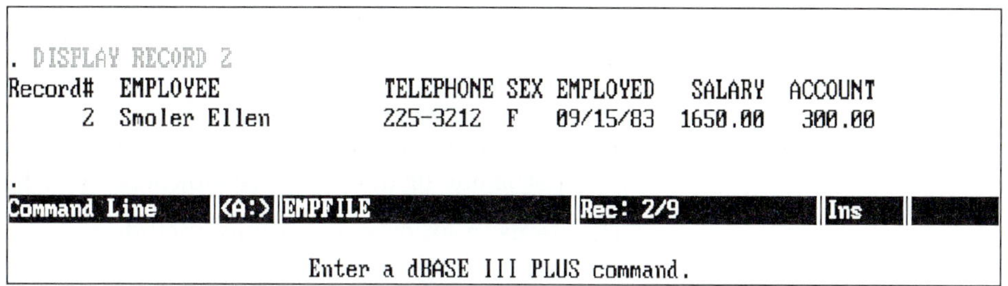

```
. DISPLAY RECORD 2
Record#  EMPLOYEE                TELEPHONE SEX EMPLOYED    SALARY  ACCOUNT
      2  Smoler Ellen            225-3212  F   09/15/83  1650.00   300.00

.
Command Line    ||<A:>||EMPFILE              ||Rec: 2/9          ||Ins  ||

                          Enter a dBASE III PLUS command.
```

The <scope> **RECORD** <n> has the same effect as typing **GOTO** 2, **DISPLAY.** Notice that the pointer remains on record 2 (Rec: 2/9 shown at the bottom of the screen).

6. Now type ||**DISPLAY NEXT** 3←┘||.

dBASE will respond by displaying the following.

```
. DISPLAY NEXT 3
Record#  EMPLOYEE                TELEPHONE SEX EMPLOYED    SALARY  ACCOUNT
      2  Smoler Ellen            225-3212  F   09/15/83  1650.00   300.00
      3  Jones David             292-3832  M   06/15/82  1550.00   225.00
      4  Sill Sally              224-4321  F   02/15/84  1507.00   150.00

.
Command Line    ||<A:>||EMPFILE              ||Rec: 4/9          ||Ins  ||

                          Enter a dBASE III PLUS command.
```

The <scope> **NEXT** <n> has the same effect as **DISPLAY, SKIP, DISPLAY** . . . <n> number of times. Notice that the record pointer is left on record 4 (Rec: 4/9).

7. Now type ||**DISPLAY REST**←┘||.

```
. DISPLAY REST
Record#  EMPLOYEE                TELEPHONE SEX EMPLOYED    SALARY  ACCOUNT
      4  Sill Sally              224-4321  F   02/15/84  1507.00   150.00
      5  Knat Michael            221-1235  M   09/15/80  1800.00   125.00
      6  Smith Paul              223-8251  M   11/15/81  1700.00   350.00
      7  Martins Mary            222-2123  F   11/01/85  1600.00   200.50
      8  Beam Sandy              225-6912  F   02/15/86  1450.00   175.00
      9  Johnson Frank           223-7928  M   03/20/90  1500.00     0.00

.
Command Line    ||<A:>||EMPFILE              ||Rec: EOF/9        ||Ins  ||

                          Enter a dBASE III PLUS command.
```

The <scope> **REST** has the same effect as **DISPLAY, SKIP, DISPLAY, SKIP** . . . until the end of the database file (EOF/9) is reached.

Using the **DISPLAY** Command with the <expression list> Parameter

The second optional parameter of the **DISPLAY** command is <expression list>. An <expression> (<exp> for short) is an item or group of items with operators whose values can be determined by dBASE III Plus. An expression list is one or more expressions separated by commas.

The items in an expression may include constants, dBASE functions, memory variable names, and/or names used to describe the fields holding database data. The operators used in an expression may include the mathematical operators (^, *, /, +, −), the relational operators (<, >, =), and the logical operators (.NOT., .AND., .OR.). When an expression contains relational operators, dBASE will evaluate the expression as being either .T. for true or .F. for false. To give you experience using expression lists, do the following.

8. Type ||**CLEAR**↵||.

CLEAR is the dBASE III Plus command used to clear the screen.

9. Next type ||**GOTO RECORD** 6↵ **DISPLAY** employee↵||.

NOTE: "employee" is a field name, so it must be typed in its entirety. It may, however, be typed in upper case or lower case.

```
. GOTO RECORD 6
. DISPLAY employee
Record#  employee
      6  Smith Paul

.
Command Line   ||<A:>||EMPFILE          ||Rec: 6/9        ||Ins  ||

                       Enter a dBASE III PLUS command.
```

dBASE will display the record number and contents of the single field, employee, for the current record. Notice that the field label over the employee's name appears exactly as typed in the expression list of the **DISPLAY** command.

10. Continue by typing ||**DISPLAY ALL** employee, telephone←||.

dBASE will respond by displaying the following.

```
. DISPLAY ALL employee,telephone
Record#  employee              telephone
      1  Pratt John            225-1234
      2  Smoler Ellen          225-3212
      3  Jones David           292-3832
      4  Sill Sally            224-4321
      5  Knat Michael          221-1235
      6  Smith Paul            223-8251
      7  Martins Mary          222-2123
      8  Beam Sandy            225-6912
      9  Johnson Frank         223-7928

.
Command Line  ||<A:>||EMPFILE          ||Rec: EOF/9      ||Ins  ||

                     Enter a dBASE III PLUS command.
```

"employee, telephone" is an example of an expression list containing two expressions (field names) separated by commas.

To make the following examples more sensible, assume that management prefers its employees to keep their account amounts less than 15 percent of their monthly salaries.

11. Type ||**DISPLAY ALL** employee, "Limit =", .15 * salary←||.

dBASE will display the following.

```
. DISPLAY ALL employee,"Limit =",.15 * salary
Record#  employee              "Limit =" .15 * salary
      1  Pratt John            Limit =       292.3500
      2  Smoler Ellen          Limit =       247.5000
      3  Jones David           Limit =       232.5000
      4  Sill Sally            Limit =       226.0500
      5  Knat Michael          Limit =       270.0000
      6  Smith Paul            Limit =       255.0000
      7  Martins Mary          Limit =       240.0000
      8  Beam Sandy            Limit =       217.5000
      9  Johnson Frank         Limit =       225.0000

.
Command Line  ||<A:>||EMPFILE          ||Rec: EOF/9      ||Ins  ||

                     Enter a dBASE III PLUS command.
```

"employee, "Limit =", .15 * salary" is an example of an expression list consisting of a field, a constant, and an expression with two items and an operator whose value can be determined.

12. Next type ‖**DISPLAY ALL** employee, **INT**(.15 * salary), **INT**(.15 * salary − account) **OFF**↵‖.

dBASE will display the following.

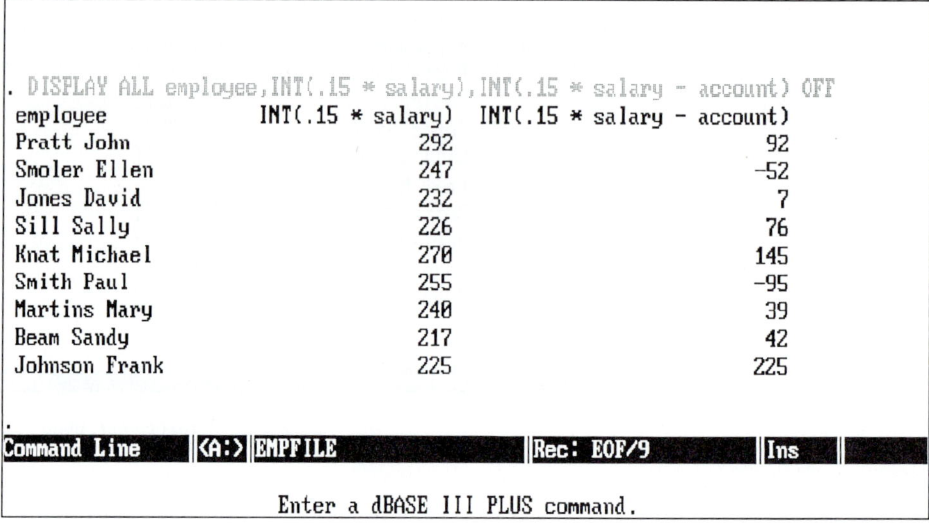

```
. DISPLAY ALL employee,INT(.15 * salary),INT(.15 * salary - account) OFF
employee                 INT(.15 * salary)  INT(.15 * salary - account)
Pratt John                             292                           92
Smoler Ellen                           247                          -52
Jones David                            232                            7
Sill Sally                             226                           76
Knat Michael                           270                          145
Smith Paul                             255                          -95
Martins Mary                           240                           39
Beam Sandy                             217                           42
Johnson Frank                          225                          225

.
Command Line    |<A:>|EMPFILE             |Rec: EOF/9          |Ins  |

                       Enter a dBASE III PLUS command.
```

In this example, the **INT** (Integer) function is used to remove trailing cents and zeros from the limit amount (**INT**(.15 * salary)) and from the amount the employee is currently under/over (−) that limit (**INT**(.15 * salary − account)).

Notice that a previously unmentioned **DISPLAY** parameter, **OFF,** may be used to stop the display of each record's record number. It also is possible to stop the display of the expression labels (first row of output) by typing the command **SET HEADING OFF.** To reestablish the display of expression labels, you type **SET HEADING ON.**

13. Now type ‖**DISPLAY ALL** employee, .15 * salary − account > 0↵‖.

dBASE will display the following.

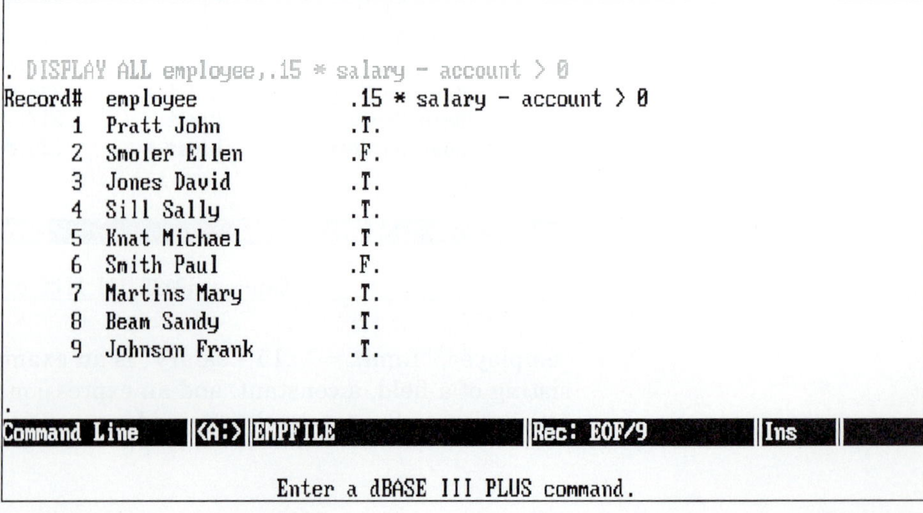

```
. DISPLAY ALL employee,.15 * salary - account > 0
Record#  employee              .15 * salary - account > 0
      1  Pratt John            .T.
      2  Smoler Ellen          .F.
      3  Jones David           .T.
      4  Sill Sally            .T.
      5  Knat Michael          .T.
      6  Smith Paul            .F.
      7  Martins Mary          .T.
      8  Beam Sandy            .T.
      9  Johnson Frank         .T.

.
Command Line    |<A:>|EMPFILE             |Rec: EOF/9          |Ins  |

                       Enter a dBASE III PLUS command.
```

Here the use of an expression containing a relational operator results in dBASE evaluating the expression as being either .T. for true or .F. for false for each record. Such an expression is referred to as being a condition.

Using the **DISPLAY** Command with the **FOR** <condition> Parameter

Using Conditions within a dBASE Command

The third parameter is [**FOR** <condition>], which allows selective execution of the command with which it is used. A <condition> is an expression that includes relational operators causing dBASE to evaluate it as either .T. for true or .F. for false. The items in the condition may include constants, dBASE functions, variable names, and/or names for the fields used to hold database data. The operators used in a condition may include the mathematical operators (**^**, *, /, +, −), the relational operators (<, >, =), and the logical operators (.NOT., .AND., .OR.).

A Change in Scope When the [**FOR** <condition>] parameter is used with a command, the default <scope> of the command becomes **ALL** records. The change in scope causes the record pointer to move to the top of the database, where the first record is evaluated for the fields of concern included in the **FOR** <condition>.

.T. and .F. The record at the top of the database will be evaluated as either .T. for true or .F. for false. If the value determined for the condition is .F., the command will not be executed for the record; dBASE will move the pointer to the next record and evaluate it.

Using Simple Conditions

14. Type and enter the following commands (printed in gray) to see how the optional parameter [**FOR** <condition>] affects the **DISPLAY** command's response (shown in black type).

```
. CLEAR
. DISPLAY FOR sex = "M"
Record#  EMPLOYEE                        TELEPHONE SEX EMPLOYED   SALARY  ACCOUNT
      1  Pratt John                      225-1234  M   06/22/82  1949.00   200.00
      3  Jones David                     292-3832  M   06/15/82  1550.00   225.00
      5  Knat Michael                    221-1235  M   09/15/80  1800.00   125.00
      6  Smith Paul                      223-8251  M   11/15/81  1700.00   350.00
      9  Johnson Frank                   223-7928  M   03/20/90  1500.00     0.00

. DISPLAY employee,telephone FOR sex = "F"
Record#  employee                        telephone
      2  Smoler Ellen                    225-3212
      4  Sill Sally                      224-4321
      7  Martins Mary                    222-2123
      8  Beam Sandy                      225-6912

. DISPLAY FOR sex = "f"
Record#  EMPLOYEE                        TELEPHONE SEX EMPLOYED   SALARY  ACCOUNT
```

No records will be displayed since you entered the record data character "f" (lower case) into the field named sex. The "M" and "F" used in the command's [**FOR** <condition>] parameter are references to data items in your database. You must refer to such items precisely, and in the same case as they exist in their fields.

15. Continue by typing and entering the commands shown in gray below.

```
. DISPLAY FOR employee = "Smith Paul"
Record#  EMPLOYEE                TELEPHONE SEX EMPLOYED   SALARY  ACCOUNT
      6  Smith Paul              223-8251  M   11/15/81  1700.00   350.00

. DISPLAY FOR employee = "Smi"
Record#  EMPLOYEE                TELEPHONE SEX EMPLOYED   SALARY  ACCOUNT
      6  Smith Paul              223-8251  M   11/15/81  1700.00   350.00

. DISPLAY FOR employee = "Sm"
Record#  EMPLOYEE                TELEPHONE SEX EMPLOYED   SALARY  ACCOUNT
      2  Smoler Ellen            225-3212  F   09/15/83  1650.00   300.00
      6  Smith Paul              223-8251  M   11/15/81  1700.00   350.00

. DISPLAY FOR employee = "S"
Record#  EMPLOYEE                TELEPHONE SEX EMPLOYED   SALARY  ACCOUNT
      2  Smoler Ellen            225-3212  F   09/15/83  1650.00   300.00
      4  Sill Sally              224-4321  F   02/15/84  1507.00   150.00
      6  Smith Paul              223-8251  M   11/15/81  1700.00   350.00
```

Although you must refer to the data items precisely, you may refer to character items in part, as long as the segment ("Smi", for instance) is meant to evaluate as .T.rue from the far left of the data field. In other words, the segment must begin at the beginning.

16. Next type

```
. DISPLAY FOR employee < "K"
Record#  EMPLOYEE                TELEPHONE SEX EMPLOYED   SALARY  ACCOUNT
      3  Jones David             292-3832  M   06/15/82  1550.00   225.00
      8  Beam Sandy              225-6912  F   02/15/86  1450.00   175.00
      9  Johnson Frank           223-7928  M   03/20/90  1500.00     0.00
```

Character data inequalities also may be used in a condition.

```
. DISPLAY FOR salary * 12 <= 18000
Record#  EMPLOYEE                TELEPHONE SEX EMPLOYED   SALARY  ACCOUNT
      8  Beam Sandy              225-6912  F   02/15/86  1450.00   175.00
      9  Johnson Frank           223-7928  M   03/20/90  1500.00     0.00
```

You may use numeric expressions with mathematical operators as items in a condition.

Converting Data Types

The data items used within a simple condition must be of the same data type. You often may need to convert one data item into another data type for use in the **FOR** <condition> parameter. Data type conversion is accomplished through using dBASE functions. Two such functions are the **DTOC** (Date-to-Character) and **CTOD** (Character-to-Date) functions. To give you experience converting data types, do the following.

17. Type and enter the command shown in gray.

```
. DISPLAY FOR employed > CTOD("01/01/84")
Record#  EMPLOYEE              TELEPHONE SEX EMPLOYED   SALARY  ACCOUNT
      4  Sill Sally            224-4321  F   02/15/84  1507.00   150.00
      7  Martins Mary          222-2123  F   11/01/85  1600.00   200.50
      8  Beam Sandy            225-6912  F   02/15/86  1450.00   175.00
      9  Johnson Frank         223-7928  M   03/20/90  1500.00     0.00
```

Here the character data "01/01/84" must be converted to date-type data with the **CTOD** (Character-to-Date) function in order to compare it with the data in the date-type field employed.

Using More Complex Conditions

Logical operators may be used with relational operators to test for more than one condition at a time.

18. Type and enter the commands shown in gray.

```
. DISPLAY FOR salary < 1600 .AND. sex = "F"
Record#  EMPLOYEE              TELEPHONE SEX EMPLOYED   SALARY  ACCOUNT
      4  Sill Sally            224-4321  F   02/15/84  1507.00   150.00
      8  Beam Sandy            225-6912  F   02/15/86  1450.00   175.00

. DISPLAY employee,salary FOR salary < 1600 .OR. salary > 1800
Record#  employee               salary
      1  Pratt John            1949.00
      3  Jones David           1550.00
      4  Sill Sally            1507.00
      8  Beam Sandy            1450.00
      9  Johnson Frank         1500.00
```

Displaying Certain Data with the **DISPLAY** Command

Use the **DISPLAY** command and its various parameters to display the described information from the database.

19. Display all fields of the second record.

```
Record#  EMPLOYEE                    TELEPHONE SEX EMPLOYED   SALARY  ACCOUNT
      2  Smoler Ellen                225-3212  F   09/15/83  1650.00   300.00
```

20. Display only the employee's name and salary for all records.

```
Record#  employee                     salary
      1  Pratt John                  1949.00
      2  Smoler Ellen                1650.00
      3  Jones David                 1550.00
      4  Sill Sally                  1507.00
      5  Knat Michael                1800.00
      6  Smith Paul                  1700.00
      7  Martins Mary                1600.00
      8  Beam Sandy                  1450.00
      9  Johnson Frank               1500.00
```

21. Display the name, gender, and date hired for all employees who make more than $1,600.00 per month.

```
Record#  employee                    sex employed
      1  Pratt John                  M   06/22/82
      2  Smoler Ellen                F   09/15/83
      5  Knat Michael                M   09/15/80
      6  Smith Paul                  M   11/15/81
```

22. Display the name, date hired, and salary of all employees who were hired before May 30, 1984.

```
Record#  employee                    employed   salary
      1  Pratt John                  06/22/82  1949.00
      2  Smoler Ellen                09/15/83  1650.00
      3  Jones David                 06/15/82  1550.00
      4  Sill Sally                  02/15/84  1507.00
      5  Knat Michael                09/15/80  1800.00
      6  Smith Paul                  11/15/81  1700.00
```

23. Display the name, date hired, and salary of all men who were hired on or before June 15, 1982.

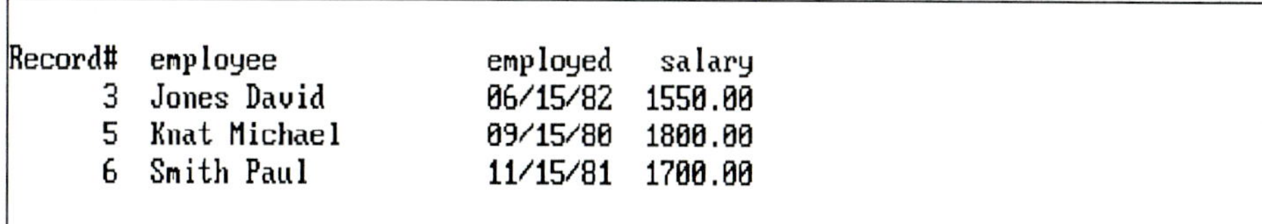

```
Record#  employee              employed   salary
      3  Jones David           06/15/82  1550.00
      5  Knat Michael          09/15/80  1800.00
      6  Smith Paul            11/15/81  1700.00
```

LESSON 7
Other Important dBASE Dot (.) Prompt Commands

The DELETE and RECALL Commands

Marking and Unmarking Records for Deletion

The **DELETE** command may be used to mark a record for deletion when you are in the dot (.) prompt command mode. The form of the **DELETE** command is

DELETE [<scope>] [**FOR** <condition>]

To unmark a record marked for deletion, the **RECALL** command may be used. Its form is

RECALL [<scope>] [**FOR** <condition>]

1. To demonstrate using the two commands, type and enter the following commands shown in gray.

```
. GO TOP
. DELETE
       1 record deleted
. DISPLAY NEXT 3
Record#  EMPLOYEE              TELEPHONE SEX EMPLOYED   SALARY  ACCOUNT
      1 *Pratt John            225-1234  M   06/22/82  1949.00   200.00
      2  Smoler Ellen          225-3212  F   09/15/83  1650.00   300.00
      3  Jones David           292-3832  M   06/15/82  1550.00   225.00
```

Notice that Record #1 still appears, but there is an asterisk next to it. The asterisk indicates that the **DELETE** command marked the record for deletion, but did not physically remove it from the database. To unmark this record, you may use the **RECALL** command.

2. Continue by typing the following commands shown in gray.

```
. GOTO 1
. RECALL
       1 record recalled
. DISPLAY NEXT 3
Record#  EMPLOYEE              TELEPHONE SEX EMPLOYED   SALARY  ACCOUNT
      1  Pratt John            225-1234  M   06/22/82  1949.00   200.00
      2  Smoler Ellen          225-3212  F   09/15/83  1650.00   300.00
      3  Jones David           292-3832  M   06/15/82  1550.00   225.00
```

3. Next type

```
. GOTO 1
. DELETE FOR employee = "Jones Da"
      1 record deleted
. DISPLAY
Record#  EMPLOYEE             TELEPHONE SEX EMPLOYED   SALARY  ACCOUNT
```

(The record pointer is left at the bottom of the database.)

```
. GO TOP
. DISPLAY NEXT 3
Record#  EMPLOYEE             TELEPHONE SEX EMPLOYED   SALARY  ACCOUNT
      1  Pratt John           225-1234  M   06/22/82  1949.00   200.00
      2  Smoler Ellen         225-3212  F   09/15/83  1650.00   300.00
      3 *Jones David          292-3832  M   06/15/82  1550.00   225.00

. DELETE FOR salary > 1600
      4 records deleted
. DISPLAY ALL
Record#  EMPLOYEE             TELEPHONE SEX EMPLOYED   SALARY  ACCOUNT
      1 *Pratt John           225-1234  M   06/22/82  1949.00   200.00
      2 *Smoler Ellen         225-3212  F   09/15/83  1650.00   300.00
      3 *Jones David          292-3832  M   06/15/82  1550.00   225.00
      4  Sill Sally           224-4321  F   02/15/84  1507.00   150.00
      5 *Knat Michael         221-1235  M   09/15/80  1800.00   125.00
      6 *Smith Paul           223-8251  M   11/15/81  1700.00   350.00
      7  Martins Mary         222-2123  F   11/01/85  1600.00   200.50
      8  Beam Sandy           225-6912  F   02/15/86  1450.00   175.00
      9  Johnson Frank        223-7928  M   03/20/90  1500.00     0.00
```

4. Continue by typing and entering the commands shown in gray.

```
. RECALL ALL
      5 records recalled
. DISPLAY ALL
Record#  EMPLOYEE             TELEPHONE SEX EMPLOYED   SALARY  ACCOUNT
      1  Pratt John           225-1234  M   06/22/82  1949.00   200.00
      2  Smoler Ellen         225-3212  F   09/15/83  1650.00   300.00
      3  Jones David          292-3832  M   06/15/82  1550.00   225.00
      4  Sill Sally           224-4321  F   02/15/84  1507.00   150.00
      5  Knat Michael         221-1235  M   09/15/80  1800.00   125.00
      6  Smith Paul           223-8251  M   11/15/81  1700.00   350.00
      7  Martins Mary         222-2123  F   11/01/85  1600.00   200.50
      8  Beam Sandy           225-6912  F   02/15/86  1450.00   175.00
      9  Johnson Frank        223-7928  M   03/20/90  1500.00     0.00
```

The **PACK** Command

To physically delete all records marked for deletion you use the **PACK** command. The **PACK** command has no parameters—its form is simply **PACK.** Once it is executed, all records marked for deletion are permanently erased from the database.

The **COUNT, SUM,** and **AVERAGE** Commands

The **COUNT, SUM,** and **AVERAGE** commands are used to provide summary data for the database. Their forms are

COUNT [<scope>] [**FOR** <condition>] [**TO** <memvar>]
SUM [<expression list>] [<scope>] [**FOR** <condition>] [**TO** <memvar>]
AVERAGE [<expression list>] [<scope>] [**FOR** <condition>] [**TO** <memvar>]

Notice the introduction of a new type of command parameter, [**TO** <memvar>].

Memory Variables

When the **COUNT, SUM,** and **AVERAGE** commands are executed, dBASE will display a number on the monitor screen. For instance, typing **SUM** account↵ with empfile in use causes dBASE to display the following.

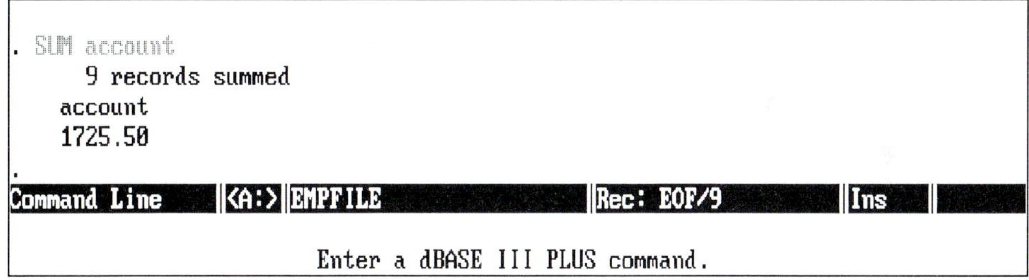

```
. SUM account
     9 records summed
   account
   1725.50
.
Command Line   |<A:>|EMPFILE            |Rec: EOF/9      |Ins  |
                        Enter a dBASE III PLUS command.
```

The number 1725.50 represents the sum of all account fields in the database. The [**TO** <memvar>] parameter of the three commands causes dBASE not only to display the number, but also to store the number in a memory location (variable) for later reference. You can consider a memory variable a single field with its own unique name, independent of the database, able to hold character-, numeric-, logical-, or date-type data. The variable's name is supplied by the user when the variable is created. Several dBASE commands use <memvar>s in their parameters.

*The **STORE TO** and = Commands*

The **STORE** command places data directly into a memory variable. Its form is

STORE <expression> **TO** <memvar>

Some examples of the **STORE** command would be

STORE 5 **TO** A
STORE 10 **TO** B
STORE A+B **TO** C
STORE "Hello There" **TO** D

Another method of directly placing data into a dBASE memory variable is to use the equal (=) sign. The dBASE commands above would then take the form

A = 5
B = 10
C = A+B
D = "Hello There"

Memory variable names must start with a letter and may be up to ten characters long. The additional characters can be letters or numbers, but no special characters or spaces should be included in the names.

The ? Command

The ? command is used to display the contents of a memory variable, the contents of a field in the current record, an expression, and/or a string or numeric constant. As an example of how the ? command works, assume the record pointer is on the first record of this database and type the following commands shown in gray.

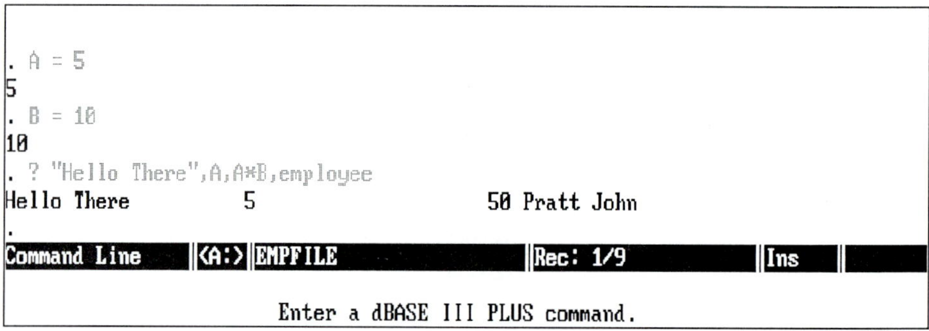

The **DISPLAY MEMORY** Command

The **DISPLAY MEMORY** command displays the name, type of data, and contents of all memory variables currently defined. With dBASE III Plus, 256 memory variables may be currently defined.

Using the **COUNT** and **SUM** Commands

5. Continue by typing and entering the following commands shown in gray.

```
. COUNT FOR sex = "M" TO x
      5 records
. COUNT FOR sex = "F" TO y
      4 records
. ? "Total men =",x
Total men =          5
. ? "Total women =",y
Total women =          4
. DISPLAY MEMORY
X           pub   N          5  (         5.00000000)
Y           pub   N          4  (         4.00000000)
    2 variables defined,      18 bytes used
  254 variables available,   5982 bytes available

.
Command Line     ||<A:>||EMPFILE                ||Rec: EOF/9         ||Ins  ||

                            Enter a dBASE III PLUS command.
```

```
. SUM salary FOR sex = "M" TO xpay
      5 records summed
     salary
   8499.00
. SUM salary FOR sex = "F" TO ypay
      4 records summed
     salary
   6207.00
. ? "Total male salaries = ",xpay
Total male salaries =       8499.00
. ? "Total female salaries = ",ypay
Total female salaries =       6207.00
.
Command Line     ||<A:>||EMPFILE                ||Rec: EOF/9         ||Ins  ||

                            Enter a dBASE III PLUS command.
```

```
. AVERAGE salary FOR sex = "M" TO xavg
      5 records averaged
  salary
 1699.80
. AVERAGE salary FOR sex = "F" TO yavg
      4 records averaged
  salary
 1551.75
. xprint = "Average male salary = "
Average male salary =
. yprint = "Average female salary = "
Average female salary =
. ? xprint,xavg
Average male salary =        1699.80
. ? yprint,yavg
Average female salary =        1551.75
.
Command Line    |<A:>|EMPFILE            |Rec: EOF/9        |Ins  |

                     Enter a dBASE III PLUS command.
```

```
. DISPLAY MEMORY
X           pub   N          5  (          5.00000000)
Y           pub   N          4  (          4.00000000)
XPAY        pub   N       8499.00  (      8499.00000000)
YPAY        pub   N       6207.00  (      6207.00000000)
XAVG        pub   N       1699.80  (      1699.80000000)
YAVG        pub   N       1551.75  (      1551.75000000)
XPRINT      pub   C  "Average male salary = "
YPRINT      pub   C  "Average female salary = "
    8 variables defined,      104 bytes used
  248 variables available,   5896 bytes available

.
Command Line    |<A:>|EMPFILE            |Rec: EOF/9        |Ins  |

                     Enter a dBASE III PLUS command.
```

The **REPLACE** Command

One highly useful dBASE command is **REPLACE,** which has the form

REPLACE [<scope>] <field> **WITH** <expression> [**FOR** <condition>]

The **REPLACE** command is most useful for making the same change to several records meeting a certain condition. For instance, to give all women in the database a 10 percent increase in salary, the command

REPLACE salary **WITH** salary + (salary * .10) **FOR** sex = "F"

could be entered. When executed, each of the female employees would receive a pay raise of 10 percent. The command says, in effect, "For each record, replace what is in the field named salary with what is there plus 10 percent of what is there, if "F" is found in the field named sex for that record."

The default <scope> is **ALL** since the **FOR** parameter is used; the <field> to replace is salary; the <expression> to replace the field salary with is "salary + (salary * .10)"; and the <condition> of the **FOR** parameter is "sex = "F"."

6. Type and enter the following commands shown in gray to see how dBASE's **REPLACE** command works.

```
. DISPLAY RECORD 6
Record#  EMPLOYEE                  TELEPHONE SEX EMPLOYED   SALARY  ACCOUNT
      6  Smith Paul                223-8251  M   11/15/81  1700.00   350.00

. REPLACE telephone WITH "244-1010"
      1 record replaced
. DISPLAY
Record#  EMPLOYEE                  TELEPHONE SEX EMPLOYED   SALARY  ACCOUNT
      6  Smith Paul                244-1010  M   11/15/81  1700.00   350.00

.
Command Line      |<A:>|EMPFILE                 |Rec: 6/9          |Ins  |

                      Enter a dBASE III PLUS command.
```

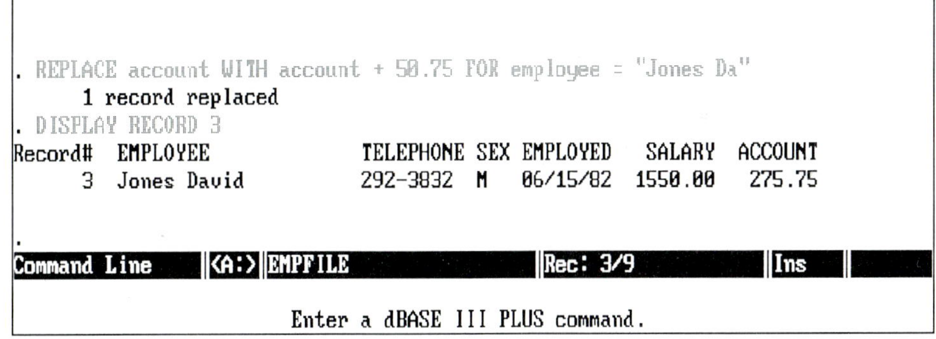

```
. REPLACE account WITH account + 50.75 FOR employee = "Jones Da"
      1 record replaced
. DISPLAY RECORD 3
Record#  EMPLOYEE                  TELEPHONE SEX EMPLOYED   SALARY  ACCOUNT
      3  Jones David               292-3832  M   06/15/82  1550.00   275.75

.
Command Line      |<A:>|EMPFILE                 |Rec: 3/9          |Ins  |

                      Enter a dBASE III PLUS command.
```

NOTE: The account amount was $225.00 before the change.

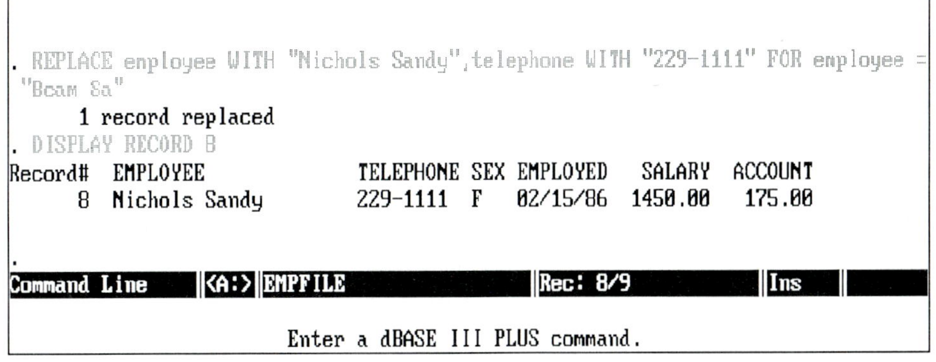

```
. REPLACE employee WITH "Nichols Sandy",telephone WITH "229-1111" FOR employee =
 "Bcam Sa"
      1 record replaced
. DISPLAY RECORD 8
Record#  EMPLOYEE                  TELEPHONE SEX EMPLOYED   SALARY  ACCOUNT
      8  Nichols Sandy             229-1111  F   02/15/86  1450.00   175.00

.
Command Line      |<A:>|EMPFILE                 |Rec: 8/9          |Ins  |

                      Enter a dBASE III PLUS command.
```

Notice that when a command is longer than the screen line of 80 characters, dBASE automatically wraps it around to the next line when the command is executed. The maximum length of a dBASE III Plus command is 254 characters.

The **LOCATE** Command

The **LOCATE** command is used to move the record pointer to the first record in the database whose data evaluate as .T.rue for the command's **FOR** <condition>. The form of the **LOCATE** command is

LOCATE [<scope>] **FOR** <condition>

If the [<scope>] is omitted or is specified as **ALL,** the search for record(s) evaluating .T.rue begins at the top of the database and continues down, record after record (sequentially), until a record that satisfies the **FOR** condition is found or until the bottom of the database is reached. If a record that satisfies the **FOR** <condition> is found, dBASE stops the record pointer on it, making it the current record, and displays its record number on the screen.

The **CONTINUE** Command

Once the **LOCATE** command has found a record that satisfies its **FOR** <condition>, another dBASE command, **CONTINUE,** may be used to locate the next record in the database that satisfies the same **FOR** <condition>. The **CONTINUE** command has no parameters.

LESSON 8
Sorting a Database

The **SORT** Command

Two different methods exist for sorting the records in a dBASE III Plus database. One method uses the **SORT** command with the form

SORT TO <new file> **ON** <field list>

When the **SORT** command is executed, dBASE creates a second database file on the disk using the records and record structure from the current database file. You then have two database files from which to choose when you enter the **USE** command.

For example, if you type ||**SORT TO** payfile **ON** salary↵|| while empfile is in use, a second database (.DBF) file will be created under the name "payfile." If you then type ||**USE** payfile↵ **DISPLAY ALL**↵||, the database would be displayed as it exists, sorted according to salary with the records of the database renumbered.

NOTE: The following screens are for illustration only. Do not enter the commands shown.

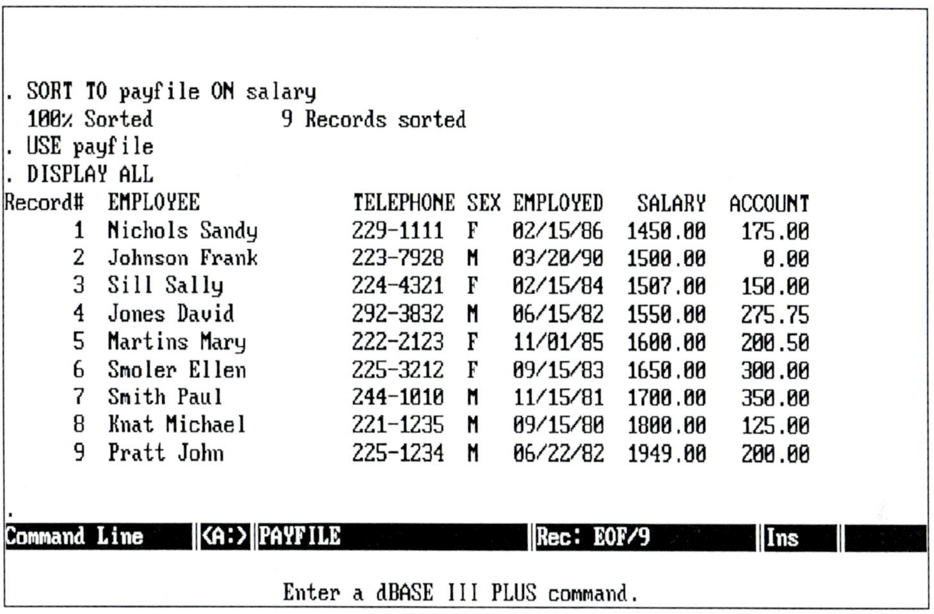

```
. SORT TO payfile ON salary
  100% Sorted          9 Records sorted
. USE payfile
. DISPLAY ALL
Record#  EMPLOYEE                 TELEPHONE SEX EMPLOYED   SALARY   ACCOUNT
      1  Nichols Sandy            229-1111  F   02/15/86  1450.00   175.00
      2  Johnson Frank            223-7928  M   03/20/90  1500.00     0.00
      3  Sill Sally               224-4321  F   02/15/84  1507.00   150.00
      4  Jones David              292-3832  M   06/15/82  1550.00   275.75
      5  Martins Mary             222-2123  F   11/01/85  1600.00   200.50
      6  Smoler Ellen             225-3212  F   09/15/83  1650.00   300.00
      7  Smith Paul               244-1010  M   11/15/81  1700.00   350.00
      8  Knat Michael             221-1235  M   09/15/80  1800.00   125.00
      9  Pratt John               225-1234  M   06/22/82  1949.00   200.00
.
Command Line     ||<A:>||PAYFILE            ||Rec: EOF/9        ||Ins  ||

                        Enter a dBASE III PLUS command.
```

The **INDEX** Command

The other method of sorting records is with the **INDEX** command, which has the form

INDEX ON <expression> **TO** <index file>

The **INDEX** command, however, does not actually sort the records in the database nor does it create an entire new database file. Instead, it creates a smaller index file which is given an .NDX file extension when it is saved onto the disk.

An index file resides in RAM with its related database and is copied into RAM when the **USE** command is given with its **INDEX** parameter. For instance, if you type **INDEX ON** salary **TO** paydex ↵, an index (.NDX) file named paydex will be created on the disk.

If you then type **USE** empfile **INDEX** paydex↵, both the database (empfile.DBF) and index (paydex.NDX) file will be read into RAM.

An Index File in RAM

Using the model of computer RAM, an index file in use with a database can be thought of as

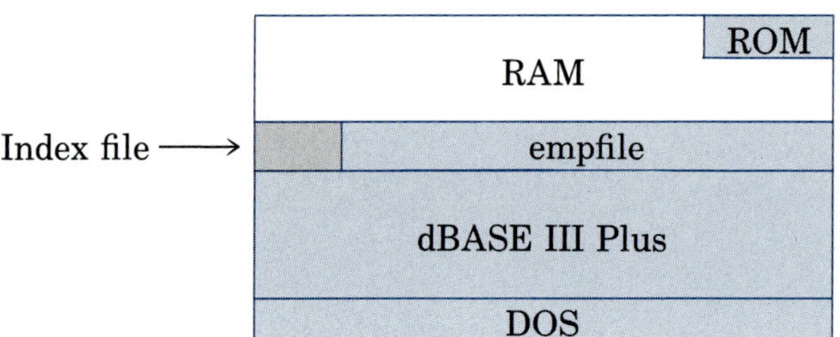

The index file is used with the database to treat the database as if it were sorted. Continuing with the example, if you then type **DISPLAY ALL**↵, the screen will display the following.

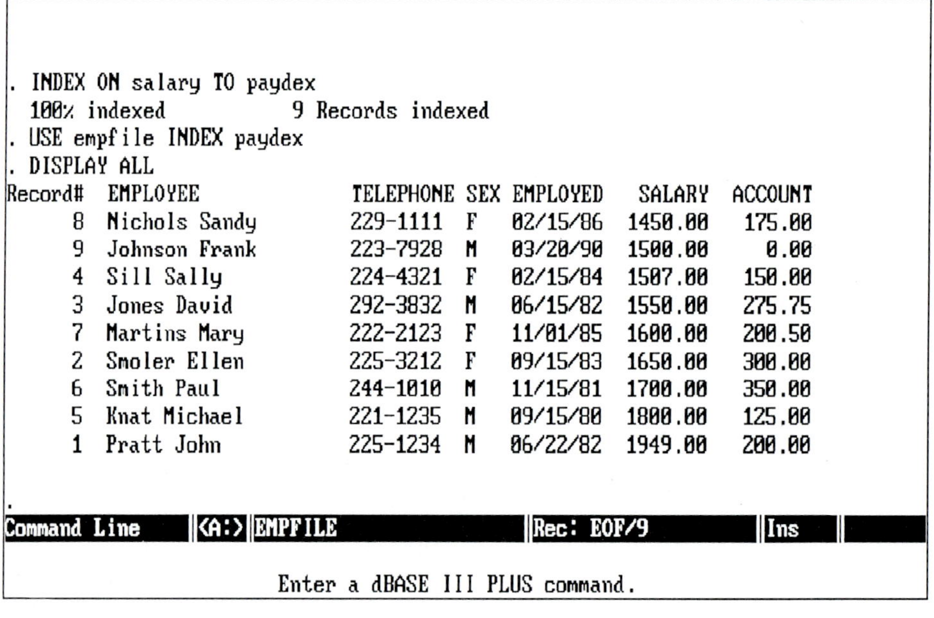

```
. INDEX ON salary TO paydex
  100% indexed          9 Records indexed
. USE empfile INDEX paydex
. DISPLAY ALL
Record#  EMPLOYEE                TELEPHONE SEX EMPLOYED   SALARY  ACCOUNT
      8  Nichols Sandy           229-1111  F   02/15/86  1450.00   175.00
      9  Johnson Frank           223-7928  M   03/20/90  1500.00     0.00
      4  Sill Sally              224-4321  F   02/15/84  1507.00   150.00
      3  Jones David             292-3832  M   06/15/82  1550.00   275.75
      7  Martins Mary            222-2123  F   11/01/85  1600.00   200.50
      2  Smoler Ellen            225-3212  F   09/15/83  1650.00   300.00
      6  Smith Paul              244-1010  M   11/15/81  1700.00   350.00
      5  Knat Michael            221-1235  M   09/15/80  1800.00   125.00
      1  Pratt John              225-1234  M   06/22/82  1949.00   200.00

.
Command Line   <A:> EMPFILE            Rec: EOF/9          Ins

                     Enter a dBASE III PLUS command.
```

Notice the record numbers have not changed; they are still in their original order in the database file empfile. An index file displays the database file *as though* it were sorted, while leaving records in their original order.

How an Index File Affects the Record Pointer

1. Type and enter the following commands shown in gray to see how dBASE's **INDEX** command works.

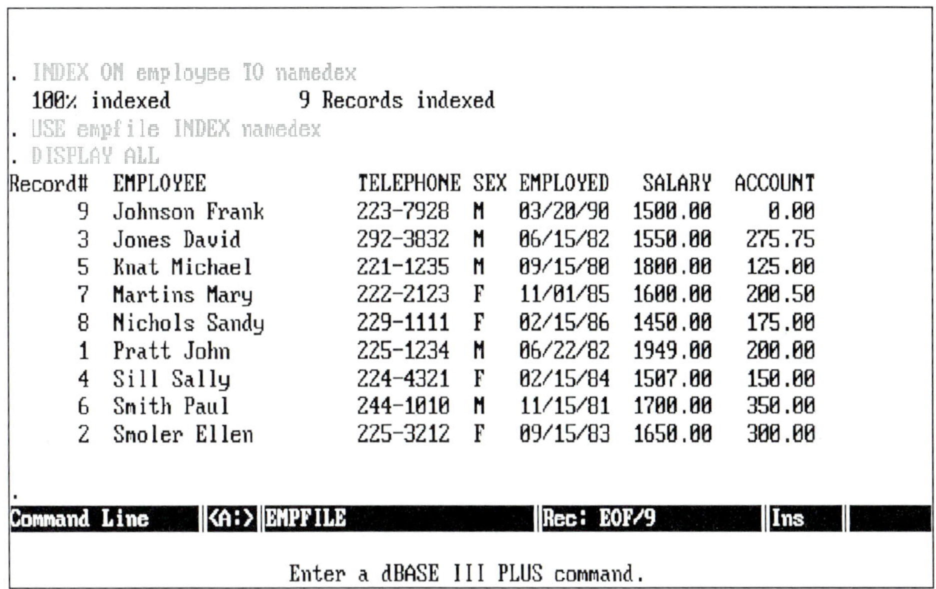

```
. INDEX ON employee TO namedex
 100% indexed            9 Records indexed
. USE empfile INDEX namedex
. DISPLAY ALL
Record#  EMPLOYEE                 TELEPHONE SEX EMPLOYED   SALARY  ACCOUNT
      9  Johnson Frank            223-7928  M   03/20/90  1500.00     0.00
      3  Jones David              292-3832  M   06/15/82  1550.00   275.75
      5  Knat Michael             221-1235  M   09/15/80  1800.00   125.00
      7  Martins Mary             222-2123  F   11/01/85  1600.00   200.50
      8  Nichols Sandy            229-1111  F   02/15/86  1450.00   175.00
      1  Pratt John               225-1234  M   06/22/82  1949.00   200.00
      4  Sill Sally               224-4321  F   02/15/84  1507.00   150.00
      6  Smith Paul               244-1010  M   11/15/81  1700.00   350.00
      2  Smoler Ellen             225-3212  F   09/15/83  1650.00   300.00

.
Command Line  ||<A:>||EMPFILE             ||Rec: EOF/9       ||Ins  ||

                     Enter a dBASE III PLUS command.
```

When you create an index file, you usually index on a <field>. This field becomes the index file's *key*. The keys in the index file are sorted and used with their corresponding record numbers to direct the record pointer to the database. It is useful to think of the record pointer as residing next to the index file, not next to the database, and the index file as being made up of a sorted list of key data with their associated record numbers.

Index File	#	#	Database File					
→ Johnson Frank	9	1	Pratt John	225-1234	M	06/22/82	1949.00	200.00
Jones David	3	2	Smoler Ellen	225-3212	F	09/15/83	1650.00	300.00
Knat Michael	5	3	Jones David	292-3832	M	06/15/82	1550.00	275.75
Martins Mary	7	4	Sill Sally	224-4321	F	02/15/84	1507.00	150.00
Nichols Sandy	8	5	Knat Michael	221-1235	M	09/15/80	1800.00	125.00
Pratt John	1	6	Smith Paul	244-1010	M	11/15/81	1700.00	350.00
Sill Sally	4	7	Martins Mary	222-2123	F	11/01/85	1600.00	200.50
Smith Paul	6	8	Nichols Sandy	229-1111	F	02/15/86	1450.00	175.00
Smoler Ellen	2	9	Johnson Frank	223-7928	M	03/20/90	1500.00	0.00

With an index file in use with a database, a command such as **GO TOP** sends the record pointer to the top of the index file rather than to the top of the database. dBASE then uses the record number located there to determine which record to make the current record. So, if a command such as **DISPLAY** is executed while the record pointer is at the top of the index file, record #9 of the database file in the example will be displayed.

The result of using a command such as **DISPLAY ALL** is that the pointer goes to the top of the index file, and dBASE displays the database file record for the record number located there, moves the record pointer down one record in the index file (**SKIP**s), and displays the database file record for the record number found there.

Index File — Database File

Index File	#	#	Database File					
Johnson Frank	9	1	Pratt John	225-1234	M	06/22/82	1949.00	200.00
Jones David	3	2	Smoler Ellen	225-3212	F	09/15/83	1650.00	300.00
Knat Michael	5	3	Jones David	292-3832	M	06/15/82	1550.00	275.75
Martins Mary	7	4	Sill Sally	224-4321	F	02/15/84	1507.00	150.00
Nichols Sandy	8	5	Knat Michael	221-1235	M	09/15/80	1800.00	125.00
Pratt John	1	6	Smith Paul	244-1010	M	11/15/81	1700.00	350.00
Sill Sally	4	7	Martins Mary	222-2123	F	11/01/85	1600.00	200.50
Smith Paul	6	8	Nichols Sandy	229-1111	F	02/15/86	1450.00	175.00
Smoler Ellen	2	9	Johnson Frank	223-7928	M	03/20/90	1500.00	0.00

The process continues until the pointer reaches the bottom of the index file, and the database records appear on the screen as if they are sorted by employee name.

Indexing on More than One Field

You may create key data for an index file based on more than one field of record data as long as the data being used are characters or converted to characters. To do this, you type **INDEX ON** <field> + <field> **TO** <index file>.

2. To demonstrate, type and enter the following commands shown in gray.

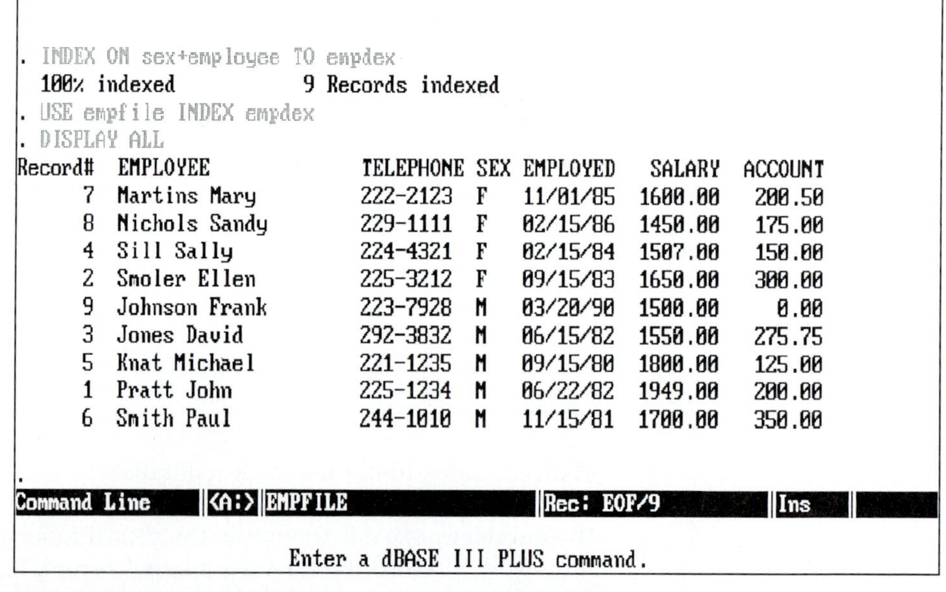

```
. INDEX ON sex+employee TO empdex
  100% indexed          9 Records indexed
. USE empfile INDEX empdex
. DISPLAY ALL
Record#  EMPLOYEE             TELEPHONE SEX EMPLOYED   SALARY  ACCOUNT
      7  Martins Mary         222-2123  F   11/01/85  1600.00   200.50
      8  Nichols Sandy        229-1111  F   02/15/86  1450.00   175.00
      4  Sill Sally           224-4321  F   02/15/84  1507.00   150.00
      2  Smoler Ellen         225-3212  F   09/15/83  1650.00   300.00
      9  Johnson Frank        223-7928  M   03/20/90  1500.00     0.00
      3  Jones David          292-3832  M   06/15/82  1550.00   275.75
      5  Knat Michael         221-1235  M   09/15/80  1800.00   125.00
      1  Pratt John           225-1234  M   06/22/82  1949.00   200.00
      6  Smith Paul           244-1010  M   11/15/81  1700.00   350.00

.
Command Line    ||<A:>||EMPFILE          ||Rec: EOF/9        ||Ins  ||

                   Enter a dBASE III PLUS command.
```

Indexing on more than one field creates an index file with its key data sorted on characters found in the first field (in this case an M or F), followed by characters found in the second field (employee's name here).

Index File

```
FMartins Mary    7
FNichols Sandy   8
FSill Sally      4
FSmoler Ellen    2
MJohnson Frank   9
MJones David     3
MKnat Michael    5
MPratt John      1
MSmith Paul      6
```

Advantages of Indexing

Automatic Updating

Indexing a database is typically the more efficient method of sorting records in a database. One of its advantages is that an index file automatically is updated for records added, deleted, or edited when it is in use with its database.

Several index files may be put into use with the database by entering their names into a list, with each name separated by commas, when you type the **USE** command

USE empfile **INDEX** paydex,namedex, . . .

All index files in use will be updated for changes made to the database, and the first index file listed is the one where the record pointer will reside.

*Faster Record Search/The **SEEK** Command*

When the commands discussed so far cause dBASE to search through the database for records, the search is conducted sequentially from the top of the database to the bottom, with each record evaluated to see if it is .T.rue for the **FOR** <condition>. In large databases, the sequential process of searching can take considerable time.

When a database is in use with an index file, dBASE can find a record very rapidly if the data item for which it is searching is key data for the index. The faster search is done with the **SEEK** command

SEEK <key expression>

For instance, if using an index file with employee names as key data in use with the database empfile, you could move the pointer to Sandy Nichols' record by typing the command

SEEK "Nicho"

The reason that **SEEK** is so much faster at locating a record is because the data through which it is searching (the index file's key data) are sorted. With sorted data the search does not have to begin at the top of the data, but can begin anywhere in the list of key data items. If the first key data item evaluated is less than the one for which dBASE is searching, dBASE can jump the pointer down several data items to make another evaluation. If the record pointer overshoots (if the second key data item is greater than the one for which dBASE is searching), the bounds have been set for finding the sought-after key data item, and the search continues in the same up and down manner until dBASE finds the data item. The result is that fewer evaluations need to be made in order to find the key data item and its record number.

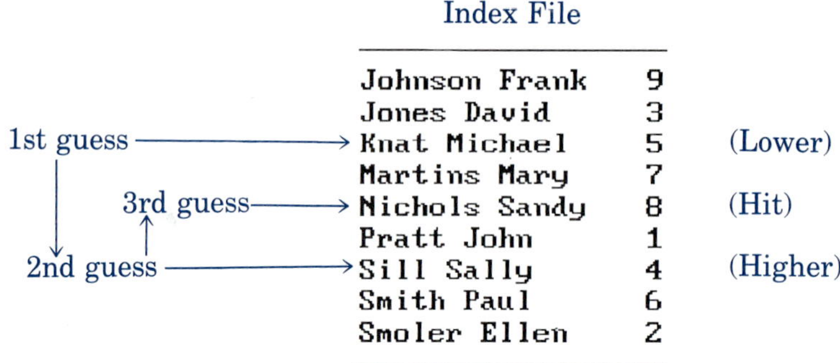

LESSON 9
Creating a dBASE III Plus Report

The **REPORT** Command

The **REPORT** command is used to generate list-type reports based on the fields of data in a database. Its form is

REPORT FORM [<form file>] [<scope>] [**FOR** <condition>] [**HEADING** <character string>] [**TO PRINT**]

The default <scope> of the **REPORT** command is **ALL.** When executed, the **REPORT** command produces a report similar to the following.

```
Page No.     1
06/15/90
                              Employee Full Report
                              ====================

                                                    Current   Account
Employee Name              Phone #  Hire Date       Salary    Balance
-------------              -------  ---------       -------   -------


Johnson Frank              223-7928 03/20/90        1500.00      0.00
Jones David                292-3832 06/15/82        1550.00    275.75
Knat Michael               221-1235 09/15/80        1800.00    125.00
Martins Mary               222-2123 11/01/85        1600.00    200.50
Nichols Sandy              229-1111 02/15/86        1450.00    175.00
Pratt John                 225-1234 06/22/82        1949.00    200.00
Sill Sally                 224-4321 02/15/84        1507.00    150.00
Smith Paul                 244-1010 11/15/81        1700.00    350.00
Smoler Ellen               225-3212 09/15/83        1650.00    300.00
*** Total ***
                                                   14706.00   1776.25

Command Line  |<A:>|EMPFILE                  |Rec: EOF/9

                     Enter a dBASE III PLUS command.
```

The report is columnar, with each column containing the evaluated results of an expression. The columns have column labels and the report has a report title. Totals and subtotals may or may not be included in the report. To produce such a report, the **REPORT** command requires that several specifications be made. A report's specifications are entered while in a dBASE full-screen, menu-driven mode, and are automatically saved by dBASE in a form file with an .FRM extension when the mode is exited by selecting the Exit menu option.

Creating a Report Form File—The **MODIFY REPORT** Command

The **MODIFY REPORT** command is used to enter the mode in which you make a report's specifications. The command's form is

MODIFY REPORT <form file>

To give you experience creating report form files for the **REPORT** command to use, you will first create the form file that produces the example report shown previously.

1. Type ||**USE** empfile **INDEX** namedex←||.

The database(s) whose data will be referred to in the report specifications must be in use prior to executing the **MODIFY REPORT** command.

2. Now type ||**MODIFY REPORT** fullrepo←||.

fullrepo will be the filename of the .FRM file for this report. The following will appear on the screen.

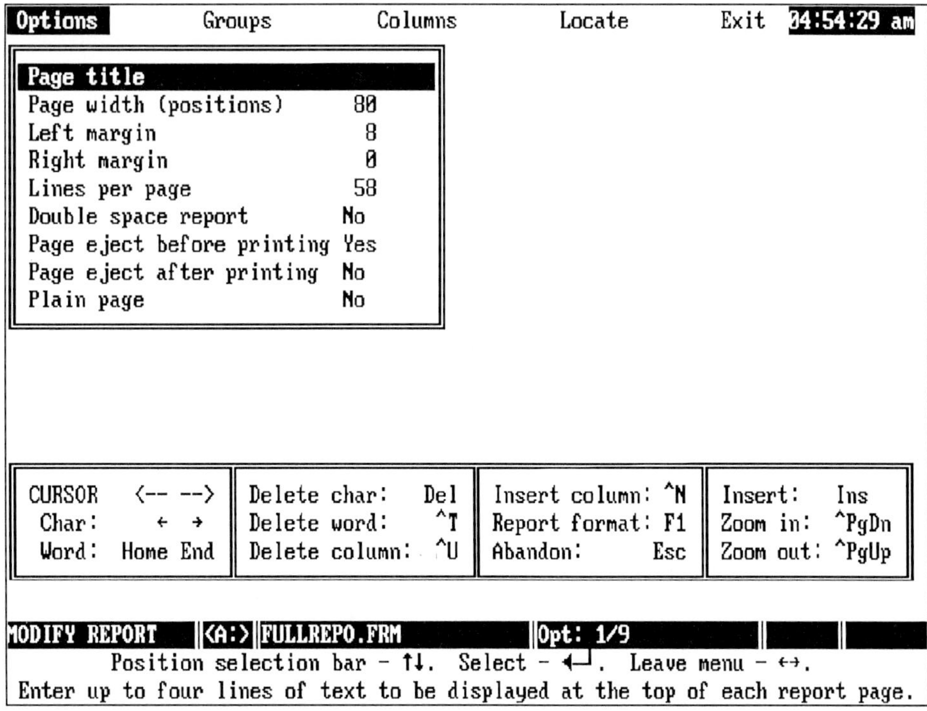

Navigating through dBASE III Plus Menus

Across the top of the screen appears a single line of menu options: Options; Groups; Columns; Locate; and Exit. This line is referred to as the menu bar. You will see one of the options highlighted with a reverse video display.

3. Press the cursor right (→) key two or three times.

Notice that as the highlight moves across the menu bar, dBASE presents a new screen below the highlighted option. The screen appearing below the menu bar option is called a pull-down menu, and is the current menu from which you may select.

To make a selection from a pull-down menu, the ↓ or ↑ keys may be used to move the highlight of the pull-down menu down or up. When the desired menu item is highlighted, the Enter key is pressed to invoke that menu operation. When a menu operation is invoked, you often are left in an editing mode for data entry. The following table of editing keystrokes may be referred to as you complete the next tutorial steps.

Action Desired	Keystrokes
Cursor Movement	
Character Left	Left ←
Character Right	Right →
Line Down	Down ↓
Line Up	Up ↑
Insert/Overwrite	Ins
Delete Characters	
Current Character	Delete (Del)
Previous Character	Backspace
Word Right of Cursor	^T
Line Right of Cursor	^Y
Save and Exit Editing Mode	^End
Columns Menu Bar Option Only	
Move to the Next Column	PgDn
Move to the Previous Column	PgUp
Delete Current Column	^U
Insert New Column	^N

Making Report Specifications

4. Move the menu bar highlight to Options and then select Page title from the pull-down menu by typing ↵.

Selecting Page title causes dBASE to provide an area on the screen into which you may enter the report title.

5. Enter the report title as shown in the following.

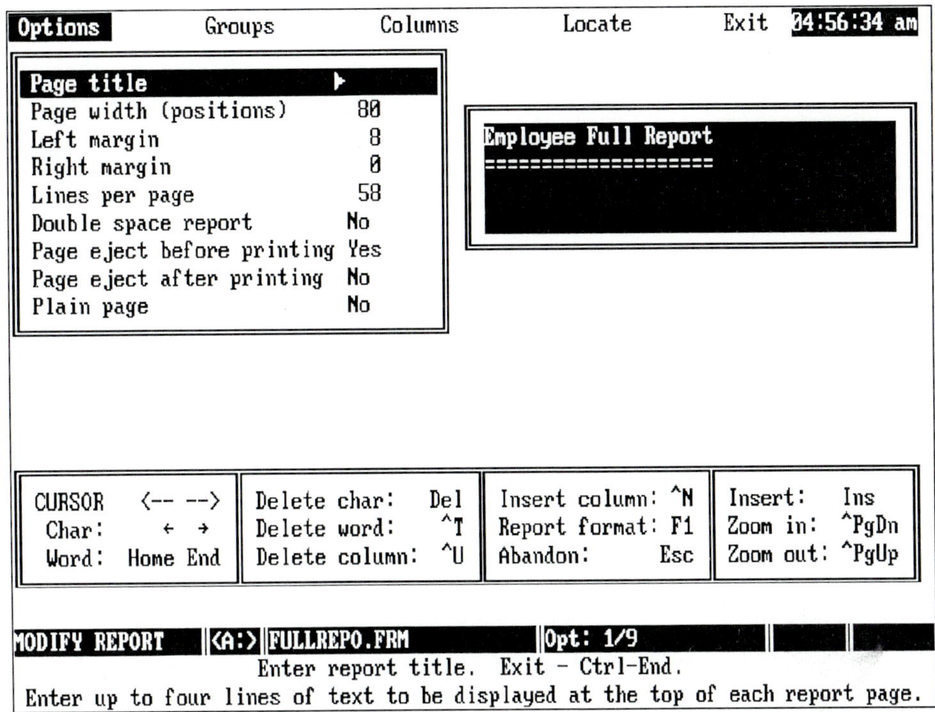

6. When done, type ||^End|| to save and exit the editing mode.
7. Move the pull-down highlight to the menu item marked "Page width (positions)" and select this item by typing ↵. Change the default answer of 80 characters to 72 characters by typing ||72↵||.

You now are ready to specify the contents of the report's columns. To do this you will use the pull-down menu provided by the Columns option of the menu bar.

8. Move the menu bar highlight to Columns.

The pull-down menu presented is for the first column of data in the report. Here you specify the contents of the column (Contents) and the column label to be used in the report (Heading).

9. Select the Contents menu item by typing ↵, and then enter the column contents of the first column by typing ||employee↵||.

Notice that the default value for Width changed from 0 to 20. Twenty characters is the field width of the field named "employee" in empfile.

When you enter the contents of a report column, dBASE checks to see if it is in the form of an expression it can evaluate. If field names are used, they must be fields found in the active database(s). If the expression is made up of a single field name, dBASE will automatically set the default width of the report column to the same width as the field to which it refers.

10. Next select the Heading item of the pull-down menu and enter the column heading as shown below.

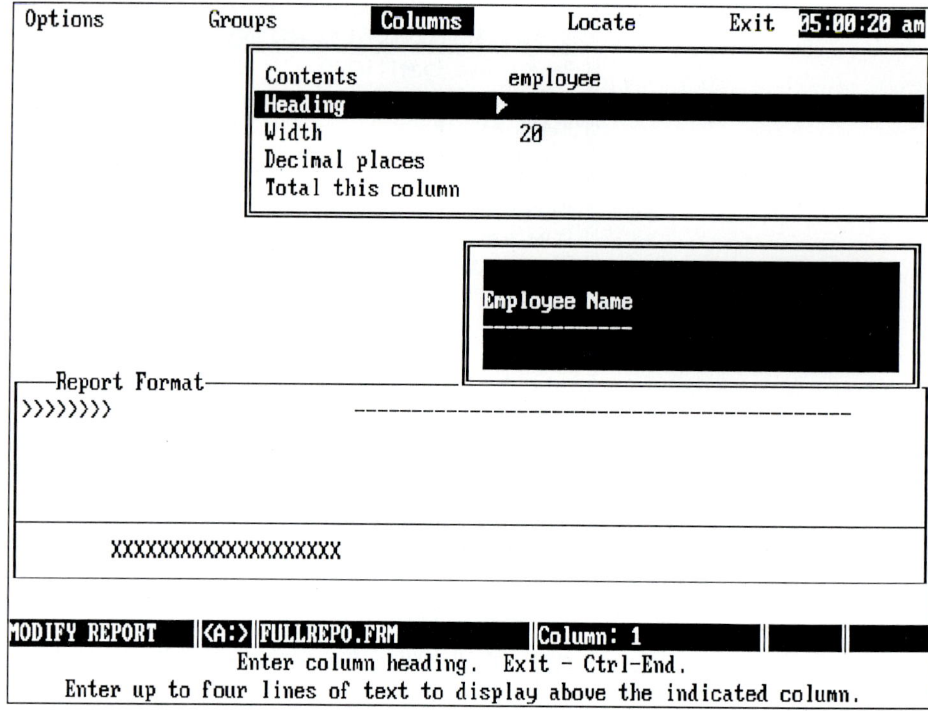

11. When done, type ||^End||.

When specifying the contents and headings of report columns, the PgDn key may be used to move to the next column and the PgUp key is used to move to a previous column.

12. Tap the PgDn key and complete the next column's specifications as shown. (Remember that you must select a menu item by typing ↵ before you enter the data.)

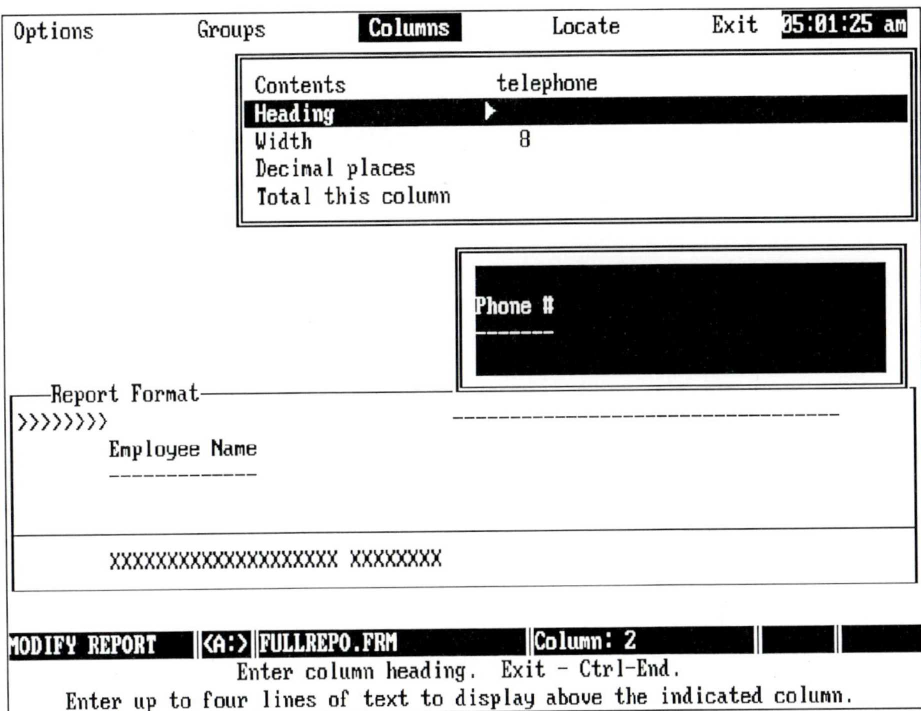

13. After entering the column heading, tap the PgDn key to move to the third column's specifications.

Before continuing, notice the area in the bottom half of the screen.

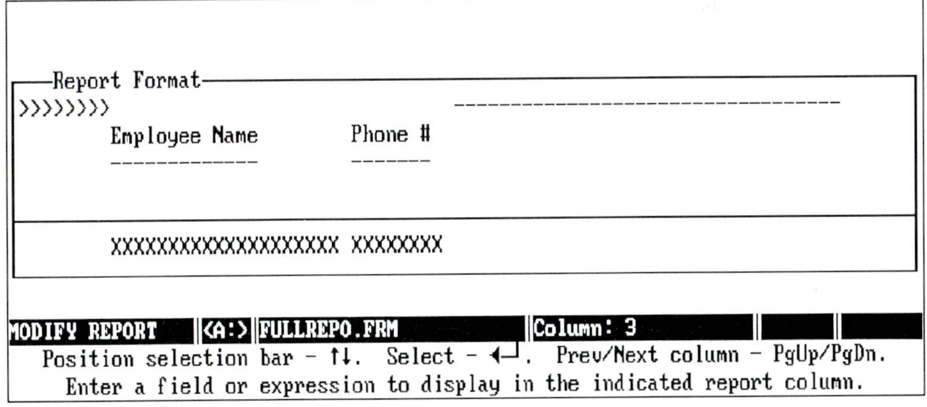

At the bottom of this area is a highlighted line (called the status bar) displaying information about the report you are creating, fullrepo, and the column you are currently on, Column 3. Over the status bar is an emerging picture representing what the finished report will look like. Shown here are the characters used by the left margin (>>>>>>>>), the specified column labels, and a mask for the characters of data included in the column.

The default width of each column in the report is based on the width of the field (or expression) specified as the contents of the column, or the width of the column heading, whichever is larger. The default value can be changed by entering a different value using the Width menu item. Within the printed report, character- or date-type data will be automatically left justified, while numeric-type data will be right justified.

14. Finish specifying the report's column contents with the following data.

Column 3:

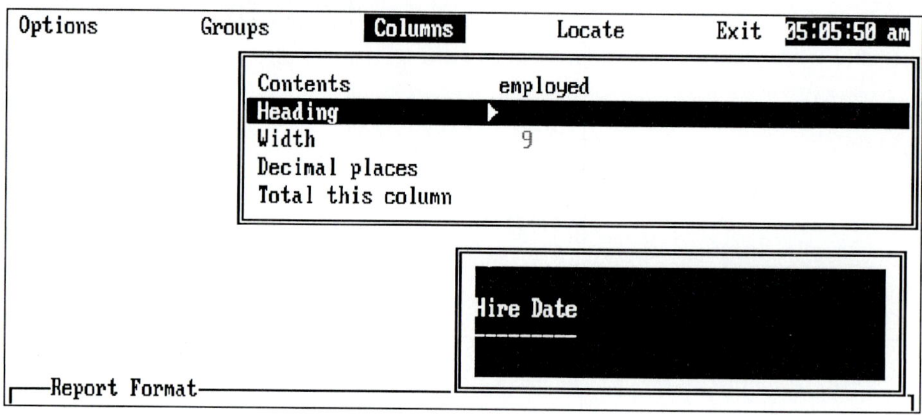

Column 4:

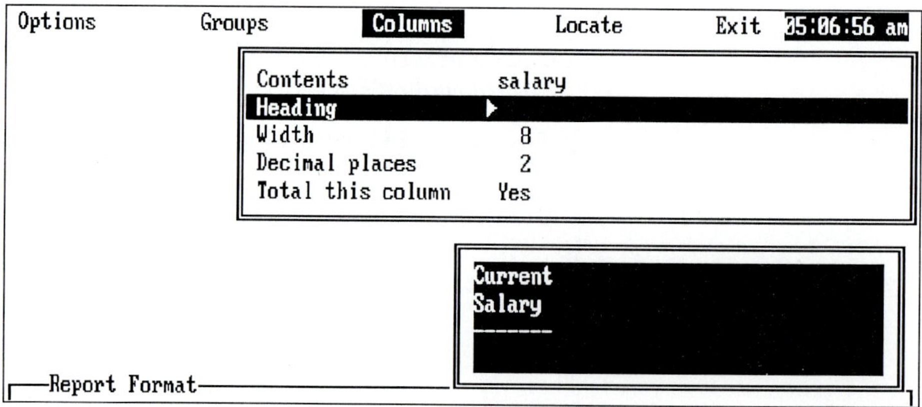

Column 5:

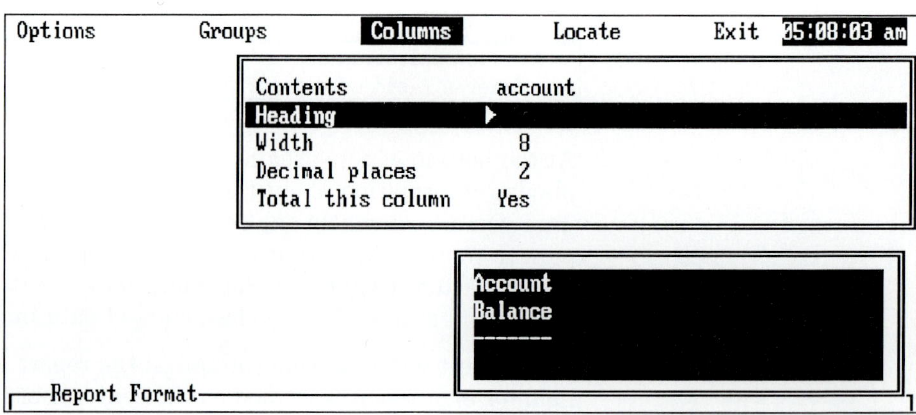

When finished entering the data for field 5, the screen should appear as follows.

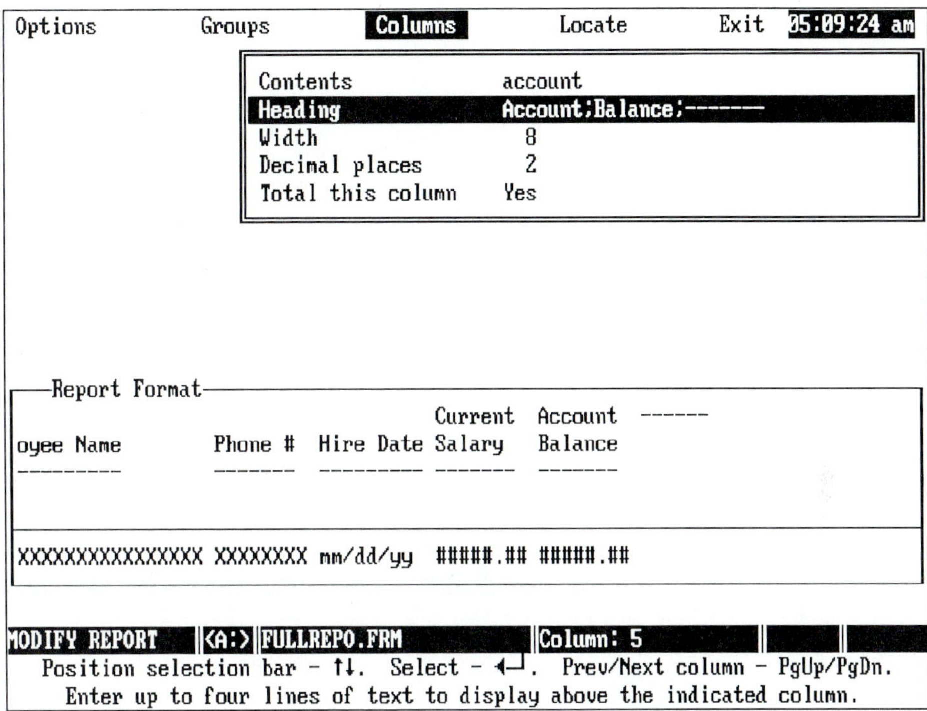

15. Move the menu bar highlight to Exit and select the Save option to save the report data and exit to the dot (.) prompt.

Running Reports

With the report specifications entered and saved in a form file, you are now able to produce the report using the **REPORT FORM** command.

16. Type ‖**REPORT FORM** fullrepo↵‖.

```
Page No.     1
06/15/90
                         Employee Full Report
                         ====================
                                          Current    Account   Account
Employee Name     Phone #     Hire Date    Salary      Limit   Balance
-------------     -------     ---------   -------    -------   -------



Johnson Frank     223-7928    03/20/90    1500.00     225.00      0.00
Jones David       292-3832    06/15/82    1550.00     232.00    275.75
Knat Michael      221-1235    09/15/80    1800.00     270.00    125.00
Martins Mary      222-2123    11/01/85    1600.00     240.00    200.50
Nichols Sandy     229-1111    02/15/86    1450.00     217.00    175.00
Pratt John        225-1234    06/22/82    1949.00     292.00    200.00
Sill Sally        224-4321    02/15/84    1507.00     226.00    150.00
Smith Paul        244-1010    11/15/81    1700.00     255.00    350.00
Smoler Ellen      225-3212    09/15/83    1650.00     255.00    350.00
*** Total ***
                                         14706.00    2204.00   1776.25

Command Line   |<A:>|EMPFILE             |Rec: EOF/9         |    |

                   Enter a dBASE III PLUS command.
```

Later you will see how to print a report on the printer.

Changing a Report's Specifications

A report's specifications may be altered by using the **MODIFY REPORT** command. To give you experience in using this command, as well as the full-screen, menu-driven mode it provides, do the following.

17. Type ‖**MODIFY REPORT** fullrepo↵‖.

NOTE: Refer to the ***MODIFY REPORT*** *editing keystrokes (see table, page D-48) to assist you in making the following changes.*

18. Make the following changes to the specifications in fullrepo.FRM.

- **a.** Change the report's Options/Left margin to 4.
- **b.** Reduce the width of the column containing employee names (Column 1) from 20 to 16.
- **c.** Increase the width of the telephone column (Column 2) to 10.
- **d.** Move to the account column (Column 5) and insert a new column into the report (type ^N to do this).
- **e.** Enter the following data into the new Column 5.

```
Options          Groups          Columns          Locate          Exit   05:32:18 am

                        Contents              INT(salary*.15)
                        Heading               Account;Limit;-------
                        Width                   9
                        Decimal places          2
                        Total this column     Yes

Report Format
                                         Current  Account    Account   --
ployee Name     Phone #     Hire Date Salary   Limit      Balance
-----------     -------     --------- -------  -------    -------

XXXXXXXXXXXXXX XXXXXXXX   mm/dd/yy  #####.## ######.## #####.##

MODIFY REPORT  |<C:>|FULLREPO.FRM              |Column: 5  |
   Position selection bar - ↑↓.  Select - ←┘.  Prev/Next column - PgUp/PgDn.
     Enter up to four lines of text to display above the indicated column.
```

19. Select the Save menu item of the Exit menu bar option to exit the **MODIFY REPORT** mode, and then type ||**REPORT FORM** full-repo←||.

The report produced should have the following form.

```
 Page No.      1
 06/15/90
                          Employee Full Report
                          ====================
                                        Current    Account  Account
 Employee Name   Phone #   Hire Date    Salary      Limit   Balance
 -------------   -------   ---------    -------    -------  -------


 Johnson Frank   223-7928  03/20/90   1500.00     225.00     0.00
 Jones David     292-3832  06/15/82   1550.00     232.00   275.75
 Knat Michael    221-1235  09/15/80   1800.00     270.00   125.00
 Martins Mary    222-2123  11/01/85   1600.00     240.00   200.50
 Nichols Sandy   229-1111  02/15/86   1450.00     217.00   175.00
 Pratt John      225-1234  06/22/82   1949.00     292.00   200.00
 Sill Sally      224-4321  02/15/84   1507.00     226.00   150.00
 Smith Paul      244-1010  11/15/81   1700.00     255.00   350.00
 Smoler Ellen    225-3212  09/15/83   1650.00     255.00   350.00
 Smoler Ellen    225-3212  09/15/83   1650.00     247.00   300.00
*** Total ***
                                     14706.00    2204.00  1776.25

Command Line   |<A:>|EMPFILE                   |Rec: EOF/9  |

                      Enter a dBASE III PLUS command.
```

Running Selective Reports

dBASE's **REPORT** command lets you be selective with your reports through the use of the **FOR** <condition> parameter of the command.

20. Type the following commands shown in gray.

```
. REPORT FORM fullrepo FOR sex = "F"
   Page No.     1
   06/15/90
                      Employee Full Report
                      ====================

                                                Current   Account   Account
   Employee Name    Phone #     Hire Date       Salary     Limit    Balance
   -------------    -------     ---------      -------   -------   -------


   Martins Mary     222-2123    11/01/85       1600.00    240.00    200.50
   Nichols Sandy    229-1111    02/15/86       1450.00    217.00    175.00
   Sill Sally       224-4321    02/15/84       1507.00    226.00    150.00
   Smoler Ellen     225-3212    09/15/83       1650.00    247.00    300.00
  *** Total ***
                                               6207.00    930.00    825.50

.
Command Line    |<A:>|EMPFILE          |Rec: EOF/9          |    |

                 Enter a dBASE III PLUS command.
```

```
. REPORT FORM fullrepo FOR employed < CTOD("01/01/83")
   Page No.     1
   06/15/90
                      Employee Full Report
                      ====================

                                                Current   Account   Account
   Employee Name    Phone #     Hire Date       Salary     Limit    Balance
   -------------    -------     ---------      -------   -------   -------


   Jones David      292-3832    06/15/82       1550.00    232.00    275.75
   Knat Michael     221-1235    09/15/80       1800.00    270.00    125.00
   Pratt John       225-1234    06/22/82       1949.00    292.00    200.00
   Smith Paul       244-1010    11/15/81       1700.00    255.00    350.00
  *** Total ***
                                               6999.00   1049.00    950.75

.
Command Line    |<A:>|EMPFILE          |Rec: EOF/9          |    |

                 Enter a dBASE III PLUS command.
```

Adding a Report Heading

Another **REPORT** command parameter, **HEADING,** may be used to further describe the report being produced.

21. Type the following command shown in gray.

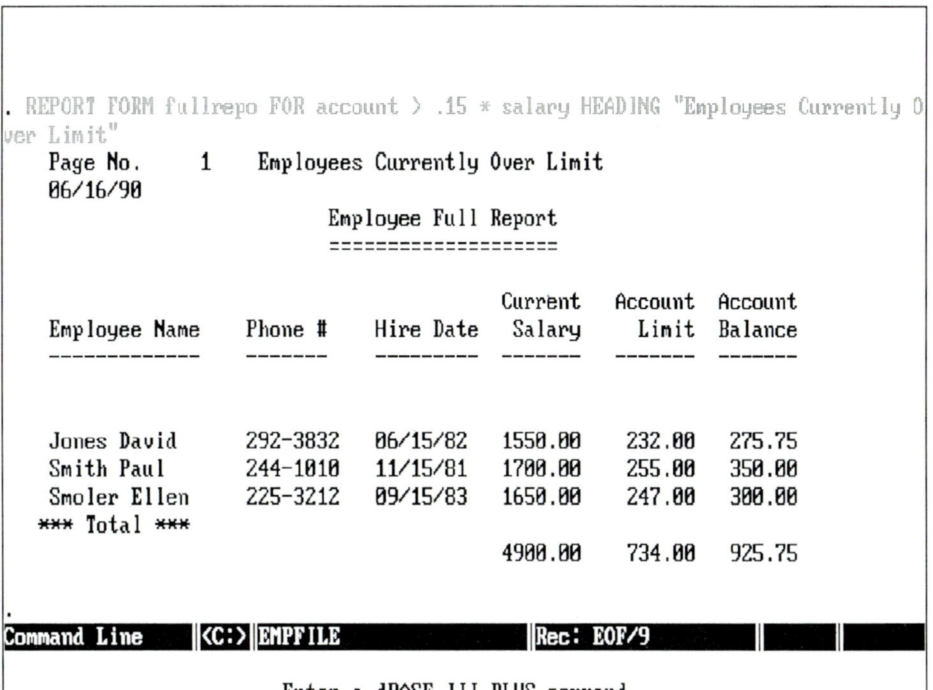

```
. REPORT FORM fullrepo FOR account > .15 * salary HEADING "Employees Currently O
ver Limit"
   Page No.     1    Employees Currently Over Limit
   06/16/90
                         Employee Full Report
                         ====================

                                        Current   Account  Account
   Employee Name    Phone #    Hire Date  Salary     Limit  Balance
   -------------    -------    ---------  -------   -------  -------


   Jones David      292-3832   06/15/82   1550.00    232.00   275.75
   Smith Paul       244-1010   11/15/81   1700.00    255.00   350.00
   Smoler Ellen     225-3212   09/15/83   1650.00    247.00   300.00
  *** Total ***
                                          4900.00    734.00   925.75

.
Command Line   ||<C:>||EMPFILE          ||Rec: EOF/9        ||    ||

                  Enter a dBASE III PLUS command.
```

Report Totals

When a column's contents are specified as numeric data, dBASE's **MODIFY REPORT** command defaults the column's "Total this column" menu item answer to "Yes." To remove report totals, you must move the pull-down menu highlight to the "Total this column" menu item and type ↵. When this is done, the answer toggles to "No" and report totals will not be printed for that column. Repeating the process will toggle the "Total this column" answer back to "Yes."

Subtotals in Reports

You can subtotal groups of data with the **REPORT** command if the database in use is currently indexed or sorted on the field(s) by which you wish to subtotal and the appropriate specifications have been made in the **MODIFY REPORT** editing mode. To give you experience with report subtotals, complete the following steps.

22. Type ||**USE** empfile **INDEX** empdex↵ **MODIFY REPORT** acctrepo↵||.
23. Use the Options menu bar option to enter the page title shown, change the page width to 65 positions, and set the left margin to 15 characters.

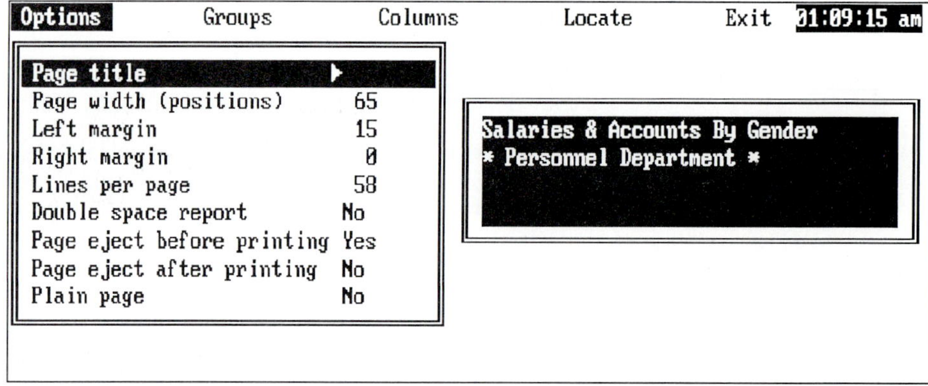

24. Move to the Groups option of the menu bar.
25. Complete this pull-down menu screen by entering the following data.

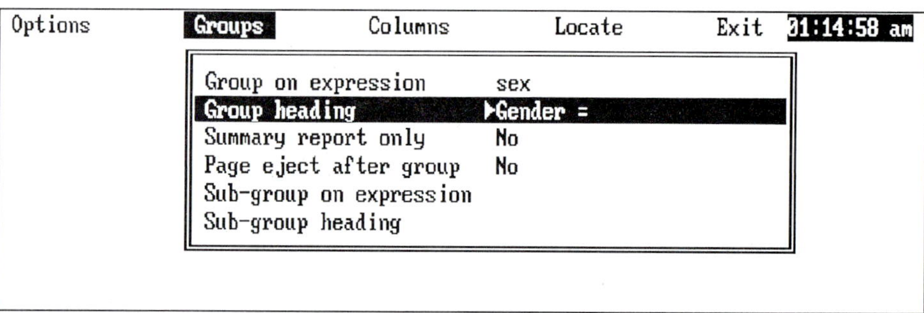

26. Move the menu bar highlight to Columns and complete the following column specifications as shown.

Column 1:

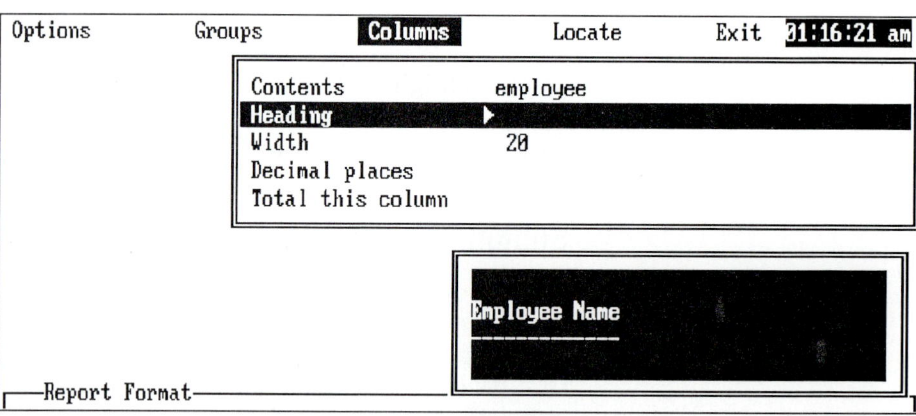

Column 2:

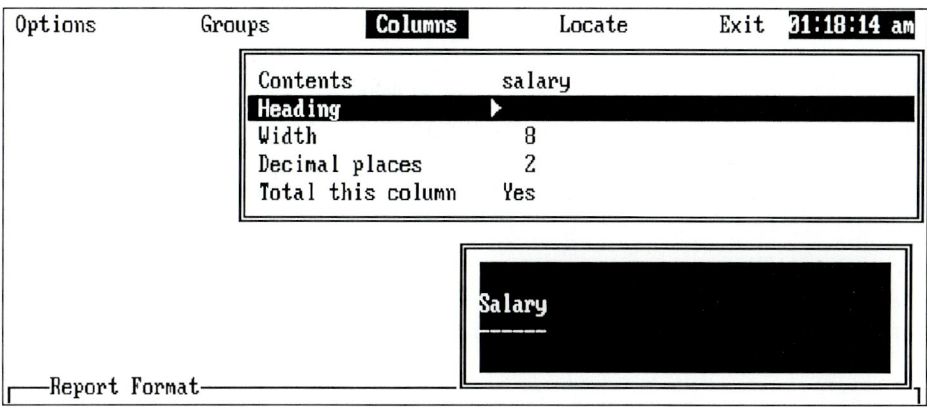

Column 3:

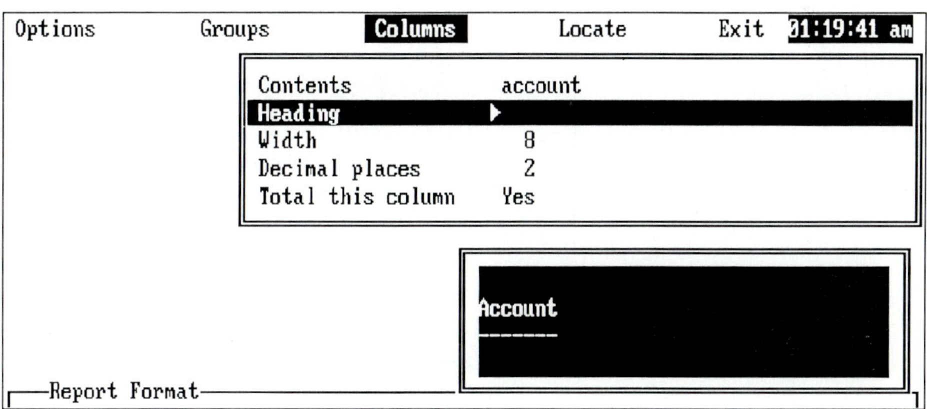

27. Save and exit the **MODIFY REPORT** mode, and then type ||**REPORT FORM** acctrepo↵|| to produce the following report.

```
        Page No.      1
        06/16/90
                  Salaries & Accounts By Gender
                     * Personnel Department *


        Employee Name            Salary  Account
        -------------            ------  -------


       ** Gender = F
        Martins Mary            1600.00   200.50
        Nichols Sandy           1450.00   175.00
        Sill Sally              1507.00   150.00
        Smoler Ellen            1650.00   300.00
       ** Subtotal **
                                6207.00   825.50

       ** Gender = M

        Johnson Frank           1500.00     0.00
        Jones David             1550.00   275.75
        Knat Michael            1800.00   125.00
        Pratt John              1949.00   200.00
        Smith Paul              1700.00   350.00
       ** Subtotal **
                                8499.00   950.75
       *** Total ***
                               14706.00  1776.25

.
Command Line      |<A:>|EMPFILE          |Rec: EOF/9    |  |

                    Enter a dBASE III PLUS command.
```

More on Column Contents

It is important to note that the contents of a report column can be any expression that dBASE is able to evaluate. In order to create such expressions, it often is necessary to convert data types within them through the use of dBASE functions.

Data Type Conversion Functions

You already have used the **CTOD** function to convert character-type data to date-type data in the tutorial. This was done so that a comparison of like data types could be made in a condition. Other dBASE functions used to convert data types include the following.

DTOC(<date variable>)

Date-to-Character-Function Converts date-type data to character-type data.

```
. DISPLAY
Record#  EMPLOYEE                 TELEPHONE SEX EMPLOYED   SALARY  ACCOUNT
      7  Martins Mary             222-2123  F   11/01/85  1600.00   200.50

. ? DTOC(employed) = "11-01-85"
.F.
. ? DTOC(employed) = "11/01/85"
.T.
.
Command Line    |<A:>|EMPFILE              |Rec: 7/9          |    |
                                                                                
                    Enter a dBASE III PLUS command.
```

STR(<numeric data> [,<length>] [,<decimals>])

Numeric-to-String Function Returns a character string converted from a numeric expression. Most useful for deleting leading spaces in output of numeric data and/or forcing the display of desired decimal places.

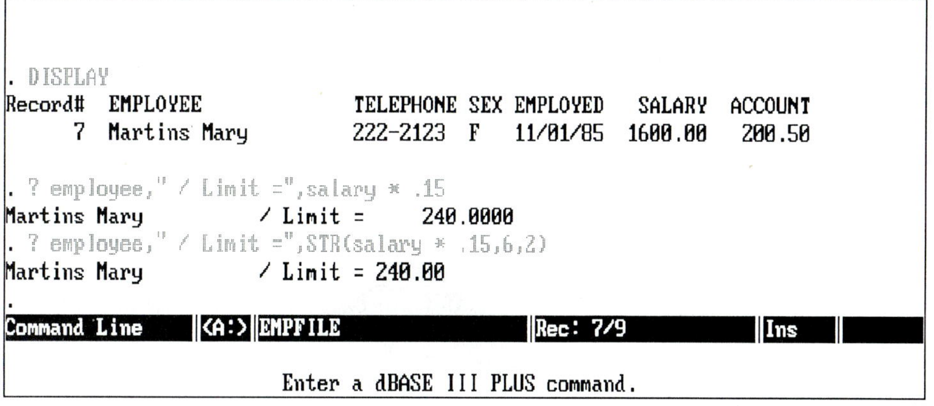

```
. DISPLAY
Record#  EMPLOYEE                 TELEPHONE SEX EMPLOYED   SALARY  ACCOUNT
      7  Martins Mary             222-2123  F   11/01/85  1600.00   200.50

. ? employee," / Limit =",salary * .15
Martins Mary           / Limit =     240.0000
. ? employee," / Limit =",STR(salary * .15,6,2)
Martins Mary           / Limit = 240.00
.
Command Line    |<A:>|EMPFILE              |Rec: 7/9          |Ins |

                    Enter a dBASE III PLUS command.
```

VAL(<character data>)

Character-to-Value Function Returns the numeric value of numbers held as strings beginning at the first character of <character data>.

```
. ? VAL("7312 S.W. Park Blvd.")
              7312.00
. ? VAL("P.O. Box 7312")
          0.00
.
Command Line    |<A:>|EMPFILE              |Rec: 7/9          |Ins |

                    Enter a dBASE III PLUS command.
```

The Immediate If Function

A useful function available with dBASE III Plus is the Immediate If function. Its form is

IIF(<condition>,<true expression>,<false expression>)

The Immediate If function returns its <true expression> if its <condition> evaluates .T.rue and returns its <false expression> if its <condition> evaluates .F.alse. This function is most useful for including conditional column output in a dBASE III Plus report.

With the **IIF** function, the <true expression> and <false expression> may be character-, numeric-, logical-, or date-type data. However, both expressions must be of the same data type.

Producing Reports with More Complex Column Contents

To give you experience using more complex expressions in report column contents, complete the following steps.

28. Type ||**USE** empfile **INDEX** namedex↵||.

29. Next type ||**AVERAGE** salary **TO** salavg↵||.

30. Type ||date = **CTOD**("06/30/90")↵||.

You may enter today's date here. Use the format mm/dd/yy.

The last two steps create two memory variables: one numeric variable named "salavg," holding the average salary, and one date-type variable named "date," holding today's date. They are variables to which the finished report specifications will refer.

31. Type ||**MODIFY REPORT** salaries ↵||.

32. Complete the report's Options, changing page width to 77, left margin to 3, and the page title, as shown.

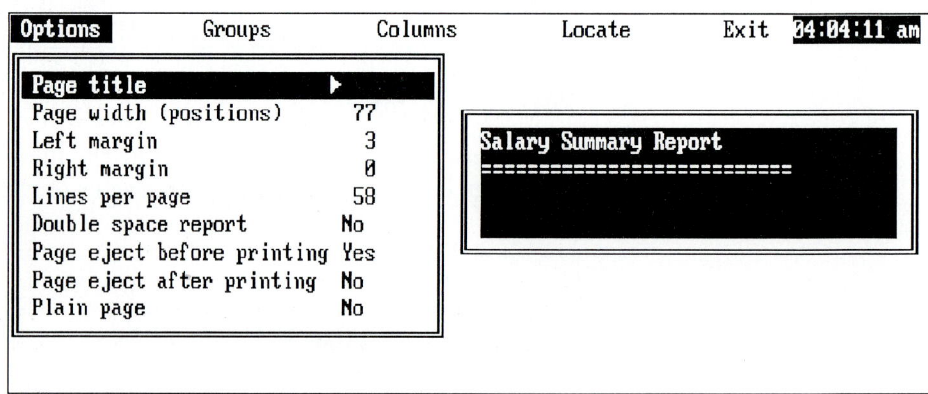

33. Move to the Columns option of the menu bar and enter the first column's data as follows.

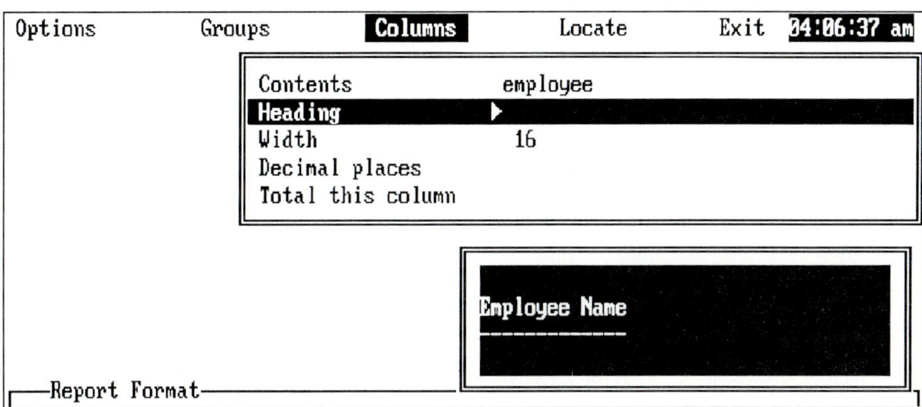

34. Type ||PgDn|| to move to the next column.

The next column's contents will be salary. This time, however, you are going to precede the displayed dollar amount (numeric data) with a dollar sign ($) (character data) in the column. To do so, you will use the **STR** function to convert salary into character data, and then concatenate (add) it to the string, "$".

35. Complete this column's data as shown.

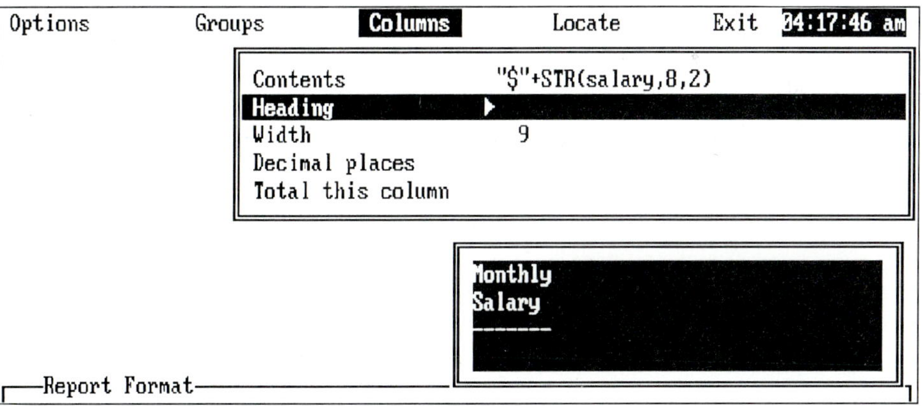

36. Type ||PgDn|| to move to the next column.

In this column (Column 3) you will enter the contents which will display the number of years each employee has worked for the company. To arrive at the final expression used, you must know that date-type data may be used in certain mathematical operations. The following are some examples of "date arithmetic."

`. date1 = CTOD("06/15/90")` `06/15/90`	Place the date-type data for June 15, 1990 into the variable "date1."
`. ? date1 + 90` `09/13/90`	Print date1 + 90. September 13, 1990 occurs 90 days after June 15, 1990.
`. date2 = CTOD("08/14/90")` `08/14/90`	Place the date-type data for August 14, 1990 into the variable "date2."
`. ? date2 - date1` `60`	Print date2 minus date1. There are 60 days between June 15 and August 14, 1990.

By using the memory variable "date," which is holding today's date, and the date field "employed," which holds the hire date for each employee, along with some date arithmetic and display formatting using the **STR** function, you are able to enter the contents for Column 3.

37. Enter the column data as shown.

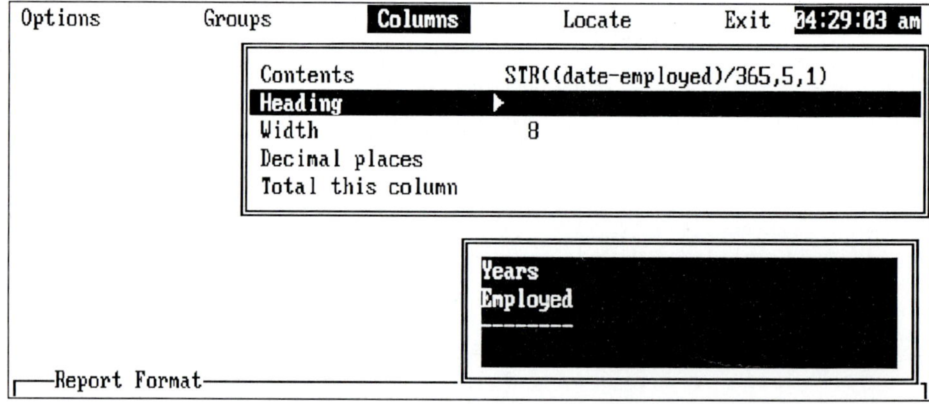

38. Type ||PgDn|| to move to Column 4.

You will enter a simple expression for column contents into column 4. Its purpose is to provide a vertical line through the report.

39. Enter the column contents as shown.

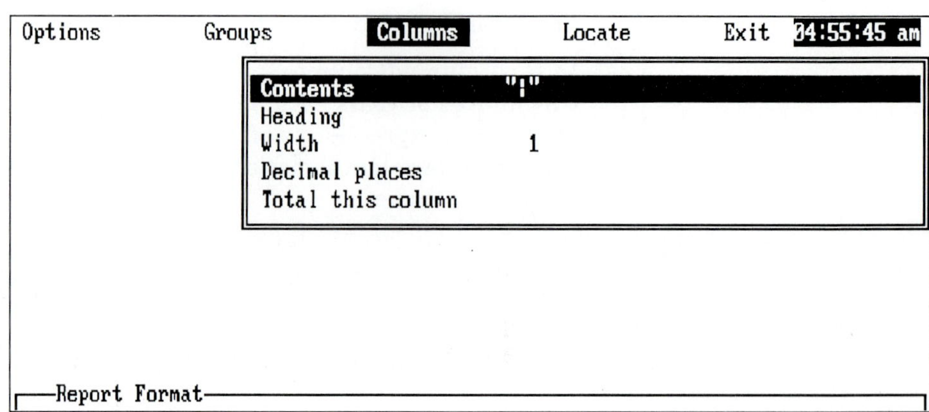

40. Type ||PgDn|| to move to the final column of the report, Column 5.

This column will have the heading "Comments" and its contents will produce the following: If the employee's salary is above or equal to the average salary, no data will be displayed in the column for that employee. However, if the employee's salary is below the average, the message "Under average salary" will be displayed in the column for that employee. The only way to produce such a column of data in a report is through using the **IIF** function.

41. Enter Column 5's contents data as

IIF(salary >= salavg, "", "Under average salary")

then enter the heading and width as shown.

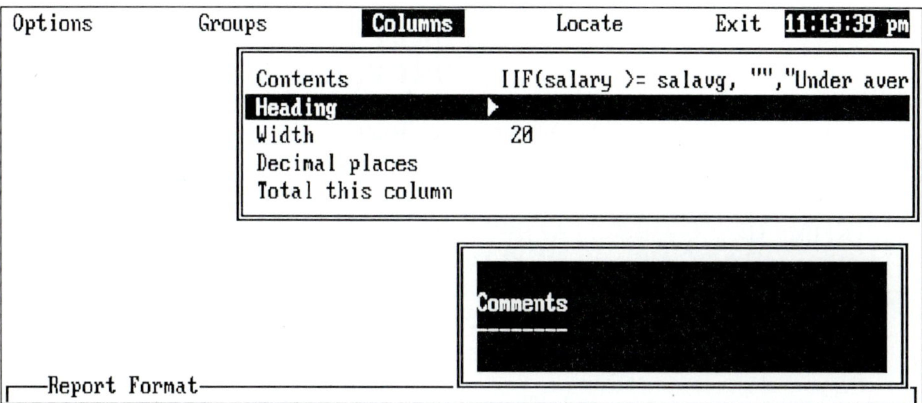

42. Save and exit the **MODIFY REPORT** mode, and then type ||**REPORT FORM** salaries↵|| to produce the following report. (Your report will not have the same figures for "Years Employed.")

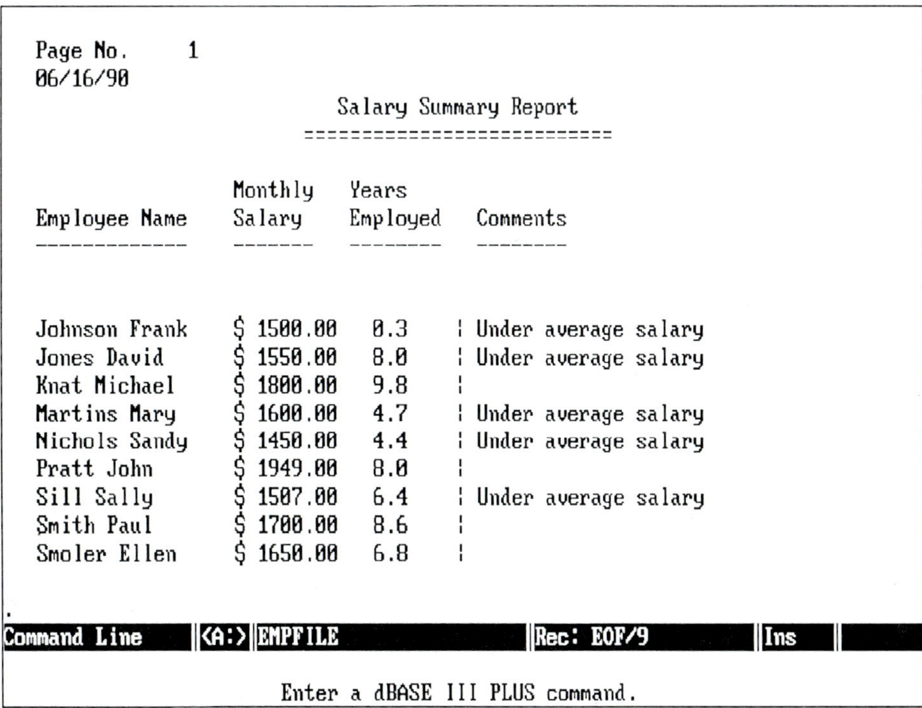

Printing Out a Report

The **REPORT** command will print a report on the printer when you include the **TO PRINT** parameter in it.

43. Make sure the printer is turned on, on-line, and connected to your computer.

NOTE: Your lab may have a shared device control switch. You will need to select your computer as the one currently connected to the printer.

44. Type and enter the following **REPORT** commands.

||**REPORT FORM** fullrepo **TO PRINT**↵||

||**REPORT FORM** salaries **TO PRINT FOR** employed < CTOD("01/01/84")↵||

||**REPORT FORM** acctrepo **TO PRINT**↵||

||**REPORT FORM** fullrepo **TO PRINT FOR** sex= "M" .AND. employed >= **CTOD**("01/01/82") **HEADING** "All Male Employees Hired After 1981"↵||

LESSON 10 Quitting dBASE III Plus

To quit dBASE and return to the DOS operating level (A>), you use the **QUIT** command. The **QUIT** command is very important since it saves all new file data that may have been created during the session. It then closes all dBASE files that may be open at the time before returning to DOS. **QUIT** is always the last command you enter when you use dBASE III Plus.

1. Type ||**QUIT**↵|| to end this dBASE session.

dBASE III Plus Command Files

AN OVERVIEW OF COMMAND FILES

In the dBASE tutorial, you used a number of dBASE commands to manipulate the data in the database empfile.DBF. You displayed records, replaced data in fields, used memory variables to store totals, created report forms, and performed other operations. dBASE executed all of the commands immediately after you entered them.

The direct mode of entering commands can be quite useful for extracting needed information or performing various operations quickly. However, as the commands to perform an operation become longer and more complex, or when certain commands or sets of commands are used repeatedly, typing and entering each command becomes a cumbersome way to accomplish tasks. At such times you may want to consider saving the command(s) in a command file.

Command files are similar to programs written in programming languages such as BASIC. A command file contains dBASE commands which dBASE will execute one after another. All of the commands you have used may be included in a command file, and several dBASE commands and command structures are normally used only in command files.

Creating a dBASE III Plus Command File

Command files are created in the Modify editing mode. To enter the Modify mode from the dot (.) prompt mode, you use the **MODIFY COMMAND** command, which has the form

MODIFY COMMAND <filename>

Command files that you create in this editing mode are stored on the disk under a filename that you supply. dBASE adds a .PRG file extension to the name to identify it as a dBASE program.

When you type the **MODIFY COMMAND** command, dBASE first looks to the default drive for a .PRG file with the same <filename> you specified. If one does not exist, it allocates space on the diskette for a new file under the name specified. If it does find a .PRG file with the specified name, it copies the file into RAM for you to edit.

Entering dBASE Commands into a Command File

When a new .PRG file is specified with the **MODIFY COMMAND** command, a blank screen is presented. Each command in the command file is typed on a single line and the Enter key ↵ is used to advance forward (down the screen) to enter the next command. Since you are in an editing mode, dBASE will not execute the commands when you enter them.

Previous lines may be edited using keystroke commands similar to the keystroke commands used in dBASE's other editing modes (**EDIT** or **BROWSE,** for example).

Saving a Command File

As with all of dBASE's editing modes, the keystroke command **^**End is used to save the .PRG file onto the diskette and return you to the dot (.) prompt mode.

Executing the Commands in a Command File

dBASE will open the command file and begin to execute the commands in it when the **DO** command is typed from the dot (.) prompt mode. The **DO** command has the basic form

DO <filename>

When the **DO** command is entered, commands in the specified file will be executed in the order that they appear, top to bottom, until the last command is completed. dBASE then will return to the dot (.) prompt mode.

The Steps for Creating a Command File

In summary, the basic steps in creating a command file are

1. Type ||**MODIFY COMMAND** <filename>↵|| to begin editing.
2. Type each command on a separate line.
3. Type ||^End|| to save the file.
4. Type ||**DO** <filename>↵|| to execute the commands in the file.

Correcting the Commands in a Command File

If you have made mistakes, you may easily edit your command file by repeating steps 1 through 3 above and using the editing keystroke commands in the following table while in the editing mode to make the necessary changes.

Keystroke	Action
Cursor right key	Moves cursor right one character.
Cursor left key	Moves cursor left one character.
Home key	Moves cursor one word to the left.
End key	Moves cursor one word to the right.
Cursor down key	Moves cursor to the next line.
Cursor up key	Moves cursor to the previous line.
PgUp key	Scrolls the screen up 17 lines.
PgDn key	Scrolls the screen down 17 lines.
Ins key	Toggles between OVERWRITE and INSERT modes.
Enter key ↵	Terminates current line. In the INSERT mode, inserts a line below the current line.
Del key	Deletes character over cursor.
← (Backspace key)	Deletes character to left of cursor.
^T	Erases word to right of cursor.
^Y	Erases current line.
^KR	Reads and inserts another file into the current file.
^END	Saves changes and returns to dot (.) prompt.
Esc	Aborts all changes made and returns to dot (.) prompt.

dBASE III PLUS EXAMPLE COMMAND FILES

The following discussion will provide a general idea of how command files may be used in conjunction with databases. It will introduce you to some of the most often used programming commands and structures through a set of example programs.

Databases and Other Files Used

The first six example programs are written to be used with the database empfile.DBF created in the dBASE tutorial. The following shows the structure of empfile.DBF and a listing of its records.

```
Structure for database: B:empfile.dbf
Number of data records:        9
Date of last update    : 07/20/90
Field  Field Name  Type        Width    Dec
    1  EMPLOYEE    Character      20
    2  TELEPHONE   Character       8
    3  SEX         Character       1
    4  EMPLOYED    Date            8
    5  SALARY      Numeric         8      2
    6  ACCOUNT     Numeric         8      2
** Total **                       54
```

```
Record#  EMPLOYEE              TELEPHONE SEX EMPLOYED  SALARY  ACCOUNT
      1  Pratt John            225-1234  M   06/22/82  1949.00  200.00
      2  Smoler Ellen          225-3212  F   09/15/83  1650.00  300.00
      3  Jones David           292-3832  M   06/15/82  1550.00  275.75
      4  Sill Sally            224-4321  F   02/15/84  1507.00  150.00
      5  Knat Michael          221-1235  M   09/15/80  1800.00  125.00
      6  Smith Paul            244-1010  M   11/15/81  1700.00  350.00
      7  Martins Mary          222-2123  F   11/01/85  1600.00  200.50
      8  Nichols Sandy         229-1111  F   02/15/86  1450.00  175.00
      9  Johnson Frank         223-7928  M   03/20/90  1500.00    0.00
```

Program #6, raises.PRG, requires that another database file for historical salary information be created and have data appended into it from empfile.DBF. The steps for creating this second database are

1. Type ||**CREATE** salhist↵||.
2. Enter the structure as shown in the following.

```
  Field Name  Type       Width  Dec        Field Name  Type      Width  Dec
  ================================        ================================
1 EMPLOYEE    Character    20
2 DATEINCR    Date          8
3 SALARY      Numeric       8    2
```

3. Type ||**USE** salhist↵||.
4. Type ||**APPEND FROM** empfile↵||.
5. Type ||**REPLACE ALL** dateincr **WITH CTOD**("01/01/90")↵||.
6. Type ||**DISPLAY ALL**↵||.

For a more complete explanation, see **APPEND FROM** in the operation and command summary (page D-153).

The database salhist.DBF should appear as follows.

```
Record#  EMPLOYEE                   DATEINCR    SALARY
      1  Pratt John                 01/01/90   1949.00
      2  Smoler Ellen               01/01/90   1650.00
      3  Jones David                01/01/90   1550.00
      4  Sill Sally                 01/01/90   1507.00
      5  Knat Michael               01/01/90   1800.00
      6  Smith Paul                 01/01/90   1700.00
      7  Martins Mary               01/01/90   1600.00
      8  Nichols Sandy              01/01/90   1450.00
      9  Johnson Frank              01/01/90   1500.00
```

Other files referred to and used in the example programs also are products of completing the dBASE tutorial. They include acctrepo.FRM, empdex.NDX, namedex.NDX, fullrepo.FRM, and salaries.FRM.

Example Program Formats

Each example program is presented in five parts.

1. A *program description* of the task that the program is designed to perform.
2. A listing with summary explanations of the *new commands and functions* used in the particular program.
3. A *program listing* of the command file.
4. Any *preliminary commands* required to execute the program successfully.
5. A *sample execution* showing what the output of that program may be.

The description prefacing each program includes an algorithm for the program. An *algorithm* is a step-by-step outline of the program's operation. Each step is described in words close to those used in everyday communication.

Example Program 1—payment.PRG

Program Description

The first sample program is designed to let the user post a payment to an employee's personal account. The intended database in use is empfile.DBF. The general algorithm for the program is

1. Present the user with the employee's name for the current record.
2. Ask the user for the amount of payment.
3. Replace the current record's "account" field with what is there minus the payment.
4. Display the new account balance and prompt the user to indicate when he/she is done viewing the screen.

New Commands and Functions Used

* <comment> dBASE considers any line beginning with an asterisk (*) a comment line and will ignore it during execution. Comments must be placed on lines separate from other commands. See **NOTE** in the operation and command summary, page D-174.

CLEAR The **CLEAR** command clears the screen at any point in a command file.

? [<exp1>[,<exp2>, . . .]] The **?** command displays "the value of" expressions which may include current fields, memory variables, and/or constants. If more than one expression follows the **?** command, the expressions must be separated by commas.

The plus (+) sign may be used to combine different character-type data items into a single character expression. The operation of combining character strings with the plus sign is called string *concatenation.*

INPUT [<expC>] **TO** <memvarN> **INPUT** pauses execution of the program after it displays a prompt defined by the character expression <expC>. The user then is allowed to type and enter a response to the prompt. The response is held in the <memvarN>. The **INPUT** command is used for numeric-type data responses.

ACCEPT [<expC>] **TO** <memvarC> **ACCEPT** is the counterpart of **INPUT.** It is used for character-type data input from the keyboard. The response will be held in the <memvarC> as a character string.

REPLACE <field1> **WITH** <exp1> [,<field2> **WITH** <exp2>, . . .] Replaces the contents of the current record's <field>s with the value of the corresponding expressions <exp>. An expression must evaluate to the same data type as the field being replaced.

RETURN Signals the end of the command file and returns control to the dot (.) prompt or program from which the program was called.

Program Listing

```
* PROGRAM:  Payment.PRG  -  to post payment to employee's account

CLEAR

?
? "       * * * Payment to Employee Account * * * "
?
? "            Employee:  " + employee
? "            Acct Bal = ",account
?

INPUT "            Enter amount of payment:  " TO pmt
REPLACE account WITH account - pmt

?
?
? "            New Balance = ",account
?
ACCEPT "When finished viewing screen, press Enter key  " TO dummy
CLEAR
RETURN
```

Preliminary Commands

```
. USE empfile

. SET TALK OFF

. LOCATE FOR employee = "Jones"

. DO payment
```

Sample Execution

```
        * * * Payment to Employee Account * * *

            Employee:  Jones David
            Acct Bal =     275.75

            Enter amount of payment: 125.00


            New Balance =     150.75

When finished viewing screen, press Enter key
```

Example Program 2—purchase.PRG

Program Description

The second example program lets the user post a purchase to an employee's personal account. The intended database in use in empfile.DBF. The second program differs from the first in that it includes two **IF . . . ELSE . . . ENDIF** structures to check certain conditions before it posts any changes to the database. The general algorithm is

1. Present the user with the employee's name and account balance for the current record.
2. Ask the user for the amount of purchase.
3. If the purchase plus the balance on the account is more than 15 percent of that employee's salary, then
   - **A.** Ask the user if the purchase is authorized by credit.

   Otherwise,
   - **A.** The purchase is automatically authorized.

   End if.
4. If the purchase is authorized, then
   - **A.** Replace the current record's field "account" with what is there plus the purchase amount.
   - **B.** Display the employee's new account balance.

   Otherwise,
   - **A.** Display a message saying that the purchase is not authorized and has not been posted.

   End if.
5. Prompt the user to indicate when he/she is done viewing the screen.

New Commands and Functions Used

IF <condition>
  any commands
ELSE
  any commands
ENDIF

The <condition> parameter of the **IF** command is a logical expression that can be evaluated as true (.T.) or false (.F.). If the <condition> evaluates true, the commands between the **IF** and the **ELSE** will be executed. If the <condition> evaluates false, the commands between the **ELSE** and the **ENDIF** will be executed.

Every **IF** command must have a corresponding **ENDIF** command to signal the end of that command structure. The **ELSE** portion of the structure and the commands following it are optional. (If the **ELSE** clause is omitted, commands between the **IF** and **ENDIF** are executed if the <condition> evaluates as true; otherwise, they are ignored.)

STORE <expression> **TO** <memvar> Places the value of the <expression> into a memory variable <memvar>. The data type of <memvar> is determined by the type of the <expression> that is stored to it (numeric, character, date, or logical).

UPPER(<expC>) The **UPPER**(<expC>) function returns the upper-case equivalent of its character string argument. It often is useful for comparisons of character strings input by a user.

Program Listing

```
* PROGRAM: Purchase.PRG - to post employee purchases on account
CLEAR
?
?
? "       * * * Employee Purchase on Account * * * "
?
? "          Employee: " + employee
? "          Acct Bal = ",account
?
INPUT "            Enter amount of desired purchase: " TO amt

IF account + amt > salary * .15
  ?
  ? "Employee's account will exceed 15% of salary with this purchase"
  ? "OK from Credit Manager required"
  ?
  ACCEPT "             OK received (y/n) ? " TO ok
ELSE
  STORE "Y" TO ok
ENDIF
?
?

IF UPPER(ok) = "Y"
  REPLACE account WITH account + amt
  ? "             New Balance = ",account
ELSE
  ? "     Approval Denied - Purchase not Posted "
ENDIF
?
ACCEPT "When finished viewing screen, press Enter key " TO dummy
CLEAR
RETURN
```

Preliminary Commands

```
. USE empfile

. SET TALK OFF

. GOTO 6

. DO purchase
```

Sample Execution

```
     * * *  Employee Purchase on Account  * * *

          Employee:  Smith Paul
          Acct Bal =     350.00

          Enter amount of desired purchase:  700

Employee's account will exceed 15% of salary with this purchase
OK from Credit Manager required

          OK received (y/n) ?  y


          New Balance =    1050.00

When finished viewing screen, press Enter key
```

Example Program 3—transact.PRG

Program Description

Example program 3 is known as a calling program. It is designed to allow the user to access either program 1, payment.PRG, or program 2, purchase.PRG, through its execution. A graphic representation of the relationship might be

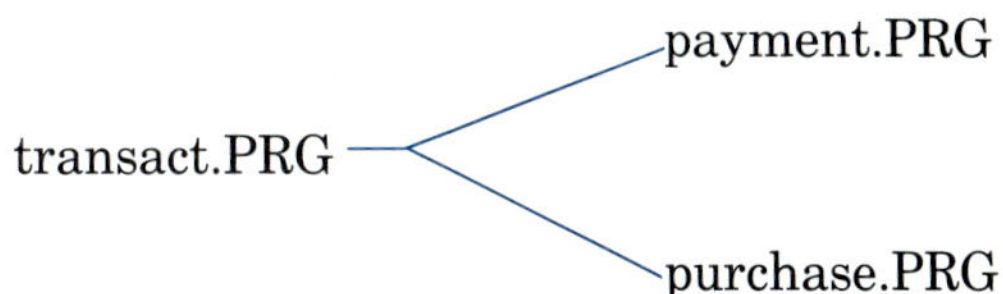

Within transact.PRG, the user is asked if the transaction to be posted is a payment or a purchase. Depending on the response, the command **DO** payment or **DO** purchase is executed. When either **DO** command is executed, dBASE starts executing the command file specified in it. When dBASE is finished with the called command file, it returns to transact.PRG and resumes execution where it left off. Example program 3 also introduces the idea of initializing the environment by including preliminary commands (to open the proper files and select a record) within the program.

Finally, transact.PRG incorporates a loop in which the posting of amounts to accounts is repeated until the user chooses to quit.

The general algorithm for program 3, transact.PRG, is

1. Initialize by setting **TALK OFF** and selecting empfile.DBF for use with its index file namedex.NDX.
2. Present the user with documentation of the program.
3. Set a <memvar> flag that will control loop processing to true.

4. Continue executing the following loop instructions until the flag is no longer true.
   - **A.** Present the user with a menu of selections to (1) Post a Purchase; (2) Post a Payment; or (3) Exit the Program.
   - **B.** Continue to prompt for a selection until a valid selection (1, 2, or 3) has been entered.
   - **C.** If the selection was either 1 or 2, then
     - **1.** Display a list of employee names in the database file.
     - **2.** Ask the user for the name of the employee of concern.
     - **3.** Search the file for the name entered and move the record pointer to that record.
     - **4.** If the name is not found or no name was entered, then
       - **a.** Ask if the user wants to continue the program.

       Otherwise,
       - **a.** If the menu selection was 1, then
         - **a1.** Execute purchase.PRG.

         Otherwise,
         - **a1.** Execute payment.PRG.

         End if.

       End if.

     Otherwise,
     - **1.** Change the <memvar> flag to no longer true.

     End if.
5. End of the loop instructions.
6. Close the files and clear the screen.

New Commands and Functions Used

SET TALK OFF and **SET STATUS OFF** Two of dBASE's **SET** commands that allow you to set features on or off. You will want to place the **SET TALK OFF** command at the beginning of your program to prevent dBASE's "talk" from cluttering up the screen. The **SET STATUS OFF** command suppresses display of the status bar at the bottom of the screen.

USE <filename> **INDEX** <index file list> Most programs will use a specific database file and sometimes a specific index file. Placing the appropriate **USE** command at the beginning of your command file ensures that the proper files are in use.

TEXT
  any data
ENDTEXT

This command structure allows you to print several lines of text without having to use a **?** command on each line.

DO WHILE <condition>
  any commands
ENDDO

This structure is used for creating loops. As long as the <condition> evaluates as true (.T.), the commands between the **DO WHILE** and **ENDDO** will be executed repeatedly, with the condition checked at the beginning of each iteration.

To end the execution of the loop, one or more items used in the <condition> must change to make the <condition> false. When this occurs, the next time the **DO WHILE** <condition> is evaluated execution of the program will resume with the command immediately following the loop's **ENDDO** command.

@ <x,y> **SAY** <exp> This command prints the evaluation of an expression <exp> starting at a specific location on the screen. The *x* value is the row number; the *y* value is the column number.

@ <x1,y1> **TO** <x2,y2> [**DOUBLE**] Draws a box on the screen with the upper-left corner defined by the <x1,y1> coordinate and the lower-right corner defined by the <x2,y2> coordinate. The box will be drawn with a single line unless the **DOUBLE** parameter is used to cause the box to be drawn with a double line.

@ <x,y> **SAY** <exp> **GET** <field / memvar> [**PICTURE** <expC>]
or
@ <x,y> **GET** <field / memvar> [**PICTURE** <expC>]

The @ **GET** command may be used alone or combined with the @ **SAY** command. It is used to input or edit the contents of a field or memory variable at a specified screen location. The @ **GET** commands are activated when the **READ** command is executed. In command files, @ **GET** is often preferable to **ACCEPT** or **INPUT** since it allows better control of screen appearance and data entry formats.

The **PICTURE** <expC> clause may be used to specify certain types of data which must be entered in the @ **GET**'s field or memory variable. In the example program, the **PICTURE** expressions use the template characters "9," "!," "X," and "Y." The "9" restricts input of character data to the characters 0 through 9, the "!" forces a character to be upper case, the "X" allows any character to be entered, and the "Y" is used with logical-type data to accept "Y" for .T. (true) and "N" for .F. (false).

READ @ **GET** commands are normally followed by a **READ** command, which causes the cursor to move to the first @ **GET** <field / memvar> for editing. The cursor may be moved to any of the active @ **GET** fields or variables. When data has been entered for all of the active @ **GET**s, execution resumes with the next command after the **READ** command.

$** (Relational Operator) The relational operator **$ is used to compare two string expressions and determine whether the first expression is a substring of the second. For example, the expression <memvarC> **$** "123" is true (.T.) if the value of <memvarC> is "1," "2," "3," "12," "23," or "123"; if it contains any other character string, the expression is false (.F.).

SEEK <exp> Searches the index file in use for the first index key that matches the expression <exp> and moves the record pointer to the corresponding record in the database file. If no index key is found for the expression, the record pointer is moved to the end of the file and the **EOF**( ) function returns .T. (true).

TRIM(<expC>) The **TRIM** function returns the character string argument with any trailing spaces removed.

EOF( ) The End-of-file function **EOF( )** is a dBASE function that returns the logical value .T. (true) when the record pointer is moved past the last record of the database file. It often is used after a search operation to determine if a record was found (end-of-file is false).

SPACE(<expN>) The **SPACE** function returns a character string of spaces with a length defined by the argument <expN>.

DO <filename> **DO** may be used to call another program from the current program. When a **RETURN** is encountered in the called program, the calling program resumes execution at the command following the **DO** <filename> command.

Program Listing

```
* PROGRAM:  Transact.PRG  -  calling program for purchase and payment programs

SET TALK OFF
SET STATUS OFF
USE empfile INDEX namedex

CLEAR
TEXT
    This program is for updating employees' personal accounts.  After
    selecting the type of transaction to post, a purchase on account or
    a payment, you will enter the name of an employee.

ENDTEXT
ACCEPT "    Press Enter to Begin " TO dummy

STORE .T. TO cont
DO WHILE cont
  CLEAR
  @  7,30 SAY "  Transaction Menu   "
  @  6,25 TO 8,55 DOUBLE
  @ 10,30 SAY " 1 - Post Purchase   "
  @ 11,30 SAY " 2 - Post Payment    "
  @ 12,30 SAY " 3 - Exit            "
  @  9,25 TO 15,55

  STORE " " TO choice
  DO WHILE .NOT. choice $ "123"
    @ 14,30 SAY " Enter Selection: " GET choice PICTURE "9"
    READ
  ENDDO

  IF choice $ "12"
    CLEAR
    ?
    ?
    DISPLAY ALL Employee OFF
    STORE SPACE(20) TO name
    @  3,30 SAY "Enter Name: " GET name PICTURE "!XXXXXXXXXXXXXXXXXXX"
    READ

    SEEK TRIM(name)
    IF EOF() .OR. name = SPACE(20)
      @ 5,30 SAY "Invalid Name Entered, Continue (Y/N) ? " GET cont PICT "Y"
      READ
    ELSE
      IF choice = "1"
        DO purchase
      ELSE
        DO payment
      ENDIF
    ENDIF
  ELSE
    STORE .F. TO cont
  ENDIF
ENDDO

USE
CLEAR
RETURN
```

Preliminary Commands

```
. DO transact
```

Sample Execution

```
This program is for updating employees' personal accounts.  After
selecting the type of transaction to post, a purchase on account or
a payment, you will enter the name of an employee.

Press Enter to Begin
```

```
                    Transaction Menu

               1 - Post Purchase
               2 - Post Payment
               3 - Exit

               Enter Selection: 1
```

```
Employee                    Enter Name: Johnson
Johnson Frank
Jones David
Knat Michael
Martins Mary
Nichols Sandy
Pratt John
Sill Sally
Smith Paul
Smoler Ellen
```

```
     *  *  *  Employee Purchase on Account  *  *  *

          Employee:  Johnson Frank
          Acct Bal =        0.00

          Enter amount of desired purchase:  800.00

Employee's account will exceed 15% of salary with this purchase
OK from Credit Manager required

          OK received (y/n) ?  n


     Approval Denied  -  Purchase not Posted

When finished viewing screen, press Enter key
```

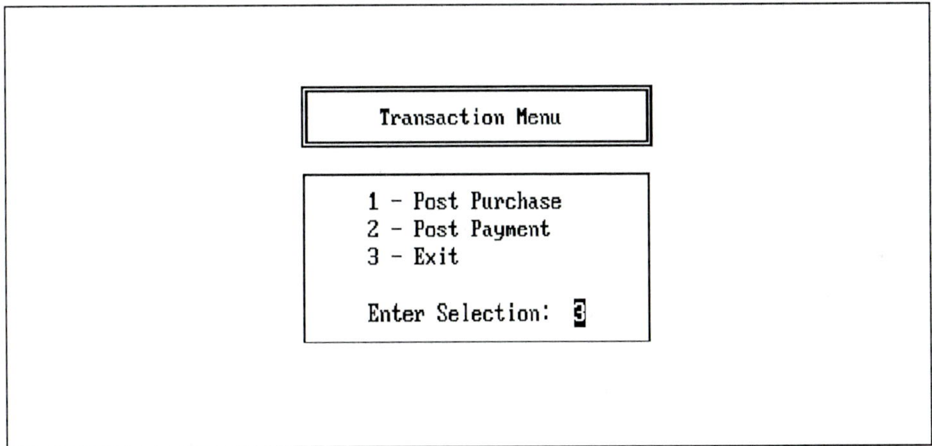

Example Programs 4 and 5— reports1.PRG and reports2.PRG

Program Description

The next two example programs also are connected to each other. Program 4, reports1.PRG, is the calling program, and program 5, reports2.PRG, is the program being called. Their relationship might be graphically depicted as

reports1.PRG⟶ reports2.PRG

Example program 4, reports1.PRG, allows the user to select the way a report will be displayed or output, and to select the report to be produced. It then conditionally initializes the appropriate output devices and calls reports2.PRG to produce the desired report. Both programs use the **DO CASE...ENDCASE** structure, which is similar to the **IF...ELSE...ENDIF** structure.

The general algorithm for example program 4, reports1.PRG, is

1. Initialize the environment by setting **TALK** and **STATUS OFF** and selecting empfile.DBF with its index file empdex.NDX as the database file for use.
2. Present the user with a menu numbered 1 through 3 with the options (1) displayed on screen, (2) sent to printer, and (3) written to a file.
3. Instruct the user to enter his/her answer.
4. Clear the screen and present to the user a second menu numbered 1 through 4 with the options (1) Salary Summary Report, (2) Salaries & Accounts by Gender, (3) Employee Full Report, and (4) All of the above.
5. Instruct the user to enter his/her answer.
6. Determine the Case for the output selection.
   - **A.** Case: the user answered "Sent to the printer."
     1. Initialize the printer for output.
     2. Do reports2.PRG.
     3. Reset the output device to the screen.
   - **B.** Case: the user answered "Written to a text file."
     1. Initialize a .TXT file.
     2. Do reports2.PRG.
     3. Close the .TXT file.
   - **C.** Otherwise: the user answered "Displayed on screen only."
     1. Do reports2.PRG. The output automatically will be sent to the screen.

   End Case.
7. Close the files.

The general algorithm for example program 5, reports2.PRG, is

1. Initialize environment for salaries.FRM.
   - **A.** Determine the average salary of all employees and store it to a memory variable.
   - **B.** Store the current system date to a memory variable.
2. Determine the Case for the report selection.
   - **A.** Case: the user selected "Salary Summary Report."
     1. Produce the report using the salaries.FRM file.
   - **B.** Case: the user selected "Salaries & Accounts by Gender."
     1. Produce the report using the acctrepo.FRM file.
   - **C.** Case: the user selected "Employee Full Report."
     1. Produce the report using the fullrepo.FRM file.
   - **D.** Otherwise: the user selected "All of the above reports."
     1. Produce the report using the salaries.FRM file, and then prompt to continue.
     2. Produce the report using the acctrepo.FRM file, and then prompt to continue.
     3. Produce the report using the fullrepo.FRM file, and then prompt to continue.

   End Case.
3. Return to the calling program reports1.PRG.

New Commands Used

DO CASE
  CASE <condition>
    <any commands>
  CASE <condition>
    <any commands>
  OTHERWISE
    <any commands>
ENDCASE

The **DO CASE...ENDCASE** command structure is useful when the <condition>s used are mutually exclusive. As soon as a <condition> is evaluated as .T. (true), only those commands following it, up to the next **CASE, OTHERWISE,** or **ENDCASE,** will be executed. Execution then resumes with the command following **ENDCASE.** The **OTHERWISE** is optional. If it is used, commands following **OTHERWISE** will be executed when none of the previous **CASE** <condition>s are evaluated as true.

DO <filename> **WITH** <expression list> The **WITH** <expression list> is used to pass values (expressions) to the program being called with the **DO** command. The receiving program must be designed to accept the values and store them to local memory variables through the **PARAMETERS** command.

PARAMETERS <memvar list> **PARAMETERS** is the command used to accept values being passed by a calling program. **PARAMETERS** must be the first executable command in the program being called.

SET PRINT ON The **SET PRINT ON** command sends the screen output to the printer. **SET PRINT OFF** is the reverse of this command.

SET ALTERNATE on / OFF and **SET ALTERNATE TO** <filename> The **SET ALTERNATE ON** command is used to send screen output to a text file on the diskette, which is given a .TXT file extension. The text file may later be edited with a word processing software.

To create and open an alternate file, use the command **SET ALTERNATE TO** <filename>. To close the alternate file, use the command without a <filename> specified.

SET ALTERNATE ON must be executed before screen output will be sent to the alternate file. **SET ALTERNATE OFF** will suspend sending output to the current text file.

Reports2.PRG uses no new commands. It provides an example of a procedure that would only be called from another program which passes a value to the memory variable "reptno" as a parameter.

The commands in this program could have been included in reports1.PRG, but they would need to have been listed three times. In this case, it is more efficient to place the commands in their own file, reports2.PRG, and call this program from three places in reports1.PRG with the single command, **DO** reports2. In addition, any other program could call reports2.PRG as long as the necessary files are in use and a parameter is passed.

Program Listings

```
*  PROGRAM:  Reports1.PRG  - to print report forms

SET TALK OFF
SET STATUS OFF
USE empfile INDEX empdex
CLEAR

@  5,10 SAY "This program allows you to print a number of reports "

@  7,20 SAY "       These reports may be:       "
@  8,15 TO 16,60
@  9,20 SAY "1 - Displayed on the screen only "
@ 11,20 SAY "2 - Sent to the printer           "
@ 13,20 SAY "3 - Written to a text file        "
STORE " " TO mode
DO WHILE .NOT. mode $ "123"
  @ 15,20 SAY "Select 1, 2, or 3 " GET mode PICTURE "9"
  READ
ENDDO
CLEAR

@  6,10 SAY "Which of the following reports would you like to use ? "
@  8,15 TO 18,60
@  9,20 SAY "1 - Salary Summary Report            "
@ 11,20 SAY "2 - Salaries and Accounts by Gender "
@ 13,20 SAY "3 - Employee Full Report             "
@ 15,20 SAY "4 - All of the above reports         "
STORE " " TO choice
DO WHILE .NOT. choice $ "1234"
  @ 17,20 SAY "Select 1, 2, 3, or 4 " GET choice PICTURE "9"
  READ
ENDDO
CLEAR

DO CASE
   CASE mode = "2"
     SET PRINT ON
     DO reports2 WITH choice
     SET PRINT OFF

   CASE mode = "3"
     SET ALTERNATE TO reports.txt
     SET ALTERNATE ON
     DO reports2 WITH choice
     SET ALTERNATE OFF
     SET ALTERNATE TO

   OTHERWISE
     DO reports2 WITH choice

ENDCASE

USE
RETURN
```

```
* PROGRAM:  Reports2.PRG  -  called from Reports1.PRG

PARAMETERS reptno
AVERAGE ALL salary TO salavg
STORE DATE() TO date

DO CASE
   CASE reptno = "1"
     REPORT FORM salaries

   CASE reptno = "2"
     REPORT FORM acctrepo

   CASE reptno = "3"
     REPORT FORM fullrepo

   OTHERWISE
     REPORT FORM salaries
     ACCEPT "Press Enter for next report " TO dummy
     REPORT FORM acctrepo
     ACCEPT "Press Enter for next report " TO dummy
     REPORT FORM fullrepo
     ACCEPT "Press Enter to continue     " TO dummy
ENDCASE
RETURN
```

Preliminary Commands

```
. DO reports1
```

Sample Execution

```
          This program allows you to print a number of reports

                          These reports may be:

                1 - Displayed on the screen only

                2 - Sent to the printer

                3 - Written to a text file

                Select 1, 2, or 3 1
```

```
Which of the following reports would you like to use ?

    1 - Salary Summary Report

    2 - Salaries and Accounts by Gender

    3 - Employee Full Report

    4 - All of the above reports

    Select 1, 2, 3, or 4  3
```

```
Page No.     1
07/23/90
                     Employee Full Report
                     ====================

                                             Current   Account  Account
Employee Name   Phone #    Hire Date   Salary    Limit   Balance
-------------   -------    ---------   -------   -------  -------


Martins Mary    222-2123   11/01/85   1600.00   240.00   200.50
Nichols Sandy   229-1111   02/15/86   1450.00   217.00   175.00
Sill Sally      224-4321   02/15/84   1507.00   226.00   150.00
Smoler Ellen    225-3212   09/15/83   1650.00   247.00   300.00
Johnson Frank   223-7928   03/20/90   1500.00   225.00     0.00
Jones David     292-3832   06/15/82   1550.00   232.00   150.75
Knat Michael    221-1235   09/15/80   1800.00   270.00   125.00
Pratt John      225-1234   06/22/82   1949.00   292.00   200.00
Smith Paul      244-1010   11/15/81   1700.00   255.00  1050.00
*** Total ***
                                     14706.00  2204.00  2351.25
```

Example Program 6—raises.PRG

Program Description

This example program is designed to maintain a second database, salhist.DBF, which is used to keep records of each employee's raises over a period of time. Included in raises.PRG are the commands and parameters used when two or more databases are put into use at the same time.

The general algorithm for the example program 6, raises.PRG, is

1. Initialize the environment by setting **TALK** and **STATUS OFF.**
2. Select work area 2 and put salhist.DBF into use there.

3. Select work area 1 and put empfile.DBF into use with its index file namedex.NDX. Leave work area 1 the current work area.
4. Set a memory variable to true for control of a loop and continue executing the following loop instructions until the memory variable is set to false.
   - **A.** Initialize the memory variables to be used and display a program description.
   - **B.** Ask the user to enter the name of the employee of concern.
   - **C.** Move empfile's record pointer to the employee's record.
   - **D.** If the end of file is encountered (the name cannot be found) or no name has been entered, then
     - **1.** Ask if the user wants to continue the program.
     - **2.** Set the loop variable to the user's response.
   - **E.** Otherwise,
     - **1.** Present a screen for the user to input the date of the raise and the percent increase.
     - **2.** Compute and display the new salary on the screen.
     - **3.** Ask the user to confirm the new salary.
     - **4.** If it is confirmed, then
       - **a.** Replace the current record's salary field with the new salary.
       - **b.** Select work area 2, salhist.DBF.
       - **c.** Move salhist's record pointer to the first record whose field "employee" matches the field "employee" of the current record in empfile.
       - **d.** Insert a blank record immediately before the current record in salhist.
       - **e.** Fill the fields in the blank record with the appropriate data.
       - **f.** Display all data in salhist for that employee.
       - **g.** Select work area 1 empfile.

       End if.
     - **5.** Ask the user if there are more salary increases to enter.
     - **6.** Set the loop variable to the user's response.

     End if.

   End of the loop instruction.
5. Close the files.

New Commands Used

SELECT <work area / alias> Ten separate work areas are available, each capable of having one database file in use. To put more than one database file into use, first select the desired work area with the **SELECT** command, and then enter the **USE** command specifying the database file to open. Independent record pointers are maintained for each database in use. Field data may be read across work areas by using aliases (the filename or a letter A through J).

CTOD(<expC>) The Character-to-Date function is used to convert character-type data to date-type data. In "raises.PRG," the **CTOD** function converts a blank date string to a date-type memory variable to be used with an @ **GET** command.

@ <x,y> CLEAR Clears the screen from the row and column specified by the <x,y> coordinate, downward and to the right.

LOCATE FOR <condition> Sets the record pointer in the current database file to the first record which evaluates as true (.T.) for the condition. If no such record is found, the record pointer will be at the end of the file.

INSERT [BLANK] [BEFORE] The **INSERT BLANK** command adds a blank record to the database in use just after the current record. This is usually done so that a subsequent **REPLACE** command can be used to store data in the new record. The **[BEFORE]** parameter is used to place the blank record immediately before the current record.

Program Listing

```
* PROGRAM: Raises.PRG - to keep records of previous salary levels

SET TALK OFF
SET STATUS OFF
SELECT 2
USE salhist
SELECT 1
USE empfile INDEX namedex

STORE .T. TO cont
DO WHILE cont
  STORE CTOD("  /  /  ") TO effdate
  STORE SPACE(20)        TO name
  STORE 0                TO increase
  CLEAR
  @ 5,15 SAY " *   *   *  Entering Salary Increases   *   *   *"
  @ 10,10 SAY "Name of Employee (Last First)  " GET name
  READ
  SEEK TRIM(name)
  IF EOF() .OR. name = SPACE(20)
    @ 15,10 SAY "Invalid name entry -- Continue (Y/N) ? " GET cont PICT "Y"
    READ
  ELSE
    @  8, 1 CLEAR
    @  8,15 SAY "EMPLOYEE"
    @  8,45 SAY "CURRENT SALARY"
    @ 10,15 SAY employee
    @ 10,45 SAY salary PICTURE "9,999.99"
    @ 15,15 SAY "Enter Effective Date (mm/dd/yy) "
    @ 15,50 GET effdate
    @ 17,15 SAY "Enter percent increase as decimal "
    @ 17,50 GET increase PICTURE "0.9999"
    READ
    @ 19,15 SAY "New Salary = "
    @ 19,30 SAY salary * (1 + increase) PICTURE "9,999.99"
    STORE " " TO ok
    DO WHILE .NOT. ok $ "YN"
      @ 19,45 SAY "Is this correct (Y/N) ? " GET ok PICTURE "!"
      READ
    ENDDO
    IF ok = "Y"
      REPLACE salary WITH salary * (1 + increase)
      SELECT 2
      LOCATE FOR employee = empfile->employee
      INSERT BLANK BEFORE
      REPLACE employee WITH empfile->employee, dateincr WITH effdate
      REPLACE salary WITH empfile->salary
      CLEAR
      @ 10,15 SAY "SALARY HISTORY"
      ?
      DISPLAY FOR employee = empfile->employee OFF
      SELECT 1
    ENDIF
    ?
    @ ROW(),15 SAY "More Salary Increases to Enter (Y/N) " GET cont PICT "Y"
    READ
  ENDIF
ENDDO
CLOSE DATABASES
RETURN
```

Preliminary Commands

```
. DO raises
```

Sample Execution

```
          *   *   *   Entering Salary Increases   *   *   *


     Name of Employee (Last First)   Sill
```

```
          *   *   *   Entering Salary Increases   *   *   *

        EMPLOYEE                      CURRENT SALARY

        Sill Sally                    1,507.00



        Enter Effective Date (mm/dd/yy)   06/15/91

        Enter percent increase as decimal  0.1000

        New Salary =    1,657.70       Is this correct (Y/N) ?  Y
```

```
            SALARY HISTORY

EMPLOYEE               DATEINCR   SALARY
Sill Sally             06/15/91  1657.70
Sill Sally             01/01/90  1507.00

            More Salary Increases to Enter (Y/N)  N
```

Example Program 7—menu.PRG

Program Description

The final example program, menu.PRG, has no new commands, structures, or functions to explain. It is the main calling program designed to allow the user to select which of the six previous sample programs he/she would like to access. It is the program that ties the other six into a system—a database management system—of programs. With it, the system can be graphically displayed as

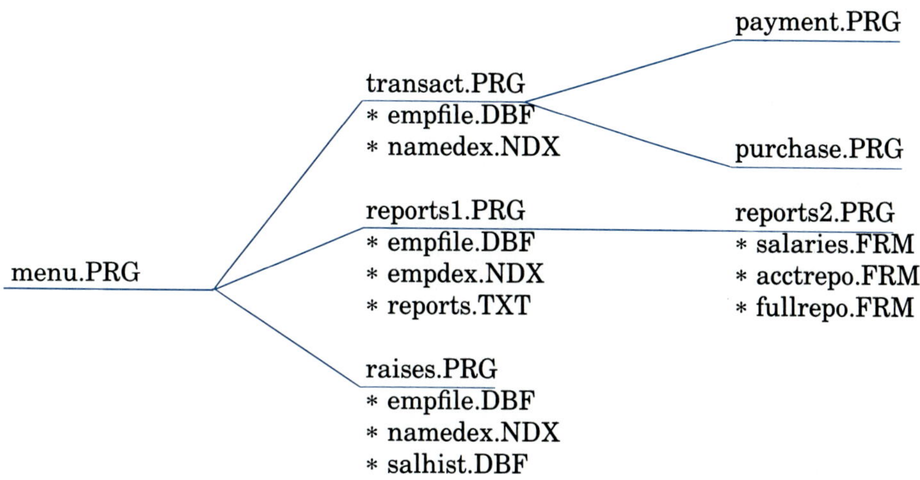

Program Listing

```
*  PROGRAM:  Menu.PRG  -  main menu to call programs

SET TALK OFF
SET STATUS OFF
STORE .T. TO contmenu

DO WHILE contmenu
  CLEAR
  @  4,15 TO  18,60 DOUBLE
  @  5,20 SAY "     *  *  *  MAIN MENU  *  *  *   "

  @  8,20 SAY " 1 - Employee Account Transactions "
  @ 10,20 SAY " 2 - Reports                       "
  @ 12,20 SAY " 3 - Salary Increases              "
  @ 14,20 SAY " 4 - Quit                          "

  STORE " " TO menchoice
  DO WHILE .NOT. menchoice $ "1234"
    @ 17,25 SAY "ENTER SELECTION  " GET menchoice PICTURE "9"
    READ
  ENDDO

  DO CASE
     CASE menchoice = "1"
       DO transact
     CASE menchoice = "2"
       DO reports1
     CASE menchoice = "3"
       DO raises
     OTHERWISE
       STORE .F. TO contmenu
  ENDCASE
ENDDO

CLOSE ALL
CLEAR
SET TALK ON
SET STATUS ON

RETURN
```

Preliminary Commands

```
. DO menu
```

Sample Execution

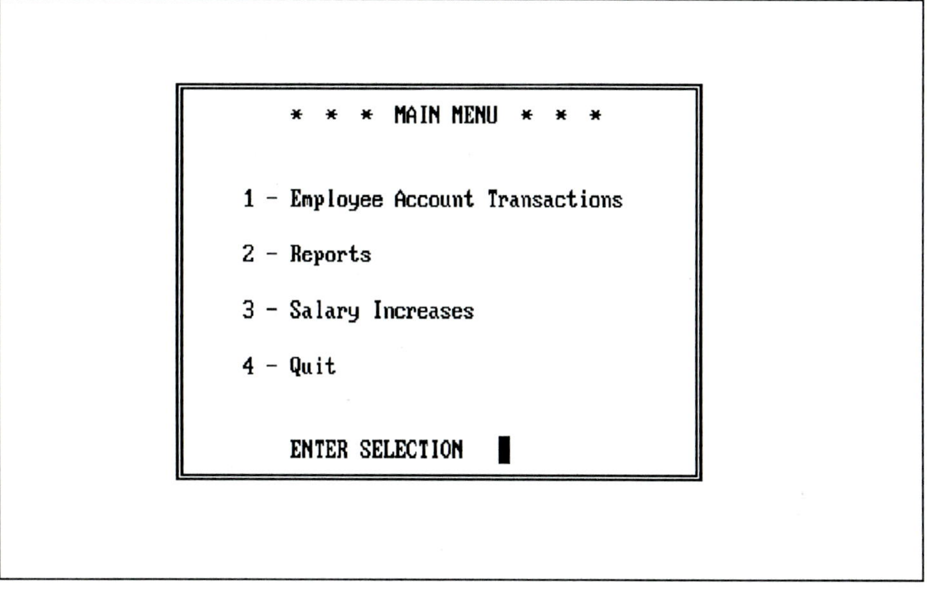

PROGRAMMING TIPS

1. If you have a command that is longer than 65 characters, dBASE's text editor (**MODIFY COMMAND**) will automatically wrap the command down to the next line as you type it in. When dBASE wraps a command, the far right side of the editing screen will not display the normal "<" character. This indicates that the Enter key was not typed at the end of the line. dBASE stops evaluating a command when it encounters an Enter key character. To remove an Enter key character that is accidentally included in an extended command, move the cursor to the end of the line and type ^T. Then type spaces until dBASE rewraps the line. dBASE command lines may actually be up to 254 characters long.
2. You may want to leave blank lines in your program to improve readability. Blank lines will not affect how the program runs; neither will indenting program lines. The practice of indenting command structures is invaluable to program debugging and readability, as demonstrated in the example dBASE command files.
3. The **MODIFY COMMAND** text editor can handle command files up to 4,096 bytes (characters) long. Files approaching this limit begin to show considerable delays in editing operations. Commands entered beyond this limit will be truncated from the file by dBASE.

dBASE is a procedural language, designed for creating interrelated programs to accomplish a processing task. The separate programs (procedures) are connected through structures of program calls and returns. This fundamental difference between dBASE and other programming languages, such as BASIC, requires that the programmer design systems that are subroutine in nature.

4. When dBASE encounters a syntax error in a program, it will display a message similar to:

```
Syntax error.
         ?
SET TALK TO OFF
Called from - A:menu.prg
Cancel, Ignore, or Suspend? (C, I, or S)
```

At this point, you may type "C" to cancel program execution and then use **MODIFY COMMAND** to open the file and correct the error. If the error is not going to have any serious effect on the rest of the program, you may type "I" to ignore the command line that produced the error and continue execution of the program.

You also may type "S" to suspend execution of the program. This allows you to execute commands from the dot (.) prompt and then continue the program. For example, you may want to view memory variable contents with the **DISPLAY MEMORY** command, store a value to a variable with the **STORE** command, or create an index file needed by the program.

When a program is suspended, memory variables created in the program will be in memory; if it is cancelled, the variables are lost. While a program is suspended, the file remains open and cannot be edited with **MODIFY COMMAND.** From the dot (.) prompt, you may type **RESUME** to continue execution of the suspended program or **CANCEL** to cancel execution and close the file.

SUSPEND is also a command that may be placed in a command file for debugging purposes. Use **SUSPEND** when you wish to check values of memory variables or the status of the environment at a certain point in the program. Other dBASE commands useful for debugging command files are **SET DEBUG on / OFF, SET ECHO on / OFF,** and **SET STEP on / OFF.**

EXERCISES

EXERCISE 1
Required Preliminary Exercise

Before completing the other dBASE III Plus exercises found in this module, you will need to create two small database files. This exercise will provide you with instructions on how to create the files.

Required Preparation

Study the explanations of the **APPEND FROM, BROWSE, CREATE, DISPLAY,** and **REPLACE** commands found in the dBASE III Plus Command Summary.

Exercise Steps

1. Load dBASE III Plus into memory.

In the tutorial lessons, you created a database that was kept intentionally simple. For instance, the data for the employees' first and last names were kept in the same field. Normally, first and last names would be placed in separate fields in the record. Additional fields for name titles (such as Mr., Ms., Ph.D, Dr., etc.), fields for middle initials, nicknames, and so on, might be considered for inclusion in the record structure. Telephone numbers often have extensions and/or area codes associated with them. In the following steps, you will create a new database file called "empinfo." The file will be used to hold address and phone information for the same group of employees. Each record also includes a special "key" field (named "empno") which is used to hold the company's employee number for that person.

2. Use the **CREATE** <filename> command to define the following record structure for the database file empinfo.

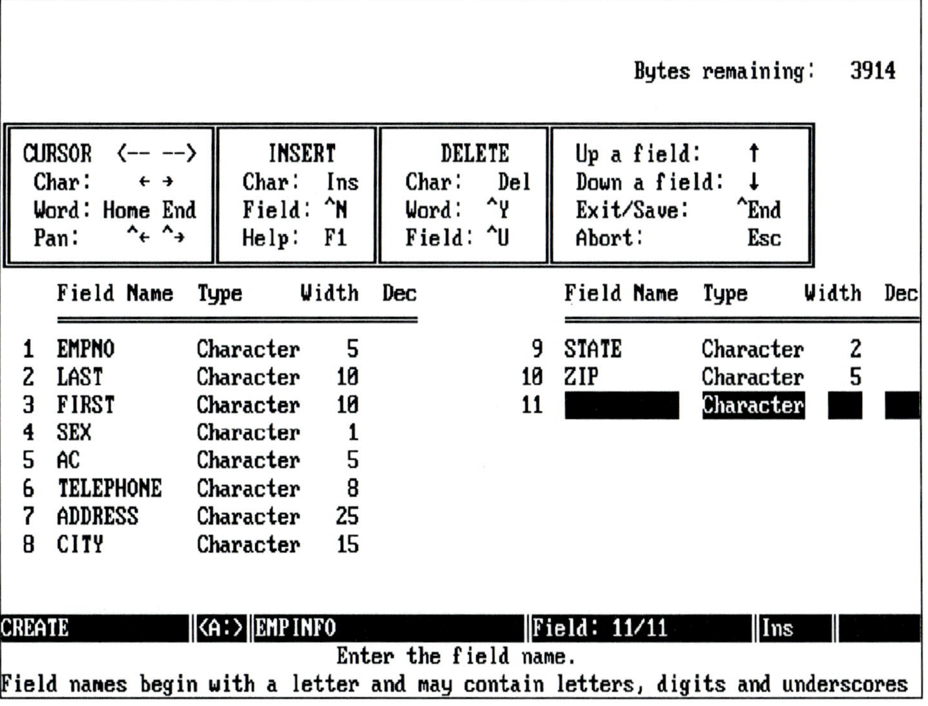

3. When finished, type ||^End,↵,N|| to complete the operation without inputting data records at this time.
4. Use the **USE** <filename> command to make empinfo the current database file. Then use the **APPEND FROM** <filename> to copy all fields having the same name in the file empfile to the current database file, empinfo.
5. Next type ||**GO TOP**||. Use the **BROWSE** command to see that the telephone numbers and gender data have been copied to empinfo.

```
EMPNO LAST------ FIRST----- SEX AC--- TELEPHONE ADDRESS-----------------
                            M         225-1234
                            F         225-3212
                            M         292-3832
                            F         224-4321
                            M         221-1235
                            M         244-1010
                            F         222-2123
                            F         229-1111
                            M         223-7928
```

6. Exit the **BROWSE** editing mode and then use the **REPLACE** [<scope>] <field> **WITH** <exp> command to replace all area code fields (ac) with the string data "(503)".
7. Use the **BROWSE** command to enter or edit the following fields of data. Notice that two of the area codes need to be changed to (206).

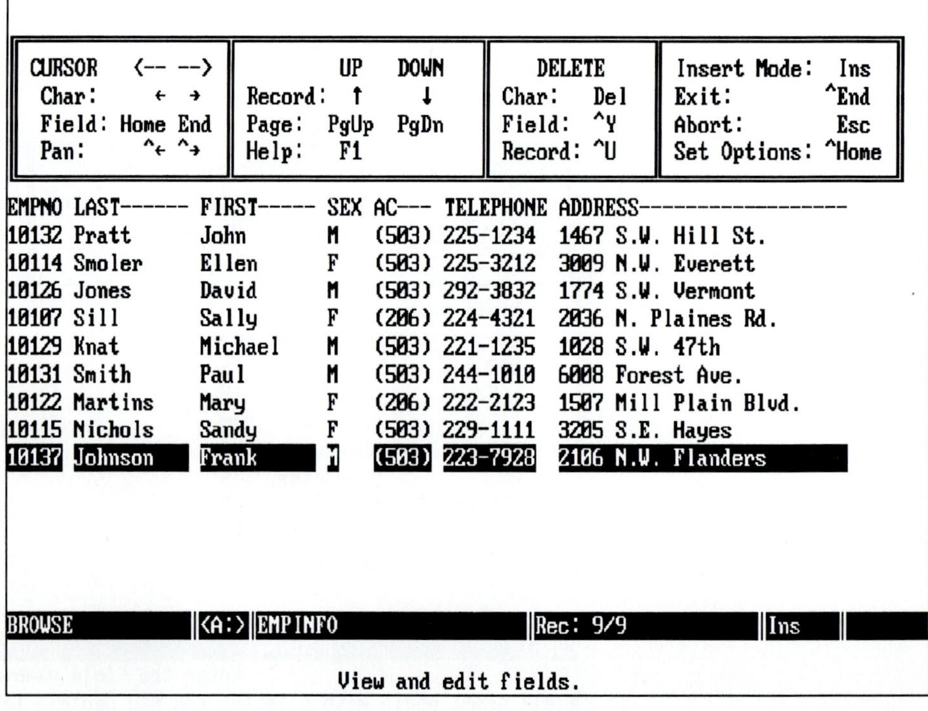

```
CURSOR     <-- -->   |        UP    DOWN  |     DELETE     | Insert Mode:    Ins
 Char:       ←   →   | Record:  ↑     ↓   | Char:    Del   | Exit:          ^End
 Field:  Home  End   | Page:  PgUp  PgDn  | Field:   ^Y    | Abort:          Esc
 Pan:       ^←  ^→   | Help:   F1         | Record:  ^U    | Set Options:  ^Home

EMPNO LAST------ FIRST----- SEX AC--- TELEPHONE ADDRESS-----------------
10132 Pratt      John       M   (503) 225-1234  1467 S.W. Hill St.
10114 Smoler     Ellen      F   (503) 225-3212  3009 N.W. Everett
10126 Jones      David      M   (503) 292-3832  1774 S.W. Vermont
10107 Sill       Sally      F   (206) 224-4321  2036 N. Plaines Rd.
10129 Knat       Michael    M   (503) 221-1235  1028 S.W. 47th
10131 Smith      Paul       M   (503) 244-1010  6008 Forest Ave.
10122 Martins    Mary       F   (206) 222-2123  1507 Mill Plain Blvd.
10115 Nichols    Sandy      F   (503) 229-1111  3205 S.E. Hayes
10137 Johnson    Frank      M   (503) 223-7928  2106 N.W. Flanders

BROWSE        ||<A:>||EMPINFO          ||Rec: 9/9          ||Ins  ||

                         View and edit fields.
```

8. Exit the **BROWSE** editing mode and use the **REPLACE** [<scope>] <field> **WITH** <exp> command to replace all city fields with the string data "Portland", all state fields with the string data "OR", and all ZIP code fields with the string data "972".
9. Now use the **BROWSE FIELDS** <field list> command to edit only the fields named first, last, city, state, and ZIP. Change the field data to reflect the following.

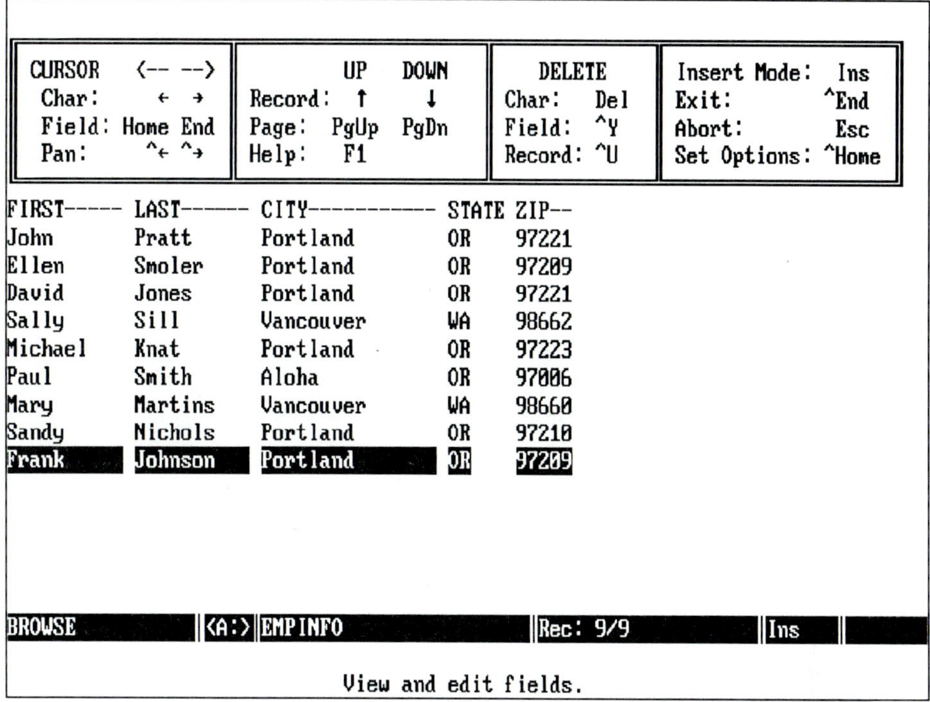

10. Exit the **BROWSE** editing mode and close the database file by typing ||**USE**↵||.
11. Now use the **CREATE** <filename> command to define the following record structure for the new database file empacct.

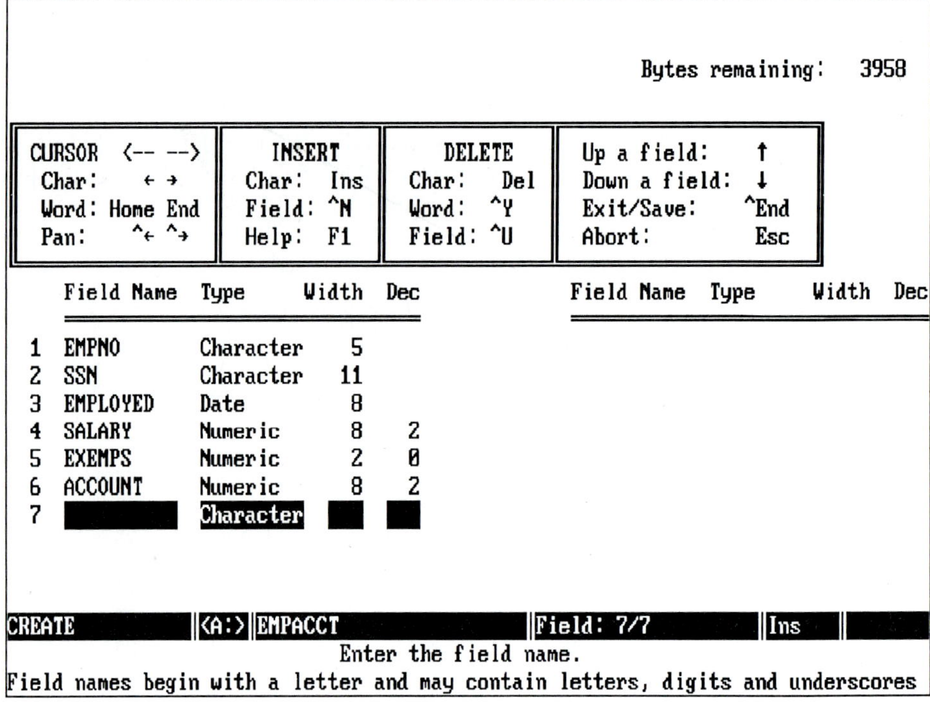

12. When finished type ||^End,↵,N|| to complete the operation without inputting data records.

13. Use the **USE** <filename> command to make empacct the current database file. Then use the **APPEND FROM** <filename> to copy all fields having the same name in the file empfile to the current database file empacct.

14. Now use the **BROWSE** editing mode to see that the fields employed, salary, and account have been copied to the new database file.

EMPNO	SSN--------	EMPLOYED	SALARY--	EXEMPS	ACCOUNT-
		06/22/82	1949.00		200.00
		09/15/83	1650.00		300.00
		06/15/82	1550.00		275.75
		02/15/84	1507.00		150.00
		09/15/80	1800.00		125.00
		11/15/81	1700.00		350.00
		11/01/85	1600.00		200.50
		02/15/86	1450.00		175.00
		03/20/90	1500.00		0.00

As a shortcut to data entry and a way to ensure that the employee numbers are exactly the same in each database, you will next put two database files into use at the same time, link the two record pointers by setting a relation to the record numbers found in each database, and then replace the empno fields in empacct with the empno fields found in empinfo. A complete explanation of the process is premature at this point; however, you may refer to the operation and command summary for more information on each of the commands used here if you desire.

15. Exit the **BROWSE** editing mode and then type the following commands.

    USE empacct↵
    SELECT 2↵
    USE empinfo↵
    SET RELATION TO RECNO() INTO empacct↵
    REPLACE ALL empacct->empno **WITH** empinfo->empno↵
    CLOSE ALL
    SELECT 1
    USE empacct

16. Now use the **BROWSE** editing mode to enter the remaining data for the empacct database file as shown here.

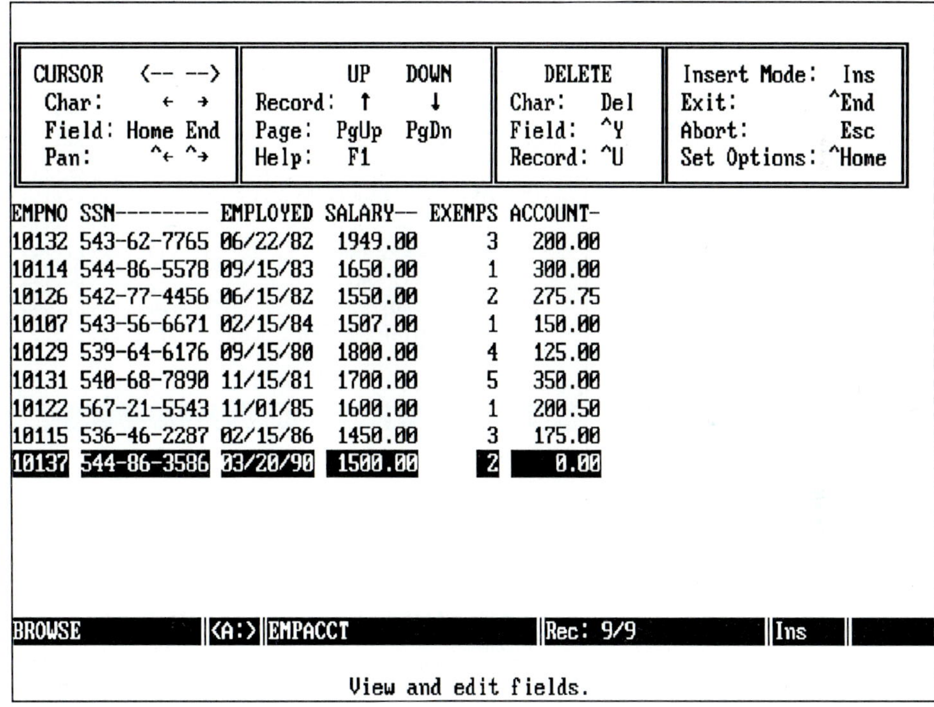

EMPNO	SSN--------	EMPLOYED	SALARY--	EXEMPS	ACCOUNT-
10132	543-62-7765	06/22/82	1949.00	3	200.00
10114	544-86-5578	09/15/83	1650.00	1	300.00
10126	542-77-4456	06/15/82	1550.00	2	275.75
10107	543-56-6671	02/15/84	1507.00	1	150.00
10129	539-64-6176	09/15/80	1800.00	4	125.00
10131	540-68-7890	11/15/81	1700.00	5	350.00
10122	567-21-5543	11/01/85	1600.00	1	200.50
10115	536-46-2287	02/15/86	1450.00	3	175.00
10137	544-86-3586	03/20/90	1500.00	2	0.00

17. Exit the **BROWSE** editing mode and then use the **DISPLAY** <scope> **TO PRINT** command to print out the contents of the database files empacct and empinfo.
18. Use the **QUIT** command to close all files and exit dBASE.

EXERCISE 2 Employee Phone Numbers

This exercise uses the empinfo database file to produce a list of employee telephone numbers that will be copied and mailed to each employee's home address.

Required Preparation

Study the explanations of the **MODIFY REPORT, MODIFY LABEL,** and **INDEX** commands as well as the **TRIM** and **IIF** functions found in the dBASE III Plus Operation and Command Summary.

Exercise Steps

1. Load dBASE III Plus into memory.
2. Use the appropriate dBASE commands to produce the following report from the indexed file empinfo.

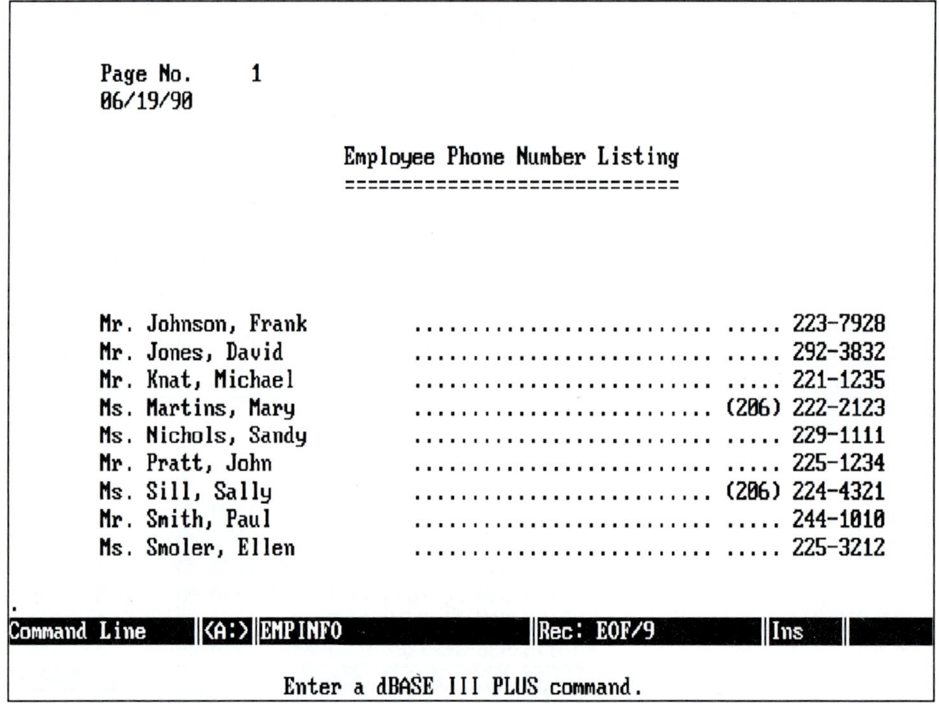

```
Page No.     1
06/19/90

                    Employee Phone Number Listing
                    =============================

Mr. Johnson, Frank      .......................... ..... 223-7928
Mr. Jones, David        .......................... ..... 292-3832
Mr. Knat, Michael       .......................... ..... 221-1235
Ms. Martins, Mary       .......................... (206) 222-2123
Ms. Nichols, Sandy      .......................... ..... 229-1111
Mr. Pratt, John         .......................... ..... 225-1234
Ms. Sill, Sally         .......................... (206) 224-4321
Mr. Smith, Paul         .......................... ..... 244-1010
Ms. Smoler, Ellen       .......................... ..... 225-3212

.
Command Line  ||<A:>||EMPINFO        ||Rec: EOF/9     ||Ins ||

                  Enter a dBASE III PLUS command.
```

3. Write down the expressions you used for each column's contents and the name you gave the .FRM file when you created it. Then, use the **REPORT FORM** <file> **TO PRINT** command to produce a printed copy of the list.
4. Use the **MODIFY LABEL** command to produce a **LABEL FORM** that will generate the following type of address labels. (Do not change Options for the label form and use the first three lines of the label to enter your expressions.)

```
Ms. Sally Sill
2036 N. Plaines Rd.
Vancouver, WA   98662


Mr. Paul Smith
6008 Forest Ave.
Aloha, OR   97006


Ms. Ellen Smoler
3009 N.W. Everett
Portland, OR   97209


.
Command Line   ||<A:>||EMPINFO          ||Rec: EOF/9      ||Ins  ||
                  Enter a dBASE III PLUS command.
```

5. Write down the expressions you used for each column's contents and the name you gave the .LBL file when you created it. Then, use the **LABEL FORM** <file> **TO PRINT** command to produce a printed copy of the list.
6. Use the **QUIT** command to close all files and exit dBASE.

EXERCISE 3 Data Entry Screens

This exercise produces a customized full-screen editing screen for use when adding or editing records of the empinfo database file.

Required Preparation

Study the explanations of the @ **SAY,** @ **GET, READ, MODIFY SCREEN,** and **SET FORMAT TO** commands found in the dBASE III Plus Operation and Command Summary.

Exercise Steps

1. Load dBASE III Plus into memory.

dBASE III Plus format (.FMT) files are used to create customized screens for data input and/or output. They contain @ **SAY,** @ **GET,** and **READ** commands only. They may be created in one of two ways: by entering the commands directly into the .FMT file through the use of dBASE's **MODIFY COMMAND** command or by using the **MODIFY SCREEN** command. In this exercise, you will first create a small test .FMT file through the use of the **MODIFY COMMAND** command.

2. Type ||**MODIFY COMMAND** test.FMT↵||. Then use the **MODIFY** text editing mode to enter the following commands.

```
Edit: A:test.fmt
CURSOR:  <-- -->  |       UP   DOWN |  DELETE      | Insert Mode:    Ins
 Char:     ← →    | Line:   ↑   ↓   | Char:   Del  | Insert line:    ^N
 Word:  Home End  | Page: PgUp PgDn | Word:   ^T   | Save: ^W  Abort:Esc
 Line:    ^← ^→   | Find:  ^KF      | Line:   ^Y   | Read file:      ^KR
 Reformat: ^KB    | Refind: ^KL     |              | Write file:     ^KW
@ 2, 4 SAY "Employee Number                  Employee Name"            <
@ 4, 4 GET empno                                                       <
@ 4,32 GET last                                                        <
@ 4,44 GET first                                                       <
@ 5,35 SAY "Last          First"                                       <
@ 1, 0 TO  6,79    DOUBLE                                              <
```

3. When finished type ||^End|| to save the file and exit the editing mode.
4. Use the **USE** <file> command to make empinfo the current database file. Then use the **SET FORMAT TO** <file> command to open the test.FMT file.

With empinfo in use and the format file in effect (open), the full-screen editing commands **EDIT, APPEND,** or **READ** will use the screen coordinates, text, and fields specified in the .FMT file to produce an editing screen.

5. Type ||**EDIT**↵|| to view the screen produced by test.FMT.

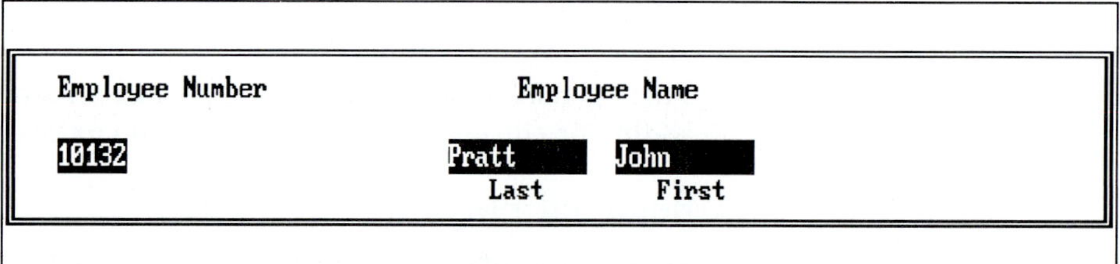

6. Type the PgDn key a few times to see the other records in the database file. Then type the Esc key to exit the editing mode.

When creating an .FMT file in this manner, you must calculate the screen coordinates for the @ **SAY** and @ **GET** commands manually, and then type them in. Another method of creating an .FMT file allows you to place text and fields on a screen and, when finished, the command used automatically generates an .FMT file with @ **SAY** and @ **GET** commands that accurately reflect the screen placement of the data.

7. Type ||**MODIFY SCREEN** empinpt↵||. The following will appear on the screen.

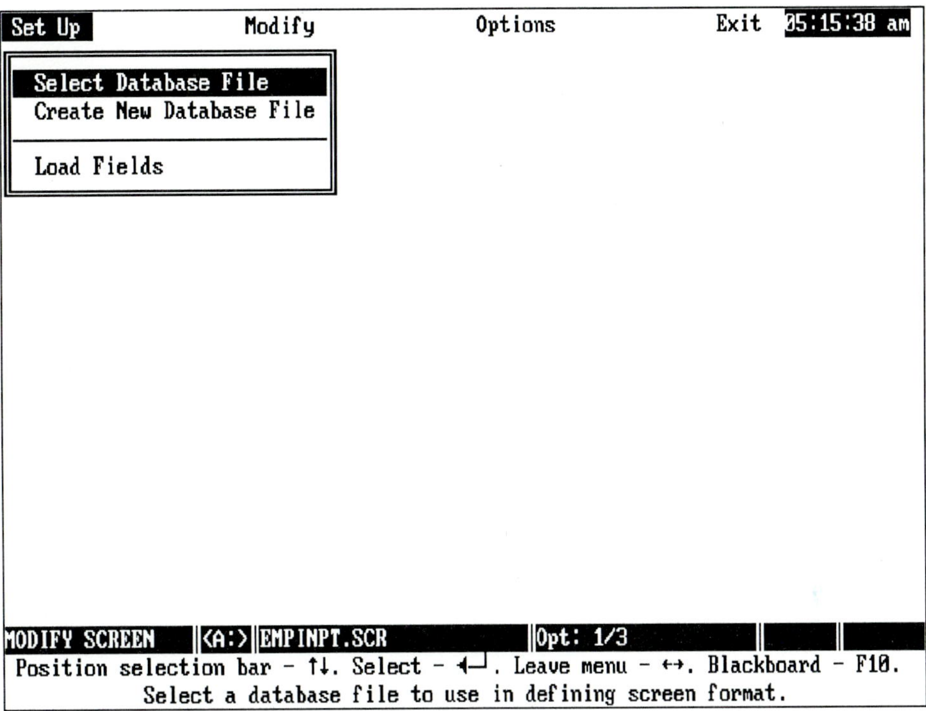

8. Type ↵ and select empinfo as the database file by moving the pull-down menu bar to its name and then typing ↵ again.
9. Use the "Load Fields" command to load all fields of the database by marking each one with ↵.

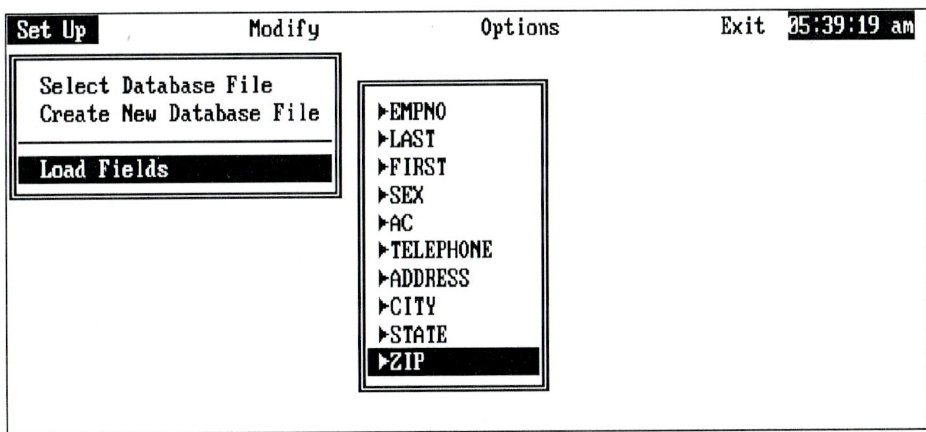

10. When finished, type ||^End|| to load the fields and automatically switch to the "blackboard" mode of the **MODIFY SCREEN** command.

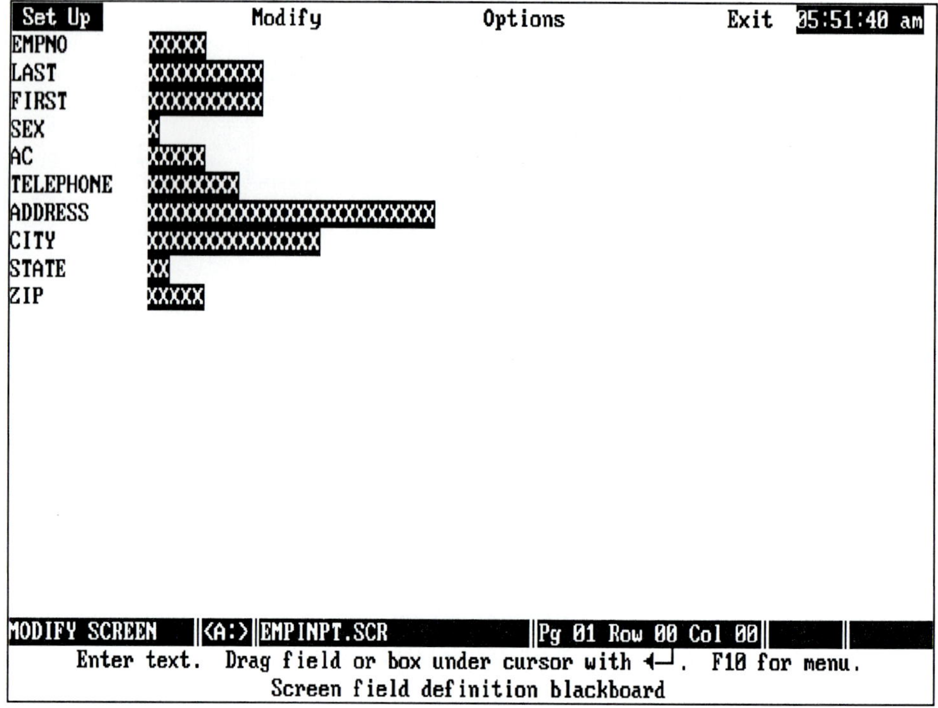

The areas on the screen shown in reverse video and filled with *X*s represent the fields that have been loaded onto the screen. dBASE places the field names next to them so that you can tell which field is which. You now are ready to begin composing the input screen. The following is a summary of editing operations available to you while in the **MODIFY SCREEN** blackboard mode.

Action Desired	Keystrokes
Cursor Movement	
Character Left	Left ←
Character Right	Right →
Field Right	End
Field Left	Home
Line Down	Down ↓
Line Up	Up ↑
Insert/Overwrite	Ins
Insert Line	^N (or ↵ with Ins ON)
Delete Line	^Y
Delete Characters	
Current Character	Delete (Del)
Previous Character	Backspace
Word Right of Cursor	^T

To move a field on the screen—Move the cursor to the field and type ↵. Then move the cursor to the new location and type ↵ again.

To abort the **MODIFY SCREEN** operation—Type F10 and then select the "Exit, Abandon" command.

In completing the next exercise step, you may find the following hints helpful. Begin by inserting 8 or 9 lines at the top of the screen and then type a field label into the blank area. Next, move to the appropriate field for the label and move it next to the label. Next, move to the field name for that field and delete it from the screen.

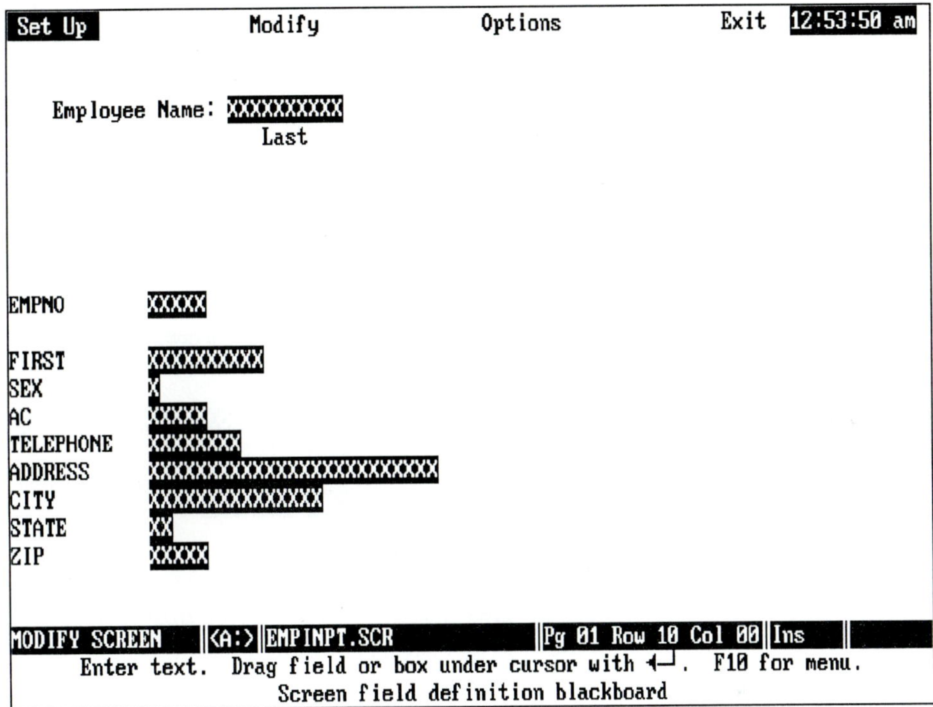

11. Use the blackboard mode of the **MODIFY SCREEN** command to compose an input screen similar to the following.

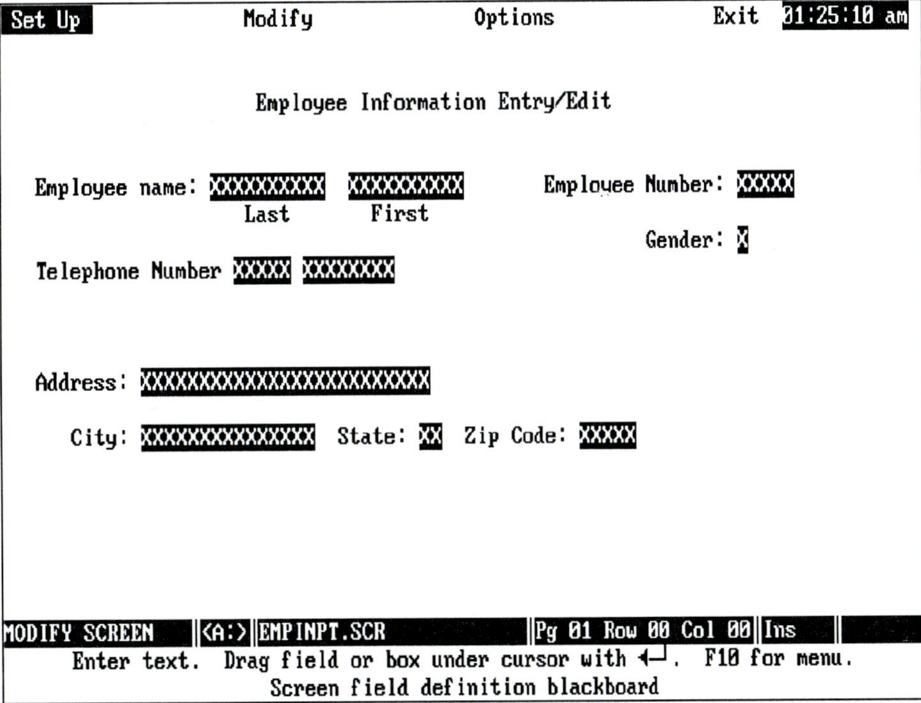

12. When finished, type F10 and then select the Options pull-down menu.

In the next step you will place a double-line box around the screen heading. To do so, you first select Option's Double bar menu item, which will automatically put you back into the blackboard mode. You then move the cursor to one corner of where you want the box drawn and type ↵. You then move the cursor to the diagonally opposite corner and type ↵ again. If you later want to change the size or shape of the block, you may move the cursor to where the box needs adjustment (somewhere on the box itself), type ↵, then move the cursor in the desired direction. When the box appears as you want it to appear, type ↵ again.

13. Place a double bar box around the heading as shown here.

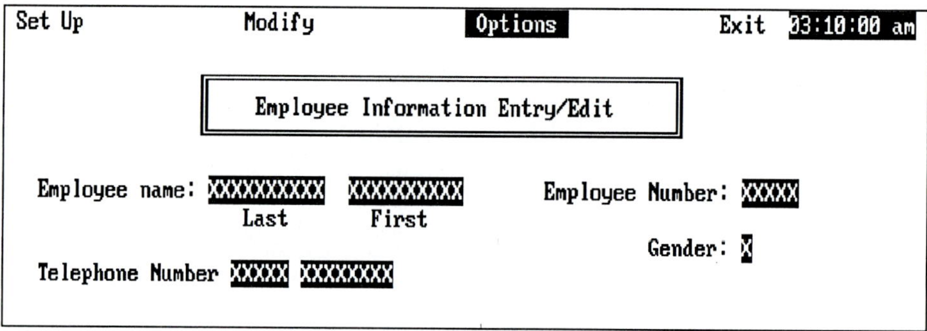

In the next steps you will add *picture clauses* to the .FMT file. A picture clause keeps the user from entering undesired data into a field when the .FMT file is used to present a screen for data entry. For instance, specifying a picture of "99999" for the employee number field will prevent the user from entering any non-number character into the field (such as typing a lower-case "l" for a number 1).

14. Move the cursor to the field for employee number and then type F10 to return to the **MODIFY SCREEN** menus. Select the "Picture Template" option of the "Modify" command and then enter five 9s into the "Picture value" area at the bottom of the screen.

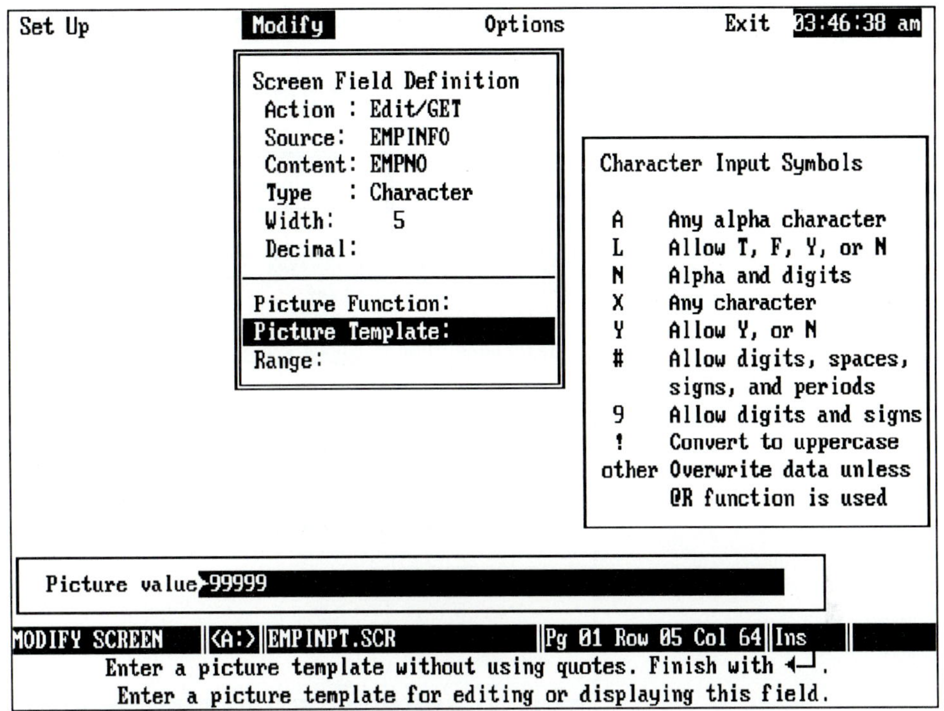

Take a moment to read the "Character Input Symbols" explanation shown on the screen. Each character in a picture clause restricts data entry in a different manner. You may notice that the character *X* allows any characters to be entered and that *X* is the default picture character used by the **MODIFY SCREEN** command.

15. Now type ||↵,F10|| to return to the blackboard mode and repeat the last steps to make the following restrictions on data entry.

- **a.** Make the ZIP code field numbers only (99999).
- **b.** Make the Gender and State fields convert to upper case (!) and (!!).
- **c.** Include parentheses in the area code field ((999)).
- **d.** Make the telephone field three numbers, a dash, then four more numbers (999–9999).

When finished, the blackboard screen should appear as follows.

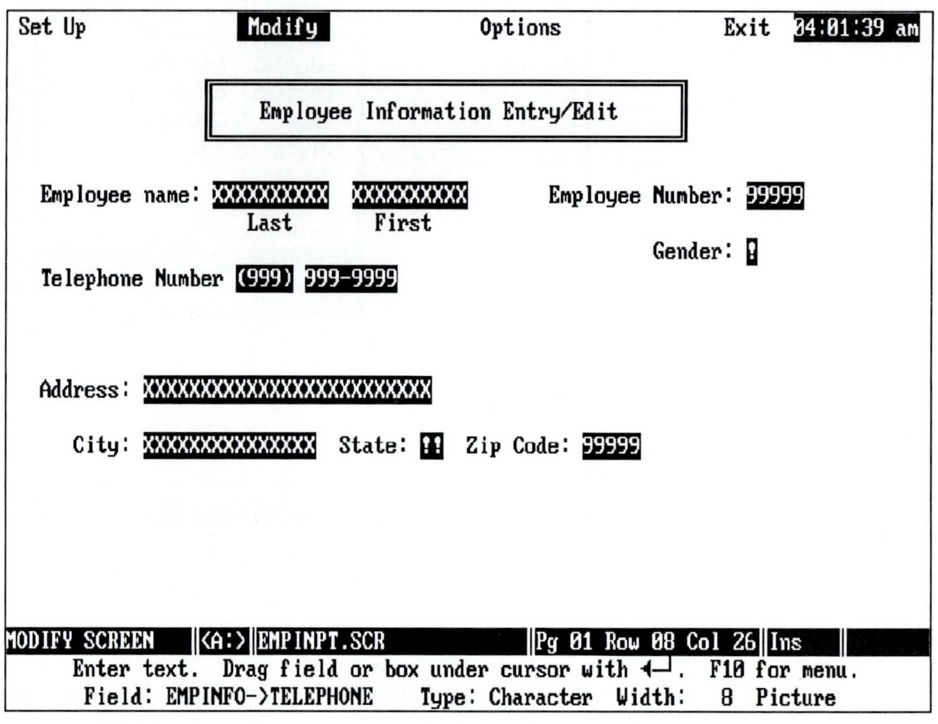

16. Now type F10 to return to the **MODIFY SCREEN** pull-down menus and select the "Exit, Save" command.
17. Next type ||**SET FORMAT TO** empinpt←┘||. Then type ||**APPEND**←┘|| to begin the operation of adding a record to the database file empinfo.
18. Enter some test data into each field presented on the screen. Try entering letters into the employee number or ZIP code fields. What happens if you try to enter lower-case letters into the gender or state fields? Notice that the user cannot forget to include the parentheses or hyphen in the telephone number.
19. When finished, type Esc to abort adding the record and then use the **TYPE** <file> **TO PRINT** command to print a copy of the empinpt.FMT file on the printer. Next, use the **QUIT** command to exit dBASE III Plus.

EXERCISE 4
Form Letters

This exercise requires that you create a dBASE command file (.PRG file) that, when executed, produces a form letter to be sent to all employees at their home addresses.

Required Preparation

Study the explanations of the **IF...ELSE...ENDIF, TEXT...ENDTEXT, DO WHILE...ENDDO** command structures, as well as the **SET MARGIN, SET PRINT, SET TALK,** and **EJECT** commands found in the dBASE III Plus Operation and Command Summary. Also study the discussion labeled "dBASE III Plus Command Files," pages D-67 through D-68.

Exercise Steps

The general algorithm for the program will be as follows.

1. Initialize: **USE** empinfo, **SET TALK OFF, SET MARGIN TO** 10.
2. Continue executing the following loop instructions until the end of the database file is reached.
   - **A.** Print two blank lines.
   - **B.** If the employee is male,
     - **a.** Print the employee's name with a "Mr." title.
   - **C.** Otherwise,
     - **a.** Print the employee's name with a "Ms." title.

     End If.
   - **D.** Print two blank lines and the letter's salutation.
   - **E.** Begin text.
     - **a.** Print the letter's text.

     End text.
   - **F.** Eject the page.
   - **G.** Move the record pointer to the next record.
3. End of loop instructions.
4. **USE, SET TALK ON, SET MARGIN TO** 0, **RETURN.**

The printed letter for the first record in the database will have the following form.

> Mr. John Pratt
> 1467 S.W. Hill St.
> Portland OR 97221
>
> Dear John:
>
> As you may already know, Philip Shear is retiring from his position as chief controller at the end of this month. There will be a reception held in the Cascade room on March 20th at 3:00 P.M. to honor his 25 years of service to the company, and to wish him well in his retirement years.
>
> Your attendance to this important company function will be greatly appreciated.
>
> R.S.V.P. (Regrets only)
>
> Sincerely,
>
> Chip Johnson
> Extension 3723
> Human Resources Department

1. Write out the commands that will be included in the command file in the order that they will occur before you begin to create the file.
2. Load dBASE III Plus into memory and use the text editing mode of the **MODIFY COMMAND** command to create the .PRG file.
3. Test the program by running it so that the output is displayed on the screen.
4. When the program is functioning correctly, use the **SET PRINT ON** command to send the output to the printer. Then run the program.
5. When finished, type ||**SET PRINT OFF**||. Then use the **TYPE** <file> **TO PRINT** command to print a copy of the program. Next, use the **QUIT** command to exit dBASE III Plus.

EXERCISE 5 Relating Database Files

The following exercise demonstrates the steps involved in bringing two or more database files into use at one time.

Required Preparation

Study the explanations of the **SEEK, SELECT,** and **SET RELATION TO** <expression> **INTO** <alias> commands found in the dBASE III Plus Operation and Command Summary.

Exercise Steps

When creating the record structure of a database, you will want to include one or more fields that uniquely identify a record. For instance, in the database empinfo.DBF there is a field named "empno", which is used to hold the employee number associated with the other data items of the same record. In such a database, you could reasonably assume that no two employees would have the same employee number. Such a field has a special relationship to the other data items in the record and is called a *unique* data item. In exercise 1 you created another database file named "empacct.DBF" which also contained a unique data item. As an intentional element of design, the data in the unique field (also named "empno") of empacct.DBF exactly matches the data found in the empno fields of the empinfo.DBF database file. In other words, the employee numbers were used in each database to uniquely identify the records in which they occurred.

While a complete discussion of concepts pertaining to the nature of data is beyond the scope of this manual, the following exercise demonstrates some basic concepts of database design and presents the steps involved in accessing more than one database file at a time.

1. Load dBASE III Plus into memory.

dBASE allows up to ten database files to be in use at the same time. Each database is opened in its own *work area.*

2. Type the following commands.

	SELECT 1↵	
	USE empinfo↵	
	SELECT 2↵	
	USE empacct↵	

At this time there are two database files in use.

3. Type the following commands to see that each database is now open in its own work area.

	SELECT 1↵	
	DISPLAY ALL↵	
	SELECT 2↵	
	DISPLAY ALL↵	

When more than one database file is in use, each maintains its own record pointer. A command that affects the position of the record pointer (such as the **DISPLAY** command) normally affects only the record pointer for the current database file (the database file residing in the currently selected work area). Commands may reference fields existing in a non-selected database by including the *alias* for the referenced field. It is recommended that you enter an alias field name in the form database file->field name. To better understand how such references can be made, type the following commands shown in gray.

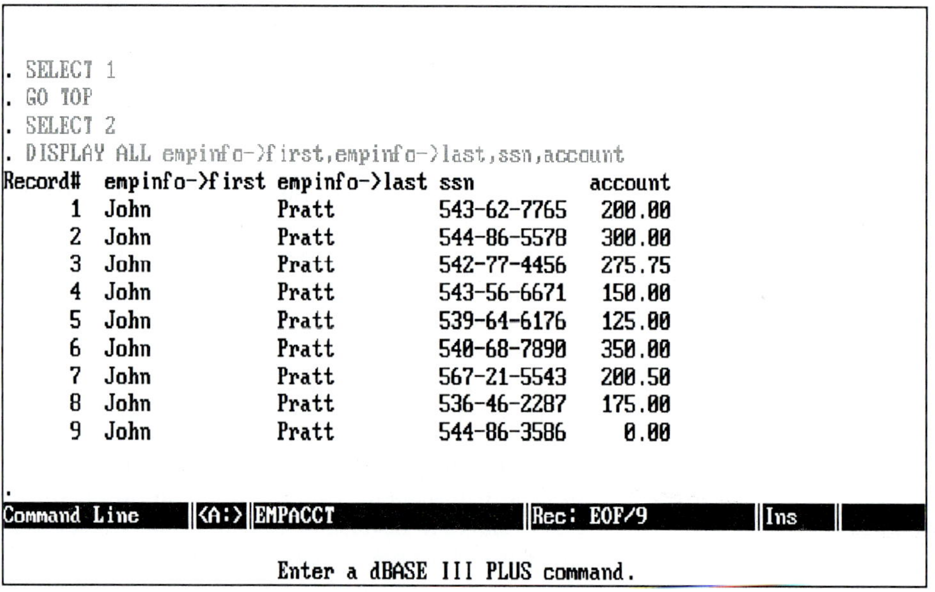

```
. SELECT 1
. GO TOP
. SELECT 2
. DISPLAY ALL empinfo->first,empinfo->last,ssn,account
Record#  empinfo->first empinfo->last ssn          account
      1  John           Pratt         543-62-7765   200.00
      2  John           Pratt         544-86-5578   300.00
      3  John           Pratt         542-77-4456   275.75
      4  John           Pratt         543-56-6671   150.00
      5  John           Pratt         539-64-6176   125.00
      6  John           Pratt         540-68-7890   350.00
      7  John           Pratt         567-21-5543   200.50
      8  John           Pratt         536-46-2287   175.00
      9  John           Pratt         544-86-3586     0.00

.
Command Line     <A:> EMPACCT             Rec: EOF/9          Ins

                       Enter a dBASE III PLUS command.
```

Notice that the **ALL** scope used in the **DISPLAY** command affected only the record pointer in the current database, empacct. The record pointer in the empinfo database remained on the first record.

As previously mentioned, the two database files share a logically related primary key, which in this case is held in the field named "empno". In the empinfo database file, the empno field holding the employee number 10126 exists in the record that holds the address information for David Jones. In the empacct database file, the empno field that holds the number 10126 exists in the record that holds the social security number, employed date, and so on, for David Jones. When two or more database files are initially designed to contain matching primary keys in this manner, it becomes possible to link the record pointers in each database so that they will point to the records having related data in them. To give you experience performing such an operation, enter the following commands shown in gray.

```
. SELECT 1
. INDEX ON empno TO nodex
 100% indexed            9 Records indexed
. USE empinfo INDEX nodex
. SELECT 2
. SET RELATION TO empno INTO empinfo
. DISPLAY ALL empinfo->first,empinfo->last,ssn,account
Record#  empinfo->first empinfo->last ssn         account
      1  John           Pratt         543-62-7765  200.00
      2  Ellen          Smoler        544-86-5578  300.00
      3  David          Jones         542-77-4456  275.75
      4  Sally          Sill          543-56-6671  150.00
      5  Michael        Knat          539-64-6176  125.00
      6  Paul           Smith         540-68-7890  350.00
      7  Mary           Martins       567-21-5543  200.50
      8  Sandy          Nichols       536-46-2287  175.00
      9  Frank          Johnson       544-86-3586    0.00

.
Command Line      ||<A:>||EMPACCT            ||Rec: EOF/9          ||Ins  ||

                   Enter a dBASE III PLUS command.
```

In the preceding steps you created a dBASE III Plus relation between the database files named "empinfo" and empacct". In such a relationship, one database is referred to as the *parent* and the other is referred to as the *child*. Here, empinfo would be considered the child database file. The child database must be in use with an index file created on the primary key data item (in this case the field empno). The **SET RELATION TO** <expression> **INTO** <database file> command is issued from the work area in which the parent database resides. The expression specified in the command references data in the parent database and reflects the same expression used to create the child's index file. When fields are used to hold a primary key in two or more database files, it is not necessary for them to have the same name as they do here (empinfo->empno and empacct->empno). For instance, if the field holding the employee numbers in empacct had been originally named "eno", the command used to set the relation would have been **SET RELATION TO** eno **INTO** empinfo. Finally, the database file specified in the command names the child database for the relation.

Once a relation has been made, the record pointer in the parent database becomes the controlling pointer. When the record pointer of the parent database is moved to a record, dBASE evaluates the relation expression and performs a **SEEK** operation on the child database file. The record pointer in the child database file will be positioned at the first record matching the **SEEK** expression. If no such record is found, the record pointer is positioned at the end of the file.

To further demonstrate the use of multiple database files, you next will create a small parent database which will use empacct as its child database. The new database will be used to hold invoice information on purchases made by employees.

4. Type the following.

||**SELECT 3**↵||

||**CREATE** emppur↵||

Next, enter the following record structure for the emppur database.

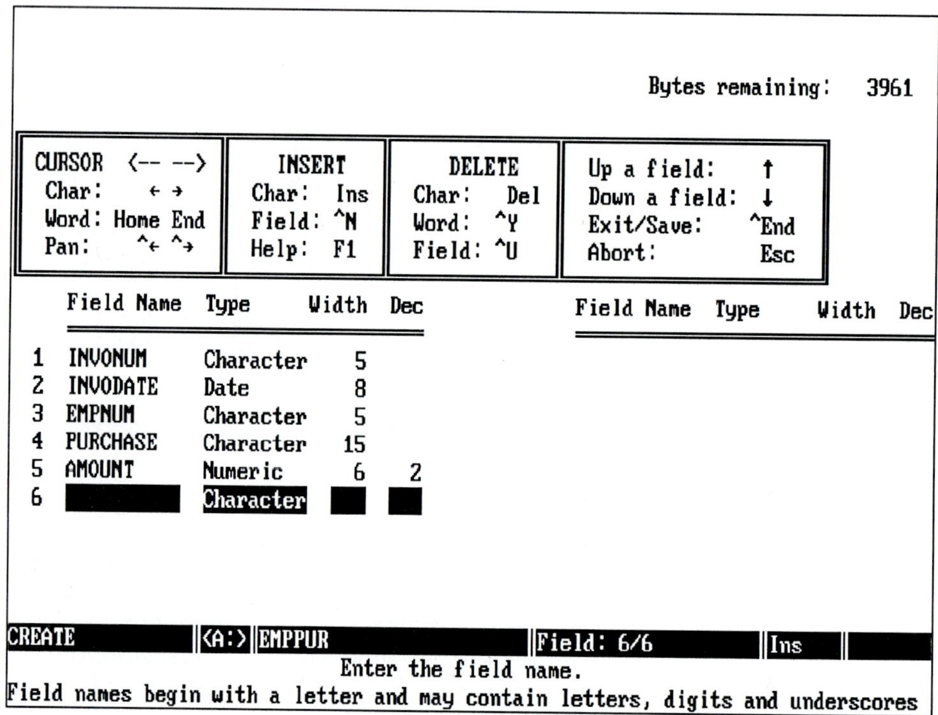
Bytes remaining: 3961

CURSOR <-- -->
Char: ← →
Word: Home End
Pan: ^← ^→

INSERT
Char: Ins
Field: ^N
Help: F1

DELETE
Char: Del
Word: ^Y
Field: ^U

Up a field: ↑
Down a field: ↓
Exit/Save: ^End
Abort: Esc

	Field Name	Type	Width	Dec
1	INVONUM	Character	5	
2	INVODATE	Date	8	
3	EMPNUM	Character	5	
4	PURCHASE	Character	15	
5	AMOUNT	Numeric	6	2
6		Character		

Field Name Type Width Dec

CREATE |<A:>|EMPPUR |Field: 6/6 |Ins

Enter the field name.

Field names begin with a letter and may contain letters, digits and underscores

5. When finished, type ||^End,↵,Y|| to end the **CREATE** operation and begin entering records.

The record structure includes a field named "invonum" to hold the invoice number (which serves as the primary key for the emppur database records), a field for the purchase date named "invodate", a field for the employee number of the employee making the purchase (named "empnum" in this database), a field for a short description of the article purchased, and a field for the dollar amount of the purchase.

6. Enter six records into the database to reflect the following information:

a. Invoice number 10012, date 03/19/90, Mary Martins (employee number 10122) purchased a barbecue on account for $69.00.

b. Invoice number 10013, date 03/21/90, Paul Smith (employee number 10131) purchased a weed trimmer on account for $59.00.

c. Invoice number 10014, date 03/21/90, Mary Martins (employee number 10122) purchased three lawn chairs on account for $89.95.

d. Invoice number 10015, date 03/22/90, Mary Martins (employee number 10122) purchased a croquet set on account for $29.95.

e. Invoice number 10016, date 03/23/90, Paul Smith (employee number 10131) purchased a hammock on account for $64.00.

f. Invoice number 10017, date 03/23/90, Frank Johnson (employee number 10137) purchased a picnic table on account for $184.00.

7. When finished, type ↵ on the next record shown (record 7) to stop inputting records.

In the next steps you will relate the parent database emppur with the child database empacct.

8. Type

	SELECT 2↵	
	INDEX ON empno **TO** actnodex↵	
	SELECT 3↵	
	USE emppur↵	
	SET RELATION TO empnum **INTO** empacct↵	

Now that all three databases are in use and their record pointers are linked, you may access the fields of related data by using alias field names. For instance, if you wanted to see the invoice number, employee name, invoice amount, and current employee account balance for every invoice record in emppur, you would type the following shown in gray.

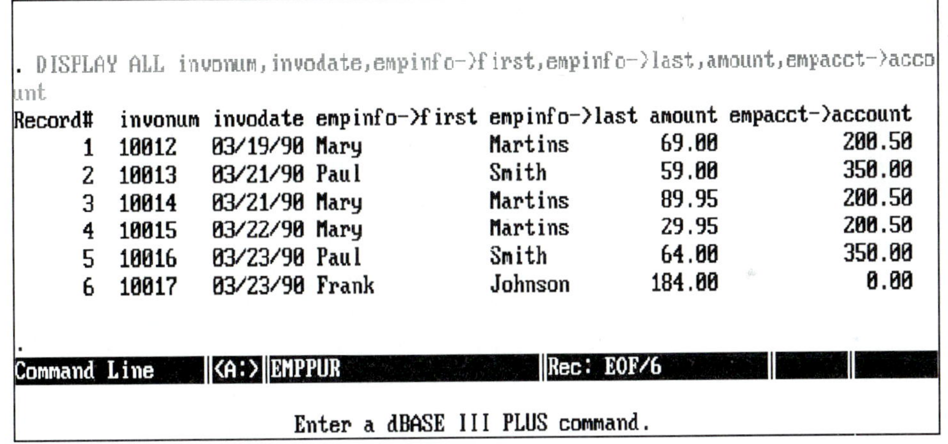

```
. DISPLAY ALL invonum,invodate,empinfo->first,empinfo->last,amount,empacct->acco
unt
Record#  invonum invodate empinfo->first empinfo->last amount empacct->account
      1  10012   03/19/90 Mary           Martins        69.00           200.50
      2  10013   03/21/90 Paul           Smith          59.00           350.00
      3  10014   03/21/90 Mary           Martins        89.95           200.50
      4  10015   03/22/90 Mary           Martins        29.95           200.50
      5  10016   03/23/90 Paul           Smith          64.00           350.00
      6  10017   03/23/90 Frank          Johnson       184.00             0.00

.
Command Line  ||<A:>||EMPPUR            ||Rec: EOF/6      ||  ||

                     Enter a dBASE III PLUS command.
```

9. Now use the **DISPLAY** <scope> <expression list> **FOR** <condition> **TO PRINT** command to produce the following printed information.

   The names, telephone numbers and invoice amounts for all employees having invoice amounts over $60.00.

```
  1  Mary      Martins    (206)    222-2123      69.00
  3  Mary      Martins    (206)    222-2123      89.95
  5  Paul      Smith      (503)    244-1010      64.00
  6  Frank     Johnson    (503)    223-7928     184.00
```

The names, telephone numbers, and invoice amounts for all employees having invoice amounts which, when added to their current account amounts, exceed 20 percent of their monthly salaries.

```
  2  Paul          Smith        (503)      244-1010          59.00
  5  Paul          Smith        (503)      244-1010          64.00
```

10. Use the **DISPLAY STATUS TO PRINT** command to produce a printed copy of the files that are currently open.

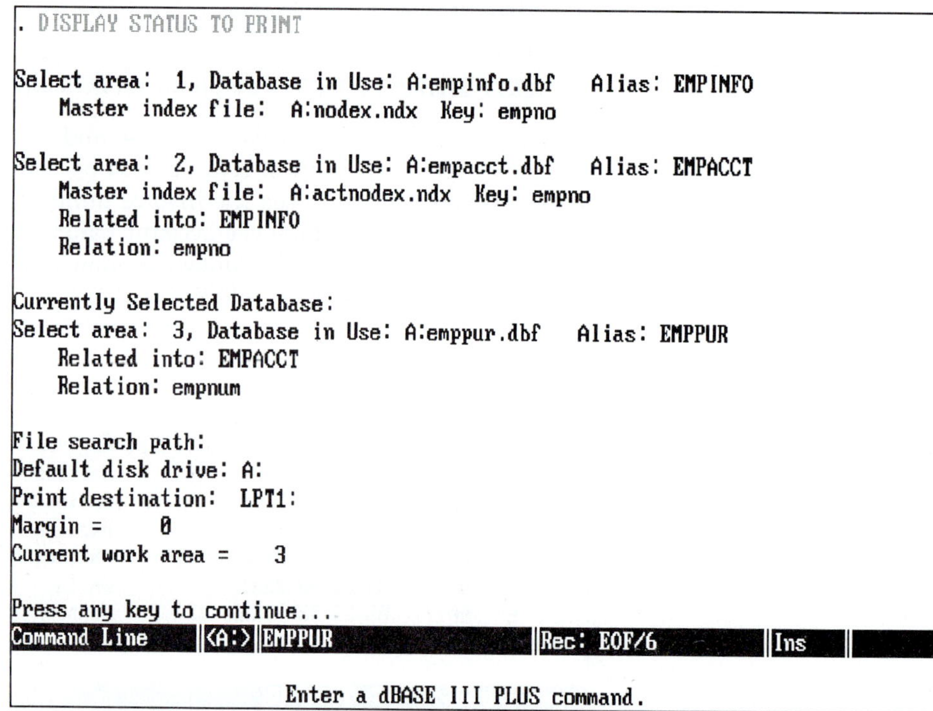

```
. DISPLAY STATUS TO PRINT

Select area:  1, Database in Use: A:empinfo.dbf   Alias: EMPINFO
    Master index file:  A:nodex.ndx  Key: empno

Select area:  2, Database in Use: A:empacct.dbf   Alias: EMPACCT
    Master index file:  A:actnodex.ndx  Key: empno
    Related into: EMPINFO
    Relation: empno

Currently Selected Database:
Select area:  3, Database in Use: A:emppur.dbf   Alias: EMPPUR
    Related into: EMPACCT
    Relation: empnum

File search path:
Default disk drive: A:
Print destination:  LPT1:
Margin =      0
Current work area =     3

Press any key to continue...
Command Line      |<A:>|EMPPUR                |Rec: EOF/6         |Ins |

                         Enter a dBASE III PLUS command.
```

11. Now use the **QUIT** command to properly exit dBASE III Plus.

EXERCISE 6
Employee Invoice Summaries

This exercise requires that you create a dBASE command file (.PRG file) that, when executed, produces invoices of purchases made during the month which will be sent to the appropriate employees at their home addresses.

Required Preparation

You will need to complete Exercise 5 before completing this exercise. Study the explanations of the **IF...ELSE...ENDIF, TEXT...ENDTEXT, DO WHILE...ENDDO** command structures, as well as the **SET MARGIN, SET PRINT, SET TALK,** and **EJECT** commands found in the dBASE III Plus Operation and Command Summary. Also study the discussion labeled "dBASE III Plus Command Files," pages D-67 through D-68.

Exercise Steps

The program will produce printed output for each employee who has had a purchase recorded in the emppur database file. The printed output for the employee named Mary Martins will appear similar to the following.

Ms. Mary Martins
1507 Mill Plain Blvd.
Vancouver WA 98660

Dear Mary:

Here is a list of your account charges for the month of March.

INVOICE #	DATE	ITEM PURCHASED	AMOUNT
10012	03/19/90	Barbecue Grill	69.00
10014	03/21/90	3 Lawn Chairs	89.95
10015	03/22/90	Croquet Set	29.95
			Total - $188.90

Our records show that with the addition of these charges your current account balance is $389.40.

The program will begin by initializing the environment, putting the following database files in use with their associated index files and relations.

Select area: 1, Database in Use: A:empinfo.dbf Alias: EMPINFO
Master index file: A:nodex.ndx Key: empno

Select area: 2, Database in Use: A:empacct.dbf Alias: EMPACCT
Master index file: A:actnodex.ndx Key: empno
Related into: EMPINFO
Relation: empno

Currently Selected Database:
Select area: 3, Database in Use: A:emppur.dbf Alias: EMPPUR
Master index file: A:innodex.ndx Key: empnum
Related into: EMPACCT
Relation: empnum

Notice that the emppur database (work area 3) needs to have an index file (named "innodex") created and in use, and, with that exception, the environment described here is the same one that existed at the conclusion of Exercise 5.

The general algorithm for the program will be

1. Initialize: Open the appropriate database files with their index files in the work areas described, and set the appropriate relations. **SET TALK OFF, SET MARGIN TO** 10.
2. Continue executing the following loop instructions until the end of the emppur database file is reached.
   - **A.** Store the field empacct->account to a variable named b.
   - **B.** Print two blank lines.
   - **C.** If the employee is male,
     - **a.** Print the employee's name with a "Mr." title.
   - **D.** Otherwise,
     - **a.** Print the employee's name with a "Ms." title.

     End If.
   - **E.** Print two blank lines and the letter's salutation.
   - **F.** Begin Text
     - **a.** Print the beginning invoice text and table headings with their underlines.

     End Text.
   - **G.** Store zero to a variable named n.
   - **H.** Store the field empnum to a variable named t.
   - **I.** Continue executing the following loop instructions until the employee number in the field empnum changes.
     - **a.** Print the fields invonum, invodate, purchase, and amount.
     - **b.** Store n plus the value in amount to the variable n.
     - **c.** Move the record pointer to the next record in emppur.
   - **J.** End of loop instructions.
   - **K.** Print the remaining invoice text, total STR(n,6,2), and balance STR(b+n,6,2), and eject the page.
3. End of loop instructions.
4. **CLOSE ALL, SET TALK ON, SET MARGIN TO** 0, **RETURN.**

1. Write out the commands that will be included in the command file, in the order that they will occur, before you begin to create the file.
2. Load dBASE III Plus into memory, put the database file emppur into use, and create an index file named "innodex" on the field empnum.
3. Use the text editing mode of the **MODIFY COMMAND** command to create the .PRG file.
4. Test the program by running it so that the output is displayed on the screen.
5. When the program is functioning correctly, use the **SET PRINT ON** command to send the output to the printer. Then run the program.
6. When finished, type ||**SET PRINT OFF**||. Then use the **TYPE** <file> **TO PRINT** command to print a copy of the program. Next use the **QUIT** command to exit dBASE III Plus.

CASES

CASE 1
University Bookstore

William Davies was recently hired to be textbook manager at the local university bookstore. Each term the bookstore receives requests from faculty members to order textbooks for their classes. Part of Bill's responsibilities includes estimating the number of used books on hand and then ordering the necessary number of new books from publishers to ensure that all students will have texts at the beginning of the term. To help facilitate the ordering process, Bill intends to create a database of textbook orders placed by faculty at the beginning of each term.

In a recent conversation with Paula Cornet, the bookstore manager, Bill said, "I think the time has come to automate at least some of the textbook ordering process around here. There are times when I need to find all orders for a certain book, or all orders made by a certain faculty member. There are other times when I need to find all orders for a particular publisher or all orders made on a certain date. The current manual system we are using makes that part of the job nearly impossible. I know that with a microcomputer database management system we could easily find the order information we are looking for when we need it.

"I realize that the person entering the order records will probably be a part-time, temporary employee and that it will probably be a different person each term. What we need is a simple, easy-to-use system, with a data entry screen that looks like the order form we receive from the faculty. It would also be nice if the system could somehow check to make sure that the employee is entering the right type of data into the right areas on the screen."

Sample Request Form

UNIVERSITY BOOKSTORE
Textbook Request Form

Department	Course #	Section	Expected Enrollment
MGMT	*335*	*002*	*45*

Instructor's Name	Phone #	Date
C. Marshall	*2724*	*02/12/90*

Term	Year
FAL	*90*

Author
L. Ingalsbe

Title	Vol	Edition
Using Computers and Applications Software		*3rd*

#Books Needed	ISBN	Publisher
45	*0-675-21097-6*	*Merrill Publishing Co.*

Data Item Descriptions

Department	Four upper-case letters (MGMT)
Course #	Three-number code (335)
Section	Three-number code (002)
Expected Enrollment	Up to three digits with no decimal (45)
Instructor's Name	Up to 25 characters (C. Marshall)
Phone #	Four-number extension (2724)
Date	Eight character date-type data (02/12/90)
Term	Three letters (FAL,WIN,SPR,SUM)
Year	Two numbers (90)
Author	Up to 25 characters (L. Ingalsbe)
Title	Up to 50 characters (Using Computers and Applications Software)
Vol	Up to three numbers
Edition	Up to four characters (3rd)
# Books Needed	Up to three digits with no decimal (45)
ISBN	13 character code (0-675-21097-6)
Publisher	Up to 35 characters (Merrill Publishing Co.)

CASE 2 Kady's Korner Market

Frank Kady has owned and operated a small grocery store for the past 27 years. Since the time that Kady's Korner Market opened as a typical neighborhood grocery store, Frank has had to make many changes to meet new consumer demands. Today he has to compete with a number of other convenience stores in the area. Frank has recently decided to start renting videotapes of movies to his customers, a service that many of the competing stores in the area offer. With his many years of experience, Frank has a good idea about what is needed to set up a rental service. However, he doesn't know much about new movies, and he has never even operated a video-cassette recorder (VCR).

Frank's nephew, Kevin, who is a sophomore at the local university, has worked for Frank every summer for the past five years. In a recent phone conversation, Frank told Kevin about his plans, and Kevin was enthusiastic about the idea. Kevin said, "I've learned quite a bit about database systems in my business courses here at college, and I think a microcomputer could really help you run the rental service."

Frank has decided to invest in a microcomputer and the software Kevin told him about. When Kevin comes back to work for him next month, Frank is going to suggest that Kevin take charge of the project and set up a record-keeping system with the microcomputer. He knows that it sometimes takes a while to get the bugs out of these systems, so he'll suggest that Kevin begin by just entering the information for the tapes the store will have in stock. Frank may be able to help Kevin decide what information would eventually be kept in the system. For the time being, though, he wants to keep track of customer rentals with a regular log book.

Frank has checked into the video rental business and collected some information. He has found that the most economical way of offering a variety of movies is to order from one of the distributors in the area that deals with private stores such as his. He can keep a stock of about 200 to 300 tapes at a time, and he may order and return tapes as desired. His system should, therefore, have the ability to add and delete titles, as well as to edit information about the titles in the system.

Frank may stock several copies of more popular movies, while keeping only one copy of movies that are less popular. He also needs to identify certain movies as new releases, for which he can charge a higher rental fee. Long movies may come on two or three separate tapes, but will be rented as one movie. Some of the information available about movies may include the production company, year made, running time in minutes, main actors and actresses, whether color or black and white, rating, and a short synopsis of the movie. He will talk to Kevin about which of this information will be kept in the system.

To have a good variety of movies available, Frank may want to put movies into categories. Some categories that he has seen used in other stores are Action, Adventure, Children's, Comedy, Drama, Foreign Films, Musicals, Mystery, Suspense, War, and Westerns. For the relatively small number of movies he will carry, Frank won't need many categories, but he would like to be able to keep track of how many tapes he has in the different categories at any one time.

Frank has obtained a list of movies scheduled for a second release this month. These movies will be available from the distributor at a reduced rate. He wants Kevin to select from the list those movies which might be good choices to start stocking. He also is relying on Kevin, who has a VCR and has seen or heard of most of the newer movies, to do some research and complete the initial list of movies to stock.

Dangerous Liaisons (1988) (R) (120 min.) Copies to Stock: ?

WARNER HOME VIDEO

Starring: Glenn Close, John Malkovich, Michelle Pfeiffer

Synopsis: Stephen Frears' film won 3 Oscars—Best Screenplay, Art Direction and Costume Design. The sexual power games played by the upper class in 18th Century France are explored, as the Marquise de Merteuil challenges her ex-lover Valmont to seduce the betrothed of her most recent lover. But Valmont has eyes for the virtuous Madame de Tourvel. Oh boy, is this going to get complicated!!!

Mississippi Burning (1988) (R) (127 min.) Copies to Stock: ?

ORION

Starring: Gene Hackman, Willem Dafoe, Frances McDormand, Brad Dourif

Synopsis: Alan Parker's intense drama about the violence and fear during the Civil Rights movement in the '60s in the deep South won an Oscar for Best Cinematography. When three freedom fighters are reported missing, two FBI agents are assigned to the case. Now they have to face the fear and prejudice of people intimidated by the Ku Klux Klan in order to solve it. This one is intense.

Cocoon—The Return (1988) (PG) (116 min.) Copies to Stock: ?

CBS/FOX

Starring: Don Ameche, Steve Guttenberg, Wilford Brimley, Jack Gilford

Synopsis: When last we saw the old folks, they were heading to the planet Antarea in a spaceship. Now they've returned to Florida for a visit, and to try to help save a captive cocoon that was discovered by Earth scientists. Holy homesickness! How will they feel now that they're back with all their loved ones? Hume Cronyn, Jessica Tandy, Maureen Stapleton and Elaine Stritch co-star.

Physical Evidence (1989) (R) (100 min.) Copies to Stock: ?

VESTRON VIDEO

Starring: Burt Reynolds, Theresa Russell, Ned Beatty, Kay Lenz

Synopsis: Joe Paris is a down-on-his-luck cop. Not only has he been suspended from the force for his overly zealous tactics, now he's being accused of first-degree murder. Can he and the beautiful attorney assigned to his case figure out what's really going on? This thriller was produced by Martin (Jagged Edge) Ransohoff, and directed by Michael (Coma) Crichton.

The Boost (1988) (R) (95 min.) Copies to Stock: ?

HBO VIDEO

Starring: James Woods, Sean Young, John Kapelos, Steven Hill

Synopsis: This yuppie couple is searching for the good life and they work hard to get to the top. But when you get to the top, the only way to go is down. Ever since Lenny and Linda Brown moved to the West Coast, he's been hotter than a pistol, selling lucrative real estate. But life in the fast lane includes the deadly lure of cocaine. Will they succumb to drugs and throw it all away?

Daffy Duck's Quackbusters (1988) (G) (76 min.) Copies to Stock: ?

WARNER HOME VIDEO

Starring: Daffy Duck, Bugs Bunny, Porky Pig, Tweety and Sylvester

Synopsis: Daffy's second full-length motion picture finds him going into the exorcism business in order to inherit a fortune. Our wisequacking friend has formed the "Ghosts 'R' Us Paranormal Agency" and the laughs won't stop. This one features his two most recent outings, "The Duxorcist" and "Night Of The Living Duck." And with classic sequences like "The Abominable Snow Rabbit," you can't miss.

Who's Harry Crumb? (1989) (PG-13) (91 min.) Copies to Stock: ?

RCA - COLUMBIA PICTURES

Starring: John Candy, Jeffrey Jones, Annie Potts, Barry Corbin

Synopsis: He's the bumblingest detective ever, that's who. The only reason he's been assigned to a kidnapping case is because his boss doesn't really want it to get solved. But Harry's a master of disguises, and he's going undercover to uncover the truth. There's more going on here than meets the eye, however. Can Crumb find the crumbs behind the crime? Paul Flaherty directed this funny farce.

NOTE: Movie listings reprinted with permission from Vidpix, *vol. 2, no. 1, July 1989.* Vidpix *is a publication of Video Marketing & Publishing, Inc.*

CASE 3 Uptown Delicatessen - Part A

Fritz Cramer owns and operates the Uptown Delicatessen, which is located in a popular shopping mall in the City Center. In addition to his regular line of deli meats and cheeses, Fritz recently began carrying a number of fresh uncooked meat items. He has found that many busy shoppers and people who work in the area find it quicker and more convenient to buy some of these items at the deli than to make an extra trip to the grocery store before going home.

Fritz has a database set up on his microcomputer, which he uses to keep track of inventory and product orders. He has created a database file on which he keeps his fresh meat master product list. The file uses a two-character field, MEATCODE, to identify the type of meat as beef (BF), chicken (CH), or pork (PO). Within each of these groupings, a two-character field, CUTCODE, is used to sequentially number the items carried. For example, beef cut 01 is used for T-bone steaks, chicken cut 01 is used for whole fryers, and chicken cut 02 is used for 8-piece cut fryers. The other fields in this file hold the number of pounds Fritz wants to keep in stock and the average selling price for each item.

The first thing Fritz wants to do is to print a form that can be used for taking a physical inventory of these items. He thinks that this can be accomplished with the database software's report form feature, although he hasn't had time to learn much about it yet. Since he often has one of his part-time employees help him take inventory, Fritz wants the inventory form to be simple, with separate sections for his three fresh meat types coinciding with the way they are separated in his cold storage room. Fritz has typed up an example of how he would like the inventory form to appear.

The Database File

FILE: meatlist.DBF

Record#	MEATCODE	CUTCODE	MEATNAME	CUTNAME	STOCKLVL	AVGPRICE
1	CH	01	CHICKEN	WHOLE FRYERS	150	1.39
2	CH	02	CHICKEN	8-PIECE CUT FRYERS	160	1.49
3	CH	03	CHICKEN	QUARTER-CUT FRYERS	120	0.89
4	BF	01	BEEF	T-BONE STEAKS	75	4.68
5	BF	02	BEEF	RIB EYE STEAKS	40	4.39
6	BF	03	BEEF	ROUND STEAKS	85	1.89
7	BF	04	BEEF	FILETS	115	4.29
8	BF	05	BEEF	SHORT RIBS	140	1.69
9	PO	01	PORK	CHOPS	115	2.89
10	PO	02	PORK	SPARE RIBS	140	1.79
11	PO	03	PORK	ROAST	60	2.69
12	PO	04	PORK	SHOULDER	50	2.09
13	BF	06	BEEF	RUMP ROAST	55	1.98
14	BF	07	BEEF	STEW MEAT	30	1.99
15	CH	04	CHICKEN	BREASTS	80	2.39
16	CH	05	CHICKEN	LEGS	40	1.49
17	CH	06	CHICKEN	THIGHS	80	1.69
18	CH	07	CHICKEN	WINGS	40	0.49
19	PO	05	PORK	CURED HAMS	180	1.89

Example Report Form Output

MEAT INVENTORY ENTRY FORM

INVENTORY DATE: ____/____/____

CODE DESCRIPTION	LBS ON HAND
MEAT TYPE: BEEF	__________
BF01 T-BONE STEAKS	__________
BF02 RIB EYE STEAKS	__________
BF03 ROUND STEAKS	__________
BF04 FILETS	__________
BF05 SHORT RIBS	__________
BF06 RUMP ROAST	__________
BF07 STEW MEAT	__________
MEAT TYPE: CHICKEN	__________
CH01 WHOLE FRYERS	__________
CH02 8-PIECE CUT FRYERS	__________
CH03 QUARTER-CUT FRYERS	__________
CH04 BREASTS	__________
CH05 LEGS	__________
CH06 THIGHS	__________
CH07 WINGS	__________

MEAT TYPE: PORK	________________
PO01 CHOPS	________________
PO02 SPARE RIBS	________________
PO03 ROAST	________________
PO04 SHOULDER	________________
PO05 CURED HAMS	________________

CASE 4 Uptown Delicatessen—Part B

Now that Fritz has an inventory form for his fresh meat items, he needs a way of entering this information into his database system. He also needs a second report that shows the number of pounds of each item he must order to bring his inventory back up to the desired stock level. To test his system, he has set up an inventory file into which he would like to enter his last two physical inventories.

Fritz's inventory file has only three fields. The first field, INVDATE, holds the inventory date. He has decided to make the second field, MEATCUT, a four-character code that is a combination of the two fields MEATCODE and CUTCODE from his master file. This will save space on his disk as well as allowing him to relate this file to the master file when he needs the full name of a particular item. The third field, LBSINV, holds the number of pounds in inventory for each item.

Since Fritz plans to train one of his employees to enter the inventory into the system from the inventory form, he wants to set up a data entry screen that will be easy to use. Since the MEATCUT code (e.g., BF01) is not at all descriptive, he wants the entry screen to display the full cut name for each fresh meat item.

After the inventory amounts have been entered, he wants to be able to produce an order sheet that shows the inventory amounts and average selling prices for each item. In another column he wants these two items multiplied to show the approximate value of his inventory for each item. The final column should show the amount he needs to order for each item, which is his stock level minus the amount he has in inventory. This column, however, should not show any negative values, since that would mean he is already overstocked for an item and shouldn't order any more. Fritz also wants the order sheet report to be organized by meat type, and he would like to see the totals for pounds on hand, value of inventory, and pounds to order for each type of meat. He has typed up an example of how he would like the order form report to appear.

The Database File

File: mtinven.DBF

Record#	INVDATE	MEATCUT	LBSINV
1	02/09/90	BF01	34
2	02/09/90	BF02	45
3	02/09/90	BF03	7
4	02/09/90	BF04	52
5	02/09/90	BF05	157
6	02/09/90	BF06	5
7	02/09/90	BF07	14
8	02/09/90	CH01	0
9	02/09/90	CH02	14
10	02/09/90	CH03	55
11	02/09/90	CH04	90
12	02/09/90	CH05	3
13	02/09/90	CH06	36
14	02/09/90	CH07	45
15	02/09/90	PO01	10
16	02/09/90	PO02	64
17	02/09/90	PO03	67
18	02/09/90	PO04	4
19	02/09/90	PO05	82
20	02/16/90	BF01	35
21	02/16/90	BF02	14
22	02/16/90	BF03	89
23	02/16/90	BF04	53
24	02/16/90	BF05	50
25	02/16/90	BF06	0
26	02/16/90	BF07	14
27	02/16/90	CH01	53
28	02/16/90	CH02	110
29	02/16/90	CH03	55
30	02/16/90	CH04	28
31	02/16/90	CH05	28
32	02/16/90	CH06	37
33	02/16/90	CH07	14
34	02/16/90	PO01	79
35	02/16/90	PO02	65
36	02/16/90	PO03	21
37	02/16/90	PO04	34
38	02/16/90	PO05	83

Example Report Form Output (Inventory Date 02/09/90)

MEAT ORDER SHEET

ITEM CODE	ITEM DESCRIPTION	POUNDS ON HAND	AVG PRICE PER POUND	VALUE OF INVENTORY	MIN LBS TO ORDER
MEAT TYPE: BEEF					
BF01	T-BONE STEAKS	34	4.68	159.12	41
BF02	RIB EYE STEAKS	45	4.39	197.55	0
BF03	ROUND STEAKS	7	1.89	13.23	78
BF04	FILETS	52	4.29	223.08	63
BF05	SHORT RIBS	157	1.69	265.33	0
BF06	RUMP ROAST	5	1.98	9.90	50
BF07	STEW MEAT	14	1.99	27.86	16
		314		896.07	248
MEAT TYPE: CHICKEN					
CH01	WHOLE FRYERS	0	1.39	0.00	150
CH02	8-PIECE CUT FRYERS	14	1.49	20.86	146
CH03	QUARTER-CUT FRYERS	55	0.89	48.95	65
CH04	BREASTS	90	2.39	215.10	0
CH05	LEGS	3	1.49	4.47	37
CH06	THIGHS	36	1.69	60.84	44
CH07	WINGS	45	0.49	22.05	0
		243		372.27	442
MEAT TYPE: PORK					
PO01	CHOPS	10	2.89	28.90	105
PO02	SPARE RIBS	64	1.79	114.56	76
PO03	ROAST	67	2.69	180.23	0
PO04	SHOULDER	4	2.09	8.36	46
PO05	CURED HAMS	82	1.89	154.98	98
		227		487.03	325
		784		1755.37	1015

CASE 5 Albright Ink Company

Leann Holmes works in the production department of Albright Ink Company, a company that manufactures and distributes inks used for printing newspapers and magazines. Albright's sells large quantities of black ink, which is manufactured in a continuous process and is usually delivered by tank trucks. The company also manufactures blue, green, red, yellow, and violet inks in a batch process and sells these inks in five-gallon containers on a much smaller scale.

Leann is primarily responsible for scheduling production runs of colored inks. She is refining the method by which sales of colored inks are forecast and would like to collect and analyze information from daily invoice records. She has spoken with John Hanson, one of the company's sales managers, who is currently receiving files from the data processing department and loading the information into his own database system. John told Leann that although he is only receiving invoice information for his own customers, he is sure that the data processing department could easily supply her with a similar file for all daily invoices. He has given her a copy of the files supplied to him for the last three days. He explained to her that the filename indicates the date for invoice information in the file—for example, the file IN112190.TXT contains invoice information for the date 11/21/90.

Leann has seen a printed copy of the contents of these files and has determined that she will have to perform some manipulation of the data to get the information she needs for her system. For example, the files contain a product code that has two letters for the ink color, followed by a four digit batch number. The files also have sales listed by invoice number. For her system, Leann is not concerned with the batch number, but wants only daily totals of each colored ink sold.

She thinks that once she has set up the structure for her file, the steps used to transfer the data from the daily text files should be routine. She would like to test a procedure using John's files before she makes her own request to the data processing department.

Items in each record of text files (.TXT):

Invoice Number, Customer Number, Product Code, Gallons Sold, Price Per Gallon, Total Dollar Amount

First two characters of product codes indicate ink colors as follows:

BK = Black
BL = Blue
GR = Green
RD = Red
VI = Violet
YL = Yellow

Contents of File: IN112190.TXT

```
"I28659", "16052", "BK8702",   4874,   15.11,   73646.14
"I28659", "16052", "BL6509",     15,   45.01,     675.15
"I28659", "16052", "YL1652",     25,   48.75,    1218.75
"I28660", "07892", "BL6509",     35,   44.95,    1573.25
"I28660", "07892", "GR1648",     10,   52.07     520.70
"I28660", "07892", "RD4586",     20,   45.55,     911.00
"I28661", "09846", "BK8703",    952,   15.12,   14394.24
"I28662", "12546", "BK8703",   4963,   15.11,   74990.93
"I28662", "12546", "BL6510",     45,   45.01,    2025.45
"I28662", "12546", "GR1648",     25,   52.07,    1301.75
"I28662", "12546", "RD4586",     20,   45.55,     911.00
"I28662", "12546", "VI0984",     15,   62.16,     932.40
"I28662", "12546", "YL1652",     20,   48.75,     975.00
"I28663", "05565", "BK8702",   2000,   15.12,   30240.00
```

Contents of File: IN112290.TXT

```
"I28664", "05629", "BK8702",    250,   16.01,    4002.50
"I28665", "10650", "BK8704",    978,   15.45,   15110.10
"I28665", "10650", "GR1648",     25,   52.03,    1300.75
"I28665", "10650", "VI0985",      5,   60.96,     304.80
"I28666", "28659", "RD4586",     35,   45.55,    1594.25
"I28667", "06350", "BK8704",   4826,   15.11,   72920.86
"I28668", "12016", "BK8705",    862,   15.12,   13033.44
"I28669", "07563", "BK8706",   3952,   15.11,   59714.72
"I28669", "07563", "BL6510",     75,   45.01,    3375.75
"I28669", "07563", "GR1648",     35,   52.07,    1822.45
"I28669", "07563", "RD4586",     45,   45.55,    2049.75
"I28669", "07563", "VI0985",     20,   61.12,    1222.40
"I28670", "09852", "BL6511",     30,   45.01,    1350.30
"I28670", "09852", "GR1648",     15,   51.93,     778.95
"I28670", "09852", "RD4586",     35,   45.45,    1590.75
"I28670", "09852", "YL1652",     10,   48.75,     487.50
"I28671", "12025", "BK8706",   4092,   15.12,   61871.04
```

Contents of File: IN112390.TXT

```
"I28972", "05654", "BK8706",    873,   15.12,   13199.76
"I28972", "05654", "GR1648",     65,   52.07,    3384.55
"I28973", "12685", "BL6511",     40,   45.01,    1800.40
"I28973", "12685", "RD4587",     25,   45.55,    1138.75
"I28974", "09846", "BK8707",   1265,   15.07,   19063.55
"I28975", "11618", "BK8707",   5650,   14.72,   83168.00
"I28975", "11618", "BL6511",     25,   44.98,    1124.50
"I28975", "11618", "GR1649",     40,   52.07,    2082.80
"I28975", "11618", "RD4587",     35,   45.55,    1594.25
"I28976", "12502", "GR1649",     25,   49.57,    1239.25
"I28976", "12502", "VI0985",     15,   62.16,     932.40
"I28976", "12502", "YL1652",     10,   48.75,     487.50
```

FILE HANDLING

HINT The following commands may be used for file maintenance operations when in dBASE's dot (.) prompt mode.

- To obtain a listing of all files on the default drive diskette, use the commands **DIR** *.* or **DISPLAY FILE LIKE** *.*.
- To erase a file on the diskette, use the commands **ERASE** <filename.ext> or **DELETE FILE** <filename.ext>.
- To rename a file, use the command **RENAME** <filename.ext> **TO** <new filename.ext>.
- To make a copy of a file, use the command **COPY FILE** [<*drive:*>]<filename.ext> **TO** [<*drive:*>]<filename.ext>.
- To display the contents of a file without opening it, use the command **TYPE** <filename.ext>.
- To produce a hard copy of the contents of a file without opening it, use the command **TYPE** <filename.ext> **TO PRINT.**

HAZARD Files that are currently open may not be erased, renamed, copied, or typed with the preceding commands.

HAZARD Do not name a database (.DBF) file with the single letter A through J. These letters are reserved as database alias names.

HAZARD dBASE III Plus allows up to 15 files (10 of which may be database files) to be open at once. However, DOS does not automatically allow that many files to be open. To use dBASE to its full capacity, the DOS disk used to load DOS must have a file named CONFIG.SYS in its root directory and the following DOS commands must be included in the file.

```
FILES = 20
BUFFERS = 24
```

The CONFIG.SYS file is an ASCII text file. You can create such a file with a word processor, dBASE's **MODIFY COMMAND** mode, or in the same manner as the .BAT file was created in the introductory Hints and Hazards.

HINT The following commands open/load and close/save the various dBASE file types.

.DBF *Database files.* The **USE** <filename> command opens a database file. To close the file, type **USE** with no <filename> specified.

.FMT *Format files.* Format files are command files with only @ **SAY,** @ **GET,** and **READ** commands in them. They may be created and saved in the **MODIFY COMMAND** mode, in which case they need to have their extensions specified in the **MODIFY COMMAND** command as <filename.FMT> (or be renamed later to have the .FMT extension). Format files may also be generated from screen files (.SCR) by the **MODIFY SCREEN** command. A format file is opened with the **SET FORMAT TO** <filename> command. Once opened, all commands that invoke full-screen editing of current database fields or memory variables will use the screen display format specified in the format file. Only one format file may be open at a time in a given work area. To close an open format file, use **SET FORMAT TO** with no <filename> specified.

.FRM *Form files.* The **REPORT FORM** command automatically opens and closes form files. Form files are created with the **MODIFY REPORT** command.

.LBL *Label files.* The **LABEL FORM** command automatically opens and closes label files. Label files are created with the **MODIFY LABEL** command.

.MEM *Memory variable files.* The **SAVE TO** <filename> creates memory variable files. They are loaded into RAM with the **RESTORE FROM** <filename> command. These commands open and close the file in a single operation. Memory variables may be erased from RAM with the **RELEASE** or **CLEAR MEMORY** commands.

.NDX *Index files.* The **INDEX ON** <expression> **TO** <filename> command creates index files and leaves them open. They also may be opened with the **USE** <filename> **INDEX** <index file list> and **SET INDEX TO** <index file list> commands. Open index files may be closed by executing either the **USE** command without the **INDEX** <index file list> clause or the **SET INDEX TO** command without the <index file list> parameter.

.PRG *Program or command files.* Command files are created and saved in the **MODIFY COMMAND** mode or with a word processing software. They are ASCII text files. A command file is loaded into RAM and executed with the **DO** <filename> command, and remains open until the program is completed. A command file may be automatically loaded and executed when dBASE is loaded by typing ||dBASE <filename>↵|| from the DOS prompt.

.TXT *Text files.* Text files are ASCII files and may be created several ways. The **COPY TO** <filename> **TYPE SDF** command creates a text file copy of the database in use. The **SET ALTERNATE TO** <filename> command creates a text file. Screen output (except editing mode output) will be written to the file after the **SET ALTERNATE ON** command is executed. **SET ALTERNATE OFF** suspends writing of screen output to the text file, but does not close the file. **SET ALTERNATE TO** with no <filename> specified closes the text file. The **LABEL FORM** and **REPORT FORM** commands will create ASCII text files (.TXT) when the [**TO FILE** <filename>] clause is included. The file is opened and closed by the command.

HINT The **CLOSE ALL** command closes/saves/erases all files currently open.

HAZARD Do not remove your files diskette from the disk drive before you type ||**QUIT**↵|| to save all data and close all files. Doing so may result in lost data and/or damaged files.

DATA PROCESSING

HINT The data held in fields and memory variables are literal values. You may not, for instance, **EDIT** a numeric field or variable as shown.

```
75+1200
```

Expressions may be used, however, to put the evaluation of such expressions into fields or variables using dBASE commands. For instance ||**STORE** account+75 **TO** macct|| or ||**REPLACE** account **WITH** account+75|| are examples of dBASE commands that use expressions to put a value into a memory variable or field.

HINT Memo fields do not hold record data, but instead hold an address used to access text data that is kept in a memo text file (.DBT) for each record having memo data. dBASE uses (opens) the .DBT file in conjunction with a database file when the database file has a record structure that includes memo fields. Memo data may be accessed for editing by placing the cursor on a memo field and typing Ctrl-PgDn when in the **EDIT** mode.

HAZARD When **MODIFY STRUCTURE** is used to remove any memo fields from a database file's structure, the memo file (.DBT) will be erased. If, however, a memo file (.DBT) is erased with another command without removing the memo field from the file structure, the database file (.DBF) may no longer be opened with the **USE** command. dBASE creates backup copies of .DBT files with a .TBK file extension. If such a file exists on your disk, use the **COPY FILE** command to recreate the .DBT file from the .TBK backup.

If no backup file exists, you may recover from this type of error as follows. Type ||**MODIFY COMMAND** <filename>.DBT↵|| specifying the database file's <filename> and a .DBT extension to recreate the memo file. Immediately type Ctrl-End to save the file, and then use the database file and **MODIFY STRUCTURE** to remove all memo fields. You will no longer have any memo data, but the rest of the database fields will be intact.

HAZARD Since the data in memo fields are not actually part of their associated record, they cannot be processed by dBASE commands. It is not possible, for instance, to search memo data for occurrences of strings; to sort or index records on memo field contents; or to perform batch replacement operations on memo data.

HINT Certain mathematical operations may be performed with date-type data. The following are some examples of "date arithmetic."

`. STORE CTOD("06/15/91") TO date1` `06/15/91`	Place the date-type data for June 15, 1991 into the variable "datel."
`. ? date1 + 90` `09/13/91`	Print datel + 90. September 13, 1991 occurs ninety days after June 15, 1991.
`. STORE CTOD("08/14/91") TO date2` `08/14/91`	Place the date-type data for August 14, 1991 into the variable "date2."
`. ? date2 - date1` `60`	Print date2 minus datel. There are 60 days between June 15, 1991 and August 14, 1991.

HINT String comparisons in expressions must be the same case as well as use the same characters in order for a condition to evaluate as .T. (true). The upper-case function, **UPPER**(<expC>), or the lower-case function, **LOWER**(<expC>), may be used to ensure that a field or variable's string data are compared in the same case. An example is shown below.

```
. LOCATE FOR UPPER(employee)="MARTINS MARY"
Record =       7
```

HAZARD Fields holding string data automatically are padded with spaces (CHR(32)s) which are evaluated as such in expressions. To remove trailing spaces, use the **TRIM** function. You also may remove leading spaces with the **LTRIM** function.

HAZARD Memory variables holding numeric data hold their data to several decimal places of accuracy (the number of decimal places varies between versions of dBASE) regardless of the number of places displayed on the screen. Fields hold numeric data to the number of places of accuracy specified when the record structure for the database was entered. Read through the following commands and their results.

```
. ? 10/3
  3.33

. STORE 10/3 TO test
  3.33

. ? test
        3.33

. ? 3.33 = test
.F.

. ? STR(test,19,15)
  3.333333333333334

. ? 3.333333333333334 = test
.T.

. REPLACE account WITH test
     1 record replaced

. ? account, STR(account,19,15)
    3.33   3.330000000000000
```

HINT You can control the number of decimal places of accuracy for numeric data held in memory variables by using the **ROUND** function.

```
. STORE ROUND(10/3,2) TO test
  3.33

. ? STR(test,19,15)
 3.330000000000000
```

HINT People with programming backgrounds often are initially confused by the dBASE commands used primarily in the dot (.) prompt mode (e.g., **DISPLAY, REPLACE, LOCATE,** and so on) and their parameters <scope>, <field list>, **FOR** <expression>, and **WHILE** <expression>. The commands are complete subroutines with all the fundamental processing operations (assignment, condition, iteration) which are called by the command when it is entered.

dBASE III PLUS FEATURES

HINT The ampersand character (&) may be used for special dBASE III Plus operations called *macro substitution*. When a character-type memory variable holds a character string that has meaning to dBASE, the name of the variable may be preceded by an & to cause dBASE to immediately substitute the contents of the variable in place of the &<memvar> in a command.

This is a very powerful feature of dBASE, but one that requires some practice to be used effectively. Following are some examples of how the macro substitution feature may be used.

- Store logical expressions as character strings to character-type memory variables so that they may then be used with dBASE commands.

```
. STORE "sex = 'F' .AND. salary >= 1650" TO cond1

. STORE "sex = 'M' .AND. salary >= 1800" TO cond2

. DISPLAY MEMORY
COND1       pub   C  "sex = 'F' .AND. salary >= 1650"
COND2       pub   C  "sex = 'M' .AND. salary >= 1800"
    2 variables defined,       64 bytes used
  254 variables available,   5936 bytes available

. DISPLAY FOR &cond1
Record#  EMPLOYEE                    TELEPHONE SEX EMPLOYED    SALARY  ACCOUNT
      2  Smoler Ellen                225-3212  F   09/15/83  1650.00   300.00
      4  Sill Sally                  224-4321  F   02/15/84  1657.70   150.00

. SET FILTER TO &cond2

. DISPLAY ALL
Record#  EMPLOYEE                    TELEPHONE SEX EMPLOYED    SALARY  ACCOUNT
      1  Pratt John                  225-1234  M   06/22/82  1949.00   200.00
      5  Knat Michael                221-1235  M   09/15/80  1800.00   125.00
      6  Smith Paul                  244-1010  M   11/15/81  2150.50  1050.00
```

- Many programming languages have the ability to define an array of variables. One variable name is used with a number defining the element of an array to use. Although dBASE III Plus does not include array capabilities, arrays can be simulated by using macro substitution to create lists of variables with similar names.

  The following command file demonstrates how an array may be simulated in dBASE III Plus.

```
* PROGRAM:  Fldarray.PRG  -  stores field employee to variables

USE empfile INDEX namedex
STORE 0 TO cntr

DO WHILE .NOT. EOF()
  STORE cntr + 1 TO cntr
  IF cntr < 10
    STORE "name" + STR(cntr,1) TO varname
  ELSE
    STORE "name" + STR(cntr,2) TO varname
  ENDIF
  STORE TRIM(employee) TO &varname
  SKIP
ENDDO

SAVE ALL LIKE name* TO names
RETURN
```

```
. DO fldarray

. RESTORE FROM names

. DISPLAY MEMORY
NAME1       pub   C  "Johnson Frank"
NAME2       pub   C  "Jones David"
NAME3       pub   C  "Knat Michael"
NAME4       pub   C  "Martins Mary"
NAME5       pub   C  "Nichols Sandy"
NAME6       pub   C  "Pratt John"
NAME7       pub   C  "Sill Sally"
NAME8       pub   C  "Smith Paul"
NAME9       pub   C  "Smoler Ellen"
    9 variables defined,      121 bytes used
  247 variables available,   5879 bytes available
```

HINT The bell that rings during data entry can be annoying. To turn off the bell from the dot (.) prompt mode, type ||**SET BELL OFF**↵||. To turn it back on, type ||**SET BELL ON**↵||.

HINT The error message "Do you want some help? (Y/N)" also can be annoying. To stop the display of this message, type ||**SET HELP OFF**↵|| and to turn it back on, type ||**SET HELP ON**↵||.

HINT The Function keys F1 through F10 are programmed by dBASE to hold the following strings:

F1	HELP;	F6	DISPLAY STATUS;
F2	ASSIST;	F7	DISPLAY MEMORY;
F3	LIST;	F8	DISPLAY;
F4	DIR;	F9	APPEND;
F5	DISPLAY STRUCTURE;	F10	EDIT;

Tapping one of these keys causes the command shown to be typed, displayed on the screen, and entered.

You may change the strings by using the **SET FUNCTION** <expN> **TO** <expC> command. For example, **SET FUNCTION** 2 **TO** "San Diego, CA" will store that city and state in the F2 key. If you want to include an Enter key character (CHR(13)) at the end of the string, add a semicolon at the end of the string "San Diego, CA;".

The Function key F1 is not programmable with the **SET FUNCTION** command.

LIMITS AND CONSTRAINTS

HINT The following are some limits and constraints to various dBASE III Plus data processing operations.

- Maximum filename length—8 characters
- Maximum field name length—10 characters
- Maximum memory variable name length—10 characters
- Maximum characters in a field, memory variable, command file line, report heading or <cstring>—254 characters

- Maximum fields to a record—128 fields
- Maximum characters to a record—4,000 characters
- Maximum current memory variables or @ **GET**s—256
- Maximum file size with **MODIFY COMMAND**—4,096 bytes

dBASE III PLUS OUTPUT

HINT To obtain a hard-copy listing of a command file, use the **TYPE** <filename.PRG> **TO PRINT** command.

HINT To obtain hard copy of screen output generated from the dot (.) prompt mode, use dBASE III Plus's output-generating commands (**DISPLAY, LIST, REPORT FORM, LABEL FORM, TYPE,** etc.) that include the [**TO PRINT**] parameter which causes an echo of screen output to the printer. For commands not having the [**TO PRINT**] parameter, follow the following steps.

1. Make sure your computer is connected and on-line to a printer that is turned on.
2. Either press and hold the Ctrl key and then type the P key, or type ||**SET PRINT ON**↵|| to toggle on the printer echo.
3. Enter the appropriate commands to generate the desired output.
4. Either press and hold the Ctrl key and then type the P key again, or type ||**SET PRINT OFF**↵|| to toggle off the printer echo.

HINT To obtain hard copy of one screen's worth of data while in an editing mode, press and hold a Shift key and then type the key marked PrtSc or Print Screen.

HAZARD If the computer's connection to the printer is not complete or the printer is not turned on, the preceding steps to obtain hard copy may result in the computer locking up until the connection is complete or the printer is turned on.

HINT When you use the **?** command to print field data on the screen, fields holding string data will be displayed with their padded spaces. To eliminate the spaces, use the **TRIM** function.

HINT When you use the **?** command to print memory variables holding numeric data, the data will be displayed with a default length of 11 characters and an accuracy of two decimal places. To control length and displayed accuracy, use the **STR** function. To control just the displayed accuracy, use the **SET DECIMALS TO** command.

HINT The ASCII text files (.TXT) produced by the **SET ALTERNATE** commands and the [**TO FILE** <filename>] clause of the **REPORT FORM** and **LABEL FORM** commands are accessible by word processing software. When text format is important and the text is a one-time product, it usually is more efficient to create a text file with the essential data in it and then use a word processing software to edit it into finished form.

STUDY QUESTIONS

1. Individual data items of a relational database are held in

   ________________.

2. Related data items of a relational database are held in

   ________________.

3. To create a database, the ________________ must be defined before any data are entered into the database.
4. Each field of the records in a database is prespecified with an unique ________________, a fixed ________________, and a certain data ________________.

5. If the length of the first field in the first record is known, is the length of the first field in the second record known? Why?

   ____

   ____

6. If the length of the data held in the first field of the first record is known, is the length of the data in the first field of the second record known? Why? ________________________________

   ____

7. Is it possible for one record in a database to have an extra field? Why?

   ____

8. dBASE III Plus has two editing modes. Direct access to data in fields or memory variables is done in the ________________ mode, and command files are created in the ________________ mode.
9. What event indicates that you are in a mode that allows direct access to data in fields or memory variables? ____________________
10. What will be the result of entering 75/100 into a numeric field of a record when you are in an editing mode? Why?

    ____

11. With a database in use, what will be the result of typing ||**DISPLAY**↵||? ________________________________
12. What are the four possible <scope>s and how do they affect the record pointer? ________________ ________________

    ________________ ________________

13. Where is the record pointer left after executing a command using the <scope> **ALL**? ____________________
14. What command parameter specifies the individual data items in each record for the command to act upon? ____________________
15. What is the default <scope> for any command using the **FOR** <expression> parameter? ____________________

Given the following database, list the record numbers of the records that will be acted on by the **DISPLAY** commands shown.

Record#	EMPLOYEE	TELEPHONE	SEX	EMPLOYED	SALARY	ACCOUNT
1	Pratt John	225-1234	M	06/22/82	1949.00	200.00
2	Smoler Ellen	225-3212	F	09/15/83	1650.00	300.00
3	Jones David	292-3832	M	06/15/82	1550.00	275.75
4	Sill Sally	224-4321	F	02/15/84	1507.50	150.00
5	Knat Michael	221-1235	M	09/15/80	1800.00	125.00
6	Smith Paul	244-1010	M	11/15/81	1700.00	350.00
7	Martins Mary	222-2123	F	11/01/85	1600.00	200.50
8	Nichols Sandy	229-1111	F	02/15/86	1450.00	175.00
9	Johnson Frank	223-7928	M	03/20/90	1500.00	0.00

16. **DISPLAY FOR** employed < **CTOD**("01/01/84") **.AND.** salary < 1600

____

17. **DISPLAY FOR DTOC**(employed) < "01/01/84" **.AND.** salary < 1600

____

18. **DISPLAY FOR** account < 200 **.AND.** account >= 300

____

19. **DISPLAY FOR** account >= 200 **.AND.** account <= 300

____

20. **DISPLAY FOR** salary < 1550 **.OR.** account > 300

____

21. **DISPLAY FOR SEX** = "F" **.AND.** salary < 1550 **.OR.** account > 300

____

22. **DISPLAY FOR SEX** = "F" **.AND.** (salary < 1550 **.OR.** account > 300)

____

23. **DISPLAY FOR 1=1**

____

24. Describe the differences between the **SORT ON** <field> **TO** <filename> command and the **INDEX ON** <expression> **TO** <filename> commands.

____

____

____

____

25. Describe the differences between the **LOCATE** command and the **SEEK** command.

____

____

____

____

Algorithm A step-by-step outline of the program's operation.

Alias An alternate name used for a database file when it is opened. It allows you to reference data from a database file that is open in an unselected work area.

Buffer A small portion of RAM that dBASE uses for temporary storage.

Catalog Files Files that maintain active lists of related files which dBASE treats as belonging to a particular group or set of files.

Child The controlled database when one database is related into another.

Close To remove the file from RAM.

Command Files Files that contain dBASE commands to be executed in sequence. Identical to program files.

Command Parameters Additions to a command that affect the way the command will be executed.

Command-Driven Software Software that responds to commands entered by the user.

Concatenation Combining two or more string data items.

Current Record The record to which the record pointer is currently pointing.

Cursor Control Keys Thc arrowed keys (up, down, left, and right) used to move the cursor.

Database Data organized in a manner that makes it possible to access specific information.

Database Files Files that hold the records and the record structure of a database.

Database Memo Files Files that hold the memo field information for databases that have a memo field.

Format Files Files that contain dBASE commands used to customize the full-screen editing presentation of fields and/or variables.

Index Files Files that point to records in a database that contain certain information, just as an index in a book points to specific pages.

Key A field in a database that is used to create an index file.

Label Form Files Files that contain user-defined specifications for producing mailing or identification labels from the data in a database.

Macro Substitution The substitution of a character-type memory variable using the & (macro) command.

Memory Variable Files Disk files in which variable names and their contents are saved.

Menu-Driven Software Software that provides menus of commands from which the user selects.

Open The condition of a file that allows changes to the contents of the file.

Parent The controlling database when one database is related into another.

Picture Clause A clause in a format file that prevents the user from entering undesired data.

Program Files Files that contain dBASE commands to be executed in sequence.

Pull-Down Menus Menus that are invoked by selecting options.

Query Files Files that contain user-defined conditions that cause dBASE to affect only certain records during processing of a database.

Record Pointer An unseen pointer that indicates which record is the current record to be processed.

Relational Database A database that contains data organized in records with fields holding related data items.

Report Form Files Files that contain user-defined specifications for producing columnar-type reports from the data in a database.

Screen Files Source files used by dBASE to produce .FMT (format) files.

Text Files Files in ASCII data format that may be processed by other software.

View Files Files that contain the set of working relationships that exist between a group of related files.

Work Area One of ten areas that may be used simultaneously for database processing in dBASE.

dBASE III PLUS OPERATION AND COMMAND SUMMARY

dBASE III PLUS QUICK REFERENCE COMMAND SUMMARY

dBASE III Plus Commands

?/?? [<exp1>[,<exp2>, . . .]]

@ <x1,y1> [**CLEAR**] [**TO** <x2,y2>] [**DOUBLE**]

@ <x,y> **GET** <field/memvar> [**PICTURE** <expC>] [**RANGE** <min>, <max>]

@ <x,y> **SAY** <exp> [**PICTURE** <expC>]

@ <x,y> **SAY** <exp> **GET** <field/memvar>

ACCEPT [<expC>] **TO** <memvarC>

APPEND

APPEND BLANK

APPEND FROM <filename> [**FOR** <condition>] [**TYPE** <file type>]

ASSIST

AVERAGE <expN list> [<scope>] [**FOR** <condition>] [**WHILE** <condition>] [**TO** <memvar list>]

BROWSE [**FIELDS** <field list>] [**LOCK** <expN>] [**FREEZE** <field>] [**NOFOLLOW**] [**NOMENU**] [**WIDTH** <expN>] [**NOAPPEND**]

CALL <module name> [**WITH** <expC> / <memvar>]

CANCEL

CHANGE [<scope>] [**FIELDS** <field list>] [**FOR** <condition>] [**WHILE** <condition>]

CLEAR

CLEAR ALL

CLEAR FIELDS

CLEAR GETS

CLEAR MEMORY

CLEAR TYPEAHEAD

CLOSE <file type> / **ALL**

CONTINUE

COPY FILE [<*drive:*>] <filename.ext> **TO** [<*drive:*>] <filename.ext>

COPY STRUCTURE TO <filename>

COPY TO <filename> [<scope>] [**FIELDS** <field list>] [**FOR** <condition>] [**WHILE** <condition>] [**TYPE** <file type>/**DELIMITED** [**WITH** <delimiter>]]

COPY TO <filename> **STRUCTURE EXTENDED**

COUNT [<scope>] [**FOR** <condition>] [**WHILE** <condition>] [**TO** <memvar>]

CREATE <filename>

CREATE <filename> **FROM** <structure extended file>

CREATE LABEL <filename>

CREATE QUERY <filename>

CREATE REPORT <filename>

CREATE VIEW FROM ENVIRONMENT

DELETE [<scope>] [**FOR** <condition>] [**WHILE** <condition>]

DELETE [**RECORD** <expN>]

DIR [<*drive:*>] [<skeleton>]

DISPLAY [<scope>] [<expression list>] [**FOR** <condition>] [**WHILE** <condition>] [**OFF**] [**TO PRINT**]

DISPLAY HISTORY [**LAST** <expN>] [**TO PRINT**]

DISPLAY MEMORY [**TO PRINT**]

DISPLAY STATUS [**TO PRINT**]

DISPLAY STRUCTURE [**TO PRINT**]

DO <filename> [**WITH** <expression list>]

DO CASE...ENDCASE

DO WHILE <condition>...**ENDDO**

EDIT [<scope>] [**FIELDS** <field list>] [**FOR** <condition>] [**WHILE** <condition>]

EJECT

ERASE <filename.extension>

EXIT

EXPORT <filename> **TYPE PFS**

FIND <literal string / &memvarC>

GO <expN> / **TOP** / **BOTTOM**

HELP [<key word>]

IF <condition>...[ELSE]...ENDIF

IMPORT FROM <filename> TYPE PFS

INDEX ON <expression> TO <index file> [UNIQUE]

INPUT [<expC>] TO <memvarN>

INSERT [BLANK] [BEFORE]

JOIN WITH <alias> TO <filename> FOR <condition> [FIELDS <field list>]

LABEL FORM <filename> [<scope>] [FOR <condition>] [WHILE <condition>] [TO PRINT / TO FILE <filename>] [SAMPLE]

LIST [<scope>] [<expression list>] [FOR <condition>] [WHILE <condition>] [TO PRINT] [OFF]

LIST HISTORY [TO PRINT]

LIST MEMORY [TO PRINT]

LIST STATUS [TO PRINT]

LIST STRUCTURE [TO PRINT]

LOAD <filename>[.<ext>]

LOCATE [<scope>] FOR <condition> [WHILE <condition>]

LOOP

MODIFY COMMAND <filename>

MODIFY LABEL <filename>

MODIFY QUERY <filename>

MODIFY REPORT <filename>

MODIFY SCREEN <filename>

MODIFY STRUCTURE

MODIFY VIEW <filename>

NOTE or *

ON ERROR / ESCAPE / KEY [<command>]

PACK

PARAMETERS <memvar list>

PRIVATE [<memvar list>] / ALL [LIKE / EXCEPT <skeleton>]

PROCEDURE <procedure name>

PUBLIC <memvar list>

QUIT

READ [SAVE]

RECALL [<scope>] [FOR <condition>] [WHILE <condition>]

REINDEX

RELEASE [<memvar list>] / ALL [LIKE / EXCEPT <skeleton>]

RELEASE MODULE

RENAME <filename.ext> TO <new filename.ext>

REPLACE [<scope>] <field1> WITH <exp1> [,<field2> WITH <exp2>, . . .] [FOR <condition>] [WHILE <condition>]

REPORT FORM [<filename>] [<scope>] [FOR <condition>] [WHILE <condition>] [PLAIN] [HEADING <expC>] [NOEJECT] [TO PRINT / TO FILE <filename>] [SUMMARY]

RESTORE FROM <filename> [ADDITIVE]

RESUME

RETRY

RETURN [TO MASTER]

RUN <command>

SAVE TO <filename> [ALL LIKE / EXCEPT <skeleton>]

SEEK <expression>

SELECT <work area / alias>

SET ALTERNATE on / OFF

SET ALTERNATE TO <filename>

SET BELL ON / off

SET CARRY on / OFF

SET CATALOG ON / off

SET CATALOG TO [<filename>]

SET CENTURY on / OFF

SET COLOR ON / off

SET COLOR TO [[<standard>] [,<enhanced>] [,<border>] [,<background>]]

SET CONFIRM on / OFF

SET CONSOLE ON / off

SET DATE [AMERICAN / ANSI / BRITISH / ITALIAN / FRENCH / GERMAN]

SET DEBUG on / OFF

SET DECIMALS TO <expN>

SET DEFAULT TO *<drive:>*

SET DELETED on / OFF

SET DELIMITER on / OFF

SET DELIMITER TO <expC> / **DEFAULT**

SET DEVICE TO PRINT / SCREEN

SET DOHISTORY on / OFF

SET ECHO on / OFF

SET ESCAPE ON / off

SET EXACT on / OFF

SET FIELDS on / OFF

SET FIELDS TO [<field list > / **ALL**]

SET FILTER TO [<condition>] [**FILE** <filename>]

SET FIXED on / OFF

SET FORMAT TO [<format file>]

SET FUNCTION <expN> **TO** <expC>

SET HEADING ON / off

SET HELP ON / off

SET HISTORY ON / off

SET HISTORY TO <expN>

SET INDEX TO [<index file list>]

SET INTENSITY ON / off

SET MARGIN TO <expN>

SET MEMOWIDTH TO <expN>

SET MENUS ON / off

SET MESSAGE TO [<expC>]

SET ORDER TO [<expN>]

SET PATH TO <path list>

SET PROCEDURE TO [<filename>]

SET PRINT on / OFF

SET RELATION TO [<key exp>/<expN> **INTO** <alias>]

SET SAFETY ON / off

SET STATUS ON / off

SET STEP on / OFF

SET TALK ON / off

SET TITLE ON / off

SET TYPEAHEAD TO <expN>

SET UNIQUE on / OFF

SET VIEW TO <filename>

SKIP [–] [<expN>]

SORT [<scope>] **ON** <field1> [**/A**] [**/C**] [**/D**] [,<field2> [**/A**] [**/C**] [**/D**]...] **TO** <new file> [**FOR** <condition>] [**WHILE** <condition>]

STORE <expression> **TO** <memvar list>

SUM <expN list> [**TO** <memvar list>] [<scope>] [**FOR** <condition>] [**WHILE** <condition>]

SUSPEND

TEXT...**ENDTEXT**

TOTAL ON <key field> **TO** <new file> [**FIELDS** <fieldN list>] [<scope>] [**FOR** <condition>] [**WHILE** <condition>]

TYPE <filename.ext> [**TO PRINT**]

UPDATE ON <key field> **FROM** <alias> **REPLACE** <field1> **WITH** <exp1> [,<field2> **WITH** <exp2>, ...] [**RANDOM**]

USE [<filename>] [**ALIAS** <name>] [**INDEX** <index file list>]

WAIT [expC] [**TO** <memvar>]

ZAP

dBASE III Plus Functions

ABS(<expN>) Absolute Value Function

ASC(<expC>) ASCII Code Function

AT(<expC1>,<expC2>) Substring Search Function

BOF( ) Beginning-of-File Function

CDOW(<expD>) Character Day of Week Function

CHR(<expN>) Character String Function

CMONTH(<expD>) Character Month Function

COL( ) Column Function

CTOD(<expC>) Character-to-Date Function

DATE( ) Date Function

DAY(<expD>) Day Function

DBF( ) Database Function

DELETED( ) Deleted Record Function

DISKSPACE( ) Disk Space Function

DOW(<expD>) Day-of-Week Function

DTOC(<expD>) Date-to-Character Function

EOF( ) End-of-File Function

ERROR( ) Error Number Function

EXP(<expN>) Exponential Function

FIELD(<expN>) Field Name Function

FILE(<expC>) File Existence Function

FKLABEL(<expN>) Function Key Label Function

FKMAX( ) Function Key Maximum Function

FOUND( ) Found Function

GETNV(<expC>) Get Environmental Variable Function

IIF(<expL>,<exptrue>,<expfalse>) Immediate IF Function

INKEY( ) Inkey Function

INT(<expN>) Integer Function

ISALPHA(<expC>) Is Alphabetic Function

ISCOLOR( ) Is Color Mode Function

ISLOWER(<expC>) Is Lowercase Function

ISUPPER(<expC>) Is Uppercase Function

LEFT(<expC>,<lenN>) Left Substring Function

LEN(<expC>) Length Function

LOG(<expN>) Logarithm Function

LOWER(<expC>) Lowercase Function

LTRIM(<expC>) Left Trim Function

LUPDATE( ) Last Update Function

MAX(<expN1>,<expN2>) Maximum Function

MESSAGE( ) Error Message Function

MIN(<expN1>,<expN2>) Minimum Function

MOD(<expN1>,<expN2>) Modulus Function

MONTH(<expD>) Month Function

NDX(<expN>) Index File Function

OS( ) Operating System Function

PCOL( ) Printer Column Function

PROW( ) Printer Row Function

READKEY( ) Read Key Function

RECCOUNT( ) Record Count Function

RECNO( ) Record Number Function

RECSIZE( ) Record Size Function

REPLICATE(<expC>,<expN>) Replicate Function

RIGHT(<expC>,<expN>) Right Substring Function

ROUND(<expN>,<decN>) Round Function

ROW( ) Row Function

RTRIM(<expC>) Right Trim Function

SPACE(<expN>) Space Function

SQRT(<expN>) Square Root Function

STR(<expN>[,<lenN>] [,<decN>]) Numeric-to-String Function

STUFF(<expC1>,<startN>,<lenN>, <expC2>) Substring Replace Function

SUBSTR(<expC>,<startN>,<lenN>) Substring Function

TIME( ) Time Function

TRANSFORM(<exp>,<pictureC>) Transform Function

TRIM(<expC>) Trim Function

TYPE(<expC>) Data-Type Function

UPPER(<expC>) Uppercase Function

VAL(<expC>) Character-to-Value Function

VERSION( ) Version Function

YEAR(<expD>) Year Function

IMPORTANT dBASE III PLUS KEYS

Control Keys (Dot (.) Prompt Mode)

Esc key	Erases the current command line or aborts a current operation.
^P	Toggles the printer on and off.
^Num Lock	Pauses operations; any key continues.
← (Backspace key)	Backspaces and deletes characters on the current line.

Editing Keystroke Commands

APPEND, CHANGE, and **EDIT** Modes

Cursor right key	Moves cursor right one character.
Cursor left key	Moves cursor left one character.
Cursor down key	Moves cursor to the next field.
Cursor up key	Moves cursor to the previous field.
PgDn key	Saves current record and advances to next record.
PgUp key	Saves current record and backs to previous record.
Ins key	Toggles between OVERWRITE and INSERT modes.
Del key	Deletes character over cursor.
← (Backspace key)	Deletes character left of cursor.
^T	Erases word to right of cursor.
^Y	Erases field to right of cursor.
^PgDn	Enter the dBASE word processor to edit a memo field.
^PgUp	Exit editing a memo field.
^U	Toggles the record *DEL* mark on and off.
^End	Saves changes and returns to dot (.) prompt.
Esc	Aborts editing of current record and returns to dot (.) prompt.

BROWSE Mode

Cursor right key	Moves cursor right one character.
Cursor left key	Moves cursor left one character.
Home key	Moves cursor to the previous field.
End key	Moves cursor to the next field.
Cursor down key	Saves current record and advances to next record.
Cursor up key	Saves current record and backs to previous record.
PgUp key	Scrolls the screen up 17 lines.
PgDn key	Scrolls the screen down 17 lines.
^Cursor right key	Pans the screen right one field.
^Cursor left key	Pans the screen left one field.
Ins key	Toggles between OVERWRITE and INSERT modes.
Del key	Deletes character over cursor.
← (Backspace key)	Deletes character left of cursor.
^T	Erases word to right of cursor.
^Y	Erases field to right of cursor.
^U	Toggles the record *DEL* mark on and off.
^End	Saves changes and returns to dot (.) prompt.
Esc	Aborts editing of current record and returns to dot (.) prompt.

MODIFY LABEL and **MODIFY REPORT** Modes

Cursor right key	Moves cursor right one character.
Cursor left key	Moves cursor left one character.
Cursor down key	Moves cursor to the next line.
Cursor up key	Moves cursor to the previous line.
PgDn key	Saves current screen and advances to next screen.
PgUp key	Saves current screen and backs to previous screen.
Ins key	Toggles between OVERWRITE and INSERT modes.

Del key	Deletes character over cursor.
← (Backspace key)	Deletes character to left of cursor.
^T	Erases word to right of cursor.
^Y	Erases field or line to right of cursor.
^U	Deletes current column or line specification.
^N	Inserts new column or line for specification.
^End	Saves changes and returns to dot (.) prompt.
Esc	Aborts all changes made and returns to dot (.) prompt.

MODIFY COMMAND and **MEMO** Field— dBASE Word Processor

Cursor right key	Moves cursor right one character.
Cursor left key	Moves cursor left one character.
Home key	Moves cursor one word to the left.
End key	Moves cursor one word to the right.
Cursor down key	Moves cursor to the next line.
Cursor up key	Moves cursor to the previous line.
PgUp key	Scrolls the screen up 17 lines.
PgDn key	Scrolls the screen down 17 lines.
Ins key	Toggles between OVERWRITE and INSERT modes.
Enter key ↵	Terminates current line. In the INSERT mode, inserts a line below the current line.
Del key	Deletes character over cursor.
← (Backspace key)	Deletes character to left of cursor.
^T	Erases word to right of cursor.
^Y	Erases current line.
^KR	Reads and inserts another file into the current file.
^End	Saves changes and returns to dot (.) prompt.
Esc	Aborts all changes made and returns to dot (.) prompt.

CONVENTIONS AND TERMINOLOGY

Conventions

BOLD UPPER CASE =	dBASE III Plus command words.
<lower case entry> =	User-supplied information.
[OPTIONAL] =	Optional command words or user-supplied information.
... =	Additional commands or parameters may be included.
/ =	Choice of mutually-exclusive command parameters.

Example

dBASE command words   Optional

DISPLAY [<scope>] [<expression list>] [**FOR** <condition>] [**WHILE** <condition>] [**OFF**] [**TO PRINT**]

User-supplied information

Either form may be used

? / **??** [<exp1>[,<exp2>,...]]

Additional parameters may be included

Terminology

<memvar>	A memory variable of any type (numeric, character, date, or logical).
<field>	The name of a field in an open database file.
<literal>	A literal expression of numeric-, character-, date-, or logical-type data. Also referred to as a constant. Logical-type data is rarely entered as a literal. Numeric-type literals are entered without quote marks (") and may consist of only numerals 0 through 9, a preceding plus (+) or minus (−) sign, and one decimal point. **Examples:** 12648.45 −56 12.7525 Character-type literals are enclosed in quote marks ("), which are referred to as delimiters. **Example:** "This is a literal string" dBASE also recognizes apostrophes (') and bracket pairs ([ ]) as literal string delimiters. This allows a character that is normally used as a delimiter to occur within the literal string. **Example:** [Enter employee's "status" code:] Date-type literals must be entered using the **CTOD** function, which converts a date character string to date-type data. The function name means character-to-date. **Example:** **CTOD**("12/25/91")
<exp> or <expression>	A valid dBASE expression of any type (numeric, character, date, or logical). Expressions may include memory variables, field names, literals, and dBASE functions.
<memvarN>, <fieldN>, or <expN>	A numeric-type memory variable, field, or expression.
<memvarC>, <fieldC>, or <expC>	A character-type memory variable, field, or expression.
<memvarD>, <fieldD>, or <expD>	A date-type memory variable, field, or expression.
<memvarL>, <fieldL>, or <expL>	A logical-type memory variable, field, or expression.
<condition>	A condition is a logical expression <expL>. A logical expression is evaluated as either true (.T.) or false (.F.). Operators in conditions may include: **Relational:** < (less than) > (greater than) = (equal to) <= (less than or equal to) >= (greater than or equal to) < > (not equal to) **Logical:** .NOT. .AND. .OR.

<memvar list>, <field list>, or <exp list>
A list of memory variables, field names, or expressions. The items in the list are delimited with commas (separated by commas).

<filename>
Name of file you wish to create or access.

<key>
An expression that is used to create index files. The expression defines the elements of a record that are used to determine the record's position in the index file.

<scope>
Specifies a range of records to be included in a command operation. <scope> has four possible values:

ALL	All records in file.
NEXT <expN>	Next group of <expN> records in file, beginning with current record.
RECORD <expN>	One record with the record number <expN>.
REST	Records in file from current record to the end of the file.

Default
Default is a term used to define an option that is taken by dBASE when not specified by the user. For example, each command that includes a <scope> parameter has a default <scope>. The default <scope> is **ALL** for some commands, while it is the current record for other commands.

[**FOR** <condition>]
Used to specify a <condition> which must be met in order for a record to be included in a command operation. When [**FOR** <condition>] is included in a command, the default <scope> automatically becomes **ALL** records in the file, and any other <scope> must be used explicitly.

[**WHILE** <condition>]
The next group of records, beginning with the current record, will be included in a command operation as long as the <condition> is evaluated as true. As soon as a record is encountered that is evaluated as false (including the current record), command operation is halted. [**WHILE** <condition>] is normally used only when a file is indexed or sorted so that all records that meet the <condition> are grouped together.

dBASE III PLUS COMMANDS

? / **??** [<exp1>[,<exp2>, ...]]

Displays the evaluation of expressions. The **?** command issues a carriage return/line feed sequence before printing the expression(s) and can be used without an expression to space down a line. The **??** command prints the expression(s) on the current line of the screen and/or printer. The expressions may be of any type and may include field names, memory variables, and literals.

. ? employee Pratt John	field
. ? limit 500	variable
. ? "Credit Available" Credit Available	literal
. ? limit-account,limit>account 300 .T.	expressions
. ? "Credit Available -",employee,limit-account Credit Available - Pratt John 300	combination

@ <x1,y1> [**CLEAR**] [**TO** <x2,y2>] [**DOUBLE**]

The @ command may be used to erase a certain portion of the screen and to draw rectangles with either single or double lines. The x and y values used with the command define a screen coordinate by row (x = 0 to 24) and column (y = 0 to 79). The command may take the following forms.

@ <x1,y1>	Clears the right side of one line on the screen starting at the coordinate specified. For example, @ 5,15 will clear line 5 only, from column 15 to the end of the line.
@ <x1,y1> **CLEAR**	Clears the bottom right portion of the screen from the coordinate specified. For example, @ 5,15 **CLEAR** will clear from row 5 downward and from column 15 to the right.
@ <x1,y1> **CLEAR TO** <x2,y2>	Clears a rectangular portion of the screen from the upper left coordinate <x1,y1> to the lower right coordinate <x2,y2>.
@ <x1,y1> **TO** <x2,y2>	Draws a rectangular box on the screen with a single line. The upper left corner of the box is defined as <x1,y1> and the lower right corner of the box is defined as <x2,y2>.
@ <x1,y1> **TO** <x2,y2> **DOUBLE**	Draws a rectangular box on the screen with a double line. The upper left corner of the box is defined as <x1,y1> and the lower right corner of the box is defined as <x2,y2>.

@ <x,y> **GET** <field/memvar> [**PICTURE** <expC>] [**RANGE** <min>,<max>]

Normally used only in command files, the @ **GET** (at get) command is used with the **READ** command to allow direct access to a field or memory variable for editing. The x and y are numeric expressions designating the screen row (x = 0 to 24) and column (y = 0 to 79) coordinates where data are to be displayed.

When the **READ** command is executed, the cursor jumps to the first field or variable placed on the screen by an @ GET command. The user then may edit the data there with all the keystroke commands of an editing mode. When finished, the edited data replace any previous data that may have been in the field or variable. (See **READ,** page D-176.)

The optional [**PICTURE** <expC>] clause may be used to control the type of data to be entered into the field or memory variable. The character expression defines a template used for data entry control. For example, the clause **PICTURE** "99,999.99" may be used for a numeric entry to include a comma thousands separator and a decimal point. It also may be used to limit data entered to numerals and plus (+) or minus (−) signs. See the dBASE help screens for a list of template characters.

The optional [**RANGE** <min>,<max>] clause may be included to control the upper and lower bounds of a numeric entry. For example, **RANGE** 60,150 will cause an error message to be displayed if an attempt is made to enter a numeric value less than 60 or greater than 150. However, if the value already held in the field or memory variable is outside of the **RANGE** specified, the Enter key may be used to leave the value unedited, and range checking will not occur.

@ <x,y> **SAY** <exp> [**PICTURE** <expC>]

Normally used only in command files, the @ **SAY** (at say) command is used to display an expression on the screen or printer at specified coordinates. When data is displayed on the screen, the x and y numeric expressions designate the screen row (x = 0 to 24) and column (y = 0 to 79) coordinates where data are to be displayed.

When data is sent to the printer, the x and y coordinates designate the printer page row and column (horizontal position) where the data is to be printed. The maximum x and y values used when printing data with an @ **SAY** will depend on the number of lines per page and characters per inch (CPI) horizontally for which the printer is set.

The [**PICTURE** <expC>] clause is used to control the way data is displayed or printed. The character expression defines a template used to format the data. For example, the clause **PICTURE** "***,***.**" will cause the value to be displayed or printed with a comma thousands separator and a decimal point, and with asterisks preceding the number if necessary (i.e., the value 2850.6 would appear as **2,850.60 when displayed or printed). See the dBASE help screens for a list of template characters.

@ <x,y> **SAY** <exp> **GET** <field/memvar>

For data entry screens, the @ **SAY** and @ **GET** commands are often combined into a single command. In this case, one set of coordinates is used to specify where the @ **SAY** expression is to be displayed, and the field or memory variable to be edited with the @ **GET** will appear immediately following the @ **SAY** expression.

The following is a portion of a command file that contains @ **SAY** and @ **GET** commands used separately and in the combined form.

```
CLEAR
STORE 0 TO amt
STORE SPACE(15) TO name

@  3,25 SAY "* * * EMPLOYEE PURCHASES * * *"
@  5, 5 SAY "Employee Name: "
@  5,25 GET name
READ

LOCATE FOR employee = TRIM(name)
IF .NOT. EOF()
  @  5,45 SAY "Record found for: " + employee
  @  9, 5 SAY "Account Balance:"
  @  9,25 SAY account PICTURE "999.99"

  @  9,45 SAY "Purchase Amount:    " GET amt PICTURE "999.99" RANGE 0,500-account
  READ

  @ 11,45 SAY "New Balance:"
  @ 11,65 SAY account+amt PICTURE "999.99"
ELSE
  @  9, 5 SAY "Record not found"
ENDIF
```

When the commands shown are executed, the screen will appear with data displayed at the appropriate screen coordinates, as follows.

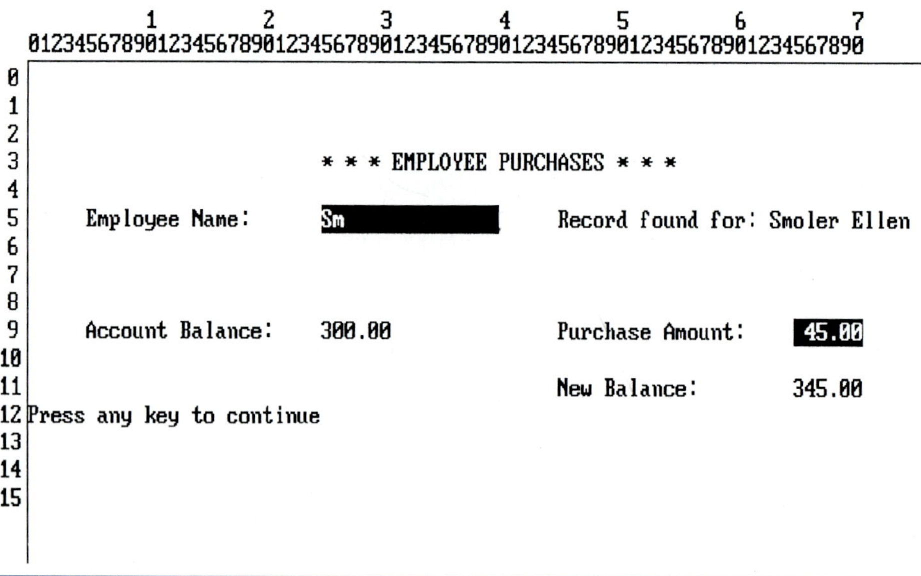

ACCEPT [<expC>] **TO** <memvarC>

Normally used in command files, this command is designed to prompt for a keyboard entry and then place the entry into a character-type memory variable. The optional [<expC>] immediately following **ACCEPT** is a character string used as a prompt to indicate the information to be entered.

```
. ACCEPT "Enter employee's name: " TO name
Enter employee's name: Martin

. ? name
Martin

. LOCATE FOR employee = name
Record =        5
```

APPEND

Appends a blank record to the database file in use and enters the record addition **(APPEND)** editing mode.

APPEND BLANK

Appends a blank record to the bottom of the database file in use.

APPEND FROM <filename> [FOR <condition>] [TYPE <file type>]

Appends records to the database file in use, either from another database file (.DBF) or from certain other types of files. If the **FROM** file is a .DBF file, any records marked for deletion in the **FROM** file will be appended and become unmarked in the file appended to. Also, if the **FROM** file is a .DBF file, only data in fields with identical field names will be appended to the file in use.

```
. CREATE deptmail
```

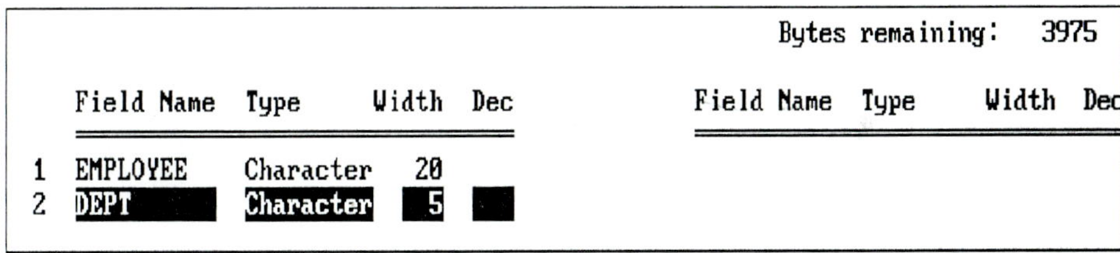

```
Bytes remaining:   3975

   Field Name  Type       Width  Dec        Field Name  Type       Width  Dec

1  EMPLOYEE    Character   20
2  DEPT        Character    5
```

```
. APPEND FROM empfile
     9 records added

. EDIT 1
```

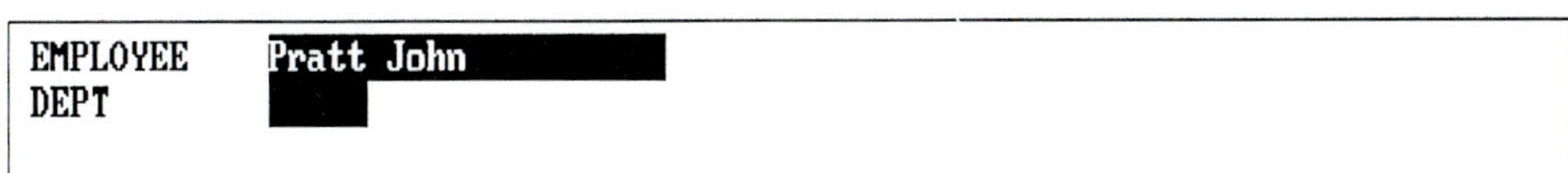

```
EMPLOYEE    Pratt John
DEPT
```

The [**FOR** <condition>] option may be used to append only records meeting a given condition. Field names used in the condition must be found in the file being appended to.

The [**TYPE** <file type>] option may be used with the following <file type> parameters to append records from other types of files.

SDF	System Data Format (ASCII files).
DIF	A VisiCalc file format.
SYLK	Multiplan spreadsheet format.
WKS	Lotus 1-2-3 spreadsheet format.

ASSIST

Provides a menu-driven mode for execution of dBASE III Plus operations.

AVERAGE <expN list> [<scope>] [**FOR** <condition>] [**WHILE** <condition>] [**TO** <memvar list>]

Computes the averages of the numeric expressions in its <expN list> for records in the database file in use and displays the results. A numeric expression is usually the name of a field. If the [**TO** <memvar list>] option is used, resulting averages are stored to memory variables specified (the two lists must have the same number of entries). The parameters [<scope>], [**FOR** <condition>], and [**WHILE** <condition>] may be used to limit the number of records included in the average calculation. Default <scope> is **ALL** records.

```
. AVERAGE salary,account FOR sex = "F" TO fsal,facct
      4 records averaged
  salary  account
 1551.75   206.38

. DISPLAY MEMORY
FSAL         pub   N        1551.75  (       1551.75000000)
FACCT        pub   N         206.38  (        206.37500000)
    2 variables defined,       18 bytes used
  254 variables available,   5982 bytes available
```

BROWSE [FIELDS <field list>] [**LOCK** <expN>] [**FREEZE** <field>] [**NOFOLLOW**] [**NOMENU**] [**WIDTH** <expN>] [**NOAPPEND**]

Enters the **BROWSE** editing mode. The optional parameter [**FIELDS** <field list>] causes dBASE to display only the fields listed for editing. The fields in the <field list> must be separated by commas. The other optional parameters that may be included when the **BROWSE** command is executed are as follows.

[**LOCK** <expN>]	Prevents the scrolling of the left-most fields when Ctrl-Left or Ctrl-Right is used to pan the screen (scroll horizontally). The <expN> defines how many fields should be prevented from scrolling.
[**FREEZE** <field>]	Allows editing of only the field specified. All other fields are displayed normally.
[**NOFOLLOW**]	Prevents the record pointer from moving with an indexed record when a field that is part of the index key is edited.
[**NOMENU**]	Prevents access to a menu bar that may otherwise be toggled on and off with the F10 key.
[**WIDTH** <expN>]	Limits the display of all character fields to the number of characters defined by <expN>. For fields longer than the width set, the cursor will scroll vertically within the field.
[**NOAPPEND**]	Prevents appending of records in the **BROWSE** mode.

The **LOCK** and **FREEZE** options also may be accessed after entering the **BROWSE** mode by typing F10 to toggle a menu bar on and off. Other options on the menu bar are to move the cursor to the top or bottom of the file or to a specific record number.

CALL <module name> [**WITH** <expC> / <memvar>]

Executes a binary file already loaded into RAM with the **LOAD** command. (See **LOAD,** page D-166.)

CANCEL

Used in a command file, stops command execution and returns to the dBASE dot (.) prompt mode. If execution of a command file was suspended after an error was detected by dBASE or with the **SUSPEND** command, the **CANCEL** command may be used from the dot (.) prompt to cancel the suspended program.

CHANGE [<scope>] [**FIELDS** <field list>] [**FOR** <condition>] [**WHILE** <condition>]

The **CHANGE** command is identical to the **EDIT** command (see **EDIT,** page D-163).

CLEAR

Clears the screen and releases any @ **GET**s that may have been active.

CLEAR ALL

Closes all database files in use and any associated files (.NDX, .DBT, .FMT, .CAT), releases all memory variables, and selects work area 1. (See **USE,** page D-191; **RELEASE,** page D-176; and **SELECT,** page D-180.)

CLEAR FIELDS

Clears any field list previously set with the **SET FIELDS TO** command in all work areas. (See **SET FIELDS TO,** page D-185.)

CLEAR GETS

Releases all active @ **GET** commands without erasing the screen.

CLEAR MEMORY

Releases all memory variables. (See also **RELEASE,** page D-176.)

CLEAR TYPEAHEAD

Used in command files, clears any characters that may be in the typeahead buffer.

CLOSE <file type> / **ALL**

Closes all files of the type specified by <file type> or **ALL** open files. The <file type> may be ALTERNATE, DATABASES, FORMAT, INDEX, or PROCEDURE.

CONTINUE

Resumes a search previously initiated with a **LOCATE** command in the currently selected work area. (See **LOCATE,** page D-166.)

COPY TO <filename> [<scope>] [**FIELDS** <field list>] [**FOR** <condition>] [**WHILE** <condition>] [**TYPE** <file type>/ **DELIMITED** [**WITH** <delimiter>]]

Copies the database in use to another .DBF file which it creates at the time the command is executed. The parameters [<scope>], [**FOR** <condition>], and [**WHILE** <condition>] may be used to limit the number of records copied. The [**FIELDS** <field list>] parameter may be used to create the new database with only specified fields included.

The [**TYPE** <file type>] parameter may be used to create and copy records to another type of file (see the **APPEND FROM** command, page D-153, for a list of <file type> parameters). The [**DELIMITED**] parameter may be used to create and copy records to an ASCII file (extension .TXT) with each record on a separate line, fields separated by commas, and character fields enclosed in double quotes ("). The double quote may be substituted with another character by using the parameter [**DELIMITED WITH** <delimiter>].

```
. COPY TO emplistm FIELDS employee,salary FOR sex = "M" DELIMITED
     5 records copied

. TYPE emplistm.txt
"Pratt John",1949.00
"Johnson Frank",1500.00
"Jones David",1550.00
"Knat Michael",1800.00
"Smith Paul",1700.00


. COPY TO emplistf FIELDS employee,salary FOR sex = "F" DELIMITED WITH '
     4 records copied

. TYPE emplistf.txt
'Martins Mary',1600.00
'Nichols Sandy',1450.00
'Sill Sally',1507.50
'Smoler Ellen',1650.00
```

COPY TO <filename> STRUCTURE EXTENDED

Converts the structure of the database file into records and copies them to the <filename> specified. The file created has four fields: FIELD_NAME, FIELD_TYPE, FIELD_LEN, and FIELD_DEC.

```
. DISPLAY STRUCTURE
Structure for database: A:EMPFILE.dbf
Number of data records:       9
Date of last update   : 07/26/90
Field  Field Name  Type        Width    Dec
    1  EMPLOYEE    Character      20
    2  TELEPHONE   Character       8
    3  SEX         Character       1
    4  EMPLOYED    Date            8
    5  SALARY      Numeric         8      2
    6  ACCOUNT     Numeric         8      2
** Total **                       54

. COPY TO stfile1 STRUCTURE EXTENDED

. USE stfile1

. LIST
Record#  FIELD_NAME FIELD_TYPE FIELD_LEN FIELD_DEC
      1  EMPLOYEE   C                 20         0
      2  TELEPHONE  C                  8         0
      3  SEX        C                  1         0
      4  EMPLOYED   D                  8         0
      5  SALARY     N                  8         2
      6  ACCOUNT    N                  8         2
```

The file created may be edited and used like any database file and the **CREATE FROM** command may later be used to create a new database file with the structure taken from the records in this file. If this is intended, care must be taken to enter valid field names, types, lengths, and decimals when editing the records of the extended file. (See **CREATE FROM,** page D-158.)

COPY FILE [<*drive:*>] <filename.ext> **TO** [<*drive:*>] <filename.ext>

Makes a copy of any type of file. The first <filename.ext> specified is copied **TO** the second <filename.ext> specified. Data is copied in blocks of 512 bytes and the size of the two files may not match exactly.

COPY STRUCTURE TO <filename>

Creates a .DBF file with the specified <filename> with a record structure that is the same as the current database. No records are copied to the new file.

COUNT [<scope>] [**FOR** <condition>] [**WHILE** <condition>] [**TO** <memvar>]

Counts the number of records in the database in use. The parameters [<scope>], [**FOR** <condition>], and [**WHILE** <condition>] may be used to limit the number of records counted. Default <scope> is **ALL** records. The [**TO** <memvar>] parameter may be used to store the results to a memory variable.

CREATE <filename>

Used to create a new database file (.DBF extension). The record structure is entered in a dBASE editing mode.

CREATE <filename> **FROM** <structure extended file>

Creates a new database file (.DBF) with a structure taken from the records of another database file that has the four fields: FIELD_NAME, FIELD_TYPE, FIELD_LEN, and FIELD_DEC. (See **COPY TO STRUCTURE EXTENDED,** page D-156.)

```
. USE stfile2

. LIST
Record#  FIELD_NAME FIELD_TYPE FIELD_LEN FIELD_DEC
      1  EMPLOYEE   C                 20         0
      2  SALARY     N                  8         2
      3  ACCOUNT    N                  8         2

. CREATE empfile2 FROM stfile2

. USE empfile2

. DISPLAY STRUCTURE
Structure for database: C:empfile2.dbf
Number of data records:       0
Date of last update   : 07/26/90
Field  Field Name  Type       Width    Dec
    1  EMPLOYEE    Character     20
    2  SALARY      Numeric        8      2
    3  ACCOUNT     Numeric        8      2
** Total **                      37
```

CREATE LABEL <filename>

Identical to **MODIFY LABEL.** (See **MODIFY LABEL,** page D-167.)

CREATE QUERY <filename>

Identical to **MODIFY QUERY.** (See **MODIFY QUERY,** page D-168.)

CREATE REPORT <filename>

Identical to **MODIFY REPORT.** (See **MODIFY REPORT,** page D-169.)

CREATE VIEW FROM ENVIRONMENT

Creates a view file (.VUE) from the files currently open. (See **MODIFY VIEW,** page D-174.)

DELETE [<scope>] [**FOR** <condition>] [**WHILE** <condition>]
and
DELETE [**RECORD** <expN>]

Marks record(s) for deletion. Records marked for deletion will not be physically removed from the database until the **PACK** command is executed. The parameters [<scope>], [**FOR** <condition>], and [**WHILE** <condition>] may be used to mark a group of records for deletion. Default scope is the current record. The parameter [**RECORD** <expN>] may be used to mark a specific record for deletion by its record number. Records also may be marked/unmarked with ^U while in edit modes. (See **RECALL,** page D-176, and **PACK,** page D-175.)

DIR [<*drive:*>] [<skeleton>]

Lists a directory of files. **DIR** with no parameters displays the names of all .DBF files on the default drive. The <*drive:*> parameter may be used to specify another disk drive. The <skeleton> parameter is used to display other types of files.

A <skeleton> is made up of filename characters and masking characters that act as "wild cards." The asterisk (*) indicates "Accept any other characters" while the question mark (?) means "Accept any single character in this position." The command **DIR** *.* will list all files on the disk.

```
.DIR *.FRM
FULLREPO.FRM        SALARIES.FRM        ACCTREPO.FRM

   5970 bytes in       3 files

352256 bytes remaining on drive.


.DIR REPORT?.PRG
REPORT1.PRG         REPORT2.PRG

   2048 bytes in       2 files

352256 bytes remaining on drive.
```

DISPLAY [<scope>] [<expression list>] [**FOR** <condition>] [**WHILE** <condition>] [**OFF**] [**TO PRINT**]

Displays information for records in the database file in use on the monitor screen. The expressions in <expression list> may be of any type and may include field names, memory variables, literal values, and functions. The parameters [<scope>], [**FOR** <condition>], and [**WHILE** <condition>] may be used to display information for a group of records. The default scope is the current record. The [**OFF**] parameter suppresses display of record numbers. The [**TO PRINT**] parameter echoes screen output to the printer.

```
. AVERAGE ALL salary TO avgsal

. DISPLAY ALL employee, sex, salary-avgsal, IIF(salary<avgsal,"<--","") OFF
 employee             sex  salary-avgsal IIF(salary<avgsal,"<--","")
 Pratt John           M           315.00
 Smoler Ellen         F            16.00
 Jones David          M           -84.00 <--
 Sill Sally           F          -127.00 <--
 Knat Michael         M           166.00
 Smith Paul           M            66.00
 Martins Mary         F           -34.00 <--
 Nichols Sandy        F          -184.00 <--
 Johnson Frank        M          -134.00 <--
```

DISPLAY HISTORY [**LAST** <expN>] [**TO PRINT**]

Displays the most recently executed commands held in the **HISTORY** buffer. dBASE sets aside a small portion of RAM (a buffer) called **HISTORY** into which it stores previously executed commands. By default, the **HISTORY** buffer holds the last 20 commands executed from the dot (.)

prompt. The buffer allows the user to back up, edit, and then reenter previous commands.

To display a previous command, the cursor up key is typed. Each time the key is typed, dBASE displays the next previous command (scrolls back through the commands in the **HISTORY** buffer). To scroll forward, the cursor down key is typed. When the desired command is displayed, the following keystrokes may be used to edit the command.

Keystroke	Action
Cursor right	Moves cursor right one character.
Cursor left	Moves cursor left one character.
Home	Moves cursor one word to the left.
End	Moves cursor one word to the right.
Ins	Toggles between overwrite and insert modes.
Del	Deletes character at cursor location.
Backspace	Deletes character to left of cursor.
^T	Deletes word to right of cursor.
^Y	Deletes line to right of cursor.
Esc	Aborts any changes made and returns cursor to beginning of command line.

The **DISPLAY HISTORY** command with the [**LAST** <expN>] parameter is used to display fewer commands than may be held in the full **HISTORY** buffer. The [**TO PRINT**] parameter echoes screen output to the printer. (See also **SET HISTORY TO,** page D-186, and **SET DOHISTORY,** page D-184.)

DISPLAY MEMORY [**TO PRINT**]

Displays names, types, and contents of all current memory variables. The [**TO PRINT**] parameter echoes screen output to the printer.

DISPLAY STATUS [**TO PRINT**]

Lists files that are open, displaying information about their relationships, **SET** command settings, function key assignments, and other current environment information. The [**TO PRINT**] parameter echoes screen output to the printer.

DISPLAY STRUCTURE [**TO PRINT**]

Displays field names, types, widths, and decimals (the record structure) of the database in use. The [**TO PRINT**] parameter echoes screen output to the printer.

DO <filename> [**WITH** <expression list>]

Opens and begins execution of the commands in the specified command file. The [**WITH** <expression list>] option is used to pass parameters (expressions) to the command files. (See **PARAMETERS,** page D-175.)

DO CASE
  CASE <condition>
    any commands
  [**CASE** <condition>]
    any commands
  [**CASE** <condition>]
    any commands
  [**OTHERWISE**]
    any commands
ENDCASE

Used only in command files, this command structure is used to select a single set of commands to execute. It is useful when the criteria for command executions are mutually exclusive. When **DO CASE** is encountered, the first **CASE** <condition> is evaluated. If evaluated as true, the commands immediately following are executed and then control passes to the first command following **ENDCASE.** If evaluated as false, the next **CASE** <condition> is evaluated. The process continues until a **CASE** <condition> is evaluated as true or **ENDCASE** is encountered. The [**OTHERWISE**] is optional and its commands are executed when none of the **CASE** <condition>s have been evaluated as true. **ENDCASE** is needed to complete the command structure.

```
USE empfile
CLEAR
STORE " " TO ans
@ 3,25 SAY "      MENU OPTIONS      "
@ 5,25 SAY "  1 - Add a Record      "
@ 6,25 SAY "  2 - Delete a Record   "
@ 7,25 SAY "  3 - Edit Records      "
@ 9,25 SAY "Enter Menu Selection:" GET ans
READ
DO CASE
   CASE ans = "1"
     APPEND
   CASE ans = "2"
     INPUT "Record number of record to delete ? " TO n
     GOTO n
     DISPLAY employee
     ACCEPT "Correct record ? (Y/N)" TO confirm
     IF UPPER(confirm) = "Y"
       DELETE
     ENDIF
   OTHERWISE
     BROWSE NOAPPEND
ENDCASE
CLEAR
RETURN
```

DO WHILE <condition>
  any commands
ENDDO

Used only in command files, the **DO WHILE...ENDDO** command structure creates a program loop. When **DO WHILE** is encountered, the <condition> is evaluated. If evaluated as true, commands between the **DO WHILE** and its **ENDDO** are executed repeatedly until the **DO WHILE**'s <condition> is no longer true.

It is important that within the loop there is something to cause the <condition> to become false at some point. Otherwise, an "endless loop" situation exists—one in which there is no exit from the **DO WHILE...ENDDO** loop. In the following example, an end-of-file condition must occur to end the loop process, and **SKIP** is the command that ensures that the record pointer will eventually reach the end of the file.

```
USE empfile
SET TALK OFF
SET PRINT ON

DO WHILE .NOT. EOF()
  IF account > .15 * salary
    ? "To: ",employee
    ? "From:  Accounting"
    ?
    ? "You have exceeded your personal account limit by"
    ? account - .15 * salary, ".  Please make arrangements"
    ? "to pay this amount as soon as possible."
    EJECT
  ENDIF
  SKIP
ENDDO

SET PRINT OFF
SET TALK ON
USE
RETURN
```

Using **LOOP** and **EXIT** in a **DO WHILE...ENDDO** Structure

The commands **LOOP** and **EXIT** have meaning only within a **DO WHILE...ENDDO** loop. **LOOP** may be used to cause command execution to jump back to the **DO WHILE** <condition> before the **ENDDO** has been reached. The <condition> then is evaluated again to determine if loop processing should continue. **EXIT** causes command execution to jump to the command immediately following the **ENDDO** command (exit the loop) regardless of the evaluation of the **DO WHILE** <condition>.

In the following example, records in the database file are to be processed until an end-of-file condition occurs. The **REPORT FORM** command used with the [**WHILE** <condition>] parameter has the effect of skipping through records of the file until the <condition> is false, at which point the record pointer will already be on the next record. The **LOOP** command is used to avoid executing the **SKIP** command at the end of the loop. The **EXIT** command is used to immediately exit the loop if more than 5 records have been found with invalid data in the sex field, whether or not the end of the file has been reached.

NOTE: The operator $ used in the command line **IF** *sex $ "MF" means "if the value of the field sex is found within the string "MF"." It is roughly equivalent to using the logical operator .OR. in the command* **IF** sex = "M" .OR. sex = "F".

```
USE empfile INDEX sexdex        && file indexed on sex field
STORE 0 TO errcount

DO WHILE .NOT. EOF()
  IF sex $ "MF"
    IF sex = "F"
      REPORT FORM salaryf TO PRINT WHILE sex = "F"
    ELSE
      REPORT FORM salarym TO PRINT WHILE sex = "M"
    ENDIF
    LOOP
  ELSE
    STORE errcount + 1 to errcount
    IF errcount > 5
      ? "Too many gender code errors encountered to produce accurate reports"
      EXIT
    ELSE
      ? "Error - Invalid gender code for " + employee
    ENDIF
  ENDIF
  SKIP
ENDDO

USE
RETURN
```

EDIT [<scope>] [**FIELDS** <field list>] [**FOR** <condition>] [**WHILE** <condition>]

Allows editing of records in the database file in use. Editing may be limited to fields specified with the [**FIELDS** <field list>] option. The parameters [<scope>], [**FOR** <condition>], and [**WHILE** <condition>] may be used to limit the number of records included for editing.

```
. EDIT FIELDS employee,account FOR account > 0
```

```
Record No.      1
EMPLOYEE     Pratt John
ACCOUNT        200.00
```

EJECT

Causes printer to form feed (page eject).

ERASE <filename.extension>

Erases a file from the diskette. **ERASE** may not be used to erase an open file.

EXIT

See "Using **LOOP** and **EXIT** in a **DO WHILE...ENDDO** Structure," page D-162.

EXPORT TO <filename> **TYPE PFS**

Copies the current dBASE database file and its open format file (.FMT), if any, to a single file named <filename> in the database format used by PFS:FILE.

FIND <literal string / &memvarC>

Used with index files, **FIND** positions the record pointer to the first database record indexed by <literal string / &memvarC>. If a literal string is used, the string is not enclosed in quotations ("), and if a character-type memory variable is used, the name of the variable is preceded by an ampersand (&). (See **SEEK,** page D-179.)

```
. USE empfile INDEX namedex

. FIND Smith P

. DISPLAY
Record#  EMPLOYEE                TELEPHONE SEX EMPLOYED   SALARY  ACCOUNT
      6  Smith Paul              244-1010  M   11/15/81  1700.00   350.00

. STORE "Johns" TO z

. FIND &z

. DISPLAY
Record#  EMPLOYEE                TELEPHONE SEX EMPLOYED   SALARY  ACCOUNT
      9  Johnson Frank           223-7928  M   03/20/90  1500.00     0.00
```

GO <expN> / **TOP** / **BOTTOM**

GO <expN> moves the record pointer to the record with the record number <expN>. **GO TOP** and **GO BOTTOM** move the record pointer to the first and last records in the file, respectively. If an index is in use, **GO TOP** and **GO BOTTOM** move the record pointer to the first and last records in the indexed order. An alternate form of the command is **GOTO.**

HELP [<key word>]

HELP invokes a menu-driven, on-line facility that provides information on various dBASE III Plus commands and operations. If a command or function is specified in the <key word> parameter, **HELP** provides a screen of summary information on that command or function.

IF <condition>
  any commands
ENDIF

Used only in command files, the **IF...ENDIF** command structure permits conditional execution of commands. If the <condition> evaluates as true, the commands between the **IF** and the **ENDIF** are executed; otherwise, the commands are ignored. Each **IF** command used must have a matching **ENDIF.**

IF <condition>
  any commands
[**ELSE**]
  any commands
ENDIF

When the optional [**ELSE**] clause is included, the structure becomes **IF...ELSE...ENDIF.** If the <condition> evaluates as true, only the commands between the **IF** and the **ELSE** are executed; otherwise, only the commands between the **ELSE** and the **ENDIF** are executed.

IMPORT FROM <filename> **TYPE PFS**

Creates a dBASE database file (.DBF) and a format file (.FMT), both having the same filename, from a PFS:FILE database file named <filename>. At the time a file is imported, dBASE creates a view file (.VUE) that relates the .DBF and .FMT files.

INDEX ON <expression> **TO** <index file> [**UNIQUE**]

Creates an index file (.NDX) for the database in use. The index file is based on key field(s) specified in the <expression>. The <expression> type may be character, numeric, or date. The [**UNIQUE**] parameter causes only the first record of several records having the same key <expression> to be included in the index file.

INPUT [<expC>] **TO** <memvarN>

Normally used in command files, this command is designed to prompt for a keyboard entry and then place the entry into a numeric-type memory variable. The optional [<expC>] immediately following **INPUT** is a character string used as a prompt to indicate the information to be entered.

```
. INPUT "Enter minimum salary to display: " TO minsal
Enter minimum salary to display: 1600

. DISPLAY FOR salary >= minsal
Record#  EMPLOYEE                 TELEPHONE SEX EMPLOYED   SALARY  ACCOUNT
      1  Pratt John               225-1234  M   06/22/82  1949.00   200.00
      2  Smoler Ellen             225-3212  F   09/15/83  1650.00   300.00
      5  Knat Michael             221-1235  M   09/15/80  1800.00   125.00
      6  Smith Paul               244-1010  M   11/15/81  1700.00   350.00
      7  Martins Mary             222-2123  F   11/01/85  1600.00   200.50
```

INSERT [**BLANK**] [**BEFORE**]

The **INSERT** command inserts a record into the database in use immediately after the current record and enters an editing mode for that record. If the [**BLANK**] parameter is used, a blank record is inserted without entering the editing mode for the record inserted. If the [**BEFORE**] parameter is used, the blank record is inserted immediately before the current record.

JOIN WITH <alias> **TO** <filename> **FOR** <condition> [**FIELDS** <field list>]

Creates a new database by combining the records of the .DBF files in use in two work areas. Records are added to a third database (specified by **TO** <filename>). Combined records are created when the **FOR** <condition> evaluates as true for the current record of the current file as it is compared to each record of the <alias> database file. That is, each record of the current file is compared to all records of the <alias> file.

LABEL FORM <filename> [<scope>] [**FOR** <condition>] [**WHILE** <condition>] [**TO PRINT** / **TO FILE** <filename>] [**SAMPLE**]

Produces labels from the specifications within a label file (.LBL). Label files are created with the **MODIFY LABEL** command. The parameters [<scope>], [**FOR** <condition>], and [**WHILE** <condition>] may be used to limit the number of records for which labels are produced. The default <scope> is **ALL** records.

The [**SAMPLE**] parameter may be used to print test labels to ensure proper label registration. The [**TO FILE** <filename>] parameter may be used to print labels in ASCII format to a diskette file. (See **MODIFY LABEL,** page D-167.)

LIST

The following **LIST** commands are identical to the **DISPLAY** commands except that there are no screen pauses and the default <scope> is **ALL** records when <scope> is part of the command syntax.

LIST [<scope>] [<expression list>] [**FOR** <condition>] [**WHILE** <condition>] [**TO PRINT**] [**OFF**]
LIST HISTORY
LIST MEMORY
LIST STATUS
LIST STRUCTURE

LOAD <filename>[.<ext>]

Loads a binary file into RAM where it may be executed with the **CALL** command.

LOCATE [<scope>] **FOR** <condition> [**WHILE** <condition>]

Moves the record pointer to the first record in the database for which the **FOR** <condition> evaluates as true. If [<scope>] is specified, moves record pointer to the first such record in <scope>. The **CONTINUE** command finds the next such record.

```
. LOCATE FOR salary <= 1500
Record =       8

. CONTINUE
Record =       9

. CONTINUE
End of LOCATE scope
```

LOOP

See "Using **LOOP** and **EXIT** in a **DO WHILE...ENDDO** Structure," page D–162.

MODIFY COMMAND <filename>

Enters dBASE's word processor editing mode to create or edit ASCII files. Normally used to edit command files (.PRG), the **MODIFY COMMAND** mode also may be used to edit .TXT and .FMT files. The maximum file size that **MODIFY COMMAND** can edit is 4,096 bytes.

MODIFY LABEL <filename>

The **MODIFY LABEL** command is used to create or edit a label form file (.LBL) to hold label specifications for use by the **LABEL FORM** command. The label specifications are entered in a dBASE editing mode similar to the **MODIFY REPORT** mode, and the file created is given a .LBL file extension by dBASE.

The **MODIFY LABEL** and **LABEL FORM** commands are primarily designed to produce mailing or identification labels on tractor-fed label stock paper. To produce such labels, the width and height of the labels, left print margin, lines and spaces between labels, and number of labels across a page must be specified. These specifications are made with the Options pull-down menu, which is the first screen the **MODIFY LABEL** command presents.

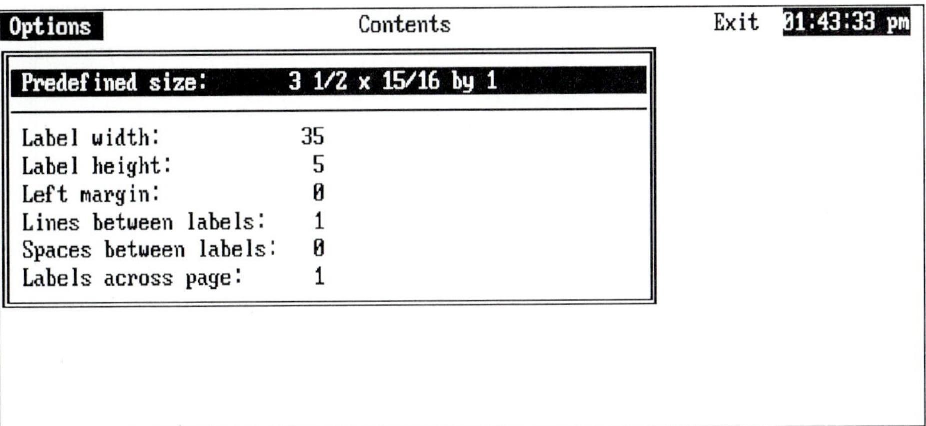

Use the cursor right key to access the Contents pull-down menu, which is used to specify the contents of each line of the label. Move the cursor to the desired line and type the Enter key ↵. Then type an expression list defining the contents for the line (separate expressions with commas if more than one is entered). To include a field name in the contents of a line, you may use the F10 key to select a field from a list in the database file in use.

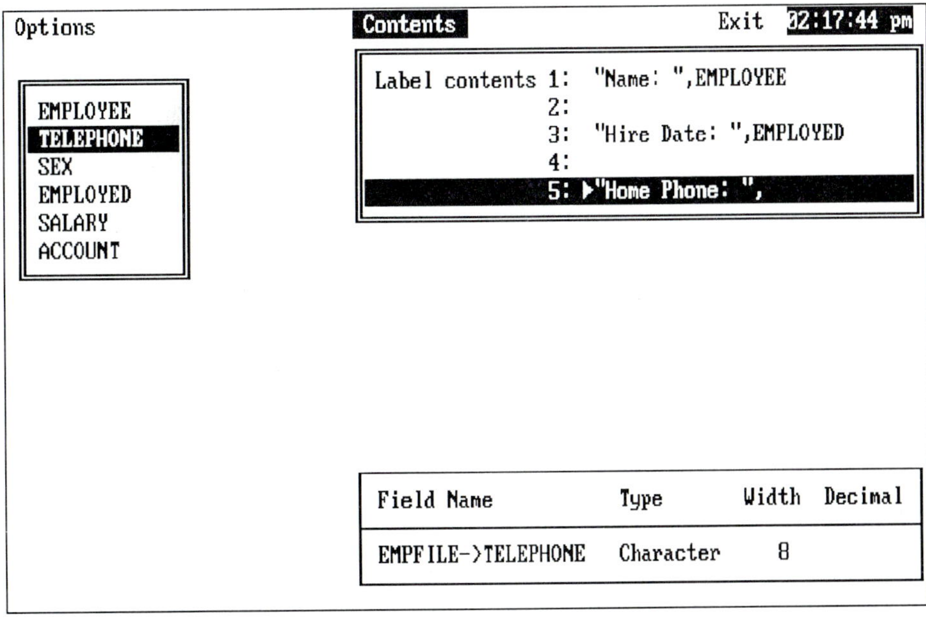

When done entering the line, type ↵. When done defining the label, use the cursor right key to access the Exit pull-down menu. Then select "Save" to save the file or "Abandon" to leave the file as it was before changes were made. To produce labels, see the **LABEL FORM** command, page D–166.

MODIFY QUERY <filename>

The **MODIFY QUERY** command is used to create or change a query file (.QRY) used with the **SET FILTER TO FILE** <filename> command. The **MODIFY QUERY** command uses a full-screen, menu-driven mode for entry of a filter expression.

To set a filter condition to limit records to all men with salaries greater than $1,600 for the database file empfile.DBF, you would first put empfile into use, and then type the **MODIFY QUERY** <filename> command.

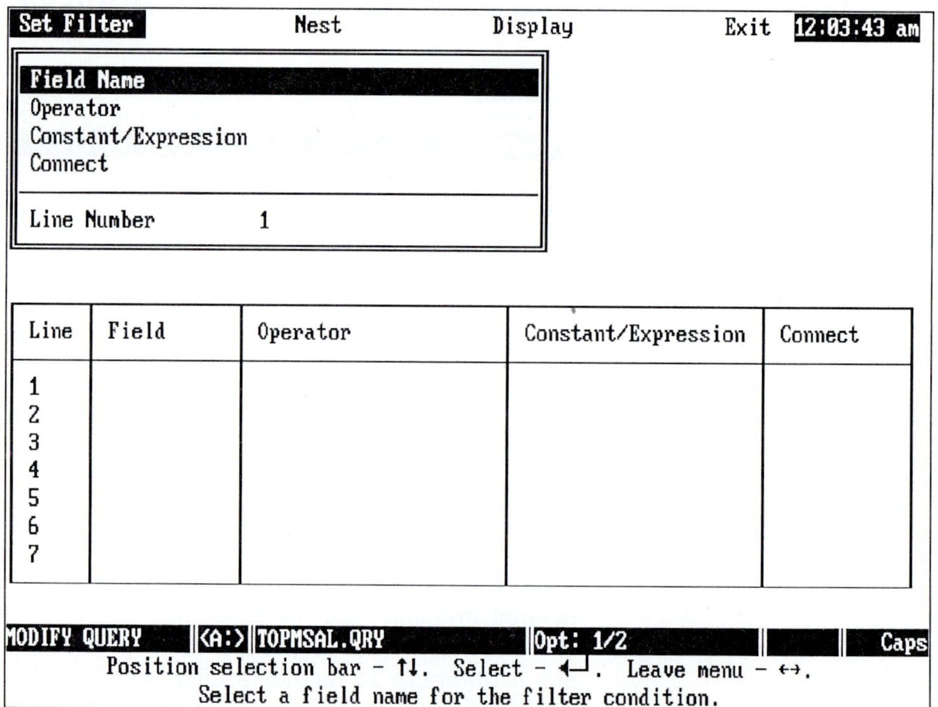

The Set Filter option of the menu bar is used to select fields, relational operators, expressions, and logical operators to form the filter condition (a logical expression). Each item and operator of the condition is selected from a menu.

```
Set Filter            Nest            Display            Exit  12:08:46 am

 Field Name            SALARY
 Operator              More than
 Constant/Expression   1600
 Connect

 Line Number           2
```

Line	Field	Operator	Constant/Expression	Connect
1	SEX	Matches	"M"	.AND.
2	SALARY	More than	1600	
3				
4				
5				
6				
7				

```
MODIFY QUERY   |<A:>|TOPMSAL.QRY          |Opt: 5/5        |   |   Caps
     Position selection bar - ↑↓.  Select - ↵.  Leave menu - ←→.
          Enter the line number of the query form to edit next.
```

When finished, the condition(s) specified are described on lines one through seven. The next option of the menu bar, Nest, is used to add parentheses to a logical expression composed of more than two conditions connected with logical operators. Here the positions for parentheses are entered so that they start or stop on a condition, with the start or stop position entered as the condition number according to the order it appears in the logical expression (1st, 2nd, 3rd, etc.).

The Display option of the **MODIFY QUERY** menu bar displays the records of the current database that pass the filter expression currently defined. The Exit option is used to save the .QRY file and return to the dot (.) prompt mode.

Once a .QRY file has been created, the **SET FILTER TO FILE** <filename> command is used to activate the filter expression in it. While the filter is active, only those records passing it will be processed by dBASE. To deactivate a filter, the **SET FILTER TO** command is used without parameters. (See **SET FILTER TO,** page D–185.)

MODIFY REPORT <filename>

The **MODIFY REPORT** command is used to create or edit a report form file (.FRM) to hold report specifications for use by the **REPORT FORM** command. See "Producing dBASE Reports," dBASE III Plus Exercises, for further information.

MODIFY SCREEN <filename>

The **MODIFY SCREEN** command serves as a dBASE program generator. The programs it generates are format files (.FMT) created from screen files (.SCR). Format files are composed of @ **SAY,** @ **GET,** and **READ** commands—commands used to format screens for data input and output.

MODIFY SCREEN uses a full-screen, menu-driven mode for data entry and provides a blank screen (called the *blackboard*) on which the input/output screen is created. The menus and blackboard are mutually-exclusive data entry modes. The F10 key is used to toggle (switch) from one mode to the other.

The **MODIFY SCREEN** menu bar provides a Set Up option for selecting the fields of data to be displayed on the finished screen. First, a database file is selected from a menu of available database files with the Select Database File option. Then the fields to be included in the screen are selected from a menu generated by the Load Fields option. (A database file also may be created with the Set Up option of **MODIFY SCREEN,** with the structure entered through the Modify option.)

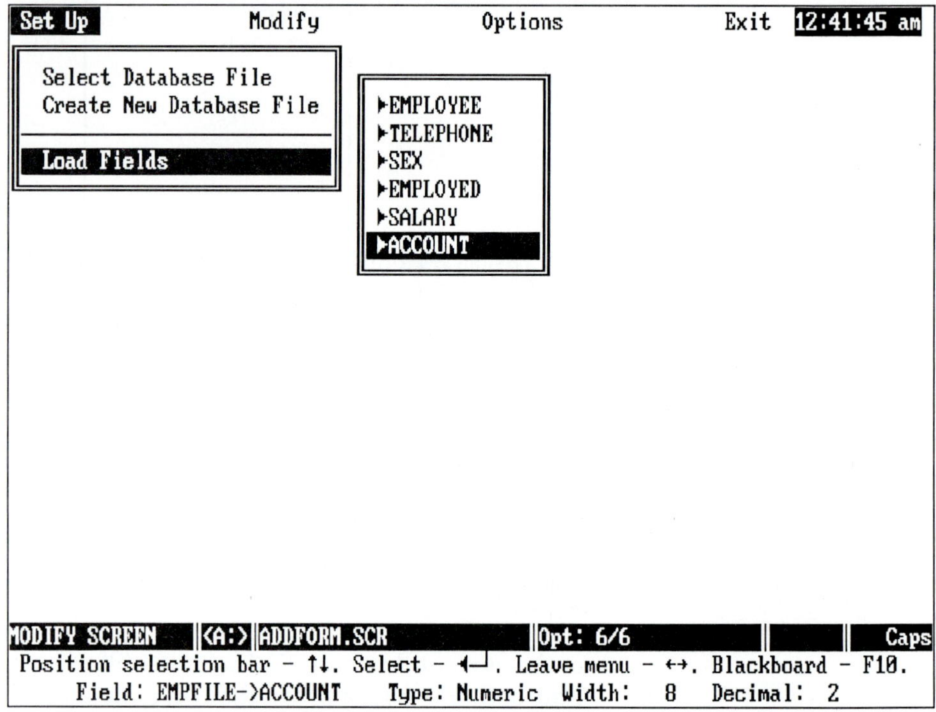

The arrow keys ↓ and ↑ are used to move through the field list displayed, and the Enter key ↵ is used to select fields to be placed on the blackboard. Selected fields are marked with an arrow and may also be unmarked with the Enter key. When the F10 key (or a character key) is typed, the selected fields are placed on the blackboard and are displayed in reverse video next to their field names. The user then is left in the blackboard mode.

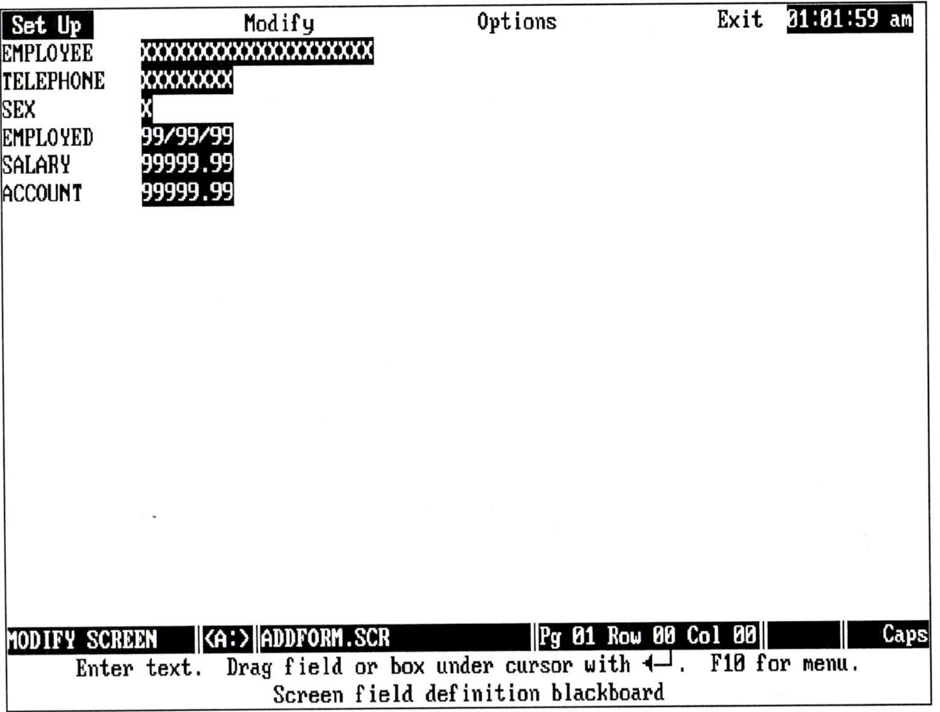

While in the blackboard mode, editing keystrokes similar to those of **MODIFY COMMAND** allow the user to enter screen text. To relocate a field currently displayed on the blackboard, move the cursor to the first character of the field and press the Enter key ↵. Then move the cursor to the new position and press the Enter key again.

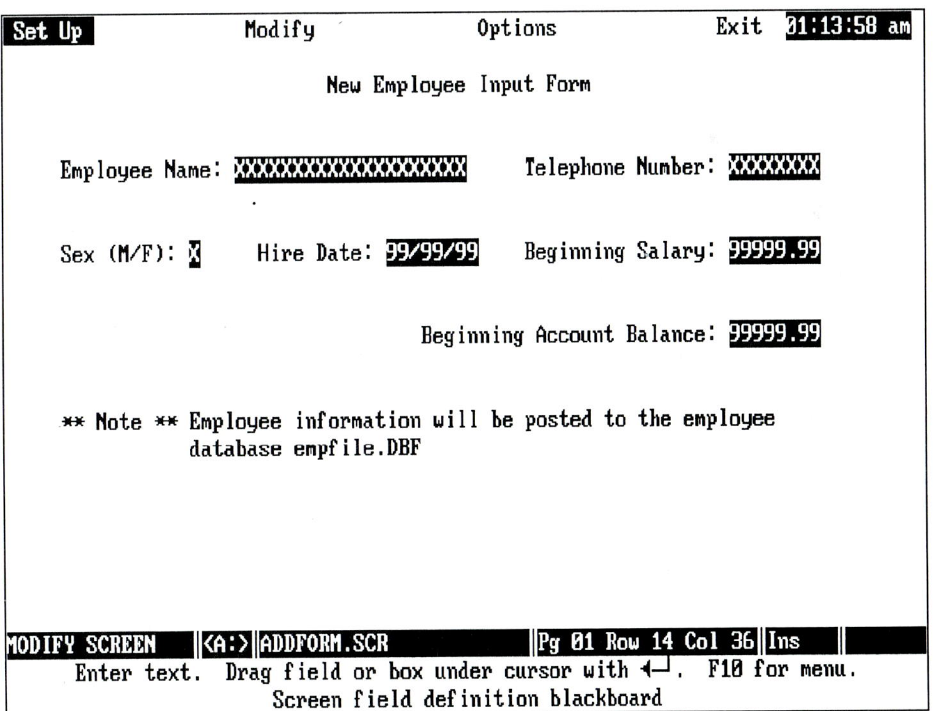

The Modify option of the menu bar is used to determine if a field will be placed on the screen with an @ **SAY** or an @ **GET** command. All fields initially placed on the blackboard are placed there as @ **GET**s. Modify also allows **PICTURE** clauses to be established for the field and permits field contents, type, width, and decimals to be altered. To modify a field, move the cursor to the first character of the field while in the blackboard mode, and then toggle to the menu mode by typing F10 and select the Modify option of the menu bar.

Options may be selected from the menu bar to draw a line or a box with single or double bars on the blackboard screen. To draw a line or box, toggle to the menu mode, select Options, and then select either Single bar or Double bar. The screen will return to the blackboard mode. Move the cursor to one corner of the area to be boxed or lined, type the Enter key ↵, move the cursor to the opposite diagonal corner of the box or the other end of the line to be drawn, and then type the Enter key again.

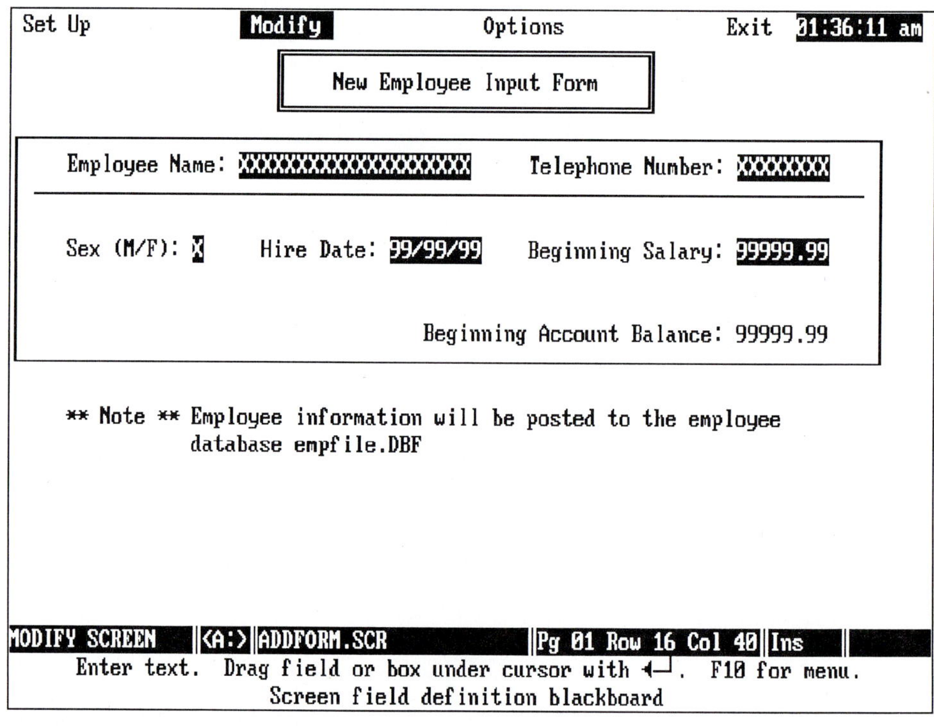

When the blackboard is finished, the Exit option of the menu bar is used to save the .SCR file and generate the .FMT file from it. Both files have the same filename. Later, if the .SCR file is altered with **MODIFY SCREEN,** a new .FMT file is produced when the Exit operation is completed. The following is a listing of the .FMT file created in this example.

```
. TYPE addform.fmt
@ 1, 28  SAY "New Employee Input Form"
@ 4,  5  SAY "Employee Name:"
@ 4, 20  GET  EMPFILE->EMPLOYEE
@ 4, 45  SAY "Telephone Number:"
@ 4, 63  GET  EMPFILE->TELEPHONE
@ 7,  5  SAY "Sex (M/F):"
@ 7, 16  GET  EMPFILE->SEX
@ 7, 22  SAY "Hire Date:"
@ 7, 33  GET  EMPFILE->EMPLOYED
@ 7, 45  SAY "Beginning Salary:"
@ 7, 63  GET  EMPFILE->SALARY
@ 10, 36  SAY "Beginning Account Balance:"
@ 10, 63  SAY  EMPFILE->ACCOUNT
@ 13,  5  SAY "** Note ** Employee information will be posted to the employee"
@ 14, 16  SAY "database empfile.DBF"
@ 0, 23  TO  2, 55   DOUBLE
@ 3,  0  TO 11, 75
@ 5,  2  TO  5, 73
```

A format file (.FMT) is activated with the **SET FORMAT TO** <filename> command. Once activated, it affects the screen displays for the **APPEND, CHANGE, EDIT, INSERT,** and **READ** commands. For instance, to add a new employee to the database empfile.DBF using the screen display created in the example, you would type the following.

```
. USE empfile
. SET FORMAT TO addform
. APPEND
```

The **APPEND** mode screen would appear as follows.

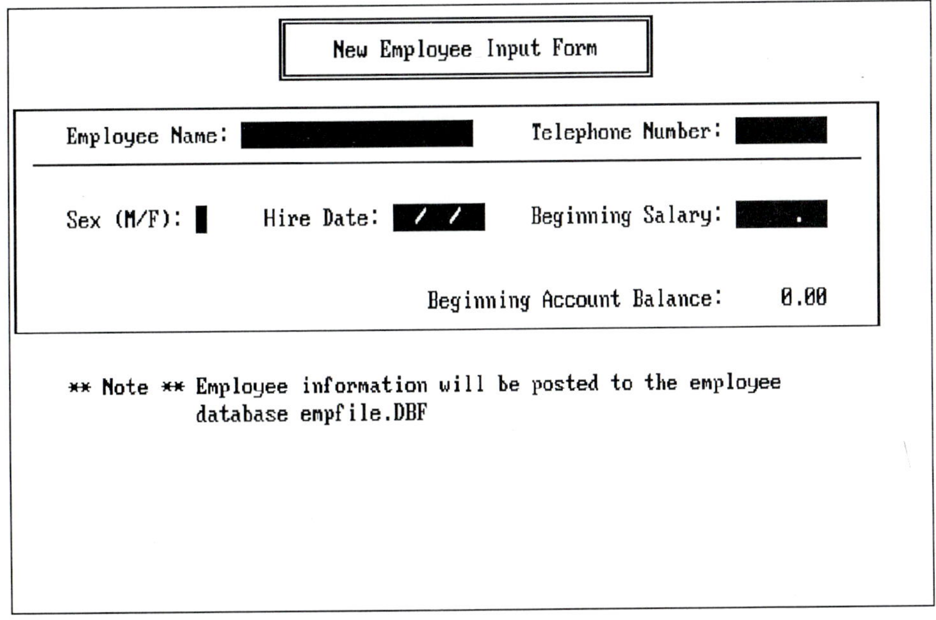

MODIFY STRUCTURE

Alters the record structure of the database in use. The **MODIFY STRUCTURE** command may be used to add new fields or delete fields from the record structure. It also may be used to rename fields or change their lengths. The modifications, however, should be done in separate steps, as listed in the following.

First, use **MODIFY STRUCTURE** to add or delete any fields necessary. Fields may be inserted with ^N or deleted with ^U. Once field additions or deletions are complete, type ^End to exit the **MODIFY STRUCTURE** editing mode.

Next, use **MODIFY STRUCTURE** to change any field names necessary, but do not add or delete any field names or change any lengths. Once field names have been changed, type ^End to exit the **MODIFY STRUCTURE** editing mode. The prompt

```
Should data be COPIED from backup for all fields? (Y/N)
```

will appear at the bottom of the screen. Type Y to leave data in fields whose names have changed or N to erase contents from these fields.

Finally, use **MODIFY STRUCTURE** to change any field widths necessary. Once the new field widths are specified, type ^End to exit the **MODIFY STRUCTURE** editing mode.

MODIFY VIEW <filename>

The **MODIFY VIEW** command is used to create view files (.VUE). View files are used to hold a set of working relationships between dBASE files. **MODIFY VIEW** uses a full-screen, menu-driven mode for data entry. The resulting file records a listing of the databases in use; their active indexes; the work areas in which the databases are in use; any relations between the databases that may exist (see **SET RELATION TO,** page D-188); and the active field list, .FMT file, and/or filter (if any) for each database in use.

Once a view file has been created, it may later be used to reinstate the environment recorded within it through the **SET VIEW TO** <filename> command. (See **SET VIEW TO,** page D-189.)

NOTE or *

Used in command files, this command allows comments to be placed in a command file. **NOTE** and * must begin a line holding a comment. To place a comment to the right of a command and on the same line, use **&&** before the comment.

ON ERROR / ESCAPE / KEY [<command>]

Used in command files, **ON ERROR / ESCAPE / KEY** may be used as an event-trapping command. The three events are **ERROR** (a dBASE error has occurred), **ESCAPE** (the Esc key has been typed), or **KEY** (any key has been typed). When one of these events occurs, and an **ON** command has already been executed for that event, the <command> specified will be executed.

The <command> is normally used to branch program execution to an error-trapping program. The program branched to should first remove the key pressed from the typeahead buffer by executing an **INKEY**() function or **READ** command. Any other commands then may be executed before returning control to the program in which the event occurred. To turn off the feature, use the **ON ERROR / ESCAPE / KEY** command with no <command> parameter.

PACK

Permanently removes (erases) all records marked for deletion in the database file in use. (See also **DELETE,** page D-158, and **RECALL,** page D-176.)

PARAMETERS <memvar list>

Used in programs (command files and procedures), receives parameters passed in the [<expression list>] clause of a **DO** <filename> [**WITH** <expression list>] command and stores each expression to a local (private) memory variable. **PARAMETERS** must be the first executable command in a program.

The number of parameters specified in the **DO** command must be the same as that specified with the **PARAMETERS** command of the program called. The <expression list> passed may include constants, memory variables, or fields. Memory variables passed as parameters will be passed back to the calling program, including any changes made to the variable in the program called. (See also **PRIVATE,** below.)

PRIVATE [<memvar list>] / [**ALL** [**LIKE** / **EXCEPT** <skeleton>]]

Used in command files, **PRIVATE** allows use of the same memory variable names as those created in a higher-level command file without affecting the contents of the higher-level command file's variables.

When a command file calls another command file with the **DO** <filename> command, all variables created in the calling program are available in the program called, and changes may be made to these variables in the calling program. Any new variables created in the program called are considered private and will disappear when control is passed back to the calling program (unless declared as **PUBLIC** variables; see **PUBLIC,** page D-176).

The **PRIVATE** command allows certain variables to be treated as private variables in the program called even though they have the same name as variables created in the calling program. The variables in the calling program thus are protected from being changed in the program called.

PROCEDURE <procedure name>

Identifies the beginning of each procedure in a procedure file. A procedure file is a command (.PRG) file that has been declared and opened as a procedure file with the **SET PROCEDURE TO** <filename> command (see page D-187).

Short program subroutines called procedures typically are found within a procedure file. Each subroutine starts with a **PROCEDURE** <procedure name> command and ends with a RETURN command. There may be up to 32 separate procedures in a procedure file.

Procedures are executed with the **DO** command in the same manner as command (.PRG) files are executed. Procedures having the same <procedure name> as that of an existing command file will take execution precedence.

PUBLIC <memvar list>

Declares memory variables as global, allowing them to be used by any program at any level. Memory variables must be declared **PUBLIC** before data are assigned to them. Public memory variables may still be protected from change in a program (command file) by being declared **PRIVATE** within that program. (See **PRIVATE,** page D-175.)

QUIT

Ends a dBASE session and returns to DOS. **QUIT** closes all files and should be typed at the end of each dBASE session to properly exit to DOS.

READ [SAVE]

Allows editing of field or memory variable contents placed on the screen with the @ **GET** command. **READ** normally clears all active @ **GET**s after data have been entered. The **[SAVE]** parameter prevents the **READ** command from clearing (deactivating) the screen's @ **GET**s when editing is finished.

Multiple screens containing @ **GET**s may be produced which allow the user to page back and forth among the screens by typing the PgUp and PgDn keys. The multiple-page screens must be generated from a .FMT file with **READ** commands inserted at the desired page breaks. (See @ **GET,** page D-150.)

RECALL [<scope>] [**FOR** <condition>] [**WHILE** <condition>]

Recalls record(s) marked for deletion ("unmarks" them). The parameters [<scope>], [**FOR** <condition>], and [**WHILE** <condition>] may be used to **RECALL** a group of records. The default <scope> is the current record. (See **DELETE,** page D-158, and **PACK,** page D-175.)

REINDEX

Updates (rebuilds) all active index (.NDX) files in the currently selected work area. (See **USE,** page D-191, and **SET INDEX TO,** page D-187.)

RELEASE [<memvar list>] / **ALL** [**LIKE** / **EXCEPT** <skeleton>]

Erases memory variables from RAM. A <skeleton> is made up of variable name characters and masking characters that act as "wild cards." The asterisk (*) indicates, "Accept all remaining characters," while the question mark (?) means, "Accept any single character in this position."

```
. DISPLAY MEMORY
MALES        pub  N          5  (          5.00000000)
MPAY         pub  N    8499.00  (       8499.00000000)
MACCT        pub  N     950.75  (        950.75000000)
FEMALES      pub  N          4  (          4.00000000)
FPAY         pub  N    6507.50  (       6507.50000000)
FACCT        pub  N     825.50  (        825.50000000)
    6 variables defined,       54 bytes used
  250 variables available,   5946 bytes available


. RELEASE ALL LIKE M*          ← MALES, MPAY, and MACCT will be released.

. RELEASE ALL LIKE MA*         ← MALES and MACCT will be released.

. RELEASE ALL LIKE ?PAY        ← MPAY and FPAY will be released.

. RELEASE ALL EXCEPT F????     ← ALL but FPAY and FACCT will be released.

. RELEASE ALL                  ← Erases all variables from RAM.
```

RELEASE MODULE <module name>

Releases a binary file placed in memory with the **LOAD** command. (See **LOAD,** page D-166.)

RENAME <filename.ext> **TO** <new filename.ext>

Used to rename any type of file on the disk from dBASE. Filename extensions must be included. An open file cannot be renamed.

```
. RENAME fullrepo.FRM TO report.FRM
```

REPLACE [<scope>] <field1> **WITH** <exp1> [,<field2> **WITH** <exp2>, . . .] [**FOR** <condition>] [**WHILE** <condition>]

Replaces contents of specified fields with the evaluation of the matching **WITH** <expression> for the records of the database in use. The parameters [<scope>], [**FOR** <condition>], and [**WHILE** <condition>] may be used to make the replacement for a group of records. The default <scope> is the current record only.

REPORT FORM [<filename>] [<scope>] [**FOR** <condition>] [**WHILE** <condition>] **[PLAIN]** **[HEADING** <expC>] **[NOEJECT]** **[TO PRINT** / **TO FILE** <filename>] **[SUMMARY]**

Creates a dBASE report from a report form file (.FRM) and the database file in use. The parameters [<scope>], [**FOR** <condition>], and [**WHILE** <condition>] may be used to limit the number of records included in the report. The default <scope> is **ALL** records. The [**HEADING** <expC>] parameter is used to include the <expC> at the top of each page. The **[PLAIN]** parameter omits page numbers, dates, and any page **[HEADING]** set. The **[NOEJECT]** parameter suppresses the initial page feed before the report is printed with **[TO PRINT]**. The [**TO FILE** <filename>] parameter produces an ASCII text file (.TXT). The **[SUMMARY]** parameter suppresses detail lines to include only total and subtotal lines in the report.

RESTORE FROM <filename> **[ADDITIVE]**

Reads memory variables and their contents into RAM after they have been saved to a memory (.MEM) file with the **SAVE** command. The **[ADDITIVE]** parameter is used to keep currently defined variables in RAM; otherwise, they are erased.

RESUME

Resumes execution of a suspended program (command file or procedure). Programs may be suspended by the **SUSPEND** command in the file, or when **SUSPEND** is selected after dBASE has detected an error.

RETRY

Similar to the **RETURN** command, **RETRY** returns control to a calling command file. With **RETURN,** command execution resumes in the calling program with the line after the last command executed, while returning control with **RETRY** causes the last command executed to be executed again. **RETRY** is most useful for error recovery within a program which uses the **ON ERROR / ESCAPE / KEY** [<command>] command. (See **ON** command, page D-174.)

RETURN [TO MASTER]

Used in command files, the **RETURN** command returns control to the command file which called it or to the dBASE dot (.) prompt. The **[TO MASTER]** parameter returns control to the highest level command file.

RUN <command>

Runs a designated DOS command or executable file (.COM or .EXE) from within dBASE.

SAVE TO <filename> **[ALL LIKE / EXCEPT** <skeleton>]

Saves currently defined memory variables in a memory file (.MEM) so that they may later be called back into RAM with the **RESTORE** command. Without optional parameters, all memory variables are saved. A <skeleton> used with **ALL LIKE** and **ALL EXCEPT** is made up of variable name characters and masking characters that act as "wild cards." The asterisk (*) indicates, "Accept all remaining characters," while the question mark (?) means, "Accept any single character in this position."

```
. DISPLAY MEMORY
MALES        pub   N          5  (          5.00000000)
MPAY         pub   N       8499.00  (       8499.00000000)
MACCT        pub   N        950.75  (        950.75000000)
FEMALES      pub   N          4  (          4.00000000)
FPAY         pub   N       6507.50  (       6507.50000000)
FACCT        pub   N        825.50  (        825.50000000)
    6 variables defined,       54 bytes used
  250 variables available,   5946 bytes available

. SAVE TO vfile ALL LIKE M*       ← MALES, MPAY, and MACCT will be
                                    saved.
. SAVE TO vfile ALL LIKE Ma*      ← MALES and MACCT will be saved.

. SAVE TO vfile ALL LIKE ?PAY     ← MPAY and FPAY will be saved.

. SAVE TO vfile ALL EXCEPT F????  ← ALL but FPAY and FACCT will be
                                    saved.
. SAVE TO vfile                   ← Saves all current variables in the
                                    specified file.
```

SEEK <expression>

Used only with files that have been indexed, **SEEK** positions the record pointer at the first database record indexed by the <expression>. **SEEK** is preferable to **FIND** because it may be used with character-type, numeric-type, or date-type index keys, as shown in the following examples. (See **INDEX,** page D-165.)

Examples of using **SEEK** with a character-type index key

```
. USE empfile

. INDEX ON employee TO namedex

. SEEK "Smith P"

. DISPLAY
Record#  EMPLOYEE                TELEPHONE SEX EMPLOYED   SALARY  ACCOUNT
      6  Smith Paul              244-1010  M   11/15/81  1700.00   350.00


. STORE "Johns" TO z

. SEEK z

. DISPLAY
Record#  EMPLOYEE                TELEPHONE SEX EMPLOYED   SALARY  ACCOUNT
      9  Johnson Frank           223-7928  M   03/20/90  1500.00     0.00
```

Examples of using **SEEK** with numeric-type index keys

```
. USE empfile

. INDEX ON salary TO saldex

. SEEK 1600

. DISPLAY WHILE salary <= 1800
Record#  EMPLOYEE                TELEPHONE SEX EMPLOYED   SALARY  ACCOUNT
      7  Martins Mary            222-2123  F   11/01/85  1600.00   200.50
      2  Smoler Ellen            225-3212  F   09/15/83  1650.00   300.00
      6  Smith Paul              244-1010  M   11/15/81  1700.00   350.00
      5  Knat Michael            221-1235  M   09/15/80  1800.00   125.00


. INDEX ON YEAR(employed) TO yeardex

. SEEK 1981

. DISPLAY WHILE YEAR(employed) < 1984
Record#  EMPLOYEE                TELEPHONE SEX EMPLOYED   SALARY  ACCOUNT
      6  Smith Paul              244-1010  M   11/15/81  1700.00   350.00
      1  Pratt John              225-1234  M   06/22/82  1949.00   200.00
      3  Jones David             292-3832  M   06/15/82  1550.00   275.75
      2  Smoler Ellen            225-3212  F   09/15/83  1650.00   300.00
```

Examples of using **SEEK** with a date-type index key

```
. USE empfile

. INDEX ON employed TO datedex

. SEEK CTOD("11/15/81")

. DISPLAY FOR sex = "M" WHILE employed < CTOD("01/01/89")
Record#  EMPLOYEE                TELEPHONE SEX EMPLOYED   SALARY  ACCOUNT
      6  Smith Paul              244-1010  M   11/15/81  1700.00   350.00
      3  Jones David             292-3832  M   06/15/82  1550.00   275.75
      1  Pratt John              225-1234  M   06/22/82  1949.00   200.00
```

SELECT <work area / alias>

dBASE III Plus allows up to ten databases to be used at the same time. When multiple databases are in use, they can be thought of as existing in separate areas of RAM called work areas. Work area 1 (or A) is the currently selected area when you first enter dBASE. To use a database file in another work area, you first must execute the **SELECT** <work area> command to select work area 2 through 10 (B through J), and then execute the **USE** <filename> command. If the **USE** <filename> **ALIAS** <name> command was used to open a database file, the alias <name> may be used with the **SELECT** command.

Each work area maintains a separate database record pointer. Commands affecting the record pointer or which write data to a database file must be executed from the work area in which the intended database for the command resides. Field data from the current record in any work area may be read by preceding the field name with an alias (A through J or alias specified with **USE**) and the characters ->. (See also **SET RELATION,** page D-188.)

```
. USE empfile

. SELECT 2
. USE deptmail ALIAS mail

. DISPLAY ALL
Record#  EMPLOYEE             DEPT
      1  Pratt John           Acct.
      2  Smoler Ellen         Sales
      3  Jones David          Sales
      4  Sill Sally           Acct.
      5  Knat Michael         Pers.
      6  Smith Paul           Acct.
      7  Martins Mary         Sctry
      8  Nichols Sandy        Sctry
      9  Johnson Frank        Sales

. GOTO 2

. ? employee,dept
Smoler Ellen         Sales

. ? A->employee,A->salary
Pratt John             1949.00

. SELECT 1

. SKIP 5
Record No.       6

. DISPLAY
Record#  EMPLOYEE             TELEPHONE SEX EMPLOYED   SALARY  ACCOUNT
      6  Smith Paul           244-1010  M   11/15/81  1700.00   350.00

. ? mail->employee,mail->dept
Smoler Ellen         Sales

. LOCATE FOR employee = mail->employee
Record =        2

. ? employee,mail->employee,mail->dept,salary
Smoler Ellen         Smoler Ellen         Sales  1650.00
```

SET

dBASE has an extensive set of operating features that can be turned on or off, or changed in other ways with **SET** commands. The **SET** commands have two general forms:

SET <parameter> **ON / OFF** or **SET** <parameter> **TO** <option>

The **SET** <parameter> **ON / OFF** commands are shown here with the normal default setting of each indicated in upper-case characters.

SET BELL ON / off (dBASE default setting is **ON**)

In addition to executing **SET** commands from the dot (.) prompt mode or from within a command file, dBASE III Plus provides a full-screen, menu-driven mode for executing many of the **SET** commands. This mode is entered from the dot prompt (.) by using the command **SET** without any parameters.

SET ALTERNATE on / OFF

ON sends all screen output (except full-screen output such as @ **SAY,** @ **GET,** and output of the editing modes) to an ASCII file on the disk. The **SET ALTERNATE ON** command must be preceded by the **SET ALTERNATE TO** <filename> command. **SET ALTERNATE OFF** discontinues output to the disk file, but does not close the file; output to the file may be resumed with **SET ALTERNATE ON.**

SET ALTERNATE TO <filename>

Creates a disk file with a .TXT extension. The file is used for saving screen output (in ASCII format) when the **SET ALTERNATE ON** command is given. **SET ALTERNATE TO** with no filename specified closes the .TXT file.

SET BELL ON / off

dBASE rings a bell at various points during data entry. **OFF** stops the ringing.

SET CARRY on / OFF

The **SET CARRY** command is used when adding records to a database in the **APPEND** or **INSERT** editing modes. When **CARRY** is **SET ON,** data in the fields of the previous record will automatically be copied into like fields of the new record presented. **OFF** leaves all fields of the new record blank.

SET CATALOG ON / off

OFF may be used to suspend updating of the current .CAT file for dBASE files being opened or created. **ON** resumes updating of the .CAT file. (See **SET CATALOG TO,** below.)

SET CATALOG TO [<filename>]

SET CATALOG TO [<filename>] may be used to create a catalog file (.CAT) or to open an existing catalog file. Catalog files are used to record information about files being used. Once the **SET CATALOG TO** [<filename>] command has been executed, the specified catalog file becomes active. Any command entered after this that opens or creates a dBASE file (with the exception of .MEM, .PRG, and .TXT files) causes the opened or created file to become listed in the active catalog file.

A catalog file is actually a database file that is automatically given a .CAT extension (instead of .DBF) at the time it is created. When a catalog file is activated with **SET CATALOG TO,** it becomes an open file in work area 10. To stop the appending of filenames to an active catalog without closing the catalog file, you may type **SET CATALOG OFF.** To resume adding filenames, type **SET CATALOG ON.** While a catalog file is active, dBASE commands that open files may be entered with a ? mark in place of the <filename> parameter to display a menu of filenames from which to select.

To close the current catalog file, use **SET CATALOG TO** with no <filename> specification.

SET CENTURY on / OFF

ON causes the display of date-type data to show all four characters for the year.

SET COLOR ON / off

SET COLOR ON / off is used to switch between color and monochrome displays for systems having both.

SET COLOR TO [[<standard>] [,<enhanced>] [,border]]

Three screen attributes may be altered with the **SET COLOR TO** command: the display of the normal <standard> screen may be changed from its default colors of white on black; the reverse video display <enhanced> of the editing modes may be changed from its default colors of black on white; and the area around the screen <border> may be changed from its default color of black.

The <standard> and <enhanced> color specifications are made in color pairs, with a forward slash (/) separating foreground/background colors. Codes used to specify colors are as follows.

Color	Code	Color	Code
Black	N	Red	R
Blue	B	Magenta	RB
Green	G	Brown	GR
Cyan	BG	White	W
Blank	X		

An asterisk (*) may be used to cause a blinking color, and a plus sign (+) may be used to cause a high-intensity color. For example, the command used to set a <standard> screen of white on blue, <enhanced> screen of bright white on red, and a magenta border would be **SET COLOR TO** W/B,W+/R,RB.

SET CONFIRM on / OFF

In editing modes, when a field or variable has been filled with data, dBASE automatically moves the cursor to the next field or variable for editing. The **SET CONFIRM ON** command disables automatic cursor movement to the next field. The Enter key ↵ must be used to proceed to the next field.

SET CONSOLE ON / off

Used only in command files, **ON** sends output to screen as normal and **OFF** suppresses most output to the screen (@ **SAY**s and @ **GET**s are still displayed).

SET DATE [AMERICAN / ANSI / BRITISH / ITALIAN / FRENCH / GERMAN]

SET DATE is used to alter the display and entry format for date-type data. The format is normally set to **AMERICAN.** For purposes of data transfer, the **ANSI** (American National Standards Institute) format is quite useful. With this format it becomes possible to convert dBASE III Plus date-type data into character-type data (using the **DTOC** function), and then transfer the data with an order of characters more usable to other software. The various formats for date-type data display are as follows.

AMERICAN	mm/dd/yy	**ITALIAN**	dd-mm-yy
ANSI	yy.mm.dd	**FRENCH**	dd/mm/yy
BRITISH	dd/mm/yy	**GERMAN**	dd.mm.yy

SET DEBUG on / OFF

ON sends output created by the **SET ECHO ON** command to the printer. **OFF** sends the output to the screen. (See **SET ECHO,** below.)

SET DECIMALS TO <expN>

Determines the minimum number of decimal places that will be displayed as a result of certain functions and calculations. Applies only to the operation of division and values returned from the functions **SQRT, LOG, EXP,** and **VAL.**

SET DEFAULT TO *<drive:>*

Makes the specified drive the default drive.

SET DELETED on / OFF

On stops dBASE from processing records that are marked for deletion during execution of commands that allow a <scope> parameter, unless the <scope> is specified as **RECORD** <n> or **NEXT** <n> and the first record of the <scope> is deleted. (See **DELETE,** page D-158.)

SET DELIMITER on / OFF

ON causes fields displayed in the editing modes to be delimited by a character string previously specified with the **SET DELIMITER TO** command, or to colons (:) if no **SET DELIMITER TO** command has been executed.

SET DELIMITER TO <expC> **/ DEFAULT**

Assigns a one-character or two-character string (<expC>) for use in delimiting fields displayed in the editing modes. To change delimiters, the **SET DELIMITER TO** <expC> and **SET DELIMITER ON** commands are used. If a two-character string such as "{ }" is used, the first character "{" appears on the left of an entry and the second character "}" appears on the right. To return to the default delimiter of colons (:), the **DEFAULT** parameter may be used.

SET DEVICE TO PRINT / SCREEN

Determines if output from @ **SAY** and @ **GET** commands will be sent to the screen (default device) or to the printer. If sent to the printer, @ **GET** commands are ignored, and any command that would cause the printer to backup causes a page eject.

SET DOHISTORY on / OFF

ON causes commands executed from within a command file (.PRG) to be stored in the **HISTORY** buffer. (See **DISPLAY HISTORY,** page D-159.)

SET ECHO on / OFF

ON displays on the screen the command currently being executed. Used during execution of command files, **SET ECHO ON** allows you to trace the execution of commands in the file. (See **SET DEBUG on / OFF,** page D-184, and **SET STEP on / OFF,** page D-189.)

SET ESCAPE ON / off

ON allows the user to interrupt execution of a command file or dot (.) prompt command with the Esc key; **OFF** disables this feature. When Esc is used to interrupt execution of a command file, the same prompt that dBASE displays when an error is encountered is displayed.

```
*** INTERRUPTED ***
Called from - A:PROGRAM1.PRG
Cancel, Ignore, or Suspend? (C, I, or S)
```

Type C to cancel execution of the program, type I to ignore the interruption and continue execution, or type S to suspend execution. If suspended, the commands **RESUME** or **CANCEL** may be used to later resume or cancel execution.

SET EXACT on / OFF

By default, dBASE allows partial matches of string comparisons in a <condition>. For instance, **DISPLAY FOR** employee = "Smit" will cause dBASE to display the record for Paul Smith in the database empfile. **EXACT ON** requires exact matches in string comparison operations. With **EXACT ON** only **DISPLAY FOR** employee = "Smith Paul" will display the record. (Notice, however, that trailing spaces do not have to be included in the item.)

SET FIELDS on / OFF

Activates or deactivates the field filter in the current work area. The **SET FIELDS TO** <field list> command is used to set a field filter and set fields **ON. OFF** deactivates the field filter and **ON** reactivates it.

SET FIELDS TO [<field list> / **ALL**]

SET FIELDS TO <field list> creates a field filter and sets fields **ON.** A field filter prevents many dBASE commands from processing fields not listed in the <field list>. The **[ALL]** parameter may be used to include all fields of the current database in the field list. **SET FIELDS TO** with no parameters removes all fields from the field list. The field filter may be turned on and off with the **SET FIELDS on / OFF** command. Several precautionary notes are listed in the dBASE III Plus manual about this command.

SET FILTER TO [<condition>] [**FILE** <filename>]

Causes the current database to appear as if it contains only certain records. The <condition> is a logical expression defining the filter. A query file (.QRY) may be created with **CREATE / MODIFY QUERY.** The file contains a filter condition which may then be put into effect with the command **SET FILTER TO FILE** <filename>. **SET FILTER TO** with no condition turns off the filter.

```
. SET FILTER TO sex = "M"

. DISPLAY ALL
Record#  EMPLOYEE                 TELEPHONE SEX EMPLOYED   SALARY  ACCOUNT
      1  Pratt John               225-1234  M   06/22/82  1949.00   200.00
      3  Jones David              292-3832  M   06/15/82  1550.00   275.75
      5  Knat Michael             221-1235  M   09/15/80  1800.00   125.00
      6  Smith Paul               244-1010  M   11/15/81  1700.00   350.00
      9  Johnson Frank            223-7928  M   03/20/90  1500.00     0.00
```

SET FIXED on / OFF

When **SET FIXED** is **ON,** all displays of numeric data contain the exact number of decimal places specified by the **SET DECIMALS** command, or two decimal places if the **SET DECIMALS** command has not been executed.

SET FORMAT TO [<format file>]

Opens a format file (.FMT) which dBASE will use to format the screen for **APPEND, CHANGE, EDIT,** and **INSERT** commands. Format files are command files that are made up of @ **SAY,** @ **GET,** and **READ** commands only. They may be created or modified by specifying the file extension (.FMT) with **MODIFY COMMAND** <filename.FMT>. Format files also may be generated along with screen files (.SCR) by using **CREATE / MODIFY SCREEN. SET FORMAT TO** closes any open format file.

SET FUNCTION <expN> **TO** <expC>

Stores the specified character string <expC> to the Function key <expN> (2 through 10). For example, **SET FUNCTION** 2 **TO** "Columbus, Ohio" stores the string to the F2 key. Each time F2 is typed, the string "Columbus, Ohio" will appear on the monitor screen at the location of the cursor just as if it had been typed. A semicolon (;) in the string has the effect of typing ↵ at that point. Type **DISPLAY STATUS** for default function key values. Function key 1 cannot be reprogrammed.

SET HEADING ON / off

OFF removes the column headings for the **DISPLAY, LIST, AVERAGE,** and **SUM** commands.

SET HELP ON / off

OFF disables the "Do you want some help? (Y/N)" message generated by syntax errors.

SET HISTORY ON / off

OFF disables the **HISTORY** buffer so dBASE will not save any previously executed commands.

SET HISTORY TO <expN>

Sets the number of commands held in the **HISTORY** buffer to <expN>. Default is 20 commands. If <expN> is smaller than the current number set, all commands in the buffer are erased. (See **DISPLAY HISTORY,** page D-159.)

SET INDEX TO [<index file list>]

Puts index files (.NDX) in use with the current database file. Records will appear in the order defined by the first index file in the list. Other index files will be updated as changes are made to the database file fields. Essentially the same as **USE** <filename> **INDEX** <index file list>. **SET INDEX TO** without a file list closes all index files in the current work area.

SET INTENSITY ON / off

OFF suppresses reverse video screen displays normally used by dBASE.

SET MARGIN TO <expN>

Sets left margin of printer to <expN> columns.

SET MEMOWIDTH TO <expN>

Adjusts the output width of memo field data to <expN> characters. The default memo output width is 50 characters.

SET MENUS ON / off

ON causes the display of keystroke command menus when in an editing mode; **OFF** suppresses the display of menus. When in an editing mode, F1 may be typed to toggle menus on or off, changing the **ON / OFF** status of **SET MENUS.**

SET MESSAGE TO [<expC>]

Causes the specified character expression [<expC>] to be displayed at the bottom line of the monitor screen. **SET MESSAGE TO** with no parameter removes the display of user-defined messages.

SET ORDER TO [<expN>]

Establishes the controlling index file from the list specified with the **USE** <filename> **INDEX** <index file list> or **SET INDEX TO** <index file list> commands. The <expN>th index file in the <index file list> becomes the controlling index when **SET ORDER TO** <expN> is executed. If <expN> is specified as 0, or **SET ORDER TO** with no <expN> is used, the database file records are processed in natural (unindexed) order. **SET ORDER TO** does not close active index files. (See **SET INDEX,** above.)

SET PATH TO <path list>

Defines alternate DOS directory paths for dBASE to search if a file specified in an operation is not found in the current directory.

SET PRINT on / OFF

ON sends all output not formatted with @ **SAY,** @ **GET,** or presented in editing modes to the printer. **OFF** stops such output to the printer.

SET PROCEDURE TO [<filename>]

Declares and opens a command file (.PRG) as a procedure file. Only one procedure file per work area may be open at one time. **SET PROCEDURE TO** with no <filename> specified may be used to close a procedure file. (See **PROCEDURE,** page D-175.)

SET RELATION TO [<key exp>/<expN> **INTO** <alias>]

Links the movement of the record pointer in the database file open in the current work area to movement of the pointer in a database file open in another work area. The second database is identified by its <alias>. An <alias> may always be specified by its letter A through J. If the **ALIAS** <name> clause was included in the **USE** command when a database file was opened, the <name> also may be used as the <alias>; otherwise, the <filename> also may be used as the <alias>.

If <key exp> is used, it corresponds to the key of the index file in use with the second database file. If an <expN> is used, it is usually entered as **RECNO**( ) and pointer movement is based on record numbers of the second database file, which must not be indexed. Only one relation may be set from each work area. Using **SET RELATION TO** with no parameters removes any relation set in the current work area.

The following example uses a key expression to set a relationship.

```
          Work Area 1                             Work Area 2
          deptmail.dbf                            mailrout.dbf  (indexed on area)

Record#  EMPLOYEE        DEPT          Record#  AREA   MANAGER         MAILCODE
      1  Pratt John      Acct.               1  Pers.  Jacobs William  103
      2  Smoler Ellen    Sales               2  Sales  Butler John     107
      3  Jones David     Sales               3  Sctry  Branden Julia   101
      4  Sill Sally      Acct.               4  Acct.  Evans Claire    106
      5  Knat Michael    Pers.
      6  Smith Paul      Acct.
      7  Martins Mary    Sctry
      8  Nichols Sandy   Sctry
      9  Johnson Frank   Sales
```

```
. SELECT 1

. SET RELATION TO dept INTO mailrout

. LOCATE FOR employee = "Smith P"
Record =       6

. ? mailrout->manager,mailrout->mailcode,"   ATTN: ",employee
Evans Claire    106    ATTN:  Smith Paul

. LIST mailrout->manager,mailrout->mailcode,"   ATTN: ",employee
Record#  mailrout->manager mailrout->mailcode "   ATTN: " employee
      1  Evans Claire       106                  ATTN:     Pratt John
      2  Butler John        107                  ATTN:     Smoler Ellen
      3  Butler John        107                  ATTN:     Jones David
      4  Evans Claire       106                  ATTN:     Sill Sally
      5  Jacobs William     103                  ATTN:     Knat Michael
      6  Evans Claire       106                  ATTN:     Smith Paul
      7  Branden Julia      101                  ATTN:     Martins Mary
      8  Branden Julia      101                  ATTN:     Nichols Sandy
      9  Butler John        107                  ATTN:     Johnson Frank
```

SET SAFETY ON / off

OFF disables the "<filename> already exists, overwrite it? (Y/N)" message.

SET STATUS ON / off

Toggles **ON / off** the status bar displayed on line 22 of the monitor screen.

SET STEP on / OFF

ON aids debugging of a command file by causing dBASE to pause after executing each command in the file.

SET TALK ON / off

dBASE displays various messages associated with the execution of certain commands. **SET TALK OFF** stops display of the messages.

SET TITLE ON / off

Toggles **ON / off** the catalog file title prompt.

SET TYPEAHEAD TO <expN>

Sets the number of characters held in the keyboard buffer to <expN>. Normally 20 characters are held.

SET UNIQUE on / OFF

When **ON,** index files (.NDX) created with **INDEX ON** <expression> **TO** <index file> will include entries for only the first record of several records having the same key <expression>. (See **INDEX ON,** page D-165.)

SET VIEW TO <filename>

Opens a view file (.VUE) and reinstates the environment specified in it. (See **MODIFY VIEW,** page D-174.)

SKIP [–] [<expN>]

Moves the record pointer up or down in the current database file. The number of records to **SKIP** is defined by <expN>. To move backward, specify the [–] parameter. The default **SKIP** value is +1.

SORT [<scope>] **ON** <field1> **[/A] [/C] [/D]** [,<field2> **[/A] [/C] [/D]** . . .] **TO** <new file> [**FOR** <condition>] [**WHILE** <condition>]

Creates a new database file (.DBF) with the same structure as the database file in use and copies records to the new file in order of the data held in the <field>(s) specified. If several fields are used (up to 10), they must be separated with commas. Sorting is done in ascending order unless specified otherwise. The parameters **[/A], [/C],** and **[/D]** are used to specify ascending order, ignore upper/lower case difference, and descending order, respectively. The parameters [<scope>], [**FOR** <condition>], and [**WHILE** <condition>] may be used to limit the number of records sorted and copied to the new file. The default <scope> is **ALL** records.

STORE <expression> **TO** <memvar list>

Stores the value of an expression to one or more memory variables.

SUM <expN list> [**TO** <memvar list>] [<scope>] [**FOR** <condition>] [**WHILE** <condition>]

Computes the sum of the expressions in the expression list for the records in the database file in use and optionally stores the sums to the memory variables in its <memvar list>. The parameters [<scope>], [**FOR** <condi-

tion>], and [**WHILE** <condition>] may be used to limit the number of records summed. The default <scope> is **ALL** records.

```
. SUM salary,account TO fsal,facct FOR sex = "F"
      4 records summed
     salary      account
    6207.00       825.50

. DISPLAY MEMORY
FSAL         pub   N        6207.00  (      6207.00000000)
FACCT        pub   N         825.50  (       825.50000000)
    2 variables defined,       18 bytes used
  254 variables available,   5982 bytes available
```

SUSPEND

Used in command files (.PRG), **SUSPEND** is a debugging command used to temporarily halt the execution of a dBASE program and return to the dot (.) prompt mode. Commands then may be used to display or modify values of memory variables, and so forth. The command file remains open while suspended. **RESUME** may be used to continue suspended program execution. **CANCEL** may be used to cancel execution of the suspended program and close the file.

TEXT
<any data>
ENDTEXT

Used in command fields, allows text to be displayed (or printed) without the use of the @ **SAY** or **?** commands. dBASE treats all data between the **TEXT** and **ENDTEXT** commands as text to be output.

TOTAL ON <key field> **TO** <new file> [**FIELDS** <fieldN list>] [<scope>] [**FOR** <condition>] [**WHILE** <condition>]

Creates a new database file (.DBF) that will have only one record for each unique <key field> in the database file in use. Numeric fields will be totalled for each unique field in the database file in use, and the record in the new database file will hold the total. In the file created, fields of a type other than numeric will hold the data from the first record with the unique field. The database file in use must be indexed or sorted on the <key field> to be specified in the **TOTAL** command.

The [**FIELDS** <fieldN list>] parameter may be used to specify the numeric fields to be totalled to the new file (otherwise all numeric fields are totalled). The parameters [<scope>], [**FOR** <condition>], and [**WHILE** <condition>] may be used to limit the number of records totalled to the new file. The default <scope> is **ALL** records.

```
. USE empfile

. INDEX ON sex TO sexdex
  100% indexed          9 Records indexed

. TOTAL ON sex TO totfile1
      9 Record(s) totalled
      2 Records generated

. USE totfile1

. LIST
Record#  EMPLOYEE                  TELEPHONE SEX EMPLOYED   SALARY  ACCOUNT
      1  Smoler Ellen              225-3212  F   09/15/83  6207.00   825.50
      2  Pratt John                225-1234  M   06/22/82  8499.00   950.75
```

TYPE <filename.ext> [**TO PRINT**]

TYPE displays the contents of an unopened file. The **[TO PRINT]** parameter echoes screen output to the printer.

UPDATE ON <key field> **FROM** <alias> **REPLACE** <field1> **WITH** <exp1> [,<field2> **WITH** <exp2>, . . .] **[RANDOM]**

Allows batch update of a presorted or indexed database.

USE [<filename>] [**ALIAS** <name>] [**INDEX** <index file list>]

Specifies a database file (.DBF) to open for processing in the current work area. A database file may be opened in each of ten work areas; however, a file may only be opened in one area at any one time. **USE** <filename> closes any previous file in use in the current work area, and sets the record pointer to the first record in the file just opened. **USE** with no parameters closes the current database.

The [**ALIAS** <name>] parameter is used to specify a <name> which may be substituted for the standard aliases (A through J) when referring to the ten work areas (see **SELECT,** page D-180.) If the **ALIAS** <name> clause is not included, the <filename> is used as the alternate alias <name>. The [**INDEX** <index file list>] parameter may be used to specify previously created index files (.NDX) that are to be opened and in use with the database file (see **INDEX ON,** page D-165).

WAIT [expC] [**TO** <memvar>]

Used in command files, the **WAIT** command pauses execution of further commands in the file until a single keyboard character is typed. The character typed (if printable) is stored in the specified memory variable.

ZAP

Removes all records from the current database. Same as using the command **DELETE ALL** followed by the command **PACK.**

---

dBASE III PLUS FUNCTIONS

A dBASE function can be described as a shorthand method of accomplishing a specific task. A function is described as returning a value. The value returned often is determined by arguments (expressions) included within the syntax of a function. The general formats for dBASE functions are

NAME(<argument>)   **NAME**(<arg1>,<arg2>, . . .)   **NAME**( )

Functions begin with the function name, which will be shown here in bold upper-case letters. This is followed by a set of parentheses. If the function requires one or more arguments, the arguments are included inside the parentheses. If more than one argument is used with a function, commas are used to separate the arguments. If no arguments are required, the parentheses are included, but left empty.

Function arguments are valid dBASE expressions, which evaluate to numeric-type, character-type, date-type, or logical-type data, and are specified as <expN>, <expC>, <expD>, or <expL>, respectively, in the function syntax. Most functions require specific types of data as arguments and return a specific type of data. Some functions, however, can accept different data types as arguments and also may return different data types depending upon the arguments used.

Some examples of function syntax are given in the following table.

Function Syntax	Function Description	Data Type Returned
VAL(<expC>)	Character to Numeric conversion	Numeric
RIGHT(<expC>,<expN>)	Right substring	Character
CTOD(<expC>)	Character to Date conversion	Date
EOF( )	End-of-file	Logical
IIF(<expL>,<exp>,<exp>)	Immediate If Function	Any

ABS(<expN>)   Data Type Returned: Numeric

Absolute Value function Returns the positive value of a positive or negative numeric argument.

```
. ? ABS(45-55)
 10
```

ASC(<expC>)   Data Type Returned: Numeric

ASCII Code Function Returns the ASCII code number of the left-most character in the string<expC>. See "ASCII Character Codes" in appendix B for character code numbers.

```
. DISPLAY
Record#  EMPLOYEE                  TELEPHONE SEX EMPLOYED   SALARY  ACCOUNT
      1  Pratt John                225-1234  M   06/22/82  1949.00   200.00

. ? ASC(employee)                  ←The ASCII code for "P" is 80.
 80

. ? ASC(sex)                       ←The ASCII code for "M" is 77.
 77

. ? CHR(ASC(sex)+32)               ←The ASCII code for any capital letter
m                                   is 32 less than its lower-case
                                    equivalent.
```

AT(<expC1>,<expC2>) Data Type Returned: Numeric

Substring Search Function Returns the integer value equal to the position in <expC2> where the substring<expC1> occurs.

```
. GOTO 7

. DISPLAY
Record#  EMPLOYEE                TELEPHONE SEX EMPLOYED   SALARY  ACCOUNT
      7  Martins Mary            222-2123  F   11/01/85  1600.00   200.50

. ? AT("Mary",employee)
         9
```

BOF( ) Data Type Returned: Logical

Beginning-of-File Function Returns .T. (true) if an attempt has been made to **SKIP** backwards past the first record in a database file. Otherwise, returns .F. (false).

```
. GO TOP

. ? RECNO()
         1

. ? BOF()
.F.

. SKIP -1
Record No.       1

. ? BOF()
.T.
```

CDOW(<expD>) Data Type Returned: Character

Character Day-of-Week Function Returns the day of the week for a date expression argument.

```
. DISPLAY
Record#  EMPLOYEE                TELEPHONE SEX EMPLOYED   SALARY  ACCOUNT
      1  Pratt John              225-1234  M   06/22/82  1949.00   200.00

. ? CDOW(employed)
Tuesday

. ? CDOW(employed + 90)
Monday
```

CHR(<expN>) Data Type Returned: Character

Character String Function Returns the ASCII character 0 through 255 specified by the <expN> argument.

```
. ? CHR(65)
A

. ? CHR(65+32)
a
```

CMONTH(<expD>) Data Type Returned: Character

Character Month Function Returns the month name for a date expression argument.

```
. DISPLAY
Record#  EMPLOYEE                TELEPHONE SEX EMPLOYED   SALARY  ACCOUNT
      1  Pratt John              225-1234  M   06/22/82  1949.00   200.00

. ? CMONTH(employed + 100)
September

. ? employed + 100
09/30/82
```

COL( ) Data Type Returned: Numeric

Column Function Returns the current screen column position of the cursor.

CTOD(<expC>) Data Type Returned: Date

Character-to-Date Function Returns a date value from a character-type argument that is a valid date representation. The character expression must be in the order mm/dd/yy, but any character can separate the numbers used.

```
. DISPLAY
Record#  EMPLOYEE                TELEPHONE SEX EMPLOYED   SALARY  ACCOUNT
      1  Pratt John              225-1234  M   06/22/82  1949.00   200.00

. ? employed = CTOD("06-22-82")
.T.

. ? CTOD("01/01/84") - employed
       558
```

DATE( ) Data Type Returned: Date

Date Function Returns the DOS system date.

```
. ? DATE()
07/19/90
```

DAY(<expD>) Data Type Returned: Numeric

Day Function Returns the day of the month of a date expression argument.

```
. DISPLAY
Record#  EMPLOYEE                TELEPHONE SEX EMPLOYED   SALARY  ACCOUNT
      1  Pratt John              225-1234  M   06/22/82  1949.00   200.00

. ? DAY(employed)
 22
```

DBF( ) Data Type Returned: Character

Database Function Returns the filename of the current database file.

```
. ? DBF()
A:empfile.dbf
```

DELETED( ) Data Type Returned: Logical

Deleted Record Function Returns .T. (true) if the current record is marked for deletion.

```
. COUNT FOR DELETED()
      1 record

. LOCATE FOR DELETED()
Record =        7

. RECALL
      1 record recalled

. ? DELETED()
.F.
```

DISKSPACE( ) Data Type Returned: Numeric

Disk Space Function Returns the number of bytes (characters) of available disk space on the current drive.

```
. SET DEFAULT TO a:

. ? DISKSPACE()
   1161216
```

DOW(<expD>) Data Type Returned: Numeric

Day-of-Week Function Returns the day of the week number from a date expression argument. Numbers begin with Sunday = 1 and end with Saturday = 7.

```
. DISPLAY
Record#  EMPLOYEE                TELEPHONE SEX EMPLOYED   SALARY  ACCOUNT
      7  Martins Mary            222-2123  F   11/01/85  1600.00   200.50

. ? DOW(employed)
 6

. ? CDOW(employed)
Friday
```

DTOC(<expD>) Data Type Returned: Character

Date-to-Character Function Converts date-type data to character-type data.

```
. DISPLAY
Record#  EMPLOYEE                TELEPHONE SEX EMPLOYED   SALARY  ACCOUNT
      9  Johnson Frank           223-7928  M   03/20/90  1500.00     0.00

. STORE DTOC(employed+180) TO reviewdate
09/16/90

. ? "Memo: "+employee+" Six month review: "+reviewdate
Memo: Johnson Frank        Six month review: 09/16/90
```

EOF( ) Data Type Returned: Logical

End-of-File Function dBASE holds a dummy record at the end of a database file which has a record number one greater than the last actual record. **EOF**( ) returns .F. (false) if the record pointer is on an actual record and returns .T. (true) if the record pointer is moved past the last actual record to the dummy record.

```
. ? RECCOUNT()
         9

. GO BOTTOM

. DISPLAY
Record#  EMPLOYEE                TELEPHONE SEX EMPLOYED   SALARY  ACCOUNT
      9  Johnson Frank           223-7928  M   03/20/90  1500.00     0.00

. ? EOF()
.F.

. SKIP
Record No.      10

. ? EOF()
.T.
```

ERROR( ) Data Type Returned: Numeric

Error Number Function Returns the dBASE III Plus error number corresponding to the error trapped with an **ON ERROR** command.

EXP(<expN>) Data Type Returned: Numeric

Exponential Function Returns the value of e^x.

```
. ? EXP(1.000)
    2.718
```

FIELD(<expN>) Data Type Returned: Character

Field Name Function Returns a field name in the current database file where <expN> is the number of the field in the database file structure.

```
. ? FIELD(4)
EMPLOYED
```

FILE(<expC>) Data Type Returned: Logical

File Existence Function Returns .T. (true) if the file specified as <expC> exists. The argument <expC> is a character string which holds a file specification "[*drive:*][*path*]*filename.ext*" where the optional [*drive:*] and [*path*], if not specified, will default to the current drive and path.

```
. STORE "empfile.dbf" TO dbfname
empfile.dbf

. ? FILE(dbfname)
.T.

. ? FILE("namedex.ndx")
.T.
```

FKLABEL(<expN>) Data Type Returned: Character

Function Key Label Function Returns the character name of a programmable function key on the current system, where <expN> specifies the number of the function key. dBASE reserves the first function key F1 for the on-line **HELP** facility. Therefore, the first programmable function key is normally F2.

FKMAX( ) Data Type Returned: Numeric

Function Key Maximum Function Returns the maximum number of programmable function keys on the current system.

FOUND( ) Data Type Returned: Logical

Found Function Returns a logical .T. (true) if the previous search operation, **FIND, SEEK, LOCATE,** or **CONTINUE,** was successful.

GETENV(<expC>) Data Type Returned: Character

Get Environmental Variable Function Returns the contents of the operating system variable specified by <expC>.

IIF(<expL>,<exptrue>,<expfalse>) Data Type Returned: Any

Immediate IF Function Returns one of two values depending on the evaluation of a condition. The condition is the <expL> argument. The <exptrue> will be returned if the condition evaluates as true; otherwise, <expfalse> will be returned. The <exptrue> and <expfalse> arguments may be of any data type, but they must both be of the same type. Most useful for including conditional field output in dBASE III Plus **REPORT**s and **LABEL**s, the **IIF** function performs the same type of operation as an **IF... ELSE... ENDIF** structure in a command file.

```
. LIST employee,IIF(account<=.15*salary,"Ok","Over Limit")
Record#  employee              IIF(account<=.15*salary,"Ok","Over Limit")
      1  Pratt John            Ok
      2  Smoler Ellen          Over Limit
      3  Jones David           Over Limit
      4  Sill Sally            Ok
      5  Knat Michael          Ok
      6  Smith Paul            Over Limit
      7  Martins Mary          Ok
      8  Nichols Sandy         Ok
      9  Johnson Frank         Ok
```

You may nest **IIF** functions to create extended conditional tests. An example might be

IIF(<expL>,<exptrue>,**IIF**(<expL>,<exptrue>,<expfalse>))

Here, the <expfalse> of the first **IIF** function is another **IIF** function. This form of nested function works in the same manner as the following **IF** structure

IF condition
  true expression
ELSE
  IF condition
    true expression
  ELSE
    false expression
  ENDIF
ENDIF

In the next example the database empfile.DBF is used. The **IIF** function is one that could be included in a **REPORT** column to produce the following results: if the account amount is less than 12 percent of salary, output nothing; if the account amount is between 12 percent and 15 percent, output "Near Limit"; if the account amount is over 15 percent of salary, output "Over Limit by" x amount. Notice the **STR** function is used to convert the second **IIF** function's <expfalse> into the same data type as all other expressions used.

IIF(account < .12 * salary,"",**IIF**(account >= .12 * salary .AND. account < .15 * salary,"Near Limit","Over Limit by "+ **STR**(account − .15 * salary,5,2)))

INKEY( ) Data Type Returned: Numeric

Inkey Function Returns an integer (the ASCII value) representing the last key typed. This function is used in command files to trap user keystrokes and branch program execution accordingly.

INT(<expN>) Data Type Returned: Numeric

Integer Function Returns the integer value of the <expN> argument.

```
. STORE account/3 TO a

. STORE INT(account/3) TO b

. STORE INT(-4.3678) TO c

. DISPLAY MEMORY
A          pub   N        66.67  (        66.66666667)
B          pub   N        66  (        66.00000000)
C          pub   N        -4  (        -4.00000000)
   3 variables defined,      27 bytes used
 253 variables available,  5973 bytes available
```

ISALPHA(<expC>) Data Type Returned: Logical

Is Alphabetic Function Returns a logical .T. (true) if the character string argument begins with any upper-case or lower-case letter A through Z.

ISCOLOR( ) Data Type Returned: Logical

Is Color Mode Function Returns a logical .T. (true) if dBASE is running in a color mode.

ISLOWER(<expC>) Data Type Returned: Logical

Is Lowercase Function Returns a logical .T. (true) if the character string argument begins with a lower-case character (a through z).

ISUPPER(<expC>) Data Type Returned: Logical

Is Uppercase Function Returns a logical .T. (true) if the character string argument begins with an upper-case character (A through Z).

LEFT(<expC>,<lenN>) Data Type Returned: Character

Left Substring Function Returns the left-most characters of the character string argument <expC>. The numeric argument <lenN> determines the length of the substring to return.

```
. DISPLAY
Record#  EMPLOYEE              TELEPHONE SEX EMPLOYED   SALARY  ACCOUNT
      7  Martins Mary          222-2123  F   11/01/85  1600.00   200.50

. STORE LEFT(employee,7) TO lastname
Martins
```

LEN(<expC>) Data Type Returned: Numeric

Length Function Returns the number of characters in the <expC> argument.

```
. DISPLAY
Record#  EMPLOYEE              TELEPHONE SEX EMPLOYED   SALARY  ACCOUNT
      7  Martins Mary          222-2123  F   11/01/85  1600.00   200.50

. ? LEN(employee)
        20

. ? LEN(TRIM(employee))
        12
```

LOG(<expN>) Data Type Returned: Numeric

Logarithm Function Returns the natural logarithm of <expN>.

```
. ? LOG(2.71828)
1.00000
```

LOWER(<expC>) Data Type Returned: Character

Lowercase Function Returns the <expC> character string with all alphabetic characters converted to lower case.

```
. DISPLAY
Record#  EMPLOYEE                TELEPHONE SEX EMPLOYED   SALARY  ACCOUNT
      7  Martins Mary            222-2123  F   11/01/85  1600.00   200.50

. ? LOWER(employee)
martins mary
```

LTRIM(<expC>) Data Type Returned: Character

Left Trim Function Returns the <expC> character string argument with any leading spaces removed.

```
. ? STR(account)
       200

. ? LTRIM(STR(account))
200
```

LUPDATE( ) Data Type Returned: Date

Last Update Function Returns the system date recorded for the last time the current database was updated.

MAX(<expN1>,<expN2>) Data Type Returned: Numeric

Maximum Function Returns the argument <expN1> or <expN2> that has the highest numeric value.

MESSAGE( ) Data Type Returned: Character

Error Message Function Returns the dBASE III Plus error message corresponding to the error trapped with an **ON ERROR** command.

```
. ON ERROR STORE MESSAGE() TO z

. sdsad
*** Unrecognized command verb.

. DISPLAY MEMORY
Z           pub   C  "*** Unrecognized command verb."
   1 variables defined,      32 bytes used
  255 variables available,   5968 bytes available
```

MIN(<expN1>,<expN2>) Data Type Returned: Numeric

Minimum Function Returns the argument <expN1> or <expN2> that has the lowest numeric value.

MOD(<expN1>, <expN2>) Data Type Returned: Numeric

Modulus Function Returns the remainder resulting from dividing the first argument <expN1> by the second argument <expN2>.

MONTH(<expD>) Data Type Returned: Numeric

Month Function Returns the month number from a date expression argument.

```
. ? MONTH(employed)
  6

. ? CMONTH(employed)
June
```

NDX(<expN>) Data Type Returned: Character

Index File Function Returns the character string *"drive:filename.ext"* for an index file in use in the current work area. The <expN> argument determines which index name to return when several are in use.

OS( ) Data Type Returned: Character

Operating System Function Returns the name of the current operating system.

PCOL( ) Data Type Returned: Numeric

Printer Column Function Returns the current column position of the printer.

PROW( ) Data Type Returned: Numeric

Printer Row Function Returns the current row position of the printer.

READKEY( ) Data Type Returned: Numeric

Read Key Function Returns an integer (the ASCII value) for the last keystroke typed while in a full-screen editing mode.

RECCOUNT( ) Data Type Returned: Numeric

Record Count Function Returns the number of records in the current database.

RECNO( ) Data Type Returned: Numeric

Record Number Function Returns the integer value equal to the current record number.

```
. GO TOP

. LIST WHILE RECNO() < 4
Record#  EMPLOYEE                     TELEPHONE SEX EMPLOYED   SALARY  ACCOUNT
      1  Pratt John                   225-1234  M   06/22/82  1949.00   200.00
      2  Smoler Ellen                 225-3212  F   09/15/83  1650.00   300.00
      3  Jones David                  292-3832  M   06/15/82  1550.00   275.75

. ? RECNO()
         4
```

RECSIZE( ) Data Type Returned: Numeric

Record Size Function Returns the record size (number of bytes) for the records in the current database.

REPLICATE(<expC>,<expN>) Data Type Returned: Character

Replicate Function Returns a character string in which the <expC> argument is repeated <expN> number of times.

```
. ? REPLICATE("<>",25)
<><><><><><><><><><><><><><><><><><><><><><><><><>
```

RIGHT(<expC>,<expN>) Data Type Returned: Character

Right Substring Function Returns the right-most characters of the character string argument <expC>. The numeric argument <expN> determines the length of the substring to return.

```
. STORE TRIM(employee) TO name
Sill Sally

. STORE RIGHT(name,5) TO fname
Sally
```

ROUND(<expN>,<decN>) Data Type Returned: Numeric

Round Function Rounds the numeric value <expN> to <decN> number of decimal places. Rounds to the left of the decimal if <decN> is negative.

```
. DISPLAY
Record#  EMPLOYEE                  TELEPHONE SEX EMPLOYED   SALARY  ACCOUNT
     3  Jones David               292-3832  M   06/15/82  1550.00   275.75

. ? ROUND(account,0)
   276.00

. ? ROUND(salary,-2)
  1600.00
```

ROW( ) Data Type Returned: Numeric

Row Function Returns the current screen row position of the cursor.

RTRIM(<expC>) Data Type Returned: Character

Right Trim Function Returns the <expC> character string argument with any trailing spaces removed. (Same as the **TRIM** function.)

SPACE(<expN>) Data Type Returned: Character

Space Function Returns a string of spaces equal in length to the <expN> argument.

```
. STORE SPACE(LEN(employee)) TO name

. @ ROW(),45 GET name
. READ
```

SQRT(<expN>) Data Type Returned: Numeric

Square Root Function Returns the square root of the <expN> argument.

STR(<expN>[,<lenN>] [,<decN>]) Data Type Returned: Character

Numeric-to-String Function Returns a character string converted from a numeric expression. The argument <expN> is returned as a character string <lenN> characters long, with <decN> number of decimal places.

Most useful for deleting leading spaces in output of numeric data and/or forcing the display of desired decimal places.

```
. DISPLAY
Record#  EMPLOYEE                TELEPHONE SEX EMPLOYED   SALARY  ACCOUNT
      7  Martins Mary            222-2123  F   11/01/85  1600.00   200.50

. ? employee," - Limit = ",salary*.15
Martins Mary           - Limit =      240.0000

. ? TRIM(employee)," - Limit = ",STR(salary*.15,6,2)
Martins Mary  - Limit =  240.00
```

STUFF(<expC1>,<startN>,<lenN>,<expC2>) Data Type Returned: Character

Substring Replace Function Replaces or inserts the second character string argument <expC2> into the first character string argument <expC1>, starting at position <startN> in <expC1>. The argument <lenN> determines how many characters in <expC1> to replace, if any. The full string <expC2> is inserted, regardless of the <lenN> being replaced.

```
. STORE "This is a test" TO string1
This is a test

. STORE STUFF(string1,10,0,"nother") TO string2
This is another test

. STORE STUFF(string2,9,7,"NOT a") TO string3
This is NOT a test
```

SUBSTR(<expC>,<startN>,<lenN>) Data Type Returned: Character

Substring Function Returns the portion of the character string <expC> argument, beginning at position <startN> and <lenN> characters in length.

```
. DISPLAY
Record#  EMPLOYEE                TELEPHONE SEX EMPLOYED   SALARY  ACCOUNT
      7  Martins Mary            222-2123  F   11/01/85  1600.00   200.50

. ? SUBSTR(employee,9,4)
Mary
```

TIME( ) Data Type Returned: Character

Time Function Returns the system time in the format hh:mm:ss.

TRANSFORM(<exp>,<pictureC>) Data Type Returned: Character

Transform Function Formats the <exp> argument using a **PICTURE** template defined by the <pictureC> argument. Using the same template characters as the @ **SAY** command, this function allows data formatting with other display commands. The <exp> argument may be of any data type.

```
. STORE account - .15 * salary TO ovrlimit
      43.2500

. ? "Your account is over the limit by $" + TRANSFORM(ovrlimit,"999.99") + "!!"
Your account is over the limit by $ 43.25!!
```

TRIM(<expC>) Data Type Returned: Character

Trim Function Returns the <expC> character string argument with any trailing spaces removed.

```
. DISPLAY
Record#  EMPLOYEE                TELEPHONE SEX EMPLOYED   SALARY  ACCOUNT
      7  Martins Mary            222-2123  F   11/01/85  1600.00   200.50

. ? employee,telephone
Martins Mary         222-2123

. ? TRIM(employee),telephone
Martins Mary 222-2123
```

TYPE(<expC>) Data Type Returned: Character

Data Type Function Returns a one-character evaluation "C," "N," "D," "L," "M," or "U" for character, numeric, date, logical, memo, or undefined, respectively, of the <expC> argument. The <expC> must be a literal string enclosed in quotes naming the data item to be checked, or a character expression that evaluates to the name of the data item.

```
. ? TYPE("employee")
C

. ? TYPE("salary")
N

. ? TYPE("account < .15 * salary")
L

. STORE "employed" TO fname

. ? TYPE(fname)
D

. ? TYPE("fname")
C

. RELEASE fname

. ? TYPE("fname")
U
```

UPPER(<expC>) Data Type Returned: Character

Uppercase Function Returns the <expC> character string with all alphabetic characters converted to upper case.

```
. DISPLAY
Record#  EMPLOYEE             TELEPHONE SEX EMPLOYED   SALARY  ACCOUNT
      7  Martins Mary         222-2123  F   11/01/85  1600.00   200.50

. ? UPPER(employee)
MARTINS MARY
```

VAL(<expC>) Data Type Returned: Numeric

Character-to-Value Function Returns the numeric value of numbers held as strings beginning at the first character of the <expC> argument.

```
. ? VAL("7312 S.W. Fulton Park Blvd.")
                     7312.00

. ? VAL("P.O. Box 7312")
          0.00
```

VERSION( ) Data Type Returned: Character

Version Function Returns the version of dBASE III Plus currently in use.

YEAR(<expD>) Data Type Returned: Numeric

Year Function Returns the year number of the <expD> date expression argument.

```
. DISPLAY
Record#  EMPLOYEE             TELEPHONE SEX EMPLOYED   SALARY  ACCOUNT
      7  Martins Mary         222-2123  F   11/01/85  1600.00   200.50

. ? YEAR(employed)
 1985
```

Data Transfer Between Applications Software

DATA TRANSFER BETWEEN APPLICATIONS

Suppose you have a report to submit that includes a Lotus 1-2-3 spreadsheet and you want the printed spreadsheet to appear in the body of a text file produced by WordPerfect. Or, maybe you have selected output produced by dBASE III Plus and want that information included in a WordPerfect text file. Perhaps you want to use the editing capabilities of WordPerfect to create a database for dBASE III Plus, or you want to use a Lotus spreadsheet to create the database for dBASE III Plus. What if you want to use WordPerfect or dBASE III Plus to create documentation or data for a Lotus 1-2-3 spreadsheet? All of this and more is possible because you can transfer data between applications software. The examples here use the applications software covered in this manual, but the fundamentals and basic procedures discussed will be similar for other applications software.

ASCII DATA FORMAT

The primary key to transferring data from one type of software to another lies in each software's ability to create and accept data stored in the American Standard Code for Information Interchange or ASCII (pronounced "as-key"). This data format standard was established specifically for the types of tasks mentioned earlier—tasks that involve the interchange of information or data.

For computer users (as opposed to computer programmers or data processing professionals) it is less important to know exactly what ASCII data formatting is than to know how it can be used and how to identify ASCII files.

NOTE: For this section's intended purpose, ASCII files are defined as files including only those characters numbered 13 and 32 to 126 inclusive.

Identifying ASCII Files

The procedure for identifying an ASCII file is straightforward. At the DOS level you use the **TYPE** command to list the contents of the file on the monitor screen. If every character of data that appears on the screen is a standard keyboard character, the file is stored in ASCII data format. If not, it is not stored in ASCII.

Software-Produced ASCII Files

Knowing whether or not you are creating an ASCII file is not as simple as identifying one after it has been created. Different software manuals, commands, and so forth, refer to ASCII files with different terminology. WordPerfect refers to the ASCII files that it creates as being *DOS Text files*. dBASE III Plus refers to ASCII files as being *SDF (System Data Format)* files.

The following is a list of the ASCII files created by the software covered in this manual. It indicates each software's ability to accept files for processing.

Lotus 1-2-3 ASCII Files

Lotus produces only its .PRN (Print files) in ASCII data format. These files are created by printing a range of the spreadsheet to a file using the /**P**rint,**F**ile command. Lotus 1-2-3 readily accepts any ASCII file into its spreadsheets through its /**F**ile,**I**mport command.

WordPerfect ASCII Files

WordPerfect will save its document files in ASCII if the proper procedures are used. The **Ctrl-F5** (Text In/Out),DOS **T**ext,**S**ave command may be used to save the current document in ASCII format.

Any ASCII format file may be directly retrieved into WordPerfect using the **Shift-F10** (Retrieve) command. The file, however, will be immediately converted to WordPerfect data format and rewritten to the current document format settings (margins, line spacing, etc.).

dBASE III Plus ASCII Files

dBASE maintains several of its file types in ASCII format. dBASE .PRG command files are stored in ASCII data format, as are its .TXT files. Its .DBF database files are not kept in ASCII, but a copy of a database in ASCII format can be easily made by using the **COPY TO** <filename> [**SDF**] command. When a copy of a database is made this way, it is given a .TXT extension. In addition, any nonediting screen output generated by a dBASE operation can be written to an ASCII file by using the **SET ALTERNATE TO** <filename> and **SET ALTERNATE ON** commands. The files created in this manner also are given a .TXT extension.

To read ASCII files into a database, the **APPEND FROM** <filename.TXT> [**TYPE SDF**] command is used. In addition, any file dBASE normally maintains in ASCII can be produced by another software and still be used by dBASE III Plus.

In general, the commands of dBASE III Plus are very effective for moving data between dBASE and other software.

DOS ASCII Files

DOS does not actually produce ASCII files itself. However, with versions of DOS 2.0+, DOS can redirect another software's output to an ASCII file as long as the software uses the DOS function calls for its output and does not generate non-ASCII characters as output. This feature of DOS (called "piping") can be most useful for canned programs written in a programming language. To cause this redirection (more accurately called an echo) of output, you use one or two greater than (>) signs followed by the ASCII file's filename when you load the software. A single > erases any previous ASCII file with the same filename, while two >s append output to any previous file with the same filename. For example, typing

```
A> C:BASICA LINPRO>>testout
```

loads IBM's BASICA programming language and the BASICA program LINPRO.BAS into RAM, and begins running the program. If the file testout does not yet exist, it is created. As the program LINPRO.BAS runs, all output that occurs on the screen is echoed to (printed to) the disk file testout. If testout previously existed, the data printed to it are appended (added at the bottom). Typing the **SYSTEM** command after the program is through executing completes the printing of data to the ASCII file and closes it.

Data Structure

Understanding the basics of data structure is the second key to transferring data between software. For software able to process both strings and numbers, data structure means incoming data is kept in units of data items. The items are separated from each other (delimited) in a way that differentiates the string-type data from the numeric-type data.

The rest of this section presents procedures for specific types of data transfer between software, and describes instances where the process may prove useful. The section provides details about how the data must be structured in each case. As you progress through the material, many principles of data structure will become apparent, enabling you to perform data transfer operations not covered.

CREATING dBASE .PRG COMMAND FILES USING WORDPERFECT

dBASE .PRG command files may be created using WordPerfect rather than the **MODIFY COMMAND** text editing mode of dBASE.

Benefits

The **MODIFY COMMAND** text editing mode (when compared to the editing mode(s) of a word processing software) is limited and often cumbersome to use. Some features of WordPerfect that are useful when creating .PRG files include the following: the **Alt-F2** (Replace) command for changing variable names throughout a program; the cut-and-paste block operations for making copies of repetitious code; the **Shift-F3** (Switch) command for easily creating two .PRG files at the same time; the **Shift-F8** (Format),**L**ine,**T**ab Set command for setting tabs appropriate for structured style; and, in certain types of .PRG files such as form letters, the **Ctrl-F2** (Spell) command for checking portions of text within the program for spelling errors.

Procedure

After loading WordPerfect, set the left margin to 0" and the right margin to 25.4" by inserting a [L/R Mar:] code at the top of the document with the **Shift-F8** (Format),**L**ine,**M**argins command. Next type the lines of the program. Make sure to end each program line with a hard return by typing ↵. When finished, use the **Ctrl-F5** (Text In/Out),DOS **T**ext,**S**ave command to save the file in ASCII format. When saving the file, include the .PRG filename extension in the specified filename.

Comments

The name you give the file must have the appropriate filename extension (.PRG) for the program to be later executed by dBASE. You either can give the file its appropriate name when you create it, or you can use the **RENAME** command of DOS to change it later. Each line of a dBASE III Plus program written in WordPerfect must end with a hard return (↵).

LOTUS 1-2-3 SPREADSHEETS INTO WORDPERFECT

When the Lotus 1-2-3 /**F**ile,**S**ave command is used, Lotus creates a non-ASCII disk file (.WK1 extension) containing the cell locations and contents of the current spreadsheet. When the Lotus 1-2-3 /**P**rint,**F**ile command is used, Lotus creates an ASCII disk file (.PRN) that contains the output (display) of the current spreadsheet.

Spreadsheet Data File (.WK1)

```
B3: 'Month
C3: "Sales
D3: "COGS
E3: "Net
B4: \-
C4: \-
D4: \-
E4: \-
B5: 'January
C5: 1250
D5: 0.65*C5
E5: +C5-D5
B6: 'February
C6: 1330
D6: 0.65*C6
E6: +C6-D6
B7: 'March
C7: 1410
D7: 0.65*C7
E7: +C7-D7
B8: 'April
C8: 1400
D8: 0.65*C8
E8: +C8-D8
```

Spreadsheet Print File (.PRN)

```
Month           Sales       COGS        Net
-------------------------------------------
January    $1,250.00    $812.50    $437.50
February   $1,330.00    $864.50    $465.50
March      $1,410.00    $916.50    $493.50
April      $1,400.00    $910.00    $490.00
```

The file shown on the left in the above example shows what a Lotus .WK1 file would look like if it were saved in ASCII format. The spreadsheet data file is used by Lotus to reconstruct a saved spreadsheet in RAM each time the file is loaded with the /**F**ile,**R**etrieve command. The .WK1 file contains the actual data entered from the keyboard or copied into other cells of the spreadsheet by the user. A file created from the same spreadsheet by using the /**F**ile,**P**rint command to print a spreadsheet to a file is shown on the right. Lotus gives such files a .PRN filename extension. This file contains the processed data, or output, generated by the software. It appears the same in this file as it appears on the monitor screen, or on paper when the spreadsheet is printed. An important difference between the two is that a Print file cannot be loaded back into a spreadsheet by Lotus. It is output that, instead of being printed on a piece of paper, was printed on the disk under its own filename in ASCII data format. If you use a word processor to open the Print file for editing, and then change one of its key values, the rest of the spreadsheet will not recalculate.

With WordPerfect, files can be merged by simply retrieving one file into another. When a file is retrieved, it will be inserted into any existing text at the location of the cursor. Any ASCII file may be inserted into a WordPerfect document in this manner.

Benefits

Using a spreadsheet to produce computed values from formulas, printing the results to a Print file, and then reading them into a WordPerfect text file has many practical applications. Corporate reports, term papers, billings, invoices, budgets, appraisals, and estimates are just some of the instances when such a procedure can be useful.

Procedure

Print the desired area of the spreadsheet to the disk with the /**P**rint,**F**ile command (you may want to set its automatic margins top, bottom, and left to zero). Load WordPerfect and then retrieve the document file into which you want to place the spreadsheet output. Move the editing cursor to the location where the spreadsheet data are to appear and then retrieve the .PRN file. Or, you may simply retrieve the .PRN file and edit around it with WordPerfect. In either case, you will need to specify the whole filename, including its extension, to retrieve the .PRN file for editing.

Comments

It is important to note that when you create a .PRN file using the /**P**rint,**F**ile command of Lotus, you must exit the command by using **Q**uit. Using the Esc key to back out of the /**P**rint commands will result in an empty .PRN file.

dBASE III PLUS DATA INTO WORDPERFECT

dBASE III Plus creates several different types of files, each of which has its own type of filename extension. The .PRG (command files) and .TXT (text files) created by dBASE III are ASCII files. As such, they may be retrieved by WordPerfect for editing and then saved onto the disk in "DOS Format" for use again by dBASE. The procedure is the same as writing a dBASE program in WordPerfect.

dBASE has commands designed specifically for creating ASCII text files (to which it gives a .TXT extension). The files contain copies of screen output created from a dBASE operation, or fields of data in a .DBF database file.

The dBASE commands used to create ASCII files of screen output are

SET ALTERNATE TO <filename>
SET ALTERNATE ON
SET ALTERNATE OFF

First, the .TXT file is created with the **SET ALTERNATE TO** <filename>. After the file is created, the command **SET ALTERNATE ON** will begin writing (echoing) all output appearing on the monitor screen (with the exception of output generated in a full-screen editing mode) to the .TXT file.

The command **SET ALTERNATE OFF** stops the writing of data to the .TXT file. The command **SET ALTERNATE TO,** without a filename specified, or the command **QUIT,** closes the .TXT file.

To create an ASCII .TXT file copy of the fields of data occurring in a database, the following command may be used.

COPY TO <filename> **TYPE SDF**

Once the .TXT file has been created, it may be opened for editing or retrieved into an existing document file with WordPerfect's **Shift-F10** (Retrieve) command.

Benefits

dBASE has commands capable of very precise formatting of output for both the screen and printer, but these commands generally are used in command files for reports produced often. When a single report requiring a specific format is needed, or before you have the time, expertise, and/or patience to write the necessary command file, letting dBASE generate the raw data and then using WordPerfect to manipulate the data into its final form can be the most effective and efficient means of producing the desired product.

Procedure

Type the dBASE commands **SET ALTERNATE TO** <filename> and **SET ALTERNATE ON,** respectively. Type the commands to generate the desired data on the monitor screen, and then use the command **SET ALTERNATE OFF** to stop writing to the .TXT file. To obtain an ASCII copy of a database, type the command **COPY TO** <filename> **TYPE SDF.** Be sure to type **QUIT** to close any .TXT files that may be left open when you are finished with dBASE.

The .TXT file may be opened for editing or retrieved into an existing document file with WordPerfect's **Shift-F10** (Retrieve) command.

Comments

dBASE III Plus seems designed to work quite effectively with word processing software, and few (if any) problems occur when these procedures are followed.

SPREADSHEETS INTO A dBASE III DATABASE

It is possible to use the spreadsheet applications to create records for a dBASE III Plus database. The dBASE command used to read an ASCII file into a database is

APPEND FROM <filename.ext> **TYPE SDF**

When dBASE appends records this way, it looks to the file being appended from for the number of characters equal to the length of the fields defined in that database's record structure. So, if the database's record structure has three fields, each nine characters long, it will append the first nine characters found in the text file into the first field of the first record, the second nine characters found into the second field of the first record, and so on. The text file must have spaces included when the data for a field does not fill the field. With spreadsheet applications this is usually not a problem. Their Print files are text files set up ideally for appending into a database. Each cell in the spreadsheet is read in as a field of data, and the cells are read from the printed spreadsheet, left to right, top to bottom. Using a previous example

Lotus .PRN File

```
Month          Sales       COGS        Net
------------------------------------------
January      1250.00     812.50     437.50
February     1330.00     864.50     465.50
March        1410.00     916.50     493.50
April        1400.00     910.00     490.00
```

an appropriate database structure would be created as

dBASE Record Structure

	Field Name	Type	Width	Dec
1	MONTH	Character	9	
2	SALES	Numeric	9	2
3	COGS	Numeric	9	2
4	NET	Numeric	9	2

Notice that the currency formatting ($ and , characters) were removed from the spreadsheet display before the Print file was created. dBASE requires that numeric data appended to fields in a database are free of such notations. Also notice that the first two rows of labels found in the .PRN file are not what you would want to (or could) enter into the first and second records of the database. Therefore, you either would (1) not print them to the file or (2) retrieve the Print file with WordPerfect, delete the first two rows (lines), and then save the file as a DOS **T**ext File.

From dBASE, after having created the database's structure, typing the command **APPEND FROM** <filename.PRN> **TYPE SDF** would result in a small database with records containing the following data.

Record No. 1

MONTH	January
SALES	1250.00
COGS	812.50
NET	437.50

Record No. 2

MONTH	February
SALES	1330.00
COGS	864.50
NET	465.50

Record No. 3

MONTH	March
SALES	1410.00
COGS	916.50
NET	493.50

Record No. 4

MONTH	April
SALES	1400.00
COGS	910.00
NET	490.00

Benefits

Many of the benefits mentioned in the previous section apply to the reading of spreadsheet Print files into dBASE as records of a database. Operations such as multilevel sorting, substring searches for reporting, and others, are operations that dBASE is designed to do. Also, the use of spreadsheet formulas and the /**C**opy commands often make creating record-type data a quick and easy process, and the ability to more easily edit a database as you create it is often desired.

Procedure

Enter the fields of data into individual spreadsheet cells so that each row in the spreadsheet contains the fields of data for one record. (This arrangement of data is called "row major," and the same organization is used for performing Lotus's /**D**ata,**Q**uery operations.) Set the column widths in the spreadsheet to be the same widths as the intended field widths in the intended database. Usually you will want to write the column width numbers down at this point since it is important that the two widths (column and field) are identical when you create the dBASE record structure. Then use the /**P**rint,**F**ile commands to set the left, top, and bottom margins to 0 and then print only the record data found in the spreadsheet out to a .PRN file.

Load dBASE III Plus. Then use the **CREATE** command to define the intended database's structure. Remember that the field widths must accurately reflect the Lotus column widths. Next use the dBASE command **APPEND FROM** <filename.PRN> **TYPE SDF** to append the spreadsheet data into the database.

Comments

It is important to note that when you create a .PRN file using the /**P**rint,**F**ile command, you must exit the /**P**rint commands by using the **Q**uit command. Using the Esc key to back out of the /**P**rint command results in an empty .PRN file on the disk.

You should note that as long as the data are organized in the same manner as a row major spreadsheet .PRN file, you can use WordPerfect and its **Ctrl-F5** (Text In/Out),DOS **T**ext,**S**ave command to create records for a dBASE database file.

WORDPERFECT FILES INTO A LOTUS 1-2-3 SPREADSHEET

To accept other software's data, Lotus's /**F**ile,**I**mport command is used. The first step in using this command is choosing the option to import a file as either **T**ext or **N**umbers.

Importing Unstructured Data

If **T**ext is specified, the file being imported into the current spreadsheet will be entered into one column of cells, beginning at the current pointer location and continuing down, with each line of the imported file entered as a Label into a cell of the column.

In the case of a WordPerfect DOS Text file, data being imported into Lotus will exist as extended labels in the spreadsheet. For instance, the previous paragraph was made into its own WordPerfect file when it was at the manuscript stage. It appeared in WordPerfect as

```
If Text is specified, the file being imported into the current
spreadsheet will be entered into one column of cells, beginning at
the current pointer location and continuing down, with each line
of the imported file entered as a Label into a cell of the column.
```

The file then was saved with the **Ctrl-F5** (Text In/Out),DOS **T**ext command (adding a .PRN extension to the name when it was saved) and WordPerfect was exited. Next, Lotus was loaded and while the spreadsheet pointer was located on cell A1, the /**F**ile,**I**mport,**T**ext command was used to import the paragraph into the spreadsheet.

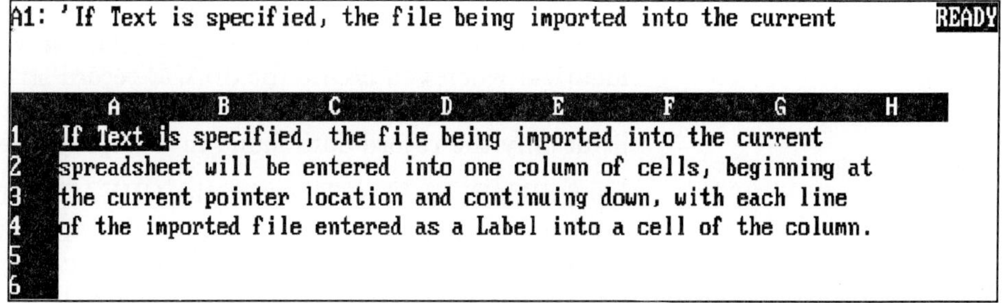

```
A1: 'If Text is specified, the file being imported into the current        READY

      A         B         C         D         E         F         G         H
1   If Text is specified, the file being imported into the current
2   spreadsheet will be entered into one column of cells, beginning at
3   the current pointer location and continuing down, with each line
4   of the imported file entered as a Label into a cell of the column.
5
6
```

The paragraph was imported one line at a time into the cells A1 through A4. Each label extends to the right of the A column as long as the spreadsheet cells to the right remained blank. If spreadsheet data had existed in cells A1 through A4 before the **I**mport command operation, they would have been replaced by the imported data.

The second step of the /**F**ile,**I**mport command requests the filename of the file to import. Lotus will only import a file if it has a .PRN filename extension. Therefore, before attempting to import a file into a Lotus spreadsheet, you may need to use the **RENAME** command of DOS (or a renaming command of another software) to make sure the file you are importing has this file extension.

Importing Structured Data

When the data being imported into the spreadsheet are intended to be separated into different cells, the /**D**ata,**P**arse command may be used after the import operation. The command makes it possible to import ASCII files with a row major organization into the spreadsheet, and then separate the fields into columns of cells having different data types. To demonstrate the operations involved in parsing data, the following example will be used. The example is based on a WordPerfect DOS Text file document listing the names, phone numbers, donations, and donation dates for companies contributing to a charity.

```
Cantrell Industries     (503) 235-7164     $1,000     03/20/90
Allstrong Inc.          (206) 643-1877     $1,500     04/15/90
Willamette Hardware     (503) 227-8739     $1,500     06/08/90
Chase Supplies          (503) 244-9983     $2,000     05/07/90
```

The file is saved as a DOS Text file under the name donors.PRN, or may be renamed later to include the .PRN extension by using DOS's **RENAME** command. The file then is imported into a Lotus spreadsheet using the /**F**ile,**I**mport,**T**ext command. Each line of the file is placed as an extended label into a cell of the A column.

```
A3: 'Cantrell Industries        (503) 235-7164      $1,000      03/20/90        READY

       A         B         C         D         E         F         G         H
1
2
3   Cantrell Industries       (503) 235-7164     $1,000     03/20/90
4   Allstrong Inc.            (206) 643-1877     $1,500     04/15/90
5   Willamette Hardware       (503) 227-8739     $1,500     06/08/90
6   Chase Supplies            (503) 244-9983     $2,000     05/07/90
7
8
```

With the pointer on the top-left cell of the data range (cell A3), the /**D**ata,**P**arse command is next entered. The menu for parsing data includes

```
Format-Line  Input-Column  Output-Range  Reset  Go  Quit
```

The first step in the example is to establish a **F**ormat-Line for parsing the data. When the **F**ormat-Line menu option is selected, the options to **C**reate or **E**dit are given. In the example, **C**reate is selected.

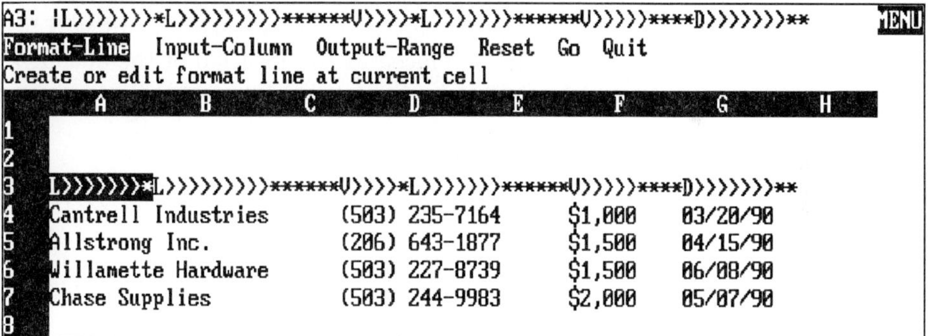

```
A3: |L>>>>>>>*L>>>>>>>>>******V>>>>*L>>>>>>>******V>>>>>****D>>>>>>>**          MENU
Format-Line  Input-Column  Output-Range  Reset  Go  Quit
Create or edit format line at current cell
       A         B         C         D         E         F         G         H
1
2
3   L>>>>>>>*L>>>>>>>>>******V>>>>*L>>>>>>>******V>>>>>****D>>>>>>>**
4   Cantrell Industries       (503) 235-7164     $1,000     03/20/90
5   Allstrong Inc.            (206) 643-1877     $1,500     04/15/90
6   Willamette Hardware       (503) 227-8739     $1,500     06/08/90
7   Chase Supplies            (503) 244-9983     $2,000     05/07/90
8
```

The line inserted by Lotus above the data is a "best guess" format-line based on the first line of data in the range. The format-line is used by Lotus to decide which data will be put in which cell and the type of data it will be (label, value, or date in this example) when the subsequent parsing is complete. The characters of the format-line shown here have the following meaning:

L	The first character of the data block is a label.
V	The first character of the data block is a value.
D	The first character of the data block is a date.
>	The character beneath is the same as the first character in the data block.
*	There is no character beneath, but one may occur in other records.

The second **F**ormat-Line option is to **E**dit. This option may be used to manually edit the characters occurring in a format-line. In the example, the format-line is edited to make the following changes. The first and second names of the companies will be put in the same cell, and the area code will be entered as a label instead of a value and will be put in the same cell as the rest of the phone number.

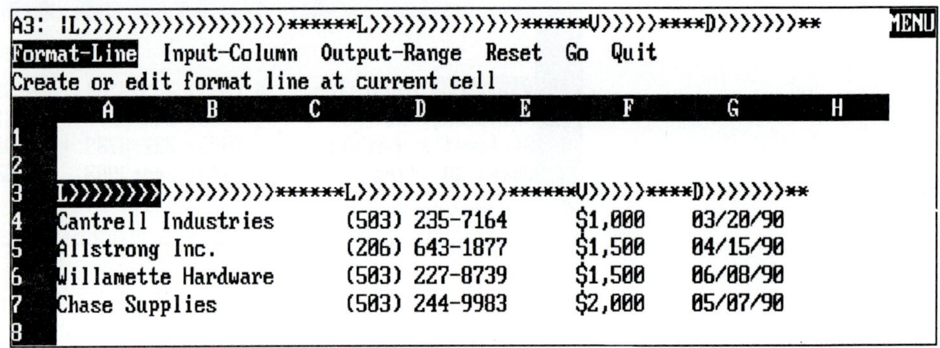

```
A3: ¦L>>>>>>>>>>>>>>>>>>>******L>>>>>>>>>>>>>>******V>>>>>****D>>>>>>>**      MENU
Format-Line  Input-Column  Output-Range  Reset  Go  Quit
Create or edit format line at current cell
      A         B         C         D         E         F         G         H
1
2
3   L>>>>>>>>>>>>>>>>>>>******L>>>>>>>>>>>>>>******V>>>>>****D>>>>>>>**
4   Cantrell Industries        (503) 235-7164        $1,000     03/20/90
5   Allstrong Inc.             (206) 643-1877        $1,500     04/15/90
6   Willamette Hardware        (503) 227-8739        $1,500     06/08/90
7   Chase Supplies             (503) 244-9983        $2,000     05/07/90
8
```

The next step is to specify the **I**nput-Column for parsing. The input-column is defined as all cells of the column containing the imported record-type data plus the cell containing the format-line. The last range to specify is the **O**utput-Range. The output-range is entered as the top-left cell of the range into which the parsed data will be copied. In this example, the output-range will be cell A10.

Once the steps have been accomplished, the **G**o command of the /**D**ata,**P**arse commands may be executed. The result will be a copy of the data originally imported, placed at the location of the output-range, with each block of data, as defined by the format-line, copied into an individual cell as a specific data type.

```
A3: ¦L>>>>>>>>>>>>>>>>>>>******L>>>>>>>>>>>>>>******V>>>>>****D>>>>>>>**     READY


      A         B         C         D         E         F         G         H
1
2
3   L>>>>>>>>>>>>>>>>>>>******L>>>>>>>>>>>>>>******V>>>>>****D>>>>>>>**
4   Cantrell Industries        (503) 235-7164        $1,000     03/20/90
5   Allstrong Inc.             (206) 643-1877        $1,500     04/15/90
6   Willamette Hardware        (503) 227-8739        $1,500     06/08/90
7   Chase Supplies             (503) 244-9983        $2,000     05/07/90
8
9
10  Cantrell (503) 235    1000      32952
11  Allstrong(206) 643    1500      32978
12  Willamett(503) 227    1500      33032
13  Chase Sup(503) 244    2000      33000
14
```

Column widths in the output-range may need to be widened to display labels, and range formatting may be necessary to add currency displays. Dates copied to the output-range are copied over as the serial number for the date. A column with such data needs to be formatted for date display.

Benefits

Large spreadsheets often require large areas of documentation explaining the assumptions of the model(s) used, and/or summarizing the information generated by the spreadsheet model(s). When such documentation is required, it may be more convenient for a person knowledgeable with WordPerfect to use that software to produce the necessary text rather than to use the relatively weak word processing capabilities of Lotus to produce the documentation. Additionally, mainframe computers often are able to provide ASCII files containing structured data that, when imported and parsed, can save a microcomputer user many hours of data input.

Procedure

Use WordPerfect to create the DOS Text file or, if necessary, edit an ASCII file provided by another software or computer system. Either name the file initially using a .PRN filename extension or rename the file later to have this extension.

After you have created the ASCII file, load Lotus 1-2-3 and the appropriate spreadsheet into RAM, move the pointer to the top-left cell of the area into which you want the file to be imported, and then use the /**F**ile,**I**mport,**T**ext command to import the file into the current spreadsheet at the location of the pointer. If necessary, use the /**D**ata,**P**arse commands to parse the imported file into separate spreadsheet cells.

Comments

The Lotus Manual states: "Many word processors generate document files which contain special characters. If you attempt to read these files using the /File Import command unpredictable results may occur. Most word processors, however, produce standard ASCII files which should be compatible with 1-2-3."

The words "unpredictable" and "should be" indicate that a more conservative approach to the procedure would be first to import the file into a blank spreadsheet and examine it for peculiar characters. If no such characters are found, continue by importing that file into the intended spreadsheet. If peculiar characters are found, try using 1-2-3's F2 edit mode to delete them, reprint the area to a .PRN file, and repeat the test.

dBASE III PLUS DATABASE RECORDS INTO A LOTUS 1-2-3 SPREADSHEET

The final data transfer operation to discuss is moving dBASE III Plus database records into a Lotus 1-2-3 spreadsheet. In this example Lotus's /**F**ile,**I**mport command will be used with the option to import **N**umbers rather than **T**ext (see "WordPerfect Files into a Lotus 1-2-3 Spreadsheet").

When the **N**umbers option of the /**F**ile,**I**mport command is used, Lotus will import an ASCII file containing both strings and numbers in it, and will automatically put the data items into separate spreadsheet cells, if the data in the imported file are structured correctly. With Lotus, the strings in the file must be delimited with quotes and the data items must be separated by commas.

Using the database created in the dBASE III Plus tutorial lessons, the **COPY TO** <filename> **TYPE SDF** command results in an ASCII file

```
Pratt John         225-1234M19820622 1949.00  200.00
Smoler Ellen       225-3212F19830915 1650.00  300.00
Jones David        292-3832M19820615 1550.00  275.75
Sill Sally         224-4321F19840215 1507.00  150.00
Knat Michael       221-1235M19800915 1800.00  125.00
Smith Paul         244-1010M19811115 1700.00  350.00
Martins Mary       222-2123F19851101 1600.00  200.50
Nichols Sandy      229-1111F19860215 1450.00  175.00
Johnson Frank      223-7928M19900320 1500.00    0.00
```

Another parameter of the dBASE **COPY** command is **DELIMITED WITH** <delimiter>. When used, it will copy the records to an ASCII file with delimiters inserted between the fields of data. When this command specifies a quote as the delimiter, as in the following

COPY TO testfile **DELIMITED WITH** "

the records in the database are copied to the ASCII file testfile.TXT in the form

```
"Pratt John","225-1234","M",19820622,1949.00,200.00
"Smoler Ellen","225-3212","F",19830915,1650.00,300.00
"Jones David","292-3832","M",19820615,1550.00,275.75
"Sill Sally","224-4321","F",19840215,1507.00,150.00
"Knat Michael","221-1235","M",19800915,1800.00,125.00
"Smith Paul","244-1010","M",19811115,1700.00,350.00
"Martins Mary","222-2123","F",19851101,1600.00,200.50
"Nichols Sandy","229-1111","F",19860215,1450.00,175.00
"Johnson Frank","223-7928","M",19900320,1500.00,0.00
```

This organization of data is suitable for importing into a Lotus spreadsheet as Numbers. However, the database field for employment date has been copied to the file as a large number representing the year, month, and day (i.e., 19820622 representing the date 06/22/82). It is typical that date-type data are among the most difficult to transfer between applications software. The general rule for making such transfers is to first convert the date-type data using the commands of the source software into character-type data. Next, make the transfer and then convert the character data back to date-type data using the commands of the destination software. In this case, the procedure would be to use the **MODIFY STRUCTURE** command of dBASE to change the field named "employed" from being date to character type. Then, use the **COPY TO** testfile **DELIMITED WITH** " command to produce the following ASCII file.

```
"Pratt John","225-1234","M","06/22/82",1949.00,200.00
"Smoler Ellen","225-3212","F","09/15/83",1650.00,300.00
"Jones David","292-3832","M","06/15/82",1550.00,275.75
"Sill Sally","224-4321","F","02/15/84",1507.00,150.00
"Knat Michael","221-1235","M","09/15/80",1800.00,125.00
"Smith Paul","244-1010","M","11/15/81",1700.00,350.00
"Martins Mary","222-2123","F","11/01/85",1600.00,200.50
"Nichols Sandy","229-1111","F","02/15/86",1450.00,175.00
"Johnson Frank","223-7928","M","03/20/90",1500.00,0.00
```

Before importing this file into a Lotus spreadsheet it must be renamed to have a .PRN extension instead of the .TXT extension. When Lotus's /**F**ile,**I**mport,**N**umbers command is executed with the pointer on cell A3, testfile specified as the file to import, and the column widths of the spreadsheet changed to make the imported data more easily read, the result is

```
A3: [W15] 'Pratt John                                                  READY

         A              B        C     D           E          F        G        H
1
2
3   Pratt John     225-1234 M   06/22/82      1949        200
4   Smoler Ellen   225-3212 F   09/15/83      1650        300
5   Jones David    292-3832 M   06/15/82      1550     275.75
6   Sill Sally     224-4321 F   02/15/84      1507        150
7   Knat Michael   221-1235 M   09/15/80      1800        125
8   Smith Paul     244-1010 M   11/15/81      1700        350
9   Martins Mary   222-2123 F   11/01/85      1600      200.5
10  Nichols Sandy  229-1111 F   02/15/86      1450        175
11  Johnson Frank  223-7928 M   03/20/90      1500          0
12
```

Each field of each record will be entered into an individual spreadsheet cell in the same data type (string or numeric) as it was held in its database field.

To convert the date labels in the spreadsheet to serial date values, you may use the /**D**ata,**P**arse command. Move the pointer to the cell D3 (the first data cell occurring in the D column) and use the /**D**ata,**P**arse,**F**ormat-Line,**C**reate command to produce the following format-line above the column

```
D3: |D>>>>>>>                                                          MENU
Format-Line  Input-Column  Output-Range  Reset  Go  Quit
Create or edit format line at current cell
         A              B        C     D           E          F        G        H
1
2
3                               D>>>>>>>>
4   Pratt John     225-1234 M   06/22/82      1949        200
5   Smoler Ellen   225-3212 F   09/15/83      1650        300
6   Jones David    292-3832 M   06/15/82      1550     275.75
7   Sill Sally     224-4321 F   02/15/84      1507        150
8   Knat Michael   221-1235 M   09/15/80      1800        125
9   Smith Paul     244-1010 M   11/15/81      1700        350
10  Martins Mary   222-2123 F   11/01/85      1600      200.5
11  Nichols Sandy  229-1111 F   02/15/86      1450        175
12  Johnson Frank  223-7928 M   03/20/90      1500          0
13
```

Next use the **I**nput-Column command to specify the format-line and all dates below it (D3..D12) as being the input-column, and then use the **O**utput-Range command to specify the cell D4 as being the output-range. Next execute the **G**o command and all date labels in the column will be converted into their serial date equivalents.

```
D3: |D>>>>>>>                                                          READY

          A              B        C      D          E        F       G        H
1
2
3                                      D>>>>>>>
4  Pratt John      225-1234 M      30124      1949      200
5  Smoler Ellen    225-3212 F      30574      1650      300
6  Jones David     292-3832 M      30117      1550   275.75
7  Sill Sally      224-4321 F      30727      1507      150
8  Knat Michael    221-1235 M      29479      1800      125
9  Smith Paul      244-1010 M      29905      1700      350
10 Martins Mary    222-2123 F      31352      1600    200.5
11 Nichols Sandy   229-1111 F      31458      1450      175
12 Johnson Frank   223-7928 M      32952      1500        0
13
```

Finally erase the format-line, widen the D column, and format the range to display the date format of your choice.

```
D4: (D1) [W12] 30124                                                   READY

          A              B        C        D            E        F        G
1
2
3
4  Pratt John      225-1234 M    22-Jun-82      1949      200
5  Smoler Ellen    225-3212 F    15-Sep-83      1650      300
6  Jones David     292-3832 M    15-Jun-82      1550   275.75
7  Sill Sally      224-4321 F    15-Feb-84      1507      150
8  Knat Michael    221-1235 M    15-Sep-80      1800      125
9  Smith Paul      244-1010 M    15-Nov-81      1700      350
10 Martins Mary    222-2123 F    01-Nov-85      1600    200.5
11 Nichols Sandy   229-1111 F    15-Feb-86      1450      175
12 Johnson Frank   223-7928 M    20-Mar-90      1500        0
13
```

Benefits

The greatest strength of a spreadsheet application is its ability to generate formula-based information for decision making. Parametric statistical analysis of an organization's internal data is an example of such information. Database management systems such as dBASE III Plus have the strengths of data maintenance, query, and record organization which are useful for reporting purposes, and provide information relevant to a different type of decision making. When the need for formula-based information from record-type data is required, this transfer of data operation may be very useful, and in fact may provide the only way to obtain the needed information.

Procedure

Use the **COPY TO** <filename> **DELIMITED WITH** ” command to create a .TXT ASCII file of the database with the fields of data properly delimited. If necessary, use the **MODIFY STRUCTURE** command to convert all date fields to character fields before creating the .TXT file. Rename the file to have a .PRN filename extension, load Lotus and the appropriate spreadsheet (if any) into RAM, and then move the spreadsheet pointer to the top-left cell of the area into which you want the records imported. Use the /**F**ile,**I**mport,**N**umbers command and specify the appropriate file to import. If necessary, use the /**D**ata,**P**arse commands to convert date labels into their serial date equivalents.

Comments

By now you should see that as long as the data are arranged in an appropriate structure, the source of the ASCII file imported as **N**umbers is not important. WordPerfect, or any software capable of producing a file with data items separated by commas and strings in quotes, could be used to create the ASCII file.

DATA TRANSFER CASE EXERCISE

PRIMARY PAINT CORPORATION

Primary Paint Corporation is a small company that manufactures paint bases for distribution to several well-known paint companies. The paint bases are made to customer specifications and come in the three primary colors (yellow, red, and blue), as well as the base tints white and black. Although small in size, Primary Paint has operated quite profitably for the last several years. A steady increase in sales and a high ratio of assets to debt have made the company a likely candidate for a corporate takeover.

Joel Wilson has worked for Primary Paint Corporation for only a few months. He originally was hired as an assistant to the shipping and receiving manager, but, when management discovered that he knew how to use the microcomputer along with several different applications software, he began being asked to do many tasks outside his normal job description.

For the most part Joel didn't mind the extra work (and recognition) he received from being the company's "computer guru," but early one Friday morning Bill Meyers, the plant supervisor, came to him with a problem that didn't readily lend itself to being solved with any one of the software with which Joel was familiar. Bill said, "Joel, there's a lot of excitement going on upstairs. Evidently Simon Harris, the owner of National Paint, is preparing a friendly takeover tender for the company. A takeover by National would almost certainly mean higher salaries and greater job security for the two of us. Anyway, Harris is coming to the plant Monday morning to ask a few questions about our operations and shipments.

"I haven't a clue about the questions he might have, but I'd like to be prepared to answer all of his questions without missing a beat. If he wants to know how many gallons of yellow paint we shipped in February, or what the dollar sales in the first quarter were for red paint, you and I need to be able to come up with the answer immediately.

"I'd also like to give Harris a one-page summary report of our year-to-date sales along with a first-quarter breakdown of gallon sales for each color of paint base. I want the report to look as professional as possible. Maybe you could include a nice table of dollar sales and a pie chart for the breakdown of first-quarter gallon sales.

"You know, Joel, it's sure good to have someone with your computer talents on our team. I'm leaving early today to get ready for a fishing trip this weekend, so I'll see you bright and early on Monday."

With that, Bill handed Joel a stack of shipping invoices and a wholesale price list and then walked out the door.

Sample Shipping Invoice

Invoice # *A1027*	Invoice Date *02/11/90*	Carrier *Freightliner*
Shipped To: *Northwest Custom Paints*		
Paint Base Color *WHITE*	Gallons Shipped *1690*	

Wholesale Price List

WHITE................$5.25/gal
YELLOW $6.00/gal
RED $6.40/gal
BLUE $6.74/gal
BLACK................$7.30/gal

> Note: In the following case exercises you will see this symbol.
>
> 
>
> It indicates an opportune time to save your files and quit the tutorial to continue later.

CASE EXERCISE 1
Creating Records of Data Using Lotus 1-2-3

When Joel sorted through the invoices he discovered that they were organized by color/tint. That is, all of the invoices for white paint base were grouped together, as were the invoices for red, yellow, and so on. You will begin solving Joel's problem by creating the dBASE invoice record data using Lotus 1-2-3.

1. Load Lotus 1-2-3 and then enter the following invoice numbers, invoice dates, and gallons shipped data into the appropriate cells. Since the invoice date data is destined to be transferred to dBASE, you will need to enter it as labels (type a single quote and then type and enter the date).

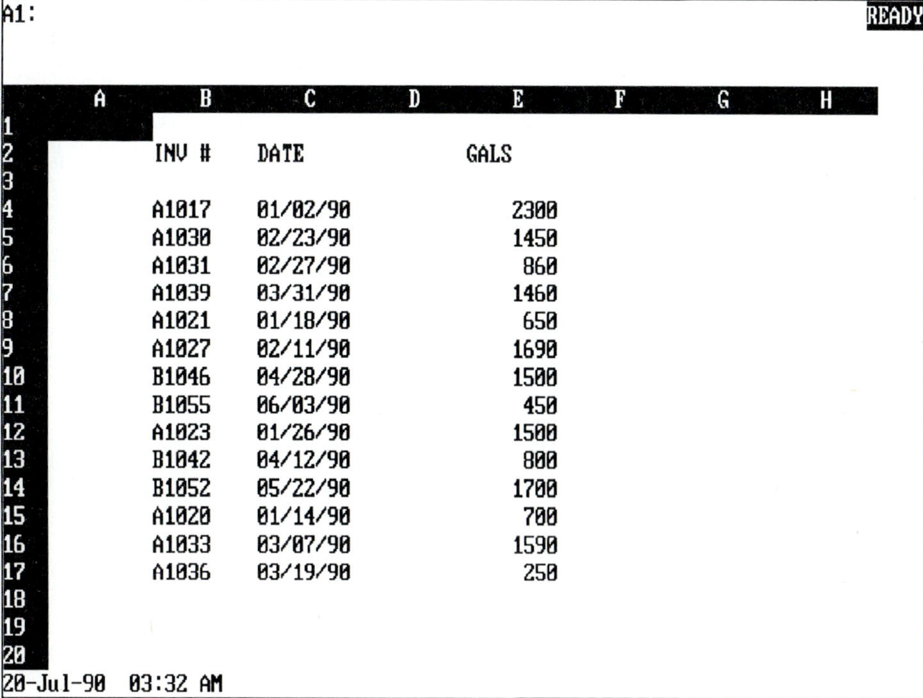

A1: READY

	A	B	C	D	E	F	G	H
1								
2		INV #	DATE		GALS			
3								
4		A1017	01/02/90		2300			
5		A1030	02/23/90		1450			
6		A1031	02/27/90		860			
7		A1039	03/31/90		1460			
8		A1021	01/18/90		650			
9		A1027	02/11/90		1690			
10		B1046	04/28/90		1500			
11		B1055	06/03/90		450			
12		A1023	01/26/90		1500			
13		B1042	04/12/90		800			
14		B1052	05/22/90		1700			
15		A1020	01/14/90		700			
16		A1033	03/07/90		1590			
17		A1036	03/19/90		250			
18								
19								
20								

20-Jul-90 03:32 AM

All of the invoice's records so far are for white paint base, which is currently priced at $5.25/gallon.

2. Move the pointer to cell D4 and enter the label WHITE. Then copy the label into the rest of the cells in that column (you may label the column COLOR). Next move to cell A4 and enter the value 5.25. Then move the pointer to cell F4 and enter the formula +E4*$A$4 and copy the formula into the remaining cells in that column. (You may label the last column EXT).

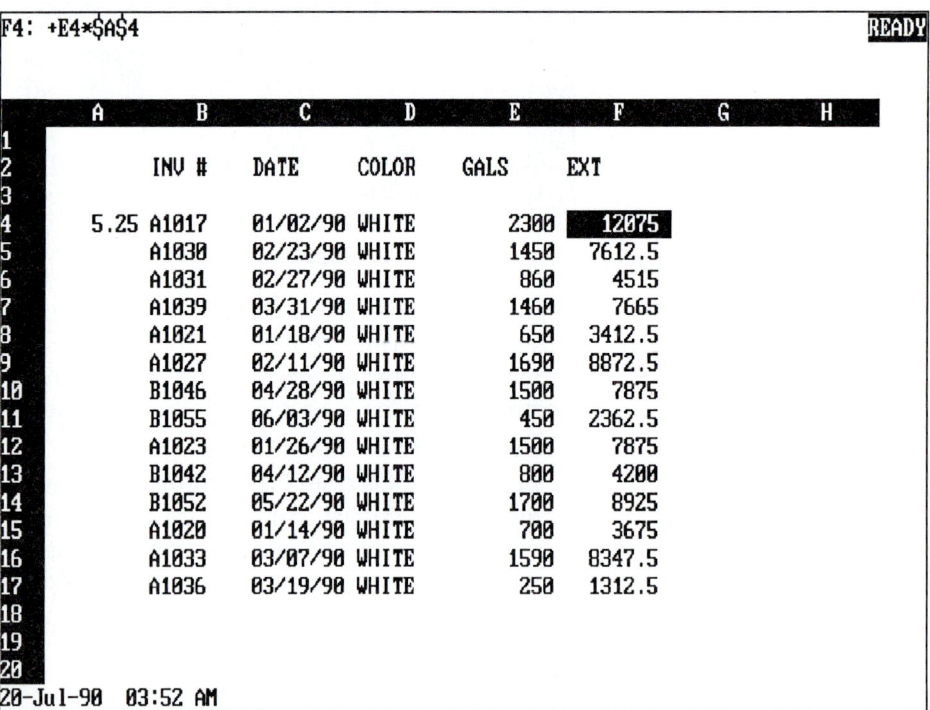

F4: +E4*$A$4 READY

	A	B	C	D	E	F	G	H
1								
2		INV #	DATE	COLOR	GALS	EXT		
3								
4	5.25	A1017	01/02/90	WHITE	2300	12075		
5		A1030	02/23/90	WHITE	1450	7612.5		
6		A1031	02/27/90	WHITE	860	4515		
7		A1039	03/31/90	WHITE	1460	7665		
8		A1021	01/18/90	WHITE	650	3412.5		
9		A1027	02/11/90	WHITE	1690	8872.5		
10		B1046	04/28/90	WHITE	1500	7875		
11		B1055	06/03/90	WHITE	450	2362.5		
12		A1023	01/26/90	WHITE	1500	7875		
13		B1042	04/12/90	WHITE	800	4200		
14		B1052	05/22/90	WHITE	1700	8925		
15		A1020	01/14/90	WHITE	700	3675		
16		A1033	03/07/90	WHITE	1590	8347.5		
17		A1036	03/19/90	WHITE	250	1312.5		
18								
19								
20								

20-Jul-90 03:52 AM

3. Now enter the records for the three primary colors in the same manner. Note that the price/gallon figures are shown in column A.

```
A37:                                                          READY

        A       B        C        D          E       F      G        H
18      6 A1038    03/27/90 YELLOW       175    1050
19        A1019    01/10/90 YELLOW       220    1320
20        B1048    05/06/90 YELLOW       155     930
21        A1028    02/15/90 YELLOW       400    2400
22        A1032    03/03/90 YELLOW       340    2040
23        B1050    05/14/90 YELLOW       650    3900
24      6.4 B1045  04/24/90 RED          165    1056
25        A1024    01/30/90 RED          230    1472
26        B1041    04/08/90 RED          200    1280
27        B1051    05/18/90 RED          275    1760
28        B1049    05/10/90 RED          150     960
29        A1029    02/19/90 RED          185    1184
30     6.75 A1034  03/11/90 BLUE         450  3037.5
31        A1022    01/22/90 BLUE         120     810
32        B1053    05/26/90 BLUE         180    1215
33        A1026    02/07/90 BLUE         210  1417.5
34        B1047    05/02/90 BLUE         200    1350
35        B1043    04/16/90 BLUE         210  1417.5
36        A1037    03/23/90 BLUE         330  2227.5
37
20-Jul-90  04:10 AM
```

4. To finish entering the database records, enter the data for the black paint base as shown here.

```
        A       B        C        D          E       F      G        H
37      7.3 A1035  03/15/90 BLACK         75   547.5
38        B1044    04/20/90 BLACK        125   912.5
39        A1018    01/06/90 BLACK        150    1095
40        B1040    04/04/90 BLACK         50     365
41        B1054    05/30/90 BLACK        140    1022
42        A1025    02/03/90 BLACK        125   912.5
43
```

CASE EXERCISE 2
Creating Lotus 1-2-3 .PRN Files

Before creating the .PRN file, you will change the spreadsheet column widths to the same lengths as the intended fields of the dBASE database.

1. Use the /**W**orksheet,**C**olumn,**S**et-Width command to make the following changes.

column B	5 characters wide
column C	8 characters wide
column D	6 characters wide
column E	5 characters wide
column F	7 characters wide

Now type the Home key and the screen should appear as

```
A1:                                                              READY

        A      B      C      D      E      F      G      H      I
1
2              INV #DATE      COLOR GALS EXT
3
4         5.25 A101701/02/90WHITE 2300   12075
5              A103002/23/90WHITE 1450 7612.5
6              A103102/27/90WHITE  860   4515
7              A103903/31/90WHITE 1460   7665
8              A102101/18/90WHITE  650 3412.5
9              A102702/11/90WHITE 1690 8872.5
10             B104604/28/90WHITE 1500   7875
11             B105506/03/90WHITE  450 2362.5
12             A102301/26/90WHITE 1500   7875
13             B104204/12/90WHITE  800   4200
14             B105205/22/90WHITE 1700   8925
15             A102001/14/90WHITE  700   3675
16             A103303/07/90WHITE 1590 8347.5
17             A103603/19/90WHITE  250 1312.5
18           6 A103803/27/90YELLOW 175   1050
19             A101901/10/90YELLOW 220   1320
20             B104805/06/90YELLOW 155    930
22-Jul-90  12:11 AM
```

2. Now use the /**F**ile,**S**ave command to save the spreadsheet under the name invrecs (for invoice records).

In the next steps you will use the /**P**rint,**F**ile command to produce an ASCII file of the spreadsheet records.

3. Type ||/**PF**|| to begin the operation, name the file invtemp, and then enter the following specifications

   Print **R**ange: B4..F42 (the record data only)

   Options - **M**argins - **L**eft = 0
   Top = 0
   Bottom = 0

Use the **Q**uit command or the Esc key to return to the /**P**rint,**F**ile menu, use the **A**lign command to set the top of page, and then use the **G**o command to begin printing the output to the file.

To successfully complete printing to a Lotus .PRN file, you **must** exit the /**P**rint,**F**ile menu with the **Q**uit command. You cannot exit the menu using the Esc key.

4. Use the **Q**uit command to end the /**P**rint,**F**ile operation and then exit Lotus 1-2-3 using the /**Q**uit command.

CASE EXERCISE 3
Viewing Lotus 1-2-3 Files from DOS

1. Change the current drive/directory to where your files are kept and use the DOS **TYPE** command to view the file invrecs.WK1.

```
A:\>TYPE invrecs.WK1
 ☻ ♠♦♠      , û *   ♦ % ☺ ☺ * ☻ ☺ * ♥ ☺ * ♦ ☺ * ♣ ☺ *  ♥ , / ☺ ☺☻ ☺  ♥ ☺  ♦ ☺
♣ ☺     ☺ ♦ q           ¶          ♦ ♦ H  ♥ ☺  ♥  ♥ ♥  ♥ ♦  ♥ ♣ ♥  ♀d
                             G ↓ /Z                  G ↓ \A           ♥
 ; ♥ ;  G ↓ \C            ♦ = ♦ =  G ↓ \X          ♥ = ♥ =  G ↓ \Z
            ↑ ↓                       ↓ ↓                       ☻
A:\>
```

What you see on the screen is an example of what a non-ASCII file may look like when viewed using DOS's **TYPE** command.

2. Now use the DOS **TYPE** command to view the ASCII file invtemp.PRN by typing ‖ **TYPE** invtemp.PRN↵ ‖.

```
B104805/06/90YELLOW 155    930
A102802/15/90YELLOW 400   2400
A103203/03/90YELLOW 340   2040
B105005/14/90YELLOW 650   3900
B104504/24/90RED    165   1056
A102401/30/90RED    230   1472
B104104/08/90RED    200   1280
B105105/18/90RED    275   1760
B104905/10/90RED    150    960
A102902/19/90RED    185   1184
A103403/11/90BLUE   450 3037.5
A102201/22/90BLUE   120    810
B105305/26/90BLUE   180   1215
A102602/07/90BLUE   210 1417.5
B104705/02/90BLUE   200   1350
B104304/16/90BLUE   210 1417.5
A103703/23/90BLUE   330 2227.5
A103503/15/90BLACK   75  547.5
B104404/20/90BLACK  125  912.5
A101801/06/90BLACK  150   1095
B104004/04/90BLACK   50    365
B105405/30/90BLACK  140   1022
A102502/03/90BLACK  125  912.5

A:\>
```

CASE EXERCISE 4
Editing a .PRN File with WordPerfect

Even though you set the top margin of the .PRN file to 0, Lotus will print three blank lines at the top of the file. Since no Lotus command is capable of preventing the three lines from appearing in the file, and the lines will create three blank records at the top of the dBASE database you will later create, you now may use WordPerfect to remove the lines from the file.

1. Load WordPerfect and then use the **Shift-F10** (Retrieve) command to retrieve the file invtemp.PRN.

```
-


A101701/02/90WHITE 2300   12075
A103002/23/90WHITE 1450 7612.5
A103102/27/90WHITE  860   4515
A103903/31/90WHITE 1460   7665
A102101/18/90WHITE  650 3412.5
A102702/11/90WHITE 1690 8872.5
B104604/28/90WHITE 1500   7875
B105506/03/90WHITE  450 2362.5
A102301/26/90WHITE 1500   7875
B104204/12/90WHITE  800   4200
B105205/22/90WHITE 1700   8925
A102001/14/90WHITE  700   3675
A103303/07/90WHITE 1590 8347.5
A103603/19/90WHITE  250 1312.5
A103803/27/90YELLOW 175   1050
A101901/10/90YELLOW 220   1320
B104805/06/90YELLOW 155    930
A102802/15/90YELLOW 400   2400
A103203/03/90YELLOW 340   2040
B105005/14/90YELLOW 650   3900
B104504/24/90RED    165   1056
A:\INVTEMP.PRN                                     Doc 1 Pg 1 Ln 1" Pos 1.1"
```

2. Type **Alt-F3** (Reveal Codes) and then use the Backspace and Del keys to remove the [HRt]s, spaces, and [Paper Sz/Typ] code that occur at the top of the file.

```
A101701/02/90WHITE 2300   12075
A103002/23/90WHITE 1450 7612.5
A103102/27/90WHITE  860   4515
A103903/31/90WHITE 1460   7665
A102101/18/90WHITE  650 3412.5
A102702/11/90WHITE 1690 8872.5
B104604/28/90WHITE 1500   7875
B105506/03/90WHITE  450 2362.5
A102301/26/90WHITE 1500   7875
B104204/12/90WHITE  800   4200
B105205/22/90WHITE 1700   8925
A:\INVTEMP.PRN                                     Doc 1 Pg 1 Ln 1" Pos 1"
{  ▲  ▲  ▲  ▲  ▲  ▲  ▲  ▲  ▲  ▲  ▲  ▲  ▲  }  ▲  ▲
A101701/02/90WHITE 2300   12075 [HRt]
A103002/23/90WHITE 1450 7612.5 [HRt]
A103102/27/90WHITE  860   4515 [HRt]
A103903/31/90WHITE 1460   7665 [HRt]
A102101/18/90WHITE  650 3412.5 [HRt]
A102702/11/90WHITE 1690 8872.5 [HRt]
B104604/28/90WHITE 1500   7875 [HRt]
B105506/03/90WHITE  450 2362.5 [HRt]
A102301/26/90WHITE 1500   7875 [HRt]
B104204/12/90WHITE  800   4200 [HRt]

Press Reveal Codes to restore screen
```

3. Next use the **Ctrl-F5** (Text In/Out),DOS **T**ext,**S**ave command to save the file in DOS Text format (ASCII) under the same name. Then exit WordPerfect *without resaving the file.*

CASE EXERCISE 5
Appending ASCII Files into a dBASE Database

You now will create a dBASE record structure for a database that will be suitable for appending the data in the .PRN file.

1. Load dBASE and use the **SET DEFAULT TO** <drive> command to cause dBASE to automatically search your files disk for any files referred to later.
2. Now type ‖ **CREATE** invos↵ ‖ and specify the following record structure for the database.

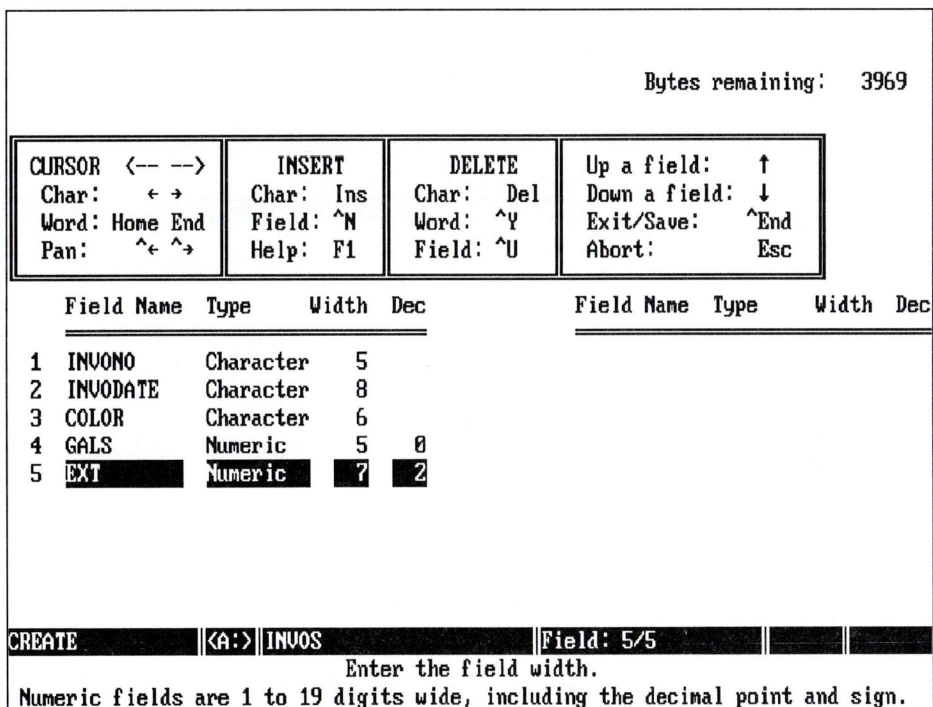

3. When finished, type ‖ **^End**↵N ‖ to complete the operation without inputting records now. Then type ‖ **USE** invos↵ ‖ to put the database in use.

Notice that the field lengths, data types, decimals, etc., specified in the record structure exactly match the structure of the data in the .PRN file.

4. Now type ‖ **APPEND FROM** invtemp.prn **TYPE SDF**↵ ‖ . Then type ‖ **DISPLAY ALL**↵ ‖ to see that the data have been appended appropriately.

```
. DISPLAY ALL
Record#  INVONO INVODATE COLOR   GALS     EXT
      1  A1017  01/02/90 WHITE   2300 12075.0
      2  A1030  02/23/90 WHITE   1450 7612.50
      3  A1031  02/27/90 WHITE    860 4515.00
      4  A1039  03/31/90 WHITE   1460 7665.00
      5  A1021  01/18/90 WHITE    650 3412.50
      6  A1027  02/11/90 WHITE   1690 8872.50
      7  B1046  04/28/90 WHITE   1500 7875.00
      8  B1055  06/03/90 WHITE    450 2362.50
      9  A1023  01/26/90 WHITE   1500 7875.00
     10  B1042  04/12/90 WHITE    800 4200.00
     11  B1052  05/22/90 WHITE   1700 8925.00
     12  A1020  01/14/90 WHITE    700 3675.00
     13  A1033  03/07/90 WHITE   1590 8347.50
     14  A1036  03/19/90 WHITE    250 1312.50
     15  A1038  03/27/90 YELLOW   175 1050.00
     16  A1019  01/10/90 YELLOW   220 1320.00
     17  B1048  05/06/90 YELLOW   155  930.00
     18  A1028  02/15/90 YELLOW   400 2400.00
     19  A1032  03/03/90 YELLOW   340 2040.00
Press any key to continue...
Command Line    ||<A:>||INVOS              ||Rec: 39/39        ||    ||

                              Enter a dBASE III PLUS command.
```

The final step in completing the data transfer operation will be to change the invodate field from its current character type to a date-type field.

5. Type ‖ **MODIFY STRUCTURE**↵ ‖ , move to the Type area for invodate, and type ‖ D ‖ to make the field a date-type field. Next type ‖ **^End**↵ ‖ to complete the modify operation.

CASE EXERCISE 6 Creating ASCII Files with dBASE

In the following steps you will create two database files designed to hold the requested summary data and then use command (.PRG) files to perform the data reduction operation.

1. Use the dBASE **CREATE** <filename> command to create the following record structure for the database file named "ytdsum" (year-to-date summary.)

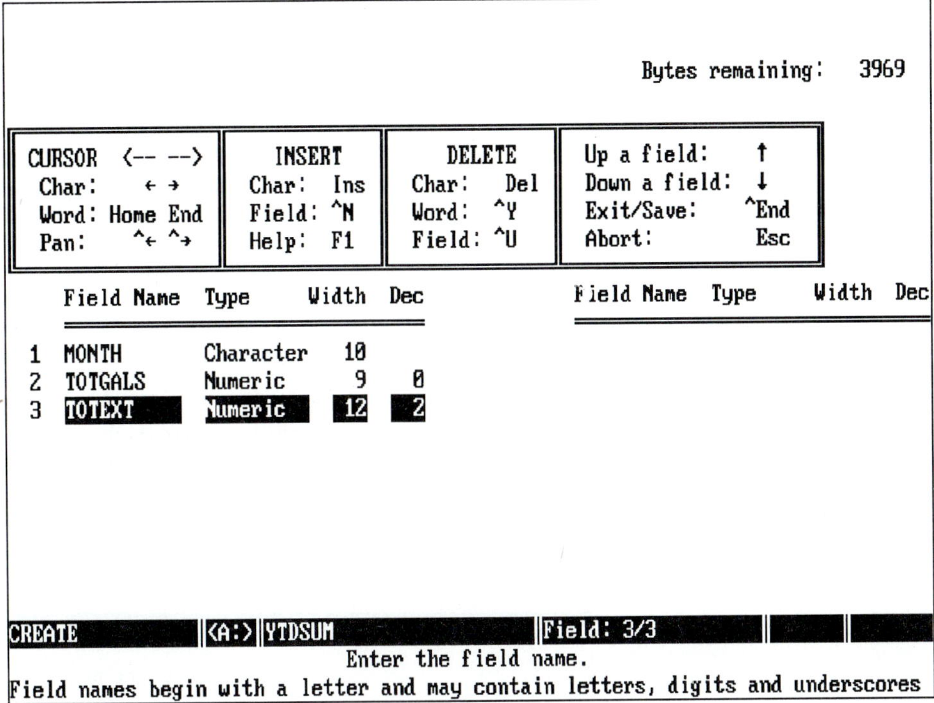

2. When finished type ‖ ^End↵N ‖ to complete the operation without inputting records now.
3. Next use the **MODIFY COMMAND** <filename> command to create the following program named "datasum."

```
Edit: A:datasum.prg

CLOSE ALL
SELECT 1
USE invos
SELECT 2
USE ytdsum
m = 1
DO WHILE m <= 5
  SELECT 2
  APPEND BLANK
  REPLACE ytdsum->month WITH CMONTH(CTOD(STR(m,2,0)+"/01/90"))
  SELECT 1
  SUM gals FOR month(invodate) = m TO total1
  SUM ext  FOR month(invodate) = m TO total2
  SELECT 2
  REPLACE ytdsum->totgals WITH total1
  REPLACE ytdsum->totext WITH total2
  m = m + 1
ENDDO
CLOSE ALL
RETURN
```

4. Use the **DO** <filename> command to execute the datasum program. Then type

	CLEAR↵	
	SELECT 1↵	
	USE ytdsum↵	
	DISPLAY ALL↵	

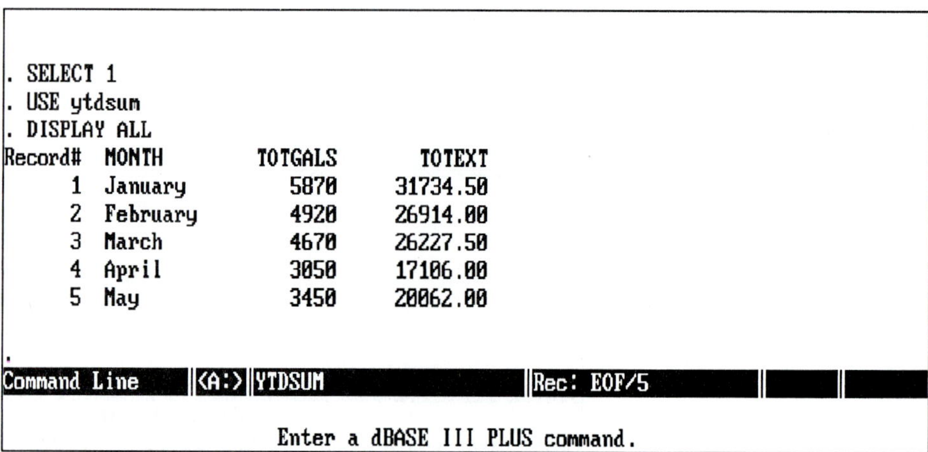

```
. SELECT 1
. USE ytdsum
. DISPLAY ALL
Record#  MONTH        TOTGALS      TOTEXT
      1  January         5870    31734.50
      2  February        4920    26914.00
      3  March           4670    26227.50
      4  April           3050    17106.00
      5  May             3450    20062.00

.
Command Line   ||<A:>||YTDSUM        ||Rec: EOF/5  ||  ||

                    Enter a dBASE III PLUS command.
```

This small table will appear in the finished report. To create an ASCII file of the screen output, you will next use the **SET ALTERNATE** commands of dBASE.

5. Type the following commands

	SET ALTERNATE TO reptin1↵	
	SET ALTERNATE ON↵	
	DISPLAY ALL↵	
	SET ALTERNATE OFF↵	
	SET ALTERNATE TO↵	

The ASCII file reptin1.TXT containing the screen output of the **DISPLAY ALL** command should now be on your files disk. To continue the exercises, you will next create a database to hold the summary information on the number of gallons sold in the first quarter for each color of paint base.

6. Use the **CREATE** <filename> command to create the following record structure for the database file quartsum.

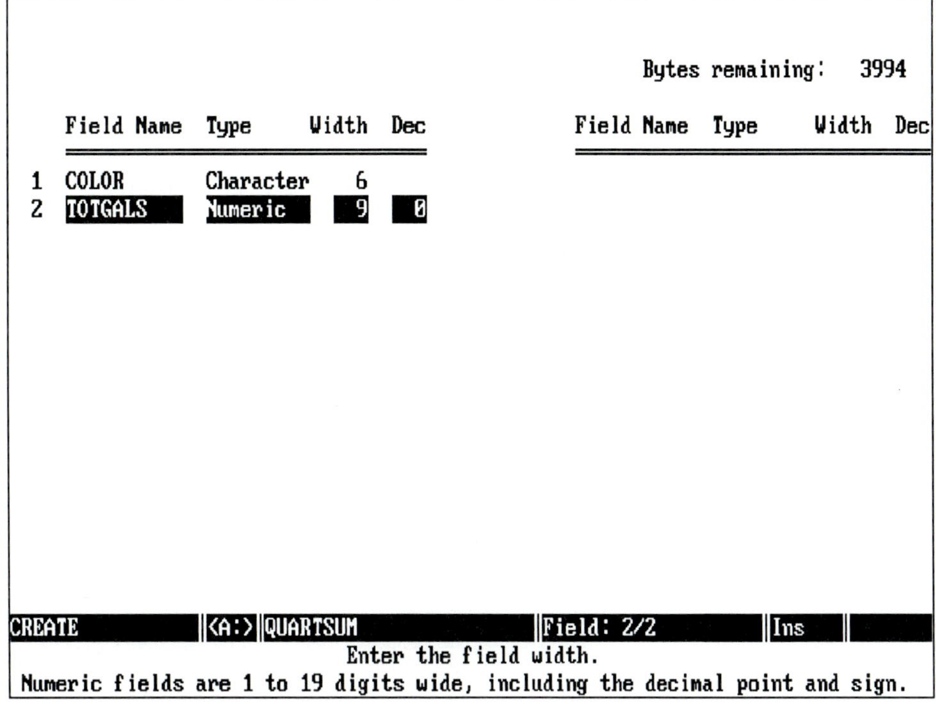

When finished creating the record structure, use the **MODIFY COMMAND** text editing mode to create the following program named "datasum2."

```
Edit: A:datasum2.prg

CLOSE ALL
SELECT 1
USE invos
SELECT 2
USE quartsum
SELECT 1
DO WHILE .NOT. EOF()
  STORE invos->color TO mcolor
  SUM gals FOR month(invodate) <= 3 WHILE invos->color = mcolor TO total1
  SELECT 2
  APPEND BLANK
  REPLACE quartsum->color WITH mcolor
  REPLACE quartsum->totgals WITH total1
  SELECT 1
ENDDO
CLOSE ALL
RETURN
```

7. Next use the **DO** <filename> command to execute the datasum2 program. Then type

	CLEAR↵	
	SELECT 1↵	
	USE quartsum↵	
	DISPLAY ALL↵	

```
. SELECT 1
. USE quartsum
. DISPLAY ALL
Record#  COLOR     TOTGALS
      1  WHITE       12450
      2  YELLOW       1135
      3  RED           415
      4  BLUE         1110
      5  BLACK         350

.
Command Line    ||<C:>||QUARTSUM              ||Rec: EOF/5      ||      ||

                          Enter a dBASE III PLUS command.
```

This data will be used to create a pie chart for the finished report. In order to transfer the data to Lotus for graphing, the **COPY TO** <filename> **DELIMITED WITH** " command will be used. Since the file is destined for a Lotus spreadsheet, and Lotus will only import an ASCII file if it has a .PRN extension, the required extension will be added to the filename when the command is executed. (dBASE would normally attach a .TXT filename extension to the file.)

8. Type || **COPY TO** spreadin.PRN **DELIMITED WITH "**↵ || .

The ASCII file named "spreadin.PRN," containing the field data of the quartsum database file, should now be on your files disk.

9. Now use the dBASE **QUIT** command to exit dBASE III Plus. Then use the DOS **TYPE** command to view the files reptin1.TXT and spreadin.PRN on the screen.

```
A:\>TYPE reptin1.txt

. DISPLAY ALL
Record#  MONTH          TOTGALS       TOTEXT
      1  January           5870     31734.50
      2  February          4920     26914.00
      3  March             4670     26227.50
      4  April             3050     17106.00
      5  May               3450     20062.00

. SET ALTERNATE OFF
A:\>
A:\>TYPE spreadin.PRN
"WHITE",12450
"YELLOW",1135
"RED",415
"BLUE",1110
"BLACK",350

A:\>
```

CASE EXERCISE 7
Importing ASCII Files into Lotus

You now are ready to create the pie chart for the report. To do so, you will import the file spreadin.PRN, created with dBASE, into a Lotus spreadsheet.

1. Load Lotus 1-2-3. Then move the pointer to cell A3 and use the /**F**ile,**I**mport,**N**umbers command to import the file spreadin.PRN into the spreadsheet. Then enter the values shown in cells C3 through C7.

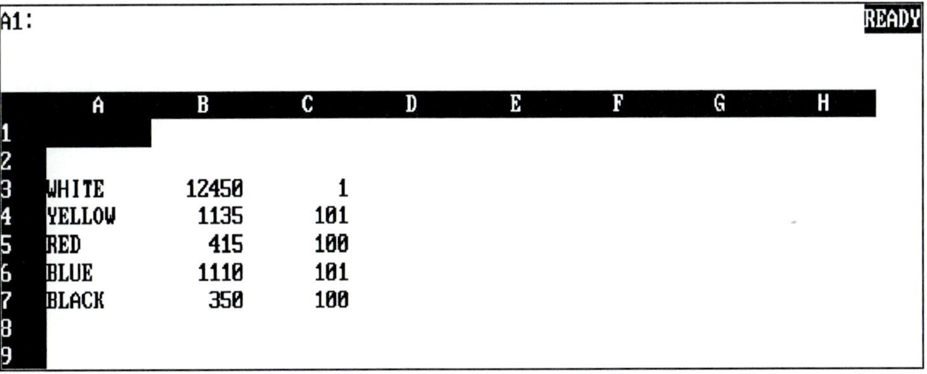

2. Now use the /**G**raph commands to create a pie chart with the following specifications.

Type = Pie
X data range = A3..A7
A data range = B3..B7
B data range = C3..C7

Then view the graph on the screen.

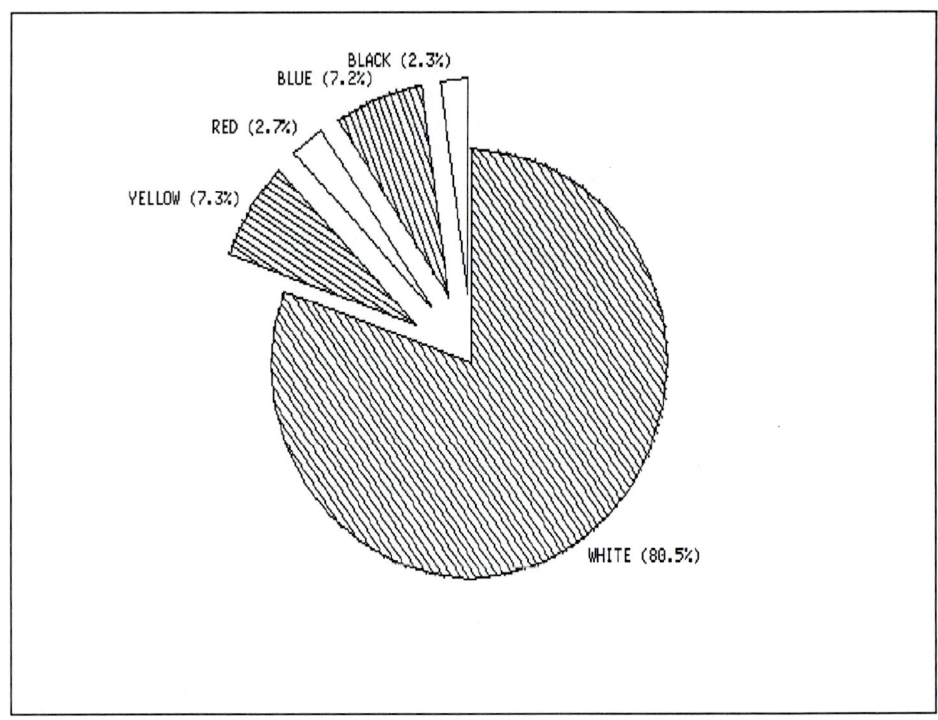

3. Now use the /**G**raph,**S**ave command to save the graph data under the name reptin2 (Lotus will automatically add a .PIC extension to the name). Then use the /**F**ile,**S**ave command to save the spreadsheet data under the name "piedata." Next use the /**Q**uit command to exit Lotus 1-2-3.

CASE EXERCISE 8
Creating the Final Report

You are now ready to create the final report using WordPerfect.

1. Load WordPerfect and then enter the following text. Center the headings and use the **Ctrl-F8** (Font),**S**ize,**L**arge command to make the company's name large font.

```
                    Primary Paint Corporation

          Year-To-Date Sales and Product Mix Report

1990 Dollar Sales

     The first five months of this year have shown a strong
     increase in sales over last year, with the expected seasonal
     down-turn occurring in April:










Typeover                                Doc 1 Pg 1 Ln 2.83" Pos 1"
```

2. Move the cursor to Ln 3″, Pos 1″ and then use the **Shift-F10** (Retrieve) command to retrieve the file reptin1.txt into the document.

```
                    Primary Paint Corporation

          Year-To-Date Sales and Product Mix Report

1990 Dollar Sales

     The first five months of this year have shown a strong
     increase in sales over last year, with the expected seasonal
     down-turn occurring in April:


. DISPLAY ALL
Record#  MONTH        TOTGALS      TOTEXT
      1  January         5870    31734.50
      2  February        4920    26914.00
      3  March           4670    26227.50
      4  April           3050    17106.00
      5  May             3450    20062.00

. SET ALTERNATE OFF^Z


Typeover                                Doc 1 Pg 1 Ln 3" Pos 1"
```

3. Next edit the retrieved data (and use the **Ctrl-F3** (Screen),**Line Draw** commands) so it appears in the document as follows.

```
                 Primary Paint Corporation

         Year-To-Date Sales and Product Mix Report

1990 Dollar Sales

     The first five months of this year have shown a strong
     increase in sales over last year, with the expected seasonal
     down-turn occurring in April:

              Month         Total       Total
                            Gallons     Dollars

              January        5870     $31,734.50
              February       4920     $26,914.00
              March          4670     $26,227.50
              April          3050     $17,106.00
              May            3450     $20,062.00

                                          Doc 1 Pg 1 Ln 1" Pos 1"
```

4. Now move the cursor to Ln 5″, Pos 1″ and type the **Alt-F9** (Graphics) command. Select the **F**igure option and then the **C**reate option. Continue by making the following specifications: **F**ilename is reptin2.PIC; **C**aption is “1st Quarter Sales (Gallons)”; **S**ize is **W**idth (auto height) 4 ″. When finished the Graphics set-up screen should appear as follows.

```
Definition: Figure

     1 - Filename                      REPTIN2.PIC (Graphic)

     2 - Caption                       Figure 1 1st Quarter Sales (Gallons...

     3 - Type                          Paragraph

     4 - Vertical Position             0"

     5 - Horizontal Position           Right

     6 - Size                          4" wide x 2.99" (high)

     7 - Wrap Text Around Box          Yes

     8 - Edit

Selection: 0
```

5. Now type **F7** (Exit) and begin entering the text shown here. Note that WordPerfect will automatically wrap the text around the figure box shown on the screen.

```
Product Percentages                 FIG 1

In the first quarter of
the year, white paint
base sustained its normal
80% of sales in gallons.

Yellow and blue paint
bases increased their
product shares slightly
with black and red bases
slipping somewhat from
last quarter's figures.

It is estimated that the
product mix will remain
relatively constant
throughout the remainder
of 1990.  However,
possible shortages of
lead chromate late in the
year may slow production of yellow paint base and create inventory
back-orders for the product at that time.
                                          Doc 1 Pg 1 Ln 8.67" Pos 5.1"
```

6. When finished, use the **Shift-F7** (Print), View Document command to preview the printed document on the screen:

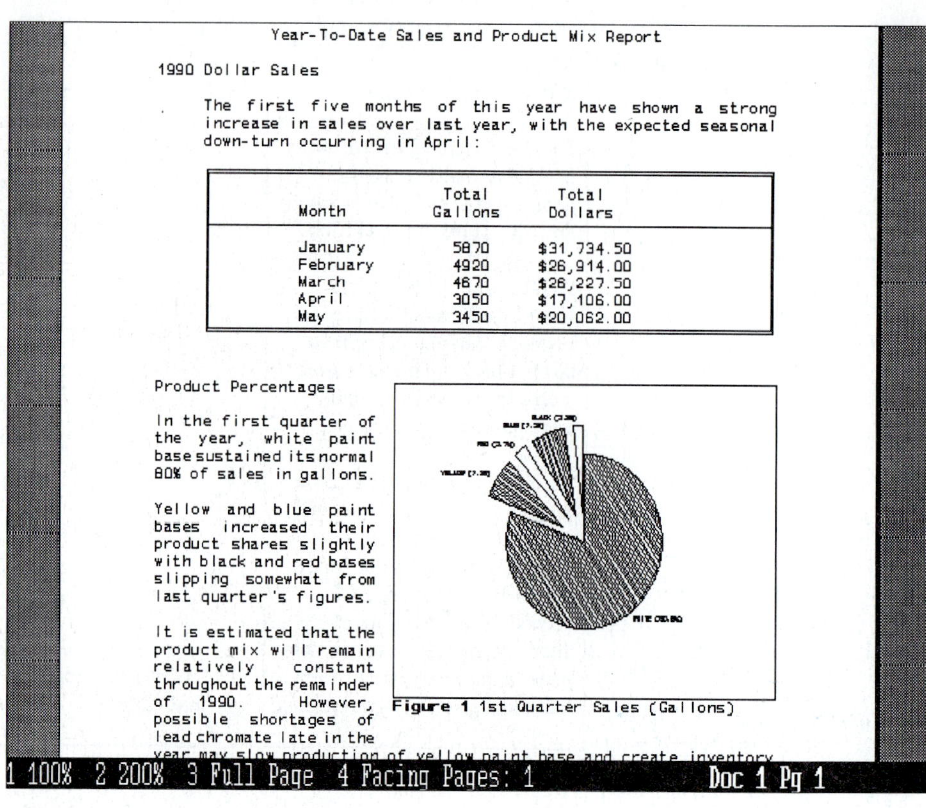

Year-To-Date Sales and Product Mix Report

1990 Dollar Sales

The first five months of this year have shown a strong increase in sales over last year, with the expected seasonal down-turn occurring in April:

Month	Total Gallons	Total Dollars
January	5870	$31,734.50
February	4920	$26,914.00
March	4670	$26,227.50
April	3050	$17,106.00
May	3450	$20,062.00

Product Percentages

In the first quarter of the year, white paint base sustained its normal 80% of sales in gallons.

Yellow and blue paint bases increased their product shares slightly with black and red bases slipping somewhat from last quarter's figures.

It is estimated that the product mix will remain relatively constant throughout the remainder of 1990. However, possible shortages of lead chromate late in the year may slow production of yellow paint base and create inventory

Figure 1 1st Quarter Sales (Gallons)

1 100% 2 200% 3 Full Page 4 Facing Pages: 1 Doc 1 Pg 1

7. Now save the document under the name "fnlrpt", print the document, and then exit WordPerfect.

BASICA

INTRODUCTION

WHY A PROGRAMMING LANGUAGE?

Unlike most other software covered in this manual, BASICA is considered a true programming language. This means that BASICA requires the user to have a knowledge of programming theory in order to use the computer as a tool.

It is generally accepted that with applications software the need for knowledge of programming theory is unnecessary. While it is true that the applications software available today may be used productively without it, it is also true that when you begin to take the applications software to the limits of their capabilities, you inevitably find that you need to understand the principles of programming theory. The macros of Lotus 1-2-3, command files of dBASE III Plus, and the Mail Merge utility used with WordPerfect are examples of application areas where the user must understand elements of programming theory.

BASIC—A Language Developed to Teach Programming Theory

BASIC is the acronym for "Beginners All Symbolic Instruction Code." It is the name for a programming language developed at Dartmouth College under the direction of professors John G. Kemeny and Thomas E. Kurtz during the academic year 1963–1964. BASIC was developed to teach beginning students the constructs of programming theory and is one of the easiest high-level languages to learn.

While it may be possible to teach programming theory by using applications software rather than a programming language, BASIC has been used to teach programming for a longer period of time, so that many excellent books, teaching techniques, and assignments on the subject have evolved. The same is not true for applications software.

Versions of BASIC

Today, more than twenty years after its conception, more than 50 versions of BASIC have been developed for use on a variety of hardware systems. While they each conform to a standard called ANSI Minimal BASIC, they often exceed the requirements of the standard in scope of commands and operations. Systemic differences between versions of BASIC often are associated with the hardware on which they are designed to be used.

The Nature of the BASICA Module

This module differs from other modules of the manual that deal with applications packages because it is assumed here that you either have previous exposure to BASIC or can refer to one of the many texts on the subject for programming concepts.

The BASICA tutorial lessons focus on the systematic differences between BASICA on the IBM PC and other versions of BASIC that you may have used or to which a text might refer. The syntax of essential commands, file handling, and editing operations are the primary focuses of the tutorial.

One of the best sources of information for the beginning or intermediate programmer can be example programs. This module has more than 40 examples of BASIC programs, shown with their output. Careful study of the programs will provide insights into programming style and techniques, as well as into BASICA statement syntax. Because such examples provide the best source for learning to use BASIC, exercises and cases have been omitted from this module.

The operation and command summary of this module does not attempt to cover all the commands and operations of BASIC. You will need to refer to an IBM BASIC manual if you intend to pursue more intense programming endeavors.

Sequential and random access data files also are introduced in this section. The knowiedge that you gain by using BASICA to create, maintain, and query these two types of data files is directly applicable to your understanding of many of the features and operations of the applications software.

BASIC for the IBM PC

Three versions of BASIC have been developed by Microsoft Corporation for the IBM PC. BASICA is the "advanced" version, and the other two versions, Cassette BASIC and Disk BASIC, are subsets of BASICA.

Cassette BASIC

Cassette BASIC is not software, but *firmware*. It is called firmware because the instruction set for Cassette BASIC is imbedded in a ROM chip inside the computer. If you turn on the computer with no diskette in the A: drive and the door open, the computer will default to this version of BASIC. It is called Cassette BASIC because you need a cassette player and interface cord to save your BASIC programs. The computer has not read DOS into memory and so does not have the instruction set that it needs to save data to a diskette.

Disk BASIC

Disk BASIC is software found on the DOS diskette (usually purchased with the computer) under the name BASIC.COM. Disk BASIC has all of the operations and commands of Cassette BASIC plus commands and operations for accessing and storing data on diskettes.

Advanced BASIC

The third version of BASIC is called Advanced BASIC. It also is found on the DOS diskette under the filename BASICA.COM. Advanced BASIC has all the operations and commands of Disk BASIC, plus advanced graphics and music commands. Advanced BASIC, or BASICA, is the version of BASIC used in the tutorial lessons and other topics of this module.

REQUIRED PREPARATION

The tutorial lessons in this module will give you experience using the commands and features of BASICA. Before you begin the "hands-on" learning experience, however, you will need to complete a few initial steps and gain some preliminary information in order to be adequately prepared.

Initial Steps

1. Obtain a floppy disk appropriate for the microcomputer you will be using to complete your course assignments. Your instructor or laboratory staff will be able to tell you which kind of disk to purchase.

   Size: ______________________

   Sides: ______________________

   Density: ______________________

2. Format your disk to the specifications of the DOS and microcomputer hardware that you will be using to complete your course assignments. Your instructor or laboratory staff will be able to tell you the steps to follow. ***Caution: Formatting a disk will erase all files that may exist on the disk.***

   Steps to Format a Disk: ______________________

   ____

   ____

   ____

   ____

   ____

   ____

3. Each time you use BASICA you will want to be sure that your files are saved on your disk. There will be certain steps to follow to ensure that your files are automatically saved on your disk. Your instructor or laboratory staff will be able to tell you the steps to follow.

   Starting a BASICA Session: ______________________

   ____

   ____

   ____

   ____

   ____

   ____

   ____

   ____

   ____

REQUIRED MATERIALS

1. An IBM DOS diskette (or hard-disk directory containing the DOS software).
2. A formatted disk (your files diskette).
3. This manual.
4. Other ____________________

TUTORIAL CONVENTIONS

During the tutorial you will create BASICA programs and use various BASICA commands and operations. The following are the conventions the tutorial's instructions will use.

↵ The bent arrow means to type the Enter key located on the right side of the keyboard.

^ This character means press and hold the Ctrl key, and then type the next key shown.

|| || Do not type the double lines; type only what is inside them.

HOW TO GET OUT OF TROUBLE

If you want to:	*Then:*
■ Erase characters being entered as a BASICA command or program line. . .	■ Tap the Backspace key (←) located just above the Enter key.
■ Stop any command operation and return to the Ok prompt. . .	■ Press and hold the Ctrl key and then type the Scroll Lock (Break) key.
■ Stop the tutorial to continue later. . .	■ Type ||SAVE"filename↵||. Watch the disk drive light to make sure the program has been saved, and then type ||SYSTEM↵|| to return to DOS.
■ Continue with the tutorial after you have stopped. . .	■ Type ||LOAD"filename↵|| after loading BASICA into RAM memory and inserting your files diskette into the A: drive.

GETTING STARTED

1. Insert the DOS diskette into the A: disk drive (the disk drive on the left) and close the disk drive door.
2. If the computer already is on, press and hold the Ctrl and Alt keys and then type the Del key. Otherwise, turn on the computer and the monitor.

In a few moments DOS will be automatically loaded.

3. Answer DOS's date and time prompts.
4. When you see the A>, type ||BASICA↵||.

The programming language BASICA is provided on the DOS Master diskette.

5. If you see the version message

```
The IBM Personal Computer Basic
Version C1.10 Copyright IBM Corp 1981
```

you do not have the correct version of BASIC loaded into memory. Repeat steps 1 through 4.

6. Remove the DOS diskette from the A: drive and then insert your files diskette into that drive. Be sure to close the disk drive door.

LESSON 1 BASICA Basics

Inherent BASICA Editing Operations

The following editing operations are almost universal for the different versions of BASIC, and they hold true for IBM's BASICA. The operations are based on the fact that each line in a BASIC program must have a line number, and that no two lines may have the same number. In addition, the computer automatically will arrange program lines by their numbers, not by the order in which they are typed.

- *Inserting a line.* Give the new program line a line number between the two line numbers of the lines above and below where it is to be inserted.
- *Deleting a line.* Type the line number of the line to be deleted and then press the Enter key.
- *Replacing a line.* Type the new line with the same line number of the line to be replaced.

Writing a BASICA Program

You will create a short BASICA program. Be sure to include all spaces, commas, quotes, etc., exactly as they are shown. If you make a mistake before you type ↵ (enter the line), use the Backspace key (←) located just above the Enter key to backspace and erase the error, and then continue typing the line correctly. If you make a mistake after typing ↵, refer to the "Inherent Editing Commands" for procedures to correct it.

1. Enter the following BASIC program.

```
10 REM Example Program #1↵
20 PRINT "This is a simple example"↵
30 PRINT↵
40 INPUT "Enter a number ",A↵
50 INPUT "Enter another number ",B↵
60 PRINT↵
70 PRINT A;" times ";B;" equals ";A*B↵
```

Viewing a BASICA Program

Clearing the Screen with ^Home

The Home key is located on the upper right side of the keyboard. When used with the Ctrl key, the Home key clears the screen and leaves the cursor in the upper left corner (home position) of the screen.

2. Type ||^Home||.

Listing a Program on the Monitor Screen

3. Now type ||**LIST**←|| to list the following program on monitor screen.

```
LIST
10 REM Example Program #1
20 PRINT "This is a simple example"
30 PRINT
40 INPUT "Enter a number ",A
50 INPUT "Enter another number ",B
60 PRINT
70 PRINT A;" times ";B;" equals ";A*B
Ok
```

4. Check once more to make certain the program is entered correctly.

Listing a Program on the Printer

To list a BASICA program on the printer you may use the **LLIST** (**LIST** with an extra *L*) command.

5. Make sure the printer is turned on, on-line, and connected to your computer. (Your lab may have a shared device control switch. You will need to select your computer as the one currently connected to the printer.)
6. Now type ||**LLIST**←||.

Listing Portions of a BASICA Program

With either the **LIST** or the **LLIST** command you can list only certain lines of a program by specifying their line numbers. To demonstrate how to specify particular lines in the **LIST** command, do the following.

7. Type ||**LIST** 20←|| (list a single line).

```
LIST 20
20 PRINT "This is a simple example"
Ok
```

8. Type ||**LIST** 20–50←|| (list a section of lines).

```
LIST 20-50
20 PRINT "This is a simple example"
30 PRINT
40 INPUT "Enter a number ",A
50 INPUT "Enter another number ",B
Ok
```

9. Type ||**LIST** 30–←|| (list from a line on).

```
LIST 30-
30 PRINT
40 INPUT "Enter a number ",A
50 INPUT "Enter another number ",B
60 PRINT
70 PRINT A;" times ";B;" equals ";A*B
Ok
```

10. Type ||**LIST** −40←|| (list up to a line).

```
LIST -40
10 REM Example Program #1
20 PRINT "This is a simple example"
30 PRINT
40 INPUT "Enter a number ",A
Ok
```

Executing a BASICA Program

As with most versions of BASIC, the **RUN** command is used to execute a BASICA program. The output of a BASICA program may be displayed on the screen, the printer, or simultaneously on both the screen and the printer.

Running a Program on the Monitor Screen

11. Type ||^Home|| to clear the screen.
12. Type ||**RUN**←||.
13. Answer the program's INPUT statement prompts by entering the numbers 25 and 4.

The output that should appear on the screen is:

```
RUN
This is a simple example

Enter a number 25
Enter another number 4

 25  times  4  equals  100
Ok
```

Running a Program on the Printer

To cause the output of a BASICA program to be sent to the printer rather than to the screen, the command **LPRINT** may be used in place of the **PRINT** command. INPUT prompts must be duplicated with **LPRINT** statements within the body of the program. For instance, to cause all of the output of the program to be printed on the printer, the program would have to be changed to the following.

```
10 REM Example Program #1
20 LPRINT "This is a simple example"
30 LPRINT
40 INPUT "Enter a number ",A
45 LPRINT "Enter a number ",A
50 INPUT "Enter another number ",B
55 LPRINT "Enter another number ",B
60 LPRINT
70 LPRINT A;" times ";B;" equals ";A*B
```

Running a Program on the Screen and the Printer

With versions of BASICA numbered 2.0 or higher it is possible to use a Ctrl-key combination to toggle on an echo of all screen output to the printer.

You press and hold the Ctrl key and then tap the key marked "PrtSc." Once toggled on, all output that appears on the screen also is sent to the printer. Output to the printer may be stopped by typing ^PrtSc again (toggle off).

If you are using a version of BASICA 2.0 +, do the following.

14. Repeat the procedure to prepare for printer output.
15. Type ||^PrtSc|| to toggle on the printer.
16. Type ||**RUN**↵||.
17. Answer the program's INPUT statement prompts with two numbers of your choice.
18. Type ||^PrtSc|| to toggle off the printer.

LESSON 2 BASICA File Operation Commands

Saving a BASICA Program—The **SAVE** Command

The **SAVE** command is used to save a copy of the BASICA program in RAM onto the diskette. This command is entered with a filename (which you specify) under which the program is saved. If a file with that name already exists on the diskette, it will be replaced by the file being saved. The computer will not hesitate or give you any message that the previous diskette file will be or has been erased.

1. Type ||**SAVE**"exone↵||.

If your files diskette is in the B: drive, the command syntax to save the program is ||**SAVE**"B:exone↵||.

2. Now type ||^Home **LIST**↵||.

```
LIST
10 REM Example Program #1
20 PRINT "This is a simple example"
30 PRINT
40 INPUT "Enter a number ",A
50 INPUT "Enter another number ",B
60 PRINT
70 PRINT A;" times ";B;" equals ";A*B
Ok
```

Notice that saving a program does not erase it from memory. It simply saves a copy of the program on the diskette.

Erasing a BASICA Program from RAM—The **NEW** Command

To erase a program from RAM you may use the **NEW** command.

3. Type ||**NEW**↵ **LIST**↵||.

Unless you have saved the program on a diskette, it will be lost when the **NEW** command is executed.

Loading a BASICA Program—The **LOAD** Command

The **LOAD** command is used to copy a BASICA program from the diskette into RAM.

4. Type ||^Home|| to clear the screen and continue by typing ||**LOAD**"exone↵ **LIST**↵||.

If your files diskette is in the B: drive, the command syntax to save the program is ||**LOAD**"B:exone↵||.

Listing the Files on a Diskette—The **FILES** Command

The **FILES** command is used to display the filenames and extensions of files on a diskette.

5. Type ||**FILES**↵||.

Erasing a Diskette File—The **KILL** Command

The **KILL** command is used to erase a file from the diskette. The file's name and extension must be specified when you use the **KILL** command.

6. Type ||**KILL**"exone.BAS↵||. Then type ||**FILES**↵||.

The file "exone.BAS" should not appear in the listing of files given by the **FILES** command.

7. Type ||**SAVE**"exone↵|| to make another diskette copy of the program now in RAM.

Renaming a Diskette File—The **NAME** Command

The **NAME** file **AS** file command is used to rename a diskette file from BASICA. Like the **KILL** command, this command requires filenames and extensions.

8. Type ||**NAME**"exone.BAS" **AS** "progone.BAS"||.
9. Now type ||**FILES**↵|| to see that the file has been renamed.

Combining BASICA Programs—The **MERGE** Command

A special BASICA file handling command, **MERGE,** may be used to combine a BASICA program from the diskette with a BASICA program in RAM (the current program). The program being merged (the one on the diskette) must have been last saved in ASCII data format, which is a standard format for data. (For more information on ASCII see Data Transfer between Applications).

To save a program file in ASCII you add a ",A after the filename when you use the **SAVE** command.

When two BASICA programs are merged, the line numbers determine how the computer will merge them together. The effect is the same as typing the program being merged from the diskette while the current program is in memory. Lines of the merged program that have the same line numbers (as lines) of the current program will replace lines in the current program. Other lines will be placed into the current program based on their line numbers.

Creating a Heading File for Merging

To gain experience in using the **MERGE** command, you will create a small BASICA program consisting of REM statements that may be merged into the beginning of any BASICA program you later create.

10. Make sure you have the file "progone" saved on your diskette, and then type ||**NEW**←|| to erase that program from RAM.
11. Create the following BASICA program, keeping the line numbers the same as shown and filling in your particular information where appropriate.

```
3 REM ****************************************
4 REM Assignment # nn
5 REM Program Name -
6 REM
7 REM Prepared for: Course name/number/section
8 REM By           : your name
9 REM Date         : mm/dd/yy
10 REM ***************************************
```

12. Save the program by typing ||**SAVE**"header",**A**←||.
13. Next load the program "progone" into memory and list it on the monitor screen.

Notice that loading a BASICA program automatically erases any program that may have been in RAM.

14. Finally, type ||**MERGE**"header←|| and then ||**LIST**←||.

```
MERGE"header
Ok
LIST
3 REM ****************************************
4 REM Assignment # nn
5 REM Program Name -
6 REM
7 REM Prepared for: Course name/number/section
8 REM By           : your name
9 REM Date         : mm/dd/yy
10 REM ***************************************
20 PRINT "This is a simple example"
30 PRINT
40 INPUT "Enter a number ",A
50 INPUT "Enter another number ",B
60 PRINT
70 PRINT A;" times ";B;" equals ";A*B
```

Notice that line 10 of the program being merged, "header," replaced line 10 of the current program, "progone," and that all other lines occur in sequence, according to line number.

LESSON 3
Current File Operations

Renumbering BASICA Program Lines—The **RENUM** Command

There will be occasions when it will be necessary or desirable to renumber the program lines in your BASICA program. The **RENUM** command is used to perform this operation.

This BASICA command has the form

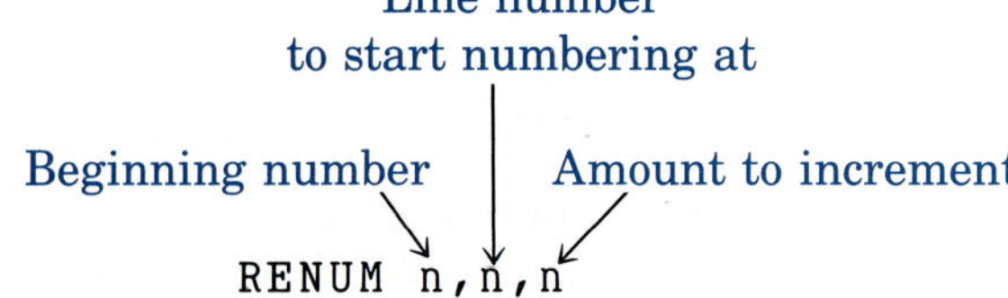

The default “beginning number” is 10; the default “line number to start numbering at” is the first line; and the default “amount to increment” is 10.

To use the **RENUM** command do the following.

1. Type ||**LIST**↵**RENUM**↵**LIST**↵||.

```
LIST
3 REM ****************************************
4 REM Assignment # nn
5 REM Program Name -
6 REM
7 REM Prepared for: Course name/number/section
8 REM By          : your name
9 REM Date        : mm/dd/yy
10 REM ***************************************
20 PRINT "This is a simple example"
30 PRINT
40 INPUT "Enter a number ",A
50 INPUT "Enter another number ",B
60 PRINT
70 PRINT A;" times ";B;" equals ";A*B
Ok
RENUM
Ok
LIST
10 REM ****************************************
20 REM Assignment # nn
30 REM Program Name -
40 REM
50 REM Prepared for: Course name/number/section
60 REM By          : your name
70 REM Date        : mm/dd/yy
80 REM ***************************************
90 PRINT "This is a simple example"
100 PRINT
110 INPUT "Enter a number ",A
120 INPUT "Enter another number ",B
130 PRINT
140 PRINT A;" times ";B;" equals ";A*B
```

2. Type ||**RENUM** ,, 1↵**LIST**↵||.

```
RENUM ,,1
Ok
LIST
10 REM ****************************************
11 REM Assignment # nn
12 REM Program Name -
13 REM
14 REM Prepared for: Course name/number/section
```

```
15 REM By            : your name
16 REM Date          : mm/dd/yy
17 REM ***************************************
18 PRINT "This is a simple example"
19 PRINT
20 INPUT "Enter a number ",A
21 INPUT "Enter another number ",B
22 PRINT
23 PRINT A;" times ";B;" equals ";A*B
```

Notice that if a single option number is used to affect the **RENUM** command, as in this case, where the number to increment was specified as 1, commas must be used to satisfy any preceding options in the command.

3. Type ||**RENUM** 100,18,20↵**LIST**↵||.

```
RENUM 100,18,20
Ok
LIST
10 REM ***************************************
11 REM Assignment # nn
12 REM Program Name -
13 REM
14 REM Prepared for: Course name/number/section
15 REM By            : your name
16 REM Date          : mm/dd/yy
17 REM ***************************************
100 PRINT "This is a simple example"
120 PRINT
140 INPUT "Enter a number ",A
160 INPUT "Enter another number ",B
180 PRINT
200 PRINT A;" times ";B;" equals ";A*B
```

Deleting Sections of a Program—The **DELETE** Command

The **DELETE** command may be used to delete lines of a BASICA program. Its syntax is similar to that of the **LIST** command.

`DELETE 20`	Deletes the single line 20
`DELETE 20-50`	Deletes the lines 20 through 50
`DELETE -30`	Deletes the lines up to 30
`DELETE 50-`	Deletes the lines 50 on

Full-Screen Editing

In addition to the inherent editing found in most versions of BASIC, IBM's BASICA has full-screen editing available for you to use.

The Full-Screen Editing Keys

The next steps of the tutorial demonstrate several control key combinations and operations you will find useful when you edit your BASICA programs. Many of the keys it references may be found on the right side of the keyboard on (or around) the numeric keypad.

Principles of Full-Screen Editing

With BASICA's full-screen editing the monitor screen acts as an "electronic message board." When you type a command or program line, you are typing a message for the computer. When you press the Enter key, you are sending that message to the computer for it to act on as a command, or to accept as a BASIC program line.

As you type, the message will begin to clutter up the message board. You already have seen how to erase the board with ^Home. But, as long as a message is still on the board, you can move the cursor back to the message and send it to the computer again by pressing the Enter key.

Four keys on the right side of the keyboard (on the numeric keypad) marked with arrows are called cursor control keys. They allow you to move the cursor anywhere on the screen.

Overwriting Characters

4. Type ||^Home **LIST**↵||.

Now your program should be listed at the top of the screen with the cursor located at the line under BASICA's "Ok" prompt.

5. Move the cursor to line 140 with the cursor-up key, and then under the *a* in the INPUT prompt with the cursor-right key.

```
140 INPUT "Enter a number ",A
                 |
                Here
```

6. Type ||the first||.

```
140 INPUT "Enter the first",A
```

Characters typed normally will overwrite existing characters when full-screen editing is being done.

Inserting Characters

7. Type the key marked "Ins."

This single key toggles on an insert mode. Notice that the cursor has become larger. This indicates that the insert mode is on. Typing the Ins key again or any noncharacter key (such as a cursor control key or the Enter key) will turn the insert mode off.

8. With the insert mode on, continue by typing || number ||.

```
140 INPUT "Enter the first number ",A
```

9. Next tap the Enter key, and then type ||^Home **LIST**↵||.

It is important to note that the computer only recognizes changes in a program line *if* the Enter key is pressed while the cursor is on that line (the cursor may be anywhere on the line). Otherwise the computer ignores any changes made. In this example, the second listing of the program would not have been updated for the changes made to line 140.

Deleting Characters

10. Move the cursor to line 100, and then to under the *T* in *This.*
11. Next tap the key marked "Del." Continue to tap this key until the program line appears as shown here.

```
100 PRINT "s a simple example"
```

The Del key is used to delete characters while full-screen editing is being done.

12. Type ‖Calculator Program↵‖.

```
100 PRINT "Calculator Program"
```

Other Full-Screen Editing Keystroke Commands

Several other keys and key combinations may be used while full-screen editing in BASICA. All of the following will work when you are originally entering a program line, or when you are editing a program line displayed on the monitor screen.

Cursor Movement

- Home key   Jumps the cursor to the top left corner of the screen.
- End key   Jumps the cursor to the last character of the line on which it is located.
- ^→   Jumps the cursor one word to the right.
- ^←   Jumps the cursor one word to the left.

Deleting

- ^End   Erases all characters to the right of the cursor.
- Esc key   Erases all characters of the line on which the cursor is located.

Controlling Screen Scroll

Screen scroll occurs when more output is going to the screen than its 24 lines can hold. With screen scroll the top lines disappear and the lines below move up as the output is generated.

When you have a long program being listed or have several lines of output from a program's execution, you often will want to temporarily halt the listing or program execution in order to view specific parts of the output. You may do this with the ^Num Lock key combination.

Typing ^Num Lock pauses BASICA operations until ^Num Lock is typed again or any other character key on the keyboard is pressed.

Interrupting BASICA Operations

The important control key combination, ^Break keys, will stop the execution of all BASICA operations including **RUN, LIST, AUTO** (the command to generate line numbers automatically), and more.

The Break key is located on the top row and far right side of the keyboard and is labeled on the top with "Scroll Lock." The front of the key is labeled "Break."

When ^Break is typed, any current operation will be interrupted and the "Ok" prompt will return.

LESSON 4 Modifying progone.BAS

You now will modify "progone.BAS" so that the program will perform any one of four computations, selected by the user, on two numbers input by the user. The purpose of this step in the tutorial is to allow you to use and build a working familiarity with many of the operations and commands discussed so far. In the lesson you will revise, run, and debug the new progone. Knowledge of the program statements used in this modified version of progone is not essential to the successful completion of this step.

The changes you will make to the program demonstrate that BASICA program lines may have several program statements on them if the statements are separated by colons, and they provide some information about command syntax and program design by example.

1. Use the commands and editing features of BASICA to modify "progone.BAS" into the following form.

```
1 REM ***************************************
2 REM Assignment # nn
3 REM Program Name -
4 REM
5 REM Prepared for: Course name/number/section
6 REM By          : your name
7 REM Date        : mm/dd/yy
8 REM ***************************************
9 REM
100 REM ----------  Menu Module -----------
110 REM
120     CLS
130     PRINT "Calculator Program"
140     PRINT "=================="
150     PRINT "1) Multiplication "
160     PRINT "2) Division       "
170     PRINT "3) Addition       "
180     PRINT "4) Subtraction    "
190     PRINT
200     INPUT "Enter the number of your choice ",C
210     REM
220     REM ------ Data Entry Module --------
230     PRINT
240     INPUT "Enter the first number ",A
250     INPUT "Enter the next  number ",B
260     PRINT
270     REM --- Process Selection Module ----
280     REM
290     ON C GOSUB 500,600,700,800
300     REM
310     REM ------- Output Module -----------
320     PRINT
330     PRINT A;C$;B;" equals ";ANSWER
340     REM
350     REM ----- Bottom of Loop Module -----
360     REM
370     PRINT:PRINT:INPUT "Continue (Y/N) ";MORE$
```

```
380 IF MORE$ = "Y" OR MORE$ = "y" THEN GOTO 120 ELSE CLS:END
390 REM
400 REM ----- Processing Subroutines -------
410 REM
500 ANSWER = A*B:C$=" times "      :RETURN
600 ANSWER = A/B:C$=" divided by ":RETURN
700 ANSWER = A+B:C$=" plus "       :RETURN
800 ANSWER = A-B:C$=" minus "      :RETURN
999 END
```

2. Run the program and test it to see if all parts of it are working. Use full-screen editing to correct any mistakes that you may have made.

LESSON 5 Programming Techniques

The remainder of the tutorial is designed to introduce you to a variety of programming techniques and to some of the peculiarities of the IBM PC and its programming language BASICA.

Using the **SAVE** Command

1. Type ||**SAVE**"progone↵||.

The first technique discussed here is brief, but important. Save your programs periodically. It is a quick operation that ultimately will save you time and frustration.

Direct Mode

Direct mode refers to the fact that most of BASICA's statements may be entered without line numbers and the computer will act on them directly.

2. To demonstrate direct mode, type the following.

```
||^Home||
||INPUT "Enter a number ",Z↵||
 Enter a number ||1234↵||
 Ok
||PRINT Z↵||
  1234
 Ok
||FOR I = 1 to 10: PRINT I;:NEXT I↵||
  1  2  3  4  5  6  7  8  9  10
 Ok
```

Using direct mode is helpful in situations when you are not sure of the syntax or would like to test the effect of a program line before you add or insert it into a program. If you are satisfied with the command's execution in direct mode, you may move the cursor to its display (still on the screen), turn on the insert mode, insert the appropriate line number at the appropriate place, and type the Enter key to enter it as a line of your program.

3. Type ||**RUN**↵ ||.

```
Calculator Program
==================
1) Multiplication
2) Division
3) Addition
4) Subtraction
```

```
Enter the number of your choice ||2↵||

Enter the first number ||10↵||
Enter the next  number ||0↵||           (meant to type 10)

Division by zero


10 divided by 0 equals 1.701412E+38

Continue (Y/N) ? ||N↵||

(screen clears)
 Ok
||PRINT A↵||
  10
 Ok
||PRINT B↵||
  0
 Ok
||PRINT A/B↵||
 Division by zero

  1.701412E+38
```

The preceding use of direct mode is helpful when unexpected results are occurring during your program's execution. You can stop the program by typing ^Break or wait until it is done executing, then print the values of the variables you suspect may be part of the problem. The values printed will be the last values held by those variables.

Tracing Program Execution

Another useful debugging technique involves the use of the **TRON** and **TROFF** commands of BASICA. These two commands turn on and off program tracing.

4. Type ||**TRON**↵**RUN**↵||.

```
[1][2][3][4][5][6][7][8][9][100][110][120] (screen clears)
[130]Calculator Program
[140]==================
[150]1) Multiplication
[160]2) Division
[170]3) Addition
[180]4) Subtraction
[190]
[200]Enter the number of your choice ||3↵||
[210][220][230]
[240]Enter the first number ||10↵||
[250]Enter the next  number ||10↵||
[260]
[270][280][290][700][300][310][320]
[330] 10  plus  10  equals  20
[340][350][360][370]

Continue (Y/N) ? ||n↵||
[380] (screen clears)
Ok
```

When program tracing is on, the line numbers of the program lines being executed are displayed on the monitor as the computer executes them. This feature allows you to track the execution of your program while it is running to determine the actual vs. desired order of program line execution.

5. Now type ||**TROFF**↵|| to turn off program tracing.

Function Keys

Ten gray keys are located on the far-left side of the keyboard. They are Function keys, often referred to as programmable or soft keys.

BASICA automatically programs each of these keys to contain a string of characters used to print entire BASICA commands on the monitor screen. The most frequently used Function keys and their strings are:

F1 (**LIST**)
F2 (**RUN**)
F3 (**LOAD"**)
F4 (**SAVE"**)

At the bottom of the monitor screen you will see a list of all Function keys and the strings they are holding.

When you press a Function key the string that it holds is placed on the monitor screen for you to enter. In some cases, an Enter keystroke is part of the string so that it is entered automatically. The strings with Enter keystrokes are displayed at the bottom of the screen with an arrow as the last character.

Function Key Commands

Several BASICA commands are associated with the Function keys, one of which allows you to reprogram the string a Function key is holding. To give you experience with Function key commands, complete the following steps.

6. Type the following.

`||^Home||`	turns off the list at the bottom of the screen.
`||KEY OFF↵||`	turns the list back on.
`||KEY ON↵||`	lists the F keys like a program is listed.
`||KEY 9, "Portland"↵||`	changes the string in F9 from KEY to Portland. Notice the list at the bottom of the screen reflects this change.

A Function key may hold up to 15 characters and the ability to assign your own characters to these keys can be very useful when you must enter repetitive data.

It may be useful to know that to add an Enter keystroke to a string, type +CHR$(13) after the string. For example typing

```
||KEY 1,"LIST"+CHR$(13)↵||
```

will program the Function key F1 to hold ||**LIST**↵||. To include a quote character in a Function key string use +CHR(34). For instance:

```
||KEY 9, "KILL"+CHR$(34)↵||
```

will program the F9 key to hold ||**KILL"**||.

The Alt Key

The key located on the bottom left side of the keyboard and labeled "Alt" is used like the Ctrl key because it is pressed and held while another key is tapped. (The convention of ||Alt-key|| will mean press and hold the Alt key and then tap the next key shown.)

The Alt key also will produce entire BASICA commands and statements when used with the alphabetic keys on the keyboard. For instance,

||Alt-P|| . . . displays **PRINT**
||Alt-I|| . . . displays **INPUT**
||Alt-G|| . . . displays **GOTO**
||Alt-D|| . . . displays **DELETE**

Generally speaking, use of the Alt key is minimal for beginning BASICA programmers. Another use—one that is both fun and appropriate for ending the tutorial—is related to using the Alt key for fancy output in your BASIC programs.

Each key on the keyboard has an ASCII code (a number) assigned to it. If you press and hold the Alt key while typing a character's code on the numeric keypad (the number keys on the right side of the keyboard), that character will appear on the screen. To demonstrate do the following.

7. Type ||Alt-65||. Capital A appears on the screen.

Approximately 128 characters are not shown on the keyboard. They are called special characters or, as a group, the extended character set. Their ASCII character codes begin at the number 127 and go to 254.

8. Type the following to view all of these special characters.

```
||^Home||
||FOR I = 127 TO 254: PRINT CHR$(I);: NEXT I↵||
```

You may print the special characters directly on the screen by using the Alt key and the numeric keypad keys.

9. Type this program line 325:

Begin in column 11

```
325       FOR I = 1 TO 12: PRINT "||Alt-177||||Alt-176||";:NEXT I:PRINT "||Alt-177||"
```

Use the Alt-key convention here rather than literally typing what is shown

10. Now ||**LIST** 310–350↵||.
11. Move the cursor to line 325 and change its line number to be 335, and then type ↵ (Enter) to enter the change.
12. Now type ||**^**Home|| and ||**LIST** 310–350↵|| again.

The last two steps illustrate a handy way to duplicate a line in a BASICA program.

13. Finally, ||**RUN**↵|| the program to see how its answer output is affected by the two new program lines.

Unfortunately, output on the screen generated by the extended ASCII character set will not print out on most printers because these characters are not accepted as part of the American Standard Code for Information Interchange.

Returning to DOS

The final steps of the tutorial follow.

14. **SAVE** progone.
15. **LLIST** the program.
16. Produce a hard-copy sample **RUN** of the program.
17. Type ||**SYSTEM**↵||.

SYSTEM is the BASICA command that erases any BASIC program that may be in RAM, and erases BASICA from RAM. You have returned to the DOS level of operation as you can tell by the A> on the screen.

ASSIGNMENT

```
LIST
10 LET A$="Example #"
20 A=1
30    PRINT A$;A
40 READ B$,B
50 DATA Example #,2
60    PRINT B$;B
70 INPUT"Type in the value for C$ :",C$
80 INPUT"                      number ";C
90    PRINT C$;C
Ok
RUN
Example # 1
Example # 2
Type in the value for C$   :Example #
                  number ? 3
Example # 3
-------------------------------------------------------------------------


LIST
10 A$="Direct assignment"
20 LET A=5
30 B=10
40 C=A+B
50 PRINT A$;A;"+";B;"=";C
Ok
RUN
Direct assignment 5 + 10 = 15
-------------------------------------------------------------------------

LIST
10    READ A$,B,C$,D
20    PRINT A$,B,C$,D
30 GOTO 10
40 DATA one,2,three,4,five,6,seven,8,nine,10,eleven,12
RUN
one            2              three          4
five           6              seven          8
nine           10             eleven         12
Out of DATA in 10
-------------------------------------------------------------------------

LIST
10 INPUT"Type in a string value :",A$
20 INPUT"Enter exactly three numbers :",A,B,C
30 PRINT A$;A;B;C
Ok
RUN
Type in a string value :This is an example
Enter exactly three numbers :4,5,6
This is an example 4  5  6
```

CONDITION

```
LIST
10 A=7:B=15
20 IF A < 10 THEN PRINT "A is less than 10":GOTO 30
25 PRINT "A is greater than 10"
30 IF A > B THEN PRINT "A is greater than B" ELSE PRINT "A is less than B"
Ok
RUN
A is less than 10
A is less than B
------------------------------------------------------------------------------

LIST
10 A=15:B=7
20 IF A < 10 THEN PRINT "A is less than 10":GOTO 30
25 PRINT "A is greater than 10"
30 IF A > B THEN PRINT "A is greater than B" ELSE PRINT "A is less than B"
RUN
A is greater than 10
A is greater than B
------------------------------------------------------------------------------

LIST
10 A=5: B=4: C=3: D=2: E=1
20 IF C > D AND C < A THEN PRINT "C lies between D and A":GOTO 30
25 PRINT"Condition NOT TRUE"
30 IF B > E OR  B = 2 THEN B= 2 * A: PRINT B;: B=2 : PRINT B:GOTO 40
35 PRINT"Condition NOT TRUE"
40 IF A > B AND C > D OR E = 5 THEN PRINT"********************":GOTO 50
45 PRINT"Condition NOT TRUE"
50 END
RUN
C lies between D and A
 10  2
********************
------------------------------------------------------------------------------

LIST
10 A=5: B=4: C=3: D=2: E=1
20 IF C < D AND C > A THEN PRINT "C lies between D and A":GOTO 30
25 PRINT"Condition NOT TRUE"
30 IF B > E OR  B = 2 THEN B= 2 * E: PRINT B;: B=2: PRINT B:GOTO 40
35 PRINT"Condition NOT TRUE"
40 IF A < B AND C < D OR E = 5 THEN PRINT"********************":GOTO 50
45 PRINT"Condition NOT TRUE"
50 END
RUN
Condition NOT TRUE
 2  2
Condition NOT TRUE
```

ITERATION

```
LIST
10 FOR X = 1 TO 5
20   PRINT X;
30 NEXT X
40 PRINT"****"
RUN
 1  2  3  4  5 ****
--------------------------------------------------------------------------

LIST
10 FOR T = 1 TO 3
20    FOR X = 1 TO 5
30      PRINT X;
40    NEXT X
50    PRINT"****";
60 NEXT T
RUN
 1  2  3  4  5 **** 1  2  3  4  5 **** 1  2  3  4  5 ****
--------------------------------------------------------------------------

LIST
10 FOR X = 1 TO 3
20    FOR Y = 1 TO 5
30      READ INFO$(X,Y)
40    NEXT Y
50 NEXT X
60 FOR X = 1 TO 3: PRINT INFO$(X,1) "....... "INFO$(X,3): NEXT X
70 DATA Allen,Greene,244-3396,Mktg.,#7763
80 DATA Carol,Lundey,236-1718,Acct.,#6658
90 DATA Terry,Bright,775-0668,Mgmt.,#7204
RUN
Allen....... 244-3396
Carol....... 236-1718
Terry....... 775-0668
--------------------------------------------------------------------------

LIST
10 HGHT = 10
20 WHILE HGHT > 1
30    BOUNCE = BOUNCE + 1
40    HGHT = HGHT * .75
50    PRINT "Bounce";BOUNCE;" - ";HGHT;TAB(25);"feet"
60 WEND
RUN
Bounce 1  -  7.5        feet
Bounce 2  -  5.625      feet
Bounce 3  -  4.21875    feet
Bounce 4  -  3.164063   feet
Bounce 5  -  2.373047   feet
Bounce 6  -  1.779785   feet
Bounce 7  -  1.334839   feet
Bounce 8  -  1.001129   feet
Bounce 9  -  .7508469   feet
```

OUTPUT

```
10 A$="This":B$="Example": A=1: B=2
20 PRINT"    5    10   15   20   25   30   35   40   45   50   55   60 ..."
30 PRINT"----!----!----!----!----!----!----!----!----!----!----!----!---- "
40 PRINT A$;"is an";B$;A;B
50 PRINT A$,"is an",B$,A,B
60 PRINT A$;TAB(10);"is an";TAB(25);B$;A;B
70 PRINT A$;SPC(10);"is an";SPC(25);B$;A;B
RUN
    5    10   15   20   25   30   35   40   45   50   55   60 ...
----!----!----!----!----!----!----!----!----!----!----!----!----
Thisis anExample 1  2
This          is an         Example        1             2
This     is an          Example 1  2
This          is an                         Example 1  2
--------------------------------------------------------------- --------

LIST
10 A$="This is one way to center a string"
20 DIS =(80-LEN(A$))/2
30 PRINT TAB(DIS);A$
RUN
                      This is one way to center a string
--------------------------------------------------------------- --------

LIST
10 INPUT " (;) includes a question mark";A
20 INPUT " (,) omits the question mark",A
RUN
 (;) includes a question mark? 1
 (,) omits the question mark 2
--------------------------------------------------------------- --------

LIST
10 PRINT RND;SPC(10);
20 PRINT CINT(RND*10);
30 PRINT CINT(RND*100);
40 PRINT CINT(RND*1000);SPC(10);
50 PRINT CINT(RND*10)/10;
60 PRINT CINT(RND*100)/100;
70 PRINT CINT(RND*1000)/1000;
Ok
RUN
 .9076439          6  19  631            .9  .74  .843
--------------------------------------------------------------- --------

LIST                *
10 FOR J = 1 TO 6    *
20   LOCATE J,20+J    *
30   PRINT "*"         *
40 NEXT J               *
RUN                      *
```

PRINT USING Statement

```
LIST
10 A=5:B=50:C=500:D=5000
20 PRINT USING "       ###   ";A;B;C;D
30 PRINT USING "   ####.##   ";A;B;C;D
40 PRINT USING "  ####,.##   ";A;B;C;D
50 PRINT USING "$####,.##    ";A;B;C;D
60 PRINT USING "$$###,.##    ";A;B;C;D
RUN
        5          50          500          %5000
     5.00       50.00       500.00      5000.00
     5.00       50.00       500.00     5,000.00
$    5.00  $    50.00  $    500.00    $5,000.00
    $5.00      $50.00      $500.00    $5,000.00
------------------------------------------------------------------------
LIST
10 Z$="TEST"
20 PRTSTRG$= "\   \#  \    \-"
30 FOR X = 1 TO 5
40    PRINT USING PRTSTRG$;Z$;X;"hello";
50 NEXT X
Ok
RUN
TEST1 hello - TEST2 hello - TEST3 hello - TEST4 hello - TEST5 hello -
------------------------------------------------------------------------
LIST
10 A = 234 :B$="OUTPUT EXAMPLE": C = 567
20 X$="     Form ###   Computer report  \                  \ No. ###.##"
30 PRINT USING X$;A,B$,C
Ok
RUN
     Form 234   Computer report  OUTPUT EXAMPLE        No. 567.00
```

*NOTE: Special formatting symbols (# . , $ \) are covered in these examples. Other formatting symbols (! * _^ + −) have special meaning when included in the* ***PRINT USING*** string. A semicolon (;) is the only ***PRINT*** separator allowed with ***PRINT USING.***

ARRAY OPERATIONS

The following examples are based on the string array A$(I,J), which is filled with data read from data statements. The data represent a database of employees working for a small retail store. In the following example, the array A$(I,J) is filled with the data:

A$(I,1)	Employee's last name
A$(I,2)	Employee's first name
A$(I,3)	Sex
A$(I,4)	Yearly salary
A$(I,5)	Department of employment
A$(I,6)	Amount owing on the company's personal account

Filling Array A$(I,J) with Data

```
100 DIM A$(15,6)
110 REM ---------------------------------------------------------
120 FOR I = 1 TO 15
130   FOR J = 1 TO 6
140    READ A$(I,J)          ' Read loop for array A$(I,J)
150   NEXT J
160 NEXT I
170 REM ---------------------------------------------------------
180 REM             Database for array A$(I,J)
190 REM
200 REM    Last        First                          Personal
210 REM    Name        Name     Sex Salary  Dept   Account
220 REM ---------------------------------------------------------
230 DATA   Hunter    , Philip , M , 12000 , 3   ,  90.00
240 DATA   Parsons   , Sharon , F , 10500 , 2   ,  50.75
250 DATA   Boronat   , Penny  , F , 16200 , 4   ,  20.50
260 DATA   Carlson   , Scott  , M , 21400 , 1   , 310.00
270 DATA   Jeli      , Krista , F ,  9500 , 3   ,   0.00
280 DATA   Carson    , Cindy  , F , 22500 , 2   ,  75.00
290 DATA   Anderson  , Jeffery, M , 10000 , 2   , 200.00
300 DATA   Harrison  , Glenys , F ,  9800 , 4   , 130.60
310 DATA   Elting    , Charles, M , 17300 , 1   ,  10.00
320 DATA   Cathcart  , Anita  , F , 19000 , 4   ,  95.50
330 DATA   Nickerson, Cheryl  , F ,  8700 , 3   , 105.10
340 DATA   Fuller    , Alice  , F , 19000 , 2   ,  45.00
350 DATA   Parks     , Larry  , M , 12600 , 4   , 180.00
360 DATA   Reeves    , Ronald , M , 18700 , 1   ,  92.50
370 DATA   Zimmerson, Dale    , M , 16300 , 1   , 330.00
380 REM ---------------------------------------------------------
390 REM Continue program here
```

NOTE: The data in these ***DATA*** *statements have been entered in columns to improve readability. When data are read from* ***DATA*** *statements they automatically are stripped of all leading and trailing spaces if quotes are not used to delimit them as part of the data.*

Once the data have been read into the array, any one or all of the following example reports may be produced. The reports demonstrate how an array may be checked for particular occurrences of data and produce outputs based on those occurrences.

Search on Single 'J' String—A$(I,3)

```
390 REM Report # 1 All male employees
395 REM ----------------------------------------------------------
400 PRINT" First        Last       Salary     Account"
410 R$ = " \           \ \         \ \      \   \      \"
415 REM ----------------------------------------------------------
420 FOR I = 1 TO 15
430   IF A$(I,3)="M" THEN PRINT USING R$; A$(I,2);A$(I,1);A$(I,4);A$(I,6)
440 NEXT I

RUN
 First        Last       Salary     Account
 Philip       Hunter     12000      90.00
 Scott        Carlson    21400      310.00
 Jeffery      Anderson   10000      200.00
 Charles      Elting     17300      10.00
 Larry        Parks      12600      180.00
 Ronald       Reeves     18700      92.50
 Dale         Zimmerson  16300      330.00
Ok
```

Search on Single 'J' String Converted to Numeric—VAL(A$I,4))

```
390 REM Report # 2 All employees making more than $15,000
400 REM per year salary.
410 REM ----------------------------------------------------------
420 PRINT" Last         First      Salary  "
430 R$ = " \          \ \         \  $##,###.## "
440 REM ----------------------------------------------------------
450 FOR I = 1 TO 15
460   IF VAL(A$(I,4))>15000 THEN PRINT USING R$; A$(I,1);A$(I,2);VAL(A$(I,4)):
470 NEXT I

RUN
 Last         First      Salary
 Boronat      Penny      $16,200.00
 Carlson      Scott      $21,400.00
 Carson       Cindy      $22,500.00
 Elting       Charles    $17,300.00
 Cathcart     Anita      $19,000.00
 Fuller       Alice      $19,000.00
 Reeves       Ronald     $18,700.00
 Zimmerson    Dale       $16,300.00
Ok
```

Search on Multiple 'J' Strings—Logical Operator AND

```
390 REM Report # 3  All Male employees making more than
400 REM $15,000 per year salary.
410 REM -------------------------------------------------------
420 PRINT " Last            First          Salary    "
430 R$ =   " \            \  \           \   $##,###.##"
440 REM -------------------------------------------------------
450 FOR I = 1 TO 15
460   IF A$(I,3)="M" AND VAL(A$(I,4))>15000 THEN PRINT USING R$;A$(I,1);
      A$(I,2);VAL(A$(I,4))
470 NEXT I

RUN
 Last          First          Salary
 Carlson       Scott          $21,400.00
 Elting        Charles        $17,300.00
 Reeves        Ronald         $18,700.00
 Zimmerson     Dale           $16,300.00
Ok
```

Search on Multiple 'J' Strings—Logical Operators AND-OR

```
390 REM Report # 4  All Male employees making more than
400 REM $15,000 per year salary or female employees making
405 REM more than $20,000 per year salary.
410 REM -------------------------------------------------------
420 PRINT " Last            First          Salary    "
430 R$ =   " \            \  \           \   $##,###.##"
440 REM -------------------------------------------------------
450 FOR I = 1 TO 15
460   IF A$(I,3)="M" AND VAL(A$(I,4))>15000 OR A $(I,3)="F"
      AND VAL(A$(I,4))>20000  THEN PRINT USING R$;A$(I,1);
      A$(I,2);VAL(A$(I,4))
470 NEXT I

RUN
 Last          First          Salary
 Carlson       Scott          $21,400.00
 Carson        Cindy          $22,500.00
 Elting        Charles        $17,300.00
 Reeves        Ronald         $18,700.00
 Zimmerson     Dale           $16,300.00
Ok
```

NOTE Since AND has precedence over OR it is not necessary to group these conditions with parentheses: (condition AND condition) OR (condition AND condition).

Search Using Substring Operations

```
390 REM Report #5- Search for data on last name fragment.
400 REM User inputs any part of the last name, beginning
410 REM with the first character. Program will search and
420 REM display information on employees whose last names
430 REM begin with that fragment
440 REM -----------------------------------------------------
450 INPUT "Enter Last Name fragment";N$
460 X=LEN(N$)
470 FOR I = 1 TO 15
480   IF LEFT$(A$(I,1),X)=N$ THEN PRINT A$(I,1);", ";A$(I,2)
490 NEXT I

RUN
Enter Last Name fragment? Carl
Carlson, Scott
Ok
RUN
Enter Last Name fragment? Car
Carlson, Scott
Carson, Cindy
Ok
RUN
Enter Last Name fragment? Ca
Carlson, Scott
Carson, Cindy
Cathcart, Anita
Ok
```

Totals and Averages

```
390 REM Report # 6  Total salaries, personal accounts &
400 REM averages.
410 REM -----------------------------------------------------
420 FOR I = 1 TO 15
430   EMPS=EMPS+1
440   TOTSALS=TOTSALS+VAL(A$(I,4))
450   TOTACCT=TOTACCT+VAL(A$(I,6))
460 NEXT I
470 REM -----------------------------------------------------
480 PRINT "  Total        Total       Average      Total       Average
490 PRINT "Employees     Salaries    Salary       Accounts     Account
500 R$ =  "  ###         $###,###    $##,###      $#,###.##    $###.##
510 PRINT USING R$;EMPS;TOTSALS;TOTSALS/EMPS;TOTACCT;TOTACCT/EMPS

RUN
  Total        Total        Average      Total       Average
Employees     Salaries     Salary       Accounts    Account
   15         $223,500     $14,900      $1,734.95   $115.66
Ok
```

Totals Using Data Cross-Indexing

```
390 REM Report #7 Total employees/personal accounts by
400 REM department
410 REM -------------------------------------------------------------
420 FOR I = 1 TO 15
430   DEPT=VAL(A$(I,5))
440   EMPS(DEPT)=EMPS(DEPT)+1
450   ACCT(DEPT)=ACCT(DEPT)+VAL(A$(I,6))
460 NEXT I
470 REM -------------------------------------------------------------
480 PRINT "            Total        Total
490 PRINT " Dept#    Employees     Accounts
500 R$ =  "  #          ##         $###.##"
510 REM -------------------------------------------------------------
520 FOR DEPT = 1 TO 4
530   PRINT USING R$;DEPT;EMPS(DEPT);ACCT(DEPT)
540 NEXT DEPT

RUN
            Total        Total
 Dept#    Employees     Accounts
  1           4         $742.50
  2           4         $370.75
  3           3         $195.10
  4           4         $426.60
Ok
```

Search for Greatest Amount A$(I,4)

```
390 REM Report # 8  Search for employee with highest
400 REM yearly salary.
410 REM -------------------------------------------------------
420 HOLD = 0
430 FOR I = 1 TO 15
440    IF VAL(A$(I,4))<= HOLD THEN GOTO 490
450    HOLD = VAL(A$(I,4))
460    FOR J = 1 TO 6
470      ANS$(J)=A$(I,J)
480    NEXT J
490 NEXT I
500 REM -------------------------------------------------------
510 PRINT " Last        First    Sex    Salary     Dept#    Account
520 R$ =  " \         \  \      \  \\  $##,###.##     \\     $###.##"
530 REM -------------------------------------------------------
540 PRINT USING R$;ANS$(1);ANS$(2);ANS$(3);VAL(ANS$(4));ANS$(5);VAL(ANS$(6))
RUN
 Last        First    Sex    Salary     Dept#    Account
 Carson      Cindy     F   $22,500.00     2      $ 75.00
Ok
```

Sorting Array A$(I,J) on Last Name A$(I,1)—Bubble sort

```
390 REM Report # 9 Database sorted on last name.
400 REM -----------------------------------------------------------------
410 FOR PASS = 1 TO 14
420   FOR I = 2 TO 15
430      IF A$(I,1)>=A$(I-1,1) THEN GOTO 470
440      FOR J = 1 TO 6
450         SWAP A$(I,J),A$(I-1,J)
460      NEXT J
470   NEXT I
480 NEXT PASS
490 REM -----------------------------------------------------------------
500 R$ = "\        \ "
510 REM -----------------------------------------------------------------
520 FOR I = 1 TO 15
530   FOR J = 1 TO 6
540     PRINT USING R$;A$(I,J);
550   NEXT J
560   PRINT
570 NEXT I
RUN
Anderson  Jeffery   M         10000     2         200.00
Boronat   Penny     F         16200     4         20.50
Carlson   Scott     M         21400     1         310.00
Carson    Cindy     F         22500     2         75.00
Cathcart  Anita     F         19000     4         95.50
Elting    Charles   M         17300     1         10.00
Fuller    Alice     F         19000     2         45.00
Harrison  Glenys    F         9800      4         130.60
Hunter    Philip    M         12000     3         90.00
Jeli      Krista    F         9500      3         0.00
Nickerson Cheryl    F         8700      3         105.10
Parks     Larry     M         12600     4         180.00
Parsons   Sharon    F         10500     2         50.75
Reeves    Ronald    M         18700     1         92.50
Zimmerson Dale      M         16300     1         330.00
Ok
```

UTILITIES

```
Function Keys Program
-----------------------
100 REM Reprograms the function keys F5-F10 then erases itself
110 REM from memory. Type [RUN"fkey] before starting to program.
120 REM ---------------------------------------------------------
130 KEY  5, "FILES"+CHR$(13)
140 KEY  6, "KILL"+CHR$(34)
150 KEY  7, "RENUM 100"
160 KEY  8, "KEY 8, "+CHR$(34)
170 KEY  9, " REM ----------"
180 KEY 10, "---------------"
190 REM ---------------------------------------------------------
200 NEW
--------------------------------------------------------------------------

Sound Effects Program
-----------------------
100 REM Each "Play string" routine produces an interesting sound effect
110 REM ---------------------------------------------------------
120 PRINT "Play string #1"
130 FOR I=1 TO 10
140    PLAY "l64 mf ml t255 n40n41n42n43 n50n51n52n53"
150 NEXT I
160 REM ---------------------------------------------------------
170 PRINT "Play string #2"
180 FOR I=1 TO 10
190    PLAY "l64 mf ml t255 n40n42n44n46n48n50n48n46n44n42n40"
200 NEXT I
210 REM ---------------------------------------------------------
220 PRINT "Play string #3"
230 FOR I=1 TO 10
240    PLAY "l64 mf ml t255 n50n60n51n61n52n62n53n63n54n64n55n65n56n66"
250 NEXT I
260 REM ---------------------------------------------------------
--------------------------------------------------------------------------

Graphics Scale Routine
-----------------------
100 REM Scale factor (S) for screen graphics LINE heights
110 REM assuming plots for array F(J), DIM F(M), on a
120 REM screen with 180 points vertical being used.
130 REM ---------------------------------------------------------
140 MIN=F(1)
150 MAX=F(1)
160 FOR J=1 TO M
170    IF F(J)>MAX THEN MAX=F(J)
180    IF F(J)<MIN THEN MIN=F(J)
190 NEXT J
200 S=180/(MAX+MIN)
210 REM ---------------------------------------------------------
220 REM  When plotting graph use:
230 REM  LINE-(horizontal position, 200 - INT(S*F(J)))
240 REM  to scale graph vertically.
```

```
Statistic Routines
------------------
100 REM Accumulations for statistics and frequency distribution
110 REM for list A(I), DIM A(N)
120 REM ---------------------------------------------------------
130 REM Calculate Range of data for list A(I)
140 REM ---------------------------------------------------------
150 MIN=A(1)
160 MAX=A(1)
170 FOR I=1 TO N
180    IF A(I)>MAX THEN MAX=A(I)
190    IF A(I)<MIN THEN MIN=A(I)
200 NEXT I
210 REM ---------------------------------------------------------
220 REM Calculate Mean (Average) for list A(I)
230 REM ---------------------------------------------------------
240 FOR I = 1 TO N
250   TOT=TOT+A(I)
260 NEXT I
270 MEAN= INT((TOT/N)*100)/100
280 REM ---------------------------------------------------------
290 REM Calculate Standard deviation for list A(I)
300 REM ---------------------------------------------------------
310 FOR I = 1 TO N
320    ER=ER+(A(I)-MEAN)^2
330 NEXT I
340 STD = INT(SQR((1/(N-1))*ER)*100)/100
350 REM ---------------------------------------------------------
360 REM Accumulate frequency of events for list A(I) given a range
370 REM MIN to MAX into the array SUBT(A)
380 REM ---------------------------------------------------------
390 FOR A = MIN TO MAX
400   FOR I = 1 TO N
410     IF CINT(A(I))=A THEN SUBT(A)=SUBT(A)+1
420   NEXT I
430 NEXT A
---------------------------------------------------------------------

Bubble Sorts / Lists - Tables
-----------------------------
100 REM   A bubble sort routine for single subscript arrays (lists)
110 REM ---------------------------------------------------------
120 FOR PASS = 1 TO 9
130   FOR I = 2 TO 10
140      IF A$(I) > A$(I-1) THEN 160   ' Bubble Sort
150      SWAP A$(I),A$(I-1)
160   NEXT I
170 NEXT PASS
180 REM ---------------------------------------------------------
```

```
100 REM Bubble sort for double subscript sorted on A$(I,2)
110 REM where A$(I=10,J=6)
120 REM ----------------------------------------------------------
130 FOR PASS = 1 TO 9
140   FOR I = 2 TO 10
150      IF A$(I,2) > A$(I-1,2) THEN 190    ' Bubble Sort
160      FOR J= 1 TO 6
170         SWAP A$(I,J),A$(I-1,J)
180      NEXT J
190   NEXT I
200 NEXT PASS
-----------------------------------------------------------------------------

Shell Sorts / Lists & Tables
----------------------------
320 N=10-1              ' N = number of A$(I)'s - 1
330 M=N
340 M=INT(M/2)
350    IF M=0 THEN GOTO 470
360    Z=1
370    K=N-M
380 I=Z
390    L=I+M
400       IF A$(I)<=A$(L) THEN GOTO 440
410       SWAP A$(I),A$(L)
420       I=I-M
430    IF I>=1 THEN GOTO 390
440 Z=Z+1
450 IF Z>K THEN GOTO 340
460 GOTO 380
470 REM - Continue program here -
-----------------------------------------------------------------------------

300 REM Shell Sort for double subscript sorted on A$(I,2) where A$(I=10,J=6)
310 REM ----------------------------------------
320 N=10-1                     ' N = number of A$(I, )'s - 1
330 M=N
340 M=INT(M/2)
350    IF M=0 THEN GOTO 480
360    Z=1
370    K=N-M
380 I=Z
390    L=I+M
400       IF A$(I,2)<=A$(L,2) THEN GOTO 440
405       FOR J= 1 TO 6
410         SWAP A$(I,J),A$(L,J)
415       NEXT J
420       I=I-M
430    IF I>=1 THEN GOTO 390
440 Z=Z+1
450 IF Z>K THEN GOTO 340
460 GOTO 380
480 REM - Continue Program Here -
```

Because it was developed as a teaching tool, BASIC is a programming language that is relatively easy to learn. It is often the first programming language to which students are exposed. One of the major weaknesses of BASIC, however, is that it is not an inherently structured programming language. Nonetheless, BASIC programs can and should be written to incorporate rules and concepts of structured programming. Structured programming is a methodology that improves both the design and testing of programs to ensure that they are error-free.

While true structured programming languages impose restrictions on the order in which lines of a program will be executed, BASIC's **GOTO** statement allows unconditional branching from any line of the program to any other line. However, if the **GOTO** statement is not used judiciously, the order of execution of the lines in a BASIC program (the program flow) may be difficult to follow for anyone reading or modifying the program (or even for the person who originally wrote it). Because of this, finding errors (or bugs) in a program may take an inordinate amount of time. Therefore, the BASIC programmer needs some knowledge of the concepts of structured programming and design.

HISTORICAL OVERVIEW

Edsger Dijkstra, one of the major proponents of structured programming, says that while the presence of "bugs," or errors, in many programming situations is merely annoying, such as in the case of fouled-up airline reservations, their presence in other situations, such as the launching and guidance of space flights, is a matter of life and death. This type of life-or-death situation occurred in 1981 when the first launching of the U.S. space shuttle was halted because errors in the software (program) caused the shuttle's computers to fall out of synchronization.

In the early days of computers, programming was more of an art than a science. Developing a quality program was mostly a hit-or-miss proposition rather than a planned goal. Programmers were given a task to program and were left on their own to come up with a solution. Three major problems which arose from this free-form method of programming were long development time, high maintenance costs, and low-quality programs (software).

Long development time resulted from programmers beginning to write programs without proper analysis of the problem and planning of the steps required to solve it. Managers found that many software projects took too long to complete, and they needed some way to increase programmer productivity.

High maintenance costs resulted from sharply rising software development costs, expecially personnel costs, as the computer age moved forward. Most of the money invested in purchasing and operating a computer system was spent on software-related costs and, in particular, on software maintenance. Many organizations were spending more than 60 percent of their time repairing and enhancing systems that were already installed. The cost of developing, testing, and maintaining programs was not only too high, it was continuing to increase. Managers needed a way to control and reduce these costs. To avoid the high costs of program maintenance, programs needed to be designed right the first time.

Low quality programs occurred because programs were too complex and had poor documentation. As a result, they were difficult to test and maintain.

Numerous errors went undetected in the testing process. In many cases, programmers lost sight of the user's requirements; consequently, the programs did not meet the user's needs.

These problems forced people to search for ways to resolve them. Edsger Dijkstra's work as well as that of others led to the development of the structured programming concept.

STRUCTURED PROGRAMMING

Structured programming is a methodology that stresses systematic design, development, and management of program development. The purpose and overall goals of structured programming are to

- decrease development time by increasing programmer productivity and reducing the time to test and debug a program.
- decrease maintenance costs by reducing errors and making programs easier to understand by reducing their complexity.
- improve the quality of software by providing programs with fewer errors.

Structured programming attempts to accomplish these goals by incorporating the following concepts.

- Use of only the sequence, selection, and repetition control structures.
- Use of top-down design and use of modules.
- Use of documentation and management control.

Control Structures

A control structure is a device in a programming language that determines the order of execution of statements in a program. In the late 1960s two mathematicians, Corrado Bohm and Guiseppe Jacopini, proved that even the most complex program logic could be expressed by the use of three control structures: sequence; selection (also called condition); and repetition (also called looping or iteration).

NOTE: Edsger Dijkstra also put forth this same theory in his article "Notes on Structured Programming."

Sequence

A sequence control structure executes statements one after another in a linear fashion. The following is an example of BASIC program code that uses only the sequence control structure.

```
100 INPUT "Enter the amount of money to be invested: ",INV
110 PRINT
120 INPUT "Enter the annual interest rate as a decimal: ",I
130 PRINT
140 INPUT "Enter the number of years for the investment: ",YRS
150 PRINT
160 PRINT "  ***************************************************"
170 PRINT "  The future value of the investment will be: ";INV*(1+I)^YRS
```

Selection

The selection control structure presents more than one processing option. The option chosen depends on the result of a decision criterion. A common selection control structure is the **IF. . .THEN. . .ELSE** structure, which is used to select one of two processing options. Another selection control structure is a case structure, which allows more than two possible processing options (the **ON** n **GOSUB** opt1, opt2, opt3. . .optN statement in BASIC).

The previous example is expanded in the following example to include a selection control structure. An **IF** statement (line 165) determines the program statements to be executed (either lines 170–180 or lines 200–210) based on the user's input (line 40).

```
10  PRINT "        1 - Calculate Compounded Interest on Single Investment "
20  PRINT "        2 - Calculate Compounded Interest on Annuity Investments"
30  PRINT
40  INPUT "        Enter 1 or 2: ",AN$
50  PRINT
60  PRINT
100 INPUT "Enter the amount of money to be invested: ",INV
110 PRINT
120 INPUT "Enter the annual interest rate as a decimal: ",I
130 PRINT
140 INPUT "Enter the number of years for the investment: ",YRS
150 PRINT
160 PRINT "  *****************************************************"
165 IF AN$="1" THEN GOSUB 170 ELSE GOSUB 200
168 END
170 PRINT "  The future value of the investment will be: ";INV*(1+I)^YRS
180 RETURN
200 PRINT "  The future value of the annuity will be: ";INV*(((1+I)^YRS-1)/I)
210 RETURN
```

Repetition

The repetition control structure is used to execute an instruction or group of instructions more than once without having to recode them. Two common repetition control structures are the **WHILE. . .WEND** and the **FOR. . .NEXT** loop structures. The program instructions to be executed repeatedly are placed within these structures, as shown in the following example.

```
5    C$ = "Y"
6    WHILE C$ = "Y" OR C$ = "y"
7      CLS
10     PRINT "        1 - Calculate Compounded Interest on Single Investment "
20     PRINT "        2 - Calculate Compounded Interest on Annuity Investments"
30     PRINT
40     INPUT "        Enter 1 or 2: ",AN$
50     PRINT
60     PRINT
100    INPUT "Enter the amount of money to be invested: ",INV
110    PRINT
120    INPUT "Enter the annual interest rate as a decimal: ",I
130    PRINT
140    INPUT "Enter the number of years for the investment: ",YRS
150    PRINT
160    PRINT "  *****************************************************"
165    IF AN$="1" THEN GOSUB 170 ELSE GOSUB 200
166    PRINT:INPUT "Would you like to calculate another investment (Y/N) ?", C$
167  WEND
168  END
```

```
170 PRINT "  The future value of the investment will be: ";INV*(1+I)^YRS
180 RETURN
200 PRINT "  The future value of the annuity will be: ";INV*(((1+I)^YRS-1)/I)
205 PRINT:INPUT "Press Enter to see yearly values",DUMMY$:PRINT
206 FOR K = 1 TO YRS
207   PRINT USING "Year ##       $######.##";K;INV*(((1+I)^K-1)/I)
208 NEXT K
210 RETURN
```

A fourth type of control structure commonly used in BASIC programs is the unconditional branch. In BASIC, the structure takes the form of a **GOTO** statement. This statement allows the execution of a program to indiscriminately jump to other points in the program. Programs designed with many of these unconditional branches can be very confusing and difficult to follow, thereby earning them the name "spaghetti code."

A poorly written BASIC program will often use the **GOTO** statement in place of the appropriate repetition control structure. For example, the previous example program could have been written using only **GOTO** statements and the **IF. . .ELSE. . .ENDIF** structure, as follows.

```
7   CLS
10  PRINT "         1 - Calculate Compounded Interest on Single Investment "
20  PRINT "         2 - Calculate Compounded Interest on Annuity Investments"
30  PRINT
40  INPUT "         Enter 1 or 2: ",AN$
50  PRINT
60  PRINT
100 INPUT "Enter the amount of money to be invested: ",INV
110 PRINT
120 INPUT "Enter the annual interest rate as a decimal: ",I
130 PRINT
140 INPUT "Enter the number of years for the investment: ",YRS
150 PRINT
160 PRINT "  *****************************************************"
165 IF AN$="1" THEN GOTO 170 ELSE GOTO 200
166 PRINT:INPUT "Would you like to calculate another investment (Y/N) ?", C$
167 IF C$="Y" OR C$="y" THEN GOTO 7
168 END
170 PRINT "  The future value of the investment will be: ";INV*(1+I)^YRS
180 GOTO 166
200 PRINT "  The future value of the annuity will be: ";INV*(((1+I)^YRS-1)/I)
205 PRINT:INPUT "Press Enter to see yearly values",DUMMY$:PRINT
206 K = 1
207 PRINT USING "Year ##       $######.##";K;INV*(((1+I)^K-1)/I)
208 K = K+1: IF K<=YRS THEN GOTO 207
210 GOTO 166
```

The program flow of this program is difficult to follow. Errors would be harder to locate in such a program. Avoiding use of the unconditional branch structure and instead using only sequence, selection, and repetition structures in a program is the first step in structured programming methodology.

Top-Down Design and Use of Modules

Structured programming also advocates the top-down approach to solving a problem. Top-down design is the process of starting with the major functions involved in a problem and dividing them into subfunctions. The subfunctions are, in turn, divided into further subfunctions, and so forth, until the problem has been broken down as much as possible. Top-down design involves three major phases:

1. Defining the output, input, and major processing steps required.
2. Breaking down and refining the major processing steps.
3. Designing the algorithms (the finite sets of step-by-step instructions that together solve the problem) and coding (writing) the program.

Phase 1—Definition

Definition involves three separate tasks. First, the desired outputs are defined. This involves determining the informational needs of those who will use the program. Second, the required inputs are defined. The input definition must include all data that will be required to produce the desired output. Finally, the major processing steps are determined. This task involves defining the processes necessary to produce the desired output from the defined inputs.

Phase 2—Refinement

In refinement each major processing step is broken down into increasingly smaller steps until they are small enough to be easily programmed within a reasonable timeframe. This method forces an examination of all aspects of a problem at one level before starting on the next level. When this phase is complete, each module, or set of processing instructions, should be easy to understand and code (include in a program). Working from the top down (from the general to the specific) rather than from the bottom up (from the specific to the general) helps the programmer avoid developing programs that are only partial solutions to problems.

A program broken into smaller modules is easier to read, test, and maintain. With the structured programming method, each module has the following features to ensure these qualities.

- *A module has only one entrance and one exit.* For example, a module written as a BASIC subroutine should have a definite beginning and end. If a subroutine is called from different parts of a program, each **GOSUB** statement used to call it should reference the same line number. The subroutine should include a single **RETURN** statement at the end of the routine.
- *After exiting a module, control returns to the module that called it (passed control to it).* For example, if module D called module G, when module G is finished executing, control returns to module D. In a BASIC subroutine there should be no **GOTO** statements which pass control to a line outside of the subroutine.
- *A module should perform only one program function.* Each discrete processing task should be included in a separate module. This allows some modules to be designed for general purpose functions.

Phase 3—Design and Coding

Design and coding involves developing the algorithm for each module and writing the corresponding program code. An algorithm is a finite set of step-by-step instructions that solves a problem. An algorithm describes the sequence, selection, and repetition control structures that will be used in the program. After the algorithm is developed, the program code is written and tested. The modules are designed and coded from the top down (main module first, then submodules).

Documentation and Management Control

Documentation is the text, diagrams, and/or charts that record the purpose or function of a particular module, step, or instruction in a program. Each step throughout the programming process should be documented. Documentation is sometimes done as an afterthought rather than as an ongoing integral part of a project. Approached in this manner, it can become an overwhelming burden of paperwork. However, if documentation guidelines are established and followed from the beginning of a project, the process will take less time and effort in the long run.

There are two good reasons to document the program development process. First, documentation leaves a clear record so that someone else using a program later can understand what was done. This record is extremely important in a business environment, because it is likely that the person who later corrects an error or modifies a program will not be the same person who originally designed and coded it. Second, documenting the steps as they are developed forces a reexamination of the actions taken. The person managing the development of the program can review documentation to control project costs and/or modify schedules. Design problems might be discovered early enough to avoid later patchwork alterations.

SUMMARY

By adhering to the discipline of structured programming when using BASIC, you will be able to develop programs that are more organized, easier to read, and easier to modify. They will also tend to be more error-free during the development process. Once you become accustomed to writing programs with structured programming techniques, you will find that the time it takes to solve a problem using BASIC will be significantly reduced.

BASICA DATA FILES

OVERVIEW OF DATA FILES

Data files are diskette files used to store data that BASICA programs may access. The data on the diskette are typically in the form of a *relational database;* that is, the data are organized in records composed of fields having related data items.

The general procedure for using data files involves having the BASICA program open a data file, read individual data items from the file into program variables, manipulate or process the data while they are held in variables, and then write the data back out to the diskette data file in its updated form.

The advantage of data files is having the means to maintain (update) the records in a database through program execution.

There are two types of data files—sequential and random. The fundamental difference between them is how the data are stored on the diskette. Sequential files use delimiters (quotes, commas, carriage returns) to separate the individual data items; random files are structured so that each data item is given a specific length in characters so the location of a data item separates it from other data items in a file.

SEQUENTIAL DATA FILES

Data Structure

Sequential data files have their string and numeric data items strung together with commas, quotes, and/or carriage returns separating them. A sequential file may be viewed as one long **DATA** statement kept on the diskette under its own filename (for example, 7765,"Example",32,"Sequential file",8867.55).

Opening a Sequential File

Before a BASICA program can access a sequential file, that file first must be opened with an **OPEN** statement in the BASICA program. A sequential file may be opened in one of three modes: output, input, or append (add to). Each sequential data file must be closed with a **CLOSE** statement before it is reopened in a different mode. The following is a summary of the syntax involved when using an **OPEN** statement to access the data in a sequential data file.

The **OPEN** Statement

OPEN *"filename"* ***FOR OUTPUT AS*** *#filenum*

This statement opens the diskette file named "filename" for data to be placed in (written to) it. If the data file already exists, any data in it automatically will be erased to prepare the file to receive a whole new set of data.

OPEN *"filename"* ***FOR APPEND AS*** *#filenum*

This statement opens the diskette file named "filename" for data to be added (appended) to it. Opening for append opens the file to receive data without erasing the file. Any data written to a file opened for append are added to the data already in the file.

OPEN "filename" FOR INPUT AS #filenum

This statement opens the diskette file named "filename" for its data to be assigned to variables in the BASICA program (read from). Opening the file for input does not erase that file.

- filename — A sequential file is first named at the time it is opened for output. The filename is enclosed in quotes, and must be eight or fewer letter/number characters in length (no commas, spaces, etc.).
- filenum — Each data file is given a number when it is opened. This number is then used to identify that file for all program statements referring to it. After a file has been closed, its filenum becomes available to identify other data files when they are opened.

NOTE: BASICA allows (by default) three data files to be open at any given time during program execution. For accessing more than three files at a time, type BASICA/F:# (where "#" is the number of files to be open at a time) when loading BASICA from the DOS (system) operating level.

Other Statements and Functions Used with Sequential Files

- **CLOSE** — Closes all data files. Option to **CLOSE** #.
- **INPUT** # — Inputs the next data item from the data file into a program variable.
- **PRINT** # — Outputs data items to a data file.
- **WRITE** # — Outputs data items and delimiters to a data file.
- **EOF** — Signals End Of File.

SEQUENTIAL FILE EXAMPLE PROGRAMS

Creating a Sequential Data File

The following example programs involve data on gallons of warehoused paint. In this example the data file "INVEN" is created by opening it for **OUTPUT.** The record data are then entered from the keyboard in the field order of color code, name, and the gallons on hand for each type of paint (each record). The set of data items entered is written to the data file #1 which is identified in the **OPEN** statement as being the file "INVEN." After each record is entered, the user has the option of entering another.

```
LIST
10  OPEN "INVEN" FOR OUTPUT AS #1
20  ANS$ = "Y"
30  WHILE ANS$ = "Y" OR ANS$ = "y"
40    INPUT "Color Code     ";TINT
50    INPUT "Brand Name     ";BRND$
60    INPUT "Gallons        ";GALS
70    WRITE #1,TINT,BRND$,GALS
80    INPUT "More (Y/N) ";ANS$
90  WEND
100 CLOSE #1
Ok
RUN
Color Code     ? 7765
```

```
Brand Name     ? Flamingo Pink
Gallons        ? 87
More (Y/N) ? y
Color Code     ? 4776
Brand Name     ? Shetland Brown
Gallons        ? 45
More (Y/N) ? y
Color Code     ?
(and so on)
```

As this program is executed the variables TINT, BRND$, and GALS temporarily hold whatever values the user inputs on the keyboard. After those values are input they are written to the data file INVEN (line 70) and the user is prompted "More (Y/N)?". If the user answers anything other than Y or y to this prompt, line 100 (**CLOSE** #1) will be executed. When the **CLOSE** #1 statement is executed the physical writing of the data items to the file will be completed. At this point the data in INVEN are stored on the diskette in the form:

```
7765,"Flamingo Pink",87,4776,"Shetland Brown",45 ...........
```

Appending to a Sequential Data File

If you wanted to add data to the existing file "INVEN," you simply would change the **OPEN** statement in the last example. An **OPEN FOR APPEND** (rather than **OPEN FOR OUTPUT**) used in line 10, will cause the program to append any data entered from the keyboard to the existing data file "INVEN."

```
10 OPEN "INVEN" FOR APPEND AS #1
```

OPEN FOR APPEND will not erase the data in "INVEN" although **OPEN FOR OUTPUT** will.

Reading a Sequential Data File

In the next example, the data file INVEN is opened for input and a report is produced showing what types and how much of each paint currently is warehoused. Note that EOF(#) is a BASICA function whose value is 0 (false) until an attempt is made to INPUT (read) past the end of a file. Its value then becomes -1 (true).

```
LIST
10 PRINT "     Color Code        Brand Name             Gallons on Hand"
20 PRINT
30 OPEN "INVEN" FOR INPUT AS #1
40 WHILE NOT EOF(1)
50   INPUT #1,TINT,BRND$,GALS
60   PRINT TAB(5);TINT;TAB(22);BRND$;TAB(55);GALS
70 WEND
80 CLOSE #1
Ok
RUN
    Color Code       Brand Name             Gallons on Hand

    7765             Flamingo Pink                       87
    4776             Shetland Brown                      45
    9953             Russian Red                         32
    5545             Coppertone Tan                      55
Ok
```

Updating a Sequential File

The next example demonstrates how a sequential file can be read into a program, altered, or updated, and then written back to the diskette in its new form.

This particular example program allows INVEN to be updated for the number of gallons on hand of each type of paint. A temporary data file TEMPFILE is used to hold the updated data; then TEMPFILE is renamed as INVEN after the new information has been written to it.

```
LIST
10  PRINT TAB(15);"GALLONS IN STOCK":PRINT
20  OPEN "INVEN" FOR INPUT AS #1
30  OPEN "TEMPFILE" FOR OUTPUT AS #2
40  WHILE NOT EOF(1)
50    INPUT #1,TINT,BRND$,GALS
60    PRINT BRND$;TAB(20):INPUT NEWGALS
70    WRITE #2,TINT,BRND$,NEWGALS
80  WEND
90  CLOSE #1,#2
100 KILL"INVEN"
110 NAME "TEMPFILE" AS "INVEN"
Ok
RUN
              GALLONS IN STOCK

Flamingo Pink      ? 55
Shetland Brown     ? 35
Russian Red        ? 28
Coppertone Tan     ? 26
Ok
```

Searching a Sequential File

The last example is an "Ordering Report" program which assumes that when stock level is below 30 gallons for any given paint, enough should be ordered to bring back up the stock level to 70 gallons.

```
LIST
10  PRINT "     Color Code      Brand Name           Gallons To Order"
20  PRINT
30  OPEN "INVEN" FOR INPUT AS #1
40  WHILE NOT EOF(1)
50    INPUT #1,TINT,BRND$,GALS
60    IF GALS < 30 THEN 70 ELSE 90
70      ORDER = 70 - GALS
80      PRINT TAB(5);TINT;TAB(22);BRND$;TAB(55);ORDER
90  WEND
100 CLOSE #1
Ok
RUN
     Color Code      Brand Name          Gallons To Order

     9953            Russian Red                       42
     5545            Coppertone Tan                    44
Ok
```

RANDOM ACCESS FILES

Data Structure

Random files are data files with their record data items set up in identical packages. Each record has a unique record number, and all data items in the record have a specified amount of record space reserved for them (called data fields).

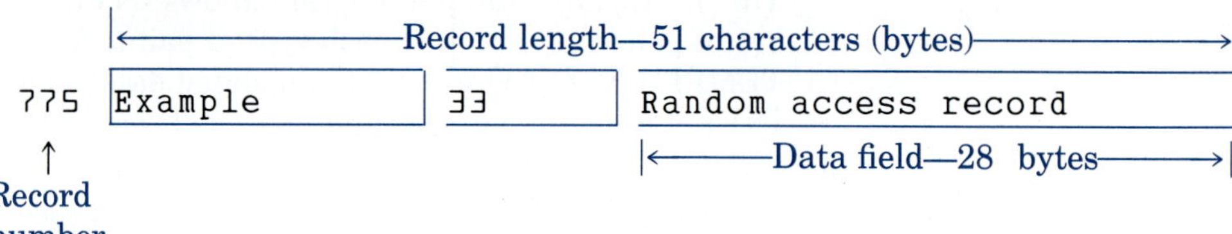

Opening a Random Data File

Before a BASIC program can access a random file, the file must be opened with an **OPEN** statement. Once opened, the random file may have data placed in it (written to), or it may have its data assigned to variables in the BASICA program (read from), with BASICA's **PUT** and **GET** statements.

The **OPEN** Statement

```
OPEN "filename" AS #filenum LEN = reclen
```

- filename — A random file is first named when it is created. The filename is enclosed in quotes, and must be eight or fewer letter/number characters in length (no commas, spaces, etc.).
- filenum — Each data file is given a number when it is opened. The number is then used to identify the file for all program statements referring to it. After a file has been closed, its filenum becomes available to identify other data files when they are opened.
- reclen — The length of the random file record is the sum of the lengths of all data fields in it.

The Random File Buffer

Data are moved in and out of a random access file through a holding space called a "random file buffer." This space is used to temporarily hold the record being written to a random file or read from a random file.

Defining the Random File Buffer

The size of the random file buffer is defined in the BASICA program by the **FIELD** statement. With this statement, each field in the buffer is given a specific length and a name.

```
FIELD #1, 15 AS A$, 8 AS B$, 28 AS C$
```

In the example above, the **FIELD** statement creates (for the random file opened as #1) a random file buffer that sets aside 15 characters for the field named A$, 8 characters for the field named B$, and 28 characters for the field named C$. The total record length becomes 51 characters (51 = 15 + 8 + 28) as defined by this statement.

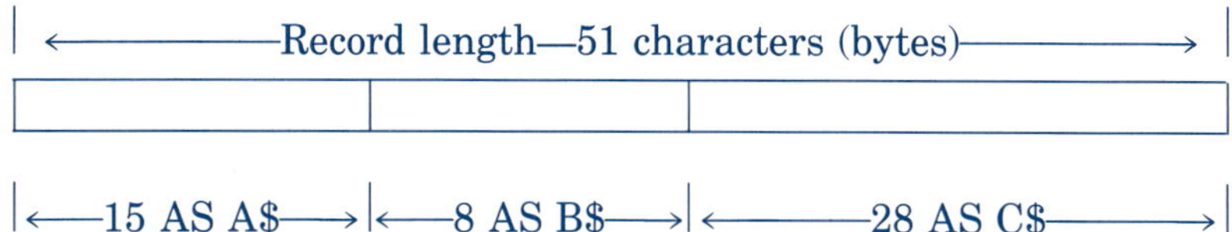

Moving Data into the Random File Buffer

Before data can be written to a random file, it must be placed in the random file buffer. Each data item is assigned to its appropriate field with the **LSET** (left justified) or **RSET** (right justified) statements. If the data item is smaller than its field, the rest of the field is packed with spaces.

Only string values may be placed in a random file buffer, so all numeric values must be converted to strings before placing them in their fields by using the MKI$, MKS$, or MKD$ (Make String) functions.

Writing Data to a Random Access File

After all data items for the record have been moved into the random file buffer, the **PUT** statement is used to write that record to the random file. The following is an example of BASIC code used to write a random file record to the diskette.

Example of Statements Used

This example starts with four program variables, the first of which (RECNO) is the integer used later as the record number.

```
RECNO = 775
TYPE$ = "Example"
AMT = 33
INFO$ = "Random access record"
```

Next the file named "RNDFILE" is opened as the #1 file and its record lengths are set at 51 characters each.

```
OPEN "RNDFILE" AS #1 LEN = 51
```

The **FIELD** statement is then used to create the random file buffer and set aside space for the three fields named A$, B$, and C$.

```
FIELD #1, 15 AS A$, 8 AS B$, 28 AS C$
```

LSETs are used to move the program variables into the random file buffer. MKS$ is used to convert AMT before moving it into its field.

```
LSET A$ = TYPE$
LSET B$ = MKS$(AMT)
LSET C$ = INFO$
```

Finally, **PUT** is used to write this record to the random file opened as #1 (RNDFILE). Notice that RECNO is used to place the record at this time.

```
PUT #1, RECNO
```

NOTE: Since BASICA and DOS block data (512 bytes at a time) before writing to a file, ***PUT*** *will not always result in an immediate writing of data to the diskette.*

In the previous example, a record with the record number 775, 51 characters long, and having three fields, would be written to the random access file, "RNDFILE."

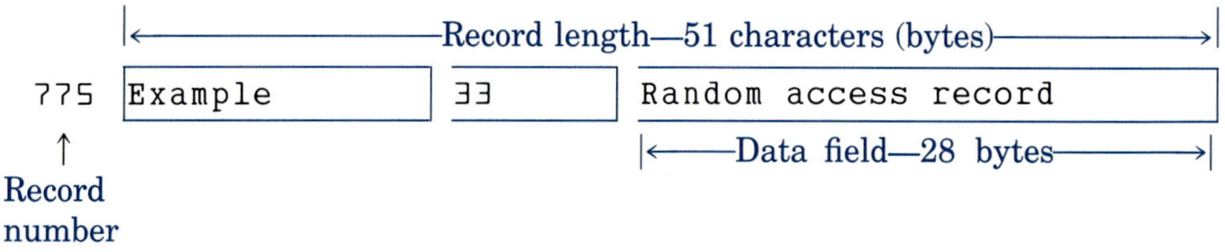

```
      |<-----------------Record length—51 characters (bytes)----------------->|
775   | Example           | 33         | Random access record                  |
 ↑                                     |<--------Data field—28 bytes--------->|
Record
number
```

If "RNDFILE" was being created in this example, it automatically would be made large enough to hold 775 records, each 51 characters long. The file "RNDFILE" would then be 38,505 bytes in size. The rest of the space would be there to hold the first 774 records. If the next record **PUT** to the file had the record number 800, the file would be enlarged to hold a total of 800 records, even though it only had two records (#775 and #800) in it.

Reading Data from a Random Access File

Once a record has been written to a random file, the **GET** statement may be used to copy it (identified by its record number) from the diskette, back into a program's random file buffer. After the **GET** statement has been executed, all numeric values previously converted to strings may be converted back to numbers with the **CVI, CVS,** or **CVD** (Convert) functions.

Example of Statements Used

If "RNDFILE" already is open and its fields declared, the following two lines are not necessary.

```
OPEN "RNDFILE" AS #1 LEN = 51
FIELD #1, 15 AS A$, 8 AS B$, 28 AS C$
```

The variable "RECNO" holds the record number.

```
RECNO = 755
```

The **GET** statement will copy the 775th record from "RNDFILE" into the random file buffer field variables A$, B$, and C$.

```
GET #1,RECNO
```

Next the program variables are assigned the values held in the field variables. **CVS** is used to convert the string in B$ to its numeric value before assigning it to AMT.

```
TYPE$ = A$
AMT = CVS(B$)
INFO$ = C$
```

When the string values in the field variables are assigned to the program string variables, they include the spaces that were packed with them before they were written to the random file. In other words, if you were to

PRINT TYPE$;AMT; INFO$;"end"

at this point, the result would be

```
Example         33 Random access record         end
```

Statements and Functions Used with Random Access Files

Statement	Function
OPEN	Opens a data file for program access.
CLOSE	Closes all data files. Option to close #(n).
FIELD	Creates a random file buffer.
LSET	Moves data items into **RSET** the random file buffer in preparation for a **PUT** statement.
PUT	Moves a data record from the random file buffer into the random file.
GET	Moves a data record from the random file to the random file buffer.
MKD$** **MKI$ **MKS$**	Convert numeric data items into string form in preparation for moving them into a random file buffer.
CVD **CVI** **CVS**	Convert random file buffer numeric items, previously converted to strings with MK$ (Make String functions), back into numeric-type variables.

EXAMPLE PROGRAMS—RANDOM ACCESS FILES

Creating a Random Access Data File

These example programs involve data on gallons of warehoused paint. In the first example, the data file "INVEN" is created and its records are written to it as they are input from the keyboard. The data items entered in each record include color code, name, and the gallons on hand for each type of paint. The color code is used as the record number. After each set of values is entered, the user has the option of entering another set of values.

```
LIST
10  OPEN "INVEN" AS #1 LEN = 24
20  FIELD #1, 20 AS A$, 4 AS B$
30  ANS$ = "Y"
40  WHILE ANS$ = "Y" OR ANS$ = "y"
50    INPUT "Color Code   ";TINT
60    INPUT "Brand Name   ";BRND$
70    INPUT "Gallons      ";GALS
80    LSET A$ = BRND$
90    LSET B$ = MKI$(GALS)
100   PUT #1,TINT
110   INPUT "More (Y/N) ";ANS$
120 WEND
130 CLOSE #1
Ok
RUN
Color Code   ? 001
Brand Name   ? Very White
Gallons      ? 122
More (Y/N) ? y
Color Code   ? 002
Brand Name   ? Bone White
Gallons      ? 65
More (Y/N) ? y
```

Reading a Random Access Data File

In the next example, the random access file "INVEN" is opened and its records are read into the program's variables. A report is produced showing what type, and how much, of each paint is currently warehoused.

```
LIST
10  OPEN "INVEN" AS #1 LEN = 24
20  FIELD #1, 20 AS A$, 4 AS B$
30  PRINT "     Color Code      Brand Name                Gallons on Hand"
40  PRINT "     ----------      ----------                ---------------"
50  P$ =  "        ####         \                    \         #####"
60  FOR TINT = 1 TO 4
70    GET #1,TINT
80    BRND$ = A$: GALS = CVI(B$)
90    PRINT USING P$;TINT,BRND$,GALS
100 NEXT TINT
110 CLOSE #1
Ok
RUN
     Color Code      Brand Name                Gallons on Hand
     ----------      ----------                ---------------
        1            Very White                     122
        2            Bone White                      65
        3            Off White                       88
        4            Bright Light White              23
Ok
```

Updating a Random Access Data File

This example demonstrates how a random access data file can be read into a program, altered, or updated, and then written back to the diskette in its corrected form. This particular example program allows "INVEN" to be updated for the number of gallons on hand of each type of paint.

```
LIST
10  OPEN "INVEN" AS #1 LEN = 24
20  FIELD #1, 20 AS A$, 4 AS B$
30  PRINT TAB(15);"GALLONS IN STOCK"
40  FOR TINT = 1 TO 4
50    GET #1,TINT
60    PRINT A$; TAB(22):INPUT NEWGALS
70    LSET B$ = MKI$(NEWGALS)
80    PUT #1,TINT
90  NEXT TINT
100 CLOSE #1
Ok
RUN
              GALLONS IN STOCK
Very White           ? 55
Bone White           ? 35
Off White            ? 28
Bright Light White   ? 26
```

In the previous example, the entire data file was updated by using the FOR NEXT loop counter "TINT" to **GET** and **PUT** each record (1 through 4). It is often the case that a random file is updated by identifying a record, and then updating only that record. For instance, suppose that "INVEN" was updated each evening by entering the number of gallons sold of the types of paint that were sold that day.

```
LIST
10   OPEN "INVEN" AS #1 LEN = 24
20   FIELD #1, 20 AS A$, 4 AS B$
30   PRINT:PRINT "INVENTORY UPDATE  (Press Enter for Color Code when done)"
50   MORE$ = "Y"
60   WHILE MORE$ = "Y"
70     PRINT: INPUT "Color Code ";TINT
80     IF TINT = 0 THEN MORE$ = "N": GOTO 150
90     GET #1,TINT
100    IF EOF(1) THEN PRINT "No record";TINT: GOTO 150
110    PRINT "Brand Name : ";A$;"  Gallons sold ";TAB(50):INPUT GALSOLD
120    GALS = CVI(B$)
130    NEWGALS = GALS - GALSOLD
140    LSET B$ = MKI$(NEWGALS)
145    PUT #1,TINT
150 WEND
160 CLOSE #1
Ok
RUN

INVENTORY UPDATE  (Press Enter for Color Code when done)

Color Code ? 2
Brand Name : Bone White             Gallons sold  ? 6

Color Code ? 6
No record 6

Color Code ? 3
Brand Name : Off White              Gallons sold  ? 4

Color Code ?
Ok
```

STUDY QUESTIONS

1. Which of the following statements are not used to assign values to a variable?
   a. **LET**
   b. **PRINT**
   c. **INPUT**
   d. **READ/DATA**
2. To delete a program line from your program you must:
   a. retype the whole line
   b. list only the line to be deleted
   c. type the line number then Enter
   d. use the removal command

What will be output if the following programs are RUN?

3.
```
10 A = 10
20 READ B
30 C = A * B
40 PRINT C
50 DATA 5
60 END
```
   a. 50
   b. 15
   c. 5
   d. 10

4.
```
10 A$ = "Computers"
15 B$ = "    and    "
20 A$ = "Business"
30 PRINT A$;B$;A$
99 END
```
   a. Computers and Business
   b. ComputersandBusiness
   c. Computers and Computers
   d. Business and Business

5.
```
10 W = 6
20 PRINT "W",W,W,"W"
99 END
```
   a. W 6 6 W
   b. 6 0 0 6
   c. 0 6 6 0
   d. W 0 0 W

6.
```
10 A = B + C
20 READ B,C
30 PRINT A
40 DATA 60,40,20
99 END
```
   a. 0
   b. nothing
   c. an error message
   d. 100 will be printed

7.
```
10 A = 32/2^3-(16/2)*4
20 PRINT A
99 END
```
   a. nothing
   b. division by zero error message
   c. 2
   d. −28

8.
```
 5 READ A
10 G2 = INT((A/3*100)/100
20 PRINT G2
30 DATA 10
99 END
```
   a. 333
   b. error message
   c. 33.3
   d. 3.33

9.
```
10 A = 5
20 READ A
30 PRINT (A+5)^2
40 DATA 2
99 END
```
   a. 49
   b. 100
   c. 25
   d. none of the above

10.
```
10 A = SQR(32/(3+5)+12)
20 PRINT A
30 END
```
   a. 256
   b. 4
   c. 16
   d. 64

11.
```
10 READ A$,B,C
20 PRINT A$
30 RESTORE
40 READ A$,B,C
50 PRINT A$,B,C
60 DATA "JACK",10,20,90
70 DATA "SUE",40,50
99 END
```

a. JACK
SUE 40 50

b. JACK
JACK 90 40

c. JACK
JACK 40 50

d. none of the above

Which of the following is the correct BASIC statement?

12. a. `10 PRINT TAB;"X"`
b. `10 PRINT TAB;15;"X"`
c. `10 PRINT (TAB 15);"X"`
d. `10 PRINT TAB(15);"X"`

13. a. `50 IF A NOT = 500 THEN 1000`
b. `50 IF A$ <> 500 THEN 1000`
c. `50 IF A$ <> "500" THEN 1000`
d. b and c are correct

14. a. `10 FOR I = 1 TO 10 STEP 5`
b. `10 FOR I = 10 TO 1 STEP -2`
c. `10 FOR I = N1 TO N2`
d. all of the above are correct

What will be output if the following programs are RUN?

15.
```
10 A = 20
20 PRINT A;
30 GOTO 50
40 PRINT "TESTING";
50 END
```

a. 20 TESTING
b. 20
c. A TESTING
d. none of the above

16.
```
10 A = 15
20 B = 10
30 IF A < B THEN 50
40 PRINT "XXX";
50 PRINT "YYY";
60 PRINT "ZZZ";
70 END
```

a. XXX
b. YYYZZZ
c. ZZZ
d. XXXYYYZZZ

17.
```
10 READ A
20 IF A < 5 THEN 50
30 PRINT A;
40 GOTO 60
50 PRINT "TESTING";
60 DATA 3,6
70 END
```

a. TESTING 6
b. TESTING
c. 3 TESTING
d. 3 6 TESTING

18.
```
10 FOR I = 1 TO 2
20    X = I + X
30    PRINT X; I;
40 NEXT I
```

a. 0 0 2 1
b. 1 1 3 2
c. 0 1 2 1
d. 0 1 1 2

19.
```
10 READ A
20  IF A = 3 THEN 70
25  IF A = 2 THEN 50
30 PRINT "XXX"
40 GOTO 100
50 PRINT "YYY"
60 GOTO 100
70 PRINT "ZZZ"
80 DATA 1
100 END
```

a. XXX
b. YYY
c. ZZZ
d. XXX
YYY
ZZZ

20.
```
10 READ A
20 ON A GOTO 30,50,70
30 PRINT "XXX"
40 GOTO 100
50 PRINT "YYY"
60 GOTO 100
70 PRINT "ZZZ"
80 DATA 3
100 END
```

a. XXX
b. YYY
c. ZZZ
d. XXX
YYY
ZZZ

21.
```
10 FOR X = 1 TO 10
20   PRINT X;
30 NEXT X
```

a. 1 2 3 4 5 6 7 8 9 10
b. 0 1 2 3 4 5 6 7 8 9 10
c. 1 2 3 4 5 6 7 8 9 10 11
d. X X X X X X X X X X

22.
```
10 FOR T = 1 TO 5
20   PRINT T;
30   IF T < 3 THEN 50
40   PRINT "XXX";
50 NEXT T
```

a. 1 2 3XXX 4XXX 5XXX
b. 1 2 3 4XXX 5XXX
c. 1XXX 2XXX 3 4 5
d. 1XXX 2XXX 3XXX 4 5

23.
```
10 FOR H = 1 TO 6
20   READ Z
30   IF Z < 25 THEN 50
40   PRINT Z;
50 NEXT H
60 DATA 10,45,18,90,73,25
```

a. 45 90 73
b. 10 18
c. 45 90 73 25
d. 10 18 25

24.
```
10 FOR I = 1 TO 6
20   READ A$(I)
30 NEXT I
40 PRINT A$(4)
50 DATA CORN FLAKES,RICE KRISPIES,HONEY O'S
60 DATA FRUIT LOOPS,CRUNCH BERRY,CHEERIOS
```

a. KRISPIES
b. FRUIT LOOPS
c. Out of data will occur
d. Subscript error will occur

25.
```
10 FOR A = 1 TO 3
20    FOR B = 1 TO 2
30       PRINT A * B;
40    NEXT B
50 NEXT A
```
a. 1 2 2 4 3 6
b. 1 1 2 2 3 3
c. 1 2 3 4 5 6
d. none of the above

26.
```
10 FOR Z = 1 TO 3 STEP 2
20    PRINT "HELLO    ";
30 NEXT Z
```
a. HELLO HELLO HELLO
b. HELLO
c. HELLO HELLO
d. none of the above

27.
```
10 READ A
20    IF A < 0 THEN 40
30 IF A = 0 THEN 10
40    A = A + 1
50    IF A >= 5 THEN 70
80 GOTO 10
70 PRINT A
80 DATA -5,-6,7,-11,0
```
a. nothing will be printed
b. −4
c. 0
d. 8

28.
```
10 READ N
20 FOR I = 1 TO N
30    READ J
40    IF J < 0 THEN 60
50    PRINT J;
60 NEXT I
70 DATA 5,1,0,-1,-2,5,6,-11
```
a. 5 1 0 5 6
b. 1 0 5
c. 5 1 0
d. 1 0 5 6

29. How many data items are required to fill the arrays in this program?
```
10 FOR I = 1 TO 10 STEP 2
20    READ B$(I),C$(I)
30    FOR J = 1 TO 5
40       READ X(I,J)
50    NEXT J
60 NEXT I
```
a. 70
b. 35
c. 15
d. 10

What will be the output of the following programs?

30.
```
10 DIM X(5,3)
20 FOR T = 1 TO 5
30    FOR U = 1 TO 3
40       READ X(T,U)
50    NEXT U
60 NEXT T
70 PRINT X(3,2)
80 DATA 1,2,3,4,5,6,7,8,9,1,2,3,4,5,6,7,8,9
```
a. 8
b. 5
c. 2
d. nothing will be printed

31.
```
10 FOR I = 1 TO 4
20    READ A$(I),A(I)
30 NEXT I
40 FOR N = 1 TO 4
50    IF A(N) < 5 THEN 70
60    PRINT A$(N);A(N);
70 NEXT N
80  DATAKATHY,4
90  DATA LUCY,6
100 DATA TOM,8
110 DATA MAGGY,2
```
a. KATHY 4 LUCY 6 TOM 8 MAGGY 2
b. LUCY 6 TOM 8
c. KATHY 4 MAGGY 2
d. nothing will be printed

32.

```
10 FOR I = 1 TO 5
20   I = I * 2
30   PRINT I;
40   I = I - 1
50   PRINT I;
60 NEXT I
70 PRINT I
```

a. 2 1 4 3 8 7 8
b. 2 1 4 3 8 7 7
c. 1 1 2 2 3 3 4 4 5 5
d. nothing will be printed

33.

```
10  FOR I = 1 TO 5
20    READ A$(I)
30  NEXT I
40  N = 2
50  PRINT A$(N * (N - 1))
60  DATA SHEILA,HENERY,JOSHUA,CARLIA,LORENZ
```

a. nothing will be printed
b. a syntax error will occur
c. JOSHUA
d. HENERY

34.

```
10 FOR K = 1 TO 5
20   READ D(K)
30   T = T + D(K)
40   C = C + 1
50 NEXT K
60 PRINT T/C;
70 DATA 10,20,30,40,50
```

a. 10 15 20 25 30
b. 30
c. 1
d. 6

35.

```
10 FOR K = 1 TO 5
20   READ D(K)
30   C(K)=D(K) * 2
40 NEXT K
50 FOR K = 1 TO 5
60   PRINT C(K);
70 NEXT K
80 DATA 10,20,30,40,50
```

a. a syntax error will occur
b. nothing will be printed
c. 0 0 0 0 100
d. 20 40 60 80 100

BASICA KEY TERMS GLOSSARY

Advanced BASIC A version of BASIC found on the DOS diskette that has all of the operations and commands of Disk BASIC plus advanced graphics and music commands.

ASCII (American Standard Code for Information Interchange) A standard Data Format that facilitates the interchange of data among various types of software and hardware.

BASIC (An Acronym) Beginner's All-purpose Symbolic Instruction Code, a programming language developed to teach beginning students the constructs of programming theory.

Cassette BASIC A version of BASIC that requires a cassette player and interface cord to save programs.

Data Files Diskette files used to store data that BASIC programs may access.

Disk BASIC A version of BASIC found on a DOS diskette—usually purchased with the computer. This version of BASIC has the operations for accessing and storing data on diskettes.

Firmware A program that is permanently held in ROM.

Random Files Files stored on a diskette that are structured so that each data item is given a specific length in characters so the location of a data item separates it from other data items in a file.

Relational Database Data organized in a database in records with fields holding related data.

Screen Scroll The vertical movement of lines of type on a monitor. As one screen of data is complete, the data at the top of the screen disappears from view to make room at the bottom of the screen for new lines of text.

Sequential Data Files Files stored on a diskette that use delimiters (quotes, commas, carriage returns) to separate the individual data items.

BASICA OPERATION AND COMMAND SUMMARY

BASICA QUICK REFERENCE COMMAND SUMMARY

ABS(x)	Returns absolute value of x
AUTO	Automatic line numbers
BEEP	Beeps the speaker
CHR$(n)	Returns ASCII character
CINT(x)	Returns x as rounded integer
CIRCLE	Draws an ellipse
CLOSE	Closes files
CLS	Clears Screen
COLOR	Alters screen output
CONT	Continues program
CV(I) (S) (D)	Converts strings to numbers
DATA	Holds data elements
DEF FN	Defines a function
DEFtype	Declares variable types
DIM	Dimensions arrays
DRAW	Draws an object
EDIT	Displays a program line
END	Terminates a program
EOF	Signals End Of File
ERASE	Eliminates arrays
FIELD	Defines file buffer
FILES	Lists diskette files
FIX(x)	Truncates x to an integer
FOR NEXT	Establishes a loop
GET	Gets a random file record
GOSUB	Passes control to subroutine
GOTO	Passes control to a line
IF	Sets a condition
INPUT	Takes data from keyboard
INPUT$	Takes data from files
INPUT$(x)	Takes x characters
INT(x)	Returns largest integer
KEY	Controls F key display
KILL	Deletes a diskette file
LEFT$(n)	Returns leftmost characters
LET	Assigns values to variables
LINE	Draws a line or box
LIST	Lists a program on screen
LLIST	Lists a program on printer
LOAD	Loads a BASICA program
LOCATE	Controls cursor position
LPRINT	Outputs to the printer
(R) (L)SET	Moves data into file buffer
MERGE	Merges ASCII file into program
**MID$**(x$,n)	Returns characters from string
MK(I) (S) (D)$	Makes strings from numbers
NAME	Renames a diskette file
NEW	Erases current program file
ON	Passes control by condition
OPEN	Opens a file
PAINT	Fills in an area on the screen
PLAY	Plays music specified by strings
PRINT	Outputs to the screen
PRINT USING	Formats output
PSET	Draws a point on the screen
PRESET	Blanks a point on the screen
PUT	Sends a record to a random file
RANDOMIZE	Reseeds random number generator
READ	Reads DATA elements
REM	Allows for remarks in program
RENUM	Renumbers a program
RESTORE	Allows DATA elements to be reREAD
RESUME	Returns control from error trap
RETURN	Returns control from subroutine
**RIGHT$**(x$,n)	Returns rightmost n characters
RND	Returns a random number
RUN	Begins program execution
SAVE	Saves a program file
SCREEN	Sets screen mode
SOUND	Generates sound through speaker
SPC(n)	Outputs n spaces
SQR(x)	Returns square root of x
STOP	Interrupts program execution
SWAP	Exchanges variable's values
SYSTEM	Exits BASICA
TAB(n)	Moves cursor to column n
TRON	Turns trace on
TROFF	Turns trace off
VAL	Returns numbers from strings
WHILE WEND	Establishes a loop
WIDTH	Sets screen character widths
WRITE#	Outputs data to a file

BASICA FILE COMMANDS

Diskette File Commands

FILES	Lists a directory of the default disk drive files on the monitor screen. (DOS (A>) equivalent is the **DIR** command).
Example Variations	
FILES"*.BAS	Lists all .BAS files on default drive.
FILES"B:	Lists all files on B: drive.
FILES"B:*.TXT	Lists all .TXT files on B: drive.
KILL"filename.ext	Erases the specified file from the diskette. (DOS (A>) equivalent is the **ERASE** command).
Example Variations	
KILL"B:progone.BAS	Erases progone.BAS from the B: drive.
KILL"*.BAS	Erases all .BAS files on default drive.
KILL"B:*.TXT	Erases all .TXT files on B: drive.
LOAD"filename	Copies the specified BASIC program (.BAS) file from the diskette into the computer's RAM.
Example Variation	
LOAD"B:progone.BAS	Loads progone.BAS from the B: drive.
MERGE"filename	Merges a program (.BAS) file, saved in ASCII, from the diskette into the program in RAM. Duplicate line numbers are replaced by lines in the file being merged.
NAME"filename.ext" **AS**"filename.ext"	Renames a diskette file. (DOS (A>) equivalent is the **RENAME** command)
RUN"filename	Loads and begins execution of the specified program (.BAS) file.
SAVE"filename	Copies the program in RAM onto the diskette under the specified filename. If a program with that filename already exists, it is replaced by the program being saved.
SAVE"filename"**,A**	Saves the specified file in ASCII.

Current File Commands

CONT	Continues program execution at the line following a break-point caused by a STOP or END statement, a ^Break, or an error.
LIST **LIST** line#-line# **LIST** -line# **LIST** line#-	Lists the lines of the program in RAM on the monitor screen. From one line to another (line#-line#), up to a line (-line#), from a line on (line#-).
LLIST	Lists the lines of the program in RAM on the printer.
NEW	Erases the current program from RAM.
RUN	Begins execution of the program in RAM.

BASICA CONTROL KEYS

KEY COMBINATIONS

^Alt-Del Reboots the DOS.

^Break Interrupts any BASICA operation.

^Home Clears the monitor screen.

^Num Lock Pauses BASICA operations.

^PrtSc Toggles ON/OFF an echo of screen output to the printer (versions of DOS 2.0 or higher).

Shift-PrtSc Prints the screen on the printer.

Alt-Key Used with alphabetic keys to print BASIC statements.

A	**AUTO**	J	(no word)	S	**SCREEN**
B	**BSAVE**	K	**KEY**	T	**THEN**
C	**COLOR**	L	**LOCATE**	U	**USING**
D	**DELETE**	M	**MOTOR**	V	**VAL**
E	**ELSE**	N	**NEXT**	W	**WIDTH**
F	**FOR**	O	**OPEN**	X	**XOR**
G	**GOTO**	P	**PRINT**	Y	(no word)
H	**HEX$**	Q	(no word)	Z	(no word)
I	**INPUT**	R	**RUN**		

OTHER CONTROL KEYS

Enter Key ↵ Enters the current line into memory for the computer to act upon.

Escape Key Erases a line from the monitor screen at current cursor position.

Num Lock Key Toggles ON/OFF ten-key numeric to cursor control keys.

Function Keys 1–10 User programmable keys that may hold up to 15 characters.

F1	**LIST**	F6	**LPT1**:"←
F2	**RUN**↵	F7	**TRON**↵
F3	**LOAD**"	F8	**TROFF**↵
F4	**SAVE**"	F9	**KEY**
F5	**CONT**↵	F10	**SCREEN** 0,0,0

To change any of these keys, type KEY #, "The string."

Type ‖+CHR$(13)‖ after the last quote to add a ↵.

Type ‖+CHR$(34)‖ after the last quote to add a quote (").

BASICA EDITING COMMANDS

AUTO

Generates line numbers, starting at 10 and increased by 10, each time the Enter key is pressed. ^Break stops automatic generation of line numbers.

An asterisk (*) following a number generated by **AUTO** indicates that a program line with that number already exists.

AUTO 100 — Starts at line 100, increased by 10.
AUTO 50,20 — Starts at line 50, increased by 20.
AUTO ,50 — Starts at line 0, increased by 50.

DELETE line#1-line#2

Deletes all lines from line#1 to line#2, inclusive. Both line#1 and line#2 must exist in the current program.

DELETE 30-100 — Deletes lines 30 through 100.
DELETE -60 — Deletes all lines up to and including 60.

EDIT line#

Displays specified program line for editing. Most useful for editing programs from hard-copy listings where several dispersed lines need correcting.

EDIT 120 — Displays line 120 for editing.

RENUM

Renumbers the current program file. Starts line numbering with 10 and renumbers by increments of 10. All referenced line numbers are changed accordingly.

RENUM ,,20	Starts with 10, increments by 20.
RENUM 100,,20	Starts with 100, increments by 20.
RENUM 100,50,20	Renumbers the program from line 50 on, starts with 100, increments of 20.

Inherent Commands

Inserting a Line

Give the new program line a line number that falls between the two line numbers of the program lines on either side of where the line is to be inserted.

Deleting a Line

Type the line number of the line to be deleted, and then press the Enter Key.

Replacing a Line

Type the new line with the same line number of the line to be replaced.

Moving a Program Line

Use the full-screen editor to change the line number of the line. This will leave two identical lines located at two different places in the new program. Type the first line number (Enter) to delete the original line.

BASICA EDITING KEYS

Any program line or command displayed on the monitor screen may be edited with BASICA's full-screen editing. The procedure is as follows.

1. Move the cursor to the position in the program or command line to be edited.
2. Make the corrections desired.
3. Press the Enter key to enter that line or command into memory.

EDITING KEYS

Enter Key Enters the line at the current cursor position (the current line) into memory.

Cursor Control Keys Moves the cursor in the direction of the cursor arrow.

Backspace Key Backspaces and erases the character to the left on the current line.

Insert Key Toggles ON Insert Mode. Any non-character key will turn OFF Insert Mode.

Delete Key Deletes the character at current cursor position.

Home Key Moves cursor to top left corner of monitor screen.

End Key Moves cursor to the end of the current line.

KEY COMBINATIONS

Ctrl-Break Exits line being edited without entering that line into memory.

Ctrl-End Erases to the end of the line from the current cursor position.

Ctrl ← or Ctrl → Moves the cursor one word to the left or the right.

BASICA COMMANDS, FUNCTIONS, AND STATEMENTS

ABS(x)	Absolute value function. Returns the absolute value of x. The following assigns the value 24 to N. LET N = ABS(12 * (−2))
AUTO	Generates line numbers, starting at 10 and increased by 10, each time the Enter key is pressed. ^Break stops Automatic generation of line numbers. An asterisk (*) following a number generated by **AUTO** indicates that a program line with that number already exists. **AUTO** 100 Starts at line 100, increased by 10. **AUTO** 50,20 Starts at line 50, increased by 20. **AUTO** ,50 Starts at line 0, increased by 50.
BEEP	Sounds the speaker (800 Hz for 1/4 second). **PRINT CHR$**(7) has the same effect.
CHR$(x)	Character string function. Returns the character equivalent of the ASCII code number x. The following prints a capital A on the monitor screen. **PRINT CHR$**(65)
CINT(x)	Convert to integer function. Returns the rounded integer value of x. The following assigns the value 6 to the variable B. **LET** B = **CINT**(17/3)
CIRCLE	(Graphics mode) Draws an ellipse on the screen. **CIRCLE**(120,80),45 The above draws a circle with its center at the screen coordinates 120, 80, and with a radius of 45. Other options allow part of the circle to be drawn and/or the aspect to be changed.
CLEAR	Sets all variables to zero or null.
CLOSE	Concludes input/output to all devices or files. Includes option to close a particular file by specifying the file number under which it was opened. For example, **CLOSE** #1,#2 closes files opened as #1 and #2.
CLS	Clears the monitor screen and returns the cursor to the Home position.
COLOR	(Black & White monitor) Sets the foreground, background, and border colors. For example, 0 = Black 7 = White 15 = Bright white **COLOR** 0, 7, 15 sets black foreground (text) on white background with a bright white border. Options include adding 16 to any number for blinking colors.

CONT — Continues program execution at the line following a break point.

CSRLIN — Cursor line function. Returns the current row number of the cursor location.

CVI(x$), **CVS**(x$), and **CVD**(x$) — (Random Files) Convert string function. Converts the string x$ to a numeric-type value as an integer **CVI**(x$), single **CVS**(x$), or double **CVD**(x$) precision numeric-type variable.

DATA — Used with the **READ** statement, the **DATA** statement holds constants to be read during execution of the program.

READ ACT,CTY$,AGE,UNIT$
DATA 653, "Port., OR",54,IBM PC

DATA statements are nonexecutable and may be placed anywhere in a program. The items in the **DATA** statement(s) are read from first to last, and are assigned in order to the variables found in the **READ** statement(s).

DEF FN — For user-defined functions. The general form is:

DEF FNvariable-name(argument) = expression

DEF — Declares variable types as integer, single-precision, double-precision, or string—INT, SNG, DBL, or STR, respectively. The following globally defines all variables starting with the letter A and the letters H through M as integer variables.

DEFINT A,H-M

DELETE line#1-line#2 — Deletes all lines from line#1 to line#2, inclusive. Both line#1 and line#2 must exist in the current program.

DELETE 30-100	Deletes lines 30 through 100.
DELETE -60	Deletes all lines up to and including 60.

DIM — Specifies the maximum values for subscript variables. Necessary for lists longer than 10 and arrays greater than 10 in any dimension. The following sets the array A$(x,y) to hold a maximum of 20 by 10 strings.

DIM A$(20,10)

Lists and arrays may only be dimensioned once.

DRAW string — (Graphics mode) Draws the object described by the defining string.

U	Move up	E	Move diagonally up and right.
D	Move down	F	Move diagonally down and right.
L	Move left	G	Move diagonally down and left.
R	Move right	H	Move diagonally up and left.

The string is composed of direction letters followed by distance numbers. The following draws a small triangle in the middle of the monitor screen.

DRAW "F20 L40 E20"

or

A$ = "F20 L40 E20"
DRAW A$

EDIT	Displays the specified program line for editing. Most useful for editing programs from hard-copy listings where several dispersed lines need to be corrected. The following displays line 120 for editing. **EDIT** 120
END	Terminates program execution and closes all files. **END** statements may be placed anywhere in the program to stop execution.
EOF(x)	(Files) End Of File function. Returns 1 (true) when an attempt is made to read past the end of the file opened as number x. Most useful when used as a condition to avoid "Input past end" errors. IF **EOF**(2) THEN . . . or WHILE NOT **EOF**(1)
FIELD	(Random Files) Defines field space for variables in a random file buffer. **FIELD** #1, 15 AS P$, 10 AS Q$ The above allocates, for the random file opened as #1, the first 15 characters (bytes) to the variable P$, and the next 10 characters to the variable Q$.
FILES	Lists a directory of the diskette files on the monitor screen.
FIX(x)	Truncates x to an integer without returning the next lowest number if x is negative.
FOR and **NEXT**	These two statements cause a series of instructions to be executed a given number of times. The general form is: **FOR** variable = x **TO** y : any program statements : **NEXT** variable "Variable" is the loop counter; x is the beginning number; y is the ending number. **STEP** option allows the loop counter variable to be increased by a value other than one (1). The following will print "Hello" 10 times on the monitor screen: **FOR** J = 1 **TO** 10 **PRINT** " Hello " **NEXT** J and this will print "Hello" twice on the monitor screen. X = 10 **FOR** Q = 1 **TO** X **STEP** 5 **PRINT** "Hello" **NEXT** Q

GET

(Random Files) Reads a record from a random file. The following reads the fifth record in the random file opened as #2.

GET #2,5

GOSUB and **RETURN**

Transfers control to a subroutine by branching to a specified line. The **RETURN** statement at the end of the subroutine returns control to the statement following the **GOSUB.** The following branches to line 1500 to perform that subroutine.

GOSUB 1500

GOTO

Causes an unconditional branch to the specified line. The following branches program execution to line 500.

GOTO 500

IF THEN and **ELSE**

Sets a condition and if the condition is true the statement(s) following the **THEN** are executed. As an option, with **ELSE** (if the condition is not true) the statements following **ELSE** are executed. Otherwise control is passed to the next program line.

IF A$ = "Y" **THEN PRINT** "Done" **ELSE PRINT** " More ": **INPUT** A2$: **GOTO** 500

If A$ equals Y then "Done" will be printed on the monitor. Otherwise, "More ?" will be printed on the monitor and the program will wait for an input. After the input is entered, control will be passed to line 500.

INKEY$

Scans the keyboard for input from the user. The following essentially "freezes" the keyboard, allowing the user to type only a Y or an N.

```
10 PRINT" Continue ? (Y/N)
20 A$=INKEY$
30 IF A$< > "Y" OR A$ < >"N" THEN 20
```

INPUT

Allows for user input from the keyboard. **INPUT** is followed by a prompt string (optional), and then an appropriate variable for the input. The following prints "Enter a number" on the monitor screen and then waits for a number to be entered from the keyboard.

INPUT "Enter a number"; A

INPUT #

(Files) Reads data from sequential files and assigns them to program variables. The following assigns two values, a numeric and a string, to two variables, DEPT and EMP$, from the sequential file opened as #1.

INPUT #1,DEPT,EMP$

INPUT$(x)

Input function. Reads x number of characters from the keyboard. With **INPUT$** it is not necessary to press Enter when answering an input prompt. The program waits until x number of characters are typed, and then continues program execution. The following assigns Q$ the single key character that is typed.

PRINT " Continue ? (Y/N)";
Q$ = **INPUT$**(1)

INSTR(x$,y$)	Instring function. Searches for the first occurrence of a substring (y$) within a string (x$) and returns the starting character position of the substring.
INT(x)	Integer function. Returns the largest integer value that is less than or equal to x. The following prints 5 and −4 on the monitor screen. **PRINT INT**(5.675) **PRINT INT**(−3.333)
KEY	Sets display of the Function keys (screen-row 25). For example, **KEY ON** or **KEY OFF** turns on or off the Function key display; **KEY LIST** lists the full contents of each Function key on the monitor screen; and **KEY** n, "string" changes the Function key n to contain the specified string.
KILL"	Erases the specified file from the diskette.
**LEFT$**(x$,n)	Left substring function. Returns the left-most n characters of the string x$. For example, A$ = "This is an example" **PRINT LEFT$**(A$,9) prints "This is a" on the monitor screen.
LEN(x$)	String Length function. Returns the number of characters in the string x$. For example, A$ = "This is an example" **PRINT LEN**(A$) prints 18 on the monitor.
LET	Assigns the value of an expression to a variable. **LET** is optional in BASICA. For example, **LET** A = 5 is the same as A = 5.
LINE	(Graphics mode) Draws a line or a box on the monitor screen. For example, **LINE** (200,50)–(300,100) draws a diagonal line from the coordinate 200, 50 to the coordinate 300, 100; and **LINE** (200,50)–(300,100),,B draws a box with its top left corner at 200, 50 and its bottom right corner at 300, 100. BF, instead of B, fills in the box with the foreground color.

LINE INPUT #n	(Files) Reads an entire line from a sequential file opened as file number n into a string variable.
LIST	Lists the lines of the current program on the monitor screen. **LIST** -line# up to a line **LIST** line#- from a line on
LLIST	Lists the lines of the current program on the printer.
LOAD"	Copies the specified file from the diskette into the computer's RAM.
LOCATE	Positions the cursor on the monitor screen by row, column. For example, **LOCATE** 12,40 positions the cursor in the middle of the screen. **LOCATE** will not work on printer output.
LPRINT	Directs output to the printer. **LPRINT** may be used with all of the options of the **PRINT** statement.
LSET and **RSET**	(Random Files) Prepares strings to be **PUT** into a random file. **LSET** or **RSET** statements must follow the **FIELD** statement for the variable(s) being (**L** or **R**) **SET**. **LSET** left justifies the string in its field; **RSET** right justifies the string. For example, **LSET** A$ = EMP$ left justifies the string EMP$ in the field defined as A$.
MERGE"	Merges a diskette file, saved in ASCII, from the diskette into the current program. Duplicate line numbers are replaced by lines in the file being merged.
**MID$**(x$,n,m)	Midstring function. Returns a portion of the string x$, m characters long, beginning at the nth character. For example, A$ = "This is an example" Z$ = **MID$**(A$,5,5) **PRINT** Z$ prints " is a" on the monitor.
MKI$**(x), **MKS$(x), and **MKD$**(x)	(Random Files) Make string function. Converts integer, double- or single-precision numeric-type variables into string-type variables.
NAME"	Renames a diskette file. For example, **NAME** "PROG1.BAS" **AS** "PROG2.BAS" renames PROG1 to PROG2.
NEW	Erases the current program from RAM.
ON ERROR GOTO	Enables (turns on) error trapping. When an error is detected, control is passed to the beginning of the error trapping subroutine specified by the line number following **GOTO.** For example,

ON ERROR GOTO 500

will pass control to line 500 if an error occurs during program execution. **RESUME** at the end of the subroutine transfers control back to the line that generated the error.

ON GOSUB and **ON GOTO**

Branches to one of several lines or subroutines, based on the value of n, where the general form is

ON n **GOSUB** line#1,line#2, ...

n is an integer that points to the line# to which control will be passed. If n = 1, then control will be passed to the first line# listed. If n = 5 then control will be passed to the fifth line# listed.

OPEN

(Files) Allows input/output to a file or device. The general form is:

OPEN "filename" **FOR** mode **AS** # fnum

Mode is necessary for sequential files and may be any of the following:

INPUT
OUTPUT
APPEND

If "**FOR** mode" is omitted, the file will be opened for random file input/output. For example,

OPEN "DATA" **FOR INPUT AS** #2

opens the sequential file named "DATA" as the #2 file for input of values from the file to the program; and

OPEN "DATA" **FOR OUTPUT AS** #3

opens the same file as the #3 file for output of values from the program to the file. **OPEN FOR OUTPUT** erases the contents of the file being opened. Further,

OPEN "DATA" **FOR APPEND AS** #3

opens DATA for output without erasing the file. Any values output are added to the end of (appended to) the file.

Once a file has been opened, it must be closed before being opened again.

PAINT

(Graphics mode) (Black & White monitor) Fills in an area on the monitor screen with a selected color. The general form is:

PAINT (x,y),color,boundary-color

x,y sets the coordinate point at which painting will begin. Color is the color that will be used to fill in the area. Boundary-color describes the color that outlines where painting is to stop.

The default foreground color is 3 in medium resolution, 1 in high resolution. Zero (0) is the background color in both resolutions. For example,

SCREEN 1
DRAW "L50 D50 R50 U50"
PAINT (130,120),3,3

sets medium resolution, draws a box on the screen, begins painting inside the box, and quits when it reaches the outline of the box.

PLAY

Plays music as specified by a string.

POS(x)

Position function. Returns the current column position of the cursor. May be used with the **CRSLN** statement to determine the exact location of the cursor.

PRINT

Displays program output on the monitor screen. **PRINT** is followed by a list of variables, constants, and/or expressions. If the list is omitted, a blank line is displayed. The items in the list are separated by: 1) A semicolon (;) which leaves no spaces between items output; 2) A space which acts in the same manner as a semicolon; or 3) a comma (,) which prints the next item in the next Print Zone (every 14 columns).

A comma or semicolon, after the last item in a **PRINT** statement, disables the automatic carriage return.

PRINT USING

Displays output on the monitor screen in a specified format. A string constant or variable, containing special formatting characters, is used to set the fields and formats for printing strings and numbers.

String fields are specified with backslashes (\). Two plus the number of spaces between the backslashes is the allowable length of a string printed in that format.

```
A$ = "This is an example"
Z$ = "    \            \     "
PRINT USING Z$; A$
This is an ex
```

If the number of spaces between the backslashes is greater than the length of the string being printed, the string is left justified and padded with spaces on the right.

Numeric fields are specified by the number sign (#). One sign is used to represent each digit position that will be displayed. A decimal point may be inserted at any position in the field. Numbers are rounded to fit in the field described, and if the number is too large to fit in its field, a percent sign (%) is output to the left of that number.

```
C  = 123.466
L$ ="                     ###.##"
PRINT USING L$;C
                     123.47
```

The dollar sign ($) may be used to the left of the numeric format to print a dollar sign to the left of the number being printed. A double dollar sign to the left causes the dollar sign to be printed to the immediate left of the number. A comma to the immediate left of the decimal in the numeric format causes a comma to be printed every third digit.

PRINT #

(Files) Writes program output to a file. **PRINT #** outputs to a file in the same manner as **PRINT** outputs to the screen, and **PRINT #** has all the same options as **PRINT** (TAB, SPC, USING, etc.). Semicolons usually are used to separate the items being output. For example,

```
PRINT #1, A$;",";B,C,D
```

outputs to the sequential file opened as #1, the values of the variables A$, B, C, and D. Notice that a comma in quotes follows a string to separate it from other items in this **PRINT #** statement.

PSET

(Graphics) Draws a point at the specified coordinates on the monitor screen. For example,

PSET (100,200)

draws a point at the screen coordinates 100, 200. **PSET** also may be used to define the starting point for a **DRAW** string.

PUT

(Random Files) Writes a record to a random file. For example,

PUT #2,5

writes the fifth record to the random file opened as #2.

RANDOMIZE number

Reseeds the random number generator. **RANDOMIZE** keeps the **RND** function from returning the same set of random numbers each time the program is executed.

The seed is the number that follows **RANDOMIZE.** Each time the seed is changed the program will generate a new set of random numbers.

READ

Reads values from **DATA** statements and assigns them to the variables listed after **READ.** For example,

READ ACT,CTY$,AGE,UNIT$
DATA 653,"Port., OR",54,IBM PC

assigns the values in the **DATA** statement, in order of their appearance, to the variables in the **READ** statements, in order of their appearance:

ACT = 653, CTY$ = Port., OR, etc.

Once a **DATA** item has been read, it is not read again during the execution of the program. Instead, a marker is set at the next **DATA** item for the next executed **READ** statement to read.

REM

Used to put explanatory notes (remarks) in a program. **REM** statements are not executed. Whatever is typed after **REM** is ignored during program execution.

RENUM

Renumbers the current program file. Starts line numbering with 10 and renumbers by increments of 10. All referenced line numbers are changed accordingly.

RENUM ,,20	Starts with 10, increments by 20.
RENUM 100,,20	Starts with 100, increments by 20.
RENUM 100,50,20	Renumbers the program from line 50 on, starts with 100, increments of 20.

RESTORE

Allows **DATA** statements to be reread. **RESTORE** sets the **READ** marker back to the beginning of the first item in the first **DATA** statement. Optionally, the marker can be set back to the first item in a particular **DATA** statement by typing the line number for the statement after **RESTORE**. For example,

RESTORE 500

sets the marker back to the first **DATA** item in line 500.

RESUME	Continues program execution after an error trapping subroutine has been completed. **RESUME** 0 — Turns off error trapping. **RESUME** NEXT — Returns control to the next line.
RETURN	Returns control, from a subroutine, to the statement following the **GOSUB** that initiated the branch to that subroutine.
**RIGHT$**(x$,n)	Right substring function. Returns the right-most n characters of the string, x$. For example, A$ = "This is an example" **PRINT RIGHT$**(A$,4) prints "mple" on the monitor.
RND	Random number function. Returns a seven-digit random number between 0 and 1, such as .6291626.
RUN	Begins execution of the BASICA program in RAM. **RUN**"filename — Loads and begins execution of the specified file. **RUN** line# — Begins program execution at the specified line number.
SAVE"	Copies the current program onto the diskette under the specified filename. If a program with that filename already exists, it is replaced by the program being saved. For example, **SAVE**"filename",A saves the specified file in ASCII format.
SCREEN	Sets the screen for text, medium resolution, or high resolution graphics. **SCREEN** 0 — Text (standard screen) 40 or 80 columns. **SCREEN** 1 — Medium resolution (320 × 200) points. **SCREEN** 2 — High resolution (640 × 200) points. **SCREEN** 1 or 2 is required for any of the statements marked (Graphics mode).
SCREEN(x,y)	Screen function. Returns the ASCII code for the character found at the screen coordinates (row = x, column = y).
SOUND	Generates sound through the speaker. **SOUND** is followed by two numbers—one for the frequency and one for the duration. For example, **SOUND** 523,3 generates a sound (roughly, middle C) for the equivalent of three clock ticks (about 1/6th of a second).
SPC(n)	Space function. Prints n number of spaces in a **PRINT** statement. For example, **PRINT SPC**(15);"Test" prints "Test" starting in the sixteenth column position on the monitor screen row.
SQR(x)	Square root function. Returns the square root of x. For example, **PRINT SQR**(16) prints 4 on the monitor.

STOP	Terminates program execution. The program will stop with a break-point message indicating the line where the **STOP** occurred. The **CONT** command will continue program execution at the line following the **STOP.**
STR$(x)	String function. Returns the string value of the numeric expression x. **STR$**(x) is the complement of **VAL**(x$).
SWAP	Exchanges the values of two variables. For example, **SWAP** A$,B$ assigns A$ the value in B$ and B$ the value in A$.
SYSTEM	Exits BASICA and returns to the DOS level of operation.
TAB(n)	Tab function. Prints spaces to the nth position in a **PRINT** statement. For example, **PRINT** "This is"; TAB(30);"a test" prints "This is," starting at the first position, then prints "a test," starting at the thirtieth position on the screen row.
TRON and **TROFF**	These two commands are used to set program execution tracing on and off.
VAL(x$)	Returns a numeric value from a string. For example, A$= "123 Example" **PRINT** VAL(A$) prints the number 123 on the monitor screen. The number to be returned must precede any characters in the string.
WHILE and **WEND**	These two statements execute a series of instructions as long as the condition of the while statement remains true. **WHILE** X => 1 | any statements | **WEND** As long as X is equal to or greater than 1, the **WEND** statement will pass control to the statement immediately following the **WHILE** statement (causing a loop). X must change in value while the loop is being executed in order to reach a value less than 1, and so stop execution of this loop.
WIDTH	Sets the character size for the monitor screen. **WIDTH** 80 (default width) Sets character size to 80 per screen row. **WIDTH** 40 Sets character size to 40 per screen row.
WRITE	Similar to **PRINT**, **WRITE** outputs to the screen the list of constants, variables and expressions that follow it. **WRITE,** however, outputs a comma between each item in the list and will print the quotes around a string constant or a string assigned to a variable.

	WRITE does not recognize the Print Zones that **PRINT** uses. A$ = "an example" B = 50 **WRITE** "This is"; A$,B "This is," "an example,"50
WRITE#	Writes output to sequential files and is preferred to **PRINT** # since commas as delimiters are automatically included.

ERROR MESSAGES

Syntax Error

- Generally caused by a misspelled statement or incorrect placement of characters. Check spelling, unmatched parentheses, and/or incorrect use of delimiters (, ; : " '.).
- Line wrap-around. **LIST** only the line with the error. If two or more lines appear, there is a line wrap-around. It probably occurred during program editing.
- If error occurs in a **DATA** statement, check the appropriate **READ** statement for correct variable type. Check if the program is trying to **READ** a string into a numeric variable.
- A reserved word may have been used as a variable name. See "Reserved Words" (p. B-76).

Subscript Out of Range

- An array element may be greater than the array can hold. Check to see if the array has been dimensioned large enough.
- Try using a **PRINT** statement to check the value of the element at the time the program generates the error. It may be more than expected.
- A space in a **TAB** function will generate this error.

Type Mismatch

- A string value occurred where a numeric value was expected. Check variables for correct names and review logic of passing values to them.

Redo from Start

- This error does not stop the execution of the program. It is generated by an **INPUT** statement expecting a particular type or number of values to be entered from the keyboard. Ctrl-Break to stop program execution and examine that line for the logic of passing values to the **INPUT** variables.

Out of Data

- There are fewer **DATA** elements than executed **READ** variable(s). Put a **PRINT** variable(s) directly after the **READ** variable(s) to determine when "out of data" occurs.

Illegal Function Call

- Probably a bad argument value in a statement or function. Usually the argument has something to do with output to the screen. Check parameters to see if they are reasonable.

RETURN without **GOSUB**

- Usually caused by directly entering a subroutine: entering it from the program lines above it, rather than through a **GOSUB.** Use a **GOTO** to pass control around that subroutine.

FOR without **NEXT** or **NEXT** without **FOR**

- Often occurs in the use of nested loops. Each **FOR** statement requires a **NEXT** statement and vice versa.
- The counter variable in **FOR** must have the same name as the variable in its matching **NEXT** statement.

Bad File Number

- The statement generating the error may refer to a file that is not currently **OPEN.**
- If the error occurs in an **OPEN** statement, the maximum number of files allowed may be currently open, or the filename may be invalid.

File Not Found

- Check spelling and proper file identification. Does the file extension need to be included in that statement?

Input Past End

- Input from a sequential file has been attempted when no data are left to input, or when no data are there. Use the **EOF** function to avoid this error.

Too Many Files

- The filename being used is probably invalid. Use eight or fewer letters or numbers only, and use no spaces, commas, periods, etc. Make sure the name starts with a letter.

Disk Media Error

- Usually indicates a diskette has gone bad.

RESERVED WORDS (BASICA VERSION 2.0 +)

ABS	DELETE	INT	OPEN	SOUND
AND	DIM	INTER$ *	OPTION	SPACE$
ASC	DRAW	IOCTL *	OR	SCP(
ATN	EDIT	IOCTL$ *	OUT	SQR
AUTO	ELSE	KEY	PAINT	STEP
BEEP	END	KILL	PEEK	STICK
BLOAD	ENVIRON *	LEFT$	PEN	STOP
BSAVE	ENVIRON$ *	LEN	PLAY	STR$
CALL	EOF	LET	PMAP *	STRIG
CDBL	EQV	LINE	POINT	STRING$ *
CHAIN	ERASE	LIST	POKE	SWAP
CHDIR *	ERDEV *	LLIST	POS	SYSTEM
CHR$	ERDEV$ *	LOAD	PRESET	TAB
CINT	ERL	LOC	PRINT	TAN
CIRCLE	ERR	LOCATE	PRINT#	THEN
CLEAR	ERROR	LOF	PSET	TIME$
CLOSE	EXP	LOG	PUT	TO
CLS	FIELD	LPOS	RANDOMIZE	TROFF
COLOR	FILES	LPRINT	READ	TRON
COM	FIX	LSET	REM	USING
COMMON	FNxxx	MERGE	RENUM	USR
CONT	FOR	MID$	RESET	VAL
COS	FRE	MKDIR *	RESTORE	VARPTR
CSNG	GET	MKD$	RESUME	VARPTR$
CSRLIN	GOSUB	MKI$	RETURN	WAIT
CVD	GOTO	MKS$	RIGHT$	WEND
CVI	HEX$	MOD	RMDIR *	WHILE
CVS	IF	MOTOR	RND	WIDTH
DATA	IMP	NAME	RSET	WINDOW *
DATE$	INKEY$	NEW	RUN	WRITE
DEF	INP	NEXT	SAVE	WRITE#
DEFDBL	INPUT	NOT	SCREEN	XOR
DEFINT	INPUT#	OCT$	SGN	
DEFSNG	INPUT$	OFF	SHELL *	
DEFSTR	INSTR	ON	SIN	

Appendices

APPENDIX A
THE BASICS OF DOS

INTRODUCTION

Before an applications software can be used with the microcomputer, DOS must be loaded (copied) into RAM. DOS performs two basic functions while the microcomputer system is in use. At the DOS operating level, before any other software has been loaded, DOS commands can be used to perform disk and file maintenance operations. At the software operating level, after an applications software has been loaded into RAM, DOS remains in RAM and allows the applications software to perform its input/output operations. Without this DOS interface, most applications software would be unable to access the microcomputer's input/output devices, such as disk drives and printers.

DOS/ROM BIOS—The Operating System

The DOS software includes a set of instructions called the IBM Basic Input/Output (or IBMBIO) which works in conjunction with a set of instructions in ROM called the ROM BIOS. Together, DOS and ROM BIOS constitute the operating system for the microcomputer.

As discussed in the "Fundamentals of Using Microcomputers" section, the operating system is what actually saves your data files onto a disk. In fact, the operating system is designed to handle all input/output device operations for the applications software currently in RAM. The operating system monitors input from the keyboard and then passes the input data to the applications software. It also sends (outputs) data obtained from the applications software to the printer. The operating system also controls the output of characters and graphics to the monitor screen.

Occasionally, an applications software will be written in such a way that it overrides the operating system and performs an input or output operation itself. Lotus 1-2-3, for instance, controls its own output to the monitor screen.

It is not obvious to the user that the operating system is the input/output device controller for the microcomputer system. The following section will explain the role of the operating system and why DOS must be present in RAM before an applications software may be used.

DOS—THE DISK FILE MAINTENANCE SOFTWARE

File maintenance is the ongoing task of keeping data files organized on the disk(s). File maintenance involves operations such as erasing files, copying files, renaming files, and grouping files together. To more fully understand the procedures used in file maintenance, the user needs to know about the microcomputer's disk operating system.

The DOS Disk

The DOS disk and the IBM manual for DOS usually come with the computer when it is purchased. While the packaging and manual suggest that a single software called DOS is on the disk, DOS is, in fact, made up of several different software files.

The software that the microcomputer automatically reads into RAM when the system unit is turned on is composed of three separate software files stored on the disk. Two of the files are "hidden" files—files that will not appear in a directory displayed by the **DIR** command. The two hidden files are named IBMBIO.COM and IBMDOS.COM. The third file, COMMAND.COM, is not a hidden file; it will appear in a **DIR** command directory. In this manual, the three files that are automatically read into RAM are referred to collectively as DOS.

DOS Commands

When the microcomputer is at the DOS operating level, the user may type and enter DOS commands. DOS commands are included in the instruction set of the DOS software. In other words, DOS commands may be entered and the command operations will be performed without the need for additional instructions (software) to be read into RAM. **DIR** is an example of a DOS command.

DOS Programs

In addition to DOS, the disk also contains several small software called DOS utility programs or DOS programs. DOS programs are not automatically present in RAM. The user must type and enter a filename while at the DOS operating level to cause a DOS program to be read into RAM and executed. One such DOS program, FORMAT.COM, is used to format a new disk. To execute the program, the user may type ‖ FORMAT A:↵ ‖ to format a disk in the A: drive. When the DOS program filename is entered, DOS reads the software into RAM memory and the screen appears similar to

```
C>FORMAT A:
Insert new diskette for drive A:
and strike ENTER when ready
```

The microcomputer now is operating at a software operating level. The following model illustrates what is being held in RAM.

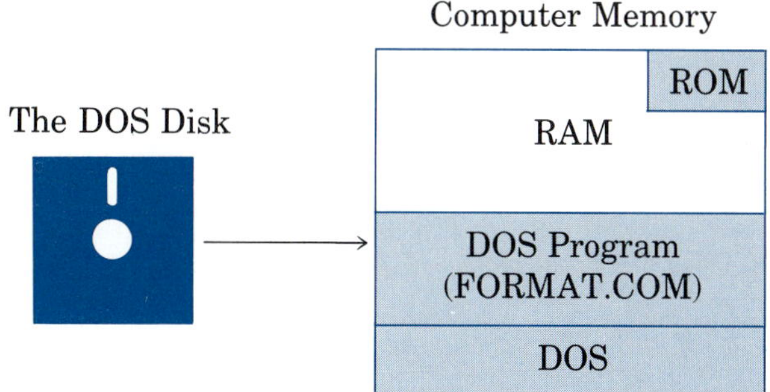

Type the filename of a DOS program: The software is copied into RAM.

DOS programs are generally not used to produce data files. They typically erase themselves from RAM when their particular function or task is complete.

The DOS Default Drive

The microcomputer searches its disk drives for DOS when it is first turned on. After finding DOS and copying it into RAM, the microcomputer's monitor screen will display an A>, B>, or C>. The letter (A, B, or C) displayed in the prompt describes the disk drive device name (A:, B:, or C:) for the drive where DOS was found. The prompt also indicates which disk drive is the current DOS *default drive*. The DOS default drive is the disk drive that DOS will automatically activate to access a disk when it is instructed to read or write data.

For instance, if you type ‖ **DIR**↵ ‖ while an A> appears on the screen, DOS will automatically read the disk in the A: drive and list its directory on the screen. If the A> is on the screen and you enter a software's filename, DOS will automatically search the disk in the A: drive to find the software file you entered.

DOS's default drive stays in effect when the microcomputer system is brought to the software operating level. That is, if the DOS default drive is A: when you use a software's command(s) to save a data file, DOS will automatically write the file onto the disk in the A: drive.

There are two ways to redirect DOS to another disk drive. The first method is to change the current default drive by entering the device name for the desired default drive. At the DOS operating level the default drive may be changed by simply typing the appropriate drive letter, then a colon, and then the Enter key (e.g., **B:**↵). At the software operating level, you must use one of the software's commands to change the DOS default drive.

The other method of redirecting DOS to another disk drive is to override the default drive by including the desired device name in the request for a DOS read/write operation. For instance, with WordPerfect you can answer the "Document to be saved:" prompt by typing ‖ B:REPORT↵ ‖ to save the data file onto the disk in the B: drive. Similarly, at the DOS operating level you can force a listing of the directory of the B: drive by typing ‖ **DIR** B:↵ ‖, or cause DOS to search the C: drive for the WordPerfect software by typing ‖ C:WP↵ ‖.

Since almost all microcomputers have more than one disk drive, the user needs to know how to direct DOS to the appropriate disk drive for its read/write operations.

Formatting a Disk

The first step in disk file maintenance is formatting the disk. All disks must be formatted before software or data files can be stored on them. The DOS program named FORMAT.COM and the microcomputer's ROM BIOS work together to format a disk. *It is important to note that formatting a disk erases all files that may have previously existed on the disk.*

Formatting a disk involves defining a series of concentric rings on the disk (called *tracks*) where the bytes of data will be stored later. The tracks are numbered and divided into sections (called *sectors*). The length of a single track within a sector is able to hold 512 bytes of data (one *block*). The sector groups then are numbered so that a sector section of track may be accessed later by referring to the side of the disk on which it occurs (side 0 or 1), its track number, and its sector group number. Adjacent segments of track called *clusters* are used by DOS in reading and writing data on the disk.

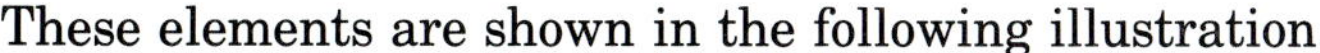

These elements are shown in the following illustration.

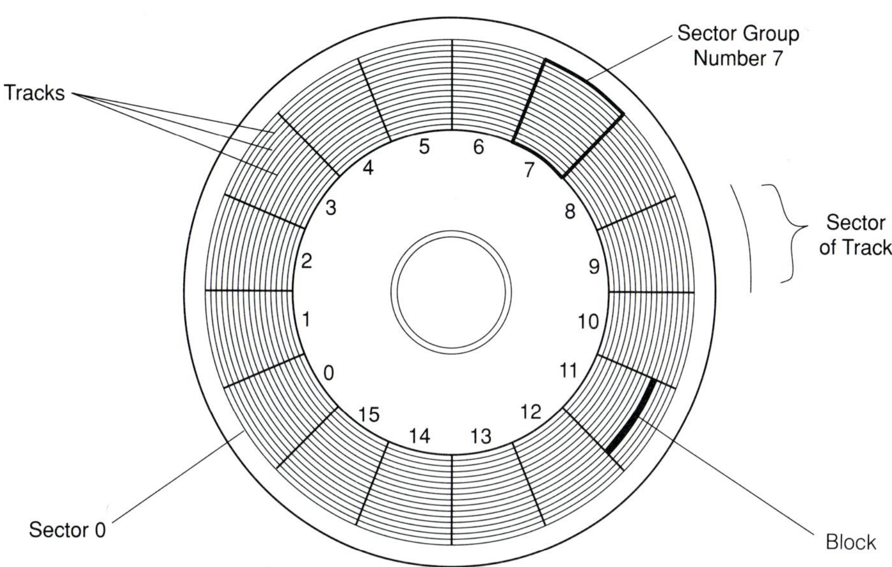

The number of tracks and sectors, as well as the size of the clusters on a disk all depend on the type of disk, the version of DOS, and the hardware being used during the format operation.

After the data storage areas of the disk are physically organized, the format operation checks each sector for errors in the magnetic medium (recording surface). If a sector error is detected, the entire track in which the error occurs is marked "bad" so that DOS will not try to save data on that track.

The format operation also reserves certain sectors of track on the disk for recording specific DOS information about the disk. The reserved sectors are collectively called the *DOS reserved area*. The first sector of data (track 0, sector 0) in the DOS reserved area is called the *boot record*. The boot record contains information about the physical format of the disk (number of tracks, number of sectors per track, number of sectors per cluster, etc.), and the version of DOS that was used to format the disk. The boot record is the first data the microcomputer copies into RAM when it reads a disk. The next information in the DOS reserved area includes the *file allocation tables* (FAT). There are usually two copies of the FAT maintained on a disk. The FAT stores the addresses (locations) of data clusters on the disk that belong to a given file. It is, in effect, a map of data locations keyed to the filenames of the files on a disk. The final major set of information contained in the DOS reserved area is the *root directory*. Every formatted disk has one root directory, and a disk may have one or more *subdirectories* of the root directory. (The root directory and subdirectories will be discussed in greater depth later.) A directory contains the list of filenames, byte sizes, and date/time stamps that are read and displayed by DOS's **DIR** command.

Creating a "Bootable" Disk

The term *bootable disk* refers to a disk that has the three files of DOS (IBMBIO.COM, IBMDOS.COM, and COMMAND.COM) stored on it. Such a disk can be used to bring the microcomputer to the DOS operating level when the system unit is turned on. A bootable disk must have the two hidden files of DOS (IBMBIO.COM and IBMDOS.COM) stored on the sectors that immediately follow the DOS reserved area. Therefore, the files must be saved on the disk in a special manner.

To make a disk bootable, the user should copy the files of DOS onto the disk during the format operation. To do so, the user follows the FORMAT program's filename and disk drive specification with a /S. /S is a *DOS switch*—an addition to a DOS command or DOS program filename that alters the way in which the command or program functions. For example, entering FORMAT A:/S will format the disk in the A: drive and then copy all three DOS files to their appropriate locations on the newly formatted disk.

Compatibility among Versions of DOS

Over time, IBM has released different versions of DOS to keep pace with the advancements in hardware technology used by the microcomputer system. The various versions of any software are numbered so that the latest version has the highest number. For instance, DOS 2.1 was released after DOS 2.0. The user needs to pay attention to which version of DOS is in use because different versions of DOS format disks differently. There are times when the version of DOS currently in RAM may not be able to read or write to a disk because the disk was previously formatted with another version of DOS.

As a general rule, a later version of DOS is able to read or write to a disk formatted with an earlier version of DOS. However, the reverse is not true. That is, an earlier version of DOS in RAM will not be able to read or write to a disk formatted with a later version of DOS.

Dividing a Disk into Subdirectories

With DOS versions 2.0 or later, the user is given the option to organize a disk into separate DOS subdirectories. A DOS subdirectory separates files on a disk into groups of files. The process of creating subdirectories is both mechanical and judgmental—while specific DOS commands are used to create and maintain subdirectories, the user must decide which subdirectories to create and which files to allocate to the subdirectories.

As mentioned earlier, each disk is assigned a directory (called the root directory) at the time it is formatted. Unless the user creates subdirectories, the disk's root directory will hold all files currently stored on the disk.

In the day-to-day use of the microcomputer, users probably will keep copies of files on floppy disks. Each disk may hold files pertaining to different areas or subjects. For instance, one disk might have data files relating to course work prepared for a business management class. The jacket of the disk might be labeled "MGMT213" to help identify the disk. Another disk might have data files relating to a literature class, and it could be labeled "ENG199." When disk files are maintained in this manner, *physical* separation is being used to organize the files.

Another method of grouping files uses DOS *logical* separation of files. With logical separation, DOS treats groups of files on a single disk as if they were stored on separate disks. A logical separation of files on a disk is possible by creating disk subdirectories. While subdirectories may (and often should) be used on a floppy disk, they become particularly important when dealing with hard disks, which have much greater storage capacities.

Preparing a Hard Disk for Subdirectories

When a microcomputer has a hard disk, it is almost always used as the system's bootable disk. Therefore, the first step in preparing a hard disk is to format the hard disk with FORMAT.COM's /S switch. To do so the user places the DOS disk purchased with the computer into the first drive (A:) and turns on the computer and its monitor. After a few moments the A> DOS prompt appears on the screen. The user next types ‖ FORMAT C:/S ‖ to read the FORMAT.COM program into RAM and begin its execution. Since the loss of all files on a hard disk could be disastrous, the program will pause and present a warning about formatting a "non-removable disk." When finished with the format operation, the screen appears similar to

```
A>FORMAT C:/S
WARNING, ALL DATA ON NON-REMOVABLE DISK
DRIVE C: WILL BE LOST!
Proceed with Format (Y/N)?y

Format complete
System transferred

  21170176 bytes total disk space
     79872 bytes used by system
    122880 bytes in bad sectors
  20967424 bytes available on disk

A>
```

These messages indicate that the disk has about 21M of disk space and that 79,872 bytes of it are being used by the three DOS files (the "system"). The format operation identified 122,880 bytes worth of bad sectors and marked them so that data cannot be saved onto the bad tracks. The remaining space (20,967,424 bytes) is available to hold software and data files.

To continue with the example, the user next types ‖ **C:↵** ‖ to change the default disk drive and then types ‖ **DIR↵** ‖ to cause the DOS **DIR** command to read the directory of the C: drive and list it on the screen.

```
C>DIR

 Volume in drive C has no label
 Directory of  C:\

COMMAND  COM    25307   3-17-87  12:00p
        1 File(s)  20967424 bytes free
```

The Disk Root Directory

The directory appearing on the screen was read from the C: disk's *root directory*—the only physical directory on a disk. The file COMMAND.COM appears in the root directory, and, although not listed by the **DIR** command, the files IBMBIO.COM and IBMDOS.COM (the two hidden files of DOS) are also present in the disk's root directory. In order for a disk to be bootable, DOS must be held in the root directory.

When a disk has subdirectories, the user should keep as few files as possible in the root directory of the disk. If the disk is to be bootable, only DOS and a few related files should appear in the root directory.

The **MD** (Make Directory) Command

The DOS command **MD** (Make Directory) is used to create a logical directory, also called a subdirectory. The next step in preparing a hard disk for use is to create a subdirectory into which the files of an applications software, in this example WordPerfect, will be copied.

The user must give a subdirectory a name at the time it is created. A conservative rule to follow when naming subdirectories is the following.

> A subdirectory name is one to eight characters long and is composed of letters and numbers only (no spaces, commas, colons, etc.).

In this example, the name used for the subdirectory will be WORDS.

The user continues by typing ‖ **MD** WORDS↵ ‖ . Although the screen gives little indication that anything has occurred, the user has, in fact, created a subdirectory named WORDS. Assume that the files of the WordPerfect software are now copied from the manufacturer's floppy disks into the WORDS subdirectory. (The process of copying files will be discussed later.)

The **CD** (Change Directory) Command

The DOS **CD** (Change Directory) command causes DOS to "change the logical disk." Here, for example, if the user were to type the DOS command ‖ **CD** WORDS↵ ‖ and then type ‖ **DIR**↵ ‖ the screen would appear similar to the following.

```
C>CD WORDS

C>DIR

 Volume in drive C has no label
 Directory of  C:\WORDS

.            <DIR>      1-17-89  12:39p
..           <DIR>      1-17-89  12:39p
WP       DRS     73688  9-16-88   3:57p
WP       EXE    251904  9-23-88   5:37p
WP       FIL    303478  9-23-88   5:37p
WPHELP   FIL     48459  9-23-88   5:37p
WPINFO   EXE      8192  9-16-88   3:50p
WPRINT1  ALL    321351  9-16-88  12:47p
WP{WP}   SET      2355  1-06-89  11:54a
WP{WP}US LEX    292109  9-16-88   3:55p
WP{WP}US SUP        87 10-22-88   6:28a
WP{WP}US THS    362269  9-16-88   4:02p
       12 File(s)  10405888 bytes free

C>
```

Notice that there are ten filenames listed here. In fact, there are several additional files not shown here that, in total, comprise the WordPerfect software. For the example's sake, however, assume that ten files constitute the entire software.

The user next types ‖ **CD**↵ ‖ and then ‖ **DIR**↵ ‖ . The following directory is read from the disk and displayed on the screen.

```
C>DIR

 Volume in drive C has no label
 Directory of  C:\

COMMAND  COM     25307   3-17-87  12:00p
WORDS        <DIR>       2-22-89   7:30a
        2 File(s)  19303532 bytes free
```

The **CD** command is used to make the root directory the current directory. Notice that the WORDS subdirectory now appears listed in the root directory. The disk's directory organization can be graphically described as follows.

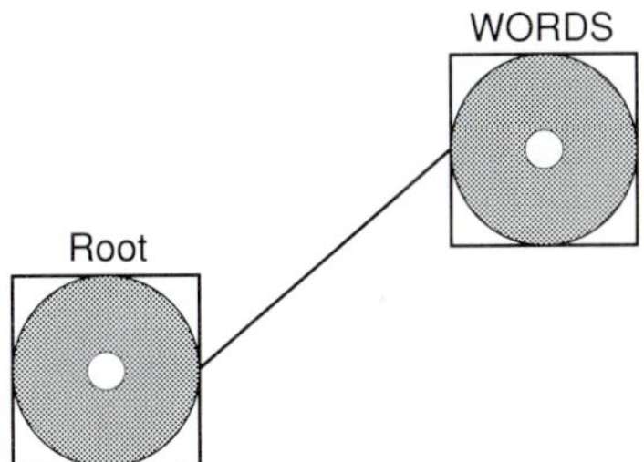

The DOS Default Directory

Like the default drive, DOS maintains a default directory (or current directory). The default directory is the directory that DOS will automatically search when it is instructed to read or write data. For instance, when the DOS command ‖ **DIR**↵ ‖ is typed while the root directory is the current directory, DOS will automatically read the directory of the root directory and display it on the screen.

There are two ways to direct DOS to another directory on the disk. The first method is to change the current default directory. At the DOS operating level, the default directory may be changed by using the **CD** (Change Directory) command. The other method of directing DOS to another directory is to override the default directory by including the directory name in the request for a DOS read/write operation. For instance, in the example, at the DOS operating level with the root directory as the current directory, the user can list the contents of the WORDS directory by typing ‖ **DIR** WORDS↵ ‖ . Like the default drive, DOS's default directory stays in effect when the microcomputer system is brought to the software operating level.

Creating Tree Structured Subdirectories

Assume that, in addition to word processing software, the user in the example intends to use a spreadsheet software and the DOS programs that come on the manufacturer's DOS disk. The user intends, however, to keep the groups of software files separated on the hard disk.

The user continues by typing ‖ **CD**\↵ ‖ to ensure that the root directory is the current directory and then types ‖ **MD** CALC↵ ‖ and ‖ **MD** DOS↵ ‖ . The user next copies the files from the manufacturers' disks into the appropriate subdirectories. The organization of directories on the hard disk can now be graphically represented as follows.

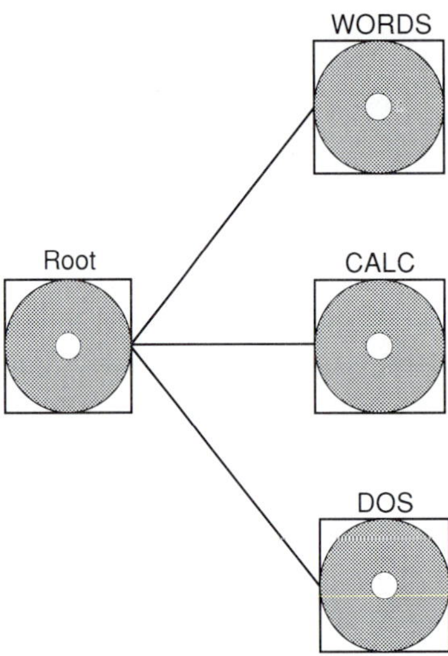

The hard disk now contains DOS in the root directory, two applications software, each in their own directories, and the DOS programs in yet another directory.

The user next is going to create three subdirectories to hold groups of data files. One subdirectory will be used for word processed data files related to a business management class, another subdirectory will hold spreadsheet data files for the same business class, and the final subdirectory will hold word processed data files for a literature class.

Using the DOS **PROMPT** Command

Before the subdirectories are created, the user types ‖ **PROMPT** pg↵ ‖ . The user then types ‖ **CD** WORDS↵ ‖ and the screen appears as follows.

```
C:\>CD WORDS

C:\WORDS>
```

The **PROMPT** command may be used to change the display of the DOS prompt. Here the command was used to cause the prompt to display the directory name of the current directory. This prompt display is most useful when subdirectories exist on a disk.

The user next types ‖ **MD** MGMT213↵ ‖ and then ‖ **MD** ENG199↵ ‖ to create the two subdirectories that will be used to hold the word processed data files. The user next types ‖ **CD**\↵ ‖ and then ‖ **CD** CALC↵ ‖ to make the spreadsheet software directory the current directory. The user then types ‖ **MD** MGMT213↵ ‖ to create the subdirectory in which the spreadsheet data files will be held.

The directory organization of the disk can now be represented as follows.

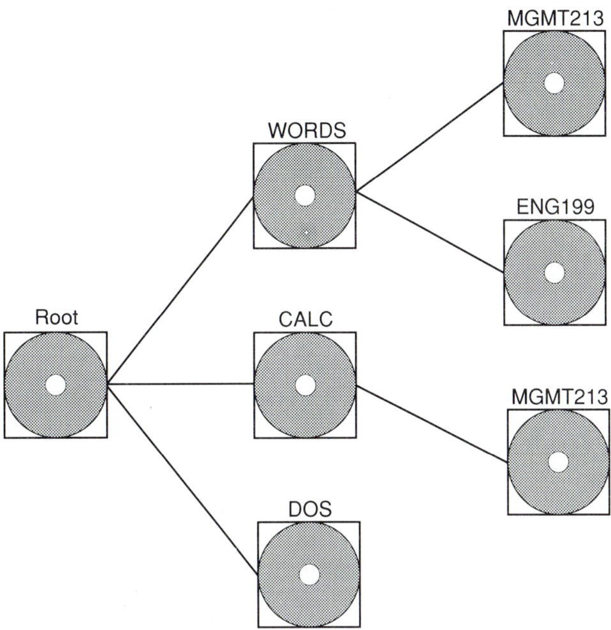

The graphic representation illustrates the concept of *hierarchical* directories—a situation where directories "belong" to each other. The relationship among directories is known as a "parent\child" relationship. Here, the parent directory WORDS has two child directories, MGMT213 and ENG199, and is itself a child directory of the root directory.

Note that there are two directories with the same name, MGMT213. This is possible only because the two directories do not have the same parent directory.

DOS Paths

A DOS path is a list of directory names describing the directories through which DOS must pass to reach a specific directory. The list of directories begins at the current directory. When there are two or more directories included in a DOS path, the directory names are separated by backslashes. For example, if the current directory is the root directory and the user wants to use the **DIR** command to list the directory of the ENG199 subdirectory, he/she types ‖ **DIR**\WORDS\ENG199↵ ‖. However, if the current directory is WORDS, he/she types ‖ **DIR** ENG199↵ ‖. Finally, if the current directory is ENG199, he/she types simply ‖ **DIR**↵ ‖. More precisely stated, the default path for a DOS read/write operation is that path which leads to the current directory. If the path the user needs extends beyond the current directory, he/she must enter the remaining directory names in their parent\child order.

It is important to note that changing the default drive does not change the "logical disk" (directory) of the previous default drive. That is, if the current directory of the C: drive is \WORDS\MGMT213 and the user changes the default drive to A: by typing ‖ **A:**↵ ‖ , the current directory of the C: drive remains the same. If the user then wanted to list the directory for the C:\WORDS\MGMT213 subdirectory, he/she would type ‖ **DIR** C:↵ ‖ .

The discussion so far has focused on how to direct DOS to the appropriate place for it to perform its read/write operation. This knowledge is essential to using DOS at both the DOS and software operating levels. When a DOS command or program is used to read, write, or otherwise affect a file on the disk, the file's filename and extension may be included in the command or program entry.

DOS Filenames and Extensions

The software and data files in a directory are stored there under a name. When the user creates a data file, he/she names the file. Rules about filenames vary among versions of DOS and the software being used. A conservative rule to follow when naming files is the following.

> A filename is one to eight characters long and is composed of letters and numbers only (no spaces, commas, colons, etc.).

A filename *extension* is composed of three characters that follow the filename. A filename's extension is often reserved for the applications software's use. Most applications software use the extension to identify the file type. For instance, when a spreadsheet created with Lotus 1-2-3 is saved, Lotus will add a WK1 extension to the filename the user gives the spreadsheet. WordPerfect is one of the few software that does not normally add extensions to filenames.

Each filename/extension combination in a directory must be unique among the filename/extensions in the directory.

When filenames and extensions are used in a DOS command or program entry, they are separated from each other by a period (.). The default filenames and extensions will vary among different DOS commands or program entries. For instance, the default scope of the **DIR** command is all files in the current or specified directory. Other DOS commands require that the filename and extension be included in the command (they have no default status).

Wild Card Characters

The user may use wild card characters in place of parts or all of the filename and/or extension included in a DOS command or program entry. Two wild card characters are the question mark (?) and the asterisk (*).

When used in a filename, a question mark has the effect of saying to DOS "accept any character here." For example, the command

DIR ?DRAFT.WK1↵

will cause DOS to list the directory for all files beginning with any single letter followed by the five letters "DRAFT" and having a WK1 extension. Examples of such files would include ADRAFT.WK1, BDRAFT.WK1, CDRAFT.WK1, and so on.

When used in a filename, the asterisk has the effect of saying to DOS "accept any remaining characters from this point on." For example, the command

DIR A*.WK1

will cause DOS to list the directory for all files beginning with the letter *A* followed by any letters and having a WK1 extension. Examples of such files would include ADRAFT1.WK1, ACCOUNTS.WK1, and ADS.WK1.

Some common uses of wild card characters and their effects include the following.

.	All files
filename.*	Same filename, any extension
*.ext	Any filename, same extension

DOS Command/Program Syntax

A DOS command or program filename (a word often in verb form) is typed with other elements (drive, path, switch, etc.) that are called *command parameters*. The way the parameters of a DOS command or program entry are put together is referred to as the command's *syntax*. Some parameters of a command or program entry may be optional; however, all parameters included must be typed according to the rules of DOS syntax. DOS identifies optional parameters by enclosing them in brackets [ ] and shows user-defined parameter entries in *italics*. For instance, the standard convention for the DOS **DIR** command is written as follows.

DIR [*d*:][*path*][*filename*[*.ext*]][/P][/W]

All parameters of the **DIR** command (other than the command name itself) are optional. The optional parameters often have default values which are used if the parameter is omitted. For instance, when using DOS commands or programs, the default [*d:*] is always the current drive and the default [*path*] is always the path that leads to the current directory.

The full command convention shown above has the [*.ext*] parameter within the brackets of [*filename*]. This means that a file extension may only be specified if a filename also is specified.

SUMMARY

The DOS software takes time and practice to learn. To help you gain experience using DOS, the following section presents a set of exercises that introduces many DOS commands and programs commonly used to perform file and disk maintenance. The exercises are followed by a brief summary of DOS commands and programs. You may want to review the summary before starting the exercises.

EXERCISES

REQUIRED PREPARATION

The exercises in this section will give you experience using the commands and features of DOS. Before you begin the "hands-on" learning experience, however, you will need to complete a few initial steps and gain some preliminary information to be adequately prepared. Your instructor or laboratory staff will be able to provide you with the following necessary information.

Initial Steps

1. Obtain a floppy disk appropriate for the microcomputer you will be using to complete this set of exercises. You need to know which kind of disk to purchase.

   Size: ____________________

   Sides: ____________________

   Density: ____________________

2. Format your disk to the specifications of the DOS and microcomputer hardware you will be using to complete this set of exercises. **Caution: Formatting a disk erases all files that may exist on the disk.**

   Steps to Format a Disk: ____________________

   ____

   ____

   ____

   ____

   ____

   ____

3. You will need to copy 40 user files that come with the instructor's manual text onto the newly formatted floppy disk. Your instructor will provide you with the files and the steps required to complete the copy operation.

   Steps to Copy Files onto the Disk: ____________________

   ____

   ____

   ____

   ____

   ____

4. To read a DOS program into RAM, you will need to know the disk drive and directory that specify where the DOS program(s) are kept.

   Drive: ____________________

   Directory: ____________________

   In these exercises, the location of the DOS programs is referred to as the *DOS directory*. When you see this expression used in an instruction, type and enter the drive\directory you have entered above. For instance, if the DOS programs are kept on the C: drive in the DOS subdirectory and you see the instruction "type *DOS directory*\CHKDSK↵," you will type ‖ C:\DOS\CHKDSK↵ ‖ .

5. Each time you use a DOS command or program to access the floppy disk, you will want to make sure that DOS is directed to the appropriate disk drive.

   Drive: ______________________

   In these exercises, the location of your floppy disk is referred to as the *files drive:*. When you see this expression used in an instruction, type and enter the drive you have entered above. For instance, if your floppy disk is to be kept in the A: drive, and you see the instruction "type DIR *files drive:*↵," you will type ‖ DIR A:↵ ‖ .

Additional Notes on the Exercises

1. DOS commands and filenames may be typed using any combination of upper- or lower-case letters. Upper-case letters are used in the examples here. DOS commands appear in bold type.
2. The term *directory* is used for both the root directory and subdirectories. When a distinction is necessary, the specific terms *root directory* and *subdirectory* are used.
3. When the **DIR** command is used during the exercises, the directory listed on your screen may show byte sizes for the files that are different from those shown in the text. This may be due to differences in floppy disks and/or in versions of DOS being used. The differences will not affect the outcome of the exercises.

REQUIRED MATERIALS

1. An IBM DOS floppy disk (or hard-disk directory containing the DOS software).
2. A formatted floppy disk with the user files on it (your files disk).
3. This manual.
4. Other ____

TUTORIAL CONVENTIONS

During the exercises you will perform many file maintenance operations using DOS commands and programs. The following are the conventions the exercise's instructions will use.

↵	The bent arrow means to type the Enter key located on the right side of the keyboard.
Key-Key	Key combinations using a hyphen indicate that you should press and hold the first key and then type the next key shown.
Key,Key	Key combinations using a comma indicate that you should type the first key and then type the second key.
‖ ‖	Do not type the double lines; type only what is inside them.

HOW TO GET OUT OF TROUBLE

If you want to:	*Then:*
■ Backspace and erase characters to the left of the cursor...	■ Type the Backspace key located on the right top side of the keyboard.
■ Abort a DOS command or program entry...	■ Type the Esc key located on the top left side of the keyboard.

GETTING STARTED

1. Load DOS from a floppy disk or hard disk, or return to the DOS operating level from the current software operating level.
2. Put your files floppy disk into the proper disk drive (drive name ________:).
3. When you see DOS's *drive:*> prompt on the screen, change the current disk drive to where your files disk is by typing ‖ *files drive:*↵ ‖ .

INTRODUCTION TO DOS COMMANDS

DOS is considered a command driven software—one in which user instructions are entered in the form of typed commands. When the microcomputer is at the DOS operating level, a DOS prompt is displayed on the screen to indicate that DOS is waiting for the user to enter a command. After the user types and enters a command, DOS performs the requested command task. When the task is complete, DOS again displays its prompt to indicate that the user can type and enter another command.

The default form of the DOS prompt is an upper-case letter that indicates the current default drive, followed by the > character (e.g., A>, B>, C>, and so forth). A similar prompt should now appear on the screen, indicating that DOS is waiting for a command to be entered. You will begin the exercise by executing a few commonly used DOS commands.

Using DOS Commands

To ensure that your screen matches the examples shown here, you will use the **PROMPT** command to set the DOS prompt to its default form. (If the prompt is already set to its default form, no action will be apparent in this step.)

1. Type ‖ **PROMPT**↵ ‖ to set the DOS prompt to its default form.

The **DIR** command is used to view a list of files in the current directory of the disk in the default drive.

2. Type ‖ **DIR↵** ‖ to list the directory of files.

```
BLSHEET1 BAK     2031  10-22-89   3:36p
CONBLNC  BAK     2827  10-30-89   3:37p
CONSTMT  BAK     2990  11-06-89   3:38p
DISCOP   BAK     2324  11-12-89   3:33p
ENTRYHLP BAK     2414  11-06-89   3:39p
FCTRANS  BAK     1348  11-21-89   3:40p
INVTS    BAK     1154  11-29-89   3:40p
MEMBDAT1 BAK    13500  11-30-89   3:42p
OPNWSNOV BAK     1002  12-15-89   3:45p
PHONEORD BAK      884  12-02-89   3:43p
RNTEQUIP BAK     1095  12-07-89   3:44p
RPTINTRO BAK     2953  12-17-89   3:46p
RPTSOFTW BAK     7054  12-20-89   3:47p
SILVINTR BAK     1553  12-21-89   3:48p
STCCURR  BAK     3082   1-03-90   3:50p
WORKCAP  BAK     1366   1-03-90   3:50p
WRSIGNAT PCX    19948  11-14-89   3:47p
BOOKVAL  PIC      429  11-14-89   3:42p
CAPEXP   PIC     5948  11-14-89   3:42p
CURRENT  PIC      462  11-14-89   3:42p
DEBTCAP  PIC      462  11-14-89   3:43p
ROA      PIC      457  11-14-89   3:43p
        40 File(s)   1302528 bytes free

A>
```

You may notice that when the directory listing reaches the bottom of the screen, the screen contents begins to scroll up and off the top of the screen. The DOS prompt should now appear below the end of the directory listing at the bottom of the screen. The **CLS** command may be used to clear the screen of all previously issued commands and screen output.

3. Type ‖ **CLS↵** ‖ to clear the screen.

After the screen is cleared, the DOS prompt is again displayed at the top of the screen. The prompt is always displayed when DOS is waiting for you to type the next command.

The **VER** command is used to display the version of DOS currently in RAM. Because different versions of DOS provide somewhat different operating features and commands, it often is useful to determine which version of DOS is currently being used.

4. Type ‖ **VER↵** ‖ to display the version of DOS being used.

The screen should now display a message similar to the following.

```
A>VER

IBM Personal Computer DOS Version  3.30

A>
```

So far, assuming you have typed all commands correctly, DOS has performed the task defined by each command. The process of entering DOS commands is quite precise—if the command is not typed in its exact form, it will generate an error message.

5. Now type ‖ **VERSION↵** ‖ , an unrecognizable command to DOS.

The screen should now display the following.

```
A>VER

IBM Personal Computer DOS Version  3.30

A>VERSION
Bad command or file name

A>
```

The message "Bad command or file name" indicates that the entry is neither a properly typed DOS command, nor a filename for a software on the disk.

User commands such as **PROMPT, VER, DIR,** and **CLS** are features included in the DOS software. When a user entry is not in the form of a DOS command, DOS will search the disk for a software file with a filename that matches the entry. If the software file is found, DOS copies it into RAM and the user is left at a software operating level. Software files are often referred to as "executable" files and have the filename extensions of "COM," "EXE," or "BAT."

The executable files that come with DOS are referred to as DOS programs. One such file, CHKDSK.COM, is a DOS program used to check disk space utilization and system memory availability. The syntax for using the CHKDSK program is

[*d:*][*path*]CHKDSK [*d:*][*path*][*filename*[*.ext*]][/F][/V]

Notice that the syntax for a DOS program usually includes two directory specifications. The first [*d:*][*path*] is used to specify the location of the CHKDSK program. The second [*d:*][*path*] is used to specify the disk location upon which the program is to perform its action.

6. Type ‖ **CLS↵** ‖ to clear the screen. Then type ‖ *DOS directory*\ CHKDSK↵ ‖ . The screen should now appear similar to the following.

```
A>C:\DOS\CHKDSK

  1457664 bytes total disk space
   155136 bytes in 40 user files
  1302528 bytes available on disk

   654336 bytes total memory
   457616 bytes free

A>
```

In this example, the first [*d:*][*path*] was used to direct DOS to the proper location of the CHKDSK program so that it could successfully read the program into RAM. Since the second [*d:*][*path*] was not entered, the CHKDSK program performed its action on the disk in the default drive.

7. Now clear the screen again by typing ‖ **CLS**↵ ‖ .

In the remainder of the exercises, feel free to execute the **CLS** command whenever you wish to clear the screen. Most of the example screens that follow will show only the screen output resulting from the most recently executed command.

The **DIR** Command

The **DIR** command is used to list the files found in a given directory on the disk in a given drive. The full format for the command is

DIR [*d:*][*path*][*filename*[*.ext*]][/P][/W]

Notice that all parameters for the **DIR** command are optional. If the drive and path are not specified, files in the current directory of the disk in the default drive are listed. If the filename and extension are not specified, all files will be included. The optional parameters [/P] and [/W] are used to modify the way in which the directory is displayed.

When the **DIR** command is executed, the following items are displayed for each file in the directory: the filename; the file extension (if any); a number indicating the size of the file in bytes; and a date and time indicating when the file was created or last modified. Following the listing is the total number of files in the directory and the number of bytes still available on the disk.

In the following steps you will practice using the **DIR** command with various specified parameters.

Using a File Specification with the **DIR** Command

If you want a directory listing to include only specific files, you can follow the **DIR** command with a space and then a specification of the files you want included. The specification may be entered to list files containing certain character patterns in the filename or file extension. The following steps will use filename specifications with the **DIR** command.

8. Type ‖ **DIR** RPTINTRO.BAK↵ ‖ to list a single file.

```
A>DIR RPTINTRO.BAK

 Volume in drive A has no label
 Directory of  A:\

RPTINTRO BAK     2953  12-17-89   3:46p
        1 File(s)   1302528 bytes free

A>
```

9. Type ‖ **DIR** RPTINTRO↵ ‖ . Two files with the same filename but with different file extensions should be listed (one has no file extension).

```
A>DIR RPTINTRO

 Volume in drive A has no label
 Directory of  A:\

RPTINTRO         2953  12-17-89   3:46p
RPTINTRO BAK     2953  12-17-89   3:46p
        2 File(s)   1302528 bytes free

A>
```

10. Now type ‖ **DIR** RPT↵ ‖ . The message "File not found" should be displayed, indicating that no file with this name is found in the current directory.

```
A>DIR RPT

 Volume in drive A has no label
 Directory of  A:\

File not found

A>
```

Using Wild Card Characters in a File Specification

The file specification may also include the characters * and ?, which are referred to as wild card characters. Wild card characters may be used in the specification of a filename or file extension, or in both.

The * is used to accept any characters in the remainder of a filename or extension. For example, the specification "TAX*.WK1" refers to all files with a name beginning "TAX" and with a file extension of "WK1." Therefore, the command **DIR** TAX*.WK1 would include files such as TAX1990.WK1 and TAXTABLE.WK1, but not files such as INC1990.WK1 (does not begin "TAX") or TAX1990.TXT (extension is not "WK1").

The ? is used to accept any character in a given position of a filename or extension. For example, the specification "???1990.WK1" refers to all files with a filename consisting of any 3 characters followed by "1990" and with the extension "WK1." Therefore, the command **DIR** ???1990.WK1 would include files such as "TAX1990.WK1" and "INC1990.WK1," but not files such as "TAX1989.WK1" or "INC1991.WK1."

The following steps incorporate the use of wild card characters in the file specification of the **DIR** command. Example screen displays are shown after each step.

11. Type ‖ **DIR** ∗.PIC↵ ‖ to list all files with the extension "PIC."

```
A>DIR *.PIC

 Volume in drive A has no label
 Directory of  A:\

BOOKVAL  PIC       429  11-14-89   3:42p
CAPEXP   PIC      5948  11-14-89   3:42p
CURRENT  PIC       462  11-14-89   3:42p
DEBTCAP  PIC       462  11-14-89   3:43p
ROA      PIC       457  11-14-89   3:43p
        5 File(s)   1302528 bytes free

A>
```

12. Type ‖ **DIR** CON∗.BAK↵ ‖ to list all files with a filename beginning "CON" and with a file extension "BAK."

```
A>DIR CON*.BAK

 Volume in drive A has no label
 Directory of  A:\

CONBLNC  BAK      2827  10-30-89   3:37p
CONSTMT  BAK      2990  11-06-89   3:38p
        2 File(s)   1302528 bytes free

A>
```

The period (.) in a file specification indicates that what follows is a file extension. To specify only files without an extension, a period must be used to indicate the end of the filename specification. If the period is omitted, DOS assumes that files with any file extension, blank or otherwise, should be included.

13. Type ‖ **DIR** CON∗.↵ ‖ to list all files beginning with "CON" and which have no file extension.

```
A>DIR CON*.

 Volume in drive A has no label
 Directory of  A:\

CONBLNC           2827  10-30-89   3:37p
CONSTMT           2990  11-06-89   3:38p
        2 File(s)   1302528 bytes free

A>
```

14. Type || **DIR** CON*.*↵ || to list all files beginning with "CON" and which have any file extension.

```
A>DIR CON*.*

 Volume in drive A has no label
 Directory of  A:\

CONBLNC          2827  10-30-89   3:37p
CONSTMT          2990  11-06-89   3:38p
CONBLNC  BAK     2827  10-30-89   3:37p
CONSTMT  BAK     2990  11-06-89   3:38p
        4 File(s)    1302528 bytes free

A>
```

In the next steps, the ? wild card character will be used to list only files with certain characters in specified positions of the filename.

15. Type || **DIR** ???R*.*↵ || to list files with the letter *R* in the fourth position of the filename and any character following the *R*, and with any file extension.

```
A>DIR ???R*.*

 Volume in drive A has no label
 Directory of  A:\

ANNRPTXT        12015  10-15-89   3:34p
ENTRYHLP         2414  11-06-89   3:39p
FCTRANS          1348  11-21-89   3:40p
ANNRPTXT BAK    12015  10-15-89   3:34p
ENTRYHLP BAK     2414  11-06-89   3:39p
FCTRANS  BAK     1348  11-21-89   3:40p
CURRENT  PIC      462  11-14-89   3:42p
        7 File(s)    1302528 bytes free

A>
```

16. Type || **DIR** ??TR*.↵ || to list files with the letters *TR* in the third and fourth positions of the filename and with no file extension.

```
A>DIR ??TR*.

 Volume in drive A has no label
 Directory of  A:\

ENTRYHLP         2414  11-06-89   3:39p
FCTRANS          1348  11-21-89   3:40p
        2 File(s)    1302528 bytes free

A>
```

Since the * masks all remaining characters in a filename or file extension, the last two examples could have included ? characters in the second part of the filename (that is, "??TR*." is equivalent to "??TR????.").

Using a Drive Specification with the **DIR** Command

Since a drive letter designation has not yet been included in the **DIR** command, all directory listings so far have assumed that the disk is in the default drive. To see a directory listing for a disk in a drive other than the default drive, the drive must be specified in the **DIR** command.

17. Use the **DIR** command to list all of the files in the current directory of your microcomputer's other disk drive. (For example, if the other drive is a C: drive, type ‖ **DIR** C:↵ ‖).
18. Now type ‖ **DIR** *DOS directory**.SYS↵ ‖ to see a listing of files with the extension "SYS" in the DOS directory.

Using Optional Switches with the **DIR** Command

The **DIR** command may be followed by /W or /P to display the directory listing differently. The W and P are referred to as switches. A switch is an option of a command or DOS program that alters the way in which the command or program works.

A directory listing is often too long to be displayed in its entirety on the screen. When the **DIR** command includes the /W switch, the listing is displayed in a wide format. When the command includes the /P switch, the command pauses when the screen is full.

19. Type ‖ **DIR**/W↵ ‖ for a wide directory listing. The screen should appear similar to the following.

```
A>DIR/W

 Volume in drive A has no label
 Directory of  A:\

ANNRPTXT        BLSHEET1        CONBLNC         CONSTMT         DISCOP
ENTRYHLP        FCTRANS         INVTS           MEMBDAT1        OPNWSNOV
PHONEORD        RNTEQUIP        RPTINTRO        RPTSOFTW        SILVINTR
STCCURR         WORKCAP         ANNRPTXT BAK    BLSHEET1 BAK    CONBLNC  BAK
CONSTMT  BAK    DISCOP   BAK    ENTRYHLP BAK    FCTRANS  BAK    INVTS    BAK
MEMBDAT1 BAK    OPNWSNOV BAK    PHONEORD BAK    RNTEQUIP BAK    RPTINTRO BAK
RPTSOFTW BAK    SILVINTR BAK    STCCURR  BAK    WORKCAP  BAK    WRSIGNAT PCX
BOOKVAL  PIC    CAPEXP   PIC    CURRENT  PIC    DEBTCAP  PIC    ROA      PIC
       40 File(s)    1302528 bytes free

A>
```

Notice that in the wide format, the filename and file extension are the only items listed for files.

20. Next type ‖ **DIR**/P↵ ‖ for a directory listing that will pause when the screen is full.

21. At the prompt "Strike a key when ready . . . ," type any key to continue the listing.

The **COPY** Command

The **COPY** command allows you to copy the contents from one or more file(s) to other file(s) having the same or different filename(s). If the copied file is to have the same filename and extension, it must be in another directory. The general syntax for the **COPY** command is

COPY [*d:*][*path*]*filename*[*.ext*] [*d:*][*path*][*filename*[*.ext*]]

There may be two file specifications included in the **COPY** command. The first specifies the source file (the file being copied from) and the second specifies the destination file (the file being copied to). Specification of the destination file is optional, but specification of the source file is required. Since every file in a directory must have a unique filename/extension combination, the filename and extension of the destination file must be different from that of the source file if the locations (drive and path) are the same.

Suppose that you want to make a second copy of the RPTINTRO file. The copy will be in the same directory as the original, so it must have a different filename. Since the copy will be used only to practice DOS file commands, you will name the copy TEMPFILE.

22. Type || **COPY** RPTINTRO TEMPFILE↵ || .
23. Next, type || **DIR**/W↵ || to see that TEMPFILE now appears in the file listing.

The **RENAME** Command

The **RENAME** command may be used to change the filename or extension of an existing file. The format of the command is

RENAME [*d:*][*path*]*filename*[*.ext*] *filename*[*.ext*]

The first file specification is for the file being renamed. The second file specification indicates the new filename and file extension. The **RENAME** command does not change the location (drive and path) of the file; it simply changes the filename or the file extension, or both.

24. Type || **RENAME** TEMPFILE TEMPREPT↵ || to change the name of TEMPFILE to TEMPREPT. Next use the **DIR** command to confirm that the file has been renamed.

The **ERASE** Command

The **ERASE** command is used to permanently remove files from a disk directory. The format of the command is

ERASE [*d:*][*path*]*filename*[*.ext*]

The TEMPREPT file will now be erased from the current directory.

25. Type || **ERASE** TEMPREPT↵ || to erase the file from the directory. Next use the **DIR** command to confirm that the file has been erased.

The specifications for filenames and file extensions used with the **COPY, RENAME,** and **ERASE** commands may also include wild card characters.

This feature is useful for copying, renaming, or deleting several files at once. In the following steps you will create several subdirectories and then copy files from one directory to another using wild card characters with the **COPY** command.

DOS SUBDIRECTORIES AND PATHS

Subdirectories are used to keep files organized by type. For instance, you may wish to keep all word processing document files in one subdirectory and all spreadsheet files in another subdirectory. The following is a partial illustration of how a disk might be organized using subdirectories.

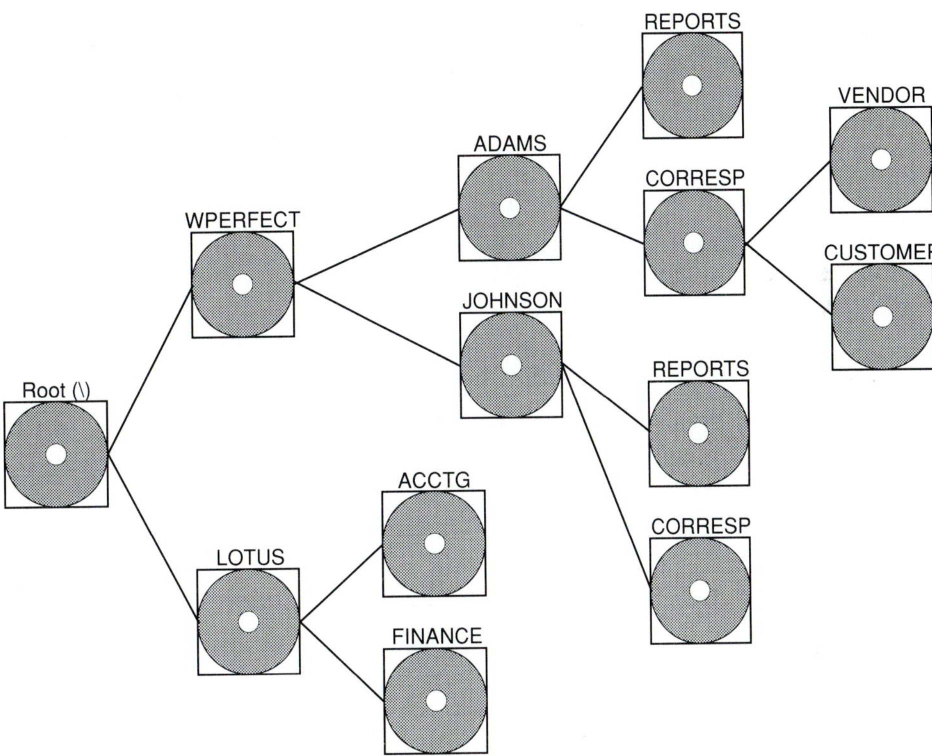

When subdirectories are used, the DOS command or program specification for a file may require that its path be included. The path identifies the directory in which the file is located. The path for the root directory is specified with a single backslash (\) character. Other directories may be specified by their path (either from the root directory or from the current directory).

In the illustration, if ADAMS were the current directory, a file ORDR1231 in the directory VENDOR could be specified as \WPERFECT\ADAMS\CORRESP\VENDOR\ORDR1231 (from the root directory) or as CORRESP\VENDOR\ORDR1231 (from the current directory). A path specification beginning with \ starts at the root directory.

The **MD** (Make Directory) Command

The command used to create a subdirectory is **MD** (Make Directory). The format for the command is

MD [*d:*]*path*

You will now use the **MD** command to make several subdirectories on your floppy disk. Many of the files on the disk are WordPerfect document files. Therefore, the first subdirectory will be named DOCFILES.

26. Type ‖ **MD** DOCFILES↵ ‖ .

DOS does not respond with a message indicating that the directory was successfully created. However, subdirectory names appear as filenames when the **DIR** command is executed. Subdirectories are designated by a <DIR> in the column where the number of bytes is displayed for files.

27. Type ‖ **DIR**↵ ‖ . The directory DOCFILES should now appear in the file listing as shown here.

```
SILVINTR BAK     1553  12-21-89   3:48p
STCCURR  BAK     3082   1-03-90   3:50p
WORKCAP  BAK     1366   1-03-90   3:50p
WRSIGNAT PCX    19948  11-14-89   3:47p
BOOKVAL  PIC      429  11-14-89   3:42p
CAPEXP   PIC     5948  11-14-89   3:42p
CURRENT  PIC      462  11-14-89   3:42p
DEBTCAP  PIC      462  11-14-89   3:43p
ROA      PIC      457  11-14-89   3:43p
DOCFILES     <DIR>      1-15-90  12:14p
       41 File(s)   1302016 bytes free

A>
```

NOTE: The <DIR> date and time displayed on your screen will reflect the DOS system date and time for the microcomputer you are using.

Now suppose that you want to have another subdirectory under the root directory for files with the extension .PIC (Lotus 1-2-3 graphics files).

28. Type ‖ **MD** PICS↵ ‖ to create a subdirectory for these files.

29. Type ‖ **DIR**↵ ‖ to verify that the subdirectory PICS was created.

The **CD** (Change Directory) Command

Once subdirectories have been created, the **CD** (Change Directory) command may be used to make a subdirectory the current directory. You now will make PICS the current directory and then copy files from the root directory to the PICS directory.

30. Type ‖ **CD** PICS↵ ‖ to make PICS the current directory. Then type the **DIR** command. The listed directory should appear as follows.

```
A>DIR

 Volume in drive A has no label
 Directory of  A:\PICS

.            <DIR>      1-15-90  12:16p
..           <DIR>      1-15-90  12:16p
        2 File(s)   1301504 bytes free

A>
```

You next will copy all files having a .PIC extension from the root directory to the current directory (PICS). First review the format for the **COPY** command

COPY [*d:*][*path*]*filename*[.*ext*] [*d:*][*path*][*filename*[.*ext*]]

Since PICS is the current directory, the source file(s) specification must include a path (\ for root directory). However, the path for the destination file(s) is (by default) the current directory, so it does not need to be specified.

31. Now type ‖ **COPY** *.PIC↵ ‖ .

As the files are copied to the PICS subdirectory, the source filenames will be listed on the screen. The **DIR** command may be used to verify that they have been copied to the current directory.

32. Type ‖ **DIR**↵ ‖ . The screen should appear similar to the following.

```
A>DIR

 Volume in drive A has no label
 Directory of  A:\PICS

.            <DIR>      1-15-90  12:16p
..           <DIR>      1-15-90  12:16p
BOOKVAL  PIC       429  11-14-89   3:42p
CAPEXP   PIC      5948  11-14-89   3:42p
CURRENT  PIC       462  11-14-89   3:42p
DEBTCAP  PIC       462  11-14-89   3:43p
ROA      PIC       457  11-14-89   3:43p
        7 File(s)   1293312 bytes free

A>
```

The PICS subdirectory listing shows two <DIR> entries: the first is a single period (.) and the second is a double period (..). Every subdirectory listing will show these two entries. The single period identifies the current directory itself; the double period identifies the parent directory, which in this case is the root directory. The . and .. directory identifiers are sometimes useful as a shorthand notation for directory names.

MULTIPLE PARENT\CHILD SUBDIRECTORIES

Next, suppose that among the WordPerfect document files, you want two further groups of files. The files with the extension .BAK are backup files for the original ("working") files on the disk. .BAK files are not intended to be modified by the user. There are also several files that begin with the letters RPT, which identifies them as parts of a report.

You now will create two additional subdirectories of the parent directory DOCFILES. One of the additional directories will be named "BAKUP" and the other will be named "REPORT." The directory structure of the disk will then appear as follows.

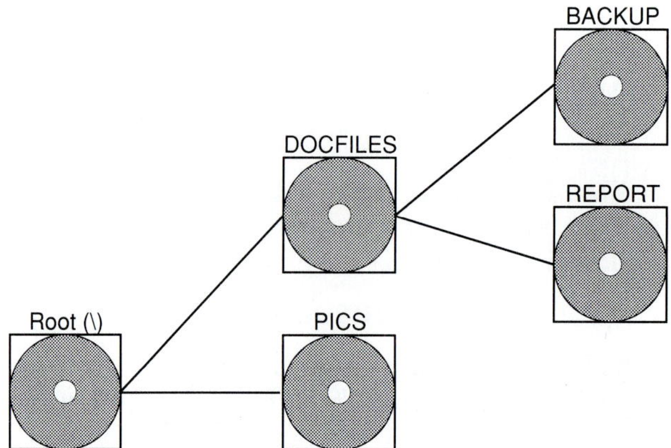

Since PICS is now the current subdirectory, the command MD BAKUP would create a directory BAKUP under the parent directory PICS, not under the correct parent directory DOCFILES. However, like most DOS commands, the **MD** command may be used with a full path specification beginning at the root directory, regardless of the current directory you are in.

33. Type ‖ **MD** \DOCFILES\BAKUP↵ ‖ to create the subdirectory BAKUP.

34. Next type ‖ **DIR** \DOCFILES↵ ‖ to verify that the directory was created.

The screen should now appear as follows.

```
A>DIR \DOCFILES

 Volume in drive A has no label
 Directory of  A:\DOCFILES

.            <DIR>       1-15-90  12:14p
..           <DIR>       1-15-90  12:14p
BAKUP        <DIR>       1-15-90   2:11p
        3 File(s)   1292800 bytes free

A>
```

A subdirectory also may be created under the parent directory DOCFILES by first making DOCFILES the current directory and then executing the **MD** command with only the new directory name. While this involves two commands and even more keystrokes, you may find it easier to keep track of where the new directory is being created if you use this method.

35. Now type ‖ **CD** \DOCFILES↵ ‖ to make DOCFILES the current directory.

36. Next type ‖ **MD** REPORT↵ ‖ to create the new directory REPORT under the current directory DOCFILES.

37. Type ‖ **DIR**↵ ‖ to verify that the directories BAKUP and REPORT now appear under the current directory (DOCFILES).

The screen should now appear as follows.

```
A>DIR

 Volume in drive A has no label
 Directory of  A:\DOCFILES

.            <DIR>      1-15-90  12:14p
..           <DIR>      1-15-90  12:14p
BAKUP        <DIR>      1-15-90   2:11p
REPORT       <DIR>      1-15-90   2:17p
        4 File(s)   1292288 bytes free

A>
```

When using the **CD** command to move among many subdirectories, you may often lose track of the current subdirectory. The **CD** command may be used without a path specification to display the name of the current directory. The **PROMPT** command also may be used with certain parameters to display the current directory as part of the DOS prompt.

38. Type ‖ **CD**↵ ‖ to display the name of the current directory. Then include the path as part of the DOS prompt by typing ‖ **PROMPT** PG↵ ‖ .

The screen should now appear as follows.

```
A>CD
A:\DOCFILES

A>PROMPT $P$G

A:\DOCFILES>
```

The $P parameter included in the **PROMPT** command is used to display the current path in the prompt. The $G parameter is used to include the > character in the prompt. Refer to the DOS command/program summary (pages 000–000) for a list of all parameters that may be used with the **PROMPT** command.

39. Now type ‖ **CD** BAKUP↵ ‖ to change the current directory to BAKUP.

The prompt should now appear as "A:\DOCFILES\BAKUP>," identifying the current directory. You now will copy all files with the extension .BAK from the root directory to the current directory.

40. Type ‖ **COPY** *.BAK↵ ‖ .

You next will copy all files having no extension from the root directory to the directory DOCFILES. Since the current directory (BAKUP) is neither the source nor target directory, the directory path must be specified for each.

41. Type || **COPY** *. \DOCFILES↵ || .

As mentioned earlier, the double period (..) is a shorthand method of identifying the parent directory of the current directory. You will now list the files in the directory DOCFILES using the double period notation.

42. Type || **DIR** ../W↵ || to list files in the parent directory DOCFILES.

The screen should now appear similar to the following.

```
A:\DOCFILES\BAKUP>DIR ../W

 Volume in drive A has no label
 Directory of  A:\DOCFILES

.               ..              BAKUP           REPORT          ANNRPTXT
BLSHEET1        CONBLNC         CONSTMT         DISCOP          ENTRYHLP
FCTRANS         INVTS           MEMBDAT1        OPNWSNOV        PHONEORD
RNTEQUIP        RPTINTRO        RPTSOFTW        SILVINTR        STCCURR
WORKCAP
       21 File(s)    1164288 bytes free

A:\DOCFILES\BAKUP>
```

Since the double period (..) identifies the parent directory DOCFILES, the other subdirectory under DOCFILES may be identified as ..\REPORT. You now will copy all files with a filename beginning "RPT" from the parent directory DOCFILES to its subdirectory REPORT using the double period notation.

43. Type || **COPY** ..\RPT*.* ..\REPORT↵ || .
44. Now change the current directory to DOCFILES by typing || **CD** ..↵ || .
45. Verify the last copy by typing || **DIR** REPORT↵ || .

The screen should now appear similar to the following.

```
A:\DOCFILES>DIR REPORT

 Volume in drive A has no label
 Directory of  A:\DOCFILES\REPORT

.            <DIR>      1-15-90   2:17p
..           <DIR>      1-15-90   2:17p
RPTINTRO         2953  12-17-89   3:46p
RPTSOFTW         7054  12-20-89   3:47p
        4 File(s)    1154048 bytes free

A:\DOCFILES>
```

The **RD** (Remove Directory) Command

You have created subdirectories on the disk to give you experience using DOS directories and path specifications. You now will remove the directories created here with the **RD** (Remove Directory) command. Before subdirectories can be removed, however, they must be emptied of all files and subdirectories. Therefore, you will begin by erasing all files in the current directory DOCFILES.

46. Type ‖ **ERASE** *.*↵ ‖ to erase all files in the current directory. At the prompt "Are you sure (Y/N)?" type ‖ Y↵ ‖ to erase the files.

The prompt "Are you sure (Y/N)?" appears when all files in a directory are about to be erased. DOS commands and programs often display this type of warning when an operation is irrevocable and many data files may be lost.

Another way of erasing all files in a directory is to use the **ERASE** command with the name of a directory.

47. Now erase all files in the directory REPORT by typing ‖ **ERASE** REPORT↵ ‖ and confirm that you want to complete the operation by typing ‖ Y↵ ‖ at the warning prompt.

The REPORT directory may now be removed with the **RD** (Remove Directory) command.

48. Type ‖ **RD** REPORT↵ ‖ to remove the directory. Then verify that the directory has been removed by typing ‖ **DIR**↵ ‖ .

If you try to remove a directory that still has files in it or has further subdirectories beneath it, a message will appear on the screen indicating that the directory may not be removed.

49. Type ‖ **RD** BAKUP↵ ‖ . The following message should be displayed.

```
A:\DOCFILES>RD BAKUP
Invalid path, not directory,
or directory not empty

A:\DOCFILES>
```

DOS normally gives messages indicating that an operation has not been successfully completed. You may have noticed, however, that messages are not normally given to indicate successful completion. Therefore, it is important to pay close attention to any messages displayed when a command is executed.

50. Type ‖ **ERASE** BAKUP↵ ‖ and respond to the warning prompt by typing ‖ Y↵ ‖ .

51. Type ‖ **RD** BAKUP↵ ‖ to remove the directory BAKUP.

You now will erase files in the PICS directory, which is a subdirectory of the root directory, and then remove the PICS directory with the **RD** command.

52. Type ‖ **ERASE** \PICS↵ ‖ and respond to the warning prompt by typing ‖ Y↵ ‖ .

53. Then type ‖ **RD** \PICS↵ ‖ to remove the directory PICS.

The final directory to be removed is the current directory DOCFILES. Although all files in the directory have been erased and the directory no longer has subdirectories beneath it, the current directory may never be removed. To remove a directory, you must first change the current directory to a previous level.

54. Type ‖ **CD**\↵ ‖ to make the root directory the current directory.

55. Then type ‖ **RD** DOCFILES↵ ‖ to remove the subdirectory DOCFILES.

A FINAL NOTE

It should be mentioned that the ability to use the wild card characters * and ? to specify groups of files has implications about how files ought to be named. If you think you might use commands with a group of files (batch operations) at any future time, you should name the files so that the group may be specified with wild card characters. You then can use DOS commands to copy all the files from one directory to another, to make backup copies of all the files, to erase all the files, and so forth.

This completes the DOS exercise. You may refer to the DOS command summary for additional information on commands used in the exercises and for several other DOS commands and programs.

DOS QUICK REFERENCE COMMAND SUMMARY

Device Names

Disk Drives	A:, B:, C:	Monitor	SCR:	Printer 2	LPT2:
Keyboard	CON:	Printer 1	LPT1:		

Commands and Programs

d: Command
Syntax: *drive letter:*

CHDIR or **CD** (Change Directory) Command
Syntax: **CD** [*d:*][*path*]

CHKDSK (Check Disk) Program
Syntax: [*d:*][*path*]CHKDSK [*d:*][*path*][*filename*[*.ext*]][/F][/V]

CLS (Clear Screen) Command
Syntax: **CLS**

COMP (Compare Files) Program
Syntax: [*d:*][*path*]COMP [*d:*][*path*][*filename*[*.ext*]]
[*d:*][*path*][*filename*[*.ext*]]

COPY (Copy Files) Command
Syntax: **COPY** [*d:*][*path*]*filename*[*.ext*] [*d:*][*path*][*filename*[*.ext*]]

DATE (Set System Date) Command
Syntax: **DATE** [*mm-dd-yy*], [*dd-mm-yy*], or [*yy-mm-dd*]

DIR (List Directory) Command
Syntax: **DIR** [*d:*][*path*][*filename*[*.ext*]][/P][/W]

DISKCOMP (Compare Floppy Disks) Program
Syntax: [*d:*][*path*]DISKCOMP [*d:*[*d:*]]

DISKCOPY (Copy Floppy Disks) Program
Syntax: [*d:*][*path*]DISKCOPY [*d:*[*d:*]]

ERASE or **DEL** (Erase Files) Command
Syntax: **ERASE** [*d:*][*path*]*filename*[*.ext*]

FORMAT (Format Disk) Program
Syntax: [*d:*][*path*]FORMAT [*d:*][/S][/1][/8][/V][/B]

LABEL (Volume Label) Program
Syntax: [*d:*][*path*]LABEL [*d:*][*volume label*]

MD or **MKDIR** (Make Directory) Command
Syntax: **MD** [*d:*]*path*

PATH (Set Search Directory) Command
Syntax: **PATH** [[*d:*]*path*[[;[*d:*]*path*]]]

PROMPT (Set System Prompt) Command
Syntax: **PROMPT** [*prompt-text*]

RENAME (Rename Files) Command
Syntax: **RENAME** [*d:*][*path*][*filename*[.*ext*]] [*filename*[.*ext*]]

RD or **RMDIR** (Remove Directory) Command
Syntax: **RD** [*d:*]*path*

SYS (System) Program
Syntax: [*d:*][*path*]SYS [*d:*]

TIME (System Time) Command
Syntax: **TIME** [*hh:mm*[*:ss*[*.xx*]]]

TYPE (Contents of File) Command
Syntax: **TYPE**[*d:*][*path*]*filename*[.*ext*]

VOL (Volume) Command
Syntax: **VOL** [*d:*]

DOS CONTROL KEYS

The following keystrokes and keystroke combinations may be used while at the DOS operating level. The convention *key-key* means press and hold the first key shown and then type the second key shown.

NOTE: Refer to the keyboards on page I-4 to help you locate the keys involved in the following keystroke combinations.

KEY COMBINATIONS

Ctrl-Alt-Del Three-key combination. Press and hold the Ctrl and Alt keys, and then tap the Del key. Erases all data from RAM and reloads DOS (reboots the system).

Ctrl-Break Interrupts a DOS command or program operation. Returns to the DOS > prompt.

Ctrl-Num Lock or Pause Pauses a DOS operation. Typing any key will resume the operation.

Ctrl-PrtScr Toggles ON/OFF an echo of screen output to the printer.

Shift-PrtScr Prints the current screen of data.

Enter key Enters the current line into memory for DOS to act upon.

Escape key Aborts the current line without entering it as a DOS command or filename.

F1 key Types out the last entry one character at a time.

F3 key Types out all of the last entry.

F6 key Types out the End of File character ^Z.

IMPORTANT DOS COMMANDS AND PROGRAMS VERSION 3.3

d:
Syntax: *drive letter:*
Type: Command

Changes the current default drive. The drive letter entry specifies the desired disk drive device to make current (usually A:, B:, or C:). The current DOS prompt indicates the letter of the current drive (i.e., A> indicates that the A: drive is the current default drive).

CHDIR or **CD** (Change Directory)
Syntax: **CD** [*d:*][*path*]
Type: Command

Changes the current directory. **CD** used by itself displays the path of the current directory on the screen. **CD**\ makes the root directory the current directory. **CD**.. makes the parent (next previous) directory the current directory.

CHKDSK (Check Disk)
Syntax: [*d:*][*path*]CHKDSK [*d:*][*path*][*filename*[.*ext*]][/F][/V]
Type: Program

The CHKDSK.COM program may be used to search the disk for errors that may have occurred after the disk was formatted, and to report on the status of used and remaining disk space.

Executing the CHKDSK.COM program provides information about the space in use on the disk being checked. The most common form of the program entry is CHKDSK *d:*. An example of the program's output is shown here.

```
C:\DOS> CHKDSK A:

  1457664 bytes total disk space
    52736 bytes in 2 hidden files
   199168 bytes in 46 user files
  1205760 bytes available on disk

   654336 bytes total memory
   457616 bytes free

C:\DOS>
```

The CHKDSK program reports on the total disk space and the disk space remaining (available) on the disk. It also reports the computer's total RAM and the RAM that is still available (total RAM less the RAM being used by DOS). Notice that the CHKDSK program can be used to determine if hidden files exist on the disk.

It is a good habit to use the CHKDSK program to check your disks periodically to avoid running out of disk space in the middle of a save operation.

If the CHKDSK program finds errors on the disk, the output of the program will contain error messages concerning lost clusters.

```
C:\DOS> CHKDSK A:

Errors found, F parameter not specified.
Corrections will not be written to disk.


3 lost clusters found in 1 chains.
Convert lost chains to files  (Y/N)?
```

If such errors occur, the CHKDSK program (with the /F switch) may be executed again to cause the program to convert the lost chains into files. The /V switch may be used to cause the CHKDSK program to display all disk files and their paths.

CHKDSK [*d:*]*.* may be used to produce a report on the disk files which has sectors that are noncontiguous (scattered).

CLS (Clear Screen)
Syntax: **CLS**
Type: Command

The **CLS** command may be used to clear the screen at the DOS operating level.

COMP (Compare Files)
Syntax: [*d:*][*path*]COMP [*d:*][*path*][*filename*[.*ext*]] [*d:*][*path*][*filename*[.*ext*]]
Type: Program

The COMP.COM program compares the contents of files to determine if they are identical. Examples of using the COMP program include the following.

COMP C:file1.ext A:file2.ext   Compares file1 on the C: drive with file2 on the A: drive.

COMP \DOCFILES\REPORT \DOCFILES\BACKUP   Compares all files in the \DOCFILES\REPORT subdirectory with the files in the \DOCFILES\BACKUP subdirectory.

COPY (Copy Files)
Syntax: **COPY** [*d:*][*path*]*filename*[.*ext*] [*d:*][*path*][*filename*[.*ext*]]
Type: Command

The **COPY** command is used primarily to copy files from one directory to another. The first file specification [*d:*][*path*]*filename*[.*ext*] defines the source file(s) to be copied. The second specification defines the destination for the copied file(s). If the second specification includes only a drive and/or path, the files are copied to the destination with the same filenames and extensions as the source files. Examples of using the **COPY** command include the following.

A> **COPY** report report.bak   Copies the file named "report" to a file named "report.bak" into the current directory. (Makes a copy with a different name into the same directory.)

A> **COPY** report.WK1 B: Copies the file named "report.WK1" from the current drive and directory into the current directory of the B: drive, under the same name.

A> **COPY** C:report.WK1   Copies the file named "report.WK1" from the current directory of the C: drive into the current directory of the A: drive, under the same name.

A> **COPY** C:\WORDS\MGMT213 B: Copies all files in the C:\WORDS\MGMT213 subdirectory into the current directory of the B: drive, under the same names.

A> **COPY** C:\WORDS\MGMT213 B:\MGMT213\BACKUP   Copies all files in the C:WORDS\MGMT213 subdirectory into the \MGMT213\BACKUP directory of the B: drive, under the same names.

A> **COPY** *.* C: Copies all files in the current directory of the A: drive into the current directory of the C: drive, under the same names.

The **COPY** command may include a hardware device as the source or destination for the copy operation. Examples would include the following.

A> **COPY** report LPT1: Copies the file named "report" to the printer (prints the file).

A> **COPY** CON:test.BAT Copies characters typed on the keyboard to a file named "test.BAT," in the current directory of the A: drive. (Allows you to create an ASCII file from DOS. Typing F6, End of File character, ends the keyboard copy operation.)

DATE (Set System Date)
Syntax: **DATE** [*mm-dd-yy*], [*dd-mm-yy*], or [*yy-mm-dd*]
Type: Command

The **DATE** command is used to change the DOS system date. *mm* specifies a month number (e.g., March = 03), *dd* specifies day number, and *yy* specifies the year number, which is entered as two numbers between 80 and 99 or four numbers between 1980 and 1999. Dashes are used to separate the numbers.

DIR (List Directory)
Syntax: **DIR** [*d:*][*path*][*filename*[*.ext*]][/P][/W]
Type: Command

The **DIR** command is used to display the directory of filenames, extensions, sizes, and date/time stamps for the files in a directory. Examples of using the **DIR** command include the following.

A> **DIR** * .WK1 Lists the directory for all files having a .WK1 extension in the current directory of the A: drive.

A> **DIR** C:\CALC\MGMT213*.PIC Lists the directory for all files having a .PIC extension in the \CALC\MGMT213 directory of the C: drive.

A> **DIR** report.WK1 Lists a directory for the single file named "report.WK1" in the current directory of the A: drive. (May be used to search a directory for a specific file.)

DISKCOMP (Compare Floppy Disks)
Syntax: [*d:*][*path*]DISKCOMP [*d:*[*d:*]]
Type: Program

The DISKCOMP program compares the contents of two floppy disks to determine if they are identical. Examples of using the DISKCOMP program include the following.

A> C:DISKCOMP A: B: Reads the DISKCOMP program from the current directory of the C: drive. The program then compares the contents of the disk in the A: drive with the contents of the disk in the B: drive.

A> C:DISKCOMP A: Reads the DISKCOMP program from the current directory of the C: drive. The program then instructs the user to first insert one disk and then the other into the A: drive in order to compare the two disks.

DISKCOPY (Copy Floppy Disks)
Syntax: [*d:*][*path*]DISKCOPY [*d:*[*d:*]]
Type: Program

The DISKCOPY program copies the contents of one floppy disk onto another floppy disk. The disk being copied from is called the source disk. The disk being copied to is called the target disk. The disks are identical when the disk copy operation is complete. The source and destination floppy disks must be of the same size and density. Examples of using the DISKCOPY program include the following.

A> C:DISKCOPY A: B: Reads the DISKCOPY program from the current directory of the C: drive. The program then copies the contents of the disk in the A: drive onto the disk in the B: drive.

A> C:DISKCOPY A: Reads the DISKCOPY program from the current directory of the C: drive. The program then instructs the user to first insert the source disk and then the target disk into the A: drive in order to perform the disk copy operation.

ERASE or **DEL** (Erase Files)
Syntax: **ERASE** [*d:*][*path*]*filename*[*.ext*]
Type: Command

The **ERASE** command is used to erase one or more files from a directory. Examples of using the **ERASE** command include the following.

A> **ERASE** report.WK1 Erases the file named "report.WK1" from the current directory of the A: drive.

A> **ERASE** *.* Erases all files in the current directory of the A: drive.

A> **ERASE** C:*.WK1 Erases all files having a WK1 extension that are in the current directory of the C: drive.

A> **ERASE** C:\WORDS\MGMT213 Erases all files in the \WORDS\MGMT213 subdirectory of the C: drive.

FORMAT (Format Disk)
Syntax: [*d:*][*path*]FORMAT [*d:*][/S][/1][/8][/V][/B]
Type: Program

The FORMAT program is used to prepare a disk for storing data. *The FORMAT program destroys all data that may already be on a disk.* The various FORMAT program switches have the following effects.

/S Copies DOS onto the disk after the format is complete.

/1 Formats only one side of the disk.

/8 Formats the disk into 8 sector groups (5 ¼″ floppy disks only).

/V Pauses after the format operation to allow you to type and enter a label for the disk. The label then will be listed by the **DIR** command when it reads a directory of the disk.

/B Formats the disk so that DOS may be copied onto it later. See the SYS program for information on copying DOS onto a disk after it has been formatted.

LABEL (Volume Label)
Syntax: [*d:*][*path*]LABEL [*d:*][*volume label*]
Type: Program

The LABEL program is used to enter a label for a disk that will be listed with the directory when the **DIR** command is used. The following example creates a label MYFILES for the disk in the A: drive. The LABEL program in the example is read from a subdirectory named DOS.

C> \DOS\LABEL A:myfiles If the disk already has a label, the LABEL program may be used to change the label. LABEL [*d:*] with no volume label specified may be used to delete a disk's label.

MD or **MKDIR** (Make Directory)
Syntax: **MD** [*d:*]*path*
Type: Command

The **MD** command is used to create a subdirectory on a disk. If the directory being created is a child of the current directory, the directory name is entered immediately after the **MD** command. For instance, if the current directory is \WORDS and you want to create a new directory ACCT335 whose parent directory is WORDS, you type ‖ C:\WORDS>**MD** ACCT335↵ ‖. However, if you want to accomplish the same task while the root directory is the current directory, you type ‖ C:\>**MD**\WORDS\ACCT335↵ ‖.

PATH (Set Search Directory)
Syntax: **PATH** [[*d:*]*path*[[;[*d:*]*path*]]]
Type: Command

The **PATH** command is used to direct DOS to another disk directory if an executable file (software or program) for which it is searching cannot be found in the current or specified directory. For instance, the command **PATH** C:CALC;C:WORDS sets a path to the two software subdirectories. If you then type a software filename command such as WP while the root directory is the current directory, DOS will first search the root directory for the software file. If the file is not found, it will next search the \CALC directory for the file. If the software file is not found there, DOS will continue its search in the \WORDS directory. DOS searches the **PATH** command's directories in the order they were entered when the **PATH** command was entered.

PROMPT (Set System Prompt)
Syntax: **PROMPT** [*prompt-text*]
Type: Command

The **PROMPT** command may be used to change the DOS prompt. Certain letters preceded by a dollar sign ($) may be used to cause the prompt to display certain system information. For instance, the command **PROMPT** pbDate-dg creates a DOS prompt similar to C:\DOS|Date-Sat 1-21-1989> (when the C: drive and the DOS directory are both current). The following is a list of letters and their displayed data that may be included in the **PROMPT** command.

Characters	DOS Prompt Display
$$	$ (dollar sign)
$t	System Time
$d	System Date
$p	The current drive and directory
$v	The version of DOS being used
$n	The current drive only
$g	> character
$l	< character
$b	| character
$q	= character

RENAME (Rename Files)
Syntax: **RENAME** [*d:*][*path*][*filename*[*.ext*]] [*filename*[*.ext*]]
Type: Command

The **RENAME** command is used to rename files in a directory. Examples of using the **RENAME** command include the following.

A> **RENAME** report report.bak   Renames the file named "report" (A: drive, current directory) to be "report.bak" (same drive and directory).

A> **RENAME** C:\WORDS\MGMT213\report report.bak   Renames the file named "report" (C: drive, \WORDS\MGMT213 directory) to be "report.bak" (same drive and directory).

A> **RENAME** *. *.bak   Renames all files having no extension to be files with the same filenames and .bak extensions.

RD or **RMDIR** (Remove Directory)
Syntax: **RD** [*d:*]*path*
Type: Command

The **RD** command is used to remove a subdirectory from a disk. Before a subdirectory can be removed, all of the files in the subdirectory must be erased (see the **ERASE** command for more information on erasing files). A directory may not be removed while it is the current directory. A preceding directory must be the current directory in order to remove a directory. A parent directory may not be removed until all child directories are removed first. A directory containing hidden files may not be removed.

SYS (System)
Syntax: [*d:*][*path*]SYS [*d:*]
Type: Program

The SYS program may be used to transfer DOS onto a disk that has been previously formatted. Unless the SYS program is executed immediately after the disk has been formatted, there is a possibility that there will not be enough room available on the disk where the hidden files of DOS must be stored. See the FORMAT program /B switch for information on how to format a disk in a way that reserves space for the hidden files.

TIME (System Time)
Syntax: **TIME** [*hh:mm*[*:ss*[*.xx*]]]
Type: Command

The **TIME** command allows you to change the system's clock time. Command entries are made: *hh* for hour, 0–23; *mm* for minute, 0–59; *ss* for second, 0–59; and *xx* for hundredths of a second, 0–99.

TYPE (Contents of File)
Syntax: **TYPE** [*d:*][*path*]*filename*[*.ext*]
Type: Command

The **TYPE** command is used to output the contents of a file to the screen. The command is most useful when the file is in ASCII data format. Any non-ASCII contents of a file will be unreadable.

VOL (Volume)
Syntax: **VOL** [*d:*]
Type: Command

The **VOL** command is used to display the volume label of a disk. See the LABEL program for information on how to label a disk volume.

DOS RELATED FILES

When DOS is first loaded into RAM (booted), the operating system will automatically look for certain files in the root directory. These files, if present, will affect the operations of the microcomputer while it is in use.

AUTOEXEC.BAT

A file given a .BAT filename extension is called a *batch file*. Batch files contain one or more DOS commands and/or executable (program) file filenames. If the filename for an existing batch file is entered at the DOS operating level, DOS will open the file and begin executing the commands/programs within the batch file in the order of their appearance.

.BAT files are ASCII files that can be created by the user with a word processing software (or any other software that will create ASCII files). They can also be created by using a method in which a variation of the DOS **COPY** command is used to create a file directly from the keyboard. This variation of the COPY command has the form

COPY CON:*filename*.BAT

The command simply designates the keyboard (CON:) as the source for the file to copy. When the command is executed, DOS pauses for you to type characters on the keyboard. When finished, you type the F6 Function key to produce the End of File (^Z) character. An example of creating such a file might appear on the screen as follows.

```
A> COPY CON:GO.BAT
C:\DOS\CHKDSK A:
PAUSE
DIR A:
PAUSE
C:\WORDS\WP
^Z
```

In this example a batch file named "GO.BAT" is created. To execute the file, the user types ‖ GO↵ ‖ at the DOS operating level. When executed, the first line in the file causes DOS to access the C:\DOS subdirectory to load the CHKDSK program and perform a CHKDSK operation on the disk in the A: DRIVE.

The next DOS command, **PAUSE,** typically is used only in batch files. The **PAUSE** command causes the computer to stop executing the commands in the batch file until the user types a key on the keyboard. When the command is executed the message

Strike a key when ready . . .

appears on the screen. The user next types a key and the computer continues by listing a directory of the files found on the disk in the A: drive (DIR A:). It then pauses again.

AUTOEXEC is a special batch file filename that DOS will automatically search for in the root directory when DOS is first booted. If a file named "AUTOEXEC.BAT" is in the directory, DOS will open the file and begin executing the commands/programs within it.

CONFIG.SYS

CONFIG.SYS is another example of a DOS-related ASCII file with a special DOS name. A CONFIG.SYS file may be created in the same manner as a .BAT file, using a software or the **COPY** CON: command. A CONFIG.SYS file also contains DOS commands/programs; however, the commands/programs contained in a CONFIG.SYS file are used to change the default input/output attributes of DOS and so may only be executed at the time when DOS is first booted. At that time DOS will open a file in the root directory named "CONFIG.SYS" and will begin executing the commands/programs within the batch file in the order of their appearance.

Having a CONFIG.SYS file in the root directory of the boot disk is particularly important with newer applications software that maintain several open files while they are being used. In such cases the CONFIG.SYS file should have the following two lines included in it.

```
FILES = 20
BUFFERS = 24
^Z
```

DEVICE = VDISK nnn

Another line you may see in a CONFIG.SYS file is used to load a DOS program (VDISK.SYS) at the time that DOS is booted. The VDISK program creates what is called a "phantom" or RAM disk drive. The program is particularly useful when the microcomputer has only one floppy disk drive in addition to its C: drive. VDISK.SYS configures a portion of the microcomputer's RAM into what is essentially a temporary disk drive. The program will assign a DOS device name (usually D:) to the RAM drive. You then can use the RAM drive (D:) for temporary storage of data while using the microcomputer.

It is important to note that the RAM drive is not a real disk drive, and any data on it will vaporize the instant the computer is turned off. Therefore, you must copy any data you want to keep onto a real disk before turning off the computer.

The RAM drive reduces the amount of RAM available for processing data. If the software you are using requires a large amount of RAM, you may not be able to use it and the RAM drive at the same time.

To use VDISK.SYS to create a RAM drive at the time the microcomputer is booted, copy the VDISK.SYS program into the root directory. You then must add the following line to your existing root directory CONFIG.SYS file, or create a root directory CONFIG.SYS file with the line in it.

DEVICE = VDISK *nnn*

The *nnn* represents the size of the RAM drive you want to create. For instance, DEVICE = VDISK 256 will create a 256K RAM disk drive.

APPENDIX B
ASCII CHARACTER CODES

The following table lists all the ASCII codes (in decimal) and their associated characters. These characters can be displayed using PRINT CHR$ (*n*), where *n* is the ASCII code. The column headed "Control Character" lists the standard interpretations of ASCII codes 0 to 31 (usually used for control functions or communications).

Each of these characters can be entered from the keyboard by pressing and holding the Alt key, then pressing the digits for the ASCII code on the numeric keypad. Note, however, that some of the codes have special meaning to the BASIC Program Editor. It uses its own interpretation for the codes and may not display the special character listed here.

ASCII Value	Character	Control Character	ASCII Value	Character	ASCII Value	Character	ASCII Value	Character
000	(null)	NUL	032	(space)	064	@	096	`
001	☺	SOH	033	!	065	A	097	a
002	☻	STX	034	"	066	B	098	b
003	♥	ETX	035	#	067	C	099	c
004	♦	EOT	036	$	068	D	100	d
005	♣	ENQ	037	%	069	E	101	e
006	♠	ACK	038	&	070	F	102	f
007	(beep)	BEL	039	'	071	G	103	g
008	◘	BS	040	(	072	H	104	h
009	(tab)	HT	041	)	073	I	105	i
010	(line feed)	LF	042	*	074	J	106	j
011	(home)	VT	043	+	075	K	107	k
012	(form feed)	FF	044	,	076	L	108	l
013	(carriage return)	CR	045	-	077	M	109	m
014	♫	SO	046	.	078	N	110	n
015	☼	SI	047	/	079	O	111	o
016	►	DLE	048	0	080	P	112	p
017	◄	DC1	049	1	081	Q	113	q
018	↕	DC2	050	2	082	R	114	r
019	‼	DC3	051	3	083	S	115	s
020	¶	DC4	052	4	084	T	116	t
021	§	NAK	053	5	085	U	117	u
022	▬	SYN	054	6	086	V	118	v
023	↨	ETB	055	7	087	W	119	w
024	↑	CAN	056	8	088	X	120	x
025	↓	EM	057	9	089	Y	121	y
026	→	SUB	058	:	090	Z	122	z
027	←	ESC	059	;	091	[	123	{
028	(cursor right)	FS	060	<	092	\	124	|
029	(cursor left)	GS	061	=	093	]	125	}
030	(cursor up)	RS	062	>	094	^	126	~
031	(cursor down)	US	063	?	095	_	127	⌂

ASCII Value	Character	ASCII Value	Character	ASCII Value	Character	ASCII Value	Character
128	Ç	160	á	192	└	224	α
129	ü	161	í	193	┴	225	β
130	é	162	ó	194	┬	226	Γ
131	â	163	ú	195	├	227	π
132	ä	164	ñ	196	─	228	Σ
133	à	165	Ñ	197	┼	229	σ
134	å	166	ª	198	╞	230	μ
135	ç	167	º	199	╟	231	τ
136	ê	168	¿	200	╚	232	Φ
137	ë	169	⌐	201	╔	233	Θ
138	è	170	¬	202	╩	234	Ω
139	ï	171	½	203	╦	235	δ
140	î	172	¼	204	╠	236	∞
141	ì	173	¡	205	═	237	Ø
142	Ä	174	«	206	╬	238	ε
143	Å	175	»	207	╧	239	∩
144	É	176	░	208	╨	240	≡
145	æ	177	▒	209	╤	241	±
146	Æ	178	▓	210	╥	242	≥
147	ô	179	│	211	╙	243	≤
148	ö	180	┤	212	╘	244	⌠
149	ò	181	╡	213	╒	245	⌡
150	û	182	╢	214	╓	246	÷
151	ù	183	╖	215	╫	247	≈
152	ÿ	184	╕	216	╪	248	°
153	Ö	185	╣	217	┘	249	•
154	Ü	186	║	218	┌	250	·
155	¢	187	╗	219	█	251	√
156	£	188	╝	220	▄	252	^{n}
157	¥	189	╜	221	▌	253	^{2}
158	Pt	190	╛	222	▐	254	■
159	ƒ	191	┐	223	▀	255	(blank 'FF')

APPENDIX C
EXPRESSIONS

Computers can be used to accomplish a wide variety of tasks, many of which may seem fairly complex. However, the computer itself deals with data in a very rudimentary fashion. It is the programming language or applications software that allows for more complex operations through the use of logical expressions. Logical expressions allow the computer to evaluate data, and then perform certain actions based upon that evaluation. To use logical expressions effectively, you must understand the order in which the computer evaluates expressions and the elements that comprise them.

This appendix covers some of the cross-software fundamentals of how computers evaluate expressions. In many cases there are general rules that may or may not be applicable to a particular software, or which may be overridden by a software's own rules. Because this appendix is a general discussion of expressions, color print has been used to call out software-specific interpretations of and exceptions to the general rules for WordPerfect, Lotus, and dBASE.

Almost all applications software include some commands and/or operations that use logical expressions. However, such expressions are used most often in database applications (dBASE). They are used less in spreadsheet applications (Lotus), and even less in word processing applications (WordPerfect). Logical expressions also tend to be used frequently in programming situations, such as those in which dBASE command files or Lotus 1-2-3 macros would be used.

To understand complex logical expressions, you must first understand the various elements that can make up such an expression: constants, variables, fields, numeric and string operators, numeric expressions, string expressions, relational operators, and logical operators.

THE TWO BASIC TYPES OF DATA: NUMERIC AND STRING

In general, computers deal with two distinct types of data, numeric and string. Numeric data are values that can be used in mathematical operations such as adding, subtracting, multiplying, and dividing. String data may also be called values; however, these values simply represent a string of characters (a group of characters arranged in a specific order). String data are typically differentiated from numeric data by the single or double quotation marks that enclose them. These quotes are referred to as delimiters. Examples of the two types of data are shown in the following.

Numeric data	String data
12	"John Smith"
45.876	"1415 S.E. 23rd Avenue"

Computer operations must make a distinction between numeric data items and string data items. The two types of data items cannot be compared to each other in an evaluation (is "John Smith" greater than 45.876?) or combined with each other to form a single item in a command or operation (print "John Smith" + 12). In other words, you cannot "mix" data types.

> Lotus sometimes refers to numeric data items as values and string data items as labels. Lotus allows you to reference string data in a numeric formula (mixed types), but will treat the item as the numeric value zero.
>
> dBASE refers to numeric data items as numeric type and string data items as character type.
>
> WordPerfect typically deals with everything as string data, and any task that performs mathematical operations must, therefore, involve some type of string-to-numeric data conversion.

OTHER TYPES OF DATA

Software sometimes provide (and appear to deal with) data types other than numeric and string. What they actually do, however, is provide a way of identifying specific numeric or string data items that are to be treated in a special manner.

For instance, logical-type data refers to a data item that may hold one of two specific values, such as true or false, yes or no, on or off, zero or non-zero. Logical data is, in fact, numeric data that is interpreted as logical-type data. Software also may appear to deal with date-type data by interpreting, displaying, or otherwise treating certain numeric or string data in a special manner.

> In dBASE you may identify data items as logical or date items. Internally, dBASE stores logical items as numeric data values 1 or 0, but presents the data to the user as .T. (true) or .F. (false), respectively. Similarly, dBASE stores date items as string data such as "19910214", but presents the data to the user in a recognizable format such as 02/14/91.
>
> In Lotus you are not required to identify data items as logical or date items, but you may treat numeric data items as either logical data or date data. Lotus will evaluate any non-zero numeric data as true and the numeric value zero as false, which is actually the way computers make logical (true/false) evaluations of data. In Lotus, you also may cause certain numeric values to be displayed in a recognizable date format. For example, the numeric value 33283 may be used to represent the date 02/14/91.

In general, when you must explicitly identify a data item as being something other than numeric or string, as is the case with dBASE, the rule about not mixing data types applies to all data types identified.

CONSTANTS, VARIABLES, AND FIELDS

Data items used in expressions may be constants, variables, or fields. Constants are values that will never change when the expression is evaluated, while fields and variables are used to identify items that may have different values each time the expression is evaluated.

Constants

A constant is an explicit value, such as the string value "John Smith" or the numeric value 12. Generally, expressions seldom consist of constant values only. Consider, for example, two numeric constants being added and compared to another numeric constant in the following question.

Is 80 + 35 greater than 100?

The evaluation of 80 + 35 will always be 115, and the answer to the question will always be yes.

Variables

The ability to store values to variables is called assignment. Assigning values to variables adds flexibility to computer operations. When a variable is created, a specific location in RAM is allocated to hold a numeric or string data item. The software keeps track of the location and allows you to choose a name with which to identify the data item. A new value may later be assigned to the same variable name, and the computer simply changes the value held in that variable's location.

For example, you might assign the value 80 to a variable named ACCOUNT and assign the value 35 to a variable named PURCHASE. The variable names then could be substituted in the previous question as follows.

Is ACCOUNT + PURCHASE greater than 100?

In this case, the evaluation of the expression depends on the current values of the variables ACCOUNT and PURCHASE. If the variables hold the values assigned above, the evaluation of ACCOUNT + PURCHASE is 115, and the answer to the question is yes. If the numeric value 50 was assigned to the variable ACCOUNT, however, the evaluation of ACCOUNT + PURCHASE would be 85 and the answer to the question would be no.

Fields

A field is one of a group of related data items constituting a record in database operations. A field name is used in an expression to identify which data item is to be evaluated for one or more records in a database. Because an expression is evaluated for only one record at a time, the value specified with a field name in any expression may vary with each record evaluated. New values can also be assigned to fields, which would change the evaluation of an expression for a record. Because of the variable nature of its data, a field can be thought of as a special type of variable. While there are some exceptions, the information held in database fields is stored on disk, while information assigned to variables is held in RAM.

Assume that ACCOUNT is the name of a numeric database field, while PURCHASE is a variable that has been assigned the value 30. Assume further that you have the following database records to consider.

Field names:	NAME	DEPT	PHONE	ACCOUNT	LIMIT
Data types:	*string*	*string*	*string*	*numeric*	*numeric*
Record 1	John Smith	acctg	221-8723	75	100
Record 2	April Miller	acctg	221-8725	42	55
Record 3	Steve Grey	sales	223-5539	90	95

Now look again at the previous example question.

Is ACCOUNT + PURCHASE greater than 100?

You can see that the evaluation of ACCOUNT + PURCHASE and the answer to the question will depend on the record to which you are referring.

LOGICAL EXPRESSIONS

A logical expression is an expression that the computer can evaluate as either true or false. The questions used in the previous examples represented simple logical expressions because they could be answered with a yes or a no. Two or more such questions may be combined into a complex logical expression, just as they could be combined into one sentence, as follows.

Is ACCOUNT + PURCHASE greater than 100?
Is NAME equal to "John Smith"?

Is ACCOUNT + PURCHASE greater than 100 and is NAME equal to "John Smith"?

Although this question could probably be answered without any ambiguity, some complex questions may be difficult to state clearly in the form of a complex logical expression. You must first understand the order in which the computer begins evaluating such an expression to arrive at its true or false determination. Complex logical expressions are evaluated in the following order.

1. All numeric and string expressions and operators are evaluated.
2. All simple logical expressions and relational operators are evaluated.
3. The complex logical expression and all logical operators are evaluated.

This order may be referred to as rules of precedence, where certain evaluation steps always precede others. To give you a clear understanding of these steps, the following sections will discuss numeric expressions, numeric operators, string expressions, string operators, relational operators, and logical operators.

Numeric Expressions

Numeric expressions are single numeric data items, or formulas that use numeric data items and numeric operators that result in single numeric values. Numeric (or arithmetic) operators commonly used in numeric expressions are shown here with their normal order of precedence. The order of precedence indicates which operations will occur first, second, third, and so on.

Operator	Operation	Order of Precedence
−	minus sign	1
^	exponentiation	2
*	multiplication	3
/	division	3
+	addition	4
−	subtraction	4

The normal order of precedence reflects the order in which you would solve a mathematical equation. In addition, parentheses ( ) may be used to override the normal order of precedence. Notice that the minus sign (−) has the highest order of precedence only when it serves to reverse the sign of a numeric value.

The following numeric expression is a formula that uses one numeric constant (.75) and a number of numeric variables (or fields).

−BALANCE/(ACCOUNT−PAYMENT)+BONUS*.75−ALLOWANCE

Assuming the values shown for each variable, the expression will be evaluated by the computer as follows.

ACCOUNT = −50
ALLOWANCE = 65
BALANCE = 2000
BONUS = 400
PAYMENT = 150

The value of each variable is placed in the equation.

−2000/(−50−150)+400*.75−65

Operations in parentheses are performed first.

−2000/−200+400*.75−65

Multiplication and division operations are performed next.

10+300−65

Addition and subtraction operations are performed last.

245

In WordPerfect all arithmetic operators have equal precedence and formulas are evaluated from left to right. The exponentiation operator (^) is not recognized by WordPerfect.

String Expressions

String expressions are single string data items, or expressions that use string data items and string operators that result in single string values. String operators, also called string concatenators, are used to add one string of characters to another. The operator commonly used to combine two string data items is the plus sign (+), as shown in the following expression.

"Please contact " +NAME+ " at " +PHONE+ " by next week."

This expression concatenates (puts together) two string variables and three string constants (also called literals). The variables and the values that have been assigned to them and the string constants are shown here.

Variables	Assigned Values	Constants
NAME	"John Smith"	"Please contact "
PHONE	"221–8723"	" at "
		" by next week."

The computer's evaluation of the previous string expression would result in the single string data item

"Please contact John Smith at 221–8723 by next week."

dBASE uses the plus sign (+) operator to concatenate strings as shown here, and also uses the minus (−) operator to concatenate strings with trailing blank spaces moved to the end of a combined string.

Lotus uses the ampersand (&) as its string concatenation operator.

dBASE also allows date expressions that use the plus (+) and minus (−) operators together with date values and numeric values. This is an exception to the rule that states that data types must not be mixed in an expression. Only certain types of operations are permitted, however. Examples of allowable dBASE date expressions, the values of variables used, and the resulting data types and values are shown here.

Variable	Data Type	Value
DAY1	date	01/14/91
DAY2	date	02/21/91
DNUM	numeric	10

Expression	Resulting Data Type	Resulting Value
DAY1 + DNUM	date	02/24/91
DAY2 − DNUM	date	02/11/91
DAY2 − DAY1	numeric	7

Relational Expressions

A relational expression is a simple logical expression—one that compares two data items of the same data type using a relational operator. Logical expressions are sometimes referred to as conditions, since they are often used to conditionally perform certain operations. The standard relational operators are shown here.

Operator	**Comparison Operation**
=	equal to
<>	not equal to
>	greater than
<	less than
>=	greater than or equal to
<=	less than or equal to

The computer evaluates a relational expression as either true or false. The following are examples of relational expressions that use constant numeric and string data items. The result of the true or false evaluation is also shown.

Relational Expression	Evaluation
12 = 45.876	false
12 > 45.876	false
45.876 >= 12	true
“John Smith” > “1415 S.E. 23rd Avenue”	true
“John Smith” = “john smith”	false
“John Smith” <> “1415 S.E. 23rd Avenue”	true

Relational operators may be used to make comparisons of two numeric data items or two string data items. When string data are compared, characters are compared according to their ASCII values. Letters at the beginning of the alphabet have lower values than letters at the end of the alphabet (“A” has the value 65 and “Z” has the value 90). Lower-case letters have values greater than upper-case letters (“a” through “z” have the values 97 through 122). Because of these ASCII values, string data items will appear in alphabetical order if they are arranged from lowest to highest.

dBASE also uses the $ sign as a relational operator; however, it is only used in comparisons of string data items. It determines whether the first data item is found within (that is, it is a substring of) the second data item. For example, “Smith” $ “John Smith” would be evaluated as true.

dBASE also uses relational operators to compare date-type data items in relational expressions such as DAY1 <= DAY2.

Recall the order in which complex logical expressions are evaluated:

1. All numeric and string expressions and operators are evaluated.
2. All simple logical expressions and relational operators are evaluated.
3. The complex logical expression and all logical operators are evaluated.

When a single relational expression is used (no logical operators are included), only the first two types of evaluation are performed to arrive at a true or false evaluation. The following variables and database records will be used in examples of the first two types of evaluation below.

Variable	Data Type	Value
PURCHASE	numeric	30
ALLOWANCE	numeric	65

Field names:	NAME	DEPT	PHONE	ACCOUNT	LIMIT
Data types:	*string*	*string*	*string*	*numeric*	*numeric*
Record 1	John Smith	acctg	221-8723	75	100
Record 2	April Miller	acctg	221-8725	42	55
Record 3	Steve Grey	sales	223-5539	90	95

Consider the following numeric relational expression and the order in which it would be evaluated for the three records of the database.

ACCOUNT+PURCHASE<=LIMIT*1.15-ALLOWANCE/2

Values of variables and database fields are placed in the expression.

Record 1	Record 2	Record 3
75+30<=100*1.5−65/2	42+30<=55*1.5−65/2	90+30<=95*1.5−65/2

Numeric expressions are evaluated according to rules of precedence for numeric operators.

1. Multiplication and division operators are evaluated.

Record 1	Record 2	Record 3
75+30<=150−32.5	42+30<=82.5−32.5	90+30<=142.5−32.5

2. Addition and subtraction operators are evaluated.

Record 1	Record 2	Record 3
105<=117.5	72<=50	120<=110

3. Relational operators are evaluated.

Record 1	Record 2	Record 3
true	false	false

Logical Operators

When logical operators are included in an expression, the expression may be referred to as a complex logical expression. Logical operators are used to combine two or more simple logical expressions (relational expressions) and/or to reverse the true or false evaluation of a logical expression. The relational operators and their normal order of precedence are shown in the following table.

Operator	Order of Precedence
NOT	1
AND	2
OR	3

The NOT operator reverses the true or false evaluation of a logical expression in the same way that a minus sign (−) reverses the sign of a positive or negative numeric value. The AND and OR operators are used to combine two logical expressions so that the result is a single true or false answer. A logical expression that combines two logical expressions with the AND operator will evaluate true only if *both* expressions combined evaluate as true. A logical expression that combines two logical expressions with the OR operator will evaluate as true if *either* of the expressions combined evaluate as true.

The following are some examples of how complex logical expressions would be evaluated when they reverse or combine simple logical expressions that have true or false evaluations as shown.

NOT Expressions	AND Expressions	OR Expressions
NOT true = false	true AND true = true	true OR true = true
NOT false = true	true AND false = false	true OR false = true
	false AND false = false	false OR false = false

When a number of logical operators are used in a longer complex expression, understanding the rules of precedence becomes very important. As in the case of numeric expressions, parentheses ( ) may be used to override the normal order of precedence for logical operators.

The following examples have no parentheses included and would, therefore, be evaluated as shown.

Expression	NOT and AND Evaluated	Result
false AND false OR true	false OR true	true
true AND true OR true AND false	true OR false	true
false OR false AND true OR true	false OR true OR false	true
NOT false OR true	true OR true	true

The same expressions yield different results if parentheses are used to override the normal order of precedence.

Expression	Parentheses Evaluated	Result
false AND (false OR true)	false AND true	false
true AND (true OR true) AND false	true AND true AND false	false
(false OR false) AND (true OR true)	false AND true	false
NOT (false OR true)	NOT true	false

The variables and database records used in the example of a simple logical expression evaluation will now be used to illustrate the evaluation of a complex logical expression.

Variable	Data Type	Value
PURCHASE	numeric	30
ALLOWANCE	numeric	65

Field names:	NAME	DEPT	PHONE	ACCOUNT	LIMIT
Data types:	*string*	*string*	*string*	*numeric*	*numeric*
Record 1	John Smith	acctg	221-8723	75	100
Record 2	April Miller	acctg	221-8725	42	55
Record 3	Steve Grey	sales	223-5539	90	95

Consider the following complex logical expression and the order in which it would be evaluated for the first record of the database.

ACCOUNT + PURCHASE < = LIMIT*1.15 – ALLOWANCE/2 OR DEPT = "sales" AND LIMIT > 75

Values of variables and database fields are placed in the expression.

Record 1
75 + 30 < = 100*1.5 – 65/2 OR "acctg" = "sales" AND 100 > 75

Numeric expressions are evaluated according to rules of precedence for numeric operators.

Record 1
105 < = 117.5 OR "acctg" = "sales" AND 100 > 75

Relational operators are evaluated.

Record 1
true OR false AND true

Logical ANDs are evaluated first.

Record 1
true OR false

Logical ORs are evaluated.

Record 1
true

Following are the same evaluation steps for records two and three of the database.

Record 2

42 + 30< = 55*1.5 – 65/2 OR "acctg" = "sales" AND 55> 75
72< = 50 OR "acctg" = "sales" AND 55>75
false OR false AND false
false OR false
false

Record 3

90 + 30< = 95*1.5 – 65/2 OR "sales" = "sales" AND 95>75
120< = 110 OR "sales" = "sales" AND 95>75
false OR true AND true
false OR true
true

Logical operators in dBASE are enclosed in periods (.) and spaces may be used to make logical expressions easier to read. The example expression above might appear in dBASE as

ACCOUNT + PURCHASE <= LIMIT*1.15 – ALLOWANCE/2 .OR.
DEPT = "sales" .AND. LIMIT > 75

Logical operators in Lotus are enclosed in score signs (#), and spaces are not allowed in logical expressions. Assuming that named ranges are used for variables, the example expression above might appear in Lotus as

ACCOUNT + PURCHASE< = LIMIT*1.15 – ALLOWANCE/2#OR#
DEPT = "sales"#AND#LIMIT>75

APPENDIX D
LOTUS 1-2-3 RELEASE 2.2 AND 3

LOTUS RELEASE 2.2

If you are using Lotus Release 2.2, you may want to take advantage of some of its new commands and features. Many of the new commands simply enhance the way other 1-2-3 commands work, while other new commands are new features of Lotus 1-2-3.

Lotus Release 2.2 is upwardly compatible with previous releases of Lotus; it consists of all the commands you may have learned with earlier versions, as well as a number of new commands. You may read through this section to determine which of the new commands and features may interest you. If you do not yet have Release 2.2, you may want to read this section to decide whether to upgrade your software.

Add-in Applications

One of the new features of Release 2.2 is the ability to use "add-in" applications with Lotus 1-2-3. An add-in application is a software that is designed to be loaded into RAM after the Lotus spreadsheet software has already been loaded. An add-in software can be thought of as an extra tool available to perform tasks for which Lotus was not specifically designed, or one that provides enhanced capabilities.

A software named ALLWAYS, for example, is an add-in application that comes with the Lotus Release 2.2 software package. ALLWAYS provides word processing and desktop publishing features that go above and beyond those found in Lotus itself. Specifically, ALLWAYS allows greater flexibility in combining text and graphics from a Lotus spreadsheet to produce a professional-looking document. Other add-in software designed to work with Lotus are also available for purchase.

Lotus Release 2.2 offers the following commands for use with add-in software applications.

/**A**dd-In, **A**ttach
Detach
Invoke
Clear
Quit

Add-In is a new command found on the Lotus main menu. When executed, the above menu of **A**dd-In commands appears. The **A**ttach command is used to load an add-in application into RAM. The **D**etach command is used to remove one add-in application from RAM, while the **C**lear command is used to remove all add-in applications from RAM.

After an add-in application has been loaded, the **I**nvoke command is used to execute the add-in application. When the add-in is loaded with the **A**ttach command, you may select **7, 8, 9,** or **10** to allow the add-in application to also be invoked (executed) by typing Alt-F7, Alt-F8, Alt-F9, or Alt-F10, respectively. If the option **N**o-Key is selected, however, the add-in application may only be executed with the /**A**dd-In,**I**nvoke command.

/**W**orksheet,**G**lobal,**D**efault,**O**ther,**A**dd-In, **S**et
Cancel
Quit

The /**W**orksheet,**G**lobal,**D**efault commands are used to set certain spreadsheet options when Lotus is first loaded. The new **A**dd-In commands are found under the **O**ther option of this menu.

The **S**et command is used to specify up to eight add-in applications that are to be loaded automatically each time Lotus is loaded. You may also specify whether an add-in application should be invoked (executed) immediately. The **C**ancel command is used to stop automatic loading of an add-in application previously specified with the **S**et command.

Linked Files

With Release 2.2, Lotus allows you to reference a cell from a spreadsheet file (.WK1) that has been previously saved on disk. In the current spreadsheet (the spreadsheet in RAM), you enter a linked file's cell reference as follows.

+<<file specification>>cell reference

The file specification entered in double angle brackets <<...>> identifies the .WK1 file where the data to be referenced is found. The specification is the filename, and may include a *drive:* letter, subdirectory name, and file extension. The cell reference may be a cell address or named range in the file on the disk.

Each time a file with linked cell references is loaded into RAM with the /**R**etrieve command, Lotus will obtain updated values from the files on disk. For example, you might have a series of spreadsheets with monthly inventory calculations. Ending inventory values for October would be beginning values for November. In the November spreadsheet you could simply reference data from the October spreadsheet. If the October file is subsequently revised, the November spreadsheet's values will be updated when the file is next retrieved.

/**F**ile,**L**ist,**L**inked

The **L**inked command has been added to the /**F**ile,**L**ist command menu. In addition to listing all **W**orksheet files (.WK1), **P**rint files (.PRN), **G**raph files (.PIC), or **O**ther files (any extension) in the current directory, you may select the **L**inked command to view a listing of spreadsheet files that are linked to the current spreadsheet.

File Administration

/**F**ile,**A**dmin, **R**eservation
Table
Link-Refresh

The /**F**ile command menu has an additional command, **A**dmin, which provides two commands for use in a network environment, and a command for creating a table of disk file information in the current spreadsheet. In a network environment, the same files may be available to users at many workstations (microcomputers attached to the network). Some precautions must, therefore, be taken to ensure that two or more users are not attempting to revise the same file at one time.

The **R**eservation command is used to issue network commands to lock and unlock a spreadsheet file. Locking a file on a network means that only one workstation has access to the file until it is subsequently unlocked. The /**F**ile,**A**dmin,**R**eservation,**G**et command is used to lock a file and the /**F**ile,**A**dmin,**R**eservation,**R**elease command is used to unlock a file.

The /**F**ile,**A**dmin,**R**efresh command is used to update all linked file cell references in the current spreadsheet. In a network environment, other users may be updating and saving files that contain data referenced in your spreadsheet through linked file references. Since this might occur after you have retrieved your file, you may use the **R**efresh command to make sure your spreadsheet is using the most recently saved data.

The /**F**ile,**A**dmin,**T**able command is used to read information from the DOS file directory and copy it to a range of cells in the current spreadsheet. Filenames will be listed alphabetically in the first column of the range specified. Adjacent columns will contain the date and time of each file's last modification, as well as each file's size in bytes. Like the /**F**ile,**L**ist command discussed previously, the /**F**ile,**A**dmin,**T**able command allows you to specify **W**orksheet, **P**rint, **G**raph, **O**ther, or **L**inked as the type of files to be listed in the table.

New File Backup Command Options

/**F**ile,**S**ave,**B**ackup and /**F**ile,**X**tract,**F**ormulas or **V**alues,**B**ackup

The **B**ackup command is a new command option on the /**F**ile,**S**ave and **F**ile,**X**tract menus. The **B**ackup command is similar to the **R**eplace command in that it saves the spreadsheet to a disk file by overwriting any existing .WK1 file with the same name. The difference is that before overwriting an existing file (the previously saved version of the file), **B**ackup will copy the file on disk to a backup file with the same filename, but with a .BAK file extension. By using the **B**ackup command, you will always have the last two saved versions of a spreadsheet file.

New Graph Commands

In addition to improving the appearance of spreadsheet graphs with Release 2.2, Lotus 1-2-3 has added some new commands to the /**G**raph command menus to make it easier to define elements of a graph.

/**G**raph,**G**roup,**C**olumnwise
Rowwise

The data ranges to be graphed (the X range and A–F ranges) may now be defined as a single range in the spreadsheet with the /**G**raph,**G**roup command. The range, however, should not contain blank rows or columns if the **G**roup command is to be used. If **R**owwise is selected, the first row in the range is used as the X range and subsequent rows as the A–F data ranges. If **C**olumnwise is selected, the first column in the range is used as the X range and subsequent columns as the A–F data ranges.

/**G**raph,**O**ptions, **L**egend,**R**ange
Data-Labels,**G**roup

The **L**egend text to be displayed on the graph for each of the data ranges A–F may now be specified individually or as a **R**ange of cells in the spreadsheet. Similarly, the text of the **D**ata-Labels used in a graph may be specified individually or as a range specified with the **G**roup command. The **D**ata-Labels,**G**roup command requires that you select **C**olumnwise or **R**owwise in the same manner as the /**G**raph,**G**roup command does.

In all cases where a single range may be specified instead of individually specifying the X range and A–F range data, specifying the range replaces all previously defined settings.

/**G**raph,**R**eset,**R**anges
Options

The /**G**raph,**R**eset command now allows you to remove all data range settings without affecting currently defined options (with the **R**anges command) or, conversely, to remove all options settings without affecting currently defined data range settings (with the **O**ptions command).

/**G**raph,**N**ame,**T**able

The /**G**raph,**N**ame command menu now includes the **T**able command, which allows you to specify a range of cells in the spreadsheet where a table of all named graphs will be created. The command is used in the same manner as the /**R**ange,**N**ame,**T**able command.

The New Undo Feature

The new function key combination Alt-F4 (UNDO) may be used to cancel all changes made to the spreadsheet since the last time it was in the READY mode. To restore the changes after using Alt-F4 (UNDO), you may type Alt-F4 (UNDO) a second time. The Undo feature may be turned on or off with the /**W**orksheet,**G**lobal,**D**efault,**O**ther,**U**ndo,**E**nable or **D**isable command.

New Macro Features

Some enhancements have been made to Lotus macros to make them more flexible and easier to construct. Some new macro commands that deal with new features of Lotus have also been added.

The Learn Feature

A macro can now be created by typing the keystrokes of the macro and having Lotus 1-2-3 record the keystrokes and keystroke equivalents in a range of cells in the spreadsheet that has been previously defined as the Learn range. The function key combination Alt-F5 (LEARN) is used to cause Lotus to begin copying subsequent keystrokes into cells of the Learn range. Typing Alt-F5 a second time turns off the Learn feature. The new commands used to specify a Learn range are discussed next.

/*Worksheet*,*Learn*,*Range*
Cancel
Erase

The **L**earn command menu is displayed by typing /**W**orksheet,**L**earn. The **R**ange command of this menu is used to specify a Learn range, which must be done before the Alt-F5 (LEARN) feature can be used. The **C**ancel command removes the Learn range specification. The **E**rase command can be used to leave the Learn range as currently defined, but to erase all cell entries in the range.

Another new macro feature allows the use of macro names up to 15 characters. Macros may still be named \A through \Z, and these macros may still be executed by pressing and holding the Alt key and typing the corresponding letter. Macros that are given longer names may be executed with the function key combination Alt-F3 (RUN). When Alt-F3 (RUN) is typed, a menu of all named ranges will appear, and the range selected will be executed as a macro.

Global Autoexec Macro Commands

/*Worksheet*,*Global*,*Default*,*Autoexec*, *Yes*
No

The autoexec macro (named \0) is a macro that will be executed automatically when a spreadsheet is loaded. The automatic execution of such macros may now be suppressed by executing the /**W**orksheet,**G**lobal,**D**efault,**A**utoexec,**N**o command. To resume automatic execution, select the **Y**es command option.

New Print Features

/**P**rint,**P**rinter or **F**ile,**O**ptions,**M**argins,**N**one

The **N**one command has been added to the menu of commands for setting page **M**argins. This command sets the right margin to 240 and all other margins (top, bottom, and left) to zero.

The /**P**rint,**P**rinter or **F**ile,**O**ptions,**H**eader and **F**ooter commands now allow you to specify a cell in the spreadsheet where the **H**eader or **F**ooter text is to be found. Instead of typing the text of the **H**eader or **F**ooter, you may type a backslash (\) and then enter a cell address or range name.

New Range Commands for Search and Replace Operations

With Release 2.2 you now have the ability to search the cells of a specified range for any occurrences of a given string of characters. The new **S**earch command appears on the /Range command menu.

/**R**ange,**S**earch,**F**ormulas
Labels
Both

After you type the /**R**ange,**S**earch command, you specify the range to be searched and the string to search for. You must then specify whether only cells containing **F**ormulas, only cells containing **L**abels, or cells containing **B**oth types of data in the specified range are to be included in the search. The next command options to appear are **F**ind or **R**eplace.

*The **F**ind Command*

The **F**ind command is used to highlight occurrences of the search string in the specified range. After selecting **F**ind, the **N**ext command is used to highlight the next occurrence of the search string (if any). The **Q**uit command is used to discontinue the search operation.

*The **R**eplace Command*

The **R**eplace command is used to replace occurrences of the search string with another string. After selecting **R**eplace, you enter the replacement string, after which the next occurrence of the search string (if any) is highlighted. For each occurrence highlighted, you are given the following command options.

Replace	To replace the highlighted search string with the replacement string and highlight the next occurrence.
All	To replace all remaining occurrences of the search string without stopping to highlight them.
Next	To leave the currently highlighted occurrence of the search string as is and highlight the next occurrence.
Quit	To discontinue the search operation.

Other New Features

Column Widths

You may now define column widths for a group of adjacent columns. The command /**W**orksheet,**C**olumn,**C**olumn-Range command allows you to define a range of columns for which the same width is to be set. Command options are then **S**et-Width to specify a new column width and **R**eset-Width to set the columns to the default column width.

Zero Label

In addition to displaying or suppressing the display of a 0 (zero) in cells with formulas evaluating to zero, you may now specify a label to be displayed in such cells. The /**W**orksheet,**G**lobal,**Z**ero command now displays three command options, **Y**es, **N**o, and **L**abel.

Formatting Negative Values

You may now determine whether cells formatted as **C**urrency or **,** (comma) will display negative values in parentheses or with a preceding – (minus) sign. The command to use is /**W**orksheet,**G**lobal,**D**efault,**O**ther,**I**nternational,**N**egative, which has the two command options, **P**arentheses and **S**ign.

Filename Indicator

In addition to setting the format for (or suppressing the display of) the date and time indicator in the lower left corner of the screen, you may now choose to display the filename of the current spreadsheet in its place. The command /**W**orksheet,**G**lobal,**D**efault,**O**ther,**C**lock has the two new command options **C**lock and **F**ilename.

Settings Sheets

While using many Lotus command menus, you will now see the spreadsheet display replaced with a screen indicating the settings you are currently selecting (such as graph settings or print settings). Lotus refers to these displays as Settings Sheets. The function key Alt-F6 (WINDOW) may be used in the MENU mode to turn the display of the Settings Sheets on and off.

LOTUS RELEASE 3

Lotus 1-2-3 Release 3 incorporates the updated commands and features of Release 2.2 discussed above along with many other commands, functions, and features specific to Release 3. Release 3 requires that your computer have greater memory capacity because of added capabilities to hold multiple spreadsheets in memory at one time. Under a DOS operating system, one megabyte of RAM is required to run Release 3, and under the OS/2 operating system, three megabytes is the required minimum (four megabytes are recommended).

Three-Dimensional Environment

The most significant change made in Lotus Release 3 is the ability to work with several spreadsheet files concurrently, which gives it the appearance of being three dimensional. The two-dimensional grids that make up the standard row and column spreadsheet can now be stacked on top of each other, and up to three grids may be displayed on the screen at one time.

Because a spreadsheet file (now a .WK3 extension) may be more than one spreadsheet deep, the spreadsheets are identified with the letters A, B, C, and so on. Cell references may now include the spreadsheet letter in addition to the column letter and row number. For example, B:A2 is the reference to cell A2 of spreadsheet B. Many commands and functions that once operated horizontally (across columns) and vertically (across rows) may now be used laterally (across spreadsheets) as well. For example the /**C**opy command may now be used as follows.

/**C**opy FROM: A:C3..A:C5 TO: B:C3..F:C5

This command will copy the contents of cells C3, C4, and C5 in spreadsheet A to the same cells in spreadsheets B, C, D, E, and F.

The ability to use the third specification (spreadsheet letter) will have a significant effect on commands, functions, range specifications, and pointer movement operations. It is beyond the scope of this discussion to outline the changes to existing commands and new commands that are designed to work with stacked spreadsheets. However, Release 3 retains the same basic spreadsheet environment and screen appearance as previous versions of Lotus, and learning to use the three-dimensional features comes easily with practice.

Multiple Files Open

In addition to allowing a single .WK3 file to comprise multiple stacked spreadsheets, Release 3 also allows more than one such file to be open at the same time. For example, you might have a spreadsheet file named INVEN.WK3 which holds monthly inventory data and another spreadsheet file named SALES.WK3 which holds monthly sales data. Each of these files could comprise multiple spreadsheets, with each stacked spreadsheet holding one month's data. Since the sales figures might be used for inventory calculations, you might want to have both of these files open at the same time, so that you could quickly view sales figures without closing the inventory file, or vice versa.

In addition, you may want to use linked file cell references in one or both of these files to reference data held in cells of the other file. Such linked file references are possible whether or not the second file is open; however, the ability to have them both open at the same time allows you to quickly switch from one file to the other to verify cell addresses and range names, or to work concurrently on the design of the two files.

New Graph Features

Release 3 provides a number of new commands and features for creating graphs. The most notable of these features allows you to view a graph on one portion of the monitor screen while viewing and modifying spreadsheet data on another portion. This feature, however, is dependent on the capabilities of your particular monitor. Other features now provide for new graph types and greater control of color, patterns, and text sizes and fonts used in graphs. Release 3 also incorporates the commands for printing graphs from the spreadsheet software itself rather than having to exit and load a separate Printgraph program.

New Database Features

Database commands and operations available in Lotus have been augmented significantly with Release 3. You may now select more than two keys for sorting data, include calculations in the output of a data extraction, obtain summary calculations for groups of records, and combine data from more than one database in extraction operations. New macro commands have been added to facilitate the creation of data entry forms for adding records to a database in Lotus. New features also provide for easier access to data files created with other software, such as the database management software dBASE III Plus.

APPENDIX E
USING VP-PLANNER PLUS WITH THIS MANUAL

VP-Planner Plus is a spreadsheet software that is very similar to Lotus 1-2-3 in its commands, functions, menus, and features. However, VP-Planner Plus provides a number of command options and spreadsheet features that are not found in Lotus 1-2-3 Version 2.01, or that are presented somewhat differently. However, because of the degree of similarity, the tutorial lessons and exercises for Lotus 1-2-3 in this manual will work equally as well with the VP-Planner Plus software.

If you are using VP-Planner Plus and you would like your screen display to more closely match the examples in this manual, you may wish to change a few of the default settings of VP-Planner Plus, as follows.

1. From the DOS prompt, load VP-Planner Plus into memory by typing ||VPP↵||. Then type the Esc key to remove any copyright message.

Your screen will appear similar to the following.

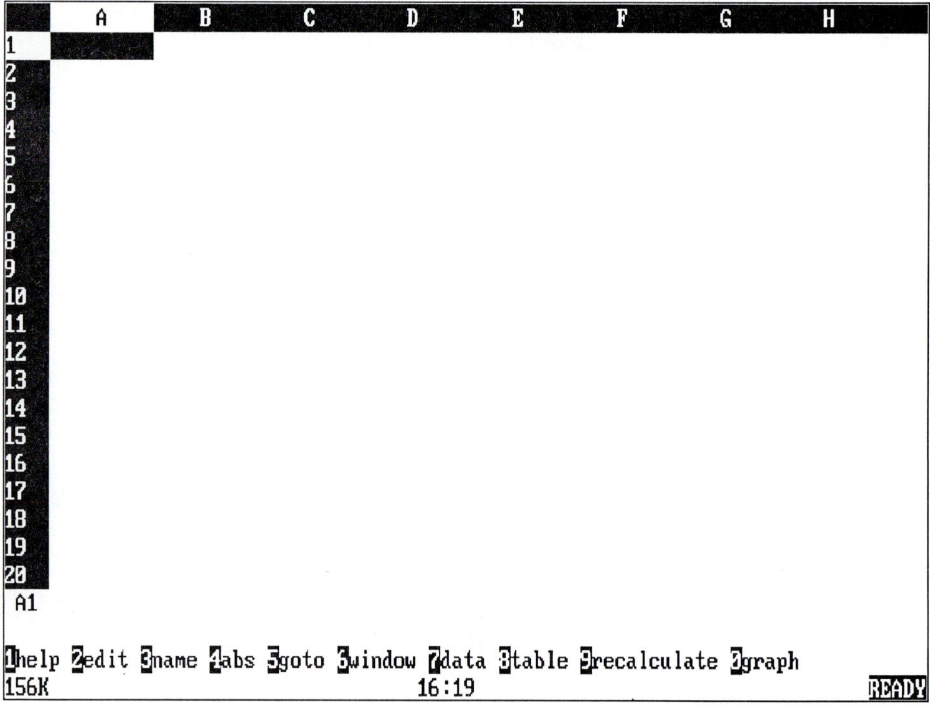

Notice that the current cell address and function key assignments are displayed at the bottom of the screen.

2. Type || / || to call the main menu of commands.

The screen will now display two pull-down menus in the spreadsheet portion of the screen, as shown here.

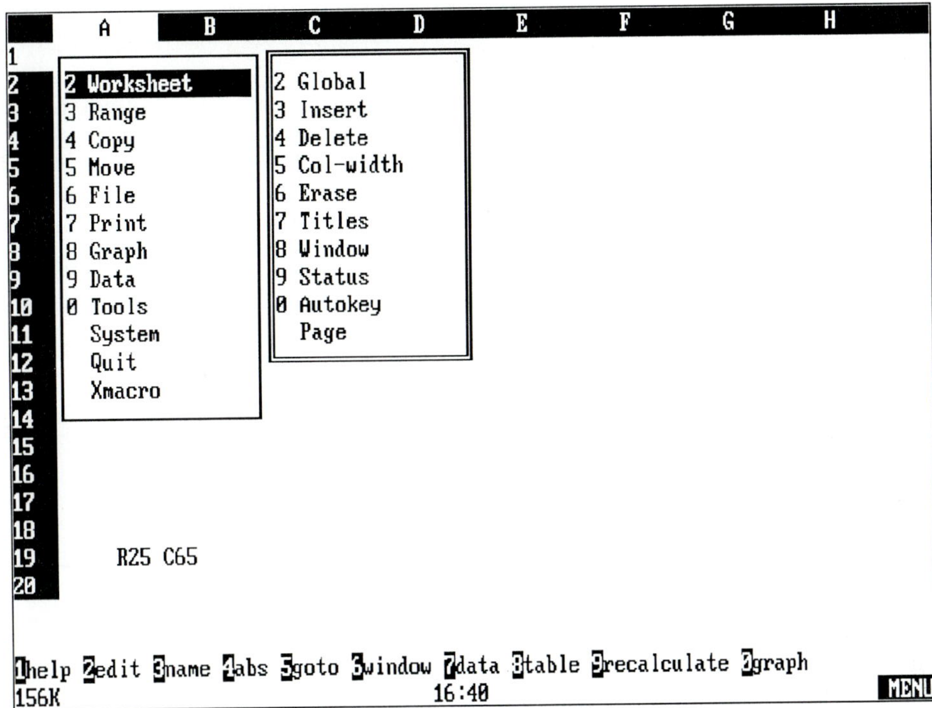

The pull-down menu on the left shows the next set of command options available, while the pull-down menu on the right shows further options for the highlighted command. To view any spreadsheet data that may be covered by the pull-down menus in the MENU mode, you may type a Shift key.

3. Continue by typing ||WGD|| to call the **W**orksheet,**G**lobal,**D**efault menu of commands.

The entire screen will now be used to display the menu, as shown in the following. Notice that numbers appear next to the menu selections on the screen. As an alternate to highlighting a menu item and typing ↵, or typing the first letter of a command, VP-Planner Plus also allows you to use the function keys F2 through F10 to select menu items.

```
2 PRINTER                6 OTHER
3 DIRECTORY                2 Screen                      4 Format
   none specified            2 FnKey#s     ON              2 Order
4 EXT-PATH                   3 Ready-menu  ON                2 D-M-Y
  2 MultiDim                 4 Trim        OFF               3 M-D-Y    X
   none specified            5 Menu-box    ON                4 Y-M-D
  3 DBF                      6 Colors                      3 Date-char  /
   none specified            7 Panel-top   OFF             4 Time-char  :
5 HARDWARE                   8 Quit                        5 Quit
  2 Video   CGA            3 Time          ON            5 Case        Ignore
    2 CGA                                                6 Autosave    0
    3 Hercules(TM)                                       7 Undo        0
    4 EGA                7 CUSTOM                        8 Quit
    5 Other              8 STATUS
  3 Colors               9 UPDATE
                         0 QUIT
                                                                      MENU
```

4. Now type ||OS|| to call the **O**ther,**S**creen menu of options.

The four options on this menu that will be changed here are options that may be set ON or OFF.

5. Type ||M|| to change the **M**enu-box option to OFF. The menu of options should now appear horizontally across the bottom of the screen.
6. Type ||F|| to change the **F**nKey#s option to OFF. The numbers that appeared next to menu options should now be absent.
7. Type ||R|| to change the **R**eady-menu option to OFF. The display of function key assignments that appeared when in the READY mode will now be suppressed when you return to the READY mode.
8. Finally, type ||P|| to change the **P**anel-top option to ON. The menu should now be shifted to the top of the screen.

You may want to save these changes so that VP-Planner Plus will use these settings the next time it is loaded. However, if you don't wish to make these changes permanent, you may make any of the above setting changes at the beginning of each work session.

9. Type ||Q|| to back up one menu level. Then type ||U|| for **U**pdate if you wish to save these changes.
10. Type ||Q|| once more to return to the READY mode.

When you type || / || to call the main menu, the top of your screen should appear similar to the following.

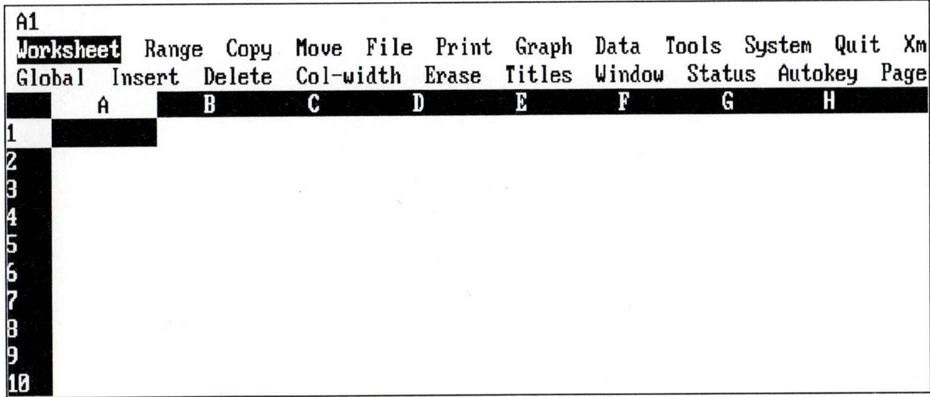

If you follow these steps, the appearance of your screens will be very similar to the examples shown in the Lotus 1-2-3 module. However, you should expect to see minor variations, as follows.

1. Some command and menu option wording may vary slightly. However, you may always enter commands by selecting the first letter. For example, when instructed to use the command /**W**orksheet,**C**olumn,**S**et-Width to set column widths, the VP-Planner Plus command wording will be /**W**orksheet,**C**ol-width,**S**et. The same set of first letters is used.
2. VP-Planner Plus does not display the current column's width at the top of the screen. The examples in this manual, however, will show a column width indicator at the top of the screen. For example, if the current column's width is 18 characters, the indicator [W18] will appear at the top of the example screen.
3. Some commands may use default settings different from those described in this manual. With VP-Planner Plus, for instance, the default scroll setting when using the /**W**indows command is **U**nsync (scrolling is not synchronized), while the default setting assumed in this manual is **S**ync (synchronized scrolling). When you notice this type of difference, simply change the appropriate setting.
4. Finally, many command options you will see on your screen are specific to VP-Planner Plus. Simply ignore those options when comparing your screen to the examples in this manual. If, however, you wish to learn more about one of these command options, select the option, and then type the F1 key (HELP) to view a help screen that explains the command's use.

INDEX

Fundamentals of Using Microcomputers

WordPerfect Version 5.0

Lotus 1-2-3 Version 2.01

dBASE III Plus

Data Transfer Between Applications Software

BASICA

Appendices